Weiss Ratings' Guide to Credit Unions

Weiss Ratings' Guide to Credit Unions

A Quarterly Compilation of Credit Union Ratings and Analyses

Fall 2017

GREY HOUSE PUBLISHING

Weiss Ratings
4400 Northcorp Parkway
Palm Beach Gardens, FL 33410
561-627-3300

Published by Grey House Publishing, Inc., located at 4919 Route 22, Amenia, NY 12501; telephone 518-789-8700. Grey House Publishing neither guarantees the accuracy of the data contained herein nor assumes any responsibility for errors, omissions or discrepancies. Grey House Publishing accepts no payment for listing; inclusion in the publication of any organization, agency, institution, publication, service or individual does not imply endorsement of the publisher.

4919 Route 22
PO Box 56
Amenia, NY 12501-0056

Edition No. 27 Fall 2017

ISBN: 978-1-68217-447-0
ISSN: 2162-8270

Contents

Terms and Conditions

This document is prepared strictly for the confidential use of our customer(s). It has been provided to you at your specific request. It is not directed to, or intended for distribution to or use by, any person or entity who is a citizen or resident of or located in any locality, state, country or other jurisdiction where such distribution, publication, availability or use would be contrary to law or regulation or which would subject Weiss Ratings or its affiliates to any registration or licensing requirement within such jurisdiction.

No part of the analysts' compensation was, is, or will be, directly or indirectly, related to the specific recommendations or views expressed in this research report.

This document is not intended for the direct or indirect solicitation of business. Weiss Ratings, LLC and its affiliates disclaims any and all liability to any person or entity for any loss or damage caused, in whole or in part, by any error (negligent or otherwise) or other circumstances involved in, resulting from or relating to the procurement, compilation, analysis, interpretation, editing, transcribing, publishing and/or dissemination or transmittal of any information contained herein.

Weiss Ratings has not taken any steps to ensure that the securities or investment vehicle referred to in this report are suitable for any particular investor. The investment or services contained or referred to in this report may not be suitable for you and it is recommended that you consult an independent investment advisor if you are in doubt about such investments or investment services. Nothing in this report constitutes investment, legal, accounting or tax advice or a representation that any investment or strategy is suitable or appropriate to your individual circumstances or otherwise constitutes a personal recommendation to you.

The ratings and other opinions contained in this document must be construed solely as statements of opinion from Weiss Ratings, LLC, and not statements of fact. Each rating or opinion must be weighed solely as a factor in your choice of an institution and should not be construed as a recommendation to buy, sell or otherwise act with respect to the particular product or company involved.

Past performance should not be taken as an indication or guarantee of future performance, and no representation or warranty, expressed or implied, is made regarding future performance. Information, opinions and estimates contained in this report reflect a judgment at its original date of publication and are subject to change without notice. Weiss Ratings offers a notification service for rating changes on companies you specify. For more information, visit WeissRatings.com or call 1-877-934-7778. The price, value and income from any of the securities or financial instruments mentioned in this report can fall as well as rise.

Date of Data Analyzed: March 31, 2017

Data Source: Call Report data provided by SNL Financial.

Welcome to Weiss Ratings
Guide to Credit Unions

Most people automatically assume their credit union will survive, year after year. However, prudent consumers and professionals realize that in this world of shifting risks, the solvency of financial institutions can't be taken for granted. After all, your credit union's failure could have a heavy impact on you in terms of lost time, lost money (in cases of deposits exceeding the federal insurance limit), tied-up deposits, lost credit lines, and the possibility of being shifted to another institution under not-so-friendly terms.

If you are looking for accurate, unbiased ratings and data to help you choose a credit union for yourself, your family, your company or your clients, Weiss Ratings' Guide to Credit Unions gives you precisely what you need.

Weiss Ratings' Mission Statement

Weiss Ratings' mission is to empower consumers, professionals, and institutions with high quality advisory information for selecting or monitoring a financial services company or financial investment.

In doing so, Weiss Ratings will adhere to the highest ethical standards by maintaining our independent, unbiased outlook and approach to advising our customers.

Why rely on Weiss Ratings?

Weiss Ratings provides fair, objective ratings to help professionals and consumers alike make educated financial decisions.

At Weiss Ratings, integrity is number one. Weiss Ratings never takes a penny from rated companies for issuing its ratings. And, we publish Weiss Safety Ratings without regard for institutions' preferences. Our analysts review and update Weiss Ratings each and every quarter, so you can be sure that the information you receive is accurate and current – providing you with advance warning of financial vulnerability early enough to do something about it.

Other rating agencies focus primarily on a company's current financial solvency and consider only mild economic adversity. Weiss Ratings also considers these issues, but in addition, our analysis covers a company's ability to deal with severe economic adversity in terms of a sharp decline in the value of its investments and a drop in the collectibility of its loans.

Our use of more rigorous standards stems from the viewpoint that a financial institution's obligations to its customers should not depend on favorable business conditions. A credit union must be able to honor its loan and deposit commitments in bad times as well as good.

Weiss's rating scale, from A to F, is easy to understand. Only a limited number of outstanding institutions receive an A (Excellent) rating, although there are many to choose from within the B (Good) category. A large group falls into the broad average range which receives C (Fair) ratings. Companies that demonstrate marked vulnerabilities receive either D (Weak) or E (Very Weak) ratings. So, there's no numbering system, star counting, or color-coding to keep track of.

How to Use This Guide

The purpose of the *Guide to Credit Unions* is to provide consumers, businesses, financial institutions, and municipalities with a reliable source of industry ratings and analysis on a timely basis. We realize that the financial safety of a credit union is an important factor to consider when establishing a relationship. The ratings and analysis in this guide can make that evaluation easier when you are considering:

- a checking, merchant banking, or other transaction account
- an investment in a certificate of deposit or savings account
- a line of credit or commercial loan
- counterparty risk

The rating for a particular company indicates our opinion regarding that company's ability to meet its obligations – not only under current economic conditions, but also during a declining economy or in an environment of increased liquidity demands.

To use this guide most effectively, we recommend you follow the steps outlined below:

Step 1 To ensure you evaluate the correct company, verify the company's exact name as it was given to you. It is also helpful to ascertain the city and state of the company's main office or headquarters since no two credit unions with the same name can be headquartered in the same city. Many companies have similar names but are not related to one another, so you will want to make sure the company you look up is really the one you are interested in evaluating.

Step 2 Turn to Section I, the Index of Credit Unions, and locate the company you are evaluating. This section contains all federally insured credit unions. It is sorted alphabetically by the name of the company and shows the main office city and state following the name for additional verification.

If you have trouble finding a particular institution or determining which is the right one, you may have an incorrect or incomplete institution name. There are often several institutions with the same or very similar names. So, make sure you have the exact name and proper spelling, as well as the city in which it is headquartered.

Step 3 Once you have located your specific company, the first column after the state shows its current Weiss Safety Rating. Turn to *About Weiss Safety Ratings* for information about what this rating means. If the rating has changed since the last edition of this guide, a downgrade will be indicated with a down triangle ▼ to the left of the company name; an upgrade will be indicated with an up triangle ▲.

Step 4 Following the current Weiss Safety Rating are two prior ratings for the company based on year-end data from the two previous years. Use this to discern the longer-term direction of the company's overall financial condition.

Step 5 The remainder of Section I, provides insight into the areas our analysts reviewed as the basis for assigning the company's rating. These areas include size, capital adequacy, asset quality, profitability, liquidity, and stability. An index within each of these categories represents a composite evaluation of that particular facet of the company's financial condition. Refer to the *Critical Ranges In Our Indexes* table for an interpretation of which index values are considered strong, good, fair, or weak. In most cases, lower-rated companies will have a low index value in one or more of the indexes shown. Bear in mind, however, that Weiss Safety Rating is the result of a complex qualitative and quantitative analysis which cannot be reproduced using only the data provided here.

Step 6 If the company you are evaluating is not highly rated and you want to find a credit union a higher rating, turn to the page in Section II that has your state's name at the top. This section contains Weiss Recommended Credit Unions (rating of A+, A, A- or B+) that have a branch office in your state. If the main office telephone number provided is not a local telephone call or to determine if a branch of the credit union is near you, consult your local telephone Yellow Pages Directory under "Credit Unions Services," or "Financial Services." Here you will find a complete list of the institution's branch locations along with their telephone numbers.

Step 7 Once you've identified a Weiss Recommended Credit Union in your local area, you can then refer back to Section I to analyze it.

Step 8 In order to use Weiss Safety ratings most effectively, we strongly recommend you consult the *Important Warnings and Cautions*. These are more than just "standard disclaimers." They are very important factors you should be aware of before using this guide. If you have any questions regarding the precise meaning of specific terms used in the guide, refer to the glossary.

Step 9 Make sure you stay up to date with the latest information available since the publication of this guide. For information on how to acquire follow-up reports, check ratings online or receive a more in-depth analysis of an individual company, call 1-877-934-7778 or visit www.weissratings.com.

About Weiss Safety Ratings

The Weiss Ratings are calculated based on a complex analysis of hundreds of factors that are synthesized into five indexes: capitalization, asset quality, profitability, liquidity and stability. Each index is then used to arrive at a letter grade rating. A weak score on any one index can result in a low rating, as financial problems can be caused by any one of a number of factors, such as inadequate capital, non-performing loans and poor asset quality, operating losses, poor liquidity, or the failure of an affiliated company.

Our **Capitalization Index** gauges the institution's capital adequacy in terms of its cushion to absorb future operating losses under adverse business and economic scenarios that may impact the company's net interest margin, securities' values, and the collectability of its loans.

Our **Asset Quality Index** measures the quality of the company's past underwriting and investment practices based on the estimated liquidation value of the company's loan and securities portfolios.

Our **Profitability Index** measures the soundness of the company's operations and the contribution of profits to the company's safety. The index is a composite of five sub-factors: 1) gain or loss on operations; 2) rates of return on assets and equity; 3) management of net interest margin; 4) generation of noninterest-based revenues; and 5) overhead expense management.

Our **Liquidity Index** evaluates a company's ability to raise the necessary cash to satisfy creditors and honor depositor withdrawals.

Finally, our **Stability Index** integrates a number of sub-factors that affect consistency (or lack thereof) in maintaining financial strength over time. These include 1) risk diversification in terms of company size and loan diversification; 2) deterioration of operations as reported in critical asset, liability, income and expense items, such as an increase in loan delinquency rates or a sharp increase in loan originations; 3) years in operation; 4) former problem areas where, despite recent improvement, the company has yet to establish a record of stable performance over a suitable period of time; and 5) relationships with holding companies and affiliates.

In order to help guarantee our objectivity, we reserve the right to publish ratings expressing our opinion of a company's financial stability based exclusively on publicly available data and our own proprietary standards for safety.

Each of these indexes is measured according to the following range of values.

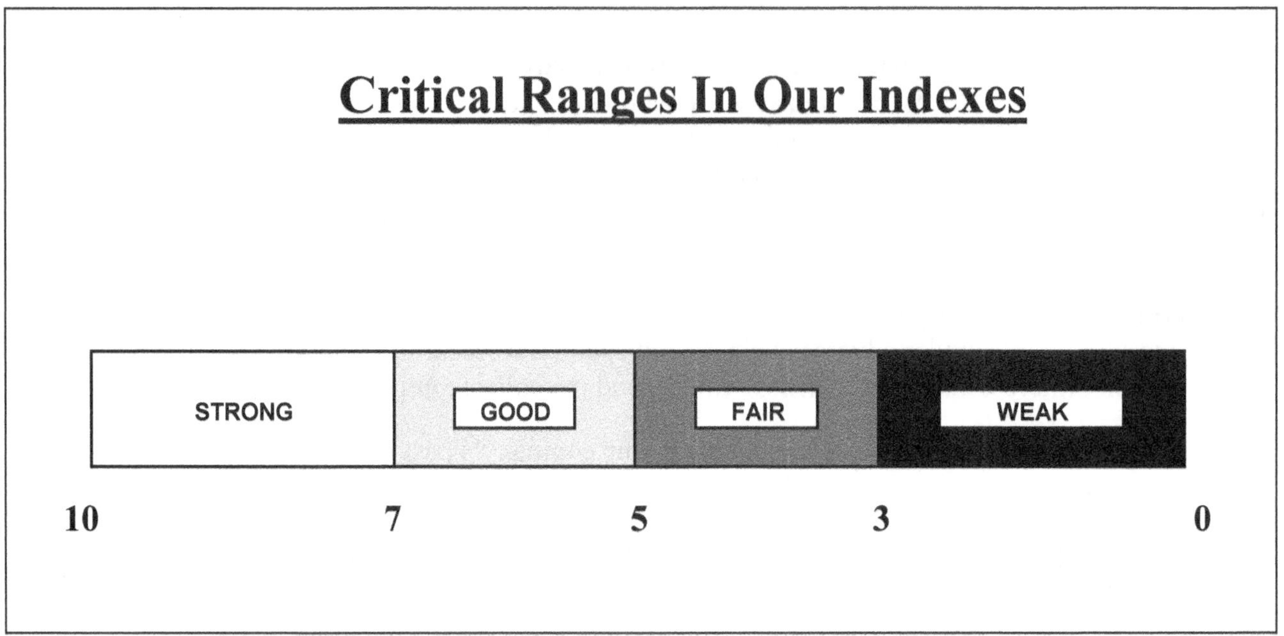

Finally, the indexes are combined to form a composite company rating which is then verified by our analysts. The resulting distribution of ratings assigned to all credit unions looks like this:

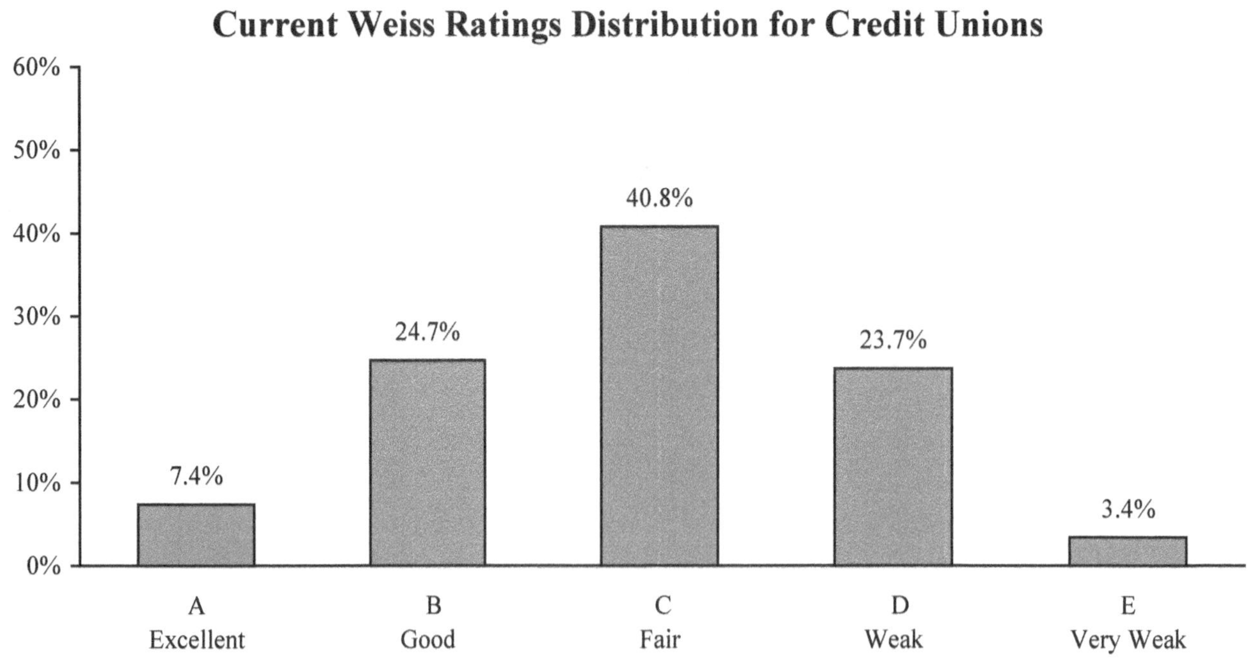

What Our Ratings Mean

A **Excellent.** The institution offers excellent financial security. It has maintained a conservative stance in its business operations and underwriting practices as evidenced by its strong equity base, high asset quality, steady earnings, and high liquidity. While the financial position of any company is subject to change, we believe that this institution has the resources necessary to deal with severe economic conditions.

B **Good.** The institution offers good financial security and has the resources to deal with a variety of adverse economic conditions. It comfortably exceeds the minimum levels for all of our rating criteria, and is likely to remain healthy for the near future. Nevertheless, in the event of a severe recession or major financial crisis, we feel that this assessment should be reviewed to make sure that the company is still maintaining adequate financial strength.

C **Fair.** The institution offers fair financial security, is currently stable, and will likely remain relatively healthy as long as the economic environment remains relatively stable. In the event of a severe recession or major financial crisis, however, we feel this company may encounter difficulties in maintaining its financial stability.

D **Weak.** The institution currently demonstrates what, in our opinion, we consider to be significant weaknesses which could negatively impact depositors or creditors. In the event of a severe recession or major financial crisis, these weaknesses could be magnified.

E **Very Weak.** The institution currently demonstrates what we consider to be significant weaknesses and has also failed some of the basic tests that we use to identify fiscal stability. Therefore, even in a favorable economic environment, it is our opinion that depositors or creditors could incur significant risks.

F **Failed.** The institution has been placed under the custodianship of regulatory authorities. This implies that it will be either liquidated or taken over by another financial institution.

\+ The **plus sign** is an indication that the institution is in the upper third of the letter grade.

\- The **minus sign** is an indication that the institution is in the lower third of the letter grade.

U **Unrated.** The institution is unrated due to the absence of sufficient data for our ratings.

Peer Comparison of Credit Union Safety Ratings

Weiss Ratings	Veribanc	Bauer Financial	IDC Financial	Bankrate.com	Lace Financial
A+, A, A-	Green, Three Stars w/ Blue Ribbon recognition	5 stars, 4 stars	201-300	1, Five stars	A+, A
B+, B, B-	Green, Three Stars w/out Blue Ribbon recognition	3 ½ stars	166-200	2, Four stars	B+
C+, C, C-	Green Two Stars, Yellow Two Stars	3 stars	126-165	3, Three stars	B, C+
D+, D, D-	Green one star, Yellow one star, Green no stars	2 stars	76-125	4, Two stars	C, D
E+, E, E-	Yellow no stars, Red no stars	1 star	1-75	5, One star	E

Important Warnings and Cautions

1. **A rating alone cannot tell the whole story.** Please read the explanatory information contained here, in the section introductions and in the appendix. It is provided in order to give you an understanding of our rating philosophy as well as to paint a more complete picture of how we arrive at our opinion of a company's strengths and weaknesses. In addition, please remember that our safety rating is not an end-all measure of an institution's safety. Rather, it should be used as a "flag" of possible troubles, suggesting a need for further research.

2. **Safety ratings shown in this directory were current as of the publication date.** In the meantime, the rating may have been updated based on more recent data. Weiss Ratings offers online reports that may be more current. For more information call 1-877-934-7778 or visit www.weissratings.com.

3. **When deciding to do business with a financial institution, your decision should be based on a wide variety of factors in addition to Weiss Safety Rating**. These include the institution's pricing of its deposit instruments and loans, the fees you will be charged, the degree to which it can help you meet your long-term planning needs, how these costs/benefits may change over the years, and what other choices are available to you given your current location and financial circumstances.

4. **Weiss Safety ratings represent our opinion of a company's insolvency risk.** As such, a high rating means we feel that the company has less chance of running into financial difficulties. A high rating is not a guarantee of solvency nor is a low rating a prediction of insolvency. Weiss Safety Ratings are not deemed to be a recommendation concerning the purchase or sale of the securities of any credit union.

5. **All firms that have the same Weiss Safety Rating should be considered to be essentially equal in safety.** This is true regardless of any differences in the underlying numbers which might appear to indicate greater strengths. Weiss Safety Rating already takes into account a number of lesser factors which, due to space limitations, cannot be included in this publication.

6. **A good rating requires consistency.** If a company is excellent on four indicators and fair on one, the company may receive a fair rating. This requirement is necessary due to the fact that fiscal problems can arise from any *one* of several causes including poor underwriting, inadequate capital resources, or operating losses.

7. **Our rating standards are more conservative than those used by other agencies.** We believe that no one can predict with certainty the economic environment of the near or long-term future. Rather, we assume that various scenarios – from the extremes of double-digit inflation to a severe recession – are within the range of reasonable possibilities over the next one or two decades. To achieve a top rating according to our standards, a company must be adequately prepared for the worst-case reasonable scenario, without impairing its current operations.

8. **We are an independent rating agency and do not depend on the cooperation of the companies we rate**. Our data is derived from quarterly financial statements filed with federal regulators. Although we seek to maintain an open line of communication with the companies being rated, we do not grant them the right to influence the ratings or stop their publication. This policy stems from the fact that this guide is designed for the protection of our customers.

9. **Inaccuracies in the data issued by the federal regulators could negatively impact the quality of a company's Safety Rating.** While we attempt to find and correct as many data errors as possible, some data errors inevitably slip through. We have no method of intercepting fraudulent or falsified data and must take for granted that all information is reported honestly to the federal regulatory agencies.

10. **There are many companies with the same or similar sounding names, despite no affiliation whatsoever.** Therefore, it is important that you have the exact name, city, and state of the institution's headquarters before you begin to research the company in this guide.

11. **This publication does not include foreign credit unions, or their U.S. branches.** Therefore, our evaluation of foreign credit unions is limited to those U.S. chartered domestic credit unions owned by foreign companies. In most cases, the U.S. operations of a foreign credit union are relatively small in relation to the overall size of the company, so you may want to consult other sources as well. In any case, do not be confused by a domestic credit union with a name which is the same as – or similar to – that of a foreign company. Even if there is an affiliation between the two, we have evaluated the U.S. institution based on its own merits.

Section I

Index of Credit Unions

An analysis of all rated

U.S. Credit Unions

Institutions are listed in alphabetical order.

Section I Contents

This section contains Weiss Safety Ratings, key rating factors, and summary financial data for all U.S. federally-insured credit unions. Companies are sorted in alphabetical order, first by company name, then by city and state.

Left Pages

1. **Institution Name** The name under which the institution was chartered. If you cannot find the institution you are interested in, or if you have any doubts regarding the precise name, verify the information with the credit union itself before proceeding. Also, determine the city and state in which the institution is headquartered for confirmation. (See columns 2 and 3.)

2. **City** The city in which the institution's headquarters or main office is located. With the adoption of intrastate and interstate branching laws, many institutions operating in your area may actually be headquartered elsewhere. So, don't be surprised if the location cited is not in your particular city.

   Also use this column to confirm that you have located the correct institution. It is possible for two unrelated companies to have the same name if they are headquartered in different cities.

3. **State** The state in which the institution's headquarters or main office is located. With the adoption of interstate branching laws, some institutions operating in your area may actually be headquartered in another state.

4. **Safety Rating** Weiss rating assigned to the institution at the time of publication. Our ratings are designed to distinguish levels of insolvency risk and are measured on a scale from A to F based upon a wide range of factors. Please see *What Our Ratings Mean* for specific descriptions of each letter grade.

   Highly rated companies are, in our opinion, less likely to experience financial difficulties than lower rated firms. See *About Weiss Safety Ratings* for more information. Also, please be sure to consider the warnings regarding the ratings' limitations and the underlying assumptions.

5. **Prior Year Safety Rating** Weiss rating assigned to the institution based on data from December 31 of the previous year. Compare this rating to the company's current rating to identify any recent changes.

6. **Safety Rating Two Years Prior** Weiss rating assigned to the institution based on data from December 31 two years ago. Compare this rating to the ratings in the prior columns to identify longer term trends in the company's financial condition.

7. Total Assets

The total of all assets listed on the institution's balance sheet, in millions of dollars. This figure primarily consists of loans, investments (such as municipal and treasury bonds), and fixed assets (such as buildings and other real estate). Overall size is an important factor which affects the company's ability to diversify risk and avoid vulnerability to a single borrower, industry, or geographic area. Larger institutions are usually, although not always, more diversified and thus less susceptible to a downturn in a particular area. Nevertheless, do not be misled by the general public perception that "bigger is better." Larger institutions are known for their inability to quickly adapt to changes in the marketplace and typically underperform their smaller brethren. If total assets are less than $1 million then it will be noted by <1 in that field column.

8. One Year Asset Growth

The percentage change in total assets over the previous 12 months. Moderate growth is generally a positive since it can reflect the maintenance or expansion of the company's market share, leading to the generation of additional revenues. Excessive growth, however, is generally a sign of trouble as it can indicate a loosening of underwriting practices in order to attract new business.

9. Commercial Loans/ Total Assets

The percentage of the institution's asset base invested in loans to businesses. Commercial loans make up a smaller portion of the typical credit union's lending portfolio compared with consumer lending. Except maybe for the largest of credit unions.

10. Consumer Loans/ Total Assets

The percentage of the institution's asset base invested in loans to consumers, primarily credit cards. Consumer lending has grown rapidly in recent years due to the high interest rates and fees institutions are able to charge. On the down side, consumer loans usually experience higher delinquency and default rates than other loans, negatively impacting earnings down the road.

11. Home Mortgage Loans/ Total Assets

The percentage of the institution's asset base invested in residential mortgage loans to consumers, excluding home equity loans. Only larger credit unions will offer home mortgage loans and typically are not involved in mortgages and mortgage-backed securities.

This type of loan typically experiences lower default rates. However, the length of the loan's term can be a subject for concern during periods of rising interest rates.

12. Securities/ Total Assets

The percentage of the institution's asset base invested in securities, including U.S. Treasury securities, mortgage-backed securities, and municipal bonds. This does not include securities the institution may be holding on behalf of individual customers. Although securities are similar to loans in that they represent obligations to pay a debt at some point in the future, they are a more liquid investment than loans and usually present less risk of default. In addition, mortgage-backed securities can present less credit risk than holding mortgage loans themselves due to the diversification of the underlying mortgages.

13. Capitalization Index

An index that measures the adequacy of the institution's capital resources to deal with potentially adverse business and economic situations that could arise. It is based on an evaluation of the company's degree of leverage compared to total assets as well as risk-adjusted assets. See the *Critical Ranges In Our Indexes* table for a description of the different critical levels presented in this index.

14. Net Worth Ratio

Net worth divided by total assets. This ratio answers the question: How much does the institution have in stockholders' equity for every dollar of assets? Thus, the Net Worth Ratio represents the amount of actual "capital cushion" the institution has to fall back on in times of trouble. We feel that this is the single most important ratio in determining financial strength because it provides the best measure of an institution's ability to withstand losses.

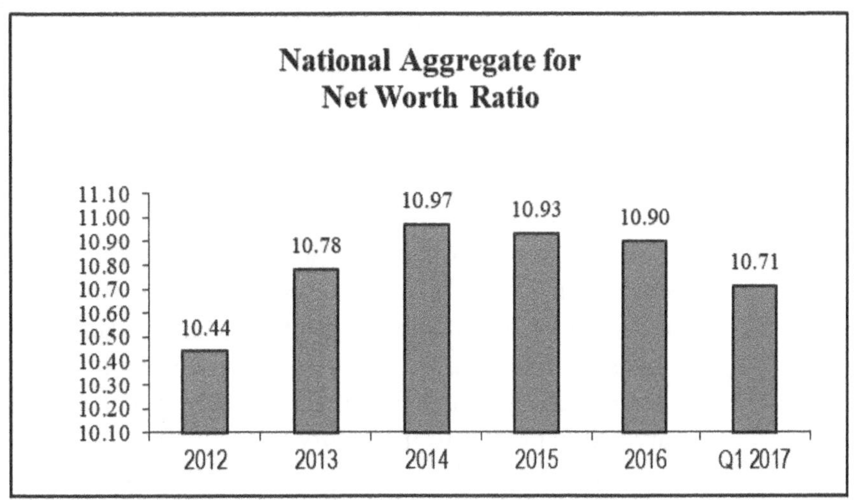

Right Pages

1. **Asset Quality Index** An index that measures the quality of the institution's past underwriting and investment practices, as well as its loss reserve coverage. See the *Critical Ranges In Our Indexes* table for a description of the different critical levels presented in this index.

2. **Nonperforming Loans/ Total Loans** The percentage of the institution's loan portfolio which is either past due on its payments by 90 days or more, or no longer accruing interest due to doubtful collectibility. This ratio is affected primarily by the quality of the institution's underwriting practices and the prosperity of the local economies where it is doing business. While only a portion of these loans will actually end up in default, a high ratio here will have several negative consequences including increased loan loss provisions, increased loan collection expenses, and decreased interest revenues.

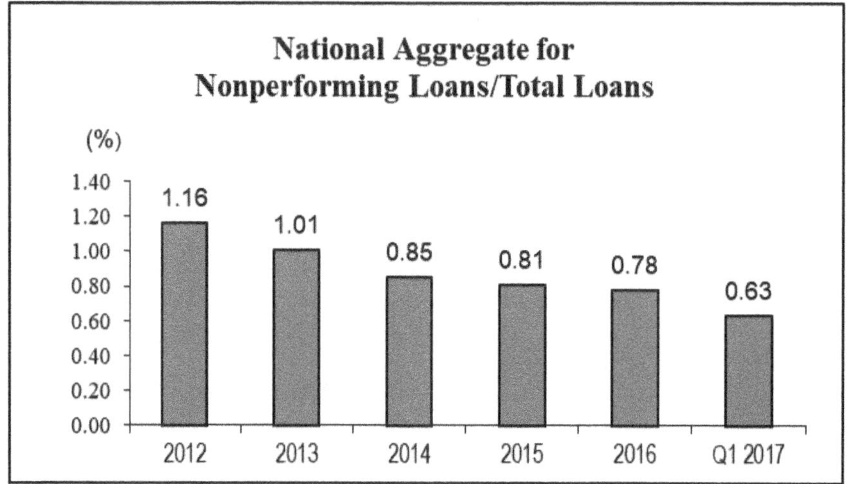

3. **Nonperforming Loans/ Capital** The percentage of past due 90 days and nonaccruing loans to the company's core (tier 1) capital plus reserve for loan losses. This ratio answers the question: If all of the credit union's significantly past due and nonaccruing loans were to go into default, how much would that eat into capital? A large percentage of nonperforming loans signal imprudent lending practices which are a direct threat to the equity of the institution.

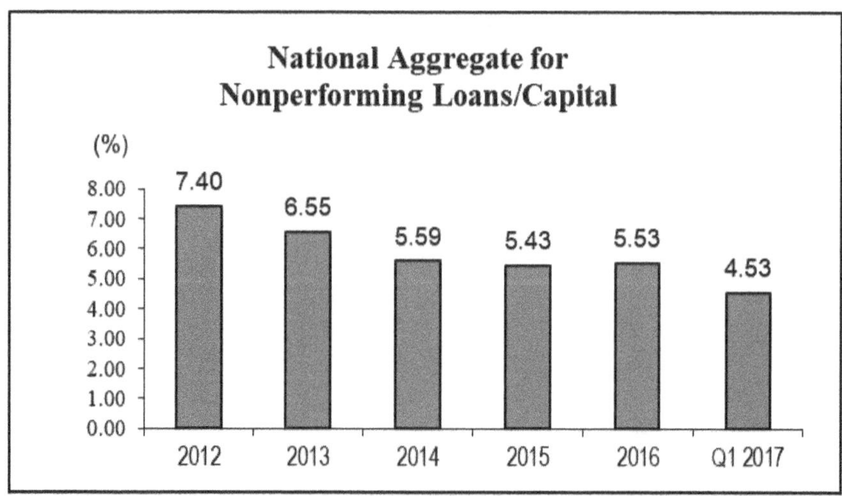

4. Net Charge-offs/ Average Loans The ratio of foreclosed loans written off the institution's books since the beginning of the year (less previous write-offs that were recovered) as a percentage of average loans for the year. This ratio answers the question: What percentage of the credit union's past loans have actually become uncollectible? Past loan charge-off experience is often a very good indication of what can be expected in the future, and high loan charge-off levels are usually an indication of poor underwriting practices.

5. Profitability Index An index that measures the soundness of the institution's operations and the contribution of profits to the company's financial strength. It is based on five sub-factors: 1) gain or loss on operations; 2) rates of return on assets and equity; 3) management of net interest margin; 4) generation of noninterest-based revenues; and 5) overhead expense management. See the Critical Ranges In Our Indexes table for a description of the different critical levels presented in this index.

6. Net Income The year-to-date net profit or loss recorded by the institution, in millions of dollars. This figure includes the company's operating profit (income from lending, investing, and fees less interest and overhead expenses) as well as nonoperating items such as capital gains on the sale of securities, income taxes, and extraordinary items.

7. Return on Assets The ratio of net income for the year (year-to-date quarterly figures are converted to a 12-month equivalent) as a percentage of average assets for the year. This ratio, known as ROA, is the most commonly used benchmark for credit union profitability since it measures the company's return on investment in a format that is easily comparable with other companies.

Historically speaking, a ratio of 1.0% or greater has been considered good performance. However, this ratio will fluctuate with the prevailing economic times. Also, larger credit unions tend to have a lower ratio.

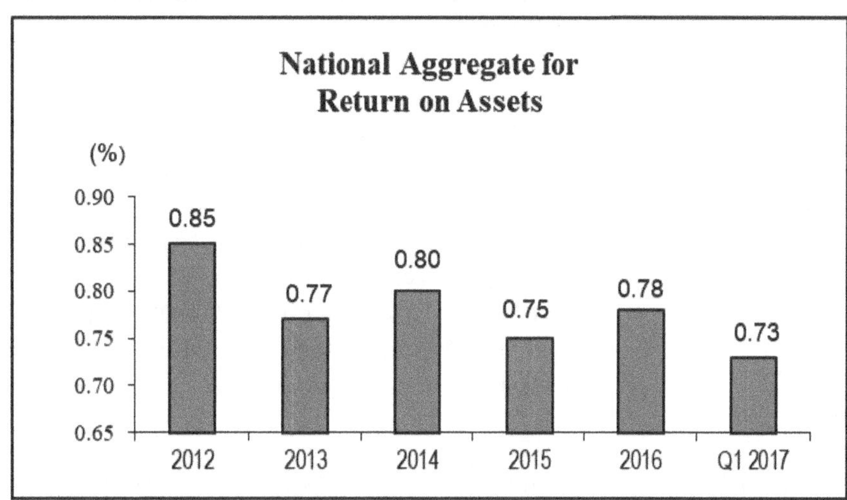

8. Return on Equity

The ratio of net income for the year (year-to-date quarterly figures are converted to a 12-month equivalent) as a percentage of average equity for the year. This ratio, known as ROE, is commonly used by a company's shareholders as a measure of their return on investment. It is not always a good measure of profitability, however, because inadequate equity levels at some institutions can result in unjustly high ROE's.

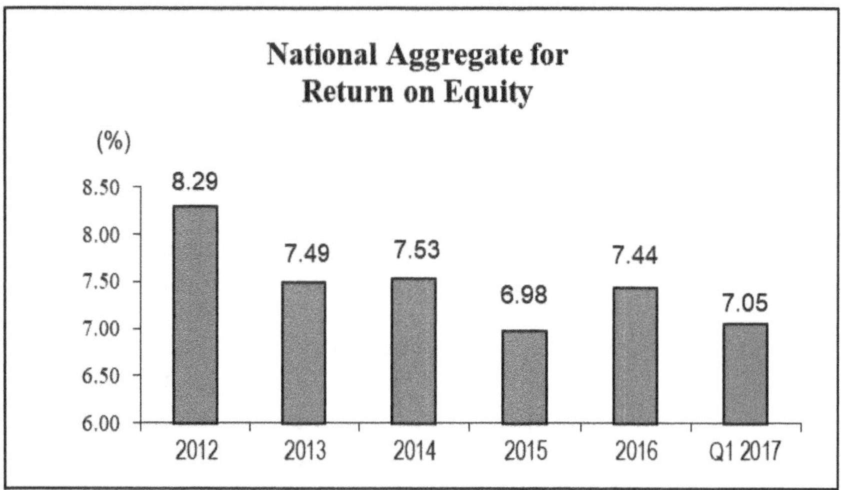

9. Net Interest Spread

The difference between the institution's interest income and interest expense for the year (year-to-date quarterly figures are converted to a 12-month equivalent) as a percentage of its average revenue-generating assets. Since the margin between interest earned and interest paid is generally where the company generates the majority of its income, this figure provides insight into the company's ability to effectively manage interest spreads.

A low Net Interest Spread can be the result of poor loan and deposit pricing, high levels of non-accruing loans, or poor asset/liability management.

10. Overhead Efficiency Ratio

Total overhead expenses as a percentage of total revenues net of interest expense. This is a common measure for evaluating an institution's ability to operate efficiently while keeping a handle on overhead expenses like salaries, rent, and other office expenses. A high ratio suggests that the company's overhead expenses are too high in relation to the amount of revenue they are generating and/or supporting. Conversely, a low ratio means good management of overhead expenses which usually results in a strong Return on Assets as well.

11. Liquidity Index

An index that measures the institution's ability to raise the necessary cash to satisfy creditors and honor depositor withdrawals. It is based on an evaluation of the company's short-term liquidity position, including its existing reliance on less stable deposit sources. See the Critical Ranges In Our Indexes table for a description of the different critical levels presented in this index.

12. Liquidity Ratio The ratio of short-term liquid assets to deposits and short-term borrowings. This ratio answers the question: How many cents can the institution easily raise in cash to cover each dollar on deposit plus pay off its short-term debts? Due to the nature of the business, it is rare (and not expected) for an established credit union to achieve 100% on this ratio. Nevertheless, it serves as a good measure of an institution's liquidity in relation to the rest of the credit union industry.

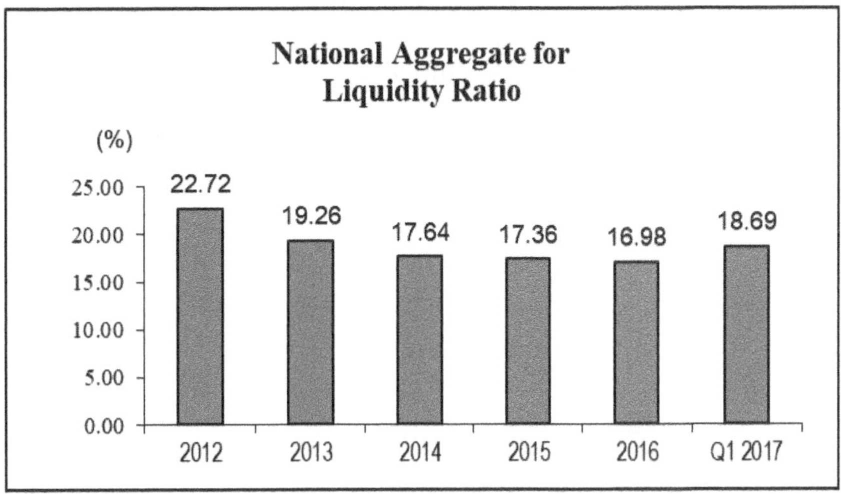

13. Hot Money Ratio The percentage of the institution's deposit base that is being funded by jumbo CDs. Jumbo CDs (high-yield certificates of deposit with principal amounts of at least $100,000) are generally considered less stable (and more costly) and thus less desirable as a source of funds.

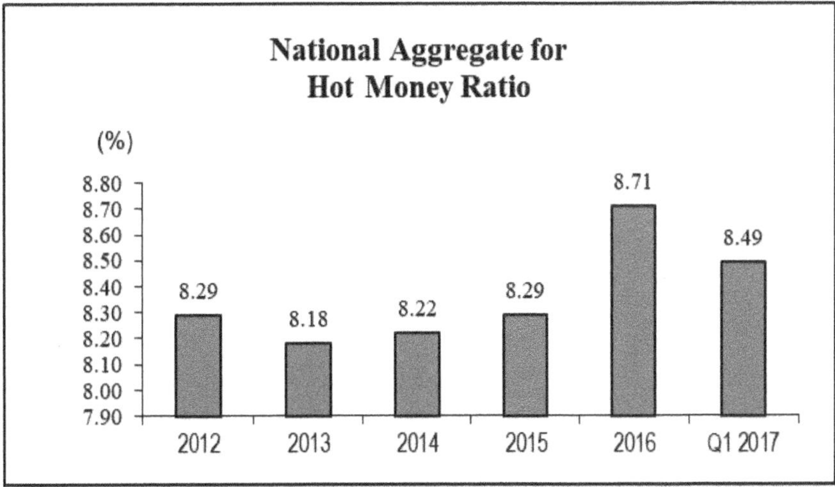

14. Stability Index

An index that integrates a number of factors such as 1) risk diversification in terms of company size and loan diversification; 2) deterioration of operations as reported in critical asset, liability, income and expense items, such as an increase in loan delinquency rates or a sharp increase in loan originations; 3) years in operation; 4) former problem areas where, despite recent improvement, the company has yet to establish a record of stable performance over a suitable period of time; and 5) relationships with affiliates. See the Critical Ranges In Our Indexes table for a description of the different critical levels presented in this index.

Name	City	State	Rating	2016 Rating	2015 Rating	Total Assets ($Mil)	One Year Asset Growth	Asset Mix (As a % of Total Assets) Commercial Loans	Consumer Loans	Mortgage Loans	Securities	Capitalization Index	Net Worth Ratio
1199 SEIU Federal Credit Union	New York	NY	C-	C-	C-	67.3	5.52	0.7	14.0	17.4	59.7	5.7	7.8
▼ 121 Financial Credit Union	Jacksonville	FL	C	C+	B-	573.2	13.65	11.2	39.3	26.5	6.5	7.1	9.1
167th TFR Federal Credit Union	Martinsburg	WV	D+	D+	D+	52.7	5.06	0.0	10.0	11.2	37.1	6.2	8.2
1st Advantage Federal Credit Union	Yorktown	VA	B	B	B	661.9	4.20	5.7	43.2	24.6	1.9	10.0	11.3
1st Bergen Federal Credit Union	Hackensack	NJ	E+	E+	D	3.1	21.45	0.0	57.9	0.0	0.0	5.8	7.8
1st Choice Credit Union	Atlanta	GA	C+	C+	C+	23.6	8.28	0.0	48.5	2.8	21.5	10.0	12.2
▲ 1st Class Express Credit Union	Waukesha	WI	C	C-	C-	2.4	-3.43	0.0	64.1	0.0	0.0	10.0	15.3
1st Community Credit Union	Sparta	WI	B-	B-	B-	145.4	10.04	10.4	22.5	40.1	2.2	8.4	9.9
1st Community Federal Credit Union	San Angelo	TX	C+	C+	B-	246.0	4.46	11.5	36.1	22.2	14.6	7.3	9.2
1st Cooperative Federal Credit Union	Cayce	SC	C	C	C	14.7	7.21	0.0	58.6	0.0	0.0	10.0	13.1
1st Ed Credit Union	Chambersburg	PA	B	B	B	122.7	-1.68	0.2	11.6	8.0	49.6	10.0	13.7
1st Financial Federal Credit Union	Wentzville	MO	C	C	C+	222.2	4.37	0.7	70.5	6.4	4.4	6.4	8.4
1st Gateway Credit Union	Camanche	IA	A-	A-	B+	137.6	6.47	3.6	33.0	40.5	0.3	9.0	10.3
▲ 1st Liberty Federal Credit Union	Great Falls	MT	C	C-	D+	176.0	8.16	1.5	32.5	11.2	35.4	8.6	10.0
1st MidAmerica Credit Union	Bethalto	IL	B+	B+	B+	697.7	4.54	5.9	65.9	11.4	1.1	8.9	10.3
1st Mississippi Federal Credit Union	Meridian	MS	A	A	A	60.8	4.27	0.7	15.0	11.3	0.8	10.0	28.1
1st Northern California Credit Union	Martinez	CA	C+	C+	C+	701.9	4.95	0.0	7.6	20.7	49.6	8.7	10.2
1st Resource Credit Union	Birmingham	AL	B-	B-	B-	36.3	7.47	0.0	40.9	41.2	0.0	8.9	10.3
1st United Services Credit Union	Pleasanton	CA	B-	B-	B-	965.1	10.35	2.5	42.4	25.6	14.3	8.1	10.0
▼ 1st University Credit Union	Waco	TX	E-	E	E	12.5	0.12	0.0	39.8	28.6	0.0	5.1	7.1
1st Valley Credit Union	San Bernardino	CA	C	C	C	40.2	3.89	0.0	17.0	22.6	32.7	8.2	10.4
2 Rivers Area Credit Union	Kankakee	IL	C+	C+	C+	16.9	5.67	0.0	41.1	0.0	0.0	10.0	15.7
20th Century Fox Federal Credit Union	Los Angeles	CA	D	D	D+	48.4	7.02	5.1	9.7	41.3	4.1	5.9	7.9
360 Federal Credit Union	Windsor Locks	CT	C	C	B-	232.5	5.39	6.4	22.6	21.1	14.8	8.3	9.9
▼ 4Front Credit Union	Traverse City	MI	B	B+	B	476.7	9.88	5.7	37.8	24.2	15.0	9.4	10.7
▲ 5 Star Community Credit Union	Mount Pleasant	IA	C-	D+	D+	30.7	8.23	7.2	21.3	30.5	11.7	7.9	9.8
540 I.B.E.W. Credit Union, Inc.	Massillon	OH	C-	C-	C-	<1	23.02	0.0	51.1	0.0	0.0	10.0	15.9
600 Atlantic Federal Credit Union	Boston	MA	B-	B-	B-	28.6	8.09	0.4	15.0	20.0	10.4	10.0	12.2
74th Street Depot Federal Credit Union	Chicago	IL	C-	C-	C-	8.8	2.30	0.0	33.2	0.0	0.0	10.0	22.3
77th Street Depot Federal Credit Union	Chicago	IL	C+	C+	C	18.6	0.76	0.0	25.7	0.0	0.0	10.0	20.2
A & S Federal Credit Union	Aliquippa	PA	B-	B-	B-	28.3	4.96	0.0	10.0	15.4	0.0	10.0	12.3
A H E Plant No 3 Federal Credit Union	Winchester	IN	C+	C+	C+	7.2	1.38	0.0	22.5	0.0	0.0	10.0	17.6
A+ Federal Credit Union	Austin	TX	B+	B+	B+	1335.4	6.47	5.1	37.7	24.8	12.6	7.2	9.2
A.A.E.C. Credit Union	Arlington Heights	IL	B+	B+	B	78.9	4.10	0.0	12.9	8.0	0.5	9.7	10.9
A.B. Federal Credit Union	Altoona	PA	C	C	C	5.6	5.60	0.0	15.8	0.0	0.0	10.0	12.3
A.B.D. Federal Credit Union	Warren	MI	D	D	D-	63.0	5.01	0.0	14.9	5.4	8.1	7.8	9.5
A.C.P.E. Federal Credit Union	Laramie	WY	D+	D+	C-	47.5	4.63	2.2	39.7	16.0	0.0	5.9	7.9
A.E.A. Federal Credit Union	Yuma	AZ	E+	E+	E	260.6	-0.88	7.3	48.4	17.5	0.5	6.0	8.0
A.U.B. Employees' Credit Union	Athens	TN	C-	C-	C-	1.7	0.53	0.0	48.9	0.0	0.0	10.0	22.1
AAA Federal Credit Union	South Bend	IN	C	C	C	61.8	2.79	0.0	16.6	15.2	10.4	10.0	11.1
AAC Credit Union	Grand Rapids	MI	A	A	A	137.6	15.31	3.4	32.1	22.0	10.2	10.0	17.7
AB&W Credit Union Inc.	Alexandria	VA	C+	C+	C	33.2	2.67	0.0	54.6	0.0	0.0	10.0	15.0
Abbeville Community Federal Credit Union	Abbeville	SC	C	C	C	7.9	6.10	0.0	53.3	0.0	0.0	10.0	15.6
Abbey Credit Union	Vandalia	OH	C	C	C	91.3	3.91	7.1	45.9	17.4	13.4	5.9	8.1
Abbott Laboratories Employees CU	Gurnee	IL	A-	A-	B+	786.4	5.50	0.0	12.7	28.4	28.0	9.7	10.8
▼ ABCO Federal Credit Union	Rancocas	NJ	C-	C	C+	230.8	2.12	8.6	20.4	13.3	16.0	5.0	7.1
Aberdeen Federal Credit Union	Aberdeen	SD	A-	A-	A-	129.3	3.48	3.2	42.8	6.3	0.0	10.0	11.6
Aberdeen Proving Ground FCU	Edgewood	MD	B	B	B-	1218.3	8.90	0.4	54.0	15.3	4.3	7.7	9.5
▼ Abilene Federal Credit Union	Abilene	TX	B-	B	B	25.2	-0.12	0.0	50.0	0.0	0.0	10.0	18.0
Abilene Teachers Federal Credit Union	Abilene	TX	B+	B+	B+	430.8	3.33	0.0	50.5	1.1	15.3	10.0	13.6
Able Federal Credit Union	Cresaptown	MD	E+	E+	E+	8.2	-6.35	0.0	48.1	1.1	12.2	5.5	7.5
▼ ABNB Federal Credit Union	Chesapeake	VA	B-	B+	B+	553.7	7.25	5.4	47.6	17.0	1.3	8.1	9.7
Abri Credit Union	Romeoville	IL	C-	C-	C-	325.1	2.08	6.5	16.6	22.2	25.8	6.5	8.8
Abyssinian Baptist Church FCU	New York	NY	D-	D-	D	<1	1.03	0.0	5.4	0.0	0.0	4.7	6.7
Academic Employees Credit Union	Columbia	MO	E+	E+	E	10.2	1.33	0.0	50.6	0.0	0.0	4.1	6.2
Academic Federal Credit Union	Briarcliff Manor	NY	D	D	D-	40.9	-2.27	2.3	20.9	20.2	25.3	5.8	8.2
▼ Acadia Federal Credit Union	Fort Kent	ME	B+	A-	B+	156.0	10.26	14.6	18.6	42.4	3.0	10.0	14.0
Acadian Federal Credit Union	Lafayette	LA	E+	E+	E+	17.2	-2.79	0.0	38.2	7.1	0.0	5.7	7.7
Acadiana Medical Federal Credit Union	Lafayette	LA	D+	D+	D+	11.0	1.37	0.0	29.6	0.0	0.0	10.0	20.0
ACBA Federal Credit Union (3226)	Pittsburgh	PA	C-	C-	C-	4.4	-3.05	0.0	47.4	0.0	0.0	10.0	22.0

Arrows denote recent upgrades ▲ or downgrades ▼

Asset Quality Index	Non-Performing Loans as a % of Total Loans	Non-Performing Loans as a % of Capital	Net Charge-Offs Avg Loans	Profitability Index	Net Income ($Mil)	Return on Assets	Return on Equity	Net Interest Spread	Overhead Efficiency Ratio	Liquidity Index	Liquidity Ratio	Hot Money Ratio	Stability Index
5.4	3.43	13.0	0.32	**3.0**	0.04	0.21	2.71	3.38	89.9	**5.0**	18.1	0.0	**3.6**
6.7	0.56	5.1	0.47	**0.9**	-0.29	-0.20	-2.19	3.88	92.5	**3.8**	14.3	4.2	**5.0**
9.7	0.15	0.4	0.24	**2.0**	0.03	0.24	2.87	2.40	91.4	**6.7**	42.0	0.4	**3.1**
5.8	1.02	10.4	0.96	**3.4**	0.08	0.05	0.43	4.73	82.8	**3.9**	14.3	3.6	**7.4**
0.7	7.98	49.0	3.99	**3.1**	0.00	0.15	1.80	6.10	89.4	**6.2**	45.0	0.0	**3.4**
7.5	0.72	2.9	0.89	**2.2**	-0.02	-0.31	-2.49	5.21	94.8	**5.0**	25.7	3.8	**5.5**
2.5	4.72	21.7	-0.38	**9.7**	0.01	2.16	14.25	7.39	64.3	**3.9**	14.0	0.0	**8.3**
9.0	0.27	2.1	-0.01	**5.5**	0.35	0.96	9.74	3.84	77.5	**3.3**	15.2	8.2	**6.6**
5.3	1.51	11.9	0.51	**2.9**	0.11	0.18	1.94	3.79	89.7	**3.0**	14.7	13.5	**5.4**
8.3	0.12	0.6	0.00	**2.3**	0.00	0.08	0.62	4.03	97.6	**4.5**	31.7	0.8	**7.0**
9.6	0.71	2.1	-0.01	**3.7**	0.17	0.55	4.07	2.29	75.9	**4.7**	29.6	3.2	**7.9**
2.7	2.42	20.4	2.22	**4.6**	0.18	0.32	3.86	5.35	74.2	**2.7**	5.3	6.4	**5.1**
5.9	0.55	11.6	0.35	**7.4**	0.31	0.93	8.96	4.57	72.5	**3.9**	20.4	6.1	**7.5**
9.7	0.29	1.2	0.04	**3.0**	0.30	0.70	6.82	2.80	89.0	**5.4**	35.5	2.3	**6.1**
6.3	0.53	4.1	0.59	**4.3**	0.70	0.41	3.92	4.12	81.2	**2.4**	9.9	13.4	**7.4**
10.0	1.01	1.4	0.85	**6.5**	0.08	0.56	1.95	3.54	83.2	**5.9**	48.4	3.4	**8.0**
10.0	0.03	0.1	0.08	**3.2**	0.44	0.25	2.45	1.68	87.1	**4.4**	24.2	10.0	**7.1**
7.9	0.20	5.0	0.10	**7.8**	0.12	1.30	12.67	4.62	63.2	**1.7**	14.6	20.2	**5.5**
9.5	0.25	2.1	0.37	**3.9**	1.01	0.43	4.34	3.01	79.4	**2.7**	13.8	15.7	**6.5**
1.7	4.11	40.0	1.78	**1.3**	-0.04	-1.35	-18.46	6.16	97.1	**3.8**	9.5	0.9	**0.0**
9.8	0.19	0.9	0.12	**2.6**	0.02	0.23	2.35	2.83	91.6	**4.8**	19.1	7.2	**4.8**
8.9	1.38	3.8	0.39	**3.8**	0.03	0.77	4.99	4.96	86.6	**5.9**	34.4	0.0	**7.0**
7.5	0.02	3.6	0.10	**1.0**	0.01	0.10	1.26	3.10	94.2	**5.0**	27.0	2.2	**2.9**
6.4	1.36	9.9	0.44	**1.3**	-0.22	-0.39	-4.06	3.69	83.9	**4.6**	19.6	3.7	**5.4**
7.7	0.46	3.5	0.32	**3.5**	0.17	0.15	1.36	4.10	89.8	**3.4**	5.5	2.6	**6.9**
6.0	0.25	6.4	0.10	**2.1**	0.01	0.09	0.96	4.05	95.2	**4.5**	18.7	0.4	**4.5**
4.9	4.39	12.6	0.00	**4.8**	0.00	0.85	5.19	4.86	80.0	**6.1**	52.1	0.0	**3.7**
10.0	0.08	0.3	0.25	**3.6**	0.03	0.44	3.57	2.40	79.9	**3.8**	37.2	14.7	**6.6**
9.8	1.38	2.0	1.76	**1.5**	-0.01	-0.23	-1.02	4.49	81.3	**5.4**	20.7	0.0	**5.6**
10.0	1.54	2.0	2.99	**3.4**	0.02	0.43	2.13	4.07	77.9	**4.7**	24.9	8.1	**6.0**
9.7	0.74	1.7	0.00	**3.3**	0.02	0.29	2.30	2.45	89.9	**6.0**	35.9	2.8	**6.9**
9.0	2.01	2.9	1.73	**3.9**	0.01	0.49	2.86	2.49	83.3	**5.9**	38.9	0.0	**8.2**
7.3	0.57	4.9	0.55	**5.1**	2.78	0.84	9.24	3.43	72.5	**3.1**	10.0	8.6	**6.7**
9.6	0.46	1.2	1.04	**5.0**	0.20	1.00	9.29	2.20	54.3	**5.4**	38.0	0.0	**5.6**
10.0	0.00	0.0	0.00	**2.5**	0.00	0.22	1.74	3.08	94.3	**5.7**	25.9	0.0	**6.8**
7.2	2.45	5.3	1.96	**2.8**	0.10	0.64	6.64	3.21	88.9	**7.2**	69.3	2.7	**3.4**
5.8	1.36	10.2	0.29	**2.6**	0.03	0.21	2.67	3.28	85.2	**4.2**	33.8	3.6	**3.8**
1.6	0.85	32.4	0.68	**5.5**	0.20	0.32	9.42	4.42	82.3	**3.4**	15.6	11.5	**4.3**
5.5	2.97	6.4	-1.37	**3.7**	0.00	0.24	1.07	5.92	91.7	**7.0**	64.3	0.0	**3.7**
9.8	0.54	1.9	0.59	**1.4**	0.03	0.17	1.51	3.14	86.7	**5.6**	44.9	1.4	**4.4**
9.5	0.63	2.1	0.35	**9.8**	0.57	1.67	9.44	4.08	62.0	**2.7**	20.0	17.6	**9.7**
5.2	1.12	9.7	0.97	**2.6**	0.04	0.44	2.91	5.94	83.2	**6.4**	40.1	0.0	**6.1**
7.0	1.24	4.7	0.00	**4.0**	0.02	0.83	5.24	6.66	85.3	**5.4**	39.3	3.5	**7.5**
5.1	0.44	5.2	0.43	**3.0**	0.10	0.43	5.45	3.01	82.4	**3.7**	17.0	6.0	**3.3**
10.0	0.14	0.6	0.19	**5.9**	1.56	0.82	7.40	2.50	68.5	**5.6**	40.2	6.5	**8.5**
6.3	1.27	9.8	1.34	**1.7**	0.05	0.09	1.29	3.41	89.0	**4.7**	21.9	1.3	**3.0**
7.0	0.80	5.9	0.26	**7.4**	0.34	1.07	10.25	3.29	69.0	**4.2**	25.0	4.0	**7.9**
5.4	0.75	7.7	0.91	**5.9**	2.60	0.87	10.75	4.42	71.8	**3.8**	16.5	4.3	**6.2**
7.5	0.81	2.2	1.09	**3.1**	-0.09	-1.37	-7.60	3.92	97.6	**4.8**	35.0	3.1	**6.8**
7.2	0.54	3.9	0.38	**4.6**	0.78	0.73	5.40	3.77	74.9	**3.7**	21.0	13.9	**7.5**
5.0	0.83	5.8	0.36	**1.0**	-0.01	-0.29	-3.90	3.67	102.7	**5.2**	41.8	0.0	**1.9**
6.1	0.56	5.0	1.69	**1.2**	-1.32	-0.96	-9.69	4.33	90.2	**3.6**	18.5	11.3	**5.8**
9.4	0.32	2.0	0.20	**2.5**	0.22	0.27	3.15	3.34	89.4	**4.2**	10.7	1.7	**5.1**
10.0	0.00	0.0	0.00	**1.0**	0.00	0.00	0.00	1.15	100.0	**7.2**	71.3	0.0	**1.0**
4.8	1.03	9.2	-0.07	**4.3**	0.02	0.76	12.32	5.22	87.2	**5.2**	27.1	0.0	**1.0**
4.7	1.85	15.2	1.12	**1.1**	-0.04	-0.38	-4.90	3.76	94.8	**4.5**	27.3	10.1	**1.6**
5.5	1.61	9.3	0.32	**5.0**	0.21	0.53	3.73	3.72	75.5	**3.6**	24.7	9.0	**8.6**
4.9	1.71	15.3	0.29	**1.1**	0.00	-0.02	-0.30	3.74	103.2	**4.9**	34.1	5.5	**1.0**
10.0	0.44	0.9	0.17	**0.8**	0.00	-0.07	-0.36	3.19	98.1	**6.0**	38.9	0.0	**6.2**
7.2	1.23	2.7	3.71	**2.7**	0.00	0.00	0.00	7.68	76.2	**4.3**	26.4	0.0	**5.6**

Name	City	State	Rating	2016 Rating	2015 Rating	Total Assets ($Mil)	One Year Asset Growth	Asset Mix (As a % of Total Assets) Commercial Loans	Consumer Loans	Mortgage Loans	Securities	Capitalization Index	Net Worth Ratio
Accentra Credit Union	Austin	MN	**C+**	C+	C+	131.7	4.97	3.4	42.1	17.2	4.1	**7.2**	9.1
▼ Access Community Credit Union	Amarillo	TX	**B-**	B+	B+	117.2	5.32	0.0	60.8	0.3	1.0	**10.0**	14.0
Access Credit Union	Broadview	IL	**C-**	C-	C-	50.8	-0.62	1.4	20.0	13.0	8.1	**10.0**	12.0
Access Federal Credit Union	Clinton	NY	**B-**	B-	B-	168.2	5.12	8.9	17.2	11.8	25.8	**6.0**	8.0
Access of Louisiana Federal Credit Union	Sulphur	LA	**D+**	D+	C	29.9	5.61	0.0	29.3	25.6	13.5	**10.0**	13.3
Acclaim Federal Credit Union	Greensboro	NC	**C**	C	C+	40.8	6.84	0.1	56.9	5.5	0.0	**7.6**	9.4
ACE Credit Union	Mason City	IA	**C**	C	C	9.8	-0.88	0.0	14.9	0.0	31.6	**10.0**	11.4
Achieva Credit Union	Dunedin	FL	**A-**	A-	A-	1524.4	7.93	6.6	45.5	19.7	1.0	**9.8**	10.9
Achieve Financial Credit Union	Berlin	CT	**C**	C	C+	133.7	3.60	0.0	27.8	22.0	7.5	**5.3**	7.4
ACIPCO Federal Credit Union	Birmingham	AL	**A**	A	A-	149.0	1.51	0.0	22.7	47.5	9.7	**10.0**	13.4
Acme Continental Credit Union	Riverdale	IL	**B**	B	B	45.8	1.71	0.0	34.8	0.2	11.1	**10.0**	17.5
ACME Federal Credit Union	Eastlake	OH	**D+**	D+	C-	14.4	5.53	0.4	20.0	10.7	0.0	**10.0**	17.5
ACMG Federal Credit Union	Solvay	NY	**C**	C	C-	62.3	6.17	0.0	35.6	10.7	10.5	**5.5**	7.5
Actors Federal Credit Union	New York	NY	**B+**	B+	B+	229.7	-0.32	9.2	5.7	28.1	0.0	**5.1**	7.1
ACU Credit Union	Abilene	TX	**C-**	C-	C-	6.3	-3.17	0.0	55.4	0.0	0.0	**10.0**	17.9
ACUME Credit Union	Moorestown	NJ	**D**	D	D-	4.6	2.93	0.0	14.6	24.3	2.4	**6.1**	8.2
Acushnet Federal Credit Union	Acushnet Center	MA	**D+**	D+	C	23.3	4.88	0.0	10.9	26.2	49.0	**6.9**	8.9
Adams County Credit Union	Monroe	IN	**C+**	C+	C+	19.0	1.72	54.9	1.1	44.0	0.0	**10.0**	19.3
▼ Adirondack Regional Federal Credit Union	Tupper Lake	NY	**C-**	C	C	47.0	7.74	0.2	22.3	18.6	15.1	**5.6**	7.6
ADM Credit Union	Decatur	IL	**C+**	C+	C+	17.3	5.47	0.0	56.7	0.0	0.0	**10.0**	14.7
▲ Advance Financial Federal Credit Union	Schererville	IN	**D+**	D	D	144.4	-1.83	0.0	46.9	18.7	22.1	**5.9**	8.0
▲ Advanced Financial Federal Credit Union	New Providence	NJ	**C**	C-	D+	96.4	25.74	9.0	5.7	22.5	34.4	**7.6**	9.4
Advancial Federal Credit Union	Dallas	TX	**B**	B	B	1431.1	10.50	11.4	33.1	33.6	1.9	**6.6**	8.6
Advantage Credit Union	Newton	IA	**A-**	A-	A-	68.5	5.77	4.9	18.8	11.4	12.7	**10.0**	15.3
Advantage Credit Union, Inc.	Mansfield	OH	**D**	D	D-	37.4	-2.38	1.7	35.0	19.1	20.3	**5.6**	7.9
Advantage Federal Credit Union	Rochester	NY	**B+**	B+	B+	302.4	21.24	0.0	46.5	9.4	19.5	**6.9**	9.2
▼ Advantage Financial Federal Credit Union	Washington	DC	**D**	D+	D+	113.4	4.21	0.0	29.8	18.8	25.6	**8.3**	10.1
Advantage One Credit Union	Morrison	IL	**D+**	D+	C	21.0	1.31	0.0	33.5	18.5	0.0	**9.2**	10.4
▼ Advantage One Credit Union	Brownstown	MI	**B**	B+	B	142.1	8.03	6.7	34.5	9.6	24.7	**8.0**	9.7
▼ Advantage Plus Federal Credit Union	Pocatello	ID	**C+**	B-	B-	133.0	9.59	1.7	28.1	22.3	0.6	**6.3**	8.3
AdvantagePlus of Indiana FCU	Terre Haute	IN	**B-**	B-	B-	23.4	8.75	0.0	50.7	0.0	0.0	**10.0**	15.8
Advantis Credit Union	Clackamas	OR	**B+**	B+	A-	1371.3	8.87	9.8	29.3	25.0	3.1	**9.3**	10.5
Adventure Credit Union	Grand Rapids	MI	**B+**	B+	B+	363.2	22.09	5.5	28.1	40.6	4.6	**10.0**	12.8
Advia Credit Union	Parchment	MI	**A-**	A-	A-	1383.9	16.76	9.0	39.9	29.0	10.6	**10.0**	11.7
AE Goetze Employees Credit Union	Lake City	MN	**D-**	D-	D	4.5	-6.10	0.0	64.1	0.0	0.0	**8.6**	10.1
Aegis Credit Union	Clinton	IA	**C+**	C+	B-	14.1	2.75	0.0	76.9	0.0	0.0	**10.0**	12.3
▲ Aero Federal Credit Union	Glendale	AZ	**C-**	D+	C-	239.7	7.66	0.0	43.4	0.2	22.2	**10.0**	13.5
▲ Aeroquip Credit Union	Jackson	MI	**B-**	C+	B-	46.3	2.06	0.3	21.5	25.8	36.4	**10.0**	14.4
Aerospace Federal Credit Union	El Segundo	CA	**C+**	C+	C+	379.9	1.79	0.3	6.6	8.5	70.7	**7.3**	9.7
Afena Federal Credit Union	Marion	IN	**C+**	C+	C+	60.9	5.09	0.0	50.2	9.5	2.6	**7.8**	9.5
Affiliated Trades Credit Union	Collegeville	PA	**C**	C	C-	29.3	3.50	0.4	10.9	5.7	41.8	**10.0**	11.6
Affinity Credit Union	Des Moines	IA	**B**	B	C+	98.9	2.01	2.7	53.9	18.5	0.0	**8.4**	9.9
Affinity Federal Credit Union	Basking Ridge	NJ	**C+**	C+	C	2739.7	11.19	18.5	11.2	57.1	6.4	**6.2**	8.4
Affinity First Federal Credit Union	Minot	ND	**A-**	A-	A-	52.2	0.06	1.2	18.0	14.9	1.1	**10.0**	12.4
Affinity One Federal Credit Union	Jamestown	NY	**C-**	C-	D+	34.8	3.73	0.0	19.7	29.4	24.3	**10.0**	13.3
Affinity Plus Federal Credit Union	Saint Paul	MN	**B**	B	B-	2010.1	8.99	0.1	39.8	26.2	1.1	**6.7**	8.7
AFGM Enterprises Federal Credit Union	Cheektowaga	NY	**C**	C	C	11.8	0.92	0.0	28.0	19.1	0.0	**10.0**	22.2
▲ AFL-CIO Employees Federal Credit Union	Washington	DC	**D**	D-	D-	53.7	0.30	0.0	23.4	26.4	18.3	**8.3**	9.9
AFLAC Federal Credit Union	Columbus	GA	**B+**	B+	B	196.1	1.44	0.0	3.8	0.0	65.8	**10.0**	16.0
Agassiz Federal Credit Union	Crookston	MN	**D**	D	D	14.0	2.71	19.0	13.4	23.0	0.0	**5.9**	7.9
Agility Financial Credit Union	Memphis	TN	**D+**	D+	D	10.2	-6.43	0.0	30.7	0.4	0.0	**9.0**	10.3
Agriculture Federal Credit Union	Washington	DC	**B-**	B-	B-	289.2	6.22	5.4	22.0	24.8	25.7	**10.0**	11.7
Air Academy Federal Credit Union	Colorado Springs	CO	**C+**	C+	C+	565.3	9.06	0.7	45.9	32.5	3.1	**6.0**	8.1
Air Force Federal Credit Union	San Antonio	TX	**C**	C	C-	385.6	2.93	0.2	58.1	11.8	5.4	**6.0**	8.0
Air Tech Credit Union	Milwaukee	WI	**C-**	C-	C-	3.4	-8.58	0.0	41.8	0.0	0.0	**10.0**	17.6
▼ Airco Federal Credit Union	Glendale	CA	**C-**	C	C	14.1	-6.19	0.0	15.6	0.0	0.0	**8.8**	10.2
Akron Federal Credit Union	Akron	CO	**D-**	D-	E+	<1	12.09	0.0	25.1	0.0	0.0	**6.2**	8.2
Akron Firefighters Credit Union	Akron	OH	**D-**	D-	D-	29.4	57.06	1.1	36.7	5.1	9.5	**6.0**	8.0
Akron Municipal Employee's Credit Union	Akron	OH	**D+**	D+	D+	6.1	2.43	0.0	30.9	0.0	36.9	**8.0**	9.7
Akron School Employees FCU	Akron	NY	**C-**	C-	D+	<1	2.56	0.0	63.5	0.0	20.6	**10.0**	17.2

Asset Quality Index	Non-Performing Loans as a % of Total Loans	Non-Performing Loans as a % of Capital	Net Charge-Offs Avg Loans	Profitability Index	Net Income ($Mil)	Return on Assets	Return on Equity	Net Interest Spread	Overhead Efficiency Ratio	Liquidity Index	Liquidity Ratio	Hot Money Ratio	Stability Index
6.4	0.85	7.8	0.32	**3.7**	0.16	0.48	5.50	3.40	83.9	**3.4**	6.2	2.0	**5.5**
8.5	0.39	2.1	0.12	**2.0**	-0.02	-0.08	-0.56	3.29	100.8	**2.6**	23.6	16.4	**8.1**
9.9	0.39	1.3	0.12	**1.1**	0.01	0.04	0.33	3.48	93.9	**4.8**	26.5	1.3	**4.5**
7.1	0.81	5.7	0.18	**3.8**	0.21	0.50	6.54	3.08	85.7	**4.6**	21.4	2.9	**5.1**
9.6	0.31	1.4	0.04	**2.0**	0.03	0.46	3.45	3.52	89.9	**4.5**	21.5	4.9	**6.3**
4.0	1.53	13.8	0.70	**5.5**	0.09	0.93	9.80	5.40	83.0	**3.8**	21.8	5.0	**4.7**
10.0	0.00	0.0	0.00	**2.6**	0.01	0.29	2.51	2.36	80.0	**7.3**	55.2	0.0	**6.1**
5.4	0.65	7.9	0.73	**6.1**	3.47	0.93	9.62	4.05	70.3	**4.0**	18.9	5.4	**7.6**
6.2	1.35	12.4	0.36	**3.4**	0.10	0.29	3.90	4.60	88.8	**4.3**	17.7	4.0	**4.4**
8.3	0.29	3.9	0.17	**7.3**	0.74	2.00	16.63	3.79	43.5	**2.5**	18.9	19.9	**8.5**
8.8	1.35	3.7	0.72	**4.2**	0.04	0.37	2.11	4.44	85.8	**5.6**	31.0	1.8	**6.2**
9.4	1.46	2.7	0.50	**1.2**	0.00	-0.06	-0.32	3.12	101.7	**6.0**	61.1	0.0	**6.5**
6.7	0.78	5.7	0.13	**4.8**	0.15	0.98	12.93	4.58	88.0	**4.6**	22.1	2.2	**3.0**
2.7	5.95	28.5	3.65	**1.7**	-0.36	-0.62	-8.77	2.57	74.6	**6.3**	45.3	3.5	**4.5**
8.6	0.60	1.8	0.34	**3.9**	0.01	0.51	2.85	2.82	79.6	**4.8**	32.3	0.0	**7.3**
10.0	0.19	1.1	0.00	**1.9**	0.00	0.00	0.00	3.76	100.0	**6.7**	57.2	0.0	**3.3**
8.3	0.09	0.4	0.00	**1.1**	-0.02	-0.33	-3.67	2.16	96.2	**4.5**	15.5	2.4	**3.7**
4.7	2.09	6.0	-0.07	**6.6**	0.05	1.16	5.94	3.08	50.9	**5.9**	50.1	3.3	**8.2**
8.5	0.31	1.7	0.61	**2.5**	-0.03	-0.30	-3.80	3.57	95.9	**5.4**	31.9	0.5	**3.5**
8.3	0.39	1.5	0.36	**3.5**	0.00	-0.02	-0.16	4.00	92.2	**5.3**	31.8	1.3	**6.6**
4.8	1.66	15.0	1.18	**1.9**	0.20	0.56	8.78	3.60	75.2	**3.1**	11.0	8.0	**2.9**
3.7	3.20	23.2	0.30	**3.4**	0.08	0.35	3.73	3.49	85.8	**5.2**	31.4	5.6	**3.5**
6.9	0.45	4.9	0.54	**4.4**	1.64	0.47	5.36	2.93	75.0	**2.8**	16.0	15.1	**6.1**
6.8	1.40	4.8	2.10	**6.4**	0.09	0.54	3.49	3.67	63.6	**4.8**	27.1	2.5	**7.5**
6.9	0.23	3.3	0.50	**1.0**	0.00	0.04	0.56	2.71	94.7	**4.1**	17.2	2.8	**2.7**
6.8	0.58	4.7	0.58	**5.7**	0.69	0.93	10.41	3.65	74.3	**2.4**	4.4	13.6	**5.9**
5.8	2.93	14.8	0.64	**0.8**	-0.16	-0.55	-5.51	3.38	96.8	**4.1**	27.3	7.4	**5.4**
7.3	0.46	2.4	0.41	**2.6**	0.02	0.47	4.40	4.43	87.6	**5.3**	34.0	1.1	**3.7**
6.9	0.93	5.7	0.95	**3.2**	-0.12	-0.33	-3.34	4.21	92.4	**4.2**	17.5	2.4	**6.0**
4.6	1.82	19.8	0.22	**3.2**	0.07	0.22	2.64	3.94	96.5	**3.6**	15.5	11.7	**5.3**
5.7	1.79	7.6	1.12	**7.8**	0.08	1.39	8.56	4.76	73.1	**4.5**	26.1	1.0	**5.7**
8.2	0.37	2.8	0.54	**5.1**	2.00	0.59	5.59	3.43	69.6	**4.0**	18.8	7.7	**8.2**
8.5	0.55	3.6	0.46	**2.1**	-0.18	-0.21	-1.62	3.54	97.2	**3.4**	11.2	7.1	**6.7**
6.4	0.95	7.3	0.60	**6.1**	2.97	0.87	7.81	3.79	74.0	**3.2**	9.0	6.3	**7.9**
2.1	2.84	20.6	3.97	**1.1**	-0.04	-3.92	-39.91	5.95	93.2	**4.6**	22.6	0.0	**3.1**
4.8	1.22	8.2	0.00	**8.2**	0.05	1.37	11.00	4.69	74.8	**4.0**	14.3	0.0	**6.8**
9.7	0.29	1.7	0.25	**1.3**	0.06	0.10	0.72	3.23	90.2	**4.4**	23.6	2.5	**7.4**
9.9	0.16	1.4	0.13	**4.3**	0.10	0.88	6.05	3.40	91.7	**4.7**	18.8	0.9	**6.5**
10.0	0.01	0.0	0.25	**3.0**	0.33	0.35	3.81	1.72	79.0	**4.8**	13.3	2.0	**5.8**
6.5	0.56	3.6	0.36	**4.6**	0.07	0.45	4.64	4.31	82.3	**3.5**	23.4	7.4	**4.5**
3.7	7.67	27.6	0.07	**1.9**	0.00	0.01	0.12	2.12	99.3	**4.3**	20.9	5.7	**5.1**
4.7	0.98	7.7	0.40	**9.2**	0.39	1.62	16.29	4.79	69.8	**3.8**	17.7	5.9	**5.3**
6.7	0.60	6.9	0.15	**3.8**	3.78	0.55	6.66	3.12	81.8	**2.6**	3.2	5.7	**6.0**
8.2	0.53	2.7	0.33	**7.3**	0.19	1.46	11.90	4.08	65.9	**3.4**	28.8	19.6	**6.2**
9.0	0.67	3.1	0.50	**0.1**	-0.07	-0.76	-5.60	4.00	103.4	**4.2**	17.1	1.2	**6.5**
6.9	0.54	5.9	0.47	**5.7**	3.44	0.70	7.95	3.67	78.8	**2.9**	9.8	6.4	**6.6**
9.8	0.66	1.6	0.38	**2.3**	0.00	0.14	0.61	2.80	87.3	**4.8**	30.9	0.0	**6.7**
9.3	0.19	1.0	0.11	**0.7**	-0.01	-0.11	-1.06	4.02	102.2	**5.1**	29.2	2.9	**3.9**
7.4	7.67	7.2	-0.07	**5.1**	0.41	0.84	5.25	1.99	51.5	**5.8**	20.4	0.0	**8.5**
7.6	0.52	3.1	0.00	**1.7**	0.01	0.23	2.91	3.46	94.3	**6.2**	43.0	0.8	**3.1**
9.2	0.60	1.8	0.59	**0.5**	-0.01	-0.43	-4.17	3.26	107.7	**5.1**	14.9	0.1	**4.9**
8.5	0.53	2.8	0.29	**3.0**	0.16	0.22	1.96	2.84	86.2	**3.4**	18.1	11.7	**7.4**
6.5	0.23	5.8	0.61	**3.4**	0.50	0.36	4.40	3.42	78.8	**3.8**	13.2	5.0	**5.8**
7.0	0.34	3.7	0.74	**2.5**	0.08	0.08	1.18	3.29	92.9	**3.0**	22.1	13.8	**3.0**
9.1	0.79	2.0	0.00	**1.0**	0.00	-0.24	-1.33	3.43	108.3	**5.3**	22.3	0.0	**6.5**
10.0	0.58	1.0	-0.62	**2.2**	0.00	0.00	0.00	2.08	100.0	**4.4**	14.2	12.0	**4.4**
4.6	2.20	19.0	0.00	**5.3**	0.00	1.40	16.90	4.79	70.0	**4.6**	24.2	0.0	**1.7**
5.5	0.47	2.7	0.24	**1.6**	0.01	0.18	2.21	4.18	95.3	**6.4**	42.0	2.1	**1.8**
7.7	1.04	3.8	0.00	**2.7**	0.00	0.14	1.37	4.51	94.9	**6.3**	39.6	0.0	**4.9**
8.5	0.00	0.0	0.00	**4.2**	0.00	0.93	5.30	3.92	71.4	**4.9**	22.7	0.0	**5.8**

Name	City	State	Rating	2016 Rating	2015 Rating	Total Assets ($Mil)	One Year Asset Growth	Asset Mix (As a % of Total Assets) Comm-ercial Loans	Cons-umer Loans	Mort-gage Loans	Secur-ities	Capital-ization Index	Net Worth Ratio
▼ AL GAR Federal Credit Union	Cumberland	MD	D+	C-	D+	34.4	1.32	0.0	32.1	10.5	9.6	10.0	16.6
▼ Alabama Central Credit Union	Birmingham	AL	C	C+	C	142.3	4.06	1.2	47.2	17.5	3.5	7.0	9.0
Alabama Credit Union	Tuscaloosa	AL	B+	B+	A-	766.5	8.72	5.3	14.6	25.5	38.8	8.0	9.9
▲ Alabama Law Enforcement Credit Union	Birmingham	AL	B-	C+	C	11.5	21.64	0.0	65.2	0.0	0.0	10.0	14.8
▲ Alabama One Credit Union	Tuscaloosa	AL	E+	E	E-	607.6	3.11	2.4	15.4	21.3	32.6	6.5	9.0
Alabama Postal Credit Union	Birmingham	AL	C+	C+	C+	8.0	-1.83	0.0	32.8	0.0	0.0	10.0	28.6
Alabama River Credit Union	Monroeville	AL	C+	C+	C	19.0	4.55	0.0	22.7	0.0	31.8	10.0	11.2
Alabama Rural Electric Credit Union	Montgomery	AL	C+	C+	C+	32.4	-2.82	5.5	41.7	0.0	0.0	10.0	11.5
Alabama State Employees Credit Union	Montgomery	AL	B	B	C+	258.1	6.08	2.9	40.0	10.5	23.1	10.0	11.0
▼ Alabama Teachers Credit Union	Gadsden	AL	B+	A-	A-	286.0	8.18	14.1	24.2	38.8	10.7	10.0	12.5
Alaska Air Group Federal Credit Union	Seatac	WA	C	C	C	69.9	11.59	0.0	19.3	9.4	19.5	10.0	14.6
Alaska District Engineers FCU	JBER	AK	D	D	D	14.0	0.75	0.0	13.5	22.1	18.4	5.3	7.3
Alaska USA Federal Credit Union	Anchorage	AK	B-	B-	B-	6802.9	6.66	8.7	63.4	10.8	4.7	6.6	9.5
Alatrust Credit Union	Birmingham	AL	B-	B-	B-	135.4	0.32	3.7	19.3	24.7	31.5	10.0	12.7
Alba Golden Federal Credit Union	Alba	TX	B	B	B	13.6	10.09	0.0	33.8	0.0	0.0	10.0	15.4
Albany City Lodge K of P 540 FCU	Albany	NY	D	D	D	1.6	-2.64	0.0	21.5	0.0	0.0	10.0	15.6
Albany Firemens Federal Credit Union	Albany	NY	C	C	C-	19.2	30.11	0.0	41.7	1.7	0.0	10.0	12.0
Albion School Employees FCU	Albion	NY	D+	D+	D+	2.2	-1.20	0.0	38.9	0.0	0.0	10.0	18.1
Alco Federal Credit Union	Wellsville	NY	B	B	B-	28.7	7.70	0.0	44.4	5.9	0.0	10.0	14.0
Alcoa Community Federal Credit Union	Benton	AR	C	C	D	42.8	2.65	0.0	48.0	4.3	30.2	9.9	10.9
▼ Alcoa Municipal Employees FCU	Alcoa	TN	D	D+	D	5.8	1.16	0.0	38.9	0.0	0.0	9.4	10.6
ALCOA Pittsburgh Federal Credit Union	Pittsburgh	PA	C	C	C	36.5	2.63	0.0	17.2	10.9	0.5	9.4	10.6
Alcoa Tenn Federal Credit Union	Alcoa	TN	B	B	C+	222.3	7.38	1.1	23.6	32.4	22.6	8.8	10.4
▼ Alcon Employees Federal Credit Union	Fort Worth	TX	B-	B	B-	28.6	-6.29	0.0	33.1	13.6	0.0	10.0	20.2
Alcose Credit Union	White Oak	PA	C-	C-	D+	17.1	0.51	0.2	29.5	2.9	0.0	10.0	13.3
▼ Alden Credit Union	Chicopee	MA	C-	C	C+	164.1	14.33	7.3	26.9	30.3	24.3	4.9	7.9
Aldersgate Federal Credit Union	Marion	IL	C+	C+	C+	5.2	15.78	0.0	85.2	0.0	0.0	10.0	11.6
Alderson FCI Federal Credit Union	Alderson	WV	C-	C-	C-	7.9	5.54	0.0	64.2	0.0	0.0	10.0	13.0
ALEC Federal Credit Union	Baton Rouge	LA	C	C	C	8.6	5.40	0.0	18.5	0.0	0.0	10.0	20.3
Alexandria Municipal Employees CU	Alexandria	LA	B-	B-	B-	22.7	4.42	0.0	31.1	10.5	0.0	10.0	12.8
Alexandria Schools Employees CU	Alexandria	MN	C	C	C	4.1	-2.40	0.0	56.3	0.0	0.0	10.0	22.9
Alexandria T&P Federal Credit Union	Alexandria	LA	C	C	C	8.0	2.31	0.0	40.3	0.0	0.0	10.0	14.9
▼ Alhambra Credit Union	Phoenix	AZ	D+	C-	C-	24.9	11.10	0.0	57.2	3.0	0.0	7.0	9.0
Align Credit Union	Lowell	MA	C-	C-	C-	606.3	8.85	6.4	9.6	43.6	29.2	10.0	11.5
Aliquippa Teachers Federal Credit Union	Aliquippa	PA	C	C	C-	<1	0.64	0.0	36.7	0.0	0.0	10.0	27.2
▲ Alive Credit Union	Jacksonville	FL	C	C-	D+	133.8	5.27	0.4	42.3	3.4	18.0	10.0	14.1
All Saints Catholic Federal Credit Union	Fort Worth	TX	D+	D+	D	<1	-2.23	0.0	32.2	0.0	0.0	10.0	18.5
All Saints Federal Credit Union	Garfield Heights	OH	C+	C+	C-	22.1	-5.97	0.0	16.9	17.4	6.1	10.0	18.6
All Souls Federal Credit Union	New York	NY	D	D	D	<1	-11.72	0.0	0.9	0.0	65.0	10.0	13.7
▲ AllCom Credit Union	Worcester	MA	B	B-	B-	68.8	-0.90	0.0	11.9	27.9	13.2	10.0	15.3
Allegacy Federal Credit Union	Winston-Salem	NC	B+	B+	B+	1295.4	6.71	8.2	27.4	18.5	5.4	8.5	10.0
▲ Allegan Community Federal Credit Union	Allegan	MI	C+	C	C-	34.8	4.42	0.4	36.0	12.3	0.0	10.0	11.6
Allegany County Teachers FCU	La Vale	MD	B	B	B	103.6	2.57	0.8	42.4	19.8	11.1	9.5	10.7
Allegany First Federal Credit Union	Fillmore	NY	D+	D+	C-	14.8	7.46	0.0	21.0	6.4	0.0	7.6	9.4
Allegent Community Federal Credit Union	Pittsburgh	PA	C-	C-	C	158.9	0.25	0.5	35.9	21.5	24.0	10.0	11.3
Allegheny Central Employees FCU	Dunbar	PA	D+	D+	D+	5.7	0.73	0.0	44.1	6.1	0.0	9.2	10.5
Allegheny Health Services Employees FCU	Pittsburgh	PA	D	D	D	12.9	5.78	0.0	17.3	0.0	9.6	6.3	8.3
Allegheny Kiski Postal FCU	New Kensington	PA	D	D	D	15.6	-1.51	0.0	20.5	5.7	0.0	10.0	16.3
Allegheny Ludlum Brackenridge FCU	Brackenridge	PA	C+	C+	C+	21.3	-3.35	0.0	19.5	0.0	0.0	10.0	17.5
Allegheny Metal Federal Credit Union	Leechburg	PA	C+	C+	B-	13.6	0.07	0.0	30.8	0.0	0.0	10.0	15.3
Allegheny Valley Federal Credit Union	Pittsburgh	PA	C-	C-	C-	12.2	-2.90	0.0	22.3	0.0	0.0	10.0	27.5
Allegiance Credit Union	Oklahoma City	OK	C+	C+	C+	263.1	0.43	2.4	41.2	16.8	9.6	6.1	8.2
Allegius Federal Credit Union	Burns Harbor	IN	C+	C+	B-	172.7	1.89	0.0	26.7	6.5	36.5	8.7	10.4
Allen Hospital Personnel Credit Union	Waterloo	IA	C-	C-	C-	5.8	3.63	0.0	70.8	0.0	0.0	10.0	17.4
Allentown Federal Credit Union	Allentown	PA	B	B	B	64.9	8.29	0.0	11.5	34.8	0.0	10.0	11.5
Alliance Blackstone Valley FCU	Pawtucket	RI	D-	D-	D	32.4	-4.51	1.3	25.1	18.5	14.5	6.2	8.2
Alliance Catholic Credit Union	Southfield	MI	A	A	A-	455.3	3.86	14.0	11.2	23.1	47.1	9.8	11.3
Alliance Credit Union	San Jose	CA	B-	B-	B	429.2	10.05	0.3	44.0	29.6	3.5	6.0	8.0
Alliance Credit Union	Fenton	MO	B	B	B	253.8	9.86	8.9	20.1	53.4	0.0	7.2	9.2
Alliance Credit Union	Lubbock	TX	B	B	B	234.2	1.80	17.4	30.1	32.1	25.7	10.0	15.0

Asset Quality Index	Non-Performing Loans as a % of Total Loans	Non-Performing Loans as a % of Capital	Net Charge-Offs Avg Loans	Profitability Index	Net Income ($Mil)	Return on Assets	Return on Equity	Net Interest Spread	Overhead Efficiency Ratio	Liquidity Index	Liquidity Ratio	Hot Money Ratio	Stability Index
8.7	0.57	1.9	1.33	**0.2**	-0.06	-0.65	-3.83	3.25	102.6	**5.1**	33.1	1.1	**6.5**
3.9	0.79	19.1	1.13	**1.9**	-0.10	-0.28	-3.42	4.88	83.6	**4.0**	19.1	4.4	**4.9**
9.0	0.50	3.7	0.24	**4.7**	0.91	0.48	4.94	2.94	84.8	**4.7**	34.0	9.4	**7.6**
7.5	0.52	2.4	0.30	**10.0**	0.11	3.80	25.82	6.96	52.4	**4.2**	41.5	14.6	**6.3**
7.3	1.14	6.4	0.30	**1.7**	0.70	0.47	5.50	2.60	87.9	**4.6**	35.1	13.7	**5.2**
7.5	4.93	5.6	6.61	**6.0**	0.01	0.61	2.12	4.65	78.3	**5.7**	37.0	0.0	**4.3**
8.8	1.93	4.5	0.71	**3.2**	0.03	0.62	5.49	3.13	84.2	**6.2**	36.8	0.6	**5.9**
9.3	0.31	1.3	0.15	**2.9**	0.03	0.31	2.69	3.29	90.2	**4.0**	28.9	7.9	**6.0**
8.0	0.56	3.9	1.02	**3.3**	0.20	0.31	2.97	4.02	84.0	**4.2**	21.3	4.1	**6.1**
6.3	1.08	6.7	0.07	**4.7**	0.45	0.63	5.05	3.51	79.6	**3.7**	24.6	9.4	**8.1**
9.9	0.00	0.0	0.19	**2.7**	0.04	0.23	1.53	3.07	88.9	**5.7**	31.7	1.5	**6.3**
9.9	0.00	0.0	0.00	**2.3**	0.00	-0.06	-0.78	3.32	99.0	**6.5**	36.5	0.0	**2.5**
4.3	1.07	12.0	0.58	**4.5**	7.56	0.45	6.09	3.27	79.4	**2.9**	13.4	10.6	**6.6**
6.5	1.36	8.0	0.47	**2.8**	0.05	0.15	1.28	3.18	92.0	**4.8**	16.6	2.1	**7.4**
7.3	2.24	7.6	1.14	**7.2**	0.02	0.44	2.88	4.27	64.0	**2.9**	17.2	28.0	**5.7**
5.4	7.69	11.3	4.11	**0.0**	0.00	-1.03	-6.56	1.85	225.0	**7.6**	70.8	0.0	**6.7**
5.0	3.29	17.0	-0.11	**4.9**	0.01	0.13	1.08	3.55	95.9	**5.0**	22.8	0.0	**6.3**
7.0	3.29	7.1	0.00	**0.6**	0.00	-0.36	-1.98	3.85	115.4	**7.1**	64.3	0.0	**7.0**
8.0	0.76	3.3	-0.11	**6.2**	0.08	1.12	7.93	4.45	85.0	**4.8**	20.1	0.0	**7.3**
5.4	0.76	5.4	1.31	**0.8**	-0.08	-0.71	-6.38	3.02	101.8	**4.3**	17.4	3.2	**5.4**
9.7	0.24	1.0	0.16	**1.0**	0.00	-0.14	-1.31	2.36	106.7	**5.5**	35.5	0.0	**5.3**
9.6	0.36	1.1	0.07	**2.4**	0.02	0.21	1.96	2.50	86.0	**5.8**	37.1	0.6	**4.9**
9.9	0.02	0.1	0.27	**5.1**	0.40	0.73	7.14	3.62	78.5	**4.6**	22.3	2.6	**7.0**
9.8	0.42	1.0	0.20	**3.2**	0.02	0.24	1.18	2.81	89.3	**5.8**	52.3	0.0	**6.5**
8.3	1.42	3.5	1.30	**1.0**	-0.01	-0.16	-1.22	3.42	96.6	**5.1**	22.0	0.0	**5.4**
6.3	1.00	8.9	0.96	**2.1**	0.02	0.06	0.85	2.99	79.7	**2.5**	13.8	19.1	**2.8**
8.1	0.00	0.0	0.00	**9.3**	0.02	1.35	11.53	3.95	61.4	**3.8**	14.1	0.0	**5.7**
1.5	6.31	33.1	0.00	**9.8**	0.03	1.68	13.10	4.11	25.0	**5.3**	30.6	0.0	**7.9**
10.0	0.00	0.0	2.31	**3.0**	0.01	0.28	1.37	3.02	89.8	**6.0**	60.2	0.0	**6.9**
8.3	1.08	4.2	0.00	**5.1**	0.04	0.67	5.13	3.53	83.1	**3.9**	22.1	11.1	**6.9**
8.1	0.00	0.0	0.00	**2.7**	0.00	0.20	0.86	2.71	92.6	**3.7**	18.8	0.0	**7.7**
6.0	1.89	8.4	0.19	**4.8**	0.01	0.61	4.07	3.82	81.8	**5.8**	42.9	0.0	**4.3**
4.8	1.07	7.6	0.57	**3.8**	0.01	0.17	1.79	5.32	90.4	**4.4**	28.3	1.7	**3.0**
9.8	0.38	2.1	0.13	**2.2**	0.47	0.31	2.78	2.90	90.9	**3.6**	10.5	6.5	**7.8**
9.8	0.00	0.0	0.00	**4.8**	0.00	2.58	9.09	11.27	50.0	**7.7**	86.0	0.0	**6.2**
9.7	0.45	1.9	0.32	**2.0**	0.08	0.24	1.73	2.36	90.3	**4.7**	22.4	2.5	**7.3**
8.9	0.00	0.0	0.00	**1.2**	0.00	0.00	0.00	4.83	120.0	**6.1**	53.4	0.0	**5.5**
10.0	0.88	1.8	1.04	**3.5**	0.04	0.71	3.82	2.72	80.6	**4.5**	28.4	4.2	**5.8**
10.0	0.00	0.0	0.00	**0.0**	0.00	-1.76	-12.12	0.00	0.0	**7.5**	92.8	0.0	**6.2**
10.0	0.13	0.4	0.17	**4.1**	0.13	0.78	5.00	2.68	76.6	**4.5**	31.8	4.7	**7.3**
6.8	0.73	6.2	0.35	**5.7**	2.31	0.73	7.16	3.95	80.6	**3.9**	17.5	7.6	**7.6**
8.0	0.77	4.2	0.73	**2.8**	0.03	0.34	2.89	3.53	90.0	**4.8**	23.9	0.0	**5.5**
8.4	0.51	3.8	0.55	**2.2**	-0.15	-0.59	-5.44	3.22	101.0	**3.9**	18.0	6.4	**7.0**
9.9	0.24	0.9	0.08	**1.5**	0.00	-0.08	-0.86	3.08	102.9	**6.7**	42.4	0.8	**3.9**
9.2	0.36	2.0	0.21	**1.3**	-0.01	-0.03	-0.29	2.26	96.1	**3.7**	11.3	7.0	**6.9**
9.4	0.23	1.3	-0.11	**2.3**	0.01	0.35	3.37	4.00	90.2	**4.6**	34.3	8.2	**4.7**
8.3	0.96	4.4	0.00	**1.4**	0.00	0.10	1.12	2.77	93.8	**6.3**	41.7	0.0	**2.9**
7.1	4.45	7.4	-0.09	**0.1**	-0.02	-0.49	-2.98	3.20	114.9	**6.2**	48.5	0.0	**6.1**
10.0	0.21	0.3	0.18	**2.5**	0.01	0.21	1.25	2.01	87.3	**5.5**	25.9	0.0	**6.8**
7.9	1.44	3.3	0.95	**2.8**	0.01	0.15	0.96	2.52	81.1	**6.0**	68.4	0.0	**6.7**
10.0	0.37	0.3	1.20	**1.0**	-0.01	-0.16	-0.60	2.14	98.4	**5.8**	38.4	3.1	**6.4**
3.0	0.87	30.2	1.55	**3.2**	0.07	0.11	1.33	4.07	78.3	**3.8**	10.9	4.2	**4.8**
7.3	1.29	6.0	0.87	**2.2**	-0.02	-0.06	-0.55	3.20	92.6	**4.6**	22.3	2.6	**5.8**
6.2	1.19	4.8	0.68	**1.9**	0.00	-0.28	-1.57	5.04	92.1	**5.1**	34.8	0.0	**6.9**
9.9	0.11	0.5	0.01	**4.1**	0.07	0.43	3.68	3.72	83.2	**5.8**	32.4	0.0	**6.3**
4.3	3.23	17.9	-0.15	**0.0**	-0.07	-0.81	-9.66	2.51	115.4	**4.8**	22.4	1.1	**2.7**
9.1	0.42	1.6	0.22	**8.8**	1.42	1.27	11.85	3.10	69.4	**4.2**	11.9	3.3	**7.8**
7.3	0.49	6.1	0.46	**3.9**	0.34	0.32	4.00	3.51	84.5	**3.1**	8.3	3.5	**4.3**
5.9	0.78	11.4	0.42	**4.9**	0.50	0.81	8.66	3.29	75.6	**2.2**	6.5	12.1	**6.1**
9.1	0.15	0.7	0.13	**4.5**	0.46	0.78	5.39	3.43	82.4	**3.2**	5.2	6.2	**8.3**

Name	City	State	Rating	2016 Rating	2015 Rating	Total Assets ($Mil)	One Year Asset Growth	Asset Mix (As a % of Total Assets): Commercial Loans	Consumer Loans	Mortgage Loans	Securities	Capitalization Index	Net Worth Ratio
Alliance Credit Union of Florida	Gainesville	FL	E+	E+	D	49.0	0.94	0.0	47.9	10.4	9.0	4.7	6.7
Alliance Niagara Federal Credit Union	Sanborn	NY	D-	D-	D-	17.0	0.12	0.0	14.7	6.6	51.1	4.9	6.9
Alliant Credit Union	Dubuque	IA	B+	B+	B-	120.3	3.77	3.7	26.2	31.7	0.0	9.9	10.9
Alliant Credit Union	Chicago	IL	B+	B+	B+	9821.3	10.12	4.0	22.4	35.2	24.8	9.4	10.6
Allied Credit Union	Stockton	CA	C+	C+	C-	24.2	1.02	0.0	12.9	9.8	0.0	10.0	12.5
Allied Federal Credit Union	Arlington	TX	C-	C-	C	92.6	9.53	0.0	35.4	1.7	14.0	4.9	6.9
Allied Healthcare Federal Credit Union	Long Beach	CA	C-	C-	C	71.8	5.01	1.3	16.8	32.9	1.2	5.4	7.4
Allied Plastics Federal Credit Union	Baton Rouge	LA	C+	C+	C	22.6	-1.37	0.0	30.9	3.1	0.0	10.0	11.5
Alloy Employees Credit Union	Waukesha	WI	D	D	D	<1	-3.81	0.0	28.1	0.0	0.0	10.0	47.5
▲ Alloy Federal Credit Union	Alloy	WV	C	C-	C-	20.6	3.06	0.0	38.0	5.9	0.0	10.0	14.0
AllSouth Federal Credit Union	Columbia	SC	A	A	A	820.2	5.93	0.1	47.1	13.4	0.8	10.0	15.0
Allsteel Credit Union	Oswego	IL	D	D	D+	23.2	0.20	0.0	25.9	17.7	2.1	10.0	16.2
allU.S. Credit Union	Salinas	CA	B+	B+	B+	42.9	11.84	0.0	21.4	0.0	37.9	10.0	13.5
Allvac Savings & Credit Union	Monroe	NC	C	C	C	8.2	8.98	0.0	32.9	0.0	0.0	10.0	14.6
▲ Allwealth Federal Credit Union	Hamilton	OH	D+	D	D-	19.8	6.03	0.0	21.3	28.0	0.0	6.3	8.3
Aloha Pacific Federal Credit Union	Honolulu	HI	B-	B-	B-	781.7	3.35	9.3	14.1	33.2	30.7	9.8	11.0
Alpena Community Credit Union	Alpena	MI	D+	D+	D+	23.7	5.63	1.0	17.4	24.6	42.0	6.0	8.1
Alpena-Alcona Area Credit Union	Alpena	MI	B+	B+	B-	337.4	8.22	0.0	22.4	18.6	1.8	7.8	9.6
Alpha Credit Union	Boston	MA	C	C	C-	31.0	4.86	0.0	16.6	7.2	4.1	10.0	13.1
▼ Alpine Community Credit Union	Alpine	TX	D+	C-	C	16.0	2.42	0.4	32.0	0.0	0.0	7.1	9.0
Alpine Credit Union	Orem	UT	B	B	B-	187.1	9.69	0.0	40.7	15.6	2.7	10.0	11.2
▼ Alps Federal Credit Union	Sitka	AK	C-	C	D+	56.2	-7.83	18.2	8.1	24.2	14.7	8.0	9.8
Alta Vista Credit Union	Redlands	CA	C	C	C	162.1	12.10	2.7	37.2	26.3	1.8	5.5	7.5
▲ Altamaha Federal Credit Union	Jesup	GA	B+	B	B	57.8	3.26	0.0	42.2	6.6	5.5	10.0	14.7
Altana Federal Credit Union	Billings	MT	A-	A-	B+	247.5	7.54	6.4	28.5	20.3	5.0	10.0	12.2
AltaOne Federal Credit Union	Ridgecrest	CA	C	C	B-	649.8	3.01	5.4	41.9	20.6	2.5	7.3	9.2
▲ Alternatives Federal Credit Union	Ithaca	NY	B-	C+	C+	102.1	2.46	3.8	9.3	50.6	0.8	6.3	8.3
▼ Altier Credit Union	Tempe	AZ	D+	C-	C+	195.7	4.79	7.5	41.2	1.9	2.3	4.9	7.0
▲ Alton Municipal Employees FCU	Alton	IL	C-	D+	D+	<1	2.70	0.0	84.7	0.0	0.0	10.0	26.9
▼ Altonized Community Federal Credit Union	Alton	IL	C+	B-	C+	36.0	-2.13	0.0	33.8	0.7	33.9	9.5	10.9
Altoona Area Employees FCU	Altoona	PA	C+	C+	C+	11.1	-1.60	0.0	31.6	0.0	0.0	9.8	10.9
Altra Federal Credit Union	Onalaska	WI	A-	A-	A-	1323.4	11.54	11.7	35.2	38.2	0.9	9.7	10.8
Altura Credit Union	Riverside	CA	A-	A-	A	1278.1	6.03	4.9	44.5	11.6	15.9	9.2	10.5
Amarillo Community Federal Credit Union	Amarillo	TX	C+	C+	B-	226.3	1.24	0.0	51.6	2.3	8.5	6.7	8.8
Amarillo Postal Employees Credit Union	Amarillo	TX	C	C	C	17.2	-1.50	1.7	34.8	8.1	0.0	10.0	15.0
Ambraw Federal Credit Union	Lawrenceville	IL	D+	D+	D	11.7	9.12	0.0	35.3	0.0	0.0	7.0	9.0
Ambridge Area Federal Credit Union	Baden	PA	C-	C-	C-	11.5	-0.70	0.0	24.9	0.0	0.0	10.0	12.2
▼ AME Church Federal Credit Union	Baton Rouge	LA	D	D+	C-	<1	-2.06	0.0	34.7	0.0	0.0	10.0	13.7
America First Federal Credit Union	Riverdale	UT	A-	A-	A-	8761.1	16.04	3.0	44.4	11.9	12.7	9.9	11.0
▲ America's Christian Credit Union	Glendora	CA	B-	C+	C	343.2	5.15	51.2	10.8	51.9	0.0	8.6	10.0
America's Credit Union	Garland	TX	C+	C+	C	242.5	-0.54	0.1	23.9	25.2	0.0	10.0	11.9
America's Federal Credit Union	Dupont	WA	B+	B+	B+	609.8	10.86	4.7	67.1	9.4	7.4	6.6	8.6
America's First Federal Credit Union	Birmingham	AL	B	B	B	1495.0	5.47	0.1	32.2	23.3	14.4	9.5	10.7
America's First Network Credit Union	Trumbull	CT	D+	D+	D+	20.4	1.56	0.0	28.0	13.5	0.0	8.0	9.6
American 1 Credit Union	Jackson	MI	A-	A-	A-	321.2	6.62	0.0	60.3	2.0	0.0	10.0	17.1
American Airlines Federal Credit Union	Fort Worth	TX	C+	C+	C+	6459.2	6.46	0.6	24.8	29.8	35.9	8.6	10.1
▼ American Baptist Association CU	Rosharon	TX	D-	D	D+	2.1	7.93	0.0	55.4	0.0	0.0	8.0	9.7
American Broadcast Employees FCU	Rockville Centre	NY	C-	C-	C-	110.2	5.80	0.7	22.1	23.6	2.9	7.7	9.5
▲ American Chemical Society FCU	Columbus	OH	C-	D+	D+	21.0	1.59	0.2	18.7	3.1	16.9	7.4	9.3
American Eagle Financial Credit Union, Inc.	East Hartford	CT	B-	B-	C+	1588.1	8.06	0.5	27.4	34.3	10.2	8.1	9.7
American First Credit Union	La Habra	CA	B+	B+	A-	679.5	14.50	10.0	14.5	39.2	18.9	7.2	9.2
American Hammered Federal Credit Union	Baltimore	MD	D	D	D	4.8	-2.73	0.0	24.3	0.0	0.0	10.0	13.7
American Heritage Federal Credit Union	Philadelphia	PA	B	B	B	1936.3	14.54	15.2	15.9	28.8	27.9	6.2	8.6
American Lake Credit Union	Lakewood	WA	B	B	C+	67.6	2.11	0.0	29.4	10.7	6.2	10.0	14.3
American Partners Federal Credit Union	Reidsville	NC	B-	B-	B	52.9	7.47	0.6	49.9	0.0	0.5	10.0	11.1
American Pride Credit Union	Altoona	PA	D+	D+	D+	16.8	-0.43	0.0	13.0	21.4	4.7	6.3	8.3
▼ American Southwest Credit Union	Sierra Vista	AZ	C+	B-	B-	221.0	7.17	6.0	32.8	18.0	29.4	6.6	8.7
American Spirit Federal Credit Union	Newark	DE	B	B	B-	61.4	-1.36	6.2	13.9	13.3	48.8	10.0	16.5
American United Family of Credit Unions, FCU	West Jordan	UT	A-	A-	A-	195.8	9.62	10.4	45.5	21.5	0.2	10.0	14.4
AmeriChoice Federal Credit Union	Mechanicsburg	PA	C-	C-	C-	177.1	4.04	8.6	17.1	21.9	7.0	6.8	8.8

Arrows denote recent upgrades ▲ or downgrades ▼

Asset Quality Index	Non-Performing Loans as a % of Total Loans	Non-Performing Loans as a % of Capital	Net Charge-Offs Avg Loans	Profitability Index	Net Income ($Mil)	Return on Assets	Return on Equity	Net Interest Spread	Overhead Efficiency Ratio	Liquidity Index	Liquidity Ratio	Hot Money Ratio	Stability Index
2.8	1.87	16.7	2.92	**1.1**	-0.10	-0.84	-12.05	5.69	87.5	**4.5**	23.4	3.4	**0.3**
6.4	1.72	7.6	0.74	**2.0**	0.01	0.12	1.69	2.82	85.1	**5.3**	29.8	0.7	**1.7**
8.7	0.30	1.9	0.11	**5.0**	0.24	0.82	7.45	3.36	80.6	**4.0**	19.6	4.0	**7.3**
8.4	0.49	3.3	0.30	**4.5**	17.30	0.72	6.71	2.12	60.1	**4.1**	26.2	4.8	**8.2**
10.0	0.78	1.9	0.07	**3.2**	0.02	0.33	2.65	2.82	90.9	**6.2**	39.3	1.7	**6.0**
6.2	1.11	7.2	0.41	**3.4**	0.09	0.40	5.73	3.34	86.6	**5.8**	34.8	1.6	**2.4**
6.1	0.34	3.4	0.08	**4.6**	0.10	0.57	7.71	3.91	84.4	**3.5**	18.6	3.5	**3.5**
9.5	0.41	1.9	-0.07	**5.5**	0.05	0.92	8.43	3.30	72.3	**3.4**	30.8	17.0	**5.6**
8.5	2.86	2.6	0.00	**0.0**	0.00	-1.33	-2.74	4.35	100.0	**5.1**	22.2	0.0	**5.3**
7.7	0.92	3.6	0.00	**2.6**	0.03	0.52	3.63	4.81	87.0	**5.9**	38.8	2.1	**5.7**
8.7	0.18	1.0	0.50	**6.7**	2.40	1.20	8.71	3.38	73.1	**5.5**	34.1	10.0	**9.2**
9.9	0.50	1.4	-0.42	**0.4**	-0.03	-0.54	-3.30	2.63	119.6	**4.7**	54.4	6.4	**5.4**
10.0	0.24	0.6	0.88	**3.3**	0.07	0.64	4.72	4.31	96.6	**5.1**	25.0	8.9	**6.2**
7.9	1.66	3.9	0.28	**3.8**	0.01	0.30	2.03	3.71	90.3	**6.7**	49.9	0.0	**6.8**
6.2	0.89	7.5	-0.03	**3.4**	0.01	0.14	1.70	4.14	98.9	**4.7**	26.7	0.6	**3.0**
9.8	0.19	1.0	0.42	**3.4**	0.76	0.39	3.60	2.95	83.1	**4.0**	9.3	3.3	**7.9**
9.9	0.07	0.4	0.36	**1.9**	-0.01	-0.10	-1.27	2.64	102.0	**4.4**	23.7	5.7	**3.7**
7.9	0.76	4.5	0.73	**5.9**	0.70	0.84	8.83	2.90	62.4	**5.2**	37.7	3.9	**6.7**
10.0	0.65	1.4	0.41	**2.4**	0.02	0.20	1.50	2.39	90.7	**6.0**	36.0	0.8	**6.0**
3.6	7.73	24.6	0.00	**3.3**	0.04	0.95	10.63	2.76	65.5	**5.8**	28.1	0.0	**3.0**
9.7	0.23	2.1	0.12	**3.9**	0.20	0.43	4.09	3.07	85.6	**3.7**	20.7	6.0	**6.7**
4.1	1.86	13.1	0.69	**1.3**	-0.34	-2.38	-24.13	4.26	90.0	**3.4**	17.7	7.0	**4.8**
7.8	0.34	4.2	0.88	**3.4**	0.23	0.59	7.61	4.48	74.2	**3.9**	16.8	5.5	**3.6**
6.6	1.82	7.6	0.84	**7.0**	0.19	1.33	8.96	4.74	77.8	**4.9**	28.7	2.4	**6.6**
8.5	0.50	2.9	0.14	**5.0**	0.36	0.59	4.79	4.22	87.3	**3.7**	13.8	8.6	**8.2**
5.5	0.81	10.5	1.15	**2.9**	0.55	0.34	3.70	4.45	81.0	**3.3**	12.0	7.3	**5.6**
6.4	0.50	8.9	0.30	**4.2**	0.12	0.46	6.94	3.93	88.0	**4.1**	21.5	4.7	**5.3**
3.1	1.67	26.7	1.17	**1.3**	-0.05	-0.10	-1.38	3.41	87.0	**3.8**	15.9	1.4	**3.8**
7.9	0.58	1.8	0.00	**4.5**	0.00	1.29	4.85	6.03	75.0	**4.2**	20.1	0.0	**4.3**
6.2	1.92	6.9	1.77	**3.2**	0.01	0.10	0.94	4.11	92.9	**5.7**	31.7	4.8	**4.6**
7.3	1.20	4.6	0.00	**3.5**	0.01	0.26	2.33	3.28	91.9	**5.4**	19.9	0.0	**5.9**
6.6	0.68	6.5	0.31	**6.5**	3.02	0.94	8.54	3.09	71.7	**3.2**	10.6	3.2	**8.8**
8.7	0.50	3.2	0.38	**6.0**	3.64	1.17	11.17	3.60	74.4	**4.6**	21.8	4.1	**7.8**
7.2	0.21	3.5	0.36	**3.2**	0.14	0.26	3.03	3.01	88.7	**3.1**	24.0	17.4	**5.2**
9.7	0.46	1.4	0.15	**2.2**	0.01	0.19	1.25	3.13	87.9	**3.5**	20.6	12.7	**6.6**
9.7	0.04	0.2	0.00	**1.2**	0.00	-0.07	-0.76	3.18	92.6	**5.8**	32.7	0.0	**4.1**
4.9	1.88	7.4	0.00	**2.0**	0.01	0.24	2.00	3.04	92.3	**4.4**	23.1	0.0	**5.8**
0.3	20.45	52.9	0.00	**2.0**	0.00	0.00	0.00	8.89	100.0	**7.1**	64.6	0.0	**6.1**
6.4	0.74	7.8	0.64	**8.6**	25.04	1.18	11.69	3.48	67.0	**4.2**	20.1	6.1	**8.7**
7.6	0.16	1.0	0.18	**7.6**	1.15	1.38	13.64	3.87	73.7	**2.6**	26.6	23.5	**7.5**
8.9	0.49	2.0	0.39	**2.6**	0.12	0.20	1.65	2.93	90.8	**5.2**	44.2	5.6	**7.4**
6.1	0.33	5.2	0.82	**3.5**	0.42	0.28	3.53	3.74	83.7	**1.7**	13.9	29.7	**5.7**
8.7	0.41	3.2	0.27	**4.0**	1.63	0.44	4.09	2.71	82.4	**5.0**	24.4	3.2	**7.8**
5.5	2.70	11.9	-0.34	**2.6**	0.01	0.10	1.02	5.37	88.3	**5.7**	24.0	0.0	**4.2**
5.7	1.59	6.5	1.37	**10.0**	1.35	1.73	9.96	6.47	67.7	**5.5**	35.2	2.3	**9.3**
9.6	0.39	2.2	0.38	**3.2**	6.95	0.43	4.30	1.66	71.8	**4.9**	35.8	2.5	**7.7**
2.4	2.20	15.6	0.00	**1.1**	-0.01	-2.42	-23.88	1.74	285.7	**5.0**	26.1	0.0	**4.8**
8.4	0.80	4.9	0.12	**1.7**	0.00	-0.01	-0.08	3.96	95.5	**5.7**	39.9	2.4	**4.9**
7.0	1.23	4.9	-0.05	**2.7**	0.03	0.59	6.42	3.01	82.9	**5.6**	34.1	1.6	**4.3**
7.6	0.64	6.1	0.29	**3.7**	2.01	0.51	5.74	3.04	79.4	**3.6**	21.5	9.1	**6.2**
8.4	0.39	3.9	-0.09	**4.5**	1.04	0.62	6.77	2.73	84.5	**4.4**	25.1	6.1	**7.3**
10.0	0.08	0.2	0.66	**0.0**	-0.01	-0.59	-4.27	2.76	126.7	**5.9**	48.6	0.0	**5.4**
7.3	0.72	5.4	0.41	**4.2**	2.21	0.47	5.55	3.13	82.8	**4.0**	23.4	8.3	**5.9**
7.3	2.02	6.5	0.91	**2.0**	-0.07	-0.40	-2.77	3.38	95.1	**5.1**	31.7	4.1	**6.4**
5.0	1.06	10.6	0.65	**4.2**	0.09	0.67	7.39	5.91	83.6	**4.9**	27.2	5.9	**4.1**
9.7	0.36	1.5	0.13	**2.0**	0.00	0.07	0.86	2.95	93.9	**6.3**	48.6	1.3	**3.8**
8.3	0.52	3.8	0.91	**3.1**	0.11	0.20	2.25	3.11	74.5	**4.2**	14.7	6.2	**5.6**
8.0	1.86	4.5	0.00	**4.0**	0.11	0.69	4.92	3.09	82.0	**4.6**	14.2	1.1	**6.5**
5.3	1.24	7.1	0.52	**10.0**	0.83	1.70	12.98	5.22	70.2	**2.3**	8.8	14.8	**9.6**
6.6	1.04	7.7	0.14	**2.2**	0.04	0.10	1.31	3.42	97.4	**4.5**	26.7	1.3	**4.8**

Name	City	State	Rating	2016 Rating	2015 Rating	Total Assets ($Mil)	One Year Asset Growth	Asset Mix (As a % of Total Assets) Commercial Loans	Consumer Loans	Mortgage Loans	Securities	Capitalization Index	Net Worth Ratio
▲ Americo Federal Credit Union	Erie	PA	C-	D+	D+	76.6	3.56	0.0	33.6	3.4	2.8	9.2	10.4
AmeriCU Credit Union	Rome	NY	B	B	B	1482.2	13.32	3.0	41.4	35.0	1.5	7.2	9.1
Amherst Federal Credit Union	Amherst	NY	C	C	C-	32.5	2.92	0.0	17.9	15.5	35.0	5.8	7.8
AMNH Employees Federal Credit Union	New York	NY	C	C	C	<1	-0.74	0.0	15.3	0.0	72.6	10.0	18.4
Amoco East Texas Federal Credit Union	Longview	TX	E+	E+	E+	4.1	-15.38	0.0	56.4	0.0	0.0	0.0	3.0
Amoco Federal Credit Union	Texas City	TX	B-	B-	B-	849.0	7.77	0.0	47.2	9.0	20.2	6.2	8.4
Amplify Credit Union	Austin	TX	B+	B+	B+	851.5	7.68	9.0	37.1	25.8	6.7	7.1	9.1
▲ Ampot Federal Credit Union	Hamilton	MS	B-	C+	C	8.2	6.86	0.0	40.8	0.2	0.0	10.0	22.0
ANCO Community Credit Union	La Salle	IL	C-	C-	C	12.1	1.77	0.0	19.8	25.1	14.6	10.0	14.3
Andalusia Mills Empls Credit Assoc FCU	Andalusia	AL	D	D	C	3.0	-7.50	0.0	21.5	0.0	0.0	10.0	23.5
Anderson County Federal Credit Union	Palestine	TX	C+	C+	C+	17.5	0.15	0.0	14.8	0.0	0.0	10.0	16.3
Anderson Federal Credit Union	Anderson	SC	C-	C-	C-	94.0	6.72	0.0	33.1	12.8	1.8	6.2	8.2
Andigo Credit Union	Schaumburg	IL	C+	C+	B-	896.7	-0.58	6.8	16.0	37.3	17.7	9.1	10.4
▼ Andovers Federal Credit Union	Andover	MA	C+	B-	B-	30.6	3.87	0.0	12.8	0.0	4.4	10.0	11.0
▼ Andrews Federal Credit Union	Suitland	MD	B-	B	B	1520.2	33.54	7.3	25.4	24.0	6.2	9.9	11.0
Andrews School Federal Credit Union	Andrews	TX	C-	C-	C-	7.4	-5.36	0.0	31.9	0.0	0.0	10.0	20.4
ANECA Federal Credit Union	Shreveport	LA	C	C	C	106.0	11.14	20.4	25.6	15.2	3.4	10.0	18.1
ANG Federal Credit Union	Birmingham	AL	D-	D-	D-	20.5	9.39	0.0	24.4	5.4	0.0	5.3	7.3
Angelina County Teachers Credit Union	Lufkin	TX	C+	C+	C+	11.9	4.03	0.0	35.9	0.0	0.0	10.0	12.8
Angelina Federal Employees Credit Union	Lufkin	TX	B	B	B-	25.8	5.16	0.0	45.9	10.9	0.0	10.0	14.9
Anheuser-Busch Employees Credit Union	Saint Louis	MO	B	B	B	1681.6	5.91	7.3	48.6	26.9	5.3	9.0	10.4
Animas Credit Union	Farmington	NM	C	C	B-	132.4	0.80	6.9	39.2	13.7	2.4	7.3	9.2
▼ Anmed Health Federal Credit Union	Anderson	SC	C-	C	C	16.1	10.13	0.0	26.5	0.0	0.0	10.0	11.7
Ann Arbor Postal Federal Credit Union	Milan	MI	C-	C-	C-	1.0	-5.49	0.0	40.4	0.0	0.0	10.0	30.5
Anoka Hennepin Credit Union	Coon Rapids	MN	B+	B+	B+	182.6	12.73	5.4	21.6	14.7	6.5	6.7	8.7
Antioch Community Federal Credit Union	Antioch	CA	C+	C+	C-	26.6	10.84	1.9	12.5	18.8	0.0	6.7	8.7
Antioch Credit Union	Cleveland	OH	C	C	D+	2.7	0.74	0.0	10.6	0.0	0.0	10.0	36.0
▲ Antioch MB Federal Credit Union	Decatur	IL	D+	D	D+	<1	83.11	0.0	0.0	0.0	0.0	10.0	15.1
AOD Federal Credit Union	Oxford	AL	B	B	B	293.6	5.10	0.3	35.0	10.5	30.7	10.0	13.2
▼ AP Federal Credit Union	Toledo	OH	D	D+	D	36.1	5.22	0.0	30.4	10.0	14.6	10.0	11.3
APC Employees Federal Credit Union	Tucson	AZ	C+	C+	C+	1.4	8.62	0.0	54.5	0.0	0.0	10.0	21.5
APCI Federal Credit Union	Allentown	PA	C+	C+	C+	562.1	5.09	0.0	10.6	31.2	45.7	7.6	9.6
Apco Employees Credit Union	Birmingham	AL	B+	B+	B	2828.7	4.48	0.0	6.7	19.6	45.2	8.1	10.8
Apex Community Federal Credit Union	Stowe	PA	B-	B-	B-	40.9	10.08	0.0	40.5	23.8	0.0	10.0	11.9
APEX Financial Credit Union	Florissant	MO	D-	D-	D-	35.9	-3.81	0.0	33.1	0.4	47.1	6.0	8.4
APL Federal Credit Union	Laurel	MD	C+	C+	C+	438.0	3.77	0.0	17.3	17.4	32.8	9.4	10.6
Appalachian Community FCU	Gray	TN	B-	B-	C	200.6	7.67	5.3	26.2	44.8	6.0	7.1	9.1
Appalachian Power Employees FCU	Huntington	WV	C-	C-	C-	7.5	-3.04	0.0	34.8	0.0	0.0	10.0	16.4
Apple Federal Credit Union	Fairfax	VA	B+	B+	B+	2366.9	9.73	11.7	25.6	38.6	9.2	7.8	9.6
AppleTree Credit Union	West Allis	WI	A	A	A	122.2	4.65	0.0	19.5	51.5	0.0	10.0	23.0
Appliance Credit Union	Cleveland	TN	C	C	C+	11.7	2.41	0.0	37.0	0.0	0.0	10.0	14.7
APS Federal Credit Union	Charleroi	PA	D-	D-	D-	8.6	3.40	0.0	65.6	0.0	0.0	5.1	7.1
Arabi Sugar Workers Federal Credit Union	New Orleans	LA	C+	C+	C+	1.4	2.23	0.0	90.7	0.0	0.0	10.0	42.7
▲ Arapahoe Credit Union	Centennial	CO	B-	C+	B	124.6	2.96	0.0	17.9	17.7	0.0	6.5	8.5
Arbor Financial Credit Union	Kalamazoo	MI	B	B	C+	512.3	13.10	5.0	20.7	43.3	5.1	6.7	8.7
Arbuckle Federal Credit Union	Ada	OK	E+	E+	E+	7.6	-14.34	3.6	70.4	0.0	0.0	5.0	7.0
ARC Federal Credit Union	Altoona	PA	C+	C+	C	81.8	7.29	0.0	19.3	20.0	15.6	5.9	7.9
Arcade Credit Union	Asheville	NC	D	D	D+	7.1	0.38	0.0	22.7	0.0	0.0	10.0	12.5
Arcadia Credit Union	Arcadia	WI	B+	B+	B+	73.5	7.33	2.3	14.7	54.9	0.0	10.0	13.1
Archer Cooperative Credit Union	Central City	NE	B-	B-	C+	60.6	8.45	72.7	5.9	61.5	0.9	9.5	10.7
Archer Heights Credit Union	Chicago	IL	C-	C-	C	17.8	-0.43	0.0	17.0	25.8	0.0	8.3	9.9
Ardent Federal Credit Union	Philadelphia	PA	C+	C+	B-	679.9	7.22	0.7	17.0	30.6	26.0	8.2	10.0
Area Community Credit Union	Grand Forks	ND	B	B	B	23.3	6.47	0.0	29.0	13.9	0.0	10.0	15.4
Area Educational Credit Union	Mattoon	IL	B-	B-	B-	25.0	2.21	0.0	23.2	0.0	0.0	10.0	21.8
▼ Argent Federal Credit Union	Chester	VA	C-	C	C-	235.0	5.96	1.9	35.1	17.9	5.2	6.7	8.7
ARH Federal Credit Union	Middlesboro	KY	B+	B+	B+	12.3	1.55	0.0	29.6	8.8	0.0	10.0	22.5
Arizona Central Credit Union	Phoenix	AZ	C	C	C	477.2	6.37	10.2	44.7	18.0	6.7	6.1	8.1
Arizona Federal Credit Union	Phoenix	AZ	A	A	A	1548.3	7.70	1.6	24.6	8.7	42.1	10.0	14.5
▲ Ark City Teachers Credit Union	Arkansas City	KS	D	D-	E+	3.5	-5.33	0.0	53.4	0.0	0.0	8.6	10.1
ARK Valley Credit Union	Arkansas City	KS	C+	C+	C	37.1	8.09	0.0	40.4	0.0	0.0	6.9	8.9

Arrows denote recent upgrades ▲ or downgrades ▼

Asset Quality Index	Non-Performing Loans as a % of Total Loans	Non-Performing Loans as a % of Capital	Net Charge-Offs Avg Loans	Profitability Index	Net Income ($Mil)	Return on Assets	Return on Equity	Net Interest Spread	Overhead Efficiency Ratio	Liquidity Index	Liquidity Ratio	Hot Money Ratio	Stability Index
6.2	1.10	5.4	0.27	**2.1**	0.04	0.23	2.21	3.17	89.2	**4.9**	26.8	0.8	**4.9**
6.9	0.68	7.0	0.36	**4.2**	1.98	0.54	5.87	3.11	77.3	**2.5**	8.1	10.9	**6.2**
8.6	0.51	2.8	0.40	**3.0**	0.03	0.35	4.41	3.12	83.7	**5.3**	23.8	0.8	**3.6**
10.0	0.00	0.0	0.00	**2.0**	0.00	0.00	0.00	3.29	87.5	**5.7**	15.1	0.0	**6.1**
0.0	21.01	279.4	3.88	**1.0**	-0.01	-0.49	-16.13	5.71	110.2	**4.6**	21.8	0.0	**1.1**
6.5	0.53	5.4	0.46	**3.4**	0.54	0.26	3.14	2.50	86.7	**4.3**	32.1	11.0	**5.8**
7.8	0.29	3.6	0.73	**4.1**	0.78	0.37	4.32	4.00	79.5	**2.9**	13.5	14.6	**6.4**
8.1	1.06	2.6	1.17	**10.0**	0.04	2.07	9.24	6.19	58.2	**4.2**	63.6	29.6	**5.7**
3.7	7.41	24.0	3.50	**0.2**	-0.01	-0.40	-2.77	2.41	118.6	**4.6**	21.4	3.0	**6.2**
9.4	2.86	3.4	-0.91	**1.9**	0.01	0.69	2.88	5.95	124.1	**7.5**	76.3	0.0	**4.8**
8.3	3.47	4.1	2.01	**3.4**	0.02	0.39	2.40	3.05	79.9	**6.1**	62.4	7.4	**6.6**
5.8	0.77	7.9	0.65	**2.7**	0.09	0.38	4.58	4.25	83.8	**4.7**	32.0	6.1	**3.2**
8.3	0.54	3.6	0.47	**3.0**	0.70	0.31	3.01	3.23	78.4	**4.1**	17.4	1.5	**6.9**
9.7	0.41	1.0	0.19	**2.5**	0.01	0.08	0.74	2.60	96.4	**4.8**	20.7	9.6	**5.7**
9.0	0.44	2.7	0.62	**2.8**	0.06	0.02	0.15	3.26	89.4	**4.7**	44.3	18.5	**7.6**
8.6	1.69	2.7	0.00	**1.8**	0.01	0.27	1.33	2.39	86.8	**6.2**	64.0	1.9	**5.8**
6.5	1.18	5.1	0.46	**2.4**	0.03	0.11	0.59	4.18	85.4	**3.4**	16.7	9.3	**5.7**
10.0	0.22	1.0	0.70	**2.5**	0.02	0.32	4.31	3.17	86.6	**5.5**	40.1	4.2	**2.3**
9.7	0.06	0.2	0.72	**5.6**	0.05	1.67	13.12	3.81	80.4	**5.0**	21.4	0.0	**6.2**
8.0	0.34	1.7	0.00	**6.2**	0.05	0.84	6.34	3.78	83.4	**4.7**	29.0	2.0	**8.2**
6.2	0.69	5.8	0.71	**4.2**	2.16	0.52	5.07	3.67	75.1	**3.3**	8.3	3.5	**7.1**
6.0	0.90	7.4	0.07	**2.8**	0.08	0.25	2.90	3.47	90.9	**5.0**	29.1	2.9	**5.0**
9.9	0.08	0.2	-0.08	**1.5**	-0.01	-0.23	-1.91	4.31	105.9	**7.5**	66.1	0.0	**6.3**
6.6	6.10	8.0	0.00	**2.0**	0.00	0.00	0.00	3.82	85.7	**6.3**	39.7	0.0	**6.3**
6.3	1.52	9.1	0.08	**5.0**	0.22	0.50	5.62	3.99	89.1	**5.4**	28.1	0.9	**5.4**
10.0	0.00	0.0	0.00	**3.1**	0.02	0.28	3.11	2.62	96.4	**6.4**	63.1	0.9	**4.0**
10.0	5.35	1.9	-1.12	**2.9**	0.00	0.60	1.62	3.00	85.2	**6.7**	45.6	0.0	**7.2**
10.0	0.00	0.0	0.00	**1.1**	0.00	0.00	0.00	0.00	0.0	**7.0**	116.1	0.0	**6.1**
9.8	0.46	1.9	0.45	**4.1**	0.48	0.66	5.04	2.42	80.1	**4.3**	17.8	3.0	**7.6**
5.7	3.09	16.3	3.15	**0.0**	-0.17	-1.96	-16.80	2.97	118.2	**5.1**	20.6	1.0	**5.0**
5.7	3.09	8.5	0.00	**10.0**	0.01	2.06	9.59	5.41	53.3	**5.3**	34.9	0.0	**5.0**
10.0	0.12	0.6	0.05	**3.2**	0.49	0.35	3.74	1.79	79.6	**4.3**	16.7	6.5	**7.0**
10.0	0.29	1.2	0.47	**5.2**	5.87	0.84	8.77	1.62	36.7	**5.8**	28.0	8.2	**6.9**
5.3	1.53	16.8	0.46	**3.7**	0.04	0.38	3.13	4.83	82.5	**4.5**	24.9	4.1	**5.5**
6.1	1.75	7.7	3.65	**0.0**	-0.13	-1.42	-17.91	3.33	111.4	**5.0**	31.5	4.6	**2.9**
10.0	0.13	0.7	0.16	**3.2**	0.45	0.41	4.67	2.40	82.0	**4.2**	17.4	6.3	**6.4**
5.6	0.73	15.9	0.93	**4.7**	0.41	0.81	9.95	4.37	70.1	**2.0**	26.4	45.7	**5.0**
6.4	4.01	9.7	0.00	**2.1**	0.00	0.05	0.32	2.62	94.9	**5.7**	26.7	0.0	**6.5**
7.0	0.58	5.3	0.56	**5.7**	4.54	0.78	8.21	3.45	69.7	**4.0**	20.2	6.0	**7.5**
9.9	0.07	0.3	0.00	**5.5**	0.22	0.73	3.19	2.12	70.3	**2.9**	13.7	6.7	**9.5**
7.5	1.55	4.8	0.44	**2.1**	0.00	0.03	0.23	2.65	91.4	**5.8**	51.2	0.0	**6.4**
5.3	0.63	6.4	0.00	**2.4**	0.00	0.10	1.32	3.49	97.4	**4.4**	18.8	0.0	**1.0**
4.5	4.88	9.9	0.00	**10.0**	0.02	4.29	9.98	10.00	55.9	**3.3**	18.3	0.0	**9.2**
9.3	0.16	1.1	0.48	**4.1**	0.30	0.97	11.52	3.76	75.7	**4.6**	26.5	6.1	**5.2**
9.7	0.16	1.3	0.19	**4.2**	0.68	0.55	6.16	3.64	83.2	**4.6**	23.4	4.9	**5.3**
7.0	0.07	0.7	1.01	**0.9**	0.00	0.00	0.00	4.07	101.1	**3.0**	11.4	8.7	**0.7**
7.0	0.83	5.0	0.05	**4.6**	0.11	0.52	6.47	3.30	84.7	**5.3**	26.9	0.3	**4.1**
10.0	0.00	0.0	-0.34	**0.6**	-0.01	-0.57	-4.49	2.73	118.5	**5.1**	26.2	0.0	**5.4**
8.2	0.62	3.8	0.00	**7.2**	0.22	1.24	9.45	4.73	68.2	**3.2**	18.1	7.4	**7.0**
5.3	0.32	2.4	0.06	**3.4**	0.05	0.31	2.97	3.85	92.4	**1.6**	7.5	16.9	**5.9**
8.5	0.58	2.6	0.05	**2.0**	-0.01	-0.20	-2.05	3.57	105.4	**4.5**	21.5	7.7	**4.4**
7.6	0.77	5.7	0.49	**3.6**	0.61	0.37	3.66	3.05	78.1	**3.1**	15.6	18.2	**6.4**
7.8	1.42	5.0	-0.09	**6.1**	0.04	0.63	4.15	3.40	83.7	**4.7**	30.8	1.6	**5.7**
10.0	1.31	1.5	-1.30	**4.3**	0.05	0.87	3.99	2.29	72.2	**6.4**	52.0	0.0	**7.4**
7.0	1.04	7.0	1.03	**1.7**	-0.10	-0.17	-1.93	4.01	90.0	**4.5**	27.7	3.0	**4.8**
9.4	0.66	1.2	0.60	**7.0**	0.04	1.19	5.22	5.66	79.7	**6.9**	51.6	0.0	**6.3**
5.7	0.63	12.0	0.90	**2.5**	0.20	0.17	2.16	4.85	87.9	**4.6**	17.6	2.2	**4.1**
10.0	0.29	0.8	0.44	**8.8**	5.65	1.50	10.30	3.28	74.5	**5.2**	23.1	1.7	**10.0**
4.7	1.66	9.9	0.96	**2.8**	0.00	0.45	4.52	2.96	76.0	**5.0**	45.0	0.0	**2.3**
9.0	0.13	0.8	0.23	**5.2**	0.07	0.76	8.36	3.78	85.2	**5.4**	47.4	6.2	**4.4**

Name	City	State	Rating	2016 Rating	2015 Rating	Total Assets ($Mil)	One Year Asset Growth	Asset Mix (As a % of Total Assets) Commercial Loans	Consumer Loans	Mortgage Loans	Securities	Capitalization Index	Net Worth Ratio
Arkansas AM&N College FCU	Pine Bluff	AR	**D-**	D-	D	2.2	-2.40	0.0	40.7	0.0	0.0	**7.0**	9.0
Arkansas Best Federal Credit Union	Fort Smith	AR	**C**	C	C+	123.9	5.12	0.0	53.9	0.0	3.2	**10.0**	13.1
Arkansas Democrat-Gazette FCU	Little Rock	AR	**C+**	C+	C+	4.4	-9.95	0.0	55.6	0.0	0.0	**10.0**	27.8
Arkansas Education Association FCU	Little Rock	AR	**C-**	C-	C-	7.4	3.54	0.0	57.5	0.0	0.0	**10.0**	13.1
Arkansas Employees Federal Credit Union	Little Rock	AR	**D-**	D-	D-	36.7	-5.21	0.8	53.7	8.1	0.0	**5.3**	7.3
Arkansas Farm Bureau FCU	Little Rock	AR	**C+**	C+	C+	9.5	0.24	0.0	40.8	0.0	0.0	**10.0**	18.0
▲ Arkansas Federal Credit Union	Jacksonville	AR	**B-**	C+	B-	1149.5	9.53	3.9	51.8	20.8	2.5	**7.5**	9.3
▲ Arkansas Health Center FCU	Benton	AR	**C**	C-	C-	7.5	-1.85	0.0	57.8	0.2	0.0	**10.0**	11.4
Arkansas Kraft Employees FCU	Morrilton	AR	**C+**	C+	C+	4.5	6.81	0.0	32.1	0.0	0.0	**10.0**	21.6
Arkansas Superior Federal Credit Union	Warren	AR	**A**	A	A-	76.3	0.09	0.0	30.7	20.2	0.0	**10.0**	19.2
Arkansas Teachers Federal Credit Union	Little Rock	AR	**D**	D	C+	1.4	-2.13	0.0	54.5	0.0	0.0	**10.0**	17.1
Arlington Community Federal Credit Union	Falls Church	VA	**B+**	B+	B+	270.4	11.10	4.4	33.6	22.1	0.6	**7.1**	9.1
Arlington Hotel Federal Credit Union	Hot Springs	AR	**D-**	D-	D	<1	-22.22	0.0	97.7	0.0	0.0	**10.0**	18.8
Arlington Municipal Federal Credit Union	Arlington	MA	**C-**	C-	D	10.0	0.86	0.0	18.7	14.7	0.0	**10.0**	19.2
Armstrong Associates FCU	Ford City	PA	**C-**	C-	D+	54.6	-0.89	0.0	25.5	0.0	0.0	**10.0**	13.0
Armstrong County Federal Employees FCU	Kittanning	PA	**C**	C	C	15.1	2.82	0.0	13.4	0.0	0.0	**10.0**	13.5
Army Aviation Center FCU	Daleville	AL	**B**	B	B	1211.4	1.88	0.3	26.8	9.9	39.3	**10.0**	12.2
Arnold Bakers Employees FCU	Greenwich	CT	**D**	D	C-	2.9	-14.08	0.0	2.4	0.0	0.0	**10.0**	26.7
Arrha Credit Union	Springfield	MA	**C**	C	C	131.0	3.96	0.4	12.9	45.3	5.9	**6.3**	8.5
Arrowhead Central Credit Union	San Bernardino	CA	**A+**	A+	A+	1138.7	8.44	5.1	32.0	5.9	39.9	**10.0**	13.5
ArrowPointe Federal Credit Union	Catawba	SC	**C+**	C+	C+	155.3	5.35	0.0	29.2	26.1	7.4	**9.5**	10.7
Arsenal Credit Union	Arnold	MO	**C+**	C+	B-	225.5	3.64	9.5	44.6	10.1	23.2	**7.0**	9.0
Artesia Credit Union	Artesia	NM	**A-**	A-	A-	96.9	1.58	0.4	35.1	11.8	0.0	**10.0**	13.4
▲ Artesian City Federal Credit Union	Albany	GA	**C**	C-	C	17.4	4.47	0.0	30.8	3.7	0.0	**10.0**	20.4
Artmet Federal Credit Union	Stoughton	MA	**D+**	D+	D+	<1	-7.85	0.0	43.2	0.0	4.6	**9.0**	10.4
ASA Federal Credit Union	Bloomfield	CT	**D**	D	D	9.1	10.20	0.0	28.9	0.0	0.0	**6.9**	8.9
Asbestos Workers Local 14 FCU	Philadelphia	PA	**D**	D	D	3.9	12.36	0.0	24.2	0.0	0.0	**6.0**	8.0
Asbestos Workers Local 53 FCU	Kenner	LA	**D**	D	D	<1	-8.58	0.0	10.2	0.0	0.0	**10.0**	24.1
Asbury Federal Credit Union	Washington	DC	**C-**	C-	C	<1	-0.26	0.0	10.2	0.0	0.0	**10.0**	18.9
Ascend Federal Credit Union	Tullahoma	TN	**A**	A	A	2052.7	9.26	5.6	32.0	30.5	19.8	**10.0**	17.1
Ascension Credit Union	Gonzales	LA	**C-**	C-	C	64.0	9.41	0.0	33.6	13.9	1.1	**6.7**	8.7
Ascentra Credit Union	Bettendorf	IA	**B+**	B+	B+	412.4	7.88	5.2	27.2	21.4	3.7	**8.2**	9.8
▼ Ash Employees Credit Union	Anna	IL	**C**	C+	C+	5.1	2.24	0.0	67.4	0.0	0.0	**10.0**	13.5
Ashland Community Federal Credit Union	Ashland	OH	**D**	D	D-	14.9	11.17	0.0	72.6	1.1	0.0	**5.6**	7.6
Ashland Credit Union	Ashland	KY	**B+**	B+	A-	216.9	11.21	0.0	37.7	13.7	15.6	**10.0**	12.3
▲ ASI Federal Credit Union	Harahan	LA	**B-**	C+	C+	326.6	2.12	7.1	35.3	13.6	21.1	**10.0**	11.2
▼ Aspire Federal Credit Union	Clark	NJ	**C-**	C	C+	173.3	-7.60	10.1	36.1	9.4	0.5	**8.2**	9.8
Assemblies of God Credit Union	Springfield	MO	**A-**	A-	B	155.5	2.63	20.3	12.8	44.8	9.0	**9.8**	11.0
Associated Credit Union	Norcross	GA	**B**	B	B	1509.2	6.56	1.8	47.9	14.4	13.7	**10.0**	11.7
Associated Credit Union of Texas	League City	TX	**A-**	A-	A	384.5	7.15	0.8	38.3	13.5	11.7	**8.3**	9.9
Associated Health Care Credit Union	Saint Paul	MN	**B-**	B-	B-	113.6	7.00	0.0	37.2	11.1	2.6	**7.6**	9.4
▼ Associated School Employees Credit Union	Austintown	OH	**D**	D+	D+	132.7	1.99	0.1	20.4	32.5	30.2	**8.7**	10.1
Associates Federal Credit Union	Windsor	CT	**C-**	C-	C-	6.9	3.67	0.0	26.1	31.1	0.0	**10.0**	16.0
Assumption Beaumont Federal Credit Union	Lumberton	TX	**D+**	D+	D	<1	-3.05	0.0	28.6	0.0	0.0	**8.3**	10.1
▲ Astera Credit Union	Lansing	MI	**C**	C-	D	144.9	-0.95	4.5	29.6	15.0	27.8	**6.2**	8.4
AT&T Employees Pittsburgh FCU	Pittsburgh	PA	**C-**	C-	C-	9.5	0.90	0.0	18.1	0.0	0.0	**10.0**	25.9
▼ Atchison Village Credit Union	Richmond	CA	**D+**	C-	C-	8.9	4.55	0.0	35.5	0.0	0.0	**10.0**	12.2
▲ Athens Area Credit Union	Athens	WI	**C+**	C	C	29.6	6.73	0.2	11.8	13.6	0.0	**10.0**	13.0
Athol Credit Union	Athol	MA	**D**	D	D-	104.5	3.62	0.4	13.3	36.8	29.7	**5.0**	7.7
ATL Federal Credit Union	Wyoming	MI	**D+**	D+	C-	12.9	2.89	0.0	45.7	10.9	22.5	**9.8**	10.9
Atlanta Federal Credit Union	Atlanta	GA	**D**	D	D+	9.8	3.27	0.0	29.8	3.9	0.0	**10.0**	18.0
Atlanta Postal Credit Union	Atlanta	GA	**C+**	C+	B-	2123.4	3.49	7.7	42.9	18.0	27.6	**10.0**	13.0
Atlantic City Electric Co Employees FCU	Mays Landing	NJ	**C+**	C+	B-	60.6	-18.01	0.0	13.2	0.2	66.4	**10.0**	11.9
Atlantic City Federal Credit Union	Lander	WY	**B+**	B+	A-	114.4	-1.32	5.2	31.4	9.7	0.0	**10.0**	12.0
Atlantic City Police FCU	Atlantic City	NJ	**C**	C	C	2.4	3.71	0.0	6.3	0.0	0.0	**10.0**	12.1
Atlantic County NJ Employees FCU	Egg Harbor Townsh	NJ	**C**	C	C-	2.6	-2.37	0.0	12.7	0.0	0.0	**10.0**	23.5
Atlantic Federal Credit Union	Kenilworth	NJ	**D+**	D+	C-	233.5	-4.40	2.6	18.5	28.2	21.8	**10.0**	16.5
Atlantic Financial Federal Credit Union	Hunt Valley	MD	**C+**	C+	C+	92.0	3.55	0.0	30.1	20.0	16.6	**8.5**	10.1
Atlantic Health Employees FCU	Summit	NJ	**C**	C	C	22.1	4.44	0.0	30.8	0.0	0.0	**9.1**	10.4
Atlantic Regional Federal Credit Union	Brunswick	ME	**A-**	A-	B+	348.4	14.77	6.8	10.7	58.0	11.3	**10.0**	12.7

Asset Quality Index	Non-Performing Loans as a % of Total Loans	Non-Performing Loans as a % of Capital	Net Charge-Offs Avg Loans	Profitability Index	Net Income ($Mil)	Return on Assets	Return on Equity	Net Interest Spread	Overhead Efficiency Ratio	Liquidity Index	Liquidity Ratio	Hot Money Ratio	Stability Index
5.8	1.70	9.4	0.00	0.0	-0.01	-1.08	-11.76	3.17	137.5	5.6	52.6	0.0	3.4
6.8	0.61	3.1	0.56	3.1	0.23	0.74	5.59	3.40	75.5	3.7	21.9	6.4	7.0
7.4	2.56	5.2	-0.77	2.8	-0.02	-1.59	-5.90	4.56	145.0	4.9	24.0	0.0	6.2
6.3	1.10	4.8	0.18	3.3	0.01	0.38	2.91	5.29	89.0	5.8	45.7	0.0	6.5
6.3	0.67	6.1	0.41	0.0	-0.08	-0.86	-11.58	2.52	127.7	4.6	29.4	2.4	1.5
9.7	0.90	2.1	0.00	3.1	0.01	0.34	1.88	1.62	67.7	6.1	48.9	0.0	7.4
6.5	0.42	4.4	0.55	3.9	1.61	0.57	6.32	3.10	74.6	3.6	15.6	9.2	6.2
7.8	0.22	1.3	-0.24	4.6	0.01	0.44	3.75	4.15	94.4	5.4	33.7	0.0	4.3
8.7	1.27	2.7	0.00	4.2	0.01	0.54	2.49	3.62	84.2	5.5	46.9	0.0	7.4
7.3	1.94	5.7	0.32	9.2	0.22	1.15	5.95	3.72	66.4	4.3	27.3	9.8	9.2
0.7	14.21	42.6	-0.50	1.4	0.00	-1.16	-6.75	8.03	122.2	6.5	51.8	0.0	5.5
7.6	0.59	5.2	0.38	4.8	0.26	0.39	4.29	4.57	85.7	3.8	12.9	6.1	6.1
0.0	26.15	73.9	0.00	0.0	0.00	-2.92	-15.38	11.35	120.0	3.6	16.7	0.0	4.9
10.0	0.36	0.8	0.00	2.1	0.01	0.56	2.93	2.84	75.8	4.8	30.1	0.0	6.5
10.0	0.44	1.4	0.20	1.8	0.04	0.26	1.98	3.10	87.8	5.5	31.2	0.9	5.5
10.0	0.08	0.1	0.61	2.0	0.00	0.03	0.20	2.66	98.7	7.2	41.8	0.0	6.8
9.5	0.43	2.1	0.56	4.1	1.72	0.58	4.71	3.01	77.0	4.0	18.4	7.2	8.0
10.0	0.72	0.4	24.63	0.1	-0.04	-4.83	-17.72	5.89	152.3	5.4	16.5	0.0	4.7
7.6	1.09	8.4	0.35	1.7	-0.02	-0.07	-0.84	3.01	97.8	2.3	8.9	17.8	5.0
9.7	0.24	0.8	0.51	8.0	2.89	1.01	8.16	3.24	76.8	5.4	25.9	1.8	10.0
9.4	0.32	2.4	0.58	3.7	0.26	0.67	7.39	4.23	85.7	3.8	22.0	10.9	5.3
8.0	0.51	3.2	0.35	4.0	0.40	0.72	7.93	3.27	87.8	3.9	9.5	1.8	5.6
9.5	0.52	2.3	0.12	7.2	0.30	1.22	9.33	2.98	59.4	4.7	41.7	0.0	7.1
9.7	0.89	1.7	1.11	2.4	0.01	0.26	1.24	4.08	89.2	6.1	53.4	4.1	6.3
9.4	0.32	1.3	0.00	1.1	0.00	-0.62	-5.80	3.34	100.0	6.8	51.8	0.0	4.7
8.3	1.24	4.4	-0.41	2.2	0.00	0.18	1.99	3.68	95.0	6.1	42.1	0.0	4.0
5.5	5.15	13.7	0.00	5.9	0.01	1.46	18.24	3.86	50.0	7.1	65.3	0.0	3.0
0.6	23.73	48.3	11.11	8.0	0.00	2.14	8.89	12.70	75.0	6.4	56.0	0.0	7.5
10.0	2.50	1.3	0.00	2.2	0.00	0.00	0.00	3.24	66.7	5.2	18.9	0.0	7.6
9.6	0.40	1.8	0.45	7.7	5.32	1.05	6.14	3.26	68.4	3.7	14.2	6.6	9.9
7.0	0.48	7.5	0.22	2.7	0.11	0.69	7.80	3.55	83.6	4.6	23.6	1.9	3.8
8.0	0.58	4.1	0.59	4.0	0.40	0.39	3.99	3.75	82.7	3.7	17.0	9.6	6.0
5.1	2.17	10.8	-0.33	3.6	0.00	0.16	1.17	4.90	98.1	4.9	38.8	0.0	6.1
5.8	0.31	3.0	1.10	2.6	0.00	0.11	1.41	4.13	95.4	4.4	20.0	2.2	2.3
7.9	0.72	4.0	0.68	4.5	0.28	0.52	4.23	3.38	75.6	3.6	20.4	8.1	7.1
5.7	2.16	11.5	0.66	5.3	0.72	0.91	8.12	4.22	82.1	4.8	22.6	1.6	7.3
1.7	4.16	39.9	1.49	0.6	-0.52	-1.20	-13.23	5.23	85.8	4.1	17.4	5.2	4.7
8.0	0.56	3.6	0.29	5.3	0.30	0.79	7.19	4.23	82.4	4.5	19.2	4.2	7.7
8.1	0.36	2.1	0.68	4.2	1.93	0.52	4.40	2.73	77.9	5.1	29.2	2.7	7.8
8.3	0.62	4.5	1.40	3.7	-0.41	-0.43	-4.56	4.58	89.1	3.5	23.6	13.5	5.7
9.7	0.08	0.6	0.42	4.3	0.17	0.60	6.60	3.46	79.3	4.7	26.9	1.3	5.5
6.4	0.99	9.1	0.13	0.7	-0.14	-0.41	-4.01	2.80	102.8	4.2	17.1	0.6	5.6
9.5	0.70	2.5	0.69	2.0	0.00	0.06	0.36	3.57	98.5	5.2	38.7	0.0	6.5
8.6	0.50	2.0	0.00	1.5	0.00	0.00	0.00	2.08	100.0	7.2	63.6	0.0	4.8
7.3	0.84	5.6	-0.35	3.1	0.29	0.82	10.09	4.20	94.0	4.2	14.2	3.6	4.3
10.0	0.21	0.2	-0.14	1.8	0.00	0.17	0.65	2.37	94.6	5.3	45.3	1.4	6.9
5.8	4.73	12.8	0.73	1.4	-0.01	-0.46	-3.66	4.87	95.0	5.1	26.0	3.4	6.7
10.0	0.13	0.3	0.00	2.9	0.04	0.60	4.60	2.21	76.8	5.7	40.9	0.0	6.7
6.5	0.74	12.2	-0.01	0.4	-0.07	-0.25	-3.54	2.61	106.3	3.1	6.1	10.2	3.8
4.2	2.57	13.5	1.00	1.8	-0.01	-0.38	-3.43	4.79	94.6	3.4	13.1	9.8	4.3
9.8	0.57	1.3	-0.09	0.4	0.00	-0.17	-0.91	3.02	105.6	6.2	62.8	0.0	5.9
9.2	0.35	2.1	0.54	2.5	1.49	0.28	2.45	2.18	75.5	2.9	20.2	14.7	7.9
7.3	4.74	7.6	-0.86	2.8	0.05	0.30	2.58	2.53	80.9	6.2	37.7	0.0	5.3
7.6	0.91	4.5	0.41	4.9	0.20	0.69	6.44	3.82	76.0	4.9	29.0	5.1	7.1
10.0	0.66	0.7	2.46	1.2	0.00	-0.17	-1.41	2.56	109.1	7.7	93.5	0.0	4.8
10.0	0.00	0.0	0.00	1.7	0.00	0.00	0.00	2.03	100.0	6.8	67.2	0.0	6.4
7.4	1.62	6.5	0.25	0.4	-0.18	-0.32	-2.03	3.45	98.9	3.3	19.6	14.9	6.7
6.5	1.14	6.2	1.29	3.9	0.12	0.51	5.05	3.67	78.2	4.7	30.7	5.7	4.1
6.8	2.07	6.9	1.07	5.3	0.04	0.64	6.15	4.01	83.0	4.6	28.7	6.5	5.0
8.3	0.54	3.2	0.05	5.3	0.63	0.74	5.76	3.60	79.8	3.0	8.8	7.6	8.6

Name	City	State	Rating	2016 Rating	2015 Rating	Total Assets ($Mil)	One Year Asset Growth	Asset Mix (As a % of Total Assets) Commercial Loans	Consumer Loans	Mortgage Loans	Securities	Capitalization Index	Net Worth Ratio
Atlas Credit Union	Hannibal	MO	C-	C-	C-	<1	-14.44	0.0	67.1	0.0	0.0	10.0	17.3
Atomic Credit Union	Piketon	OH	B	B	B-	284.0	7.49	9.8	29.3	32.1	6.5	6.4	8.4
Atrium Credit Union, Inc.	Middletown	OH	C+	C+	C+	8.7	3.61	0.0	30.9	11.7	0.0	10.0	12.4
Attica-Wyoming Correctional Empls FCU	Attica	NY	C+	C+	C	14.5	-0.21	0.0	19.1	0.0	52.7	10.0	14.2
Attleboro ME Federal Credit Union	Attleboro	MA	C	C	D+	18.8	8.47	0.0	17.0	5.0	0.0	10.0	11.3
Auburn Community Federal Credit Union	Auburn	NY	C+	C+	C	91.3	7.35	0.0	11.3	0.0	49.7	7.0	9.0
Auburn University Federal Credit Union	Auburn	AL	C+	C+	C+	178.7	5.42	1.5	15.7	16.9	42.4	9.5	10.9
Audubon Federal Credit Union	Owensboro	KY	C-	C-	D+	22.1	3.77	0.0	39.2	18.9	0.0	8.1	9.7
Augusta County Federal Credit Union	Verona	VA	B-	B-	B-	24.3	2.54	0.2	36.3	0.0	8.1	10.0	15.5
Augusta Health Care Credit Union	Fishersville	VA	B-	B-	C+	11.8	-1.16	0.0	41.2	0.0	45.5	10.0	11.7
Augusta Metro Federal Credit Union	Augusta	GA	C-	C-	C+	118.1	4.72	0.0	68.8	4.0	0.1	7.6	9.4
Augusta VAH Federal Credit Union	Augusta	GA	B-	B-	C	69.7	1.29	0.0	48.4	3.4	3.0	10.0	13.9
▼ Aurgroup Financial Credit Union	Fairfield	OH	D+	C-	C-	154.9	2.92	4.3	33.8	24.9	11.1	5.9	8.1
Aurora Credit Union	Milwaukee	WI	A-	A-	B+	52.8	4.26	0.0	6.9	81.1	0.0	10.0	12.1
Aurora Federal Credit Union	Aurora	CO	A	A	A	92.9	9.16	3.1	22.6	15.3	1.0	10.0	16.3
Aurora Firefighters' Credit Union	Aurora	IL	D	D	D+	2.0	7.57	0.0	51.1	0.0	0.0	9.0	10.3
Aurora Policemen Credit Union	Aurora	IL	B	B	B	16.4	4.40	0.0	19.3	0.0	0.0	10.0	13.4
Aurora Postal Employees Credit Union	Aurora	IL	C-	C-	C-	2.1	1.36	0.0	53.2	0.0	0.0	10.0	19.4
Aurora Schools Federal Credit Union	Aurora	CO	C+	C+	C+	110.2	8.07	0.7	15.4	39.0	7.9	8.2	9.8
Austin City Employees Credit Union	Austin	MN	C	C	C	9.6	-0.93	0.0	32.6	8.0	10.3	10.0	12.3
Austin Federal Credit Union	Austin	TX	D	D	D+	33.8	9.88	0.0	21.8	9.6	9.2	4.6	6.7
Austin Telco Federal Credit Union	Austin	TX	A	A	A	1429.2	4.44	9.3	17.9	28.4	37.6	10.0	12.4
▼ Auto Club Federal Credit Union	Cerritos	CA	D	D+	D+	28.6	2.11	0.1	32.9	12.6	10.1	5.5	7.5
Auto-Owners Associates Credit Union	Lansing	MI	B-	B-	C+	35.6	6.61	0.0	18.1	0.0	29.3	10.0	11.3
▲ Autotruck Financial Credit Union	Louisville	KY	B+	B	B-	141.0	8.47	0.5	24.1	6.1	2.7	10.0	11.0
Avadian Credit Union	Hoover	AL	B	B	B	756.0	17.14	6.4	29.9	20.0	18.7	8.8	10.2
Avanti Federal Credit Union	Watertown	SD	C	C	C	18.1	5.69	2.3	23.1	11.5	1.0	10.0	11.2
Aventa Credit Union	Colorado Springs	CO	B+	B+	A-	176.1	8.02	2.5	49.9	15.5	1.9	8.7	10.2
▼ Avenue Baptist Brotherhood FCU	Shreveport	LA	D+	C-	D+	<1	-14.44	0.0	13.2	0.0	0.0	10.0	27.9
Avestar Credit Union	Waterloo	WI	C-	C-	D+	24.8	8.55	2.8	22.9	42.8	0.0	6.7	8.7
AVH Federal Credit Union	Natrona Heights	PA	C	C	C	5.3	3.12	0.0	17.9	0.0	0.0	10.0	28.3
Avista Corp. Credit Union	Spokane	WA	B+	B+	B+	63.0	7.32	0.0	18.4	32.8	30.1	10.0	14.5
Avoyelles Parish School Board Empls FCU	Marksville	LA	D	D	D	2.9	-2.98	0.0	19.2	0.0	0.0	10.0	22.0
▲ Awakon Federal Credit Union	Onaway	MI	B-	C+	C+	104.5	9.22	3.8	24.7	22.6	12.1	7.7	9.5
Azalea City Credit Union	Mobile	AL	C+	C+	C+	25.1	25.32	0.8	49.4	7.5	0.0	10.0	15.5
Azura Credit Union	Topeka	KS	B-	B-	C+	487.8	80.28	1.1	42.0	10.0	28.5	8.6	10.0
B E T Federal Credit Union	Yonkers	NY	D-	D-	D-	7.7	0.32	0.0	8.4	0.0	0.0	5.2	7.2
B N A Federal Credit Union	Arlington	VA	D	D	D	16.4	-8.36	0.0	8.2	0.0	18.2	10.0	11.4
B P S Federal Credit Union	Beeville	TX	C	C	C	4.0	-4.86	0.0	14.3	0.0	0.0	10.0	41.0
B&V Credit Union	Overland Park	KS	B-	B-	C+	66.7	0.40	0.0	15.7	0.0	24.0	10.0	11.7
B-M S Federal Credit Union	New Brunswick	NJ	C	C	C	113.6	0.93	0.0	4.5	7.4	65.0	10.0	13.5
B. Braun Federal Credit Union	Allentown	PA	D+	D+	D	2.7	1.62	0.0	28.4	0.0	0.0	6.3	8.3
▼ B.C.S. Community Credit Union	Wheat Ridge	CO	D+	C-	C+	24.4	-2.37	0.0	25.8	29.1	0.0	10.0	17.7
B.E.A. Credit Union	Bethalto	IL	C	C	C-	3.8	3.76	0.0	73.4	0.0	0.0	10.0	15.7
B.M.H. Federal Credit Union	Cleveland	TN	D+	D+	D+	3.0	-1.74	0.0	29.0	0.0	0.0	10.0	21.2
▼ B.O.N.D. Community Federal Credit Union	Atlanta	GA	D+	C-	C-	43.8	8.93	2.8	11.1	22.2	0.0	6.3	8.3
B.S. And C.P. Hospitals Employees FCU	Bronx	NY	B-	B-	B-	1.1	3.32	0.0	64.5	0.0	0.0	10.0	32.3
Bacharach Employees Federal Credit Union	New Kensington	PA	D	D	D	<1	-0.51	0.0	15.5	0.0	0.0	10.0	37.6
Back Mountain Federal Credit Union	Trucksville	PA	C	C	C	12.4	3.00	0.0	16.7	0.0	74.9	10.0	13.4
Badger Credit Union	Peshtigo	WI	C+	C+	C+	15.1	1.13	0.0	32.6	31.9	0.0	10.0	15.3
▼ Badger-Globe Credit Union	Neenah	WI	C+	B-	C+	44.2	2.22	0.0	23.6	26.8	0.0	10.0	12.9
Badlands Federal Credit Union	Glendive	MT	C-	C-	C	28.3	1.18	0.0	22.1	0.0	0.0	7.2	9.2
Baker Federal Credit Union	Phillipsburg	NJ	D-	D-	D	39.5	5.88	0.2	53.6	0.0	2.3	4.9	7.0
Baker Hughes Federal Credit Union	Houston	TX	D+	D+	C-	17.4	-12.01	0.0	17.3	0.0	0.0	8.6	10.1
Baker's Federal Credit Union	Omaha	NE	C	C	C	7.9	-0.33	0.0	39.8	0.0	4.3	10.0	14.2
Bakersfield City Employees FCU	Bakersfield	CA	C-	C-	C-	32.6	5.70	1.3	25.2	13.2	32.1	6.3	8.3
Baldwin County Federal Credit Union	Bay Minette	AL	B-	B-	B-	22.2	9.84	0.6	24.6	9.2	0.7	10.0	11.9
Ball State Federal Credit Union	Muncie	IN	D+	D+	D+	96.4	4.17	0.8	38.4	19.2	5.4	5.5	7.5
Baltimore County Employees FCU	Towson	MD	C	C	C	382.9	5.22	0.0	23.6	11.7	42.3	6.7	8.7
▼ Baltimore Washington FCU	Glen Burnie	MD	D-	D	D-	9.6	10.01	0.0	33.0	5.8	48.8	6.0	8.0

Asset Quality Index	Non-Performing Loans as a % of Total Loans	Non-Performing Loans as a % of Capital	Net Charge-Offs Avg Loans	Profitability Index	Net Income ($Mil)	Return on Assets	Return on Equity	Net Interest Spread	Overhead Efficiency Ratio	Liquidity Index	Liquidity Ratio	Hot Money Ratio	Stability Index
8.2	0.00	0.0	0.00	**3.2**	0.00	0.86	4.88	3.62	100.0	**3.9**	8.1	0.0	**6.7**
7.8	0.44	4.1	0.28	**4.9**	0.50	0.73	8.43	4.32	85.4	**4.1**	22.5	6.2	**5.8**
8.9	0.98	3.8	0.00	**4.1**	0.01	0.42	3.36	3.64	89.7	**5.7**	52.3	0.0	**6.6**
10.0	0.61	1.0	0.00	**3.2**	0.02	0.45	3.14	2.34	76.5	**6.8**	50.9	0.0	**7.2**
10.0	0.68	1.5	0.78	**1.7**	0.00	-0.04	-0.38	2.48	92.0	**6.2**	47.1	0.0	**6.2**
10.0	0.06	0.2	0.07	**3.2**	0.09	0.39	4.26	3.10	87.7	**5.8**	31.3	0.7	**4.7**
9.7	0.38	1.5	-0.23	**3.4**	0.29	0.65	6.35	2.69	81.1	**4.9**	34.0	7.7	**5.8**
6.6	0.79	5.3	0.14	**3.7**	0.04	0.69	7.14	3.59	84.2	**4.4**	18.7	1.0	**3.7**
8.6	0.79	2.1	0.74	**5.2**	0.04	0.72	4.60	2.78	60.0	**5.4**	26.5	0.0	**7.7**
7.7	0.88	3.3	0.45	**8.9**	0.05	1.65	14.48	3.34	55.4	**4.5**	24.0	5.1	**6.0**
4.8	1.23	10.1	1.41	**2.0**	-0.01	-0.03	-0.29	4.18	84.9	**4.2**	19.1	3.5	**4.9**
4.7	2.03	10.5	1.02	**3.3**	0.03	0.18	1.29	4.88	83.5	**4.7**	29.5	3.4	**6.2**
7.1	0.90	6.9	0.75	**0.9**	-0.17	-0.45	-5.55	3.44	98.8	**3.8**	17.2	7.3	**4.5**
9.9	0.15	1.1	-0.02	**9.4**	0.16	1.19	9.89	3.53	76.6	**3.0**	6.1	0.4	**7.3**
9.9	0.50	1.5	0.57	**8.1**	0.22	0.95	5.80	3.55	72.9	**5.9**	59.5	5.4	**9.2**
4.5	1.69	9.1	0.00	**3.0**	0.00	0.80	7.69	4.48	77.8	**5.6**	34.9	0.0	**2.3**
10.0	0.18	0.3	0.00	**2.6**	0.01	0.12	0.91	2.40	94.0	**6.7**	57.5	0.0	**7.6**
7.8	1.08	2.9	-0.36	**3.3**	0.00	0.77	3.96	4.39	80.0	**5.2**	35.2	0.0	**6.3**
8.9	0.38	2.6	0.23	**2.7**	0.05	0.18	1.82	2.77	93.1	**3.9**	20.6	8.4	**6.1**
9.9	0.00	0.0	0.00	**2.7**	0.00	0.17	1.35	3.31	95.1	**5.1**	42.3	0.0	**6.6**
6.8	1.20	6.4	0.13	**2.2**	0.00	0.05	0.71	2.30	98.0	**5.8**	50.1	0.5	**2.5**
9.7	0.10	0.5	0.04	**7.2**	3.58	1.01	8.58	2.11	64.2	**2.9**	10.1	17.9	**9.1**
8.4	0.35	2.1	0.84	**0.9**	-0.02	-0.25	-3.35	3.36	94.4	**4.2**	26.2	6.7	**2.3**
10.0	0.33	1.1	0.00	**3.9**	0.05	0.62	5.22	1.95	74.8	**6.5**	44.8	1.8	**6.6**
9.5	0.53	1.6	0.36	**5.4**	0.35	1.04	9.24	2.91	76.0	**6.5**	44.6	1.7	**7.3**
7.2	0.57	6.3	0.74	**3.3**	0.31	0.16	1.72	3.69	85.6	**3.8**	22.1	10.5	**6.3**
6.3	0.85	5.2	0.00	**3.1**	0.02	0.34	2.97	3.41	89.2	**4.3**	23.8	7.6	**6.1**
7.3	0.41	2.8	0.96	**2.7**	-0.04	-0.10	-0.97	4.30	88.7	**3.4**	16.1	11.5	**5.9**
9.3	0.00	0.0	0.00	**0.1**	0.00	-0.88	-3.13	2.99	133.3	**6.7**	96.7	0.0	**5.1**
8.3	0.36	2.6	0.02	**5.2**	0.04	0.69	7.88	3.96	85.9	**4.3**	31.5	5.1	**4.3**
10.0	1.67	1.3	4.91	**2.3**	0.00	-0.08	-0.27	2.93	80.0	**7.2**	80.0	0.0	**6.3**
9.3	0.65	2.8	0.00	**4.4**	0.09	0.60	4.05	2.19	71.7	**4.2**	15.7	0.0	**8.1**
8.4	7.47	6.7	0.66	**0.0**	-0.01	-0.70	-3.12	2.97	127.3	**5.3**	30.6	0.0	**5.3**
6.7	0.90	6.9	0.33	**4.3**	0.18	0.70	7.32	4.61	82.5	**4.7**	21.4	2.6	**5.1**
4.2	3.35	17.2	1.40	**9.0**	0.09	1.51	9.71	6.63	65.2	**2.1**	17.3	28.3	**6.6**
9.1	0.48	2.7	0.52	**3.9**	0.67	0.56	5.51	3.12	80.3	**4.5**	29.8	4.9	**5.6**
10.0	0.60	0.9	0.00	**2.1**	0.00	0.16	2.16	1.06	83.3	**5.6**	20.4	0.0	**1.7**
10.0	1.94	1.6	0.00	**0.7**	0.00	-0.07	-0.64	1.81	104.0	**5.5**	11.9	0.0	**4.3**
9.8	0.18	0.1	0.36	**1.9**	0.00	0.10	0.24	1.60	86.7	**6.4**	66.5	0.0	**7.2**
10.0	0.56	1.1	1.18	**3.8**	0.09	0.51	4.53	1.61	67.7	**5.0**	22.6	0.0	**5.4**
10.0	0.09	0.1	0.19	**1.9**	0.03	0.10	0.80	1.85	91.5	**6.4**	36.8	1.8	**7.6**
10.0	0.26	0.9	0.00	**3.7**	0.00	0.61	7.17	2.68	62.5	**7.4**	59.7	0.0	**3.0**
6.8	3.14	10.3	0.36	**0.6**	-0.02	-0.30	-1.66	4.04	107.6	**3.9**	24.2	12.2	**5.2**
6.1	1.02	4.5	0.85	**9.5**	0.02	2.20	14.17	4.42	48.7	**4.4**	15.2	0.0	**5.0**
10.0	0.23	0.3	-1.70	**0.5**	0.00	-0.40	-1.89	3.61	115.8	**7.3**	70.0	0.0	**5.1**
5.7	1.58	7.4	0.80	**1.2**	-0.03	-0.24	-2.86	3.34	106.0	**6.3**	60.6	0.0	**3.3**
8.5	0.00	0.0	0.00	**10.0**	0.02	6.84	21.53	12.39	28.0	**5.7**	50.9	0.0	**6.3**
9.1	0.00	0.0	0.00	**0.0**	0.00	-6.28	-16.22	8.79	200.0	**7.5**	86.9	0.0	**5.6**
7.2	6.32	8.2	0.18	**2.6**	0.00	0.13	0.96	1.46	89.2	**5.4**	30.0	0.0	**5.7**
9.5	0.00	0.0	0.00	**2.5**	0.00	-0.08	-0.52	3.87	102.2	**3.6**	25.6	13.2	**6.8**
6.6	1.99	8.8	0.35	**2.4**	0.00	0.04	0.28	3.23	88.3	**4.4**	31.5	2.1	**6.5**
7.5	1.83	5.3	0.16	**2.8**	0.04	0.60	6.37	2.30	80.7	**6.2**	37.0	0.0	**3.9**
2.0	2.38	29.5	0.89	**3.2**	0.07	0.74	10.65	6.11	79.7	**3.9**	14.7	3.0	**1.7**
7.7	2.08	4.2	-0.11	**1.1**	-0.01	-0.33	-3.20	2.34	111.6	**4.8**	21.4	4.9	**2.9**
9.8	0.00	0.0	0.40	**3.0**	0.01	0.26	1.80	3.10	91.1	**4.9**	18.5	0.0	**7.4**
8.3	0.02	0.1	1.15	**2.6**	0.02	0.22	2.66	3.08	92.7	**4.9**	33.9	9.9	**3.7**
9.8	0.44	1.5	0.04	**3.6**	0.02	0.39	2.95	3.73	89.5	**4.9**	19.4	5.7	**6.2**
5.2	1.15	12.2	0.43	**2.7**	0.04	0.18	2.39	4.04	89.3	**4.3**	21.7	4.4	**2.9**
9.9	0.37	2.1	0.13	**3.0**	0.30	0.32	4.02	2.46	86.7	**4.6**	22.6	2.3	**4.7**
9.8	0.28	1.4	0.11	**1.8**	0.00	0.17	2.09	2.66	94.9	**4.9**	21.3	0.0	**1.7**

Name	City	State	Rating	2016 Rating	2015 Rating	Total Assets ($Mil)	One Year Asset Growth	Asset Mix (As a % of Total Assets) Commercial Loans	Consumer Loans	Mortgage Loans	Securities	Capitalization Index	Net Worth Ratio
Bangor Federal Credit Union	Bangor	ME	**B-**	B-	B-	149.4	9.37	0.5	26.9	25.1	0.0	**6.8**	8.8
Bank-Fund Staff Federal Credit Union	Washington	DC	**B**	B	B-	4601.2	6.10	0.3	4.5	47.5	31.3	**9.9**	11.0
Banner Federal Credit Union	Phoenix	AZ	**C**	C	C	61.2	3.02	0.0	38.1	0.0	48.5	**8.8**	10.3
Baptist Credit Union	San Antonio	TX	**D+**	D+	C-	35.9	5.82	8.2	45.7	18.2	0.0	**6.4**	8.4
Baptist Health Federal Credit Union	Little Rock	AR	**B+**	B+	B+	29.8	3.13	0.0	54.6	0.0	0.0	**10.0**	16.2
Baptist Health South Florida FCU	Miami	FL	**B+**	B+	B+	59.2	4.35	0.0	53.6	2.6	0.0	**10.0**	12.3
Bar-Cons Federal Credit Union	Columbus	IN	**C+**	C+	C-	36.2	7.55	0.0	32.7	6.0	0.2	**7.1**	9.0
▼ Baraboo Municipal Employees Credit Union	Baraboo	WI	**D+**	C-	C-	1.8	1.52	0.0	47.9	0.0	0.0	**10.0**	18.0
Baraga County Federal Credit Union	L'Anse	MI	**C-**	C-	D	37.0	5.41	0.0	18.3	2.0	56.2	**5.6**	8.2
Bard Employees Federal Credit Union	New Providence	NJ	**D+**	D+	C-	17.5	-2.80	7.5	7.0	13.8	14.6	**8.3**	9.9
Bardes Employees Federal Credit Union	Cincinnati	OH	**D**	D	D+	<1	5.03	0.0	48.5	0.0	37.5	**7.9**	10.5
Barksdale Federal Credit Union	Bossier City	LA	**B-**	B-	B-	1302.1	4.29	1.7	32.1	14.8	26.7	**8.2**	9.8
Barstow Community Credit Union	Barstow	CA	**C-**	C-	C	8.9	2.33	0.0	31.3	0.0	0.0	**10.0**	11.7
Barton Plant Employees FCU	Luling	LA	**B-**	B-	B-	18.8	0.03	0.0	31.9	8.8	0.0	**10.0**	19.4
BASF Chattanooga Federal Credit Union	Chattanooga	TN	**D+**	D+	D+	3.0	-6.57	0.0	47.4	0.0	0.0	**10.0**	15.1
Bashas' Associates Federal Credit Union	Tempe	AZ	**C-**	C-	D-	17.5	8.53	0.0	28.6	0.0	0.0	**7.4**	9.3
▲ Baton Rouge City Parish Employees FCU	Baton Rouge	LA	**C+**	C	C-	52.1	9.78	0.0	31.3	4.4	0.0	**10.0**	15.0
Baton Rouge Fire Department FCU	Baton Rouge	LA	**A-**	A-	A-	53.1	13.95	0.0	49.5	20.1	0.0	**10.0**	17.3
Baton Rouge Telco Federal Credit Union	Baton Rouge	LA	**B+**	B+	B+	296.9	5.53	0.0	57.2	23.1	0.7	**9.3**	10.5
Battery Employees Federal Credit Union	Attica	IN	**D**	D	D+	1.4	-5.33	0.0	37.0	0.0	0.0	**10.0**	22.1
Baxter Credit Union	Vernon Hills	IL	**A-**	A-	A-	2803.7	10.24	2.1	33.3	40.6	1.2	**8.0**	9.7
Bay Area Credit Union	Oregon	OH	**B**	B	B	62.9	6.58	0.3	37.8	14.2	5.9	**10.0**	12.8
Bay Atlantic Federal Credit Union	Vineland	NJ	**C-**	C-	C	58.9	3.84	0.2	23.6	5.5	13.1	**5.5**	7.5
▲ Bay Cities Credit Union	Hayward	CA	**C+**	C	C	74.6	7.67	0.0	29.5	0.0	0.0	**6.0**	8.0
Bay Credit Union	Panama City	FL	**C**	C	C	84.6	1.24	0.0	43.8	14.4	20.6	**8.2**	9.8
Bay Federal Credit Union	Capitola	CA	**B**	B	B	890.2	13.03	0.2	28.2	18.4	25.6	**6.2**	8.5
Bay Ridge Federal Credit Union	Brooklyn	NY	**D+**	D+	C-	203.5	0.58	60.6	11.0	32.8	1.1	**7.5**	9.3
Bay Ridge Lodge No. 632 FCU	Marlboro	NJ	**B-**	B-	C+	<1	0.00	0.0	32.2	0.0	0.0	**10.0**	52.9
Bay Shore Credit Union	Marinette	WI	**B**	B	B	29.5	2.70	0.0	33.4	8.1	0.0	**10.0**	17.0
Baycel Federal Credit Union	Bay City	TX	**A-**	A-	A-	57.5	9.22	0.0	31.5	9.0	0.4	**10.0**	16.2
▼ Bayer Credit Union	Kansas City	MO	**E+**	D-	D	7.5	6.89	0.0	32.2	0.0	1.3	**6.4**	8.4
Bayer Heritage Federal Credit Union	Proctor	WV	**B-**	B-	B	452.5	12.64	4.7	28.6	36.6	4.2	**6.8**	8.9
Baylands Federal Credit Union	West Point	VA	**D+**	D+	D+	74.5	3.62	0.0	31.4	27.0	12.5	**6.3**	8.5
Baylor Health Care System Credit Union	Dallas	TX	**B+**	B+	B+	72.8	8.38	0.0	31.4	7.1	32.5	**10.0**	16.4
Bayonne City Empls Federal Credit Unions	Bayonne	NJ	**C**	C	C	5.6	2.53	0.0	29.5	0.0	0.0	**10.0**	22.8
Bayonne Hospital Employees FCU	Bayonne	NJ	**C-**	C-	C-	5.3	-3.79	0.0	16.8	0.0	0.1	**10.0**	14.4
Bayonne School Employees FCU	Bayonne	NJ	**D**	D	C-	5.5	6.83	0.0	11.8	0.0	0.0	**4.4**	6.4
▼ Bayou City Federal Credit Union	Houston	TX	**D**	D+	D	26.0	1.76	0.0	30.0	0.0	0.0	**5.7**	7.8
Bayou Federal Credit Union	Baton Rouge	LA	**C**	C	C	76.0	7.34	0.4	50.2	15.2	0.2	**10.0**	12.9
▲ BCBST Employees Credit Union	Chattanooga	TN	**B**	B-	B-	11.2	-1.11	0.0	18.2	11.8	0.0	**10.0**	18.0
BCM Federal Credit Union	Houston	TX	**D+**	D+	D	39.1	1.22	0.3	28.7	6.6	0.6	**5.3**	7.3
Beach Municipal Federal Credit Union	Virginia Beach	VA	**B-**	B-	B	118.4	4.93	0.3	34.6	6.3	4.1	**10.0**	11.8
▼ Beacon Community Credit Union	Louisville	KY	**B-**	B+	B+	63.7	8.83	0.1	25.9	6.2	42.3	**9.0**	10.3
Beacon Credit Union	Wabash	IN	**B**	B	B	1200.8	3.59	65.7	2.0	59.8	12.8	**10.0**	14.6
Beacon Credit Union, Incorporated	Lynchburg	VA	**C+**	C+	B-	163.4	-0.93	2.5	67.0	3.7	0.0	**6.5**	8.5
▼ Beacon Federal Credit Union	La Porte	TX	**C**	C+	B-	152.7	3.49	0.0	42.2	6.8	15.3	**5.4**	7.5
▼ Beacon Mutual Federal Credit Union	Lima	OH	**E+**	D-	D	14.5	9.76	0.0	26.2	0.0	37.2	**5.4**	7.4
▼ Bear Paw Credit Union	Havre	MT	**C-**	C	C	118.6	2.26	1.0	25.9	17.5	0.0	**6.0**	8.0
Beaumont Community Credit Union	Beaumont	TX	**C**	C	C	28.7	1.60	0.0	33.0	0.4	0.0	**9.8**	10.8
Beauregard School Employees FCU	Deridder	LA	**C**	C	C+	21.6	1.54	0.0	50.8	0.0	0.5	**10.0**	12.8
Beaver Avenue Federal Credit Union	Pittsburgh	PA	**E+**	E+	E+	4.7	-4.25	0.0	89.8	0.0	0.0	**6.3**	8.3
Beaver County Times Federal Credit Union	Beaver	PA	**C-**	C-	C-	<1	-2.88	0.0	41.9	0.0	0.0	**10.0**	56.1
Beaver Falls Pennsylvania Teachers FCU	Wampum	PA	**C-**	C-	C	2.6	7.14	0.0	66.4	0.0	0.0	**10.0**	16.1
Beaver Valley Federal Credit Union	Beaver Falls	PA	**C**	C	C	75.6	3.52	0.5	12.2	10.8	0.0	**10.0**	15.8
Becco Buffalo Federal Credit Union	Tonawanda	NY	**C-**	C-	C-	1.4	-12.02	0.0	24.8	0.0	25.1	**10.0**	14.7
Beckstrand & Associates Credit Union	Salt Lake City	UT	**C+**	C+	C+	<1	-12.11	0.0	0.0	0.0	0.0	**10.0**	53.7
Bedco Hospital Federal Credit Union	Everett	PA	**C-**	C-	C-	2.3	-1.03	0.0	65.4	0.0	0.0	**10.0**	14.2
▼ Bedford VA Federal Credit Union	Bedford	MA	**D+**	C-	C	3.3	-0.18	0.0	33.4	0.0	0.0	**10.0**	23.5
Bee Federal Credit Union	Salisbury	MD	**C+**	C+	C	7.4	0.31	0.0	23.4	0.0	0.0	**10.0**	22.7
▼ Beehive Federal Credit Union	Rexburg	ID	**B+**	A-	A-	241.2	11.97	0.1	32.0	31.8	4.5	**9.7**	10.9

Asset Quality Index	Non-Performing Loans as a % of Total Loans	Non-Performing Loans as a % of Capital	Net Charge-Offs Avg Loans	Profitability Index	Net Income ($Mil)	Return on Assets	Return on Equity	Net Interest Spread	Overhead Efficiency Ratio	Liquidity Index	Liquidity Ratio	Hot Money Ratio	Stability Index
8.7	0.36	2.8	0.17	**3.8**	0.22	0.60	6.77	3.15	86.0	**3.0**	18.7	11.2	**5.8**
9.6	0.48	2.4	0.14	**5.0**	9.36	0.82	7.53	2.19	59.6	**4.6**	29.3	7.8	**8.3**
8.4	0.75	3.0	0.44	**2.5**	0.02	0.11	1.03	2.69	89.4	**5.3**	29.0	0.0	**4.9**
6.2	0.34	4.4	0.25	**0.3**	-0.07	-0.78	-9.09	4.37	110.0	**5.0**	36.0	5.1	**3.5**
7.8	1.05	3.7	-0.11	**6.3**	0.07	0.97	6.01	3.64	81.7	**5.5**	40.4	1.7	**7.9**
6.6	1.43	7.8	1.42	**8.2**	0.18	1.26	10.18	5.92	77.3	**4.3**	15.1	1.7	**5.8**
8.5	0.76	4.1	-0.02	**3.3**	0.05	0.53	5.62	3.48	88.2	**5.1**	26.7	1.1	**4.6**
5.4	3.37	9.1	0.00	**0.6**	0.00	-0.65	-3.67	4.42	113.3	**6.6**	57.8	0.0	**5.4**
8.2	0.64	2.3	1.07	**2.3**	0.04	0.41	5.41	2.64	78.0	**5.1**	15.3	2.3	**3.2**
3.3	4.24	24.0	0.45	**1.2**	0.01	0.27	2.79	2.86	90.7	**4.8**	28.6	5.9	**3.4**
8.8	0.00	0.0	0.00	**0.9**	0.00	0.00	0.00	4.03	111.1	**4.8**	15.1	0.0	**5.1**
7.0	0.97	5.4	0.73	**3.1**	0.84	0.26	2.65	2.98	83.1	**4.1**	16.5	9.6	**6.6**
8.3	0.13	0.5	2.57	**2.5**	0.00	0.14	1.15	4.99	97.7	**6.3**	66.3	5.1	**6.6**
9.7	0.49	1.1	-0.10	**4.2**	0.03	0.54	2.75	2.94	83.3	**5.0**	36.2	0.0	**7.2**
4.7	3.85	13.6	1.00	**3.4**	0.01	0.84	5.41	5.06	69.2	**6.2**	41.9	0.0	**5.6**
9.6	0.47	1.4	0.00	**2.4**	0.01	0.19	1.97	3.81	97.2	**6.4**	47.2	0.0	**3.9**
9.8	0.41	1.1	0.12	**2.7**	0.05	0.35	2.31	2.60	86.6	**6.1**	50.1	0.0	**7.0**
8.3	0.34	1.8	0.08	**9.8**	0.21	1.58	9.19	4.18	63.4	**4.0**	19.0	2.8	**8.0**
6.0	0.58	5.9	0.42	**4.3**	0.51	0.69	6.65	2.71	71.2	**1.8**	17.6	21.6	**7.1**
6.2	8.20	13.1	-0.80	**0.3**	0.00	-0.58	-2.68	5.25	107.1	**6.5**	42.8	0.0	**4.7**
8.7	0.31	3.2	0.47	**8.4**	7.92	1.17	11.90	3.45	73.6	**2.9**	10.5	9.2	**7.9**
7.1	1.07	5.9	0.23	**3.6**	0.05	0.33	2.73	3.98	91.6	**3.8**	16.7	2.7	**6.7**
6.2	1.23	7.8	0.59	**3.4**	0.05	0.37	4.83	3.72	88.5	**4.9**	19.4	1.0	**2.8**
9.9	0.28	1.2	0.33	**4.3**	0.12	0.67	8.30	3.50	84.5	**4.8**	27.0	1.5	**3.5**
8.2	0.32	2.4	0.56	**1.9**	0.03	0.12	1.37	4.23	94.2	**3.6**	14.9	7.1	**3.6**
7.0	0.85	6.3	0.22	**6.6**	1.97	0.90	11.00	3.57	80.4	**4.6**	15.8	2.8	**6.2**
0.1	3.65	28.6	0.24	**2.2**	0.02	0.04	0.41	3.70	71.5	**1.1**	12.8	47.4	**6.6**
10.0	0.00	0.0	0.00	**8.7**	0.00	4.55	8.70	13.33	0.0	**8.6**	146.3	0.0	**6.3**
9.6	0.59	1.7	-0.03	**3.9**	0.04	0.48	2.80	3.08	85.1	**5.2**	35.4	1.1	**7.4**
7.1	1.85	6.7	0.39	**8.8**	0.23	1.58	9.85	3.21	53.8	**4.1**	23.9	9.4	**8.5**
6.5	1.70	7.8	1.06	**0.0**	-0.01	-0.78	-8.74	3.25	104.6	**6.2**	53.0	1.2	**3.1**
6.4	0.81	7.1	0.54	**2.6**	0.05	0.05	0.50	3.04	86.3	**3.5**	23.0	10.5	**5.5**
4.1	1.76	16.3	0.04	**2.8**	0.05	0.29	3.89	3.51	92.4	**3.3**	11.0	7.3	**3.0**
8.7	1.58	4.1	0.57	**5.2**	0.13	0.69	4.66	3.12	75.7	**5.1**	28.5	0.0	**7.3**
10.0	0.00	0.0	0.00	**2.8**	0.00	0.29	1.26	2.91	89.5	**5.3**	18.0	0.0	**7.1**
10.0	0.00	0.0	9.58	**1.9**	0.00	0.00	0.00	2.81	89.5	**5.1**	25.7	0.0	**5.3**
8.0	1.68	3.1	0.00	**5.8**	0.01	1.16	16.33	2.02	43.5	**6.6**	65.9	0.0	**2.3**
6.1	1.92	8.2	1.51	**0.9**	-0.02	-0.35	-4.54	3.46	98.8	**5.0**	26.1	4.9	**2.1**
7.2	0.41	4.9	0.06	**2.5**	0.04	0.22	2.08	3.90	92.9	**4.0**	18.3	3.3	**5.6**
10.0	0.53	0.9	0.00	**5.7**	0.03	1.09	5.81	4.13	72.4	**7.2**	55.7	0.0	**7.2**
6.0	2.06	11.1	0.89	**3.5**	0.05	0.48	6.68	3.19	79.6	**5.8**	64.8	0.0	**2.2**
6.5	1.98	10.6	0.32	**3.4**	0.12	0.42	3.85	4.05	88.0	**5.1**	24.7	1.8	**6.9**
8.2	0.68	2.4	0.87	**1.6**	-0.04	-0.23	-2.10	3.28	94.7	**4.8**	27.8	8.6	**4.7**
5.7	0.63	4.4	0.01	**3.9**	1.29	0.43	3.11	2.88	83.4	**2.2**	10.2	17.7	**9.3**
5.1	0.87	7.4	1.40	**3.1**	0.02	0.04	0.52	5.31	73.6	**2.9**	17.1	16.3	**4.3**
8.4	0.37	3.4	1.10	**1.2**	-0.14	-0.37	-4.85	3.74	91.0	**4.4**	15.2	3.8	**3.9**
5.3	2.18	10.0	1.22	**0.9**	-0.01	-0.41	-5.15	3.11	90.8	**5.8**	35.4	0.8	**2.6**
7.7	1.47	8.4	0.31	**1.1**	-0.10	-0.32	-3.97	2.84	104.5	**5.7**	42.9	6.6	**5.0**
9.1	0.41	1.4	1.01	**1.1**	-0.02	-0.27	-2.43	1.83	92.5	**3.8**	49.6	20.4	**5.6**
4.8	2.05	9.9	0.00	**3.4**	0.03	0.50	3.92	1.90	72.3	**4.1**	12.5	0.0	**5.9**
1.2	3.64	34.2	5.08	**1.8**	-0.04	-3.02	-35.21	5.73	50.8	**3.1**	8.9	0.0	**1.0**
9.8	0.79	0.6	0.00	**1.5**	0.00	0.00	0.00	3.25	100.0	**6.1**	46.6	0.0	**6.8**
8.4	0.06	0.2	0.00	**1.3**	-0.01	-0.93	-5.67	4.70	124.0	**5.0**	36.9	0.0	**6.8**
10.0	0.58	1.2	0.19	**1.8**	-0.03	-0.15	-0.99	4.86	102.5	**7.8**	74.8	1.5	**6.6**
8.7	0.56	1.0	0.00	**1.1**	0.00	-0.29	-1.99	2.77	114.3	**6.2**	28.4	0.0	**6.6**
10.0	0.00	0.0	0.00	**1.8**	0.00	0.00	0.00	0.00	0.0	**9.3**	171.0	0.0	**7.3**
7.9	0.79	3.4	0.00	**3.6**	0.00	0.35	2.45	8.88	94.6	**5.9**	40.4	0.0	**6.2**
9.5	0.00	0.0	-0.35	**0.8**	-0.01	-0.99	-4.15	4.60	130.8	**6.6**	66.8	0.0	**6.0**
9.0	0.91	1.0	7.94	**6.6**	0.02	0.92	4.07	3.16	70.9	**5.1**	20.1	0.0	**5.0**
8.5	0.51	3.7	0.07	**5.2**	0.45	0.75	6.90	2.97	80.1	**3.4**	14.7	6.5	**7.6**

Name	City	State	Rating	2016 Rating	2015 Rating	Total Assets ($Mil)	One Year Asset Growth	Asset Mix (As a % of Total Assets) Comm-ercial Loans	Cons-umer Loans	Mort-gage Loans	Secur-ities	Capital-ization Index	Net Worth Ratio
Befit Financial Federal Credit Union	Vacaville, CA	CA	**D+**	D+	C	39.0	-3.39	10.4	29.0	22.0	0.0	**7.1**	9.1
▲ BEKA Federal Credit Union	Rome	GA	**D**	D-	D	6.9	-0.98	0.0	52.1	0.0	0.0	**10.0**	12.0
Belco Community Credit Union	Harrisburg	PA	**B**	B	C+	470.9	3.35	10.1	33.4	11.6	9.8	**7.9**	9.6
Belen Railway Employees Credit Union	Belen	NM	**B+**	B+	B	29.5	5.14	2.7	31.8	22.6	0.0	**10.0**	13.3
Bell Credit Union	Hutchinson	KS	**C+**	C+	C-	11.7	2.42	0.9	54.3	1.8	0.0	**10.0**	13.6
BellCo Credit Union	Greenwood Village	CO	**A**	A	A	4345.6	18.02	10.3	36.5	21.2	1.3	**7.2**	9.1
Bellco Federal Credit Union	Wyomissing	PA	**C-**	C-	D-	114.9	4.44	4.1	21.1	19.4	20.6	**7.1**	9.1
Belle River Community Credit Union	Casco	MI	**C-**	C-	C-	21.0	-2.49	0.0	9.6	13.4	0.0	**6.8**	8.8
Bellwether Community Credit Union	Manchester	NH	**C-**	C-	C-	487.9	13.20	2.0	32.8	24.6	22.3	**7.4**	9.7
Belmont Municipal Federal Credit Union	Belmont	MA	**C+**	C+	C+	4.2	13.24	0.0	25.8	0.0	0.0	**10.0**	13.1
▲ Belton Federal Credit Union	Belton	TX	**D+**	D	D	4.3	-0.35	0.0	34.7	0.0	9.4	**10.0**	11.4
Ben E. Keith Employees FCU	Fort Worth	TX	**C+**	C+	C+	9.2	7.86	0.0	47.3	0.0	0.0	**10.0**	15.3
Benchmark Federal Credit Union	West Chester	PA	**D+**	D+	C	237.0	0.03	0.0	26.8	33.5	10.9	**10.0**	12.7
Bent River Community Credit Union	Davenport	IA	**C-**	C-	D+	20.0	-7.46	9.2	20.7	29.5	16.6	**10.0**	13.1
Benton County Schools Credit Union	Corvallis	OR	**C**	C	C-	49.6	5.26	0.0	10.5	33.7	1.0	**5.8**	7.8
Berea Federal Credit Union	Brooklyn	NY	**C**	C	C+	<1	-5.17	0.0	19.1	0.0	19.1	**10.0**	16.4
Berean Credit Union	Chicago	IL	**C-**	C-	C-	<1	2.59	0.0	0.0	0.0	0.0	**10.0**	18.5
▲ Bergen Division Federal Credit Union	Toms River	NJ	**B-**	C+	C+	10.1	8.25	0.0	42.6	0.0	0.0	**10.0**	17.3
Berkeley Community Federal Credit Union	Moncks Corner	SC	**C+**	C+	C	11.1	1.72	0.0	50.0	0.3	0.0	**10.0**	17.5
Berkeley County Public Schools FCU	Martinsburg	WV	**E+**	E+	E+	5.7	9.53	0.0	40.2	0.0	0.0	**3.7**	5.7
▼ Berrien Teachers Federal Credit Union	Nashville	GA	**D+**	C-	C	1.3	2.72	0.0	42.1	0.0	0.0	**10.0**	13.9
Berylco Employees' Credit Union	Hamburg	PA	**C-**	C-	C-	2.5	-5.15	0.0	11.9	0.0	0.0	**10.0**	40.7
Bessemer System Federal Credit Union	Greenville	PA	**C**	C	C	39.0	-1.27	0.0	29.9	7.4	0.6	**10.0**	14.3
Besser Credit Union	Alpena	MI	**B**	B	B-	73.3	7.05	0.9	20.4	15.4	25.6	**8.5**	10.2
Best Financial Credit Union	Muskegon	MI	**A**	A	A	85.6	5.68	0.4	26.2	14.9	18.2	**10.0**	20.6
Best Reward Credit Union	Brook Park	OH	**C-**	C-	C-	155.5	0.30	2.7	10.0	2.1	52.3	**10.0**	11.9
Bethany Baptist Christian FCU	Chester	PA	**C**	C	D+	<1	-4.00	0.0	0.0	0.0	0.0	**10.0**	20.8
Bethel A.M.E. Church Credit Union	Chicago	IL	**C-**	C-	D+	<1	-7.58	0.0	1.6	0.0	0.0	**10.0**	16.4
Bethel Baptist Church East Credit Union	Detroit	MI	**C**	C	D+	<1	6.08	0.0	12.4	0.0	0.0	**10.0**	12.9
▼ Bethlehem 1st Federal Credit Union	Bethlehem	PA	**C-**	C	C-	51.8	4.71	0.5	10.1	5.5	48.9	**9.1**	10.4
Bethpage Federal Credit Union	Bethpage	NY	**B**	B	B	6982.2	5.06	14.0	6.7	46.5	22.4	**6.7**	8.7
Beulah Federal Credit Union	Brooklyn	NY	**D+**	D+	C-	<1	-1.69	0.0	10.3	0.0	0.0	**5.4**	7.4
Beverly Bus Garage Federal Credit Union	Evergreen Park	IL	**C**	C	C	4.0	4.24	0.0	79.3	0.0	0.0	**10.0**	42.2
Beverly Hills City Employees FCU	Beverly Hills	CA	**B-**	B-	B-	21.0	-2.01	0.0	24.0	3.0	10.2	**10.0**	12.0
Beverly Municipal Federal Credit Union	Beverly	MA	**C**	C	C-	10.9	-0.05	0.0	25.9	17.1	23.3	**10.0**	18.0
BFG Federal Credit Union	Akron	OH	**D**	D	D+	153.6	-0.89	0.3	31.8	17.5	26.0	**9.7**	10.9
BHCU	Ridley Park	PA	**B+**	B+	B+	139.2	5.13	4.6	10.1	35.5	38.6	**10.0**	16.1
Bi-County PTC Federal Credit Union	Warren	MI	**D-**	D-	D+	9.0	5.71	1.9	32.9	8.8	23.2	**5.7**	7.7
Big Bethel A.M.E. Church FCU	Atlanta	GA	**D+**	D+	D-	<1	12.76	0.0	8.3	0.0	0.0	**7.7**	9.5
Big Island Federal Credit Union	Hilo	HI	**C+**	C+	C+	95.9	7.09	0.5	25.2	14.8	1.0	**6.9**	8.9
Big Sky Federal Credit Union	Billings	MT	**C-**	C-	C-	8.6	3.77	0.0	24.6	0.0	0.0	**8.6**	10.1
Big Spring Education Employees FCU	Big Spring	TX	**B+**	B+	B	47.7	4.74	0.0	34.3	0.1	0.0	**10.0**	13.6
▼ Billerica Municipal Employees CU	Billerica	MA	**D+**	C-	D+	14.5	-1.02	0.0	12.3	8.7	0.0	**10.0**	21.3
Billings Federal Credit Union	Billings	MT	**A**	A	A	137.4	7.16	2.1	29.2	31.8	0.0	**10.0**	12.3
Biloxi Teachers Federal Credit Union	Biloxi	MS	**C-**	C-	C-	10.0	2.87	0.0	24.8	0.0	0.0	**9.3**	10.5
Binsy Federal Credit Union	Memphis	TN	**D+**	D+	D+	1.7	10.59	0.0	61.9	0.0	0.0	**10.0**	17.0
Birmingham-Bloomfield Credit Union	Birmingham	MI	**C**	C	C+	66.7	6.07	25.5	18.4	17.9	0.2	**5.8**	7.8
Bison Federal Credit Union	Shawnee	OK	**C+**	C+	C	38.9	1.17	0.3	13.4	0.0	36.8	**7.0**	9.3
Bitterroot Community FCU	Darby	MT	**D**	D	D	11.3	18.05	0.0	30.2	0.0	39.3	**5.4**	7.4
Bivins Federal Credit Union	Masterson	TX	**D**	D	D	7.1	-6.03	0.0	38.7	0.0	0.0	**10.0**	14.3
Black Hills Federal Credit Union	Rapid City	SD	**A-**	A-	A-	1162.7	6.12	9.9	15.4	32.5	16.3	**10.0**	11.5
Blackhawk Area Credit Union	Savanna	IL	**C-**	C-	D+	34.8	3.80	0.0	21.6	28.9	0.0	**6.6**	8.6
Blackhawk Community Credit Union	Janesville	WI	**B**	B	B	488.0	12.84	8.9	25.7	28.3	17.9	**6.3**	8.4
▼ Blackhawk Federal Credit Union	Beaver Falls	PA	**D+**	C-	C+	14.3	-5.97	0.0	17.3	0.1	2.1	**10.0**	11.7
Blackstone River Federal Credit Union	Woonsocket	RI	**C+**	C+	C+	53.2	4.14	0.0	22.4	5.6	1.4	**6.2**	8.2
Blair County Federal Credit Union	Altoona	PA	**B-**	B-	C+	53.8	2.95	0.0	15.5	4.7	30.9	**10.0**	17.3
▲ Blaw-Knox Credit Union	Mattoon	IL	**B-**	C+	C	10.4	3.30	0.0	48.9	0.0	0.0	**10.0**	16.2
Bloomfield Fire & Police FCU	Bloomfield	NJ	**C-**	C-	C-	6.6	1.41	0.0	62.4	0.0	0.0	**10.0**	15.8
Bloomington Municipal Credit Union	Bloomington	IL	**B-**	B-	B-	25.2	2.89	0.0	31.5	0.0	0.0	**10.0**	12.1
Bloomington Postal Employees CU	Bloomington	IL	**C+**	C+	B-	22.7	3.02	0.0	35.3	0.0	0.0	**10.0**	14.1

Asset Quality Index	Non-Performing Loans as a % of Total Loans	Non-Performing Loans as a % of Capital	Net Charge-Offs Avg Loans	Profitability Index	Net Income ($Mil)	Return on Assets	Return on Equity	Net Interest Spread	Overhead Efficiency Ratio	Liquidity Index	Liquidity Ratio	Hot Money Ratio	Stability Index
8.5	0.15	1.1	0.90	1.2	-0.04	-0.39	-4.28	3.98	106.2	4.3	12.4	1.8	3.5
2.8	3.49	19.4	2.61	2.2	0.01	0.76	6.40	5.40	103.6	4.6	31.9	5.1	4.8
5.9	1.29	10.6	0.67	4.5	0.71	0.62	7.06	4.06	78.8	3.6	8.4	3.7	5.4
8.0	1.38	6.1	0.76	8.3	0.09	1.18	8.79	4.42	69.5	3.7	27.7	15.0	7.0
5.8	1.18	5.7	0.36	3.5	0.02	0.73	5.29	4.12	83.6	3.1	16.9	9.6	6.8
7.6	0.52	4.4	0.67	6.6	5.39	0.53	5.49	3.87	58.7	4.0	33.1	20.8	7.2
7.0	1.16	8.1	0.27	2.0	0.04	0.12	1.35	3.61	94.9	4.6	19.0	1.6	5.1
10.0	0.00	0.0	0.14	2.3	0.00	0.02	0.22	2.06	98.5	5.7	47.8	3.4	3.7
9.7	0.23	1.7	0.37	2.0	0.20	0.17	1.75	2.80	86.3	2.0	4.8	19.9	5.4
10.0	0.06	0.2	2.40	5.0	0.01	0.68	5.15	3.72	77.4	6.2	58.6	0.0	7.0
10.0	0.26	0.8	0.54	1.8	0.01	0.66	5.77	3.17	82.4	5.2	17.6	0.0	4.4
7.1	1.43	4.6	0.17	6.5	0.02	0.97	6.26	3.91	71.6	5.3	39.7	0.0	5.0
9.6	0.41	2.1	0.38	1.0	0.03	0.04	0.33	3.18	92.1	3.9	20.5	4.7	6.8
8.2	0.41	1.8	1.60	1.7	-0.01	-0.14	-1.07	3.14	103.7	3.4	26.3	12.3	6.2
10.0	0.08	0.5	0.00	2.9	0.03	0.23	2.91	2.62	91.3	5.2	33.5	2.8	3.7
4.0	14.29	16.7	0.00	7.1	0.00	3.70	23.53	9.76	0.0	7.9	72.8	0.0	6.6
10.0	0.00	0.0	0.00	1.5	0.00	0.00	0.00	0.00	0.0	7.9	72.2	0.0	6.0
7.6	2.31	5.5	3.99	6.8	0.00	0.08	0.46	4.96	53.5	6.0	58.5	0.0	5.7
5.0	2.33	10.1	0.40	5.4	0.01	0.22	1.24	6.99	84.8	6.4	53.3	3.0	7.3
6.0	1.43	10.0	0.00	3.8	0.01	0.57	10.06	3.11	87.3	6.2	36.6	0.0	1.0
3.7	7.47	22.6	0.00	2.8	0.00	0.00	0.00	4.22	100.0	5.6	23.3	0.0	6.7
10.0	0.00	0.0	0.00	1.6	0.00	0.00	0.00	1.55	100.0	5.9	47.2	0.0	5.9
10.0	0.15	0.4	0.16	1.8	0.00	0.04	0.29	2.38	95.6	4.7	20.5	0.9	6.6
7.1	0.65	3.5	-0.05	4.0	0.08	0.42	4.20	3.20	83.9	5.7	30.8	0.0	5.2
9.8	0.55	1.6	0.14	6.7	0.25	1.17	5.61	3.55	71.2	5.0	25.5	2.1	7.2
9.2	1.17	3.0	0.25	1.2	0.00	0.01	0.07	2.16	97.9	5.8	33.6	0.3	6.9
7.6	16.67	5.9	0.00	3.2	0.00	0.00	0.00	0.00	0.0	7.3	45.6	0.0	5.2
10.0	0.00	0.0	0.00	1.5	0.00	0.00	0.00	0.00	0.0	7.3	56.9	0.0	6.4
10.0	0.00	0.0	0.00	3.1	0.00	0.66	5.06	2.64	75.0	6.4	28.8	0.0	5.7
8.3	0.27	0.7	0.03	2.0	-0.01	-0.07	-0.70	2.65	102.8	6.0	36.7	1.3	4.5
6.3	1.08	9.2	0.22	5.3	14.54	0.84	9.97	2.52	67.5	2.4	13.1	15.3	7.9
10.0	0.00	0.0	0.00	4.9	0.00	2.26	30.77	3.67	50.0	8.0	93.8	0.0	3.0
4.7	3.84	7.3	5.49	10.0	0.04	4.22	9.98	12.43	67.2	4.0	23.7	0.0	7.9
9.1	0.98	3.0	0.56	3.7	0.01	0.25	2.10	3.60	86.9	4.5	20.7	5.4	5.6
9.9	0.69	1.7	0.47	3.2	0.03	1.03	5.73	3.35	90.2	4.6	21.9	0.0	5.6
9.5	0.15	2.1	0.21	1.4	0.04	0.09	1.06	3.29	95.7	4.6	18.0	1.8	4.8
9.8	0.53	1.6	0.34	3.5	0.11	0.31	1.82	2.97	84.0	3.8	13.3	5.6	7.5
9.5	0.22	1.2	-0.25	1.5	-0.01	-0.27	-3.45	4.82	103.3	5.6	35.3	0.0	2.9
5.3	6.98	8.8	0.00	8.4	0.00	1.25	12.12	3.14	50.0	7.5	95.2	0.0	3.7
9.7	0.18	1.2	0.14	5.1	0.21	0.86	9.75	3.60	78.8	4.7	17.9	0.5	4.2
9.4	0.00	1.6	0.00	2.7	0.00	0.19	1.85	2.91	93.3	5.1	30.6	1.2	5.6
9.6	0.23	1.1	2.56	7.8	0.16	1.37	10.07	3.94	64.1	6.8	61.9	0.6	6.7
10.0	0.23	0.2	0.00	0.8	-0.01	-0.36	-1.68	2.09	104.4	5.9	43.6	0.0	6.8
6.9	1.14	8.4	0.48	6.9	0.30	0.87	7.04	4.53	76.6	1.9	13.0	22.4	8.5
6.9	1.35	4.3	2.01	2.5	-0.02	-0.65	-6.08	2.25	100.0	7.2	60.6	0.0	4.7
4.9	2.29	8.7	1.00	2.7	0.00	0.00	0.00	4.88	87.5	4.6	35.7	0.0	5.7
7.9	0.28	2.5	-0.01	3.8	0.10	0.59	7.76	3.17	84.3	3.7	13.9	1.0	3.7
7.9	1.33	4.4	0.14	3.8	0.03	0.35	3.83	2.77	88.9	5.2	40.4	10.0	4.7
5.4	0.83	4.2	0.00	3.4	0.01	0.18	2.41	3.88	96.1	4.6	19.4	5.7	2.3
3.1	10.11	30.1	0.12	1.7	0.00	0.06	0.39	2.57	84.1	3.6	24.4	13.0	5.7
9.5	0.30	1.7	0.04	5.1	1.91	0.66	5.82	3.12	81.7	3.7	21.0	12.5	8.9
6.2	0.12	9.4	0.00	1.9	-0.01	-0.14	-1.81	4.03	102.4	5.2	34.3	1.2	3.3
7.4	0.50	4.7	0.23	4.0	0.25	0.21	2.64	3.20	93.2	3.9	11.3	3.6	4.6
7.3	3.17	9.0	1.66	0.7	-0.03	-0.83	-7.15	3.13	107.1	6.6	43.5	1.1	4.4
9.1	0.17	0.9	0.63	3.4	0.05	0.41	4.96	3.02	82.3	6.0	37.2	0.5	4.1
10.0	0.51	0.7	0.89	3.7	0.06	0.48	2.76	2.23	75.5	6.7	44.8	0.0	7.2
8.0	0.83	2.7	0.21	7.0	0.03	1.08	6.67	4.73	69.1	4.5	16.3	0.0	5.7
5.3	3.35	12.2	0.57	2.9	-0.04	-2.54	-15.77	4.66	112.9	4.9	29.9	0.0	6.8
9.9	0.56	1.6	0.27	4.8	0.04	0.56	4.61	2.60	76.5	5.4	38.0	1.4	6.4
8.4	1.98	4.9	-0.14	2.7	0.01	0.11	0.75	2.16	89.4	4.9	17.7	0.0	6.6

Name	City	State	Rating	2016 Rating	2015 Rating	Total Assets ($Mil)	One Year Asset Growth	Asset Mix (As a % of Total Assets) Comm-ercial Loans	Cons-umer Loans	Mort-gage Loans	Secur-ities	Capital-ization Index	Net Worth Ratio
Blucurrent Credit Union	Springfield	MO	B+	B+	B+	176.0	9.60	11.4	40.6	20.9	0.0	7.6	9.4
Blue Chip Federal Credit Union	Harrisburg	PA	B+	B+	B	29.5	-0.41	0.0	33.7	7.7	1.4	10.0	14.3
Blue Cross & Blue Shield of Maine FCU	South Portland	ME	D+	D+	D+	6.1	-4.18	0.0	16.5	0.0	0.0	10.0	20.1
Blue Eagle Credit Union	Roanoke	VA	B+	B+	A-	150.3	7.49	0.1	33.9	18.5	0.0	10.0	12.5
Blue Federal Credit Union	Cheyenne	WY	B+	B+	B+	932.9	54.72	17.4	33.6	20.6	1.4	8.0	9.7
Blue Flame Credit Union	Mobile	AL	C-	C-	C-	8.5	0.51	1.1	34.5	7.2	0.0	10.0	14.0
▼ Blue Flame Credit Union	Charlotte	NC	C+	B-	B-	37.1	8.47	0.0	37.9	5.4	0.0	10.0	15.8
Blue Mountain Credit Union	College Place	WA	B-	B-	B	31.3	0.04	2.4	54.2	25.7	0.0	10.0	12.2
Blue Water Federal Credit Union	Port Huron	MI	C+	C+	B-	14.1	-0.31	0.0	21.1	7.0	3.6	10.0	17.4
Bluegrass Community Federal Credit Union	Ashland	KY	E+	E+	E+	8.4	3.15	0.0	67.8	0.0	3.9	4.4	6.4
BlueOx Credit Union	Battle Creek	MI	C	C	C+	146.9	14.86	3.9	15.8	14.8	30.0	7.3	9.4
Bluescope Employees' Credit Union	Kansas City	MO	D	D	D	1.7	2.18	0.0	86.5	0.0	0.0	9.1	10.4
Bluestem Community Credit Union	El Dorado	KS	D	D	D	11.1	-0.02	0.0	34.3	1.2	2.0	6.6	8.7
Bluffton Motor Works/Franklin Electric Empls CU	Bluffton	IN	C	C	C	1.3	-16.91	0.0	16.2	0.0	0.0	10.0	19.1
BMI Federal Credit Union	Dublin	OH	C+	C+	C+	455.8	4.86	0.8	20.1	39.4	22.1	7.2	9.1
Boeing Employees Credit Union	Tukwila	WA	A	A	A	17159.5	14.08	6.3	19.7	27.5	25.0	9.0	10.5
Boise Fire Department Credit Union	Boise	ID	C-	C-	C-	9.1	3.54	0.0	68.4	0.0	0.0	10.0	12.4
Bootstrap Federal Credit Union	New York	NY	D-	D-	D-	<1	-11.02	0.0	4.6	0.0	0.0	5.9	7.9
Bopti Federal Credit Union	San Pedro	CA	A-	A-	A-	71.8	6.33	0.0	23.9	5.5	28.2	10.0	16.0
▼ Border Federal Credit Union	Del Rio	TX	B+	A-	A	146.2	-1.95	0.0	30.6	25.8	11.4	10.0	13.0
Borger Federal Credit Union	Borger	TX	C+	C+	C+	18.1	-1.51	0.0	43.8	0.0	0.0	10.0	11.5
▲ Borinquen Community Federal Credit Union	Aguadilla	PR	C-	D+	D-	18.0	-1.99	0.0	27.9	20.9	9.7	9.7	10.8
Borinquen Sur Federal Credit Union	Penuelas	PR	D	D	D+	9.8	-2.13	0.0	24.7	21.0	0.0	7.8	9.6
Bossier Federal Credit Union	Bossier City	LA	C+	C+	C	177.4	4.19	0.0	33.0	3.7	18.3	8.8	10.2
▼ Boston Customs Federal Credit Union	Boston	MA	D+	C-	C-	2.7	2.65	0.0	33.5	0.0	0.0	10.0	12.5
Boston Firefighters Credit Union	Dorchester	MA	A-	A-	A-	260.2	10.75	1.0	18.6	44.4	9.9	10.0	11.3
Bothwell Hospital Employees Credit Union	Sedalia	MO	D-	D-	D-	2.3	8.90	0.0	62.4	0.0	8.7	4.9	7.0
Boulder Dam Credit Union	Boulder City	NV	A-	A-	A-	601.3	8.64	4.9	2.9	27.5	60.1	8.9	10.4
Boulevard Federal Credit Union	Amherst	NY	B-	B-	C+	34.3	0.45	0.0	24.5	8.0	0.0	10.0	13.3
Bourns Employees Federal Credit Union	Riverside	CA	B+	B+	A-	46.4	24.20	1.6	15.3	37.2	7.3	10.0	13.9
▼ Bowater Employees Credit Union	Calhoun	TN	C	C+	C	154.8	4.79	0.0	33.5	10.0	13.2	7.5	9.3
Box Butte Public Employees FCU	Alliance	NE	C	C	C	5.3	1.90	0.0	39.0	1.2	0.0	10.0	15.3
Box Elder County Federal Credit Union	Brigham City	UT	A	A	A	120.1	11.19	0.0	40.9	5.7	9.8	10.0	21.4
Boyds Federal Credit Union	Boyds	MD	C-	C-	D+	1.8	-11.68	0.0	12.6	7.7	69.8	10.0	12.4
Boys Town Federal Credit Union	Boys Town	NE	E+	E+	E+	3.3	1.84	0.0	36.6	0.0	0.0	5.3	7.3
BP Federal Credit Union	Houston	TX	B-	B-	B-	142.6	-2.42	0.0	25.5	28.8	23.6	5.5	8.0
Bradford Area Federal Credit Union	Bradford	PA	C-	C-	C-	7.4	-5.23	0.0	33.3	0.0	0.0	10.0	19.9
▲ Bradford Area School Employees FCU	Bradford	PA	C-	D+	D+	1.0	10.98	0.0	65.7	0.0	0.0	10.0	18.6
Bradken Credit Union	Atchison	KS	D+	D+	C-	7.7	-5.32	0.0	40.3	0.0	0.0	10.0	15.4
Bragg Mutual Federal Credit Union	Fayetteville	NC	C-	C-	D+	53.9	6.91	0.0	33.1	0.4	13.3	10.0	12.5
Brainerd BN Credit Union	Brainerd	MN	C+	C+	C+	73.8	6.59	2.3	11.9	38.6	0.0	10.0	11.1
Branch 6000 NALC Credit Union	Amityville	NY	E+	E+	E+	9.0	-1.29	0.0	29.6	5.2	28.0	3.8	7.2
▲ Brantwood Credit Union	Brantwood	WI	D+	D	D+	5.3	5.85	0.0	42.9	0.0	0.0	10.0	13.9
▼ Brassies Credit Union	Anniston	AL	D+	C-	C-	5.1	-5.86	0.0	27.4	8.6	0.0	10.0	16.5
Brazos Community Credit Union	Alvin	TX	C+	C+	C	16.1	3.53	0.0	66.0	4.2	0.0	10.0	22.6
Brazos Valley Schools Credit Union	Katy	TX	C+	C+	C+	701.4	3.37	0.0	18.9	10.6	51.8	6.5	8.5
Brazosport Teachers Federal Credit Union	Clute	TX	B+	B+	B+	40.2	-0.44	0.0	33.8	0.0	11.2	10.0	15.7
Breco Federal Credit Union	Baton Rouge	LA	D	D	C-	50.5	3.61	0.3	40.5	3.0	14.2	7.3	9.2
▼ Brentwood Baptist Church FCU	Houston	TX	D-	D	D-	1.1	2.82	0.0	66.4	0.0	0.0	6.6	8.6
Brewer Federal Credit Union	Brewer	ME	C	C	C+	55.9	8.67	2.8	34.3	16.3	0.0	7.7	9.5
Brewery Credit Union	Milwaukee	WI	B+	B+	B	44.0	1.74	6.4	37.2	22.4	0.0	10.0	19.1
Brewster Federal Credit Union	Brewster	OH	B	B	B	22.2	6.38	0.4	45.0	1.2	0.0	10.0	14.0
▲ Brewton Mill Federal Credit Union	Brewton	AL	D	D-	D+	21.7	-3.69	0.0	49.6	1.6	0.0	7.3	9.2
Bridge Credit Union	Columbus	OH	B	B	B	87.4	6.38	5.1	37.8	14.7	0.0	9.0	10.4
Bridgeport City Employees FCU	Bridgeport	CT	C-	C-	C-	30.4	1.90	0.0	22.2	7.9	0.0	10.0	23.6
Bridgeport Fairfield Teachers FCU	Bridgeport	CT	C	C	C	5.8	-5.21	0.0	39.4	0.0	0.0	10.0	27.3
Bridgeport Police Federal Credit Union	Bridgeport	CT	B-	B-	B-	18.4	6.04	0.0	37.1	0.0	0.0	10.0	12.8
▲ Bridgeport Post Office FCU	Bridgeport	CT	C-	D+	C-	4.2	3.88	0.0	27.3	0.0	9.4	10.0	30.6
Bridgeton Onized Federal Credit Union	Vineland	NJ	D-	D-	D	42.5	-1.46	0.0	41.1	0.2	4.9	4.4	6.5
Bridgewater Credit Union	Bridgewater	MA	C-	C-	C	355.1	4.65	6.2	28.4	37.8	18.8	8.4	10.0

Asset Quality Index	Non-Performing Loans as a % of Total Loans	Non-Performing Loans as a % of Capital	Net Charge-Offs Avg Loans	Profitability Index	Net Income ($Mil)	Return on Assets	Return on Equity	Net Interest Spread	Overhead Efficiency Ratio	Liquidity Index	Liquidity Ratio	Hot Money Ratio	Stability Index
7.8	0.44	3.9	0.80	**6.3**	0.32	0.73	8.81	5.20	73.3	**3.2**	17.8	5.6	**6.3**
8.5	0.96	3.2	0.70	**8.6**	0.09	1.24	8.72	4.79	74.4	**5.5**	30.7	0.3	**6.8**
10.0	0.23	0.7	0.00	**0.2**	-0.01	-0.81	-3.92	2.61	124.4	**4.9**	38.7	0.0	**6.7**
8.6	0.54	3.5	0.73	**4.1**	0.11	0.29	2.61	4.44	82.8	**3.8**	20.7	5.6	**7.8**
6.2	0.60	6.5	0.35	**5.9**	1.83	0.80	8.21	3.69	78.3	**2.3**	7.3	12.5	**6.3**
8.6	0.14	1.3	1.00	**2.5**	0.00	0.14	1.01	4.00	94.9	**5.4**	36.8	0.0	**6.8**
9.8	0.02	0.1	0.75	**2.4**	0.00	0.01	0.07	4.07	94.1	**6.4**	46.8	0.8	**6.5**
7.3	0.34	2.8	0.09	**4.8**	0.08	0.96	8.08	4.53	74.5	**2.8**	6.1	6.1	**6.3**
10.0	0.00	0.0	0.23	**1.3**	-0.01	-0.14	-0.81	3.02	101.0	**5.2**	46.6	0.0	**6.7**
0.7	4.26	37.4	0.29	**4.5**	0.03	1.42	22.22	7.49	69.6	**4.0**	14.6	1.3	**3.0**
9.8	0.55	2.6	0.10	**3.1**	0.09	0.25	2.71	3.02	93.4	**5.1**	24.8	3.1	**5.6**
4.6	0.89	7.0	0.00	**3.2**	0.00	0.24	2.27	4.03	106.7	**3.9**	13.3	0.0	**2.3**
7.3	0.62	5.4	0.09	**1.1**	0.00	0.04	0.42	3.79	94.4	**6.2**	45.5	0.0	**3.6**
8.3	7.04	5.4	0.00	**2.1**	0.00	0.00	0.00	2.94	100.0	**5.7**	27.0	0.0	**5.9**
8.7	0.32	3.9	0.18	**3.4**	0.33	0.29	3.19	2.89	89.6	**3.6**	18.4	3.4	**5.9**
9.7	0.27	1.6	0.26	**9.5**	54.47	1.30	12.60	3.01	60.4	**4.1**	16.9	4.6	**9.3**
3.7	3.84	18.7	0.00	**3.1**	0.00	0.18	1.42	3.01	87.3	**5.2**	37.2	0.0	**3.0**
10.0	0.00	0.0	0.00	**0.5**	0.00	0.00	0.00	1.53	100.0	**7.9**	95.0	0.0	**2.9**
9.3	1.16	2.2	0.48	**8.1**	0.23	1.31	8.21	2.85	55.4	**4.7**	17.6	0.0	**6.9**
8.0	1.35	6.4	0.97	**3.7**	0.04	0.10	0.76	5.06	87.3	**4.4**	29.9	10.7	**8.0**
9.5	0.21	1.8	-0.04	**3.1**	0.02	0.47	4.05	3.94	87.2	**5.1**	37.5	4.2	**5.7**
8.2	0.65	3.0	-0.17	**2.4**	0.02	0.51	4.76	3.82	88.6	**5.7**	27.2	0.0	**4.8**
4.6	3.27	16.3	1.85	**2.1**	0.01	0.20	2.13	4.54	82.0	**5.5**	28.7	0.0	**3.8**
5.9	2.11	10.3	1.10	**3.4**	0.19	0.43	4.17	3.46	82.7	**4.7**	20.2	5.0	**5.8**
9.9	0.00	0.0	0.00	**1.0**	-0.01	-0.76	-5.95	2.40	150.0	**6.1**	45.3	0.0	**4.9**
9.9	0.10	0.6	0.06	**5.8**	0.58	0.90	7.90	3.42	73.0	**3.4**	24.3	11.9	**8.3**
8.2	0.00	0.0	0.51	**0.9**	0.00	-0.37	-5.03	5.27	100.0	**5.1**	30.7	0.0	**2.5**
7.6	1.67	6.5	0.01	**6.4**	1.25	0.84	8.19	2.49	67.1	**5.4**	30.1	0.0	**7.7**
8.2	1.51	4.4	-0.17	**4.0**	0.05	0.61	4.60	3.73	87.3	**4.6**	25.9	2.6	**5.8**
7.2	1.22	4.3	0.94	**8.3**	0.15	1.44	9.23	2.78	72.8	**4.5**	33.0	10.6	**7.0**
5.8	1.63	12.2	0.57	**2.0**	-0.03	-0.08	-0.80	3.61	92.9	**4.0**	22.2	4.1	**5.7**
9.6	0.00	0.0	0.00	**4.8**	0.01	0.62	4.01	3.89	83.3	**5.1**	22.4	0.0	**7.9**
9.5	0.28	0.8	0.22	**9.5**	0.54	1.84	8.47	3.30	57.9	**4.1**	31.3	7.1	**10.0**
10.0	0.00	0.0	0.00	**2.8**	0.00	0.66	5.31	2.63	81.8	**5.4**	27.6	0.0	**5.7**
7.5	0.57	2.7	2.99	**2.7**	0.00	0.25	3.32	4.12	84.6	**5.2**	11.9	0.0	**1.0**
9.8	0.25	2.0	0.10	**3.9**	0.15	0.45	5.62	2.83	78.2	**4.5**	13.7	1.8	**5.0**
6.5	2.81	5.3	0.00	**3.3**	0.00	0.11	0.54	4.42	98.4	**6.9**	61.2	0.0	**6.1**
4.8	3.27	11.8	0.00	**4.7**	0.00	0.81	4.23	4.23	77.8	**5.1**	37.8	0.0	**3.7**
4.8	5.35	13.2	12.99	**1.3**	-0.15	-7.58	-47.28	4.78	96.1	**5.7**	24.9	0.0	**5.4**
8.4	0.11	3.0	0.75	**6.2**	0.26	1.97	15.82	4.95	70.4	**4.9**	24.6	0.2	**5.5**
9.8	0.05	0.7	-0.01	**3.1**	0.06	0.34	3.09	2.58	87.0	**4.1**	39.7	8.0	**6.3**
6.2	2.01	11.4	0.38	**0.9**	-0.01	-0.27	-4.54	3.67	107.3	**6.0**	34.2	0.0	**1.4**
1.4	8.69	44.4	1.13	**6.1**	0.02	1.23	8.85	3.57	63.0	**3.5**	19.0	0.0	**7.6**
6.2	2.97	13.0	0.00	**1.2**	-0.01	-0.69	-4.28	3.38	133.3	**4.8**	29.0	0.0	**5.4**
7.9	0.42	1.4	1.39	**3.7**	-0.02	-0.51	-2.20	4.80	81.1	**3.7**	20.7	7.7	**6.6**
9.6	0.64	2.3	0.50	**3.5**	0.90	0.52	6.09	2.70	80.8	**5.3**	29.2	10.5	**5.6**
9.8	0.63	1.7	0.30	**5.3**	0.07	0.66	4.20	2.77	78.2	**5.3**	40.9	8.6	**7.4**
5.9	1.62	9.5	0.04	**0.9**	0.00	0.03	0.34	4.12	91.2	**5.0**	27.9	5.7	**2.9**
2.3	3.07	20.4	-0.50	**3.7**	0.00	-1.47	-16.67	5.98	75.0	**5.5**	35.0	0.0	**1.0**
5.2	0.93	8.5	0.25	**2.9**	0.03	0.22	2.27	4.46	86.3	**3.7**	19.9	8.8	**4.2**
6.2	2.83	9.9	1.17	**8.1**	0.09	0.82	4.25	5.08	75.1	**3.1**	39.6	27.6	**7.7**
9.7	0.39	1.4	0.58	**5.9**	0.04	0.74	5.18	4.24	87.8	**5.0**	29.0	4.2	**8.4**
3.2	1.41	17.4	-0.09	**4.1**	0.04	0.73	8.12	3.89	74.6	**3.2**	21.7	10.9	**3.0**
8.3	0.30	1.8	0.36	**4.9**	0.15	0.70	6.60	4.14	84.8	**4.6**	31.9	7.4	**6.4**
10.0	0.04	0.1	-0.04	**1.9**	0.02	0.23	0.95	3.29	94.0	**5.7**	46.9	0.6	**6.4**
7.3	4.85	6.7	1.01	**4.3**	0.01	0.41	1.52	7.75	78.6	**7.4**	83.7	0.0	**6.0**
9.1	0.56	1.6	0.12	**5.1**	0.03	0.56	4.26	3.51	80.5	**5.0**	49.9	6.4	**7.1**
8.6	3.17	3.0	1.25	**2.5**	0.00	0.29	0.94	3.67	83.3	**6.1**	49.1	0.0	**5.6**
2.5	2.91	32.3	1.39	**4.5**	0.06	0.52	8.15	5.79	86.6	**4.5**	22.7	5.1	**1.7**
8.0	0.42	3.6	0.95	**1.5**	0.01	0.01	0.11	2.54	96.4	**3.2**	10.9	6.9	**6.4**

							One	Asset Mix (As a % of Total Assets)					
Name	City	State	Rating	2016 Rating	2015 Rating	Total Assets ($Mil)	One Year Asset Growth	Commercial Loans	Consumer Loans	Mortgage Loans	Securities	Capitalization Index	Net Worth Ratio
BrightStar Credit Union	Sunrise	FL	**A-**	A-	B+	455.0	4.04	0.3	34.5	10.0	29.5	**9.5**	10.8
Brightview Federal Credit Union	Ridgeland	MS	**D**	D	D	27.1	-2.98	0.7	19.1	1.4	5.2	**10.0**	12.3
▲ Bristol Virginia School System FCU	Bristol	VA	**C**	C-	C	<1	-3.97	0.0	35.7	0.0	0.0	**10.0**	26.3
Brockport Federal Credit Union	Brockport	NY	**D+**	D+	D-	9.7	8.77	0.0	27.8	31.1	4.6	**7.1**	9.1
Brokaw Credit Union	Weston	WI	**C-**	C-	D+	52.9	3.39	2.7	24.9	21.1	6.1	**6.1**	8.1
Bronco Federal Credit Union	Franklin	VA	**C**	C	C-	183.7	2.32	5.0	29.2	26.6	2.5	**5.4**	7.4
Brookland Federal Credit Union	West Columbia	SC	**E+**	E+	E+	3.3	-7.16	0.0	68.9	0.0	0.0	**5.3**	7.3
Brookline Municipal Credit Union	Brookline	MA	**C+**	C+	C+	39.3	-3.01	0.0	4.7	28.7	5.3	**10.0**	11.7
Brooklyn Cooperative FCU	Brooklyn	NY	**D+**	D+	D	23.4	0.02	12.0	17.1	42.2	0.0	**7.3**	9.2
Brooks Community Federal Credit Union	Brooks	MN	**D-**	D-	D-	2.6	-2.60	0.0	15.4	2.2	0.0	**8.3**	9.9
Brosnan Yard Federal Credit Union	Macon	GA	**C**	C	D+	2.6	0.00	0.0	74.9	0.0	0.0	**10.0**	17.7
Brotherhood Credit Union	Lynn	MA	**D+**	D+	D+	110.7	3.21	0.0	3.9	30.7	17.8	**10.0**	26.7
Broward HealthCare Federal Credit Union	Fort Lauderdale	FL	**C**	C	C+	72.3	6.30	0.0	21.9	3.4	47.5	**7.2**	9.8
Brown County Employees Credit Union	Green Bay	WI	**C-**	C-	C-	17.4	-4.72	0.0	7.9	28.7	0.0	**10.0**	20.3
Brown-Forman Employees Credit Union	Louisville	KY	**B-**	B-	B-	11.8	1.72	0.0	37.4	5.2	0.0	**10.0**	12.3
▼ Brownfield Federal Credit Union	Brownfield	TX	**D+**	C-	C	12.8	-3.97	0.0	37.3	0.0	0.0	**10.0**	29.5
▲ Brownsville City Employees FCU	Brownsville	TX	**C**	C-	C-	6.7	-1.05	0.0	56.9	0.0	0.0	**10.0**	23.5
Brunot Island Federal Credit Union	Burgettstown	PA	**C-**	C-	D+	4.4	-4.89	0.0	18.6	0.0	0.0	**10.0**	24.1
Brunswick County Teachers FCU	Lawrenceville	VA	**D+**	D+	D	<1	-9.13	0.0	30.2	0.0	0.0	**10.0**	30.0
▲ BSE Credit Union	Middleburg Heights	OH	**D**	D-	D-	18.4	3.61	0.0	25.6	0.0	37.3	**5.4**	7.4
▼ Buckeye Community Federal Credit Union	Perry	FL	**C+**	B-	B-	93.6	17.68	5.2	27.4	8.5	5.9	**9.4**	10.6
▲ Buckeye State Credit Union Inc.	Akron	OH	**D**	D-	D-	86.1	-6.78	9.2	51.5	2.2	1.1	**4.4**	6.4
Bucks County Employees Credit Union	Doylestown	PA	**C+**	C+	C+	37.5	5.38	0.0	0.0	0.0	0.0	**6.9**	9.0
Buffalo Conrail Federal Credit Union	Cheektowaga	NY	**C**	C	C	42.0	2.88	0.1	14.7	9.0	24.6	**10.0**	19.7
Buffalo Cooperative Federal Credit Union	Buffalo	NY	**E+**	E+	E+	6.1	-2.63	0.0	25.3	24.6	0.0	**5.6**	7.6
Buffalo Metropolitan FCU	Buffalo	NY	**B**	B	B	105.2	8.65	0.0	38.1	18.3	0.0	**9.8**	10.9
Buffalo Police Federal Credit Union	Buffalo	NY	**C**	C	C	10.2	6.92	0.0	42.8	0.0	0.0	**10.0**	13.7
▼ Buffalo Service Credit Union	Buffalo	NY	**C+**	B-	C+	54.7	3.79	0.0	15.5	4.8	46.5	**8.7**	10.2
Building Trades Federal Credit Union	Maple Grove	MN	**B**	B	B	133.2	5.86	3.5	23.5	22.6	23.4	**10.0**	11.9
Bulab Employees Federal Credit Union	Memphis	TN	**C-**	C-	C-	3.7	-12.49	0.0	82.4	0.0	0.0	**10.0**	20.0
▼ Bull Dog Federal Credit Union	Hagerstown	MD	**D**	D+	D	150.1	8.12	9.6	26.2	3.5	48.3	**5.3**	7.4
Bull's Eye Credit Union	Wisconsin Rapids	WI	**B**	B	C+	151.6	5.47	1.8	28.1	20.7	10.9	**8.1**	9.8
▼ Burbank City Federal Credit Union	Burbank	CA	**C+**	B-	B-	323.6	12.88	3.5	20.2	29.3	10.5	**5.6**	7.6
Burlington Municipal Employees CU	Burlington	IA	**D**	D	D+	5.6	13.90	0.0	56.9	0.0	34.1	**7.2**	9.2
Burlington Municipal Employees FCU	Burlington	MA	**D-**	D-	D-	9.7	6.79	0.0	29.6	0.0	3.2	**5.8**	7.9
Burlington Northern Santa Fe Railway CU	Cicero	IL	**D+**	D+	D	7.2	-1.97	0.0	23.5	0.0	0.0	**10.0**	18.1
Burlington Northtown Community CU	North Kansas City	MO	**B-**	B-	B-	13.1	3.88	0.0	29.7	0.0	0.0	**10.0**	15.9
▲ Burns & McDonnell Credit Union	Kansas City	MO	**C-**	D+	D	21.6	-1.32	0.0	41.8	1.2	0.0	**5.5**	7.5
Business & Industrial FCU	Columbus	IN	**D+**	D+	D+	38.2	5.05	0.1	32.3	0.0	0.0	**10.0**	13.2
Butler Armco Employees Credit Union	Butler	PA	**A**	A	A	333.7	7.00	0.0	24.6	24.5	0.3	**10.0**	15.3
Butler County Teachers FCU	Butler	PA	**C-**	C-	C-	27.9	2.42	0.0	11.9	7.7	1.3	**5.9**	7.9
▲ Butler Heritage Federal Credit Union	Middletown	OH	**C-**	D+	C-	13.5	11.76	0.0	18.8	17.1	0.0	**7.8**	9.5
Butte Community Federal Credit Union	Butte	MT	**D**	D	D+	21.5	5.77	0.0	34.8	0.0	0.0	**6.4**	8.4
BVA Federal Credit Union	Belle Vernon	PA	**C-**	C-	C-	27.8	-3.83	0.0	9.2	14.1	30.9	**8.6**	10.1
BVMSN Federal Credit Union	Walnutport	PA	**C-**	C-	C-	2.2	-5.63	0.0	18.4	0.0	35.9	**10.0**	14.9
Bykota Federal Credit Union	Brooklyn	NY	**D+**	D+	D	1.6	1.57	0.0	0.0	0.0	0.0	**7.3**	9.3
C & N W Proviso Credit Union	Northlake	IL	**D**	D	D	2.8	-0.83	0.0	41.2	0.0	0.0	**8.5**	10.0
▼ C & R Credit Union	Clay Center	KS	**D**	D+	D	4.1	6.27	0.0	69.4	0.0	0.0	**7.5**	9.4
C B S Employees Federal Credit Union	Studio City	CA	**C**	C	C	19.6	2.67	0.0	18.7	1.7	2.5	**10.0**	12.7
C C M H Federal Credit Union	Parkersburg	WV	**D+**	D+	D+	4.9	4.98	0.0	70.5	0.0	0.0	**10.0**	11.1
▲ C C S E Federal Credit Union	Salamanca	NY	**B-**	C+	B	38.3	7.62	0.0	20.9	3.6	0.0	**8.7**	10.1
C O Federal Credit Union	Charleston	SC	**B-**	B-	B-	2.6	20.01	0.0	31.7	0.0	0.0	**10.0**	15.6
▲ C T A C And M Federal Credit Union	Oak Park	IL	**D+**	D	C-	2.0	-0.80	0.0	46.6	0.0	0.0	**10.0**	11.6
C T A F C Federal Credit Union	Chicago	IL	**C-**	C-	C-	<1	-2.96	0.0	24.4	0.0	0.0	**10.0**	17.0
C&H Sugar Employees Federal Credit Union	Crockett	CA	**D**	D	D	9.6	-2.21	0.0	22.4	0.0	0.0	**10.0**	21.6
C&O United Credit Union	Edgewood	KY	**C-**	C-	D	16.7	4.76	0.0	17.5	2.5	0.0	**9.0**	10.4
C-B-W Schools Federal Credit Union	Sidman	PA	**B**	B	B	107.9	1.69	0.0	6.4	11.5	39.3	**10.0**	29.3
C-E Federal Credit Union	Houston	TX	**E+**	E+	D-	17.9	4.28	0.0	56.0	0.0	16.4	**4.9**	6.9
C-F LA Credit Union	Donaldsonville	LA	**C**	C	C	9.5	2.81	0.0	35.7	0.0	0.0	**10.0**	11.8
▲ C-Plant Federal Credit Union	Paducah	KY	**A**	A-	A-	214.8	2.96	7.3	32.5	17.4	0.0	**10.0**	11.3

Asset Quality Index	Non-Performing Loans as a % of Total Loans	Non-Performing Loans as a % of Capital	Net Charge-Offs Avg Loans	Profitability Index	Net Income ($Mil)	Return on Assets	Return on Equity	Net Interest Spread	Overhead Efficiency Ratio	Liquidity Index	Liquidity Ratio	Hot Money Ratio	Stability Index
8.7	0.64	3.7	0.82	**7.0**	0.78	0.70	6.86	3.82	85.0	**4.0**	7.5	3.1	**7.0**
10.0	0.62	1.4	1.33	**0.0**	-0.08	-1.23	-9.85	2.54	126.1	**6.6**	75.6	4.6	**4.9**
6.8	4.21	4.8	0.00	**4.7**	0.00	0.00	0.00	5.71	100.0	**7.4**	92.4	0.0	**4.3**
8.2	0.13	1.0	1.44	**3.7**	-0.02	-0.99	-10.75	5.48	81.4	**3.0**	9.9	8.4	**3.0**
5.2	1.60	11.8	0.08	**2.9**	0.07	0.55	6.81	3.17	87.6	**5.0**	27.3	2.6	**3.7**
3.7	1.72	21.4	0.57	**3.4**	0.17	0.38	5.07	4.07	88.2	**4.2**	22.2	4.5	**4.4**
0.7	3.98	35.9	2.43	**3.1**	0.00	-0.49	-6.50	6.04	88.7	**4.5**	25.1	1.2	**3.3**
8.7	1.35	4.0	-0.06	**2.7**	0.02	0.25	2.01	2.36	89.3	**5.4**	39.4	5.8	**6.0**
4.1	1.81	15.8	-0.05	**5.3**	0.04	0.76	9.74	5.33	91.5	**4.3**	16.6	1.2	**3.0**
4.7	5.91	16.1	0.00	**0.0**	-0.01	-1.80	-18.18	3.57	100.0	**6.6**	34.5	0.0	**3.1**
8.2	0.40	1.6	-0.60	**3.4**	0.00	0.31	1.76	7.18	97.5	**5.0**	36.3	0.0	**7.1**
10.0	0.79	0.8	0.02	**1.0**	-0.02	-0.07	-0.17	2.10	102.2	**4.2**	37.6	12.1	**7.9**
9.2	0.35	1.3	1.50	**2.4**	0.05	0.26	2.81	2.83	89.5	**5.1**	15.1	1.8	**4.5**
10.0	0.74	1.3	-0.36	**1.2**	-0.01	-0.11	-0.56	2.24	109.9	**6.0**	71.1	0.0	**6.6**
9.6	0.11	0.5	0.00	**3.4**	0.01	0.31	2.48	4.32	92.5	**4.5**	35.6	3.9	**6.2**
9.2	2.40	3.2	0.08	**0.8**	-0.01	-0.35	-1.17	3.48	107.3	**5.3**	40.6	0.0	**6.9**
8.5	0.77	1.9	0.00	**5.3**	0.03	1.51	6.41	4.47	68.8	**5.7**	48.6	0.0	**4.3**
7.7	6.48	5.9	0.00	**1.7**	0.00	0.27	1.12	2.38	88.9	**7.3**	63.9	0.0	**6.7**
6.4	6.67	7.2	0.00	**0.3**	0.00	-1.32	-4.42	16.00	111.1	**8.0**	94.3	0.0	**4.8**
9.6	0.18	0.8	0.58	**2.5**	0.02	0.35	4.76	3.39	90.5	**5.2**	24.8	0.0	**2.3**
6.2	0.80	5.3	0.22	**2.3**	-0.01	-0.04	-0.41	4.30	96.2	**4.4**	19.1	4.5	**4.7**
4.3	1.15	12.8	0.88	**2.4**	0.22	1.02	15.99	4.39	77.3	**4.4**	18.5	0.4	**1.5**
10.0	1.01	0.9	0.51	**2.9**	0.03	0.31	3.47	0.77	50.8	**5.3**	12.8	0.0	**3.4**
10.0	0.50	1.1	-0.02	**2.7**	0.04	0.34	1.69	2.76	86.9	**6.6**	47.2	0.0	**7.1**
7.2	0.32	2.9	0.13	**2.6**	0.00	-0.13	-2.46	3.60	101.3	**5.0**	25.3	0.0	**1.0**
6.7	0.73	6.0	0.40	**5.1**	0.15	0.59	6.19	4.83	84.9	**4.1**	15.8	1.2	**5.5**
8.9	1.49	4.7	0.00	**2.5**	0.01	0.32	2.31	3.46	89.4	**6.3**	50.3	0.0	**6.4**
10.0	0.18	0.6	0.46	**2.6**	0.01	0.05	0.46	3.33	97.1	**6.0**	45.4	1.2	**6.4**
9.7	0.24	1.8	0.53	**3.0**	0.09	0.26	2.17	3.49	86.3	**4.1**	18.3	4.5	**7.9**
7.6	0.36	1.5	-0.51	**2.3**	0.00	0.31	1.63	3.49	90.9	**3.4**	18.9	6.8	**6.7**
8.1	0.79	4.2	0.84	**0.9**	-0.01	-0.01	-0.18	2.85	88.0	**5.7**	51.2	0.0	**3.3**
6.3	1.54	8.6	0.15	**4.2**	0.18	0.47	4.35	3.48	81.1	**4.4**	23.5	0.8	**6.8**
7.9	0.42	3.5	1.21	**2.8**	-0.02	-0.03	-0.36	3.56	77.8	**4.0**	30.9	16.2	**4.0**
6.5	0.33	2.0	0.00	**4.1**	0.01	0.65	7.11	2.86	75.7	**4.3**	17.5	0.0	**2.3**
9.2	0.39	1.8	0.00	**1.5**	0.00	-0.17	-2.12	4.50	107.4	**6.9**	50.3	0.0	**2.6**
10.0	1.36	1.7	0.00	**1.0**	0.00	-0.11	-0.61	2.67	104.0	**6.7**	63.1	0.0	**5.6**
9.2	0.61	1.7	1.54	**3.0**	0.00	0.03	0.19	4.05	84.7	**6.0**	39.0	0.0	**7.0**
9.7	0.07	0.5	0.07	**7.4**	0.08	1.42	19.70	2.80	56.4	**4.5**	19.0	1.0	**3.3**
9.9	0.25	0.7	0.03	**1.1**	-0.01	-0.05	-0.40	2.41	101.4	**5.9**	34.9	1.2	**6.7**
9.8	0.48	2.0	0.13	**6.0**	0.66	0.81	5.43	3.62	70.5	**6.0**	39.1	1.8	**9.2**
7.6	1.48	4.2	-0.06	**1.7**	0.01	0.07	0.91	0.88	90.2	**5.0**	22.8	0.0	**3.3**
9.2	0.62	2.3	-0.08	**2.8**	0.02	0.49	5.01	3.02	84.1	**5.7**	30.7	0.8	**4.1**
4.4	1.96	13.5	0.76	**2.2**	0.01	0.26	3.11	3.93	90.1	**4.2**	18.2	4.4	**4.2**
4.3	4.31	17.6	1.72	**2.7**	0.00	0.01	0.14	3.23	104.6	**5.0**	32.1	3.1	**4.4**
10.0	0.00	0.0	0.00	**1.9**	0.00	0.18	1.20	1.48	87.5	**5.5**	38.1	0.0	**7.0**
9.7	0.64	0.6	0.00	**2.6**	0.00	0.51	5.63	2.64	62.5	**6.4**	25.1	0.0	**4.9**
1.7	10.29	38.1	-0.33	**3.8**	0.00	0.44	4.36	6.23	91.7	**6.8**	60.0	0.0	**5.8**
7.5	0.00	0.0	-0.26	**2.7**	0.00	0.20	2.07	6.48	97.0	**3.8**	17.3	6.7	**2.3**
10.0	0.02	0.0	0.00	**1.9**	0.00	0.06	0.48	2.47	98.0	**6.9**	66.8	6.5	**6.7**
5.8	0.98	5.9	0.00	**3.6**	0.01	0.60	5.12	4.15	90.0	**4.8**	26.9	0.0	**6.6**
8.5	0.61	2.7	-0.02	**6.3**	0.12	1.31	12.77	3.58	85.3	**5.5**	27.3	1.2	**5.0**
6.1	2.84	7.4	-0.36	**10.0**	0.02	2.76	17.35	7.82	61.0	**6.7**	55.8	0.0	**5.7**
3.8	4.56	16.2	-0.41	**2.8**	0.01	1.02	8.73	14.44	86.1	**7.0**	59.0	0.0	**5.0**
5.2	3.82	7.7	1.15	**4.1**	0.00	0.00	0.00	4.55	88.9	**6.7**	50.6	0.0	**3.7**
10.0	0.38	0.5	0.00	**0.0**	-0.03	-1.42	-6.51	3.03	139.4	**5.5**	43.1	0.0	**5.1**
7.6	1.21	3.2	-0.09	**2.1**	0.01	0.22	2.09	3.48	95.6	**7.0**	57.1	0.8	**4.6**
10.0	0.09	0.1	-0.04	**4.1**	0.14	0.51	1.79	1.87	72.2	**5.6**	42.1	2.5	**8.5**
6.9	0.32	2.7	-0.19	**2.3**	0.01	0.16	2.27	3.85	100.9	**4.1**	11.8	1.5	**1.0**
9.6	0.00	0.0	0.00	**2.9**	0.01	0.26	2.15	2.06	86.4	**5.5**	45.5	0.0	**6.3**
8.5	0.49	3.1	0.25	**7.5**	0.54	1.02	9.05	2.85	69.2	**3.7**	33.6	16.4	**8.4**

Name	City	State	Rating	2016 Rating	2015 Rating	Total Assets ($Mil)	One Year Asset Growth	Asset Mix (As a % of Total Assets) Comm-ercial Loans	Cons-umer Loans	Mort-gage Loans	Secur-ities	Capital-ization Index	Net Worth Ratio
▼ C-T Waco Federal Credit Union	Waco	TX	**D-**	D	D	7.3	9.20	0.0	48.3	0.0	0.0	**8.8**	10.2
▲ C.U.P. Federal Credit Union	Provo	UT	**C-**	D+	D+	6.5	7.75	0.0	40.4	3.5	0.0	**10.0**	14.9
Caano Employees Federal Credit Union	Kenner	LA	**E+**	E+	D	3.2	11.97	0.0	45.7	0.0	6.7	**7.1**	9.1
Cable Federal Credit Union	Marion	IN	**D+**	D+	D+	1.1	-13.88	0.0	67.9	0.0	0.0	**10.0**	21.7
Cabot & NOI Employees Credit Union	Pampa	TX	**C-**	C-	C-	30.4	-3.76	0.0	67.5	9.5	0.0	**8.2**	9.8
Cabot Boston Credit Union	Boston	MA	**D+**	D+	D+	7.2	3.44	0.0	32.6	0.0	10.4	**10.0**	16.2
Cabot Employees Credit Union	Franklin	LA	**C+**	C+	C	1.9	-2.87	0.0	47.7	0.0	5.1	**10.0**	19.9
Cabot Employees Credit Union	Ville Platte	LA	**D**	D	D	<1	-5.86	0.0	22.4	0.0	0.0	**10.0**	14.4
Cabrillo Credit Union	San Diego	CA	**B+**	B+	B+	270.0	13.73	0.6	34.0	11.8	0.0	**8.6**	10.0
▼ Cabway Telco Federal Credit Union	Huntington	WV	**C**	C+	C	4.8	-6.62	0.0	41.0	0.0	0.0	**10.0**	24.4
CACL Federal Credit Union	Pottsville	PA	**B+**	B+	B	104.1	14.22	5.2	18.9	25.0	5.9	**8.4**	9.9
Caddo Parish Teachers FCU	Shreveport	LA	**B**	B	B	12.1	0.65	0.0	44.4	0.0	0.0	**10.0**	24.5
▼ Cadets Federal Credit Union	Buffalo	NY	**C-**	C	C	11.9	0.55	0.0	11.4	14.9	1.6	**10.0**	12.5
Cadmus Credit Union Incorporated	Richmond	VA	**D**	D	D	2.1	1.72	0.0	36.7	0.0	0.0	**10.0**	20.2
CAHP Credit Union	Sacramento	CA	**B+**	B+	B+	196.7	20.17	0.1	71.4	0.0	0.0	**6.3**	8.3
Cal Poly Federal Credit Union	Pomona	CA	**E**	E	E+	13.9	4.53	0.0	35.3	0.0	0.0	**3.8**	5.8
Cal State L.A. Federal Credit Union	Los Angeles	CA	**B-**	B-	B-	51.3	15.48	0.4	18.9	26.8	0.0	**8.2**	9.8
▲ Cal-Com Federal Credit Union	Port Lavaca	TX	**C**	C-	C+	140.0	0.00	0.0	66.1	0.0	0.0	**7.5**	9.3
Cal-Ed Federal Credit Union	Coal Center	PA	**C**	C	C-	25.5	-1.56	0.0	11.2	0.0	0.0	**10.0**	12.8
Calcasieu Parish Employees FCU	Lake Charles	LA	**B-**	B-	C+	13.5	-2.44	0.0	47.2	0.0	22.1	**10.0**	16.2
Calcasieu Teachers & Employees CU	Lake Charles	LA	**C**	C	C	38.0	1.26	0.5	17.3	4.8	0.0	**10.0**	13.3
Calcite Credit Union	Rogers City	MI	**B+**	B+	B+	70.7	9.25	0.1	25.7	19.3	32.8	**10.0**	11.6
Calcoe Federal Credit Union	Yakima	WA	**C-**	C-	D+	28.1	0.34	0.0	53.6	11.4	11.7	**7.5**	9.4
CalCom Federal Credit Union	Torrance	CA	**B+**	B+	B	63.5	1.11	0.0	33.1	27.0	7.6	**10.0**	14.2
▲ Calhoun-Liberty Employees Credit Union	Blountstown	FL	**B**	B-	C+	40.1	9.33	0.0	28.6	20.9	2.0	**10.0**	11.6
California Adventist FCU	Glendale	CA	**B**	B	B-	51.5	4.56	0.0	6.9	23.4	55.3	**10.0**	11.9
California Agribusiness Credit Union	Buena Park	CA	**D+**	D+	D+	30.0	3.17	1.1	37.9	11.8	26.3	**6.1**	8.1
California Bear Credit Union	Los Angeles	CA	**C**	C	C+	114.5	1.00	0.0	21.3	11.1	35.4	**4.7**	7.0
California Coast Credit Union	San Diego	CA	**A-**	A-	A-	2328.0	11.16	12.4	38.2	30.4	14.7	**9.9**	11.0
▲ California Community Credit Union	Sacramento	CA	**C+**	C	C+	61.6	3.30	0.7	21.0	11.0	0.0	**10.0**	12.0
California Credit Union	Glendale	CA	**B+**	B+	B+	3030.9	98.09	12.4	16.1	37.1	11.1	**9.7**	10.9
California Lithuanian Credit Union	Santa Monica	CA	**A**	A	A	116.5	4.06	40.1	0.1	62.4	1.2	**10.0**	13.8
California State & Federal Empls #20 CU	Eureka	CA	**B**	B	B	135.4	5.53	1.3	16.4	16.7	31.7	**10.0**	13.7
Call Federal Credit Union	Richmond	VA	**C-**	C-	C+	400.4	4.42	0.0	25.2	18.5	35.1	**8.2**	10.3
Caltech Employees Federal Credit Union	La Cañada Flintridg	CA	**B+**	B+	B+	1555.8	8.93	2.2	3.8	18.4	67.6	**8.1**	9.7
Calvary Baptist of Pacoima FCU	San Fernando	CA	**C**	C	C	<1	9.45	0.0	9.4	0.0	0.0	**8.6**	10.1
Cambridge Firefighters FCU	Cambridge	MA	**B-**	B-	B-	10.9	4.80	0.7	30.0	22.3	0.0	**10.0**	20.1
Cambridge Municipal Employees FCU	Cambridge	MA	**D**	D	D	9.7	3.57	0.0	14.2	0.0	0.0	**10.0**	20.3
Cambridge Teachers Federal Credit Union	Cambridge	MA	**D+**	D+	D+	31.7	2.23	0.0	13.1	2.2	35.6	**7.6**	9.4
CAMC Federal Credit Union	Charleston	WV	**B+**	B+	A-	67.9	7.67	0.0	15.0	21.1	0.0	**10.0**	21.9
▼ Camden Firemen's Credit Union	Moorestown	NJ	**D+**	C-	D+	<1	-10.85	0.0	80.7	0.0	0.0	**10.0**	12.2
Camden Police Federal Credit Union	Camden	NJ	**E+**	E+	E+	<1	0.13	0.0	37.2	0.0	0.0	**5.4**	7.6
Camino Federal Credit Union	Montebello	CA	**C**	C	C	151.6	3.97	1.1	16.3	25.3	8.9	**8.0**	9.8
Camp Shelby Federal Credit Union	Hattiesburg	MS	**B**	B	B-	18.7	6.25	0.0	49.2	0.0	0.0	**10.0**	18.8
Campbell Employees Federal Credit Union	Cherry Hill	NJ	**C-**	C-	D+	156.6	2.55	4.4	15.8	4.1	51.5	**8.6**	10.2
Campco Federal Credit Union	Gillette	WY	**B**	B	B	105.5	5.42	0.0	43.9	8.9	0.0	**7.2**	9.1
Campus Credit Union	Wichita	KS	**B-**	B-	C+	29.5	-2.96	0.3	53.9	6.7	0.0	**10.0**	12.8
Campus Federal Credit Union	Baton Rouge	LA	**C-**	C-	C	614.3	10.19	9.9	32.3	29.3	15.4	**6.4**	8.4
Campus USA Credit Union	Jonesville	FL	**A-**	A-	A-	1590.7	11.44	6.2	43.2	28.3	12.3	**10.0**	12.0
▼ Canaan Credit Union	Urbana	IL	**B-**	B	B-	<1	6.39	0.0	30.8	0.0	0.0	**10.0**	11.3
Canals & Trails Credit Union	Lockport	IL	**C-**	C-	C-	23.6	6.50	0.0	22.6	5.2	0.0	**6.7**	8.7
Canandaigua Federal Credit Union	Canandaigua	NY	**D+**	D+	C-	24.3	6.86	0.0	22.5	17.8	38.4	**9.9**	10.9
Cando Credit Union	Walbridge	OH	**E+**	E+	E+	8.7	5.20	0.0	38.1	0.0	0.0	**4.8**	6.8
▼ Cannon Federal Credit Union	Clovis	NM	**D**	D+	C-	65.4	2.79	0.0	48.0	2.8	2.4	**5.2**	7.2
Canoga Postal Federal Credit Union	Canoga Park	CA	**C+**	C+	C+	1.0	1.00	0.0	32.9	0.0	0.0	**10.0**	27.8
Canton Police & Firemen's Credit Union	Canton	OH	**D-**	D-	D-	8.5	1.37	0.0	35.0	0.0	22.4	**5.1**	7.1
Canton School Employees FCU	Canton	OH	**B-**	B-	B-	238.5	10.80	0.8	46.0	6.8	5.8	**6.7**	8.8
Canyon State Credit Union	Phoenix	AZ	**C+**	C+	C+	198.5	9.87	0.0	30.6	17.2	34.7	**6.9**	9.1
Cape Regional Credit Union	Cape Girardeau	MO	**D**	D	D	15.1	3.41	0.0	37.1	0.0	0.0	**5.1**	7.1
Capital Area Federal Credit Union	Augusta	ME	**B+**	B+	B+	35.4	13.82	0.4	35.3	30.8	0.0	**10.0**	13.9

Asset Quality Index	Non-Performing Loans as a % of Total Loans	Non-Performing Loans as a % of Capital	Net Charge-Offs Avg Loans	Profitability Index	Net Income ($Mil)	Return on Assets	Return on Equity	Net Interest Spread	Overhead Efficiency Ratio	Liquidity Index	Liquidity Ratio	Hot Money Ratio	Stability Index
3.0	2.67	18.0	0.31	**0.4**	-0.01	-0.74	-6.94	5.55	105.6	**5.3**	35.5	3.2	**3.9**
9.4	0.00	0.0	0.73	**1.9**	0.01	0.37	2.49	3.79	89.8	**3.7**	21.3	9.2	**7.0**
2.7	5.89	28.2	0.00	**0.3**	-0.01	-1.02	-10.77	4.48	124.2	**6.2**	49.6	0.0	**2.6**
6.4	0.28	0.8	0.00	**2.6**	0.00	0.38	1.75	5.82	100.0	**5.8**	47.1	0.0	**5.8**
2.0	3.26	26.9	0.68	**4.1**	0.06	0.76	7.71	4.66	71.3	**3.6**	13.8	0.0	**4.4**
10.0	0.23	0.6	0.00	**0.6**	-0.01	-0.34	-2.05	3.29	114.3	**5.5**	38.0	2.6	**6.0**
8.3	1.33	3.1	0.00	**4.2**	0.00	0.41	2.13	1.99	90.9	**5.3**	25.7	0.0	**8.5**
5.7	6.29	11.6	0.00	**0.0**	0.00	-0.73	-4.88	2.56	100.0	**7.0**	81.5	0.0	**6.3**
9.9	0.13	1.4	0.50	**3.2**	0.16	0.24	2.41	3.54	91.1	**4.7**	21.6	2.3	**6.3**
7.3	2.74	5.0	4.80	**3.7**	-0.01	-0.73	-3.09	4.59	64.6	**5.4**	36.3	0.0	**7.1**
6.0	0.75	11.2	0.22	**7.5**	0.26	1.04	10.25	4.19	75.3	**2.6**	22.9	20.2	**6.8**
8.2	1.75	4.2	0.33	**8.3**	0.06	1.91	7.71	5.31	70.5	**5.2**	29.2	1.4	**6.3**
5.3	0.56	3.1	0.75	**1.5**	-0.05	-1.58	-12.39	4.22	94.6	**3.2**	12.3	12.4	**6.2**
9.6	1.06	2.1	0.00	**0.0**	-0.01	-1.93	-9.43	7.51	135.3	**6.1**	47.8	7.6	**5.4**
7.9	0.09	0.9	0.24	**8.4**	0.44	0.94	10.83	5.28	82.5	**2.3**	18.2	27.6	**6.0**
8.6	0.26	2.0	0.12	**1.7**	0.00	0.00	0.00	3.28	99.3	**5.1**	33.3	0.0	**1.0**
8.7	0.22	1.6	0.22	**6.7**	0.09	0.70	6.92	4.78	82.8	**4.4**	16.2	2.8	**5.0**
6.2	0.42	4.7	0.88	**4.1**	0.32	0.93	11.76	2.66	72.8	**3.5**	27.8	12.1	**4.3**
1.7	14.04	38.7	0.04	**2.0**	-0.01	-0.08	-0.61	3.63	102.2	**5.2**	31.3	5.5	**5.9**
8.0	0.21	0.8	0.00	**5.0**	0.03	0.79	4.99	3.37	76.8	**4.0**	12.0	0.0	**7.9**
10.0	0.18	0.5	0.38	**2.7**	0.02	0.25	1.91	2.96	89.1	**7.0**	62.8	0.0	**6.5**
9.5	0.35	2.7	0.10	**5.2**	0.11	0.60	5.23	3.51	77.2	**4.6**	18.6	1.9	**6.5**
5.1	0.96	6.5	1.40	**2.9**	0.02	0.23	2.45	5.91	78.6	**3.8**	13.9	6.6	**4.3**
8.4	0.72	3.7	0.44	**5.5**	0.09	0.58	4.37	4.72	79.9	**4.0**	20.1	6.3	**6.5**
9.4	0.09	0.4	0.05	**5.1**	0.11	1.09	9.25	4.45	75.4	**4.5**	18.0	3.2	**6.5**
9.7	0.60	1.6	0.39	**4.2**	0.07	0.55	4.59	2.07	74.4	**4.9**	26.7	8.8	**6.2**
9.7	0.17	1.0	0.23	**2.7**	0.03	0.38	4.65	3.33	85.0	**4.1**	16.2	3.0	**3.1**
7.3	1.04	5.3	0.49	**2.4**	0.04	0.13	1.92	3.42	91.1	**5.7**	30.1	3.6	**2.9**
9.4	0.24	1.6	0.07	**5.9**	3.78	0.67	5.92	2.91	78.3	**3.1**	14.1	10.4	**8.4**
10.0	0.09	0.2	0.60	**2.7**	0.01	0.08	0.65	4.04	97.2	**7.1**	53.4	2.5	**6.1**
7.5	0.39	3.9	0.18	**3.0**	0.90	0.16	1.75	3.12	91.3	**3.9**	15.6	7.0	**5.7**
8.9	0.00	0.0	0.00	**8.6**	0.33	1.14	8.28	2.10	42.1	**2.9**	45.8	25.6	**9.9**
10.0	0.05	0.1	0.09	**4.4**	0.26	0.76	5.56	2.52	56.6	**6.9**	40.8	0.0	**8.5**
9.5	0.39	2.0	0.52	**1.9**	0.13	0.13	1.32	3.08	88.3	**4.8**	21.0	0.5	**5.7**
10.0	0.03	0.1	0.06	**4.6**	2.71	0.71	7.07	1.61	56.3	**5.2**	26.4	0.0	**7.5**
4.4	7.69	15.8	0.00	**3.0**	0.00	0.00	0.00	9.30	100.0	**7.9**	82.4	0.0	**3.0**
9.9	0.34	1.0	0.00	**5.4**	0.03	0.96	4.80	3.49	69.9	**5.3**	42.0	0.0	**7.9**
10.0	0.19	0.2	0.00	**0.0**	-0.02	-0.63	-3.06	2.91	128.9	**7.3**	66.3	0.0	**6.8**
9.9	0.42	1.1	0.31	**1.5**	-0.01	-0.08	-0.81	2.12	104.8	**4.0**	22.2	18.3	**4.0**
10.0	0.23	0.6	0.00	**4.5**	0.09	0.54	2.40	2.42	82.0	**5.7**	39.4	1.6	**7.8**
5.6	1.85	10.4	0.00	**3.7**	0.00	-2.42	-19.05	8.82	100.0	**2.3**	21.9	50.9	**3.0**
5.5	3.20	10.8	-5.84	**2.9**	0.00	1.07	14.55	5.23	120.0	**5.9**	47.6	0.0	**1.0**
10.0	0.18	0.9	0.44	**2.7**	0.05	0.13	1.35	4.04	91.0	**5.4**	29.6	3.3	**5.7**
8.4	0.37	1.7	0.72	**7.9**	0.07	1.50	7.96	4.32	66.7	**4.9**	28.2	0.0	**6.3**
9.7	0.84	2.3	0.78	**2.4**	0.09	0.23	2.19	2.46	80.9	**6.1**	32.0	0.0	**5.5**
6.4	0.97	6.5	0.74	**5.6**	0.11	0.40	4.38	3.89	75.0	**3.1**	21.1	14.9	**5.4**
4.7	2.22	11.9	1.99	**4.1**	0.03	0.36	2.86	4.68	66.2	**4.6**	32.2	5.2	**5.6**
7.6	0.47	4.1	0.40	**2.3**	0.21	0.14	1.64	3.24	90.7	**3.8**	16.8	4.5	**5.7**
8.8	0.26	1.8	0.60	**5.9**	3.62	0.94	8.01	3.33	66.2	**2.1**	12.5	18.6	**8.7**
1.7	17.97	39.7	0.00	**8.5**	0.00	1.01	8.51	12.12	83.3	**7.8**	77.8	0.0	**8.4**
8.1	0.57	3.8	-0.32	**3.9**	0.02	0.38	4.31	3.00	84.5	**4.9**	25.1	1.0	**3.7**
5.2	2.10	12.3	-0.07	**1.1**	0.00	-0.03	-0.30	2.95	100.5	**5.0**	22.2	1.0	**4.9**
1.7	4.65	35.1	2.04	**0.4**	-0.04	-1.76	-24.26	7.03	110.9	**5.5**	43.5	1.6	**1.5**
3.0	2.45	17.4	2.34	**0.1**	-0.18	-1.11	-15.02	4.43	74.4	**4.6**	22.3	5.5	**2.4**
9.5	2.05	2.4	0.00	**2.9**	0.00	0.00	0.00	5.16	100.0	**7.2**	90.5	0.0	**7.7**
6.2	1.31	8.0	0.49	**0.3**	-0.01	-0.43	-5.71	4.50	105.9	**5.4**	26.9	0.0	**2.8**
5.7	1.00	6.6	1.84	**3.9**	0.19	0.33	3.72	5.23	83.8	**3.4**	20.5	10.4	**5.2**
9.7	0.29	2.3	0.38	**2.8**	0.13	0.28	3.03	3.24	90.3	**4.2**	28.0	5.3	**6.0**
9.1	0.21	1.4	0.00	**2.4**	0.00	0.11	1.49	2.90	97.5	**5.9**	53.7	0.0	**2.3**
7.3	1.63	8.3	-0.01	**9.2**	0.10	1.21	8.53	4.99	71.3	**4.4**	26.9	3.7	**8.7**

Name	City	State	Rating	2016 Rating	2015 Rating	Total Assets ($Mil)	One Year Asset Growth	Comm-ercial Loans	Cons-umer Loans	Mort-gage Loans	Secur-ities	Capital-ization Index	Net Worth Ratio
								Asset Mix (As a % of Total Assets)					
Capital Area Realtors FCU	Rockville	MD	**D**	D	C-	11.8	14.10	5.8	24.2	22.0	0.0	**6.2**	8.2
▲ Capital Area Taiwanese FCU	Boyds	MD	**C**	C-	D	11.9	12.73	5.2	0.0	49.1	4.8	**6.0**	8.0
Capital Communications FCU	Albany	NY	**A-**	A-	A	1448.3	12.25	10.3	22.0	52.8	3.1	**9.2**	10.5
Capital Credit Union	Bismarck	ND	**A-**	A-	A-	455.1	9.52	23.5	18.1	23.1	5.1	**10.0**	11.0
Capital Credit Union	Green Bay	WI	**A-**	A-	B+	1258.0	7.93	6.1	25.8	45.6	3.6	**10.0**	12.1
Capital Educators Federal Credit Union	Meridian	ID	**B-**	B-	B	581.7	11.78	4.3	52.4	26.8	0.3	**5.5**	7.5
Capitol Credit Union	Austin	TX	**C-**	C-	D+	126.1	1.59	0.0	49.1	7.3	8.5	**4.9**	6.9
Capitol View Credit Union	Des Moines	IA	**B**	B	B	34.8	4.74	2.4	29.5	6.0	0.0	**10.0**	14.7
▼ Caprock Federal Credit Union	Lamesa	TX	**C+**	B-	B-	29.1	1.92	0.0	53.2	10.2	5.1	**10.0**	13.5
Caprock Santa Fe Credit Union	Slaton	TX	**A-**	A-	A-	42.3	1.47	0.0	41.6	0.0	1.7	**10.0**	30.5
Capstone Federal Credit Union	Aliso Viejo	CA	**C+**	C+	C-	40.0	-1.66	0.0	19.5	11.7	19.1	**7.2**	9.1
Carbondale Highway Credit Union	Carbondale	IL	**C-**	C-	C-	4.9	1.20	0.0	57.7	0.0	0.0	**10.0**	14.8
Carco Federal Credit Union	Denton	MD	**C-**	C-	C-	5.2	6.16	0.0	29.4	0.0	60.3	**10.0**	11.7
Cardinal Credit Union, Inc.	Mentor	OH	**B**	B	C+	248.2	28.35	3.2	38.1	19.7	6.1	**10.0**	11.1
Carey Poverello Federal Credit Union	Carey	OH	**C-**	C-	C	21.2	6.05	0.0	20.0	6.9	38.8	**10.0**	13.2
Caribe Federal Credit Union	San Juan	PR	**B+**	B+	B+	342.6	5.88	5.4	53.2	12.6	22.4	**10.0**	13.1
Carle Employees Federal Credit Union	Urbana	IL	**D-**	D-	D-	16.0	3.46	0.0	38.1	0.0	0.0	**5.3**	7.3
Carmel Brotherhood Federal Credit Union	Cincinnati	OH	**D**	D	D+	<1	-27.41	0.0	15.8	0.0	0.0	**7.3**	9.2
Carnegie Mellon University FCU	Pittsburgh	PA	**D+**	D+	D	11.4	-1.01	0.0	22.0	0.0	52.0	**5.8**	8.3
Carolina Collegiate Federal Credit Union	Columbia	SC	**B+**	B+	B+	91.1	2.08	7.8	28.1	10.7	0.2	**10.0**	13.3
▼ Carolina Community Federal Credit Union	Charlotte	NC	**C-**	C	D	39.2	-2.37	1.2	39.9	13.6	18.0	**8.7**	10.1
▼ Carolina Federal Credit Union	Cherryville	NC	**C-**	C	B-	49.0	10.34	0.3	48.9	0.0	3.6	**8.3**	9.9
Carolina Foothills Federal Credit Union	Spartanburg	SC	**A-**	A-	B-	106.1	5.39	5.6	36.7	16.4	0.5	**9.0**	10.3
Carolina Trust Federal Credit Union	Myrtle Beach	SC	**B+**	B+	B+	231.2	8.00	1.5	37.1	10.0	10.8	**7.2**	9.2
Carolinas Telco Federal Credit Union	Charlotte	NC	**B-**	B-	B	450.4	10.86	0.0	22.8	16.3	43.4	**10.0**	15.0
▲ Carpenters Federal Credit Union	Saint Paul	MN	**B-**	C+	C	28.2	13.09	0.0	21.8	7.3	1.8	**6.3**	8.3
▲ Carter Federal Credit Union	Springhill	LA	**C**	C-	C+	267.7	2.05	13.0	30.4	37.8	1.1	**6.3**	8.3
Carville Employees Federal Credit Union	Carville	LA	**C**	C	C-	10.5	1.79	0.0	48.4	16.0	0.0	**10.0**	13.5
Cascade Central Credit Union	Hood River	OR	**B+**	B+	B+	66.6	12.24	5.3	9.7	24.6	23.0	**10.0**	11.2
Cascade Community Federal Credit Union	Roseburg	OR	**A-**	A-	B	212.9	10.29	1.1	22.6	14.9	0.1	**10.0**	12.0
▼ Cascade Federal Credit Union	Kent	WA	**B+**	A-	B+	290.3	4.56	0.0	7.0	15.3	34.1	**10.0**	12.1
Casco Federal Credit Union	Gorham	ME	**C+**	C+	C+	61.7	10.40	7.7	20.4	44.1	0.0	**6.8**	8.8
▼ CASE Credit Union	Lansing	MI	**B-**	B	B	286.2	10.50	13.5	45.3	25.2	9.9	**6.8**	9.0
CASE Federal Credit Union	Tyler	TX	**C**	C	C	5.1	2.64	0.0	26.9	0.0	0.0	**10.0**	13.7
Casebine Community Credit Union	Burlington	IA	**C-**	C-	B-	34.2	-0.67	9.4	23.4	10.5	3.0	**10.0**	15.0
Castparts Employees Federal Credit Union	Portland	OR	**B+**	B+	B+	59.9	2.95	0.0	36.7	3.7	3.3	**10.0**	13.1
Catholic & Community Credit Union	Belleville	IL	**B+**	B+	B-	120.7	3.95	0.6	59.3	1.5	23.6	**8.9**	10.4
Catholic Credit Union	Avon Lake	OH	**C**	C	C	10.3	-0.98	2.0	16.2	0.0	23.3	**9.0**	10.4
Catholic Family Credit Union	Kansas City	MO	**D**	D	D	13.1	7.02	0.0	23.0	0.0	1.0	**6.4**	8.4
Catholic Family Federal Credit Union	Wichita	KS	**D+**	D+	C-	30.5	3.36	0.6	41.9	14.3	2.3	**7.1**	9.1
Catholic Federal Credit Union	Saginaw	MI	**C**	C	C+	352.5	3.35	0.3	21.9	31.9	27.0	**9.9**	10.9
Catholic United Financial Credit Union	Saint Paul	MN	**D+**	D+	D-	16.7	1.94	0.0	44.6	6.6	0.6	**10.0**	13.0
Catholic Vantage Financial FCU	Livonia	MI	**C+**	C+	C+	98.5	11.60	8.0	26.5	24.5	17.8	**5.7**	7.7
Catholics United Credit Union	South Hutchinson	KS	**C+**	C+	D+	<1	3.27	0.0	38.9	0.0	0.0	**10.0**	13.6
Cattaraugus County Employees FCU	Little Valley	NY	**C-**	C-	C-	11.0	1.95	0.0	35.3	6.7	29.9	**7.8**	9.5
CBC Federal Credit Union	Oxnard	CA	**B-**	B-	C+	468.0	1.91	4.7	21.0	21.2	39.2	**7.5**	9.8
CBI Federal Credit Union	Plainfield	IL	**D+**	D+	D+	20.0	1.79	0.0	27.1	19.2	3.9	**6.5**	8.5
CCAC Federal Credit Union	Pittsburgh	PA	**C-**	C-	C-	4.7	5.51	0.0	38.8	0.0	0.0	**10.0**	11.1
CCC Van Wert Credit Union	Van Wert	OH	**C**	C	C-	<1	-3.32	0.0	48.7	0.0	0.0	**10.0**	37.8
CDC Federal Credit Union	Atlanta	GA	**C+**	C+	C+	299.5	4.78	0.1	16.0	4.7	58.1	**5.3**	7.8
CDSC Louisiana Federal Credit Union	Coushatta	LA	**C+**	C+	C+	17.7	-2.69	0.0	25.0	25.1	0.0	**10.0**	19.5
Cecil County School Employees FCU	Elkton	MD	**D**	D	D	29.4	6.54	0.2	34.4	0.0	15.8	**5.2**	7.2
Cedar Falls Community Credit Union	Cedar Falls	IA	**A**	A	A	113.4	10.94	5.5	31.3	27.6	8.8	**10.0**	14.9
Cedar Point Federal Credit Union	Lexington Park	MD	**B-**	B-	C+	462.5	4.51	7.3	13.6	20.5	33.5	**7.8**	9.6
Cedars-Sinai Federal Credit Union	Los Angeles	CA	**B**	B	B-	27.7	10.08	0.0	18.1	0.0	1.8	**10.0**	13.1
Celco Federal Credit Union	Narrows	VA	**B**	B	B	106.5	3.62	2.0	14.5	21.8	20.6	**10.0**	19.6
CEMC Employees Credit Union	Clarksville	TN	**D**	D	D	2.6	7.23	0.0	58.0	0.0	0.0	**10.0**	21.5
▲ Cen Tex Manufacturing Credit Union	Brownwood	TX	**C-**	D+	D	9.7	7.23	0.0	49.0	0.0	0.0	**10.0**	11.7
Cencap Federal Credit Union	Hartford	CT	**C-**	C-	C	58.5	6.28	0.0	56.9	0.0	2.5	**6.6**	8.6
Cenla Federal Credit Union	Alexandria	LA	**B+**	B+	B+	115.6	3.29	0.0	27.0	8.2	43.1	**10.0**	13.3

Asset Quality Index	Non-Performing Loans as a % of Total Loans	Non-Performing Loans as a % of Capital	Net Charge-Offs Avg Loans	Profitability Index	Net Income ($Mil)	Return on Assets	Return on Equity	Net Interest Spread	Overhead Efficiency Ratio	Liquidity Index	Liquidity Ratio	Hot Money Ratio	Stability Index
6.7	0.47	4.3	0.00	**3.7**	0.01	0.48	5.80	3.53	81.3	**4.6**	23.4	0.0	**3.0**
10.0	0.00	0.0	0.00	**6.6**	0.03	0.96	11.88	2.12	47.2	**4.2**	155.1	39.2	**4.3**
5.8	1.54	12.2	0.33	**5.7**	2.81	0.79	7.51	3.66	75.7	**2.3**	3.5	8.9	**8.6**
6.9	0.64	4.4	0.08	**8.9**	1.64	1.45	13.37	3.96	71.5	**3.1**	8.6	6.5	**7.6**
7.8	0.39	3.6	0.21	**5.9**	3.23	1.05	8.31	3.43	72.4	**3.4**	9.5	4.5	**9.1**
5.0	0.76	10.9	0.35	**4.3**	0.73	0.51	7.62	3.15	82.8	**2.2**	1.8	9.2	**4.5**
8.5	0.12	1.8	0.27	**3.3**	0.09	0.27	3.99	3.33	89.3	**4.8**	23.3	0.2	**3.0**
7.6	0.97	6.1	0.07	**3.7**	0.02	0.18	1.18	3.48	85.4	**5.1**	32.5	2.2	**7.3**
6.2	0.96	6.6	0.96	**2.1**	-0.08	-1.09	-7.99	5.53	103.9	**2.7**	18.2	23.0	**6.2**
8.7	1.89	2.7	1.10	**10.0**	0.25	2.40	7.87	5.40	48.0	**5.2**	52.3	17.2	**8.0**
10.0	0.19	0.7	0.09	**3.1**	0.04	0.45	4.88	2.53	80.5	**4.9**	27.4	1.6	**3.7**
7.8	0.46	2.2	0.00	**2.1**	0.00	0.25	1.66	4.09	94.7	**5.1**	28.4	0.0	**7.0**
3.7	8.67	22.7	1.35	**5.7**	0.01	1.09	9.26	2.19	50.0	**4.8**	18.0	0.0	**6.4**
8.6	0.47	3.6	0.44	**3.9**	0.27	0.43	3.91	4.04	85.0	**3.8**	18.0	3.4	**6.3**
10.0	0.04	0.1	0.22	**1.0**	0.01	0.13	1.01	3.25	90.4	**6.4**	52.4	0.0	**6.2**
7.4	0.33	2.9	0.28	**4.0**	0.40	0.47	3.61	3.13	72.7	**3.0**	20.1	10.9	**8.2**
6.1	1.69	9.1	0.19	**2.3**	0.01	0.26	3.45	2.31	84.4	**5.4**	35.1	0.1	**1.7**
0.3	18.33	52.4	0.00	**3.7**	0.00	0.00	0.00	5.41	150.0	**6.3**	30.3	0.0	**3.0**
9.2	0.48	1.5	0.30	**3.0**	0.01	0.25	3.15	2.62	91.0	**6.0**	33.8	0.0	**3.2**
8.3	0.47	2.7	0.90	**3.7**	0.02	0.09	0.69	4.47	92.3	**5.2**	26.0	1.8	**6.3**
6.3	0.48	3.0	1.53	**2.1**	-0.11	-1.16	-10.96	4.64	106.9	**4.4**	31.0	9.8	**5.1**
3.8	1.73	14.1	1.20	**2.5**	0.03	0.29	2.82	5.28	75.4	**3.5**	32.0	27.0	**3.5**
8.7	0.45	2.7	0.32	**7.8**	0.45	1.72	16.70	4.73	72.7	**4.5**	25.0	2.9	**6.8**
9.8	0.20	1.7	0.29	**5.3**	0.42	0.74	8.06	3.35	82.4	**5.0**	25.3	2.3	**6.0**
9.9	0.53	1.8	0.17	**4.6**	1.04	0.97	6.94	2.89	71.7	**4.5**	20.1	2.1	**7.7**
9.9	0.04	0.2	-0.57	**8.8**	0.09	1.25	15.34	2.44	76.1	**5.1**	37.6	0.0	**5.4**
3.7	1.51	19.4	0.93	**5.3**	0.99	1.48	22.06	3.63	62.5	**2.1**	18.4	22.7	**4.5**
4.3	2.90	14.4	0.29	**3.7**	0.01	0.43	3.11	4.61	83.1	**4.6**	24.8	0.0	**6.3**
7.9	0.20	0.8	0.24	**5.4**	0.11	0.68	5.93	2.75	72.2	**5.7**	35.4	2.1	**6.1**
9.9	0.02	0.1	0.01	**5.8**	0.50	0.95	7.83	2.71	70.8	**4.7**	24.0	2.7	**8.4**
10.0	0.56	1.2	0.21	**4.9**	0.42	0.58	4.86	1.61	67.1	**4.5**	26.9	7.5	**7.5**
6.6	0.52	4.2	0.30	**4.0**	0.06	0.42	4.67	4.33	90.8	**3.7**	11.8	3.9	**4.3**
4.7	1.09	9.4	1.31	**4.5**	0.19	0.28	3.07	4.67	82.1	**3.1**	5.0	6.4	**5.0**
9.4	0.44	1.0	0.00	**3.5**	0.01	0.47	3.46	2.49	88.2	**6.1**	59.7	0.0	**7.3**
9.6	0.15	0.4	0.03	**2.2**	0.03	0.30	2.04	3.99	92.7	**5.3**	27.5	0.0	**5.4**
9.3	0.42	2.6	0.28	**5.9**	0.13	0.88	6.70	3.53	76.1	**4.6**	28.8	5.1	**7.1**
6.9	0.55	3.6	1.26	**4.6**	0.18	0.59	5.76	2.91	71.1	**3.5**	4.0	1.8	**6.3**
10.0	0.34	1.0	0.00	**2.8**	0.00	0.08	0.75	2.79	98.6	**6.1**	38.2	0.0	**4.4**
6.0	3.30	12.0	0.29	**1.4**	0.00	0.06	0.73	2.50	96.7	**5.8**	63.3	0.0	**3.4**
3.2	4.37	30.7	0.93	**4.1**	0.00	0.05	0.58	4.33	80.2	**4.7**	24.1	2.9	**4.2**
8.4	0.43	3.6	0.28	**3.2**	0.40	0.46	4.20	3.29	84.0	**4.1**	16.2	3.0	**7.0**
9.7	0.41	1.9	0.00	**1.1**	-0.01	-0.12	-0.92	2.56	99.4	**4.4**	30.1	0.0	**5.3**
6.1	0.91	6.4	0.77	**3.8**	0.11	0.47	5.99	3.42	76.0	**4.7**	18.7	0.3	**3.3**
9.8	0.00	0.0	0.00	**3.7**	0.00	0.00	0.00	8.16	100.0	**7.3**	74.4	0.0	**9.0**
6.9	0.92	5.1	0.00	**3.1**	0.01	0.26	2.70	3.02	90.9	**5.3**	32.6	0.0	**5.4**
7.7	1.33	7.0	0.56	**3.7**	0.48	0.42	4.47	3.48	79.1	**4.2**	32.4	7.7	**6.2**
5.7	1.70	11.9	0.00	**3.5**	0.03	0.58	6.84	3.21	81.0	**4.5**	17.0	1.5	**3.0**
6.8	2.11	8.5	-0.19	**0.9**	-0.01	-0.43	-3.84	3.68	97.4	**5.0**	27.1	2.5	**5.8**
7.9	2.39	3.1	0.00	**3.6**	0.00	-1.28	-3.28	8.02	125.0	**6.9**	67.2	0.0	**5.8**
9.5	0.73	2.7	0.42	**3.8**	0.30	0.41	5.64	2.48	87.1	**5.0**	19.2	0.7	**3.7**
5.2	4.94	14.9	0.07	**8.2**	0.06	1.37	7.11	3.41	60.7	**4.0**	19.8	0.0	**7.6**
6.1	1.11	5.7	1.09	**1.8**	0.01	0.08	1.14	3.72	87.3	**4.6**	15.8	4.5	**2.4**
8.8	0.64	3.3	0.20	**8.3**	0.30	1.09	7.64	2.91	69.9	**3.2**	26.5	13.2	**9.8**
8.6	0.78	3.7	0.09	**3.7**	0.55	0.48	5.00	2.83	86.3	**5.0**	25.9	4.0	**6.0**
10.0	0.60	0.8	0.00	**4.9**	0.05	0.67	4.98	2.73	75.8	**5.6**	20.7	1.2	**6.3**
8.9	1.00	3.0	0.13	**3.6**	0.11	0.42	2.45	3.37	85.3	**5.2**	19.0	0.0	**8.1**
7.6	1.27	3.9	0.00	**0.3**	-0.01	-0.95	-4.29	4.94	124.0	**5.0**	40.0	6.7	**5.6**
6.3	1.31	5.9	0.58	**5.8**	0.02	1.00	8.50	5.12	83.1	**3.9**	34.5	12.9	**4.3**
1.7	4.23	29.5	2.53	**2.6**	-0.30	-2.04	-22.51	5.75	96.9	**2.9**	28.5	20.3	**3.7**
7.1	1.45	5.6	0.83	**3.9**	0.12	0.43	3.64	3.35	73.3	**4.2**	10.2	4.1	**7.7**

Name	City	State	Rating	2016 Rating	2015 Rating	Total Assets ($Mil)	One Year Asset Growth	Asset Mix (As a % of Total Assets) Comm-ercial Loans	Cons-umer Loans	Mort-gage Loans	Secur-ities	Capital-ization Index	Net Worth Ratio
Census Federal Credit Union	Washington	DC	**C**	C	D+	57.8	-1.76	0.0	9.4	7.3	70.7	**10.0**	17.1
Cent Credit Union	Mason City	IA	**B**	B	B	47.7	12.43	0.4	31.1	34.7	6.5	**10.0**	15.1
▲ Centerville Clinics Employees FCU	Fredericktown	PA	**C**	C-	D	<1	8.15	0.0	18.0	0.0	0.0	**10.0**	21.5
▼ Centex Citizens Credit Union	Mexia	TX	**B+**	A-	A-	65.5	3.69	0.7	44.8	15.3	0.6	**10.0**	20.6
Centra Credit Union	Columbus	IN	**A**	A	A-	1425.9	6.63	10.9	28.1	27.3	19.7	**10.0**	11.9
Central Coast Federal Credit Union	Seaside	CA	**C-**	C-	C	137.8	6.91	0.9	10.9	21.4	41.9	**5.2**	8.0
Central Communications Credit Union	Independence	MO	**D**	D	D+	50.5	2.00	1.5	20.1	8.9	53.5	**5.9**	8.9
Central Credit Union of Florida	Pensacola	FL	**B+**	B+	B+	155.9	6.08	0.0	31.5	16.0	1.3	**10.0**	11.1
Central Credit Union of Illinois	Bellwood	IL	**C+**	C+	C+	92.2	2.84	0.0	40.4	24.7	0.0	**6.6**	8.6
▼ Central Credit Union of Maryland	Baltimore	MD	**D+**	C-	C-	21.7	3.07	0.0	32.3	0.0	13.5	**10.0**	11.6
Central Florida Educators FCU	Lake Mary	FL	**C+**	C+	C+	1760.7	7.14	1.5	25.6	21.3	39.5	**9.0**	10.5
Central Hanna Employees Credit Union	Keewatin	MN	**D**	D	D+	3.5	-3.37	0.0	39.4	0.0	0.0	**10.0**	21.6
Central Illinois Credit Union	Champaign	IL	**C-**	C-	C-	18.1	5.89	0.0	43.5	0.0	0.0	**6.5**	8.5
Central Jersey Federal Credit Union	Woodbridge	NJ	**D-**	D-	E	79.1	5.29	2.0	14.1	12.0	14.8	**3.8**	5.8
Central Jersey Police & Fire FCU	Hamilton	NJ	**B+**	B+	B+	29.0	9.51	0.0	27.0	18.4	46.7	**10.0**	13.8
Central Kansas Credit Union	Hutchinson	KS	**D-**	D-	D-	36.2	-2.01	0.3	43.5	9.1	4.8	**5.0**	7.0
Central Kansas Education Credit Union	Salina	KS	**C-**	C-	C-	2.7	3.84	0.0	70.4	0.0	0.0	**10.0**	25.8
Central Keystone Federal Credit Union	Sunbury	PA	**B**	B	B	41.7	4.38	0.0	18.2	26.6	16.2	**10.0**	17.5
Central Maine Federal Credit Union	Lewiston	ME	**C**	C	C	92.3	1.91	0.5	11.4	29.8	0.0	**10.0**	12.3
▲ Central Minnesota Credit Union	Melrose	MN	**B+**	B	B	986.5	7.04	58.7	9.1	42.2	1.6	**10.0**	15.0
Central Missouri Community Credit Union	Warrensburg	MO	**C**	C	C	102.9	4.17	0.0	29.4	22.1	8.7	**5.8**	7.8
Central Nebraska Federal Credit Union	Grand Island	NE	**D+**	D+	C-	8.7	2.63	0.0	40.7	0.0	0.0	**8.9**	10.2
▼ Central Oklahoma Federal Credit Union	Davenport	OK	**C-**	C	C+	29.5	-4.92	3.9	16.6	43.5	0.0	**10.0**	16.7
Central One Federal Credit Union	Shrewsbury	MA	**B**	B	B	459.0	7.00	9.2	18.2	40.3	1.1	**7.7**	9.5
Central Soya Federal Credit Union	Decatur	IN	**C**	C	C+	24.2	-3.51	0.0	14.2	0.0	0.0	**10.0**	18.5
▼ Central State Credit Union	Stockton	CA	**C**	C+	C-	186.8	5.16	7.2	41.0	11.5	22.8	**5.5**	7.8
Central Sunbelt Federal Credit Union	Laurel	MS	**A**	A	A	216.5	2.19	0.0	28.4	5.7	31.1	**10.0**	14.5
Central Susquehanna Community FCU	Danville	PA	**C**	C	C	25.1	-0.21	0.0	15.4	13.0	53.5	**10.0**	14.7
▼ Central Texas Teachers Credit Union	Corsicana	TX	**D**	D+	D+	13.3	3.17	0.0	21.9	0.0	64.9	**10.0**	11.4
Central Valley Federal Credit Union	Arnold	PA	**E+**	E+	D	2.2	8.05	0.0	55.3	0.0	0.0	**4.2**	6.2
Central Vermont Medical Center Inc., CU	Berlin	VT	**B**	B	B	11.9	7.31	0.0	41.4	0.0	0.0	**10.0**	20.6
Central Virginia Federal Credit Union	Lynchburg	VA	**C+**	C+	C+	131.8	8.22	0.2	20.7	14.5	0.0	**6.2**	8.2
Central Willamette Community CU	Albany	OR	**B**	B	B	270.9	10.30	5.5	45.8	9.8	5.2	**7.3**	9.2
Central Wisconsin Credit Union	Plover	WI	**C**	C	C+	36.3	6.06	0.2	14.1	45.9	0.0	**9.1**	10.4
▲ CentralAlliance Credit Union	Neenah	WI	**B+**	B	B-	78.1	1.97	13.3	5.8	32.1	23.8	**10.0**	20.0
Centric Federal Credit Union	West Monroe	LA	**B-**	B-	B-	159.3	10.45	10.8	35.1	25.7	1.2	**6.4**	8.4
Centris Federal Credit Union	Omaha	NE	**C+**	C+	B-	689.6	12.11	5.2	40.8	31.5	2.1	**6.0**	8.0
Century Credit Union	Saint Louis	MO	**A**	A	A	97.0	7.40	0.7	25.9	20.8	0.0	**10.0**	17.1
▼ Century Employees' Savings Fund CU	Hickory	NC	**D+**	C-	C-	9.1	5.03	0.0	32.3	9.5	0.0	**10.0**	31.3
Century Federal Credit Union	Cleveland	OH	**B-**	B-	C+	379.8	5.41	0.8	16.0	40.1	26.5	**7.2**	9.2
Century Heritage Federal Credit Union	Pittsburgh	PA	**C**	C	C-	121.6	1.24	4.9	38.5	27.0	18.6	**10.0**	12.3
CES Credit Union	Mount Vernon	OH	**B-**	B-	B-	137.2	4.92	0.0	27.1	18.1	0.9	**6.4**	8.4
CFCU Community Credit Union	Ithaca	NY	**B+**	B+	A	1045.3	6.67	7.7	16.5	41.4	12.5	**10.0**	12.8
CGR Credit Union	Macon	GA	**A**	A	A	89.3	1.41	0.0	29.6	3.9	15.2	**10.0**	15.7
CHA-TEL Federal Credit Union	Charleston	WV	**C**	C	C-	11.6	3.69	1.2	51.8	0.0	22.3	**7.8**	9.6
Chabot Federal Credit Union	Dublin	CA	**B**	B	B	69.9	-1.33	0.0	1.9	14.0	21.3	**10.0**	14.2
▲ Chadron Federal Credit Union	Chadron	NE	**C**	C-	C	10.3	1.26	0.0	43.5	10.4	0.0	**10.0**	12.4
▲ Chadwick Federal Credit Union	Norwood	MA	**E**	E-	E-	24.4	5.29	0.0	17.1	18.1	0.0	**3.9**	5.9
Chaffey Federal Credit Union	Upland	CA	**B+**	B+	B	139.2	10.87	5.7	22.9	21.4	17.7	**6.1**	8.4
Champaign County School Employees CU	Champaign	IL	**D**	D	D	14.1	5.50	0.0	31.9	0.0	0.0	**5.5**	7.5
▼ Champaign Postal Credit Union	Champaign	IL	**D**	D+	C-	2.5	1.30	0.0	55.0	0.0	0.0	**10.0**	16.9
Champion Community Credit Union	Courtland	AL	**C-**	C-	C	52.4	-2.75	0.6	25.5	26.6	0.0	**10.0**	11.9
Champion Credit Union	Canton	NC	**A-**	A-	B+	238.4	9.60	3.6	28.1	50.2	0.0	**10.0**	11.8
Champion Credit Union	Toledo	OH	**C-**	C-	C-	52.9	4.79	0.0	19.6	10.6	7.9	**10.0**	11.8
Champion Federal Credit Union	Cambridge	OH	**D**	D	C-	5.4	-0.11	0.0	25.1	0.0	0.0	**10.0**	12.3
Changing Seasons Federal Credit Union	Hampden	ME	**C-**	C-	C-	22.5	0.85	0.0	30.1	34.7	0.0	**8.3**	9.9
▼ Charleston County Teachers FCU	Charleston	SC	**D+**	C-	D+	1.6	-0.88	0.0	57.7	0.0	0.0	**9.6**	10.7
Charleston Federal Credit Union	Charleston	WV	**D+**	D+	D+	9.8	5.66	0.0	47.3	0.0	0.0	**8.7**	10.2
Charleston Postal Federal Credit Union	Charleston	WV	**D-**	D-	D	4.1	-5.36	0.0	74.2	0.0	0.0	**7.5**	9.3
Charlotte Fire Department Credit Union	Charlotte	NC	**C-**	C-	C	47.2	2.01	1.5	30.6	6.7	34.3	**10.0**	12.2

Asset Quality Index	Non-Performing Loans as a % of Total Loans	Non-Performing Loans as a % of Capital	Net Charge-Offs Avg Loans	Profitability Index	Net Income ($Mil)	Return on Assets	Return on Equity	Net Interest Spread	Overhead Efficiency Ratio	Liquidity Index	Liquidity Ratio	Hot Money Ratio	Stability Index
7.6	5.16	6.0	0.29	**2.4**	0.05	0.36	2.15	2.15	85.9	**5.1**	12.4	3.5	**6.8**
8.1	0.73	3.6	0.17	**5.5**	0.08	0.70	4.46	3.76	83.9	**4.3**	20.9	0.0	**7.6**
9.6	3.09	3.0	0.00	**3.8**	0.00	0.93	4.12	5.85	50.0	**7.7**	70.3	0.0	**7.1**
8.5	1.02	3.5	0.77	**4.7**	0.07	0.43	2.14	5.70	81.0	**4.8**	31.7	8.1	**7.4**
9.5	0.24	1.4	0.29	**6.9**	3.76	1.08	8.98	2.46	70.6	**3.7**	19.2	8.9	**8.9**
10.0	0.10	0.5	0.17	**2.2**	0.08	0.25	3.37	2.95	93.1	**5.1**	25.5	4.9	**4.8**
9.6	0.29	1.4	0.24	**1.2**	-0.01	-0.06	-0.83	2.73	104.2	**4.4**	6.9	2.7	**2.4**
8.1	0.58	3.5	0.65	**3.6**	0.09	0.23	2.04	4.61	89.7	**5.5**	38.4	7.0	**6.8**
6.6	0.72	5.2	0.80	**3.3**	0.05	0.20	2.27	4.17	85.3	**4.0**	16.9	0.7	**4.4**
9.1	1.46	4.3	0.00	**0.4**	-0.06	-1.10	-9.14	2.75	126.1	**5.4**	52.7	0.0	**5.0**
9.6	0.33	2.1	1.29	**2.7**	2.01	0.47	4.52	3.32	80.3	**4.3**	10.5	2.1	**6.6**
5.7	4.92	11.0	-0.69	**0.2**	-0.01	-0.59	-2.67	3.75	139.3	**5.3**	35.0	0.0	**5.0**
9.7	0.13	0.7	0.00	**2.7**	0.02	0.34	3.93	2.63	91.3	**5.9**	47.0	0.0	**3.8**
4.2	2.24	18.7	0.91	**2.7**	0.10	0.54	9.21	3.99	85.9	**6.2**	37.0	0.3	**1.4**
9.1	0.34	1.2	0.58	**7.0**	0.10	1.34	9.94	3.03	56.4	**4.3**	15.5	0.0	**7.5**
5.4	1.45	12.1	0.52	**1.7**	-0.01	-0.09	-1.26	3.28	95.3	**4.5**	21.9	0.0	**2.5**
8.4	0.21	0.6	0.83	**3.9**	0.00	0.45	1.72	4.15	86.7	**4.2**	23.1	0.0	**6.9**
7.8	1.60	5.2	0.12	**4.8**	0.07	0.71	4.02	2.75	71.9	**4.3**	26.4	4.9	**7.6**
10.0	0.04	0.2	0.04	**2.8**	0.08	0.33	2.70	2.47	87.7	**5.5**	46.6	3.7	**6.0**
5.0	0.63	4.3	0.03	**6.9**	2.34	0.96	6.39	3.87	76.7	**2.8**	18.5	13.5	**10.0**
6.8	0.78	7.5	0.46	**2.9**	0.01	0.03	0.35	3.75	91.7	**4.2**	19.4	5.5	**4.1**
7.7	0.71	2.9	-0.11	**3.0**	0.00	0.19	1.79	4.60	95.7	**6.1**	37.4	0.0	**4.9**
3.3	5.60	24.4	0.40	**1.3**	0.01	0.15	0.89	4.60	102.4	**4.8**	46.3	8.0	**5.2**
7.2	0.54	4.9	0.13	**4.4**	0.48	0.43	4.65	3.22	86.6	**2.8**	9.1	8.3	**6.6**
9.0	2.36	2.6	1.34	**2.2**	0.01	0.15	0.81	1.90	91.9	**6.3**	50.9	0.0	**7.1**
8.9	0.28	2.5	0.77	**1.9**	-0.06	-0.14	-1.79	3.69	89.4	**4.8**	21.5	1.2	**4.3**
9.0	1.00	2.9	1.85	**6.9**	0.51	0.97	6.58	4.38	71.8	**6.0**	36.6	3.7	**7.9**
10.0	0.30	0.6	0.68	**0.9**	-0.03	-0.42	-2.80	2.48	103.8	**5.3**	20.3	0.7	**6.8**
9.8	0.38	0.9	1.73	**0.1**	-0.02	-0.63	-5.53	2.86	97.9	**5.2**	37.5	5.2	**4.2**
6.5	0.32	2.4	-0.97	**0.4**	0.00	-0.18	-2.90	4.53	96.0	**5.2**	29.4	0.0	**2.9**
8.3	1.19	2.7	0.55	**10.0**	0.05	1.63	7.90	5.39	59.2	**6.0**	66.8	0.0	**7.0**
8.9	0.42	2.5	0.36	**3.3**	0.08	0.25	2.95	3.37	90.1	**5.3**	27.9	1.0	**4.8**
6.0	0.47	4.7	0.54	**6.1**	0.59	0.89	9.64	3.85	74.2	**3.7**	11.0	2.1	**6.3**
10.0	0.00	0.0	0.00	**2.5**	0.03	0.29	2.77	3.36	91.6	**4.0**	20.1	3.6	**5.4**
8.6	0.06	3.6	0.01	**5.1**	0.20	1.04	5.21	3.17	66.9	**5.3**	28.5	2.3	**7.9**
6.0	0.85	7.9	0.74	**6.3**	0.32	0.83	9.68	5.04	80.1	**3.1**	25.0	19.8	**5.5**
6.1	0.71	9.1	0.38	**3.1**	0.35	0.21	3.03	3.79	89.6	**2.8**	8.7	8.0	**4.6**
8.9	0.88	3.1	0.45	**8.2**	0.28	1.18	6.85	3.13	64.2	**4.1**	26.2	5.4	**8.1**
9.9	0.67	1.4	0.91	**0.8**	-0.01	-0.53	-1.68	3.46	105.4	**6.0**	72.5	1.9	**6.4**
8.8	0.52	3.5	0.51	**3.3**	0.32	0.34	3.71	2.67	81.2	**3.9**	23.7	3.7	**5.8**
8.4	0.49	2.9	0.23	**2.3**	0.07	0.24	1.99	3.07	91.0	**3.6**	23.0	3.3	**7.5**
9.9	0.17	1.0	0.31	**4.2**	0.22	0.63	7.51	3.06	83.1	**4.9**	25.6	0.7	**4.9**
7.4	1.13	5.8	0.34	**4.7**	1.78	0.68	5.32	3.47	75.0	**4.4**	28.1	13.2	**8.7**
10.0	0.34	0.9	0.50	**8.7**	0.24	1.10	6.83	3.47	79.2	**6.0**	48.2	9.9	**8.2**
8.0	0.26	1.6	-0.29	**6.3**	0.03	1.03	10.65	4.03	73.4	**5.0**	18.4	0.0	**5.0**
10.0	0.04	0.1	-0.05	**2.7**	0.04	0.20	1.53	1.86	90.9	**4.4**	23.3	6.0	**6.7**
8.5	0.58	3.2	0.80	**5.5**	0.02	0.71	5.71	5.19	79.2	**4.4**	31.7	5.3	**6.2**
6.9	0.39	2.9	0.40	**1.9**	0.01	0.09	1.40	2.70	96.7	**5.5**	37.9	1.4	**0.7**
8.5	0.62	4.6	0.16	**5.1**	0.23	0.68	8.23	2.92	78.8	**3.9**	17.4	8.3	**5.8**
9.1	0.51	2.1	0.18	**2.4**	0.01	0.26	3.42	2.87	91.0	**6.5**	66.6	0.0	**2.3**
8.6	0.36	1.2	0.00	**0.0**	-0.01	-1.81	-10.30	2.40	153.9	**5.3**	29.3	0.0	**5.4**
7.2	0.82	5.2	0.59	**2.1**	0.05	0.35	2.97	3.48	87.7	**4.0**	22.9	11.6	**5.8**
6.6	0.57	8.2	0.21	**5.3**	0.40	0.69	5.75	4.29	79.8	**2.5**	10.2	13.2	**7.8**
6.2	3.27	12.1	-0.16	**2.2**	0.03	0.24	2.19	3.01	93.1	**5.2**	35.2	0.9	**5.8**
6.1	6.74	14.5	-0.27	**0.5**	-0.01	-0.68	-5.43	2.70	127.3	**7.4**	64.5	0.0	**5.2**
4.5	2.21	16.3	-0.02	**1.7**	0.01	0.11	1.08	3.96	97.7	**4.1**	27.6	0.6	**3.9**
5.6	0.61	3.4	1.60	**3.0**	0.00	-0.77	-7.02	11.44	106.5	**6.0**	40.1	0.0	**4.9**
3.9	2.52	11.8	1.63	**4.8**	0.01	0.54	5.28	3.46	65.8	**4.9**	20.2	0.0	**3.0**
4.6	1.14	7.5	2.62	**3.1**	0.00	0.19	2.09	7.06	75.0	**4.5**	20.0	0.0	**2.3**
8.8	0.63	2.4	0.00	**1.7**	0.01	0.04	0.35	3.40	103.1	**3.9**	34.3	20.3	**5.3**

Name	City	State	Rating	2016 Rating	2015 Rating	Total Assets ($Mil)	One Year Asset Growth	Asset Mix (As a % of Total Assets) Comm-ercial Loans	Cons-umer Loans	Mort-gage Loans	Secur-ities	Capital-ization Index	Net Worth Ratio
▼ Charlotte Metro Federal Credit Union	Charlotte	NC	**A-**	A	A	441.3	17.92	11.5	27.6	36.8	0.0	**8.5**	10.0
Charlottesville Postal FCU	Charlottesville	VA	**E+**	E+	E+	6.2	-0.11	0.0	30.8	26.2	0.0	**5.1**	7.1
Charter Oak Federal Credit Union	Waterford	CT	**B-**	B-	B	1012.3	5.62	13.4	17.4	56.6	8.1	**7.7**	9.5
Chartway Federal Credit Union	Virginia Beach	VA	**C+**	C+	C+	2165.6	1.16	0.6	53.2	14.7	6.1	**6.1**	8.1
Chattahoochee Federal Credit Union	Valley	AL	**C+**	C+	C	15.8	3.44	0.0	45.1	1.9	0.0	**10.0**	12.6
▼ Chattanooga Area Schools FCU	Chattanooga	TN	**C+**	B-	C+	150.0	0.98	0.0	21.7	8.7	41.0	**10.0**	15.1
Chattanooga Federal Employees CU	Chattanooga	TN	**B-**	B-	B	45.5	-2.52	0.0	24.3	22.6	0.0	**10.0**	17.8
Chattanooga First Federal Credit Union	Chattanooga	TN	**C+**	C+	C-	22.2	3.38	0.0	21.2	31.3	9.0	**10.0**	22.5
Chaves County School Employees CU	Roswell	NM	**B**	B	B	24.6	4.47	0.0	30.1	0.0	11.1	**10.0**	17.6
Cheektowaga Community FCU	Cheektowaga	NY	**C-**	C-	C-	11.9	1.42	0.0	22.8	16.9	5.4	**10.0**	13.4
Chelsea Employees Federal Credit Union	Chelsea	MA	**D+**	D+	D+	14.2	7.88	0.0	36.0	0.0	0.0	**6.8**	8.8
Chem Family Credit Union	Anniston	AL	**C+**	C+	C+	6.6	4.08	0.0	3.5	4.1	43.2	**10.0**	17.0
Chemcel Federal Credit Union	Bishop	TX	**B-**	B-	B	110.9	1.63	0.0	41.6	5.0	10.6	**9.5**	10.6
Chemco Credit Union	McIntosh	AL	**C-**	C-	D+	5.0	-10.92	0.0	34.2	1.0	0.0	**10.0**	14.6
Chemco Federal Credit Union	Louisville	KY	**E+**	E+	D-	20.0	-2.64	0.0	33.6	10.4	0.0	**6.0**	8.0
Chen-Del-O Federal Credit Union	Franklin	NY	**D+**	D+	D	26.2	1.07	0.0	20.3	0.0	58.2	**7.5**	9.4
Cheney Federal Credit Union	Cheney	WA	**B-**	B-	B-	94.5	6.59	0.0	16.8	19.4	7.3	**9.5**	10.7
Cherokee County Federal Credit Union	Rusk	TX	**B+**	B+	B+	31.6	3.66	0.0	60.4	1.0	0.0	**10.0**	22.7
Cherokee County Teachers FCU	Rusk	TX	**C+**	C+	C+	13.5	0.04	0.0	44.8	0.0	6.0	**10.0**	16.7
▲ Cherokee Strip Credit Union	Ponca City	OK	**D+**	D	D	74.6	-1.94	0.0	42.3	7.1	27.5	**4.8**	6.8
Cheshire County Federal Credit Union	Keene	NH	**C**	C	D+	17.8	5.35	0.0	28.9	4.3	0.0	**8.1**	9.7
Chessie Federal Credit Union	Cumberland	MD	**C-**	C-	C	264.6	2.84	1.4	29.8	30.9	2.7	**6.1**	8.1
▼ Chesterfield Federal Credit Union	North Chesterfield	VA	**D+**	C-	C-	91.6	8.97	0.0	48.3	5.2	20.2	**4.9**	6.9
Cheswick Atomic Division FCU	Cheswick	PA	**D+**	D+	D+	6.3	1.05	0.0	20.9	0.0	0.0	**10.0**	22.9
Chevron Federal Credit Union	Oakland	CA	**A-**	A-	A-	3172.5	8.30	1.5	6.5	68.3	8.2	**9.4**	10.6
Cheyenne-Laramie County Employees FCU	Cheyenne	WY	**D+**	D+	C-	23.2	7.96	0.0	21.2	1.1	0.0	**8.9**	10.2
▼ CHHE Federal Credit Union	Huntington	WV	**C-**	C	C	20.6	15.75	0.0	27.5	0.0	0.0	**7.2**	9.1
Chicago Area Office Federal Credit Union	Chicago	IL	**C+**	C+	C+	10.5	-2.00	0.0	25.7	0.0	0.0	**10.0**	19.4
▲ Chicago Avenue Garage FCU	Chicago	IL	**D+**	D	D+	6.1	-9.41	0.0	22.3	0.0	0.0	**10.0**	39.2
Chicago Central & Commerce Credit Union	Waterloo	IA	**C**	C	C	6.9	-2.53	0.0	22.1	0.0	0.0	**10.0**	21.1
Chicago Faucet Federal Credit Union	Des Plaines	IL	**C-**	C-	C-	<1	3.96	0.0	75.4	0.0	0.0	**10.0**	46.0
Chicago Fire Officers' Association CU	Chicago	IL	**C+**	C+	C+	9.9	2.47	0.0	40.9	0.0	0.0	**10.0**	14.9
Chicago Firefighter's Credit Union	Chicago	IL	**B**	B	B	54.9	2.11	0.0	42.4	0.0	0.0	**10.0**	11.3
Chicago Fireman's Association CU	Chicago	IL	**C+**	C+	C+	18.5	4.76	0.0	51.5	0.0	0.0	**10.0**	13.5
Chicago Municipal Employees Credit Union	Chicago	IL	**D+**	D+	D+	39.6	2.60	0.0	20.2	21.1	0.0	**10.0**	12.8
Chicago Patrolmen's Federal Credit Union	Chicago	IL	**C+**	C+	C	391.2	2.85	2.5	31.8	19.7	24.4	**6.7**	8.8
Chicago Post Office Employees CU	Chicago	IL	**B-**	B-	B-	18.7	2.43	0.0	52.3	0.0	0.0	**10.0**	25.7
Chief Financial Federal Credit Union	Rochester Hills	MI	**A-**	A-	A-	156.2	1.68	5.0	35.2	11.2	0.0	**10.0**	12.5
Children's Medical Center FCU	Cincinnati	OH	**B+**	B+	B+	36.8	2.88	0.0	44.4	19.3	0.0	**10.0**	14.1
Chiphone Federal Credit Union	Elkhart	IN	**C-**	C-	C-	89.7	1.76	0.0	18.4	18.1	26.9	**10.0**	13.8
Chippewa County Credit Union	Sault Sainte Marie	MI	**C-**	C-	C	30.5	5.13	0.5	25.5	23.6	25.8	**7.7**	9.5
Chiropractic Federal Credit Union	Farmington	MI	**C+**	C+	C+	27.4	4.08	5.7	29.1	7.5	0.0	**10.0**	14.4
▼ Chivaho Federal Credit Union	Chillicothe	OH	**C-**	C	C+	26.7	5.83	0.0	19.7	15.6	0.0	**10.0**	16.3
▲ Chocolate Bayou Community FCU	Alvin	TX	**C+**	C	C	111.9	2.43	0.0	31.5	10.4	17.2	**6.6**	8.6
Choctaw Federal Credit Union	Choctaw	MS	**C-**	C-	C-	2.3	-1.69	0.0	73.3	0.0	0.0	**10.0**	26.6
Choice One Community FCU	Plains Township	PA	**C**	C	C	96.7	4.32	2.7	39.6	27.0	0.0	**6.3**	8.3
Choptank Electric Coop Employees FCU	Denton	MD	**B-**	B-	B-	2.9	0.10	0.0	24.2	0.0	15.5	**10.0**	20.1
▼ Christ the King Parish FCU	Kansas City	KS	**D+**	C-	D+	1.7	-0.65	0.0	40.7	0.0	0.0	**10.0**	12.1
Christian Community Credit Union	San Dimas	CA	**B+**	B+	A-	643.9	1.22	43.3	6.0	70.8	0.0	**10.0**	12.0
Christian Financial Credit Union	Roseville	MI	**A-**	A-	A-	375.6	6.58	12.7	28.1	32.8	14.9	**8.6**	10.1
Christiansted Federal Credit Union	Christiansted	VI	**B**	B	B	21.5	0.41	0.0	28.3	0.0	0.0	**10.0**	20.4
Christo Rey Federal Credit Union	Ney	OH	**C-**	C-	D+	1.9	-2.02	0.0	22.9	0.0	0.0	**10.0**	12.4
Chrome Federal Credit Union	Washington	PA	**B+**	B+	A-	171.1	25.49	3.2	36.0	22.1	2.4	**10.0**	12.1
Chula Vista City Employees FCU	Chula Vista	CA	**D-**	D-	D-	2.9	1.38	0.0	54.7	0.0	0.0	**5.7**	7.7
Church of the Master FCU	New York	NY	**C**	C	C	<1	3.87	0.0	12.5	0.0	0.0	**10.0**	13.6
Churchill County Federal Credit Union	Fallon	NV	**B+**	B+	B+	47.1	1.47	0.0	35.2	0.0	12.1	**10.0**	17.7
Cincinnati Employees Credit Union	Harrison	OH	**B-**	B-	B-	28.0	4.31	0.0	25.5	2.4	48.1	**10.0**	11.4
Cincinnati HealthCare Associates FCU	Cincinnati	OH	**D-**	D-	D	21.1	5.26	0.0	29.3	0.0	0.0	**6.1**	8.1
Cincinnati Interagency FCU	Cincinnati	OH	**C+**	C+	C	28.9	3.47	0.0	38.0	0.3	0.0	**10.0**	12.0
Cincinnati Ohio Police FCU	Cincinnati	OH	**B-**	B-	C+	115.6	4.66	4.8	24.0	15.7	11.0	**10.0**	11.4

Asset Quality Index	Non-Performing Loans as a % of Total Loans	Non-Performing Loans as a % of Capital	Net Charge-Offs Avg Loans	Profitability Index	Net Income ($Mil)	Return on Assets	Return on Equity	Net Interest Spread	Overhead Efficiency Ratio	Liquidity Index	Liquidity Ratio	Hot Money Ratio	Stability Index
7.5	0.70	5.0	0.61	7.2	0.91	0.85	8.37	3.85	78.6	4.0	23.0	10.5	7.4
9.9	0.00	0.0	-0.33	0.5	-0.01	-0.38	-5.42	3.71	111.3	3.8	20.5	5.0	2.3
8.9	0.20	1.8	0.15	4.3	2.20	0.88	9.29	2.94	73.7	3.1	3.6	4.2	7.2
5.6	0.87	7.8	0.63	3.7	1.72	0.32	3.82	3.15	79.2	2.8	12.8	13.8	5.6
8.3	0.44	1.9	0.74	3.9	0.02	0.42	3.24	4.11	92.6	4.5	28.1	2.7	6.4
9.7	0.14	0.3	-0.02	2.3	0.16	0.44	2.89	1.52	70.8	4.4	31.2	8.0	8.1
7.8	1.30	5.4	-0.09	4.0	0.08	0.70	3.98	2.84	76.5	4.9	54.8	4.3	6.9
8.7	0.42	1.3	0.32	3.5	0.02	0.40	1.76	3.21	86.1	3.1	34.5	18.9	6.9
10.0	0.00	0.0	0.00	3.0	0.01	0.23	1.30	2.30	92.1	5.7	27.5	0.0	7.8
4.6	3.44	18.1	-0.14	3.5	0.01	0.33	2.53	4.33	69.6	4.5	23.9	0.0	5.6
7.5	0.78	4.3	0.17	1.4	0.00	0.00	0.00	3.16	97.7	4.4	14.2	0.0	4.1
10.0	0.00	0.0	0.00	3.5	0.01	0.63	4.45	2.11	66.7	5.8	27.1	0.0	7.2
7.5	0.96	5.2	0.89	3.7	0.13	0.47	4.40	3.00	78.5	4.5	24.8	6.0	6.3
9.2	0.00	0.0	1.14	1.6	0.00	0.32	2.17	4.05	87.9	7.1	67.1	0.0	5.3
5.7	1.81	12.5	0.00	1.2	0.00	0.04	0.50	3.58	98.5	5.5	36.4	2.0	2.3
7.3	1.52	5.5	-0.29	1.3	0.00	-0.02	-0.16	2.56	88.1	4.9	25.4	0.1	3.7
8.4	0.59	2.3	0.03	3.3	0.10	0.41	3.87	1.95	81.2	4.4	24.8	4.4	5.7
7.2	0.77	3.2	0.96	4.7	0.06	0.79	3.48	4.83	69.2	5.2	49.3	5.6	6.0
7.0	0.94	5.3	1.60	3.7	0.04	1.18	7.18	4.11	68.3	5.2	22.8	0.0	5.8
3.4	2.16	24.4	5.70	5.0	0.16	0.89	14.25	4.48	68.4	5.1	24.1	1.8	1.8
6.1	2.31	9.4	-0.26	2.8	0.00	0.02	0.23	3.50	92.5	6.0	54.5	0.0	5.3
6.8	0.71	7.5	0.31	2.1	0.11	0.17	2.19	3.28	89.7	4.1	22.6	4.0	4.2
4.9	0.91	7.6	0.49	2.2	0.00	0.02	0.25	3.85	91.0	4.6	17.1	1.4	2.6
10.0	0.00	0.0	0.00	0.8	0.00	0.00	0.00	2.00	103.9	5.9	46.6	0.0	5.9
9.8	0.18	1.7	0.04	7.1	7.60	0.98	9.04	2.70	62.3	3.3	19.3	12.7	9.2
8.6	0.57	1.4	0.83	1.3	0.00	-0.07	-0.67	3.63	101.2	7.6	66.3	0.5	4.8
7.5	1.16	4.2	1.52	4.2	0.03	0.55	5.80	4.12	77.1	6.0	34.9	1.4	3.6
9.0	2.46	3.6	1.91	4.0	0.02	0.66	3.34	5.06	86.9	5.6	32.3	0.6	6.3
7.3	10.25	5.5	3.85	1.5	0.00	0.13	0.33	5.50	92.9	5.3	27.8	0.0	4.7
9.2	2.62	4.0	0.00	3.9	0.01	0.60	2.78	4.42	85.5	6.2	52.4	0.0	7.3
8.4	0.00	0.0	0.00	1.8	0.00	0.00	0.00	3.65	100.0	6.0	56.4	0.0	6.3
9.7	0.50	1.4	0.37	2.3	0.00	0.00	0.00	4.16	99.0	4.8	27.1	0.0	6.5
9.8	0.00	0.0	0.07	4.5	0.06	0.44	3.89	4.09	75.1	5.9	33.1	0.1	5.6
7.0	1.06	4.2	0.23	5.8	0.05	1.02	7.59	4.10	73.3	5.0	30.9	0.0	5.7
7.8	1.05	4.7	2.12	1.7	0.01	0.12	0.95	5.22	84.3	4.7	19.7	2.8	5.5
6.4	0.88	9.4	1.16	3.7	0.33	0.34	3.89	3.71	82.7	4.2	19.2	5.6	5.0
8.6	0.34	0.6	0.90	5.4	0.18	3.86	15.17	7.48	86.0	5.7	55.8	5.8	6.6
7.7	0.63	4.1	0.74	6.1	0.32	0.83	6.57	4.57	77.3	1.6	10.2	28.7	8.3
9.7	0.26	1.2	0.00	5.2	0.07	0.75	5.34	2.25	71.9	4.7	22.9	0.0	7.6
8.6	0.98	3.1	1.36	1.8	0.01	0.02	0.16	3.25	87.4	4.8	20.3	1.1	6.2
3.4	2.81	25.3	0.52	0.7	-0.02	-0.32	-3.29	3.88	98.6	4.4	20.5	1.5	3.7
8.4	0.20	3.3	-0.02	3.3	0.02	0.34	2.34	3.58	88.5	3.8	12.2	2.6	6.7
8.3	1.26	3.3	0.47	0.5	-0.02	-0.36	-2.29	2.83	108.8	4.9	23.1	0.0	5.8
7.6	0.67	4.7	0.78	4.1	0.27	0.99	11.99	3.26	75.5	4.6	21.7	2.6	5.0
4.8	2.65	7.1	2.90	10.0	0.10	18.21	68.94	9.73	33.5	5.0	29.3	0.0	6.9
4.2	2.00	19.0	0.11	3.3	0.10	0.43	5.17	3.49	90.2	3.8	14.1	0.9	3.8
10.0	1.00	1.2	0.00	8.4	0.01	1.10	5.51	2.45	52.9	4.8	14.2	0.0	5.7
7.1	1.49	5.8	0.00	0.6	0.00	-0.48	-3.94	2.60	137.5	6.4	43.7	0.0	5.8
7.0	0.43	5.1	0.27	4.9	1.35	0.84	7.03	3.61	86.4	3.3	18.4	12.4	8.6
6.5	1.26	8.1	0.71	6.6	0.70	0.76	7.49	3.98	80.9	4.3	20.1	4.6	7.5
10.0	1.21	1.9	0.12	4.5	0.03	0.60	2.93	3.72	80.7	5.9	50.1	9.1	6.8
7.8	3.08	5.9	0.00	1.5	0.00	-0.22	-1.74	1.52	116.7	5.7	29.9	0.0	6.7
7.8	0.58	3.7	0.50	3.0	0.03	0.07	0.57	4.18	94.6	2.7	14.8	15.9	7.2
8.4	0.06	0.5	0.48	0.0	-0.01	-1.40	-17.78	4.43	122.2	4.8	22.6	0.0	3.0
10.0	0.00	0.0	0.00	2.3	0.00	0.00	0.00	0.52	100.0	6.7	93.9	0.0	7.4
9.7	0.65	1.9	0.04	8.0	0.19	1.62	9.25	2.59	36.7	4.6	26.6	0.0	7.9
8.1	1.12	4.6	0.00	3.2	0.02	0.25	2.14	2.08	88.8	3.6	24.7	10.8	5.9
7.0	1.03	4.1	3.36	0.6	-0.06	-1.07	-12.74	4.20	91.2	6.4	52.9	0.6	2.5
9.7	0.18	0.7	-0.09	3.2	0.01	0.13	1.04	3.42	81.8	5.3	43.4	0.5	6.0
9.9	0.08	0.4	-0.05	3.3	0.11	0.37	3.25	2.74	89.3	3.9	32.0	12.7	7.2

Name	City	State	Rating	2016 Rating	2015 Rating	Total Assets ($Mil)	One Year Asset Growth	Asset Mix (As a % of Total Assets): Commercial Loans	Consumer Loans	Mortgage Loans	Securities	Capitalization Index	Net Worth Ratio
Cinco Family Financial Center CU	Cincinnati	OH	D+	D+	D+	117.5	0.41	6.2	16.2	14.6	1.2	5.4	7.5
Cinfed Federal Credit Union	Cincinnati	OH	A-	A-	B+	404.1	7.62	15.7	22.6	46.3	6.7	9.5	10.7
Cit-Co Federal Credit Union	Sheridan	WY	D+	D+	C-	12.9	1.19	1.3	77.4	0.0	0.0	7.4	9.3
Citadel Federal Credit Union	Exton	PA	B+	B+	B+	2836.1	10.57	4.1	38.1	44.7	2.3	7.7	9.4
Cities Credit Union	Vadnais Heights	MN	C-	C-	C-	30.4	10.48	0.1	30.6	2.8	4.1	6.0	8.0
▲ Citizens Choice Federal Credit Union	Natchez	MS	D+	D	D	1.1	3.36	0.0	49.5	0.0	0.0	10.0	31.9
Citizens Community Credit Union	Fort Dodge	IA	A	A	A	196.5	2.02	0.1	67.3	2.7	0.0	10.0	14.2
▼ Citizens Community Credit Union	Devils Lake	ND	C-	C	B+	201.3	8.31	51.1	8.0	40.0	0.0	8.4	9.9
▼ Citizens Equity First Credit Union	Peoria	IL	B+	A-	B+	5832.0	5.33	7.7	22.4	39.8	18.2	9.0	10.4
▼ Citizens Federal Credit Union	Big Spring	TX	C-	C	C+	131.7	4.53	0.1	16.9	0.0	62.6	7.8	10.3
City & County Credit Union	Saint Paul	MN	B+	B+	B+	508.9	8.13	6.9	29.8	17.7	25.3	8.8	10.4
City & County Employees Credit Union	Fargo	ND	C	C	C-	14.0	7.07	0.0	32.5	0.0	0.0	7.0	9.0
City & Police Federal Credit Union	Jacksonville	FL	C+	C+	C	71.3	6.93	1.3	29.6	10.8	36.2	6.5	9.1
▼ City and County Employees FCU	Albert Lea	MN	C+	B-	B-	18.6	12.51	0.0	22.7	0.0	0.0	10.0	11.7
▲ City Center Credit Union	Provo	UT	C	C-	D+	11.6	32.43	2.3	40.3	37.8	0.0	8.4	9.9
City Co Federal Credit Union	Pittsburgh	PA	C-	C-	D+	21.4	2.13	0.0	35.5	4.7	0.0	9.7	10.8
City Credit Union	Tuscaloosa	AL	C+	C+	C+	17.6	-2.30	0.0	34.7	7.5	0.0	10.0	21.8
City Credit Union	Independence	MO	C	C	C+	36.3	5.80	0.3	38.2	1.3	0.0	7.1	9.1
▼ City Credit Union	Dallas	TX	B+	A-	A-	384.2	7.47	0.0	45.5	9.8	6.7	9.9	10.9
City Employees Credit Union	Knoxville	TN	A-	A-	A-	77.8	3.16	3.2	20.0	9.4	0.0	10.0	19.4
City Federal Credit Union	Amarillo	TX	C+	C+	C-	33.2	5.87	4.7	37.2	7.7	0.0	7.9	9.6
City of Birmingham General Employees CU	Birmingham	AL	C+	C+	C+	8.8	8.07	0.0	62.7	5.2	0.0	10.0	13.6
City of Boston Credit Union	Boston	MA	B	B	B	381.7	10.16	0.0	22.5	49.5	10.1	10.0	12.3
▼ City of Clarksburg Federal Credit Union	Clarksburg	WV	D	D+	C	10.5	4.63	0.0	73.8	0.0	0.0	10.0	13.8
City of Deer Park Federal Credit Union	Deer Park	TX	C-	C-	C-	5.7	1.32	0.0	39.1	0.8	0.0	10.0	17.0
City of Fairbanks Federal Credit Union	Fairbanks	AK	D	D	D+	2.0	-12.29	0.0	21.5	0.0	0.0	10.0	17.0
City of Fairmont Federal Credit Union	Fairmont	WV	D	D	D	1.2	-1.05	0.0	61.2	0.0	0.0	9.1	10.4
▼ City of Firsts Community FCU	Kokomo	IN	D+	C-	C	31.7	13.70	0.0	18.9	1.8	0.0	5.8	7.8
City of Mckeesport Employees FCU	McKeesport	PA	D	D	D+	1.2	2.01	0.0	16.4	0.0	0.0	10.0	22.6
City of Schenectady Employees FCU	Schenectady	NY	E+	E+	E+	4.2	-3.97	0.0	42.0	0.0	49.8	6.1	8.1
▲ City of Ukiah Employees Credit Union	Ukiah	CA	D	D-	D	3.4	-8.04	0.0	33.9	0.0	0.0	10.0	11.0
City Public Service/IBEW FCU	San Antonio	TX	C+	C+	C+	41.7	2.61	0.0	23.6	8.1	31.5	10.0	11.8
City Trust Federal Credit Union	Fort Wayne	IN	C-	C-	D+	9.6	2.97	0.5	20.5	5.4	0.0	10.0	12.0
City-County Employees Credit Union	Clearwater	FL	C+	C+	C+	21.3	13.10	0.0	60.8	0.0	0.0	10.0	12.8
▲ Citymark Federal Credit Union	Wilkes-Barre	PA	B-	C+	C	39.3	4.24	0.2	29.4	40.0	9.7	10.0	13.7
Civil Service Employees Association CU	Cleveland	OH	C-	C-	D+	6.3	-1.93	0.0	66.0	1.9	0.0	10.0	18.4
Clackamas Community Federal Credit Union	Milwaukie	OR	A-	A-	B+	347.5	17.39	5.2	39.7	19.8	5.7	7.5	9.3
▼ Clairton Works Federal Credit Union	Elizabeth	PA	D+	C-	C-	13.5	3.94	0.0	20.1	0.0	0.0	9.8	10.8
Clarence Community & Schools FCU	Clarence	NY	D+	D+	D+	21.9	8.52	0.0	24.0	16.5	25.1	6.5	8.5
Clarion Federal Credit Union	Clarion	PA	A-	A-	B+	81.6	9.64	8.8	30.8	33.4	15.4	10.0	11.7
Clarity Credit Union	Nampa	ID	D+	D+	D+	71.3	8.75	0.0	49.8	0.6	0.0	4.9	6.9
Clark County Credit Union	Las Vegas	NV	A	A	A-	684.4	13.82	10.3	30.0	24.3	10.9	10.0	11.7
Clarke Educators Federal Credit Union	Grove Hill	AL	C+	C+	C+	3.6	-0.58	0.0	55.0	0.0	0.0	10.0	24.1
▼ Clarksburg Area Postal Employees FCU	Clarksburg	WV	D+	C-	C	14.3	5.03	0.4	27.9	39.6	0.1	8.3	9.9
Class Act Federal Credit Union	Louisville	KY	C	C	C+	201.0	5.39	0.0	33.7	12.9	0.3	8.0	9.6
Classic Federal Credit Union	Amelia	OH	D+	D+	C+	41.9	3.50	0.7	35.1	9.1	0.0	0.9	4.1
Clearchoice Federal Credit Union	Wyomissing	PA	E+	E+	E+	16.7	-1.92	0.0	40.1	20.7	0.6	4.1	6.1
Clearpath Federal Credit Union	Glendale	CA	C+	C+	B-	111.4	11.53	26.1	37.4	15.6	11.3	9.0	10.4
Clearview Federal Credit Union	Moon Township	PA	B-	B-	B-	1141.8	9.46	4.6	38.3	13.4	14.6	7.5	9.7
▼ Cleveland Church of Christ FCU	Cleveland	OH	D	D+	D+	<1	15.86	0.8	22.1	0.0	0.0	10.0	19.4
Cleveland Heights Teachers Credit Union, Inc.	Cleveland	OH	C	C	C	7.6	1.22	0.0	22.0	5.9	45.4	10.0	19.6
Cleveland Police Credit Union, Inc.	Cleveland	OH	D+	D+	C-	34.8	-0.71	0.4	18.1	21.2	18.9	6.9	8.9
Cleveland Selfreliance FCU	Parma	OH	C+	C+	C+	89.5	-0.70	6.4	0.7	27.2	12.2	10.0	16.7
Cleveland-Bradley County Teachers FCU	Cleveland	TN	B	B	B	48.8	4.85	0.0	13.3	20.1	36.8	10.0	12.2
Clifford-Jacobs Employees Credit Union	Champaign	IL	C+	C+	C	1.8	-5.70	0.0	29.0	0.0	0.0	10.0	26.3
Clifton NJ Postal Employees FCU	Clifton	NJ	C	C	C-	2.9	-5.34	0.0	22.1	0.0	74.9	10.0	38.5
Clifty Creek Employees FCU	Madison	IN	C+	C+	C+	12.1	-2.23	0.0	59.8	0.0	0.0	10.0	19.1
Clinchfield Federal Credit Union	Erwin	TN	B+	B+	B+	82.0	-0.33	0.5	21.7	35.7	14.0	10.0	12.6
▼ Cloverbelt Credit Union	Wausau	WI	B+	A-	B+	226.1	9.17	5.9	21.2	41.2	16.8	10.0	12.6
CM Members Federal Credit Union	Columbus	MS	C-	C-	D+	11.5	-2.88	0.0	33.5	0.0	0.0	10.0	16.4

Asset Quality Index	Non-Performing Loans as a % of Total Loans	Non-Performing Loans as a % of Capital	Net Charge-Offs Avg Loans	Profitability Index	Net Income ($Mil)	Return on Assets	Return on Equity	Net Interest Spread	Overhead Efficiency Ratio	Liquidity Index	Liquidity Ratio	Hot Money Ratio	Stability Index
7.3	0.61	4.7	0.24	**1.8**	0.04	0.12	1.65	3.36	95.7	**5.5**	32.3	0.0	**3.8**
6.3	1.07	8.3	0.89	**4.7**	0.51	0.52	4.77	3.82	70.3	**4.0**	20.5	5.7	**8.0**
4.3	1.03	9.2	0.07	**4.2**	0.01	0.34	3.72	3.81	89.9	**3.1**	9.8	6.0	**3.0**
8.8	0.28	2.7	0.48	**6.4**	7.65	1.09	11.57	3.07	68.5	**1.4**	6.7	18.4	**7.1**
7.0	0.66	4.6	0.10	**2.6**	0.00	0.03	0.33	3.53	98.4	**4.3**	9.9	0.8	**3.3**
5.6	5.49	9.0	0.00	**3.7**	0.01	2.31	7.04	13.40	85.2	**6.4**	47.9	0.0	**3.7**
7.1	0.65	3.2	1.19	**7.3**	0.45	0.92	6.46	5.05	77.6	**4.4**	23.0	3.9	**8.2**
0.0	6.79	47.5	0.57	**2.2**	-0.93	-1.87	-18.23	3.77	97.9	**2.4**	23.8	28.3	**8.3**
8.9	0.33	2.7	0.33	**4.8**	15.45	1.08	11.45	3.03	61.4	**3.9**	22.4	10.1	**7.7**
8.1	1.32	3.4	5.01	**1.8**	-0.05	-0.16	-1.62	2.88	83.9	**5.3**	21.4	8.2	**5.1**
7.3	1.01	5.8	0.50	**2.5**	-0.07	-0.06	-0.55	3.18	94.7	**4.7**	22.8	1.8	**5.8**
8.6	0.48	2.4	0.00	**3.4**	0.01	0.29	3.19	3.22	85.7	**6.0**	41.3	0.0	**4.8**
6.5	0.94	5.1	0.83	**3.6**	0.07	0.41	4.88	3.50	86.6	**4.2**	9.4	2.9	**3.5**
10.0	0.41	1.0	-0.08	**2.3**	0.00	-0.04	-0.37	2.20	101.5	**5.5**	26.5	0.0	**6.3**
5.6	0.83	9.0	0.57	**10.0**	0.07	2.62	26.82	7.03	61.3	**1.1**	13.1	27.1	**5.0**
6.4	1.70	7.6	0.38	**3.3**	0.04	0.75	7.01	4.03	82.1	**5.0**	33.3	0.0	**4.5**
9.7	0.00	0.0	0.10	**2.9**	0.02	0.46	2.09	3.59	87.8	**5.4**	43.4	1.5	**6.2**
6.9	0.78	4.3	0.66	**3.1**	0.02	0.27	2.93	4.04	84.2	**4.8**	31.1	4.3	**3.3**
6.6	0.59	4.4	1.18	**4.9**	0.48	0.51	4.81	4.21	73.2	**4.2**	27.3	7.7	**7.6**
10.0	0.03	0.1	0.21	**6.5**	0.23	1.18	6.06	2.86	67.4	**5.0**	43.4	2.8	**7.8**
5.8	1.37	9.3	0.24	**4.3**	0.04	0.49	5.05	4.31	79.0	**4.0**	30.1	11.2	**4.9**
5.5	1.61	7.6	1.18	**3.7**	-0.02	-0.69	-5.03	6.29	96.0	**4.5**	17.9	0.0	**7.5**
7.2	1.01	6.5	0.64	**3.5**	0.14	0.15	1.17	4.12	81.5	**2.6**	18.5	13.5	**7.2**
0.0	10.71	55.4	1.12	**7.5**	0.02	0.89	6.38	3.91	64.6	**4.5**	20.6	0.0	**7.3**
9.7	0.31	0.8	0.32	**1.3**	0.00	-0.14	-0.82	4.28	103.9	**6.1**	46.0	0.0	**6.2**
5.8	5.28	14.0	1.71	**0.0**	-0.01	-1.54	-9.20	4.46	147.1	**6.4**	50.4	0.0	**5.4**
2.8	3.20	16.3	0.00	**2.7**	0.00	0.00	0.00	5.15	66.7	**4.2**	27.2	0.0	**2.3**
8.2	0.73	2.5	1.54	**1.3**	-0.04	-0.55	-6.54	2.84	95.5	**6.6**	37.6	0.0	**2.6**
10.0	2.59	1.8	0.00	**0.2**	0.00	-0.70	-3.02	6.40	133.3	**8.3**	95.6	0.0	**5.6**
5.3	2.37	15.0	0.00	**0.0**	-0.01	-0.97	-11.66	3.67	117.1	**4.7**	7.1	0.0	**2.6**
9.6	0.07	0.2	0.00	**0.0**	-0.01	-0.90	-8.36	2.98	132.0	**4.9**	29.5	0.0	**5.6**
10.0	0.41	1.3	0.27	**2.8**	0.05	0.43	3.87	3.27	87.9	**4.7**	18.8	3.3	**5.3**
10.0	0.47	1.1	0.00	**1.4**	0.00	0.04	0.35	2.55	98.5	**6.5**	82.6	0.0	**6.5**
8.4	0.00	0.0	0.46	**4.1**	0.02	0.36	2.79	4.45	85.6	**4.2**	17.8	1.7	**6.8**
8.6	0.43	4.2	-0.01	**7.9**	0.17	1.73	12.66	3.94	58.2	**3.7**	20.4	2.3	**5.8**
6.7	1.06	3.9	1.52	**4.7**	0.01	0.83	4.48	9.83	82.6	**5.1**	35.8	2.2	**3.7**
8.2	0.36	3.5	0.34	**5.9**	0.64	0.77	7.99	4.55	77.5	**4.7**	20.1	1.6	**6.2**
9.4	0.60	1.5	1.05	**0.8**	-0.01	-0.31	-2.86	2.69	103.5	**6.0**	36.7	0.0	**4.3**
6.6	1.16	7.9	-0.03	**2.0**	0.01	0.09	1.07	3.37	98.0	**4.4**	20.4	2.4	**4.1**
9.0	0.35	2.2	0.03	**5.0**	0.17	0.83	7.01	2.93	70.9	**3.7**	14.0	5.7	**7.0**
4.5	1.22	10.0	1.85	**3.9**	0.18	1.03	14.96	5.33	77.8	**4.4**	19.5	1.3	**2.2**
7.7	0.23	3.6	0.61	**9.6**	2.98	1.79	15.23	4.73	60.5	**5.7**	34.2	3.2	**8.7**
8.1	0.34	0.8	2.77	**5.1**	0.01	0.78	3.22	7.98	74.5	**6.5**	52.4	0.0	**4.3**
3.7	2.69	20.4	0.00	**1.3**	-0.03	-0.89	-8.98	2.55	131.1	**3.5**	5.7	0.0	**4.9**
8.4	0.60	3.6	0.80	**3.1**	0.04	0.07	0.80	4.85	83.8	**5.6**	34.8	3.4	**5.3**
7.6	0.35	2.9	0.20	**4.9**	0.19	1.86	47.19	5.78	71.0	**4.8**	31.7	7.9	**1.9**
6.3	0.79	7.4	1.23	**2.2**	-0.12	-2.92	-44.24	4.76	84.8	**4.3**	17.3	2.5	**0.3**
8.1	0.09	0.8	0.96	**3.6**	0.10	0.38	3.58	3.83	81.9	**3.7**	12.1	5.2	**6.6**
9.3	0.31	2.5	0.46	**4.3**	1.90	0.68	7.28	3.75	75.7	**3.5**	16.0	5.5	**6.4**
9.9	0.00	0.0	0.00	**0.0**	0.00	-1.73	-7.84	11.59	100.0	**8.2**	92.0	0.0	**4.8**
9.6	1.53	2.2	5.47	**2.6**	0.00	0.05	0.27	3.51	79.7	**5.9**	48.3	1.7	**5.9**
5.5	1.55	11.0	1.03	**2.1**	-0.02	-0.17	-1.92	3.62	90.5	**5.0**	26.7	2.7	**3.2**
7.8	2.92	6.0	0.37	**2.1**	0.05	0.20	1.21	3.21	83.4	**5.9**	66.9	20.9	**6.6**
9.7	0.50	2.1	-0.09	**3.5**	0.05	0.42	3.44	2.76	84.4	**5.0**	24.5	6.4	**6.3**
10.0	0.18	0.2	-4.94	**3.4**	0.00	0.00	0.00	4.91	100.0	**7.0**	87.2	0.0	**5.9**
10.0	0.74	0.5	-0.56	**2.5**	0.00	0.14	0.37	3.29	95.8	**4.9**	32.7	0.0	**7.8**
8.0	0.18	1.2	0.18	**4.6**	0.02	0.69	3.67	3.18	73.7	**3.3**	16.7	6.0	**7.6**
8.3	0.71	3.4	0.25	**3.9**	0.10	0.47	3.77	3.15	85.3	**3.3**	24.0	11.3	**6.5**
9.6	0.05	0.3	0.05	**4.8**	0.31	0.56	4.36	2.73	81.2	**2.5**	13.2	15.3	**8.8**
9.5	0.51	1.3	0.79	**0.8**	-0.01	-0.18	-1.05	3.42	94.5	**5.6**	52.4	1.1	**6.1**

	Name	City	State	Rating	2016 Rating	2015 Rating	Total Assets ($Mil)	One Year Asset Growth	Asset Mix (As a % of Total Assets) Comm-ercial Loans	Cons-umer Loans	Mort-gage Loans	Secur-ities	Capital-ization Index	Net Worth Ratio
	CMC-FCPI Employees Federal Credit Union	Scranton	PA	**D-**	D-	D-	7.4	2.69	0.0	52.8	0.0	22.0	**7.7**	9.5
	CME Federal Credit Union	Columbus	OH	**C**	C	B-	279.1	2.62	4.5	31.6	30.7	7.3	**5.2**	7.2
	CN/IC Employees Credit Union	Memphis	TN	**C-**	C-	C-	7.7	-0.23	0.0	37.8	0.1	0.0	**10.0**	19.0
▼	Co-Lib Credit Union	Saint Louis	MO	**D+**	C-	D+	1.0	-1.36	0.1	37.8	0.0	0.0	**10.0**	11.2
	CO-NE Federal Credit Union	Julesburg	CO	**C-**	C-	C-	4.5	13.61	0.0	31.3	20.2	0.0	**10.0**	13.0
▼	CO-OP Credit Union	Black River Falls	WI	**B+**	A-	A-	308.1	6.04	10.8	13.1	63.7	0.0	**10.0**	12.5
	Co-Op Credit Union of Montevideo	Montevideo	MN	**A**	A	A-	178.8	7.56	37.7	14.6	26.9	8.3	**10.0**	14.0
	Co-op Toledo Credit Union, Inc.	Maumee	OH	**D-**	D-	D	10.9	7.53	0.0	44.3	0.0	1.8	**5.5**	7.5
▲	Co-Operative Credit Union	Coffeyville	KS	**D+**	D	D	20.1	0.00	0.0	61.1	7.9	0.0	**10.0**	13.4
	Co-Operative Federal Credit Union	Woodridge	NY	**D+**	D+	D	6.3	-11.10	0.0	14.2	0.0	5.3	**10.0**	13.9
	Coast 2 Coast Financial Credit Union	Tampa	FL	**B-**	B-	B-	20.1	6.32	1.0	34.2	20.4	0.0	**10.0**	11.0
	Coast Central Credit Union	Eureka	CA	**A-**	A-	B+	1321.1	9.40	9.7	14.5	26.0	44.3	**9.3**	11.0
	Coast Guard Employees Credit Union	New Orleans	LA	**D**	D	C-	5.4	1.44	0.0	24.6	0.0	0.0	**10.0**	21.0
	Coast Line Credit Union	South Portland	ME	**A-**	A-	A-	55.9	11.13	0.0	17.5	35.3	0.0	**10.0**	15.9
▲	Coast-Tel Federal Credit Union	Salinas	CA	**D**	D-	E+	19.1	14.60	0.0	37.1	0.0	0.0	**5.0**	7.0
	Coast360 Federal Credit Union	Maite	GU	**B+**	B+	B	363.5	4.24	10.0	38.4	32.9	8.7	**10.0**	14.3
	Coastal Bend Post Office FCU	Victoria	TX	**B-**	B-	B-	16.4	-1.79	0.0	31.7	0.0	55.3	**10.0**	15.5
	Coastal Community And Teachers CU	Corpus Christi	TX	**C**	C	C-	287.9	0.45	0.1	48.7	11.0	11.9	**8.7**	10.3
	Coastal Community Federal Credit Union	Galveston	TX	**C+**	C+	C+	69.1	3.41	0.0	37.0	26.8	5.5	**6.9**	8.9
	Coastal Credit Union	Biloxi	MS	**C**	C	C-	9.6	8.26	0.0	61.5	2.2	0.0	**10.0**	18.5
	Coastal Federal Credit Union	Raleigh	NC	**B+**	B+	B+	2897.9	9.19	10.2	39.7	29.0	3.1	**8.7**	10.1
	Coastal Teachers Federal Credit Union	Port Lavaca	TX	**E+**	E+	E+	5.2	-0.78	0.0	46.2	0.0	0.0	**6.1**	8.1
	CoastHills Credit Union	Lompoc	CA	**B+**	B+	B+	1043.7	11.52	11.6	41.5	37.1	5.2	**6.8**	8.8
	Coastland Federal Credit Union	Metairie	LA	**C**	C	C	107.0	-4.75	0.0	16.5	31.6	1.9	**10.0**	12.4
	Coastline Federal Credit Union	Jacksonville	FL	**C**	C	C	133.4	6.06	0.6	36.5	14.8	8.9	**6.6**	8.7
	Cobblestone Country Federal Credit Union	Albion	NY	**E+**	E+	E+	10.4	6.65	0.0	36.6	0.0	0.0	**4.6**	6.6
	Coburn Credit Union	Beaumont	TX	**C**	C	C	7.7	-0.27	0.0	31.6	0.0	0.0	**10.0**	13.4
	Coca-Cola Federal Credit Union	Atlanta	GA	**C+**	C+	C+	208.5	5.39	0.0	26.0	28.4	24.9	**5.4**	7.9
	Cochise Credit Union	Willcox	AZ	**B**	B	B	33.1	5.56	0.0	49.2	0.5	0.0	**10.0**	14.4
	Cochran County Schools FCU	Morton	TX	**C**	C	C	6.1	14.27	0.0	45.3	0.0	0.0	**10.0**	12.4
	Coconino Federal Credit Union	Flagstaff	AZ	**C**	C	C+	73.3	8.74	0.0	43.3	0.0	31.9	**6.6**	8.6
	Code Credit Union	Dayton	OH	**B-**	B-	B-	120.9	3.21	9.2	41.0	10.0	0.0	**10.0**	11.7
	Coffee County Teachers FCU	Douglas	GA	**C+**	C+	C+	3.7	2.28	0.0	28.7	0.0	0.0	**10.0**	14.4
▲	Cogic Credit Union	Lafayette	LA	**D-**	E+	E+	<1	3.69	0.0	22.4	0.0	0.0	**7.4**	9.3
	Colfax Power Plant Employees FCU	Springdale	PA	**D+**	D+	D+	8.5	4.55	0.0	51.0	0.0	0.0	**9.9**	10.9
	Colfax School Employees Credit Union	Raton	NM	**D**	D	C-	<1	-0.67	0.0	79.1	0.0	0.0	**10.0**	16.5
	College & University Credit Union	Chicago	IL	**D-**	D-	D	1.1	-1.99	0.0	18.2	0.0	0.0	**8.6**	10.2
	Collegedale Credit Union	Collegedale	TN	**D+**	D+	C-	43.9	3.83	9.6	7.4	25.8	0.0	**6.2**	8.2
	Collins Community Credit Union	Cedar Rapids	IA	**B-**	B-	B	1090.7	16.48	13.3	24.7	40.7	6.2	**6.6**	8.6
	Colorado Credit Union	Littleton	CO	**A-**	A-	B+	171.3	13.18	7.3	23.4	15.8	1.0	**7.7**	9.5
	Coloramo Federal Credit Union	Grand Junction	CO	**B+**	B+	B+	94.4	7.54	0.0	26.5	6.8	8.9	**10.0**	12.1
	Colquitt County Teachers FCU	Moultrie	GA	**C**	C	C+	7.0	3.97	0.0	61.4	0.0	0.0	**10.0**	19.8
▲	Colton Federal Credit Union	Colton	CA	**D+**	D	D	6.5	5.85	0.0	20.8	0.0	0.0	**10.0**	13.0
	Columbia Credit Union	Columbia	MO	**D-**	D-	D-	21.6	-1.25	2.1	38.5	6.9	0.0	**5.1**	7.1
▼	Columbia Credit Union	Vancouver	WA	**A-**	A	A	1256.1	7.49	13.2	36.4	30.9	9.7	**10.0**	11.5
	Columbia Greene Federal Credit Union	Hudson	NY	**D+**	D+	C-	31.0	8.21	0.0	29.1	18.9	12.4	**5.0**	7.0
	Columbia Post Office Credit Union	Columbia	SC	**B-**	B-	B	34.2	0.31	0.0	19.4	0.0	2.9	**10.0**	12.9
	Columbiana County School Employees CU	Lisbon	OH	**C+**	C+	C+	9.3	-2.99	0.0	24.7	0.0	35.9	**10.0**	15.9
	Columbine Federal Credit Union	Centennial	CO	**C**	C	C	59.4	7.05	3.5	25.7	16.5	8.5	**6.6**	8.8
	Columbus Club Federal Credit Union	San Fernando	CA	**D+**	D+	D+	7.0	0.52	0.0	3.8	0.0	0.0	**10.0**	14.0
▼	Columbus Metro Federal Credit Union	Columbus	OH	**C**	C+	B-	241.7	2.54	0.3	64.3	9.2	0.0	**8.5**	10.0
	Columbus United Federal Credit Union	Columbus	NE	**C+**	C+	C	62.7	4.96	7.1	49.8	17.8	8.8	**8.8**	10.2
	Comanche County Federal Credit Union	Lawton	OK	**B-**	B-	B-	24.8	4.67	0.0	26.4	4.5	2.8	**10.0**	14.7
	Combined Employees Credit Union	Warner Robins	GA	**C-**	C-	C-	11.6	-2.47	0.2	60.8	0.0	0.0	**10.0**	12.1
	Combined Federal Credit Union	Hot Springs	AR	**D**	D	D	6.7	-3.45	0.0	45.0	0.0	0.0	**10.0**	14.0
	Commfirst Federal Credit Union	Jackson	MS	**B-**	B-	C+	10.8	0.91	0.0	52.1	0.2	0.4	**10.0**	14.4
▼	Commodore Perry Federal Credit Union	Oak Harbor	OH	**D**	D+	D+	40.1	9.69	6.3	37.8	20.4	1.5	**6.1**	8.1
▲	Common Cents Federal Credit Union	Beaumont	TX	**C+**	C	C+	26.8	6.43	0.0	37.1	0.0	0.0	**10.0**	14.3
	Commonwealth Central Credit Union	San Jose	CA	**B+**	B+	B+	494.2	5.31	10.9	24.5	28.2	4.5	**7.2**	9.2
	CommonWealth Credit Union	Bourbonnais	IL	**C**	C	C	82.7	6.37	1.2	50.3	23.1	0.0	**7.8**	9.6

Asset Quality Index	Non-Performing Loans as a % of Total Loans	Non-Performing Loans as a % of Capital	Net Charge-Offs Avg Loans	Profitability Index	Net Income ($Mil)	Return on Assets	Return on Equity	Net Interest Spread	Overhead Efficiency Ratio	Liquidity Index	Liquidity Ratio	Hot Money Ratio	Stability Index
1.5	4.99	28.7	1.07	**3.2**	0.00	0.22	2.30	6.26	90.2	**5.3**	26.3	0.0	**4.0**
7.0	0.68	5.9	0.73	**2.9**	0.43	0.62	8.37	4.14	76.4	**3.6**	19.1	10.7	**3.3**
9.3	1.15	2.5	-0.11	**2.6**	0.01	0.26	1.36	4.62	87.0	**5.6**	47.2	0.0	**5.0**
3.7	9.07	26.5	0.00	**1.6**	0.00	-0.78	-6.90	3.88	66.7	**7.0**	59.6	0.0	**5.2**
7.4	0.00	0.3	0.42	**4.5**	0.00	0.36	2.77	5.74	92.3	**4.2**	33.1	10.2	**4.3**
6.2	1.14	8.7	0.03	**4.7**	0.45	0.58	4.65	3.15	83.9	**2.5**	6.3	8.3	**8.3**
7.6	0.38	1.8	0.04	**9.5**	0.64	1.46	10.32	3.63	64.2	**4.3**	26.4	1.0	**9.7**
1.7	7.66	35.8	4.32	**0.4**	-0.05	-1.67	-21.58	4.06	93.0	**4.1**	21.3	6.1	**0.3**
5.0	2.39	12.7	1.47	**1.8**	0.03	0.52	3.88	5.59	90.7	**4.6**	26.8	1.9	**5.9**
6.4	4.55	8.4	0.00	**0.6**	0.00	-0.19	-1.36	1.91	110.7	**5.9**	40.9	0.0	**5.7**
9.6	0.08	0.4	0.00	**5.8**	0.02	0.49	4.37	3.72	89.7	**4.9**	34.4	5.6	**5.7**
9.8	0.24	1.1	0.15	**6.0**	3.28	1.01	9.68	2.45	64.2	**4.7**	26.1	10.0	**8.4**
10.0	0.37	0.4	0.31	**1.1**	0.00	0.22	1.06	2.88	94.3	**6.0**	32.8	0.0	**5.0**
10.0	0.36	1.3	0.00	**6.0**	0.12	0.88	5.54	2.68	70.5	**3.8**	23.8	5.0	**7.9**
8.9	0.02	0.2	0.10	**5.6**	0.03	0.54	7.51	3.39	91.9	**6.3**	41.0	0.7	**3.2**
7.6	0.67	3.9	0.47	**5.0**	0.57	0.63	4.52	4.68	80.4	**3.6**	8.8	4.1	**7.8**
7.9	1.58	3.4	0.35	**3.7**	0.01	0.31	2.05	2.90	50.4	**3.9**	17.9	15.5	**6.6**
4.3	1.63	12.0	2.41	**1.0**	-0.35	-0.48	-5.29	4.23	66.3	**4.2**	14.1	2.4	**5.4**
5.4	1.68	13.0	0.68	**4.8**	0.12	0.67	7.60	4.17	77.9	**2.8**	17.6	21.6	**4.2**
6.9	1.10	4.4	0.00	**7.1**	0.03	1.12	6.15	5.69	83.9	**3.2**	28.3	17.7	**5.0**
7.6	0.41	4.1	0.09	**5.1**	5.74	0.80	8.22	3.56	72.0	**3.9**	17.1	5.6	**7.5**
5.9	0.61	4.1	0.13	**2.7**	0.01	0.45	5.70	3.80	88.2	**5.2**	30.4	0.0	**1.7**
6.6	0.72	6.8	0.33	**5.5**	1.55	0.61	6.83	3.42	76.8	**1.6**	9.8	22.5	**7.0**
10.0	0.07	0.3	0.05	**2.3**	0.06	0.21	1.69	3.46	91.4	**5.8**	33.4	4.7	**6.9**
9.3	0.09	2.2	0.12	**3.4**	0.15	0.46	5.15	2.89	87.4	**4.1**	19.5	8.4	**5.3**
6.0	0.73	6.9	1.16	**2.7**	0.00	0.12	1.75	4.40	90.0	**5.4**	29.7	0.0	**1.0**
7.2	1.83	6.1	1.72	**4.2**	0.01	0.31	2.35	2.22	46.3	**4.7**	36.0	0.0	**3.7**
8.2	0.54	4.1	0.19	**3.4**	0.22	0.45	5.90	3.33	83.9	**4.9**	15.8	0.2	**4.7**
8.1	0.42	2.0	0.12	**5.8**	0.06	0.76	5.16	3.71	82.4	**4.6**	30.2	3.0	**7.8**
2.7	4.87	20.4	-0.24	**8.9**	0.02	1.62	12.97	6.35	70.9	**5.5**	42.7	0.0	**6.5**
5.7	0.33	3.0	0.78	**2.8**	0.01	0.03	0.32	3.63	84.0	**4.6**	21.4	3.4	**4.2**
7.2	1.21	6.4	0.32	**2.9**	0.14	0.48	4.11	2.87	81.3	**3.6**	18.3	5.5	**7.3**
8.5	2.96	6.4	0.30	**6.2**	0.01	1.11	7.63	4.58	76.9	**5.8**	22.9	0.0	**5.0**
0.3	21.59	54.3	0.00	**4.6**	0.01	7.30	66.67	4.06	60.0	**7.3**	76.3	0.0	**5.4**
2.7	4.13	19.0	0.44	**2.6**	0.01	0.48	4.33	3.05	82.1	**5.9**	47.8	0.0	**2.3**
8.0	0.85	2.6	0.00	**0.1**	0.00	-1.36	-8.00	6.48	125.0	**5.2**	33.5	0.0	**6.3**
6.4	4.85	8.2	0.00	**0.3**	0.00	-0.36	-3.48	2.72	116.7	**6.0**	58.1	0.0	**3.1**
5.6	1.40	10.0	0.15	**1.4**	0.00	0.03	0.33	3.32	99.5	**4.8**	39.0	12.8	**3.2**
8.3	0.26	2.9	0.27	**3.4**	1.06	0.39	4.74	3.08	83.6	**2.1**	11.0	18.9	**5.5**
9.8	0.15	1.2	0.14	**8.7**	0.59	1.41	14.72	3.82	75.4	**4.2**	26.2	6.3	**7.6**
10.0	0.23	1.3	0.13	**4.3**	0.16	0.67	5.53	2.89	83.4	**5.0**	30.0	2.3	**6.4**
6.7	0.90	3.0	0.33	**5.0**	0.02	0.92	4.68	4.45	79.8	**4.2**	31.5	0.0	**4.3**
10.0	0.00	0.0	-0.56	**1.1**	0.00	0.06	0.48	2.26	117.7	**5.6**	23.4	0.0	**5.4**
9.5	0.08	1.4	0.49	**2.4**	0.01	0.20	2.86	4.17	78.3	**4.1**	18.9	0.0	**2.0**
8.7	0.25	2.3	0.37	**5.1**	1.20	0.38	3.36	3.55	79.6	**4.1**	12.6	2.4	**8.8**
4.9	1.95	15.3	0.09	**2.2**	0.00	0.00	0.00	4.32	84.7	**4.9**	30.3	0.6	**1.7**
9.2	1.59	2.4	0.59	**3.6**	0.05	0.54	4.20	1.91	67.3	**4.8**	12.1	0.0	**5.4**
9.8	1.75	2.6	1.18	**3.9**	0.01	0.39	2.45	3.17	86.4	**5.8**	39.5	0.0	**7.0**
5.7	0.75	6.1	0.22	**3.1**	0.05	0.33	3.87	3.72	89.2	**3.4**	12.5	6.8	**3.8**
10.0	2.90	1.2	0.00	**0.2**	-0.01	-0.63	-4.46	2.03	134.4	**5.3**	20.1	0.0	**4.9**
7.1	0.40	3.6	0.48	**2.7**	0.11	0.18	1.95	2.42	84.0	**2.6**	20.1	19.1	**5.4**
6.3	0.37	2.7	0.31	**3.7**	0.08	0.51	4.97	4.18	82.1	**3.4**	16.0	3.9	**4.8**
10.0	0.07	0.2	0.29	**4.0**	0.04	0.65	4.41	2.58	79.8	**5.7**	37.4	0.5	**7.2**
5.3	1.46	7.8	0.30	**1.1**	-0.03	-0.94	-7.62	7.43	104.8	**3.9**	34.2	15.5	**4.8**
5.7	2.09	8.0	2.16	**0.0**	-0.03	-1.58	-10.94	5.58	109.2	**5.6**	41.7	0.0	**5.1**
8.4	0.10	0.4	0.59	**7.2**	0.03	1.00	6.75	4.39	80.7	**5.9**	36.0	0.0	**6.3**
4.6	0.91	9.0	0.69	**2.3**	-0.04	-0.43	-5.50	5.70	96.3	**3.6**	11.4	3.7	**2.8**
6.2	0.54	2.8	0.91	**6.2**	0.13	1.97	13.71	6.00	78.7	**2.8**	18.2	15.5	**5.7**
8.9	0.36	3.1	0.26	**3.8**	0.38	0.31	3.39	3.93	86.0	**4.7**	25.1	2.9	**5.8**
6.9	0.27	2.2	0.01	**2.6**	0.06	0.28	3.10	3.34	91.4	**3.9**	22.3	11.2	**4.5**

Name	City	State	Rating	2016 Rating	2015 Rating	Total Assets ($Mil)	One Year Asset Growth	Asset Mix (As a % of Total Assets) Comm-ercial Loans	Cons-umer Loans	Mort-gage Loans	Secur-ities	Capital-ization Index	Net Worth Ratio
Commonwealth Credit Union	Frankfort	KY	**B+**	B+	A	1141.3	6.78	2.3	33.8	25.1	14.9	**10.0**	15.5
Commonwealth One Federal Credit Union	Alexandria	VA	**C+**	C+	C+	338.2	4.35	4.6	27.7	27.7	14.0	**8.1**	9.9
▲ Commonwealth Utilities Employees CU	Marion	MA	**B-**	C+	C	42.8	2.48	0.0	13.7	6.7	3.9	**10.0**	14.5
Communication Federal Credit Union	Oklahoma City	OK	**B**	B	B+	1112.3	5.36	0.0	57.7	8.8	14.0	**10.0**	14.0
▼ Communities of Abilene FCU	Abilene	TX	**C-**	C	C+	138.4	3.74	0.0	18.4	15.5	31.2	**5.5**	8.0
Community & Teachers FCU	East Providence	RI	**C-**	C-	D	26.7	5.62	5.4	6.7	45.5	0.0	**6.3**	8.3
Community 1st Credit Union	Ottumwa	IA	**B**	B	B	607.0	5.60	15.8	24.5	45.2	0.0	**6.7**	8.7
▼ Community 1st Credit Union	Dupont	WA	**C-**	C	C-	113.5	2.05	0.1	57.8	7.0	3.6	**10.0**	15.3
Community 1st Federal Credit Union	Miles City	MT	**C**	C	C	29.0	0.80	14.7	14.4	32.8	0.9	**6.9**	8.9
Community Alliance Credit Union	Novi	MI	**C-**	C-	C	108.4	0.86	1.9	58.3	15.1	1.6	**6.0**	8.0
▼ Community Choice Credit Union	Commerce City	CO	**B-**	B	B-	57.8	-0.21	0.2	39.2	12.2	0.0	**10.0**	12.3
▲ Community Choice Credit Union	Johnston	IA	**B+**	B	B	473.2	5.30	10.0	45.0	20.8	3.9	**8.5**	10.0
Community Choice Credit Union	Farmington Hills	MI	**B+**	B+	B+	882.5	14.59	11.4	35.2	23.4	7.1	**6.5**	8.5
Community Credit Union	Lewiston	ME	**B-**	B-	B-	54.1	13.20	3.8	27.7	32.4	0.0	**9.4**	10.6
Community Credit Union	New Rockford	ND	**B**	B	B	169.7	3.73	15.7	0.3	8.4	61.8	**10.0**	13.6
Community Credit Union of Florida	Rockledge	FL	**A**	A	A-	607.5	9.83	11.2	31.5	33.7	3.6	**10.0**	11.5
Community Credit Union of Lynn	Lynn	MA	**C+**	C+	B	145.6	6.90	16.6	30.7	34.9	3.5	**10.0**	11.6
Community Credit Union of New Milford, Inc.	New Milford	CT	**E**	E	E+	12.1	12.66	0.0	23.5	0.0	5.2	**4.3**	6.3
▲ Community Credit Union of Southern Humboldt	Garberville	CA	**A-**	B+	B	92.3	5.03	5.3	8.6	49.8	1.4	**10.0**	11.2
Community Federal Credit Union	Chicago	IL	**C-**	C-	D+	<1	30.79	0.0	15.1	0.0	0.0	**9.2**	10.7
Community Financial Credit Union	Plymouth	MI	**A**	A	A	790.9	11.81	9.0	32.4	36.6	1.3	**10.0**	12.3
Community Financial Credit Union	Springfield	MO	**C**	C	C-	65.8	4.30	0.4	42.0	11.6	9.4	**6.8**	8.9
Community Financial Services FCU	Roselle	NJ	**D**	D	D	40.0	1.16	10.4	11.1	10.3	14.4	**10.0**	16.5
Community First Credit Union	Santa Rosa	CA	**B-**	B-	C+	240.5	7.60	0.0	52.4	8.1	26.8	**5.4**	7.4
▼ Community First Credit Union	Hannibal	MO	**E+**	D-	D-	7.2	2.08	0.0	56.7	8.1	0.0	**7.0**	9.0
▲ Community First Credit Union	Ashtabula	OH	**C**	C-	C-	77.7	4.73	5.0	16.9	9.0	36.2	**10.0**	13.9
Community First Credit Union	Appleton	WI	**A**	A	A	2700.4	11.86	15.8	13.1	61.8	0.0	**10.0**	12.6
Community First Credit Union of Florida	Jacksonville	FL	**A**	A	A	1476.0	8.64	4.1	32.6	28.8	21.9	**10.0**	12.7
Community First Federal Credit Union	Lakeview	MI	**C-**	C-	C-	48.6	18.65	0.0	29.3	54.6	0.0	**5.2**	7.2
Community First Guam FCU	Hagatna	GU	**B-**	B-	B	121.0	9.05	23.9	26.7	36.3	0.8	**9.3**	10.6
▲ Community Focus Federal Credit Union	Brownstown	MI	**C+**	C	C-	54.7	3.86	0.0	14.7	10.0	23.0	**10.0**	15.2
Community Healthcare Credit Union, Inc.	Manchester	CT	**D-**	D-	E+	11.2	19.39	0.0	55.5	0.0	0.0	**5.2**	7.2
Community Healthcare FCU	Everett	WA	**D+**	D+	D	14.3	20.17	0.0	34.7	0.0	0.0	**6.3**	8.3
Community Link Federal Credit Union	Huntington	IN	**B-**	B-	C+	19.5	1.43	6.0	20.9	35.7	24.8	**10.0**	13.2
Community One Credit Union, Inc.	North Canton	OH	**C-**	C-	C-	75.6	4.85	0.3	28.1	8.9	30.3	**6.2**	8.2
Community Plus Federal Credit Union	Rantoul	IL	**D-**	D-	D-	19.3	-0.89	0.8	39.0	16.0	0.0	**4.8**	6.8
Community Powered Federal Credit Union	Bear	DE	**D+**	D+	D	129.5	4.15	1.1	15.9	13.6	45.2	**8.1**	10.9
▲ Community Promise Federal Credit Union	Kalamazoo	MI	**C-**	D+	C-	<1	35.67	0.0	53.2	0.0	0.0	**10.0**	19.8
Community Regional Credit Union	Kingston	PA	**D**	D	D	19.3	-3.67	0.0	15.7	11.1	0.0	**8.3**	9.8
Community Resource Credit Union	Baytown	TX	**B**	B	B	443.5	10.59	6.0	56.1	21.4	2.8	**6.9**	8.9
Community Resource Federal Credit Union	Latham	NY	**B+**	B+	B+	85.8	11.89	0.0	27.0	24.9	4.3	**10.0**	11.7
Community Service Credit Union	Huntsville	TX	**B**	B	B	95.2	2.42	1.5	56.6	3.1	4.2	**8.3**	9.9
Community South Credit Union	Chipley	FL	**B+**	B+	A-	113.6	2.18	4.9	42.2	24.3	10.6	**10.0**	13.9
Community Spirit Credit Union	Lawrenceburg	IN	**C-**	C-	C	14.7	3.88	0.0	42.5	2.7	33.6	**10.0**	15.5
Community Star Credit Union	Elyria	OH	**C+**	C+	C+	71.7	8.82	4.6	40.1	11.0	0.0	**6.6**	8.6
Community Trust Credit Union	Gurnee	IL	**C+**	C+	C	221.7	5.80	0.1	15.0	30.5	12.5	**6.0**	8.0
▼ Community United Credit Union	Strongsville	OH	**C-**	C	C+	11.8	1.36	0.0	38.3	3.8	13.0	**10.0**	15.6
▼ Community United Federal Credit Union	Waycross	GA	**F**	E-	C+	25.3	17.39	0.2	12.7	47.1	0.0	**1.6**	4.5
Community West Credit Union	Kentwood	MI	**B+**	B+	B+	187.0	5.92	0.1	48.9	16.9	1.3	**9.1**	10.4
CommunityAmerica Credit Union	Lenexa	KS	**A-**	A-	A-	2478.0	9.70	1.8	24.0	23.8	24.4	**10.0**	12.4
CommunityWide Federal Credit Union	South Bend	IN	**B-**	B-	B-	393.9	0.03	0.2	75.3	6.1	7.3	**10.0**	16.1
▼ CommunityWorks Federal Credit Union	Greenville	SC	**C-**	C	C+	2.4	-2.12	0.0	43.8	0.0	0.0	**10.0**	13.3
Compass Federal Credit Union	Oswego	NY	**A-**	A-	A-	55.9	42.68	0.0	22.2	17.1	5.4	**10.0**	15.1
▼ Compass Financial Federal Credit Union	Medley	FL	**C+**	B-	B	26.8	2.65	0.0	61.8	2.5	0.1	**10.0**	14.9
Complex Community Federal Credit Union	Odessa	TX	**B+**	B+	B+	457.4	0.44	0.0	32.0	17.5	22.8	**8.2**	10.0
Comtrust Federal Credit Union	Chattanooga	TN	**C+**	C+	C+	367.8	1.67	1.2	13.7	10.6	50.8	**10.0**	11.0
Comunidad Latina Federal Credit Union	Santa Ana	CA	**C**	C	C	4.7	10.95	0.0	59.9	0.0	0.0	**10.0**	15.1
Concho Educators Federal Credit Union	San Angelo	TX	**C**	C	C	75.2	0.32	0.5	18.3	5.6	41.5	**6.5**	9.5
Concho Valley Credit Union	San Angelo	TX	**C**	C	C	17.6	3.61	0.0	22.4	18.0	0.0	**8.8**	10.2
Concora Wabash Federal Credit Union	Wabash	IN	**D+**	D+	C-	1.1	4.35	0.0	77.8	0.0	0.0	**10.0**	18.5

Asset Quality Index	Non-Performing Loans as a % of Total Loans	Non-Performing Loans as a % of Capital	Net Charge-Offs Avg Loans	Profitability Index	Net Income ($Mil)	Return on Assets	Return on Equity	Net Interest Spread	Overhead Efficiency Ratio	Liquidity Index	Liquidity Ratio	Hot Money Ratio	Stability Index
7.9	0.79	3.8	1.03	**5.0**	1.56	0.55	3.87	4.28	70.3	**3.8**	12.3	5.2	**8.6**
9.5	0.30	2.1	0.29	**4.1**	0.40	0.49	4.91	3.51	86.3	**3.8**	15.4	6.6	**6.1**
8.5	2.49	4.4	0.35	**3.5**	0.06	0.56	3.83	2.27	77.5	**5.2**	29.9	3.1	**6.1**
6.7	0.55	4.2	1.18	**4.9**	2.59	0.95	6.85	3.71	59.6	**2.6**	17.9	22.9	**7.6**
8.2	0.47	3.0	1.15	**2.0**	0.10	0.28	3.73	3.99	75.3	**4.4**	14.6	5.4	**3.6**
9.9	0.09	0.7	0.00	**3.0**	0.02	0.26	3.49	3.65	93.2	**4.9**	34.9	6.6	**3.5**
6.4	0.47	5.9	0.19	**4.0**	0.40	0.27	3.01	3.77	88.2	**2.7**	12.1	12.9	**6.3**
6.6	0.97	4.7	0.38	**0.9**	-0.06	-0.23	-1.48	3.09	97.8	**3.9**	17.4	8.7	**7.5**
5.8	0.57	4.0	0.12	**2.9**	0.00	0.01	0.16	3.88	97.1	**4.2**	24.6	4.4	**4.7**
4.2	1.14	12.7	0.96	**1.9**	0.00	0.00	0.05	5.54	84.5	**2.9**	11.5	11.4	**4.1**
9.8	0.39	1.4	0.59	**2.8**	0.11	0.77	5.33	4.31	82.7	**5.2**	37.4	6.9	**5.8**
8.0	0.38	3.6	0.57	**5.7**	1.14	0.98	9.71	4.39	78.5	**4.4**	16.3	0.6	**6.5**
7.7	0.40	3.9	0.40	**3.3**	0.86	0.40	4.70	3.54	88.9	**3.6**	12.3	4.9	**5.5**
6.1	0.50	5.5	0.06	**3.6**	0.08	0.60	5.47	4.26	94.5	**4.1**	26.1	6.2	**4.6**
8.6	4.31	5.0	0.00	**4.3**	0.21	0.49	3.56	1.22	58.5	**3.9**	23.8	15.6	**8.6**
8.5	0.24	1.9	0.91	**9.0**	2.13	1.42	13.35	4.35	64.0	**3.9**	17.4	6.1	**9.7**
7.8	0.43	3.7	0.41	**1.3**	-0.17	-0.49	-4.11	4.09	103.2	**2.0**	15.2	24.9	**6.8**
7.2	0.75	3.7	0.00	**2.4**	0.01	0.38	5.87	3.24	98.5	**5.7**	25.8	0.9	**0.7**
8.2	0.69	3.7	0.15	**9.1**	0.39	1.65	15.22	4.48	68.6	**4.2**	12.0	3.3	**7.1**
7.0	3.23	4.6	0.00	**1.8**	0.00	0.00	0.00	10.26	100.0	**8.4**	94.0	0.0	**4.7**
6.1	1.24	9.1	0.36	**7.4**	1.71	0.88	7.11	3.82	74.9	**2.4**	5.4	8.2	**9.5**
7.9	0.24	2.4	0.65	**2.4**	0.01	0.08	0.90	3.52	86.1	**4.3**	17.9	2.0	**3.6**
5.0	7.11	19.5	0.02	**0.4**	-0.02	-0.18	-1.09	3.16	101.5	**4.4**	17.2	2.6	**6.3**
5.4	0.93	9.5	0.61	**4.0**	0.33	0.56	7.37	4.34	75.7	**3.8**	9.1	2.2	**4.1**
5.7	0.39	3.0	3.31	**0.0**	-0.03	-1.66	-18.26	3.17	95.0	**3.5**	5.9	0.0	**3.6**
9.8	0.68	1.7	0.71	**2.1**	0.03	0.18	1.27	2.84	85.7	**4.5**	18.5	2.3	**6.3**
9.3	0.24	1.7	0.08	**9.5**	9.28	1.40	11.41	2.96	56.6	**3.5**	18.4	10.9	**10.0**
9.4	0.36	1.9	0.68	**6.6**	2.73	0.76	5.92	3.14	71.5	**3.8**	16.6	6.9	**9.4**
4.7	1.13	14.2	0.06	**9.8**	0.18	1.52	21.44	5.10	76.7	**1.7**	3.8	13.2	**3.7**
5.0	0.45	14.2	1.03	**4.0**	0.11	0.38	4.50	5.63	76.6	**2.3**	19.9	31.5	**6.0**
10.0	0.31	0.6	0.03	**3.1**	0.08	0.62	4.00	3.38	85.6	**5.5**	26.4	1.2	**6.9**
2.7	2.64	22.1	-0.22	**4.5**	0.02	0.55	7.51	4.59	85.9	**4.2**	29.4	0.0	**1.7**
4.9	2.68	14.9	0.28	**8.1**	0.18	5.18	64.85	5.26	7.0	**5.5**	28.0	0.0	**3.2**
8.6	0.23	1.1	0.00	**6.3**	0.03	0.65	4.86	4.03	85.6	**2.9**	13.3	17.2	**5.7**
6.5	1.27	7.3	1.12	**3.7**	0.06	0.30	4.07	4.48	83.3	**4.6**	29.0	8.4	**2.7**
6.3	0.73	6.0	0.11	**0.4**	-0.02	-0.49	-6.96	3.67	102.5	**5.0**	31.7	1.4	**2.3**
8.6	0.89	3.5	0.60	**1.1**	0.05	0.15	1.55	2.81	93.9	**4.5**	15.1	9.9	**4.7**
6.2	2.45	6.1	3.38	**8.7**	0.02	15.01	74.19	11.27	61.2	**6.5**	51.2	0.0	**5.0**
3.6	4.30	27.5	0.00	**1.4**	0.00	0.02	0.21	2.66	97.9	**5.6**	55.7	0.7	**3.4**
6.0	0.48	4.9	0.56	**4.9**	0.62	0.58	7.01	4.18	82.8	**2.9**	8.5	7.1	**5.1**
6.7	1.10	7.8	0.49	**4.5**	0.08	0.39	3.28	4.35	85.7	**2.5**	24.5	17.9	**5.5**
5.2	0.32	4.2	0.75	**4.3**	0.07	0.30	3.04	4.66	84.8	**3.6**	14.3	6.4	**4.4**
5.1	1.83	11.4	2.27	**8.7**	0.52	1.85	14.17	6.45	65.2	**2.7**	11.5	13.6	**7.8**
5.6	2.89	8.5	0.72	**2.3**	0.02	0.50	3.18	3.59	81.2	**5.0**	24.3	0.0	**5.0**
5.6	0.87	9.6	0.32	**2.4**	-0.07	-0.42	-4.78	3.86	104.8	**3.6**	18.4	10.3	**3.7**
9.4	0.30	2.3	0.20	**3.5**	0.23	0.42	5.23	3.19	87.5	**5.1**	25.4	4.2	**4.7**
9.7	0.67	2.2	0.52	**1.1**	-0.01	-0.24	-1.53	4.05	100.0	**5.6**	34.7	1.3	**6.2**
0.3	6.47	55.1	2.45	**3.0**	-1.21	-19.96	-277.77	4.46	200.0	**5.3**	42.7	9.6	**0.0**
6.1	0.78	5.4	0.64	**4.0**	0.22	0.48	4.49	3.72	83.6	**3.7**	20.4	7.7	**7.3**
8.5	0.65	4.4	0.56	**5.0**	3.43	0.56	4.59	2.74	82.8	**3.9**	14.6	5.3	**8.9**
4.0	2.48	13.9	2.56	**8.7**	1.13	1.15	7.22	4.99	37.6	**1.2**	11.2	27.4	**8.8**
6.6	1.54	7.7	3.42	**3.2**	0.00	-0.66	-8.33	10.25	95.4	**5.5**	117.7	45.0	**5.4**
9.4	0.33	1.2	0.77	**10.0**	0.20	1.42	9.52	4.65	66.0	**4.6**	27.4	8.1	**8.7**
5.9	0.85	5.7	2.58	**2.2**	-0.06	-0.96	-6.15	6.47	92.4	**3.5**	34.5	22.8	**6.3**
8.5	0.56	3.3	0.87	**2.5**	0.38	0.34	3.43	3.18	79.0	**3.8**	17.3	12.8	**5.8**
9.8	0.51	1.5	0.12	**2.4**	0.11	0.12	1.04	1.86	93.3	**5.5**	25.1	4.3	**7.1**
8.3	0.71	2.7	1.28	**9.1**	0.03	2.88	18.55	5.75	57.7	**2.7**	64.0	61.7	**5.0**
9.1	0.35	1.6	0.05	**2.9**	0.06	0.33	3.89	2.76	89.4	**4.2**	16.8	14.8	**4.2**
9.9	0.21	0.9	0.00	**2.6**	0.01	0.14	1.34	2.89	93.2	**4.7**	49.5	10.9	**4.8**
6.5	0.00	0.0	0.00	**1.5**	0.00	0.00	0.00	4.24	111.1	**4.7**	24.9	0.0	**7.0**

								Asset Mix (As a % of Total Assets)					
Name	City	State	Rating	2016 Rating	2015 Rating	Total Assets ($Mil)	One Year Asset Growth	Comm-ercial Loans	Cons-umer Loans	Mort-gage Loans	Secur-ities	Capital-ization Index	Net Worth Ratio
Concord Federal Credit Union	Brooklyn	NY	**C+**	C+	C+	9.1	2.24	0.0	2.6	0.0	10.8	**10.0**	17.9
Concordia Parish School Employees FCU	Ferriday	LA	**E+**	E+	E+	3.7	-0.29	0.0	52.8	0.0	0.0	**7.3**	9.2
CONE Credit Union	Neenah	WI	**C+**	C+	C+	30.7	0.34	4.5	10.8	33.6	0.0	**10.0**	11.2
Congressional Federal Credit Union	Oakton	VA	**C**	C	C+	927.1	7.18	0.0	17.9	29.0	34.6	**6.3**	8.3
▼ Connect Credit Union	Fort Lauderdale	FL	**C**	C+	B-	77.4	7.63	0.0	25.0	4.9	35.6	**9.1**	10.6
Connected Credit Union	Augusta	ME	**B**	B	B-	38.5	6.15	0.6	24.8	27.1	0.0	**9.8**	10.9
Connecticut Community Credit Union, Inc.	Pawcatuck	CT	**E+**	E+	D-	20.3	2.03	0.0	33.1	0.0	0.0	**4.1**	6.1
▼ Connecticut Federal Credit Union	North Haven	CT	**D-**	D	D	7.9	4.94	0.0	6.7	0.0	0.0	**7.0**	9.0
Connecticut Labor Department FCU	Wethersfield	CT	**C**	C	C-	13.0	-5.03	0.0	22.7	8.2	0.0	**10.0**	14.7
Connecticut Postal Federal Credit Union	New Britain	CT	**B-**	B-	C+	14.0	0.14	0.0	28.0	8.2	0.0	**10.0**	16.8
Connecticut State Empls Credit Union, Inc.	Hartford	CT	**C**	C	C	1803.5	3.69	0.0	2.4	15.1	56.7	**6.1**	8.1
Connecticut Transit Federal Credit Union	Hartford	CT	**E+**	E+	E+	1.1	-8.92	0.0	57.0	0.0	0.0	**4.1**	6.1
Connection Credit Union	Silverdale	WA	**C+**	C+	C	31.5	6.15	0.0	35.9	15.8	12.2	**10.0**	12.3
▲ Connections Credit Union	Pocatello	ID	**C-**	D+	D	154.4	5.51	4.4	25.8	27.5	2.5	**5.9**	7.9
Connects Federal Credit Union	Richmond	VA	**C-**	C-	C-	76.9	-2.62	0.0	36.4	0.0	12.6	**5.6**	7.9
Connex Credit Union, Inc.	North Haven	CT	**B-**	B-	B	514.5	13.34	0.7	39.9	24.2	10.1	**10.0**	11.0
Connexus Credit Union	Wausau	WI	**B+**	B+	B	1614.8	20.87	0.5	31.8	11.6	0.5	**7.4**	9.2
Conservation Employees Credit Union	Jefferson City	MO	**B**	B	B	110.3	4.63	2.4	26.2	30.4	12.5	**7.9**	9.8
Consol Employees Credit Union	Canonsburg	PA	**D+**	D+	D+	14.8	-8.16	0.0	19.6	0.0	14.5	**10.0**	14.8
Consolidated Controls Corporation FCU	Bethel	CT	**C-**	C-	C-	1.1	-1.79	0.0	75.4	0.0	0.0	**10.0**	17.9
Consolidated Federal Credit Union	Portland	OR	**B+**	B+	B+	220.0	7.14	12.0	20.7	30.6	0.0	**10.0**	13.7
Consolidated Hub-Co Federal Credit Union	Aberdeen	SD	**E+**	E+	E+	6.0	7.00	0.0	39.4	0.0	0.0	**5.2**	7.2
Constellation Federal Credit Union	Reston	VA	**B-**	B-	B-	212.6	1.92	1.3	5.7	38.3	15.2	**10.0**	14.6
Construction Federal Credit Union	Bingham Farms	MI	**B-**	B-	C+	20.8	-5.61	4.1	6.8	32.1	7.8	**10.0**	15.6
Construction Industries Credit Union	Lincoln	NE	**C-**	C-	C-	2.0	15.86	0.0	60.2	0.0	0.0	**10.0**	13.7
Consumer Credit Union	Greeneville	TN	**B-**	B-	B-	399.5	6.54	9.7	19.4	49.1	15.7	**9.1**	10.8
Consumer Healthcare Federal Credit Union	Pittsburgh	PA	**C+**	C+	C	20.1	-2.01	0.0	9.3	2.7	0.0	**10.0**	15.4
Consumer's Federal Credit Union	Gregory	SD	**D**	D	D+	13.2	3.93	16.6	28.7	13.9	0.0	**5.7**	7.7
Consumers Cooperative Credit Union	Gurnee	IL	**B-**	B-	B	1106.6	18.88	9.4	33.8	17.5	24.5	**5.8**	7.9
Consumers Cooperative FCU	Alliance	NE	**B+**	B+	B	26.9	6.27	0.6	56.0	4.2	0.0	**10.0**	18.8
Consumers Credit Union	Denison	IA	**C+**	C+	C+	6.9	5.52	0.0	44.3	0.0	0.0	**10.0**	12.9
Consumers Credit Union	Kalamazoo	MI	**A-**	A-	A-	859.0	25.88	7.1	46.1	30.1	0.0	**7.2**	9.1
Consumers Federal Credit Union	Brooklyn	NY	**C+**	C+	C+	61.6	1.08	20.6	4.4	71.4	0.0	**10.0**	13.4
Consumers Professional Credit Union	Lansing	MI	**B+**	B+	B	74.1	0.14	5.2	18.0	39.1	0.0	**10.0**	15.6
Consumers Union Employees FCU	Yonkers	NY	**C**	C	C	3.6	-19.98	0.0	21.4	0.0	0.0	**10.0**	17.3
Container Mutual Credit Union	Fernandina Beach	FL	**C**	C	C	7.5	3.01	0.0	41.2	7.3	0.0	**10.0**	35.6
▲ Continental Employees FCU	Pineville	LA	**D+**	D	D	1.3	17.43	0.0	38.3	0.0	0.0	**10.0**	22.0
Cooperative Center Federal Credit Union	Berkeley	CA	**D+**	D+	D	118.5	4.42	1.1	42.6	17.9	4.6	**4.6**	6.6
▼ Cooperative Employees Credit Union	Anadarko	OK	**D+**	C-	C-	6.9	-4.96	0.0	64.8	0.0	4.3	**10.0**	13.4
▼ Cooperative Extension Service FCU	Little Rock	AR	**C-**	C	C	5.3	0.88	0.0	56.7	0.0	0.0	**10.0**	23.8
▼ Cooperative Teachers Credit Union	Tyler	TX	**B+**	A-	A	106.6	15.73	0.0	26.9	40.1	15.2	**10.0**	12.3
Coopers Cave Federal Credit Union	Glens Falls	NY	**D**	D	D+	14.0	9.07	0.0	15.4	0.0	15.7	**6.0**	8.0
Coosa Pines Federal Credit Union	Childersburg	AL	**B+**	B+	B+	240.3	1.15	0.7	23.8	23.9	29.9	**10.0**	13.0
Coosa Valley Credit Union	Rome	GA	**B-**	B-	B	301.6	59.65	6.9	40.0	15.9	13.1	**6.0**	8.1
Copoco Community Credit Union	Bay City	MI	**D-**	D-	D-	102.0	0.39	0.9	42.6	20.2	15.5	**5.2**	7.4
Copper & Glass Federal Credit Union	Glassport	PA	**C**	C	C	8.7	-0.29	0.0	41.9	0.0	0.0	**10.0**	13.7
▲ Copper Basin Federal Credit Union	Copperhill	TN	**D**	D-	D-	30.1	5.22	0.2	28.5	28.8	0.0	**5.2**	7.2
Coral Community Federal Credit Union	Fort Lauderdale	FL	**C-**	C-	C-	31.9	7.40	0.0	36.2	1.6	30.8	**7.0**	9.1
CORE Credit Union	Statesboro	GA	**C+**	C+	C+	74.9	8.96	5.5	30.3	34.8	1.7	**7.1**	9.1
▼ Core Federal Credit Union	East Syracuse	NY	**B**	B+	B+	110.8	5.51	9.5	7.6	4.6	8.4	**8.8**	10.2
CorePlus Federal Credit Union	Norwich	CT	**C-**	C-	C-	204.5	2.55	2.6	29.3	21.6	14.4	**5.4**	7.5
Corner Post Federal Credit Union	Wilkes-Barre	PA	**C-**	C-	D+	84.7	-0.28	0.0	12.8	5.2	36.5	**7.6**	9.4
Corner Stone Credit Union	Lancaster	TX	**D-**	D-	D	21.4	-5.54	0.0	64.6	4.1	0.0	**4.3**	6.4
▲ Cornerstone Community Credit Union	Stamford	CT	**C-**	D+	D	50.5	53.24	0.0	15.8	21.5	0.0	**10.0**	11.8
Cornerstone Community Credit Union	Des Moines	IA	**C-**	C-	C	22.3	0.53	10.8	31.7	22.5	20.9	**9.1**	10.4
Cornerstone Community FCU	Lockport	NY	**C-**	C-	C	419.8	8.99	0.2	23.7	5.9	23.9	**4.9**	6.9
Cornerstone Community Financial CU	Auburn Hills	MI	**A-**	A-	A-	280.9	4.21	6.9	52.0	16.8	2.8	**10.0**	11.8
▲ Cornerstone Credit Union	Freeport	IL	**C**	C-	C+	114.8	6.39	1.6	47.8	6.6	10.0	**9.0**	10.3
Cornerstone Federal Credit Union	Carlisle	PA	**C+**	C+	C+	109.1	3.42	8.7	15.6	24.5	11.4	**8.3**	9.9
Cornerstone Financial Credit Union	Nashville	TN	**B-**	B-	B-	331.0	10.77	1.0	53.0	16.6	5.8	**7.8**	9.5

Arrows denote recent upgrades ▲ or downgrades ▼

Asset Quality Index	Non-Performing Loans as a % of Total Loans	Non-Performing Loans as a % of Capital	Net Charge-Offs Avg Loans	Profitability Index	Net Income ($Mil)	Return on Assets	Return on Equity	Net Interest Spread	Overhead Efficiency Ratio	Liquidity Index	Liquidity Ratio	Hot Money Ratio	Stability Index
10.0	0.22	0.1	0.00	**2.2**	0.00	0.09	0.49	1.68	93.9	**5.7**	20.0	0.0	**6.8**
0.7	6.50	42.3	1.46	**3.8**	0.01	0.75	8.24	7.18	65.5	**5.0**	37.4	0.0	**3.3**
9.3	0.17	1.0	0.00	**2.8**	0.02	0.30	2.70	2.51	87.3	**4.0**	24.0	0.0	**5.9**
7.7	0.92	6.1	0.28	**3.0**	1.47	0.64	7.58	3.12	81.4	**4.6**	32.4	7.0	**5.4**
6.8	0.56	3.1	1.97	**1.9**	0.05	0.26	2.46	3.41	92.9	**4.3**	16.8	2.2	**5.1**
9.5	0.07	0.9	0.14	**2.4**	-0.01	-0.12	-1.05	3.47	102.8	**4.5**	25.3	1.7	**6.4**
7.3	0.68	4.1	0.38	**0.2**	-0.03	-0.53	-8.29	2.64	111.5	**6.3**	48.2	0.8	**1.7**
8.3	3.14	2.6	0.64	**0.0**	-0.01	-0.67	-7.22	2.51	117.5	**6.1**	19.3	0.0	**2.9**
9.6	0.32	0.7	0.19	**2.4**	0.01	0.18	1.26	3.63	88.1	**5.5**	24.9	0.0	**5.5**
8.2	2.52	5.6	0.38	**2.9**	0.01	0.26	1.54	2.19	85.3	**6.1**	43.2	2.6	**7.0**
10.0	0.13	0.4	0.12	**2.8**	1.75	0.39	4.98	1.10	54.9	**7.2**	50.3	1.6	**5.5**
0.0	7.79	60.5	3.69	**0.0**	0.00	-0.74	-11.76	10.04	109.1	**4.7**	34.7	14.8	**1.7**
5.6	1.15	9.4	1.43	**2.9**	0.02	0.26	2.07	6.36	82.0	**4.5**	22.3	3.0	**5.7**
6.8	0.63	5.3	0.46	**2.2**	0.07	0.19	2.39	3.49	90.7	**4.3**	19.7	5.0	**4.0**
6.2	1.53	8.1	1.01	**1.6**	0.01	0.03	0.41	3.28	89.9	**4.7**	19.2	3.2	**2.3**
8.4	0.52	3.6	0.31	**3.8**	0.57	0.45	4.02	2.89	81.5	**2.3**	8.8	15.4	**7.0**
6.2	1.04	7.0	0.25	**8.2**	7.63	1.96	19.09	3.28	60.9	**2.7**	17.2	18.4	**7.7**
9.0	0.34	2.6	0.11	**3.6**	0.12	0.44	4.76	2.82	88.5	**3.9**	15.0	4.0	**6.4**
10.0	1.01	1.4	0.13	**0.4**	-0.01	-0.22	-1.46	2.62	109.3	**6.7**	41.4	0.0	**4.7**
8.3	0.00	0.0	0.00	**2.6**	0.00	0.37	2.03	5.64	85.7	**4.0**	29.9	0.0	**7.0**
9.6	0.22	1.0	0.14	**3.7**	0.19	0.35	2.49	2.89	91.5	**3.7**	24.6	4.6	**8.7**
4.4	1.89	13.9	0.47	**2.4**	0.00	-0.13	-1.84	5.01	81.6	**5.6**	36.4	0.0	**1.0**
8.8	0.47	2.9	0.01	**3.5**	0.25	0.48	3.27	2.92	83.0	**4.2**	24.0	7.9	**8.2**
10.0	0.21	0.5	0.00	**3.3**	0.02	0.33	2.10	2.90	89.6	**4.9**	32.6	9.1	**7.1**
5.0	2.81	12.2	0.00	**1.8**	0.00	0.00	0.00	4.45	94.4	**5.7**	34.8	0.0	**6.5**
9.6	0.04	1.6	-0.01	**3.7**	0.51	0.52	4.93	2.05	82.5	**2.7**	9.5	14.8	**7.0**
9.4	2.56	3.0	0.64	**2.8**	0.01	0.27	1.69	1.96	81.3	**6.5**	46.2	0.0	**6.6**
6.2	0.36	2.7	0.36	**5.1**	0.03	1.06	13.68	3.13	73.8	**4.1**	36.3	15.8	**3.0**
7.7	0.57	4.6	0.36	**4.3**	1.80	0.67	8.76	3.29	82.1	**3.3**	18.4	11.1	**5.3**
6.9	1.30	4.6	0.50	**9.8**	0.13	1.94	10.35	4.49	49.0	**3.0**	44.7	32.2	**8.9**
9.7	0.00	0.0	0.00	**5.1**	0.01	0.59	4.49	5.67	90.6	**5.9**	59.4	13.0	**5.0**
8.0	0.14	1.4	0.21	**8.7**	2.43	1.16	12.61	3.44	73.7	**1.6**	3.9	16.7	**8.1**
1.7	3.35	43.9	-0.03	**5.3**	0.16	1.01	7.77	3.17	74.3	**1.5**	8.9	25.6	**7.1**
8.2	0.54	4.2	0.34	**4.1**	0.06	0.33	2.08	3.68	83.2	**2.9**	26.4	23.0	**7.2**
10.0	0.00	0.0	0.00	**5.3**	0.01	1.01	5.90	2.19	50.0	**6.2**	58.6	0.0	**5.0**
9.4	1.63	2.4	0.00	**2.5**	-0.01	-0.64	-1.80	3.15	103.5	**5.6**	59.9	0.0	**7.1**
7.4	0.24	0.7	5.21	**1.2**	-0.01	-3.62	-14.67	5.36	178.6	**4.8**	36.0	0.0	**5.1**
3.7	1.39	22.0	0.96	**1.7**	0.01	0.03	0.72	3.85	87.5	**4.6**	24.5	0.9	**2.0**
5.7	1.16	7.1	-0.07	**2.5**	0.01	0.40	3.05	4.45	91.2	**2.7**	8.3	3.5	**6.4**
8.2	0.52	1.3	1.18	**1.3**	-0.01	-0.61	-2.53	4.19	105.5	**6.0**	53.7	0.0	**7.2**
9.0	0.50	2.9	0.29	**4.2**	0.09	0.35	2.73	3.35	86.4	**3.9**	10.9	0.0	**8.0**
9.1	0.06	0.3	0.30	**1.2**	0.00	-0.06	-0.72	3.25	96.8	**6.2**	34.9	0.0	**2.1**
8.3	0.69	3.8	0.71	**4.5**	0.42	0.70	5.59	3.32	77.4	**4.6**	23.7	3.7	**7.5**
6.1	0.64	7.9	0.86	**4.3**	0.39	0.54	6.45	4.45	79.8	**4.2**	15.0	5.3	**3.7**
5.4	0.46	12.6	1.92	**0.2**	-0.15	-0.59	-9.69	4.44	90.7	**4.1**	12.5	2.9	**2.0**
3.5	7.57	28.6	0.86	**2.8**	-0.03	-1.39	-9.98	4.56	113.4	**5.5**	37.3	0.0	**5.7**
3.4	0.29	24.6	0.13	**3.4**	0.04	0.50	6.85	4.85	85.1	**4.8**	26.4	4.3	**2.3**
7.5	0.49	2.3	1.26	**1.8**	0.02	0.27	2.91	3.54	89.6	**5.2**	22.2	2.2	**3.6**
5.9	0.78	6.9	0.16	**6.5**	0.20	1.10	12.37	5.23	80.0	**3.9**	19.2	7.5	**4.5**
6.3	2.42	8.9	0.06	**3.4**	0.06	0.21	2.03	3.68	74.0	**6.8**	46.2	0.5	**7.3**
8.3	0.43	3.8	0.38	**2.9**	0.14	0.27	3.65	3.21	90.3	**3.8**	16.3	5.6	**4.0**
8.7	1.51	3.4	0.68	**1.9**	0.01	0.03	0.30	2.12	98.7	**5.7**	27.2	0.7	**3.8**
3.1	1.89	15.6	0.79	**1.7**	0.03	0.53	8.31	6.25	89.1	**4.1**	18.2	5.0	**0.0**
7.8	1.45	6.4	0.44	**2.0**	-0.01	-0.06	-0.58	4.03	97.1	**5.0**	21.3	1.0	**2.9**
5.4	1.22	11.6	0.49	**2.4**	0.01	0.09	0.86	3.15	92.7	**2.2**	9.7	21.2	**5.0**
7.5	0.63	4.8	0.75	**1.0**	-0.09	-0.09	-1.25	3.07	87.1	**4.2**	16.9	1.4	**3.4**
5.9	0.69	5.1	0.41	**5.5**	0.33	0.48	4.05	3.16	85.8	**3.1**	15.2	12.3	**7.0**
5.5	1.29	8.3	0.75	**3.1**	0.11	0.38	3.73	4.69	85.0	**4.6**	24.4	5.3	**5.4**
7.4	1.33	8.1	0.07	**2.2**	-0.01	-0.05	-0.51	2.97	98.2	**4.7**	22.1	3.0	**5.9**
7.2	0.42	4.0	0.23	**4.5**	0.54	0.67	7.97	3.84	81.6	**3.7**	16.4	3.6	**5.4**

Name	City	State	Rating	2016 Rating	2015 Rating	Total Assets ($Mil)	One Year Asset Growth	Asset Mix (As a % of Total Assets) Commercial Loans	Consumer Loans	Mortgage Loans	Securities	Capitalization Index	Net Worth Ratio
Corning Federal Credit Union	Corning	NY	**B-**	B-	B-	1353.8	10.98	9.4	27.3	25.9	15.0	**6.6**	8.8
Corning Glass Works Harrodsburg FCU	Harrodsburg	KY	**D+**	D+	C-	5.4	-7.60	0.0	19.9	0.0	0.0	**10.0**	17.3
Corporate America Family Credit Union	Elgin	IL	**B+**	B+	B+	626.4	0.44	0.0	26.6	26.4	28.0	**10.0**	15.8
▼ Corpus Christi Postal Employees CU	Corpus Christi	TX	**C+**	B-	B-	15.0	0.42	0.0	42.1	0.0	0.0	**10.0**	14.9
Corpus Christi S.P. Credit Union	Corpus Christi	TX	**D**	D	D	2.8	-9.01	0.0	68.6	0.0	0.0	**10.0**	22.3
Correctional Workers FCU	El Reno	OK	**C-**	C-	D+	10.6	-2.95	0.0	20.8	17.0	0.0	**10.0**	11.3
▲ Corrections Federal Credit Union	Soledad	CA	**C-**	D+	D	14.6	7.09	0.0	66.7	0.0	0.0	**6.8**	8.8
Corry Area Schools Federal Credit Union	Corry	PA	**D+**	D+	D-	4.7	7.80	0.0	29.8	10.0	0.0	**8.1**	9.7
▼ Corry Federal Credit Union	Corry	PA	**C+**	B-	B-	48.1	7.26	0.0	25.2	14.5	0.6	**8.9**	10.3
Corry Jamestown Credit Union	Corry	PA	**B-**	B-	B-	19.5	10.24	0.0	21.6	7.8	0.0	**10.0**	11.2
▲ Cosden Federal Credit Union	Big Spring	TX	**D+**	D	D+	39.0	0.71	0.0	22.4	0.1	0.0	**10.0**	12.5
▼ Coshocton Federal Credit Union	Coshocton	OH	**D**	D+	C-	1.7	-6.29	0.0	49.9	2.5	0.0	**8.9**	10.3
▼ Cosmopolitan Federal Credit Union	Chicago	IL	**D**	D+	D+	<1	-18.03	0.0	38.0	0.0	0.0	**6.0**	8.0
Coteau Valley Federal Credit Union	Sisseton	SD	**C-**	C-	C-	9.6	0.20	2.8	31.9	16.5	0.0	**10.0**	11.4
Cottonwood Community FCU	Cottonwood	ID	**B**	B	B	86.2	3.00	36.9	8.4	41.9	0.0	**10.0**	18.1
Coulee Dam Federal Credit Union	Coulee Dam	WA	**B-**	B-	B	138.1	5.66	5.0	39.4	7.3	30.7	**5.5**	7.7
Councill Federal Credit Union	Normal	AL	**C-**	C-	C	3.1	-11.28	0.0	44.1	0.0	0.0	**10.0**	16.0
Country Federal Credit Union	Macclenny	FL	**C+**	C+	C	73.9	10.65	5.1	30.4	16.8	11.3	**6.1**	8.1
Country Heritage Credit Union	Buchanan	MI	**B+**	B+	B+	39.3	1.77	19.0	1.2	64.6	19.3	**10.0**	16.6
Countryside Federal Credit Union	East Syracuse	NY	**A-**	A-	B+	153.1	8.24	7.1	9.1	61.4	1.8	**10.0**	12.9
County Credit Union	Saint Louis	MO	**C**	C	C+	19.7	5.60	0.0	27.9	7.9	0.0	**10.0**	17.0
County Credit Union	Kenosha	WI	**C+**	C+	C	14.1	3.78	0.0	19.7	19.7	0.0	**10.0**	12.2
▲ County Educators Federal Credit Union	Roselle Park	NJ	**D+**	D	C-	104.6	6.14	0.0	9.0	0.0	0.0	**7.8**	9.5
County Federal Credit Union	Presque Isle	ME	**A-**	A-	B+	231.1	8.71	5.1	34.1	27.1	4.4	**9.8**	10.9
▼ County Schools Federal Credit Union	Ventura	CA	**C-**	C	D+	56.7	7.54	5.0	32.0	29.6	0.9	**5.4**	7.4
County-City Credit Union	Jefferson	WI	**D+**	D+	D	25.9	4.61	5.0	20.4	28.0	0.0	**5.9**	7.9
Covantage Credit Union	Antigo	WI	**A**	A	A	1436.8	8.82	19.2	19.7	44.1	13.1	**10.0**	11.2
Cove Federal Credit Union	Edgewood	KY	**B+**	B+	B+	62.7	10.41	0.0	44.5	17.4	0.0	**10.0**	13.7
Covenant Savings Federal Credit Union	Killeen	TX	**D**	D	E+	2.7	2.69	0.0	57.3	0.0	0.0	**6.1**	8.1
Coventry Credit Union	Coventry	RI	**C+**	C+	C+	266.3	4.73	0.1	1.6	25.8	1.1	**6.8**	8.8
Coventry Teachers Federal Credit Union	Coventry	RI	**D**	D	D	2.9	-1.32	0.0	42.1	0.0	0.0	**10.0**	21.4
Covington Schools Federal Credit Union	Andalusia	AL	**B**	B	B	17.3	-1.11	0.0	28.8	8.7	0.0	**10.0**	34.0
▼ Cowboy Country Federal Credit Union	Premont	TX	**C-**	C	C+	14.8	-0.69	0.0	49.1	0.0	0.0	**10.0**	12.0
Coweta Cities & County Employees FCU	Newnan	GA	**B-**	B-	B-	20.1	7.98	0.0	33.4	0.0	0.0	**10.0**	15.2
Coxsackie Correctional Employees FCU	Coxsackie	NY	**C+**	C+	C+	3.5	0.06	0.0	44.2	0.0	0.0	**10.0**	28.3
CP Federal Credit Union	Jackson	MI	**B+**	B+	B+	436.1	5.32	3.4	27.2	28.6	12.8	**10.0**	11.1
▼ CPM Federal Credit Union	North Charleston	SC	**A-**	A	A-	324.3	8.90	0.1	21.5	22.6	6.1	**9.8**	10.9
cPort Credit Union	Portland	ME	**B**	B	B-	193.4	7.98	6.8	16.4	45.1	2.0	**7.4**	9.3
Craftmaster Federal Credit Union	Towanda	PA	**C+**	C+	C	10.5	5.77	0.0	46.6	0.0	0.0	**10.0**	17.5
Craig Credit Union	Selma	AL	**C-**	C-	D	12.9	3.68	0.0	23.4	2.8	0.0	**10.0**	12.7
Crane Credit Union	Odon	IN	**A-**	A-	A-	528.7	6.78	8.8	27.1	33.1	19.2	**10.0**	13.4
Cranston Municipal Employees CU	Cranston	RI	**C-**	C-	C	58.8	2.38	0.0	9.0	3.1	36.5	**10.0**	19.9
Crayola LLC Employees FCU	Easton	PA	**C**	C	C	8.4	4.80	0.0	6.8	27.9	18.3	**10.0**	16.2
CRCH Employees Federal Credit Union	Roanoke	VA	**C**	C	C	4.8	0.86	0.0	65.9	0.0	0.0	**10.0**	15.1
Credit Human Federal Credit Union	San Antonio	TX	**C+**	C+	B-	2975.7	6.69	0.0	40.6	5.9	0.0	**10.0**	11.6
▼ Credit Union 1	Anchorage	AK	**B+**	A-	A	1003.8	3.50	0.4	40.7	24.3	5.0	**10.0**	11.8
Credit Union 1	Rantoul	IL	**C+**	C+	C+	837.9	6.79	0.5	24.9	21.6	21.8	**6.5**	8.5
▼ Credit Union Advantage	Southfield	MI	**C**	C+	B-	29.3	7.63	0.0	18.3	8.8	56.9	**9.9**	11.0
Credit Union for Robertson County	Springfield	TN	**B**	B	B	52.6	10.12	0.1	42.1	14.9	2.4	**10.0**	11.3
Credit Union of America	Wichita	KS	**A-**	A-	A-	766.2	12.51	2.0	53.6	17.4	1.2	**10.0**	12.3
Credit Union of Atlanta	Atlanta	GA	**B-**	B-	B-	65.9	-4.23	0.0	32.9	1.5	28.1	**8.6**	10.4
▲ Credit Union of Colorado, A FCU	Denver	CO	**B-**	C+	C+	1434.5	8.03	0.4	28.3	21.1	19.8	**8.9**	10.3
Credit Union of Denver	Lakewood	CO	**A**	A	A	722.4	9.33	2.7	31.4	15.8	32.8	**10.0**	11.3
Credit Union of Dodge City	Dodge City	KS	**C-**	C-	C	74.4	5.71	1.1	67.9	2.3	0.3	**6.3**	8.3
Credit Union of Emporia	Emporia	KS	**B-**	B-	B-	23.0	3.34	0.4	30.2	11.9	0.0	**10.0**	12.2
Credit Union of Georgia	Woodstock	GA	**A-**	A-	A-	288.0	9.28	0.4	30.5	10.0	21.0	**7.3**	9.5
Credit Union of Leavenworth County	Lansing	KS	**D-**	D-	D-	7.6	-0.08	0.0	33.0	7.0	0.0	**6.4**	8.5
Credit Union of New Jersey	Ewing	NJ	**C**	C	C	347.0	4.41	10.1	27.8	40.9	0.5	**5.8**	7.8
Credit Union of Ohio	Hilliard	OH	**C-**	C-	C-	149.4	11.10	0.0	23.9	13.5	5.9	**8.0**	9.7
Credit Union Of Richmond Incorporated	Richmond	VA	**B+**	B+	B-	75.5	0.34	0.0	25.3	12.7	29.1	**10.0**	16.4

Asset Quality Index	Non-Performing Loans as a % of Total Loans	Non-Performing Loans as a % of Capital	Net Charge-Offs Avg Loans	Profitability Index	Net Income ($Mil)	Return on Assets	Return on Equity	Net Interest Spread	Overhead Efficiency Ratio	Liquidity Index	Liquidity Ratio	Hot Money Ratio	Stability Index
9.2	0.25	2.1	0.12	**4.5**	2.33	0.70	8.09	2.97	78.9	**4.1**	17.0	4.7	**6.5**
6.2	8.38	9.2	13.38	**1.0**	-0.05	-3.58	-20.10	2.81	72.2	**6.0**	43.0	0.0	**6.3**
9.0	1.08	3.9	0.96	**3.4**	0.39	0.25	1.61	3.97	85.9	**4.4**	20.1	3.1	**8.3**
9.7	0.10	0.4	-0.12	**2.2**	-0.02	-0.49	-3.86	4.59	103.5	**6.3**	49.1	0.0	**7.4**
6.0	0.18	0.5	10.22	**0.0**	-0.09	-12.57	-53.01	6.24	129.8	**5.0**	30.0	0.0	**4.7**
9.8	0.25	1.0	-0.08	**1.8**	0.00	0.08	0.67	2.38	96.8	**5.4**	40.3	0.0	**5.4**
6.8	0.06	1.5	0.22	**5.9**	0.03	0.91	10.07	6.47	87.2	**4.4**	20.3	3.0	**3.7**
3.3	5.91	23.6	0.96	**2.8**	-0.02	-1.31	-12.90	3.69	125.0	**6.9**	58.5	0.0	**2.3**
7.0	0.70	3.7	0.44	**3.1**	0.03	0.24	2.27	3.45	85.9	**3.6**	19.9	10.2	**4.7**
7.2	2.09	8.0	0.26	**2.7**	-0.01	-0.19	-1.64	3.56	101.0	**5.6**	32.1	1.3	**5.9**
9.8	0.70	1.5	1.94	**0.9**	0.01	0.10	0.82	2.69	94.2	**5.2**	39.0	5.1	**4.9**
3.3	2.74	11.9	6.48	**2.5**	-0.03	-6.67	-58.38	7.27	91.7	**6.0**	36.9	0.0	**2.3**
2.8	10.53	25.0	-19.05	**9.5**	0.00	15.38	200.00	0.00	50.0	**7.5**	71.7	0.0	**2.3**
6.6	0.58	9.3	-0.22	**4.2**	0.01	0.43	3.70	4.04	89.4	**4.8**	35.8	0.0	**3.7**
4.7	2.60	12.1	0.03	**9.8**	0.31	1.46	8.13	3.76	60.4	**3.1**	23.2	6.6	**8.9**
7.8	0.63	4.7	0.65	**3.6**	0.07	0.22	3.17	4.09	85.8	**4.9**	25.6	2.2	**4.0**
8.6	0.84	2.3	1.64	**2.7**	0.00	-0.13	-0.82	4.65	80.0	**6.2**	50.9	0.0	**5.4**
6.4	0.48	4.1	0.44	**8.8**	0.20	1.12	13.61	4.80	72.9	**2.5**	24.8	25.6	**4.2**
9.4	0.00	0.0	-0.04	**9.4**	0.14	1.42	8.76	3.48	55.1	**2.3**	19.4	25.7	**8.0**
8.3	0.86	6.0	-0.01	**6.6**	0.43	1.14	8.86	2.70	55.1	**1.9**	13.0	14.1	**9.1**
9.9	0.58	1.7	1.19	**2.2**	-0.01	-0.16	-0.95	3.94	88.2	**5.1**	36.1	0.0	**6.2**
10.0	0.06	0.2	0.31	**2.8**	0.01	0.20	1.64	2.81	93.6	**5.7**	37.3	0.0	**6.6**
10.0	0.48	1.0	0.29	**3.0**	0.23	0.91	9.87	2.44	75.3	**6.3**	38.3	1.0	**4.2**
7.6	0.48	4.1	0.12	**5.4**	0.42	0.74	6.80	3.33	77.8	**3.9**	25.0	6.4	**7.8**
6.5	0.58	5.4	1.82	**3.0**	0.01	0.08	1.05	4.56	80.0	**3.3**	17.7	9.0	**3.5**
9.4	0.02	0.2	-0.02	**3.3**	0.04	0.67	8.29	3.96	86.7	**4.3**	18.4	0.5	**3.5**
8.7	0.34	2.4	0.19	**8.3**	4.15	1.18	10.55	3.01	62.7	**3.2**	11.6	7.5	**9.2**
9.3	0.28	2.0	0.41	**6.5**	0.21	1.39	9.94	3.99	75.5	**3.4**	23.8	6.9	**6.9**
8.3	0.00	0.0	0.00	**6.1**	0.01	1.06	12.96	5.04	82.9	**5.4**	36.4	0.0	**3.0**
5.1	1.20	11.2	0.07	**3.5**	0.27	0.41	4.67	2.86	88.1	**4.1**	18.3	7.5	**5.4**
9.7	0.82	1.6	0.00	**0.0**	-0.01	-0.99	-4.46	2.14	157.1	**5.3**	38.0	0.0	**6.1**
9.6	0.09	0.1	0.39	**5.3**	0.04	0.95	2.80	3.14	56.3	**6.4**	57.1	0.0	**7.3**
3.2	3.57	18.3	0.84	**4.1**	0.01	0.30	2.49	3.17	79.0	**2.3**	20.0	20.1	**5.5**
9.6	0.08	0.2	0.09	**5.0**	0.04	0.85	5.54	3.24	74.3	**6.0**	48.9	0.7	**7.9**
8.9	1.17	2.1	0.22	**7.4**	0.01	1.27	4.49	5.71	59.4	**6.6**	52.6	0.0	**5.0**
7.9	0.61	4.0	0.46	**4.5**	0.59	0.56	5.29	3.92	83.4	**4.4**	21.1	2.3	**6.1**
8.6	1.22	5.8	1.65	**5.7**	0.33	0.42	3.97	3.26	84.9	**5.0**	29.4	5.8	**6.2**
9.3	0.30	2.6	0.14	**5.0**	0.36	0.75	8.07	4.25	81.9	**4.4**	21.6	3.6	**6.1**
6.9	1.34	4.7	0.41	**6.2**	0.03	1.01	5.71	3.64	60.9	**4.9**	45.9	5.9	**5.7**
5.4	7.18	17.2	10.39	**1.5**	0.00	0.03	0.24	6.58	97.3	**7.1**	47.5	0.0	**5.5**
8.9	0.36	2.4	0.20	**5.2**	1.08	0.84	6.19	3.27	72.8	**3.9**	17.8	5.5	**9.5**
10.0	0.19	0.1	-0.09	**1.3**	0.06	0.42	1.93	1.94	80.4	**5.8**	46.3	10.7	**6.7**
10.0	0.00	0.0	-0.74	**3.1**	0.01	0.55	3.27	2.94	80.0	**6.6**	44.7	0.0	**7.2**
4.4	3.37	14.4	3.57	**6.3**	0.01	0.58	3.89	7.07	59.0	**3.9**	16.0	2.6	**3.7**
3.5	2.06	18.2	0.46	**2.4**	1.07	0.15	1.40	3.73	84.5	**1.5**	9.0	18.7	**6.6**
7.1	0.88	5.9	1.30	**4.4**	1.05	0.42	3.57	4.72	75.9	**4.0**	17.3	7.2	**6.9**
6.2	1.32	11.5	0.59	**3.8**	0.96	0.47	5.46	3.28	89.4	**5.4**	33.4	2.8	**5.7**
7.3	1.57	4.5	0.74	**2.5**	0.02	0.24	2.12	2.82	88.4	**5.0**	14.7	2.2	**5.1**
7.8	0.57	4.5	0.50	**5.7**	0.09	0.67	5.88	5.28	85.8	**4.1**	29.3	8.5	**5.9**
6.1	0.76	5.2	0.52	**9.1**	2.28	1.22	9.80	3.74	66.0	**3.0**	16.8	13.0	**9.4**
6.6	1.71	6.1	3.38	**4.3**	0.01	0.06	0.61	5.09	94.2	**6.8**	48.6	3.0	**3.9**
9.9	0.21	1.3	0.41	**4.3**	2.38	0.67	6.44	3.58	80.9	**5.5**	34.0	5.2	**7.1**
8.3	0.82	4.1	0.45	**5.9**	1.59	0.89	7.97	3.09	67.0	**3.4**	12.5	10.3	**8.4**
5.2	0.57	6.6	0.31	**3.5**	0.08	0.42	4.89	4.88	84.8	**3.9**	19.1	7.8	**3.9**
9.7	0.33	1.3	0.07	**5.4**	0.05	0.83	6.75	2.91	72.3	**5.0**	30.8	4.2	**6.9**
9.9	0.12	0.8	0.15	**7.0**	0.61	0.87	9.42	3.68	80.5	**5.2**	22.3	0.7	**6.7**
7.6	1.03	5.6	0.47	**0.0**	-0.02	-0.95	-11.04	3.17	127.4	**4.9**	23.5	0.0	**3.8**
3.6	2.12	24.4	0.94	**3.4**	0.29	0.34	4.37	4.56	83.1	**2.6**	5.3	6.0	**4.4**
8.2	1.15	4.9	0.52	**1.7**	0.00	0.01	0.08	3.26	94.9	**4.9**	28.2	5.2	**5.2**
7.1	2.36	6.8	0.45	**5.0**	0.13	0.72	4.79	3.92	86.1	**6.5**	51.7	0.0	**6.9**

Name	City	State	Rating	2016 Rating	2015 Rating	Total Assets ($Mil)	One Year Asset Growth	Asset Mix (As a % of Total Assets) Commercial Loans	Consumer Loans	Mortgage Loans	Securities	Capitalization Index	Net Worth Ratio
Credit Union of Southern California	Anaheim	CA	A	A	A	1218.9	16.54	9.2	16.1	29.6	34.2	10.0	12.2
Credit Union Of Texas	Dallas	TX	B+	B+	B+	1361.2	4.01	20.5	37.3	14.9	2.0	6.4	8.5
Credit Union of the Berkshires	Pittsfield	MA	D+	D+	C	21.3	0.49	0.0	21.8	1.1	3.6	10.0	13.3
Credit Union of the Rockies	Golden	CO	B	B	B-	96.7	1.96	1.1	24.7	10.8	24.7	10.0	11.3
Credit Union of Vermont	Rutland	VT	B+	B+	B+	44.1	12.50	0.0	22.2	29.4	0.0	10.0	11.1
▼ Credit Union One	Ferndale	MI	B-	B	B	1133.8	6.69	1.1	46.3	15.5	12.9	6.4	8.5
Credit Union One	North Jackson	OH	C	C	C+	12.8	4.72	0.0	20.2	0.0	13.3	10.0	14.4
Credit Union One of the Oklahoma	Oklahoma City	OK	C	C	D	38.4	-2.42	0.0	65.9	0.1	3.8	10.0	11.8
Credit Union South	Gulfport	MS	D-	D-	D+	8.3	-5.26	0.0	45.4	5.3	0.0	8.3	9.9
Credit Union West	Glendale	AZ	B+	B+	B+	659.7	9.84	2.4	44.1	9.3	10.6	9.3	10.6
Creighton Federal Credit Union	Omaha	NE	C	C	C	51.2	-2.03	2.0	12.2	40.6	3.5	8.0	9.6
Crescent Credit Union	Brockton	MA	B	B	B	431.7	0.02	5.9	22.4	41.3	5.0	10.0	14.0
Criers Federal Credit Union	Monroe Township	NJ	C	C	C	1.7	-1.00	0.0	4.8	0.0	0.0	10.0	21.2
CRMC Employee's Credit Union	Douglas	GA	C+	C+	C+	2.5	5.21	0.0	32.5	0.0	0.0	10.0	18.2
Cross Roads Credit Union	Kansas City	MO	C-	C-	C	4.5	-5.01	0.0	47.7	0.0	0.0	10.0	15.4
Cross Valley Federal Credit Union	Wilkes-Barre	PA	C	C	D+	159.9	2.02	3.3	15.7	13.8	31.3	4.5	6.7
Crossroads Community FCU	Cheektowaga	NY	C-	C-	C-	67.3	6.50	0.0	14.6	15.1	11.1	10.0	11.9
Crossroads Credit Union	Goessel	KS	C-	C-	C	9.5	5.51	9.9	27.1	12.6	0.0	10.0	13.5
CrossRoads Financial FCU	Portland	IN	C+	C+	C	55.3	7.78	0.0	28.5	10.4	1.8	5.8	7.8
Crouse Federal Credit Union	Syracuse	NY	C-	C-	C-	17.0	9.78	0.0	34.6	0.0	2.3	8.5	10.0
Crouse Hinds Employees FCU	Syracuse	NY	D-	D-	D-	6.4	3.31	0.0	24.9	0.0	0.0	6.1	8.1
Crow Wing Power Credit Union	Brainerd	MN	C+	C+	C	79.7	4.39	0.0	8.4	44.5	0.0	5.7	7.7
CS Credit Union	Catawba	NC	B-	B-	B-	32.1	5.25	0.7	14.4	16.2	40.0	10.0	12.7
▲ CSD Credit Union	Kansas City	MO	C+	C	C+	41.6	5.67	0.0	17.2	12.6	0.0	10.0	12.5
CSE Federal Credit Union	Lake Charles	LA	B	B	B-	305.1	2.87	7.4	24.3	35.2	6.4	10.0	12.8
CSP Employees Federal Credit Union	Enfield	CT	C-	C-	D+	9.5	8.08	0.0	20.1	0.0	0.0	10.0	14.1
CSX Chicago Terminal Credit Union	Calumet City	IL	C-	C-	C-	4.9	-16.32	0.0	22.4	0.0	0.0	10.0	21.2
CT1 Media Credit Union	Hartford	CT	D+	D+	D	1.4	-8.30	0.0	57.4	0.0	0.0	10.0	18.4
CTA South Federal Credit Union	Chicago	IL	C	C	C-	1.3	6.94	0.0	21.8	0.0	0.0	10.0	34.1
CTECU	Bellaire	TX	D+	D+	D	37.3	-15.34	0.3	13.2	8.7	0.0	10.0	13.6
CU Community Credit Union	Springfield	MO	A+	A+	A	107.0	5.72	12.7	18.4	20.7	15.3	10.0	15.8
CU Hawaii Federal Credit Union	Hilo	HI	B+	B+	C+	277.9	6.34	4.5	21.4	21.7	22.4	10.0	11.7
Cuba Credit Union	Cuba	NM	C+	C+	C+	14.8	7.04	0.1	15.1	20.2	0.0	10.0	14.4
Cumberland County Federal Credit Union	Falmouth	ME	B+	B+	B+	234.8	12.97	0.0	23.7	25.3	24.6	8.7	10.2
Cumberland Municipal Employees FCU	Cumberland Hill	RI	C-	C-	C-	8.0	4.88	0.0	28.5	0.0	0.0	10.0	18.1
Curtis Federal Credit Union	Sandy Hook	CT	C	C	C-	<1	7.65	0.0	10.1	0.0	0.0	10.0	21.1
Cusa Federal Credit Union	Covington	LA	B	B	B-	32.8	2.41	0.2	40.3	29.8	11.3	10.0	11.5
Cutting Edge Federal Credit Union	Milwaukie	OR	C+	C+	C	45.5	10.01	1.1	30.9	19.8	22.6	8.9	10.3
CVPH Employees Federal Credit Union	Plattsburgh	NY	D	D	C-	8.6	-5.18	0.0	58.4	0.0	0.0	7.8	9.5
CWV TEL Federal Credit Union	Clarksburg	WV	C	C	C-	27.5	7.50	0.0	30.8	9.7	0.0	10.0	15.2
Cy-Fair Federal Credit Union	Houston	TX	B-	B-	B-	228.3	3.71	0.1	55.6	17.3	5.6	6.5	8.7
Cyprus Federal Credit Union	West Jordan	UT	A-	A-	A-	828.3	7.63	9.5	50.5	18.8	5.4	10.0	11.0
D'PUC Credit Union	Chicago	IL	D+	D+	D+	4.1	-1.38	0.0	14.8	0.0	0.0	10.0	12.1
Dacotah Federal Credit Union	Rapid City	SD	D	D	D	10.2	1.80	0.0	37.7	7.7	0.0	6.6	8.6
Dade County Federal Credit Union	Sweetwater	FL	B+	B+	B+	729.4	5.89	6.9	39.9	9.0	27.2	9.6	11.2
Daijo Federal Credit Union	Los Angeles	CA	C	C	C-	1.6	-19.38	0.0	16.5	0.0	0.0	10.0	17.6
Dairyland Power Credit Union	La Crosse	WI	B-	B-	B-	14.4	9.59	0.0	29.2	31.5	0.0	10.0	17.2
Dairypak Employees Credit Union	Olmsted Falls	OH	B-	B-	C+	<1	-5.06	0.0	69.3	0.0	0.0	10.0	51.0
Dakota Plains Credit Union	Edgeley	ND	C	C	C+	74.2	8.34	42.0	18.8	36.6	0.0	6.5	8.5
▼ Dakota Plains Federal Credit Union	Lemmon	SD	C	C+	C+	54.8	6.72	29.9	29.3	18.1	0.0	6.7	8.7
Dakota Star Federal Credit Union	Rapid City	SD	C	C	C	24.0	3.72	6.3	34.9	12.1	0.0	8.2	9.8
Dakota Telco Federal Credit Union	Fargo	ND	C	C	C	21.7	1.88	0.0	2.6	0.0	80.6	10.0	11.5
Dakota West Credit Union	Watford City	ND	B	B	B+	248.2	-0.72	47.6	3.8	33.3	27.8	10.0	11.3
Dakotaland Federal Credit Union	Huron	SD	A-	A-	B+	308.8	6.53	20.3	20.8	31.5	4.5	9.2	10.4
Dale Employees Federal Credit Union	Columbus	NE	B+	B+	B+	26.1	2.90	0.2	11.0	16.0	0.0	10.0	20.0
Dallas Federal Credit Union	Dallas	TX	D	D	D	54.6	2.17	1.7	60.2	7.8	0.0	5.7	7.7
Dallas U.P. Employees Credit Union	Dallas	TX	B	B	B-	19.3	8.53	0.0	41.4	0.0	21.5	10.0	24.8
Danbury Cyanamid Employees Credit Union	Danbury	CT	D	D	D	6.6	1.99	0.0	15.0	0.0	0.0	10.0	23.2
Dane County Credit Union	Madison	WI	B-	B-	B-	174.1	12.28	0.6	39.2	20.5	1.9	7.0	9.0
Daniels-Sheridan Federal Credit Union	Scobey	MT	B+	B+	B	54.2	-3.26	27.1	14.2	9.7	2.9	10.0	16.5

Asset Quality Index	Non-Performing Loans as a % of Total Loans	Non-Performing Loans as a % of Capital	Net Charge-Offs Avg Loans	Profitability Index	Net Income ($Mil)	Return on Assets	Return on Equity	Net Interest Spread	Overhead Efficiency Ratio	Liquidity Index	Liquidity Ratio	Hot Money Ratio	Stability Index
9.5	0.47	2.2	0.40	**5.8**	2.64	0.88	8.86	3.27	79.0	**4.3**	11.8	5.7	**8.1**
7.1	0.53	5.7	0.68	**4.7**	0.89	0.26	3.11	4.22	83.6	**3.1**	10.5	9.0	**5.4**
7.2	4.04	8.9	0.43	**0.7**	-0.02	-0.32	-2.39	2.47	106.5	**5.9**	33.8	1.1	**5.7**
9.7	0.19	1.4	0.30	**4.4**	-0.01	-0.04	-0.37	3.45	98.1	**4.6**	19.7	4.3	**5.9**
10.0	0.00	0.0	0.00	**5.7**	0.10	0.90	7.98	2.90	69.9	**4.5**	40.9	7.5	**6.5**
4.9	1.30	10.4	0.79	**3.4**	0.64	0.23	2.71	3.54	77.9	**4.2**	13.7	4.3	**5.6**
10.0	1.32	2.1	0.00	**0.6**	-0.02	-0.65	-4.31	3.52	113.1	**6.4**	43.2	0.0	**6.4**
5.8	1.08	7.0	0.73	**2.6**	0.04	0.39	3.31	3.82	86.9	**4.1**	22.5	0.6	**5.3**
4.5	1.58	8.0	-0.08	**0.1**	-0.03	-1.21	-12.08	7.16	121.3	**6.0**	44.2	0.0	**4.7**
9.3	0.07	0.9	0.32	**4.2**	0.86	0.53	5.47	3.81	83.2	**3.4**	9.7	4.5	**6.8**
4.6	0.39	2.3	0.03	**2.9**	0.02	0.16	1.62	2.90	93.7	**4.2**	29.2	10.9	**4.8**
7.4	0.89	5.2	0.03	**4.6**	0.61	0.57	4.05	2.93	82.4	**2.7**	10.4	8.7	**8.7**
7.7	8.81	6.9	0.00	**2.5**	0.00	0.47	2.25	1.04	50.0	**5.7**	33.8	0.0	**6.8**
9.7	1.20	2.3	0.00	**6.5**	0.01	1.14	6.19	3.53	57.9	**6.0**	48.2	0.0	**5.0**
8.5	0.17	0.6	0.00	**0.3**	-0.01	-1.00	-6.29	3.72	115.6	**5.9**	45.3	0.0	**5.0**
6.3	1.41	8.2	2.80	**3.3**	0.12	0.31	4.66	3.19	80.9	**5.6**	32.4	0.0	**2.3**
10.0	0.56	1.7	0.22	**2.0**	0.04	0.21	1.75	2.41	89.0	**6.1**	44.0	1.5	**6.2**
5.0	4.10	14.2	0.00	**4.3**	0.02	0.76	5.66	3.29	76.8	**5.1**	42.0	0.0	**3.7**
8.9	0.24	2.1	0.21	**5.7**	0.11	0.85	10.59	3.88	81.1	**4.9**	20.6	0.2	**4.2**
7.2	1.06	3.7	0.26	**2.2**	0.01	0.12	1.17	3.00	85.1	**5.8**	37.1	1.7	**4.4**
9.3	0.36	1.7	0.00	**2.6**	0.00	0.13	1.54	2.47	91.2	**5.5**	28.7	0.0	**2.3**
10.0	0.00	0.0	-0.01	**3.6**	0.08	0.40	5.18	2.18	82.7	**4.1**	27.8	6.3	**3.8**
6.5	3.37	10.1	0.16	**4.4**	0.03	0.43	3.41	4.10	84.1	**5.2**	41.7	13.8	**6.2**
10.0	0.38	1.3	0.00	**4.0**	0.09	0.84	6.78	2.67	75.2	**4.8**	24.4	0.0	**6.0**
8.3	0.57	3.2	0.38	**4.8**	0.82	1.10	8.58	3.73	72.4	**4.2**	15.9	2.5	**7.6**
10.0	1.19	1.7	0.00	**1.5**	0.00	-0.09	-0.60	3.03	104.0	**6.0**	32.1	0.0	**6.8**
7.4	8.42	8.8	0.00	**4.2**	0.01	0.70	3.02	3.29	79.1	**5.3**	43.3	0.0	**5.9**
2.2	9.05	27.7	0.00	**0.9**	0.00	-0.57	-3.03	3.86	142.9	**6.4**	47.6	0.0	**6.6**
3.5	9.20	19.2	4.43	**5.7**	0.00	0.63	1.84	10.33	92.9	**5.0**	31.8	0.0	**7.8**
10.0	0.40	0.7	0.00	**1.1**	0.00	-0.01	-0.08	2.01	98.9	**4.6**	27.0	6.5	**5.8**
9.4	0.13	0.4	0.86	**8.0**	0.24	0.90	5.84	4.09	67.9	**6.1**	36.0	3.3	**9.7**
9.2	0.53	2.7	-0.02	**3.4**	0.28	0.41	3.46	3.14	84.9	**5.0**	28.3	4.0	**8.1**
6.1	1.91	10.1	0.12	**3.7**	0.01	0.35	2.46	3.50	85.7	**6.0**	52.6	5.2	**7.5**
8.5	0.56	3.2	0.24	**5.0**	0.33	0.57	5.49	2.95	79.8	**4.2**	24.8	9.1	**7.3**
8.8	1.65	2.7	2.27	**1.5**	-0.01	-0.49	-2.77	2.85	79.6	**3.3**	37.6	43.0	**6.8**
9.0	5.97	4.4	0.00	**1.7**	0.00	0.00	0.00	2.58	100.0	**7.2**	74.8	0.0	**6.2**
6.4	0.74	5.0	0.35	**7.0**	0.08	0.95	8.26	3.86	71.9	**3.3**	10.9	7.2	**6.3**
6.3	0.73	4.6	0.10	**3.7**	0.06	0.53	5.09	3.69	85.8	**4.3**	17.8	2.1	**4.7**
8.2	0.00	0.0	0.07	**1.2**	0.00	-0.14	-1.47	3.07	100.0	**5.6**	33.5	0.0	**3.3**
9.9	0.24	0.7	0.46	**2.5**	0.02	0.31	2.02	2.95	81.3	**5.3**	26.4	0.0	**6.7**
5.8	0.87	8.8	0.51	**4.5**	0.21	0.37	4.29	4.32	86.5	**3.7**	9.5	1.5	**4.9**
7.6	0.15	1.4	0.40	**7.1**	1.98	0.98	9.22	3.50	74.1	**3.4**	14.9	8.1	**8.6**
8.1	4.98	6.2	0.00	**0.7**	0.00	-0.30	-2.43	4.13	106.5	**7.7**	75.7	0.0	**6.0**
6.3	0.65	5.9	-0.19	**1.6**	-0.01	-0.35	-4.08	5.94	109.3	**4.4**	24.0	7.3	**3.3**
9.3	0.40	2.3	0.59	**4.2**	1.09	0.62	6.11	4.32	83.6	**4.3**	11.8	3.1	**6.8**
8.8	3.95	3.9	-3.67	**2.9**	0.00	0.00	0.00	4.42	300.0	**8.4**	99.2	0.0	**5.0**
9.5	0.46	1.8	0.00	**5.9**	0.03	0.90	5.20	3.70	75.6	**4.9**	32.4	1.1	**7.9**
7.9	2.88	3.5	0.00	**6.7**	0.00	0.00	0.00	9.68	100.0	**6.1**	73.5	0.0	**5.0**
5.4	0.31	3.3	0.09	**4.3**	0.07	0.37	4.35	3.98	87.1	**2.5**	20.8	21.7	**4.3**
8.0	0.06	1.4	0.15	**2.6**	0.00	0.00	0.00	4.20	96.4	**3.4**	9.6	5.6	**4.9**
6.6	0.30	3.2	0.17	**5.1**	0.03	0.44	4.45	4.25	90.6	**3.8**	20.1	2.2	**4.3**
10.0	0.00	0.0	0.00	**2.4**	0.01	0.24	2.10	1.16	74.5	**6.8**	54.0	0.0	**5.5**
3.3	1.55	14.3	0.00	**8.5**	0.74	1.19	11.02	4.06	70.8	**4.1**	14.9	6.2	**8.4**
6.5	0.78	6.9	0.41	**6.0**	0.46	0.60	5.89	3.49	85.3	**4.0**	19.1	6.7	**8.1**
10.0	0.00	0.0	0.14	**3.0**	0.01	0.14	0.69	2.02	93.2	**5.7**	37.9	4.5	**7.2**
4.8	0.90	8.1	0.99	**1.5**	0.01	0.04	0.48	4.11	87.0	**3.7**	15.2	0.2	**2.6**
9.3	1.94	3.2	0.10	**5.1**	0.02	0.32	1.26	4.14	66.4	**5.2**	31.5	0.0	**7.3**
7.7	8.86	6.4	0.00	**0.0**	-0.02	-1.30	-5.47	2.53	135.0	**6.0**	38.2	0.0	**5.3**
6.0	1.47	12.3	0.29	**4.6**	0.30	0.71	7.77	4.39	80.0	**3.2**	9.0	5.0	**5.5**
5.6	3.29	10.0	-0.10	**3.8**	0.05	0.36	2.19	3.12	95.2	**5.5**	43.3	2.0	**7.5**

Name	City	State	Rating	2016 Rating	2015 Rating	Total Assets ($Mil)	One Year Asset Growth	Asset Mix (As a % of Total Assets) Commercial Loans	Consumer Loans	Mortgage Loans	Securities	Capitalization Index	Net Worth Ratio
Dannemora Federal Credit Union	Plattsburgh	NY	B+	B+	A-	173.0	8.51	0.3	21.2	17.8	29.8	10.0	12.5
Danvers Municipal Federal Credit Union	Danvers	MA	C-	C-	C-	7.9	4.98	0.0	38.0	0.0	0.0	10.0	34.4
Danville City Employees FCU	Danville	VA	D+	D+	D+	25.0	2.04	0.0	18.2	7.9	0.0	10.0	21.3
DATCU Credit Union	Corinth	TX	A	A	A	908.9	8.85	0.3	57.9	14.1	0.9	10.0	14.3
Davenport Police Department Credit Union	Davenport	IA	C	C	C	4.3	1.14	0.0	11.1	14.6	47.4	10.0	13.3
Daviess County Teachers FCU	Owensboro	KY	C	C	C	43.8	7.79	0.0	32.0	26.6	0.0	7.9	9.6
Davison Employees Federal Credit Union	Sulphur	LA	D	D	D	2.9	-0.10	0.0	58.9	0.0	0.0	10.0	25.5
Dawson Co-op Credit Union	Dawson	MN	B	B	B	152.5	8.24	62.0	8.8	29.3	0.7	10.0	15.6
Day Air Credit Union	Kettering	OH	A	A	A	353.3	6.59	6.7	51.9	16.6	14.3	10.0	13.2
Day-Met Credit Union, Inc.	Dayton	OH	D+	D+	C-	90.9	3.90	8.2	45.3	27.1	8.2	8.2	9.8
Dayton Firefighters Federal Credit Union	Dayton	OH	B-	B-	B-	58.2	9.45	4.1	35.3	14.3	14.3	8.6	10.2
DC Federal Credit Union	Washington	DC	B-	B-	B-	58.0	2.50	6.4	42.9	16.8	16.8	7.9	9.7
DCH Credit Union	Tuscaloosa	AL	C+	C+	C+	30.9	2.14	0.0	26.0	8.0	28.7	10.0	13.0
De Soto Mo-Pac Credit Union	De Soto	MO	C+	C+	C+	15.4	9.52	0.0	54.5	0.9	0.0	8.8	10.2
Dearborn County Hospital FCU	Lawrenceburg	IN	C	C	C-	15.7	3.03	0.0	25.7	0.0	0.0	8.9	10.2
Deca Credit Union	Cincinnati	OH	C-	C-	C-	5.4	8.74	0.0	41.5	0.0	0.0	10.0	18.7
Decatur Earthmover Credit Union	Forsyth	IL	D+	D+	C-	270.7	-1.65	0.0	27.7	15.9	29.1	9.0	10.5
Decatur Medical Dental Credit Union	Decatur	IL	C-	C-	C-	13.5	1.18	0.0	46.1	0.0	29.1	8.6	10.1
Decatur Policemen Credit Union	Decatur	IL	C-	C-	C-	4.5	4.84	0.0	70.5	0.0	0.0	10.0	12.9
▼ Decatur Postal Credit Union	Decatur	IL	C-	C	C	8.9	-4.53	0.0	22.9	0.0	0.0	10.0	12.8
Decatur Stanolind Credit Union	Decatur	IL	D	D	D	3.1	-11.45	0.0	17.8	0.0	0.1	10.0	20.6
Dedham Town Employees FCU	Dedham	MA	D+	D+	D+	8.6	2.95	0.0	41.4	0.0	0.0	10.0	11.9
Deepwater Industries FCU	Deepwater	NJ	D	D	D	89.5	2.23	0.0	16.3	16.1	12.1	6.3	8.3
Deer Lodge County School Employees FCU	Anaconda	MT	D+	D+	D+	5.4	9.69	0.0	22.8	0.0	0.0	6.4	8.4
Deer River Cooperative Credit Union	Deer River	MN	C+	C+	C-	18.1	8.04	0.0	14.9	32.4	0.0	8.0	9.7
Deer Valley Credit Union	Phoenix	AZ	C+	C+	C+	229.3	2.93	0.0	38.5	20.5	17.7	6.6	8.7
Deere Employees Credit Union	Moline	IL	B+	B+	B+	851.5	8.98	0.0	29.0	46.9	0.0	6.2	8.2
Defense Logistics Federal Credit Union	Picatinny Arsenal	NJ	E+	E+	E+	<1	-10.37	0.0	62.2	0.0	16.9	5.8	7.8
Dekalb County Credit Union	Dekalb	IL	E+	E+	D-	6.2	2.12	0.0	32.2	0.0	0.0	5.6	7.6
Del Met Federal Credit Union	Muncie	IN	C-	C-	C-	10.2	2.89	0.0	19.0	0.0	0.0	10.0	15.0
Del Norte Credit Union	Santa Fe	NM	B+	B+	B+	576.5	8.33	0.0	47.4	12.8	7.2	10.0	11.1
Del Rio S.P. Credit Union	Del Rio	TX	D	D	D	4.4	-21.16	0.0	15.1	0.0	0.0	10.0	34.8
Del-One Federal Credit Union	Dover	DE	B	B	B	442.0	15.98	1.8	48.7	23.0	2.7	7.7	9.5
Delancey Street Federal Credit Union	San Francisco	CA	C-	C-	D+	<1	25.95	0.0	0.0	0.0	71.9	10.0	32.7
Delaware Alliance Federal Credit Union	New Castle	DE	C+	C+	C+	21.9	1.58	0.0	22.7	4.9	0.0	10.0	13.9
Delaware River & Bay Authority Empls FCU	New Castle	DE	C	C	C	6.3	-3.11	0.0	0.0	0.0	6.3	10.0	12.9
▼ Delaware State Police FCU	Georgetown	DE	C+	B-	C+	126.0	3.61	0.2	17.8	15.8	40.4	8.5	10.2
Delco Postal Credit Union	Upper Darby	PA	D-	D-	E+	14.9	2.64	0.0	14.5	27.1	0.0	5.3	7.3
Delmar OCF Federal Credit Union	Feura Bush	NY	D	D	D	1.1	-9.12	0.0	22.1	0.0	0.0	10.0	11.7
Delmarva Power Southern Division FCU	Salisbury	MD	B-	B-	B-	17.2	3.11	0.0	14.9	1.4	0.0	10.0	18.7
Delta Community Credit Union	Atlanta	GA	A	A	A-	5544.2	7.50	2.7	39.7	33.7	13.2	10.0	11.4
Delta County Credit Union	Escanaba	MI	B	B	B	133.2	5.43	0.6	23.4	21.1	30.5	8.9	10.4
Delta County Federal Credit Union	Delta	CO	C+	C+	C+	54.5	11.27	0.6	6.3	20.3	0.0	6.5	8.5
Delta Credit Union	Greenville	MS	C	C	C-	5.6	4.96	0.0	38.5	0.0	0.0	10.0	22.8
Delta Refining Company Employees FCU	Memphis	TN	C	C	C	4.6	-5.37	0.0	33.2	0.0	0.0	10.0	18.2
Delta Schools Federal Credit Union	Antioch	CA	C+	C+	C+	39.3	11.22	0.1	17.7	11.7	0.3	6.9	8.9
Deming Schools Employees Credit Union	Deming	NM	C	C	C	4.8	1.77	0.0	49.2	0.0	0.0	10.0	18.8
Democracy Federal Credit Union	Alexandria	VA	C-	C-	D+	155.6	-0.84	4.6	23.3	22.7	24.3	8.6	10.4
▲ Democrat P&L Federal Credit Union	Little Rock	AR	C	C-	C-	1.9	-2.00	0.0	51.2	0.0	0.0	10.0	19.3
Demopolis Federal Credit Union	Demopolis	AL	E+	E+	E+	<1	9.65	0.0	61.1	0.0	0.0	5.4	7.4
Denali Federal Credit Union	Anchorage	AK	B-	B-	B-	659.9	7.53	6.3	66.1	11.2	0.9	6.0	8.0
Dennison Federal Credit Union	Coopersville	MI	D	D	D+	<1	-35.86	0.0	62.0	0.0	0.0	10.0	19.2
Denocos Federal Credit Union	Crescent City	CA	D	D	D	6.7	-3.37	0.0	16.7	0.0	0.0	7.4	9.3
Denver Community Credit Union	Denver	CO	B+	B+	A-	315.1	6.55	9.2	24.9	17.8	15.6	10.0	12.9
Denver Fire Department FCU	Denver	CO	B-	B-	C+	146.6	0.93	4.7	8.4	30.6	35.7	10.0	12.4
Department of Commerce FCU	Washington	DC	C+	C+	B-	437.3	18.17	0.0	13.5	35.1	39.8	6.4	8.4
▲ Department of Corrections Credit Union	Baton Rouge	LA	A	A-	A-	81.5	1.10	0.0	39.8	14.3	0.6	10.0	17.5
Department of Labor Federal Credit Union	Washington	DC	A-	A-	B+	87.1	-0.13	0.0	22.6	26.3	31.0	10.0	12.7
Department of Public Safety FCU	Oklahoma City	OK	C-	C-	C-	27.2	0.99	0.0	30.7	0.0	0.6	10.0	17.4
Department of the Interior FCU	Washington	DC	C+	C+	C+	179.1	6.01	6.9	26.0	38.2	9.1	9.1	10.5

Arrows denote recent upgrades ▲ or downgrades ▼

Asset Quality Index	Non-Performing Loans as a % of Total Loans	Non-Performing Loans as a % of Capital	Net Charge-Offs Avg Loans	Profitability Index	Net Income ($Mil)	Return on Assets	Return on Equity	Net Interest Spread	Overhead Efficiency Ratio	Liquidity Index	Liquidity Ratio	Hot Money Ratio	Stability Index
9.4	0.42	2.6	0.05	**4.7**	0.23	0.54	4.32	3.51	85.5	**5.1**	19.6	0.5	**8.4**
9.8	0.00	0.0	0.00	**2.0**	0.01	0.26	0.74	2.16	87.5	**4.8**	34.5	0.0	**7.1**
10.0	0.04	0.1	0.05	**1.3**	0.00	-0.03	-0.15	2.53	100.6	**5.9**	43.1	2.6	**6.3**
7.4	0.38	3.0	0.33	**7.9**	2.86	1.27	8.90	3.46	63.2	**3.2**	10.3	5.1	**9.1**
9.9	0.00	0.0	0.00	**2.8**	0.00	0.28	2.11	2.48	88.5	**5.1**	34.7	0.0	**7.2**
9.8	0.10	0.7	0.00	**3.1**	0.06	0.51	5.28	3.48	84.8	**5.0**	26.9	0.5	**4.8**
8.4	0.22	0.5	0.00	**0.0**	-0.01	-1.38	-5.32	5.94	134.5	**6.2**	49.3	0.0	**6.3**
3.8	1.63	7.5	-0.10	**9.5**	0.72	1.87	12.19	3.34	42.2	**3.3**	21.1	6.3	**10.0**
6.3	0.74	4.9	0.36	**7.9**	0.84	0.97	7.63	3.34	71.1	**3.2**	8.6	4.7	**9.2**
5.1	0.97	7.3	0.33	**1.6**	0.06	0.26	2.70	3.48	86.8	**3.0**	14.8	8.4	**4.2**
6.9	0.70	4.4	0.41	**4.1**	0.08	0.54	5.24	3.22	77.5	**3.6**	25.0	12.9	**5.4**
5.2	1.40	10.5	1.25	**7.3**	0.25	1.80	20.62	5.95	66.7	**4.1**	20.0	8.8	**4.7**
7.2	2.10	7.6	0.25	**4.3**	0.07	0.89	6.92	3.65	84.1	**4.6**	37.7	17.7	**5.4**
5.2	0.70	5.1	0.00	**8.7**	0.05	1.40	13.75	3.16	63.4	**4.0**	16.3	0.0	**5.0**
10.0	0.00	0.0	-0.08	**2.7**	0.01	0.21	2.00	2.47	93.1	**5.6**	30.5	0.0	**5.2**
8.6	1.99	5.0	0.32	**1.8**	0.00	0.15	0.79	3.02	97.0	**6.1**	53.6	0.0	**6.7**
7.7	1.04	5.3	0.99	**1.3**	0.04	0.06	0.67	3.18	86.7	**5.0**	25.3	5.1	**4.6**
6.0	1.12	5.3	0.00	**2.9**	0.01	0.39	3.85	2.83	78.0	**5.2**	29.0	0.0	**4.9**
6.4	1.18	6.5	0.00	**2.8**	0.00	0.27	2.08	1.48	78.6	**4.8**	26.2	0.0	**6.5**
10.0	0.74	1.3	-0.19	**1.4**	-0.02	-0.99	-7.71	2.41	83.0	**6.3**	56.1	0.0	**5.7**
10.0	1.71	1.5	0.00	**0.0**	-0.02	-2.29	-11.18	1.49	272.7	**6.6**	65.0	0.0	**6.1**
8.2	1.27	4.3	-0.23	**1.2**	-0.01	-0.57	-4.67	4.24	96.3	**3.9**	21.7	16.8	**4.7**
5.8	1.55	9.2	0.80	**0.7**	-0.08	-0.37	-5.07	3.59	108.4	**4.9**	20.8	4.7	**2.5**
9.9	0.00	0.0	0.00	**3.4**	0.01	0.37	4.40	2.73	85.3	**5.7**	30.8	0.0	**3.0**
8.5	0.11	0.7	-0.07	**4.1**	0.03	0.58	6.00	3.86	84.7	**5.0**	32.0	0.0	**5.2**
8.6	0.42	3.1	0.34	**3.4**	0.15	0.26	3.00	3.52	88.6	**4.2**	12.5	2.2	**5.5**
9.7	0.14	1.5	0.21	**5.8**	2.08	0.99	12.15	2.45	70.5	**3.2**	15.0	8.2	**6.3**
5.4	1.19	9.7	0.00	**3.5**	0.00	0.48	6.06	4.86	100.0	**4.4**	12.6	0.0	**1.7**
9.9	0.00	0.0	-0.14	**0.3**	0.00	-0.19	-2.55	2.66	108.0	**5.4**	25.0	0.0	**2.5**
8.4	2.87	4.2	1.77	**1.1**	-0.01	-0.43	-2.88	1.81	108.5	**5.4**	29.8	0.0	**6.6**
7.7	0.36	2.5	0.62	**4.4**	0.61	0.43	3.79	3.69	77.2	**4.9**	27.8	7.1	**7.9**
10.0	1.92	0.9	0.00	**0.0**	-0.01	-1.09	-3.10	2.83	124.1	**5.4**	30.7	0.0	**6.2**
5.8	0.68	6.4	0.82	**5.2**	0.64	0.59	6.68	4.07	76.2	**3.2**	14.3	8.6	**5.6**
10.0	0.00	0.0	0.00	**1.5**	0.00	0.00	0.00	1.37	100.0	**7.8**	76.9	0.0	**6.3**
9.2	0.10	0.2	-0.22	**2.2**	0.01	0.09	0.66	3.43	97.8	**5.6**	25.8	0.0	**6.6**
10.0	0.43	0.2	-0.85	**4.5**	0.01	0.51	3.94	1.38	63.2	**5.6**	22.4	0.0	**4.3**
5.7	3.49	16.9	1.18	**2.9**	0.03	0.09	0.98	3.22	84.8	**5.0**	30.4	5.5	**5.7**
6.0	0.90	10.4	0.18	**3.0**	0.02	0.54	7.38	5.49	87.0	**6.1**	39.1	0.0	**1.7**
9.5	0.78	1.6	16.00	**0.0**	-0.01	-2.65	-21.88	2.75	240.0	**6.7**	42.0	0.0	**6.2**
9.3	3.63	3.6	-0.25	**3.7**	0.02	0.35	1.87	1.82	80.0	**5.8**	35.7	0.0	**6.9**
8.8	0.36	2.8	0.60	**5.9**	9.02	0.67	5.80	3.31	69.1	**3.5**	10.1	2.0	**9.1**
7.0	1.31	7.8	0.31	**4.2**	0.18	0.55	5.29	3.45	79.1	**3.9**	20.5	10.2	**6.9**
8.8	0.03	0.1	-0.02	**3.2**	0.05	0.36	4.19	2.79	85.1	**5.3**	25.9	4.2	**3.9**
7.3	3.33	5.9	1.84	**2.0**	-0.01	-0.58	-2.50	4.32	97.1	**5.4**	47.5	0.0	**7.2**
9.9	0.00	0.0	-0.24	**3.5**	0.01	0.44	2.40	2.17	83.3	**5.3**	62.0	2.7	**7.4**
10.0	0.22	0.9	0.20	**3.0**	0.03	0.26	2.88	3.01	93.1	**5.2**	32.6	1.1	**3.6**
7.0	2.30	6.2	-0.31	**7.3**	0.02	1.84	9.93	4.90	59.3	**4.9**	44.8	0.0	**5.0**
7.5	1.26	6.3	0.95	**2.1**	0.02	0.04	0.43	3.89	91.8	**4.2**	19.0	8.8	**5.4**
8.4	0.19	0.6	-0.37	**4.0**	0.00	0.86	4.48	3.66	100.0	**3.9**	43.6	8.5	**7.3**
0.7	5.46	41.2	3.04	**1.7**	0.00	0.00	0.00	12.93	90.9	**5.8**	36.5	0.0	**2.8**
3.9	1.16	13.9	1.83	**4.2**	1.08	0.66	8.33	5.72	69.0	**3.1**	8.6	5.1	**4.7**
0.7	15.54	44.8	0.00	**6.2**	0.00	1.31	6.78	4.63	100.0	**5.8**	48.6	0.0	**7.2**
7.6	2.01	3.7	0.00	**0.8**	0.00	-0.25	-2.58	2.06	106.3	**5.6**	44.5	0.0	**3.4**
9.8	0.03	0.3	0.48	**3.5**	0.34	0.43	3.34	3.26	81.4	**4.6**	34.1	9.0	**7.4**
9.9	0.02	0.1	0.01	**5.4**	1.67	4.62	41.09	2.28	25.6	**4.4**	20.4	5.2	**7.6**
9.5	0.41	2.4	0.48	**3.4**	0.35	0.32	3.61	2.84	82.5	**4.2**	64.6	13.6	**5.0**
9.3	0.71	2.4	0.37	**8.8**	0.29	1.44	8.16	5.87	79.7	**5.6**	45.6	4.3	**7.5**
7.7	1.59	6.3	1.38	**6.5**	0.14	0.64	5.13	3.88	79.4	**4.4**	18.7	2.5	**5.8**
9.9	0.38	0.7	0.39	**0.3**	0.00	-0.01	-0.08	2.46	96.0	**5.2**	33.0	5.6	**6.2**
8.1	0.43	4.0	0.34	**3.1**	0.11	0.24	2.39	3.62	87.7	**3.8**	23.2	5.3	**6.2**

Name	City	State	Rating	2016 Rating	2015 Rating	Total Assets ($Mil)	One Year Asset Growth	Asset Mix (As a % of Total Assets)				Capital-ization Index	Net Worth Ratio
								Comm-ercial Loans	Cons-umer Loans	Mort-gage Loans	Secur-ities		
Derry Area Federal Credit Union	Derry	PA	C-	C-	C-	9.6	10.14	0.0	41.3	11.0	0.0	10.0	12.6
Dertown School Federal Credit Union	Latrobe	PA	C	C	C	8.8	5.03	0.0	37.0	27.8	25.7	10.0	33.7
Des Moines County Postal Credit Union	Burlington	IA	C-	C-	C-	2.4	0.59	0.0	68.7	0.0	19.9	10.0	20.1
Des Moines Fire Department Credit Union	Des Moines	IA	C-	C-	C-	4.7	-6.72	0.0	68.5	0.0	0.0	10.0	17.7
Des Moines Metro Credit Union	Des Moines	IA	C+	C+	C+	52.6	0.54	4.3	18.8	18.5	0.0	10.0	12.0
Des Moines Police Officers Credit Union	Des Moines	IA	A-	A-	A-	68.5	30.86	1.6	32.2	17.5	12.2	10.0	13.7
Des Moines Water Works Credit Union	Des Moines	IA	D	D	D	1.5	-8.26	0.0	54.2	0.0	0.0	10.0	12.1
Desco Federal Credit Union	Portsmouth	OH	B-	B-	B-	291.6	3.55	15.0	11.3	39.8	20.1	9.0	10.6
Deseret First Federal Credit Union	Salt Lake City	UT	C+	C+	C+	591.5	9.10	4.3	32.0	24.3	12.8	4.6	6.7
Desert Communities Federal Credit Union	Needles	CA	E	E	E+	27.6	12.47	0.0	19.9	4.1	5.6	3.9	5.9
Desert Sage Federal Credit Union	Nampa	ID	D+	D+	C-	1.3	-10.74	0.0	55.3	0.0	0.0	10.0	16.6
Desert Schools Federal Credit Union	Phoenix	AZ	A	A	A	4253.2	6.56	4.8	16.9	17.2	47.2	10.0	11.7
Desert Valleys Federal Credit Union	Ridgecrest	CA	D	D	D	35.1	18.07	0.8	39.1	4.9	0.0	3.6	5.6
Desertview Federal Credit Union	Huntington	UT	B-	B-	B-	33.5	0.83	1.1	26.9	12.6	36.5	10.0	12.2
Destinations Credit Union	Baltimore	MD	C-	C-	D+	61.3	-0.12	0.0	33.6	7.9	22.4	10.0	13.0
▲ Detour Drummond Community Credit Union	Drummond Island	MI	B	B-	C+	32.5	1.61	0.9	11.0	36.9	32.5	10.0	12.3
Devils Slide Federal Credit Union	Morgan	UT	B-	B-	C+	11.4	6.87	0.0	45.6	0.0	0.0	10.0	13.6
DEXSTA Federal Credit Union	Wilmington	DE	B-	B-	B-	283.7	10.51	0.0	47.3	2.4	22.2	6.5	8.7
Dexter Public Schools Credit Union	Dexter	MO	D-	D-	D	4.5	-0.60	0.0	36.0	0.0	0.0	7.6	9.4
DFCU Financial	Dearborn	MI	A-	A-	A-	4552.2	7.98	0.7	4.7	13.2	67.6	8.9	11.0
Diablo Valley Federal Credit Union	Concord	CA	C+	C+	C-	37.7	3.94	6.3	18.3	28.6	1.9	6.0	8.1
▼ Dial Credit Union	Montgomery	IL	D-	D	C-	9.9	1.89	0.0	22.1	0.0	20.2	9.2	11.6
Diamond Credit Union	Pottstown	PA	B+	B+	A-	573.8	11.22	3.0	45.8	17.6	4.9	8.5	10.0
Diamond Lakes Federal Credit Union	Malvern	AR	C+	C+	C-	70.7	0.90	0.1	50.1	7.7	0.4	9.8	10.9
▲ Diamond Valley Federal Credit Union	Evansville	IN	C+	C	D+	142.8	3.21	0.0	27.1	16.8	0.3	7.6	9.4
Diebold Federal Credit Union	North Canton	OH	D	D	C-	21.5	16.85	2.6	45.6	18.3	0.0	5.4	7.4
Digital Federal Credit Union	Marlborough	MA	A-	A-	A-	7983.9	11.89	10.3	36.5	29.4	2.4	7.1	9.1
Dill Federal Credit Union	Roxboro	NC	D	D	D	1.1	2.79	0.0	39.4	0.0	0.0	10.0	39.8
Dillard's Federal Credit Union	Little Rock	AR	D-	D-	D-	27.0	-1.58	0.5	30.7	10.9	2.3	7.2	9.2
Dillon Credit Union	Hutchinson	KS	B-	B-	C+	39.4	1.43	0.0	36.3	24.4	0.0	10.0	15.3
Dillonvale Federal Credit Union	Dillonvale	OH	D	D	D	1.1	-1.50	0.0	47.1	0.0	0.0	10.0	29.3
Direct Federal Credit Union	Needham	MA	B+	B+	A	555.7	12.59	0.0	23.9	34.1	0.4	10.0	13.7
Directions Credit Union	Sylvania	OH	C+	C+	C+	705.3	6.45	17.4	29.2	30.0	4.2	5.9	8.0
Directors Choice Credit Union	Albany	NY	C	C	C+	8.9	20.98	38.1	11.9	1.7	0.0	10.0	14.7
Discovery Federal Credit Union	Wyomissing	PA	B-	B-	C+	133.3	2.37	9.7	15.9	5.0	34.7	10.0	11.2
District #6 Federal Credit Union	Hornell	NY	D	D	D	17.5	-0.53	0.0	25.5	0.0	0.0	7.3	9.2
District 05 DOTD Federal Credit Union	Monroe	LA	D+	D+	C-	7.9	-0.69	0.0	30.5	8.0	0.0	10.0	18.8
District 08 Federal Credit Union	Alexandria	LA	D-	D-	E+	7.8	-2.69	0.0	27.6	12.4	0.0	6.1	8.1
District 123 Federal Credit Union	Oak Lawn	IL	C+	C+	C+	3.2	-1.66	0.0	13.8	0.0	0.0	10.0	19.6
▲ District 58 Federal Credit Union	Chase	LA	C-	D+	C-	5.4	3.84	0.0	49.9	0.0	0.0	10.0	14.1
District 62 Highway Federal Credit Union	Hammond	LA	C	C	C+	5.2	6.81	0.0	59.8	2.1	0.0	10.0	16.8
District 8 Highway Employees CU	Springfield	MO	B-	B-	B-	17.0	2.95	0.0	31.7	4.3	0.0	10.0	15.4
District Of Columbia Fire Department FCU	Washington	DC	C-	C-	C-	7.5	1.30	0.0	38.4	0.0	0.0	10.0	16.0
▲ District of Columbia Teachers FCU	Washington	DC	B	B-	B-	46.9	2.87	0.0	16.1	10.4	42.0	10.0	12.1
District One Highway Credit Union	Saint Joseph	MO	B	B	B-	26.8	3.56	0.0	18.7	0.0	0.0	10.0	13.6
▼ Diversified Credit Union	Minneapolis	MN	C	C+	C+	36.5	11.89	1.5	25.3	4.0	0.0	7.7	9.5
Diversified General Federal Credit Union	Logansport	IN	C-	C-	C-	9.5	4.19	0.0	52.6	0.0	0.0	8.0	9.6
Diversified Members Credit Union	Detroit	MI	B-	B-	B-	426.6	-0.36	13.4	8.8	16.6	53.5	10.0	19.2
Division #6 Highway Credit Union	Chesterfield	MO	C-	C-	C-	14.1	1.84	0.0	28.4	15.5	0.0	10.0	16.0
▼ Division 10 Highway Employees' CU	Sikeston	MO	C	C+	C	11.4	-4.29	0.0	31.9	0.0	0.0	10.0	23.5
Division 726 Federal Credit Union	Staten Island	NY	C+	C+	C-	10.6	4.01	0.4	65.6	0.0	0.0	10.0	14.3
Division 819 Transit Employees CU	Irvington	NJ	C+	C+	C-	19.7	-1.83	0.0	22.9	0.0	63.8	9.8	11.0
Dixie Craft Employees Credit Union	Goodwater	AL	D+	D+	D+	2.5	1.83	0.0	47.7	1.8	0.0	10.0	14.6
▲ Dixie Line Credit Union	Nashville	TN	B-	C+	C	10.4	8.16	0.0	63.9	0.0	0.0	10.0	17.8
Dixies Federal Credit Union	Darlington	SC	B	B	B	42.9	1.86	1.1	32.9	24.9	0.0	10.0	19.6
Doches Credit Union	Nacogdoches	TX	B-	B-	B-	44.1	5.39	0.1	37.4	6.3	0.0	10.0	12.6
▼ DOCO Credit Union	Albany	GA	B-	B	B	231.7	3.48	7.4	40.0	14.9	3.3	8.8	10.2
▲ Doe Run Federal Credit Union	Brandenburg	KY	C	C-	D+	10.2	5.18	0.0	52.2	5.7	0.0	10.0	11.1
Dominion Credit Union	Richmond	VA	B	B	B-	293.8	8.37	0.0	24.7	19.8	47.5	9.9	11.1
Domino Federal Credit Union	Texarkana	TX	B	B	B	60.3	3.57	0.0	35.7	21.6	0.0	10.0	14.0

Asset Quality Index	Non-Performing Loans as a % of Total Loans	Non-Performing Loans as a % of Capital	Net Charge-Offs Avg Loans	Profitability Index	Net Income ($Mil)	Return on Assets	Return on Equity	Net Interest Spread	Overhead Efficiency Ratio	Liquidity Index	Liquidity Ratio	Hot Money Ratio	Stability Index
9.2	0.16	0.6	0.00	2.0	0.01	0.21	1.67	3.43	90.9	5.5	47.9	1.7	6.4
9.6	0.00	0.0	0.00	5.3	0.02	0.92	2.73	2.72	64.3	3.8	12.0	1.8	5.0
8.5	0.12	0.4	0.00	2.8	0.00	0.67	3.37	3.79	81.0	4.0	29.4	0.0	6.9
8.5	0.25	1.1	0.00	2.3	0.00	0.34	1.93	3.11	85.7	3.8	29.8	0.0	6.8
7.9	0.37	4.5	0.29	3.0	0.04	0.33	2.73	2.99	87.4	5.4	34.5	0.9	6.0
9.7	0.26	1.2	0.00	5.1	0.05	0.29	2.06	3.34	91.6	4.5	22.9	1.9	7.7
3.6	2.96	14.9	1.89	2.8	0.00	0.26	2.16	4.34	91.7	5.6	35.6	0.0	5.9
7.7	0.80	6.3	0.18	3.4	0.23	0.30	3.45	3.10	89.6	4.3	26.9	7.8	6.3
7.0	0.70	7.1	0.70	4.6	0.72	0.50	7.51	3.73	77.1	3.9	13.5	6.0	4.4
5.4	2.77	13.6	1.28	0.3	-0.03	-0.43	-7.03	3.46	103.5	5.7	26.9	1.7	0.9
5.0	1.32	5.7	0.00	3.7	0.00	0.31	1.94	7.37	96.8	4.3	21.9	0.0	3.7
8.6	0.70	3.7	0.23	8.9	15.19	1.47	12.86	2.68	69.1	4.5	15.8	2.2	9.2
7.2	0.48	4.2	0.30	5.2	0.09	1.00	17.77	5.09	86.9	4.6	25.4	8.0	1.3
5.9	3.12	11.1	0.35	4.1	0.04	0.44	3.54	3.61	82.7	5.0	37.7	3.2	7.0
8.1	1.01	4.0	0.93	1.3	-0.02	-0.10	-0.78	3.74	91.2	4.0	23.4	7.1	5.8
6.8	1.06	8.6	-0.05	7.2	0.12	1.52	12.42	3.44	82.1	4.4	21.9	8.6	6.3
7.9	0.15	0.7	0.31	5.5	0.02	0.66	4.94	3.86	77.8	3.9	37.4	26.4	7.6
6.6	0.84	5.3	0.81	3.7	0.29	0.41	4.77	3.74	80.5	4.9	27.8	2.3	4.4
6.6	1.62	7.3	0.00	0.6	0.00	-0.27	-2.84	1.45	107.1	5.4	54.8	0.0	3.8
10.0	0.17	0.4	0.11	6.4	14.66	1.32	12.42	2.14	54.5	4.9	10.6	2.8	7.9
9.8	0.15	1.1	0.19	3.4	0.03	0.36	4.38	4.08	92.2	5.9	38.1	1.6	4.1
6.8	2.79	5.9	0.36	0.0	-0.02	-0.94	-8.74	3.01	133.3	6.2	53.5	4.5	3.5
7.3	0.41	3.5	0.57	3.9	0.43	0.31	3.01	3.69	85.5	3.7	19.0	11.2	6.4
5.4	0.69	4.8	0.40	3.4	0.07	0.40	3.67	3.34	87.6	3.7	19.2	2.7	5.9
9.3	0.37	2.5	0.36	3.5	0.15	0.43	4.48	3.31	87.5	4.9	26.3	3.7	5.5
6.3	0.30	3.4	0.07	3.4	0.02	0.39	5.05	4.27	88.9	3.0	26.6	12.8	2.3
7.5	0.50	4.4	0.35	8.4	22.96	1.18	12.86	3.05	57.4	3.9	15.4	2.7	8.6
9.9	0.47	0.5	1.90	0.0	-0.01	-2.25	-5.59	4.15	175.0	6.4	43.9	0.0	5.3
7.5	0.86	4.0	0.03	1.3	0.02	0.25	2.76	2.67	92.2	5.0	27.1	1.3	3.2
8.7	0.62	2.9	0.38	3.8	0.03	0.33	2.13	3.58	84.3	4.4	22.7	3.0	7.1
2.5	13.10	24.9	0.00	0.7	0.00	-0.72	-2.43	5.47	108.3	5.8	45.2	0.0	5.4
9.0	0.59	3.7	-0.01	4.8	0.88	0.65	4.63	2.82	87.0	1.8	10.0	18.4	8.1
8.4	0.24	3.1	0.22	3.2	0.65	0.38	4.68	3.30	85.5	3.3	10.8	3.6	5.2
3.9	2.13	10.5	-1.70	8.0	0.07	3.30	22.27	2.96	42.5	2.5	34.0	40.1	7.3
9.9	0.21	0.9	0.08	3.6	0.11	0.33	2.95	2.99	86.9	4.5	31.7	4.7	7.1
4.5	3.25	17.7	-0.05	0.5	-0.02	-0.43	-5.27	2.27	106.5	4.6	22.2	0.0	2.7
9.0	0.95	2.5	-0.30	1.6	0.00	0.05	0.27	3.63	112.3	5.1	32.3	6.3	5.6
8.0	0.44	2.5	0.22	3.0	0.00	0.15	1.91	4.01	96.3	5.7	39.2	0.0	1.7
10.0	0.22	0.2	0.00	3.7	0.01	0.64	3.21	2.25	73.3	5.8	37.9	0.0	7.5
2.7	4.20	20.8	0.31	6.9	0.06	4.22	30.56	4.33	55.3	5.0	33.2	0.0	6.6
7.3	1.21	4.8	0.34	5.1	0.01	0.54	3.24	3.92	74.4	4.9	24.3	0.0	4.3
9.8	0.10	0.5	-0.53	6.4	0.09	2.01	13.20	2.41	74.4	4.9	21.9	1.5	6.3
6.9	3.28	7.6	4.26	3.7	0.00	0.21	1.33	11.65	76.5	7.4	69.4	0.0	6.3
7.5	2.02	6.3	0.11	5.6	0.10	0.89	7.74	3.83	94.6	6.0	46.2	0.0	6.2
10.0	0.10	0.2	0.06	3.9	0.04	0.53	3.86	1.86	62.4	4.9	16.6	0.0	6.6
4.1	1.90	14.2	0.69	4.5	0.07	0.79	8.08	4.99	79.4	3.1	20.9	10.6	3.5
8.0	0.31	1.8	0.15	6.2	0.02	0.71	7.08	3.91	89.1	4.9	35.2	1.2	3.7
9.9	0.62	0.8	0.39	2.8	0.24	0.23	1.16	2.87	90.2	5.3	32.8	5.6	7.5
9.8	0.37	1.1	0.28	1.3	0.00	-0.09	-0.53	2.53	96.6	4.7	19.6	0.3	6.7
9.8	0.27	0.5	1.19	1.9	0.00	-0.11	-0.45	3.11	92.0	5.1	35.9	0.0	7.1
6.7	1.56	6.4	2.54	3.5	0.01	0.27	1.84	5.46	79.0	5.2	27.7	0.0	6.8
6.9	3.32	6.9	0.87	4.1	0.04	0.81	7.54	3.48	63.0	5.8	29.5	0.0	4.0
2.7	6.22	20.5	4.19	1.8	0.00	-0.68	-4.44	4.65	71.9	5.8	57.6	0.0	5.7
6.6	0.59	3.7	0.98	9.5	0.03	1.32	7.42	5.24	74.0	2.9	34.3	36.3	5.7
7.7	0.69	4.3	0.92	5.5	0.06	0.56	2.87	6.18	84.9	5.2	36.4	4.3	7.3
8.4	0.66	3.2	0.99	3.2	0.04	0.34	2.67	3.44	83.8	4.5	40.0	7.0	6.2
5.1	1.37	15.3	0.82	2.3	0.11	0.19	1.83	4.99	88.2	5.0	35.0	7.8	5.9
4.6	1.92	10.8	0.35	6.3	0.03	1.18	10.74	6.38	80.9	5.0	35.0	1.1	5.8
9.7	0.48	2.0	0.19	4.1	0.44	0.60	5.47	2.28	74.9	4.2	29.5	4.8	7.1
8.2	0.99	4.8	0.45	4.3	0.07	0.48	3.37	4.24	81.9	4.6	38.4	7.5	6.9

Name	City	State	Rating	2016 Rating	2015 Rating	Total Assets ($Mil)	One Year Asset Growth	Asset Mix (As a % of Total Assets) Commercial Loans	Consumer Loans	Mortgage Loans	Securities	Capitalization Index	Net Worth Ratio
Dor Wic Federal Credit Union	Salisbury	MD	**C+**	C+	C+	8.7	2.26	0.0	31.5	0.0	58.7	**10.0**	20.4
Dort Federal Credit Union	Grand Blanc	MI	**A**	A	A	764.0	9.10	4.2	31.8	28.5	13.0	**10.0**	17.1
▼ Dover Federal Credit Union	Dover	DE	**C**	C+	B-	465.0	5.50	6.4	39.0	7.2	21.6	**6.0**	8.1
Dover-Phila Federal Credit Union	Dover	OH	**A-**	A-	A	446.6	6.79	0.4	18.7	18.3	31.6	**10.0**	13.8
Dow Bucks County Federal Credit Union	Bristol	PA	**B-**	B-	B-	15.1	-0.89	0.5	23.5	28.2	27.3	**10.0**	16.5
Dow Chemical Employees' Credit Union	Midland	MI	**C-**	C-	C	1646.2	4.77	0.0	20.5	24.5	40.7	**8.8**	10.2
Dow Great Western Credit Union	Antioch	CA	**B-**	B-	C+	47.2	6.71	0.0	12.4	23.6	0.0	**8.4**	10.0
Dow Jones Employees Federal Credit Union	Princeton	NJ	**D+**	D+	C-	12.9	-3.07	0.0	13.5	26.2	0.0	**10.0**	12.1
Dowagiac Area Federal Credit Union	Dowagiac	MI	**E+**	E+	D	18.2	5.23	0.0	20.0	21.9	0.0	**5.9**	7.9
Dowell Federal Credit Union	Tulsa	OK	**B-**	B-	B-	34.9	2.96	0.0	54.8	2.3	0.0	**10.0**	11.3
Down East Credit Union	Baileyville	ME	**C+**	C+	C	172.1	14.72	0.5	47.5	17.2	0.0	**5.6**	7.6
Downey Federal Credit Union	Downey	CA	**B-**	B-	B-	212.7	5.04	0.0	14.6	16.6	24.2	**9.8**	11.4
Downriver Community Federal Credit Union	Ecorse	MI	**C+**	C+	C+	157.7	3.64	6.4	14.2	23.5	29.4	**5.9**	8.2
Doy Federal Credit Union	Youngstown	OH	**B+**	B+	B+	49.2	5.68	0.0	3.1	37.9	6.6	**10.0**	14.9
Dresser Alexandria Federal Credit Union	Pineville	LA	**D**	D	D+	5.5	-4.22	0.0	33.8	0.0	0.0	**10.0**	20.2
Du Pont Employees Credit Union	Fort Madison	IA	**C**	C	C	3.7	5.86	0.0	70.3	0.0	18.5	**10.0**	16.8
Dubois-Pike Federal Credit Union	Jasper	IN	**C+**	C+	C	30.0	8.69	0.3	17.1	25.0	0.0	**6.4**	8.4
Dubuque Postal Employees Credit Union	Dubuque	IA	**C**	C	C	4.4	3.52	0.0	17.5	0.0	12.5	**10.0**	11.5
DuGood Federal Credit Union	Beaumont	TX	**B+**	B+	B+	286.9	8.28	4.6	24.4	33.0	4.8	**10.0**	11.8
Dugway Federal Credit Union	Dugway	UT	**D+**	D+	C-	3.2	-5.95	0.0	56.9	0.0	0.0	**10.0**	24.4
Duke University Federal Credit Union	Durham	NC	**C+**	C+	B-	137.5	7.61	0.0	27.9	8.3	19.8	**5.1**	7.3
Duluth Fire Department Credit Union	Duluth	MN	**C**	C	C	4.7	-0.72	0.0	42.8	0.0	0.0	**10.0**	20.4
Duluth Police Department Employees CU	Duluth	MN	**C+**	C+	C-	10.4	-1.94	0.0	27.7	0.0	0.0	**10.0**	11.1
Duluth Teachers Credit Union	Duluth	MN	**B**	B	B-	108.7	5.88	3.0	14.9	31.6	2.2	**6.8**	8.8
Dunlop Employees Federal Credit Union	Buffalo	NY	**C-**	C-	C-	14.0	-0.91	0.0	21.5	11.1	0.0	**10.0**	13.3
Dupaco Community Credit Union	Dubuque	IA	**A**	A	A	1551.6	12.65	18.3	24.8	20.4	25.6	**10.0**	14.3
Dupage County Employees Credit Union	Wheaton	IL	**D+**	D+	D+	17.9	9.73	0.0	34.2	0.0	0.0	**5.9**	7.9
DuPage Credit Union	Naperville	IL	**B**	B	B-	353.6	8.76	0.0	36.0	4.4	8.9	**5.7**	7.7
Dupont Community Credit Union	Waynesboro	VA	**B+**	B+	B+	1127.3	8.00	8.9	20.2	43.5	8.5	**8.0**	9.8
Duq Lite Employees Federal Credit Union	Beaver Falls	PA	**E+**	E+	E+	1.3	-10.09	0.0	76.4	0.0	0.0	**6.4**	8.4
Dutch Point Credit Union	Wethersfield	CT	**B**	B	B-	299.8	14.71	0.0	20.9	15.6	27.6	**8.8**	10.2
DuTrac Community Credit Union	Dubuque	IA	**B**	B	B	656.1	4.02	9.4	30.6	34.6	19.0	**10.0**	12.1
Dynamic Federal Credit Union	Celina	OH	**A-**	A-	A-	37.2	5.09	0.5	34.4	6.2	23.8	**10.0**	16.5
E E South Texas Credit Union	Corpus Christi	TX	**C-**	C-	C-	7.0	-4.08	0.0	7.3	0.0	0.0	**10.0**	17.7
E M O T Federal Credit Union	Abilene	TX	**B-**	B-	B-	10.6	2.89	0.0	23.8	0.0	0.0	**10.0**	25.7
E-Central Credit Union	Pasadena	CA	**A-**	A-	A	163.0	1.99	10.6	13.3	41.2	16.1	**10.0**	17.8
E.S.A. Credit Union	Boise	ID	**D-**	D-	D-	6.6	11.04	0.8	18.9	14.6	0.0	**5.6**	7.6
E.S.C.U. Federal Credit Union	Holland	OH	**C-**	C-	C-	4.9	2.10	0.0	44.6	1.7	0.0	**10.0**	17.3
E.W. #401 Credit Union	Reno	NV	**D-**	D-	D	11.7	24.18	0.0	12.2	7.1	53.6	**5.5**	7.6
Eagle Can Employees Federal Credit Union	Wellsburg	WV	**C**	C	C-	<1	-0.86	0.0	27.3	0.0	0.0	**10.0**	19.2
▼ Eagle Community Credit Union	Lake Forest	CA	**C+**	B-	B-	243.3	8.48	5.3	31.0	17.9	32.9	**5.8**	8.2
Eagle Express Federal Credit Union	Jackson	MS	**B-**	B-	B	62.6	-1.19	0.0	22.8	3.1	6.1	**10.0**	20.3
Eagle Federal Credit Union	Atchison	KS	**E+**	E+	E+	2.0	4.10	0.0	52.5	0.0	0.0	**4.9**	7.0
▲ Eagle Louisiana Federal Credit Union	Baton Rouge	LA	**B-**	C+	C+	112.7	6.88	0.2	70.1	6.8	0.0	**10.0**	11.1
▲ Eagle One Federal Credit Union	Claymont	DE	**C-**	D+	B-	63.9	2.70	6.7	34.0	14.5	5.7	**8.9**	10.2
Earthmover Credit Union	Oswego	IL	**A**	A	A	260.3	3.94	0.9	31.6	6.3	17.8	**10.0**	16.7
East Alabama Community FCU	Opelika	AL	**B-**	B-	B-	14.4	1.66	0.0	46.5	0.1	0.0	**10.0**	17.2
East Allen Federal Credit Union	New Haven	IN	**C-**	C-	C-	14.2	5.72	0.0	12.5	3.3	43.6	**6.4**	8.4
East Baton Rouge Teachers FCU	Baton Rouge	LA	**D+**	D+	D	4.3	16.09	0.0	51.0	0.5	0.0	**10.0**	14.0
East Central Mississippi Credit Union	Newton	MS	**C**	C	C	5.3	5.82	0.0	27.4	1.5	0.0	**10.0**	11.9
East Chicago Firemen's Credit Union	East Chicago	IN	**C**	C	C-	<1	-3.71	0.0	7.9	0.0	0.0	**10.0**	17.0
East County Schools Federal Credit Union	El Cajon	CA	**C+**	C+	C+	110.0	7.78	9.2	12.4	32.1	24.2	**6.3**	8.3
East End Baptist Tabernacle FCU	Bridgeport	CT	**D**	D	D+	<1	-6.47	0.0	9.2	0.0	0.0	**10.0**	13.1
East End Food Cooperative FCU	Pittsburgh	PA	**D-**	D-	E+	<1	0.81	0.0	27.6	0.0	0.0	**6.8**	8.8
East Feliciana Teachers FCU	Clinton	LA	**E+**	E+	D-	<1	-4.32	0.0	63.2	0.0	0.0	**5.1**	7.1
East Haven Municipal Employees CU	East Haven	CT	**C-**	C-	D+	2.6	3.59	0.0	21.0	0.0	0.0	**10.0**	13.3
▲ East Idaho Credit Union	Idaho Falls	ID	**C+**	C	C	273.0	3.72	0.0	56.4	12.1	12.7	**8.0**	9.8
▼ East Ohio Gas Cleveland Operating FCU	Cleveland	OH	**D**	D+	D+	1.5	1.33	0.0	62.3	0.0	0.0	**10.0**	22.4
East Ohio Gas Youngstown Division Empls FCU	Youngstown	OH	**C+**	C+	C	3.8	3.26	0.0	45.6	0.0	17.6	**10.0**	21.0
East Orange Firemens FCU	East Orange	NJ	**C**	C	C-	8.6	5.67	0.0	50.5	0.0	0.0	**10.0**	20.5

Asset Quality Index	Non-Performing Loans as a % of Total Loans	Non-Performing Loans as a % of Capital	Net Charge-Offs Avg Loans	Profitability Index	Net Income ($Mil)	Return on Assets	Return on Equity	Net Interest Spread	Overhead Efficiency Ratio	Liquidity Index	Liquidity Ratio	Hot Money Ratio	Stability Index
9.6	1.46	2.5	0.00	**5.2**	0.02	0.83	4.01	2.58	69.1	**4.7**	15.5	0.0	**5.0**
7.3	1.27	5.5	0.72	**8.7**	2.02	1.08	6.28	4.46	71.4	**4.3**	20.7	4.4	**9.8**
6.8	0.88	6.9	1.21	**1.6**	0.00	0.00	0.01	4.23	89.6	**4.4**	23.3	5.8	**3.9**
8.5	1.22	3.8	0.19	**5.2**	0.94	0.86	6.36	2.40	67.2	**5.1**	33.0	3.3	**8.6**
8.4	1.96	6.6	0.00	**4.2**	0.02	0.53	3.19	2.54	76.3	**4.1**	8.8	0.0	**7.9**
9.9	0.16	0.9	0.16	**1.8**	0.58	0.15	1.40	1.38	87.3	**4.2**	19.9	4.6	**7.1**
10.0	0.00	0.0	0.06	**4.4**	0.07	0.57	5.66	2.50	80.2	**4.6**	22.1	3.8	**5.3**
7.6	2.74	9.8	-0.07	**1.3**	0.00	0.03	0.26	2.41	92.5	**4.1**	14.9	4.2	**5.5**
3.2	4.68	31.1	0.47	**1.3**	-0.01	-0.20	-2.51	2.54	102.6	**5.8**	49.2	0.0	**3.4**
6.8	0.75	3.8	0.74	**3.5**	0.03	0.38	3.36	2.54	78.0	**2.9**	40.0	21.8	**5.6**
3.8	0.98	13.5	0.46	**6.6**	0.45	1.07	14.03	4.70	79.4	**2.8**	7.5	8.6	**5.3**
8.3	0.87	3.1	0.76	**3.3**	0.15	0.29	2.66	2.66	77.7	**4.4**	23.0	8.3	**7.2**
8.8	0.61	3.6	0.48	**3.0**	0.08	0.21	2.76	3.39	90.1	**5.1**	26.5	2.7	**4.1**
10.0	0.35	1.0	0.10	**5.8**	0.10	0.80	5.32	1.91	52.3	**5.4**	59.4	0.0	**8.1**
6.6	4.07	8.3	3.03	**0.0**	-0.05	-3.26	-15.79	4.03	165.3	**5.2**	32.1	0.0	**5.5**
8.4	0.00	0.0	0.00	**4.0**	0.01	0.76	4.52	2.85	64.0	**4.2**	17.2	0.0	**7.4**
9.4	0.23	1.5	-0.02	**3.7**	0.02	0.22	2.54	2.83	92.0	**3.8**	18.2	8.7	**5.0**
10.0	0.00	0.0	0.00	**2.4**	0.00	0.00	0.00	1.71	100.0	**5.9**	39.1	0.0	**6.2**
9.6	0.23	1.3	0.25	**4.8**	0.44	0.63	5.22	3.32	82.2	**4.2**	25.1	7.5	**7.9**
5.0	3.77	10.2	0.00	**3.0**	0.00	0.38	1.56	6.74	95.2	**4.8**	50.4	15.1	**6.3**
7.9	0.65	5.1	0.56	**3.1**	0.11	0.34	4.62	3.71	84.2	**5.9**	35.3	1.9	**3.9**
9.4	1.24	2.8	0.00	**3.1**	0.00	0.34	1.68	2.37	84.6	**4.5**	49.3	8.8	**7.4**
9.8	0.41	1.3	0.00	**4.0**	0.02	0.58	5.23	1.81	62.8	**4.7**	14.1	0.0	**5.9**
8.2	0.17	3.7	0.33	**4.4**	0.14	0.50	5.71	2.96	81.3	**3.8**	21.9	2.5	**6.2**
10.0	0.29	0.9	0.00	**1.7**	0.00	0.09	0.65	2.40	94.7	**6.1**	54.1	0.0	**5.7**
7.8	0.90	3.9	0.34	**9.5**	5.77	1.51	10.60	3.42	62.7	**4.0**	14.2	8.7	**10.0**
9.9	0.03	0.1	0.06	**1.9**	0.01	0.14	1.69	2.09	93.7	**5.5**	26.6	0.0	**3.5**
8.0	0.58	4.7	0.18	**5.5**	0.53	0.61	7.84	4.10	87.3	**5.1**	21.0	0.7	**5.3**
8.2	0.37	3.7	0.33	**4.3**	1.67	0.60	6.53	3.45	78.4	**3.8**	11.9	4.0	**6.9**
4.0	1.10	10.0	0.00	**0.5**	0.00	-0.63	-7.48	3.81	120.0	**4.7**	21.6	0.0	**1.7**
8.9	0.57	2.5	0.31	**4.1**	0.43	0.58	5.47	2.96	82.5	**4.9**	23.5	4.4	**6.9**
7.7	0.56	4.2	0.16	**3.9**	0.87	0.53	4.50	2.77	83.1	**3.0**	18.7	10.3	**8.3**
9.9	0.59	1.9	0.08	**9.3**	0.13	1.40	8.72	3.79	72.5	**4.9**	34.5	0.0	**8.0**
10.0	0.00	0.0	0.00	**0.6**	-0.01	-0.39	-2.25	1.06	135.3	**6.8**	91.4	0.0	**6.7**
9.8	0.39	0.4	0.00	**4.6**	0.02	0.68	2.66	2.25	66.7	**5.0**	31.0	0.0	**7.3**
9.6	0.16	0.5	0.35	**4.5**	0.21	0.53	2.95	3.63	91.0	**4.2**	29.1	10.5	**8.2**
9.5	0.18	0.8	0.87	**2.3**	0.01	0.44	5.58	3.53	101.6	**5.5**	28.7	0.0	**1.0**
7.7	1.77	4.7	0.87	**2.5**	0.00	0.16	0.95	3.63	88.6	**6.7**	65.7	0.0	**6.9**
10.0	0.04	0.1	-0.31	**0.8**	0.00	0.00	0.00	2.56	101.3	**5.6**	29.3	8.5	**2.7**
6.4	7.98	10.9	0.00	**4.6**	0.00	0.59	3.03	4.07	100.0	**5.6**	17.8	0.0	**4.3**
7.6	0.05	4.9	0.67	**3.1**	0.07	0.12	1.55	3.28	89.5	**4.3**	19.9	5.5	**4.8**
9.5	1.38	2.7	0.37	**3.4**	0.08	0.54	2.95	3.27	83.3	**4.7**	26.6	4.0	**6.6**
4.1	1.09	9.9	0.00	**2.5**	0.00	0.21	2.96	4.46	95.8	**4.4**	35.1	0.0	**1.0**
7.7	0.49	3.4	0.32	**3.5**	0.15	0.55	4.96	4.57	84.6	**2.7**	15.2	11.0	**6.5**
5.5	1.80	11.5	1.22	**2.2**	0.04	0.25	2.44	5.10	84.8	**4.1**	21.7	9.2	**4.6**
8.6	0.73	3.6	0.39	**9.1**	1.09	1.72	10.28	3.62	64.2	**4.4**	24.6	5.5	**8.2**
8.8	0.22	0.6	0.53	**4.3**	0.01	0.23	1.29	4.20	93.4	**6.1**	38.6	0.0	**7.0**
10.0	0.24	0.5	0.00	**2.1**	0.00	0.12	1.33	1.96	92.6	**6.3**	51.0	2.3	**3.7**
5.2	3.63	10.5	-2.74	**3.0**	0.01	0.58	4.04	11.54	94.2	**6.8**	58.5	0.0	**5.0**
9.6	0.85	2.5	0.64	**3.3**	0.00	-0.24	-1.91	5.18	99.0	**6.6**	50.7	0.0	**5.5**
10.0	0.00	0.0	0.00	**2.0**	0.00	0.00	0.00	2.82	83.3	**5.8**	24.1	0.0	**6.2**
9.0	0.09	0.7	0.05	**3.4**	0.17	0.60	7.34	3.04	81.3	**3.6**	21.4	5.4	**5.5**
3.7	28.57	21.1	0.00	**3.7**	0.00	3.13	26.67	0.00	100.0	**8.3**	105.6	0.0	**4.9**
5.7	4.62	13.8	4.47	**2.0**	0.00	0.00	0.00	3.01	95.2	**5.6**	16.7	0.0	**1.7**
2.2	3.53	21.4	6.70	**0.0**	0.00	-3.02	-40.00	9.57	116.7	**5.7**	39.7	0.0	**4.0**
7.4	6.41	10.0	1.44	**1.7**	0.00	0.16	1.16	2.37	100.0	**6.5**	61.3	0.0	**6.4**
8.0	0.30	2.7	0.50	**3.6**	0.39	0.57	5.94	3.51	81.4	**3.6**	7.3	1.9	**5.1**
5.8	2.63	6.9	0.00	**0.0**	-0.01	-1.84	-8.07	2.12	200.0	**5.4**	49.1	0.0	**5.6**
8.6	0.52	1.1	0.95	**4.2**	0.00	0.43	2.03	2.14	76.5	**5.3**	27.5	0.0	**7.7**
5.2	3.72	8.5	2.83	**7.7**	0.04	1.89	9.15	5.40	60.4	**5.3**	33.9	0.0	**4.3**

Name	City	State	Rating	2016 Rating	2015 Rating	Total Assets ($Mil)	One Year Asset Growth	Asset Mix (As a % of Total Assets) Comm-ercial Loans	Cons-umer Loans	Mort-gage Loans	Secur-ities	Capital-ization Index	Net Worth Ratio
East Orange Veterans Hospital FCU	East Orange	NJ	**C+**	C+	C+	16.0	8.57	0.0	33.0	0.0	0.0	**10.0**	11.0
East River Federal Credit Union	Madison	SD	**B-**	B-	B-	31.6	0.88	0.0	44.6	8.2	15.5	**7.9**	9.8
East Texas Professional Credit Union	Longview	TX	**A+**	A+	A+	584.3	2.70	1.2	35.7	19.8	11.5	**10.0**	18.6
East Traverse Catholic FCU	Traverse City	MI	**C**	C	C-	61.8	20.08	1.3	41.2	23.2	8.8	**5.8**	7.8
▼ Eastern Indiana Federal Credit Union	New Castle	IN	**D+**	C-	D+	27.1	7.69	0.0	24.6	4.4	0.0	**5.5**	7.5
▼ Eastern Kentucky Federal Credit Union	Prestonsburg	KY	**D**	D+	C-	4.3	10.18	0.0	69.2	0.0	0.0	**10.0**	19.0
Eastern Maine Medical Center FCU	Bangor	ME	**C+**	C+	C	51.9	2.10	0.0	15.2	11.5	6.3	**8.0**	9.6
Eastern Panhandle Federal Credit Union	Martinsburg	WV	**D-**	D-	D-	15.8	0.62	0.0	44.4	1.4	0.0	**5.1**	7.1
Eastern Utah Community FCU	Price	UT	**B-**	B-	B-	119.8	2.95	6.4	26.5	21.0	14.4	**7.5**	9.3
Eastex Credit Union	Evadale	TX	**B**	B	B	78.5	10.55	0.0	42.1	0.5	2.2	**9.3**	10.5
Eastman Credit Union	Kingsport	TN	**A**	A	A	3818.3	12.49	7.6	23.6	51.8	2.2	**10.0**	12.9
Eastmill Federal Credit Union	East Millinocket	ME	**B-**	B-	B-	62.6	1.28	0.5	12.7	5.9	5.6	**10.0**	18.8
▼ Eastpointe Community Credit Union	Eastpointe	MI	**D-**	D	D-	9.8	6.07	0.0	39.8	0.0	34.3	**6.5**	8.5
▲ Eaton Employees Credit Union	Spencer	IA	**D-**	E+	E+	2.3	-22.76	0.0	60.6	0.0	0.0	**9.7**	10.8
▲ Eaton Employees Credit Union	Eden Prairie	MN	**C-**	D+	D+	2.6	-8.97	1.1	62.5	0.0	0.0	**10.0**	11.3
Eaton Employees Federal Credit Union	Denver	CO	**D+**	D+	D+	<1	4.52	0.0	31.4	0.0	0.0	**10.0**	17.3
Eaton Family Credit Union, Inc.	Euclid	OH	**C+**	C+	C+	63.9	6.56	5.3	22.0	19.7	24.6	**8.0**	10.0
EBSCO Federal Credit Union	Birmingham	AL	**C-**	C-	D	12.0	1.48	0.0	34.0	19.1	0.0	**7.4**	9.3
ECCO Credit Union	Milton	FL	**B-**	B-	B-	23.2	0.52	7.5	11.3	33.9	0.0	**10.0**	16.9
ECM Credit Union	Ridgeland	MS	**B-**	B-	B-	22.1	3.91	5.2	33.3	0.0	2.1	**10.0**	11.7
eCO Credit Union	Birmingham	AL	**C**	C	C	136.0	3.33	0.0	26.4	15.0	40.0	**8.3**	10.5
▲ ECU Credit Union	Largo	FL	**D+**	D	D	39.6	7.85	0.0	40.3	5.8	20.3	**10.0**	13.0
Ecusta Credit Union	Brevard	NC	**D+**	D+	C-	59.7	2.40	0.0	18.2	11.2	51.7	**9.9**	10.9
Ed-Med Federal Credit Union	Ogdensburg	NY	**C-**	C-	C-	24.7	5.07	0.0	28.3	0.0	43.5	**7.6**	9.4
Eddy Federal Credit Union	Carlsbad	NM	**C+**	C+	C-	54.8	-4.92	0.0	38.5	0.0	0.0	**10.0**	12.5
Eddy Paper Employees Credit Union	White Pigeon	MI	**D**	D	C-	<1	-16.48	0.0	69.5	0.0	0.0	**10.0**	14.2
Eddyville Cooperative Credit Union	Eddyville	NE	**C**	C	C	1.9	7.71	0.0	12.2	0.8	0.0	**10.0**	17.8
Edge Federal Credit Union	Liverpool	NY	**C**	C	C+	47.8	7.43	1.3	11.2	8.5	4.9	**8.8**	10.2
Edinburg Teachers Credit Union	Edinburg	TX	**B+**	B+	A-	90.4	3.93	0.0	15.8	0.0	68.3	**10.0**	23.5
▲ Edison Credit Union	Kansas City	MO	**D**	D-	D-	29.9	2.85	0.0	12.9	12.2	5.2	**7.8**	9.5
Edison Credit Union	Springfield	OH	**C-**	C-	D+	4.5	1.56	2.1	50.4	0.0	0.0	**10.0**	11.4
Edisto Federal Credit Union	Orangeburg	SC	**C+**	C+	C+	25.7	2.68	0.0	26.2	14.2	0.0	**10.0**	12.5
Education Credit Union	Amarillo	TX	**A**	A	A	251.5	4.29	0.0	45.2	20.7	5.6	**10.0**	13.3
Education First Credit Union	Ogden	UT	**C+**	C+	C+	31.0	7.98	2.6	35.3	18.2	0.0	**7.4**	9.2
Education First Credit Union, Inc.	Westerville	OH	**C-**	C-	D	98.4	2.56	2.5	33.7	25.5	0.0	**7.1**	9.0
Education First Federal Credit Union	Beaumont	TX	**B+**	B+	A-	363.5	3.97	3.3	28.8	14.9	16.7	**10.0**	11.6
Education Personnel Federal Credit Union	Danville	IL	**B-**	B-	B-	52.0	6.20	0.3	18.2	11.0	3.8	**10.0**	11.9
Education Plus Credit Union	Monroe	MI	**A**	A	A-	113.8	8.43	0.4	26.7	5.4	30.1	**10.0**	15.2
Educational & Governmental Employees FCU	Hartsdale	NY	**C+**	C+	C	54.3	3.10	0.0	20.4	5.4	15.9	**9.4**	10.9
Educational Community Alliance CU	Toledo	OH	**C-**	C-	D	44.9	7.03	0.0	28.2	4.1	29.1	**8.7**	10.2
▼ Educational Community Credit Union	Springfield	MO	**D+**	C-	C-	59.8	3.10	0.0	36.0	9.0	7.0	**6.1**	8.3
Educational Employees Credit Union	Fresno	CA	**A**	A	A	2860.7	8.35	0.3	24.3	13.0	41.5	**10.0**	12.1
Educational Systems Federal Credit Union	Greenbelt	MD	**B+**	B+	B+	941.7	9.80	0.0	34.0	19.4	22.5	**6.9**	9.2
Educators Credit Union	Waco	TX	**B+**	B+	A	394.6	2.35	0.0	22.4	8.6	30.6	**10.0**	15.8
Educators Credit Union	Racine	WI	**A-**	A-	A-	1747.0	5.20	2.8	18.8	45.0	8.5	**10.0**	11.4
Edwards Federal Credit Union	Edwards AFB	CA	**C**	C	C+	193.1	6.67	5.5	15.6	17.0	38.8	**5.2**	7.2
EECU	Fort Worth	TX	**A**	A	A	2028.6	7.76	9.1	53.9	12.0	6.8	**10.0**	11.5
▲ EFCU Financial Federal Credit Union	Baton Rouge	LA	**B**	B-	C+	387.7	14.54	2.4	57.8	17.1	1.5	**7.4**	9.3
Effingham Highway Credit Union	Effingham	IL	**D-**	D-	D+	5.2	7.09	0.0	65.3	0.0	0.0	**8.4**	9.9
Eglin Federal Credit Union	Fort Walton Beach	FL	**B**	B	B-	1833.5	8.33	0.0	18.7	15.5	44.2	**9.9**	10.9
Eight Federal Credit Union	Rossford	OH	**C+**	C+	C	12.8	7.36	0.0	34.0	0.0	17.9	**10.0**	14.8
El Monte Community Credit Union	El Monte	CA	**C**	C	C-	28.8	13.09	0.0	20.3	10.2	6.8	**6.2**	8.2
El Paso Area Teachers FCU	El Paso	TX	**B**	B	B	638.6	5.51	2.0	51.0	4.9	21.1	**10.0**	11.6
El Reno R.I.L. Credit Union	El Reno	OK	**C**	C	C	46.6	5.70	0.3	13.5	5.4	15.4	**6.2**	8.3
▲ ELCA Federal Credit Union	Chicago	IL	**C-**	D	D	3.6	231.02	0.0	48.2	0.0	0.0	**10.0**	61.1
ELCO Federal Credit Union	Elberton	GA	**C+**	C+	C	3.0	3.38	0.0	65.3	0.0	0.0	**10.0**	19.8
Electchester Federal Credit Union	Flushing	NY	**D-**	D-	D	<1	-14.07	0.0	49.1	0.0	0.0	**10.0**	32.0
ElecTel Cooperative Federal Credit Union	Raleigh	NC	**B**	B	B	50.7	16.02	0.0	54.5	0.0	0.0	**9.7**	10.8
Electric Cooperatives FCU	Little Rock	AR	**D+**	D+	D+	13.5	2.43	0.0	48.8	0.0	0.0	**7.2**	9.2
Electric Energy Incorporated Empls CU	Metropolis	IL	**D**	D	D+	2.0	-1.40	0.0	58.5	0.0	20.1	**10.0**	16.8

Asset Quality Index	Non-Performing Loans as a % of Total Loans	Non-Performing Loans as a % of Capital	Net Charge-Offs Avg Loans	Profitability Index	Net Income ($Mil)	Return on Assets	Return on Equity	Net Interest Spread	Overhead Efficiency Ratio	Liquidity Index	Liquidity Ratio	Hot Money Ratio	Stability Index
5.5	3.43	10.6	0.07	**5.5**	0.03	0.74	6.69	5.42	76.7	**5.8**	45.3	13.3	**5.0**
9.1	0.06	0.4	-0.08	**4.6**	0.03	0.44	4.52	4.06	91.3	**4.3**	17.6	2.5	**5.0**
9.0	0.45	1.8	0.28	**9.3**	1.82	1.27	6.80	3.55	66.3	**3.9**	22.7	6.6	**10.0**
5.8	0.69	6.6	0.12	**4.2**	0.09	0.57	7.19	4.13	79.9	**3.9**	11.1	2.3	**3.2**
9.8	0.22	1.1	0.16	**1.3**	-0.02	-0.23	-2.93	2.50	104.7	**5.6**	34.1	1.7	**3.6**
2.7	4.27	20.9	2.93	**2.9**	-0.09	-8.29	-41.47	5.60	93.2	**4.1**	21.9	0.0	**2.3**
9.2	0.46	2.0	0.05	**2.9**	0.03	0.21	2.16	2.66	90.9	**6.1**	52.5	2.5	**5.4**
5.0	1.76	13.3	-0.04	**3.3**	0.01	0.21	2.84	3.28	94.2	**4.8**	16.6	0.0	**1.7**
8.2	0.36	2.7	0.03	**3.9**	0.18	0.62	6.58	3.32	83.7	**4.1**	27.5	6.5	**6.2**
7.1	0.50	3.4	0.38	**4.8**	0.10	0.51	4.71	3.62	85.8	**4.0**	17.7	6.5	**5.0**
9.5	0.06	0.9	0.20	**9.6**	13.72	1.47	11.44	3.58	58.6	**2.4**	19.3	20.1	**9.7**
10.0	0.12	0.2	0.15	**3.3**	0.06	0.36	1.87	2.17	86.6	**5.3**	42.3	2.8	**7.4**
6.7	0.83	4.4	1.07	**1.9**	0.00	0.09	0.96	4.36	91.3	**5.5**	31.1	0.0	**1.7**
0.7	6.93	41.4	-0.43	**1.9**	0.00	0.17	1.62	5.24	91.7	**4.6**	23.9	0.0	**3.8**
6.4	0.88	4.4	0.63	**2.9**	0.00	0.32	2.79	5.73	95.0	**5.4**	33.2	0.0	**6.4**
5.5	9.22	18.5	0.00	**1.0**	0.00	0.00	0.00	2.37	100.0	**7.0**	80.4	0.0	**6.2**
5.4	1.71	9.3	1.58	**3.0**	0.02	0.12	1.16	4.57	80.7	**3.6**	19.4	13.6	**4.7**
9.7	0.00	0.0	0.00	**1.7**	0.00	0.07	0.72	2.75	98.0	**6.1**	49.3	0.0	**4.5**
9.7	0.00	0.0	0.00	**5.0**	0.04	0.65	3.90	2.70	73.2	**5.0**	29.4	0.0	**7.9**
9.1	0.91	2.9	0.68	**3.4**	0.01	0.24	2.01	2.49	79.0	**5.7**	31.8	0.0	**6.5**
8.1	0.73	3.9	1.06	**3.1**	0.12	0.35	4.04	3.32	84.0	**4.6**	14.9	1.3	**4.4**
7.6	1.36	5.0	0.40	**1.1**	0.02	0.17	1.25	3.40	91.0	**4.5**	19.6	0.0	**5.8**
10.0	0.06	0.2	0.43	**1.8**	0.01	0.05	0.49	2.97	95.5	**5.5**	22.4	0.8	**5.2**
8.1	0.59	2.1	0.57	**3.7**	0.01	0.15	1.56	1.84	73.2	**4.5**	38.7	9.9	**4.6**
8.9	0.32	1.7	1.31	**1.3**	-0.02	-0.12	-0.93	3.27	90.7	**5.4**	55.8	14.1	**5.5**
0.7	12.59	50.0	4.69	**5.0**	0.00	1.27	9.52	9.30	80.0	**5.7**	35.8	0.0	**4.9**
6.5	3.99	9.1	0.00	**6.3**	0.02	4.04	23.46	12.93	55.0	**7.4**	85.1	1.8	**5.0**
8.9	0.85	2.8	0.17	**2.2**	0.03	0.22	2.06	3.43	91.6	**6.1**	32.4	0.0	**4.7**
9.5	2.51	2.0	-0.22	**3.7**	0.04	0.16	0.66	3.53	89.5	**5.4**	12.7	1.3	**6.5**
8.4	0.63	2.8	0.32	**0.9**	-0.01	-0.10	-0.98	3.61	99.4	**4.7**	21.4	0.4	**4.3**
5.3	2.10	9.8	-0.33	**2.6**	0.00	-0.18	-1.56	3.96	103.6	**4.9**	43.0	8.2	**5.7**
6.3	2.56	10.1	0.07	**3.4**	0.03	0.41	3.26	4.59	96.4	**5.0**	56.2	20.4	**5.8**
6.4	0.89	4.7	1.49	**4.0**	0.01	0.02	0.13	5.60	78.9	**2.8**	16.3	14.4	**8.1**
6.5	0.90	6.4	-0.06	**4.3**	0.04	0.49	5.21	4.06	85.4	**4.6**	28.1	6.5	**4.9**
6.0	0.81	8.3	0.40	**2.3**	0.02	0.07	0.87	4.37	95.1	**3.3**	16.9	7.3	**3.3**
7.0	1.03	6.0	0.94	**4.0**	0.35	0.39	4.10	3.83	83.0	**4.1**	19.3	7.9	**5.8**
10.0	0.13	0.4	0.02	**3.6**	0.06	0.49	4.08	2.19	84.7	**5.1**	27.4	0.0	**6.3**
7.4	1.52	5.5	0.25	**9.5**	0.42	1.49	9.71	3.62	61.6	**4.7**	26.0	3.2	**9.5**
9.0	0.85	2.1	-0.11	**2.9**	0.03	0.20	1.88	3.01	89.7	**5.9**	32.5	1.4	**4.6**
9.5	0.43	2.0	0.40	**2.3**	0.03	0.31	2.99	3.80	90.8	**4.5**	21.9	1.0	**4.4**
3.4	3.63	26.3	1.71	**1.3**	-0.18	-1.21	-14.51	3.79	89.7	**4.9**	17.8	1.1	**3.5**
10.0	0.19	0.7	0.38	**5.9**	4.89	0.70	5.95	2.88	77.2	**5.0**	25.9	11.3	**8.5**
8.0	0.67	4.3	0.52	**4.6**	0.80	0.35	3.90	2.91	83.1	**4.3**	28.4	8.2	**5.4**
10.0	0.34	1.0	0.32	**4.5**	0.55	0.56	3.52	2.85	71.6	**6.4**	44.1	7.5	**8.4**
7.5	0.73	5.0	0.56	**5.5**	3.46	0.81	7.05	3.27	75.5	**3.6**	13.0	4.1	**8.2**
7.1	0.62	3.2	0.59	**2.4**	0.19	0.39	5.39	3.19	84.9	**5.6**	31.5	2.0	**3.3**
8.3	0.20	1.6	0.49	**6.6**	4.55	0.91	8.26	3.05	66.7	**3.8**	21.5	11.3	**8.6**
8.3	0.12	1.5	0.22	**5.0**	0.95	0.98	11.20	3.32	75.1	**3.6**	17.2	8.0	**5.3**
2.9	2.79	17.2	0.00	**3.0**	0.01	0.70	7.02	3.15	79.1	**4.1**	29.9	0.0	**2.3**
9.9	0.39	1.5	0.27	**4.3**	3.09	0.68	6.66	2.20	72.5	**5.6**	32.1	3.6	**7.2**
9.6	0.07	0.2	0.15	**2.6**	0.01	0.29	1.90	3.01	88.5	**5.8**	46.2	3.7	**7.2**
10.0	0.26	1.1	0.44	**3.6**	0.02	0.32	3.76	3.60	92.1	**5.7**	34.1	5.2	**2.9**
7.0	0.64	3.9	0.89	**3.6**	0.60	0.38	3.20	3.55	76.5	**3.5**	17.6	14.2	**7.6**
8.0	0.46	3.1	-0.04	**3.3**	0.03	0.26	3.15	1.97	89.7	**5.4**	53.1	15.5	**3.5**
8.8	0.00	0.0	0.00	**9.5**	0.76	99.15	168.20	2.54	6.9	**7.0**	146.1	0.0	**6.3**
6.7	1.78	6.2	0.00	**10.0**	0.02	2.21	11.05	5.90	58.5	**5.2**	40.8	0.0	**5.0**
1.1	16.11	23.0	7.21	**0.0**	-0.01	-7.53	-23.88	8.62	233.3	**7.0**	70.2	0.0	**4.8**
7.1	0.45	2.6	-0.07	**6.6**	0.11	0.91	8.06	4.33	81.0	**5.2**	39.9	6.2	**5.9**
5.7	0.57	3.3	0.22	**5.2**	0.04	1.23	13.18	4.43	86.4	**5.2**	37.1	1.7	**3.7**
8.4	0.08	0.3	0.00	**0.3**	-0.01	-1.02	-6.10	6.53	118.5	**4.7**	15.5	0.0	**5.0**

Name	City	State	Rating	2016 Rating	2015 Rating	Total Assets ($Mil)	One Year Asset Growth	Asset Mix (As a % of Total Assets) Comm-ercial Loans	Cons-umer Loans	Mort-gage Loans	Secur-ities	Capital-ization Index	Net Worth Ratio
Electric Machinery Employees CU	Minneapolis	MN	**C**	C	C-	8.7	-2.05	0.0	43.7	3.3	12.0	**10.0**	23.2
Electric Service Credit Union	Nashville	TN	**C-**	C-	C+	63.6	-0.09	0.0	54.5	3.7	3.3	**10.0**	12.3
Electric Utilities Credit Union	Big Spring	TX	**D+**	D+	C-	6.4	-2.10	0.0	29.8	0.0	0.0	**10.0**	12.5
Electrical Federal Credit Union	Arvada	CO	**C**	C	C	36.9	3.34	1.7	35.3	11.2	11.4	**6.8**	8.8
Electrical Workers Local 130 FCU	Metairie	LA	**D-**	D-	D	5.0	-2.03	0.0	36.8	1.0	0.1	**8.0**	9.8
Electrical Workers Local 58 Credit Union	Detroit	MI	**C+**	C+	C	13.0	10.41	0.5	31.2	0.0	37.0	**10.0**	12.0
Electrical Workers No. 22 FCU	Omaha	NE	**D+**	D+	D	9.8	2.03	0.0	29.8	0.0	0.0	**8.2**	9.8
Electrical Workers No. 558 FCU	Sheffield	AL	**B-**	B-	B-	23.9	2.74	0.0	45.8	3.1	0.0	**10.0**	20.1
Electricians' Local 349 Credit Union	Miami	FL	**D**	D	D	4.2	0.53	0.0	26.8	0.7	0.0	**10.0**	18.4
Electro Savings Credit Union	Saint Louis	MO	**B-**	B-	B	164.9	6.50	1.3	52.2	2.4	15.2	**7.8**	9.7
Electrogas Credit Union	Alton	IL	**D**	D	D	<1	-8.27	0.0	45.2	0.0	0.0	**10.0**	36.5
Electrus Federal Credit Union	Brooklyn Center	MN	**C**	C	C	59.2	5.26	1.5	23.2	3.2	48.8	**10.0**	17.0
▲ Elektra Federal Credit Union	New York	NY	**B**	B-	B-	41.2	7.03	0.0	7.8	0.0	3.4	**10.0**	14.3
Element Federal Credit Union	Charleston	WV	**C+**	C+	B-	31.2	0.72	0.0	73.2	0.0	0.0	**10.0**	11.5
Elements Financial Federal Credit Union	Indianapolis	IN	**B+**	B+	A-	1450.5	10.19	0.7	25.9	34.6	9.4	**6.2**	8.2
▲ Elevations Credit Union	Boulder	CO	**A**	A-	A-	1854.3	12.66	5.6	12.7	40.0	10.1	**8.5**	10.0
Elevator Credit Union	Olive Branch	MS	**B-**	B-	B-	15.1	5.53	0.0	31.3	0.0	0.0	**10.0**	14.5
ELGA Credit Union	Burton	MI	**A-**	A-	A-	543.3	18.45	6.5	41.4	28.9	1.7	**10.0**	13.0
Elgin Mental Health Center Credit Union	Elgin	IL	**C**	C	C-	5.6	-5.58	0.0	24.1	0.0	0.8	**10.0**	13.7
Elite Community Credit Union	Bourbonnais	IL	**C-**	C-	C-	14.1	-0.72	0.0	56.9	3.6	1.4	**10.0**	13.5
Elizabeth (N.J.) Firemen's FCU	Elizabeth	NJ	**D-**	D-	D-	9.3	11.01	0.0	23.3	0.0	0.0	**5.9**	7.9
Elizabeth Police Department Employee FCU	Elizabeth	NJ	**D+**	D+	D+	2.6	-5.28	0.0	31.4	0.0	0.0	**10.0**	36.4
Elizabeth Postal Employees Credit Union	Elizabeth	NJ	**C**	C	C	<1	-4.20	0.0	29.1	0.0	0.0	**10.0**	27.9
Elko Federal Credit Union	Elko	NV	**B+**	B+	B	157.4	6.56	6.9	11.8	12.5	16.0	**8.4**	9.9
Elliott Community Federal Credit Union	Jeannette	PA	**C+**	C+	C+	34.7	3.61	0.0	27.3	9.4	0.0	**10.0**	11.1
Ellis County Teachers & Employees FCU	Waxahachie	TX	**C+**	C+	C+	14.2	6.10	0.0	43.3	0.0	0.0	**10.0**	12.0
Ellis Credit Union	Ellis	KS	**C**	C	C	5.3	-11.41	7.3	31.4	0.1	0.0	**10.0**	17.6
Ellisville State School Employees CU	Ellisville	MS	**D+**	D+	C	2.5	-0.16	0.0	14.6	0.0	0.0	**10.0**	23.7
Elm River Credit Union	Kindred	ND	**B**	B	B	22.3	4.11	40.8	11.7	40.5	0.0	**10.0**	15.9
Ely Area Credit Union	Ely	MN	**B**	B	B-	39.1	68.32	0.0	14.7	7.7	0.0	**10.0**	12.8
EM Federal Credit Union	Mesa	AZ	**D+**	D+	D+	8.1	5.72	0.0	37.4	0.0	55.3	**10.0**	18.5
Embark Federal Credit Union	Great Falls	MT	**C**	C	B-	104.6	6.84	0.1	27.4	13.7	23.3	**8.9**	10.3
Embarrass Vermillion FCU	Aurora	MN	**B**	B	B-	32.3	7.38	0.0	27.6	38.3	0.0	**10.0**	12.3
▲ EME Credit Union	Easton	PA	**D+**	D	D+	1.6	-3.78	0.0	22.8	0.0	0.0	**10.0**	13.4
▲ Emerald Coast Federal Credit Union	Port Saint Joe	FL	**D+**	D	D	47.4	3.92	1.5	30.3	17.4	0.0	**5.6**	7.6
Emerald Credit Association FCU	Greenwood	SC	**D+**	D+	D	6.5	4.01	0.0	53.8	0.0	0.0	**6.7**	8.7
▲ Emerald Credit Union, Inc.	Garfield Heights	OH	**C**	C-	D-	42.8	-3.01	2.7	23.4	19.5	22.1	**7.8**	9.5
Emergency Responders Credit Union	Winston-Salem	NC	**C+**	C+	C+	21.0	8.94	0.0	43.6	1.0	0.3	**10.0**	11.7
▲ Emery Federal Credit Union	Cincinnati	OH	**B**	B-	B	156.8	0.29	7.5	22.7	31.3	10.7	**9.8**	10.9
Emory Alliance Credit Union	Decatur	GA	**C+**	C+	C+	154.7	8.15	3.6	20.4	9.3	23.4	**5.0**	7.4
Empire Branch 36 Natl Assoc of Le Carr CU	New York	NY	**E+**	E+	D	5.1	-4.00	0.0	53.0	0.0	0.0	**8.0**	9.7
▼ Empire ONE Federal Credit Union	West Seneca	NY	**D+**	C-	C-	74.4	0.29	0.0	18.5	16.5	0.7	**9.7**	10.8
Empirt 207 Federal Credit Union	New York	NY	**C-**	C-	C-	4.5	4.91	0.0	58.4	0.0	0.0	**10.0**	26.8
▲ Employee Resources Credit Union	Lawrenceburg	TN	**C**	C-	C-	87.9	6.20	0.0	59.4	8.7	0.0	**6.2**	8.2
Employees Choice Federal Credit Union	El Cajon	CA	**C-**	C-	C-	18.6	9.75	0.0	21.4	15.5	0.0	**6.5**	8.5
Employees Credit Union	Estherville	IA	**A-**	A-	A-	93.8	6.32	3.3	33.8	10.0	0.0	**10.0**	19.9
Employees Credit Union	Dallas	TX	**D+**	D+	C-	67.8	1.72	0.6	45.6	3.7	1.5	**7.7**	9.5
Employees Federal Credit Union	Tulsa	OK	**D-**	D-	D-	21.9	-1.52	1.8	31.3	9.3	1.8	**5.9**	7.9
Employees First Credit Union	Logan	UT	**C**	C	C	1.8	-2.23	0.0	15.4	0.0	0.5	**10.0**	26.5
Employees United Federal Credit Union	Paris	TX	**B-**	B-	B-	11.0	6.30	0.0	28.7	0.0	0.0	**10.0**	27.3
Employment Security Credit Union	Jefferson City	MO	**C+**	C+	C+	69.1	1.99	0.0	19.5	7.3	52.9	**10.0**	12.0
▲ Emporia State Federal Credit Union	Emporia	KS	**B**	B-	B-	79.0	5.00	3.8	16.6	45.8	5.1	**8.0**	9.7
Empower Credit Union	West Allis	WI	**C-**	C-	C	94.8	-1.54	1.3	6.3	46.9	5.8	**10.0**	17.9
Empower Federal Credit Union	Syracuse	NY	**A-**	A-	B+	1625.5	9.06	7.8	30.1	17.5	8.0	**7.9**	9.7
Empowerment Community Development FCU	Houston	TX	**D-**	D-	D-	1.6	-1.70	0.0	46.1	0.0	0.0	**6.3**	8.3
▲ Encentus Federal Credit Union	Tulsa	OK	**C**	C-	D+	27.3	-5.48	0.0	38.6	9.9	0.0	**10.0**	12.3
Enchanted Mountains Federal Credit Union	Allegany	NY	**D+**	D+	D+	12.9	4.12	0.0	15.9	18.6	0.2	**6.8**	8.8
Encompass Federal Credit Union	Tipton	IN	**B+**	B+	A-	173.7	5.97	0.5	34.7	29.1	0.0	**10.0**	11.3
Encompass Niagara Federal Credit Union	Niagara Falls	NY	**C-**	C-	D+	16.6	-1.91	0.0	51.2	11.5	9.0	**10.0**	11.1
Encore Federal Credit Union	Des Plaines	IL	**C**	C	C	33.0	-4.04	0.0	11.1	0.0	54.6	**10.0**	17.1

Asset Quality Index	Non-Performing Loans as a % of Total Loans	Non-Performing Loans as a % of Capital	Net Charge-Offs Avg Loans	Profitability Index	Net Income ($Mil)	Return on Assets	Return on Equity	Net Interest Spread	Overhead Efficiency Ratio	Liquidity Index	Liquidity Ratio	Hot Money Ratio	Stability Index
9.3	1.00	2.2	0.26	**5.5**	0.02	0.96	4.16	3.81	82.7	**4.2**	25.8	1.9	**5.0**
5.6	1.60	9.7	4.66	**1.1**	-0.02	-0.14	-1.17	4.66	88.7	**3.6**	18.9	13.5	**4.9**
5.3	5.27	19.2	2.17	**0.7**	-0.03	-1.90	-14.81	2.68	104.4	**5.7**	61.3	0.0	**5.0**
6.0	2.04	11.9	0.67	**4.7**	0.05	0.59	6.71	3.60	75.4	**4.2**	27.2	3.1	**4.3**
6.5	1.36	5.4	0.20	**0.5**	-0.01	-0.64	-6.56	3.88	114.0	**5.3**	33.6	0.0	**3.1**
9.8	0.00	0.0	0.00	**2.7**	0.01	0.26	2.06	2.65	91.7	**5.0**	28.2	0.0	**6.1**
10.0	0.00	0.0	0.11	**2.5**	0.01	0.37	3.75	3.09	89.8	**5.3**	21.4	0.0	**4.9**
8.4	0.42	1.4	0.03	**4.6**	0.04	0.64	3.18	2.73	75.0	**4.5**	53.5	5.5	**7.7**
10.0	1.25	2.0	0.00	**0.1**	0.00	-0.38	-2.06	3.17	112.1	**6.5**	51.6	0.0	**6.2**
5.1	1.47	10.8	0.95	**3.3**	0.08	0.20	2.24	3.65	88.2	**3.7**	16.0	7.2	**5.0**
8.7	0.23	0.3	0.00	**0.0**	0.00	-0.83	-2.29	1.90	128.6	**5.6**	41.1	0.0	**6.2**
9.6	0.19	0.4	0.02	**2.6**	0.03	0.17	1.00	2.19	93.0	**5.5**	39.3	0.9	**7.2**
10.0	1.83	1.0	-0.73	**4.4**	0.10	1.02	7.13	1.96	85.4	**5.1**	17.9	0.0	**6.3**
3.7	2.47	19.0	1.84	**3.9**	0.03	0.38	3.25	5.61	73.0	**2.5**	17.5	19.4	**5.4**
9.7	0.23	2.1	0.31	**4.1**	2.26	0.65	7.73	2.60	78.6	**3.7**	21.2	9.5	**5.7**
9.7	0.34	2.4	0.11	**9.0**	5.68	1.25	12.33	3.71	75.9	**4.4**	19.8	2.0	**8.1**
9.7	0.60	1.3	2.61	**3.3**	0.00	0.08	0.55	3.31	64.8	**5.2**	16.9	0.0	**7.6**
6.2	1.18	7.6	0.54	**10.0**	3.78	2.90	21.97	5.03	57.4	**3.8**	13.9	1.5	**9.1**
9.9	0.58	1.0	0.00	**2.8**	0.00	0.22	1.57	4.37	85.3	**5.9**	33.8	0.0	**5.4**
8.2	0.07	0.4	0.20	**1.7**	0.00	0.12	0.84	4.41	97.7	**4.4**	17.6	0.9	**6.5**
6.6	2.03	6.6	-0.16	**2.0**	0.00	-0.09	-1.09	3.05	101.4	**5.4**	32.0	5.4	**1.7**
8.9	4.72	3.8	-1.94	**0.4**	0.00	-0.61	-1.66	4.66	113.3	**6.2**	109.0	0.0	**5.2**
9.1	4.25	4.1	0.00	**4.7**	0.00	0.55	1.97	5.10	88.9	**6.4**	60.0	0.0	**4.3**
8.9	1.15	4.1	0.06	**5.8**	0.38	0.97	9.73	4.14	83.8	**6.9**	51.8	4.7	**7.5**
7.2	0.68	8.1	0.09	**1.5**	-0.02	-0.27	-2.39	3.79	106.0	**6.7**	49.0	2.6	**6.0**
9.5	0.40	1.6	0.11	**3.5**	0.02	0.54	4.48	2.87	76.5	**5.2**	29.2	0.0	**6.3**
6.5	3.17	9.4	0.56	**4.4**	0.01	0.38	2.15	3.14	85.0	**5.3**	37.5	0.0	**4.3**
9.9	0.27	0.2	0.00	**1.6**	0.00	0.16	0.68	4.29	95.0	**7.8**	88.4	0.0	**5.9**
8.2	0.02	0.1	0.00	**7.5**	0.06	0.99	6.36	4.28	75.1	**4.0**	25.7	8.2	**6.3**
10.0	0.19	0.6	-0.14	**4.5**	0.05	0.51	3.94	2.87	84.8	**5.3**	33.0	0.0	**6.2**
9.4	1.50	3.0	0.13	**1.3**	0.00	0.20	1.07	2.84	91.2	**4.6**	23.6	0.0	**6.5**
9.7	0.37	1.8	0.41	**2.5**	0.10	0.41	3.89	3.57	86.8	**4.8**	29.2	2.6	**4.1**
7.0	0.92	7.3	0.07	**6.9**	0.08	1.02	8.24	4.87	79.9	**4.4**	34.0	0.4	**6.3**
9.9	1.31	2.3	0.00	**1.2**	0.00	0.00	0.00	3.01	100.0	**7.1**	84.7	0.0	**5.3**
5.6	1.08	10.7	0.39	**3.1**	0.08	0.68	10.70	4.22	84.3	**4.9**	30.7	4.2	**3.0**
8.4	0.13	0.9	0.00	**3.8**	0.00	0.25	2.83	5.55	94.6	**5.8**	42.3	3.8	**3.0**
7.1	0.76	3.8	1.52	**4.3**	0.13	1.20	12.91	4.42	78.8	**4.5**	19.0	1.6	**3.8**
7.8	0.82	4.8	0.19	**4.8**	0.05	0.85	7.43	3.84	78.6	**4.3**	23.3	1.7	**6.2**
9.4	0.22	1.3	0.21	**4.7**	0.19	0.49	4.52	3.16	86.3	**3.5**	22.1	9.7	**6.8**
7.7	0.73	5.4	0.48	**3.6**	0.11	0.28	3.93	3.91	88.1	**5.3**	29.5	0.9	**3.6**
0.9	6.81	30.4	0.00	**0.8**	0.00	-0.16	-1.63	7.84	101.9	**5.0**	21.6	0.0	**4.8**
7.9	0.64	2.6	0.37	**1.1**	-0.04	-0.21	-1.89	2.92	98.7	**5.1**	30.9	0.2	**4.9**
7.1	1.56	3.3	0.00	**3.5**	0.00	0.09	0.33	10.65	65.1	**6.5**	56.3	0.0	**7.2**
3.2	1.08	12.1	1.65	**4.7**	0.13	0.61	7.37	4.78	69.9	**3.3**	23.8	18.0	**3.5**
9.8	0.30	1.4	-0.11	**3.5**	0.02	0.42	4.85	3.08	87.4	**4.9**	25.5	2.2	**4.1**
7.3	1.85	5.8	0.41	**9.8**	0.49	2.15	10.72	3.81	40.0	**5.2**	45.7	0.1	**9.0**
7.1	0.53	3.1	0.33	**1.3**	-0.01	-0.08	-0.81	3.20	96.8	**4.6**	28.7	0.0	**3.9**
4.4	2.27	15.8	0.14	**2.8**	0.03	0.63	7.82	5.55	86.7	**4.7**	25.8	6.6	**1.7**
9.9	0.34	0.2	5.16	**0.7**	0.00	-0.46	-1.72	3.43	114.3	**5.4**	29.1	0.0	**6.9**
9.8	0.89	1.1	0.32	**6.8**	0.03	1.14	4.15	4.95	71.9	**6.9**	68.0	0.0	**6.3**
10.0	0.21	0.5	0.06	**2.8**	0.05	0.28	2.43	2.28	89.9	**5.4**	26.1	1.0	**6.2**
7.0	0.48	3.4	0.03	**5.8**	0.18	0.90	9.14	3.06	75.8	**3.2**	16.0	11.8	**5.6**
9.0	0.96	3.4	0.01	**1.5**	0.03	0.13	0.71	2.72	95.7	**3.7**	23.1	9.6	**6.2**
7.2	0.61	5.2	0.60	**6.1**	3.26	0.82	8.44	4.33	76.9	**3.8**	12.0	4.8	**7.9**
2.4	3.58	26.8	0.00	**3.1**	0.00	0.76	13.64	3.94	76.9	**6.0**	53.9	0.0	**1.0**
7.1	0.54	5.3	0.28	**2.2**	0.03	0.37	3.00	3.24	89.7	**5.2**	36.6	1.8	**5.2**
8.8	0.24	1.0	0.39	**1.7**	0.00	-0.03	-0.35	2.97	100.0	**5.3**	37.8	4.4	**3.8**
5.5	2.18	13.8	1.83	**4.4**	0.18	0.41	3.59	4.61	69.6	**2.6**	30.8	20.7	**6.2**
4.8	1.96	10.9	1.91	**1.4**	-0.04	-1.02	-8.96	4.61	89.3	**4.9**	31.4	0.7	**4.8**
10.0	0.00	0.0	-0.08	**2.2**	0.01	0.13	0.78	1.66	96.6	**6.1**	30.7	0.0	**7.3**

	Name	City	State	Rating	2016 Rating	2015 Rating	Total Assets ($Mil)	One Year Asset Growth	Comm-ercial Loans	Cons-umer Loans	Mort-gage Loans	Secur-ities	Capital-ization Index	Net Worth Ratio
	Energize Credit Union	Oklahoma City	OK	**C-**	C-	C	25.7	0.74	0.0	72.5	0.0	0.0	**9.7**	10.8
	Energy Capital Credit Union	Houston	TX	**C+**	C+	C+	231.1	1.16	0.0	42.0	10.8	9.4	**6.6**	8.8
	Energy Credit Union	West Roxbury	MA	**D+**	D+	D+	79.8	-1.72	0.1	12.9	34.5	33.2	**10.0**	18.7
	Energy One Federal Credit Union	Tulsa	OK	**C**	C	C-	253.9	-1.63	4.5	27.9	17.9	11.4	**5.2**	7.3
	Energy People Federal Credit Union	Tabernacle	NJ	**C+**	C+	C+	16.5	2.98	0.0	39.6	28.0	0.0	**10.0**	18.7
	Energy Plus Credit Union	Indianapolis	IN	**B-**	B-	B-	33.3	4.97	0.0	48.7	4.4	0.0	**10.0**	13.9
	Energy Services Federal Credit Union	Saint Cloud	MN	**C**	C	C	10.5	4.19	0.0	32.7	1.4	0.0	**10.0**	15.9
	Enfield Community Federal Credit Union	Enfield	CT	**D+**	D+	D+	29.2	6.23	0.0	23.3	1.5	22.7	**5.2**	7.2
	Engineers Federal Credit Union	Little Rock	AR	**D+**	D+	D	3.8	-1.67	0.0	37.6	0.0	0.0	**8.0**	9.7
▼	Enlighten Federal Credit Union	Jackson	TN	**C-**	C	C-	14.8	4.47	0.0	25.8	1.2	17.4	**9.0**	10.3
	Enrichment Federal Credit Union	Oak Ridge	TN	**C**	C	C	451.5	5.78	8.4	18.4	35.5	19.5	**8.1**	10.0
	Ent Credit Union	Colorado Springs	CO	**A**	A	A	4851.2	10.77	4.0	26.3	41.9	8.1	**10.0**	12.8
	Enterprise Credit Union	Enterprise	KS	**D-**	D-	E+	1.2	2.83	0.0	69.2	0.0	0.0	**6.8**	8.9
	Enterprise Credit Union	Brookfield	WI	**D+**	D+	D	27.9	1.45	0.0	16.6	1.4	28.4	**5.5**	8.0
	Entertainment Industries FCU	Brooklyn	NY	**E**	E	E-	15.6	3.80	8.0	19.1	41.3	0.0	**6.9**	8.9
	Entrust Financial Credit Union	Richmond	VA	**C-**	C-	C-	77.3	-3.63	2.8	30.1	16.2	4.6	**5.9**	7.9
	Envision Credit Union	Tallahassee	FL	**B**	B	B-	481.3	5.38	12.1	33.5	26.0	15.8	**6.7**	8.8
	Envista Credit Union	Topeka	KS	**B+**	B+	B+	338.5	9.17	4.0	56.5	19.6	2.9	**7.4**	9.4
	EP Federal Credit Union	Washington	DC	**C-**	C-	C	64.5	-2.33	0.1	22.3	21.5	36.9	**5.8**	8.2
	EPB Employees Credit Union	Chattanooga	TN	**D-**	D-	D	28.9	-1.46	0.0	24.1	6.3	18.3	**7.5**	9.3
	Epiphany Federal Credit Union	Brooklyn	NY	**D**	D	D	<1	-9.04	0.0	13.3	0.0	0.0	**10.0**	17.9
	Episcopal Community Federal Credit Union	Los Angeles	CA	**E+**	E+	E+	4.9	-5.16	0.0	40.1	0.0	3.1	**5.4**	7.4
	EQT Federal Credit Union	Pittsburgh	PA	**C-**	C-	C-	40.4	-0.52	0.0	4.4	0.0	0.0	**9.9**	10.9
	Equishare Credit Union	Wichita	KS	**C-**	C-	C-	33.4	13.23	0.0	62.3	11.4	0.0	**8.1**	9.7
	Equitable Federal Credit Union	Akron	OH	**D+**	D+	C-	7.3	-5.37	0.0	32.6	0.0	32.9	**10.0**	14.5
▲	Erie City Employees Federal Credit Union	Erie	PA	**D+**	D	D+	8.0	-12.19	0.0	36.0	0.0	0.0	**10.0**	18.4
	Erie Community Credit Union	Erie	PA	**C+**	C+	C+	114.0	1.80	0.0	40.3	0.5	3.6	**6.2**	8.3
▼	Erie Community Federal Credit Union	Sandusky	OH	**D+**	C-	D+	26.4	5.09	14.4	18.9	22.9	20.2	**6.7**	8.8
	Erie County Employees Credit Union	Buffalo	NY	**C+**	C+	C+	26.3	5.64	0.0	20.5	13.2	13.8	**10.0**	11.8
	Erie Federal Credit Union	Erie	PA	**B**	B	B	480.2	6.32	6.2	19.8	18.5	38.2	**9.6**	10.7
	Erie Firefighters Federal Credit Union	Erie	PA	**D-**	D-	D-	8.4	0.39	0.0	25.0	0.9	0.0	**6.9**	8.9
	Erie Lackawanna Railroad Company Empls FCU	Hoboken	NJ	**C+**	C+	C+	8.2	16.42	0.0	53.7	0.0	0.0	**10.0**	26.2
▼	Erie Metro Federal Credit Union	Blasdell	NY	**C-**	C	C	36.6	13.87	0.0	20.8	13.2	0.0	**9.4**	10.6
	Erie Police Federal Credit Union	Erie	PA	**C**	C	C+	2.5	4.35	0.0	42.5	0.0	0.0	**10.0**	20.4
	Erie T.P.E. Federal Credit Union	Erie	PA	**D+**	D+	D+	2.3	-3.58	0.0	45.4	9.5	0.0	**10.0**	30.1
	Erie Times Federal Credit Union	Erie	PA	**D**	D	D	6.7	0.54	0.0	14.9	0.0	0.0	**10.0**	16.4
	ERRL Federal Credit Union	Wyndmoor	PA	**D-**	D-	E+	1.6	6.55	0.0	30.8	0.0	0.0	**6.7**	8.7
	Escondido Federal Credit Union	Escondido	CA	**B-**	B-	C+	44.8	9.01	0.2	22.4	5.5	0.0	**7.7**	9.5
	ESL Federal Credit Union	Rochester	NY	**A+**	A+	A+	6224.5	7.71	7.0	14.3	8.2	42.8	**10.0**	15.3
	Espeeco Federal Credit Union	Bakersfield	CA	**C-**	C-	D	8.7	-0.39	3.7	30.5	12.8	4.3	**10.0**	18.2
	Esquire-GoodFellowship FCU	Brooklyn	NY	**D**	D	D	<1	-10.25	0.0	18.1	0.0	0.0	**10.0**	29.5
▼	Essential Federal Credit Union	Plaquemine	LA	**B-**	B+	B+	358.2	17.08	2.7	34.8	13.5	0.0	**5.1**	7.1
	Essex County NJ Employees FCU	Newark	NJ	**C-**	C-	D+	6.7	-1.26	0.0	36.1	0.0	0.0	**10.0**	11.9
▼	Essex County Teachers FCU	Bloomfield	NJ	**E+**	D-	D	14.6	0.95	1.6	34.8	10.1	0.0	**5.2**	7.2
▼	Estacado Federal Credit Union	Hobbs	NM	**C-**	C	C-	58.5	-2.38	0.0	42.1	0.0	17.5	**9.9**	10.9
▼	Ethicon Suture Credit Union	Chicago	IL	**D+**	C-	C-	1.1	0.64	0.0	71.2	0.0	0.0	**10.0**	11.0
	Etma Federal Credit Union	Louisville	TN	**C+**	C+	C+	17.6	6.80	0.0	35.7	17.3	0.0	**10.0**	13.9
	ETS Credit Union	Eldora	IA	**B-**	B-	B-	2.8	11.18	0.0	25.2	0.0	0.0	**10.0**	14.7
▲	Evangelical Christian Credit Union	Brea	CA	**C-**	D+	D-	808.3	-12.07	60.3	11.6	58.0	10.7	**5.9**	7.9
▼	Evanston Firemens Credit Union	Evanston	IL	**C**	C+	C+	1.9	3.49	0.0	26.5	0.0	0.0	**10.0**	15.1
	Evansville Federal Credit Union	Evansville	IN	**B+**	B+	B+	70.0	5.54	3.3	25.5	28.4	0.0	**10.0**	11.9
	Evansville Firefighters FCU	Evansville	IN	**C+**	C+	C+	24.2	16.01	0.0	37.4	22.0	0.0	**9.8**	10.8
	Evansville Teachers Federal Credit Union	Evansville	IN	**B+**	B+	B+	1371.1	8.44	2.5	35.3	29.0	1.7	**7.2**	9.2
	Ever $ Green Federal Credit Union	Rochester	NY	**C+**	C+	C+	32.9	0.08	0.5	18.6	4.0	22.9	**8.2**	9.8
	Everence Federal Credit Union	Lancaster	PA	**B-**	B-	C+	179.5	13.15	14.5	12.7	33.8	7.9	**5.3**	7.4
	Everett Credit Union	Everett	MA	**C**	C	C	46.3	1.33	0.0	5.5	52.5	16.8	**10.0**	13.8
	Everglades Federal Credit Union	Clewiston	FL	**B+**	B+	B	37.5	9.38	0.0	35.6	15.0	0.0	**10.0**	11.9
	Evergreen Credit Union	Portland	ME	**B-**	B-	C+	269.8	10.54	10.5	10.7	32.4	4.7	**6.4**	8.5
	Evergreen Credit Union	Neenah	WI	**B**	B	B	35.9	3.87	0.0	32.5	29.5	0.0	**10.0**	12.2
	Evergreen Park Schools FCU	Evergreen Park	IL	**C+**	C+	C	12.2	-0.55	0.0	21.1	0.0	0.0	**10.0**	12.4

Asset Mix columns (Comm-ercial Loans, Cons-umer Loans, Mort-gage Loans, Secur-ities) are "Asset Mix (As a % of Total Assets)".

Asset Quality Index	Non-Performing Loans as a % of Total Loans	Non-Performing Loans as a % of Capital	Net Charge-Offs Avg Loans	Profitability Index	Net Income ($Mil)	Return on Assets	Return on Equity	Net Interest Spread	Overhead Efficiency Ratio	Liquidity Index	Liquidity Ratio	Hot Money Ratio	Stability Index
5.2	0.63	4.3	-0.08	**2.4**	0.01	0.22	2.02	2.88	85.4	**3.0**	17.4	7.4	**5.5**
7.1	0.30	3.5	0.47	**3.3**	0.26	0.45	5.48	3.45	79.0	**3.7**	10.3	1.5	**4.8**
10.0	0.31	0.9	-0.03	**0.7**	-0.02	-0.09	-0.48	2.90	110.2	**3.8**	11.5	4.9	**6.5**
5.3	1.36	19.7	0.24	**3.0**	0.23	0.38	5.15	2.99	85.3	**4.3**	21.3	5.9	**3.8**
9.5	0.00	0.0	0.13	**2.8**	0.01	0.22	1.17	3.62	90.6	**3.7**	13.7	3.0	**7.4**
7.9	0.56	2.8	0.41	**3.9**	0.05	0.55	3.89	4.42	85.1	**4.2**	22.8	3.2	**7.0**
9.5	0.76	2.2	0.17	**2.2**	0.01	0.19	1.21	3.24	90.2	**4.7**	18.7	0.0	**6.8**
6.7	0.97	6.5	0.46	**3.6**	0.04	0.53	7.27	3.60	86.3	**4.6**	15.1	1.0	**3.2**
9.9	0.07	0.3	0.00	**2.0**	0.00	0.21	2.20	2.28	85.7	**4.7**	15.0	0.0	**4.7**
9.9	0.07	0.2	0.83	**2.3**	0.01	0.14	1.31	3.04	89.8	**7.2**	53.0	0.0	**4.8**
9.6	0.04	0.5	0.22	**3.1**	0.35	0.31	3.17	2.98	87.9	**4.2**	12.6	3.7	**6.4**
9.7	0.20	1.3	0.16	**7.3**	10.41	0.87	6.94	2.53	65.8	**4.0**	18.9	5.9	**9.4**
0.0	9.08	71.3	0.00	**5.1**	0.01	1.73	19.61	7.20	80.0	**3.7**	10.5	0.0	**4.3**
8.9	0.32	1.9	0.14	**2.0**	0.01	0.19	2.88	3.28	91.1	**5.4**	17.9	0.0	**1.7**
0.3	11.80	127.4	0.11	**1.8**	0.00	0.05	0.81	5.53	87.2	**4.5**	19.5	0.0	**2.7**
6.4	1.05	6.4	0.46	**2.2**	0.02	0.09	1.12	3.55	93.0	**4.8**	25.2	2.0	**2.8**
6.7	0.65	6.5	0.45	**6.1**	0.83	0.71	8.36	4.41	85.2	**4.1**	14.1	1.4	**4.7**
5.4	0.67	7.6	0.68	**3.9**	0.14	0.17	1.77	3.26	80.7	**2.6**	9.0	9.9	**6.5**
8.8	0.33	2.2	0.20	**2.0**	0.03	0.21	2.74	2.90	90.8	**4.2**	14.9	3.5	**2.8**
6.4	1.68	6.4	0.82	**0.0**	-0.04	-0.50	-5.32	2.88	104.9	**4.7**	23.1	0.7	**3.1**
9.6	0.00	0.0	0.00	**0.0**	0.00	-5.23	-28.57	4.17	300.0	**7.9**	87.1	0.0	**5.0**
4.3	1.98	15.8	-0.41	**1.8**	0.00	0.08	1.54	4.89	98.4	**5.6**	22.7	0.0	**0.6**
10.0	2.42	1.0	1.11	**1.9**	0.01	0.05	0.45	1.04	87.3	**5.6**	37.5	0.0	**4.6**
2.4	1.35	21.5	1.99	**2.0**	-0.02	-0.22	-2.42	5.92	76.8	**4.3**	19.4	1.1	**3.4**
8.5	0.86	2.9	2.82	**0.5**	-0.03	-1.42	-9.74	3.22	94.4	**4.1**	23.2	10.4	**4.7**
7.9	1.60	3.6	2.08	**1.9**	0.01	0.54	3.00	3.52	75.4	**4.8**	39.9	0.0	**5.2**
3.4	2.38	25.7	1.27	**1.9**	-0.07	-0.24	-2.82	4.49	81.2	**4.7**	25.1	3.2	**5.0**
5.5	1.43	7.5	0.13	**0.7**	-0.03	-0.53	-5.85	3.35	107.6	**4.7**	26.8	4.8	**3.7**
9.7	0.45	1.3	0.13	**2.5**	0.02	0.26	2.19	2.72	91.0	**5.1**	15.8	0.0	**6.2**
9.0	0.57	2.8	0.45	**3.9**	0.49	0.41	3.78	2.91	81.5	**4.2**	31.0	6.0	**7.0**
7.4	1.55	4.6	1.77	**3.0**	0.01	0.33	3.76	2.77	71.2	**5.2**	23.4	0.0	**2.3**
7.7	1.35	2.8	2.01	**10.0**	0.06	3.02	11.37	6.92	42.6	**4.1**	39.3	13.0	**5.7**
8.4	0.68	2.7	1.13	**1.6**	-0.02	-0.19	-1.75	3.24	94.6	**5.3**	25.8	0.0	**5.1**
9.8	0.61	1.3	0.00	**2.7**	0.00	0.00	0.00	3.64	100.0	**5.9**	43.2	0.0	**7.1**
5.9	2.13	4.8	2.20	**0.7**	-0.01	-1.55	-5.24	4.89	104.4	**5.2**	41.7	0.0	**5.2**
10.0	0.76	1.0	0.27	**0.0**	-0.01	-0.37	-2.17	3.36	105.5	**6.5**	45.5	0.0	**5.8**
10.0	0.00	0.0	0.00	**1.1**	0.00	0.00	0.00	3.02	110.0	**5.3**	22.5	0.0	**3.5**
10.0	0.30	1.1	0.31	**3.6**	0.05	0.49	5.03	2.83	74.4	**6.0**	38.6	4.7	**5.3**
9.9	0.58	1.7	0.46	**9.5**	25.59	1.67	11.05	3.31	50.7	**4.9**	27.1	7.9	**10.0**
9.5	0.70	1.7	1.07	**0.0**	-0.02	-0.84	-4.73	3.24	129.7	**6.8**	59.9	1.1	**6.1**
9.4	6.25	3.7	0.00	**0.0**	0.00	-2.22	-7.48	5.97	300.0	**8.6**	114.6	0.0	**5.7**
4.8	1.01	11.9	0.49	**2.8**	0.27	0.31	4.22	4.11	82.4	**2.1**	13.5	20.4	**3.7**
9.8	0.52	1.5	0.47	**1.9**	0.00	0.12	1.01	7.38	98.8	**5.1**	19.1	0.0	**5.7**
4.1	2.65	18.2	1.78	**1.5**	-0.05	-1.36	-17.57	4.51	94.2	**5.4**	29.4	0.0	**1.0**
6.2	1.33	6.0	0.93	**1.9**	-0.01	-0.06	-0.56	4.19	87.9	**4.2**	27.3	8.4	**4.8**
2.7	3.87	23.5	0.00	**4.1**	0.00	0.73	6.61	7.12	80.0	**5.3**	30.0	0.0	**5.2**
9.0	0.34	1.6	0.00	**3.3**	0.01	0.23	1.64	3.70	94.1	**4.6**	25.2	2.8	**7.4**
9.9	0.00	0.0	0.00	**7.4**	0.01	1.02	6.85	3.24	56.3	**6.6**	36.4	0.0	**5.7**
4.9	0.93	7.5	0.08	**2.1**	0.84	0.41	5.29	3.28	81.5	**2.5**	28.2	32.5	**5.2**
10.0	0.00	0.0	0.00	**1.0**	-0.01	-2.76	-17.69	3.72	186.7	**6.2**	46.4	0.0	**7.3**
8.4	0.54	3.1	-0.01	**5.7**	0.10	0.56	4.63	3.56	90.0	**4.0**	20.9	6.3	**6.4**
8.2	0.27	1.5	0.17	**4.1**	0.02	0.30	2.59	3.26	92.4	**4.8**	25.9	1.6	**6.0**
8.6	0.33	2.9	0.29	**6.1**	3.34	1.01	10.80	3.35	79.1	**3.1**	18.5	16.4	**7.5**
7.6	0.39	1.9	0.24	**3.7**	0.03	0.40	4.12	3.23	84.1	**4.4**	12.7	4.4	**5.8**
6.4	1.30	9.9	0.05	**4.1**	0.18	0.42	5.57	3.71	89.4	**4.7**	34.6	1.6	**5.1**
8.0	0.63	3.0	0.00	**2.6**	0.02	0.20	1.45	3.10	94.3	**3.4**	12.7	6.8	**6.7**
8.4	0.40	2.6	1.17	**3.7**	0.00	-0.02	-0.18	4.57	79.2	**5.0**	31.6	7.9	**6.2**
8.3	0.51	3.6	0.26	**3.9**	0.31	0.48	5.55	3.27	84.0	**4.9**	20.3	1.3	**5.4**
7.4	0.94	5.8	0.00	**6.1**	0.07	0.74	5.98	3.91	84.1	**3.3**	15.3	5.4	**6.9**
10.0	0.55	1.0	0.00	**3.6**	0.03	0.82	6.66	2.01	58.3	**5.8**	49.3	0.0	**5.0**

Name	City	State	Rating	2016 Rating	2015 Rating	Total Assets ($Mil)	One Year Asset Growth	Asset Mix (As a % of Total Assets): Commercial Loans	Consumer Loans	Mortgage Loans	Securities	Capitalization Index	Net Worth Ratio
▼ EvergreenDIRECT Credit Union	Tumwater	WA	**B-**	B	B	57.2	6.60	1.0	42.7	10.1	12.0	**10.0**	11.5
Everman Parkway Credit Union	Fort Worth	TX	**D+**	D+	D	5.0	5.88	0.0	66.3	0.0	25.9	**10.0**	29.1
Everyone's Federal Credit Union	Tucumcari	NM	**B+**	B+	B	31.1	9.47	9.1	25.9	4.1	0.0	**10.0**	14.3
▼ Evolve Federal Credit Union	El Paso	TX	**C-**	C	C+	317.6	-5.04	0.0	49.5	16.8	15.3	**9.6**	10.9
Evonik Employees Federal Credit Union	Theodore	AL	**C-**	C-	D+	7.8	4.91	0.0	47.4	0.0	0.0	**8.6**	10.0
EWA Federal Credit Union	Ewa Beach	HI	**C+**	C+	C	13.3	2.12	0.0	25.0	0.0	0.0	**10.0**	22.4
EWEB Employees Federal Credit Union	Eugene	OR	**C-**	C-	C-	25.4	10.68	1.3	19.0	19.9	0.0	**5.9**	7.9
▲ Excel Federal Credit Union	Norcross	GA	**C+**	C	C	106.1	8.30	17.7	26.9	33.9	0.0	**8.5**	10.0
Express Credit Union	Seattle	WA	**C-**	C-	C-	11.5	-2.43	0.0	76.0	4.0	0.0	**9.5**	10.7
Express-News Federal Credit Union	San Antonio	TX	**C-**	C-	C-	7.4	-1.13	0.0	27.6	13.0	0.0	**10.0**	11.5
Extra Credit Union	Warren	MI	**B**	B	B-	224.3	7.10	0.1	24.4	15.0	32.4	**6.5**	8.7
F C Federal Credit Union	Cherry Hill	NJ	**D**	D	D	<1	-6.42	0.0	4.7	2.3	0.0	**10.0**	30.8
F C I Federal Credit Union	Littleton	CO	**D**	D	D	4.7	-7.72	0.0	33.7	0.0	0.0	**10.0**	22.0
F C S Federal Credit Union	Floydada	TX	**B+**	B+	B+	12.2	3.32	0.0	33.7	0.0	0.0	**10.0**	30.9
F&A Federal Credit Union	Monterey Park	CA	**A**	A	A	1586.7	6.89	0.0	6.3	4.7	73.1	**10.0**	15.0
F.C.I. Ashland Federal Credit Union	Ashland	KY	**C-**	C-	C-	4.9	-0.82	0.0	66.7	0.0	0.0	**10.0**	21.7
FAA Federal Credit Union	Memphis	TN	**B-**	B-	C+	109.1	-0.28	0.0	21.4	12.1	4.2	**9.9**	11.0
▼ FAB Church Federal Credit Union	Savannah	GA	**D+**	C-	C-	<1	-5.18	0.0	24.8	0.0	0.0	**10.0**	22.7
Fairfax City Federal Credit Union	Fairfax	VA	**C**	C	D+	2.2	-4.49	0.0	49.2	0.0	0.0	**10.0**	11.6
Fairfax County Federal Credit Union	Fairfax	VA	**A-**	A-	A-	406.3	18.14	0.4	6.0	10.6	9.3	**7.9**	9.7
Fairfield Federal Credit Union	Pine Bluff	AR	**C**	C	C	87.8	2.14	0.0	24.2	16.5	0.0	**10.0**	19.8
Fairleigh Dickinson University FCU	Madison	NJ	**C-**	C-	C-	12.4	-0.76	0.0	27.3	5.4	0.0	**9.8**	10.9
Fairmont Federal Credit Union	Fairmont	WV	**B-**	B-	B	343.8	4.72	3.9	27.4	37.3	3.5	**7.1**	9.1
Fairmont School Employees FCU	Fairmont	MN	**D+**	D+	C-	2.2	0.74	0.0	69.0	0.0	0.0	**10.0**	13.1
Fairmont Village Credit Union	East Saint Louis	IL	**D**	D	C-	2.0	-8.44	0.0	41.8	0.0	0.0	**10.0**	17.9
Fairport Federal Credit Union	Fairport	NY	**C**	C	C	39.9	4.40	0.0	26.5	0.0	0.0	**6.0**	8.0
Fairwinds Credit Union	Orlando	FL	**B+**	B+	B	2168.4	9.35	8.3	24.2	34.4	24.7	**7.8**	9.7
Faith Community United Credit Union	Cleveland	OH	**C+**	C+	B-	13.5	-0.83	11.7	48.8	10.2	3.7	**10.0**	18.7
▼ Faith Cooperative Federal Credit Union	Dallas	TX	**C-**	C	C	1.1	126.18	0.0	60.7	0.0	0.0	**8.1**	9.8
Faith Tabernacle Baptist FCU	Stamford	CT	**D-**	D-	E+	<1	-5.95	0.0	5.7	0.0	0.0	**9.6**	11.4
Fall River Municipal Credit Union	Fall River	MA	**C**	C	C	204.1	1.21	3.1	11.0	41.9	30.8	**10.0**	12.7
Fallon County Federal Credit Union	Baker	MT	**C-**	C-	C+	11.6	4.53	0.0	20.9	11.6	0.0	**7.3**	9.2
▼ Falls Catholic Credit Union	Cuyahoga Falls	OH	**C**	C+	B	44.5	3.77	3.4	23.0	5.4	13.9	**10.0**	14.4
Families & Schools Together FCU	Hanford	CA	**A-**	A-	A-	150.8	6.80	23.4	31.7	35.7	8.1	**9.0**	10.4
Families First Federal Credit Union	Casper	WY	**C-**	C-	C-	5.6	-0.12	0.0	46.4	24.6	0.0	**10.0**	15.1
Family 1st Federal Credit Union	New Castle	PA	**C**	C	C	12.2	0.68	0.0	59.6	0.0	0.0	**10.0**	12.2
Family 1st Of Texas Federal Credit Union	Fort Worth	TX	**C**	C	C	13.9	-5.08	0.0	68.1	4.2	0.0	**10.0**	14.4
Family Advantage Federal Credit Union	Spring Hill	TN	**B-**	B-	C+	60.3	13.35	0.0	38.4	7.7	0.0	**6.0**	8.0
▼ Family Community Credit Union	Charles City	IA	**C+**	B-	C+	19.0	5.69	0.0	21.2	0.0	0.0	**10.0**	11.8
Family Credit Union	Davenport	IA	**A-**	A-	A-	155.0	4.52	1.5	25.8	19.9	30.9	**10.0**	12.4
▼ Family Financial Credit Union	Norton Shores	MI	**B-**	B	B	107.6	5.64	0.1	32.7	13.7	30.0	**10.0**	13.1
Family First Credit Union	Hapeville	GA	**C**	C	B	97.1	4.99	2.0	36.6	9.1	0.5	**10.0**	12.5
Family First Credit Union	Saginaw	MI	**D-**	D-	D	78.0	-3.49	1.3	27.3	21.6	27.9	**7.5**	9.5
Family First Federal Credit Union	Great Falls	MT	**D-**	D-	E+	13.9	6.09	0.0	24.9	5.0	0.0	**5.2**	7.2
Family First of NY Federal Credit Union	Rochester	NY	**B+**	B+	B+	188.9	10.57	10.0	20.9	21.9	1.0	**9.0**	10.3
Family Focus Federal Credit Union	Omaha	NE	**B+**	B+	B+	33.0	7.59	0.0	45.5	21.2	0.0	**10.0**	13.6
Family Horizons Credit Union	Indianapolis	IN	**C**	C	C	88.3	-1.94	0.0	64.0	13.3	8.5	**9.8**	10.8
Family Savings Credit Union	Rainbow City	AL	**B+**	B+	A-	405.9	10.53	0.1	45.7	17.0	4.6	**9.5**	10.7
Family Security Credit Union	Decatur	AL	**A**	A	A	625.9	9.09	0.4	39.3	5.1	15.1	**10.0**	13.6
Family Trust Federal Credit Union	Rock Hill	SC	**B+**	B+	B+	474.2	12.25	0.9	30.6	30.1	1.1	**6.5**	8.5
Fannin County Teachers FCU	Bonham	TX	**C+**	C+	C+	9.1	4.59	0.0	58.2	0.0	0.0	**10.0**	20.4
Fannin Federal Credit Union	Bonham	TX	**B**	B	B-	36.5	14.11	0.0	48.5	0.0	0.0	**9.0**	10.4
Far Rockaway Postal Federal Credit Union	Far Rockaway	NY	**C-**	C-	C-	<1	-28.24	0.0	73.6	0.0	0.0	**10.0**	27.5
▼ Fargo Federal Employee FCU	Fargo	ND	**D+**	C-	C-	5.0	1.94	0.0	24.2	0.0	0.0	**8.8**	10.2
Fargo Public Schools FCU	Fargo	ND	**B-**	B-	B-	38.9	9.76	0.0	16.4	18.6	0.0	**10.0**	12.4
Fargo VA Federal Credit Union	Fargo	ND	**C+**	C+	C	10.4	6.46	0.0	38.3	0.0	0.0	**10.0**	11.6
Farm Bureau Family Credit Union	Lansing	MI	**C-**	C-	D+	19.3	2.94	0.0	25.9	0.0	0.0	**6.7**	8.7
Farm Credit Employees FCU	Saint Paul	MN	**C**	C	C-	13.7	3.72	0.0	42.4	11.1	0.0	**8.2**	9.8
Farmers Branch City Employees FCU	Farmers Branch	TX	**D**	D	D+	5.0	-4.89	0.0	28.8	0.0	0.0	**10.0**	19.5
Farmers Credit Union	Hays	KS	**D+**		D	13.8	-2.36	17.6	8.3	9.4	0.0	**10.0**	11.3

Asset Quality Index	Non-Performing Loans as a % of Total Loans	Non-Performing Loans as a % of Capital	Net Charge-Offs Avg Loans	Profitability Index	Net Income ($Mil)	Return on Assets	Return on Equity	Net Interest Spread	Overhead Efficiency Ratio	Liquidity Index	Liquidity Ratio	Hot Money Ratio	Stability Index
9.6	0.28	1.9	1.05	**2.5**	-0.11	-0.81	-6.94	4.71	95.1	**4.6**	18.2	0.5	**5.5**
8.2	0.80	1.8	0.24	**2.0**	0.00	0.16	0.55	4.15	96.3	**4.0**	22.1	0.0	**6.0**
9.1	0.22	0.7	0.53	**4.9**	0.02	0.27	1.80	3.88	94.2	**4.9**	31.2	9.6	**7.5**
5.1	1.67	11.2	1.51	**2.0**	0.35	0.44	4.37	3.39	72.9	**2.4**	11.4	19.8	**4.3**
8.8	0.00	0.0	0.21	**6.6**	0.02	1.25	12.42	3.90	66.3	**5.3**	24.1	0.0	**4.3**
9.8	1.03	1.3	0.42	**2.3**	0.00	0.12	0.54	2.91	93.3	**5.1**	28.6	0.0	**6.9**
9.9	0.08	0.5	0.00	**3.4**	0.02	0.39	4.83	2.88	87.5	**5.7**	33.8	0.9	**3.8**
8.5	0.44	2.7	0.17	**3.5**	0.15	0.58	5.09	3.37	89.9	**4.6**	34.8	5.7	**6.9**
6.6	0.61	5.4	0.90	**2.7**	0.01	0.17	1.63	6.43	91.1	**2.9**	18.5	11.8	**4.6**
8.7	0.63	3.6	0.25	**1.0**	0.00	-0.22	-1.89	3.83	102.9	**5.6**	37.4	0.0	**6.1**
7.8	0.83	4.6	1.23	**5.0**	0.39	0.71	8.31	4.68	75.7	**4.8**	16.1	1.7	**5.1**
10.0	0.00	0.0	0.00	**0.0**	0.00	-1.79	-5.80	3.07	300.0	**8.8**	128.4	0.0	**6.2**
9.8	0.00	0.0	-0.45	**0.0**	-0.02	-1.81	-8.14	3.57	148.8	**5.5**	32.1	0.0	**5.6**
9.8	0.50	0.6	0.66	**9.2**	0.04	1.42	4.59	2.86	45.1	**4.6**	16.9	0.0	**7.0**
10.0	0.21	0.3	-0.01	**6.8**	4.57	1.16	7.94	1.64	46.2	**4.2**	9.7	12.2	**9.6**
5.4	3.95	11.6	0.00	**1.8**	0.00	0.08	0.37	3.04	94.1	**4.7**	34.6	0.0	**6.6**
9.9	0.18	0.6	0.04	**3.4**	0.11	0.41	3.67	2.69	86.9	**5.5**	54.8	3.9	**6.8**
1.7	38.71	42.9	161.19	**2.4**	0.00	0.00	0.00	11.76	50.0	**8.2**	95.1	0.0	**5.9**
8.5	0.00	0.0	0.00	**2.8**	0.00	0.00	0.00	5.61	100.0	**5.5**	24.9	0.0	**6.3**
8.6	0.38	3.0	0.32	**8.9**	1.77	1.73	19.39	4.17	52.4	**2.8**	21.6	15.2	**7.5**
7.0	2.11	5.3	0.40	**4.4**	0.22	1.00	5.01	3.36	85.8	**4.7**	30.7	0.5	**6.5**
6.3	1.47	8.2	0.15	**2.6**	0.01	0.29	2.69	3.72	91.9	**4.0**	20.6	3.8	**5.4**
8.2	0.24	2.9	0.14	**4.0**	0.33	0.40	4.83	3.38	88.6	**4.7**	24.6	1.6	**5.8**
4.7	1.73	9.8	0.00	**4.4**	0.01	1.08	8.42	3.54	68.4	**3.7**	23.5	0.0	**3.7**
5.1	5.11	12.6	0.00	**1.2**	0.00	-0.61	-3.37	5.78	111.8	**6.1**	60.5	0.0	**4.8**
10.0	0.02	0.1	0.00	**3.3**	0.04	0.43	5.44	2.82	83.6	**5.3**	35.8	1.0	**4.0**
7.0	0.36	6.8	0.20	**6.2**	5.25	0.99	10.29	3.12	77.2	**3.8**	10.4	3.1	**7.2**
5.3	1.91	6.3	2.51	**6.8**	0.11	3.40	18.36	7.93	74.9	**4.4**	24.4	0.0	**5.0**
0.0	8.33	52.3	6.13	**9.5**	0.01	1.88	18.87	3.89	82.8	**6.7**	76.3	0.0	**6.2**
0.0	34.72	119.1	0.00	**6.8**	0.00	5.26	47.06	7.02	33.3	**6.8**	60.7	0.0	**5.0**
9.8	0.18	0.9	0.14	**2.2**	0.05	0.10	0.83	2.61	95.7	**3.3**	6.6	8.6	**7.0**
6.2	1.04	5.0	1.74	**3.2**	0.01	0.48	5.21	5.21	87.2	**5.0**	53.0	21.7	**4.9**
1.7	15.06	46.3	1.50	**5.1**	0.08	0.70	4.82	3.64	72.9	**5.1**	37.3	6.7	**6.3**
7.0	0.30	5.1	0.39	**9.3**	0.52	1.40	13.42	3.96	67.0	**4.4**	18.1	1.4	**7.5**
8.0	0.35	1.9	0.16	**1.6**	0.00	-0.14	-0.94	4.07	101.6	**3.7**	12.5	0.0	**6.9**
4.7	2.29	12.0	0.35	**2.7**	0.01	0.37	2.96	3.19	90.8	**4.0**	25.4	11.3	**6.2**
6.5	1.01	5.2	1.07	**2.4**	0.00	0.03	0.20	6.30	85.6	**3.5**	11.5	3.5	**5.4**
6.9	0.55	3.5	0.77	**9.6**	0.20	1.33	16.49	4.59	68.3	**5.7**	36.9	2.8	**3.9**
10.0	0.33	1.1	0.00	**2.3**	-0.03	-0.62	-5.14	2.68	110.6	**6.1**	49.7	0.0	**6.1**
9.0	0.60	3.0	0.30	**5.3**	0.30	0.80	6.36	3.35	78.4	**4.2**	18.6	4.6	**7.5**
9.1	0.65	2.6	-0.03	**3.2**	0.06	0.23	1.74	3.09	93.7	**4.1**	17.4	6.0	**8.0**
7.1	0.99	7.3	0.98	**2.0**	-0.01	-0.03	-0.23	4.72	91.0	**4.9**	33.8	3.9	**5.1**
7.7	0.57	3.1	0.51	**0.4**	-0.06	-0.29	-3.17	3.29	95.0	**3.5**	14.0	15.8	**2.9**
7.1	0.46	4.3	0.22	**2.6**	0.02	0.53	7.31	3.85	85.2	**5.7**	35.1	1.6	**1.7**
8.7	0.43	3.2	0.26	**4.5**	0.20	0.42	4.02	3.93	85.5	**3.1**	13.3	8.4	**7.0**
6.9	0.72	3.9	0.29	**5.7**	0.04	0.52	3.75	4.46	80.2	**3.5**	19.5	5.7	**7.9**
8.4	0.12	0.9	0.33	**2.8**	0.08	0.36	3.20	2.86	90.5	**3.5**	8.0	2.8	**5.5**
5.2	1.10	8.6	1.01	**5.3**	0.58	0.59	5.42	5.18	80.2	**4.4**	21.1	5.9	**6.9**
8.9	0.48	2.7	0.38	**6.8**	1.36	0.90	6.74	2.88	73.8	**4.7**	24.6	7.7	**9.3**
7.5	0.56	5.0	0.55	**5.8**	0.62	0.53	6.66	4.00	83.0	**4.1**	26.1	10.6	**5.8**
7.9	0.53	1.9	0.00	**6.7**	0.02	0.92	4.56	4.26	62.9	**4.0**	25.0	0.0	**5.0**
8.1	0.00	1.0	0.48	**9.0**	0.17	1.89	18.40	4.81	61.4	**5.0**	28.9	2.4	**5.9**
2.7	9.16	20.2	0.00	**2.7**	0.00	-1.92	-7.77	7.29	133.3	**5.1**	42.8	0.0	**5.2**
7.1	0.61	2.5	9.05	**3.3**	0.01	0.87	8.71	2.84	65.6	**5.2**	19.0	3.0	**3.0**
10.0	0.09	0.3	0.51	**3.4**	0.04	0.45	3.58	2.67	84.4	**5.1**	23.9	2.7	**7.1**
8.7	0.92	4.4	0.00	**4.3**	0.01	0.46	3.99	3.54	89.7	**5.1**	23.6	0.0	**6.6**
8.6	0.49	2.2	0.15	**3.5**	0.02	0.36	4.07	2.90	85.7	**5.5**	28.1	0.0	**3.9**
9.6	0.11	0.8	0.00	**3.8**	0.01	0.37	3.88	3.33	85.9	**4.4**	24.0	2.7	**5.2**
9.7	0.66	1.3	0.00	**0.0**	-0.02	-1.27	-6.48	2.96	147.2	**4.6**	33.3	13.5	**6.4**
9.1	0.27	0.8	0.00	**0.8**	0.00	-0.06	-0.51	2.76	102.3	**6.5**	66.1	0.0	**4.8**

	Name	City	State	Rating	2016 Rating	2015 Rating	Total Assets ($Mil)	One Year Asset Growth	Comm-ercial Loans	Cons-umer Loans	Mort-gage Loans	Secur-ities	Capital-ization Index	Net Worth Ratio
									Asset Mix (As a % of Total Assets)					
▼	Farmers Federal Credit Union	Jacksonville	FL	**C**	C+	C+	13.7	5.56	0.0	12.1	14.4	0.0	**10.0**	13.6
	Farmers Insurance Group FCU	Los Angeles	CA	**B+**	B+	A-	761.6	6.61	51.2	22.4	28.7	2.2	**10.0**	13.1
	Farmway Credit Union	Beloit	KS	**B+**	B+	B+	88.3	2.57	44.1	15.8	33.3	0.0	**10.0**	22.7
	FASNY Federal Credit Union	Albany	NY	**C-**	C-	C	13.4	9.12	9.0	16.7	10.8	0.0	**8.8**	10.2
	Fasson Employees Federal Credit Union	Painesville	OH	**C+**	C+	C	13.0	0.34	0.0	19.7	0.0	8.1	**10.0**	17.1
	Fayette County School Employees CU	Uniontown	PA	**B-**	B-	B-	17.2	5.32	0.0	39.0	0.3	1.5	**10.0**	15.8
▲	Fayette Federal Credit Union	Mount Hope	WV	**C**	C-	C-	9.1	-12.48	0.0	13.2	0.0	0.0	**10.0**	18.6
▼	Fayette Federal Employees FCU	Uniontown	PA	**C**	C+	C-	12.5	1.60	0.0	33.4	1.2	0.0	**10.0**	12.3
	Fayetteville Postal Credit Union	Fayetteville	NC	**D-**	D-	D-	8.6	12.60	1.2	44.6	0.0	0.0	**5.8**	7.8
	FCI Federal Credit Union	Texarkana	TX	**D**	D	D+	6.7	-13.58	0.0	68.2	0.0	0.0	**10.0**	16.1
	FD Community Federal Credit Union	Waterbury	CT	**B-**	B-	C+	76.2	6.77	2.2	27.0	16.9	0.0	**7.7**	9.5
▼	FedChoice Federal Credit Union	Lanham	MD	**C**	C+	B-	389.0	7.29	9.0	21.0	8.3	40.1	**8.9**	10.2
	Fedco Credit Union	Jefferson City	MO	**D-**	D-	D-	5.8	6.86	0.0	12.5	0.0	0.0	**5.3**	7.3
	FEDCom Credit Union	Grand Rapids	MI	**B-**	B-	B	67.7	11.30	3.6	30.7	12.1	6.5	**8.8**	10.2
	Federal Employees Credit Union	Birmingham	AL	**C+**	C+	C+	19.0	16.65	0.0	31.2	5.5	0.0	**10.0**	17.0
	Federal Employees Credit Union	Monroe	LA	**B**	B	B	17.7	-1.48	0.0	54.5	0.8	0.0	**10.0**	30.9
	Federal Employees Credit Union	Texarkana	TX	**D**	D	D+	3.9	-8.06	0.0	33.4	0.0	0.0	**10.0**	17.2
	Federal Employees Newark FCU	Newark	NJ	**D**	D	C-	14.4	5.05	0.0	15.6	0.0	0.0	**10.0**	18.5
	Federal Employees of Chippewa County CU	Sault Sainte Marie	MI	**D+**	D+	D+	11.2	2.77	0.0	58.8	0.9	0.0	**6.3**	8.3
	Federal Employees West FCU	Los Angeles	CA	**D-**	D-	D	11.6	-1.82	0.0	22.2	0.0	6.3	**5.6**	7.6
	Federal Family Federal Credit Union	Salt Lake City	UT	**C+**	C+	C+	28.7	-2.74	0.6	17.4	24.1	11.0	**10.0**	16.0
	Federal Life Employees Credit Union	Riverwoods	IL	**C-**	C-	C-	<1	-2.03	0.0	3.1	0.0	0.0	**10.0**	11.6
▲	Federated Employees Credit Union	Owatonna	MN	**B**	B-	B-	44.6	1.66	0.0	29.0	5.3	5.6	**10.0**	14.1
	FEDEX Employees Credit Association FCU	Memphis	TN	**A-**	A-	A-	456.7	9.16	0.0	23.4	15.6	30.6	**10.0**	15.5
▼	FedFinancial Federal Credit Union	Silver Spring	MD	**D+**	C-	C-	75.8	1.79	0.0	15.0	1.9	0.0	**6.0**	8.0
	Fedmont Federal Credit Union	Montgomery	AL	**B-**	B-	B-	13.3	4.12	0.0	32.8	0.4	4.0	**10.0**	14.2
	FedONE Federal Credit Union	Laguna Niguel	CA	**C**	C	D+	20.2	-0.22	0.0	24.1	0.0	40.2	**10.0**	11.3
	Fedstar Credit Union	College Station	TX	**B-**	B-	B-	26.4	-0.99	0.0	37.5	8.2	0.0	**10.0**	11.2
	Fedstar Federal Credit Union	Roanoke	VA	**C-**	C-	D+	14.7	15.36	0.0	69.9	0.1	0.0	**6.8**	8.8
	Fedtrust Federal Credit Union	Memphis	TN	**E+**	E+	D-	40.4	-2.37	2.1	26.7	33.4	0.0	**4.5**	6.5
	Feliciana Federal Credit Union	Zachary	LA	**C+**	C+	C-	25.4	-3.27	1.2	34.0	20.5	8.8	**10.0**	19.5
	Fellowship Baptist Church Credit Union	Chicago	IL	**C-**	C-	C	<1	15.14	0.0	19.2	0.0	0.0	**9.5**	10.6
▼	Fellowship Credit Union	Lamar	CO	**C**	C+	C+	24.5	103.62	5.9	24.2	30.3	0.0	**9.7**	10.8
	Fellowship Credit Union	Windcrest	TX	**C+**	C+	C+	20.9	9.63	2.1	33.4	14.9	0.0	**10.0**	21.9
	Fergus Federal Credit Union	Lewistown	MT	**B+**	B+	B+	65.8	3.74	8.7	31.2	12.8	0.0	**10.0**	11.5
	Ferguson Federal Credit Union	Monticello	MS	**A-**	A-	B+	66.9	11.62	0.0	37.0	22.0	21.9	**10.0**	16.3
▲	Ferko Maryland Federal Credit Union	Frederick	MD	**D+**	D	C-	33.3	0.41	0.0	27.5	0.0	0.0	**7.6**	9.4
	Fiafe Federal Credit Union	Baltimore	MD	**C+**	C+	C+	8.4	-2.37	0.0	19.4	0.0	0.0	**10.0**	28.1
	Fibre Federal Credit Union	Longview	WA	**B-**	B-	B	1021.3	7.09	11.7	27.5	28.2	25.3	**10.0**	12.3
	Fidelis Catholic Federal Credit Union	Arvada	CO	**C+**	C+	C+	89.8	3.61	1.5	13.0	23.1	1.1	**7.1**	9.0
▲	Fidelis Federal Credit Union	New York	NY	**C-**	D+	D+	<1	-2.06	0.0	27.3	0.0	0.0	**10.0**	27.6
	Fieldale Credit Union	Cornelia	GA	**C**	C	C	9.7	3.51	0.0	8.2	2.7	0.0	**10.0**	13.5
	Fieldstone Credit Union	Bradley	IL	**B-**	B-	B	45.6	1.97	0.0	30.7	16.0	0.0	**10.0**	11.2
	Filer Credit Union	Manistee	MI	**B+**	B+	B+	139.1	8.65	0.2	16.8	28.2	40.7	**10.0**	11.7
▼	Financial 1st Federal Credit Union	Williamsport	PA	**E+**	D-	D	4.4	0.75	0.0	51.6	0.0	0.0	**6.7**	8.7
	Financial Advantage Federal Credit Union	Homestead	PA	**C-**	C-	C-	9.7	-1.95	0.0	14.5	0.0	37.3	**10.0**	11.8
	Financial Benefits Credit Union	Alameda	CA	**D**	D	D+	20.2	5.14	0.0	2.8	0.0	0.0	**5.5**	7.5
	Financial Builders Federal Credit Union	Kokomo	IN	**A-**	A-	A-	92.5	5.34	0.2	38.3	23.1	2.5	**10.0**	12.4
	Financial Center Credit Union	Stockton	CA	**A-**	A-	A-	474.2	8.51	0.0	31.6	1.9	47.6	**10.0**	19.5
	Financial Center First Credit Union	Indianapolis	IN	**B-**	B-	B-	536.1	3.79	4.7	32.9	30.3	1.8	**10.0**	12.0
	Financial Educators Federal Credit Union	Daytona Beach	FL	**B**	B	C+	17.8	1.32	1.7	32.8	8.1	32.2	**10.0**	13.1
	Financial Federal Credit Union	Miami	FL	**D+**	D+	C-	51.1	-6.30	0.0	19.6	3.4	4.2	**10.0**	16.1
▲	Financial Health Federal Credit Union	Indianapolis	IN	**B-**	C+	D+	31.9	10.00	0.0	42.4	0.2	5.3	**10.0**	11.2
	Financial Horizons Credit Union	Hawthorne	NV	**B+**	B+	B+	179.7	2.58	6.2	28.7	19.4	23.8	**8.3**	10.3
	Financial One Credit Union	Coon Rapids	MN	**B-**	B-	B-	101.7	13.93	18.7	27.2	13.7	0.0	**6.2**	8.2
	Financial Partners Credit Union	Downey	CA	**B**	B	B-	1237.6	9.95	12.5	22.3	39.9	9.9	**7.4**	9.3
	Financial Partners Credit Union	Springfield	IL	**D+**	D+	D	8.6	-1.50	0.0	42.9	0.0	0.0	**7.6**	9.4
	Financial Partners Federal Credit Union	Woodburn	IN	**D+**	D+	C-	31.6	9.97	0.0	33.4	8.3	16.8	**5.9**	7.9
	Financial Plus Credit Union	West Des Moines	IA	**C+**	C+	B-	172.7	1.91	6.8	21.1	11.9	33.4	**9.3**	10.6
	Financial Plus Credit Union	Ottawa	IL	**A-**	A-	A-	318.3	8.94	0.6	36.1	15.4	10.9	**10.0**	12.3

Asset Quality Index	Non-Performing Loans as a % of Total Loans	Non-Performing Loans as a % of Capital	Net Charge-Offs Avg Loans	Profitability Index	Net Income ($Mil)	Return on Assets	Return on Equity	Net Interest Spread	Overhead Efficiency Ratio	Liquidity Index	Liquidity Ratio	Hot Money Ratio	Stability Index
10.0	0.12	0.5	0.37	**1.3**	-0.01	-0.15	-1.07	2.92	104.1	**5.8**	32.4	0.0	**6.4**
5.0	0.70	4.4	0.78	**4.4**	0.10	0.05	0.39	4.90	90.4	**3.1**	13.0	7.2	**9.0**
7.9	0.79	2.4	0.01	**4.9**	0.16	0.74	3.25	3.89	80.2	**4.0**	23.0	3.2	**7.7**
6.2	1.29	6.0	0.12	**3.6**	0.02	0.66	6.20	3.20	76.2	**5.0**	38.1	4.2	**5.2**
9.9	0.04	0.0	0.00	**2.9**	0.01	0.25	1.44	2.01	88.5	**5.8**	35.3	1.4	**7.0**
9.5	0.83	2.2	0.32	**4.2**	0.02	0.50	3.12	3.01	78.2	**5.1**	13.2	0.0	**7.3**
10.0	0.00	0.0	0.00	**2.0**	0.01	0.26	1.43	2.03	84.4	**5.6**	33.3	0.0	**6.4**
9.7	0.69	2.3	1.73	**1.8**	-0.01	-0.29	-2.32	3.37	79.6	**5.7**	38.1	1.3	**6.1**
4.1	2.07	17.3	1.29	**2.5**	0.01	0.52	6.63	6.22	89.0	**5.8**	46.0	6.2	**1.0**
4.2	2.30	12.3	2.12	**0.0**	-0.06	-3.21	-20.25	5.04	115.7	**3.4**	12.2	0.0	**5.3**
6.6	0.67	6.2	0.42	**3.9**	0.05	0.29	3.00	3.64	85.5	**4.1**	23.1	1.8	**4.8**
8.0	1.00	3.8	0.58	**2.4**	0.11	0.11	1.03	3.31	89.1	**5.6**	57.1	3.9	**6.7**
10.0	0.00	0.0	0.00	**2.6**	0.00	0.28	3.84	0.63	50.0	**6.6**	80.7	0.0	**1.7**
5.6	0.59	4.2	0.30	**3.2**	0.02	0.13	1.22	4.07	92.3	**4.4**	26.7	1.5	**5.3**
7.0	1.70	4.4	2.26	**4.4**	0.03	0.67	3.86	3.87	76.6	**6.1**	40.9	0.0	**6.3**
6.9	2.12	4.8	-0.13	**9.8**	0.08	1.84	6.04	4.35	62.4	**3.6**	32.1	8.1	**6.3**
9.7	0.00	0.0	1.25	**0.3**	0.00	-0.41	-2.37	3.34	107.1	**5.6**	41.0	0.0	**4.8**
9.5	1.01	3.5	-0.04	**2.3**	0.02	0.59	3.15	3.85	87.0	**4.0**	15.9	0.0	**5.5**
7.8	0.06	0.5	0.00	**4.6**	0.02	0.84	9.97	4.02	77.6	**4.1**	20.5	3.1	**3.7**
10.0	0.22	0.8	0.12	**3.2**	0.05	1.74	23.47	3.13	69.6	**5.5**	47.0	3.3	**2.3**
10.0	0.32	1.1	0.21	**2.8**	0.01	0.18	1.36	2.70	93.1	**4.3**	25.6	3.5	**6.8**
10.0	0.00	0.0	0.00	**1.5**	0.00	0.00	0.00	0.63	100.0	**7.5**	62.9	0.0	**5.8**
9.9	0.00	0.0	0.00	**4.0**	0.06	0.56	3.90	2.47	78.8	**5.1**	21.5	0.3	**7.1**
9.3	0.33	1.3	0.45	**5.1**	0.79	0.70	4.51	3.54	78.6	**5.5**	25.3	2.0	**8.0**
9.2	0.49	1.5	0.42	**1.4**	-0.04	-0.19	-2.36	2.45	102.2	**4.7**	16.8	2.9	**3.4**
7.0	2.47	7.2	4.57	**3.2**	0.00	0.12	0.86	3.96	82.9	**6.4**	65.7	0.0	**6.3**
9.8	0.68	1.6	1.28	**1.0**	-0.02	-0.47	-4.19	2.69	92.8	**5.9**	40.2	0.0	**5.5**
8.2	0.56	2.6	1.77	**3.1**	0.00	0.02	0.14	2.95	80.4	**4.2**	27.6	11.9	**5.7**
8.2	0.12	1.1	0.20	**4.2**	0.01	0.30	3.40	5.06	88.0	**3.9**	10.5	0.0	**3.7**
1.7	3.14	37.7	0.34	**0.5**	-0.05	-0.54	-8.09	3.55	109.0	**4.5**	31.7	5.0	**0.0**
9.7	0.16	0.5	-0.15	**3.1**	0.02	0.35	1.82	5.58	86.7	**5.1**	29.1	2.6	**6.8**
0.3	31.58	70.0	-2.96	**2.5**	0.00	0.00	0.00	3.40	75.0	**7.5**	61.0	0.0	**4.8**
6.0	0.51	6.1	-0.08	**2.5**	-0.02	-0.27	-2.41	5.54	105.5	**5.6**	35.6	0.0	**5.2**
9.6	0.20	0.5	0.04	**2.9**	0.01	0.26	1.13	3.14	89.6	**5.2**	37.7	6.0	**7.4**
5.7	1.70	9.0	0.14	**4.7**	0.07	0.43	3.96	3.56	83.0	**4.3**	20.7	7.1	**6.5**
6.1	2.21	9.9	0.72	**9.7**	0.24	1.44	8.99	5.33	61.2	**4.0**	12.7	0.0	**7.6**
6.9	2.06	5.8	0.83	**1.7**	0.02	0.19	2.05	2.83	72.8	**7.4**	58.6	0.0	**3.1**
10.0	2.51	2.0	0.00	**5.7**	0.02	0.86	3.07	2.21	57.8	**5.3**	40.4	0.0	**5.0**
9.4	0.11	1.1	0.38	**3.7**	1.42	0.57	4.62	3.24	81.6	**3.7**	11.3	4.5	**8.5**
9.2	0.31	1.8	0.20	**4.0**	0.13	0.58	6.40	3.08	79.8	**3.9**	16.3	4.1	**4.4**
6.7	8.79	8.3	0.00	**4.0**	0.00	1.23	4.35	2.58	100.0	**5.3**	35.4	0.0	**3.7**
10.0	0.00	0.0	0.30	**1.9**	0.00	0.04	0.31	0.56	84.6	**6.3**	98.3	0.0	**6.6**
7.4	1.07	5.7	1.21	**3.6**	0.04	0.39	3.38	3.46	83.1	**4.9**	31.5	2.0	**5.3**
9.4	0.26	1.1	0.43	**4.9**	0.28	0.81	7.15	2.46	70.8	**4.4**	17.9	2.7	**7.6**
8.4	0.26	1.4	0.00	**0.3**	-0.01	-0.56	-6.23	5.48	109.8	**5.6**	28.0	0.0	**2.7**
8.8	1.88	3.8	0.00	**2.0**	0.00	0.16	1.40	2.80	82.6	**5.4**	39.9	0.0	**5.2**
8.1	0.00	0.0	0.00	**0.7**	-0.03	-0.57	-7.61	4.83	115.5	**5.0**	27.0	3.8	**3.1**
8.8	0.54	3.3	0.28	**7.1**	0.18	0.80	6.25	4.26	85.4	**3.1**	16.8	10.0	**7.0**
9.9	0.47	0.9	0.83	**6.1**	1.50	1.29	6.59	3.72	65.3	**5.4**	23.9	1.0	**7.8**
8.5	0.36	2.3	0.31	**3.6**	0.45	0.34	2.80	3.81	86.1	**4.0**	21.3	8.8	**8.1**
8.4	0.24	0.9	-0.20	**9.8**	0.20	4.50	36.18	4.38	71.9	**4.7**	20.4	1.7	**6.3**
9.9	0.73	1.4	1.26	**0.7**	-0.04	-0.31	-1.95	2.52	90.6	**5.7**	39.5	0.3	**5.3**
5.6	3.57	16.8	1.65	**8.9**	0.14	1.76	15.61	6.78	87.2	**5.7**	36.1	6.4	**5.6**
9.5	0.23	1.7	0.35	**4.5**	0.25	0.57	5.72	3.38	75.6	**4.1**	19.8	6.6	**7.3**
5.6	0.65	6.6	0.64	**7.3**	0.24	0.96	11.57	4.98	77.3	**1.9**	5.2	13.7	**5.2**
8.7	0.55	4.1	0.34	**3.7**	1.12	0.36	3.84	3.03	88.0	**2.9**	16.5	16.2	**7.3**
9.6	0.20	1.0	2.66	**1.2**	-0.02	-0.95	-9.83	4.58	86.9	**4.7**	18.7	2.2	**3.7**
7.5	0.54	3.3	1.15	**1.2**	0.00	0.04	0.48	3.14	96.3	**4.6**	19.4	1.3	**3.0**
7.0	0.95	6.6	0.55	**3.4**	0.20	0.48	4.47	2.91	85.2	**5.3**	19.5	1.4	**6.4**
7.6	1.11	5.4	0.34	**5.9**	0.70	0.90	7.22	3.39	73.4	**4.9**	26.1	2.9	**9.0**

Name	City	State	Rating	2016 Rating	2015 Rating	Total Assets ($Mil)	One Year Asset Growth	Asset Mix (As a % of Total Assets) Comm-ercial Loans	Cons-umer Loans	Mort-gage Loans	Secur-ities	Capital-ization Index	Net Worth Ratio
Financial Plus Credit Union	Flint	MI	**B+**	B+	A-	529.2	10.98	7.8	44.7	12.8	16.2	**10.0**	13.2
Financial Resources Federal Credit Union	Bridgewater	NJ	**C+**	C+	C+	479.6	4.89	13.0	14.3	42.5	15.9	**6.4**	8.5
Financial Security Credit Union	Carlsbad	NM	**B**	B	B	43.7	5.43	0.0	51.5	0.0	0.0	**10.0**	12.1
Financial Trust Federal Credit Union	Cheektowaga	NY	**B**	B	B	75.7	7.36	1.3	20.3	19.8	1.3	**10.0**	11.8
FinancialEdge Community Credit Union	Bay City	MI	**C+**	C+	C	92.8	4.80	2.8	20.8	33.4	11.0	**8.1**	9.7
Finans Federal Credit Union	Hammond	IN	**E+**	E+	D-	10.4	-0.58	0.0	32.0	3.6	0.0	**6.9**	8.9
Finest Federal Credit Union	New York	NY	**D**	D	D	5.1	2.54	0.0	68.2	0.0	19.6	**10.0**	15.4
▼ Finex Credit Union	East Hartford	CT	**D**	D+	D+	82.7	2.86	0.0	24.9	20.3	0.0	**6.3**	8.3
Finger Lakes Federal Credit Union	Geneva	NY	**B-**	B-	B-	117.0	6.60	0.1	39.6	24.0	5.9	**6.3**	8.3
Finger Lakes Health Care FCU	Elmira	NY	**C+**	C+	C	26.0	2.82	0.0	29.1	6.3	0.0	**10.0**	13.3
Fire Department Credit Union	Superior	WI	**D**	D	D	1.1	-11.05	0.0	43.1	0.0	0.0	**10.0**	17.6
Fire Fighters Credit Union	Tulsa	OK	**B**	B	B	38.6	5.70	0.0	49.0	0.0	0.0	**10.0**	15.4
Fire Police City County FCU	Fort Wayne	IN	**C+**	C+	C+	120.9	5.43	0.2	30.0	31.8	0.0	**8.9**	10.2
Firefighters Community Credit Union	Cleveland	OH	**D+**	D+	D+	250.2	5.33	0.0	37.9	20.5	3.3	**7.5**	9.4
Firefighters Credit Union	Indianapolis	IN	**B**	B	C+	64.9	3.76	0.3	28.2	3.1	41.0	**10.0**	12.0
Firefighters Credit Union	Salt Lake City	UT	**B-**	B-	B-	39.3	8.32	0.0	36.3	15.4	3.3	**10.0**	11.6
Firefighters Credit Union	Onalaska	WI	**B+**	B+	B	80.6	6.87	19.1	14.9	49.1	0.0	**10.0**	13.5
Firefighters First Federal Credit Union	Los Angeles	CA	**B+**	B+	B+	1211.2	10.75	11.2	17.2	50.4	0.3	**7.6**	9.4
Firefly Federal Credit Union	Burnsville	MN	**B+**	B+	B+	1158.1	8.01	5.5	40.7	26.7	7.1	**8.1**	9.7
Firelands Federal Credit Union	Bellevue	OH	**B-**	B-	B	264.6	5.20	2.5	52.0	12.9	7.9	**8.7**	10.2
Fireman's Credit Union	Birmingham	AL	**B-**	B-	B-	5.3	6.43	0.0	59.4	0.0	0.0	**10.0**	30.2
Firestone Federal Credit Union	Akron	OH	**C+**	C+	C+	208.0	3.20	0.0	2.4	10.8	63.1	**10.0**	17.1
Firestone Lake Charles FCU	Sulphur	LA	**C+**	C+	C-	11.0	-3.78	0.0	21.9	0.0	0.0	**10.0**	11.0
First Abilene Federal Credit Union	Abilene	TX	**B-**	B-	B-	70.5	2.34	0.0	56.5	3.0	0.0	**8.5**	10.0
First Alliance Credit Union	Rochester	MN	**B**	B	B-	170.2	6.76	6.4	32.2	21.3	15.0	**9.5**	10.8
▼ First American Credit Union	Casa Grande	AZ	**D+**	C-	C+	106.7	-4.58	4.6	41.9	10.8	12.6	**5.2**	7.4
First Area Credit Union	Saginaw	MI	**B-**	B-	B-	30.6	8.82	5.1	34.3	15.0	17.3	**10.0**	11.3
▼ First Area Federal Credit Union	Lewistown	PA	**D**	D+	D	18.3	1.42	0.0	19.0	1.6	49.2	**6.8**	8.8
First Atlantic Federal Credit Union	Eatontown	NJ	**C**	C	C-	238.0	4.94	4.3	19.6	29.2	10.5	**6.3**	8.3
▼ First Baptist Church (Stratford) FCU	Stratford	CT	**E+**	D-	D	<1	8.78	0.0	0.7	0.0	0.0	**5.4**	7.4
First Baptist Church FCU	East Elmhurst	NY	**D**	D	D	<1	5.05	0.0	4.8	0.0	0.0	**10.0**	18.9
▼ First Baptist Church of Darby FCU	Darby	PA	**C+**	B-	C	<1	4.29	0.0	9.6	0.0	0.0	**10.0**	24.7
First Baptist Church of Vienna (VA) FCU	Vienna	VA	**C**	C	C	1.4	0.00	0.0	0.4	0.6	0.0	**9.3**	10.5
First Basin Credit Union	Odessa	TX	**B+**	B+	B+	216.4	4.15	8.6	33.9	39.6	4.6	**8.2**	9.8
First Bristol Federal Credit Union	Bristol	CT	**D**	D	D+	90.4	3.22	0.0	11.3	19.8	11.7	**9.0**	10.3
First California Federal Credit Union	Fresno	CA	**D+**	D+	D	87.8	5.01	0.0	34.7	7.8	32.9	**7.3**	9.2
First Capital Federal Credit Union	York	PA	**B**	B	B	194.4	9.14	8.4	22.2	25.9	3.9	**6.8**	8.8
First Carolina People's Credit Union	Goldsboro	NC	**C-**	C-	D+	29.8	2.25	0.4	12.0	55.2	0.0	**7.2**	9.2
First Castle Federal Credit Union	Covington	LA	**D+**	D+	C	70.4	-3.15	0.6	59.8	16.2	0.2	**6.5**	8.5
▲ First Central Credit Union	Waco	TX	**A-**	B+	B+	81.1	9.62	0.0	39.7	15.1	7.6	**10.0**	11.9
First Century Federal Credit Union	Sioux Falls	SD	**C-**	C-	C-	20.1	1.39	24.6	12.6	18.1	10.4	**9.1**	10.4
▼ First Cheyenne Federal Credit Union	Cheyenne	WY	**D**	D+	D+	29.1	5.89	0.0	33.5	13.6	0.0	**6.0**	8.0
First Choice America Community FCU	Weirton	WV	**C+**	C+	C+	441.2	3.82	5.1	4.4	19.6	11.8	**10.0**	13.9
First Choice Community Credit Union	Niles	OH	**C+**	C+	B-	27.9	2.47	0.1	7.8	10.9	60.4	**10.0**	12.6
First Choice Community Credit Union	Knoxville	TN	**C+**	C+	C+	38.2	3.16	0.0	27.8	14.1	0.0	**10.0**	15.7
First Choice Credit Union	West Palm Beach	FL	**B-**	B-	B-	108.4	5.39	0.2	19.2	9.4	42.6	**6.7**	9.4
First Choice Credit Union	Ottawa	IL	**C-**	C-	C	12.6	0.33	0.0	19.5	4.7	0.0	**10.0**	11.4
First Choice Credit Union	Marshfield	WI	**B**	B	B	33.9	7.63	0.0	20.7	18.1	9.5	**10.0**	14.7
▼ First Choice Credit Union, Inc.	Coldwater	OH	**C**	C+	C+	17.6	10.83	0.0	16.3	19.2	18.8	**9.4**	10.6
First Choice Federal Credit Union	New Castle	PA	**D**	D	D+	45.1	4.22	0.8	51.2	0.0	5.4	**5.5**	7.5
First Choice Financial FCU	Gloversville	NY	**B+**	B+	A-	99.4	5.95	0.0	19.7	21.7	23.9	**10.0**	12.0
First Citizens' Federal Credit Union	Fairhaven	MA	**C**	C	B-	727.0	5.24	8.4	44.0	35.2	3.7	**7.9**	9.6
First City Credit Union	Los Angeles	CA	**B-**	B-	B-	634.7	8.91	0.0	37.9	7.7	31.6	**9.7**	10.9
First Class American Credit Union	Fort Worth	TX	**C+**	C+	C	51.2	3.80	0.0	38.6	4.8	0.0	**7.0**	9.0
First Class Community Credit Union	West Des Moines	IA	**C-**	C-	C-	76.4	5.70	1.0	29.1	6.0	32.5	**6.2**	8.4
First Class Federal Credit Union	Allentown	PA	**B+**	B+	B+	29.4	1.40	0.0	11.7	59.3	0.0	**10.0**	16.2
First Coast Community Credit Union	Palatka	FL	**B-**	B-	B-	114.8	4.89	0.0	19.6	5.7	28.0	**10.0**	11.2
▲ First Coast Federal Credit Union	Jacksonville	FL	**C**	C-	D+	8.5	5.48	0.0	60.8	0.1	0.0	**10.0**	14.4
First Commerce Credit Union	Tallahassee	FL	**A-**	A-	A-	546.1	9.94	10.5	30.9	27.0	2.9	**10.0**	11.6
First Commonwealth Federal Credit Union	Bethlehem	PA	**B+**	B+	B+	672.4	7.51	5.5	21.6	31.1	26.9	**8.6**	10.4

Asset Quality Index	Non-Performing Loans as a % of Total Loans	Non-Performing Loans as a % of Capital	Net Charge-Offs Avg Loans	Profitability Index	Net Income ($Mil)	Return on Assets	Return on Equity	Net Interest Spread	Overhead Efficiency Ratio	Liquidity Index	Liquidity Ratio	Hot Money Ratio	Stability Index
7.0	0.83	5.1	0.66	**4.9**	0.87	0.68	5.09	3.76	73.3	**4.0**	13.5	2.9	**7.8**
6.6	0.96	7.5	0.61	**2.2**	0.04	0.04	0.43	3.22	93.7	**4.3**	19.4	1.5	**5.7**
6.3	0.89	4.2	0.95	**5.1**	0.03	0.30	2.43	5.30	87.3	**4.6**	31.5	13.6	**6.3**
8.4	0.83	4.2	-0.51	**3.8**	0.08	0.45	3.72	3.04	83.0	**4.4**	30.2	2.1	**6.6**
6.8	0.51	3.8	0.20	**3.3**	0.09	0.38	3.81	4.32	89.8	**4.5**	19.6	2.7	**4.7**
3.5	5.22	19.4	-0.31	**1.6**	0.01	0.27	3.04	3.14	96.1	**5.0**	22.2	1.1	**3.3**
7.7	0.72	2.9	2.68	**0.0**	-0.09	-7.05	-42.56	5.38	223.9	**4.3**	10.3	0.0	**5.0**
5.2	0.93	7.6	0.17	**1.0**	-0.06	-0.28	-3.37	3.88	105.8	**4.4**	17.3	1.1	**3.5**
7.9	0.48	4.2	0.38	**3.8**	0.12	0.40	4.74	3.78	84.3	**3.7**	9.0	0.6	**5.6**
9.8	0.20	0.7	0.27	**3.2**	0.04	0.55	4.08	2.51	83.6	**5.2**	24.3	0.0	**7.2**
6.5	2.59	6.6	0.00	**0.0**	-0.01	-2.14	-12.44	3.79	200.0	**6.9**	60.0	0.0	**5.2**
8.0	0.71	2.7	0.36	**3.6**	0.02	0.17	1.08	4.62	90.0	**5.5**	47.4	5.6	**6.9**
8.1	0.66	4.6	0.48	**3.1**	0.02	0.07	0.66	4.09	90.4	**3.8**	23.5	3.8	**6.5**
5.6	1.84	14.2	0.68	**1.6**	-0.05	-0.08	-0.85	3.92	90.7	**3.8**	18.9	4.0	**5.6**
9.5	0.92	2.9	0.05	**3.7**	0.00	-0.01	-0.05	2.91	101.4	**5.3**	26.9	1.1	**5.7**
9.4	0.43	2.3	0.05	**3.5**	0.03	0.32	2.73	2.92	90.9	**4.1**	17.4	4.8	**6.4**
6.2	1.11	6.7	0.02	**5.3**	0.09	0.43	3.19	3.61	89.2	**1.9**	8.9	18.3	**7.7**
9.1	0.24	2.0	0.01	**3.5**	1.00	0.34	3.52	3.24	90.4	**3.2**	19.6	16.4	**6.8**
7.7	0.46	3.9	0.56	**4.8**	2.20	0.77	7.86	3.21	72.2	**2.9**	8.8	8.5	**7.0**
5.6	0.84	7.3	1.17	**3.7**	0.17	0.26	2.87	4.00	80.2	**3.2**	13.9	7.7	**5.1**
8.3	1.04	2.0	0.75	**10.0**	0.06	4.23	14.10	7.25	31.3	**5.1**	25.3	0.0	**5.7**
10.0	1.52	1.2	-0.20	**2.9**	0.14	0.27	1.57	1.09	70.9	**5.2**	24.9	2.1	**7.3**
8.6	0.62	1.6	1.96	**2.9**	0.00	0.15	1.33	3.06	67.9	**6.0**	64.3	0.0	**5.4**
5.1	0.76	7.0	0.24	**3.6**	0.05	0.29	2.91	3.40	88.1	**4.3**	20.2	4.2	**5.1**
7.8	0.69	4.5	0.21	**4.7**	0.25	0.59	5.49	3.81	84.3	**3.8**	10.6	1.3	**7.4**
5.6	1.35	11.2	2.07	**1.2**	-0.35	-1.34	-17.96	3.81	97.1	**3.4**	27.9	18.2	**3.3**
7.7	0.69	3.9	0.28	**3.9**	0.06	0.77	6.85	4.02	78.0	**4.6**	19.9	2.3	**5.8**
10.0	0.26	1.0	0.00	**0.8**	-0.01	-0.22	-2.48	3.16	105.9	**5.6**	21.1	0.0	**4.3**
7.5	0.76	6.3	0.07	**3.3**	0.27	0.45	5.44	3.05	84.9	**3.5**	12.3	6.2	**5.5**
3.7	8.77	21.7	0.00	**0.9**	0.00	-1.44	-18.18	4.71	200.0	**8.0**	85.2	0.0	**4.9**
9.0	15.79	5.0	0.00	**0.3**	0.00	0.00	0.00	1.65	100.0	**7.8**	104.0	0.0	**5.6**
8.2	14.29	5.3	0.00	**3.9**	0.00	0.00	0.00	0.00	0.0	**8.8**	120.0	0.0	**7.2**
9.9	0.00	0.0	0.00	**3.7**	0.00	0.59	5.63	2.94	62.5	**6.7**	32.4	0.0	**5.0**
8.3	0.23	3.5	0.71	**5.1**	0.25	0.48	4.79	4.53	77.6	**4.1**	21.8	5.5	**5.9**
6.4	1.52	7.4	0.85	**1.0**	0.00	-0.02	-0.17	3.68	98.8	**5.4**	29.0	3.3	**4.4**
8.1	0.24	2.2	0.40	**1.3**	0.01	0.04	0.51	2.76	91.9	**4.3**	24.2	9.5	**3.3**
8.7	0.49	3.5	0.18	**4.8**	0.44	0.92	11.00	3.61	79.2	**5.0**	25.5	1.2	**5.9**
5.9	1.02	10.8	0.33	**2.6**	0.02	0.28	3.09	4.33	93.1	**4.1**	28.6	12.6	**4.4**
2.9	1.34	16.7	0.29	**3.1**	0.03	0.18	2.06	4.00	89.2	**2.2**	20.9	27.9	**4.0**
6.5	1.53	8.3	0.26	**8.6**	0.26	1.33	10.98	5.26	84.4	**4.6**	26.6	6.4	**7.0**
4.6	1.74	10.3	0.00	**5.8**	0.05	0.93	8.92	4.18	79.5	**4.8**	38.1	2.6	**4.3**
6.3	1.19	9.5	0.10	**0.0**	-0.08	-1.07	-13.10	4.07	106.6	**4.9**	41.3	10.8	**2.6**
9.9	0.20	0.8	0.05	**3.1**	0.38	0.35	2.50	1.97	84.8	**5.4**	42.9	3.7	**8.1**
7.6	3.81	6.6	0.51	**2.6**	0.01	0.10	0.80	2.38	96.6	**3.9**	30.1	25.9	**5.1**
10.0	0.16	0.7	0.15	**2.6**	0.03	0.26	1.67	3.36	93.3	**5.1**	30.1	3.8	**7.2**
8.4	0.72	3.0	0.19	**4.1**	0.13	0.48	5.42	2.53	87.4	**5.4**	30.4	1.0	**5.6**
9.1	1.98	4.6	1.05	**0.3**	-0.02	-0.69	-5.80	2.51	118.3	**6.0**	33.1	1.0	**4.5**
7.4	1.02	4.1	0.03	**3.5**	0.03	0.34	2.26	3.31	87.4	**5.3**	35.6	1.1	**7.5**
10.0	0.16	0.6	0.30	**2.4**	0.00	0.05	0.46	2.53	95.3	**4.9**	24.1	0.0	**4.9**
6.3	0.40	3.3	0.14	**1.1**	0.00	0.02	0.24	2.74	92.9	**4.4**	23.9	1.6	**3.3**
8.2	1.02	4.2	0.35	**5.2**	0.16	0.64	5.38	3.33	81.0	**5.3**	26.2	0.9	**6.6**
8.0	0.40	4.1	0.16	**3.0**	0.75	0.41	4.30	2.93	82.8	**2.5**	9.6	13.2	**6.7**
9.8	0.24	1.2	0.68	**3.5**	0.67	0.43	3.90	2.90	79.2	**4.9**	27.0	6.1	**7.6**
9.2	0.19	1.3	0.00	**3.5**	0.02	0.18	2.00	3.85	96.5	**4.5**	28.4	4.1	**4.6**
7.9	0.61	3.2	0.69	**2.4**	0.03	0.14	1.74	3.55	96.3	**5.3**	23.2	0.4	**3.4**
7.8	1.24	5.4	0.00	**3.8**	0.06	0.76	4.64	4.26	78.2	**5.2**	28.0	0.0	**7.5**
8.6	1.29	4.4	0.57	**2.7**	0.04	0.14	1.19	3.25	93.8	**5.5**	33.9	2.3	**6.7**
8.4	0.29	1.3	-0.22	**4.5**	0.02	0.92	6.22	5.02	84.1	**5.0**	34.4	3.0	**4.3**
6.2	1.45	8.9	0.70	**5.1**	0.74	0.56	4.71	3.81	79.8	**3.9**	24.3	11.8	**8.5**
8.5	0.53	3.3	0.59	**6.0**	1.40	0.85	8.35	3.59	72.8	**4.1**	10.3	3.5	**7.3**

								Asset Mix (As a % of Total Assets)					
Name	City	State	Rating	2016 Rating	2015 Rating	Total Assets ($Mil)	One Year Asset Growth	Comm-ercial Loans	Cons-umer Loans	Mort-gage Loans	Secur-ities	Capital-ization Index	Net Worth Ratio
First Community Credit Union	Chesterfield	MO	B-	B-	C+	2325.5	6.62	1.3	35.3	16.1	25.3	6.4	8.6
First Community Credit Union	Jamestown	ND	A-	A-	A	585.2	6.83	56.5	16.4	44.1	7.8	10.0	13.6
First Community Credit Union	Coquille	OR	B	B	B	1007.9	9.67	9.7	19.2	32.1	12.4	8.8	10.2
First Community Credit Union	Houston	TX	B	B	B	1273.5	7.61	11.1	51.8	26.1	10.7	6.4	8.5
First Community Credit Union of Beloit	Beloit	WI	A	A	A	135.3	4.89	0.6	66.9	5.2	0.0	10.0	12.9
First Connecticut Credit Union, Incorporated	Wallingford	CT	D-	D-	D-	37.7	-2.43	0.0	79.0	0.0	0.0	4.6	6.6
First County Federal Credit Union	Muncie	IN	D-	D-	D-	16.8	3.77	0.0	51.3	0.6	3.2	5.0	7.0
▼ First Credit Union	Chandler	AZ	C	C+	B-	467.6	6.77	0.3	54.5	6.2	8.9	6.2	8.2
First Credit Union of Scranton	Scranton	PA	E+	E+	E+	17.9	-4.67	0.0	9.0	10.3	12.6	4.6	6.6
First Eagle Federal Credit Union	Owings Mills	MD	C	C	C	95.2	0.90	0.0	37.2	10.3	23.5	6.5	8.5
First Education Federal Credit Union	Cheyenne	WY	C-	C-	C-	57.7	5.61	0.3	18.7	10.8	1.8	5.0	7.0
▼ First Entertainment Credit Union	Hollywood	CA	B-	B+	B+	1411.6	8.80	5.5	15.2	31.9	31.4	6.1	8.2
First Family Federal Credit Union	Henryetta	OK	C+	C+	B-	82.5	7.91	0.0	74.1	0.0	0.0	7.0	9.0
First Federal Credit Union	Hiawatha	IA	A-	A-	B+	121.4	6.62	4.5	17.9	51.0	11.0	9.8	10.9
First Financial Credit Union	Chicago	IL	C	C	C+	77.1	8.01	0.0	34.6	19.0	3.5	8.4	10.0
First Financial Credit Union	Albuquerque	NM	C-	C-	C-	528.6	6.28	6.3	57.0	12.5	6.8	5.5	7.5
First Financial Federal Credit Union	West Covina	CA	B	B	B-	556.2	22.10	1.2	25.9	36.0	5.5	5.5	7.5
First Financial Federal Credit Union	Toms River	NJ	C-	C-	C-	192.7	3.73	9.9	21.7	15.4	8.5	4.8	6.9
First Financial of Maryland FCU	Lutherville	MD	B+	B+	A-	1007.6	2.18	0.3	12.6	17.1	46.9	10.0	20.4
First Flight Federal Credit Union	Cary	NC	B	B	B	198.5	6.36	1.0	51.7	12.5	0.0	10.0	12.1
First Florida Credit Union	Jacksonville	FL	B+	B+	B+	852.5	17.69	1.2	29.9	17.9	33.9	10.0	14.9
First Frontier Federal Credit Union	Lynbrook	NY	D+	D+	D	<1	18.11	0.0	54.9	0.0	0.0	9.2	10.4
First General Credit Union	Muskegon	MI	D	D	C-	60.9	-5.09	0.0	36.4	5.1	10.6	10.0	15.6
▼ First Heritage Federal Credit Union	Painted Post	NY	B-	B	B	444.7	3.91	6.6	30.0	16.0	24.3	9.9	11.2
First Illinois Credit Union	Danville	IL	D+	D+	D	50.9	2.50	0.0	34.5	16.1	0.0	5.2	7.2
First Imperial Credit Union	El Centro	CA	B	B	B	101.2	10.91	1.8	56.0	9.6	3.1	8.7	10.2
▼ First Jersey Credit Union	Wayne	NJ	D-	D	D	111.1	-18.56	13.6	21.3	8.8	8.4	4.4	6.5
First Legacy Community Credit Union	Charlotte	NC	C-	C-	C	35.7	2.91	5.4	15.7	28.2	4.2	10.0	15.6
First Lincoln Federal Credit Union	Lincoln	NE	C	C	C	18.7	4.41	0.0	34.8	9.0	0.0	10.0	14.2
▲ First Miami University Student FCU	Oxford	OH	D-	E+	E+	<1	68.51	0.0	33.8	0.0	0.0	10.0	53.9
First Missouri Credit Union	Saint Louis	MO	B+	B+	B+	64.8	5.23	4.0	50.5	11.0	5.0	10.0	11.6
First Nebraska Credit Union	Omaha	NE	B+	B+	A-	123.6	4.89	0.0	24.8	27.6	18.5	10.0	16.1
First Neshoba Federal Credit Union	Philadelphia	MS	D+	D+	D	16.0	6.22	0.0	21.4	0.0	0.0	10.0	14.2
First New York Federal Credit Union	Albany	NY	C	C	C	314.6	6.24	7.3	16.8	24.6	19.6	7.2	9.2
First Northern Credit Union	Chicago	IL	C-	C-	D+	331.0	1.09	0.0	20.6	17.6	26.8	5.3	7.3
▲ First NRV Federal Credit Union	Radford	VA	C-	D+	D+	18.0	9.66	0.0	24.1	0.9	0.0	6.6	8.6
First Ohio Community FCU	North Canton	OH	D	D	D-	34.9	1.22	0.0	48.5	6.3	0.0	6.4	8.4
First Oklahoma Federal Credit Union	Tulsa	OK	C-	C-	C	35.6	3.01	0.0	51.1	14.4	0.0	6.7	8.7
First Pace Credit Union	West Saint Paul	MN	C	C	C	8.9	-3.61	0.0	38.7	0.0	24.5	10.0	19.4
First Pennsylvania Township Empls FCU	King of Prussia	PA	E+	E+	D-	1.8	14.24	0.0	50.3	0.0	0.0	6.5	8.5
First Peoples Community FCU	Cumberland	MD	B+	B+	A-	395.5	7.82	20.9	15.1	50.7	1.6	10.0	11.8
First Pioneers Federal Credit Union	Lafayette	LA	B	B	B	26.1	0.07	0.0	40.1	18.7	9.4	10.0	13.6
First Point Federal Credit Union	Hamilton	NJ	C	C	C-	23.0	-2.41	0.0	9.9	0.0	57.4	10.0	11.3
First Priority Credit Union	East Boston	MA	B-	B-	B-	108.6	-0.61	10.5	3.1	49.4	11.3	10.0	17.5
First Priority Credit Union	Abilene	TX	D	D	D-	14.8	1.52	0.0	27.4	5.8	0.0	6.4	8.4
First Priority Federal Credit Union	Barboursville	WV	B-	B-	B	57.6	2.65	0.8	27.8	19.9	0.0	10.0	11.2
First Reliance Federal Credit Union	Athens	GA	C	C	C	13.0	1.81	0.0	32.0	6.9	0.0	9.5	10.7
▼ First Security Credit Union	Lincolnwood	IL	D-	D	D-	8.1	23.74	0.0	91.4	0.0	0.0	5.4	7.4
First Service Credit Union	Houston	TX	C+	C+	C-	671.7	10.01	0.0	57.9	7.0	7.2	7.2	9.3
First Service Federal Credit Union	Groveport	OH	C	C	C	150.8	3.86	10.0	29.4	18.1	0.7	6.9	8.9
First Source Federal Credit Union	New Hartford	NY	B+	B+	B+	489.1	9.80	2.4	33.7	41.3	0.2	8.1	9.7
First South Financial Credit Union	Bartlett	TN	A+	A+	A+	545.1	5.51	1.6	37.9	20.0	8.4	10.0	27.2
First Street Federal Credit Union	DeRidder	LA	B+	B+	B+	39.2	3.84	0.0	38.0	0.0	37.8	10.0	14.8
First Technology Federal Credit Union	Mountain View	CA	A-	A-	A-	9810.8	12.68	5.5	20.1	42.0	20.5	8.1	9.7
First Trust Credit Union	Michigan City	IN	B-	B-	B-	111.4	6.67	1.3	11.4	16.3	0.0	8.1	9.8
▼ First Tulsa Federal Credit Union	Tulsa	OK	C	C+	C+	12.6	1.92	0.0	50.7	14.4	0.0	10.0	13.9
First U.S. Community Credit Union	Sacramento	CA	B+	B+	B+	356.6	4.76	3.1	15.6	31.2	24.5	9.1	10.4
▼ First United Credit Union	Grandville	MI	C+	B-	C+	34.5	19.47	0.9	56.3	14.8	1.4	7.5	9.3
First United Credit Union	Tyler	TX	C-	C-	D+	2.9	-0.68	1.7	73.3	0.0	0.0	10.0	27.9
▼ First Unity Federal Credit Union	McComb	MS	E-	E	E+	2.9	74.22	0.0	70.0	0.0	0.0	0.0	2.9

Asset Quality Index	Non-Performing Loans as a % of Total Loans	Non-Performing Loans as a % of Capital	Net Charge-Offs Avg Loans	Profitability Index	Net Income ($Mil)	Return on Assets	Return on Equity	Net Interest Spread	Overhead Efficiency Ratio	Liquidity Index	Liquidity Ratio	Hot Money Ratio	Stability Index
7.7	0.46	4.9	0.62	3.9	2.78	0.49	5.91	2.75	76.5	4.7	20.4	3.4	5.6
6.1	0.35	2.1	0.12	9.8	2.25	1.57	11.51	4.13	64.0	2.7	10.1	13.1	10.0
8.9	0.22	2.0	0.04	4.8	1.70	0.69	6.96	3.00	82.2	5.0	24.9	3.8	7.2
7.6	0.27	2.5	0.50	5.2	2.46	0.78	9.29	3.18	73.1	2.9	7.6	6.8	6.5
6.8	0.55	3.7	0.20	7.5	0.32	0.96	7.51	3.21	77.4	1.8	16.3	21.1	9.8
6.3	0.30	3.7	0.18	1.1	-0.01	-0.11	-1.60	3.77	102.9	3.0	7.0	2.3	1.7
8.5	0.14	1.1	0.00	1.0	-0.01	-0.15	-2.04	3.73	95.8	4.0	18.9	5.3	2.1
6.4	0.30	5.3	1.04	2.7	0.16	0.14	1.87	4.34	82.6	4.4	14.5	1.1	4.2
9.5	0.45	2.0	-0.44	1.4	0.00	0.07	1.02	3.05	95.0	5.5	16.5	0.0	1.9
8.0	0.43	2.8	0.26	2.7	0.04	0.18	2.03	3.00	92.5	4.5	26.5	4.9	4.0
7.9	0.65	3.4	0.06	3.0	0.05	0.34	4.77	3.02	91.3	5.2	18.6	3.3	2.8
7.6	0.99	6.1	0.36	1.6	-1.99	-0.57	-6.86	2.79	76.5	4.4	16.2	5.5	6.0
4.8	0.99	8.9	0.67	4.7	0.11	0.52	6.05	4.74	84.2	2.7	23.4	22.7	3.3
6.8	1.35	9.6	0.74	8.3	0.44	1.47	13.56	2.92	81.8	2.5	12.2	14.9	7.0
6.7	0.87	5.0	1.39	3.1	0.12	0.61	6.04	5.12	70.2	4.0	23.8	9.1	4.9
5.1	0.71	7.7	0.85	2.1	0.28	0.22	2.86	4.00	82.6	3.7	10.6	4.8	4.3
8.6	0.30	3.9	0.58	3.8	0.37	0.28	3.56	4.56	81.6	3.9	18.9	8.1	4.6
1.7	3.07	37.8	1.02	1.9	0.18	0.39	5.96	4.50	87.5	3.9	11.1	2.0	2.4
10.0	0.24	0.4	0.47	2.9	0.47	0.19	0.93	2.36	87.2	5.9	30.4	1.9	8.4
6.4	0.39	4.2	0.28	4.9	0.50	1.02	8.36	3.56	80.7	3.5	23.6	13.0	7.5
9.8	0.50	1.8	0.39	4.3	1.48	0.71	4.56	2.76	76.0	4.1	12.8	5.2	8.5
2.6	6.07	14.3	0.00	5.5	0.00	1.82	17.39	1.80	33.3	6.9	63.3	0.0	6.5
7.3	1.66	5.1	0.69	0.0	-0.17	-1.11	-7.04	3.37	115.0	4.8	37.6	9.4	4.8
9.3	0.46	2.5	0.37	3.4	0.11	0.10	0.87	2.91	86.2	4.0	17.6	9.3	7.3
7.5	0.48	3.5	0.07	3.1	0.06	0.47	6.37	3.85	93.6	5.1	27.6	0.4	2.8
5.5	1.24	8.2	0.76	6.1	0.12	0.48	4.87	5.30	80.8	3.0	19.7	19.3	5.6
0.3	5.80	52.0	4.98	0.0	-0.85	-2.98	-44.87	3.83	98.8	3.3	18.2	11.9	4.0
1.7	12.36	40.2	7.02	2.8	-0.09	-0.97	-6.13	5.43	118.3	6.4	49.6	2.7	5.0
7.4	1.09	4.2	-0.35	3.8	0.02	0.45	3.17	3.71	89.1	4.2	19.4	2.8	6.8
6.2	0.84	0.5	0.00	7.1	0.34	260.74	732.61	5.90	4.4	8.4	137.8	0.0	4.3
5.6	1.03	7.3	1.13	5.7	0.17	1.06	9.09	4.76	72.8	3.6	11.1	1.4	5.7
9.9	0.11	0.5	0.12	3.9	0.06	0.21	1.27	4.05	95.7	3.8	6.5	2.2	8.8
9.8	0.36	0.7	0.36	0.3	-0.02	-0.48	-3.32	3.54	111.4	7.3	55.9	0.0	6.1
9.9	0.30	1.9	0.29	3.3	0.17	0.21	2.32	3.57	87.6	4.5	19.3	0.8	6.1
9.8	0.26	1.7	0.42	2.3	0.14	0.17	2.28	3.05	91.1	5.0	23.5	1.1	4.1
8.8	0.28	1.2	0.56	3.5	0.02	0.44	5.15	3.96	89.6	5.6	24.3	0.0	4.0
8.3	0.09	0.7	0.41	0.5	-0.03	-0.30	-3.53	2.64	98.2	4.0	24.7	3.2	3.3
5.1	0.83	6.2	-0.02	3.7	0.04	0.43	4.96	4.18	77.2	1.8	12.6	28.1	3.6
9.5	0.02	1.0	0.37	2.0	0.00	0.09	0.47	3.27	96.0	4.2	20.5	6.9	6.2
4.0	2.20	13.5	0.81	2.4	0.00	0.22	2.58	2.53	80.0	5.4	48.6	0.0	1.0
5.3	1.63	13.9	0.14	5.1	0.71	0.74	6.13	3.27	75.1	3.6	17.3	8.0	8.0
7.5	1.58	7.0	0.02	6.5	0.08	1.23	9.00	4.74	80.3	4.9	27.7	1.7	6.2
8.5	1.18	4.1	0.24	2.0	0.01	0.10	0.93	2.46	95.6	4.3	13.7	5.2	5.2
9.8	0.25	0.9	0.02	3.2	0.07	0.28	1.59	4.16	92.2	4.8	24.5	3.9	7.8
7.7	0.47	2.1	0.00	2.9	0.03	0.74	8.82	2.56	79.1	5.7	45.7	4.2	3.3
9.0	0.33	1.4	0.24	2.8	0.04	0.25	2.24	3.41	94.4	4.6	23.9	2.8	5.7
6.1	1.07	9.6	0.30	3.3	0.01	0.29	2.60	4.60	91.0	5.9	37.3	1.9	5.1
2.1	2.91	26.1	0.91	2.9	0.01	0.30	4.04	6.97	55.2	3.5	14.5	0.0	1.0
5.8	0.70	5.9	2.09	3.5	-0.18	-0.11	-1.18	4.33	66.2	2.6	19.2	24.4	5.6
9.3	0.16	1.4	0.22	2.4	0.06	0.16	1.82	3.14	92.7	4.8	22.6	3.7	5.7
7.3	0.56	5.6	0.62	7.3	1.19	0.99	10.16	4.55	67.3	3.3	9.5	2.4	7.3
9.7	0.16	0.4	0.82	9.5	2.38	1.77	6.45	2.37	60.6	4.4	34.8	5.8	10.0
9.5	0.10	0.3	0.00	3.2	0.04	0.43	2.91	2.34	82.7	5.0	21.7	0.0	6.8
9.6	0.24	1.9	0.32	7.8	25.83	1.07	10.43	2.78	66.5	3.1	9.0	7.4	9.0
7.7	1.81	5.5	1.24	4.1	0.13	0.46	4.57	2.63	89.6	5.5	34.6	0.9	6.2
4.7	1.71	8.8	1.16	2.7	-0.02	-0.58	-4.09	4.45	82.9	4.0	15.6	4.8	6.6
7.8	0.24	4.9	0.07	4.5	0.67	0.76	7.28	3.30	76.7	4.3	19.0	5.6	7.0
4.7	1.05	8.2	0.83	5.1	0.01	0.15	1.49	6.04	75.1	1.9	17.3	18.0	4.3
8.1	0.57	1.6	0.00	1.6	0.00	0.00	0.00	3.67	100.0	4.5	29.8	0.0	6.9
0.0	0.86	72.4	0.00	6.7	0.02	2.60	272.00	7.68	67.9	4.1	33.5	0.0	4.5

							One	Asset Mix (As a % of Total Assets)					
Name	City	State	Rating	2016 Rating	2015 Rating	Total Assets ($Mil)	Year Asset Growth	Comm-ercial Loans	Cons-umer Loans	Mort-gage Loans	Secur-ities	Capital-ization Index	Net Worth Ratio
FirstEnergy Choice Federal Credit Union	Greensburg	PA	C	C	C	53.0	-4.47	0.0	14.4	0.1	54.9	10.0	16.2
FirstEnergy Family Credit Union, Inc.	Akron	OH	C	C	C	42.7	0.70	0.0	30.2	0.0	10.7	10.0	12.6
FirstLight Federal Credit Union	El Paso	TX	B-	B-	B-	1012.2	6.29	11.0	48.9	29.0	3.7	6.2	8.3
Firstmark Credit Union	San Antonio	TX	C+	C+	B	1056.7	3.47	4.0	38.6	30.2	18.5	6.7	8.9
▼ Fisher Scientific Employees FCU	Pittsburgh	PA	D+	C-	D+	2.3	-6.04	0.0	61.5	0.0	0.0	10.0	12.3
Fitzsimons Federal Credit Union	Aurora	CO	C-	C-	C	182.8	3.85	10.6	18.8	25.2	19.5	10.0	11.3
Five County Credit Union	Bath	ME	B-	B-	C+	240.5	6.13	5.6	16.7	45.9	0.0	6.2	8.2
Five Star Credit Union	Dothan	AL	A-	A-	B+	387.7	2.64	12.3	31.1	22.2	15.4	9.1	10.5
FivePoint Credit Union	Nederland	TX	A-	A-	A-	563.7	7.66	9.6	41.9	23.4	4.6	10.0	11.7
FLAG Credit Union	Tallahassee	FL	C-	C-	C	39.6	6.16	1.5	41.0	7.6	0.0	7.5	9.4
Flagship Community Federal Credit Union	Port Huron	MI	D-	D-	D-	22.7	17.55	16.7	27.3	41.8	0.0	4.5	6.5
Flasher Community Credit Union	Flasher	ND	D+	D+	D+	11.4	2.22	13.4	6.8	28.4	0.0	6.0	8.0
Fleur De Lis Federal Credit Union	Metairie	LA	D+	D+	C-	14.9	-4.22	0.0	29.9	0.0	15.7	8.8	10.3
Flint Area School Employees Credit Union	Flint	MI	B	B	B	406.3	3.93	0.3	12.2	5.3	64.3	10.0	15.1
Flint Federal Credit Union	Reynolds	GA	D+	D+	C	2.7	0.95	0.0	22.9	3.1	0.0	10.0	23.1
Flint River Employees FCU	Oglethorpe	GA	C	C	C	2.0	6.77	0.0	32.7	0.0	0.0	10.0	24.2
Floodwood Area Credit Union	Floodwood	MN	C	C	C	18.9	-0.89	1.7	12.8	25.9	35.9	10.0	15.8
Florence Federal Credit Union	Florence	AL	C+	C+	C	52.0	-0.11	0.0	7.0	20.6	22.5	10.0	11.4
Florida A&M University FCU	Tallahassee	FL	E-	E-	E+	20.4	2.32	0.2	40.0	16.7	0.0	5.4	7.4
Florida Central Credit Union	Tampa	FL	D+	D+	C	455.4	7.04	1.1	54.9	11.0	8.5	6.6	8.7
Florida Credit Union	Gainesville	FL	A-	A-	B	914.1	14.10	8.2	53.4	18.6	0.0	8.0	9.7
Florida Customs Federal Credit Union	Tampa	FL	C	C	C	9.9	2.98	0.0	33.4	0.0	0.0	10.0	16.9
Florida Department of Transportation CU	Tallahassee	FL	C	C	C	49.6	-0.07	0.9	21.2	5.2	36.0	10.0	17.5
▲ Florida Hospital Credit Union	Altamonte Springs	FL	B	B-	B-	48.7	1.45	0.0	34.6	6.2	4.3	9.5	10.6
Florida Rural Electric Credit Union	Tallahassee	FL	C	C	B-	29.6	3.48	0.0	29.3	3.4	14.7	10.0	19.6
Florida State Employees FCU	Pensacola	FL	D-	D-	D-	26.9	-2.08	0.0	32.1	3.3	0.0	5.3	7.3
Florida State University Credit Union	Tallahassee	FL	B+	B+	B+	200.4	11.84	11.3	59.2	13.6	0.0	7.4	9.2
Florida West Coast Credit Union	Brandon	FL	B-	B-	B-	92.9	2.02	0.0	31.9	0.0	38.4	8.1	9.9
Florist Federal Credit Union	Roswell	NM	C-	C-	C-	9.4	18.77	4.6	33.4	10.5	0.0	10.0	12.7
Flowers Employees Credit League CU	Thomasville	GA	B	B	B	26.6	3.22	0.0	51.8	0.0	0.0	10.0	26.3
Fluke Employees Federal Credit Union	Everett	WA	C-	C-	D+	2.9	-1.38	0.0	50.5	0.0	0.0	10.0	18.5
FME Federal Credit Union	Saint Clair Shores	MI	C+	C+	C+	73.8	1.02	1.0	13.5	22.0	12.2	10.0	12.5
Fo Me Bo Company Federal Credit Union	Wabash	IN	C-	C-	C-	3.6	5.03	0.0	45.0	0.0	0.0	10.0	14.4
Focus Credit Union	Wauwatosa	WI	D	D	D	46.8	9.19	0.1	67.0	2.5	0.0	4.8	6.8
▼ Focus Federal Credit Union	Toledo	OH	D-	D	D-	9.5	16.15	0.0	41.7	0.6	6.8	6.6	8.6
▼ Focus Federal Credit Union	Oklahoma City	OK	D	D+	C-	111.1	4.18	0.0	48.6	21.1	8.1	5.5	7.6
Focus First Federal Credit Union	Rochester	NY	D	D	D	17.1	0.71	0.0	46.3	0.0	0.0	10.0	41.8
FOGCE Federal Credit Union	Eutaw	AL	C+	C+	C+	1.4	-3.79	0.0	28.7	0.0	0.0	10.0	21.3
▼ Fond Du Lac Credit Union	Fond du Lac	WI	C	C+	C+	62.5	7.95	0.0	37.7	30.7	0.0	7.0	9.0
▼ Fontana Federal Credit Union	Fontana	CA	C-	C	C	14.2	7.43	0.0	31.9	0.0	0.0	10.0	11.4
Food Industries Credit Union	Springfield	OR	C+	C+	C+	23.5	0.29	1.7	18.2	32.2	0.0	10.0	22.4
Foothill Federal Credit Union	Arcadia	CA	A	A	A	399.1	9.49	6.4	19.3	23.4	36.0	10.0	12.0
Foothills Credit Union	Lakewood	CO	C+	C+	B	97.6	9.70	11.8	19.6	41.2	0.5	7.4	9.3
Foothills Federal Credit Union	Loudon	TN	B-	B-	B-	48.2	8.34	2.9	28.1	12.1	0.0	9.9	11.0
Forest Area Federal Credit Union	Fife Lake	MI	B+	B+	B+	105.4	4.23	0.4	14.6	22.2	12.9	10.0	14.2
Formica-Evendale Federal Credit Union	Evendale	OH	C-	C-	C-	1.9	-2.58	0.0	59.9	0.0	0.0	10.0	26.1
▲ Forrest County Teachers FCU	Hattiesburg	MS	C-	D+	C-	<1	1.18	0.0	37.6	0.0	0.0	10.0	16.3
Fort Bayard Federal Credit Union	Silver City	NM	D	D	D+	4.5	-2.37	0.0	63.6	0.0	0.0	10.0	20.7
Fort Billings Federal Credit Union	Gibbstown	NJ	D	D	D	62.7	1.67	0.0	10.7	9.6	55.0	8.4	9.9
Fort Bragg Federal Credit Union	Fayetteville	NC	C+	C+	C+	398.3	3.67	0.4	28.4	12.0	17.4	9.1	10.6
Fort Community Credit Union	Fort Atkinson	WI	A-	A-	A-	234.7	5.55	6.9	27.7	23.2	22.1	10.0	13.7
Fort Dix Federal Credit Union	Joint Base MDL	NJ	D	D	D+	9.7	1.30	0.0	20.2	0.0	0.0	10.0	12.7
Fort Dodge Family Credit Union	Fort Dodge	IA	B+	B+	B+	29.8	6.36	0.0	35.4	0.0	14.2	10.0	11.3
Fort Financial Federal Credit Union	Fort Wayne	IN	B-	B-	B-	234.4	5.23	0.0	45.0	16.4	0.0	6.4	8.4
Fort Knox Federal Credit Union	Radcliff	KY	A+	A+	A+	1427.1	7.40	4.2	32.3	22.9	11.9	10.0	15.6
Fort Lee Federal Credit Union	Prince George	VA	B-	B-	C+	173.1	4.59	0.0	41.0	6.0	27.3	7.9	9.8
Fort Ligonier Federal Credit Union	Bolivar	PA	C+	C+	C+	3.0	6.15	0.0	35.3	0.0	0.0	10.0	14.1
Fort McClellan Credit Union	Anniston	AL	B+	B+	B+	235.7	7.62	0.0	20.9	10.6	0.4	10.0	12.8
▼ Fort McPherson Credit Union	Atlanta	GA	D+	C-	C-	24.1	8.39	1.1	28.0	5.4	4.4	6.8	8.8
Fort Meade Credit Union	Fort Meade	MD	E-	E-	E	32.2	1.00	0.0	9.9	8.9	15.1	3.5	5.5

Asset Quality Index	Non-Performing Loans as a % of Total Loans	Non-Performing Loans as a % of Capital	Net Charge-Offs Avg Loans	Profitability Index	Net Income ($Mil)	Return on Assets	Return on Equity	Net Interest Spread	Overhead Efficiency Ratio	Liquidity Index	Liquidity Ratio	Hot Money Ratio	Stability Index
10.0	0.15	0.2	0.06	**2.4**	0.04	0.30	1.93	2.23	87.2	**5.3**	33.9	1.4	**7.2**
9.9	0.00	0.0	-0.03	**1.8**	0.02	0.14	1.12	2.12	92.7	**4.6**	26.2	0.0	**6.6**
5.5	0.53	5.8	1.18	**3.8**	0.91	0.37	4.40	4.16	70.5	**3.2**	12.9	11.8	**5.9**
7.1	0.51	6.3	0.65	**3.7**	0.74	0.29	3.57	3.52	81.8	**2.4**	15.3	16.7	**5.3**
8.1	0.28	1.3	2.42	**0.5**	-0.01	-2.44	-19.24	5.41	106.3	**5.4**	33.9	0.0	**5.5**
9.2	0.52	2.5	0.31	**2.3**	0.20	0.45	3.95	3.36	84.8	**4.0**	19.3	4.3	**6.6**
7.2	0.56	6.0	0.35	**4.4**	0.41	0.70	8.45	4.38	84.2	**3.1**	19.7	11.3	**5.3**
6.2	1.08	9.0	0.64	**9.9**	1.34	1.39	14.20	4.67	71.2	**3.6**	20.7	14.4	**8.1**
6.7	0.83	5.5	0.84	**4.6**	0.11	0.08	0.68	4.76	85.0	**2.9**	15.0	17.3	**8.6**
5.9	0.94	6.9	1.05	**2.0**	0.00	0.01	0.11	4.18	93.0	**5.4**	38.0	3.4	**3.1**
3.1	1.20	19.6	0.20	**5.7**	0.05	0.84	12.71	4.30	74.3	**3.9**	12.0	0.0	**1.0**
5.9	1.16	8.0	0.00	**4.7**	0.02	0.60	7.96	4.20	81.0	**6.1**	46.2	0.0	**3.0**
5.5	1.09	12.9	-0.40	**1.3**	-0.01	-0.19	-1.84	3.97	110.2	**5.3**	38.2	8.0	**4.5**
10.0	0.73	1.1	0.13	**4.6**	0.73	0.72	4.98	2.12	71.1	**5.1**	21.5	1.7	**8.1**
10.0	0.00	0.0	0.00	**1.0**	0.00	-0.15	-0.65	2.61	106.7	**6.5**	89.0	0.0	**5.9**
9.6	0.00	0.0	0.00	**3.9**	0.00	0.61	2.45	4.26	84.2	**6.5**	81.7	0.0	**7.3**
6.2	4.43	12.9	0.00	**2.5**	0.02	0.32	2.01	2.96	88.4	**5.4**	30.1	0.0	**6.6**
9.5	0.30	0.8	-0.03	**3.1**	0.06	0.45	3.95	2.16	79.2	**4.4**	28.5	7.8	**5.5**
1.7	5.36	47.8	-0.09	**2.2**	0.03	0.59	9.38	4.99	102.1	**4.6**	22.3	3.0	**0.0**
5.8	0.52	5.4	1.15	**1.2**	0.02	0.01	0.18	3.38	83.5	**4.0**	11.9	2.3	**3.5**
6.3	0.35	4.1	0.69	**8.2**	2.20	0.99	10.07	4.77	71.1	**2.3**	17.2	24.4	**7.5**
8.8	1.80	3.7	0.34	**3.3**	0.01	0.44	2.64	3.95	81.9	**4.7**	25.7	8.1	**6.1**
8.4	0.30	3.5	-0.21	**1.5**	0.01	0.06	0.33	3.24	98.6	**5.0**	15.5	4.4	**6.5**
9.9	0.18	0.7	0.25	**5.4**	0.12	0.98	9.22	3.66	78.9	**5.5**	26.6	0.0	**5.1**
9.2	0.08	0.2	0.07	**1.7**	-0.01	-0.19	-0.95	3.69	105.9	**5.5**	38.3	4.3	**6.7**
4.2	3.46	17.4	1.61	**1.5**	0.02	0.24	3.26	3.26	96.0	**4.7**	21.6	10.1	**1.9**
4.4	0.88	11.3	0.75	**5.4**	0.36	0.73	7.94	4.79	76.8	**3.8**	11.5	0.6	**5.4**
9.4	0.18	0.8	0.68	**3.5**	0.06	0.25	2.59	3.01	90.3	**5.1**	27.7	4.7	**5.0**
7.5	1.15	4.5	0.00	**2.5**	-0.01	-0.27	-2.00	3.59	103.6	**3.4**	31.1	22.7	**6.8**
7.5	1.11	2.7	1.43	**5.0**	0.05	0.74	2.76	5.64	73.3	**5.5**	44.2	3.1	**6.9**
8.7	0.07	0.2	0.27	**1.2**	0.00	-0.14	-0.76	3.61	91.7	**4.8**	29.0	0.0	**6.3**
10.0	0.11	0.8	-0.01	**2.1**	0.02	0.11	0.83	2.75	96.8	**4.9**	28.1	2.9	**6.1**
8.7	0.00	0.0	0.00	**2.4**	0.00	0.35	2.34	2.74	84.2	**5.8**	36.1	0.0	**7.2**
4.6	0.78	8.5	0.19	**3.5**	0.03	0.26	3.78	3.97	92.0	**4.3**	19.3	2.0	**2.3**
5.5	2.01	11.3	0.58	**0.9**	-0.04	-1.59	-16.79	5.33	106.7	**4.7**	35.0	5.8	**2.8**
5.9	0.50	6.1	0.93	**0.9**	-0.06	-0.21	-2.82	3.40	95.0	**4.0**	12.9	3.2	**4.1**
8.8	0.01	0.0	-0.05	**0.0**	-0.08	-1.95	-4.67	1.88	202.5	**3.3**	41.8	20.7	**5.6**
9.8	0.44	0.7	0.00	**3.4**	0.00	-0.29	-1.39	3.55	107.1	**5.2**	19.7	0.0	**6.8**
9.2	0.15	1.2	0.37	**2.5**	0.00	-0.03	-0.29	3.26	87.8	**4.3**	19.5	2.2	**4.5**
8.9	1.19	3.9	1.43	**0.6**	-0.02	-0.61	-5.17	3.58	122.8	**4.9**	37.6	9.7	**6.3**
9.9	0.06	0.2	0.00	**4.0**	0.04	0.59	2.67	3.27	82.9	**4.3**	33.0	5.4	**7.0**
9.8	0.18	0.8	0.11	**7.6**	1.01	1.03	8.94	2.85	71.8	**4.0**	14.3	7.5	**8.9**
6.7	0.61	4.6	0.08	**4.9**	0.33	1.36	14.65	3.62	68.2	**3.3**	18.8	8.7	**4.7**
8.2	0.36	1.6	0.33	**3.3**	0.03	0.24	2.13	3.50	84.2	**4.2**	22.2	12.7	**5.9**
8.8	0.86	3.6	0.11	**3.0**	0.08	0.32	2.25	3.19	96.6	**4.0**	18.9	8.2	**7.7**
8.5	0.00	0.0	0.00	**1.3**	0.00	0.00	0.00	4.71	105.6	**5.0**	49.2	11.3	**6.0**
7.9	0.99	2.2	17.54	**2.5**	-0.01	-12.26	-69.57	12.20	128.6	**7.1**	65.7	0.0	**5.0**
4.2	2.09	6.8	7.96	**0.6**	0.00	-0.09	-0.43	9.18	71.6	**4.8**	26.8	0.0	**5.0**
7.7	1.15	4.0	0.54	**0.6**	-0.04	-0.28	-2.72	2.49	97.3	**4.5**	19.2	5.0	**4.5**
7.9	1.09	5.1	0.31	**3.8**	0.45	0.46	4.41	2.95	84.5	**4.9**	30.6	6.7	**6.0**
7.1	1.29	6.0	0.05	**7.8**	0.77	1.33	9.81	3.12	68.5	**4.4**	14.2	2.7	**8.6**
8.2	0.25	0.7	0.66	**1.0**	0.01	0.29	2.27	3.49	87.6	**4.8**	18.3	0.0	**5.1**
7.2	1.85	7.4	-0.33	**5.3**	0.04	0.52	4.54	3.77	79.0	**6.1**	39.1	2.1	**6.3**
5.8	0.82	7.6	0.38	**3.6**	0.25	0.43	5.72	3.67	85.9	**4.4**	19.5	3.5	**4.9**
8.7	0.48	2.8	0.79	**9.0**	4.30	1.22	8.14	3.10	51.4	**2.5**	16.3	22.3	**10.0**
8.4	0.67	4.0	0.70	**3.6**	0.20	0.47	5.45	3.21	80.7	**4.6**	24.0	5.2	**5.2**
10.0	0.00	0.0	0.00	**3.6**	0.00	0.55	3.83	1.84	71.4	**4.7**	23.8	0.0	**7.4**
8.5	0.94	3.6	0.70	**4.8**	0.38	0.66	5.12	2.60	65.8	**4.2**	26.0	13.9	**7.8**
7.5	0.75	4.9	1.10	**1.3**	-0.04	-0.65	-7.25	4.83	102.4	**6.6**	46.7	0.0	**3.1**
3.0	9.44	30.9	0.12	**0.1**	-0.06	-0.77	-13.80	3.11	113.7	**6.7**	39.3	0.0	**0.0**

Name	City	State	Rating	2016 Rating	2015 Rating	Total Assets ($Mil)	One Year Asset Growth	Asset Mix (As a % of Total Assets) Commercial Loans	Consumer Loans	Mortgage Loans	Securities	Capitalization Index	Net Worth Ratio
Fort Morgan Schools Federal Credit Union	Fort Morgan	CO	**C**	C	C-	4.1	-2.40	0.0	45.4	22.6	0.0	**10.0**	18.1
Fort Peck Community Federal Credit Union	Fort Peck	MT	**C+**	C+	C+	11.4	4.26	0.0	22.4	26.2	0.0	**10.0**	12.1
Fort Roots Federal Credit Union	North Little Rock	AR	**C-**	C-	D+	4.7	0.17	0.0	47.5	0.0	0.0	**10.0**	13.6
Fort Sill Federal Credit Union	Fort Sill	OK	**C**	C	C	285.7	4.76	0.0	32.2	3.7	24.6	**7.4**	9.5
Fort Smith Dixie Cup FCU	Fort Smith	AR	**B-**	B-	B-	13.9	3.98	0.0	24.3	0.4	0.0	**10.0**	23.6
▲ Fort Smith Municipal Employees FCU	Fort Smith	AR	**D+**	D	D+	2.1	-15.39	0.0	28.1	0.0	0.0	**10.0**	11.3
Fort Smith Teachers Federal Credit Union	Fort Smith	AR	**C**	C	C-	13.0	8.82	0.0	19.0	0.0	0.0	**10.0**	17.2
Fort Worth City Credit Union	Fort Worth	TX	**A-**	A-	A-	183.8	9.86	0.1	22.1	14.3	8.1	**10.0**	12.0
Fort Worth Community Credit Union	Bedford	TX	**C-**	C-	C-	880.6	4.01	0.0	62.4	6.2	13.5	**7.0**	9.0
Fortera Federal Credit Union	Clarksville	TN	**B+**	B+	A-	541.8	6.75	1.0	49.4	17.6	8.2	**10.0**	13.4
Fortress Federal Credit Union	Marion	IN	**D+**	D+	D+	16.9	-1.50	0.0	61.4	1.6	0.0	**10.0**	16.2
FORUM Credit Union	Fishers	IN	**B-**	B-	B	1388.7	19.57	7.6	49.2	19.6	3.4	**7.9**	9.6
Forward Financial Credit Union	Niagara	WI	**C+**	C+	C+	74.0	6.76	3.8	23.1	38.4	0.0	**10.0**	11.4
Foundation Credit Union	Springfield	MO	**B-**	B-	B	64.4	0.62	0.6	12.5	32.7	4.5	**10.0**	13.7
Founders Federal Credit Union	Lancaster	SC	**A-**	A-	A-	2111.8	10.03	0.5	40.0	35.1	8.0	**10.0**	13.6
Fountain Valley Credit Union	Fountain Valley	CA	**D+**	D+	D+	2.1	1.91	0.0	36.0	0.0	0.0	**10.0**	17.5
Four Corners Federal Credit Union	Kirtland	NM	**C**	C	B-	27.9	1.10	0.0	28.1	0.0	0.0	**10.0**	12.7
▼ Four Flags Area Credit Union	Niles	MI	**D**	D+	D	4.4	8.42	0.0	50.2	0.0	11.4	**8.7**	10.1
Four Points Federal Credit Union	Omaha	NE	**B**	B	B	116.5	-1.56	0.9	17.2	25.9	41.4	**10.0**	13.2
Four Seasons Federal Credit Union	Opelika	AL	**C**	C	D+	52.3	7.00	2.3	27.4	1.9	1.0	**6.8**	8.8
Fourth Ward Federal Credit Union	Amite	LA	**C-**	C-	C-	<1	10.01	0.0	20.2	7.2	0.0	**10.0**	11.6
Fox Communities Credit Union	Appleton	WI	**A-**	A-	A-	1353.5	15.76	20.9	18.3	61.9	2.6	**8.9**	10.3
Fox Valley Credit Union	Aurora	IL	**C-**	C-	C-	20.0	-3.70	0.0	27.6	12.1	4.3	**10.0**	13.9
Frankenmuth Credit Union	Frankenmuth	MI	**A-**	A-	B+	493.3	17.20	6.5	42.3	17.4	1.4	**9.6**	10.8
Frankfort Community Federal Credit Union	Frankfort	MI	**C-**	C-	C-	12.1	8.14	0.0	32.3	0.0	0.0	**10.0**	13.2
Franklin First Federal Credit Union	Greenfield	MA	**D+**	D+	D+	60.1	3.05	0.0	21.0	23.1	9.9	**5.5**	7.5
▲ Franklin Johnstown Federal Credit Union	Johnstown	PA	**D+**	D	D+	32.0	4.24	0.0	23.5	0.2	6.4	**10.0**	11.6
Franklin Mint Federal Credit Union	Broomall	PA	**B-**	B-	B-	1045.9	6.88	8.1	31.0	27.9	8.1	**5.6**	7.8
Franklin Regional Schools FCU	Jeannette	PA	**D+**	D+	D+	3.2	4.54	0.0	55.8	0.0	1.6	**10.0**	11.3
Franklin Trust Federal Credit Union	Hartford	CT	**C**	C	C	45.8	3.71	0.0	26.6	3.7	0.0	**8.8**	10.2
Franklin-Oil Region Credit Union	Franklin	PA	**B-**	B-	B-	37.9	1.62	0.0	41.1	1.8	0.0	**10.0**	11.3
Franklin-Somerset Federal Credit Union	Skowhegan	ME	**A-**	A-	B+	89.7	6.12	1.9	24.0	23.9	0.0	**10.0**	11.6
Fraternal Order of Police Credit Union	Tulsa	OK	**C**	C	D+	37.7	1.57	0.0	47.0	0.0	0.0	**7.9**	9.6
FRB Federal Credit Union	Washington	DC	**C+**	C+	C+	83.8	5.80	0.4	19.7	12.6	21.8	**6.5**	8.5
Frederiksted Federal Credit Union	Frederiksted	VI	**C-**	C-	C-	12.9	8.06	0.0	27.7	9.3	0.0	**10.0**	12.2
Freedom Community Credit Union	Fargo	ND	**D**	D	E+	27.9	10.08	0.0	25.3	16.0	0.0	**5.6**	7.6
Freedom Credit Union	Springfield	MA	**B-**	B-	C+	488.0	-6.23	9.9	5.2	50.8	27.4	**10.0**	15.0
Freedom Credit Union	Warminster	PA	**A-**	A-	B+	768.0	8.60	1.6	23.3	29.7	23.6	**8.4**	10.1
Freedom Credit Union	Provo	UT	**B**	B	B-	33.5	14.91	3.9	44.8	16.4	12.4	**9.3**	10.6
Freedom Federal Credit Union	Bel Air	MD	**C+**	C+	C	318.5	12.70	6.8	61.5	19.9	6.0	**5.9**	7.9
Freedom First Credit Union	Dayton	OH	**C+**	C+	C+	34.9	4.69	0.0	42.5	0.0	0.0	**7.5**	9.3
Freedom First Federal Credit Union	McConnell AFB	KS	**C-**	C-	D+	33.7	4.13	0.0	14.1	0.0	8.6	**10.0**	14.1
Freedom First Federal Credit Union	Roanoke	VA	**A-**	A-	B+	476.1	14.79	24.3	29.2	36.8	4.2	**8.0**	9.7
Freedom Northwest Credit Union	Kamiah	ID	**A-**	A-	A-	91.3	20.89	1.5	17.0	60.3	4.6	**10.0**	11.3
Freedom United Federal Credit Union	Rochester	PA	**B-**	B-	B-	62.4	5.22	0.0	17.3	1.1	3.4	**10.0**	15.6
FreeStar Financial Credit Union	Clinton Township	MI	**B+**	B+	B+	199.0	7.23	3.8	34.8	31.2	11.8	**8.5**	10.1
Freestone Credit Union	Teague	TX	**C**	C	C	40.1	-0.06	0.0	24.4	24.3	10.7	**8.0**	9.7
Fremont Federal Credit Union	Fremont	OH	**A**	A	A	204.4	12.40	9.0	21.5	25.4	24.6	**10.0**	13.2
▼ Fremont First Central FCU	Fremont	NE	**D+**	C-	C	41.3	3.42	0.0	13.9	19.1	0.0	**7.6**	9.4
▼ Fresno Fire Department Credit Union	Fresno	CA	**D+**	C-	C-	35.7	1.75	0.0	18.7	3.0	0.0	**10.0**	12.9
Fresno Grangers Federal Credit Union	Fresno	CA	**B**	B	B-	17.4	7.60	21.3	1.4	45.4	0.0	**10.0**	23.7
Fresno Police Department Credit Union	Fresno	CA	**B**	B	B-	50.4	2.53	0.0	23.0	13.1	8.0	**10.0**	18.9
Freudenberg-Nok Employees Credit Union	Bristol	NH	**C-**	C-	C-	2.9	5.31	0.0	27.2	0.0	0.0	**10.0**	23.0
Frick Tri-County Federal Credit Union	Uniontown	PA	**B**	B	B	86.8	4.35	0.0	15.4	11.1	38.5	**8.2**	9.8
Friendly Federal Credit Union	Aliquippa	PA	**B**	B	B	52.1	1.42	0.0	21.4	23.0	31.9	**10.0**	17.3
Friends and Family Credit Union	Massillon	OH	**C-**	C-	C-	87.5	9.26	0.0	46.3	24.2	0.4	**5.8**	7.8
▼ Friends Federal Credit Union	Norman	OK	**D**	D+	D+	8.2	-8.33	0.0	33.4	0.0	0.0	**10.0**	13.4
Friends First Credit Union	Owensboro	KY	**E+**	E+	E+	6.0	0.76	0.0	36.7	0.0	0.0	**4.8**	6.9
▼ Frio County Federal Credit Union	Pearsall	TX	**C**	C+	B-	6.6	2.57	0.0	49.6	0.0	0.0	**10.0**	21.6
Friona Texas Federal Credit Union	Friona	TX	**B-**	B-	B-	12.5	-0.43	0.0	15.4	11.4	0.0	**10.0**	18.5

Asset Quality Index	Non-Performing Loans as a % of Total Loans	Non-Performing Loans as a % of Capital	Net Charge-Offs Avg Loans	Profitability Index	Net Income ($Mil)	Return on Assets	Return on Equity	Net Interest Spread	Overhead Efficiency Ratio	Liquidity Index	Liquidity Ratio	Hot Money Ratio	Stability Index
8.7	0.14	0.5	0.00	**4.3**	0.01	0.78	4.34	2.95	69.0	**4.9**	38.9	0.0	**6.8**
7.4	1.58	7.3	0.00	**6.0**	0.03	1.14	9.41	4.66	75.0	**4.9**	27.3	5.0	**5.7**
7.4	0.00	0.0	0.00	**1.2**	0.00	-0.17	-1.25	3.75	101.7	**5.3**	38.7	0.0	**6.8**
9.6	0.44	2.1	0.70	**3.0**	0.33	0.47	4.94	2.85	83.0	**5.2**	28.5	3.3	**5.2**
8.5	3.25	3.8	0.31	**3.8**	0.01	0.38	1.59	2.32	80.3	**5.1**	46.4	7.0	**7.4**
9.1	0.00	0.0	0.00	**2.1**	0.00	0.18	1.72	6.71	72.0	**6.6**	54.6	0.0	**3.6**
10.0	0.00	0.0	0.00	**1.9**	0.00	0.13	0.72	2.41	97.0	**6.0**	42.7	0.0	**6.8**
9.9	0.10	0.4	0.17	**5.2**	0.41	0.90	8.08	2.79	73.4	**4.4**	17.2	4.3	**8.0**
7.7	0.31	3.2	0.68	**2.3**	0.47	0.22	2.39	3.04	81.0	**3.8**	12.7	7.6	**5.8**
6.5	0.74	4.4	1.19	**4.5**	0.67	0.50	3.74	3.85	71.4	**3.1**	14.2	10.5	**8.3**
5.2	2.56	9.4	-0.03	**1.0**	0.01	0.19	1.17	5.65	74.0	**4.3**	36.5	8.1	**5.0**
7.2	0.33	3.3	0.42	**3.9**	1.97	0.59	5.97	2.84	79.1	**3.0**	21.5	17.9	**7.0**
6.0	2.14	11.8	0.24	**2.6**	0.02	0.10	0.86	3.85	94.3	**4.7**	36.6	4.1	**5.8**
10.0	0.50	1.7	-0.01	**3.1**	0.05	0.31	2.24	2.14	84.8	**4.4**	18.4	0.0	**6.6**
8.1	0.66	4.0	1.06	**5.1**	3.18	0.62	4.45	4.67	75.1	**3.5**	17.9	9.1	**7.6**
9.1	0.34	0.8	0.00	**0.2**	0.00	-0.52	-3.21	2.80	130.8	**5.4**	34.6	0.0	**6.5**
9.9	0.27	0.6	-0.09	**0.9**	0.01	0.08	0.56	2.49	98.5	**6.1**	135.6	18.9	**5.2**
4.9	1.12	6.5	0.45	**1.3**	0.00	-0.10	-0.90	4.15	98.5	**4.8**	19.4	0.0	**4.3**
9.9	0.03	0.2	0.04	**4.1**	0.18	0.62	5.02	2.44	77.3	**3.5**	1.9	5.6	**8.0**
5.5	0.64	11.5	1.16	**2.9**	0.02	0.13	1.48	5.15	95.4	**5.0**	22.8	8.1	**3.4**
5.7	4.95	14.6	0.00	**5.4**	0.01	3.07	27.27	11.36	30.0	**7.5**	70.6	0.0	**4.3**
8.8	0.13	2.0	0.06	**6.5**	3.13	0.96	8.75	2.91	74.7	**3.0**	10.0	4.6	**9.0**
6.2	4.99	13.8	1.04	**2.1**	0.00	0.02	0.14	3.60	96.9	**4.9**	22.1	0.7	**5.8**
5.3	1.59	13.1	0.56	**8.8**	1.33	1.10	10.11	4.86	72.0	**2.9**	8.6	8.9	**8.7**
8.8	0.98	3.7	0.00	**2.5**	0.01	0.30	2.26	3.00	90.4	**5.0**	33.6	0.0	**6.2**
7.6	0.38	2.8	0.43	**1.8**	0.01	0.05	0.72	3.26	92.0	**3.4**	18.3	11.1	**3.1**
9.4	0.99	2.8	0.60	**0.8**	-0.01	-0.11	-0.97	3.56	97.5	**6.7**	41.0	0.9	**5.5**
7.3	0.55	5.3	0.55	**3.2**	0.58	0.23	2.94	3.43	88.4	**3.5**	16.2	10.0	**5.9**
8.4	0.00	0.0	1.80	**1.3**	0.00	0.00	0.00	3.22	104.2	**4.1**	13.7	0.0	**6.0**
3.3	2.53	34.4	1.07	**4.5**	0.09	0.81	10.93	6.38	80.7	**5.6**	38.6	2.6	**4.2**
7.2	0.89	5.2	1.05	**4.8**	0.04	0.47	4.11	5.23	76.1	**4.5**	29.5	7.9	**5.6**
6.9	0.95	5.7	0.40	**7.7**	0.21	0.97	8.35	3.92	72.6	**4.1**	22.6	6.3	**6.4**
7.3	0.42	2.6	0.12	**2.3**	0.03	0.30	3.70	2.71	86.9	**4.8**	23.2	4.7	**3.5**
6.2	1.91	8.7	0.57	**2.7**	0.05	0.24	2.80	2.88	83.8	**5.5**	32.8	2.9	**4.0**
3.6	5.54	23.8	0.60	**1.1**	-0.02	-0.57	-4.54	4.51	113.2	**5.5**	32.5	0.0	**6.2**
5.3	1.38	11.1	0.17	**2.0**	0.00	0.04	0.57	3.16	98.6	**4.5**	22.5	0.0	**2.6**
9.1	0.47	2.0	0.03	**3.3**	0.69	0.56	3.82	3.14	84.8	**3.3**	22.1	8.3	**7.9**
9.1	0.54	3.1	0.54	**6.8**	2.04	1.07	10.87	3.14	68.1	**4.2**	28.3	13.9	**7.5**
8.3	0.19	2.5	0.02	**8.0**	0.11	1.35	13.58	3.68	68.2	**3.6**	22.5	9.8	**5.6**
5.9	0.61	6.4	0.51	**3.2**	0.29	0.37	4.70	3.65	80.9	**2.4**	8.5	10.7	**4.3**
6.9	0.54	3.3	0.18	**5.0**	0.06	0.72	7.59	3.15	82.3	**4.6**	31.5	1.2	**5.2**
10.0	0.99	1.1	0.30	**1.8**	0.02	0.19	1.35	2.29	89.5	**6.2**	35.2	3.9	**6.4**
6.7	0.65	5.9	0.52	**5.8**	0.78	0.68	7.24	3.79	78.7	**3.5**	16.7	10.3	**5.5**
7.2	1.04	8.6	0.03	**10.0**	0.44	2.03	17.68	4.63	62.0	**2.8**	7.1	7.1	**7.9**
10.0	0.54	1.4	0.13	**3.3**	0.07	0.44	2.81	2.45	83.2	**5.3**	33.8	0.5	**7.2**
6.8	0.52	5.9	0.72	**4.2**	0.16	0.33	3.24	3.70	80.8	**3.0**	14.1	9.1	**6.6**
7.4	0.46	2.7	0.29	**3.3**	0.03	0.29	3.01	3.83	91.8	**4.4**	20.4	6.2	**5.1**
7.0	1.35	6.7	0.36	**6.0**	0.35	0.71	5.28	3.59	83.9	**3.5**	21.7	11.6	**8.7**
8.9	0.51	2.2	0.05	**1.1**	-0.01	-0.05	-0.52	3.04	101.5	**5.8**	33.6	0.0	**4.4**
10.0	0.45	1.1	0.00	**0.5**	-0.04	-0.43	-3.30	2.26	119.1	**5.4**	43.7	1.5	**6.3**
9.5	0.00	1.1	0.00	**4.8**	0.03	0.78	3.20	3.17	64.2	**6.6**	54.4	0.0	**7.6**
9.6	1.24	2.7	0.79	**3.2**	0.02	0.13	0.67	3.16	92.7	**6.9**	55.4	3.1	**6.9**
9.9	0.00	0.0	0.91	**1.2**	0.00	-0.15	-0.61	2.83	109.1	**7.3**	66.8	0.0	**7.1**
6.4	1.47	7.6	1.15	**4.5**	0.08	0.39	4.10	3.05	71.5	**4.6**	20.4	6.9	**4.2**
7.3	2.25	6.4	0.35	**3.8**	0.07	0.51	2.94	2.90	74.7	**4.2**	16.0	2.3	**7.0**
6.6	0.24	2.6	0.27	**2.6**	0.05	0.24	3.08	3.41	88.6	**3.3**	14.1	10.9	**3.4**
6.6	3.26	10.6	10.35	**0.0**	-0.08	-3.94	-28.42	4.69	104.8	**6.0**	48.3	0.0	**4.9**
5.2	1.59	12.2	0.59	**4.1**	0.01	0.76	10.86	4.58	84.2	**6.0**	53.7	4.4	**1.0**
4.9	1.56	9.2	0.00	**5.9**	0.00	0.00	0.00	6.01	100.0	**3.7**	13.1	0.0	**4.3**
9.5	2.21	3.4	0.00	**4.0**	0.02	0.75	4.01	3.36	80.2	**5.5**	44.1	2.5	**7.6**

Name	City	State	Rating	2016 Rating	2015 Rating	Total Assets ($Mil)	One Year Asset Growth	Asset Mix (As a % of Total Assets) Comm-ercial Loans	Cons-umer Loans	Mort-gage Loans	Secur-ities	Capital-ization Index	Net Worth Ratio
Froid Federal Credit Union	Froid	MT	**C-**	C-	D+	<1	1.81	0.0	18.7	0.0	0.0	**10.0**	14.0
Front Royal Federal Credit Union	Front Royal	VA	**B**	B	B-	60.5	6.84	0.0	17.0	3.4	0.0	**10.0**	12.9
Frontier Community Credit Union	Leavenworth	KS	**B+**	B+	B+	129.3	6.46	1.5	25.9	22.4	3.9	**10.0**	12.4
Frontier Financial Credit Union	Reno	NV	**C-**	C-	D	83.3	8.33	0.0	50.3	16.0	0.5	**6.3**	8.3
FRSA Credit Union	Winter Park	FL	**D+**	D+	D+	5.0	-9.91	4.9	80.5	0.0	0.0	**9.7**	10.8
Ft. Randall Federal Credit Union	Pickstown	SD	**C**	C	C-	21.2	8.18	2.3	38.1	10.9	0.0	**7.0**	9.0
Fulda Area Credit Union	Fulda	MN	**B+**	B+	A-	108.5	15.58	28.6	16.7	41.5	2.6	**8.3**	9.9
Funeral Service Credit Union	Springfield	IL	**D+**	D+	D+	9.0	-2.07	71.3	17.2	0.0	0.0	**10.0**	17.5
▲ G P M Federal Credit Union	San Antonio	TX	**C**	C-	C	1.7	-5.94	0.0	38.5	0.0	0.0	**10.0**	18.7
G.A.P. Federal Credit Union	Johnstown	PA	**C+**	C+	C+	45.7	3.54	0.0	25.8	7.9	2.9	**10.0**	12.0
▼ G.E.M. Federal Credit Union	Minot	ND	**D+**	C-	C-	24.7	2.72	0.0	27.4	0.4	0.0	**6.3**	8.3
G.H.S. Federal Credit Union	Greenville	SC	**C+**	C+	C+	44.0	8.81	0.0	31.4	0.5	0.0	**7.1**	9.0
G.P.O. Federal Credit Union	New Hartford	NY	**B+**	B+	A-	249.4	4.08	8.0	27.6	3.5	8.3	**7.5**	9.3
Gabriels Community Credit Union	Lansing	MI	**B-**	B-	B-	14.2	0.25	1.3	39.4	22.7	0.0	**10.0**	11.8
GAF Linden Employees FCU	Parsippany	NJ	**C-**	C-	C-	4.4	-17.61	0.0	22.4	5.0	0.0	**10.0**	12.8
Galaxy Federal Credit Union	Franklin	PA	**B**	B	B	55.0	-0.18	0.9	20.9	0.0	0.4	**10.0**	15.6
▼ Gale Credit Union	Galesburg	IL	**D+**	C-	C+	27.8	1.04	0.0	39.0	6.0	1.6	**10.0**	12.7
Galesburg Burlington Credit Union	Galesburg	IL	**B**	B	B	44.1	-1.79	0.0	33.5	4.3	0.0	**10.0**	27.4
Gallatin Steam Plant Credit Union	Gallatin	TN	**D+**	D+	C-	5.1	-6.07	0.0	36.9	0.0	0.0	**10.0**	19.3
Gallup Federal Credit Union	Omaha	NE	**B-**	B-	B-	17.5	-4.68	0.0	20.0	10.1	0.0	**10.0**	12.2
Galveston Government Employees CU	La Marque	TX	**E+**	E+	E+	6.5	2.76	2.1	53.3	2.5	0.0	**4.8**	6.8
Galveston School Employees FCU	Galveston	TX	**D-**	D-	E+	3.5	-4.34	0.0	62.7	0.0	0.0	**7.7**	9.5
Garden City Teachers FCU	Garden City	KS	**D**	D	D+	12.2	3.05	0.0	36.9	6.5	0.0	**5.3**	7.3
Garden Island Federal Credit Union	Lihue	HI	**C+**	C+	C	93.9	3.38	0.1	15.2	6.9	20.0	**10.0**	14.2
Garden Savings Federal Credit Union	Parsippany	NJ	**C+**	C+	B	355.9	9.11	3.5	28.2	19.7	20.3	**7.5**	9.5
▲ Garden State Federal Credit Union	Moorestown	NJ	**C**	C-	D+	28.7	3.71	0.0	11.2	30.1	9.6	**7.5**	9.3
Gardiner Federal Credit Union	Gardiner	ME	**B+**	B+	B+	46.7	10.08	0.0	29.9	29.2	0.0	**10.0**	12.2
Garland County Educators' FCU	Hot Springs	AR	**D+**	D+	C-	3.7	3.67	0.0	49.3	0.0	0.0	**8.5**	10.0
Gary Firefighters Association FCU	Gary	IN	**C+**	C+	C+	2.0	1.01	0.0	43.2	0.0	0.0	**10.0**	35.0
Gary Municipal Employees FCU	Gary	IN	**C+**	C+	C+	<1	1.60	0.0	25.6	0.0	0.0	**10.0**	50.6
▼ Gary Police Department Employees FCU	Gary	IN	**C-**	C	C-	1.7	-3.00	0.0	0.0	0.0	0.0	**10.0**	45.3
Gas & Electric Credit Union	Rock Island	IL	**B+**	B+	B+	73.8	1.47	0.0	24.4	28.3	22.1	**10.0**	11.3
Gas & Electric Employees Credit Union	Mason City	IA	**B-**	B-	B-	5.2	-7.74	0.0	50.9	0.0	0.0	**10.0**	31.9
▼ Gates Chili Federal Credit Union	Rochester	NY	**D-**	D	D-	23.9	7.17	0.0	18.5	11.6	2.7	**4.7**	6.7
▲ Gateway Credit Union	Clarksville	TN	**E+**	E	E-	11.5	0.57	1.6	39.1	18.9	0.0	**4.6**	6.7
Gateway Metro Federal Credit Union	Swansea	IL	**C-**	C-	C-	181.3	4.17	0.0	31.4	27.8	17.5	**5.8**	7.8
▼ GCA Federal Credit Union	Lake Charles	LA	**D+**	C-	D+	5.1	-3.68	0.0	15.8	0.0	0.0	**10.0**	23.3
GCS Credit Union	Granite City	IL	**B-**	B-	C+	335.2	5.66	0.1	63.9	15.0	0.0	**10.0**	11.7
GEA Employees Federal Credit Union	Pearisburg	VA	**C-**	C-	C-	1.6	-3.66	0.0	29.9	0.0	0.0	**10.0**	28.5
Geauga Credit Union, Inc.	Burton	OH	**C-**	C-	C-	37.7	7.85	7.7	11.9	5.4	34.1	**9.3**	10.5
Geco Federal Credit Union	Harvey	LA	**D-**	D-	D-	1.0	-11.95	0.0	22.0	0.0	0.0	**7.5**	9.3
GECU	El Paso	TX	**B**	B	B	2615.6	6.94	1.9	65.9	17.8	3.2	**7.1**	9.1
GEICO Federal Credit Union	Chevy Chase	MD	**C-**	C-	C+	141.4	2.01	0.0	10.3	20.2	18.1	**6.4**	8.4
Geismar Complex Federal Credit Union	Geismar	LA	**C**	C	C-	28.7	9.09	0.0	24.7	18.9	0.0	**5.7**	7.7
GEMC Federal Credit Union	Tucker	GA	**B-**	B-	B-	120.3	6.14	6.4	40.6	13.2	0.0	**8.3**	9.9
GENCO Federal Credit Union	Waco	TX	**B+**	B+	B+	289.1	3.98	0.8	53.3	7.3	5.3	**10.0**	11.7
General Credit Union	Fort Wayne	IN	**B-**	B-	C+	86.7	3.81	0.5	31.1	26.8	11.8	**7.4**	9.4
General Electric Credit Union	Cincinnati	OH	**B+**	B+	B+	2810.9	17.93	2.2	60.3	20.1	0.7	**7.2**	9.2
General Electric Employees FCU	Milford	CT	**C-**	C-	C	213.4	4.04	2.0	18.4	11.9	29.6	**5.5**	8.0
▲ General Portland Peninsular Empls FCU	Paulding	OH	**D+**	D	D+	<1	0.49	0.0	56.5	0.0	0.0	**10.0**	15.0
▼ Generations Community FCU	San Antonio	TX	**C**	C+	C+	591.6	-5.33	4.2	46.5	14.4	16.9	**6.7**	8.7
▲ Generations Credit Union	Rockford	IL	**D+**	D	C-	19.0	3.91	0.0	29.0	18.0	0.1	**10.0**	14.8
▲ Generations Credit Union	Olympia	WA	**D+**	D	D-	32.6	14.08	0.2	14.2	17.6	0.1	**5.8**	7.8
▲ Generations Family Federal Credit Union	Saginaw	MI	**C-**	D+	D+	31.6	-1.74	2.1	20.0	8.6	52.7	**10.0**	11.2
▼ Generations Federal Credit Union	La Porte	IN	**D**	D+	D+	10.0	8.96	0.0	29.4	0.0	0.0	**7.1**	9.1
Genesee Co-Op Federal Credit Union	Rochester	NY	**D+**	D+	D	20.3	15.41	0.0	17.6	34.4	0.0	**5.5**	7.5
Genesee Valley Federal Credit Union	Geneseo	NY	**C+**	C+	C+	76.1	4.23	2.8	19.4	37.5	0.0	**6.8**	8.8
Genesis Employees Credit Union	Zanesville	OH	**C**	C	C	13.5	2.09	0.0	54.4	0.0	0.0	**10.0**	11.4
GenFed Financial Credit Union	Akron	OH	**B+**	B+	B+	234.6	0.59	0.4	26.1	31.6	1.1	**10.0**	15.6
Genisys Credit Union	Auburn Hills	MI	**A**	A	A	2348.4	13.31	3.5	30.6	16.1	33.4	**10.0**	14.4

Asset Quality Index	Non-Performing Loans as a % of Total Loans	Non-Performing Loans as a % of Capital	Net Charge-Offs Avg Loans	Profitability Index	Net Income ($Mil)	Return on Assets	Return on Equity	Net Interest Spread	Overhead Efficiency Ratio	Liquidity Index	Liquidity Ratio	Hot Money Ratio	Stability Index
7.6	0.16	0.7	0.00	**3.7**	0.00	0.45	3.17	7.92	57.1	**4.9**	21.7	0.0	**7.1**
10.0	0.73	1.3	0.87	**3.5**	0.05	0.33	2.51	2.28	84.2	**5.9**	63.5	0.9	**6.1**
9.4	0.38	2.5	0.50	**2.1**	-0.03	-0.09	-0.67	3.42	92.6	**4.3**	24.8	1.6	**7.4**
2.1	1.84	27.0	0.18	**5.8**	0.18	0.87	10.35	3.89	81.2	**4.2**	16.9	0.7	**4.0**
6.0	0.36	2.4	1.22	**4.3**	0.00	0.00	0.00	6.04	84.4	**4.3**	24.7	0.0	**3.7**
8.3	0.25	1.8	0.15	**4.8**	0.03	0.52	5.71	4.29	91.0	**4.4**	21.7	0.0	**4.3**
5.5	1.03	8.7	0.20	**4.8**	0.06	0.23	2.29	4.08	92.1	**3.0**	18.1	13.5	**6.7**
5.5	0.00	0.0	0.00	**1.6**	0.00	0.00	0.00	2.78	101.7	**2.6**	13.0	12.7	**7.3**
8.5	0.00	0.0	0.00	**3.5**	0.00	0.73	3.87	2.49	75.0	**6.3**	75.0	0.0	**6.5**
9.7	0.40	1.3	0.51	**3.1**	0.07	0.61	4.91	3.70	78.3	**6.0**	37.0	0.3	**6.6**
5.8	2.24	11.9	2.46	**2.5**	-0.05	-0.86	-10.22	3.08	83.7	**5.4**	26.5	0.5	**2.3**
10.0	0.14	0.5	0.26	**4.4**	0.11	0.98	10.82	2.87	73.9	**5.7**	29.9	0.3	**4.5**
3.3	4.43	24.9	1.08	**4.2**	0.66	1.08	11.54	3.68	69.7	**4.1**	23.8	4.8	**6.4**
9.7	0.24	1.4	0.75	**5.3**	0.03	0.74	6.22	5.81	85.1	**4.7**	25.6	0.0	**6.3**
10.0	0.58	1.2	1.63	**2.8**	0.00	0.18	1.45	2.80	89.7	**5.4**	21.9	0.0	**5.7**
10.0	0.45	1.1	0.00	**4.0**	0.08	0.60	3.83	2.40	73.0	**5.3**	40.4	4.7	**7.3**
5.0	3.94	13.0	4.81	**0.6**	-0.23	-3.35	-25.21	3.68	82.1	**5.0**	24.8	0.0	**5.1**
9.7	1.79	2.5	0.71	**5.0**	0.08	0.73	2.71	2.91	66.8	**5.2**	30.9	0.0	**7.0**
9.4	0.29	0.6	0.00	**2.7**	0.01	0.55	2.87	3.06	178.6	**6.6**	69.6	7.2	**7.0**
8.7	0.00	0.0	0.03	**1.9**	-0.02	-0.44	-3.55	3.91	106.3	**4.6**	28.8	7.3	**6.9**
4.5	0.38	4.0	-0.08	**1.2**	-0.01	-0.78	-10.84	5.72	113.4	**4.4**	28.1	3.4	**1.0**
4.1	2.55	15.3	-0.36	**2.9**	0.00	0.45	4.88	7.30	93.6	**4.5**	40.6	6.5	**2.3**
9.7	0.05	0.3	0.07	**0.7**	-0.02	-0.63	-8.41	4.12	113.2	**5.9**	37.4	0.9	**2.4**
9.4	1.80	2.9	-0.05	**2.6**	0.06	0.24	1.67	2.36	89.2	**4.5**	29.1	8.9	**6.3**
5.9	2.04	13.2	0.71	**2.9**	0.07	0.07	0.80	3.55	82.3	**2.6**	20.2	20.6	**5.8**
6.2	1.14	6.6	-0.74	**3.2**	0.03	0.42	4.49	3.71	83.4	**5.3**	40.9	0.5	**3.5**
9.5	0.47	2.7	0.18	**8.0**	0.13	1.10	8.90	4.27	72.5	**4.5**	25.9	5.1	**6.8**
7.7	0.04	0.3	0.35	**2.3**	0.00	0.22	2.16	5.69	97.7	**5.5**	38.7	0.0	**4.8**
7.5	3.91	4.8	0.00	**7.7**	0.01	1.21	3.45	10.58	78.8	**7.4**	86.6	0.0	**5.0**
8.9	8.77	4.3	0.00	**3.7**	0.00	0.00	0.00	6.04	125.0	**8.5**	150.2	0.0	**6.9**
4.3	11.95	11.8	-3.08	**0.9**	-0.02	-3.86	-8.48	5.94	183.3	**7.4**	99.8	0.0	**6.4**
8.4	0.59	3.4	0.50	**3.9**	0.08	0.44	4.28	2.89	82.2	**4.5**	22.2	4.4	**5.7**
8.6	0.39	0.7	0.00	**9.0**	0.02	1.21	3.88	2.65	52.9	**4.3**	15.8	0.0	**5.7**
9.8	0.08	0.5	0.04	**2.7**	0.02	0.27	4.01	2.87	90.2	**4.8**	19.6	0.0	**1.7**
6.7	0.53	4.6	0.45	**3.7**	0.01	0.42	6.31	4.18	91.0	**3.4**	24.5	16.4	**1.4**
6.2	1.49	11.2	0.75	**1.6**	0.13	0.29	3.62	2.94	82.0	**4.6**	23.9	1.0	**3.1**
7.3	7.69	6.1	0.00	**0.1**	-0.01	-0.64	-2.70	2.60	124.2	**6.8**	68.6	0.0	**6.0**
7.4	0.38	3.1	0.65	**3.7**	0.50	0.60	5.11	4.08	80.1	**3.5**	10.0	3.3	**6.8**
7.6	5.13	5.5	0.00	**2.1**	0.00	-0.26	-0.90	3.70	110.0	**7.1**	54.8	0.0	**7.2**
6.8	1.12	3.7	0.21	**1.9**	0.01	0.10	0.91	3.13	89.2	**5.5**	35.5	0.3	**5.3**
1.7	15.18	37.7	0.00	**1.1**	0.00	-0.37	-4.08	7.72	140.0	**7.9**	79.5	0.0	**1.0**
5.1	0.92	8.9	1.12	**4.6**	2.29	0.36	3.88	4.26	73.1	**2.2**	9.8	14.5	**6.7**
8.9	0.68	3.1	1.57	**2.3**	0.04	0.10	1.19	2.57	91.4	**5.4**	31.8	6.6	**5.4**
8.9	0.06	1.7	0.34	**4.1**	0.05	0.68	8.77	3.21	78.2	**5.7**	42.7	0.0	**3.8**
9.2	0.12	0.8	0.14	**4.3**	0.22	0.76	7.53	3.66	78.8	**4.4**	29.4	1.7	**6.6**
8.4	0.33	1.7	0.46	**3.9**	0.35	0.49	4.11	2.70	82.2	**4.2**	22.0	6.2	**7.3**
9.6	0.10	0.9	0.20	**4.0**	0.11	0.51	5.44	3.43	84.1	**4.5**	20.8	1.2	**4.1**
5.5	0.56	5.4	0.92	**5.3**	5.28	0.75	8.16	1.53	44.1	**0.9**	9.6	39.3	**7.3**
6.6	1.77	10.5	0.36	**2.4**	0.11	0.22	2.96	3.05	88.9	**4.7**	15.4	2.4	**3.6**
7.5	0.58	2.1	0.00	**0.8**	0.00	0.00	0.00	3.14	125.0	**5.1**	20.0	0.0	**6.1**
4.8	1.01	9.0	3.06	**1.2**	-1.61	-1.05	-14.48	4.06	76.4	**2.3**	11.8	24.0	**5.1**
9.5	0.89	3.0	-0.52	**1.2**	0.01	0.30	2.00	3.29	87.5	**3.8**	18.1	6.6	**5.7**
4.7	0.55	10.1	1.24	**6.0**	0.59	7.48	103.99	4.26	31.8	**4.6**	27.7	1.8	**2.7**
7.8	0.83	2.7	0.38	**1.5**	0.01	0.14	1.26	3.15	92.3	**4.5**	13.5	2.5	**5.2**
7.6	1.00	3.6	-0.12	**1.7**	0.00	-0.13	-1.32	3.30	102.2	**6.2**	46.9	0.0	**4.6**
8.0	0.16	1.7	0.00	**3.6**	0.02	0.36	6.72	3.86	92.0	**5.2**	33.8	1.1	**3.0**
9.1	0.18	1.4	0.11	**5.0**	0.21	1.14	13.01	3.92	81.2	**4.4**	25.4	3.3	**5.0**
5.1	2.20	11.0	0.37	**2.4**	-0.01	-0.15	-1.31	3.44	98.6	**5.5**	43.1	0.0	**6.3**
9.3	0.37	1.8	0.37	**3.1**	0.14	0.24	1.60	3.55	89.4	**4.5**	24.6	4.3	**7.9**
9.1	0.62	2.5	0.75	**9.5**	9.26	1.63	11.37	3.07	50.7	**4.0**	11.2	4.9	**10.0**

Name	City	State	Rating	2016 Rating	2015 Rating	Total Assets ($Mil)	One Year Asset Growth	Asset Mix (As a % of Total Assets) Commercial Loans	Consumer Loans	Mortgage Loans	Securities	Capitalization Index	Net Worth Ratio
Genuine Parts Credit Union	Norcross	GA	C	C	C	9.5	2.67	0.0	29.9	0.0	0.0	10.0	26.9
Georgetown Kraft Credit Union	Georgetown	SC	A-	A-	A-	105.0	7.95	1.3	31.7	16.2	2.9	10.0	13.2
Georgetown University Alumni & Student FCU	Washington	DC	D	D	D	16.3	-0.17	0.0	8.2	0.0	67.6	5.2	7.4
Georgia Guard Credit Union	Macon	GA	D+	D+	D	4.4	2.09	0.0	47.9	2.2	0.0	8.8	10.2
Georgia Heritage Federal Credit Union	Savannah	GA	B-	B-	B	97.2	10.04	0.0	56.7	8.4	0.0	10.0	11.6
Georgia Power Macon Federal Credit Union	Macon	GA	D+	D+	D	3.4	-2.09	0.0	61.4	0.0	0.0	8.6	10.0
Georgia Power Northwest FCU	Rome	GA	D+	D+	D+	58.0	10.43	0.0	33.3	1.1	0.9	6.0	8.0
Georgia Power Valdosta FCU	Valdosta	GA	C-	C-	C	24.7	-1.48	0.0	40.1	7.6	2.6	9.8	10.9
▼ Georgia United Credit Union	Duluth	GA	B+	A-	A-	1279.6	14.00	3.9	32.4	19.0	16.0	10.0	11.3
Georgia's Own Credit Union	Atlanta	GA	B-	B-	B-	2229.3	5.36	5.0	34.5	23.5	11.1	9.0	10.4
GeoVista Federal Credit Union	Hinesville	GA	B	B	B	140.2	4.48	0.0	42.9	8.2	4.6	6.7	8.8
Gerber Federal Credit Union	Fremont	MI	B-	B-	B	140.9	4.30	0.1	18.4	25.8	20.5	9.6	10.8
Germania Credit Union	Brenham	TX	C-	C-	C-	11.1	11.73	0.0	42.6	0.0	0.0	10.0	12.4
Gesa Credit Union	Richland	WA	B+	B+	B+	1826.8	9.25	10.9	55.1	20.6	2.3	7.2	9.1
▼ GESB Sheet Metal Workers FCU	Portage	IN	D-	D	E+	9.1	6.33	0.0	41.1	9.5	0.0	6.6	8.6
GFA Federal Credit Union	Gardner	MA	C+	C+	C+	489.3	5.21	3.9	14.0	28.3	36.8	8.4	10.3
GGW Federal Credit Union	New Orleans	LA	C	C	C	<1	1.57	0.0	61.3	0.0	0.0	10.0	32.1
▼ GHA Federal Credit Union	Greenwich	CT	D+	C-	C	25.6	6.59	0.0	17.2	0.0	8.9	7.7	9.5
▼ GHS Federal Credit Union	Binghamton	NY	B-	B	B+	146.7	3.85	0.5	33.4	21.1	6.1	8.2	9.8
Gibbons & Reed Employees FCU	Salt Lake City	UT	C-	C-	C-	5.0	2.69	0.0	38.7	0.0	0.0	10.0	17.1
Gibbs Aluminum Federal Credit Union	Henderson	KY	C+	C+	C	5.6	1.27	0.0	53.4	0.0	0.0	10.0	31.9
▼ Gideon Federal Credit Union	Waukegan	IL	D-	D	D+	<1	2.88	0.0	17.1	0.0	0.0	6.4	8.4
▲ Gilt Edge Employees Federal Credit Union	Norman	OK	C+	C	D+	2.0	-4.67	0.0	35.2	0.0	0.0	10.0	13.9
Girard Credit Union, Inc.	Girard	OH	C-	C-	D+	1.9	-4.40	0.0	46.4	0.0	0.0	10.0	18.2
Glacial Lakes Educational Employees FCU	Watertown	SD	D	D	D	1.1	3.47	0.0	38.8	0.0	0.0	6.3	8.3
Glacier Hills Credit Union	West Bend	WI	B+	B+	B	117.2	5.48	0.9	33.4	23.5	1.1	7.8	9.5
Glamorgan Employees Federal Credit Union	Lynchburg	VA	C+	C+	C	1.1	6.90	0.0	62.6	0.0	0.0	10.0	36.5
Glamour Community Federal Credit Union	Quebradillas	PR	D+	D+	D	3.1	2.59	0.0	58.9	0.0	0.0	7.9	9.6
Glass Cap Federal Credit Union	Connellsville	PA	B-	B-	B-	29.8	6.51	0.0	38.5	22.6	0.0	9.5	10.7
Glass City Federal Credit Union	Maumee	OH	C+	C+	C	211.4	1.31	13.5	31.7	18.4	18.2	8.0	9.9
Glatco Credit Union	Spring Grove	PA	C+	C+	C	42.1	4.57	0.0	10.7	3.7	0.0	10.0	13.0
Glendale Area Schools Credit Union	Glendale	CA	A-	A-	B	346.5	-2.43	0.6	15.3	5.0	47.0	10.0	13.8
Glendale Federal Credit Union	Glendale	CA	C+	C+	C+	87.3	38.23	0.0	20.5	15.0	11.2	10.0	12.8
Glendive BN Federal Credit Union	Glendive	MT	B+	B+	B+	28.4	-2.79	0.0	12.1	24.7	0.0	10.0	14.4
Glenview Credit Union	Glenview	IL	D	D	D-	14.6	0.78	0.0	13.7	0.8	0.0	5.2	7.2
▼ Global 1 Federal Credit Union	Pennsauken	NJ	D	D+	C-	7.5	-4.04	0.0	30.6	17.2	0.0	5.8	7.8
▼ Global Credit Union	Spokane	WA	C	C+	C-	415.0	4.84	10.3	40.3	25.0	6.1	6.4	8.4
▼ Gloucester Fire Department Credit Union	Gloucester	MA	C+	B-	B-	<1	-1.74	0.0	53.6	0.0	0.0	10.0	39.9
Gloucester Municipal Credit Union	Gloucester	MA	C	C	C-	2.0	0.10	0.0	28.7	0.0	0.0	10.0	19.7
Glover Federal Credit Union	Honolulu	HI	C	C	C	4.3	-6.46	0.0	4.5	0.0	1.8	10.0	14.9
Glynn County Federal Employees CU	Brunswick	GA	C	C	C+	19.9	4.25	0.0	29.0	1.2	0.0	10.0	18.6
GNC Community Federal Credit Union	New Castle	PA	B+	B+	B+	77.5	2.12	0.0	31.3	0.8	40.2	10.0	15.0
▲ Go Federal Credit Union	Dallas	TX	C-	D+	C-	126.2	0.63	17.1	36.3	22.0	1.4	5.2	7.2
Goetz Credit Union	Saint Joseph	MO	A-	A-	B+	57.7	7.29	0.0	37.1	9.4	0.0	10.0	12.7
▼ Gogebic County Federal Credit Union	Bessemer	MI	C-	C	C	21.9	23.02	0.0	32.1	0.0	0.0	6.3	8.3
Gold Coast Federal Credit Union	West Palm Beach	FL	C+	C+	B-	171.0	7.18	0.0	37.9	3.6	0.8	8.0	9.7
GOLD Credit Union	Allentown	PA	C+	C+	B-	128.3	3.72	0.4	24.0	26.2	18.7	10.0	14.2
Golden 1 Credit Union	Sacramento	CA	A	A	A	11069.5	9.63	1.0	41.7	23.0	17.5	10.0	11.3
Golden Circle Credit Union, Inc.	Massillon	OH	D+	D+	D+	90.7	1.55	7.9	40.7	9.2	9.0	10.0	15.8
Golden Eagle Federal Credit Union	Tulsa	OK	D	D	D	16.9	-1.76	0.0	44.4	0.0	0.0	10.0	13.1
▼ Golden Plains Credit Union	Garden City	KS	B-	B	B	592.6	7.24	1.9	77.9	4.0	0.0	8.3	9.9
Golden Rule Community Credit Union	Ripon	WI	D+	D+	D+	28.1	3.66	0.0	25.1	16.6	0.0	5.9	7.9
Golden Triangle Federal Credit Union	Groves	TX	B	B	B	29.2	2.62	0.0	27.0	6.4	0.0	10.0	15.2
Golden Valley Federal Credit Union	Manteca	CA	C	C	C	27.5	5.08	0.0	18.4	3.7	0.0	8.4	9.9
Goldenwest Federal Credit Union	Ogden	UT	A	A	A	1372.6	16.44	14.0	31.6	25.8	9.3	10.0	13.3
Goldmark Federal Credit Union	Attleboro	MA	C-	C-	C-	31.2	4.07	0.0	4.1	18.9	0.0	10.0	11.8
▼ Golmar Federal Credit Union	Cataño	PR	C	C+	C+	<1	-80.43	0.0	13.7	0.0	0.0	10.0	93.2
Good Counsel Federal Credit Union	Brooklyn	NY	D-	D-	D	<1	0.93	0.0	0.9	0.0	0.0	9.5	10.7
Good Neighbors Federal Credit Union	Depew	NY	B-	B-	B-	48.3	7.81	0.0	21.9	9.4	39.8	7.9	9.6
Good Samaritan Federal Credit Union	Sioux Falls	SD	B-	B-	B-	25.7	1.40	0.0	33.6	0.0	0.0	10.0	21.0

Asset Quality Index	Non-Performing Loans as a % of Total Loans	Non-Performing Loans as a % of Capital	Net Charge-Offs Avg Loans	Profitability Index	Net Income ($Mil)	Return on Assets	Return on Equity	Net Interest Spread	Overhead Efficiency Ratio	Liquidity Index	Liquidity Ratio	Hot Money Ratio	Stability Index
10.0	0.21	0.2	-0.85	**3.2**	0.02	0.73	2.68	4.81	78.6	**5.2**	42.3	0.0	**6.3**
7.6	0.91	4.5	0.03	**5.2**	0.13	0.52	4.34	4.58	90.0	**4.4**	24.0	8.1	**7.0**
10.0	0.12	0.2	0.00	**0.6**	-0.02	-0.59	-8.11	2.16	125.0	**7.0**	51.7	0.0	**1.3**
5.7	0.93	6.1	-0.33	**3.8**	0.01	0.65	6.31	4.86	89.0	**5.4**	24.7	0.0	**3.0**
6.2	0.78	5.8	0.43	**4.0**	0.15	0.62	5.25	4.16	79.8	**3.6**	27.2	12.0	**5.6**
2.8	3.23	19.0	0.00	**4.6**	0.00	0.36	3.51	5.85	92.3	**5.5**	40.8	3.3	**2.3**
9.9	0.07	0.4	0.18	**1.3**	-0.03	-0.19	-2.32	2.91	101.7	**6.1**	54.6	1.2	**3.1**
5.4	1.99	11.0	1.00	**3.1**	0.02	0.35	3.14	4.07	81.9	**3.5**	37.8	28.7	**5.1**
9.4	0.24	1.8	0.17	**5.0**	1.78	0.57	5.07	3.11	84.0	**4.4**	18.9	3.1	**8.0**
8.6	0.38	3.0	0.80	**3.5**	2.94	0.54	5.23	3.46	74.0	**3.8**	11.5	2.8	**7.7**
6.1	1.83	10.7	1.76	**5.5**	0.21	0.62	6.91	5.09	79.2	**5.5**	32.7	2.7	**5.4**
8.2	0.26	4.4	0.46	**2.4**	-0.02	-0.05	-0.45	3.06	94.2	**4.4**	20.8	3.0	**6.7**
9.1	0.08	0.4	0.00	**1.4**	0.00	0.00	0.00	2.72	102.7	**4.4**	35.2	4.9	**6.4**
6.4	0.37	4.6	0.52	**5.2**	2.80	0.62	6.97	3.49	74.8	**2.9**	11.1	7.4	**6.2**
4.7	2.43	16.4	0.99	**3.4**	0.00	-0.18	-2.03	3.62	88.7	**3.9**	7.9	0.0	**1.7**
8.7	0.45	2.8	0.17	**3.0**	0.25	0.21	2.07	2.32	89.8	**3.4**	22.8	11.6	**6.5**
2.0	12.42	23.0	0.00	**8.7**	0.00	1.57	4.86	10.39	66.7	**6.4**	57.0	0.0	**7.9**
6.3	2.81	7.0	3.75	**1.6**	-0.10	-1.55	-15.96	2.96	75.7	**4.8**	21.6	1.3	**3.7**
6.6	1.15	8.9	0.60	**1.6**	-0.04	-0.12	-1.31	3.97	91.3	**4.5**	25.0	2.7	**5.7**
6.4	4.14	11.0	-0.34	**3.2**	0.00	0.31	1.88	3.49	86.4	**5.6**	62.4	0.0	**6.7**
8.6	1.02	1.7	0.13	**6.2**	0.01	0.74	2.25	3.86	74.1	**6.2**	60.6	0.0	**5.0**
10.0	0.00	0.0	0.00	**1.2**	0.00	0.00	0.00	8.00	100.0	**8.4**	90.1	0.0	**2.8**
6.9	3.39	8.4	1.47	**8.4**	0.01	2.40	17.45	3.88	72.2	**6.1**	63.0	0.0	**5.0**
5.0	3.73	10.7	3.51	**2.6**	0.00	0.41	2.32	2.46	72.7	**4.5**	34.9	0.0	**6.8**
9.7	0.00	0.0	0.00	**1.5**	0.00	0.00	0.00	3.07	116.7	**5.1**	13.7	0.0	**4.2**
8.0	0.60	4.0	0.11	**5.7**	0.23	0.80	8.50	3.35	82.1	**4.4**	18.5	0.8	**6.8**
7.3	0.98	1.6	0.00	**8.4**	0.01	2.30	6.11	10.00	70.0	**6.2**	53.1	0.0	**5.0**
8.5	0.00	0.0	0.00	**3.0**	0.00	0.39	4.11	5.37	91.9	**5.6**	38.4	0.0	**3.0**
8.1	0.31	2.1	0.50	**4.7**	0.04	0.51	5.41	3.96	82.5	**4.7**	24.3	0.0	**4.9**
7.4	0.76	4.9	0.50	**3.8**	0.19	0.37	3.62	3.64	83.5	**4.0**	10.5	2.8	**6.2**
10.0	0.36	0.6	0.21	**3.1**	0.04	0.35	2.65	2.34	83.7	**6.9**	46.7	0.8	**6.8**
10.0	0.40	0.7	0.31	**4.9**	0.56	0.66	4.76	2.42	61.3	**5.9**	51.3	16.4	**7.9**
9.8	0.86	2.5	0.43	**2.5**	0.02	0.11	0.86	3.24	96.7	**4.5**	24.9	7.4	**6.0**
10.0	0.00	0.0	-0.07	**5.1**	0.04	0.60	4.13	3.18	78.5	**5.1**	31.5	5.5	**7.4**
10.0	0.17	0.7	0.10	**3.1**	0.01	0.33	4.59	2.85	90.7	**4.9**	22.9	3.4	**2.2**
5.2	3.14	16.6	-0.24	**0.0**	-0.02	-0.87	-10.77	4.43	119.5	**5.0**	23.0	0.0	**2.9**
7.2	0.20	4.4	0.60	**2.5**	0.07	0.07	0.80	3.82	91.1	**3.2**	7.7	3.7	**4.9**
8.7	0.00	0.0	0.00	**5.0**	0.00	0.00	0.00	6.35	87.5	**5.0**	21.6	0.0	**5.0**
10.0	0.00	0.0	0.00	**2.6**	0.00	0.40	2.04	4.74	94.4	**5.6**	24.4	0.0	**6.5**
10.0	0.00	0.0	0.00	**2.3**	0.00	0.00	0.00	1.06	110.0	**6.4**	47.2	0.0	**7.1**
8.4	1.63	3.4	0.00	**2.6**	0.02	0.40	2.06	3.30	89.4	**5.9**	44.3	0.0	**6.2**
7.4	1.79	5.9	0.36	**2.7**	0.03	0.16	1.04	2.82	94.2	**5.1**	21.0	3.4	**6.3**
9.4	0.08	2.1	0.41	**2.4**	0.17	0.55	7.59	3.74	88.0	**3.0**	9.0	5.8	**3.3**
9.3	0.14	0.6	0.76	**5.9**	0.08	0.58	4.74	4.20	70.5	**6.3**	41.1	0.0	**6.7**
6.7	1.37	5.6	0.97	**3.8**	0.02	0.43	4.85	3.78	78.0	**7.0**	51.6	0.0	**3.5**
9.8	0.04	0.6	0.54	**3.2**	0.16	0.38	3.91	2.33	82.4	**6.0**	40.3	1.1	**5.8**
9.9	0.46	1.9	0.06	**2.5**	0.07	0.23	1.62	2.73	89.1	**4.4**	22.8	4.1	**8.1**
9.4	0.34	2.1	0.41	**5.6**	23.88	0.88	7.74	3.04	68.6	**4.2**	18.7	4.9	**9.5**
8.3	0.93	3.5	0.05	**1.4**	0.02	0.09	0.57	3.06	97.1	**4.0**	24.6	2.4	**6.8**
8.2	0.84	3.1	0.10	**0.0**	-0.03	-0.64	-4.85	3.05	113.9	**5.3**	36.3	4.9	**5.2**
4.7	0.62	9.8	0.45	**3.7**	0.40	0.27	2.77	3.47	80.5	**1.9**	6.4	14.5	**7.2**
7.1	0.30	3.3	0.08	**2.9**	0.02	0.30	3.79	4.24	88.4	**5.7**	47.7	1.9	**2.9**
9.7	0.17	0.5	0.07	**3.7**	0.02	0.22	1.58	3.55	95.2	**5.8**	39.3	1.7	**7.3**
9.9	0.29	0.7	0.57	**2.7**	0.01	0.16	1.62	2.60	94.0	**6.0**	37.0	2.7	**4.5**
8.8	0.39	2.5	0.29	**9.2**	4.01	1.22	9.05	3.21	74.8	**3.4**	20.2	8.3	**10.0**
10.0	0.00	0.0	0.03	**0.8**	-0.01	-0.08	-0.65	2.24	102.0	**5.1**	54.1	6.7	**5.6**
10.0	0.00	0.0	0.00	**2.6**	0.00	0.00	0.00	0.00	0.0	**4.0**	NA	0.0	**6.5**
8.2	16.67	2.2	0.00	**0.2**	0.00	0.00	0.00	0.00	0.0	**9.1**	108.8	0.0	**3.7**
7.6	0.69	3.1	0.04	**5.1**	0.12	1.01	10.48	3.21	70.6	**4.6**	20.6	2.6	**4.9**
9.8	0.45	0.8	0.08	**3.6**	0.04	0.56	2.60	2.14	75.7	**5.4**	54.1	0.0	**7.5**

Name	City	State	Rating	2016 Rating	2015 Rating	Total Assets ($Mil)	One Year Asset Growth	Asset Mix (As a % of Total Assets): Commercial Loans	Consumer Loans	Mortgage Loans	Securities	Capitalization Index	Net Worth Ratio
Good Street Baptist Church FCU	Dallas	TX	**D-**	D-	D	<1	-7.36	0.0	28.1	0.0	0.0	**5.5**	7.5
Goodyear Employees Credit Union	Akron	OH	**C-**	C-	C-	4.4	-2.47	0.0	39.7	0.0	8.1	**10.0**	21.7
Goodyear San Angelo Federal Credit Union	San Angelo	TX	**C**	C	C	2.2	35.18	0.0	78.5	0.0	0.0	**9.6**	10.7
Gorman-Rupp & Associates Credit Union	Mansfield	OH	**D+**	D+	D+	8.6	-1.80	0.0	61.9	0.7	0.0	**10.0**	11.3
Gorton's of Gloucester Employees FCU	Gloucester	MA	**C**	C	C-	<1	-11.20	0.0	50.3	0.0	0.0	**10.0**	19.8
Government Employees FCU	Austin	TX	**D+**	D+	D+	135.1	0.53	0.0	15.6	20.7	14.0	**6.2**	8.3
Government Printing Office FCU	Washington	DC	**D**	D	D+	37.4	-5.29	0.0	43.7	0.0	0.0	**10.0**	12.3
Governmental Employees Credit Union	La Crosse	WI	**C+**	C+	C+	67.5	5.47	3.5	28.7	38.9	8.6	**7.8**	9.5
Gowanda Area Federal Credit Union	Gowanda	NY	**C-**	C-	C-	19.1	4.69	0.0	21.5	6.7	0.0	**6.6**	8.6
Goya Foods Employees FCU	Jersey City	NJ	**B-**	B-	C+	11.1	8.60	0.0	0.0	0.0	85.3	**10.0**	14.7
▼ GP Community Federal Credit Union	Plattsburgh	NY	**D-**	D	C-	6.7	0.45	0.0	38.5	12.7	0.0	**7.7**	9.5
GP Louisiana Federal Credit Union	Zachary	LA	**C+**	C+	C+	41.5	8.65	0.0	57.4	0.2	16.8	**8.1**	9.8
GPA Credit Union	Garden City	GA	**C+**	C+	C+	13.5	1.93	0.0	32.0	0.0	2.6	**10.0**	18.5
GPCE Credit Union	Pensacola	FL	**C-**	C-	C-	45.2	5.98	0.0	33.7	4.2	0.4	**6.3**	8.3
▲ GR Consumers Credit Union	Wyoming	MI	**B**	B-	C+	42.9	3.99	0.0	17.1	7.2	9.6	**10.0**	15.3
Grace Congregational Church FCU	New York	NY	**D**	D	D	<1	-15.23	0.0	9.2	0.0	59.7	**10.0**	37.9
Graco Federal Credit Union	Alma	MI	**D+**	D+	D+	18.0	2.65	0.0	34.8	0.0	0.0	**5.6**	7.6
▼ Granco Federal Credit Union	Ephrata	WA	**D**	D+	C	62.2	10.23	0.2	32.1	29.1	5.3	**8.4**	9.9
Grand Central Terminal Employees FCU	New York	NY	**C+**	C+	C+	8.1	-1.28	0.0	22.2	2.9	1.5	**10.0**	14.0
▲ Grand County Credit Union	Moab	UT	**C-**	D+	D+	28.2	15.62	0.0	56.8	5.9	0.0	**6.9**	8.9
Grand Heritage Federal Credit Union	La Porte	IN	**D**	D	D	16.2	-0.07	0.0	21.5	12.1	0.0	**5.2**	7.2
Grand Junction Federal Credit Union	Grand Junction	CO	**A-**	A-	A-	62.4	4.30	3.7	24.1	20.8	18.1	**10.0**	17.5
▲ Grand Prairie Credit Union	Grand Prairie	TX	**C**	C-	C-	16.4	3.63	0.0	29.7	11.3	0.0	**8.6**	10.1
Grand Trunk Battle Creek Employees FCU	Battle Creek	MI	**B**	B	B	34.4	7.09	0.0	35.2	7.4	0.0	**10.0**	14.4
Granite Federal Credit Union	Salt Lake City	UT	**B+**	B+	B	418.5	6.57	9.0	33.1	35.8	16.5	**8.2**	9.9
Granite Furniture Employees FCU	Woods Cross	UT	**C-**	C-	C-	<1	34.90	0.0	88.8	0.0	0.0	**10.0**	37.7
Granite Hills Credit Union	Barre	VT	**C**	C	C+	41.3	3.93	0.0	10.8	10.8	31.7	**10.0**	12.3
Granite State Credit Union	Manchester	NH	**C+**	C+	C+	387.9	3.49	8.4	30.4	34.7	5.3	**5.7**	7.7
▼ Graphic Arts Credit Union	Shreveport	LA	**C**	C+	C+	1.6	0.25	0.0	61.7	0.0	0.0	**10.0**	40.9
Gratiot Community Credit Union	Alma	MI	**C+**	C+	C+	34.2	9.76	0.0	32.1	14.4	17.7	**6.4**	8.5
Great Basin Federal Credit Union	Reno	NV	**B+**	B+	A-	163.7	14.39	5.0	40.6	17.6	2.0	**7.5**	9.3
▼ Great Erie Federal Credit Union	Orchard Park	NY	**B-**	B	B-	82.2	5.70	4.1	23.6	14.4	4.9	**8.1**	9.8
Great Falls Regional FCU	Lewiston	ME	**C**	C	C	28.5	8.35	0.7	12.2	14.6	0.0	**10.0**	17.0
Great Horizons Federal Credit Union	Munster	IN	**D+**	D+	C-	3.3	-0.69	0.0	51.8	0.0	0.0	**10.0**	18.6
Great Lakes Credit Union	North Chicago	IL	**C-**	C-	C-	789.9	6.84	6.1	32.2	27.2	10.3	**7.0**	9.1
Great Lakes Credit Union, Inc.	Sylvania	OH	**D+**	D+	C-	28.6	6.37	2.7	43.9	1.4	33.0	**6.2**	8.7
Great Lakes Federal Credit Union	Bay City	MI	**C+**	C+	C	42.2	5.23	0.4	11.2	32.4	40.1	**9.4**	10.8
Great Lakes First Federal Credit Union	Escanaba	MI	**C+**	C+	C-	71.0	5.20	0.0	23.9	19.9	30.7	**8.2**	10.1
Great Lakes Members Credit Union	Dearborn	MI	**C-**	C-	C	9.8	-2.94	10.3	21.6	21.3	31.7	**10.0**	27.2
Great Meadow Federal Credit Union	Granville	NY	**B-**	B-	C+	28.3	10.71	0.0	56.6	6.9	15.2	**10.0**	14.5
▲ Great Neck School Employees FCU	Great Neck	NY	**C+**	C	C	3.7	-0.35	0.0	42.5	0.0	0.0	**10.0**	26.5
Great Northwest Federal Credit Union	Aberdeen	WA	**A**	A	A-	136.7	8.73	9.1	26.1	19.3	3.3	**10.0**	13.1
Great Plains Federal Credit Union	Joplin	MO	**C**	C	C+	293.3	2.15	0.1	15.7	12.5	43.0	**10.0**	16.7
Great River Federal Credit Union	Saint Cloud	MN	**C+**	C+	C+	173.6	6.03	2.0	22.7	25.1	14.4	**9.2**	10.4
Greater Abbeville Federal Credit Union	Abbeville	SC	**B**	B	B	19.2	14.21	0.0	62.9	0.0	0.0	**10.0**	16.7
Greater Alliance Federal Credit Union	Paramus	NJ	**C**	C	D+	194.4	9.77	8.6	21.4	31.1	0.5	**6.4**	8.4
▼ Greater Centennial Federal Credit Union	Mount Vernon	NY	**D**	D+	C-	<1	-10.14	0.0	9.7	0.0	0.0	**4.6**	6.6
Greater Central Texas FCU	Killeen	TX	**D**	D	D	24.9	0.74	11.0	10.0	13.7	27.3	**5.1**	7.1
Greater Chautauqua Federal Credit Union	Falconer	NY	**C**	C	C+	64.0	4.03	0.8	32.6	20.1	5.9	**6.8**	8.8
Greater Christ Baptist Church CU	Detroit	MI	**D**	D	D	<1	-7.62	0.0	26.0	0.0	0.8	**10.0**	23.5
Greater Cincinnati Credit Union	Cincinnati	OH	**D+**	D+	D+	96.9	2.58	0.0	14.6	26.8	0.0	**4.3**	7.4
▲ Greater Eastern Credit Union	Johnson City	TN	**B-**	C+	C+	52.9	3.42	2.3	23.3	26.6	0.0	**10.0**	14.6
▼ Greater Galilee Baptist Credit Union	Milwaukee	WI	**E+**	D-	D	<1	-21.55	0.0	51.4	0.0	0.0	**2.9**	5.0
Greater Hartford Police FCU	Hartford	CT	**D-**	D-	D	23.5	5.88	0.0	42.5	1.3	20.0	**5.6**	7.6
▼ Greater Iowa Credit Union	Ames	IA	**C+**	B-	B-	411.5	10.61	6.4	43.5	24.5	8.5	**6.6**	8.6
Greater KC Public Safety Credit Union	Kansas City	MO	**C**	C	D+	128.9	8.39	1.0	35.0	23.6	15.1	**8.7**	10.4
Greater Kentucky Credit Union, Inc.	Lexington	KY	**C**	C	B-	74.4	4.76	0.0	60.3	11.5	0.0	**7.5**	9.4
Greater Kinston Credit Union	Kinston	NC	**C**	C	D+	11.7	2.28	0.7	19.9	49.2	0.0	**8.4**	9.9
Greater Latrobe Schools FCU	New Alexandria	PA	**C**	C	C	2.4	0.81	0.0	37.1	0.0	0.0	**10.0**	12.2
▼ Greater Metro Federal Credit Union	Long Island City	NY	**C-**	C	C+	88.2	0.71	6.2	6.5	14.0	28.4	**10.0**	12.7

Asset Quality Index	Non-Performing Loans as a % of Total Loans	Non-Performing Loans as a % of Capital	Net Charge-Offs Avg Loans	Profitability Index	Net Income ($Mil)	Return on Assets	Return on Equity	Net Interest Spread	Overhead Efficiency Ratio	Liquidity Index	Liquidity Ratio	Hot Money Ratio	Stability Index
0.3	19.32	97.1	7.50	**0.0**	-0.02	-7.14	-86.96	7.69	233.3	**7.3**	67.5	0.0	**4.1**
9.9	0.00	0.0	0.23	**1.7**	0.00	0.09	0.44	2.76	96.9	**6.0**	64.1	0.0	**6.6**
8.0	0.00	0.0	0.00	**5.0**	0.00	0.57	5.22	2.92	75.0	**4.2**	18.1	0.0	**4.3**
5.8	0.90	4.6	0.21	**4.5**	0.01	0.66	5.80	7.56	86.6	**2.9**	30.1	28.1	**3.7**
8.6	0.64	1.6	0.00	**1.7**	0.00	-0.43	-2.14	4.91	100.0	**5.1**	17.8	0.0	**6.3**
10.0	0.07	0.3	0.01	**1.3**	0.00	0.00	-0.04	2.19	100.1	**4.9**	23.9	1.1	**4.8**
5.9	2.98	11.0	0.57	**2.3**	0.09	0.92	7.47	4.05	95.4	**4.1**	17.7	5.4	**4.7**
5.7	1.09	9.8	0.30	**3.6**	0.04	0.26	2.68	3.26	86.2	**3.3**	13.0	7.6	**5.3**
10.0	0.09	0.3	0.00	**3.2**	0.02	0.43	4.90	2.17	82.6	**6.8**	67.0	0.0	**4.0**
10.0	0.24	0.2	0.00	**3.8**	0.02	0.66	4.45	1.69	59.1	**5.6**	30.2	0.0	**6.3**
9.4	0.00	0.0	0.00	**0.2**	-0.02	-1.49	-14.95	5.36	128.6	**6.1**	41.9	0.0	**4.5**
5.2	0.85	5.3	1.07	**5.5**	0.08	0.73	7.48	4.14	67.1	**2.4**	13.6	26.3	**5.0**
9.9	0.77	1.4	0.41	**2.3**	0.00	0.00	0.00	3.25	100.0	**5.9**	51.1	5.1	**7.4**
9.5	0.11	0.6	0.20	**2.3**	0.00	0.02	0.24	3.59	99.4	**6.3**	48.7	3.0	**4.0**
10.0	0.57	1.0	0.03	**4.5**	0.10	0.97	6.22	3.23	76.3	**5.5**	36.7	0.0	**7.2**
9.3	15.79	3.8	0.00	**0.5**	0.00	0.00	0.00	0.00	0.0	**8.4**	125.6	0.0	**4.8**
9.0	0.23	1.2	0.22	**3.6**	0.01	0.32	4.11	3.61	89.7	**5.5**	28.8	0.0	**3.2**
6.3	0.91	6.1	0.17	**0.7**	-0.08	-0.53	-5.74	4.35	115.4	**4.1**	23.9	7.6	**3.7**
8.5	2.30	4.3	1.25	**7.6**	0.01	0.54	3.91	4.91	88.5	**5.5**	20.4	0.0	**5.0**
1.9	1.92	21.5	0.33	**6.6**	0.12	1.74	19.46	5.56	73.7	**3.7**	12.9	5.6	**4.1**
10.0	0.20	0.9	0.57	**1.2**	0.00	0.03	0.34	3.32	97.6	**5.3**	12.6	0.0	**2.5**
9.4	0.33	1.1	0.34	**8.0**	0.17	1.10	6.26	3.46	63.4	**4.4**	27.4	5.5	**7.9**
8.8	0.30	2.1	-0.05	**3.3**	0.02	0.48	4.86	3.52	89.3	**5.0**	22.4	0.0	**4.7**
9.6	0.24	0.7	0.29	**2.7**	0.01	0.14	0.97	3.27	92.7	**4.6**	28.3	1.4	**7.2**
8.1	0.38	2.7	0.32	**5.6**	0.93	0.90	9.19	3.31	71.5	**3.2**	6.6	5.6	**6.8**
7.4	0.00	0.0	0.00	**5.4**	0.00	1.46	3.70	4.18	62.5	**2.6**	2.6	0.0	**4.3**
10.0	0.12	0.3	0.00	**1.8**	0.01	0.11	0.89	2.65	96.4	**6.2**	35.6	1.0	**6.2**
7.3	0.57	5.6	0.11	**2.9**	0.20	0.21	2.75	3.96	94.9	**3.7**	9.1	2.7	**4.9**
8.5	0.39	0.6	0.00	**4.6**	0.00	0.00	0.00	6.13	100.0	**4.2**	11.8	0.0	**4.3**
8.6	0.39	2.4	0.24	**4.0**	0.03	0.30	3.49	3.86	84.1	**5.1**	23.8	1.4	**4.5**
8.7	0.41	3.2	0.35	**4.9**	0.24	0.59	6.32	4.00	85.5	**4.4**	20.7	1.1	**5.6**
7.9	0.45	3.1	0.20	**3.5**	0.06	0.27	2.75	3.14	86.0	**4.1**	15.0	0.8	**4.6**
9.9	0.86	1.5	0.09	**2.6**	0.02	0.23	1.33	2.69	93.8	**6.3**	49.1	0.5	**7.0**
4.7	1.72	9.8	0.33	**2.4**	0.00	0.00	0.00	4.51	94.3	**4.7**	34.6	0.0	**6.8**
6.3	1.20	9.7	0.81	**2.5**	0.20	0.10	1.10	3.53	85.4	**3.5**	11.2	6.3	**6.1**
6.1	1.06	8.0	0.82	**0.0**	-0.04	-0.60	-7.18	3.52	107.3	**4.1**	10.4	3.2	**3.2**
3.7	4.20	20.4	0.56	**2.9**	0.03	0.33	3.04	3.21	103.4	**4.5**	14.1	3.0	**5.6**
7.4	0.81	3.8	0.04	**3.6**	0.10	0.56	5.69	3.78	85.4	**4.9**	20.5	4.8	**4.8**
9.7	0.00	0.0	0.00	**0.0**	-0.04	-1.57	-5.68	3.25	152.1	**5.6**	36.9	0.0	**6.2**
8.3	0.22	1.0	0.31	**3.7**	0.03	0.37	2.23	5.36	90.6	**3.7**	15.4	4.5	**6.7**
9.8	0.76	1.2	0.00	**7.0**	0.01	1.45	5.31	6.48	67.5	**7.2**	77.1	0.0	**5.7**
8.7	0.74	3.5	0.23	**5.6**	0.17	0.51	3.85	3.99	87.5	**5.3**	34.6	1.5	**8.4**
10.0	0.51	1.1	0.46	**1.9**	0.15	0.20	1.21	2.29	81.9	**4.7**	31.2	11.4	**7.4**
9.8	0.15	0.9	0.10	**3.2**	0.16	0.37	3.50	3.22	89.5	**4.2**	22.6	1.4	**6.8**
5.2	1.55	6.7	1.30	**10.0**	0.10	2.17	12.92	9.34	69.6	**5.0**	33.6	4.9	**8.3**
3.3	2.60	26.2	0.49	**3.3**	-0.02	-0.04	-0.48	4.22	90.9	**3.9**	21.4	10.2	**4.9**
1.7	36.00	37.5	0.00	**3.5**	0.00	1.57	23.53	15.38	66.7	**8.7**	98.3	0.0	**1.0**
8.9	0.16	0.6	0.59	**1.8**	0.00	0.06	0.90	2.97	95.2	**5.5**	24.6	0.5	**1.7**
5.2	1.80	12.7	0.32	**2.9**	0.05	0.30	3.35	3.92	89.6	**4.7**	27.6	3.2	**3.9**
6.3	8.74	10.7	0.00	**0.0**	-0.01	-8.19	-33.55	2.80	566.7	**6.2**	71.2	0.0	**5.3**
6.4	0.61	4.8	-0.01	**2.0**	0.03	0.12	1.58	4.24	96.6	**4.6**	20.9	2.9	**3.0**
9.9	0.21	1.1	0.49	**3.6**	0.05	0.36	2.44	3.88	86.9	**4.5**	22.4	6.7	**7.0**
0.0	14.50	65.5	0.00	**1.4**	-0.01	-22.61	-273.68	11.94	100.0	**6.4**	48.3	0.0	**6.6**
5.8	1.59	9.8	1.29	**2.6**	0.03	0.51	6.53	4.28	86.7	**4.9**	29.5	5.6	**1.7**
7.8	0.43	4.1	0.81	**3.0**	0.02	0.02	0.27	3.83	80.8	**3.1**	6.8	6.6	**5.4**
9.1	0.56	3.7	0.08	**2.4**	0.02	0.06	0.58	3.73	94.9	**3.7**	14.0	9.6	**6.1**
3.5	1.44	16.0	1.67	**2.7**	-0.06	-0.31	-3.27	4.28	73.9	**3.3**	23.5	13.0	**4.0**
8.9	0.38	2.8	0.65	**5.9**	0.05	1.61	16.24	6.13	80.0	**3.2**	30.0	34.1	**4.6**
7.3	1.58	5.6	0.00	**3.6**	0.00	0.35	2.79	4.66	85.0	**5.7**	29.6	0.0	**6.7**
2.4	10.57	32.4	-0.09	**1.4**	0.05	0.24	2.17	2.43	88.1	**4.6**	25.2	10.6	**5.2**

Name	City	State	Rating	2016 Rating	2015 Rating	Total Assets ($Mil)	One Year Asset Growth	Asset Mix (As a % of Total Assets) Comm-ercial Loans	Cons-umer Loans	Mort-gage Loans	Secur-ities	Capital-ization Index	Net Worth Ratio
Greater Nevada Credit Union	Carson City	NV	**A-**	A-	A-	716.0	18.48	7.9	24.1	23.9	11.1	**7.6**	9.4
Greater New Mt. Moriah Baptist Church CU	Detroit	MI	**D+**	D+	C-	<1	12.75	0.0	53.0	0.0	0.0	**10.0**	51.3
Greater New Orleans Federal Credit Union	Metairie	LA	**B-**	B-	C+	113.2	2.64	14.5	48.6	15.3	3.9	**10.0**	13.8
Greater Niagara Federal Credit Union	Niagara Falls	NY	**B-**	B-	B-	50.9	12.02	0.0	21.6	16.8	23.0	**9.9**	10.9
Greater Niles Community FCU	Niles	MI	**C**	C	C-	56.8	3.15	0.0	11.0	42.6	0.0	**6.4**	8.4
Greater Pittsburgh Federal Credit Union	Pittsburgh	PA	**C+**	C+	C-	43.4	2.40	0.0	22.5	0.0	0.0	**7.7**	9.5
Greater Pittsburgh Police FCU	Pittsburgh	PA	**B+**	B+	B+	68.1	4.38	0.0	43.8	0.4	5.8	**10.0**	15.5
Greater Salem Employees FCU	Salem	MA	**D-**	D-	D	13.3	6.54	0.0	22.2	11.5	1.5	**5.7**	7.7
Greater Springfield Credit Union	Springfield	MA	**A**	A	A	164.8	8.47	0.0	8.3	31.4	17.1	**10.0**	13.0
Greater Texas Federal Credit Union	Austin	TX	**B-**	B-	C+	597.8	5.16	4.4	32.8	23.9	19.5	**5.7**	8.0
Greater Valley Credit Union	Fresno	CA	**C**	C	C	31.6	5.09	5.0	19.5	9.6	0.0	**10.0**	13.3
Greater Waterbury Healthcare FCU	Waterbury	CT	**C+**	C+	C+	12.1	1.14	0.0	19.1	0.0	0.0	**10.0**	18.1
Greater Watertown Federal Credit Union	Watertown	CT	**D-**	D-	E+	18.3	4.38	0.0	21.9	0.1	0.0	**5.2**	7.2
Greater Wayne Community FCU	Rittman	OH	**D**	D	D	16.5	15.20	0.0	61.7	5.2	0.0	**5.7**	7.7
Greater Woodlawn Federal Credit Union	Blasdell	NY	**B**	B	B	127.5	4.60	0.0	5.3	23.5	0.0	**10.0**	19.2
▼ Greater Wyoming Federal Credit Union	Casper	WY	**D-**	D	C-	22.4	-5.86	0.2	32.0	9.8	0.0	**8.6**	10.1
▼ Greece Community Federal Credit Union	Rochester	NY	**E+**	D-	E+	9.4	3.58	0.0	26.8	1.1	0.0	**5.2**	7.2
Green Country Federal Credit Union	Sand Springs	OK	**D+**	D+	C-	60.6	5.36	13.8	32.0	25.9	8.6	**6.2**	8.3
▲ Green Mountain Credit Union	South Burlington	VT	**C**	C-	D+	47.5	6.88	6.0	15.6	49.3	0.0	**5.6**	7.6
Green River Area Federal Credit Union	Owensboro	KY	**C+**	C+	C+	40.5	-1.18	0.0	29.5	12.3	0.0	**10.0**	20.1
▲ Green River Basin Federal Credit Union	Green River	WY	**E+**	E	E	12.4	0.82	0.0	37.3	0.6	0.0	**4.7**	6.7
Greenbelt Federal Credit Union	Greenbelt	MD	**C**	C	C	29.6	6.32	0.0	13.1	11.6	4.2	**8.1**	9.7
Greeneville City Employees' Credit Union	Greeneville	TN	**B-**	B-	B-	9.8	-1.63	0.0	61.5	0.0	0.0	**10.0**	25.3
Greeneville Works Empls Savings Assoc CU	Greeneville	TN	**B-**	B-	B-	2.2	5.19	0.0	52.3	0.0	0.0	**10.0**	35.9
Greensboro Municipal FCU	Greensboro	NC	**B**	B	B-	52.3	7.59	0.0	45.1	6.1	12.6	**10.0**	11.2
Greensboro Postal Credit Union	Greensboro	NC	**C-**	C-	D+	22.9	-0.01	0.0	9.8	21.3	0.0	**10.0**	22.1
▲ Greensburg Teachers Credit Union	Greensburg	PA	**C**	C-	C-	7.0	-0.20	0.0	13.1	0.0	80.9	**10.0**	13.3
Greenup County Federal Credit Union	Russell	KY	**D+**	D+	D+	5.1	-3.74	0.0	37.0	0.0	49.2	**8.1**	9.7
Greenville Federal Credit Union	Greenville	SC	**A-**	A-	A-	221.8	8.73	8.8	23.0	30.8	11.4	**9.3**	10.5
Greenville Heritage Federal Credit Union	Greenville	SC	**A**	A	A	94.6	9.55	0.0	39.1	30.9	0.0	**10.0**	14.9
Greenwich Municipal Employees FCU	Greenwich	CT	**C-**	C-	C-	24.7	6.66	0.0	16.1	0.0	43.8	**6.4**	8.4
Greenwood Credit Union	Warwick	RI	**B-**	B-	B-	463.1	7.25	10.6	56.6	18.0	9.5	**7.0**	9.0
▲ Greenwood Municipal Federal Credit Union	Greenwood	SC	**B**	B-	B	39.9	3.94	0.0	32.9	1.9	0.0	**10.0**	13.6
Greylock Federal Credit Union	Pittsfield	MA	**C+**	C+	C+	1116.8	2.56	6.0	19.5	40.5	10.6	**8.2**	9.8
Griffith Institute Employees FCU	Springville	NY	**C-**	C-	C	3.6	5.67	0.0	33.9	0.0	50.4	**10.0**	11.0
▲ Groton Municipal Employees FCU	Groton	CT	**D**	D-	E+	6.7	5.73	0.0	35.0	0.0	0.0	**6.7**	8.7
Group Service Employees FCU	Tulsa	OK	**C**	C	C	11.7	2.21	0.0	85.8	0.0	0.0	**10.0**	15.9
Grove City Area Federal Credit Union	Grove City	PA	**B-**	B-	B-	82.9	5.29	0.0	24.1	2.5	32.9	**10.0**	11.9
Grow Financial Federal Credit Union	Tampa	FL	**C+**	C+	B-	2378.7	6.44	3.0	54.2	20.9	6.5	**7.8**	9.6
GRS Employees Federal Credit Union	West Henrietta	NY	**E+**	E+	E+	2.9	-0.87	0.0	59.1	0.0	0.0	**4.5**	6.5
GSA Federal Credit Union	Washington	DC	**C-**	C-	C-	34.8	0.50	0.0	50.7	9.8	29.2	**8.9**	10.2
GTE Federal Credit Union	Tampa	FL	**C+**	C+	C+	1899.5	4.07	5.6	40.3	20.0	0.0	**6.0**	8.0
Guadalupe Center Federal Credit Union	Kansas City	MO	**D+**	D+	D+	2.9	6.21	0.0	73.4	0.0	0.0	**10.0**	14.3
▲ Guadalupe Credit Union	Santa Fe	NM	**A-**	B+	A-	161.2	12.51	1.1	29.9	36.5	0.0	**10.0**	11.5
Guadalupe Parish Credit Union	Antonito	CO	**B**	B	B-	27.5	11.23	8.9	5.2	51.4	0.0	**10.0**	26.2
Guardian 1st Federal Credit Union	Fort Worth	TX	**E+**	E+	E+	5.2	3.52	0.0	49.3	0.0	0.0	**4.1**	6.1
Guardian Credit Union	Montgomery	AL	**B**	B	B	399.1	16.92	0.3	50.1	15.0	11.1	**8.0**	9.7
Guardian Credit Union	West Milwaukee	WI	**D-**	D-	E+	228.5	3.76	3.5	30.9	15.9	0.2	**3.9**	5.9
Guardians Credit Union	West Palm Beach	FL	**A**	A	A	149.7	7.01	0.0	38.6	5.9	0.3	**10.0**	12.0
GUCO Credit Union	Greenville	NC	**C+**	C+	C+	13.1	-0.06	0.0	46.8	0.5	0.0	**10.0**	12.8
Guernsey Community Federal Credit Union	Guernsey	WY	**D+**	D+	D+	1.8	0.34	0.0	16.6	25.5	0.0	**6.4**	8.4
Gulf Coast Community FCU	Gulfport	MS	**A-**	A-	A-	103.2	10.83	0.3	35.7	14.6	3.7	**10.0**	16.1
Gulf Coast Educators FCU	Pasadena	TX	**A**	A	A	686.8	5.50	0.1	28.7	12.7	46.2	**10.0**	16.9
Gulf Coast Federal Credit Union	Mobile	AL	**C**	C	C	34.7	3.91	0.0	25.4	10.4	0.0	**10.0**	13.3
Gulf Coast Federal Credit Union	Corpus Christi	TX	**C+**	C+	C+	205.8	9.13	0.0	43.0	41.2	0.0	**7.8**	9.5
Gulf Credit Union	Groves	TX	**C-**	C-	C-	254.6	2.45	4.8	33.1	16.2	26.5	**4.2**	6.8
Gulf Shore Federal Credit Union	Texas City	TX	**D-**	D-	D-	14.1	10.10	0.0	44.0	0.0	0.0	**5.1**	7.1
Gulf States Credit Union	Maitland	FL	**B**	B	B	29.9	3.78	1.3	26.2	9.7	0.0	**10.0**	14.7
▲ Gulf Trust Credit Union	Pascagoula	MS	**B**	B-	C+	25.3	0.19	0.0	28.2	23.0	0.0	**10.0**	14.6
Gulf Winds Federal Credit Union	Pensacola	FL	**B+**	B+	B+	660.7	8.58	0.1	31.8	21.6	20.4	**10.0**	11.2

Asset Quality Index	Non-Performing Loans as a % of Total Loans	Non-Performing Loans as a % of Capital	Net Charge-Offs Avg Loans	Profitability Index	Net Income ($Mil)	Return on Assets	Return on Equity	Net Interest Spread	Overhead Efficiency Ratio	Liquidity Index	Liquidity Ratio	Hot Money Ratio	Stability Index
7.2	0.57	4.8	0.30	**7.1**	1.47	0.84	8.84	4.45	84.8	**4.6**	18.0	2.3	**7.7**
3.9	9.29	10.6	0.00	**5.0**	0.00	1.22	2.26	9.09	50.0	**6.9**	103.8	0.0	**3.7**
6.6	0.44	3.6	0.48	**4.0**	0.18	0.66	4.75	4.36	83.1	**3.5**	15.5	8.1	**7.1**
9.8	0.25	1.0	0.52	**3.9**	0.08	0.61	5.43	3.33	83.6	**5.3**	23.6	0.7	**4.9**
8.0	0.48	3.8	-0.02	**2.9**	0.04	0.25	2.94	3.26	99.0	**3.5**	13.7	3.8	**4.2**
9.0	0.61	2.0	-0.06	**4.7**	0.11	1.01	10.64	2.92	69.4	**5.3**	30.0	0.4	**4.4**
9.5	0.03	0.1	0.56	**5.1**	0.20	1.19	7.70	3.38	57.3	**4.7**	22.2	0.0	**6.8**
6.3	1.47	6.9	0.00	**1.5**	0.00	-0.09	-1.16	3.23	102.0	**5.3**	24.6	0.0	**3.4**
10.0	0.01	0.0	0.01	**9.3**	0.57	1.41	11.19	2.19	49.8	**3.6**	14.6	9.7	**9.4**
9.6	0.29	2.2	0.18	**3.8**	0.67	0.46	5.92	3.03	82.0	**4.5**	16.2	2.2	**5.4**
7.4	0.76	6.8	0.00	**1.9**	0.00	0.03	0.19	2.28	98.1	**5.0**	27.6	8.2	**6.1**
9.5	0.84	0.9	-0.97	**2.6**	0.01	0.27	1.46	2.55	82.1	**5.7**	27.5	0.0	**6.1**
6.9	0.45	5.1	0.61	**1.8**	0.01	0.11	1.53	3.58	97.0	**5.3**	25.7	1.3	**1.7**
3.3	1.58	15.2	0.12	**5.1**	0.04	0.88	11.49	5.31	81.0	**3.8**	15.6	5.7	**2.3**
10.0	0.38	0.6	0.09	**4.3**	0.22	0.70	3.59	2.71	67.1	**6.8**	67.2	9.1	**8.4**
7.4	0.21	3.1	0.72	**0.2**	-0.05	-0.87	-8.59	3.33	106.3	**4.1**	11.8	4.3	**3.2**
6.2	0.88	6.1	2.35	**2.0**	0.00	0.13	1.79	4.19	95.7	**5.2**	30.1	0.0	**1.0**
2.8	1.94	19.7	0.69	**5.1**	0.11	0.75	9.59	4.92	79.5	**3.9**	14.9	7.2	**3.2**
6.4	0.35	3.7	0.03	**10.0**	0.23	1.98	26.84	4.95	63.2	**1.9**	22.5	31.2	**3.4**
9.9	0.27	0.7	-0.02	**3.3**	0.05	0.51	2.65	3.09	84.1	**5.7**	36.9	1.4	**7.3**
8.8	0.34	2.4	-0.07	**2.1**	0.01	0.40	5.85	3.21	100.0	**5.1**	38.5	3.6	**1.7**
10.0	0.28	0.8	-0.21	**3.1**	0.03	0.38	3.92	2.74	85.5	**6.7**	45.8	0.0	**4.4**
8.0	0.11	0.3	0.11	**8.9**	0.03	1.39	5.52	3.14	56.3	**3.7**	28.1	0.0	**5.7**
8.0	0.16	0.9	1.55	**7.6**	0.00	0.57	1.56	5.25	80.8	**5.6**	71.8	0.0	**5.0**
6.1	1.14	6.7	0.20	**6.7**	0.12	0.90	7.97	5.24	82.0	**4.2**	18.3	6.0	**5.8**
10.0	0.01	1.2	0.00	**1.3**	-0.01	-0.10	-0.47	2.38	104.0	**6.0**	43.5	0.0	**6.8**
10.0	0.00	0.0	0.00	**2.5**	0.01	0.51	3.90	1.88	71.9	**5.0**	23.2	0.0	**6.6**
5.0	2.37	8.6	-0.37	**1.0**	0.00	0.08	0.80	2.33	96.4	**5.1**	30.6	0.0	**3.9**
8.0	0.68	3.9	0.34	**8.2**	0.61	1.13	10.64	4.20	74.6	**4.6**	18.4	2.3	**7.9**
9.6	0.18	1.0	0.70	**7.2**	0.18	0.78	5.17	4.54	85.6	**3.7**	18.6	8.6	**7.9**
8.6	0.03	0.1	0.00	**4.5**	0.06	1.01	11.88	2.85	68.2	**4.9**	17.9	0.6	**3.7**
6.8	0.31	3.4	0.03	**3.6**	0.44	0.38	4.25	2.00	84.3	**1.4**	11.2	22.2	**6.3**
9.8	0.17	0.5	0.39	**4.3**	0.07	0.71	5.44	3.58	84.6	**5.4**	50.3	6.2	**6.5**
7.3	0.90	7.1	0.23	**3.0**	1.37	0.49	5.08	2.85	81.6	**2.6**	7.1	10.4	**6.6**
5.0	2.52	8.1	0.00	**5.5**	0.01	0.90	8.12	2.15	52.9	**5.3**	22.7	0.0	**3.7**
8.0	0.47	2.4	0.00	**4.0**	0.01	0.66	7.67	4.48	84.7	**5.4**	29.5	0.0	**2.3**
6.8	0.63	3.3	0.74	**2.3**	-0.01	-0.35	-2.15	4.98	89.9	**3.4**	10.5	0.0	**6.3**
8.7	1.09	4.6	0.21	**3.8**	0.09	0.46	3.84	2.77	81.4	**5.2**	31.0	0.5	**6.0**
6.7	0.47	4.2	0.87	**3.5**	1.66	0.28	2.93	3.61	80.4	**3.8**	16.5	5.5	**6.5**
3.6	0.83	8.2	4.79	**0.3**	-0.01	-0.70	-10.58	5.78	111.8	**5.1**	33.2	7.0	**1.4**
5.6	0.88	5.2	0.51	**2.3**	0.01	0.11	1.12	3.02	91.2	**4.1**	19.4	0.0	**4.2**
5.6	1.24	12.7	0.83	**3.8**	1.40	0.30	3.92	3.66	80.8	**3.9**	15.3	4.9	**5.2**
2.6	4.21	20.8	-0.19	**4.5**	0.00	0.29	1.93	6.11	98.0	**4.2**	27.5	0.0	**7.2**
5.8	1.78	12.6	0.79	**7.8**	2.08	5.32	52.72	5.94	47.1	**3.7**	28.5	15.0	**6.4**
9.7	0.07	0.2	0.00	**5.0**	0.06	0.86	3.23	3.22	78.5	**3.0**	19.3	16.7	**7.6**
2.9	1.61	13.9	0.71	**0.7**	-0.02	-1.51	-23.31	5.84	114.1	**5.1**	17.1	0.0	**1.5**
5.7	0.80	6.1	1.34	**4.6**	0.51	0.53	5.59	4.98	75.2	**2.5**	22.5	19.2	**5.5**
1.7	1.73	37.8	1.33	**2.1**	0.23	0.41	6.88	3.88	84.4	**4.2**	15.6	1.5	**2.4**
9.5	0.14	0.6	1.13	**7.9**	0.38	1.03	8.45	5.44	77.8	**6.2**	40.1	0.2	**8.0**
8.7	0.40	1.5	0.25	**2.2**	0.00	0.09	0.72	2.59	95.4	**3.4**	25.2	12.5	**6.1**
5.8	1.19	6.6	1.50	**0.0**	-0.04	-9.66	-100.00	5.94	116.7	**4.1**	45.5	31.0	**4.6**
5.8	2.26	10.8	1.56	**9.5**	0.34	1.34	8.30	7.61	71.1	**3.4**	21.7	13.8	**8.2**
9.9	0.27	0.8	0.75	**7.2**	1.98	1.18	7.35	3.28	62.1	**3.1**	21.7	19.6	**9.5**
6.9	2.73	11.3	0.86	**2.5**	0.03	0.35	2.60	3.45	83.7	**5.1**	38.9	10.5	**6.2**
3.2	1.95	25.9	1.64	**3.0**	-0.06	-0.11	-1.32	4.16	64.1	**1.2**	12.4	43.0	**5.2**
7.8	0.17	4.0	0.48	**1.7**	0.04	0.06	1.29	3.10	98.0	**4.4**	13.3	3.1	**1.9**
6.8	0.68	4.5	0.00	**1.7**	0.00	0.00	0.00	3.04	100.0	**5.5**	30.3	0.0	**1.7**
8.7	0.77	2.4	0.34	**3.9**	0.02	0.31	2.10	3.87	91.4	**5.5**	34.6	2.0	**7.0**
8.6	0.45	3.4	0.27	**4.3**	0.04	0.63	4.35	3.78	83.0	**3.3**	25.0	15.4	**7.0**
9.5	0.29	1.9	0.48	**4.6**	1.25	0.78	7.21	3.05	75.8	**4.4**	25.1	7.7	**8.3**

Name	City	State	Rating	2016 Rating	2015 Rating	Total Assets ($Mil)	One Year Asset Growth	Asset Mix (As a % of Total Assets) Comm-ercial Loans	Cons-umer Loans	Mort-gage Loans	Secur-ities	Capital-ization Index	Net Worth Ratio
Gundersen Credit Union	La Crosse	WI	**B-**	B-	B	42.6	3.16	0.0	19.7	42.1	16.7	**10.0**	13.5
▼ Guthrie Federal Credit Union	Sayre	PA	**B-**	B	B	72.5	7.35	0.0	24.0	33.8	19.1	**8.7**	10.4
H A L E Federal Credit Union	Indianapolis	IN	**C+**	C+	C+	<1	-10.53	0.0	53.2	0.0	0.0	**10.0**	18.1
H E Telephone Federal Credit Union	Rochelle Park	NJ	**C**	C	C+	45.6	6.12	0.4	14.3	21.5	4.4	**10.0**	12.4
H M S A Employees Federal Credit Union	Honolulu	HI	**B**	B	B-	71.1	3.79	0.0	6.8	0.0	18.1	**10.0**	11.2
▼ H&H Federal Credit Union	Stinnett	TX	**C-**	C	C-	49.3	0.95	0.0	33.6	4.8	0.0	**10.0**	16.1
H.B.I. Employees Credit Union	Saint Paul	MN	**C-**	C-	C-	7.8	-3.01	0.0	19.4	6.6	0.0	**10.0**	12.5
H.E.B. Federal Credit Union	San Antonio	TX	**B-**	B-	B-	167.6	2.44	0.2	24.4	34.8	10.1	**10.0**	13.9
H.P.C. Credit Union	Alpena	MI	**B**	B	B	123.7	4.16	1.5	8.1	26.9	16.4	**10.0**	13.0
Habersham Federal Credit Union	Clarkesville	GA	**B-**	B-	B-	20.1	15.26	0.0	39.3	8.0	10.2	**10.0**	14.6
Hale County Teachers FCU	Plainview	TX	**C-**	C-	D	7.2	-5.66	0.0	66.9	1.7	0.0	**9.8**	10.8
Halifax County Community FCU	South Boston	VA	**C**	C	D+	6.1	-9.54	0.0	10.2	17.2	0.1	**10.0**	13.1
HALLCO Community Credit Union	Gainesville	GA	**C+**	C+	C	79.5	11.11	0.8	47.6	4.4	16.0	**6.2**	8.2
Halliburton Employees FCU	Duncan	OK	**B+**	B+	B+	150.4	-2.48	0.0	68.4	0.7	14.3	**8.6**	10.1
▲ Hamakua Coast Community FCU	Pepeekeo	HI	**C-**	D+	D+	15.9	4.37	0.3	34.5	2.0	5.1	**10.0**	15.9
Hamilton Federal Credit Union	Novato	CA	**D**	D	D	22.4	-5.02	0.6	6.3	28.0	0.0	**10.0**	15.2
▼ Hamilton Horizons Federal Credit Union	Hamilton	NJ	**E-**	E	E+	25.6	1.79	0.0	28.6	1.9	23.4	**4.9**	6.9
Hamlet Federal Credit Union	Hamlet	NC	**C-**	C-	C	17.6	7.59	0.0	32.1	8.8	0.0	**8.7**	10.2
Hammond Firefighters Association CU	Hammond	IN	**C**	C	C	1.5	-2.03	0.0	28.2	0.0	0.0	**10.0**	22.6
Hampton Roads Catholic FCU	Virginia Beach	VA	**D-**	D-	D-	5.6	1.05	0.0	23.7	7.1	0.0	**5.5**	7.5
Hampton Roads Educators' Credit Union, Inc.	Hampton	VA	**D**	D	D	33.1	5.17	0.0	36.3	0.0	0.0	**4.7**	6.7
▲ Hampton V. A. Federal Credit Union	Hampton	VA	**D+**	D	D	7.4	-0.19	0.0	25.9	0.4	1.4	**10.0**	11.8
Hancock Federal Credit Union	Findlay	OH	**C**	C	C+	82.0	6.07	11.3	30.6	26.6	5.3	**8.9**	10.3
Hancock School Employees FCU	Weirton	WV	**C**	C	C	18.2	7.44	0.0	10.0	0.0	0.0	**10.0**	12.5
Hanesbrands Credit Union	Winston-Salem	NC	**D**	D	D	48.0	-3.05	0.0	13.5	14.0	23.0	**10.0**	11.7
Hanin Federal Credit Union	Los Angeles	CA	**C+**	C+	B-	27.9	5.18	1.5	60.4	6.6	0.0	**8.1**	9.8
Hanscom Federal Credit Union	Hanscom AFB	MA	**B**	B	B-	1205.9	6.07	1.9	33.2	17.9	3.1	**8.6**	10.1
HAPO Community Credit Union	Richland	WA	**B**	B	B	1536.0	7.15	0.6	64.4	15.5	0.0	**6.3**	8.3
Happy Valley Credit Union	Elizabethton	TN	**B**	B	B	30.3	0.15	0.0	43.3	7.6	0.0	**10.0**	17.8
HAR-CO Credit Union	Bel Air	MD	**C+**	C+	C+	193.0	-0.48	0.4	18.3	26.5	18.0	**7.4**	9.3
Harbor Area Postal Employees FCU	Lomita	CA	**D**	D	D	20.4	2.85	0.0	10.9	18.9	47.6	**10.0**	11.0
Harbor Beach Community FCU	Harbor Beach	MI	**D+**	D+	D+	4.1	-6.97	0.0	27.6	0.0	0.0	**10.0**	11.8
Harbor Credit Union	Green Bay	WI	**C**	C	C	112.7	1.38	1.9	20.4	30.8	0.2	**7.9**	9.6
HarborLight Credit Union	Whitehall	MI	**C**	C	D+	106.6	9.44	0.0	18.2	25.3	8.6	**8.4**	10.0
Harborstone Credit Union	Lakewood	WA	**B**	B	B	1224.5	6.30	10.9	30.4	26.6	20.8	**10.0**	11.3
▼ Hardin County Hospital Employees CU	Savannah	TN	**D-**	D	C-	1.2	6.86	0.0	25.6	0.0	0.0	**7.8**	9.5
Harris County Federal Credit Union	Houston	TX	**A**	A	A	153.1	3.67	0.0	35.4	9.9	14.1	**10.0**	14.8
▼ Harris Employees Credit Union	Cordele	GA	**D+**	C-	C-	1.1	-21.31	0.0	21.5	8.6	0.0	**10.0**	19.5
Harrison County Federal Credit Union	Nutter Fort	WV	**C-**	C-	C-	14.1	-0.20	0.0	26.7	0.0	0.0	**10.0**	16.0
▼ Harrison County POE Federal Credit Union	Biloxi	MS	**D**	D+	C	6.0	1.48	0.0	55.0	0.0	0.0	**10.0**	19.7
Harrison District No. Two FCU	Colorado Springs	CO	**D**	D	D	14.1	7.94	0.0	24.3	15.2	41.1	**10.0**	11.7
▲ Harrison Police & Firemen's FCU	Harrison	NJ	**C-**	D+	D	20.6	1.58	0.4	14.5	0.0	0.0	**7.9**	9.6
▼ Harrison Teachers Federal Credit Union	Harrison	NY	**D-**	D	D	2.3	-8.07	0.0	0.0	0.0	0.0	**8.4**	9.9
Hartford Federal Credit Union	Hartford	CT	**C+**	C+	C+	96.5	2.36	0.0	11.6	9.4	0.5	**10.0**	12.7
▼ Hartford Firefighters FCU	Hartford	CT	**C**	C+	C	20.6	5.76	0.0	21.4	9.1	0.0	**10.0**	11.8
▼ Hartford Healthcare Federal Credit Union, Inc.	Hartford	CT	**C**	C+	C+	37.2	4.72	0.0	34.2	17.2	0.0	**7.3**	9.2
Harvard Community Credit Union	Harvard	IL	**C+**	C+	C	13.6	-4.00	0.0	29.8	16.2	0.0	**10.0**	11.6
Harvard University Employees CU	Cambridge	MA	**B+**	B+	B+	599.2	13.89	0.7	11.1	53.3	5.8	**6.6**	8.6
Harvest Federal Credit Union	Heath	OH	**B-**	B-	B-	28.6	8.49	0.4	30.3	18.4	0.9	**10.0**	13.2
Harvester Financial Credit Union	Indianapolis	IN	**C-**	C-	C-	53.6	0.62	0.0	23.7	17.7	29.2	**7.2**	9.1
▲ Harvesters Federal Credit Union	Cantonment	FL	**C**	C-	C-	153.3	4.01	11.1	43.4	27.7	0.4	**6.3**	8.4
Hastings Federal Credit Union	Hastings	NE	**C**	C	C+	29.3	10.59	0.3	32.3	9.2	0.0	**7.6**	9.4
Haulpak Federal Credit Union	Peoria	IL	**D+**	D+	D	2.2	-8.86	0.0	48.9	0.0	0.0	**10.0**	23.6
Haverhill Fire Department Credit Union	Haverhill	MA	**C-**	C-	C	17.5	1.44	0.0	12.9	13.6	1.2	**10.0**	12.3
Hawaii Central Federal Credit Union	Honolulu	HI	**B+**	B+	B	264.3	1.79	2.1	15.7	16.2	34.0	**9.8**	10.9
Hawaii Community Federal Credit Union	Kailua-Kona	HI	**B-**	B-	B-	493.8	7.94	7.8	8.3	35.4	39.8	**7.0**	9.0
▲ Hawaii County Employees FCU	Hilo	HI	**B**	B-	C+	90.9	6.15	3.9	14.5	9.1	22.7	**10.0**	15.4
▲ Hawaii Federal Credit Union	Honolulu	HI	**A-**	B+	B	88.8	7.24	0.0	52.0	5.8	0.6	**10.0**	11.0
▲ Hawaii First Federal Credit Union	Kamuela	HI	**C+**	C	D+	41.2	7.75	0.0	16.4	15.9	0.0	**8.1**	9.7
Hawaii Law Enforcement FCU	Honolulu	HI	**C-**	C-	C-	163.8	3.50	1.4	20.3	6.4	33.6	**8.3**	10.0

Asset Quality Index	Non-Performing Loans as a % of Total Loans	Non-Performing Loans as a % of Capital	Net Charge-Offs Avg Loans	Profitability Index	Net Income ($Mil)	Return on Assets	Return on Equity	Net Interest Spread	Overhead Efficiency Ratio	Liquidity Index	Liquidity Ratio	Hot Money Ratio	Stability Index
9.8	0.08	0.4	0.01	**3.4**	0.05	0.51	3.71	2.79	83.2	**4.3**	18.6	0.0	**6.9**
8.2	0.36	2.2	0.46	**3.5**	0.04	0.23	2.24	3.74	87.3	**4.5**	22.1	4.5	**5.3**
8.2	0.97	2.9	0.00	**5.9**	0.01	2.71	15.04	6.22	100.0	**7.4**	110.1	0.0	**5.0**
10.0	0.37	1.4	0.42	**1.9**	0.01	0.06	0.49	3.34	85.3	**4.9**	35.6	8.5	**5.4**
10.0	1.08	1.6	0.00	**4.0**	0.13	0.72	6.43	1.39	59.1	**5.3**	27.8	0.0	**5.8**
8.3	1.05	3.3	0.39	**1.2**	-0.03	-0.22	-1.36	2.51	102.5	**5.2**	60.2	3.2	**7.0**
9.0	0.71	3.6	-0.14	**2.2**	0.00	0.05	0.41	2.81	100.0	**6.1**	61.1	1.6	**6.3**
9.9	0.16	0.7	0.00	**3.6**	0.16	0.39	2.79	3.80	91.4	**4.8**	39.4	12.8	**8.3**
9.9	0.12	2.0	-0.03	**3.7**	0.14	0.46	3.53	2.18	78.0	**5.7**	40.0	2.9	**8.0**
9.6	0.12	0.4	0.15	**4.7**	0.03	0.62	4.10	5.48	88.9	**5.8**	38.8	1.0	**7.2**
6.7	0.59	4.2	0.00	**5.4**	0.01	0.78	7.25	4.26	81.2	**3.0**	23.7	14.9	**3.7**
8.6	1.98	4.2	0.22	**5.7**	0.02	1.15	9.11	3.54	73.9	**6.0**	41.9	0.0	**4.3**
5.2	0.77	6.7	0.47	**6.7**	0.13	0.66	8.00	3.71	80.7	**4.7**	22.8	0.0	**4.3**
6.2	0.68	5.0	0.48	**3.1**	0.08	0.21	2.04	2.35	82.1	**3.1**	9.3	8.1	**5.7**
9.8	0.50	1.2	-0.19	**2.0**	0.02	0.56	3.51	3.15	105.3	**5.1**	30.7	2.4	**5.8**
10.0	0.59	1.6	-0.05	**0.3**	-0.02	-0.41	-3.07	2.50	143.1	**5.2**	50.6	8.1	**4.8**
5.1	1.49	14.4	2.74	**1.4**	-0.01	-0.21	-2.92	4.95	91.1	**3.5**	4.6	2.6	**0.3**
3.2	5.56	24.7	-0.11	**2.9**	0.01	0.12	1.12	4.83	97.6	**6.7**	53.1	3.6	**4.8**
10.0	0.47	0.5	0.00	**4.4**	0.00	0.53	2.37	4.16	83.3	**7.0**	51.1	0.0	**7.8**
8.7	0.54	2.6	0.00	**2.0**	0.00	0.07	0.96	3.13	95.6	**5.5**	31.7	0.0	**1.7**
7.8	0.23	2.1	1.20	**1.8**	-0.01	-0.17	-4.37	5.07	94.9	**5.5**	22.2	0.0	**1.0**
7.5	3.66	8.3	0.76	**1.3**	0.00	0.22	1.85	4.83	95.5	**7.4**	63.9	0.0	**5.0**
5.4	0.90	8.4	-0.05	**2.8**	0.05	0.23	2.23	3.53	93.5	**4.0**	17.4	4.7	**5.5**
10.0	1.09	0.9	0.00	**2.7**	0.02	0.40	3.20	2.49	82.7	**5.1**	9.7	0.0	**6.7**
6.8	1.79	8.6	0.93	**0.6**	0.00	0.00	0.00	2.65	95.6	**5.8**	34.3	3.0	**4.2**
5.3	0.74	5.1	0.43	**4.4**	0.02	0.29	3.12	6.91	92.9	**3.9**	54.9	43.6	**5.0**
9.3	0.34	2.9	0.22	**4.6**	2.08	0.69	6.89	2.96	74.1	**3.5**	14.2	3.3	**7.4**
7.6	0.20	2.8	0.51	**4.3**	1.39	0.37	4.80	3.64	81.6	**2.0**	11.2	19.6	**5.8**
7.9	1.07	3.3	0.21	**4.7**	0.04	0.58	3.29	3.57	86.9	**4.2**	15.4	5.5	**6.8**
9.3	0.29	2.2	0.43	**2.6**	0.06	0.13	1.40	3.66	93.5	**4.9**	23.9	2.2	**5.5**
10.0	0.22	0.8	0.35	**0.1**	-0.04	-0.71	-6.36	2.76	116.4	**4.4**	33.6	14.4	**5.6**
8.5	1.13	2.9	-0.32	**0.5**	0.00	-0.39	-3.32	2.62	96.2	**4.8**	23.8	5.0	**4.7**
9.0	0.35	2.2	0.07	**3.1**	0.09	0.32	3.31	2.94	93.1	**4.8**	28.5	0.4	**5.6**
8.8	0.70	3.4	0.28	**2.3**	0.02	0.07	0.72	3.24	92.3	**4.7**	24.2	3.5	**6.0**
8.2	0.55	3.3	0.58	**3.9**	1.24	0.41	3.55	3.33	76.6	**3.9**	11.3	4.1	**7.7**
8.1	1.19	3.0	-1.14	**0.0**	0.00	-1.32	-13.45	4.12	157.1	**7.6**	80.5	0.0	**4.7**
8.5	1.08	3.8	0.91	**8.1**	0.37	0.97	7.11	3.99	67.4	**4.4**	24.6	8.8	**8.7**
6.2	7.77	15.7	-2.99	**0.7**	0.00	-0.68	-3.65	3.14	110.0	**5.8**	60.6	0.0	**7.0**
10.0	0.66	1.1	0.32	**1.1**	0.00	-0.11	-0.70	2.30	103.9	**5.6**	21.8	0.0	**6.6**
2.6	8.93	24.1	3.79	**3.1**	-0.01	-0.93	-4.58	6.70	83.5	**2.9**	24.8	18.8	**2.3**
9.2	0.86	2.9	1.06	**0.3**	-0.01	-0.15	-1.21	2.98	103.3	**5.7**	42.3	1.7	**5.6**
6.0	3.29	10.9	-0.11	**3.4**	0.02	0.35	3.66	3.06	88.3	**4.3**	26.3	8.6	**5.0**
1.7	15.21	36.9	0.00	**1.5**	0.00	-0.37	-3.43	5.50	118.2	**7.7**	73.4	0.0	**4.0**
10.0	0.17	0.6	0.31	**2.9**	0.06	0.24	1.84	3.20	94.4	**4.8**	26.3	1.9	**6.4**
10.0	0.03	0.1	0.40	**1.7**	0.00	-0.04	-0.33	3.35	100.6	**5.2**	19.6	0.0	**6.0**
4.5	2.33	17.8	0.73	**3.4**	0.00	0.01	0.12	5.64	86.6	**4.1**	19.4	2.4	**4.5**
7.3	1.66	6.2	2.44	**5.3**	0.02	0.72	6.16	5.05	86.2	**5.1**	22.8	0.0	**5.0**
8.7	0.48	4.5	0.12	**6.4**	1.39	0.95	10.88	4.15	73.0	**3.0**	9.4	3.7	**7.1**
5.4	3.90	16.5	0.20	**3.8**	0.04	0.57	4.27	3.32	86.0	**4.2**	25.8	2.2	**6.4**
7.6	0.49	2.5	0.05	**1.9**	0.02	0.11	1.23	3.31	95.6	**4.9**	31.7	2.2	**4.2**
6.9	0.28	6.0	0.38	**2.8**	0.17	0.44	5.97	3.44	84.8	**4.4**	20.3	2.3	**4.0**
9.8	0.11	0.5	-0.06	**3.4**	0.03	0.42	4.37	3.64	89.2	**6.3**	45.8	0.8	**4.5**
7.9	0.82	1.7	-0.36	**1.7**	0.00	0.18	0.76	4.75	91.7	**5.7**	54.4	0.0	**5.0**
8.5	0.52	1.6	0.29	**1.4**	0.00	0.09	0.75	3.03	96.2	**5.1**	26.1	4.1	**5.9**
7.2	1.15	6.6	0.71	**5.1**	0.14	0.21	2.45	3.13	85.6	**3.6**	13.2	11.3	**6.4**
8.1	0.64	4.0	0.16	**3.6**	0.46	0.38	4.12	2.54	87.8	**4.4**	17.8	0.9	**6.0**
10.0	0.25	0.5	0.37	**4.2**	0.19	0.85	5.45	2.62	78.2	**5.6**	32.7	2.0	**7.0**
5.5	1.40	8.0	1.55	**10.0**	0.32	1.48	13.37	5.20	67.3	**3.6**	28.0	13.8	**6.3**
5.7	0.43	3.0	0.40	**8.8**	0.17	1.70	17.80	7.19	78.0	**4.3**	19.5	0.0	**5.5**
10.0	0.12	0.9	0.30	**2.5**	0.11	0.27	2.70	2.97	83.3	**4.2**	13.1	5.3	**6.4**

Name	City	State	Rating	2016 Rating	2015 Rating	Total Assets ($Mil)	One Year Asset Growth	Asset Mix (As a % of Total Assets) Commercial Loans	Consumer Loans	Mortgage Loans	Securities	Capitalization Index	Net Worth Ratio
▼ Hawaii Pacific Federal Credit Union	Honolulu	HI	**D**	D+	D+	51.2	5.82	9.4	19.0	33.8	27.9	**6.5**	9.1
Hawaii Schools Federal Credit Union	Honolulu	HI	**C**	C	C-	66.0	-1.51	0.0	11.0	5.2	37.1	**10.0**	11.6
Hawaii State Federal Credit Union	Honolulu	HI	**B**	B	B	1503.7	5.41	2.5	19.0	15.6	34.3	**10.0**	11.1
Hawaiian Airlines Federal Credit Union	Honolulu	HI	**D-**	D-	D-	21.2	6.54	0.0	29.9	0.0	3.5	**5.3**	7.3
Hawaiian Electric Employees FCU	Honolulu	HI	**C**	C	C-	36.0	0.48	0.0	18.4	8.6	0.0	**10.0**	15.5
Hawaiian Tel Federal Credit Union	Honolulu	HI	**A-**	A-	A-	610.7	7.95	11.4	8.1	34.6	31.8	**10.0**	12.1
HawaiiUSA Federal Credit Union	Honolulu	HI	**B+**	B+	B+	1624.9	5.46	5.3	18.5	16.7	41.2	**10.0**	11.1
▼ Haxtun Community Federal Credit Union	Haxtun	CO	**D-**	D	C-	7.6	34.75	0.0	23.0	30.9	0.0	**6.1**	8.1
Haynes Community Federal Credit Union	Kokomo	IN	**B-**	B-	C	27.1	6.45	2.3	40.3	24.2	0.5	**10.0**	12.5
Hayward Community Credit Union	Hayward	WI	**C-**	C-	C-	69.9	8.23	9.5	8.2	44.9	27.8	**8.5**	10.0
Hazleton School Employees Credit Union	Hazleton	PA	**B+**	B+	B+	28.0	7.43	0.0	6.6	25.2	25.2	**10.0**	13.5
HB Telco Federal Credit Union	Huron	SD	**D**	D	D	4.9	3.83	0.0	60.4	0.0	0.0	**7.2**	9.1
HEA Federal Credit Union	Warner Robins	GA	**C+**	C+	D+	25.8	1.89	1.1	42.1	4.5	0.0	**7.9**	9.6
Health & Education Federal Credit Union	Lexington	KY	**C+**	C+	C+	85.0	4.81	0.0	21.4	9.2	7.2	**10.0**	12.0
Health Alliance Federal Credit Union	Somerville	MA	**D+**	D+	D+	3.8	2.40	0.0	50.4	0.0	0.0	**8.2**	9.8
Health Care Credit Union	Oshkosh	WI	**C-**	C-	C-	17.2	5.79	0.0	28.7	32.5	0.6	**7.6**	9.4
Health Care Family Credit Union	Richmond Heights	MO	**A-**	A-	B	58.9	3.94	0.2	24.1	13.1	8.8	**10.0**	13.0
Health Care Idaho Credit Union	Boise	ID	**B-**	B-	B-	13.3	6.88	0.0	29.6	0.0	0.0	**10.0**	11.6
▼ Health Care of New Jersey FCU	Mount Holly	NJ	**D**	D+	C	6.8	-1.56	0.0	34.2	0.0	0.0	**10.0**	12.4
Health Care Professionals FCU	Richmond	IN	**B**	B	B	24.3	8.38	0.0	32.1	0.0	7.2	**10.0**	15.1
Health Center Credit Union	Augusta	GA	**D+**	D+	C-	52.6	3.72	0.9	37.4	20.3	2.8	**7.3**	9.2
Health Credit Union	Birmingham	AL	**C+**	C+	C+	19.8	-2.81	0.0	27.6	9.4	0.0	**10.0**	24.3
▲ Health Employees Federal Credit Union	Albany	NY	**B**	B-	C	32.7	4.12	0.0	18.9	9.2	0.0	**10.0**	15.2
Health Facilities Federal Credit Union	Florence	SC	**B**	B	C-	30.2	11.59	2.4	33.9	2.4	0.8	**9.8**	10.9
Health Systems Credit Union	Knoxville	TN	**E+**	E+	E+	6.2	-1.35	0.0	21.8	26.6	0.0	**5.5**	7.5
Healthcare 1st Federal Credit Union	Cumberland	MD	**E+**	E+	E+	9.0	5.72	0.0	33.4	0.0	2.2	**5.5**	7.5
Healthcare Associates Credit Union	Naperville	IL	**B+**	B+	A-	333.3	5.10	3.8	26.8	20.2	36.0	**10.0**	13.8
Healthcare Employees FCU	Princeton	NJ	**C+**	C+	C	111.6	9.39	0.0	26.1	6.7	1.5	**6.0**	8.0
Healthcare Financial FCU	New Haven	CT	**C**	C	B-	57.9	2.19	0.0	14.3	4.3	34.0	**9.8**	11.3
HealthCare First Credit Union	Johnstown	PA	**C-**	C-	C	89.7	51.17	0.0	26.6	7.1	13.7	**7.7**	9.4
▼ Healthcare Plus Federal Credit Union	Aberdeen	SD	**D**	D+	C-	48.7	2.61	2.2	48.4	18.6	0.0	**5.5**	7.5
Healthcare Services Credit Union	Chattanooga	TN	**C-**	C-	C+	20.1	-4.52	0.0	49.5	0.0	0.0	**10.0**	13.4
Healthcare Systems Federal Credit Union	Fairfax	VA	**C+**	C+	C	72.3	12.94	10.2	32.2	2.7	26.5	**6.5**	8.8
▼ HealthNet Federal Credit Union	Cordova	TN	**D+**	C-	C-	53.0	3.30	0.0	25.1	2.0	0.3	**9.9**	10.9
▼ HealthPlus Federal Credit Union	Jackson	MS	**E+**	D-	D-	6.7	-0.96	0.0	53.5	0.0	0.0	**6.4**	8.4
HealthShare Credit Union	Greensboro	NC	**C**	C	C+	33.5	2.34	1.2	34.9	7.5	0.0	**10.0**	12.5
Heard A.M.E. Federal Credit Union	Roselle	NJ	**D+**	D+	D-	<1	-1.38	0.0	20.0	0.0	0.0	**8.9**	10.7
Heart Center Federal Credit Union	Roslyn	NY	**C+**	C+	C+	18.3	8.12	0.6	19.1	2.0	14.7	**10.0**	12.2
Heart O' Texas Federal Credit Union	Waco	TX	**D-**	D-	D	57.6	3.36	0.2	27.9	9.2	0.0	**5.2**	7.2
▼ Heart of Louisiana Federal Credit Union	Pineville	LA	**B-**	B+	B+	108.5	4.91	6.4	32.6	18.1	0.5	**10.0**	11.6
▲ Heartland Area Federal Credit Union	Omaha	NE	**C-**	D+	D+	21.8	-0.90	0.0	21.0	14.5	0.0	**10.0**	24.5
Heartland Community Credit Union	Kansas City	MO	**E+**	E+	E+	8.3	1.58	0.0	47.1	0.0	0.0	**6.6**	8.6
Heartland Credit Union	Springfield	IL	**B+**	B+	B+	279.6	5.97	0.0	68.6	3.3	0.0	**9.0**	10.4
Heartland Credit Union	Hutchinson	KS	**B**	B	B	284.5	3.04	20.9	31.1	43.8	5.2	**7.7**	9.5
Heartland Credit Union	Inver Grove Heights	MN	**B-**	B-	B	114.8	2.35	0.0	34.5	16.8	6.1	**7.9**	9.6
Heartland Credit Union	Madison	WI	**B**	B	B-	256.8	8.35	18.3	26.9	39.9	0.0	**8.2**	9.8
Heartland Federal Credit Union	Dayton	OH	**D+**	D+	D+	106.7	-1.08	1.2	36.4	10.0	26.5	**10.0**	12.1
▲ Heekin Can Employees Credit Union	Cincinnati	OH	**C-**	D+	D	<1	-2.57	0.0	44.8	0.0	0.0	**10.0**	42.4
Heights Auto Workers Credit Union	Chicago Heights	IL	**D+**	D+	C-	39.7	1.96	0.0	11.8	2.7	0.0	**10.0**	14.1
Heights Community Federal Credit Union	Bethlehem	PA	**E-**	E-	E-	11.9	4.91	0.0	18.4	19.3	0.0	**5.3**	7.3
Helco Federal Credit Union	Hilo	HI	**C+**	C+	B	42.0	2.92	1.1	19.0	1.1	0.0	**10.0**	17.3
Helena Community Credit Union	Helena	MT	**B**	B	B	193.6	3.96	0.5	30.6	13.1	14.9	**10.0**	11.2
HEMA Federal Credit Union	Silver Spring	MD	**D**	D	D+	14.7	1.82	0.0	32.0	0.0	52.5	**8.5**	10.0
Hemingford Community FCU	Hemingford	NE	**C-**	C-	C-	6.7	8.41	5.0	26.2	7.9	0.0	**8.3**	9.9
Hempfield Area Federal Credit Union	Greensburg	PA	**C**	C	C-	6.4	2.03	0.0	19.0	0.0	0.0	**10.0**	12.2
Henderson State University FCU	Arkadelphia	AR	**C+**	C+	C+	10.4	-1.42	0.0	53.2	0.0	0.0	**10.0**	14.8
Henrico Federal Credit Union	Henrico	VA	**C+**	C+	B-	248.1	14.77	0.0	38.3	9.9	8.4	**5.7**	7.7
▼ Hercules Credit Union	Salt Lake City	UT	**C**	C+	B-	67.4	6.18	0.6	16.8	8.8	15.2	**9.3**	10.5
Hereford Texas Federal Credit Union	Hereford	TX	**B+**	B+	B	50.5	2.52	6.5	65.7	0.0	0.0	**10.0**	20.0
Heritage Community Credit Union	Sacramento	CA	**C-**	C-	C	204.8	-0.23	3.8	43.1	22.1	0.9	**7.4**	9.3

Asset Quality Index	Non-Performing Loans as a % of Total Loans	Non-Performing Loans as a % of Capital	Net Charge-Offs Avg Loans	Profitability Index	Net Income ($Mil)	Return on Assets	Return on Equity	Net Interest Spread	Overhead Efficiency Ratio	Liquidity Index	Liquidity Ratio	Hot Money Ratio	Stability Index
5.5	1.82	12.8	0.67	**0.5**	-0.14	-1.07	-12.21	3.28	103.9	**3.6**	11.5	5.9	**3.7**
10.0	0.22	0.6	-0.10	**2.0**	0.01	0.08	0.69	2.24	95.8	**4.3**	14.8	3.7	**5.7**
10.0	0.20	1.0	0.41	**3.6**	1.36	0.37	3.29	3.33	80.1	**5.2**	25.5	2.9	**7.6**
8.7	0.57	2.3	0.25	**1.6**	0.00	0.08	1.03	2.41	97.1	**5.3**	22.8	0.0	**2.1**
10.0	0.06	0.1	-0.04	**2.7**	0.04	0.42	2.73	2.22	93.0	**4.8**	21.9	0.7	**6.4**
9.6	0.16	0.6	0.19	**4.9**	1.20	0.79	6.50	2.62	75.9	**4.3**	22.5	8.9	**9.3**
9.9	0.33	1.2	0.62	**4.5**	2.03	0.51	4.57	3.21	77.4	**5.5**	23.7	2.2	**8.2**
5.8	1.08	7.4	0.35	**2.3**	-0.01	-0.55	-6.44	4.17	112.7	**4.3**	52.2	30.0	**1.7**
8.0	0.52	3.8	0.16	**5.1**	0.05	0.70	7.15	4.62	84.5	**4.1**	18.1	0.0	**5.5**
3.3	2.71	20.4	0.00	**2.4**	0.02	0.11	1.03	3.79	95.9	**2.9**	20.7	18.3	**5.0**
9.0	1.42	3.7	0.00	**5.5**	0.06	0.83	6.10	2.84	54.2	**7.1**	49.7	0.0	**7.5**
5.2	0.71	5.2	-0.11	**2.9**	0.00	0.08	0.90	3.61	90.2	**4.2**	14.8	0.0	**2.3**
6.5	0.70	6.5	-0.12	**4.3**	0.05	0.76	7.83	3.53	79.6	**5.3**	33.5	2.1	**5.2**
10.0	0.36	1.3	0.05	**3.5**	0.11	0.52	4.72	2.68	88.7	**6.2**	42.0	0.0	**5.3**
7.2	0.05	0.2	0.43	**3.7**	0.00	0.43	4.31	4.91	82.2	**5.2**	35.3	0.0	**3.0**
7.7	0.61	4.3	0.00	**2.6**	0.01	0.31	3.24	4.08	92.4	**4.7**	23.6	0.0	**4.9**
10.0	0.30	1.6	0.15	**6.3**	0.11	0.77	5.94	3.65	85.9	**3.4**	22.4	10.2	**6.8**
10.0	0.10	0.3	2.33	**3.6**	-0.04	-1.33	-11.20	2.37	113.8	**5.2**	32.7	0.0	**6.4**
8.2	1.07	3.3	0.85	**0.1**	-0.02	-1.09	-8.39	3.83	93.9	**6.5**	62.5	0.0	**5.0**
9.8	0.09	0.2	0.94	**7.0**	0.07	1.12	7.25	3.41	80.7	**5.5**	32.9	2.2	**6.3**
4.6	1.11	14.9	0.13	**2.6**	0.08	0.59	6.33	4.50	93.1	**4.8**	23.5	3.6	**3.3**
8.5	2.42	4.3	1.16	**3.1**	0.01	0.12	0.50	3.62	93.0	**4.4**	27.6	9.0	**6.4**
10.0	0.43	0.9	-0.44	**4.2**	0.05	0.65	4.56	2.73	80.3	**5.8**	40.4	0.0	**6.7**
9.3	0.13	0.4	1.60	**4.4**	0.01	0.16	1.47	4.25	96.6	**6.3**	39.2	2.3	**5.3**
6.4	0.00	8.3	0.13	**0.1**	-0.01	-0.79	-10.26	3.28	119.6	**5.1**	18.9	0.0	**3.0**
5.6	2.04	11.1	0.84	**1.4**	-0.01	-0.55	-7.11	3.98	104.4	**5.2**	27.2	1.3	**1.0**
9.7	0.50	1.9	0.47	**4.1**	0.33	0.40	2.95	3.43	85.0	**4.3**	12.8	1.1	**8.0**
6.8	0.54	9.0	-0.04	**3.6**	0.13	0.49	5.95	3.08	86.0	**4.9**	28.6	0.0	**5.0**
7.5	1.27	3.4	0.02	**1.3**	0.00	-0.01	-0.13	3.18	100.3	**5.9**	31.7	1.0	**5.6**
6.9	0.77	3.6	0.02	**2.3**	0.06	0.26	2.75	2.45	90.0	**5.2**	25.9	2.8	**3.7**
3.4	1.60	14.4	0.41	**3.0**	0.05	0.39	5.16	3.74	92.6	**2.9**	14.7	11.8	**2.3**
5.9	1.62	6.4	1.50	**2.2**	0.00	0.04	0.30	4.76	87.3	**5.9**	45.6	1.5	**5.8**
6.3	0.74	4.9	0.35	**4.7**	0.10	0.58	6.76	4.06	84.8	**3.7**	13.2	7.7	**4.0**
9.9	0.45	1.2	0.05	**1.5**	0.00	-0.02	-0.14	2.34	99.3	**6.0**	44.5	0.7	**5.5**
3.3	2.15	12.6	1.25	**1.0**	0.00	0.00	0.00	7.86	91.9	**5.5**	25.6	0.0	**1.0**
9.3	0.73	2.8	0.63	**0.7**	-0.03	-0.30	-2.39	3.14	97.9	**5.0**	22.7	0.0	**5.8**
10.0	0.00	0.0	0.00	**1.6**	0.00	0.00	0.00	4.17	100.0	**8.0**	88.1	0.0	**4.6**
9.5	1.33	2.8	0.59	**2.5**	0.01	0.11	0.90	2.58	87.3	**5.3**	39.7	6.9	**5.8**
7.1	0.17	3.3	-0.08	**0.7**	-0.02	-0.13	-1.83	3.65	103.6	**5.9**	41.9	2.2	**2.2**
6.2	1.22	6.9	2.24	**1.2**	-0.15	-0.56	-4.67	4.99	86.8	**4.8**	27.6	0.8	**6.3**
10.0	0.18	0.3	0.15	**1.3**	0.01	0.11	0.45	2.39	95.5	**5.0**	37.3	2.7	**6.6**
1.8	4.75	27.8	0.67	**4.7**	0.01	0.64	7.34	5.35	88.5	**6.1**	51.3	0.0	**1.0**
8.4	0.07	0.5	0.35	**4.5**	0.31	0.46	4.36	3.40	81.1	**4.2**	19.3	2.1	**7.1**
6.7	0.51	5.0	0.18	**5.0**	0.42	0.60	6.33	3.52	84.1	**2.3**	6.9	12.7	**7.6**
7.9	0.56	3.4	0.21	**3.5**	0.08	0.30	3.02	3.09	90.1	**4.2**	19.0	3.0	**6.6**
7.0	0.58	5.0	0.17	**4.3**	0.28	0.45	5.03	4.01	88.1	**3.7**	13.4	6.9	**6.2**
7.9	1.05	5.2	0.64	**0.6**	-0.01	-0.03	-0.26	3.07	94.6	**4.4**	20.5	1.0	**5.3**
8.1	1.97	2.5	2.83	**1.5**	0.00	0.00	0.00	4.87	100.0	**5.1**	25.7	0.0	**5.7**
9.1	3.32	3.5	0.82	**1.5**	0.00	0.02	0.13	2.76	99.6	**7.1**	51.4	1.0	**5.5**
1.7	6.86	38.7	0.37	**2.4**	0.00	0.07	0.93	3.60	100.0	**6.1**	42.8	0.0	**0.3**
10.0	0.28	0.7	0.20	**3.0**	0.05	0.43	2.48	2.41	81.0	**3.0**	17.3	25.4	**6.7**
9.3	0.25	1.7	0.44	**3.3**	0.16	0.34	3.04	2.98	83.9	**3.6**	12.4	7.4	**7.2**
7.5	1.17	3.7	1.78	**0.8**	0.00	0.03	0.27	3.37	99.1	**5.5**	22.9	0.0	**3.2**
9.9	0.00	0.0	0.00	**2.6**	0.01	0.38	3.68	3.28	86.3	**6.1**	44.2	0.0	**5.3**
9.8	1.15	2.1	0.00	**3.7**	0.01	0.50	4.09	1.80	69.2	**5.8**	42.2	0.0	**6.4**
5.6	1.74	8.7	0.05	**8.6**	0.04	1.61	11.06	3.66	72.0	**2.3**	31.1	29.4	**7.9**
7.9	0.57	4.5	0.22	**3.5**	0.23	0.38	5.52	3.04	86.7	**4.4**	29.8	6.1	**3.6**
9.7	0.34	1.5	-0.01	**2.6**	0.02	0.11	1.23	2.67	95.2	**4.5**	21.5	3.0	**4.9**
7.7	0.42	1.5	0.28	**8.8**	0.14	1.16	5.74	5.40	73.8	**3.8**	25.7	13.0	**7.0**
6.0	1.16	10.2	2.12	**2.3**	0.30	0.58	6.29	3.02	79.2	**3.5**	13.5	2.0	**5.0**

Name	City	State	Rating	2016 Rating	2015 Rating	Total Assets ($Mil)	One Year Asset Growth	Asset Mix (As a % of Total Assets) Commercial Loans	Consumer Loans	Mortgage Loans	Securities	Capitalization Index	Net Worth Ratio
Heritage Credit Union	Madison	WI	**B**	B	B	323.5	9.30	1.5	28.0	31.1	2.1	**10.0**	12.0
Heritage Family Federal Credit Union	Rutland	VT	**B+**	B+	B+	451.3	13.24	10.7	26.7	30.5	1.6	**7.8**	9.5
Heritage Federal Credit Union	Newburgh	IN	**B-**	B-	B-	562.4	8.87	0.0	46.0	14.8	6.7	**8.2**	9.8
Heritage Grove Federal Credit Union	Salem	OR	**B-**	B-	B-	114.9	10.17	3.3	25.3	14.5	13.6	**6.3**	8.3
Heritage South Community Credit Union	Shelbyville	TN	**A**	A	A	187.6	9.63	10.5	31.9	19.9	4.8	**10.0**	14.5
Heritage South Credit Union	Sylacauga	AL	**B**	B	B-	118.7	8.34	2.0	27.0	32.4	7.5	**9.6**	10.8
Heritage Trust Federal Credit Union	Summerville	SC	**B**	B	B	583.3	10.25	0.5	23.7	20.0	22.2	**7.6**	9.5
Heritage USA Federal Credit Union	Midland	TX	**D-**	D-	D+	50.6	-4.39	0.0	45.8	0.0	14.3	**4.9**	7.0
▲ Heritage Valley Federal Credit Union	York	PA	**C-**	D+	C	82.7	6.08	0.0	28.4	7.8	1.8	**8.0**	9.7
Hermantown Federal Credit Union	Hermantown	MN	**B**	B	B-	140.6	6.81	2.4	34.2	13.6	1.9	**9.2**	10.4
Hershey Federal Credit Union	Hummelstown	PA	**C-**	C-	C-	64.1	6.69	11.5	22.5	29.1	0.0	**5.5**	7.5
Hershey Robinson Employees Credit Union	Robinson	IL	**C+**	C+	B-	2.6	1.94	0.0	69.2	0.0	0.0	**10.0**	23.9
HFS Federal Credit Union	Hilo	HI	**B-**	B-	C+	538.1	5.18	0.3	15.6	13.2	44.5	**8.1**	9.7
Hi-Land Credit Union	Salt Lake City	UT	**A-**	A-	A-	51.7	7.64	2.2	11.7	30.0	28.4	**10.0**	16.6
Hialeah Municipal Employees FCU	Hialeah	FL	**B-**	B-	B-	11.3	3.79	0.0	36.6	0.0	22.2	**10.0**	33.4
Hibbing Cooperative Credit Union	Hibbing	MN	**C**	C	C	75.4	5.38	0.0	9.9	5.9	13.0	**10.0**	11.4
Hickam Federal Credit Union	Honolulu	HI	**C+**	C+	C+	579.8	5.28	0.6	15.8	16.4	22.7	**7.6**	9.4
Hidden River Credit Union	Pottsville	PA	**D+**	D+	D	141.1	19.78	0.0	13.0	10.0	15.8	**7.0**	9.0
High Desert Community Credit Union	Aztec	NM	**C+**	C+	C+	12.2	13.31	7.7	45.5	21.7	3.0	**9.2**	10.5
High Peaks Federal Credit Union	Dillon	MT	**D**	D	D	22.4	2.38	0.0	21.5	2.6	0.0	**6.1**	8.1
High Sierra Credit Union	Bishop	CA	**C+**	C+	C+	13.0	-2.96	0.0	22.0	0.0	63.6	**10.0**	13.4
High Street Baptist Church FCU	Roanoke	VA	**D+**	D+	D	1.9	7.26	0.0	25.3	0.0	0.0	**9.9**	10.9
Highmark Federal Credit Union	Rapid City	SD	**C+**	C+	C+	111.2	1.62	21.1	28.3	25.1	0.2	**6.3**	8.3
Highway Alliance Credit Union	Jefferson City	MO	**C+**	C+	C	22.1	5.29	0.0	31.6	16.5	0.0	**10.0**	11.7
Highway District 19 Employees CU	Atlanta	TX	**D+**	D+	D+	12.0	-1.29	0.0	31.6	0.4	0.0	**10.0**	12.0
Highway District 2 Credit Union	Fort Worth	TX	**D+**	D+	C	6.0	-2.66	0.0	37.1	0.0	0.0	**10.0**	19.5
▲ Highway District 21 Federal Credit Union	Pharr	TX	**B-**	C+	C+	41.6	1.59	0.0	39.0	0.0	0.0	**10.0**	15.8
Highway District 9 Credit Union	Waco	TX	**C**	C	C	4.7	-2.20	0.0	31.0	2.4	0.0	**10.0**	20.4
Highway Employees Credit Union	Tyler	TX	**C**	C	C	1.6	2.48	0.0	46.6	0.0	0.0	**10.0**	25.7
Highway Federal Credit Union	Pittston	PA	**C+**	C+	C+	23.5	5.60	0.0	34.6	14.6	15.3	**10.0**	15.5
Hilco Federal Credit Union	Kerrville	TX	**E+**	E+	E+	7.8	-11.42	1.2	38.8	0.0	0.0	**4.6**	6.6
Hill District Federal Credit Union	Pittsburgh	PA	**E+**	E+	E+	4.8	8.84	0.0	34.0	0.0	0.0	**6.1**	8.1
Hillcrest Federal Credit Union	Tulsa	OK	**D**	D	D	13.6	-2.31	0.0	45.1	0.0	0.0	**10.0**	15.0
Hiway Federal Credit Union	Saint Paul	MN	**B+**	B+	A-	1098.9	5.88	3.2	21.9	36.8	22.7	**9.5**	10.7
▲ HMC (NJ) Federal Credit Union	Flemington	NJ	**C-**	D+	D	6.2	3.88	0.0	23.2	0.0	0.0	**10.0**	11.8
Hobart Indiana School Employees FCU	Hobart	IN	**D-**	D-	E+	2.2	5.55	0.0	53.9	0.0	0.0	**7.0**	9.0
Hoboken New Jersey Police FCU	Hoboken	NJ	**C-**	C-	D+	9.4	5.38	0.0	20.8	0.0	0.0	**10.0**	21.6
Hoboken School Employees FCU	Hoboken	NJ	**B**	B	B	50.4	8.20	0.0	4.8	39.5	0.0	**10.0**	26.7
Hockley County School Employees CU	Levelland	TX	**C+**	C+	B-	31.5	-1.56	0.0	54.8	0.0	11.7	**10.0**	12.2
Holley Credit Union	Paris	TN	**B**	B	B	53.8	9.47	0.0	64.9	0.1	2.1	**10.0**	11.1
HollyFrontier Employee's Credit Union	West Bountiful	UT	**C+**	C+	C+	6.8	4.80	0.0	90.3	2.1	0.0	**10.0**	17.7
▼ Holsey Temple Federal Credit Union	Philadelphia	PA	**D**	D+	D+	<1	-9.09	0.0	13.3	0.0	0.0	**10.0**	40.0
Holston Methodist Federal Credit Union	Knoxville	TN	**D-**	D-	E+	14.9	2.72	8.6	43.5	25.7	0.0	**5.1**	7.1
Holy Family Memorial Credit Union	Manitowoc	WI	**C**	C	C	14.8	1.52	0.0	19.9	33.3	0.0	**9.0**	10.3
Holy Family Parma Federal Credit Union	Parma	OH	**C**	C	C	21.5	2.98	0.0	5.1	3.5	52.1	**10.0**	14.2
Holy Ghost Parish Credit Union	Dubuque	IA	**C-**	C-	C-	27.9	1.68	0.0	1.0	0.0	0.0	**10.0**	11.1
Holy Redeemer Community of SE Wisconsin CU	Milwaukee	WI	**C-**	C-	D+	<1	-31.52	0.0	9.6	0.0	0.0	**10.0**	17.9
Holy Rosary Church Federal Credit Union	Wilkes-Barre	PA	**D**	D	D+	<1	-6.27	0.0	40.8	0.0	0.0	**10.0**	17.7
Holy Rosary Credit Union	Kansas City	MO	**E+**	E+	D-	22.1	10.12	1.3	20.2	8.1	0.0	**4.8**	6.8
Holy Rosary Credit Union	Rochester	NH	**B**	B	B	258.5	9.23	3.1	21.8	34.3	3.7	**6.9**	8.9
Holy Trinity Baptist FCU	Philadelphia	PA	**B**	B	B-	<1	-8.70	0.0	28.6	0.0	0.0	**10.0**	23.8
Holyoke Community Federal Credit Union	Holyoke	CO	**C-**	C-	D+	30.8	-3.46	1.1	17.9	57.3	0.0	**6.5**	8.5
Holyoke Credit Union	Holyoke	MA	**C+**	C+	B-	184.5	12.61	6.4	18.1	33.1	14.9	**7.7**	9.5
Holyoke Postal Credit Union	Holyoke	MA	**D+**	D+	C-	3.3	-4.54	0.0	9.9	0.0	0.0	**10.0**	22.4
Home Town Federal Credit Union	Owatonna	MN	**B-**	B-	B-	136.2	12.01	0.0	49.7	12.5	4.2	**7.5**	9.4
▲ Homefield Credit Union	North Grafton	MA	**C-**	D+	D	144.2	6.10	11.9	13.3	35.5	16.2	**7.3**	9.4
Homeland Credit Union	Chillicothe	OH	**B+**	B+	A-	392.3	4.09	0.5	15.1	10.5	51.9	**10.0**	17.6
▼ Homeport Federal Credit Union	Corpus Christi	TX	**D-**	D	D	15.5	-4.31	0.0	42.4	0.9	0.0	**9.1**	10.4
Homestead Federal Credit Union	Billings	MT	**C-**	C-	C	5.1	35.79	0.0	73.5	0.0	0.0	**9.7**	10.8
HOMETOWN Credit Union	Shenandoah	IA	**C**	C	C+	2.5	-3.23	0.0	64.2	0.0	0.0	**10.0**	24.5

Asset Quality Index	Non-Performing Loans as a % of Total Loans	Non-Performing Loans as a % of Capital	Net Charge-Offs Avg Loans	Profitability Index	Net Income ($Mil)	Return on Assets	Return on Equity	Net Interest Spread	Overhead Efficiency Ratio	Liquidity Index	Liquidity Ratio	Hot Money Ratio	Stability Index
9.6	0.28	2.2	0.14	**4.5**	0.52	0.65	5.63	3.39	81.8	**3.2**	13.6	8.5	**7.9**
6.5	0.69	7.0	0.49	**5.4**	0.73	0.65	7.80	4.78	78.3	**3.8**	14.3	4.9	**6.1**
6.7	0.55	4.6	0.47	**3.7**	0.65	0.47	4.73	3.17	78.3	**4.2**	21.9	7.1	**7.3**
7.6	0.62	5.6	0.10	**4.6**	0.18	0.64	7.45	3.33	82.5	**5.4**	31.4	3.0	**4.7**
6.7	1.40	7.5	0.35	**10.0**	0.75	1.64	11.30	5.60	72.1	**2.7**	17.1	18.6	**9.2**
7.1	0.61	6.3	0.32	**4.2**	0.19	0.64	6.68	4.68	79.7	**3.9**	17.7	8.8	**6.4**
7.3	0.52	5.9	0.83	**4.2**	0.64	0.45	4.74	3.98	83.5	**4.1**	17.6	3.7	**6.3**
6.2	0.19	2.5	0.67	**2.9**	0.10	0.82	11.73	3.78	93.3	**5.0**	26.5	3.0	**1.0**
7.6	0.57	3.4	0.34	**2.1**	0.02	0.12	1.34	4.23	95.3	**4.6**	19.7	0.3	**3.5**
6.9	0.98	6.2	0.22	**5.2**	0.26	0.74	7.04	4.30	83.4	**4.3**	18.3	2.1	**7.1**
7.5	0.41	3.1	-0.04	**2.2**	0.01	0.05	0.67	3.36	97.6	**4.4**	23.1	0.7	**3.2**
7.9	1.04	2.8	0.00	**6.8**	0.01	1.57	6.42	5.54	64.3	**5.5**	35.9	0.0	**5.0**
7.6	1.33	4.8	0.32	**4.1**	0.77	0.58	5.96	2.96	79.5	**5.5**	23.3	3.4	**7.1**
10.0	0.02	0.1	-0.05	**7.8**	0.15	1.13	6.84	2.47	56.0	**2.7**	29.3	31.5	**8.3**
9.9	0.00	0.0	0.64	**4.9**	0.02	0.61	1.81	4.13	82.4	**4.8**	28.0	0.0	**7.6**
8.4	1.77	3.8	0.28	**2.5**	0.03	0.13	1.28	2.25	89.1	**7.5**	67.2	0.0	**4.8**
10.0	0.33	1.6	0.41	**3.6**	0.86	0.60	6.39	2.46	73.5	**4.0**	26.4	15.9	**6.2**
7.7	1.47	6.3	0.17	**1.7**	0.06	0.18	1.99	2.21	91.0	**5.1**	29.1	3.1	**5.5**
4.9	0.86	6.6	0.04	**7.6**	0.06	2.11	20.13	4.04	53.0	**3.2**	13.5	4.6	**8.0**
6.7	0.84	3.9	0.32	**1.8**	0.02	0.43	5.32	3.10	85.8	**5.4**	29.6	0.0	**1.7**
9.9	0.27	1.0	0.00	**3.7**	0.02	0.55	4.16	2.54	88.8	**5.3**	38.5	0.0	**6.0**
10.0	0.00	0.0	0.00	**1.2**	0.00	0.00	0.00	2.83	100.0	**6.5**	64.2	2.8	**6.3**
5.5	0.72	7.6	0.36	**3.4**	0.10	0.35	4.50	3.96	92.3	**2.7**	10.7	9.1	**4.9**
9.7	0.53	2.3	0.14	**3.0**	0.02	0.33	2.80	2.72	80.0	**4.3**	19.7	4.2	**5.9**
9.6	0.06	0.7	0.00	**0.4**	-0.01	-0.37	-3.05	2.65	111.7	**5.8**	42.5	0.0	**5.4**
9.9	0.00	0.0	0.71	**0.8**	0.00	-0.19	-1.02	2.82	107.1	**5.5**	52.7	0.0	**6.3**
7.9	1.34	4.3	0.00	**3.4**	0.05	0.47	3.00	1.94	74.2	**3.3**	47.1	25.3	**7.3**
9.5	0.42	0.7	0.00	**3.5**	0.01	0.60	2.95	3.12	76.5	**5.0**	30.9	0.0	**6.8**
7.9	0.27	0.7	1.83	**3.5**	0.00	-0.25	-0.96	5.65	85.7	**4.0**	31.0	8.7	**7.4**
6.7	2.76	8.5	1.91	**5.2**	0.03	0.47	2.98	4.91	69.9	**5.5**	36.0	5.8	**5.0**
6.2	0.71	5.0	0.42	**0.0**	-0.04	-1.78	-25.93	5.20	133.7	**3.7**	30.1	15.0	**1.2**
0.3	4.98	61.8	-0.18	**2.2**	0.00	0.35	10.67	5.68	90.4	**6.5**	44.2	0.0	**1.5**
7.6	0.76	2.5	0.69	**0.3**	-0.02	-0.45	-2.93	3.08	108.3	**5.0**	44.9	0.0	**5.7**
9.8	0.19	1.3	0.13	**4.5**	1.45	0.54	5.29	2.85	86.7	**4.1**	24.1	6.3	**7.7**
10.0	0.00	0.0	0.54	**1.6**	0.00	0.26	2.20	2.69	85.0	**5.1**	20.7	0.0	**5.6**
4.3	1.91	10.8	0.00	**4.1**	0.00	0.55	6.09	3.97	75.0	**6.5**	49.0	0.0	**2.3**
6.2	3.96	12.1	-0.18	**4.5**	0.01	0.51	2.37	3.95	86.5	**2.7**	22.0	16.3	**3.7**
9.5	1.27	2.2	-0.03	**3.8**	0.03	0.28	1.01	2.41	88.2	**4.1**	30.4	10.0	**7.5**
5.8	0.63	5.3	1.40	**3.4**	0.03	0.36	2.94	4.10	84.4	**1.6**	8.2	35.9	**4.9**
7.5	0.31	1.9	0.18	**6.1**	0.11	0.86	7.64	4.43	73.3	**4.4**	20.2	3.2	**6.3**
6.4	0.82	4.2	0.50	**9.4**	0.03	1.57	8.74	4.77	59.7	**1.2**	8.8	25.2	**5.0**
1.0	100.00	28.6	0.00	**0.8**	0.00	0.00	0.00	0.00	0.0	**8.6**	152.6	0.0	**4.8**
5.5	0.29	6.5	-0.14	**2.4**	0.00	0.03	0.38	4.95	100.0	**3.6**	16.5	4.3	**1.7**
9.6	0.10	0.7	0.00	**2.8**	0.01	0.14	1.31	3.20	94.3	**4.2**	14.8	0.8	**5.4**
8.0	5.32	5.2	0.66	**1.9**	0.00	0.07	0.52	1.60	96.3	**5.1**	27.6	3.8	**7.2**
10.0	0.30	0.0	0.00	**1.9**	0.02	0.23	2.07	0.92	74.6	**5.9**	43.7	0.0	**5.3**
9.2	4.96	4.2	0.00	**2.1**	0.00	0.00	0.00	8.33	100.0	**8.5**	100.3	0.0	**5.6**
6.9	4.10	7.7	0.00	**0.0**	0.00	-3.95	-21.43	10.26	200.0	**7.3**	66.3	0.0	**6.2**
6.5	1.11	6.4	0.37	**2.4**	0.03	0.48	7.01	4.30	92.2	**6.2**	44.3	0.0	**1.0**
9.4	0.19	2.0	0.27	**5.4**	0.48	0.75	8.40	3.42	80.4	**2.9**	13.5	12.7	**6.6**
10.0	0.00	0.0	0.00	**6.2**	0.00	0.00	0.00	0.00	0.0	**8.0**	93.8	0.0	**5.7**
6.2	0.89	8.8	0.10	**2.0**	0.00	-0.01	-0.15	3.70	100.4	**3.0**	26.0	16.6	**4.4**
9.7	0.10	0.7	0.21	**3.5**	0.16	0.36	3.76	3.14	89.4	**3.1**	22.6	17.4	**6.6**
10.0	0.00	0.0	0.00	**1.3**	0.00	0.12	0.55	1.71	100.0	**6.0**	27.2	0.0	**6.6**
8.4	0.10	0.9	-0.01	**4.3**	0.21	0.64	6.60	3.21	86.3	**4.2**	17.1	1.2	**5.8**
8.5	0.48	3.4	-0.02	**2.1**	0.09	0.24	2.58	3.15	93.1	**3.5**	12.0	12.2	**5.3**
9.9	0.89	1.7	0.49	**4.4**	0.48	0.49	2.91	2.20	75.3	**4.4**	21.3	10.7	**8.1**
5.7	1.96	9.2	3.16	**0.0**	-0.10	-2.49	-23.04	4.42	119.4	**5.2**	30.9	4.5	**4.5**
2.5	1.54	12.2	2.49	**3.7**	-0.02	-1.51	-13.48	5.84	85.9	**1.0**	8.9	32.9	**2.3**
2.2	13.21	32.0	-0.23	**8.2**	0.01	1.14	4.68	7.48	76.5	**3.9**	43.3	25.3	**7.7**

Name	City	State	Rating	2016 Rating	2015 Rating	Total Assets ($Mil)	One Year Asset Growth	Asset Mix (As a % of Total Assets) Comm-ercial Loans	Cons-umer Loans	Mort-gage Loans	Secur-ities	Capital-ization Index	Net Worth Ratio
Hometown Credit Union	Kulm	ND	**B**	B	B+	104.6	2.30	78.3	4.3	45.1	0.5	**10.0**	14.4
Hometown Federal Credit Union	Peru	IN	**B-**	B-	B-	23.7	4.06	0.7	50.4	0.0	0.0	**10.0**	15.3
Homewood Federal Credit Union	Homewood	IL	**D-**	D-	D-	2.9	-7.72	0.0	32.9	0.0	0.0	**8.1**	9.7
Honda Federal Credit Union	Torrance	CA	**B+**	B+	A-	762.2	5.23	0.1	35.9	29.1	15.8	**7.4**	9.6
Honea Federal Credit Union	Fort Shafter	HI	**D+**	D+	C-	23.1	-9.29	0.0	13.0	5.4	0.2	**9.5**	10.8
Honeywell Philadelphia Division FCU	Fort Washington	PA	**D**	D	D+	31.0	8.05	0.0	4.9	0.0	42.9	**7.1**	9.1
Honolulu Federal Credit Union	Honolulu	HI	**C+**	C+	C	253.6	2.61	1.3	22.9	23.2	27.0	**10.0**	11.2
Honolulu Fire Department FCU	Honolulu	HI	**C**	C	C	70.8	3.59	0.0	29.9	6.4	15.5	**8.7**	10.3
Honor Credit Union	Berrien Springs	MI	**A**	A	A	734.9	7.72	11.9	32.4	32.3	11.3	**9.6**	10.8
Hoosier Hills Credit Union	Bedford	IN	**B**	B	B	500.7	11.00	30.0	12.4	56.4	6.7	**7.7**	9.4
Hoosier United Credit Union	Indianapolis	IN	**D**	D	D	21.6	0.75	0.0	26.7	0.0	15.3	**6.2**	8.2
Hope Federal Credit Union	Jackson	MS	**D-**	D-	D	205.0	11.26	31.9	3.8	68.0	9.7	**9.6**	10.7
Hope Federal Credit Union	Bridgeport	WV	**B**	B	B	34.8	1.76	0.0	27.0	0.0	7.1	**10.0**	15.5
Hopes Employees Federal Credit Union	Jamestown	NY	**C-**	C-	D+	<1	4.78	0.0	57.3	0.0	0.0	**9.5**	10.6
Hopewell Chemical Federal Credit Union	Hopewell	VA	**C**	C	C-	38.3	11.14	0.0	38.4	0.0	0.0	**7.0**	9.0
Hopewell Federal Credit Union	Heath	OH	**C+**	C+	C+	87.8	7.93	9.7	17.1	35.0	6.2	**6.7**	8.7
Hopkins County Teachers FCU	Madisonville	KY	**C+**	C+	C+	11.3	3.75	0.0	16.2	4.8	0.0	**10.0**	17.5
Horizon Credit Union	Macon	MO	**B**	B	B-	27.9	1.93	0.8	57.5	0.4	26.4	**10.0**	12.2
Horizon Credit Union	Kingsport	TN	**C+**	C+	C	46.4	2.17	0.0	32.1	22.1	0.0	**9.9**	10.9
Horizon Credit Union	Spokane Valley	WA	**B+**	B+	B	940.1	14.06	0.2	23.0	15.2	0.3	**9.4**	10.6
Horizon Federal Credit Union	Williamsport	PA	**D+**	D+	C-	72.9	9.84	0.0	35.0	15.5	21.0	**7.6**	9.4
Horizon Utah Federal Credit Union	Farmington	UT	**B**	B	B	139.9	7.10	3.5	25.0	17.2	9.6	**9.1**	10.4
Horizons Federal Credit Union	Binghamton	NY	**B-**	B-	B-	108.7	4.05	0.0	24.7	22.0	19.7	**10.0**	11.6
Horizons North Credit Union	Northglenn	CO	**B-**	B-	C-	83.0	10.80	18.4	29.7	12.7	0.4	**6.4**	8.4
Hornell Erie Federal Credit Union	Hornell	NY	**D+**	D+	D	4.5	-4.87	0.0	51.6	0.0	0.0	**10.0**	12.3
▲ Hotel & Travel Industry FCU	Honolulu	HI	**D+**	D	D+	33.3	-0.33	2.7	24.2	12.9	12.6	**6.4**	8.8
Houston Belt & Terminal FCU	Humble	TX	**C+**	C+	C	4.2	-1.93	0.0	44.9	0.0	0.0	**10.0**	24.1
Houston Federal Credit Union	Sugar Land	TX	**B-**	B-	B-	619.7	5.29	0.0	42.0	12.5	6.3	**5.8**	7.8
▼ Houston Highway Credit Union	Houston	TX	**D-**	D	D+	57.8	-6.64	0.3	36.8	26.5	9.4	**5.2**	7.3
Houston Metropolitan Employees FCU	Houston	TX	**B-**	B-	C+	53.8	7.01	0.0	58.0	5.5	6.0	**9.3**	10.5
Houston Musicians Federal Credit Union	Houston	TX	**C-**	C-	C-	5.5	9.08	10.9	12.9	0.0	0.0	**10.0**	11.8
Houston Police Federal Credit Union	Houston	TX	**A**	A	A	679.8	7.64	0.0	42.2	7.9	33.0	**10.0**	13.5
Houston Texas Fire Fighters FCU	Houston	TX	**B+**	B+	B+	259.2	0.91	0.1	35.6	8.3	12.9	**10.0**	14.5
Howard County Education FCU	Ellicott City	MD	**D**	D	D	21.4	2.88	0.0	54.6	8.9	13.8	**7.2**	9.1
Howard County School Employees FCU	Kokomo	IN	**C**	C	C	32.2	-2.12	0.0	21.8	2.3	0.0	**10.0**	11.7
Howard University Employees FCU	Washington	DC	**D**	D	D	10.3	-1.48	0.0	17.7	6.1	0.0	**10.0**	19.0
HOYA Federal Credit Union	Washington	DC	**D-**	D-	D	20.8	-4.24	0.0	40.9	0.3	1.7	**5.9**	7.9
▼ HSM Federal Credit Union	Hickory	NC	**E+**	D-	D+	4.9	3.20	0.0	57.4	0.0	0.0	**7.9**	9.6
HTM Area Credit Union	Troy	OH	**B**	B	B	25.4	7.50	2.3	57.2	4.4	20.8	**10.0**	15.3
HTM Credit Union	Haverhill	MA	**C+**	C+	C+	20.3	4.36	0.0	17.0	21.4	3.9	**10.0**	15.7
Hub-Co Credit Union	Keokuk	IA	**C**	C	C	18.0	4.33	0.0	34.7	9.4	15.5	**9.2**	10.4
HUD Federal Credit Union	Washington	DC	**D+**	D+	D-	46.3	-2.16	0.0	24.9	16.6	15.8	**6.8**	8.8
Hudson Heritage Federal Credit Union	Middletown	NY	**B-**	B-	C+	361.3	6.11	0.3	41.2	23.0	2.5	**8.1**	9.7
Hudson River Community Credit Union	Corinth	NY	**A-**	A-	A-	231.7	8.42	1.0	31.3	41.7	0.1	**10.0**	12.3
Hudson River Financial FCU	Mohegan Lake	NY	**C-**	C-	C-	54.1	8.01	0.0	10.9	19.3	39.0	**5.5**	7.9
Hudson Valley Federal Credit Union	Poughkeepsie	NY	**B+**	B+	B+	4605.8	3.80	7.8	24.5	16.5	34.1	**8.3**	10.4
Hughes Federal Credit Union	Tucson	AZ	**B+**	B+	B+	1068.6	20.53	0.0	60.8	0.0	0.0	**7.5**	9.4
Hulman Field Technicians FCU	Terre Haute	IN	**C-**	C-	C-	8.1	-2.63	0.0	31.4	0.0	0.0	**10.0**	16.4
Huntington Beach City Employees CU	Huntington Beach	CA	**C+**	C+	C+	57.5	5.73	0.4	10.3	1.3	19.9	**8.1**	9.7
▼ Huntington C&O Railway Employees FCU	Huntington	WV	**C-**	C	C+	39.7	15.89	0.0	72.4	11.9	0.0	**9.3**	10.5
Huntington County Federal Credit Union	Huntington	IN	**C-**	C-	C-	3.6	-1.99	0.0	57.2	0.0	0.0	**10.0**	11.9
Huntington West Virginia Firemen's FCU	Huntington	WV	**C-**	C-	C	3.9	1.90	0.0	58.9	0.0	0.0	**10.0**	17.7
Huntingtonized Federal Credit Union	Huntington	WV	**B+**	B+	B	30.5	8.41	0.4	31.8	22.1	0.0	**10.0**	15.4
Hurd Employees Credit Union	Greeneville	TN	**C+**	C+	C+	3.1	4.15	0.0	72.9	0.0	0.0	**10.0**	42.4
Huron Area Education FCU	Huron	SD	**D**	D	D	13.4	-2.16	1.2	21.6	28.2	9.8	**5.4**	7.4
Huron C&NW Federal Credit Union	Huron	SD	**E+**	E+	E+	5.6	-7.26	0.0	71.2	0.0	0.0	**5.3**	7.3
Hurricane Creek Federal Credit Union	Benton	AR	**B**	B	B	29.2	8.16	0.0	54.1	0.7	16.9	**10.0**	13.8
Hutchinson Government Employees CU	Hutchinson	KS	**C**	C	C	22.0	3.81	0.4	61.0	15.7	0.0	**10.0**	11.6
Hutchinson Postal and Community CU	Hutchinson	KS	**D+**	D+	D+	4.0	1.06	0.0	60.3	0.0	0.0	**10.0**	22.8
I B E W Local 56 Federal Credit Union	Erie	PA	**E+**	E+	E+	8.7	2.83	0.0	25.5	0.0	0.0	**5.2**	7.2

Asset Quality Index	Non-Performing Loans as a % of Total Loans	Non-Performing Loans as a % of Capital	Net Charge-Offs Avg Loans	Profitability Index	Net Income ($Mil)	Return on Assets	Return on Equity	Net Interest Spread	Overhead Efficiency Ratio	Liquidity Index	Liquidity Ratio	Hot Money Ratio	Stability Index
4.5	0.48	2.9	0.45	**9.8**	0.41	1.55	11.11	3.91	49.3	**1.5**	8.8	19.3	**10.0**
5.5	2.08	9.7	-0.07	**10.0**	0.15	2.58	16.80	5.89	64.4	**3.7**	10.1	1.2	**9.5**
6.1	1.97	7.0	0.00	**1.2**	0.00	0.28	2.86	3.01	95.0	**5.5**	41.1	0.0	**3.2**
9.7	0.22	2.0	0.14	**4.0**	0.55	0.29	3.15	3.65	91.3	**3.6**	11.6	9.3	**6.6**
7.9	0.92	3.2	0.33	**1.9**	0.01	0.13	1.30	2.04	93.3	**3.8**	19.6	10.5	**4.2**
5.4	10.12	12.7	0.00	**0.9**	-0.01	-0.07	-0.72	2.14	103.5	**6.5**	35.7	0.0	**3.1**
8.7	0.78	4.4	-0.01	**2.2**	0.07	0.11	1.03	2.98	88.3	**4.5**	13.9	0.9	**7.1**
9.0	0.23	1.2	1.17	**2.6**	0.03	0.19	1.82	3.12	92.8	**4.6**	22.0	1.4	**5.7**
8.7	0.27	2.3	0.37	**7.4**	2.25	1.25	11.63	3.93	72.8	**3.3**	12.1	8.3	**8.1**
6.9	0.30	3.8	0.30	**5.0**	1.01	0.82	8.68	3.75	80.2	**2.6**	7.6	10.5	**6.2**
7.6	0.99	3.6	0.86	**2.2**	0.01	0.10	1.14	2.37	93.1	**5.9**	44.9	0.0	**3.0**
0.3	4.59	102.5	0.64	**2.4**	0.06	0.12	5.02	3.69	92.9	**1.6**	14.8	48.8	**4.7**
10.0	0.21	0.4	0.00	**4.6**	0.07	0.81	5.21	2.39	62.6	**6.3**	53.9	0.0	**6.9**
6.5	0.29	1.5	0.00	**1.9**	0.00	-1.37	-12.50	8.19	142.9	**6.3**	45.4	0.0	**4.8**
7.7	0.87	4.3	0.12	**3.0**	0.02	0.18	1.98	3.16	89.9	**5.0**	21.8	2.4	**4.1**
9.1	0.15	1.2	0.10	**4.1**	0.15	0.70	9.27	3.40	81.4	**3.9**	12.7	3.4	**3.6**
10.0	0.00	0.0	0.00	**3.3**	0.01	0.29	1.62	2.17	87.3	**6.2**	48.3	0.0	**7.1**
8.5	0.23	1.1	0.25	**4.9**	0.04	0.59	4.74	4.23	83.5	**4.0**	15.5	6.0	**7.1**
4.3	1.21	19.2	0.05	**2.8**	0.02	0.16	1.43	4.61	96.8	**3.1**	13.7	13.1	**5.3**
7.8	0.37	3.5	0.28	**5.1**	1.91	0.83	7.77	3.88	71.8	**3.3**	14.0	11.5	**7.5**
7.4	0.59	4.3	0.12	**1.6**	-0.01	-0.07	-0.75	3.75	100.8	**4.0**	16.6	0.4	**4.3**
9.0	0.35	1.7	0.56	**3.8**	0.14	0.40	3.78	3.48	83.7	**4.4**	19.8	2.4	**7.1**
7.9	0.84	4.1	0.82	**2.8**	0.05	0.18	1.50	3.19	90.2	**4.0**	23.9	7.4	**7.3**
9.3	0.10	0.8	0.33	**3.5**	0.06	0.29	3.45	3.68	87.2	**4.3**	16.3	1.4	**3.9**
6.2	1.30	5.3	0.00	**2.5**	0.01	0.53	4.39	3.70	85.0	**4.3**	13.1	0.0	**5.3**
8.7	0.29	1.8	0.37	**1.5**	0.01	0.14	1.97	2.98	93.9	**4.4**	14.3	0.7	**2.8**
9.4	0.00	0.0	1.58	**8.2**	0.01	0.86	3.61	5.06	72.9	**4.6**	27.0	0.0	**5.7**
8.8	0.35	3.2	0.40	**5.1**	1.17	0.76	9.84	2.79	72.1	**4.5**	27.1	7.3	**5.1**
3.5	1.43	16.6	1.22	**0.6**	-0.22	-1.47	-24.28	4.87	99.7	**2.6**	11.2	17.4	**0.7**
6.3	0.57	4.2	0.32	**5.4**	0.06	0.45	5.21	6.04	86.0	**4.0**	13.3	5.0	**4.5**
8.6	0.52	1.9	0.60	**1.7**	0.00	-0.07	-0.61	4.45	100.0	**4.4**	57.0	16.1	**6.8**
8.6	0.89	3.6	0.70	**7.9**	1.69	1.02	7.66	2.48	55.7	**4.6**	12.0	1.5	**9.6**
9.5	0.23	1.0	0.33	**3.5**	0.19	0.30	2.03	3.23	87.1	**4.8**	39.2	7.7	**7.9**
5.8	0.61	4.1	0.64	**1.5**	-0.01	-0.09	-1.02	4.54	91.7	**4.2**	20.9	1.3	**3.4**
10.0	0.72	1.8	0.00	**2.6**	0.02	0.21	1.81	1.27	83.0	**4.7**	27.6	2.9	**5.8**
8.8	0.38	1.1	0.07	**0.0**	-0.05	-1.92	-9.84	3.73	152.7	**5.3**	32.7	0.0	**5.0**
3.7	4.27	21.9	0.39	**0.3**	-0.01	-0.09	-1.22	3.47	97.8	**4.6**	28.6	2.4	**2.0**
1.6	3.70	29.8	4.58	**0.0**	-0.03	-2.54	-24.79	5.73	85.4	**4.0**	36.7	7.8	**4.6**
7.9	0.61	2.6	0.36	**9.8**	0.12	1.97	12.71	3.96	57.6	**4.3**	20.3	2.8	**7.0**
10.0	0.02	0.1	0.00	**2.5**	0.00	0.08	0.50	3.02	96.7	**5.4**	25.9	0.0	**7.3**
6.6	1.92	9.1	0.05	**2.6**	0.01	0.27	2.56	3.29	90.8	**5.3**	33.3	0.0	**5.0**
6.6	1.39	6.6	0.81	**1.6**	0.02	0.13	1.48	3.30	91.2	**5.5**	40.9	0.0	**3.2**
7.2	0.77	6.7	0.55	**3.4**	0.14	0.16	1.59	4.45	84.9	**3.1**	7.8	3.2	**6.6**
7.3	0.76	5.3	0.34	**5.7**	0.52	0.91	7.32	4.68	79.8	**3.5**	16.3	8.3	**8.2**
9.6	0.00	0.0	0.17	**2.5**	0.02	0.14	1.76	3.20	93.9	**4.7**	18.2	2.0	**3.5**
7.5	0.87	5.3	1.05	**4.9**	7.99	0.71	7.11	3.18	60.6	**2.6**	9.4	17.8	**7.2**
5.8	0.40	4.8	0.87	**6.9**	1.85	0.72	7.49	4.50	65.5	**3.4**	23.3	15.8	**7.4**
9.3	1.16	2.7	0.39	**1.6**	0.00	0.05	0.30	2.42	89.4	**5.5**	27.7	0.0	**6.9**
10.0	0.00	0.0	0.52	**2.7**	0.03	0.22	2.23	2.55	93.6	**6.9**	48.3	1.4	**5.5**
1.8	3.01	24.5	2.39	**5.3**	0.09	0.89	8.44	5.63	52.7	**2.9**	10.4	4.3	**4.7**
8.0	0.32	1.9	0.00	**4.4**	0.01	0.67	5.74	4.52	87.8	**4.7**	29.9	0.0	**4.3**
6.7	0.72	2.7	0.00	**4.8**	0.01	0.51	2.89	5.33	87.0	**4.6**	27.7	0.0	**4.3**
8.0	0.81	3.2	1.06	**8.6**	0.07	0.95	6.09	7.20	82.7	**5.2**	28.3	0.0	**7.0**
5.4	3.44	6.4	0.90	**6.9**	0.00	0.26	0.62	4.49	81.1	**3.2**	19.0	0.0	**4.3**
4.4	2.60	16.7	-0.26	**3.6**	0.01	0.42	5.67	3.03	89.2	**4.2**	26.6	0.8	**2.3**
2.0	3.98	29.4	-0.17	**6.8**	0.02	1.56	22.39	4.55	65.6	**3.3**	7.8	0.0	**1.0**
8.2	0.28	1.7	0.10	**6.7**	0.08	1.10	7.83	3.49	73.8	**3.9**	20.3	4.5	**7.7**
4.2	2.26	14.3	1.39	**3.6**	0.00	-0.05	-0.47	5.11	71.9	**3.7**	24.3	10.4	**5.9**
5.6	2.94	7.6	3.55	**0.8**	-0.03	-2.73	-11.64	6.52	98.4	**4.6**	39.6	14.7	**6.6**
5.2	2.67	15.0	0.00	**1.9**	0.00	0.19	2.58	2.57	93.2	**5.0**	30.7	0.0	**1.0**

Name	City	State	Rating	2016 Rating	2015 Rating	Total Assets ($Mil)	One Year Asset Growth	Asset Mix (As a % of Total Assets) Commercial Loans	Consumer Loans	Mortgage Loans	Securities	Capitalization Index	Net Worth Ratio
I C Federal Credit Union	Indiana	PA	C-	C-	C-	3.0	-1.09	0.0	52.3	0.0	0.0	10.0	12.4
I C S Federal Credit Union	Elma	NY	E+	E+	E+	1.9	3.93	0.0	39.3	0.0	0.0	3.8	5.8
▼ I F F Employees Federal Credit Union	Hazlet	NJ	D	D+	D-	14.7	15.90	0.0	10.7	15.0	1.4	5.5	7.5
I H Mississippi Valley Credit Union	Moline	IL	C+	C+	C+	1123.1	11.03	9.3	50.1	19.1	9.5	6.6	8.8
I R E B Federal Credit Union	Brooklyn	NY	C	C	C-	3.8	-5.09	0.0	22.1	0.0	0.0	10.0	13.7
I W U Federal Credit Union	Bloomington	IL	C	C	C-	3.1	-2.93	0.0	13.6	0.0	0.0	10.0	12.6
I-C Federal Credit Union	Fitchburg	MA	B-	B-	B-	519.0	2.06	5.2	22.3	36.6	6.9	9.4	10.6
I.B.E.W. Local #146 Credit Union	Decatur	IL	C-	C-	D+	3.6	-4.14	0.0	37.3	0.0	0.0	8.3	9.9
I.B.E.W. Local #681 Credit Union	Wichita Falls	TX	D	D	D+	<1	-0.56	0.0	54.6	0.0	0.0	10.0	13.5
I.B.E.W. LU 66 Federal Credit Union	Pasadena	TX	D+	D+	D+	6.4	7.08	0.0	66.5	0.0	0.0	7.8	9.5
I.B.E.W.-Local No. 5 FCU	Pittsburgh	PA	C	C	C	11.0	2.51	0.0	9.4	0.0	73.1	10.0	11.1
I.L.A. Local 1235 Federal Credit Union	Newark	NJ	C-	C-	C-	7.5	0.01	0.0	58.6	0.0	0.0	10.0	17.6
I.L.W.U. Credit Union	Wilmington	CA	A-	A-	A	248.4	10.83	2.8	28.0	23.2	17.1	9.4	10.7
▼ I.M. Detroit District Credit Union	Detroit	MI	C	C+	C+	1.7	17.78	0.0	1.9	0.0	0.0	10.0	14.0
I.U. 7 Federal Credit Union	New Kensington	PA	C+	C+	C+	22.1	5.21	0.0	19.0	27.3	25.5	10.0	13.4
IAA Credit Union	Bloomington	IL	A-	A-	B+	236.7	7.66	0.0	22.7	31.6	3.6	9.2	10.4
IAM Community Federal Credit Union	Daleville	AL	D	D	D	32.5	-3.39	0.0	34.7	16.9	20.8	6.6	8.6
Iberia Parish Federal Credit Union	New Iberia	LA	D	D	D	<1	3.51	0.0	47.5	0.0	0.0	10.0	55.2
▲ Iberville Federal Credit Union	Plaquemine	LA	C	C-	C-	5.9	1.58	0.0	38.3	0.0	0.0	10.0	15.0
▲ IBEW & United Workers FCU	Portland	OR	C	C-	C-	76.3	5.44	1.3	25.9	9.8	6.1	5.6	7.6
IBEW 116 Federal Credit Union	Fort Worth	TX	D	D	D	4.5	9.29	0.0	38.3	0.0	0.0	5.7	7.7
IBEW 141 Federal Credit Union	Wheeling	WV	D	D	D	2.2	-1.27	0.0	17.8	0.0	0.0	8.8	10.3
IBEW 175 Federal Credit Union	Chattanooga	TN	C+	C+	C-	5.6	14.78	0.0	60.1	0.0	0.0	10.0	13.3
▼ IBEW 26 Federal Credit Union	Lanham	MD	D-	D	D-	27.1	0.88	0.0	29.5	0.0	34.0	5.4	7.4
IBEW 317 Federal Credit Union	Huntington	WV	D+	D+	D+	23.3	4.05	0.0	12.6	24.5	0.0	8.4	9.9
IBEW 76 Federal Credit Union	Tacoma	WA	C	C	C	25.8	-7.65	0.0	12.5	10.0	0.0	10.0	12.4
▼ IBEW 968 Federal Credit Union	Parkersburg	WV	C-	C	C	4.5	-9.87	0.0	19.1	4.5	15.4	10.0	15.5
▼ IBEW Community Federal Credit Union	Beaumont	TX	D	D+	C-	14.5	2.21	0.0	47.8	9.2	0.0	7.9	9.6
IBEW Local Union 712 FCU	Beaver	PA	E+	E+	D-	6.8	-2.92	0.0	32.5	0.0	0.0	6.9	9.0
IBEW Local Union 80 Federal Credit Union	Chesapeake	VA	D+	D+	D-	1.2	-2.62	0.0	25.7	0.0	0.0	8.2	9.8
IBEW LU 278 Federal Credit Union	Corpus Christi	TX	D+	D+	C-	2.4	-8.42	0.0	40.4	0.0	0.0	5.8	7.8
IBEW/SJ Cascade Federal Credit Union	Salem	OR	C	C	D+	12.6	8.94	0.0	38.3	25.0	0.0	7.9	9.6
IBM Southeast Employees' Credit Union	Delray Beach	FL	A-	A-	A-	979.3	6.28	2.4	31.1	27.5	12.1	9.8	10.9
▼ ICI America Federal Credit Union	New Castle	DE	D	D+	D+	2.7	-3.67	0.0	38.4	0.0	0.0	9.5	10.6
Icon Credit Union	Boise	ID	B+	B+	A	277.2	4.14	2.2	51.0	16.7	0.4	10.0	12.6
Idaho Central Credit Union	Chubbuck	ID	A-	A-	A-	3010.0	24.10	7.6	43.9	32.5	0.0	6.6	8.6
Idaho State University FCU	Pocatello	ID	B-	B-	B-	179.8	10.42	0.0	43.1	17.0	1.3	6.5	8.5
Idaho United Credit Union	Boise	ID	E+	E+	D	34.3	9.76	0.0	55.3	20.4	0.0	4.0	6.0
IDB-IIC Federal Credit Union	Washington	DC	A-	A-	A-	557.8	3.10	1.8	2.1	61.6	11.7	10.0	11.8
Ideal Credit Union	Woodbury	MN	B+	B+	B	685.2	7.27	2.7	29.3	36.2	1.7	8.5	10.0
IEC Federal Credit Union	Springfield	IL	D	D	D+	11.4	-0.43	11.1	49.3	0.0	0.0	10.0	13.7
IH Credit Union, Inc.	Springfield	OH	B-	B-	C+	301.3	1.47	3.7	28.3	21.2	35.7	10.0	16.6
ILA 1351 Federal Credit Union	La Porte	TX	C+	C+	C	14.3	2.66	0.0	30.4	0.0	12.8	10.0	16.6
ILA 28 Federal Credit Union	Pasadena	TX	B-	B-	B-	6.4	4.72	0.0	27.8	0.0	0.0	10.0	24.7
Illiana Financial Credit Union	Calumet City	IL	B	B	B	239.6	12.11	3.4	25.1	12.8	37.4	10.0	13.8
Illinois Community Credit Union	Sycamore	IL	A-	A-	A-	81.4	2.36	0.6	38.8	7.1	3.6	10.0	14.6
Illinois Educators Credit Union	Springfield	IL	C	C	C	55.1	4.51	0.0	55.7	0.7	5.8	7.4	9.3
Illinois State Credit Union	Normal	IL	B	B	B-	120.9	8.11	0.6	41.0	20.7	2.6	6.8	8.9
Illinois State Police FCU	Springfield	IL	D+	D+	D+	104.8	2.75	0.5	27.2	6.2	0.0	4.9	6.9
Illinois Valley Credit Union	Peru	IL	C+	C+	C	26.8	6.24	0.0	34.7	14.3	1.3	9.2	10.5
Imeco Federal Credit Union	South Bend	IN	D	D	D	9.0	-1.66	0.0	35.5	22.3	0.0	10.0	13.8
Immaculate Conception Fall River FCU	Fall River	MA	E+	E+	E+	1.2	-17.91	0.0	17.0	32.4	0.0	0.0	2.6
Immaculate Heart of Mary Credit Union	Lafayette	LA	D	D	D+	<1	-1.49	0.0	15.9	0.0	0.0	10.0	24.9
Impact Credit Union, Inc.	Clyde	OH	C+	C+	C+	134.2	1.66	6.5	28.4	22.4	3.7	8.1	9.8
Imperial Credit Union	Springfield	IL	D-	D-	D-	<1	15.79	0.0	11.4	0.0	0.0	7.1	9.1
Incenta Federal Credit Union	Englewood	OH	C-	C-	D	89.1	3.88	0.1	24.2	19.1	1.5	8.1	9.8
Independence Federal Credit Union	Independence	MO	D-	D-	E+	3.0	13.67	0.0	65.9	0.0	0.0	6.5	8.5
Independence Teachers Credit Union	Independence	MO	C	C	C	16.2	10.56	0.0	19.2	0.0	0.0	7.3	9.2
Independent Federal Credit Union	Anderson	IN	D+	D+	D+	71.2	2.82	0.0	35.0	17.6	0.0	5.4	7.4
Indiana Heartland Federal Credit Union	Kokomo	IN	D+	D+	D+	15.9	28.34	0.0	72.7	0.4	0.0	7.1	9.0

Asset Quality Index	Non-Performing Loans as a % of Total Loans	Non-Performing Loans as a % of Capital	Net Charge-Offs Avg Loans	Profitability Index	Net Income ($Mil)	Return on Assets	Return on Equity	Net Interest Spread	Overhead Efficiency Ratio	Liquidity Index	Liquidity Ratio	Hot Money Ratio	Stability Index
8.6	0.42	1.7	0.48	**2.0**	0.00	0.28	2.15	4.31	96.3	**5.8**	35.6	0.0	**4.6**
6.3	0.76	6.1	0.00	**2.4**	0.00	0.22	3.60	3.13	80.0	**6.3**	39.7	0.0	**1.0**
6.5	2.07	8.2	-0.09	**1.8**	0.00	0.03	0.36	3.97	98.8	**7.6**	66.0	0.0	**3.2**
5.8	0.52	6.1	0.33	**3.9**	1.67	0.60	7.06	3.34	79.6	**2.7**	7.6	11.4	**5.9**
9.1	1.59	2.7	2.10	**3.5**	0.00	0.42	3.11	4.05	75.0	**5.3**	22.3	0.0	**5.7**
10.0	0.00	0.0	0.00	**3.3**	0.00	0.40	3.13	1.23	62.5	**6.8**	70.1	0.0	**5.3**
7.1	0.83	6.5	0.13	**3.8**	0.52	0.40	3.81	3.03	86.4	**4.1**	18.9	5.2	**7.6**
9.5	0.00	0.0	0.00	**3.2**	0.00	0.45	4.56	3.46	90.0	**5.1**	21.6	0.0	**5.5**
8.4	0.19	0.8	1.48	**0.1**	0.00	-0.91	-6.67	4.04	100.0	**5.3**	25.6	0.0	**6.0**
4.0	0.56	4.8	0.78	**8.0**	0.01	0.75	7.91	6.76	84.5	**3.9**	13.9	0.0	**3.0**
7.0	6.70	8.4	5.06	**1.7**	0.00	-0.11	-0.98	2.30	50.9	**6.0**	35.3	0.0	**6.0**
8.6	0.00	0.0	0.00	**1.7**	-0.02	-0.87	-4.80	5.09	91.6	**4.3**	15.1	0.0	**6.6**
4.7	3.84	18.5	0.32	**3.7**	-0.17	-0.28	-2.59	3.99	76.5	**4.1**	26.9	10.9	**8.3**
10.0	0.00	0.0	63.16	**0.9**	-0.01	-3.00	-19.12	2.71	0.0	**9.0**	113.3	0.0	**5.6**
6.3	1.88	7.4	0.20	**2.9**	0.01	0.13	0.95	2.49	93.6	**2.8**	20.3	24.6	**6.4**
7.9	0.81	5.0	0.06	**6.5**	0.56	0.96	9.11	2.99	66.8	**4.1**	27.7	10.0	**7.7**
5.7	1.38	9.4	0.58	**0.8**	-0.09	-1.08	-12.29	3.29	124.8	**3.8**	15.4	10.0	**3.1**
5.2	8.16	6.7	0.00	**0.0**	0.00	-1.85	-3.46	9.64	122.2	**6.5**	89.2	0.0	**5.2**
9.7	0.08	0.2	-0.31	**2.7**	0.00	0.28	1.83	5.36	96.3	**6.2**	45.1	0.0	**6.3**
7.5	0.21	2.2	0.25	**3.1**	0.07	0.36	4.79	3.55	92.6	**5.6**	32.0	0.2	**3.2**
9.8	0.00	0.0	0.00	**2.0**	0.00	0.18	2.33	5.71	94.1	**6.5**	47.7	3.7	**1.7**
4.4	7.73	13.3	0.00	**1.0**	0.00	-0.37	-3.57	3.17	107.7	**6.9**	49.6	0.0	**5.9**
5.4	3.01	14.2	0.11	**8.8**	0.03	1.98	14.92	6.81	62.7	**3.5**	33.6	21.3	**5.0**
8.8	0.41	1.7	0.83	**0.0**	-0.09	-1.39	-18.46	4.03	109.0	**6.2**	39.4	0.0	**2.0**
3.7	5.04	20.1	2.64	**3.4**	0.03	0.59	5.92	2.36	66.4	**4.7**	13.3	0.0	**3.0**
9.7	0.26	0.5	1.65	**0.7**	-0.06	-0.99	-7.93	2.24	101.3	**5.8**	40.1	0.7	**5.2**
10.0	0.97	1.6	0.00	**1.1**	0.00	-0.33	-2.29	4.98	112.0	**7.7**	70.2	0.0	**6.8**
3.7	1.17	9.8	0.00	**0.9**	0.00	0.06	0.58	3.47	89.9	**3.3**	23.8	8.4	**3.9**
6.0	2.10	9.3	0.00	**1.0**	0.00	0.12	1.31	3.08	94.6	**6.4**	51.1	0.0	**3.5**
8.0	0.00	0.0	1.24	**5.3**	0.00	0.00	0.00	5.63	81.8	**6.9**	53.4	0.0	**3.7**
3.0	3.31	19.5	5.87	**1.9**	-0.02	-2.96	-35.60	5.82	123.1	**6.4**	49.4	0.0	**1.0**
7.2	0.69	5.1	0.04	**5.5**	0.03	0.84	8.73	4.23	79.6	**4.1**	21.5	0.0	**4.3**
8.4	0.38	3.6	0.29	**6.8**	2.40	1.00	10.37	3.94	72.7	**4.1**	19.4	4.9	**7.2**
5.6	3.99	11.3	0.00	**0.0**	0.00	-0.30	-2.83	3.14	109.5	**5.6**	51.5	0.0	**5.0**
8.2	0.26	1.6	0.29	**4.2**	0.37	0.54	4.37	2.82	83.0	**2.0**	13.3	19.9	**7.5**
7.8	0.37	3.9	0.11	**7.9**	7.09	0.97	11.36	2.63	67.1	**1.0**	2.8	22.7	**8.1**
6.0	1.14	10.0	0.49	**4.1**	0.21	0.48	5.61	3.90	88.6	**4.0**	19.6	7.6	**5.0**
4.7	0.34	8.8	0.29	**2.2**	0.05	0.59	9.57	4.76	86.0	**3.9**	12.7	2.7	**1.0**
10.0	0.00	0.0	0.01	**5.7**	1.19	0.86	7.34	2.27	63.0	**3.5**	25.3	13.4	**9.0**
8.2	0.48	3.8	0.21	**5.2**	1.45	0.87	9.34	3.38	76.6	**3.7**	19.6	10.1	**7.2**
8.0	0.20	0.9	0.59	**0.0**	-0.03	-0.99	-7.16	2.44	123.4	**4.2**	28.6	5.7	**6.2**
9.7	0.50	2.1	0.69	**3.4**	0.28	0.37	2.27	3.13	77.0	**3.9**	15.4	4.6	**7.8**
9.9	0.34	0.8	0.21	**2.4**	0.01	0.36	2.19	3.84	90.6	**5.8**	43.0	0.0	**7.1**
9.7	0.87	1.3	-0.17	**8.4**	0.02	1.46	5.92	4.03	66.1	**5.1**	39.0	0.0	**5.7**
7.6	1.58	5.3	0.91	**3.6**	0.22	0.37	2.66	3.48	80.6	**3.9**	13.5	9.0	**7.3**
9.5	0.37	2.2	0.50	**6.7**	0.03	0.13	0.91	3.67	105.7	**3.3**	14.3	7.9	**7.3**
5.4	0.63	4.2	1.50	**3.2**	0.05	0.35	3.66	4.22	81.1	**3.8**	12.1	1.3	**4.0**
7.9	0.51	4.2	0.69	**4.4**	0.11	0.37	4.15	4.95	81.9	**4.6**	24.9	4.3	**5.7**
8.5	0.63	3.7	0.47	**1.5**	0.01	0.03	0.39	2.63	91.3	**4.6**	23.1	2.4	**3.5**
6.4	1.52	7.0	1.58	**5.5**	0.06	0.89	8.49	4.62	74.3	**5.0**	33.6	3.7	**5.1**
9.8	0.24	1.0	0.00	**0.2**	0.00	-0.18	-1.29	2.73	105.9	**4.1**	21.2	0.0	**6.5**
1.7	4.11	50.0	0.00	**0.0**	-0.02	-6.62	-200.00	8.38	229.4	**6.5**	46.7	0.0	**1.4**
8.2	4.64	4.2	0.00	**0.3**	0.00	-0.47	-1.86	2.02	100.0	**6.1**	66.5	0.0	**6.7**
7.9	0.31	3.3	0.26	**3.5**	0.15	0.47	5.06	4.13	86.3	**4.4**	17.7	1.6	**6.1**
10.0	0.00	0.0	0.00	**3.9**	0.00	0.00	0.00	0.00	100.0	**8.7**	100.0	0.0	**3.7**
8.1	0.58	2.7	0.14	**2.2**	0.03	0.13	1.34	3.00	92.8	**4.8**	19.2	0.0	**4.5**
0.7	5.09	38.4	0.00	**7.8**	0.01	0.94	11.11	6.56	89.7	**5.7**	37.2	0.0	**4.1**
9.4	0.86	1.9	-0.13	**2.4**	0.01	0.23	2.43	1.77	86.5	**7.0**	45.1	0.0	**4.4**
7.0	0.69	5.2	0.22	**0.5**	-0.09	-0.51	-6.67	2.90	108.5	**4.4**	19.8	1.7	**2.7**
1.4	3.32	32.9	0.53	**10.0**	0.07	1.84	20.00	5.01	68.0	**3.0**	11.0	9.2	**5.7**

Name	City	State	Rating	2016 Rating	2015 Rating	Total Assets ($Mil)	One Year Asset Growth	Asset Mix (As a % of Total Assets) Comm-ercial Loans	Cons-umer Loans	Mort-gage Loans	Secur-ities	Capital-ization Index	Net Worth Ratio
Indiana Lakes Federal Credit Union	Warsaw	IN	**C+**	C+	C+	19.8	-3.35	2.7	12.1	33.4	0.0	**10.0**	13.0
Indiana Members Credit Union	Indianapolis	IN	**B-**	B-	B-	1765.2	9.41	7.6	18.0	27.3	26.8	**8.9**	10.2
Indiana State University FCU	Terre Haute	IN	**C**	C	C-	90.8	9.05	3.3	35.6	22.2	4.7	**8.1**	9.7
Indiana University Credit Union	Bloomington	IN	**A-**	A-	A-	934.4	8.19	19.9	17.1	45.0	17.7	**10.0**	12.6
Indianapolis Post Office Credit Union	Indianapolis	IN	**C-**	C-	C-	57.8	1.65	0.0	14.9	0.0	14.8	**10.0**	19.6
Indianapolis' Newspaper FCU	Indianapolis	IN	**D+**	D+	D+	7.8	0.40	0.0	74.2	0.0	0.0	**10.0**	13.0
Indianhead Credit Union	Spooner	WI	**C+**	C+	C+	54.5	19.02	0.0	16.6	22.8	0.0	**8.5**	10.0
Industrial Credit Union of Whatcom County	Bellingham	WA	**C+**	C+	C	236.0	9.80	4.5	27.2	26.0	26.9	**5.3**	7.5
Industrial Employees Credit Union	Centerville	IA	**C+**	C+	C+	8.8	-4.83	0.0	34.7	5.7	0.0	**10.0**	14.9
Industrial Federal Credit Union	Lafayette	IN	**C**	C	C+	191.6	5.12	0.5	31.7	15.7	0.0	**8.2**	9.8
Infinity Federal Credit Union	Westbrook	ME	**C**	C	C	335.1	7.12	0.0	11.4	41.8	21.8	**6.6**	9.3
Infirmary Federal Credit Union	Mobile	AL	**B**	B	B	20.0	8.17	8.0	22.9	4.0	31.6	**10.0**	16.3
InFirst Federal Credit Union	Alexandria	VA	**C+**	C+	C+	174.3	3.09	2.8	34.0	30.4	10.8	**8.0**	9.8
Infuze Credit Union	Fort Leonard Wood	MO	**C-**	C-	C	227.9	1.42	1.5	49.7	10.6	15.5	**7.0**	9.1
Ingersoll-Rand Federal Credit Union	Athens	PA	**C+**	C+	C+	59.2	-1.62	0.0	15.8	8.5	37.0	**10.0**	20.6
Inland Federal Credit Union	El Cajon	CA	**D+**	D+	D+	12.0	1.38	0.0	47.2	28.9	0.0	**6.1**	8.1
Inland Motor Employees FCU	Radford	VA	**C-**	C-	C-	2.3	6.83	0.0	35.8	0.0	0.0	**10.0**	17.4
Inland Valley Federal Credit Union	Fontana	CA	**C-**	C-	C-	44.0	5.21	0.1	23.9	18.5	0.2	**5.6**	7.6
Inner Lakes Federal Credit Union	Westfield	NY	**C-**	C-	C-	83.2	5.93	0.1	18.9	7.8	26.6	**4.9**	7.1
Innovations Federal Credit Union	Panama City	FL	**C+**	C+	C+	190.1	10.90	8.5	32.0	29.7	3.1	**6.6**	8.6
INOVA Federal Credit Union	Elkhart	IN	**C**	C	C+	336.4	8.58	6.8	47.0	30.8	0.0	**5.9**	7.9
▼ Insight Credit Union	Orlando	FL	**C-**	C	B-	579.3	0.86	9.4	29.3	13.7	12.8	**6.6**	8.9
Inspire Federal Credit Union	Bristol	PA	**B-**	B-	B-	136.4	17.43	2.8	18.1	25.2	0.0	**5.3**	7.3
Inspirus Credit Union	Tukwila	WA	**B+**	B+	B-	1234.5	10.20	0.2	30.8	21.4	15.1	**7.7**	9.6
Integra First Federal Credit Union	Powers	MI	**C**	C	C	100.7	1.75	0.0	15.7	30.6	21.7	**6.7**	8.8
Integris Federal Credit Union	Oklahoma City	OK	**C-**	C-	C-	12.6	-3.12	0.0	37.7	0.0	0.0	**10.0**	12.2
Integrity Federal Credit Union	Barberton	OH	**D**	D	C-	44.2	9.59	0.0	25.7	9.1	5.9	**6.7**	8.7
IntegrUS Credit Union	Dubuque	IA	**D-**	D-	D	27.2	34.65	3.0	53.0	19.3	0.0	**6.1**	8.1
Inter-American Federal Credit Union	Brooklyn	NY	**D**	D	D-	<1	-3.00	0.0	0.0	0.0	0.5	**9.0**	10.3
▼ Intercorp Credit Union	Amarillo	TX	**D**	D+	D+	4.6	-12.75	0.0	51.3	0.0	0.0	**10.0**	16.2
Internal Revenue Employees FCU	Greensboro	NC	**C+**	C+	C	20.9	-4.30	0.0	8.6	11.7	0.0	**10.0**	14.2
Internal Revenue Federal Credit Union	New Orleans	LA	**C+**	C+	C-	12.5	1.74	0.0	26.5	9.4	0.0	**10.0**	17.4
International UAW Federal Credit Union	Detroit	MI	**D+**	D+	C	24.6	2.58	0.0	9.2	11.3	0.0	**8.1**	9.7
Internationalites Federal Credit Union	Carlsbad	NM	**B-**	B-	B	11.4	8.24	0.0	36.8	0.0	0.0	**10.0**	14.7
Interra Credit Union	Goshen	IN	**B-**	B-	B	952.0	13.64	34.3	24.9	40.3	7.1	**8.6**	10.2
Interstate Unlimited FCU	Jesup	GA	**A**	A	A-	138.3	15.45	0.0	60.1	10.5	9.8	**10.0**	15.3
▼ InTouch Credit Union	Plano	TX	**D**	D+	D+	805.2	3.28	1.8	53.2	19.8	5.1	**7.0**	9.2
Investex Credit Union	Humble	TX	**B-**	B-	B	191.1	2.17	0.0	42.8	8.0	28.2	**8.4**	10.0
Iowa Heartland Credit Union	Mason City	IA	**C+**	C+	C+	23.7	3.39	0.0	37.1	12.5	24.6	**10.0**	18.1
IQ Credit Union	Vancouver	WA	**A-**	A-	B+	955.4	11.04	13.1	38.0	18.9	9.4	**7.2**	9.1
IRCO Community Federal Credit Union	Phillipsburg	NJ	**D**	D	D	76.2	0.08	0.0	17.3	21.1	21.9	**7.1**	9.1
Iron County Community Credit Union	Hurley	WI	**C**	C	C+	24.5	2.75	0.2	33.2	20.1	0.0	**10.0**	12.2
Iron Mountain Kingsford Community FCU	Kingsford	MI	**C-**	C-	C-	94.3	5.37	0.9	18.7	15.0	5.2	**10.0**	13.2
Iron Workers Federal Credit Union	Pittsburgh	PA	**D-**	D-	D-	6.0	-1.54	1.2	21.3	30.0	12.6	**6.6**	8.7
IRS Buffalo Federal Credit Union	Buffalo	NY	**E+**	E+	E+	4.6	0.55	0.0	61.2	15.3	0.0	**5.9**	7.9
IRSE Credit Union	Springfield	IL	**C-**	C-	D+	9.2	3.98	0.0	37.2	0.0	0.0	**9.9**	11.0
Irvin Works Federal Credit Union	West Mifflin	PA	**C+**	C+	B-	21.8	0.25	0.0	37.8	7.8	0.0	**10.0**	25.9
▼ Irving City Employees FCU	Irving	TX	**C+**	B-	C+	57.9	1.60	0.0	39.5	4.3	0.0	**10.0**	12.0
Isabella Community Credit Union	Mount Pleasant	MI	**B-**	B-	B-	122.5	4.07	1.8	26.4	18.3	16.1	**6.4**	8.4
Island Federal Credit Union	Hauppauge	NY	**B-**	B-	B-	1314.3	18.02	0.5	6.8	25.8	44.5	**5.4**	8.4
▲ Israel Memorial AME Federal Credit Union	Newark	NJ	**D+**	D	D	<1	-11.57	0.0	15.2	0.0	0.0	**10.0**	33.3
▼ Israel Methcomm Federal Credit Union	Chicago	IL	**D**	D+	D+	1.5	17.69	0.0	7.0	0.0	0.0	**5.3**	7.3
Issaquena County Federal Credit Union	Mayersville	MS	**D+**	D+	C-	1.2	-0.08	0.0	31.6	0.0	0.0	**10.0**	13.3
Italo-American Federal Credit Union	Glendale	NY	**B**	B	B	19.9	7.01	7.3	0.0	71.3	0.0	**10.0**	12.1
iTrust Federal Credit Union	Memphis	TN	**C+**	C+	C+	19.8	2.86	0.0	35.6	0.0	0.0	**10.0**	11.1
IUPAT D.C. 21 Federal Credit Union	Philadelphia	PA	**D+**	D+	D	1.8	11.36	0.0	0.0	0.0	0.0	**5.8**	7.8
J D M H Federal Credit Union	Jeannette	PA	**D+**	D+	C-	4.8	-1.01	0.0	54.6	0.0	0.0	**10.0**	38.8
J.C. Federal Employees Credit Union	Jefferson City	MO	**C**	C	C	3.2	16.58	0.0	42.5	0.0	0.0	**10.0**	14.6
Jack Daniel Employees Credit Union	Lynchburg	TN	**B-**	B-	B-	30.6	6.27	0.0	29.0	23.3	6.5	**8.0**	9.7
Jackson Acco Credit Union	Jackson	MS	**C-**	C-	C	2.9	3.00	0.0	66.6	0.0	0.0	**10.0**	19.2

Arrows denote recent upgrades ▲ or downgrades ▼

Asset Quality Index	Non-Performing Loans as a % of Total Loans	Non-Performing Loans as a % of Capital	Net Charge-Offs Avg Loans	Profitability Index	Net Income ($Mil)	Return on Assets	Return on Equity	Net Interest Spread	Overhead Efficiency Ratio	Liquidity Index	Liquidity Ratio	Hot Money Ratio	Stability Index
7.2	2.02	7.8	0.43	**2.6**	0.02	0.30	2.35	2.76	88.7	**4.6**	16.9	0.3	**6.1**
9.6	0.07	0.4	0.10	**3.8**	1.94	0.45	4.32	2.30	83.2	**5.4**	28.3	6.0	**7.7**
8.8	0.14	1.2	0.20	**3.3**	0.11	0.51	5.15	3.26	84.6	**4.1**	18.2	2.8	**4.9**
9.3	0.18	1.0	0.12	**6.2**	2.38	1.04	8.16	3.08	71.1	**4.3**	17.7	2.5	**9.5**
10.0	0.46	0.4	1.55	**1.1**	-0.02	-0.15	-0.81	1.48	105.4	**4.9**	17.2	0.0	**6.3**
6.5	0.76	4.5	-1.31	**2.2**	0.01	0.41	3.17	4.05	118.1	**4.1**	27.6	0.0	**5.1**
6.7	0.56	4.6	0.31	**3.5**	0.04	0.32	3.22	4.48	89.7	**6.4**	44.1	1.2	**4.5**
5.6	2.03	16.5	0.51	**4.5**	0.45	0.77	10.71	3.36	82.1	**5.1**	35.0	0.9	**4.7**
9.7	0.00	0.0	0.00	**3.6**	0.01	0.41	2.75	3.44	88.9	**5.5**	29.2	0.0	**7.3**
6.8	1.27	7.8	0.41	**2.6**	0.12	0.26	2.60	4.50	92.7	**5.0**	27.5	2.1	**5.5**
8.2	0.33	4.1	0.14	**2.5**	0.18	0.22	2.57	3.36	89.7	**2.8**	5.8	11.9	**5.9**
9.9	0.03	0.1	-0.32	**4.9**	0.04	0.86	5.09	3.20	86.8	**5.6**	29.8	3.3	**6.7**
6.1	1.15	9.8	0.33	**3.3**	0.19	0.44	4.77	3.79	84.4	**3.1**	18.2	12.9	**5.8**
6.1	0.62	6.2	0.17	**2.0**	0.11	0.19	2.16	3.42	86.1	**3.1**	14.7	11.3	**5.2**
8.7	2.06	3.1	0.48	**2.6**	0.02	0.15	0.77	2.99	89.6	**6.7**	50.7	0.3	**7.2**
6.7	0.25	2.3	0.21	**5.1**	0.03	0.87	10.86	4.80	82.2	**3.9**	17.0	0.0	**3.0**
9.7	1.23	2.5	0.00	**2.1**	0.00	0.00	0.00	4.55	100.0	**5.4**	16.7	0.0	**6.0**
8.1	0.39	2.3	1.78	**2.5**	0.00	-0.02	-0.24	3.33	81.6	**4.6**	34.7	11.7	**3.4**
6.9	0.71	5.0	0.53	**4.1**	0.11	0.55	7.90	2.88	77.1	**5.5**	32.2	1.3	**2.7**
7.3	0.46	4.9	0.62	**3.4**	0.24	0.51	5.76	5.00	84.2	**4.4**	18.6	2.1	**4.9**
4.1	1.27	16.2	1.09	**4.1**	0.76	0.93	11.66	4.37	70.8	**2.6**	14.4	14.9	**4.9**
5.8	0.85	9.2	1.48	**1.1**	0.06	0.04	0.46	3.82	78.3	**5.0**	24.4	2.8	**4.9**
7.7	0.47	4.8	0.33	**6.1**	0.62	1.86	25.41	3.81	64.3	**4.5**	21.5	2.9	**4.1**
9.1	0.29	2.2	0.30	**5.2**	2.62	0.86	8.92	3.04	69.2	**3.9**	14.0	0.5	**6.7**
9.9	0.27	1.6	0.02	**2.4**	0.06	0.23	2.58	2.68	92.0	**5.3**	37.7	7.5	**4.8**
9.9	0.00	0.0	0.00	**1.6**	0.00	0.03	0.26	2.59	96.6	**6.5**	68.2	1.2	**5.8**
4.9	0.68	2.8	1.98	**0.6**	-0.04	-0.35	-3.95	3.13	88.6	**5.0**	21.6	0.3	**3.2**
1.8	2.55	28.2	1.19	**4.6**	0.05	0.69	8.32	5.90	69.6	**2.2**	12.1	15.0	**3.9**
4.3	13.97	18.1	-14.08	**1.9**	0.00	0.00	0.00	3.70	100.0	**8.3**	93.6	0.0	**4.1**
6.9	0.99	3.4	0.00	**0.1**	-0.01	-1.04	-6.45	4.59	102.1	**3.2**	30.4	20.3	**5.6**
9.8	1.75	2.6	0.18	**2.7**	0.02	0.36	2.56	1.48	70.5	**5.1**	31.7	0.0	**6.4**
10.0	0.29	0.6	0.58	**2.9**	0.02	0.49	2.76	2.86	87.0	**6.2**	59.8	0.0	**6.3**
9.2	0.30	0.7	0.99	**1.5**	0.01	0.12	1.17	2.82	92.0	**6.0**	27.2	0.0	**3.3**
8.6	0.42	3.1	1.92	**2.9**	0.00	0.00	0.00	3.74	96.8	**7.3**	65.7	0.0	**7.0**
8.2	0.29	2.3	0.16	**4.4**	1.31	0.56	5.48	3.56	82.4	**2.7**	9.9	12.2	**7.3**
6.3	0.84	5.1	0.63	**9.5**	0.45	1.35	8.40	4.02	68.4	**2.2**	15.5	20.3	**9.3**
6.1	0.74	6.0	0.78	**0.9**	0.64	0.32	3.53	3.25	87.0	**3.9**	11.7	2.3	**5.5**
8.1	0.67	3.8	0.54	**4.0**	0.15	0.31	3.34	3.57	85.9	**4.3**	9.6	2.9	**5.5**
9.0	1.50	4.4	0.00	**2.5**	0.00	0.03	0.19	3.50	97.5	**5.0**	30.1	0.8	**7.3**
8.8	0.21	2.1	0.31	**8.5**	3.19	1.36	15.75	3.99	67.5	**4.7**	20.8	2.1	**7.4**
6.4	0.98	8.4	0.32	**1.2**	-0.01	-0.04	-0.66	3.59	92.6	**4.6**	20.6	1.1	**2.7**
5.2	2.95	18.1	-0.07	**4.8**	0.06	0.92	7.55	4.32	79.5	**5.2**	36.3	0.0	**6.1**
9.6	0.34	1.4	0.32	**1.7**	0.00	-0.01	-0.10	2.94	96.8	**6.9**	63.3	1.2	**6.7**
3.2	6.08	32.1	1.15	**0.3**	-0.03	-2.05	-23.35	3.62	96.7	**4.9**	33.2	2.3	**3.5**
4.1	1.11	10.8	1.74	**3.1**	0.00	0.35	4.47	4.45	86.2	**3.5**	16.1	0.0	**1.0**
8.8	0.42	1.5	0.00	**2.0**	0.00	0.04	0.40	2.62	98.4	**5.3**	35.4	0.0	**5.5**
9.7	0.54	1.1	3.75	**1.4**	-0.06	-1.02	-4.01	3.91	88.3	**4.9**	41.1	2.1	**6.3**
9.7	0.20	0.8	0.30	**2.5**	0.08	0.55	4.53	2.59	84.4	**5.2**	31.6	2.4	**6.1**
8.4	0.50	3.4	0.37	**3.5**	0.11	0.36	4.30	3.45	86.9	**5.1**	27.5	1.7	**5.6**
9.2	0.46	3.3	0.13	**3.1**	1.06	0.33	4.81	2.10	79.2	**2.3**	7.1	25.5	**5.3**
5.6	20.45	11.0	0.00	**1.7**	0.00	0.84	2.56	1.90	100.0	**5.6**	20.0	0.0	**4.7**
6.7	2.45	10.3	0.00	**1.4**	0.00	0.29	3.74	3.47	83.3	**7.1**	53.8	0.0	**1.0**
1.7	18.20	38.2	5.80	**6.1**	0.01	2.29	17.50	5.30	50.0	**6.7**	79.2	0.0	**7.0**
9.9	0.19	1.1	0.00	**9.0**	0.07	1.35	11.66	2.46	38.7	**2.5**	24.0	23.4	**6.3**
8.5	1.05	3.6	1.27	**2.2**	0.00	0.04	0.37	4.75	97.4	**4.1**	19.4	12.9	**5.2**
9.9	0.39	0.7	0.00	**3.4**	0.00	0.45	5.67	3.47	71.4	**8.0**	89.4	0.0	**3.0**
5.0	5.93	9.1	-0.28	**3.7**	0.01	0.76	1.93	4.23	81.6	**5.3**	44.5	0.0	**3.7**
5.5	5.88	17.3	0.00	**4.9**	0.01	0.89	6.07	4.29	70.4	**6.3**	48.1	0.0	**4.3**
9.2	0.22	1.4	-0.02	**7.0**	0.08	1.07	11.16	3.16	76.7	**3.0**	30.7	18.7	**5.6**
4.8	3.19	11.7	0.57	**3.1**	0.00	0.00	0.00	7.29	90.2	**4.2**	29.1	0.0	**6.9**

Name	City	State	Rating	2016 Rating	2015 Rating	Total Assets ($Mil)	One Year Asset Growth	Asset Mix (As a % of Total Assets) Commercial Loans	Consumer Loans	Mortgage Loans	Securities	Capitalization Index	Net Worth Ratio
Jackson Area Federal Credit Union	Jackson	MS	**B**	B	B	72.5	2.90	0.0	38.1	0.0	0.0	**10.0**	11.8
Jackson Community Federal Credit Union	Jackson	MI	**C+**	C+	C	26.0	3.30	0.0	35.6	22.7	19.2	**10.0**	13.2
Jackson County Cooperative Credit Union	Seymour	IN	**C+**	C+	C+	21.6	3.56	73.7	4.5	29.5	0.0	**10.0**	16.2
Jackson County Federal Credit Union	Edna	TX	**D-**	D-	D-	6.0	-2.07	0.0	59.5	12.1	0.0	**6.5**	8.5
Jackson County Teachers Credit Union	Marianna	FL	**B+**	B+	B+	27.3	4.11	0.0	45.5	0.0	8.9	**10.0**	24.9
Jackson County Teachers FCU	Edna	TX	**C**	C	C	7.4	-4.26	0.0	41.7	8.7	0.0	**10.0**	12.0
Jackson River Community Credit Union	Covington	VA	**C**	C	C	79.9	2.11	0.0	15.7	6.4	48.9	**9.0**	10.8
Jacksonville Firemen's Credit Union	Jacksonville	FL	**C-**	C-	C+	35.5	11.18	1.3	18.9	17.2	4.8	**7.4**	9.3
Jacksonville Postal & Professional CU	Jacksonville	FL	**C**	C	C+	45.1	3.14	0.0	17.3	15.7	1.2	**10.0**	18.4
JACL Credit Union	Glendale	AZ	**D**	D	D	<1	-6.42	0.0	49.0	0.0	0.0	**10.0**	19.7
Jaco Federal Credit Union	Ruston	LA	**C**	C	C	13.0	-3.24	0.0	14.0	32.2	0.0	**10.0**	16.5
▲ JACOM Credit Union	Los Angeles	CA	**C**	C-	D+	78.5	0.29	9.1	11.8	10.3	8.0	**10.0**	14.2
▲ Jafari No-Interest Credit Union	Houston	TX	**C+**	D		<1	560.00	0.0	10.1	0.0	0.0	**10.0**	29.2
James Ward Jr. Federal Credit Union	Jennings	LA	**C-**	C-	C-	2.2	3.93	0.0	50.7	7.8	0.0	**10.0**	25.6
Jamestown Area Community FCU	Jamestown	NY	**C**	C	C-	51.2	4.33	0.0	28.0	13.8	0.0	**5.2**	7.2
Jamestown Post Office Employees CU	Jamestown	NY	**C-**	C-	D+	4.9	5.87	0.0	22.4	0.0	0.0	**10.0**	12.8
JAX Federal Credit Union	Jacksonville	FL	**B+**	B+	B	386.2	7.79	0.4	44.4	14.8	8.4	**8.7**	10.2
Jax Glidco Employees FCU	Jacksonville	FL	**E+**	E+	E+	2.1	-8.06	0.0	47.5	0.0	0.0	**3.6**	5.6
Jax Metro Credit Union	Jacksonville	FL	**B-**	B-	C+	43.6	6.97	1.9	33.5	7.2	33.5	**9.7**	11.2
Jay Bee Employees Federal Credit Union	Bethlehem	PA	**C**	C	C	1.4	-7.88	0.0	35.5	0.0	29.0	**10.0**	13.6
Jeanne D'Arc Credit Union	Lowell	MA	**B-**	B-	C+	1272.1	6.21	20.5	10.4	62.2	3.4	**6.1**	8.1
Jeep Country Federal Credit Union	Holland	OH	**B**	B	C+	64.0	2.09	0.0	31.1	10.4	32.4	**10.0**	16.9
Jeff Davis Teachers Federal Credit Union	Jennings	LA	**C**	C	C	3.4	-2.00	0.0	22.7	0.0	0.0	**10.0**	18.5
Jefferson Community Federal Credit Union	Madison	IN	**C-**	C-	D+	12.4	8.82	0.0	38.1	9.1	0.0	**5.8**	7.8
Jefferson County Federal Credit Union	Louisville	KY	**C**	C	C	128.0	3.70	2.1	16.9	18.1	12.0	**10.0**	12.8
Jefferson County Teachers Credit Union	Monticello	FL	**C**	C	C	9.6	2.75	0.0	35.8	0.0	45.0	**10.0**	13.7
▲ Jefferson Credit Union	Hoover	AL	**C**	C-	D+	68.2	1.49	0.6	33.0	13.3	14.5	**7.7**	9.5
Jefferson Financial Federal Credit Union	Metairie	LA	**B+**	B+	B	504.3	22.15	12.7	33.4	32.8	0.0	**8.3**	9.8
Jefferson Parish Employees FCU	New Orleans	LA	**B+**	B+	B+	97.8	4.47	0.0	36.7	7.4	0.3	**10.0**	13.9
Jemez Valley Credit Union	Jemez Springs	NM	**B**	B	B	21.6	2.27	0.0	16.3	34.4	0.0	**10.0**	14.3
Jersey Central Federal Credit Union	Cranford	NJ	**C**	C	C+	18.7	5.01	0.0	58.4	0.0	0.0	**10.0**	21.0
Jersey City Firemen Federal Credit Union	Jersey City	NJ	**B**	B	B-	11.6	10.55	0.0	26.1	0.0	0.0	**10.0**	41.5
Jersey City Police Federal Credit Union	Jersey City	NJ	**C**	C	C+	9.3	-4.24	0.0	20.2	0.0	0.0	**10.0**	14.3
Jersey Shore Federal Credit Union	Northfield	NJ	**C-**	C-	C-	147.3	0.56	9.9	10.6	19.9	28.5	**5.6**	7.6
Jessop Community Federal Credit Union	Washington	PA	**D+**	D+	D+	32.5	-2.91	0.0	14.8	1.7	24.0	**7.3**	9.2
JetStream Federal Credit Union	Miami Lakes	FL	**A**	A	A-	191.3	4.67	10.6	51.4	16.8	6.7	**10.0**	12.4
JM Associates Federal Credit Union	Jacksonville	FL	**A**	A	A	120.5	5.89	0.0	26.3	4.3	48.1	**10.0**	13.4
▼ John Wesley Ame Zion Church FCU	Washington	DC	**C-**	C	C+	<1	-13.33	0.0	9.2	0.0	0.0	**7.4**	9.2
Johns Hopkins Federal Credit Union	Baltimore	MD	**A-**	A-	A-	429.9	7.51	0.0	17.6	22.6	28.4	**10.0**	11.2
Johnsonville TVA Employees Credit Union	Camden	TN	**B+**	B+	B+	96.3	5.93	0.1	35.1	6.8	1.5	**10.0**	13.9
Johnstown School Employees FCU	Johnstown	PA	**C+**	C+	C+	8.4	-3.86	1.1	31.9	4.2	56.7	**10.0**	18.1
Joliet Firefighters Credit Union	Joliet	IL	**D+**	D+	D+	6.7	1.23	0.0	43.2	0.0	0.0	**7.0**	9.0
▼ Joliet Municipal Employees FCU	Joliet	IL	**D+**	C-	C-	7.6	-0.40	0.0	51.7	0.0	0.0	**9.2**	10.5
Jones Methodist Church Credit Union	San Francisco	CA	**D**	D	D	<1	-4.38	0.0	7.8	0.0	22.0	**10.0**	22.2
Joplin Metro Credit Union	Joplin	MO	**B-**	B-	B-	29.4	5.99	0.0	48.5	0.0	0.0	**8.1**	9.7
Jordan Federal Credit Union	Sandy	UT	**C+**	C+	C+	264.5	6.32	4.7	23.4	25.0	16.3	**6.4**	8.5
Josten Employees Credit Union	Owatonna	MN	**D+**	D+	C-	1.2	-6.36	0.0	80.0	0.0	0.0	**10.0**	31.2
▲ Journey Federal Credit Union	Saint Johns	MI	**C**	C-	C	112.6	9.64	0.1	21.8	12.1	20.8	**7.7**	9.4
▼ Joy Employees Federal Credit Union	Bluefield	VA	**D+**	C-	C	1.5	-33.10	0.0	67.2	0.0	0.0	**10.0**	20.8
JPFCE Federal Credit Union	Jackson	MS	**C-**	C-	C	1.2	9.85	0.0	54.3	0.0	0.0	**10.0**	19.5
JSC Federal Credit Union	Houston	TX	**B-**	B-	B-	2014.5	3.79	0.1	17.1	7.2	60.6	**9.3**	10.5
▼ JSTC Employees Federal Credit Union	Johnstown	PA	**C-**	C	C	24.0	-2.35	0.0	24.3	5.2	0.0	**10.0**	14.2
Judd's Federal Credit Union	Gaithersburg	MD	**D**	D	D+	2.0	-6.73	0.0	39.5	0.0	44.6	**10.0**	16.5
Judicial & Justice Federal Credit Union	New Orleans	LA	**D+**	D+	D+	2.1	-4.20	0.0	37.5	0.0	0.0	**10.0**	12.5
▲ Junction Bell Federal Credit Union	Grand Junction	CO	**D+**	D	D-	20.7	3.08	2.1	15.6	10.7	52.0	**9.8**	10.9
Junior College Federal Credit Union	Perkinston	MS	**D+**	D+	C-	1.7	-5.81	0.0	31.7	0.0	0.0	**10.0**	18.9
Justice Federal Credit Union	Chantilly	VA	**B+**	B+	A-	706.7	2.69	0.2	35.6	25.7	19.1	**9.2**	10.6
K G C Federal Credit Union	Knox	PA	**D**	D	D-	5.8	6.96	0.0	50.1	0.0	0.0	**6.9**	8.9
K I T Federal Credit Union	Louisville	KY	**D+**	D+	D+	16.9	26.33	0.0	49.6	11.7	0.0	**6.3**	8.3
K&E Employees Federal Credit Union	Hoboken	NJ	**D**	D	D+	<1	-22.70	0.0	26.4	0.0	0.0	**10.0**	13.8

Arrows denote recent upgrades ▲ or downgrades ▼

Asset Quality Index	Non-Performing Loans as a % of Total Loans	Non-Performing Loans as a % of Capital	Net Charge-Offs Avg Loans	Profitability Index	Net Income ($Mil)	Return on Assets	Return on Equity	Net Interest Spread	Overhead Efficiency Ratio	Liquidity Index	Liquidity Ratio	Hot Money Ratio	Stability Index
7.8	1.14	5.0	0.72	**3.9**	0.09	0.51	4.24	5.47	76.0	**7.0**	53.7	1.9	**5.9**
6.5	1.34	9.1	0.39	**2.7**	0.00	0.03	0.23	5.13	96.8	**4.0**	14.6	2.8	**6.4**
6.5	0.03	0.1	0.00	**5.1**	0.05	0.96	6.00	4.60	79.3	**4.4**	40.6	12.6	**5.0**
8.1	0.00	0.0	0.00	**1.9**	0.00	0.07	0.78	2.80	95.4	**3.3**	12.7	6.6	**1.7**
7.7	0.43	2.3	1.44	**8.7**	0.10	1.54	7.10	6.34	68.0	**4.8**	27.8	6.4	**7.0**
9.7	0.00	0.0	0.00	**2.0**	0.00	0.16	1.35	1.97	89.2	**4.4**	23.6	0.0	**6.2**
9.1	0.66	1.9	0.25	**2.2**	0.02	0.08	0.85	2.09	94.4	**5.7**	31.5	1.5	**4.7**
5.7	1.26	6.6	0.09	**1.7**	0.03	0.31	3.30	4.84	92.2	**6.8**	57.2	5.5	**2.9**
10.0	0.24	0.5	0.32	**2.2**	0.02	0.19	1.02	3.16	89.0	**6.3**	54.9	10.9	**6.7**
8.7	0.00	0.0	0.00	**0.0**	0.00	-2.96	-14.68	2.19	300.0	**6.7**	60.5	0.0	**6.2**
4.6	4.76	18.0	0.40	**3.7**	0.01	0.34	2.06	3.67	83.2	**5.2**	41.4	0.0	**7.2**
10.0	0.72	1.7	0.00	**2.1**	0.05	0.26	2.00	3.20	88.2	**7.0**	53.9	4.1	**6.5**
10.0	0.00	0.0	0.00	**9.5**	0.01	4.17	14.07	1.27	57.9	**8.5**	127.3	0.0	**3.7**
6.0	2.76	6.4	0.00	**5.6**	0.01	1.11	4.34	5.16	81.5	**4.6**	51.1	0.0	**4.3**
9.5	0.33	2.0	0.27	**2.7**	0.02	0.18	2.51	3.56	95.0	**5.6**	30.5	0.0	**2.9**
9.4	1.57	2.9	0.00	**1.4**	0.00	0.00	0.00	3.10	97.4	**5.6**	33.9	0.0	**5.4**
9.0	0.35	2.5	0.28	**4.9**	0.52	0.54	5.31	3.77	82.9	**4.3**	19.8	2.7	**6.7**
8.7	0.10	0.8	0.00	**0.0**	-0.02	-3.12	-51.61	3.72	188.9	**5.8**	34.0	0.0	**0.7**
5.5	0.26	11.3	0.21	**4.6**	0.09	0.82	7.59	3.92	79.8	**4.2**	18.5	3.8	**6.2**
9.7	0.52	1.6	0.00	**2.2**	0.00	0.30	2.13	3.06	88.9	**5.6**	32.8	0.0	**6.2**
7.1	0.55	5.4	0.26	**3.9**	1.75	0.56	6.82	2.97	78.9	**2.4**	17.5	16.0	**6.1**
7.3	2.43	6.8	0.96	**3.3**	0.03	0.18	1.09	4.89	95.1	**4.8**	12.7	1.8	**6.7**
8.6	2.86	3.9	0.00	**3.3**	0.00	0.37	1.90	2.26	77.8	**6.5**	47.2	0.0	**7.6**
9.4	0.08	0.5	-0.13	**4.5**	0.02	0.75	9.21	3.76	88.5	**6.3**	38.9	0.0	**3.5**
9.9	0.79	2.2	0.69	**2.1**	0.04	0.13	0.96	2.52	83.2	**5.2**	38.0	5.4	**7.7**
8.4	1.19	3.8	0.00	**4.4**	0.01	0.54	3.98	3.79	82.4	**3.1**	18.3	17.6	**4.3**
4.1	2.88	18.4	2.62	**2.9**	0.04	0.23	2.39	5.08	81.6	**4.4**	26.5	9.7	**4.0**
7.2	0.68	5.4	0.43	**5.4**	0.97	0.78	7.91	4.34	76.9	**4.4**	24.7	9.8	**6.2**
7.6	1.41	5.3	1.16	**4.8**	0.10	0.43	3.59	4.90	89.4	**5.8**	44.8	4.5	**6.8**
8.5	0.79	3.1	0.20	**4.3**	0.02	0.32	2.21	3.87	93.1	**3.5**	33.9	11.5	**7.8**
7.7	0.76	2.6	1.16	**2.7**	0.01	0.30	1.43	7.59	89.7	**4.2**	15.4	2.0	**5.8**
9.6	3.76	2.3	-2.69	**7.6**	0.03	1.08	2.59	4.05	70.4	**5.8**	50.0	5.4	**6.3**
10.0	0.21	0.3	1.02	**4.8**	0.02	0.94	6.65	2.82	65.7	**5.1**	7.5	0.0	**6.8**
8.0	0.78	5.6	0.12	**2.5**	0.07	0.20	2.71	3.26	93.6	**4.8**	29.7	3.8	**4.4**
5.2	4.20	15.2	0.00	**1.6**	0.01	0.14	1.47	2.33	94.6	**5.3**	27.8	3.5	**3.7**
6.5	0.71	5.1	0.65	**8.7**	0.57	1.20	9.64	5.65	70.3	**3.3**	12.7	5.7	**8.4**
9.8	0.62	1.7	0.60	**7.3**	0.44	1.48	11.82	3.34	69.8	**6.0**	45.6	2.7	**8.2**
10.0	0.00	0.0	0.00	**0.0**	0.00	-6.35	-57.14	0.00	0.0	**7.9**	91.5	0.0	**4.2**
10.0	0.29	1.4	0.11	**5.4**	0.77	0.72	6.45	3.00	81.6	**4.8**	22.8	1.4	**7.7**
9.4	0.45	1.7	0.06	**4.5**	0.16	0.66	4.97	2.91	79.4	**5.4**	39.8	1.7	**7.4**
9.9	0.48	1.1	0.48	**3.1**	0.00	0.10	0.53	2.29	95.7	**4.6**	22.4	0.0	**7.6**
9.8	0.07	0.3	0.00	**4.4**	0.01	0.42	4.64	2.24	80.0	**4.6**	19.5	0.0	**3.0**
6.9	0.53	2.6	-0.20	**3.1**	0.01	0.53	5.03	3.39	83.6	**2.7**	17.2	23.3	**3.0**
3.7	66.67	31.6	0.00	**0.0**	0.00	-1.82	-8.42	2.72	200.0	**8.6**	113.7	0.0	**5.2**
6.0	0.79	4.8	0.81	**3.3**	-0.03	-0.42	-4.17	5.61	83.3	**5.7**	36.0	0.4	**5.1**
9.2	0.38	2.8	0.15	**2.8**	0.15	0.22	2.84	3.48	90.0	**4.6**	21.5	5.6	**4.5**
7.6	1.13	2.8	0.00	**1.5**	0.00	-0.33	-1.05	4.53	108.3	**4.6**	28.7	0.0	**5.8**
8.4	0.71	3.6	0.36	**3.7**	0.25	0.94	9.68	3.31	79.4	**5.0**	21.4	1.8	**5.3**
0.0	18.45	54.9	-0.35	**2.8**	-0.01	-3.17	-14.81	5.56	52.9	**5.4**	35.0	0.0	**6.8**
6.0	1.63	5.9	0.90	**3.0**	0.00	0.34	1.71	6.81	95.0	**5.1**	40.9	0.0	**7.4**
10.0	0.30	0.9	0.28	**4.2**	3.32	0.67	6.32	1.69	67.3	**5.1**	21.5	6.8	**7.2**
9.0	0.13	0.4	3.42	**0.0**	-0.09	-1.51	-10.52	3.37	99.5	**6.0**	70.4	5.4	**6.2**
9.6	0.43	1.2	0.00	**0.2**	-0.01	-1.00	-6.08	3.66	123.5	**4.8**	26.3	0.0	**5.5**
7.1	2.69	7.9	0.00	**1.8**	0.00	0.20	1.56	4.66	105.6	**5.8**	33.2	0.0	**5.2**
10.0	0.00	0.0	-0.06	**1.7**	0.01	0.15	1.70	2.73	95.1	**5.3**	28.2	2.2	**4.5**
8.1	2.84	4.5	0.00	**0.6**	-0.01	-2.67	-13.71	3.50	128.6	**4.7**	16.4	0.0	**4.7**
8.6	0.49	3.3	0.45	**5.1**	1.04	0.59	5.69	4.11	80.4	**3.6**	9.9	7.3	**6.9**
5.1	1.43	8.3	0.00	**5.8**	0.02	1.28	14.17	4.20	78.8	**5.9**	43.2	0.0	**2.3**
2.8	1.48	18.8	1.78	**10.0**	0.07	1.69	19.33	6.39	64.4	**4.0**	31.4	15.7	**4.3**
3.7	7.71	26.3	0.00	**0.0**	-0.01	-5.95	-33.99	3.34	137.5	**3.3**	49.9	15.5	**5.5**

Name	City	State	Rating	2016 Rating	2015 Rating	Total Assets ($Mil)	One Year Asset Growth	Asset Mix (As a % of Total Assets) Commercial Loans	Consumer Loans	Mortgage Loans	Securities	Capitalization Index	Net Worth Ratio
K.C. Area Credit Union	Kansas City	MO	C-	C-	C	11.8	131.85	0.0	32.9	0.0	0.0	10.0	14.5
▲ K.U.M.C. Credit Union	Kansas City	KS	C-	D+	D+	28.5	3.38	0.0	13.8	1.2	0.0	6.7	8.7
KAH Credit Union	Keokuk	IA	C-	C-	D+	1.8	-0.39	0.0	33.1	0.0	0.0	10.0	29.6
▼ Kahuku Federal Credit Union	Kahuku	HI	D-	D	D-	5.8	1.79	0.0	79.4	0.0	0.0	7.7	9.5
Kahului Federal Credit Union	Kahului	HI	C-	C-	C	58.2	2.53	1.2	9.4	17.3	32.8	10.0	15.1
Kaiperm Diablo Federal Credit Union	Walnut Creek	CA	C+	C+	C+	73.4	2.78	1.5	28.9	14.8	21.8	10.0	12.7
KaiPerm Northwest Federal Credit Union	Portland	OR	B	B	B	81.9	9.20	3.1	17.1	17.4	29.5	8.3	9.9
Kalamazoo Building Trades Credit Union	Kalamazoo	MI	D	D	D	2.8	-5.21	0.0	54.6	0.0	24.5	10.0	12.6
▲ Kaleida Health Federal Credit Union	Buffalo	NY	C-	D+	D	14.3	4.24	0.0	42.6	0.0	32.5	6.4	8.4
KALSEE Credit Union	Kalamazoo	MI	B+	B+	B	173.0	2.96	6.1	45.7	18.3	10.5	8.9	10.5
Kamehameha Federal Credit Union	Honolulu	HI	C-	C-	C-	37.5	1.34	0.0	9.1	9.9	5.8	10.0	12.6
Kan Colo Credit Union	Hoisington	KS	D+	D+	D+	<1	-3.46	0.0	44.1	0.0	0.0	10.0	14.4
Kane County Teachers Credit Union	Elgin	IL	B-	B-	C+	226.7	5.93	2.0	21.4	12.5	23.0	9.6	10.9
Kankakee County Federal Employees FCU	Kankakee	IL	D+	D+	C-	4.9	-2.96	0.0	16.6	0.0	0.0	10.0	17.2
Kankakee Federation of Teachers CU	Kankakee	IL	D	D	D+	8.4	3.74	0.0	67.3	0.0	0.0	10.0	13.1
Kankakee Terminal Belt Credit Union	Kankakee	IL	D+	D+	C-	6.1	8.05	0.0	69.8	0.0	0.0	8.7	10.1
Kansas Air Guard Credit Union	Topeka	KS	C	C	C	5.3	-0.43	0.0	63.7	0.0	0.0	10.0	15.1
Kansas Blue Cross-Blue Shield CU	Topeka	KS	B+	B+	B+	40.9	6.55	0.0	29.8	19.8	4.3	10.0	14.4
Kansas City Credit Union	Kansas City	MO	B-	B-	C	32.9	4.45	0.0	17.6	4.2	22.2	10.0	11.6
Kansas City Kansas Firemen & Police CU	Kansas City	KS	B-	B-	B-	14.4	7.24	0.0	53.9	0.0	0.0	10.0	17.6
Kansas City P&G Employees Credit Union	Kansas City	KS	D+	D+	D+	4.7	10.36	0.0	56.6	0.0	0.0	10.0	23.4
Kansas State University FCU	Manhattan	KS	B-	B-	B-	80.0	4.63	0.0	37.2	11.7	8.7	8.1	9.7
▲ Kansas Teachers Community Credit Union	Pittsburg	KS	B+	B	B	94.1	9.42	0.0	44.5	19.1	9.1	10.0	11.1
Kase Federal Credit Union	Vandergrift	PA	D+	D+	C-	1.3	-3.36	0.0	41.7	0.0	0.0	10.0	14.0
▼ Kaskaskia Valley Community Credit Union	Centralia	IL	D-	D	D	22.6	75.76	0.0	49.5	0.0	0.0	4.7	6.7
Katahdin Federal Credit Union	Millinocket	ME	B-	B-	C+	75.0	5.87	0.8	26.9	33.7	12.3	10.0	12.3
Kauai Community Federal Credit Union	Lihue	HI	B+	B+	B+	470.6	7.48	0.5	23.4	17.9	29.1	8.2	9.8
Kauai Government Employees FCU	Lihue	HI	B-	B-	C+	118.6	5.42	1.1	29.8	30.9	10.9	7.2	9.2
Kauai Teachers Federal Credit Union	Lihue	HI	C-	C-	D+	28.8	-0.78	0.0	10.4	8.7	10.9	7.6	9.5
KBR Heritage Federal Credit Union	Houston	TX	C+	C+	C+	89.4	-4.67	0.1	17.3	6.5	31.3	10.0	12.3
KC Fairfax Federal Credit Union	Kansas City	KS	D+	D+	D+	9.4	2.98	0.0	32.6	2.4	0.0	10.0	12.7
Kearny Municipal Employees FCU	Kearny	NJ	C	C	C	9.4	-2.30	0.0	13.2	0.0	60.7	10.0	15.8
Keesler Federal Credit Union	Biloxi	MS	A	A	A	2532.0	6.46	1.9	37.0	17.0	28.0	10.0	14.2
▲ Kekaha Federal Credit Union	Kekaha	HI	C	C-	C-	20.1	1.28	0.0	10.5	40.8	2.0	10.0	20.0
Kelco Federal Credit Union	Cumberland	MD	B	B	B	50.5	-0.14	3.9	15.2	28.5	0.0	10.0	13.9
Kellogg Community Credit Union	Battle Creek	MI	A	A	A	507.8	6.65	6.3	16.2	33.5	18.2	10.0	14.2
Kellogg Memphis Employees FCU	Memphis	TN	C-	C-	D	4.7	-1.16	0.0	64.7	0.0	0.0	10.0	26.3
Kellogg Midwest Federal Credit Union	Omaha	NE	B-	B-	B-	47.3	-3.64	0.0	24.3	9.1	23.0	10.0	20.2
Kelly Community Federal Credit Union	Tyler	TX	B+	B+	B+	99.8	0.22	2.1	29.4	35.6	6.8	10.0	11.5
Kemba Charleston Federal Credit Union	Dunbar	WV	C	C	C	40.2	0.13	0.0	26.3	2.9	5.0	10.0	20.2
Kemba Credit Union	West Chester	OH	A	A	A	801.8	5.73	1.3	52.8	21.3	1.4	10.0	12.7
Kemba Delta Federal Credit Union	Memphis	TN	B-	B-	B-	24.1	-0.05	0.0	51.2	0.1	0.0	10.0	23.5
KEMBA Financial Credit Union	Gahanna	OH	A	A	A	1184.8	10.26	6.2	38.4	23.2	6.7	10.0	11.4
▲ Kemba Indianapolis Credit Union	Indianapolis	IN	B-	C+	C+	70.4	1.46	0.0	20.3	12.6	12.6	10.0	14.9
Kemba Louisville Credit Union	Louisville	KY	B	B	B	53.0	4.83	0.0	21.5	5.9	2.7	10.0	18.9
Kemba Peoria Credit Union	Peoria	IL	C-	C-	D	10.4	5.19	0.0	37.2	0.0	0.0	9.5	10.7
KEMBA Roanoke Federal Credit Union	Salem	VA	C+	C+	C	62.5	3.34	0.0	20.3	5.6	0.0	10.0	15.8
Kenmore NY Teachers Federal Credit Union	Buffalo	NY	C-	C-	C	43.6	10.19	0.0	10.6	22.9	37.6	5.7	7.7
Kennaford Federal Credit Union	Bedford	PA	C	C	C	6.3	-1.58	0.0	25.4	0.0	0.0	10.0	20.5
▼ Kennametal Orwell Employees FCU	Orwell	OH	C-	C	C+	<1	-0.31	0.0	39.8	0.0	0.0	10.0	24.0
Kennedy Veterans Administration Empls FCU	Memphis	TN	B-	B-	C+	26.6	16.73	0.0	39.0	0.0	0.0	9.8	10.8
Kenosha Police & Firemen's Credit Union	Kenosha	WI	C-	C-	C	9.6	-0.80	0.0	25.1	0.0	1.6	10.0	33.1
Kenowa Community Federal Credit Union	Wyoming	MI	B-	B-	B-	21.0	6.22	0.0	29.7	14.4	0.0	10.0	13.1
Kent County Credit Union	Grand Rapids	MI	C+	C+	C-	46.5	4.26	0.0	31.0	2.0	25.0	7.7	9.5
Kent Hospital Federal Credit Union	Warwick	RI	D+	D+	D+	14.5	2.31	0.0	44.3	0.4	0.0	6.8	8.8
Kentucky Employees Credit Union	Frankfort	KY	C	C	B-	77.2	3.28	2.3	32.5	31.7	3.2	8.7	10.1
Kentucky Telco Credit Union	Louisville	KY	A-	A-	A	392.5	8.24	0.9	52.9	10.4	3.1	10.0	11.3
▼ Kern Federal Credit Union	Bakersfield	CA	C	C+	B+	247.0	6.28	0.0	42.5	24.0	0.4	10.0	12.2
Kern Schools Federal Credit Union	Bakersfield	CA	B+	B+	A-	1494.6	5.99	3.9	20.3	37.1	19.9	7.9	9.6
Kerr County Federal Credit Union	Kerrville	TX	D+	D+	D+	63.7	9.34	0.4	61.9	0.0	0.0	5.6	7.6

Asset Quality Index	Non-Performing Loans as a % of Total Loans	Non-Performing Loans as a % of Capital	Net Charge-Offs Avg Loans	Profitability Index	Net Income ($Mil)	Return on Assets	Return on Equity	Net Interest Spread	Overhead Efficiency Ratio	Liquidity Index	Liquidity Ratio	Hot Money Ratio	Stability Index
8.7	0.89	2.3	1.21	3.6	0.00	0.10	0.68	4.95	98.5	4.9	25.6	0.0	5.4
9.5	0.04	0.1	0.48	2.6	0.04	0.51	5.86	2.92	83.9	5.1	25.6	2.7	2.7
6.7	8.02	9.0	0.00	4.6	0.01	1.14	3.80	3.87	61.5	7.1	73.5	0.0	4.3
0.0	7.99	50.4	2.77	3.5	-0.09	-6.27	-60.40	6.70	78.5	2.2	16.0	33.6	6.4
10.0	0.32	0.7	0.28	1.3	-0.02	-0.15	-0.96	2.55	103.1	4.4	24.5	6.8	7.1
9.4	0.00	0.0	0.09	2.7	0.06	0.35	2.72	2.19	84.7	4.1	28.7	6.2	6.5
9.4	0.39	1.6	0.05	5.0	0.13	0.66	6.28	3.02	80.1	6.1	55.2	2.7	6.7
8.5	0.00	0.0	0.00	0.0	-0.01	-1.80	-14.33	2.81	154.6	4.0	22.6	0.0	6.2
8.0	0.42	2.5	-0.05	6.4	0.03	0.79	9.42	3.79	73.7	5.0	26.8	0.0	3.7
6.0	0.88	5.7	1.17	2.9	-0.05	-0.12	-1.19	4.69	84.3	3.6	17.4	4.7	5.7
10.0	0.08	0.2	0.00	1.6	0.00	0.02	0.17	2.45	96.6	4.9	23.2	3.3	5.2
3.7	8.40	21.8	-2.05	2.0	0.00	0.46	3.20	3.02	85.7	5.1	25.9	0.0	5.0
7.8	1.34	6.0	0.55	3.8	0.25	0.46	4.19	3.59	79.0	4.7	16.6	0.5	6.5
9.9	0.48	2.2	0.00	1.2	0.00	0.08	0.47	2.67	100.0	7.3	84.5	5.0	5.5
3.0	3.77	19.6	0.20	3.2	0.02	0.95	7.33	2.43	60.4	4.1	25.3	0.0	3.0
4.4	1.72	11.1	0.00	3.4	0.00	0.27	2.58	6.72	92.8	4.9	27.7	0.0	3.0
8.1	0.00	0.0	0.00	2.4	0.00	0.08	0.50	2.76	97.3	5.1	55.9	0.0	6.9
9.6	0.55	2.1	0.32	5.2	0.07	0.75	5.07	2.65	70.8	3.4	38.1	15.3	7.6
10.0	0.10	1.3	0.61	3.9	0.07	0.84	7.37	3.02	88.1	6.3	43.9	0.0	5.4
8.6	0.73	2.0	2.32	4.2	0.02	0.53	3.02	4.31	61.2	4.4	15.7	0.0	6.4
8.0	0.18	0.5	0.60	0.4	0.00	-0.34	-1.46	2.95	108.1	4.9	26.7	0.0	6.1
6.7	0.83	4.9	0.59	4.7	0.09	0.46	4.71	3.63	80.5	4.8	20.7	0.9	4.8
8.9	0.31	3.2	0.09	5.4	0.23	1.01	9.11	3.04	74.3	4.0	17.5	5.1	6.1
6.4	2.56	8.0	0.00	0.3	0.00	-0.61	-4.30	6.40	118.2	7.1	61.9	0.0	6.8
4.8	0.93	8.1	0.26	2.6	-0.01	-0.24	-3.44	4.14	101.6	5.0	28.0	0.5	0.7
7.1	0.94	5.4	0.07	4.2	0.13	0.71	5.83	3.93	89.3	3.6	14.1	4.5	6.1
7.4	0.63	5.9	0.91	4.7	0.45	0.39	4.25	3.58	67.2	4.1	17.9	9.9	6.6
6.2	1.26	9.3	0.60	5.7	0.50	1.70	18.47	3.84	59.4	2.8	18.6	14.9	6.0
7.9	1.15	3.4	0.10	1.8	0.00	0.03	0.30	2.46	98.9	5.2	30.9	7.7	3.5
9.8	1.09	2.2	-0.04	2.1	0.02	0.08	0.66	1.95	89.7	6.2	41.6	0.0	6.0
7.4	2.11	5.9	5.54	0.4	-0.04	-1.87	-14.45	5.06	97.8	6.1	56.2	1.5	5.0
7.9	6.05	5.0	6.64	2.7	0.00	0.17	1.08	1.72	68.6	6.0	26.8	0.0	7.4
8.9	0.58	3.1	0.61	7.4	7.26	1.16	8.64	2.96	61.6	4.0	23.6	12.9	9.5
7.9	2.08	5.4	0.20	2.1	0.03	0.58	2.68	2.97	87.7	5.7	43.6	1.3	6.4
7.0	3.95	13.5	0.21	3.4	0.03	0.21	1.56	2.88	80.5	5.0	43.8	1.2	6.5
9.8	0.31	1.5	0.04	9.5	2.14	1.72	12.08	3.15	64.3	3.8	16.5	6.4	9.2
3.9	7.71	18.4	-0.13	6.2	0.01	1.20	4.58	4.99	78.7	3.9	46.6	11.4	3.7
10.0	0.57	1.1	0.02	2.9	0.06	0.49	2.38	2.89	85.5	4.8	30.9	1.1	7.0
8.8	0.43	2.6	0.63	5.8	0.23	0.93	8.10	4.16	74.4	3.9	25.6	3.7	6.0
9.8	0.64	1.9	-0.05	2.1	0.02	0.16	0.79	3.11	94.0	4.1	18.6	6.4	6.7
8.2	0.21	2.1	0.27	5.9	1.70	0.86	7.36	2.69	69.9	3.0	15.3	10.4	9.5
8.7	0.32	0.8	1.21	3.9	0.01	0.22	0.92	3.73	89.1	5.5	41.2	1.2	6.3
9.3	0.36	2.3	0.41	9.4	4.11	1.46	12.36	3.73	63.0	3.8	26.9	15.1	8.9
8.9	1.29	3.7	0.47	3.7	0.11	0.63	4.14	3.50	84.2	4.4	18.2	6.0	6.5
10.0	1.20	2.0	0.33	3.9	0.05	0.37	1.92	3.23	87.4	5.8	44.3	3.3	6.8
7.5	0.57	3.3	0.84	2.5	0.01	0.36	3.27	3.97	92.4	5.3	34.7	3.3	5.2
9.7	0.93	2.3	1.29	2.0	-0.01	-0.04	-0.24	2.99	90.3	5.2	23.8	0.0	6.6
7.0	0.68	3.2	-0.05	2.8	0.01	0.12	1.56	2.46	94.9	5.1	19.4	0.0	3.5
9.8	0.86	1.3	0.00	3.1	0.01	0.51	2.48	2.36	75.8	5.5	29.4	0.0	7.1
9.8	0.00	0.0	0.94	1.4	0.00	-0.41	-1.70	9.26	110.0	7.4	74.1	0.0	6.8
9.4	0.47	1.8	0.04	4.0	0.02	0.28	2.51	2.78	93.6	4.4	21.2	11.3	4.3
9.9	0.21	0.2	-0.14	1.6	0.01	0.21	0.63	1.78	92.7	5.5	41.4	0.0	7.1
9.5	0.19	0.8	0.28	4.6	0.02	0.40	3.08	5.13	90.5	6.4	45.1	0.0	6.8
7.2	1.16	4.6	0.44	3.8	0.05	0.45	4.74	3.64	86.2	4.9	24.4	0.0	4.3
7.3	0.87	4.6	0.00	3.6	0.01	0.39	4.41	4.48	88.3	5.1	23.5	0.0	4.0
7.3	0.42	2.6	0.69	2.9	0.06	0.32	3.11	4.04	84.1	2.9	27.9	19.0	4.3
8.3	0.33	2.0	0.46	5.0	0.78	0.80	7.08	2.67	77.6	3.7	28.2	12.1	7.2
9.1	0.30	2.4	0.58	1.9	-0.13	-0.21	-1.66	3.67	90.5	4.0	19.6	5.2	7.0
9.5	0.30	2.1	0.45	4.1	3.43	0.95	9.96	3.21	76.6	4.2	16.6	3.1	6.2
2.7	1.10	16.7	1.26	3.9	0.04	0.25	3.50	5.39	77.5	4.4	31.2	6.5	2.8

	Name	City	State	Rating	2016 Rating	2015 Rating	Total Assets ($Mil)	One Year Asset Growth	Asset Mix (As a % of Total Assets) Comm-ercial Loans	Cons-umer Loans	Mort-gage Loans	Secur-ities	Capital-ization Index	Net Worth Ratio
▼	KeyPoint Credit Union	Santa Clara	CA	**B-**	B	B-	1157.4	10.73	13.4	21.9	49.0	10.7	**5.9**	8.0
▲	Keys Federal Credit Union	Key West	FL	**D+**	D	D-	137.1	7.26	2.8	36.1	19.2	2.9	**5.7**	7.8
	Keystone Credit Union	Tyler	TX	**D**	D	D+	36.2	-1.78	0.0	19.7	29.8	0.0	**10.0**	26.2
▼	Keystone United Methodist FCU	Cranberry Township	PA	**D**	D+	D+	18.2	2.70	5.5	26.5	10.1	0.0	**6.9**	8.9
	KH Network Credit Union	Dayton	OH	**B-**	B-	B	54.6	6.18	3.4	38.4	25.4	5.7	**9.1**	10.4
	Kief Protective Mutual Benefit Assoc CU	Bloomfield	CT	**D+**	D+	D	1.2	-2.29	0.0	25.9	4.3	0.0	**10.0**	19.2
	Kilgore Shell Employees FCU	Kilgore	TX	**D+**	D+	C-	2.7	13.54	0.0	27.7	0.0	0.0	**10.0**	13.0
	Kilowatt Community Credit Union	Jefferson City	MO	**E+**	E+	E+	7.2	0.53	0.0	53.2	0.0	0.0	**5.1**	7.1
▼	Kimberly Clark Credit Union	Memphis	TN	**B+**	A-	A	111.6	3.24	0.0	49.7	10.7	16.7	**10.0**	22.6
	Kinecta Federal Credit Union	Manhattan Beach	CA	**C+**	C+	B-	4025.7	2.45	18.2	35.3	44.8	1.8	**6.1**	8.1
	Kinetic Federal Credit Union	Columbus	GA	**C-**	C-	B-	396.2	27.10	5.4	58.5	8.9	5.8	**9.0**	10.4
	Kings Federal Credit Union	Hanford	CA	**B+**	B+	A-	111.6	10.41	0.0	61.8	2.9	16.6	**10.0**	14.8
	Kings Peak Credit Union	Roosevelt	UT	**D-**	D-	D+	12.5	2.24	1.6	45.9	1.4	0.0	**5.8**	7.8
	Kingsport Press Credit Union	Kingsport	TN	**B-**	B-	B-	69.0	3.10	3.0	18.7	23.8	2.0	**10.0**	12.0
	Kingston TVA Employees Credit Union	Harriman	TN	**C-**	C-	C-	2.2	3.45	0.0	61.0	0.0	0.0	**10.0**	24.5
	Kingsville Area Educators FCU	Kingsville	TX	**D-**	D-	D+	20.7	-2.14	0.0	24.2	0.0	0.0	**5.9**	7.9
▼	KINZUA Federal Credit Union	Warren	PA	**D+**	C-	D+	8.8	-0.70	0.0	31.6	0.3	3.4	**10.0**	18.3
▼	Kirtland Federal Credit Union	Albuquerque	NM	**B+**	A-	A-	783.6	4.95	0.9	32.5	24.2	27.8	**10.0**	12.9
	Kit Tel Federal Credit Union	Kittanning	PA	**D+**	D+	C-	<1	4.67	0.0	24.4	0.0	0.0	**10.0**	24.3
	Kitsap Credit Union	Bremerton	WA	**A-**	A-	B+	1155.6	7.17	4.5	56.5	11.2	15.7	**8.5**	10.3
	Klamath Public Employees FCU	Klamath Falls	OR	**C-**	C-	C-	38.7	5.83	0.0	25.5	3.1	17.8	**7.4**	9.3
	Knoll Employees Credit Union	East Greenville	PA	**C-**	C-	C	8.1	5.70	0.0	19.1	14.2	10.0	**10.0**	15.7
	Knox County Employees Credit Union	Knoxville	TN	**C-**	C-	C-	9.8	12.64	0.0	45.2	0.0	0.0	**10.0**	16.6
	Knox County Teachers FCU	Knoxville	TN	**C+**	C+	C+	26.6	4.11	0.0	23.3	15.0	0.0	**10.0**	11.6
	Knoxville Firefighters FCU	Knoxville	TN	**B-**	B-	B	27.0	-0.55	0.0	26.1	20.7	0.0	**10.0**	14.4
	Knoxville Law Enforcement FCU	Knoxville	TN	**C+**	C+	B-	25.4	5.04	0.0	29.5	18.8	0.0	**10.0**	14.4
	Knoxville Teachers Federal Credit Union	Knoxville	TN	**B-**	B-	B	205.9	3.89	5.6	10.0	33.4	34.9	**10.0**	11.0
	Knoxville TVA Employees Credit Union	Knoxville	TN	**B+**	B+	B+	1753.3	10.29	8.4	47.6	29.1	0.0	**6.9**	8.9
	Kohler Credit Union	Kohler	WI	**B**	B	B	341.9	6.35	5.7	29.1	38.6	1.2	**7.1**	9.1
	Kokomo Heritage Federal Credit Union	Kokomo	IN	**D+**	D+	C-	10.8	8.72	0.4	51.7	0.0	0.0	**9.5**	10.7
▼	Kone Employees Credit Union	Moline	IL	**C**	C+	C	20.7	5.27	0.0	36.1	0.0	0.0	**7.0**	11.0
	Kootenai Valley Federal Credit Union	Libby	MT	**D**	D	D	4.4	6.54	0.0	41.5	0.0	0.0	**8.1**	9.7
	Korean American Catholics FCU	Flushing	NY	**E+**	E+	E-	26.4	10.55	1.9	8.0	21.3	0.0	**4.8**	6.8
	Korean Catholic Federal Credit Union	Olney	MD	**C-**	C-	D+	2.1	15.13	0.0	22.9	0.0	0.0	**10.0**	14.2
	Kraftcor Federal Credit Union	Hawesville	KY	**C+**	C+	C+	15.6	-0.42	0.0	28.2	13.6	0.0	**10.0**	11.3
	Kraftman Federal Credit Union	Bastrop	LA	**B-**	B-	C+	111.8	2.64	0.1	13.4	13.7	50.7	**10.0**	14.9
▲	Kraftsman Federal Credit Union	Hopewell	VA	**D+**	D	D+	6.9	-7.51	0.0	10.5	0.0	0.0	**10.0**	19.2
	Kraton Belpre Federal Credit Union	Belpre	OH	**C**	C	C	7.0	8.53	0.0	33.8	0.0	0.0	**10.0**	13.2
	KRD Federal Credit Union	McCook	NE	**C+**	C+	C-	13.6	-4.08	0.0	63.1	7.0	0.0	**10.0**	12.2
	KSW Federal Credit Union	Waterville	ME	**B-**	B-	B-	59.3	6.34	0.2	32.9	37.3	0.0	**8.7**	10.1
	Kuakini Medical and Dental FCU	Honolulu	HI	**C+**	C+	B-	41.9	-4.13	0.0	6.1	6.1	45.5	**10.0**	12.8
▲	KUE Federal Credit Union	Lexington	KY	**B**	B-	B-	44.7	2.69	0.0	15.5	10.2	11.0	**10.0**	12.2
	KV Federal Credit Union	Augusta	ME	**C+**	C+	C+	82.5	32.46	0.0	18.7	24.0	0.0	**8.7**	10.1
	Kyger Creek Credit Union	Cheshire	OH	**C+**	C+	C+	16.8	0.10	0.0	41.8	21.1	26.5	**10.0**	17.7
	L C E Federal Credit Union	Painesville	OH	**D+**	D+	D	38.4	0.99	0.0	23.5	13.8	31.2	**5.0**	7.2
▼	L C Municipal Federal Credit Union	Lake Charles	LA	**D+**	C-	D	1.2	5.32	0.0	30.4	0.0	8.1	**10.0**	15.5
	L G & W Federal Credit Union	Memphis	TN	**A-**	A-	B	91.8	-0.42	0.0	16.9	13.8	23.5	**10.0**	20.3
	L&N Employees Credit Union	Birmingham	AL	**C-**	C-	C	9.6	-3.51	0.0	33.5	29.8	0.0	**10.0**	20.2
	L&N Federal Credit Union	Louisville	KY	**A-**	A-	A-	1122.7	8.47	11.3	7.7	53.4	17.4	**9.0**	10.3
	L'Oreal USA Federal Credit Union	Clark	NJ	**C+**	C+	B-	27.8	6.29	0.0	18.8	23.4	13.2	**10.0**	18.9
▼	L. A. Electrical Workers Credit Union	Pasadena	CA	**D+**	C-	D+	43.8	-2.16	0.0	9.0	0.0	48.8	**10.0**	21.5
	L.A. Healthcare Federal Credit Union	Los Angeles	CA	**D**	D	D	15.8	-2.83	0.0	39.0	0.0	0.0	**5.3**	7.3
	L.E.O. Credit Union	Painesville	OH	**B-**	B-	B-	14.1	-4.30	0.0	28.1	0.0	55.0	**10.0**	17.0
	La Capitol Federal Credit Union	Baton Rouge	LA	**B-**	B-	B-	509.5	5.49	1.7	43.8	16.2	10.1	**10.0**	12.2
	La Crosse-Burlington Credit Union	La Crosse	WI	**C-**	C-	C-	6.8	-0.63	0.0	33.7	2.8	0.0	**10.0**	13.9
	LA Financial Federal Credit Union	Pasadena	CA	**C-**	C-	C-	385.1	4.58	3.1	23.0	36.5	16.5	**5.8**	8.0
▼	La Joya Area Federal Credit Union	La Joya	TX	**B-**	B	B-	52.7	-4.76	0.0	36.5	3.7	0.0	**9.8**	10.9
	La Loma Federal Credit Union	Loma Linda	CA	**D+**	D+	D	78.5	4.92	3.5	17.8	13.2	27.2	**3.9**	6.0
	LA Mission Federal Credit Union	San Fernando	CA	**D**	D	D+	7.0	-1.95	0.0	10.0	0.0	0.0	**6.0**	8.1
	La Terre Federal Credit Union	Houma	LA	**D-**	D-	D	25.1	-0.27	0.0	48.4	0.0	0.0	**8.8**	10.2

Asset Quality Index	Non-Performing Loans as a % of Total Loans	Non-Performing Loans as a % of Capital	Net Charge-Offs Avg Loans	Profitability Index	Net Income ($Mil)	Return on Assets	Return on Equity	Net Interest Spread	Overhead Efficiency Ratio	Liquidity Index	Liquidity Ratio	Hot Money Ratio	Stability Index
9.2	0.19	2.1	0.23	**3.6**	0.74	0.26	3.25	3.03	88.5	**3.1**	5.2	4.5	**5.6**
6.8	0.26	6.5	0.83	**9.4**	0.41	1.21	15.68	5.67	70.2	**4.4**	21.1	4.9	**4.9**
9.6	0.69	1.4	1.37	**0.0**	-0.08	-0.92	-3.52	2.59	90.0	**4.9**	34.9	0.0	**5.5**
7.0	0.37	2.8	0.04	**1.5**	-0.01	-0.16	-1.73	4.15	103.8	**3.8**	24.2	12.7	**4.1**
8.7	0.19	1.2	0.66	**3.3**	0.01	0.08	0.78	3.84	89.5	**3.6**	22.3	6.6	**4.9**
5.4	10.15	17.4	0.00	**1.6**	0.00	0.35	1.80	3.28	87.5	**6.6**	81.0	0.0	**6.4**
7.0	0.00	0.0	0.00	**3.7**	0.01	1.19	9.28	3.25	95.0	**4.9**	27.5	0.0	**3.7**
3.3	1.27	12.0	1.60	**1.2**	-0.01	-0.74	-10.02	4.86	94.2	**4.9**	29.9	0.0	**1.0**
8.5	0.45	1.3	0.44	**4.8**	0.16	0.59	2.58	4.24	82.0	**4.0**	23.5	9.1	**8.0**
7.3	0.43	4.6	0.68	**3.1**	2.60	0.26	3.22	3.06	82.8	**1.7**	5.5	17.8	**5.5**
5.0	1.08	9.3	1.46	**2.3**	0.10	0.10	0.96	4.60	82.0	**4.0**	20.5	8.5	**4.8**
8.1	0.52	2.5	0.38	**4.1**	0.12	0.43	3.00	3.26	75.0	**3.3**	19.0	15.5	**7.1**
2.7	1.55	13.2	2.19	**0.9**	-0.01	-0.31	-3.67	4.76	105.6	**5.5**	33.9	0.0	**0.3**
7.8	0.35	4.3	0.20	**3.4**	0.06	0.34	2.82	2.50	84.7	**4.8**	61.4	8.3	**6.1**
7.8	0.00	0.0	-0.94	**5.1**	0.01	2.09	8.30	5.32	60.0	**4.8**	29.3	0.0	**4.3**
5.6	3.81	13.9	5.42	**0.0**	-0.09	-1.75	-21.44	3.56	107.5	**5.1**	18.0	1.9	**2.8**
9.2	1.63	2.9	-0.14	**0.5**	-0.02	-0.98	-5.20	3.35	133.3	**6.4**	55.2	0.0	**5.9**
8.0	0.63	3.7	0.74	**4.7**	1.12	0.58	4.44	2.87	72.4	**3.3**	11.8	11.9	**9.0**
10.0	0.00	0.0	0.00	**1.3**	0.00	0.00	0.00	2.84	75.0	**6.5**	40.1	0.0	**7.1**
8.1	0.18	2.2	0.49	**5.4**	1.74	0.61	6.13	3.99	76.7	**3.6**	12.8	5.0	**7.4**
9.2	0.01	0.0	0.58	**2.3**	0.02	0.20	2.12	3.30	87.8	**5.3**	31.6	4.6	**4.2**
8.6	0.00	0.0	0.00	**1.2**	-0.01	-0.25	-1.57	2.43	111.1	**4.8**	28.3	0.0	**7.1**
8.3	0.30	0.9	0.00	**2.9**	0.01	0.41	2.47	3.21	95.6	**5.5**	37.8	0.0	**6.5**
8.3	0.76	2.9	0.56	**2.8**	0.02	0.23	1.95	3.04	91.1	**6.4**	48.4	0.0	**5.9**
9.8	0.00	0.0	0.06	**3.7**	0.05	0.66	4.65	3.39	79.9	**4.8**	23.8	3.0	**6.9**
9.0	0.21	0.7	0.03	**2.9**	0.02	0.35	2.42	3.33	93.4	**5.2**	37.5	10.7	**6.6**
7.8	0.22	2.9	0.51	**4.5**	0.38	0.74	6.71	2.75	75.9	**4.5**	17.7	0.0	**6.7**
8.0	0.14	1.5	0.27	**5.9**	3.92	0.92	10.77	2.99	71.4	**2.8**	14.1	12.9	**6.7**
7.7	0.45	4.1	0.09	**4.7**	0.46	0.55	6.25	3.75	88.7	**3.5**	7.5	0.7	**5.9**
1.8	2.85	21.3	0.52	**3.2**	0.00	0.04	0.35	4.75	88.4	**3.1**	31.1	25.4	**5.6**
9.8	0.15	0.6	-0.05	**3.2**	0.02	0.41	3.71	2.98	87.1	**5.1**	30.3	0.0	**5.7**
4.9	1.74	10.1	0.00	**3.4**	0.01	0.48	4.67	5.73	93.1	**5.4**	37.5	0.0	**2.3**
9.9	0.27	1.2	-0.05	**0.9**	-0.01	-0.11	-1.71	2.83	104.0	**5.7**	22.1	0.0	**0.8**
9.5	0.00	0.0	0.00	**1.9**	0.00	0.20	1.36	4.84	100.0	**7.2**	62.9	0.0	**6.4**
9.1	0.47	2.3	0.05	**2.6**	0.01	0.23	2.05	2.71	91.2	**4.6**	28.3	2.2	**6.2**
8.2	2.07	4.8	0.19	**3.8**	0.16	0.59	4.13	2.54	78.5	**4.3**	16.6	11.9	**8.1**
8.5	4.27	2.6	-8.73	**2.5**	0.02	0.98	5.20	2.17	108.3	**5.2**	30.1	0.0	**5.0**
9.7	0.11	0.3	0.00	**3.8**	0.01	0.70	5.23	2.88	73.3	**5.1**	22.9	0.0	**6.8**
4.7	1.49	9.4	0.60	**5.9**	0.02	0.52	4.38	4.80	72.0	**3.2**	11.4	8.6	**6.5**
6.9	0.27	2.8	0.00	**4.5**	0.10	0.68	7.14	3.95	81.2	**2.7**	12.2	11.5	**5.0**
10.0	0.29	0.4	0.00	**2.9**	0.04	0.36	2.84	1.79	78.7	**4.8**	22.4	4.4	**6.2**
10.0	0.11	0.3	0.14	**3.9**	0.08	0.71	5.78	2.54	71.2	**5.8**	33.7	1.1	**6.5**
9.2	0.14	1.1	0.08	**3.4**	0.07	0.33	3.27	3.20	88.0	**5.2**	30.7	2.7	**5.0**
7.6	1.52	5.5	0.00	**4.2**	0.03	0.59	3.36	2.20	73.3	**2.9**	20.2	13.4	**7.7**
8.8	0.36	2.1	0.15	**3.0**	0.04	0.38	5.37	3.03	88.2	**5.1**	25.4	0.1	**2.6**
9.4	1.05	2.5	3.33	**0.4**	-0.01	-4.56	-28.43	6.36	88.2	**6.9**	55.4	0.0	**5.5**
10.0	0.06	0.1	0.27	**5.7**	0.19	0.81	3.95	3.77	69.0	**6.1**	42.4	6.8	**7.6**
6.3	0.00	10.9	0.00	**3.0**	0.00	0.09	0.54	5.99	98.6	**4.9**	31.7	2.9	**6.9**
9.0	0.32	2.6	0.17	**6.9**	2.79	1.02	9.76	3.19	71.4	**4.1**	22.1	7.6	**8.5**
8.8	1.19	2.9	0.52	**3.2**	0.04	0.51	2.67	4.67	84.5	**6.8**	49.1	0.5	**6.2**
9.5	2.33	1.6	4.14	**0.3**	-0.06	-0.56	-2.63	1.76	92.4	**4.9**	9.3	0.0	**6.8**
6.9	0.91	4.6	3.03	**4.8**	0.02	0.43	5.91	4.58	82.8	**5.4**	27.4	0.0	**2.2**
7.8	3.92	7.0	0.73	**4.0**	0.02	0.56	3.36	3.30	80.2	**5.1**	27.5	1.7	**7.1**
7.6	0.69	4.1	0.90	**3.5**	0.78	0.62	5.68	3.86	79.6	**4.3**	13.3	2.2	**7.2**
6.8	2.89	8.7	0.00	**1.9**	0.00	0.00	0.00	3.53	98.2	**7.0**	64.7	0.0	**6.7**
9.8	0.17	1.6	0.26	**2.0**	0.18	0.19	2.37	3.12	91.6	**4.4**	17.6	4.1	**4.5**
5.2	2.89	15.0	0.31	**3.3**	0.02	0.15	1.33	5.34	90.2	**4.7**	22.7	7.3	**5.2**
8.2	0.20	1.2	0.43	**2.5**	0.02	0.12	1.98	3.36	93.7	**6.2**	34.9	0.0	**2.0**
6.7	5.01	7.2	0.00	**0.0**	-0.06	-3.40	-39.40	2.67	250.0	**7.2**	45.8	0.0	**2.7**
2.9	2.77	17.1	0.59	**0.4**	-0.05	-0.73	-6.98	5.27	99.1	**5.9**	38.3	0.0	**4.7**

Name	City	State	Rating	2016 Rating	2015 Rating	Total Assets ($Mil)	One Year Asset Growth	Asset Mix (As a % of Total Assets) Comm-ercial Loans	Cons-umer Loans	Mort-gage Loans	Secur-ities	Capital-ization Index	Net Worth Ratio
Labor Credit Union	Neenah	WI	**D-**	D-	E+	1.8	3.80	0.0	37.2	34.6	0.0	**6.3**	8.3
Labor Management Federal Credit Union	Lewisport	KY	**C+**	C+	C+	26.1	11.68	0.0	40.8	20.0	0.0	**10.0**	12.9
Lafayette Federal Credit Union	Rockville	MD	**B-**	B-	C+	504.3	2.62	9.0	7.2	57.9	5.6	**6.9**	8.9
Lafayette Schools' Federal Credit Union	Lafayette	LA	**B+**	B+	A-	206.4	5.61	0.1	24.4	28.8	4.5	**10.0**	11.5
LAFCU	Lansing	MI	**B-**	B-	B	654.6	5.92	5.0	33.4	7.2	22.7	**10.0**	11.3
Lake Chem Community Federal Credit Union	Benton	KY	**C+**	C+	C+	56.5	2.73	0.0	30.7	0.0	0.0	**7.3**	9.2
▼ Lake Community Federal Credit Union	Hartville	OH	**D-**	D	D	22.1	5.91	0.0	49.3	3.2	0.0	**6.1**	8.1
Lake County Educational FCU	Painesville	OH	**D**	D	D	20.4	3.28	0.0	31.1	9.1	30.5	**5.5**	7.7
Lake Erie Community Federal Credit Union	Girard	PA	**D-**	D-	D-	4.8	4.97	0.0	41.1	0.0	0.0	**6.1**	8.1
Lake Huron Credit Union	Saginaw	MI	**C+**	C+	C+	50.8	8.86	1.5	38.5	24.0	2.0	**7.9**	9.6
Lake Michigan Credit Union	Grand Rapids	MI	**A**	A	A	5063.2	15.79	5.9	10.6	47.6	7.5	**10.0**	11.4
Lake Shore Federal Credit Union	Angola	NY	**C**	C	C	16.1	8.92	0.0	32.1	6.9	0.0	**7.6**	9.4
▼ Lake Superior Credit Union	Ontonagon	MI	**E+**	D-	D-	6.1	2.92	0.0	31.8	0.0	14.0	**5.6**	7.6
Lake Trust Credit Union	Brighton	MI	**C+**	C+	C+	1838.9	5.94	9.2	24.3	30.6	7.7	**7.8**	9.6
Lakehurst Naval Federal Credit Union	Lakehurst	NJ	**B-**	B-	C	27.3	3.88	0.0	15.6	15.3	3.8	**8.9**	10.3
Lakelands Federal Credit Union	Greenwood	SC	**C-**	C-	C-	12.9	15.00	0.0	37.1	0.0	0.0	**8.7**	10.1
Lakes Area Federal Credit Union	Grand Rapids	MN	**E-**	E-	E-	24.4	2.89	1.3	29.0	18.9	2.6	**3.6**	5.6
▼ Lakes Community Credit Union	Lake Orion	MI	**D+**	C-	C	93.4	-0.03	0.1	36.9	19.2	18.5	**9.6**	10.8
Lakes Federal Credit Union	Monticello	IN	**C**	C	D+	19.6	1.06	0.0	27.8	10.1	0.0	**7.4**	9.3
Lakeshore Community Credit Union	Avon Lake	OH	**D-**	D-	D	28.1	1.97	0.0	13.9	22.5	14.4	**5.9**	7.9
Lakeshore Federal Credit Union	Muskegon	MI	**C+**	C+	C	28.4	8.20	0.0	10.5	18.8	35.9	**10.0**	14.6
Lakeside Employees Credit Union	New Johnsonville	TN	**D+**	D+	D+	39.3	1.47	0.0	28.1	2.5	0.0	**10.0**	13.6
Lakeview Federal Credit Union	Ashtabula	OH	**B-**	B-	B-	95.9	1.34	8.7	6.3	34.3	16.9	**10.0**	12.2
Lakewood Credit Union	Rib Lake	WI	**B-**	B-	B-	12.5	2.79	0.0	12.0	23.9	0.0	**10.0**	13.8
Lakewood Fire Fighters Credit Union, Inc.	Lakewood	OH	**C-**	C-	C-	1.6	-3.12	0.0	28.6	0.0	0.0	**10.0**	20.5
Lakota Federal Credit Union	Kyle	SD	**D+**	D+	C-	5.1	37.18	0.0	48.8	0.0	0.0	**6.4**	8.4
LaMoure Credit Union	Lamoure	ND	**B+**	B+	B	26.8	5.43	32.0	21.6	12.9	0.0	**10.0**	11.2
Lampco Federal Credit Union	Anderson	IN	**D**	D	D-	56.1	-1.32	0.0	35.1	1.7	0.0	**7.4**	9.3
Lan-fair Federal Credit Union	Lancaster	OH	**C**	C	C	55.5	4.53	0.0	4.6	6.4	32.7	**9.6**	10.7
Lanai Federal Credit Union	Lanai City	HI	**C+**	C+	C+	27.8	6.97	0.0	2.5	0.0	0.0	**10.0**	11.4
Lancaster Pennsylvania Firemen FCU	Lancaster	PA	**C-**	C-	D+	<1	9.68	0.0	42.1	0.0	0.0	**8.1**	9.7
▲ Lancaster Red Rose Credit Union	Lancaster	PA	**B-**	C+	C+	64.7	-2.13	0.0	13.2	3.9	56.6	**9.0**	10.3
Lanco Federal Credit Union	Lancaster	PA	**C**	C	C	89.3	10.03	11.0	19.0	19.9	23.0	**4.9**	7.0
Land of Lincoln Credit Union	Decatur	IL	**B+**	B+	B+	234.9	3.12	4.8	41.5	11.4	0.6	**9.2**	10.5
Landings Credit Union	Tempe	AZ	**C+**	C+	B-	160.1	8.40	3.4	31.5	11.4	10.6	**5.9**	8.0
Landmark Credit Union	Fairfield	AL	**C+**	C+	C+	42.1	-5.61	1.0	14.4	50.8	16.5	**10.0**	13.4
Landmark Credit Union	Danville	IL	**C**	C	B-	86.2	5.13	0.1	24.1	7.8	0.9	**7.8**	9.5
Landmark Credit Union	New Berlin	WI	**B+**	B+	B	3370.4	12.07	11.5	44.3	29.4	3.1	**7.1**	9.1
Lane Memorial Federal Credit Union	Zachary	LA	**E+**	E+	E+	1.4	-0.14	0.0	80.3	0.0	0.0	**6.2**	8.2
Laneco Federal Credit Union	Eugene	OR	**D-**	D-	D	17.2	9.99	0.0	25.4	0.0	0.0	**4.8**	6.8
Langley Federal Credit Union	Newport News	VA	**B**	B	B	2384.9	8.15	4.9	48.7	20.6	9.5	**10.0**	11.2
Langston Bag Company Empl Savings Assoc CU	Memphis	TN	**C**	C	C	<1	-8.00	0.0	26.1	0.0	0.0	**10.0**	28.3
Lanier Federal Credit Union	Oakwood	GA	**B**	B	B	33.7	6.04	0.0	45.6	4.6	0.0	**7.9**	9.6
▼ Lansing Postal Community Credit Union	Lansing	MI	**C**	C+	C+	22.4	-0.58	0.0	30.0	14.7	0.0	**10.0**	12.1
LaPorte Community Federal Credit Union	La Porte	IN	**B**	B	B-	36.8	14.33	0.0	41.5	8.3	0.0	**10.0**	11.5
Laramie Plains Community FCU	Laramie	WY	**C-**	C-	C	46.2	3.94	2.1	58.9	10.9	0.0	**7.2**	9.1
Laredo Federal Credit Union	Laredo	TX	**B+**	B+	B+	136.1	1.27	0.6	14.7	13.3	23.8	**7.1**	9.2
Laredo Fire Department FCU	Laredo	TX	**C+**	C+	C+	12.2	4.85	0.0	77.3	0.0	0.0	**10.0**	11.3
Las Colinas Federal Credit Union	Irving	TX	**C-**	C-	C-	73.2	3.18	0.0	53.5	5.2	0.6	**5.8**	7.8
Las Vegas Up Employees FCU	Las Vegas	NV	**C-**	C-	D+	4.0	-7.40	0.0	38.8	0.0	47.9	**10.0**	34.9
Lassen County Federal Credit Union	Susanville	CA	**B-**	B-	B-	73.9	6.59	7.7	36.8	3.2	23.9	**10.0**	16.4
▼ Last Federal Credit Union	Long Island City	NY	**C**	C+	C+	<1	4.49	0.0	0.0	0.0	0.0	**10.0**	29.6
Latah Credit Union	Moscow	ID	**C**	C	C	92.5	6.26	5.0	14.8	21.6	12.2	**6.4**	8.6
Latino Community Credit Union	Durham	NC	**A-**	A-	A-	252.2	16.29	0.8	29.6	55.0	0.0	**10.0**	11.9
▲ Latitude 32 Federal Credit Union	Charleston	SC	**C+**	C	C+	52.2	0.33	0.0	70.8	1.0	0.0	**8.4**	10.0
Latrobe Area Hospital FCU	Latrobe	PA	**D-**	D-	D+	11.1	0.32	0.0	35.6	0.0	0.0	**8.4**	9.9
Latrobe Federal Credit Union	Latrobe	PA	**B-**	B-	B-	11.1	4.23	0.0	26.9	4.7	0.0	**10.0**	12.0
Latvian Cleveland Credit Union	Lakewood	OH	**B**	B	B	31.5	1.50	6.5	1.7	53.2	26.5	**10.0**	14.2
Latvian Credit Union	Minneapolis	MN	**C-**	C-	C-	4.5	-6.50	0.0	39.9	25.4	0.0	**10.0**	12.1
▼ Latvian Federal Credit Union	Melville	NY	**D**	D+	C-	3.9	-2.37	0.0	0.0	15.7	0.3	**10.0**	14.7

Asset Quality Index	Non-Performing Loans as a % of Total Loans	Non-Performing Loans as a % of Capital	Net Charge-Offs Avg Loans	Profitability Index	Net Income ($Mil)	Return on Assets	Return on Equity	Net Interest Spread	Overhead Efficiency Ratio	Liquidity Index	Liquidity Ratio	Hot Money Ratio	Stability Index
6.9	1.13	10.7	0.00	**2.2**	0.00	0.23	2.70	3.88	87.5	**4.2**	27.3	0.0	**1.7**
9.5	0.39	2.0	-0.12	**4.4**	0.06	0.97	7.33	3.27	70.8	**4.3**	26.4	6.4	**5.7**
5.5	0.76	13.2	0.58	**2.5**	0.05	0.04	0.44	3.47	95.2	**2.8**	10.5	7.8	**5.9**
6.7	1.27	8.1	0.59	**4.3**	0.26	0.50	4.65	3.43	82.5	**4.2**	24.8	8.9	**7.0**
7.9	0.65	3.8	0.87	**3.3**	0.33	0.21	1.85	3.44	85.5	**4.5**	22.7	4.2	**7.5**
7.4	0.05	3.4	0.43	**2.9**	0.00	0.00	0.00	3.81	92.2	**3.8**	21.3	9.4	**4.8**
4.8	1.07	8.5	0.74	**1.2**	-0.02	-0.34	-3.99	4.05	105.6	**5.9**	38.4	0.0	**3.5**
9.7	0.13	0.8	0.24	**2.4**	0.00	0.08	1.05	3.45	93.9	**4.4**	14.9	2.1	**3.2**
6.2	1.07	5.8	3.09	**3.7**	0.00	0.09	1.02	4.88	92.6	**5.7**	37.6	0.0	**2.3**
4.6	1.30	11.8	0.57	**5.8**	0.05	0.41	4.21	4.57	79.6	**4.1**	36.3	14.4	**4.5**
9.7	0.11	0.7	0.05	**9.0**	18.08	1.46	12.85	2.72	67.8	**4.8**	28.0	8.2	**10.0**
7.7	0.78	3.6	0.33	**5.1**	0.03	0.71	7.46	3.76	78.5	**6.4**	35.0	0.0	**4.3**
9.2	0.38	1.9	0.00	**0.7**	-0.01	-0.47	-6.03	3.02	110.5	**5.8**	53.6	8.1	**1.8**
7.1	0.61	4.6	0.43	**3.2**	1.39	0.31	3.13	3.56	84.9	**3.9**	12.1	3.4	**6.9**
7.8	1.22	5.2	-0.18	**5.0**	0.05	0.71	7.84	3.16	78.6	**4.8**	24.0	1.4	**4.6**
5.9	1.25	9.7	0.32	**1.6**	0.00	-0.03	-0.30	3.89	100.0	**5.1**	34.4	3.3	**4.1**
1.7	1.38	43.6	2.98	**0.5**	-0.15	-2.41	-40.87	5.67	83.4	**2.7**	15.8	15.4	**0.0**
5.8	1.16	8.1	0.36	**1.5**	0.01	0.03	0.24	3.45	89.0	**4.0**	16.3	1.5	**5.0**
8.4	0.69	2.8	0.00	**4.8**	0.03	0.67	7.11	2.76	79.3	**5.4**	31.5	0.0	**4.0**
5.8	1.07	5.4	0.00	**0.3**	-0.05	-0.75	-11.19	2.82	122.0	**5.7**	49.3	3.1	**1.9**
10.0	0.35	0.9	0.04	**3.2**	0.02	0.27	1.85	2.51	91.4	**5.8**	41.0	3.6	**7.5**
8.8	0.26	0.7	0.67	**1.3**	0.00	0.04	0.30	2.44	96.3	**5.7**	43.7	2.0	**5.9**
9.4	0.62	2.7	0.02	**3.2**	0.08	0.31	2.72	2.76	83.8	**4.8**	37.7	2.7	**6.3**
10.0	0.15	0.4	0.08	**3.5**	0.01	0.39	2.80	2.98	84.0	**5.7**	27.2	0.0	**7.5**
6.9	6.31	7.8	0.00	**3.5**	0.00	0.00	0.00	1.13	100.0	**6.6**	91.3	0.0	**6.7**
3.1	3.65	14.5	1.48	**10.0**	0.03	2.55	30.24	8.41	74.8	**5.7**	156.6	63.3	**3.0**
8.5	0.08	0.4	0.00	**8.0**	0.07	1.08	9.58	4.17	64.8	**5.3**	43.6	14.3	**6.9**
3.1	2.61	20.7	0.50	**1.0**	0.00	0.02	0.33	4.02	93.7	**4.4**	21.8	4.5	**3.2**
6.3	1.24	9.4	0.38	**2.9**	0.04	0.26	2.43	2.85	88.5	**7.0**	50.1	5.7	**5.6**
10.0	0.00	0.0	0.00	**2.6**	0.02	0.22	1.90	1.52	86.7	**5.2**	17.4	0.0	**5.9**
5.2	2.38	9.2	3.64	**3.7**	0.00	-0.92	-8.99	13.48	112.5	**7.0**	59.9	0.0	**3.0**
6.3	2.85	9.7	0.27	**4.1**	0.10	0.63	6.02	2.83	81.0	**5.0**	32.4	0.2	**4.9**
7.4	0.41	3.4	0.69	**3.4**	0.12	0.55	7.78	4.34	81.0	**5.3**	25.9	0.1	**2.6**
8.3	0.57	3.4	0.59	**4.3**	0.22	0.39	3.63	4.33	86.2	**4.5**	27.4	5.5	**6.5**
6.4	0.69	7.7	-0.24	**2.8**	0.11	0.28	3.47	4.48	94.1	**5.2**	28.5	2.7	**4.0**
5.8	1.31	14.3	0.43	**3.8**	0.05	0.44	3.93	4.34	91.3	**2.4**	15.9	25.6	**4.9**
7.4	1.02	4.2	0.38	**3.0**	0.05	0.26	2.64	2.83	88.8	**6.0**	31.5	0.9	**4.3**
6.6	0.64	6.3	0.30	**8.9**	10.33	1.25	14.12	2.73	61.3	**2.4**	9.0	10.2	**7.5**
7.6	0.09	0.8	0.68	**1.8**	0.00	-0.28	-3.39	6.46	108.0	**3.2**	17.8	8.2	**1.0**
9.8	0.00	0.0	0.00	**1.5**	0.01	0.14	2.06	2.48	94.2	**5.8**	38.0	0.0	**2.2**
6.0	0.91	6.1	1.00	**4.7**	4.44	0.76	6.83	3.25	69.4	**3.6**	18.2	10.5	**7.4**
10.0	0.00	0.0	0.00	**3.7**	0.00	0.00	0.00	9.30	0.0	**5.6**	18.2	0.0	**4.7**
7.2	0.48	4.5	0.19	**8.1**	0.08	0.92	9.63	4.52	79.8	**5.4**	42.9	2.2	**5.8**
8.1	1.04	6.4	0.11	**2.0**	-0.01	-0.09	-0.86	3.55	102.2	**5.2**	26.1	1.3	**5.0**
8.9	0.24	1.2	0.52	**6.0**	0.09	1.05	8.91	4.20	81.9	**4.5**	28.2	5.7	**6.0**
4.6	0.36	5.4	0.86	**2.0**	0.00	0.03	0.28	4.11	89.0	**2.7**	11.1	12.0	**3.4**
8.5	0.44	3.9	0.25	**3.2**	0.11	0.31	3.99	2.92	91.9	**4.6**	29.8	6.2	**5.0**
7.4	0.42	2.9	0.64	**3.7**	0.01	0.47	4.10	5.69	82.1	**2.1**	20.6	26.3	**6.2**
6.8	0.30	2.3	-0.06	**2.8**	0.07	0.42	5.20	2.88	88.3	**4.7**	32.3	3.2	**3.2**
9.4	1.68	1.8	1.28	**1.2**	0.00	-0.29	-0.86	5.79	98.3	**6.2**	72.6	0.0	**5.0**
9.5	0.29	1.2	-0.01	**3.4**	0.06	0.34	2.07	3.01	90.2	**4.5**	22.6	6.5	**7.7**
10.0	0.00	0.0	0.00	**1.9**	0.00	0.00	0.00	0.00	0.0	**9.4**	140.0	0.0	**7.9**
6.3	0.49	5.5	0.07	**2.8**	0.05	0.20	3.00	3.09	92.9	**5.1**	31.6	3.9	**3.9**
6.6	0.96	8.0	0.26	**9.5**	1.03	1.66	14.65	5.76	69.1	**1.8**	22.6	47.2	**9.5**
7.4	0.23	2.0	0.18	**3.5**	0.09	0.68	6.83	3.41	84.7	**3.8**	21.3	4.7	**4.7**
7.8	1.05	3.7	-1.02	**1.7**	0.02	0.55	5.47	3.26	101.1	**4.9**	15.5	0.0	**3.3**
9.0	1.26	3.5	0.00	**2.8**	0.00	0.11	0.90	3.01	95.3	**6.9**	54.0	0.0	**6.1**
9.5	0.69	2.8	-0.02	**4.0**	0.04	0.50	3.51	2.11	70.9	**4.3**	30.3	8.0	**6.7**
9.1	0.33	2.1	0.00	**2.3**	0.00	-0.27	-2.20	4.27	110.2	**2.6**	14.6	14.3	**6.1**
9.3	2.36	3.0	3.66	**0.0**	-0.01	-1.22	-8.25	1.10	209.1	**5.5**	43.5	0.0	**5.1**

Name	City	State	Rating	2016 Rating	2015 Rating	Total Assets ($Mil)	One Year Asset Growth	Asset Mix (As a % of Total Assets) Comm-ercial Loans	Cons-umer Loans	Mort-gage Loans	Secur-ities	Capital-ization Index	Net Worth Ratio
Latvian Heritage Federal Credit Union	Grand Rapids	MI	D-	D-	D	4.8	-3.40	0.0	13.0	40.5	0.0	5.7	7.7
Lauderdale County Teachers Credit Union	Florence	AL	B-	B-	B-	28.6	-2.76	0.0	9.2	24.9	0.0	10.0	12.2
▲ Lauhoff Employees Credit Union	Danville	IL	C-	D+	D	5.6	-3.18	0.0	57.0	0.0	0.0	10.0	17.0
Launch Federal Credit Union	Merritt Island	FL	B-	B-	B-	852.1	10.34	0.0	23.0	14.5	39.4	8.6	10.6
Lawilifie Credit Union	Baton Rouge	LA	D+	D+	C-	2.7	-2.97	0.0	28.0	0.0	0.0	10.0	18.6
Lawrence Memorial Hospital Employee FCU	New London	CT	B-	B-	B-	29.9	5.54	0.0	25.4	0.0	0.0	10.0	18.1
LBS Financial Credit Union	Westminster	CA	B+	B+	A	1381.0	9.40	0.0	41.3	15.7	10.5	10.0	13.0
LCO Federal Credit Union	Hayward	WI	E+	E+	E+	1.4	-21.96	0.0	93.4	0.0	0.0	7.7	9.5
LCRA Credit Union	Austin	TX	D	D	D+	22.0	-2.75	0.0	44.8	6.9	0.0	10.0	12.3
Le Roy Federal Credit Union	Le Roy	NY	D+	D+	D	12.4	15.12	0.0	24.1	5.9	6.8	5.0	7.0
Leadco Community Credit Union	Park Hills	MO	C-	C-	C-	21.2	4.75	0.0	45.0	1.1	0.0	9.9	10.9
Leaders Credit Union	Jackson	TN	A	A	A	313.1	10.08	1.2	50.0	14.5	5.2	10.0	12.1
Leahi Federal Credit Union	Honolulu	HI	E+	E+	E+	1.9	-0.16	0.0	68.6	0.0	0.0	3.0	5.0
Leatherstocking Region FCU	Cooperstown	NY	C+	C+	C+	50.1	9.71	0.0	22.8	4.3	32.0	7.2	9.3
Lebanon Federal Credit Union	Lebanon	PA	B	B	B	216.1	7.58	8.5	22.0	36.5	17.8	9.2	10.6
Lee County Mosquito Control Credit Union	Lehigh Acres	FL	C+	C+	C+	<1	-2.17	0.0	13.3	0.0	0.0	10.0	39.0
▼ Lee Federal Credit Union	Washington	DC	C	C+	B-	9.6	-7.39	0.0	0.8	25.5	67.3	10.0	20.7
Leeco Credit Union	Keokuk	IA	B-	B-	B-	4.1	11.17	0.0	43.2	0.0	0.0	10.0	17.8
▼ Lefors Federal Credit Union	Lefors	TX	D	D+	D+	5.3	6.60	0.0	34.4	10.8	0.0	10.0	15.0
Legacy Community Federal Credit Union	Birmingham	AL	B	B	B	433.5	3.73	2.3	29.9	20.2	27.0	10.0	13.5
Legacy Credit Union	Joplin	MO	B-	B-	B-	18.2	2.78	0.0	17.1	12.2	0.0	10.0	11.4
Legacy Federal Credit Union	Portland	OR	C-	C-	C-	50.2	7.93	0.0	21.4	4.2	8.3	8.6	10.1
Lehigh County Employees FCU	Allentown	PA	B-	B-	C+	18.2	9.72	0.0	8.1	20.9	5.4	9.9	10.9
Lehigh Valley Educators Credit Union	Allentown	PA	B+	B+	B+	317.7	3.12	0.0	13.5	0.8	57.6	10.0	16.1
▼ Lehrer Interests Credit Union	Garwood	TX	C-	C	C	2.1	2.29	0.0	8.2	0.0	0.0	10.0	21.4
Lenco Credit Union	Adrian	MI	C+	C+	C-	78.5	3.11	0.0	25.7	20.7	17.0	6.2	8.2
Lennox Employees Credit Union	Marshalltown	IA	C+	C+	C	40.1	4.16	1.7	42.9	1.4	32.5	10.0	13.8
Leominster Credit Union	Leominster	MA	C	C	C	653.0	5.18	2.4	23.5	31.4	25.6	6.6	8.6
Leominster Employees FCU	Leominster	MA	C	C	C	18.8	6.29	0.0	36.7	16.5	0.0	8.6	10.1
▲ LES Federal Credit Union	Baton Rouge	LA	C	C-	C	35.6	8.50	0.0	44.4	7.3	0.0	7.8	9.5
Lesco Federal Credit Union	Latrobe	PA	C+	C+	C+	71.4	3.83	0.0	18.6	4.8	0.0	10.0	17.6
Letcher County Teachers Credit Union	Whitesburg	KY	C	C	C-	1.1	5.71	0.0	41.7	0.0	0.0	10.0	20.3
LeTourneau Federal Credit Union	Longview	TX	C+	C+	B-	22.6	-0.61	0.0	8.5	0.4	0.0	10.0	22.6
▼ Lewis Clark Credit Union	Lewiston	ID	C+	B-	B	96.2	57.94	0.6	39.3	1.4	0.0	6.2	8.2
Lewiston Municipal Federal Credit Union	Lewiston	ME	B-	B-	C	24.0	8.57	0.0	14.3	32.3	0.0	9.6	10.7
Lewiston Porter Federal Credit Union	Youngstown	NY	C+	C+	C+	11.0	2.32	0.0	11.6	23.7	0.0	10.0	11.3
Lexington Avenue Federal Credit Union	Rochester	NY	E+	E+	D-	15.3	-7.55	0.0	68.2	0.4	2.3	6.1	8.1
Lexington MA Federal Credit Union	Lexington	MA	D+	D+	D+	10.9	7.95	0.0	31.7	3.0	0.0	8.8	10.2
Lexington Postal Credit Union	Lexington	KY	C-	C-	D	21.8	5.74	0.0	23.1	13.8	2.5	10.0	13.1
Leyden Credit Union	Franklin Park	IL	C-	C-	C-	84.9	5.30	0.0	11.2	11.4	17.7	6.0	8.2
LGE Community Credit Union	Marietta	GA	A-	A-	A-	1221.8	10.43	2.2	46.1	29.4	11.0	9.9	11.0
▼ Liberty Bay Credit Union	Braintree	MA	D+	C-	C-	646.8	-1.84	2.8	11.6	39.6	24.0	10.0	14.9
Liberty County Teachers FCU	Liberty	TX	C-	C-	D+	16.5	0.81	0.0	36.8	5.4	0.0	6.7	8.7
Liberty First Credit Union	Lincoln	NE	A-	A-	A-	231.5	11.43	8.8	33.1	33.6	0.0	9.5	10.7
▲ Liberty Savings Federal Credit Union	Jersey City	NJ	C+	C	C-	92.0	4.98	0.0	49.7	4.0	0.0	10.0	11.0
▼ LibertyOne Credit Union	Arlington	TX	C+	B-	B-	121.8	8.93	0.0	44.9	12.2	10.8	9.5	10.7
Library of Congress Federal Credit Union	Hyattsville	MD	A	A	A	239.2	4.10	0.0	19.8	31.6	18.4	10.0	14.6
Life Credit Union	Nashville	TN	B	B	B	34.2	7.19	0.0	39.9	18.1	0.3	10.0	11.4
▼ LiFE Federal Credit Union	Denton	TX	C-	C	C	20.9	64.41	36.2	28.7	35.9	0.0	9.7	10.8
Lifetime Federal Credit Union	Richardson	TX	B+	B+	B+	41.5	8.26	0.0	30.4	10.2	16.8	10.0	15.0
▼ LifeWay Credit Union	Nashville	TN	C-	C	C+	47.0	-2.79	0.0	13.1	23.3	14.3	7.5	9.4
▼ Light Commerce Credit Union	Houston	TX	C-	C	C	2.8	4.06	0.0	57.2	0.0	0.0	10.0	18.9
Lighthouse Community Credit Union	Vancouver	WA	D	D	D+	11.3	0.93	0.0	38.6	14.9	0.0	7.2	9.2
Limestone Federal Credit Union	Manistique	MI	B-	B-	B-	47.7	6.62	1.2	26.9	44.7	0.0	10.0	11.3
▲ Limoneira Federal Credit Union	Santa Paula	CA	C	C-	D+	5.3	6.53	0.0	39.3	0.0	0.0	9.7	10.8
Lincoln County Credit Union	Libby	MT	A	A	A	110.9	1.98	2.9	8.5	26.1	20.0	10.0	19.9
Lincoln Maine Federal Credit Union	Lincoln	ME	B	B	B	61.7	8.83	0.1	33.2	26.2	0.0	9.2	10.5
▼ Lincoln National Federal Credit Union	Greensboro	NC	D	D+	D+	15.9	-9.66	0.0	12.5	11.9	54.7	10.0	14.7
Lincoln Park Community Credit Union	Lincoln Park	MI	D+	D+	C-	53.5	0.84	0.0	4.2	2.6	80.6	10.0	16.3
Lincoln S.D.A. Credit Union	Lincoln	NE	D	D	D	11.4	-3.82	0.0	11.2	6.9	0.0	10.0	20.0

Asset Quality Index	Non-Performing Loans as a % of Total Loans	Non-Performing Loans as a % of Capital	Net Charge-Offs Avg Loans	Profitability Index	Net Income ($Mil)	Return on Assets	Return on Equity	Net Interest Spread	Overhead Efficiency Ratio	Liquidity Index	Liquidity Ratio	Hot Money Ratio	Stability Index
3.2	4.37	28.7	-0.13	**5.4**	0.01	1.06	14.25	3.69	69.6	**4.2**	14.9	0.0	**1.7**
9.3	0.48	2.8	0.00	**3.1**	0.02	0.21	1.73	2.28	89.0	**4.6**	27.5	7.9	**6.6**
8.5	0.35	1.1	0.38	**1.4**	0.00	-0.07	-0.42	4.52	102.9	**5.0**	31.5	0.0	**6.0**
9.7	0.43	1.7	1.27	**4.0**	1.45	0.69	6.81	3.40	73.0	**5.4**	16.8	1.0	**6.3**
9.9	0.00	0.0	0.00	**0.6**	0.00	-0.59	-3.16	4.10	120.0	**6.8**	44.2	0.0	**6.7**
10.0	0.02	0.0	0.26	**3.4**	0.03	0.37	2.00	2.32	88.5	**5.8**	52.3	0.5	**7.3**
9.2	0.15	1.0	0.13	**4.9**	2.37	0.70	5.68	3.08	77.1	**4.0**	23.8	12.8	**8.6**
0.7	1.81	41.0	0.81	**3.6**	0.02	4.20	266.67	10.45	82.0	**2.6**	0.7	0.0	**1.7**
8.7	0.19	0.9	0.66	**0.2**	-0.02	-0.37	-3.08	2.78	106.1	**3.9**	14.5	2.5	**5.4**
9.9	0.11	0.8	-0.06	**4.3**	0.02	0.59	8.43	3.76	86.9	**5.8**	35.4	0.0	**3.1**
4.0	1.77	10.2	0.10	**2.8**	0.00	0.00	0.00	3.56	92.5	**5.0**	39.8	0.2	**4.8**
6.4	0.58	4.1	0.57	**8.2**	0.84	1.10	8.97	3.90	75.4	**1.5**	7.1	22.7	**9.0**
0.7	4.97	37.9	0.00	**1.8**	-0.04	-7.31	-122.81	8.15	114.3	**5.5**	35.0	0.0	**2.9**
6.7	1.52	6.6	0.54	**4.5**	0.09	0.69	7.52	2.97	73.2	**5.4**	35.6	2.7	**4.4**
9.0	0.35	2.1	0.29	**5.0**	0.33	0.63	5.94	3.70	80.8	**3.7**	15.5	4.1	**7.0**
10.0	0.00	0.0	0.00	**3.4**	0.00	0.00	0.00	2.30	50.0	**7.7**	140.5	0.0	**6.7**
10.0	0.00	0.0	0.00	**1.9**	0.00	0.00	0.00	1.02	100.0	**6.0**	90.9	0.0	**6.9**
7.3	2.19	5.9	0.60	**7.1**	0.01	0.80	4.44	6.91	77.5	**6.7**	53.5	0.0	**5.0**
7.9	1.32	4.6	0.00	**0.3**	-0.01	-0.99	-6.53	4.56	110.2	**5.5**	41.5	0.0	**5.9**
7.8	0.36	5.3	0.55	**3.7**	0.52	0.48	3.93	2.84	82.2	**4.5**	19.5	3.7	**8.1**
9.9	0.37	1.1	0.00	**3.5**	0.02	0.42	3.70	2.22	78.3	**5.2**	25.7	0.0	**6.2**
8.0	1.21	3.1	0.15	**3.1**	0.07	0.53	5.17	2.38	71.9	**6.9**	51.5	0.8	**5.0**
10.0	0.07	0.2	-0.07	**4.8**	0.04	0.88	7.90	3.15	70.3	**7.3**	59.3	0.0	**6.6**
10.0	0.74	1.3	0.28	**4.5**	0.50	0.63	3.98	2.36	70.3	**5.7**	42.3	2.6	**8.0**
10.0	0.00	0.0	0.00	**1.5**	0.00	-0.19	-0.91	0.69	125.0	**6.7**	68.8	0.0	**7.4**
9.9	0.09	0.6	-0.12	**5.8**	0.22	1.14	13.86	3.15	71.9	**4.8**	28.4	2.4	**4.1**
8.4	0.40	2.8	0.99	**2.9**	0.02	0.21	1.52	3.32	88.2	**4.3**	12.6	0.3	**6.9**
9.2	0.25	2.2	0.09	**2.7**	0.23	0.14	1.46	2.52	93.3	**2.7**	1.2	11.9	**7.0**
6.0	1.82	10.2	-0.14	**4.7**	0.03	0.55	5.52	3.59	82.3	**4.0**	22.8	9.4	**4.3**
6.4	0.93	5.8	0.83	**2.9**	0.05	0.50	5.36	3.87	81.7	**4.6**	44.0	4.1	**4.3**
10.0	0.23	0.7	0.98	**2.3**	0.02	0.09	0.48	2.46	83.3	**5.7**	41.4	6.5	**6.7**
9.8	0.22	0.4	0.00	**4.6**	0.00	1.15	5.45	5.03	75.0	**6.1**	71.5	0.0	**6.9**
10.0	0.23	0.1	0.00	**2.2**	0.00	0.04	0.16	2.21	99.4	**5.9**	49.5	2.5	**6.6**
5.8	0.60	5.4	0.82	**3.7**	0.05	0.21	2.69	4.40	88.3	**3.9**	26.9	12.7	**3.7**
10.0	0.00	0.0	0.06	**6.0**	0.06	0.98	9.28	3.20	71.8	**3.7**	39.9	21.1	**5.7**
5.4	2.50	11.2	0.41	**3.9**	0.01	0.40	3.54	2.96	85.7	**4.8**	22.1	0.6	**6.3**
0.7	3.64	36.8	2.21	**1.5**	0.00	0.10	1.30	5.94	76.2	**2.2**	11.2	13.8	**0.0**
9.9	0.23	0.9	0.34	**1.9**	0.00	0.00	0.00	3.53	98.8	**6.0**	36.8	0.0	**4.5**
9.1	0.10	0.3	0.40	**1.9**	0.01	0.18	1.40	3.32	92.7	**6.1**	37.8	0.0	**6.8**
9.4	0.49	1.6	0.09	**2.2**	0.02	0.09	1.07	2.96	93.1	**6.6**	36.0	1.5	**2.9**
8.5	0.11	0.9	0.33	**5.7**	2.34	0.78	7.05	2.91	74.3	**3.3**	8.7	3.8	**8.2**
8.8	0.65	3.1	0.11	**0.6**	-1.46	-0.90	-6.21	2.75	134.5	**3.0**	6.9	10.0	**8.2**
9.2	0.04	0.3	0.38	**4.6**	0.02	0.52	6.32	4.00	87.9	**5.0**	30.5	0.0	**4.2**
6.6	1.03	7.4	0.40	**7.6**	0.61	1.07	9.98	4.66	76.6	**2.4**	11.0	18.2	**7.6**
3.8	3.11	12.8	3.81	**5.0**	0.24	1.10	9.73	8.25	75.3	**6.3**	45.0	0.0	**6.0**
8.9	0.30	1.9	0.56	**3.2**	0.07	0.24	2.22	2.48	83.0	**3.1**	10.5	8.9	**6.9**
9.4	0.56	2.8	0.46	**6.4**	0.58	0.98	6.68	3.03	61.4	**3.7**	18.8	9.4	**8.6**
7.1	1.18	7.3	0.16	**4.0**	0.03	0.39	3.41	5.11	94.1	**3.9**	21.3	6.7	**5.7**
8.5	0.13	1.0	0.20	**0.7**	-0.06	-1.14	-9.99	4.52	118.3	**2.2**	19.7	27.8	**5.9**
9.5	0.42	1.1	0.14	**4.7**	0.05	0.47	3.09	2.55	73.5	**5.1**	29.2	1.6	**7.2**
6.3	1.56	6.5	4.03	**0.2**	0.00	-0.01	-0.09	2.55	100.3	**5.0**	37.1	0.9	**4.1**
4.9	2.01	10.3	-0.19	**2.7**	-0.01	-1.00	-5.33	5.05	67.4	**4.5**	32.5	11.2	**7.9**
5.2	1.23	8.9	0.49	**2.3**	0.01	0.46	5.05	5.41	100.6	**4.7**	26.9	0.0	**4.1**
7.7	0.64	5.3	-0.14	**6.4**	0.15	1.25	11.05	4.37	73.2	**2.5**	16.8	21.8	**6.2**
9.9	0.00	0.0	0.00	**5.4**	0.02	1.22	11.43	3.86	65.3	**4.3**	33.0	14.6	**4.3**
9.9	0.80	1.9	0.05	**7.5**	0.31	1.14	5.70	2.70	59.8	**5.6**	30.4	1.8	**9.6**
6.3	0.70	5.2	0.09	**5.0**	0.13	0.83	7.88	3.24	78.4	**3.9**	18.2	5.1	**6.2**
10.0	0.24	0.4	-0.10	**0.2**	-0.02	-0.43	-2.90	1.75	123.9	**5.3**	33.7	0.0	**5.8**
10.0	0.40	0.2	0.30	**0.4**	-0.05	-0.34	-2.10	1.74	113.6	**5.8**	31.3	0.0	**5.9**
10.0	0.00	0.0	0.00	**0.0**	-0.02	-0.70	-3.51	2.11	122.6	**5.3**	29.1	7.4	**5.9**

Name	City	State	Rating	2016 Rating	2015 Rating	Total Assets ($Mil)	One Year Asset Growth	Asset Mix (As a % of Total Assets) Commercial Loans	Consumer Loans	Mortgage Loans	Securities	Capitalization Index	Net Worth Ratio
Lincoln Sudbury Town Employee FCU	Sudbury	MA	**D**	D	D	5.2	-1.92	0.0	21.0	12.6	0.0	**10.0**	12.5
Lincoln USDA Federal Credit Union	Lincoln	NE	**C-**	C-	C-	5.9	-1.49	0.7	50.4	0.0	0.0	**10.0**	11.9
LincOne Federal Credit Union	Lincoln	NE	**D**	D	D	132.2	6.34	0.2	24.4	4.4	0.0	**6.8**	8.8
Linde Employees Federal Credit Union	Bridgewater	NJ	**E+**	E+	E+	6.3	-1.68	0.0	36.6	0.0	46.7	**1.9**	4.6
▲ Linden New Jersey Police & Firemen FCU	Linden	NJ	**B-**	C+	B-	10.3	3.40	0.0	10.9	0.0	81.0	**10.0**	15.2
▼ Link Federal Credit Union	Indianapolis	IN	**E-**	E	D-	18.1	-10.25	0.9	60.2	2.4	0.0	**5.1**	7.1
Linkage Credit Union	Waco	TX	**C**	C	C	14.8	14.52	0.3	40.1	0.0	0.0	**10.0**	14.4
Linn Area Credit Union	Cedar Rapids	IA	**B**	B	B	419.2	14.88	5.3	40.3	24.4	5.6	**6.5**	8.6
Linn-Co Federal Credit Union	Lebanon	OR	**B-**	B-	B-	98.2	11.11	0.5	36.2	1.5	0.0	**9.1**	10.4
Linton Federal Credit Union	Tonawanda	NY	**C-**	C-	C-	6.7	2.60	0.0	57.0	0.0	0.0	**10.0**	19.3
LinXus Credit Union	Machesney Park	IL	**C+**	C+	C	18.6	3.06	0.0	27.8	0.0	0.0	**10.0**	13.3
▼ Lion Federal Credit Union	El Dorado	AR	**C**	C+	B-	14.5	4.41	0.0	50.9	0.0	0.0	**10.0**	15.6
Lion's Share Federal Credit Union	Salisbury	NC	**C-**	C-	C-	43.7	-4.71	0.0	65.9	0.0	0.0	**6.9**	9.0
▲ Lisbon Community Federal Credit Union	Lisbon	ME	**B-**	C+	C+	108.3	11.28	4.5	16.6	33.4	0.0	**8.7**	10.1
▼ Lisbon Farmers Union Credit Union	Lisbon	ND	**D**	D+	D	4.5	-2.82	7.5	11.2	29.8	0.0	**10.0**	66.3
Listerhill Credit Union	Muscle Shoals	AL	**B+**	B+	B+	752.6	7.47	13.1	33.5	36.2	7.3	**9.5**	10.7
Lithium Federal Credit Union	Bessemer City	NC	**C**	C	D+	9.1	4.21	0.0	38.8	0.0	0.0	**10.0**	17.0
Little Giant Federal Credit Union	McKees Rocks	PA	**D**	D	D+	9.4	0.17	0.0	20.8	0.0	29.8	**10.0**	12.8
Little Rock Fire Department FCU	Little Rock	AR	**B**	B	B	11.4	1.80	0.0	54.3	0.0	0.0	**10.0**	18.5
Littlefield School Employees FCU	Littlefield	TX	**C+**	C+	C+	1.2	-0.91	0.0	22.1	0.0	0.0	**10.0**	13.1
▼ Livingston Parish Federal Credit Union	Denham Springs	LA	**C**	C+	C+	14.3	-1.54	0.0	23.5	7.9	0.0	**10.0**	17.8
LM Federal Credit Union	Baltimore	MD	**C**	C	C-	35.9	5.15	0.0	32.8	2.9	0.0	**5.3**	7.3
LOC Federal Credit Union	Farmington	MI	**C**	C	C	208.9	9.59	4.7	19.2	17.0	24.4	**5.0**	7.1
Local #673 Credit Union	Mentor	OH	**C-**	C-	D	1.7	-5.03	0.0	64.0	0.0	5.1	**10.0**	13.7
Local 1233 Federal Credit Union	Newark	NJ	**B-**	B-	C+	10.1	4.83	0.0	44.3	0.0	0.0	**10.0**	17.5
Local 142 Federal Credit Union	San Antonio	TX	**D-**	D-	D-	8.3	-5.76	0.0	34.8	0.0	0.0	**8.0**	9.7
Local 20 IBEW Federal Credit Union	Grand Prairie	TX	**E+**	E+	E+	6.9	0.45	0.0	38.0	0.0	0.0	**4.7**	6.8
Local 229 IBEW Federal Credit Union	York	PA	**E+**	E+	E+	1.6	4.98	0.0	64.2	0.0	0.0	**4.9**	6.9
Local 24 Employees Federal Credit Union	Houston	TX	**B-**	B-	B-	11.1	-3.29	0.0	25.6	0.1	0.0	**10.0**	15.8
Local 265 IBEW Federal Credit Union	Lincoln	NE	**D+**	D+	D+	3.1	-21.37	0.0	55.6	2.9	0.0	**10.0**	12.8
Local 355 Maryland Federal Credit Union	Baltimore	MD	**C+**	C+	C+	4.2	-5.55	0.0	12.5	0.0	11.2	**10.0**	24.6
Local 41 I.B.E.W. Federal Credit Union	Orchard Park	NY	**C-**	C-	D+	10.3	1.59	0.0	25.3	21.4	0.0	**8.2**	9.8
Local 461 Federal Credit Union	Macon	GA	**D**	D	D	<1	6.64	0.0	59.4	0.0	0.0	**10.0**	18.7
Local 50 Plumbers & Steamfitters FCU	Northwood	OH	**D+**	D+	D+	8.8	8.93	0.0	46.7	0.0	0.0	**10.0**	11.6
▲ Local 520 UA Federal Credit Union	Harrisburg	PA	**C-**	D+	D+	7.7	-2.68	0.0	31.3	0.0	0.0	**10.0**	19.9
Local 606 Electrical Workers FCU	Orlando	FL	**C+**	C+	C+	8.2	1.30	0.0	4.3	16.5	0.0	**10.0**	15.4
Local 697 Federal Credit Union	Merrillville	IN	**C**	C	C-	35.3	1.83	0.0	16.6	5.8	53.7	**10.0**	18.6
Local 804 Federal Credit Union	Long Island City	NY	**D**	D	D	19.8	-9.67	1.6	10.3	24.4	0.0	**10.0**	23.8
Local Credit Union	Sterling Heights	MI	**C-**	C-	C-	95.9	0.51	0.9	31.3	10.9	42.7	**10.0**	14.2
Local Federal Credit Union	Dallas	TX	**C+**	C+	C+	22.6	0.77	0.0	57.9	3.3	0.0	**10.0**	17.9
Local Government Federal Credit Union	Raleigh	NC	**B+**	B+	B+	1877.6	11.00	4.1	39.4	27.6	4.6	**6.7**	8.9
Local No. 317 I.A.F.F. Credit Union	Charleston	WV	**D+**	D+	D+	7.6	5.64	0.0	41.9	0.0	0.0	**6.5**	8.5
Local Union 1186 IBEW FCU	Honolulu	HI	**D+**	D+	D+	14.9	3.35	0.0	11.3	0.0	35.8	**10.0**	12.2
Local Union 392 Federal Credit Union	Cincinnati	OH	**C-**	C-	C	11.4	6.63	0.0	57.4	0.4	0.0	**10.0**	13.9
Lockport Schools Federal Credit Union	Lockport	NY	**C-**	C-	D+	14.0	15.79	0.0	18.4	13.3	15.0	**6.6**	8.6
LOCO Credit Union	Alamogordo	NM	**B+**	B+	B+	47.2	8.65	0.0	37.0	0.4	4.3	**10.0**	13.6
Locoga Federal Credit Union	Valdosta	GA	**D-**	D-	D	4.8	3.19	0.0	34.2	0.0	0.0	**5.7**	7.7
Locomotive & Control Employees FCU	Erie	PA	**B-**	B-	B-	18.7	2.56	0.0	9.9	16.2	0.0	**10.0**	19.1
Logan Cache Rich Federal Credit Union	Logan	UT	**B-**	B-	B-	24.2	9.92	0.0	29.4	7.0	0.0	**10.0**	13.0
▲ Logan County School Employees FCU	Logan	WV	**C-**	D+	C-	1.4	0.00	0.0	15.9	0.0	0.0	**10.0**	11.7
Logan Medical Federal Credit Union	Logan	UT	**B**	B	B	21.5	6.68	0.5	31.8	21.9	1.2	**10.0**	15.4
Logix Federal Credit Union	Burbank	CA	**A**	A	A	4887.8	9.20	12.8	21.2	60.2	6.0	**10.0**	16.3
▼ Lomto Federal Credit Union	Woodside	NY	**D+**	C-	C+	236.5	-7.68	86.1	0.3	3.4	2.7	**4.0**	6.0
Lone Star Credit Union	Dallas	TX	**B-**	B-	B-	121.6	4.89	0.8	39.3	22.4	2.0	**5.1**	7.1
Long Beach City Employees FCU	Signal Hill	CA	**B-**	B-	B-	307.3	1.97	0.8	7.5	21.7	53.1	**8.9**	10.8
Long Beach Firemen's Credit Union	Long Beach	CA	**A+**	A+	A+	183.2	4.61	8.7	1.9	53.8	1.6	**10.0**	18.6
Long Beach Teachers Federal Credit Union	Long Beach	NY	**C-**	C-	D	4.1	-0.70	0.0	22.0	0.0	0.0	**10.0**	20.0
Long Island City Postal Employees FCU	Long Island City	NY	**D+**	D+	D+	3.1	-5.50	0.0	3.5	0.0	26.6	**10.0**	20.3
▲ Long Island Community FCU	Port Jefferson	NY	**E+**	E	E+	19.9	3.48	0.0	6.6	20.8	0.0	**6.1**	8.1
Long Island Realtors FCU	West Babylon	NY	**D+**	D+	C	15.4	7.53	0.0	37.1	24.6	0.0	**7.6**	9.4

Arrows denote recent upgrades ▲ or downgrades ▼

Asset Quality Index	Non-Performing Loans as a % of Total Loans	Non-Performing Loans as a % of Capital	Net Charge-Offs Avg Loans	Profitability Index	Net Income ($Mil)	Return on Assets	Return on Equity	Net Interest Spread	Overhead Efficiency Ratio	Liquidity Index	Liquidity Ratio	Hot Money Ratio	Stability Index
3.4	10.79	30.5	-0.21	**1.3**	0.00	0.23	1.87	2.51	93.1	**5.5**	70.9	10.8	**5.5**
8.1	0.54	2.8	0.00	**2.0**	0.00	0.07	0.57	3.44	90.7	**4.1**	36.7	2.9	**5.6**
8.1	1.15	5.2	0.09	**1.3**	0.07	0.21	2.32	2.84	92.8	**4.7**	32.3	0.6	**5.3**
3.7	2.85	20.1	0.65	**1.6**	0.00	0.00	0.00	3.99	100.0	**5.4**	23.6	0.0	**0.4**
8.7	5.31	3.7	-0.35	**4.9**	0.02	0.74	4.88	1.80	55.8	**5.9**	34.9	0.0	**7.7**
2.7	2.67	21.7	0.88	**1.0**	-0.02	-0.46	-6.53	5.41	91.4	**4.4**	20.2	3.4	**0.0**
7.2	1.61	5.5	0.32	**2.2**	0.00	-0.11	-0.75	4.10	95.3	**3.0**	26.0	20.0	**6.4**
6.1	0.89	9.1	0.22	**4.1**	0.47	0.45	5.32	3.36	84.7	**3.0**	7.4	7.0	**5.5**
3.9	2.04	14.3	1.70	**5.2**	0.08	0.32	3.02	6.93	69.5	**3.7**	18.7	8.1	**5.1**
6.1	1.70	5.8	0.00	**2.1**	0.00	0.12	0.63	2.61	95.0	**5.0**	39.3	0.0	**6.9**
10.0	0.30	0.7	-0.07	**2.7**	0.02	0.43	3.24	2.77	85.3	**5.3**	36.2	0.0	**6.0**
3.3	3.71	17.4	-0.15	**4.0**	0.01	0.34	2.13	4.99	76.6	**4.1**	11.0	0.0	**7.0**
4.1	1.36	10.3	1.61	**3.3**	0.01	0.11	1.23	5.94	82.3	**3.9**	18.9	7.4	**4.3**
9.1	0.30	2.2	0.12	**4.1**	0.17	0.65	6.37	3.39	81.0	**4.9**	36.9	3.5	**6.6**
9.4	0.43	1.6	0.00	**0.0**	-0.02	-1.78	-2.68	3.38	180.0	**7.7**	136.7	0.0	**6.5**
6.5	0.74	7.1	0.62	**4.7**	1.46	0.79	8.28	4.26	80.2	**3.7**	17.5	7.8	**6.8**
9.3	0.66	2.1	0.16	**1.8**	-0.01	-0.27	-1.56	4.21	104.7	**4.8**	39.5	4.4	**6.5**
7.7	1.44	2.6	-1.37	**0.0**	-0.04	-1.81	-13.73	2.89	152.6	**5.8**	25.0	0.0	**4.7**
7.8	0.32	1.2	-0.10	**9.1**	0.04	1.56	8.43	3.93	56.7	**4.7**	26.6	0.0	**6.3**
8.8	0.76	2.5	0.00	**5.0**	0.00	0.68	5.13	4.53	72.7	**5.5**	20.8	0.0	**4.3**
3.7	6.04	20.1	6.16	**2.1**	-0.01	-0.31	-1.73	4.94	101.8	**7.4**	70.4	0.0	**6.8**
9.9	0.07	1.0	0.03	**3.5**	0.04	0.43	5.86	3.10	86.3	**5.0**	30.1	0.7	**3.5**
8.8	0.22	2.6	0.12	**3.5**	0.26	0.51	9.21	2.90	83.5	**5.0**	21.8	0.8	**3.3**
8.2	0.00	0.0	1.61	**1.0**	0.00	-0.23	-1.62	4.06	105.6	**4.7**	30.5	0.0	**6.8**
9.8	0.00	0.0	0.26	**9.8**	0.04	1.53	8.72	5.94	69.1	**5.9**	34.3	0.0	**6.3**
6.1	1.76	6.3	1.31	**0.9**	0.00	0.05	0.50	3.71	100.0	**4.7**	41.9	10.8	**3.7**
4.9	1.36	8.4	-0.13	**0.2**	-0.01	-0.47	-6.78	3.67	104.8	**4.9**	37.2	0.0	**1.5**
8.5	0.10	0.9	0.00	**3.0**	0.00	0.52	7.48	4.41	83.3	**4.9**	23.5	0.0	**1.0**
8.1	4.66	7.3	0.00	**4.7**	0.01	0.18	1.14	3.83	95.1	**6.1**	33.1	0.0	**7.9**
5.8	1.34	6.5	0.00	**2.1**	0.00	0.13	1.02	3.12	104.8	**4.6**	20.8	0.0	**5.5**
7.6	2.53	1.3	8.92	**3.1**	-0.02	-1.43	-5.79	3.65	86.7	**6.8**	54.2	0.0	**5.5**
9.7	0.00	0.0	0.29	**2.2**	0.00	-0.12	-1.20	3.44	94.6	**4.4**	32.6	0.0	**5.2**
8.2	0.00	0.0	0.00	**0.1**	0.00	-0.85	-4.35	6.45	113.3	**5.3**	41.8	0.0	**5.5**
6.8	0.84	3.7	0.00	**1.1**	0.00	0.00	0.00	3.10	96.2	**5.9**	43.2	0.0	**6.3**
5.7	6.72	14.6	-0.47	**3.6**	0.01	0.67	3.40	3.43	85.5	**5.7**	58.0	0.0	**6.5**
9.9	0.24	0.4	0.00	**3.9**	0.01	0.60	3.82	2.08	51.2	**5.5**	38.9	0.0	**7.2**
6.7	7.17	10.5	-0.22	**1.8**	0.00	0.02	0.13	2.41	88.7	**5.4**	45.4	0.0	**6.2**
7.2	3.07	4.9	2.73	**0.1**	-0.01	-0.28	-1.19	2.96	107.7	**4.6**	31.6	6.3	**5.0**
9.7	0.72	2.4	0.35	**1.7**	0.05	0.19	1.34	2.66	88.3	**3.6**	23.5	14.7	**6.7**
5.4	2.61	9.6	0.34	**2.9**	-0.01	-0.16	-0.89	8.96	99.4	**5.3**	46.0	8.8	**6.7**
5.7	1.17	10.7	1.05	**4.7**	1.11	0.25	2.76	4.50	67.9	**4.1**	16.4	5.9	**6.6**
9.2	0.37	1.6	0.00	**6.1**	0.03	1.54	18.38	3.76	52.5	**5.5**	41.5	0.0	**3.7**
6.2	2.10	2.2	-0.43	**0.4**	-0.01	-0.35	-2.87	1.38	131.0	**6.3**	32.8	0.0	**5.3**
7.3	0.15	0.7	1.05	**2.6**	0.02	0.64	4.56	4.31	72.7	**3.9**	11.2	1.1	**5.4**
10.0	0.27	1.1	0.81	**2.1**	0.01	0.18	2.00	3.12	92.4	**5.9**	25.2	0.0	**3.7**
7.8	1.48	5.0	2.15	**9.8**	0.15	1.31	10.39	5.08	63.1	**4.2**	24.6	9.2	**7.8**
7.9	0.60	2.5	-0.71	**1.2**	0.00	-0.26	-3.23	4.27	97.7	**7.4**	82.0	0.0	**1.0**
8.8	2.93	4.2	0.08	**3.4**	0.02	0.43	2.25	2.33	81.1	**5.3**	38.7	1.7	**7.4**
9.8	0.08	0.3	0.00	**4.7**	0.03	0.57	4.34	2.41	73.6	**4.6**	19.7	0.0	**7.2**
7.9	4.39	5.8	0.00	**2.0**	0.00	0.57	4.82	3.79	75.0	**7.4**	59.9	0.0	**5.3**
7.7	1.48	5.8	0.00	**6.9**	0.06	1.04	6.69	2.85	65.5	**4.0**	28.3	2.3	**5.7**
9.1	0.41	2.3	0.42	**9.2**	15.39	1.27	8.01	3.36	61.9	**2.4**	8.3	9.1	**9.0**
0.0	20.55	167.3	5.53	**1.5**	0.46	0.78	15.93	2.78	90.4	**1.0**	7.9	30.9	**5.3**
9.3	0.19	2.0	0.30	**3.7**	0.09	0.28	3.95	4.05	92.2	**3.4**	12.0	7.6	**3.4**
9.1	1.02	3.2	0.21	**2.9**	0.11	0.14	1.50	1.85	89.8	**5.7**	24.4	0.0	**6.5**
9.9	0.01	0.0	-0.01	**9.2**	0.59	1.29	6.94	2.08	37.1	**4.2**	20.5	0.0	**9.9**
9.7	1.47	2.0	0.00	**1.8**	0.00	0.10	0.49	3.38	92.6	**7.3**	89.2	0.0	**6.9**
9.9	5.43	1.1	0.00	**0.7**	0.00	-0.13	-0.63	2.21	106.3	**5.6**	36.4	0.0	**5.2**
3.7	4.56	21.4	0.00	**1.1**	0.01	0.16	1.99	2.91	95.7	**4.7**	16.7	2.5	**3.3**
2.8	4.95	33.4	-0.04	**2.7**	0.01	0.26	2.78	2.42	88.8	**4.5**	16.8	0.0	**5.0**

Name	City	State	Rating	2016 Rating	2015 Rating	Total Assets ($Mil)	One Year Asset Growth	Asset Mix (As a % of Total Assets) Commercial Loans	Consumer Loans	Mortgage Loans	Securities	Capitalization Index	Net Worth Ratio
Long Island State Employees FCU	Hauppauge	NY	**C-**	C-	C-	13.9	4.60	0.0	21.4	0.0	0.0	**6.8**	8.8
Long Reach Federal Credit Union	Middlebourne	WV	**C**	C	C+	57.1	12.13	0.0	40.9	18.6	0.0	**6.0**	8.0
Longshore Federal Credit Union	Hoquiam	WA	**D**	D	D	5.1	8.67	0.0	47.2	0.0	7.3	**7.5**	9.3
Longshoremen's Local Four FCU	Vancouver	WA	**B**	B	B	27.0	2.84	0.0	20.8	10.4	0.0	**10.0**	18.6
Longview Consolidated Credit Union	Longview	TX	**C**	C	B-	10.1	1.26	0.0	73.8	0.0	0.0	**10.0**	20.6
Longview Federal Credit Union	White Oak	TX	**C-**	C-	C-	4.0	-2.21	0.0	41.2	0.0	0.0	**10.0**	17.6
Lonza Federal Credit Union	Williamsport	PA	**C-**	C-	D+	<1	-3.35	0.0	46.3	0.0	0.0	**10.0**	18.4
▲ Lormet Community Federal Credit Union	Amherst	OH	**C+**	C	C-	158.3	5.26	0.0	61.1	0.6	11.3	**10.0**	11.4
Los Alamos Schools Credit Union	Los Alamos	NM	**B-**	B-	C+	18.2	12.43	1.5	23.8	25.8	0.0	**10.0**	12.3
Los Angeles Federal Credit Union	Glendale	CA	**B+**	B+	B+	911.2	5.60	3.1	19.0	34.9	28.3	**10.0**	11.9
▼ Los Angeles Lee Federal Credit Union	Los Angeles	CA	**C-**	C	D+	<1	-7.23	0.0	30.1	0.0	0.0	**10.0**	24.1
Los Angeles Police Federal Credit Union	Van Nuys	CA	**B-**	B-	B-	903.9	3.93	2.1	21.3	34.6	20.1	**10.0**	11.9
▲ Louchem Federal Credit Union	Louisville	KY	**C+**	C	D+	26.3	2.94	2.1	43.1	15.6	0.0	**8.0**	9.7
Loudoun Credit Union	Leesburg	VA	**C-**	C-	C-	41.3	3.12	0.0	39.3	0.0	0.0	**7.1**	9.1
▼ Louise Mills Federal Credit Union	Merrimac	MA	**D**	D+	D+	9.4	14.59	0.0	23.4	31.2	0.0	**10.0**	11.6
Louisiana Baptist Federal Credit Union	Alexandria	LA	**D-**	D-	D-	4.5	3.11	0.0	63.0	0.0	0.0	**7.9**	9.6
Louisiana Catholic Federal Credit Union	Shreveport	LA	**C-**	C-	C	25.7	-0.74	0.3	25.6	10.9	0.0	**9.1**	10.4
Louisiana Central Credit Union	Harahan	LA	**E-**	E-	D-	13.2	0.61	0.0	60.5	0.0	0.0	**5.5**	7.5
Louisiana Federal Credit Union	Laplace	LA	**A-**	A-	A-	227.0	6.19	6.4	50.2	21.0	4.4	**9.3**	10.5
Louisiana Machinery Employees FCU	Monroe	LA	**C**	C	C	5.0	-1.31	0.0	71.3	0.0	0.0	**10.0**	16.7
Louisiana USA Federal Credit Union	Baton Rouge	LA	**B**	B	B-	81.6	7.65	0.0	27.2	14.5	21.7	**10.0**	11.0
▲ Louisville Federal Credit Union	Louisville	KY	**B**	B-	B-	33.9	-0.21	0.0	21.6	18.7	0.9	**10.0**	16.3
Louisville Gas & Electric Company CU	Louisville	KY	**B+**	B+	B+	40.0	5.88	0.0	32.6	0.9	0.0	**10.0**	13.3
▲ Louisville Metro Police Officers CU	Louisville	KY	**C**	C-	D+	27.9	9.62	0.0	54.0	0.0	0.0	**9.8**	10.9
▲ Loup Employees Credit Union	Gonzales	LA	**B-**	C+	C+	10.5	2.43	0.0	29.7	0.6	0.0	**10.0**	18.5
Louvah Federal Credit Union	Louisville	KY	**D-**	D-	D	3.5	8.34	0.0	58.8	5.7	0.0	**7.2**	9.2
Louviers Federal Credit Union	Newark	DE	**C**	C	C-	291.7	0.32	0.0	4.4	8.3	73.1	**6.5**	10.3
Love Gospel Assembly FCU	Bronx	NY	**D**	D	C-	<1	-42.86	0.0	26.7	0.0	0.0	**3.0**	5.0
Lovers Lane Credit Union	Saint Joseph	MO	**C-**	C-	C-	6.0	5.67	0.0	66.4	0.0	0.0	**10.0**	11.9
Lowell Firefighters Credit Union	Lowell	MA	**C+**	C+	C+	17.1	-2.25	0.0	33.0	8.8	0.0	**10.0**	17.7
▼ Lowell Municipal Employees FCU	Lowell	MA	**E+**	D-	D-	6.7	-10.89	0.0	26.5	0.0	0.0	**6.0**	8.0
Lower Columbia Longshoremen's FCU	Longview	WA	**C+**	C+	C+	71.7	5.61	0.1	16.6	28.7	0.0	**8.2**	9.8
Lower East Side People's FCU	New York	NY	**C+**	C+	C	52.6	15.84	26.8	4.1	63.7	0.0	**8.6**	10.1
Lower Valley Credit Union	Sunnyside	WA	**C**	C	B-	112.8	12.09	0.7	62.8	16.2	2.0	**8.2**	9.8
Lowland Credit Union	Morristown	TN	**D+**	D+	C-	93.0	4.10	0.4	41.4	7.9	2.4	**6.7**	8.8
Loyola University Employees FCU	Maywood	IL	**C+**	C+	C+	48.0	0.90	0.0	13.4	0.0	23.4	**9.9**	11.3
LPS Employees Federal Credit Union	Lincoln	NE	**B**	B	B	46.8	8.01	0.0	16.8	1.0	9.5	**10.0**	12.4
LU 354 IBEW Federal Credit Union	Salt Lake City	UT	**C+**	C+	B-	24.1	6.12	0.4	47.6	11.3	11.9	**10.0**	13.1
Lubbock Teachers Federal Credit Union	Lubbock	TX	**C**	C	C	18.3	4.66	0.0	25.8	0.0	21.9	**10.0**	17.8
Lubbock Telco Federal Credit Union	Lubbock	TX	**C-**	C-	C-	6.0	1.29	0.0	27.9	0.0	0.0	**10.0**	25.8
Lubrizol Employees' Credit Union	Deer Park	TX	**B-**	B-	B-	44.1	7.38	0.0	42.1	0.2	0.0	**10.0**	11.9
Lufkin Federal Credit Union	Lufkin	TX	**B+**	B+	B+	33.9	2.93	0.2	26.7	17.5	0.0	**10.0**	21.0
Lufthansa Employees Federal Credit Union	East Meadow	NY	**B-**	B-	B-	97.3	1.37	0.0	1.5	6.1	11.0	**10.0**	14.3
Luso Federal Credit Union	Ludlow	MA	**B-**	B-	B-	217.7	4.01	4.9	4.9	73.2	2.2	**8.3**	9.9
Luso-American Credit Union	Peabody	MA	**B-**	B-	C+	90.8	6.88	12.2	7.3	42.9	18.5	**10.0**	13.6
Lutheran Federal Credit Union	Saint Louis	MO	**D**	D	D	13.6	94.34	0.3	22.5	23.3	10.3	**10.0**	21.4
Luzerne County Federal Credit Union	Wilkes-Barre	PA	**D+**	D+	D+	16.6	1.35	0.0	17.5	2.7	40.9	**8.0**	9.7
Lynchburg Municipal Employees FCU	Lynchburg	VA	**B**	B	B	22.4	2.79	0.0	33.2	7.3	0.0	**10.0**	18.1
Lynn Co Federal Credit Union	Tahoka	TX	**D**	D	D	<1	-5.82	0.0	35.7	0.0	0.0	**10.0**	25.4
Lynn Firemens Federal Credit Union	Lynn	MA	**C+**	C+	C-	12.2	-5.91	0.0	20.9	23.8	0.0	**10.0**	18.7
Lynn Municipal Employees Credit Union	Lynn	MA	**C+**	C+	C+	2.4	-0.25	0.0	42.6	0.0	0.0	**10.0**	23.9
Lynn Police Credit Union	Lynn	MA	**C+**	C+	C	11.8	-2.00	0.0	22.7	0.0	4.7	**10.0**	22.6
Lynn Teachers Credit Union	Lynn	MA	**C**	C	C-	5.1	-1.15	0.0	24.3	0.0	0.0	**10.0**	14.1
M & C Menlo Park Federal Credit Union	Iselin	NJ	**D-**	D-	E+	1.6	-8.16	0.0	25.4	0.0	0.0	**7.7**	9.5
M A Ford Employees Credit Union	Davenport	IA	**D+**	D+	C-	1.7	9.18	0.0	33.5	0.0	0.0	**10.0**	12.5
M E C O Federal Credit Union	Hondo	TX	**C**	C	C	5.7	-0.05	0.0	45.3	0.0	0.0	**10.0**	16.7
M G & E Credit Union	Madison	WI	**C-**	C-	C-	3.7	7.55	0.0	68.3	0.0	0.0	**10.0**	12.7
▲ M G Employees Federal Credit Union	Hilliard	OH	**C**	C-	C-	3.1	0.68	0.0	46.1	0.4	0.0	**10.0**	27.8
M O Federal Credit Union	Huron	SD	**B-**	B-	B	26.4	2.49	1.3	33.4	28.8	0.0	**10.0**	13.4
M. C. T. Federal Credit Union	Amsterdam	NY	**C-**	C-	D+	53.2	3.27	0.0	6.5	4.6	0.0	**6.7**	8.7

Asset Quality Index	Non-Performing Loans as a % of Total Loans	Non-Performing Loans as a % of Capital	Net Charge-Offs Avg Loans	Profitability Index	Net Income ($Mil)	Return on Assets	Return on Equity	Net Interest Spread	Overhead Efficiency Ratio	Liquidity Index	Liquidity Ratio	Hot Money Ratio	Stability Index
7.1	1.38	4.7	-0.19	5.9	0.03	0.90	10.31	3.74	79.1	5.1	24.4	0.0	3.7
5.5	0.77	8.0	1.21	3.7	-0.04	-0.32	-3.86	4.80	68.5	4.0	24.2	7.4	3.4
3.9	3.06	15.8	0.00	2.8	0.00	0.16	1.67	5.01	93.1	6.0	42.2	0.0	2.3
9.9	0.68	1.4	0.15	4.2	0.04	0.57	3.03	3.27	80.7	5.0	24.7	3.7	7.5
7.5	0.64	2.4	0.15	3.0	0.00	0.12	0.58	4.37	95.4	2.3	25.1	19.5	7.1
7.1	1.68	4.9	0.00	4.4	0.01	1.12	6.32	4.34	86.1	4.4	11.0	0.0	4.3
8.7	0.00	0.0	-1.06	1.8	0.00	0.00	0.00	5.20	100.0	6.7	55.8	0.0	6.7
8.5	0.24	1.5	0.20	2.7	0.14	0.36	3.33	2.18	86.5	4.2	17.6	4.8	6.4
9.8	0.00	0.0	-0.04	4.5	0.03	0.73	5.96	3.94	78.6	5.2	47.5	8.8	6.6
9.5	0.21	1.1	0.75	3.4	0.96	0.43	3.60	3.30	80.1	3.4	8.0	7.7	8.1
7.7	0.00	0.0	0.00	1.8	0.00	0.00	0.00	2.01	100.0	7.0	74.3	0.0	6.4
9.8	0.18	1.0	0.22	2.7	0.26	0.12	0.99	3.76	89.3	3.9	21.4	13.2	8.3
7.7	0.28	2.8	0.48	3.7	0.03	0.47	4.74	4.56	85.3	4.6	26.1	3.2	4.3
7.9	0.58	2.6	0.83	1.8	0.00	0.04	0.43	3.20	86.0	5.4	29.5	1.5	3.9
9.9	0.00	0.0	0.00	0.0	-0.02	-0.77	-6.53	3.11	115.2	3.7	27.0	0.0	5.5
4.5	0.40	3.0	0.00	3.2	0.01	0.54	5.59	4.35	84.8	4.7	28.0	0.0	2.3
5.7	1.03	6.0	0.42	2.4	0.00	0.05	0.45	3.47	113.8	4.9	25.1	5.4	4.2
2.2	3.20	24.4	0.73	4.5	0.03	0.79	10.59	4.91	84.4	3.6	13.4	4.3	1.0
6.9	0.40	3.2	0.70	7.8	0.58	1.06	9.93	4.75	76.7	3.7	15.1	5.9	7.6
7.7	0.64	3.0	-0.10	5.0	0.01	0.79	4.77	4.29	81.1	2.4	22.2	19.1	4.3
8.4	0.57	2.8	0.07	3.3	0.05	0.27	2.41	4.10	92.8	5.2	25.8	2.5	6.2
10.0	0.36	1.0	-0.18	5.1	0.10	1.14	7.00	2.74	71.7	4.7	29.6	6.1	7.2
9.0	1.16	3.6	0.85	4.3	0.07	0.69	5.05	2.73	75.0	4.8	30.9	9.2	7.4
4.4	1.54	8.1	1.08	9.4	0.12	1.75	16.03	5.37	63.9	4.5	30.9	8.6	6.2
9.8	0.36	0.8	0.00	3.4	0.01	0.27	1.45	3.03	88.1	6.0	38.8	0.0	7.7
2.3	0.44	20.4	1.42	2.1	-0.01	-0.92	-9.85	5.84	102.4	4.5	12.3	0.0	1.0
10.0	0.96	1.9	0.03	2.8	0.23	0.33	3.74	1.99	83.6	4.6	11.3	3.6	5.1
2.5	12.50	20.0	0.00	0.7	0.00	0.00	0.00	14.29	100.0	7.6	63.8	0.0	4.8
5.4	0.96	5.5	-0.18	6.6	0.02	1.16	9.66	5.51	70.3	5.2	29.6	0.0	4.3
8.6	0.93	2.8	-0.04	3.0	0.01	0.26	1.46	3.82	90.4	4.8	26.7	2.3	7.0
6.8	2.23	7.3	0.00	0.0	-0.06	-3.88	-44.84	3.45	-2000.0	6.7	40.2	0.0	3.4
7.9	0.96	4.8	-0.01	3.6	0.09	0.52	5.28	3.22	90.6	4.7	32.0	5.4	5.5
4.4	0.42	12.7	0.82	3.8	0.05	0.42	5.72	5.35	93.3	4.7	26.3	1.9	5.0
2.7	1.30	22.5	1.08	5.6	0.17	0.61	6.23	7.38	81.1	2.2	16.1	16.0	5.7
7.7	0.31	2.9	0.28	1.8	0.04	0.17	1.93	2.86	91.7	4.0	13.5	4.0	3.1
8.8	1.95	2.4	0.87	2.2	0.03	0.21	1.92	2.08	85.9	5.0	18.8	0.0	4.4
10.0	0.42	1.2	0.17	4.6	0.08	0.65	5.20	2.20	65.5	4.6	13.7	2.7	6.7
7.2	0.12	0.7	-0.18	6.1	0.06	0.99	7.54	3.38	74.9	3.3	19.6	11.6	5.7
7.2	4.24	6.2	1.45	2.0	0.01	0.24	1.36	3.33	79.3	6.6	50.4	5.8	5.9
9.9	0.10	0.1	0.00	1.8	0.00	0.27	1.03	4.68	89.5	7.3	61.6	0.0	6.8
9.5	0.53	2.0	-0.16	3.4	0.06	0.53	4.45	2.95	89.5	5.0	22.8	0.0	6.7
9.6	0.68	2.3	0.66	5.2	0.02	0.28	1.30	3.20	82.9	4.9	31.3	0.4	7.1
10.0	0.06	0.0	0.00	2.8	0.06	0.26	1.81	0.58	63.4	5.6	38.1	0.8	7.2
7.5	0.79	6.5	0.02	4.3	0.32	0.60	6.03	2.56	78.5	1.0	13.4	35.1	6.9
9.8	0.33	1.6	0.11	2.8	0.07	0.31	2.27	3.08	88.9	3.2	16.8	9.7	7.3
10.0	0.00	0.0	0.00	0.0	-0.22	-6.45	-28.87	3.26	300.9	6.7	52.3	1.4	5.3
5.8	3.77	13.5	0.19	1.0	-0.01	-0.17	-1.74	2.73	104.7	6.2	40.1	0.0	3.8
9.9	0.30	0.7	0.00	6.7	0.08	1.50	8.20	3.67	60.4	5.7	38.2	0.0	6.3
8.9	0.36	0.6	9.56	0.0	-0.01	-5.10	-19.51	5.90	214.3	6.9	62.6	0.0	5.9
10.0	0.18	0.6	0.05	2.8	0.01	0.26	1.41	2.93	91.5	4.3	27.8	1.1	6.6
9.0	1.75	3.0	-0.37	4.7	0.00	0.17	0.69	7.44	93.1	6.9	54.2	0.0	9.3
8.4	3.88	6.0	0.00	3.8	0.02	0.58	2.54	1.92	70.4	3.3	35.1	21.6	7.0
10.0	0.32	0.5	0.30	2.2	0.01	0.41	2.80	5.31	85.7	7.6	76.6	0.0	5.3
3.1	7.20	29.2	0.00	1.9	0.00	0.24	2.56	3.45	100.0	4.7	12.8	0.0	1.7
3.7	11.27	26.5	0.00	2.4	0.00	0.00	0.00	2.45	80.0	7.4	66.4	0.0	5.7
8.5	0.28	0.8	0.00	4.8	0.01	0.86	5.08	3.86	79.0	5.5	57.1	2.5	7.8
8.3	0.08	0.4	0.00	3.9	0.00	0.44	3.45	3.61	90.0	4.3	31.7	0.0	7.3
5.1	6.15	10.9	0.00	6.5	0.01	1.40	5.12	6.27	54.8	6.7	57.0	0.0	4.3
9.8	0.22	1.1	0.00	3.0	0.01	0.21	1.59	2.97	92.1	3.7	22.1	4.1	6.7
8.6	1.11	1.6	1.32	2.5	0.04	0.29	3.28	2.07	82.3	6.2	33.9	1.1	3.9

Name	City	State	Rating	2016 Rating	2015 Rating	Total Assets ($Mil)	One Year Asset Growth	Asset Mix (As a % of Total Assets) Commercial Loans	Consumer Loans	Mortgage Loans	Securities	Capitalization Index	Net Worth Ratio
▲ M.A.B.C. Federal Credit Union	Philadelphia	PA	**C**	C-	C	<1	-0.72	0.0	16.1	0.0	0.0	**10.0**	13.1
M.E. Employees Credit Union	Wausau	WI	**C**	C	C	11.7	9.99	0.0	24.5	49.8	0.0	**10.0**	15.1
M.O.S.E.S. Federal Credit Union	North Reading	MA	**C-**	C-	C-	1.8	-0.17	0.0	42.1	0.0	0.0	**10.0**	17.7
▲ M.P.D. Community Credit Union	Nashville	TN	**C+**	C	C	27.1	5.79	0.0	51.2	12.7	0.0	**7.1**	9.1
▼ M.W.P.H. Grand Lodge of Illinois FCU	Chicago	IL	**D-**	D	D	<1	-3.30	0.0	2.6	0.0	0.0	**9.7**	10.8
MAC Federal Credit Union	Fairbanks	AK	**A-**	A-	A-	106.0	1.27	0.5	61.9	3.2	3.8	**10.0**	16.6
Machinists-Boilermakers FCU	Gladstone	OR	**E+**	E+	E+	4.2	-1.59	0.0	65.7	0.0	0.0	**6.5**	8.5
Macon Firemen's Credit Union	Macon	GA	**B-**	B-	B-	4.7	1.18	0.0	58.6	0.0	0.0	**10.0**	26.8
Macon-Bibb Employees Credit Union	Macon	GA	**C**	C	D+	3.2	17.67	0.0	66.4	0.0	0.0	**10.0**	11.4
Madco Credit Union	Edwardsville	IL	**D**	D	D+	1.7	1.96	0.0	33.1	0.0	0.0	**8.0**	9.7
▼ Madison County Federal Credit Union	Anderson	IN	**D**	D+	D+	74.0	4.96	0.3	24.9	16.8	21.0	**4.9**	6.9
Madison Credit Union	Madison	WI	**C-**	C-	D+	41.5	5.63	0.5	24.8	17.7	40.4	**7.0**	9.0
Madison Education Association CU	Madison	FL	**C+**	C+	C	5.2	3.95	0.0	40.5	0.0	0.0	**10.0**	16.7
Madison Fire Department Credit Union	Madison	WI	**C-**	C-	D+	3.4	-7.49	0.0	70.1	0.0	0.0	**10.0**	17.8
Magnify Credit Union	Mulberry	FL	**C+**	C+	C+	79.2	4.31	6.9	18.9	26.6	11.3	**10.0**	11.9
▼ Magnolia Federal Credit Union	Jackson	MS	**B-**	B	B-	144.2	2.04	0.0	44.3	2.4	7.7	**10.0**	14.1
▲ Mahoning Valley Federal Credit Union	Youngstown	OH	**D+**	D	D	1.2	-20.53	0.0	18.3	0.0	8.7	**10.0**	33.2
Maine Family Federal Credit Union	Lewiston	ME	**B-**	B-	B-	152.5	11.07	0.3	24.2	19.2	7.7	**7.3**	9.2
Maine Highlands Federal Credit Union	Dexter	ME	**B-**	B-	C	110.7	7.55	2.0	17.9	49.7	9.5	**6.5**	8.5
Maine Media Federal Credit Union	South Portland	ME	**C-**	C-	C-	4.8	8.06	0.0	34.8	22.4	0.0	**10.0**	20.9
▲ Maine Savings Federal Credit Union	Hampden	ME	**B**	B-	C+	344.4	10.18	12.3	13.7	41.3	2.9	**6.1**	8.2
Maine Solutions Federal Credit Union	South Portland	ME	**C**	C	C	15.5	1.81	0.0	25.2	36.5	0.0	**10.0**	12.2
Maine State Credit Union	Augusta	ME	**B**	B	B	393.2	5.08	1.5	25.8	29.0	19.6	**10.0**	13.3
Mainstreet Federal Credit Union	Lenexa	KS	**C**	C	C+	433.0	7.45	0.0	27.0	13.0	31.7	**6.0**	8.4
Malden Federal Credit Union	Malden	MA	**C**	C	C-	24.5	1.93	0.0	8.5	9.6	0.0	**10.0**	17.1
Malheur Federal Credit Union	Ontario	OR	**B+**	B+	B	126.2	10.83	10.2	28.7	25.2	10.3	**6.9**	8.9
Mamta Federal Credit Union	Larchmont	NY	**D+**	D+	D+	13.0	2.28	0.0	10.2	0.0	0.0	**5.9**	7.9
Manatee Community Federal Credit Union	Bradenton	FL	**B+**	B+	B+	46.5	47.02	0.0	53.7	0.0	0.0	**10.0**	15.0
▼ Manchester Federal Credit Union	Manchester-by-the-	MA	**D+**	C-	C-	1.7	-4.56	0.0	30.3	0.0	0.0	**10.0**	12.8
Manchester Municipal FCU	Manchester	CT	**C+**	C+	C	21.7	2.23	0.0	38.1	0.0	0.4	**8.3**	9.8
Manistique Federal Credit Union	Manistique	MI	**C**	C	C-	25.6	4.89	0.0	23.0	20.0	25.2	**7.8**	9.5
Manville Area Federal Credit Union	Manville	NJ	**C**	C	C	29.2	-0.01	0.0	8.3	50.1	0.0	**8.6**	10.1
Maple Federal Credit Union	Lafayette	LA	**B+**	B+	B+	32.0	7.75	0.0	41.4	0.0	0.0	**10.0**	12.0
Mapleton Public Schools FCU	Denver	CO	**C+**	C+	C+	2.5	1.53	0.0	22.5	0.0	0.0	**10.0**	14.0
Marathon County Employees Credit Union	Wausau	WI	**B-**	B-	B-	25.8	8.48	0.0	34.3	40.2	0.0	**10.0**	15.2
Marathon Republic Federal Credit Union	Texas City	TX	**D+**	D+	D+	7.9	1.19	0.0	41.1	0.0	0.0	**10.0**	11.0
Marblehead Municipal FCU	Marblehead	MA	**C-**	C-	C	9.3	3.16	0.0	45.9	0.0	0.0	**10.0**	17.6
Marin County Federal Credit Union	San Rafael	CA	**C+**	C+	C+	69.6	7.09	0.0	19.3	0.0	55.9	**7.0**	9.0
Marine Credit Union	La Crosse	WI	**B**	B	B-	704.2	9.24	3.1	27.8	42.2	1.6	**9.9**	10.9
▼ Marine Federal Credit Union	Jacksonville	NC	**C-**	C	C-	731.5	0.71	7.4	46.4	17.5	10.9	**5.9**	8.0
Marion and Polk Schools Credit Union	Salem	OR	**B**	B	B	653.3	13.68	9.9	25.8	27.5	5.2	**5.7**	7.7
Marion Community Credit Union	Marion	OH	**C**	C	C+	66.7	9.42	3.7	40.3	12.1	21.2	**7.9**	9.9
Marion County School Employees FCU	Fairmont	WV	**C-**	C-	C	9.8	2.61	0.0	25.3	0.0	0.0	**10.0**	17.0
MariSol Federal Credit Union	Phoenix	AZ	**B+**	B+	C+	38.0	6.07	0.0	28.1	18.1	0.0	**10.0**	11.4
▲ Market USA Federal Credit Union	Laurel	MD	**A-**	B+	B	103.5	4.12	5.7	39.7	10.3	7.2	**10.0**	19.5
Maroon Financial Credit Union	Chicago	IL	**C**	C	C	43.2	3.02	0.0	14.0	30.8	16.8	**6.7**	8.8
Marquette Community Federal Credit Union	Marquette	MI	**C**	C	C	75.2	6.62	0.4	21.4	2.7	39.2	**6.0**	8.0
▼ Marriott Employees Federal Credit Union	Bethesda	MD	**C**	C+	C+	190.3	5.33	0.0	29.6	12.9	12.4	**9.4**	10.7
Marshall Community Credit Union	Marshall	MI	**A**	A	A	185.3	9.74	10.3	15.6	48.4	11.1	**10.0**	16.9
Marshall County Federal Credit Union	Moundsville	WV	**C-**	C-	C-	14.8	10.19	0.0	38.7	0.0	0.0	**5.9**	7.9
Marshall T&P Employees FCU	Marshall	TX	**B-**	B-	B-	11.7	2.30	0.0	54.5	0.0	0.0	**10.0**	18.1
Marshfield Medical Center Credit Union	Marshfield	WI	**C**	C	C	65.7	5.72	0.4	12.9	32.0	32.2	**5.3**	7.8
Marshland Community Federal Credit Union	Brunswick	GA	**B+**	B+	B+	140.8	2.26	1.9	21.5	16.7	24.6	**9.3**	10.7
Martin County Cooperative Credit Union	Loogootee	IN	**B-**	B-	C+	12.7	6.17	2.3	13.9	58.1	0.0	**10.0**	13.3
Martin Luther King Credit Union	Houston	TX	**D+**	D+	C	<1	-3.48	0.0	31.2	0.0	0.0	**10.0**	43.3
Martinsburg VA Center FCU	Kearneysville	WV	**C+**	C+	C	13.6	2.39	0.0	26.7	0.7	0.0	**9.4**	10.6
Martinsville DuPont Employees CU	Martinsville	VA	**B-**	B-	B-	309.5	10.37	4.9	23.3	31.7	24.1	**10.0**	14.4
Marvel City Federal Credit Union	Bessemer	AL	**C**	C	C	7.4	4.24	0.0	20.7	8.6	0.0	**10.0**	14.7
Maryknoll of Los Angeles FCU	Los Angeles	CA	**D-**	D-	D+	1.1	4.41	0.0	23.5	0.0	10.9	**6.9**	8.9
Maryland Postal Federal Credit Union	Gaithersburg	MD	**C-**	C-	C-	2.5	-8.73	0.0	68.1	0.0	25.3	**10.0**	13.0

Asset Quality Index	Non-Performing Loans as a % of Total Loans	Non-Performing Loans as a % of Capital	Net Charge-Offs Avg Loans	Profitability Index	Net Income ($Mil)	Return on Assets	Return on Equity	Net Interest Spread	Overhead Efficiency Ratio	Liquidity Index	Liquidity Ratio	Hot Money Ratio	Stability Index
10.0	0.00	0.0	0.00	**2.5**	0.00	0.00	0.00	4.30	100.0	**7.9**	95.0	0.0	**7.7**
9.4	0.51	2.5	0.14	**1.7**	0.00	0.00	0.00	3.39	101.1	**4.8**	27.1	0.0	**6.8**
9.3	1.17	2.8	0.00	**1.9**	0.00	0.44	2.55	9.56	85.7	**6.8**	50.1	0.0	**5.6**
6.9	0.00	0.0	-0.04	**6.9**	0.11	1.72	18.93	4.37	81.9	**4.5**	23.0	3.4	**4.5**
8.5	11.11	2.5	0.00	**0.3**	0.00	-1.17	-10.26	0.00	200.0	**7.0**	46.8	0.0	**4.0**
5.3	1.44	8.6	3.27	**8.7**	0.63	2.43	15.19	7.69	44.0	**3.7**	26.2	12.9	**8.1**
4.8	0.55	4.8	0.44	**1.6**	0.01	0.48	5.67	5.62	91.4	**3.4**	12.0	0.0	**1.0**
8.4	0.38	0.8	3.58	**7.3**	0.01	0.94	3.49	5.83	69.2	**5.2**	48.7	0.0	**5.0**
4.8	1.46	11.6	0.91	**10.0**	0.01	1.73	14.69	8.17	76.4	**5.3**	40.3	3.9	**4.3**
5.1	3.67	13.2	11.90	**0.0**	-0.01	-1.99	-19.16	4.54	150.0	**7.1**	67.4	0.0	**5.7**
6.9	0.27	3.9	1.01	**1.7**	-0.06	-0.36	-5.63	3.81	98.5	**5.3**	32.6	0.3	**1.8**
8.3	0.41	1.9	0.68	**2.4**	0.01	0.13	1.40	3.01	87.7	**4.5**	18.1	0.3	**3.7**
7.4	2.23	6.1	0.00	**6.2**	0.01	1.01	6.05	3.39	72.1	**4.3**	23.0	0.0	**4.3**
7.9	0.00	0.0	0.15	**3.9**	0.01	0.71	3.97	3.78	77.4	**3.7**	30.6	0.0	**6.6**
8.0	0.33	4.6	0.82	**3.2**	0.04	0.19	1.58	3.60	91.6	**4.3**	24.5	4.2	**5.7**
7.2	1.89	7.6	2.64	**2.6**	0.05	0.15	1.09	6.89	80.7	**5.2**	28.9	3.1	**7.1**
10.0	0.40	0.3	0.00	**2.1**	0.00	0.97	3.16	3.51	170.0	**6.0**	35.4	0.0	**4.9**
9.7	0.25	1.8	0.07	**3.7**	0.16	0.43	4.53	2.91	84.9	**5.0**	27.7	3.6	**5.6**
6.9	0.70	7.7	0.06	**4.6**	0.20	0.72	8.46	4.40	86.1	**3.1**	14.0	7.8	**5.5**
8.4	0.27	1.0	0.00	**3.0**	0.00	0.09	0.40	4.32	100.0	**4.9**	30.1	0.0	**6.9**
9.5	0.16	1.8	0.03	**5.9**	0.75	0.89	10.84	3.85	73.6	**3.4**	16.8	7.9	**6.0**
9.8	0.04	0.2	-0.04	**1.7**	0.01	0.19	1.47	2.83	94.6	**3.6**	21.0	4.9	**6.3**
9.5	0.28	1.7	0.51	**4.4**	0.45	0.47	4.00	3.54	78.7	**4.4**	17.1	5.1	**8.0**
9.9	0.21	1.7	0.27	**2.9**	0.35	0.33	4.05	2.95	86.1	**4.6**	15.1	1.4	**4.9**
10.0	0.00	0.0	-0.03	**1.9**	0.01	0.21	1.24	2.50	92.1	**4.7**	32.1	0.0	**7.2**
7.4	0.58	3.9	0.55	**5.5**	0.06	0.20	2.14	4.50	87.2	**4.5**	24.7	4.4	**6.9**
10.0	0.00	0.0	0.88	**2.2**	0.00	0.12	1.56	1.70	91.5	**6.0**	25.6	0.0	**3.8**
5.6	1.75	7.7	4.85	**3.2**	-0.20	-1.78	-11.27	5.06	75.3	**3.0**	37.1	22.2	**6.3**
9.3	0.60	1.4	0.00	**0.9**	0.00	-0.24	-1.90	2.63	100.0	**5.3**	22.2	0.0	**6.0**
9.4	0.21	1.2	-0.03	**4.2**	0.02	0.30	3.00	3.16	91.9	**4.4**	10.5	0.0	**6.0**
6.7	0.95	4.8	-0.03	**3.6**	0.03	0.45	4.62	3.38	84.4	**6.2**	44.5	0.4	**5.0**
6.3	1.53	9.1	0.00	**3.4**	0.02	0.31	3.14	2.53	88.1	**4.2**	40.6	5.4	**5.1**
8.3	0.55	2.3	0.57	**3.5**	0.03	0.32	2.61	3.27	85.1	**5.3**	39.5	1.7	**7.0**
10.0	0.00	0.0	0.62	**3.5**	0.00	0.65	4.68	2.88	68.8	**5.4**	40.9	0.0	**7.4**
7.3	0.93	4.7	-0.06	**5.6**	0.04	0.66	4.31	4.15	85.1	**4.0**	18.0	1.0	**7.2**
8.0	1.08	4.9	-0.10	**1.3**	0.00	0.00	0.00	3.85	100.0	**4.6**	12.5	0.0	**5.4**
8.6	0.02	0.1	0.00	**2.4**	0.01	0.39	2.22	3.05	85.0	**5.3**	40.2	0.0	**7.0**
9.6	0.16	0.6	0.46	**3.9**	0.10	0.56	6.12	2.69	79.9	**5.2**	24.5	2.0	**3.9**
5.1	2.55	17.3	0.85	**8.1**	1.39	0.80	7.29	6.93	76.2	**2.7**	19.9	20.0	**9.2**
5.3	0.89	7.7	1.74	**0.7**	-1.02	-0.56	-7.04	4.12	79.8	**4.3**	18.4	6.2	**4.9**
8.9	0.17	1.7	0.17	**7.4**	1.89	1.20	15.22	4.26	75.0	**4.4**	19.1	1.6	**5.9**
8.0	0.10	2.6	0.33	**2.9**	0.02	0.11	1.12	2.89	89.5	**4.1**	18.7	9.4	**4.5**
9.8	1.51	2.5	0.00	**1.4**	0.00	-0.13	-0.72	2.78	100.0	**6.1**	45.3	1.9	**6.7**
8.8	1.08	4.8	0.51	**6.2**	0.06	0.64	5.60	4.48	82.9	**4.9**	22.7	0.0	**6.1**
8.4	1.03	3.1	0.87	**5.9**	0.26	1.03	5.24	4.40	78.3	**4.6**	25.4	1.8	**7.3**
9.6	0.29	1.7	0.36	**3.7**	0.06	0.53	6.01	3.47	88.8	**4.7**	34.9	9.4	**4.1**
6.7	1.50	6.4	0.52	**2.7**	0.05	0.25	3.06	2.87	87.0	**5.6**	24.8	0.2	**3.6**
8.3	0.56	4.1	0.81	**2.3**	0.03	0.06	0.54	3.43	94.5	**5.2**	28.0	1.8	**6.5**
6.5	1.53	7.1	0.32	**9.8**	0.63	1.39	8.22	3.66	71.2	**3.2**	12.6	8.6	**9.7**
9.9	0.00	0.0	0.21	**4.2**	0.02	0.67	8.36	3.94	75.7	**7.2**	57.5	0.0	**3.4**
8.1	0.26	1.0	0.15	**8.4**	0.05	1.62	9.04	4.15	57.1	**2.5**	37.7	22.6	**6.3**
10.0	0.05	0.3	0.00	**2.5**	0.03	0.17	2.25	2.37	93.0	**4.6**	20.8	3.4	**3.5**
8.1	0.78	4.3	0.55	**4.0**	0.15	0.42	3.99	3.56	86.0	**4.8**	22.1	4.5	**6.2**
6.7	1.77	10.1	0.00	**8.1**	0.04	1.09	8.35	3.18	66.4	**2.2**	14.6	16.2	**5.7**
3.1	30.84	23.7	0.00	**4.7**	0.00	1.27	3.01	7.31	75.0	**7.2**	99.4	0.0	**5.8**
10.0	0.00	0.0	0.00	**2.8**	0.01	0.15	1.38	2.70	101.0	**5.5**	30.2	1.8	**4.5**
8.6	0.67	3.2	0.73	**3.8**	0.36	0.48	3.33	3.66	78.5	**3.8**	13.6	4.0	**7.3**
10.0	0.66	1.4	0.33	**3.2**	0.00	0.22	1.47	4.01	89.4	**5.6**	54.0	5.0	**6.5**
5.5	4.09	12.3	0.00	**1.5**	0.00	0.00	0.00	2.44	100.0	**6.6**	75.8	12.0	**4.6**
8.4	0.00	0.0	-0.23	**1.8**	0.00	-0.47	-3.65	5.35	125.8	**3.8**	19.8	0.0	**4.4**

Name	City	State	Rating	2016 Rating	2015 Rating	Total Assets ($Mil)	One Year Asset Growth	Asset Mix (As a % of Total Assets) Commercial Loans	Consumer Loans	Mortgage Loans	Securities	Capitalization Index	Net Worth Ratio
▼ Maryvale Schools Federal Credit Union	Cheektowaga	NY	**C-**	C	C-	8.7	0.78	0.0	21.5	8.8	0.0	**10.0**	16.2
Maryville Municipal Credit Union	Maryville	TN	**B**	B	B	15.8	5.87	0.0	13.5	6.4	0.0	**10.0**	14.5
Mason County School Employees CU	Ludington	MI	**C+**	C+	C+	6.4	7.42	0.0	27.6	0.0	0.0	**10.0**	17.4
Mass Bay Credit Union	South Boston	MA	**C+**	C+	C+	246.4	10.37	1.6	14.4	46.4	13.7	**8.0**	9.9
Massachusetts Family Credit Union	Lynn	MA	**B-**	B-	B-	22.4	5.18	0.0	17.6	30.3	0.0	**10.0**	16.0
Massachusetts Institute of Technology FCU	Cambridge	MA	**B-**	B-	B-	535.7	9.22	0.0	13.6	41.3	5.8	**5.3**	7.5
MassMutual Federal Credit Union	Springfield	MA	**B-**	B-	C+	259.5	4.65	0.0	11.7	21.5	30.7	**8.8**	10.2
Masters, Mates & Pilots FCU	Linthicum Heights	MD	**D**	D	D+	1.9	-1.07	0.0	45.9	0.0	0.0	**5.3**	7.3
▲ Matadors Community Credit Union	Chatsworth	CA	**A**	A-	B	205.1	12.06	0.7	30.2	14.7	0.0	**10.0**	11.0
▼ Matagorda County Credit Union	Bay City	TX	**C-**	C	C-	27.0	6.20	0.0	28.5	7.3	0.0	**9.8**	10.9
Matanuska Valley Federal Credit Union	Palmer	AK	**B+**	B+	B+	480.9	3.15	16.5	15.1	30.4	36.5	**9.4**	11.0
Materion Federal Credit Union	Elmore	OH	**B-**	B-	B-	20.1	12.77	1.1	41.5	12.6	3.2	**10.0**	14.4
Maternity B.V.M. Credit Union	Bourbonnais	IL	**C**	C	C+	11.8	3.86	0.0	34.9	0.0	0.0	**10.0**	11.2
Matson Employees Federal Credit Union	Oakland	CA	**B+**	B+	B+	31.4	-0.96	0.0	8.6	1.3	0.0	**10.0**	23.1
▼ Mattel Federal Credit Union	El Segundo	CA	**D**	D+	D	26.6	5.29	0.0	19.7	17.2	5.1	**6.6**	8.6
Maui County Federal Credit Union	Wailuku	HI	**A**	A	A	276.9	4.75	0.9	9.4	30.8	32.5	**10.0**	14.2
▼ Maui Federal Credit Union	Kahului	HI	**B+**	A-	B	100.8	3.22	2.8	11.6	14.9	41.2	**10.0**	15.2
Maui Teachers Federal Credit Union	Wailuku	HI	**B**	B	B	33.3	-5.34	0.0	5.7	0.0	28.7	**10.0**	13.2
▲ Maumee Educators Federal Credit Union	Maumee	OH	**C-**	D+	C-	2.5	-1.51	0.0	37.6	0.0	15.2	**10.0**	14.9
Maumee Valley Credit Union	Toledo	OH	**C-**	C-	C	21.4	3.89	0.1	36.8	0.0	0.0	**10.0**	12.0
MAWC Credit Union	Saint Louis	MO	**C-**	C-	C-	2.5	-0.24	0.0	60.4	0.0	0.0	**10.0**	11.7
Max Credit Union	Montgomery	AL	**B+**	B+	A-	1291.9	7.76	13.1	31.8	19.8	27.3	**10.0**	13.5
Mayo Employees Federal Credit Union	Rochester	MN	**A-**	A-	A-	870.7	9.11	0.0	15.9	17.1	27.4	**8.4**	10.2
Mazuma Credit Union	Overland Park	KS	**B+**	B+	B+	588.2	2.11	3.5	29.3	31.9	13.0	**7.2**	9.3
▼ MBFT Federal Credit Union	Thurmont	MD	**D+**	C-	C	<1	0.82	0.0	24.6	0.0	4.1	**10.0**	33.1
McAlester AAP Federal Credit Union	McAlester	OK	**B-**	B-	C+	13.2	-2.40	0.0	14.9	0.0	0.0	**10.0**	23.7
McBryde Federal Credit Union	Eleele	HI	**B+**	B+	A-	89.7	1.84	0.1	7.0	1.3	80.9	**10.0**	23.3
McCabe Hamilton & Renny FCU	Honolulu	HI	**C**	C	C	6.6	3.24	0.0	48.1	0.0	24.8	**10.0**	13.2
McClatchy Employees Credit Union	Sacramento	CA	**C**	C	C	15.5	-1.28	0.0	15.4	9.7	21.8	**10.0**	12.7
▼ McComb Federal Credit Union	McComb	MS	**D**	D+	D+	11.8	-10.47	0.0	25.2	1.0	0.0	**6.8**	8.8
McCone County Federal Credit Union	Circle	MT	**B+**	B+	B+	74.0	10.62	44.2	3.8	39.3	0.0	**10.0**	12.4
▼ McCoy Federal Credit Union	Orlando	FL	**B-**	B	B	565.5	6.34	1.3	33.3	11.8	25.0	**6.7**	9.0
▼ McDonald Community Federal Credit Union	McDonald	OH	**D**	D+	D	4.3	-1.41	0.0	12.7	0.0	68.1	**10.0**	19.0
McDowell Cornerstone Credit Union	Marion	NC	**C**	C	C+	27.2	-0.26	0.0	8.8	33.8	0.0	**10.0**	17.7
▼ McDowell County Federal Credit Union	Welch	WV	**C**	C+	C-	<1	2.38	0.0	0.0	0.0	0.0	**10.0**	32.6
▲ McGraw Hill Federal Credit Union	East Windsor	NJ	**C-**	D+	D+	388.3	5.68	0.0	36.3	20.9	9.6	**10.0**	11.4
McIntosh Chemical Federal Credit Union	McIntosh	AL	**C**	C	C-	22.7	4.50	0.0	20.6	6.2	0.0	**10.0**	15.4
McKeesport Area Public School Empls FCU	McKeesport	PA	**C+**	C+	C+	3.5	-1.16	0.0	59.9	0.0	0.0	**10.0**	19.1
McKeesport Bell Federal Credit Union	McKeesport	PA	**D**	D	D-	10.3	-1.24	0.0	12.7	0.0	0.0	**8.3**	9.9
McKeesport Congregational FCU	McKeesport	PA	**D+**	D+	C	<1	-1.00	0.0	42.0	0.0	0.0	**10.0**	16.4
▼ McKesson Employees Federal Credit Union	San Francisco	CA	**D+**	C-	C	28.9	0.28	2.8	32.1	24.0	16.2	**6.1**	8.1
McKesson Federal Credit Union	Stratford	CT	**C-**	C-	C-	24.4	-0.87	0.0	12.4	12.8	0.8	**8.6**	10.1
McLennan County Employees FCU	Waco	TX	**B**	B	B	19.6	2.81	0.0	24.9	0.0	0.0	**10.0**	25.1
McMurrey Federal Credit Union	Tyler	TX	**C+**	C+	C	22.6	-4.04	0.0	40.7	20.0	0.0	**10.0**	12.9
McNairy County Employees Credit Union	Adamsville	TN	**C-**	C-	C-	1.4	5.16	0.0	52.0	0.0	0.0	**10.0**	32.0
McNeese Federal Credit Union	Lake Charles	LA	**C-**	C-	D+	15.4	-4.00	0.0	25.0	0.0	0.0	**10.0**	12.8
McPherson Community Federal Credit Union	Tryon	NE	**E+**	E+	E+	<1	-12.01	0.0	28.1	20.2	0.0	**4.0**	6.1
McPherson Cooperative Credit Union	McPherson	KS	**C-**	C-	C	33.7	0.94	0.0	35.9	17.0	1.5	**7.7**	9.4
MCT Credit Union	Port Neches	TX	**B+**	B+	B+	266.0	5.64	8.0	27.6	30.4	12.2	**9.0**	10.5
▲ MCU Financial Center Credit Union	Racine	WI	**D**	D-	D-	24.0	-3.91	0.0	65.8	6.2	0.0	**6.7**	8.7
MDU Employees Federal Credit Union	Glendive	MT	**C**	C	C	4.7	2.88	0.0	42.6	0.0	0.0	**10.0**	13.0
▼ MEA Credit Union	White Heath	IL	**D**	D+	D+	<1	16.46	0.0	47.5	0.0	0.0	**6.0**	8.0
Mead Coated Board Federal Credit Union	Phenix City	AL	**B**	B	B	53.7	4.58	0.0	10.7	4.9	16.9	**10.0**	14.5
Meadow Gold Employees Credit Union	Salt Lake City	UT	**C-**	C-	C-	4.9	6.07	0.0	48.3	0.0	0.0	**10.0**	22.7
Meadow Grove Federal Credit Union	Meadow Grove	NE	**C+**	C+	C+	4.8	4.89	3.8	12.6	32.5	0.0	**10.0**	14.3
Meadowland Credit Union	Sheboygan Falls	WI	**D+**	D+	D+	20.8	11.60	0.0	24.3	34.2	0.0	**6.5**	8.5
▲ Meadows Credit Union	Palatine	IL	**C**	C-	C-	122.7	7.32	1.2	25.6	26.2	1.2	**4.2**	6.3
▼ MECU	Atlanta	GA	**D**	D+	D	4.6	7.83	0.0	37.1	0.0	0.0	**10.0**	31.5
Med Park Credit Union	Grand Forks	ND	**B-**	B-	C+	18.7	7.94	0.0	27.5	0.0	0.0	**10.0**	11.1
Med5 Federal Credit Union	Rapid City	SD	**C+**	C+	C+	63.0	8.16	2.3	47.6	5.8	0.0	**6.4**	8.4

Asset Quality Index	Non-Performing Loans as a % of Total Loans	Non-Performing Loans as a % of Capital	Net Charge-Offs Avg Loans	Profitability Index	Net Income ($Mil)	Return on Assets	Return on Equity	Net Interest Spread	Overhead Efficiency Ratio	Liquidity Index	Liquidity Ratio	Hot Money Ratio	Stability Index
10.0	0.06	0.1	0.00	**1.6**	0.00	-0.14	-0.85	2.33	86.1	**5.6**	23.4	0.0	**7.0**
10.0	0.00	0.0	0.00	**3.5**	0.01	0.33	2.29	2.97	87.1	**7.3**	51.4	0.0	**7.5**
10.0	0.05	0.1	0.00	**4.4**	0.01	0.58	3.26	1.72	64.0	**5.3**	33.2	0.0	**7.7**
8.4	0.56	4.2	0.11	**3.1**	0.18	0.30	3.13	3.46	93.3	**3.1**	12.3	12.1	**5.8**
10.0	0.28	1.2	0.57	**4.1**	0.02	0.38	2.36	3.58	87.4	**2.7**	34.9	46.6	**7.8**
6.4	1.03	12.0	0.08	**4.8**	0.87	0.66	9.01	3.54	80.2	**2.8**	4.9	3.7	**6.0**
9.6	0.56	2.6	0.14	**4.1**	0.34	0.56	5.22	2.29	74.3	**5.1**	34.5	5.2	**7.0**
2.6	3.78	22.0	0.00	**4.7**	0.00	0.64	8.57	2.50	79.0	**5.2**	54.8	0.0	**1.0**
8.9	0.04	0.3	0.17	**10.0**	1.26	2.48	22.93	6.46	54.8	**3.3**	20.2	14.2	**7.8**
9.3	0.51	1.9	0.50	**2.2**	0.01	0.10	0.96	3.00	85.5	**5.9**	31.8	0.0	**5.5**
6.5	0.86	7.3	0.17	**4.9**	0.77	0.64	6.13	3.36	82.3	**4.2**	27.1	2.9	**7.6**
9.3	0.38	1.8	0.03	**8.4**	0.05	1.09	7.37	3.99	75.6	**4.7**	30.0	4.1	**6.3**
6.7	3.01	10.8	0.00	**2.5**	0.01	0.28	2.42	2.32	87.5	**4.8**	19.8	0.0	**6.1**
10.0	0.48	0.2	0.51	**2.6**	0.01	0.17	0.72	1.88	91.5	**5.1**	9.0	0.0	**6.2**
7.9	0.31	1.6	1.78	**0.9**	-0.02	-0.34	-3.85	2.93	112.6	**5.2**	33.6	4.5	**3.8**
7.2	2.16	7.0	0.27	**7.4**	0.64	0.92	6.64	3.16	69.2	**4.5**	19.0	5.6	**9.1**
10.0	0.39	0.7	-0.07	**4.9**	0.19	0.76	5.08	2.69	71.2	**5.0**	36.6	12.2	**8.1**
10.0	0.54	0.8	0.00	**4.4**	0.04	0.51	4.04	2.10	68.3	**5.3**	15.7	0.0	**6.2**
6.5	0.53	1.3	0.00	**2.7**	0.00	0.32	2.17	2.74	81.3	**5.1**	23.8	0.0	**6.7**
9.3	0.46	2.1	0.72	**1.9**	0.00	0.00	0.00	3.12	100.0	**3.5**	22.2	8.4	**5.5**
8.5	0.00	0.0	0.80	**2.1**	0.00	0.00	0.00	3.26	90.0	**4.3**	32.9	0.0	**5.9**
7.2	1.05	5.1	0.54	**4.6**	2.28	0.72	5.31	3.24	76.9	**4.2**	16.7	5.7	**8.5**
10.0	0.05	0.2	0.07	**6.3**	2.01	0.95	9.37	2.30	66.8	**4.5**	20.0	3.9	**8.5**
5.9	1.39	11.8	1.23	**6.5**	2.24	1.54	17.09	4.10	68.0	**3.6**	15.0	5.3	**6.3**
10.0	0.00	0.0	0.00	**0.0**	0.00	-1.33	-3.94	6.94	133.3	**8.3**	105.8	0.0	**5.4**
9.6	0.02	0.4	1.04	**3.5**	0.02	0.46	1.93	2.97	83.3	**6.1**	42.0	0.0	**7.1**
9.6	5.94	2.6	2.95	**3.5**	0.10	0.44	1.89	1.57	51.2	**5.3**	25.3	0.0	**6.3**
6.5	1.39	5.2	0.72	**3.7**	0.00	-0.06	-0.46	4.70	93.7	**5.9**	47.5	0.0	**6.6**
9.9	0.33	2.0	0.10	**0.9**	-0.01	-0.28	-2.22	1.70	113.9	**5.0**	27.4	0.0	**5.9**
7.0	1.12	3.5	1.30	**1.0**	0.00	0.03	0.38	7.45	107.8	**7.7**	70.1	0.0	**2.8**
4.3	3.11	15.2	0.03	**6.9**	0.16	0.87	7.03	3.45	67.5	**3.3**	30.7	19.0	**7.4**
8.1	0.64	3.6	1.50	**3.5**	0.09	0.07	0.77	3.68	82.9	**4.6**	20.7	7.9	**5.7**
10.0	0.00	0.0	0.00	**0.0**	-0.01	-0.67	-3.46	2.26	133.3	**6.4**	43.0	0.0	**6.8**
7.2	1.80	7.4	1.18	**1.8**	0.00	0.00	0.00	3.61	84.1	**6.3**	50.9	1.5	**6.1**
9.2	0.00	0.0	0.00	**2.0**	0.00	0.00	0.00	28.57	0.0	**8.3**	110.3	0.0	**5.8**
7.5	0.75	5.7	0.23	**1.4**	0.04	0.04	0.38	3.05	90.7	**3.4**	12.7	9.7	**7.1**
8.2	2.69	6.0	0.27	**1.7**	-0.01	-0.09	-0.57	2.15	94.2	**5.9**	38.4	0.0	**6.1**
8.1	0.86	2.7	0.00	**9.5**	0.02	1.83	9.71	4.22	54.3	**4.7**	44.6	0.0	**5.7**
6.7	4.37	7.4	0.90	**0.5**	0.00	-0.12	-1.18	2.10	106.5	**6.7**	46.5	0.5	**4.4**
2.5	12.00	28.9	0.00	**5.4**	0.00	2.70	16.33	3.36	0.0	**6.5**	62.9	0.0	**7.6**
5.8	1.33	11.2	0.41	**3.0**	0.01	0.19	2.22	4.12	90.7	**4.3**	17.2	1.8	**3.2**
10.0	0.19	0.5	0.00	**2.2**	0.01	0.10	0.98	2.25	95.5	**5.7**	56.7	6.2	**4.6**
9.9	0.24	1.1	-0.13	**4.1**	0.02	0.35	1.38	2.75	76.9	**6.0**	72.7	10.1	**6.9**
7.9	0.46	2.9	0.36	**3.3**	0.02	0.42	3.74	2.85	91.4	**2.5**	33.8	22.3	**6.1**
8.5	0.00	0.0	0.00	**1.4**	0.00	-0.30	-0.90	4.93	100.0	**6.2**	67.9	0.0	**7.2**
10.0	0.07	0.2	0.00	**1.7**	0.00	0.08	0.61	2.28	95.5	**5.4**	33.3	0.0	**6.2**
9.9	0.00	0.0	0.00	**0.4**	0.00	-0.62	-10.00	3.87	116.7	**5.2**	17.7	0.0	**0.9**
9.6	0.10	0.6	0.00	**2.1**	0.01	0.11	1.12	3.40	97.0	**3.8**	24.4	11.5	**4.3**
7.1	0.55	4.3	0.11	**4.4**	0.49	0.74	8.11	4.09	84.5	**4.3**	18.7	3.5	**6.0**
6.7	0.38	3.3	0.00	**1.7**	0.01	0.15	1.73	2.58	94.8	**4.1**	16.3	2.0	**3.9**
9.8	0.00	0.0	0.20	**2.6**	0.01	0.52	3.97	2.67	79.3	**5.2**	48.6	0.0	**6.5**
8.7	0.00	0.0	0.00	**2.3**	0.00	0.00	0.00	4.71	100.0	**6.9**	56.8	0.0	**4.0**
6.6	2.56	3.2	0.77	**4.1**	0.07	0.55	3.81	1.18	54.0	**5.0**	24.1	0.0	**7.4**
8.1	0.03	0.1	0.26	**2.9**	0.00	0.33	1.44	4.33	92.9	**4.1**	19.1	3.2	**6.6**
9.2	0.73	2.6	0.00	**4.8**	0.01	0.42	2.91	3.54	87.0	**5.6**	49.5	3.1	**7.9**
7.7	0.26	2.0	0.00	**3.1**	0.02	0.40	4.57	3.73	86.2	**3.5**	14.0	9.3	**3.0**
6.0	1.00	14.3	0.14	**3.8**	0.12	0.41	6.47	3.23	90.0	**3.9**	10.5	0.3	**3.0**
9.8	0.11	0.1	-0.61	**0.0**	-0.01	-0.78	-2.46	3.36	114.8	**5.7**	40.3	0.0	**6.4**
9.8	0.05	0.2	-0.04	**5.0**	0.04	0.87	7.78	3.22	71.2	**5.8**	33.4	0.7	**6.3**
5.6	0.06	3.7	0.25	**5.4**	0.04	0.26	3.02	3.77	89.2	**2.6**	16.8	19.0	**4.3**

Name	City	State	Rating	2016 Rating	2015 Rating	Total Assets ($Mil)	One Year Asset Growth	Asset Mix (As a % of Total Assets) Commercial Loans	Consumer Loans	Mortgage Loans	Securities	Capitalization Index	Net Worth Ratio
Medford Municipal Employees FCU	Medford	MA	**C**	C	C	7.1	3.14	0.0	26.9	0.0	0.0	**10.0**	20.3
Media City Community Credit Union	Burbank	CA	**B**	B	B	32.4	0.00	2.9	19.5	16.1	17.9	**10.0**	13.3
▼ Media Members Federal Credit Union	Conshohocken	PA	**C**	C+	B-	43.0	0.78	0.0	11.9	14.2	10.5	**10.0**	23.8
Medical Employees of Staten Island FCU	Staten Island	NY	**E+**	E+	E+	2.9	-6.35	0.0	52.9	0.0	0.0	**4.9**	6.9
Medina County Federal Credit Union	Wadsworth	OH	**C+**	C+	C	75.4	5.98	2.6	26.2	13.0	33.4	**9.6**	11.0
▼ Medisys Employees Federal Credit Union	Jamaica	NY	**D+**	C-	C-	28.9	4.67	9.3	12.4	0.0	0.0	**8.2**	9.8
Meijer Credit Union	Grand Rapids	MI	**C**	C	C-	64.2	3.49	1.7	33.0	23.1	7.5	**8.5**	10.1
Melrose Credit Union	Briarwood	NY	**F**	E-	B-	1707.8	-11.29	90.1	0.0	26.4	3.0	**0.6**	3.8
Melrose First Federal Credit Union	Melrose	MA	**D+**	D+	C	10.9	6.66	0.0	17.7	30.0	0.0	**10.0**	16.8
MEM Federal Credit Union	Pittsburgh	PA	**C-**	C-	C-	20.5	9.75	0.0	20.9	0.0	0.0	**7.8**	9.5
Member One Federal Credit Union	Roanoke	VA	**B+**	B+	B+	863.3	10.92	0.4	60.5	9.8	3.1	**7.3**	9.2
Member Preferred Federal Credit Union	Fort Worth	TX	**C+**	C+	C	11.6	9.70	0.0	74.3	0.0	0.0	**10.0**	11.4
▼ MemberFocus Community Credit Union	Dearborn	MI	**C-**	C	D+	103.5	3.65	0.0	15.5	9.4	55.9	**8.6**	10.6
Members "FIRST" Community Credit Union	Quincy	IL	**A-**	A-	A-	55.0	8.24	0.0	37.5	27.0	0.0	**10.0**	16.9
Members 1st Credit Union	Redding	CA	**C**	C	C+	179.4	6.08	1.2	55.6	10.8	12.7	**8.2**	9.8
Members 1st Credit Union	Saint Louis	MO	**C**	C	C	42.3	4.98	4.7	18.1	15.2	0.0	**6.9**	8.9
Members 1st Credit Union	Brattleboro	VT	**C**	C	D+	15.3	0.99	0.0	26.2	19.8	0.0	**8.0**	9.6
Members 1st Federal Credit Union	Mechanicsburg	PA	**B**	B	B	3550.3	12.63	13.5	37.5	24.6	10.0	**6.5**	8.6
Members 1st of NJ Federal Credit Union	Vineland	NJ	**D+**	D+	D	54.9	3.76	0.5	29.4	1.1	15.3	**5.7**	7.7
Members Advantage Community Credit Union	Barre	VT	**B+**	B+	B	123.2	9.10	0.0	20.7	13.5	0.0	**7.9**	9.6
▼ Members Advantage Credit Union	Michigan City	IN	**C-**	C	C	96.3	4.01	0.0	21.6	15.3	44.5	**8.3**	10.3
Members Alliance Credit Union	Rockford	IL	**B-**	B-	C+	193.3	5.11	0.0	31.8	13.6	1.0	**5.9**	7.9
Members Choice Credit Union	Peoria	IL	**B-**	B-	B-	120.1	2.97	0.0	35.5	4.6	2.5	**10.0**	13.8
Members Choice Credit Union	Ashland	KY	**B+**	B+	A-	208.5	-0.88	0.3	29.0	24.8	22.0	**10.0**	11.2
Members Choice Credit Union	Greenville	OH	**B+**	B+	B+	20.5	5.67	0.0	22.9	24.3	0.0	**10.0**	18.7
▼ Members Choice Credit Union	Houston	TX	**B-**	B	B-	551.6	4.52	3.7	19.3	38.4	11.2	**6.4**	8.7
Members Choice Federal Credit Union	Bloomington	IN	**D-**	D-	D-	14.7	-0.27	0.5	29.6	10.6	0.0	**5.4**	7.4
▲ Members Choice Financial Credit Union	Danville	PA	**C**	C-	C	148.1	11.14	8.8	32.9	35.7	8.6	**5.9**	8.0
Members Choice of Central Texas FCU	Waco	TX	**B+**	B+	A-	194.5	5.53	0.9	60.4	25.4	3.8	**10.0**	11.4
Members Choice WV Federal Credit Union	Charleston	WV	**B+**	B+	B+	86.6	1.96	1.4	20.5	3.3	0.0	**10.0**	17.9
Members Community Credit Union	Muscatine	IA	**C+**	C+	C+	58.6	3.73	4.1	22.5	27.3	1.2	**7.1**	9.1
Members Cooperative Credit Union	Cloquet	MN	**B+**	B+	B+	648.6	4.71	10.2	38.7	23.8	5.6	**10.0**	12.2
Members Credit Union	Cos Cob	CT	**D**	D	D	28.4	1.59	0.0	23.8	0.0	0.0	**4.9**	6.9
Members Credit Union	Winston-Salem	NC	**C+**	C+	C+	289.0	5.05	0.0	38.0	1.0	35.7	**8.7**	10.1
Members Credit Union	Cleburne	TX	**C+**	C+	C	79.6	5.20	1.1	41.3	0.9	0.0	**6.3**	8.3
Members Exchange Credit Union	Ridgeland	MS	**A**	A	A	108.4	8.58	0.5	38.9	0.5	0.2	**10.0**	16.7
▼ Members Financial Federal Credit Union	Midland	TX	**E+**	D-	D-	44.9	-4.44	0.0	68.2	0.0	0.0	**4.0**	6.0
▲ Members First Credit Union	Midland	MI	**A-**	B+	B	408.0	8.67	7.2	28.3	21.1	11.1	**9.3**	10.6
Members First Credit Union	Corpus Christi	TX	**A+**	A+	A+	128.9	3.74	0.7	26.1	14.5	8.4	**10.0**	18.5
Members First Credit Union	Brigham City	UT	**B+**	B+	B+	117.4	9.26	1.3	45.3	5.8	18.5	**8.8**	10.2
Members First Credit Union	Madison	WI	**B-**	B-	B-	22.1	1.56	0.0	47.7	29.1	0.0	**10.0**	12.6
Members First Credit Union of Florida	Pensacola	FL	**B-**	B-	B-	184.7	4.83	0.0	24.8	17.8	6.0	**10.0**	13.6
Members First Credit Union of N.H.	Manchester	NH	**C**	C	C	173.5	2.98	9.7	13.7	43.9	23.1	**6.5**	8.7
Members First Of Maryland FCU	Baltimore	MD	**D-**	D-	D-	29.2	-7.32	0.0	40.4	21.2	14.7	**8.0**	9.7
Members Heritage Credit Union Inc.	Lexington	KY	**B-**	B-	B-	372.2	5.40	2.2	31.9	13.4	14.3	**10.0**	12.0
Members Plus Credit Union	Medford	MA	**B-**	B-	B-	236.0	7.18	1.2	6.0	50.0	24.0	**10.0**	15.1
Members Preferred Credit Union	Idaho Falls	ID	**B**	B	B-	25.7	15.84	0.0	59.9	14.4	0.0	**10.0**	12.0
Members Source Credit Union	Merrillville	IN	**C+**	C+	C+	79.3	4.38	1.7	18.3	13.5	53.7	**9.8**	10.9
Members Trust Federal Credit Union	Mason	OH	**B-**	B-	B-	24.4	-8.81	0.0	31.1	22.5	0.0	**10.0**	15.9
Members Trust of the Southwest FCU	Houston	TX	**B**	B	B-	113.8	13.90	15.8	20.9	24.9	6.2	**7.1**	9.1
Members United Credit Union	Albany	GA	**B+**	B+	B	64.7	4.95	0.0	49.1	6.1	3.9	**10.0**	14.0
Members' Advantage Credit Union	Wisconsin Rapids	WI	**A**	A	A-	104.4	6.93	8.9	24.2	29.2	0.0	**10.0**	16.8
MEMBERS1st Community Credit Union	Marshalltown	IA	**B-**	B-	C	160.3	5.44	4.4	29.7	13.7	11.1	**8.5**	10.0
MembersFirst Credit Union	Decatur	GA	**C+**	C+	B	189.8	4.59	12.7	45.9	16.3	5.7	**9.6**	10.7
MembersFirst CT Federal Credit Union	Meriden	CT	**B-**	B-	C+	73.5	15.17	0.0	16.2	12.6	2.0	**8.9**	10.3
MemberSource Credit Union	Houston	TX	**C**	C	C	206.5	-1.86	0.0	39.7	6.0	7.6	**5.6**	7.6
▼ MembersOwn Credit Union	Lincoln	NE	**D**	D+	D+	102.8	-0.81	0.0	23.9	3.1	48.1	**5.7**	8.4
Memorial Credit Union	Chattanooga	TN	**C-**	C-	C-	7.8	0.32	0.0	40.2	2.0	0.0	**10.0**	16.5
▼ Memorial Credit Union	Houston	TX	**C**	C+	C-	74.3	3.83	0.0	73.7	5.2	0.0	**7.7**	9.5
Memorial Employees Federal Credit Union	Hollywood	FL	**C+**	C+	B-	63.4	1.80	0.0	26.3	0.6	49.7	**8.4**	10.6

Asset Quality Index	Non-Performing Loans as a % of Total Loans	Non-Performing Loans as a % of Capital	Net Charge-Offs Avg Loans	Profitability Index	Net Income ($Mil)	Return on Assets	Return on Equity	Net Interest Spread	Overhead Efficiency Ratio	Liquidity Index	Liquidity Ratio	Hot Money Ratio	Stability Index
10.0	0.42	0.6	0.00	**3.7**	0.01	0.57	2.78	3.20	81.8	**5.3**	49.0	0.0	**6.7**
9.8	0.48	1.6	0.23	**4.0**	0.05	0.64	4.82	3.19	77.7	**4.2**	28.0	6.4	**6.2**
9.9	1.71	2.2	0.96	**1.2**	-0.05	-0.46	-1.91	2.49	116.1	**5.5**	27.5	0.0	**6.5**
4.4	1.71	11.5	1.03	**2.2**	0.00	0.42	6.09	5.42	90.0	**5.0**	50.0	0.0	**1.0**
9.9	0.29	1.2	-0.01	**3.7**	0.10	0.55	5.10	2.86	81.6	**5.2**	25.8	0.6	**5.4**
7.5	2.35	4.9	0.00	**1.0**	-0.02	-0.21	-2.11	3.13	85.9	**6.5**	55.9	5.0	**4.5**
6.9	0.62	3.9	0.54	**2.8**	0.01	0.06	0.56	4.69	92.2	**4.6**	21.2	0.6	**5.1**
0.0	33.71	242.9	0.41	**0.0**	-38.19	-8.76	-215.31	1.50	62.0	**0.5**	10.6	50.4	**6.0**
10.0	0.05	0.2	-0.08	**0.9**	0.00	0.00	0.00	3.14	100.0	**4.6**	23.9	1.3	**6.5**
7.0	1.56	5.1	0.00	**2.0**	0.00	0.00	0.00	2.99	100.0	**6.5**	41.4	1.3	**4.7**
6.0	0.71	6.6	0.93	**5.2**	1.52	0.72	7.90	3.69	68.6	**2.1**	13.7	20.4	**6.2**
4.6	1.47	9.5	1.60	**3.7**	0.00	-0.14	-1.21	5.47	70.6	**3.3**	34.3	25.4	**7.6**
9.7	0.75	2.6	0.37	**1.6**	0.00	0.00	0.04	2.69	97.4	**4.7**	20.5	1.4	**5.4**
9.0	0.46	2.7	0.38	**10.0**	0.30	2.25	13.24	5.36	65.0	**4.8**	31.2	3.5	**9.4**
8.5	0.07	0.6	0.06	**3.2**	0.24	0.54	5.29	3.14	86.8	**3.7**	11.9	4.1	**5.5**
9.2	0.24	1.7	-0.01	**3.9**	0.06	0.57	6.45	3.17	83.7	**4.4**	19.4	0.3	**4.3**
6.5	0.69	4.7	-0.04	**5.0**	0.01	0.24	2.45	5.21	95.7	**4.0**	32.1	13.0	**4.3**
7.0	0.50	5.4	0.46	**6.9**	9.22	1.06	13.77	3.60	70.6	**3.3**	12.6	8.2	**6.1**
6.7	0.72	5.1	0.08	**2.8**	0.04	0.30	3.82	5.08	94.3	**4.8**	20.1	0.0	**2.6**
7.9	1.21	5.4	0.32	**5.1**	0.19	0.64	6.53	3.72	82.0	**5.4**	33.0	2.2	**6.8**
8.4	0.48	2.0	0.21	**2.1**	0.01	0.02	0.21	2.74	96.1	**4.5**	13.4	2.6	**4.7**
6.2	1.60	11.1	0.40	**4.4**	0.26	0.55	6.83	3.62	81.1	**4.5**	18.2	0.7	**4.8**
8.9	1.07	3.5	0.53	**3.4**	0.12	0.42	3.01	3.04	80.8	**5.2**	32.1	2.4	**7.7**
7.0	1.49	7.5	2.10	**2.9**	-0.21	-0.40	-3.49	3.56	64.4	**4.0**	18.2	10.4	**6.0**
9.9	0.43	1.2	0.15	**5.5**	0.03	0.65	3.46	2.91	81.3	**4.9**	38.0	2.3	**8.2**
7.9	0.45	3.5	0.32	**3.4**	0.42	0.31	3.66	4.17	85.6	**4.1**	14.4	3.5	**6.0**
7.0	0.38	2.6	-0.05	**1.3**	0.00	0.06	0.74	3.53	101.8	**5.2**	32.5	0.0	**2.0**
3.7	1.21	21.8	0.08	**2.9**	0.16	0.43	5.38	3.28	83.1	**3.9**	21.0	6.2	**4.6**
7.0	0.20	3.5	1.47	**3.2**	-0.08	-0.17	-1.45	4.51	78.4	**1.5**	10.8	23.6	**6.8**
10.0	0.68	1.3	0.68	**3.8**	0.08	0.35	1.94	2.16	83.9	**5.1**	33.2	3.1	**7.2**
7.9	0.19	1.4	-0.07	**4.4**	0.07	0.46	5.00	3.74	89.5	**4.6**	24.3	2.8	**5.0**
7.1	0.63	4.5	0.43	**4.0**	0.94	0.59	4.70	3.72	77.9	**3.2**	12.8	11.2	**7.9**
8.4	0.08	0.8	-0.08	**3.2**	0.02	0.24	3.50	4.34	95.6	**4.5**	23.8	0.0	**2.3**
8.7	0.56	3.4	0.99	**3.9**	0.40	0.57	5.40	3.38	78.5	**5.0**	21.8	1.6	**5.5**
6.4	1.01	5.8	0.62	**3.1**	0.05	0.25	2.93	3.38	90.5	**5.5**	45.1	4.5	**3.8**
8.0	1.20	3.9	2.01	**9.5**	0.34	1.29	7.58	6.07	70.4	**4.1**	37.2	18.9	**9.2**
3.0	0.92	11.9	1.34	**0.7**	0.00	-0.03	-0.45	4.30	90.4	**4.0**	22.9	8.7	**0.0**
8.6	0.46	2.4	0.95	**6.4**	1.00	1.00	9.44	4.86	75.7	**4.4**	22.2	3.9	**6.8**
9.8	0.36	1.1	0.86	**7.6**	0.36	1.13	6.33	3.17	68.4	**4.8**	26.9	3.8	**8.8**
8.4	0.10	0.6	0.00	**4.4**	0.15	0.51	4.91	3.49	86.0	**4.3**	14.3	3.5	**6.7**
7.3	0.33	2.2	0.50	**6.9**	0.05	0.91	7.29	4.92	85.4	**1.4**	9.4	27.4	**5.7**
9.4	0.31	1.7	0.87	**2.7**	0.08	0.18	1.42	3.81	89.0	**5.5**	33.4	3.8	**7.4**
9.4	0.13	1.7	0.07	**2.3**	0.08	0.18	2.10	3.06	94.2	**3.6**	18.6	6.1	**5.6**
7.0	0.46	3.2	1.50	**0.0**	-0.08	-1.09	-10.98	3.75	108.5	**4.2**	28.1	0.0	**3.2**
9.2	0.40	2.1	0.73	**3.6**	0.47	0.51	4.83	3.58	82.5	**5.2**	33.1	4.9	**5.9**
8.8	1.16	5.1	0.03	**3.4**	0.30	0.51	3.45	2.99	83.4	**3.4**	11.5	6.4	**8.3**
8.1	0.36	2.3	0.66	**10.0**	0.14	2.26	18.62	5.36	58.5	**3.6**	14.3	3.7	**6.3**
9.9	0.26	0.8	-0.12	**2.1**	0.02	0.10	0.93	2.48	94.3	**4.8**	23.5	0.8	**5.1**
8.3	0.38	4.4	0.00	**3.0**	0.02	0.32	1.96	3.36	89.1	**4.8**	26.0	1.8	**6.8**
5.9	0.68	6.5	0.41	**4.9**	0.22	0.79	10.38	3.06	77.7	**2.5**	13.0	16.4	**5.5**
6.5	0.89	5.4	0.44	**7.6**	0.16	0.98	6.89	4.57	74.2	**3.0**	17.0	13.9	**7.1**
9.2	0.45	1.9	0.09	**9.3**	0.35	1.35	7.99	3.73	69.5	**3.6**	15.8	3.8	**9.9**
7.4	0.30	5.1	0.10	**4.4**	0.29	0.74	7.37	2.83	77.5	**4.3**	23.7	2.3	**6.4**
6.9	0.33	4.1	0.36	**3.7**	0.25	0.54	4.98	3.84	83.5	**4.2**	23.0	4.4	**6.0**
9.3	0.30	1.0	0.72	**3.7**	0.09	0.50	4.85	2.89	79.5	**5.7**	34.1	1.6	**4.7**
8.8	0.40	3.3	0.87	**2.1**	0.06	0.12	1.51	3.32	88.9	**4.4**	19.7	4.5	**4.3**
8.7	0.64	3.4	0.35	**0.6**	-0.04	-0.17	-2.21	2.51	99.7	**4.2**	26.9	6.6	**4.2**
9.6	0.52	1.9	-0.21	**1.9**	0.00	-0.05	-0.31	4.42	101.1	**5.4**	37.2	0.0	**6.2**
5.4	0.43	4.7	0.66	**2.3**	0.01	0.06	0.63	5.10	91.1	**3.8**	13.4	3.8	**3.8**
8.3	0.75	2.4	0.93	**3.5**	0.06	0.41	4.09	3.08	86.1	**5.1**	16.6	0.4	**4.5**

Name	City	State	Rating	2016 Rating	2015 Rating	Total Assets ($Mil)	One Year Asset Growth	Asset Mix (As a % of Total Assets): Commercial Loans	Consumer Loans	Mortgage Loans	Securities	Capitalization Index	Net Worth Ratio
Memorial Federal Credit Union	Gulfport	MS	**C+**	C+	C+	9.0	2.97	0.0	32.2	0.0	0.0	**10.0**	22.8
Memorial Health Credit Union	Savannah	GA	**C+**	C+	C+	19.6	7.95	0.0	30.8	6.6	0.1	**10.0**	17.1
Memphis City Employees Credit Union	Memphis	TN	**A-**	A-	A-	267.4	3.37	0.6	24.3	15.4	34.9	**10.0**	18.4
Memphis Municipal Employees FCU	Memphis	TN	**C+**	C+	C+	14.3	3.80	0.0	30.2	0.5	0.0	**10.0**	30.1
Menlo Survey Federal Credit Union	Menlo Park	CA	**B**	B	B-	61.9	-0.22	0.6	7.0	30.6	0.0	**10.0**	11.8
Menominee Area Credit Union	Menominee	MI	**C-**	C-	C	9.5	4.61	0.0	39.0	0.0	0.0	**10.0**	15.8
▼ Merced Municipal Employees Credit Union	Merced	CA	**D-**	D	D+	2.1	4.91	0.0	71.6	0.0	0.0	**8.0**	9.6
Merced School Employees FCU	Merced	CA	**B+**	B+	A-	482.8	5.81	0.3	21.2	9.7	45.3	**7.2**	9.6
Mercer County Community FCU	Hermitage	PA	**C-**	C-	C-	78.0	5.93	0.0	20.0	1.6	3.8	**6.0**	8.0
Mercer County Improvement Authority FCU	Hamilton	NJ	**C**	C	C	<1	12.33	0.0	46.3	0.0	0.0	**10.0**	21.0
Mercer County NJ Teachers FCU	Hamilton Square	NJ	**D-**	D-	D	30.9	1.36	0.0	10.5	0.0	11.2	**4.6**	6.6
Mercer County West Virginia Teachers FCU	Bluefield	WV	**D+**	D+	D-	8.7	3.72	0.0	76.3	0.0	0.0	**9.2**	10.4
Mercer Credit Union	Aledo	IL	**D**	D	D	2.4	-12.69	0.0	78.5	0.0	0.0	**10.0**	13.0
Merck Employees Federal Credit Union	Rahway	NJ	**B-**	B-	B-	2022.1	3.76	0.0	0.9	5.9	83.8	**9.3**	10.7
Merck Sharp & Dohme Federal Credit Union	Chalfont	PA	**B-**	B-	B-	573.7	5.89	1.7	11.7	10.8	28.5	**6.7**	8.8
Merco Credit Union	Merced	CA	**B-**	B-	B-	106.5	7.07	0.0	29.5	11.2	3.3	**6.9**	8.9
Mercy Credit Union	Springfield	MO	**C**	C	D+	63.4	18.15	0.0	48.1	1.1	6.2	**6.5**	8.5
Mercy Federal Credit Union	Savannah	GA	**C+**	C+	C+	7.7	-0.32	0.0	42.6	0.0	0.0	**10.0**	15.5
Mercy Health Partners FCU	Toledo	OH	**C-**	C-	C	21.9	4.31	0.0	24.7	10.7	26.7	**10.0**	13.6
Merho Federal Credit Union	Johnstown	PA	**C**	C	C	48.6	8.36	0.0	15.1	4.6	0.9	**8.3**	9.8
Meriden Postal Employees FCU	Southington	CT	**D**	D	D	<1	-8.85	0.0	26.3	0.0	0.0	**10.0**	25.0
Meridia Community Federal Credit Union	Hamburg	NY	**A-**	A-	A-	67.6	8.48	0.0	32.8	10.0	0.0	**10.0**	11.7
Meridian Credit Union	Ottumwa	IA	**B+**	B+	B+	28.4	-8.64	4.5	18.1	17.2	39.8	**10.0**	14.7
Meridian Mississippi Air Natl Guard FCU	Meridian	MS	**C+**	C+	C+	19.1	12.30	0.0	19.5	10.9	0.0	**8.2**	9.8
Meridian Mutual Federal Credit Union	Meridian	MS	**B**	B	B-	38.2	5.28	0.0	12.0	12.7	0.0	**10.0**	12.5
Meridian Trust Federal Credit Union	Cheyenne	WY	**B**	B	B	347.5	6.54	6.6	32.7	27.3	1.9	**9.6**	10.7
Meritrust Credit Union	Wichita	KS	**B+**	B+	B+	1266.6	9.91	2.8	63.8	17.6	0.7	**7.5**	9.4
Meriwest Credit Union	San Jose	CA	**B+**	B+	B+	1404.2	8.73	9.3	21.5	36.0	18.1	**6.6**	8.7
Merrimack Valley Federal Credit Union	Lawrence	MA	**B-**	B-	B-	600.5	4.49	4.4	8.6	30.4	26.6	**8.0**	9.9
Merritt Federal Credit Union	Wilton	CT	**D**	D	D+	13.3	-8.08	0.0	23.6	30.5	10.4	**10.0**	11.6
Mesquite Credit Union	Mesquite	TX	**D**	D	D-	31.2	3.89	0.0	44.4	9.1	0.0	**5.4**	7.4
Messiah Baptist Church FCU	East Orange	NJ	**D+**	D+	D+	<1	-13.33	0.0	7.2	0.0	4.5	**10.0**	11.8
Messiah Baptist-Jubilee FCU	Brockton	MA	**C**	C	C-	<1	10.28	0.0	19.4	0.0	0.0	**10.0**	13.3
▼ Met Tran Federal Credit Union	Houston	TX	**D+**	C-	C-	8.9	2.40	0.0	28.8	0.0	0.0	**10.0**	16.4
METCO Credit Union	Cedar Rapids	IA	**B**	B	B-	31.9	7.18	6.9	23.5	19.1	0.0	**10.0**	11.3
Methodist Healthcare FCU	Cordova	TN	**A-**	A-	A-	38.0	5.34	0.0	23.0	0.3	0.6	**10.0**	15.2
Methodist Hospital Employees FCU	Dallas	TX	**C-**	C-	C-	9.4	4.20	0.0	34.7	0.0	0.0	**8.5**	10.0
▼ Methuen Federal Credit Union	Methuen	MA	**D+**	C-	D+	23.3	3.35	0.0	25.7	3.4	4.5	**10.0**	12.3
Metrex Federal Credit Union	Kenilworth	NJ	**C+**	C+	C	5.1	-0.35	0.0	59.5	0.0	0.0	**10.0**	19.1
Metro Community Federal Credit Union	Huntington	WV	**C-**	C-	C-	30.4	2.82	0.0	25.9	5.5	0.4	**6.4**	8.4
Metro Credit Union	Chelsea	MA	**B-**	B-	C+	1702.6	12.85	9.3	25.4	36.8	6.6	**6.7**	8.8
Metro Credit Union	Springfield	MO	**B-**	B-	B-	58.8	6.21	2.9	21.4	6.4	0.0	**10.0**	11.3
▲ Metro Employees Credit Union	Lexington	KY	**B+**	B	B-	27.9	8.69	0.0	35.4	10.7	1.8	**10.0**	11.1
Metro Federal Credit Union	Arlington Heights	IL	**C-**	C-	D	43.3	7.42	0.1	19.4	19.8	15.5	**5.2**	7.2
Metro Health Services FCU	Omaha	NE	**A**	A	A	324.4	11.82	1.7	39.0	15.7	5.7	**10.0**	11.0
Metro Medical Credit Union	Dallas	TX	**B-**	B-	C+	75.1	7.36	0.0	11.9	8.2	69.2	**10.0**	11.4
Metro North Federal Credit Union	Jacksonville	FL	**C+**	C+	B-	17.3	5.54	0.0	17.7	26.1	0.0	**10.0**	18.0
Metro North Federal Credit Union	Waterford	MI	**D+**	D+	D+	46.2	7.21	0.0	36.1	8.5	28.8	**5.7**	7.7
▲ Metro Wire Federal Credit Union	Plains	PA	**C**	C-	D+	4.6	-1.56	0.0	9.3	0.0	74.5	**10.0**	12.2
Metropolitan "L" Federal Credit Union	Oak Park	IL	**C**	C	C	7.3	-0.41	0.0	28.1	0.0	0.0	**10.0**	19.1
Metropolitan Church Federal Credit Union	Suffolk	VA	**C+**	C+	C+	8.7	4.41	0.0	31.4	0.0	0.0	**10.0**	32.8
Metropolitan District Employees CU	Hartford	CT	**C+**	C+	C+	25.1	1.17	0.0	21.2	33.6	5.7	**10.0**	13.9
Metropolitan Federal Credit Union	Kansas City	MO	**D**	D	D	10.4	1.93	0.0	17.3	0.0	0.0	**10.0**	17.9
Metropolitan Services Credit Union	Saint Paul	MN	**D+**	D+	D	9.1	5.83	0.0	33.8	18.4	6.3	**6.7**	9.0
Metropolitan Teachers Credit Union	Nashville	TN	**D**	D	D	2.9	-5.71	0.0	23.6	0.0	9.9	**10.0**	32.5
MetroWest Community Federal Credit Union	Framingham	MA	**C**	C	C-	99.5	4.75	0.0	23.3	2.6	18.6	**8.8**	10.3
▼ Metrum Community Credit Union	Centennial	CO	**B+**	A-	A-	65.6	5.93	0.0	27.4	27.5	0.0	**10.0**	13.2
▲ Miami Federal Credit Union	Miami	FL	**B**	B-	B	33.7	2.00	0.8	23.5	21.1	0.0	**10.0**	14.2
Miami Firefighters Federal Credit Union	Miami	FL	**B-**	B-	C	95.6	5.73	0.5	21.1	23.9	13.5	**6.8**	8.9
Miami Postal Service Credit Union	Miami	FL	**C+**	C+	B	129.5	4.43	0.0	30.8	0.5	34.0	**9.8**	11.2

Asset Quality Index	Non-Performing Loans as a % of Total Loans	Non-Performing Loans as a % of Capital	Net Charge-Offs Avg Loans	Profitability Index	Net Income ($Mil)	Return on Assets	Return on Equity	Net Interest Spread	Overhead Efficiency Ratio	Liquidity Index	Liquidity Ratio	Hot Money Ratio	Stability Index
9.7	1.72	2.6	0.24	**5.1**	0.02	1.08	4.69	3.09	62.0	**4.9**	30.9	0.0	**5.0**
9.3	0.75	2.1	0.70	**3.6**	0.01	0.13	0.72	5.08	94.0	**5.0**	29.3	4.5	**6.3**
10.0	0.25	0.6	0.47	**5.4**	0.54	0.81	4.82	3.07	75.7	**4.7**	20.4	5.0	**8.1**
9.8	1.96	2.1	0.91	**5.1**	0.03	0.94	3.09	4.60	82.1	**6.4**	63.3	3.9	**6.0**
10.0	0.18	0.7	0.03	**3.6**	0.06	0.42	3.51	2.47	84.4	**6.0**	56.5	2.5	**6.3**
8.3	1.14	3.1	1.14	**1.3**	-0.01	-0.35	-2.14	3.57	107.5	**6.3**	53.7	0.0	**6.9**
3.2	2.20	15.1	2.96	**2.1**	0.00	0.40	3.98	5.14	88.9	**4.3**	31.3	0.0	**1.7**
10.0	0.53	1.8	0.24	**5.1**	0.80	0.68	7.29	3.09	80.7	**5.6**	25.3	4.4	**6.0**
9.9	0.08	0.4	0.13	**2.1**	0.03	0.15	1.79	2.30	91.6	**5.4**	26.1	0.3	**3.8**
7.8	2.02	4.2	1.99	**3.7**	0.00	-0.97	-4.49	12.17	100.0	**6.9**	66.3	0.0	**7.2**
5.5	1.70	12.5	0.78	**1.9**	0.00	-0.03	-0.72	2.51	89.1	**6.1**	46.3	0.0	**1.5**
5.1	0.51	3.8	0.86	**7.4**	0.05	2.16	20.39	6.74	58.7	**4.1**	16.3	0.0	**3.7**
4.3	1.97	11.9	-0.20	**2.4**	0.00	0.32	2.55	2.69	87.5	**3.6**	15.0	0.0	**6.0**
10.0	0.99	0.8	0.02	**3.4**	1.97	0.39	3.75	0.65	35.9	**5.3**	19.6	0.0	**7.5**
9.9	0.34	1.8	0.18	**3.3**	0.45	0.33	3.64	2.85	86.1	**5.6**	28.8	5.1	**6.6**
10.0	0.34	1.6	0.46	**3.9**	0.08	0.32	3.56	3.19	89.9	**5.5**	44.8	2.0	**5.5**
6.2	0.61	4.0	0.13	**2.3**	0.03	0.19	2.16	2.91	90.7	**5.8**	35.7	0.0	**3.8**
8.6	1.14	3.5	-0.36	**6.4**	0.02	0.89	5.74	5.03	84.8	**6.1**	65.7	6.8	**5.0**
7.9	1.91	5.2	0.29	**1.5**	0.00	-0.06	-0.40	2.98	97.2	**6.0**	38.9	1.4	**6.6**
9.6	0.44	1.5	0.32	**2.7**	0.05	0.44	4.38	2.25	80.6	**4.6**	11.9	1.3	**4.8**
7.8	4.82	4.7	0.00	**0.0**	0.00	-1.28	-5.06	4.00	150.0	**7.1**	51.8	0.0	**5.2**
9.7	0.31	2.1	0.07	**6.6**	0.17	1.00	8.49	3.91	76.5	**4.3**	13.8	0.2	**6.8**
7.7	2.75	7.1	-0.07	**2.9**	0.01	0.17	1.16	3.24	89.9	**5.3**	26.4	2.8	**6.7**
9.9	0.07	0.3	0.17	**3.7**	0.02	0.45	4.52	2.43	84.6	**5.9**	47.5	0.9	**5.1**
10.0	0.18	1.1	0.19	**5.1**	0.10	1.09	10.41	4.37	75.7	**7.4**	65.5	2.9	**5.4**
7.6	0.49	4.0	0.41	**4.7**	0.48	0.56	5.22	3.32	74.2	**3.2**	11.2	6.6	**7.3**
5.8	0.65	7.1	1.11	**4.1**	1.00	0.31	3.47	3.71	69.4	**1.8**	16.4	25.2	**6.8**
7.9	0.36	3.9	0.08	**5.1**	3.25	0.95	13.81	2.96	77.2	**3.1**	11.4	7.4	**5.5**
8.4	0.77	4.6	0.07	**4.3**	0.91	0.61	6.34	2.80	78.8	**4.1**	18.4	10.4	**7.3**
7.3	1.35	6.2	0.35	**1.0**	0.00	0.03	0.26	3.79	103.9	**4.9**	39.0	2.9	**4.7**
7.7	0.27	2.6	0.45	**2.5**	0.03	0.41	5.62	3.22	91.3	**4.7**	23.7	0.0	**1.9**
3.7	11.11	14.8	0.00	**2.6**	0.00	0.00	0.00	0.00	100.0	**7.5**	56.9	0.0	**5.1**
9.8	0.00	0.0	0.00	**2.8**	0.00	0.00	0.00	1.81	100.0	**6.2**	54.7	0.0	**7.1**
9.9	0.58	1.1	1.87	**0.0**	-0.05	-2.23	-13.23	4.27	132.4	**6.2**	47.1	0.0	**5.2**
8.7	0.22	3.6	0.00	**4.9**	0.06	0.76	6.70	4.15	79.8	**4.6**	26.5	1.7	**6.3**
9.7	1.41	2.6	1.55	**5.2**	0.06	0.63	4.09	3.64	81.4	**6.0**	39.2	1.4	**6.6**
5.1	2.98	14.0	0.47	**2.8**	0.00	0.13	1.27	3.58	95.4	**6.0**	58.1	0.0	**2.3**
10.0	0.15	0.6	0.00	**0.6**	-0.01	-0.19	-1.52	3.18	105.6	**5.3**	32.8	0.0	**6.4**
8.3	0.00	0.0	-0.12	**5.8**	0.01	0.55	2.89	4.99	89.5	**4.8**	39.4	0.0	**4.3**
6.8	1.14	5.3	0.60	**2.5**	0.01	0.08	0.94	2.94	97.0	**5.6**	41.5	6.6	**3.8**
9.6	0.10	1.0	0.02	**3.8**	2.49	0.60	6.90	2.55	80.7	**2.8**	6.7	6.7	**6.4**
9.9	0.45	1.6	0.13	**3.1**	0.05	0.37	3.52	2.99	86.2	**5.0**	20.7	0.4	**5.1**
9.7	0.21	1.0	0.11	**6.7**	0.08	1.20	10.64	4.21	79.8	**5.2**	40.2	5.4	**6.5**
9.0	0.32	2.1	0.21	**3.1**	0.05	0.48	6.69	3.49	87.5	**4.9**	18.7	0.7	**2.8**
8.1	0.62	3.6	0.54	**7.4**	0.72	0.91	8.18	4.14	80.8	**4.5**	34.7	9.1	**8.0**
10.0	0.67	1.3	-0.10	**3.5**	0.07	0.38	3.27	1.91	86.8	**5.6**	35.0	1.7	**6.1**
9.7	0.36	1.0	-0.14	**2.6**	0.02	0.45	2.45	3.06	90.5	**4.9**	52.4	5.3	**6.9**
7.0	0.66	4.5	0.13	**1.6**	-0.03	-0.23	-2.93	3.54	104.7	**5.0**	24.2	0.2	**2.9**
9.9	1.68	2.3	-1.46	**3.5**	0.01	0.61	4.85	2.50	77.4	**5.3**	27.2	0.0	**4.8**
9.5	2.18	3.3	0.00	**3.0**	0.01	0.33	1.71	4.17	93.6	**5.6**	47.4	0.0	**5.9**
7.3	2.76	5.2	0.37	**9.5**	0.03	1.50	4.53	8.21	78.5	**5.5**	51.5	4.8	**5.7**
9.7	0.42	1.7	0.69	**2.7**	0.02	0.29	2.07	2.93	88.8	**4.1**	14.8	4.0	**6.9**
10.0	0.97	1.1	0.20	**0.0**	-0.03	-1.32	-7.23	1.97	155.8	**7.3**	54.9	0.0	**6.4**
9.4	0.00	0.0	0.00	**4.4**	0.01	0.53	6.13	4.26	89.6	**4.1**	12.5	0.0	**3.0**
10.0	1.56	1.2	-1.80	**0.0**	-0.01	-1.53	-4.68	4.22	136.4	**7.6**	90.8	0.0	**4.7**
8.4	0.51	2.4	0.25	**2.0**	0.02	0.07	0.73	2.43	95.9	**3.7**	22.6	13.8	**4.3**
9.9	0.35	1.6	0.18	**5.0**	0.09	0.58	4.36	3.13	78.8	**4.1**	30.6	8.3	**7.1**
9.6	0.22	0.9	0.38	**4.1**	0.07	0.87	5.99	3.70	81.1	**5.0**	27.7	0.0	**6.2**
9.2	0.27	1.6	0.03	**4.3**	0.18	0.75	8.40	3.08	75.2	**4.5**	19.3	2.6	**5.3**
7.0	1.50	7.2	3.42	**5.2**	0.40	1.26	11.70	3.82	43.6	**4.4**	15.0	10.1	**5.7**

Name	City	State	Rating	2016 Rating	2015 Rating	Total Assets ($Mil)	One Year Asset Growth	Asset Mix (As a % of Total Assets) Commercial Loans	Consumer Loans	Mortgage Loans	Securities	Capitalization Index	Net Worth Ratio
Miami University Community FCU	Oxford	OH	**C+**	C+	C	62.2	1.30	3.1	15.0	32.9	20.0	**8.3**	9.9
Michael Baker International FCU	Moon Township	PA	**C+**	C+	C+	8.0	4.97	0.0	53.2	0.0	0.0	**10.0**	16.6
Michigan Coastal Credit Union	Muskegon	MI	**D+**	D+	C	18.2	10.59	0.0	38.1	21.5	10.4	**6.6**	8.6
▲ Michigan Columbus Federal Credit Union	Livonia	MI	**B-**	C+	C-	45.3	-1.46	1.0	11.9	27.6	40.7	**9.3**	10.5
Michigan Educational Credit Union	Plymouth	MI	**B-**	B-	B-	785.1	5.67	0.0	23.5	24.5	31.7	**10.0**	11.9
Michigan First Credit Union	Lathrup Village	MI	**A-**	A-	A-	816.6	3.81	7.8	24.3	21.9	21.4	**10.0**	14.7
▼ Michigan Legacy Credit Union	Pontiac	MI	**C+**	B	B	180.5	4.45	0.7	20.9	13.6	43.3	**8.3**	10.3
Michigan One Community Credit Union	Ionia	MI	**B-**	B-	C	110.2	7.80	0.7	61.3	5.2	2.7	**6.7**	8.7
Michigan Schools and Government CU	Clinton Township	MI	**A**	A	A-	1750.0	10.90	4.9	35.5	30.5	14.2	**10.0**	11.9
Michigan State University FCU	East Lansing	MI	**A-**	A-	A-	3570.0	10.44	10.1	26.7	30.8	16.1	**9.1**	10.5
Michigan Tech Employees FCU	Houghton	MI	**C+**	C+	C-	77.5	14.30	0.1	18.5	12.5	36.6	**5.2**	7.6
Mico Employees Credit Union	North Mankato	MN	**C-**	C-	C	2.0	-5.27	0.0	44.8	0.0	0.0	**10.0**	15.5
▼ Mid American Credit Union	Wichita	KS	**C+**	B-	B-	284.0	2.04	3.4	72.3	13.1	0.0	**7.5**	9.3
Mid Carolina Credit Union	Lugoff	SC	**C**	C	C	131.5	7.04	0.3	58.0	11.2	7.7	**10.0**	13.3
Mid Delta Credit Union	Indianola	MS	**C**	C	C	1.8	0.06	0.0	32.0	0.0	0.0	**10.0**	29.9
Mid East Tennessee Community CU	Decatur	TN	**E+**	E+	E+	9.4	14.36	0.0	70.2	0.0	0.0	**5.7**	7.7
Mid Minnesota Federal Credit Union	Baxter	MN	**B+**	B+	B+	323.6	9.28	9.7	48.9	17.9	0.8	**8.8**	10.2
Mid Oregon Federal Credit Union	Bend	OR	**B-**	B-	B	267.0	18.04	10.3	26.7	18.8	0.1	**6.0**	8.0
▲ Mid Plains Credit Union	Glasco	KS	**C**	C-	C	1.7	6.19	0.0	77.5	0.0	0.0	**10.0**	11.7
▼ Mid-Atlantic Federal Credit Union	Germantown	MD	**D+**	C-	C	315.7	1.47	6.0	15.0	29.1	5.0	**3.8**	5.9
Mid-Cities Credit Union	Compton	CA	**D+**	D+	C	21.0	-6.78	0.0	45.7	14.2	0.0	**10.0**	12.5
Mid-Hudson Valley Federal Credit Union	Kingston	NY	**C-**	C-	C-	975.6	8.41	8.6	24.9	27.6	22.7	**6.9**	9.0
▼ Mid-Illini Credit Union	Bloomington	IL	**D+**	C-	D+	56.5	12.48	1.8	77.4	5.1	0.0	**5.3**	7.3
Mid-Island Federal Credit Union	Christiansted	VI	**C-**	C-	C-	9.7	7.68	0.0	32.6	1.7	0.0	**9.4**	10.6
Mid-Kansas Credit Union	Moundridge	KS	**D+**	D+	D+	52.6	4.96	15.8	8.5	19.8	19.8	**8.1**	10.1
Mid-State Federal Credit Union	Carteret	NJ	**C-**	C-	D+	17.2	-0.22	8.2	8.8	10.6	0.0	**10.0**	11.3
▼ Mid-Tex Federal Credit Union	Brownwood	TX	**D-**	D	D	23.7	6.86	0.0	50.1	1.2	0.0	**5.2**	7.2
▼ Midcoast Federal Credit Union	Freeport	ME	**B+**	A-	A-	161.3	6.91	3.9	18.9	36.7	12.7	**10.0**	12.1
▲ Middle Tennessee Federal Credit Union	Cookeville	TN	**C**	C-	D+	33.1	8.99	0.0	38.7	14.4	0.0	**7.1**	9.1
Middlesex County New Jersey Empls FCU	New Brunswick	NJ	**C**	C	C	9.4	3.39	0.0	23.2	0.0	0.0	**10.0**	17.4
Middlesex-Essex Postal Employees FCU	North Reading	MA	**C**	C	C-	5.1	-2.82	0.0	37.9	0.0	0.0	**10.0**	29.0
Middletown Area Schools Credit Union	Middletown	OH	**C-**	C-	D+	7.7	3.80	0.0	54.4	0.0	0.0	**10.0**	12.8
MIDFLORIDA Credit Union	Lakeland	FL	**A-**	A-	A-	2901.6	16.51	13.2	42.4	24.9	7.8	**8.6**	10.1
Midland Co-Op Credit Union	Minneapolis	MN	**D+**	D+	D+	10.0	-1.00	0.0	26.9	5.7	0.0	**8.9**	10.3
Midland Credit Union	Urbandale	IA	**B-**	B-	B-	52.5	8.54	4.7	30.2	30.2	16.7	**10.0**	12.9
Midland Municipal Employees Credit Union	Midland	TX	**C-**	C-	C-	18.5	1.98	0.0	14.0	0.0	68.9	**7.7**	9.5
Midsouth Community Federal Credit Union	Macon	GA	**A-**	A-	B+	252.7	5.00	1.3	52.9	4.5	17.6	**10.0**	11.8
MidUSA Credit Union	Middletown	OH	**C-**	C-	C-	210.9	4.03	6.8	36.7	21.6	10.6	**8.3**	10.0
MidValley Federal Credit Union	Murray	UT	**D**	D	D	5.7	-0.70	0.0	6.9	29.2	0.0	**10.0**	31.8
Midway Federal Credit Union	Winchester	VA	**C-**	C-	C-	12.2	-5.15	0.0	16.5	4.6	28.0	**10.0**	16.1
Midwest America Federal Credit Union	Fort Wayne	IN	**A-**	A-	B+	564.0	7.36	14.5	38.6	26.1	6.2	**10.0**	13.3
Midwest Carpenters & MillWrights FCU	Hobart	IN	**C**	C	C	98.3	1.86	0.2	27.1	15.3	29.8	**6.6**	8.6
Midwest Community Credit Union	Sioux City	IA	**C-**	C-	C-	30.1	4.74	0.3	13.7	4.1	44.0	**6.1**	8.1
▼ Midwest Community Federal Credit Union	Defiance	OH	**D+**	C-	C-	161.2	6.82	6.9	16.3	22.1	19.6	**6.5**	8.5
Midwest Credit Union	Florissant	MO	**D**	D	D+	10.7	-5.58	0.0	38.0	0.0	0.0	**10.0**	17.9
Midwest Family Federal Credit Union	Portage	IN	**D+**	D+	D+	30.0	7.36	0.0	22.9	13.6	5.8	**4.8**	6.8
Midwest Members Federal Credit Union	Wood River	IL	**C**	C	C-	127.2	7.94	0.1	64.4	12.6	0.0	**7.1**	9.1
▲ Midwest Operating Engineers Credit Union	Countryside	IL	**C+**	C	C	54.5	8.09	0.0	19.7	8.0	0.0	**6.2**	8.2
Midwest Regional Credit Union	Kansas City	KS	**C-**	C-	D+	63.7	4.45	0.0	27.9	14.7	0.0	**6.8**	8.8
Midwestern State University Credit Union	Wichita Falls	TX	**D**	D	D	6.2	-5.10	0.0	21.3	5.6	0.0	**10.0**	15.3
Mil-Way Federal Credit Union	Texarkana	AR	**C+**	C+	C+	120.8	3.06	0.0	40.9	8.9	0.0	**8.9**	10.3
Mile High Federal Credit Union	Butte	MT	**C+**	C+	B-	23.3	3.84	0.0	24.2	0.0	0.0	**10.0**	13.7
Miles City Federal Credit Union	Miles City	MT	**C**	C	C-	3.3	-1.60	0.0	37.3	0.0	0.0	**10.0**	17.0
Milford Memorial Federal Credit Union	Milford	DE	**C-**	C-	C-	3.9	8.10	0.0	36.5	0.0	0.0	**9.3**	10.6
Mill City Credit Union	Minnetonka	MN	**B-**	B-	B-	338.8	4.30	0.0	19.9	30.2	18.7	**9.5**	10.7
Mill Town Credit Union	Everett	WA	**B**	B	B	50.5	1.44	0.0	30.2	4.0	0.0	**10.0**	23.4
Millard County Credit Union	Fillmore	UT	**B-**	B-	B-	33.9	6.34	4.1	32.1	13.5	2.5	**10.0**	11.2
Millbury Federal Credit Union	Millbury	MA	**C-**	C-	C-	320.9	4.53	10.9	12.2	54.2	7.4	**5.5**	7.6
Milledgeville Community Credit Union	Milledgeville	IL	**D-**	D-	D-	4.3	-0.68	0.0	26.5	0.0	0.0	**6.5**	8.6
Miller Transporters Federal Credit Union	Jackson	MS	**C-**	C-	C-	3.4	-1.98	0.0	30.5	0.0	0.9	**10.0**	18.1

Asset Quality Index	Non-Performing Loans as a % of Total Loans	Non-Performing Loans as a % of Capital	Net Charge-Offs Avg Loans	Profitability Index	Net Income ($Mil)	Return on Assets	Return on Equity	Net Interest Spread	Overhead Efficiency Ratio	Liquidity Index	Liquidity Ratio	Hot Money Ratio	Stability Index
9.3	0.32	1.7	0.06	**3.3**	0.07	0.43	4.40	3.01	85.0	**4.6**	30.2	6.3	**4.8**
8.7	0.00	0.0	0.37	**3.1**	0.00	0.20	1.21	3.44	93.1	**5.7**	36.8	0.0	**7.4**
6.7	0.50	3.6	0.64	**5.2**	0.03	0.74	8.50	4.63	81.3	**3.0**	20.0	21.7	**3.6**
7.5	0.54	2.3	0.30	**5.2**	0.09	0.78	7.45	3.02	73.1	**4.3**	11.1	2.5	**4.7**
10.0	0.28	1.3	0.14	**3.8**	0.78	0.41	3.31	2.81	84.6	**4.5**	19.2	3.5	**8.2**
6.8	1.64	7.2	1.68	**4.9**	1.18	0.59	4.08	5.42	79.8	**4.3**	13.2	4.0	**8.5**
7.8	1.33	5.2	0.73	**1.7**	-0.26	-0.59	-5.63	3.72	101.6	**4.8**	16.7	1.1	**5.8**
5.4	0.83	7.5	0.60	**4.0**	0.09	0.34	3.87	3.46	80.1	**3.5**	14.3	6.7	**6.6**
9.2	0.20	1.5	0.46	**8.9**	6.57	1.54	12.79	3.97	57.2	**3.0**	9.7	10.1	**8.8**
8.8	0.39	2.8	0.42	**6.5**	8.48	0.97	9.59	3.63	68.9	**3.0**	10.8	10.1	**7.6**
7.7	0.43	3.5	0.19	**4.8**	0.18	0.94	12.83	3.40	79.3	**4.8**	16.2	3.2	**3.4**
9.5	0.00	0.0	0.00	**1.2**	0.00	-0.20	-1.31	1.91	100.0	**6.3**	43.4	0.0	**6.7**
5.4	0.45	5.6	1.45	**2.4**	-0.46	-0.66	-6.95	4.07	85.4	**1.1**	6.9	24.4	**5.5**
7.6	0.39	2.6	0.53	**1.7**	-0.06	-0.17	-1.42	3.50	93.6	**3.5**	7.2	3.6	**7.4**
9.8	0.16	0.2	1.19	**2.3**	0.00	-0.46	-1.51	5.10	100.0	**7.0**	66.7	0.0	**6.6**
0.0	4.93	59.1	2.95	**6.6**	0.01	0.21	3.16	9.97	55.3	**1.6**	17.1	51.9	**3.7**
4.7	0.80	9.2	0.31	**3.6**	0.22	0.27	2.67	4.09	90.9	**3.0**	5.4	3.2	**6.5**
6.7	0.19	7.1	0.28	**4.2**	0.21	0.33	4.01	3.95	87.4	**3.9**	11.7	1.8	**4.9**
4.7	1.25	8.2	0.59	**9.4**	0.01	1.70	14.66	4.67	56.3	**4.5**	20.4	0.0	**4.3**
6.0	1.13	14.9	0.42	**0.6**	-0.06	-0.07	-1.25	4.17	94.6	**4.6**	23.5	4.8	**1.4**
4.7	3.64	13.5	2.81	**0.9**	-0.32	-6.21	-46.08	6.48	128.3	**4.7**	37.1	5.0	**4.7**
5.9	1.24	10.5	0.64	**2.7**	0.68	0.28	3.35	3.57	81.5	**3.7**	10.9	6.0	**5.4**
4.1	1.07	11.6	0.89	**2.7**	-0.03	-0.23	-3.11	5.75	87.5	**2.4**	7.1	10.0	**2.3**
5.3	4.49	16.4	-0.11	**3.8**	0.00	0.17	1.54	5.67	96.8	**6.7**	42.6	0.0	**3.7**
3.5	4.63	17.7	0.19	**1.6**	-0.01	-0.10	-1.02	2.60	102.1	**4.3**	15.3	2.6	**4.5**
8.8	0.17	0.8	0.00	**1.9**	0.00	0.07	0.61	3.25	89.7	**3.3**	20.1	15.1	**4.9**
3.9	1.19	10.4	0.91	**3.0**	-0.01	-0.17	-2.33	4.74	89.2	**5.1**	28.2	1.3	**1.7**
8.6	0.60	3.9	0.21	**4.5**	0.16	0.40	3.65	4.04	87.7	**3.7**	9.7	3.2	**7.9**
6.7	0.80	6.8	0.53	**7.5**	0.10	1.30	14.08	4.77	70.9	**5.3**	28.9	0.6	**4.1**
9.6	2.40	3.2	0.86	**1.8**	-0.01	-0.30	-1.71	3.96	108.3	**5.4**	24.2	0.0	**6.3**
9.8	1.49	1.9	0.00	**4.3**	0.01	0.84	2.97	3.55	69.1	**4.9**	22.7	0.0	**7.3**
5.9	1.44	6.7	0.51	**4.2**	0.01	0.70	5.33	4.65	81.9	**5.0**	26.9	0.0	**3.7**
8.4	0.36	3.1	0.30	**8.2**	11.01	1.59	16.81	3.14	60.1	**3.7**	14.5	7.1	**7.5**
9.7	0.19	0.8	0.00	**1.6**	0.00	0.04	0.39	2.52	96.7	**5.1**	36.8	0.0	**5.0**
9.6	0.16	1.8	0.00	**3.6**	0.06	0.48	3.69	3.60	87.5	**4.1**	27.9	8.6	**7.1**
7.6	1.71	3.7	0.40	**2.0**	0.00	-0.09	-0.91	1.46	82.8	**5.1**	18.5	0.0	**4.6**
7.5	0.35	3.2	1.34	**5.9**	0.57	0.92	7.87	3.57	74.4	**3.6**	11.1	10.7	**7.6**
6.5	1.26	8.9	0.77	**2.5**	0.14	0.27	2.75	3.23	80.6	**3.4**	13.1	12.2	**5.8**
7.2	5.89	7.6	0.00	**0.0**	-0.02	-1.06	-3.30	2.62	141.7	**5.0**	33.4	2.7	**6.0**
9.0	2.81	4.9	0.00	**1.1**	0.00	0.00	0.00	2.81	100.0	**4.9**	20.7	0.0	**5.0**
9.0	0.23	1.3	0.22	**5.3**	1.12	0.80	6.00	3.12	78.5	**3.6**	17.7	5.8	**9.3**
7.0	0.98	5.3	0.48	**2.3**	0.03	0.14	1.61	2.17	94.1	**4.0**	24.1	5.9	**3.7**
7.2	0.28	1.0	0.19	**2.5**	0.01	0.10	1.16	2.36	96.5	**5.8**	28.2	0.0	**3.9**
9.5	0.30	1.8	0.03	**1.3**	-0.12	-0.31	-3.58	3.20	102.9	**3.6**	21.1	11.4	**5.3**
8.7	1.03	2.5	3.54	**0.0**	-0.03	-1.26	-7.73	3.34	113.2	**6.1**	51.0	0.0	**5.3**
6.4	1.50	9.9	0.50	**0.5**	-0.05	-0.63	-8.92	3.40	95.1	**5.4**	34.7	2.5	**2.2**
7.1	0.24	2.5	0.31	**3.3**	0.17	0.55	7.20	3.27	84.5	**3.6**	12.5	5.9	**5.0**
9.1	0.25	0.8	1.38	**5.2**	0.18	1.34	16.15	2.66	99.4	**5.7**	32.2	2.8	**4.0**
5.8	2.17	11.5	2.28	**0.9**	-0.07	-0.42	-4.60	3.19	88.9	**5.7**	42.4	1.3	**3.5**
9.8	0.68	1.6	0.00	**0.0**	-0.02	-1.02	-6.32	2.20	137.5	**4.9**	36.0	0.0	**5.7**
9.2	0.09	0.9	0.09	**3.5**	0.12	0.40	3.89	3.34	87.9	**3.9**	20.8	9.3	**6.8**
9.4	0.38	1.0	3.44	**2.1**	0.00	-0.07	-0.50	2.77	84.4	**5.5**	34.4	1.1	**7.0**
9.5	0.00	0.0	0.00	**2.2**	0.00	0.12	0.71	3.78	97.2	**5.1**	14.9	0.0	**7.4**
8.8	0.77	2.6	1.36	**2.0**	0.00	0.11	0.97	4.23	86.1	**5.4**	29.4	0.0	**4.2**
10.0	0.08	0.4	0.20	**3.3**	0.20	0.24	2.26	2.89	88.4	**3.7**	25.9	11.9	**7.1**
8.2	0.98	2.8	0.29	**5.2**	0.12	0.95	4.07	3.83	78.6	**4.1**	25.7	2.2	**6.7**
9.0	0.34	2.7	0.06	**4.5**	0.07	0.79	7.68	3.62	74.5	**5.6**	38.2	0.0	**5.2**
3.3	1.13	27.9	0.03	**2.5**	0.08	0.10	1.33	3.17	97.1	**2.8**	9.1	11.1	**4.9**
5.9	2.79	9.1	-1.47	**0.5**	0.00	0.00	0.00	2.60	100.0	**5.6**	29.6	0.0	**2.9**
7.2	2.33	9.4	0.00	**2.2**	0.00	-0.12	-0.65	3.77	84.4	**5.2**	25.8	0.0	**6.7**

	Name	City	State	Rating	2016 Rating	2015 Rating	Total Assets ($Mil)	One Year Asset Growth	Asset Mix (As a % of Total Assets) Comm-ercial Loans	Cons-umer Loans	Mort-gage Loans	Secur-ities	Capital-ization Index	Net Worth Ratio
	Mills42 Federal Credit Union	Lowell	MA	**C**	C	C	18.9	-5.58	0.0	43.7	21.9	0.0	**9.4**	10.6
	Millstream Area Credit Union	Findlay	OH	**B**	B	B	40.4	1.61	0.4	32.7	13.3	6.8	**10.0**	11.1
▼	Minerva Area Federal Credit Union	Minerva	OH	**D+**	C-	C-	8.9	3.59	0.0	36.8	0.3	0.0	**8.4**	9.9
▼	Mingo County Education FCU	Williamson	WV	**C**	C+	C+	2.4	12.50	0.0	80.4	0.0	0.0	**10.0**	17.2
	Mini-Cassia Employees Credit Union	Burley	ID	**C**	C	C	<1	-1.42	0.0	45.9	0.0	0.0	**10.0**	14.6
	Minnco Credit Union	Cambridge	MN	**B+**	B+	B+	272.8	11.73	1.7	31.4	8.1	24.5	**8.0**	9.8
	Minnequa Works Credit Union	Pueblo	CO	**A-**	A-	B+	179.2	2.14	1.4	18.2	11.1	22.8	**10.0**	12.1
	Minnesota Catholic Credit Union	Little Canada	MN	**D+**	D+	D+	31.3	8.43	5.1	21.8	14.1	5.1	**6.3**	8.3
	Minnesota Ore Operations Employees CU	Hibbing	MN	**D+**	D+	D	8.1	-0.02	0.0	21.6	0.0	6.4	**10.0**	18.6
	Minnesota Power Employees Credit Union	Duluth	MN	**B-**	B-	B-	96.5	2.41	10.2	17.4	26.9	16.9	**10.0**	16.5
	Minnesota Valley Federal Credit Union	Mankato	MN	**A-**	A-	A-	148.2	16.35	1.1	21.6	12.2	15.9	**7.5**	9.4
	Minot Area Schools Federal Credit Union	Minot	ND	**D-**	D-	D-	10.0	2.90	0.7	32.2	0.0	0.0	**6.0**	8.0
	Mint Valley Federal Credit Union	Longview	WA	**C-**	C-	C-	18.6	12.33	0.0	35.5	7.3	0.0	**10.0**	14.0
	Minuteman Federal Credit Union	Rapid City	SD	**D+**	D+	D+	16.1	8.34	0.0	50.3	0.3	0.0	**7.4**	9.3
	Mission City Federal Credit Union	Santa Clara	CA	**C+**	C+	C+	97.0	15.48	0.0	21.1	21.2	13.6	**5.4**	7.7
	Mission Federal Credit Union	San Diego	CA	**A**	A	A	3307.9	11.65	8.2	27.7	34.9	22.2	**10.0**	11.8
	Mississippi Central Federal Credit Union	Morton	MS	**D**	D	D+	3.3	0.39	0.0	59.5	0.0	0.0	**10.0**	15.7
	Mississippi College Employees CU	Clinton	MS	**C+**	C+	C	2.9	9.31	0.0	28.0	0.0	0.0	**10.0**	13.8
	Mississippi DHS Federal Credit Union	Jackson	MS	**C**	C	C	7.8	0.75	0.0	35.3	0.0	0.0	**10.0**	16.5
	Mississippi Farm Bureau Employees CU	Jackson	MS	**C-**	C-	C-	14.5	3.36	0.0	22.3	0.0	0.0	**10.0**	12.7
▼	Mississippi Federal Credit Union	Jackson	MS	**B+**	A-	A-	120.6	6.22	0.1	27.0	17.8	5.4	**10.0**	11.8
	Mississippi Highway Safety Patrol FCU	Jackson	MS	**C+**	C+	C-	10.9	-0.56	0.0	30.5	0.0	0.0	**10.0**	20.0
	Mississippi National Guard FCU	Jackson	MS	**D**	D	D	17.9	7.34	0.0	67.8	0.0	0.0	**7.4**	9.3
	Mississippi Public Employees CU	Jackson	MS	**C+**	C+	C+	24.1	3.74	0.0	22.5	0.0	0.2	**10.0**	15.2
	Missoula Federal Credit Union	Missoula	MT	**B**	B	B-	486.5	9.38	10.0	18.1	14.3	50.3	**7.5**	9.4
▼	Missouri Baptist Credit Union	Jefferson City	MO	**D-**	D	E+	7.5	21.54	0.0	38.1	0.0	0.0	**6.1**	8.1
	Missouri Central Credit Union	Lee's Summit	MO	**C**	C	C+	54.8	11.30	0.2	24.2	1.0	3.2	**9.0**	10.3
▲	Missouri Credit Union	Columbia	MO	**B-**	C+	C	324.1	8.35	0.0	52.8	9.4	7.9	**7.4**	9.3
	Missouri Electric Cooperatives Empls' CU	Jefferson City	MO	**B+**	B+	A-	170.9	3.77	0.6	24.2	12.4	37.2	**8.0**	9.9
	Missouri Valley Federal Credit Union	Saint Peters	MO	**C-**	C-	C-	36.9	5.61	0.0	48.6	0.1	0.1	**6.6**	8.7
	MM Employees Federal Credit Union	Missoula	MT	**D+**	D+	D+	1.3	3.80	0.0	65.7	0.0	0.0	**8.1**	9.7
	MNCPPC Federal Credit Union	College Park	MD	**C+**	C+	D+	12.8	3.05	0.0	35.4	0.0	28.0	**10.0**	11.8
	Mobile Educators Credit Union	Mobile	AL	**C+**	C+	C	82.8	3.92	0.0	9.2	2.7	21.5	**8.1**	9.8
	Mobile Government Employees Credit Union	Mobile	AL	**C**	C	C+	22.1	0.40	0.0	9.3	14.0	0.0	**10.0**	14.6
	Mobile Postal Employees Credit Union	Mobile	AL	**C+**	C+	C+	11.0	1.10	0.0	47.1	0.0	0.0	**10.0**	14.4
	Mobility Credit Union	Irving	TX	**D**	D	D+	182.7	9.57	5.0	46.9	21.4	4.3	**6.0**	8.1
	Mobiloil Federal Credit Union	Beaumont	TX	**A**	A	A	696.2	18.68	15.3	44.5	28.9	2.7	**10.0**	11.6
	MOCSE Federal Credit Union	Modesto	CA	**C+**	C+	C+	289.3	10.63	0.0	30.2	4.1	41.4	**5.3**	7.3
	Modern Employees Federal Credit Union	Owensboro	KY	**C-**	C-	C-	6.0	4.56	0.0	35.2	26.3	0.0	**10.0**	21.4
	Modesto's First Federal Credit Union	Modesto	CA	**D+**	D+	C	31.9	5.45	0.0	20.6	0.9	16.2	**10.0**	12.4
	Moffat County Schools FCU	Craig	CO	**C-**	C-	C	4.6	-0.70	0.0	35.9	0.0	0.0	**10.0**	12.1
	Mohave Community Federal Credit Union	Kingman	AZ	**D+**	D+	D+	34.9	9.33	0.0	57.3	0.0	0.0	**5.0**	7.0
	Mohawk Progressive Federal Credit Union	Schenectady	NY	**D-**	D-	D-	9.3	3.68	0.0	25.6	11.6	16.3	**6.3**	8.3
	Mohawk Valley Federal Credit Union	Marcy	NY	**B-**	B-	B-	35.6	6.72	0.0	32.2	7.6	0.0	**10.0**	12.3
	Mojave Plant Employees FCU	Mojave	CA	**C-**	C-	D+	2.2	17.49	0.0	23.5	0.0	0.0	**9.2**	10.4
	Mokelumne Federal Credit Union	Stockton	CA	**B+**	B+	B	50.9	3.60	0.0	29.0	1.7	16.0	**10.0**	12.4
	Molex Employees Federal Credit Union	Lisle	IL	**D+**	D+	D	8.6	5.00	0.0	57.3	0.0	0.0	**6.9**	8.9
	Moline Municipal Credit Union	Moline	IL	**B+**	B+	B+	33.1	2.19	0.0	27.9	35.4	0.0	**10.0**	15.5
▲	Molokai Community Federal Credit Union	Kaunakakai	HI	**C-**	D+	D+	24.9	3.21	0.0	32.6	0.0	7.6	**7.5**	9.4
	Mon Valley Community FCU	Allenport	PA	**B+**	B+	A-	153.4	0.66	4.0	3.9	21.9	13.5	**10.0**	23.1
	Monad Federal Credit Union	Pasco	WA	**D+**	D+	D+	14.3	3.23	0.7	19.3	8.2	0.0	**6.4**	8.4
▲	Monarch Federal Credit Union	Miamisburg	OH	**C-**	D+	D+	9.7	-5.39	0.0	39.4	9.1	35.4	**10.0**	20.6
	Money Federal Credit Union	Syracuse	NY	**B**	B	B	42.4	3.51	0.0	29.6	27.6	20.4	**10.0**	13.5
	Money One Federal Credit Union	Largo	MD	**B+**	B+	B+	126.4	4.17	9.2	49.3	15.0	0.6	**10.0**	12.1
▼	Monmouth County Postal Employees CU	Red Bank	NJ	**D+**	C-	C-	25.6	-1.37	0.0	7.8	0.0	8.0	**10.0**	18.4
	Monmouth Federal Credit Union	Monmouth	ME	**E+**	E+	E+	20.0	3.03	0.0	28.1	11.9	0.0	**5.2**	7.2
▲	Monroe County Community Credit Union	Monroe	MI	**B-**	C+	B-	203.4	11.04	15.3	20.6	26.7	15.5	**5.7**	7.7
	Monroe County Teachers FCU	Key West	FL	**C**	C	C-	28.7	-0.03	0.0	51.2	19.6	0.0	**6.9**	9.0
	Monroe Education Employees FCU	Monroeville	AL	**D**	D	D+	5.2	1.94	0.0	44.5	0.0	0.0	**6.5**	8.5
▲	Monroe Telco Federal Credit Union	West Monroe	LA	**C**	C-	C-	43.2	0.19	0.1	25.7	3.1	0.2	**7.2**	9.2

Asset Quality Index	Non-Performing Loans as a % of Total Loans	Non-Performing Loans as a % of Capital	Net Charge-Offs Avg Loans	Profitability Index	Net Income ($Mil)	Return on Assets	Return on Equity	Net Interest Spread	Overhead Efficiency Ratio	Liquidity Index	Liquidity Ratio	Hot Money Ratio	Stability Index
9.7	0.10	0.8	-0.03	**3.7**	0.02	0.46	4.42	4.14	90.5	**2.0**	12.4	24.7	**5.1**
6.7	0.94	5.6	-0.06	**5.0**	0.02	0.24	2.06	4.72	95.2	**4.6**	24.6	2.8	**6.5**
6.3	1.20	6.1	0.00	**1.9**	-0.02	-0.76	-7.20	5.89	104.9	**6.6**	57.2	0.0	**4.2**
0.0	18.63	87.4	2.44	**10.0**	0.02	4.11	24.18	10.92	49.1	**4.9**	46.7	0.0	**9.1**
7.6	0.87	3.3	0.00	**2.8**	0.00	0.00	0.00	5.67	80.0	**6.2**	45.0	0.0	**6.9**
9.0	0.25	2.6	0.15	**6.5**	0.74	1.12	11.45	2.89	74.7	**4.5**	13.7	2.0	**6.4**
8.2	1.48	4.5	0.10	**5.5**	0.34	0.77	6.79	2.72	77.1	**4.9**	30.6	3.3	**7.4**
5.9	0.41	7.7	0.25	**2.9**	0.03	0.39	5.44	3.58	90.6	**4.7**	39.5	1.8	**3.2**
10.0	0.05	0.1	0.00	**1.2**	0.00	0.05	0.26	2.40	95.7	**5.1**	32.8	0.0	**6.8**
9.4	0.03	0.1	0.00	**2.7**	-0.01	-0.02	-0.13	3.67	100.6	**4.6**	23.0	2.6	**7.5**
7.8	0.92	5.4	0.11	**7.3**	0.28	0.78	8.13	2.73	79.1	**4.1**	13.5	2.7	**7.6**
9.7	0.00	0.0	0.00	**2.1**	0.00	0.04	0.50	2.33	98.4	**5.7**	36.7	0.0	**3.5**
7.9	0.63	2.2	0.60	**2.0**	0.01	0.22	1.59	4.20	92.0	**5.5**	45.3	13.4	**5.3**
3.7	1.30	10.8	-0.03	**4.0**	0.02	0.37	4.04	4.34	75.3	**1.9**	20.1	34.7	**3.0**
9.7	0.18	1.4	0.40	**2.3**	0.02	0.10	1.34	3.08	84.0	**3.3**	14.9	12.0	**3.3**
9.6	0.14	0.9	0.27	**6.8**	6.50	0.80	6.75	2.72	73.9	**3.7**	20.0	5.5	**9.0**
2.0	8.02	25.9	8.19	**1.7**	0.00	-0.24	-1.53	9.14	100.0	**5.1**	30.1	0.0	**5.0**
10.0	0.49	1.0	-1.01	**7.6**	0.02	2.36	17.39	3.73	42.3	**4.8**	6.4	0.0	**5.7**
9.2	0.77	1.9	0.98	**4.0**	0.01	0.31	1.85	6.10	88.2	**5.9**	53.3	6.5	**6.6**
10.0	0.15	0.3	0.80	**1.1**	-0.01	-0.22	-1.74	1.83	93.9	**5.2**	33.2	0.0	**6.2**
9.0	0.68	3.1	1.20	**4.6**	0.12	0.41	3.47	3.81	78.8	**5.0**	36.6	7.9	**7.7**
9.8	0.05	0.1	0.00	**2.9**	0.01	0.37	1.83	3.22	90.4	**5.3**	33.7	0.0	**6.6**
0.7	4.39	35.2	0.14	**8.7**	0.08	1.84	20.04	4.72	65.4	**3.7**	8.0	0.0	**4.2**
9.4	1.25	1.9	0.41	**1.6**	-0.02	-0.38	-2.40	4.09	107.2	**7.0**	49.2	0.0	**6.3**
7.3	0.94	5.5	1.05	**4.2**	0.59	0.49	5.19	3.20	72.2	**4.5**	20.4	2.6	**6.8**
8.9	0.30	2.7	0.00	**2.9**	0.00	0.22	2.64	4.22	86.8	**4.5**	19.3	0.0	**1.7**
8.1	0.66	2.8	0.15	**2.5**	0.04	0.26	2.48	2.88	89.0	**4.7**	27.1	0.8	**4.4**
7.8	0.31	2.7	0.63	**5.0**	0.82	1.03	11.13	4.40	72.2	**4.5**	17.9	1.2	**6.1**
9.9	0.09	0.5	0.19	**5.6**	0.40	0.96	9.82	2.33	60.4	**3.6**	5.7	4.4	**6.2**
5.1	0.99	6.8	0.73	**2.9**	0.03	0.35	4.03	3.88	84.6	**4.6**	24.7	0.3	**3.6**
8.2	0.00	0.0	0.00	**2.6**	0.00	0.00	0.00	4.75	100.0	**5.4**	30.7	0.0	**5.4**
9.7	0.37	1.3	-0.13	**4.8**	0.03	0.85	7.21	3.59	73.5	**6.4**	49.3	0.0	**5.3**
10.0	0.29	0.4	0.69	**3.2**	0.07	0.33	3.30	2.39	89.7	**6.5**	36.6	0.0	**4.7**
9.5	1.61	2.7	4.21	**0.9**	-0.02	-0.38	-2.60	1.86	89.0	**6.2**	41.5	0.0	**6.8**
3.9	4.10	18.1	0.75	**5.6**	0.01	0.30	2.04	5.27	94.6	**4.6**	19.4	0.0	**6.6**
4.8	0.97	12.5	0.35	**1.0**	0.03	0.07	0.91	2.98	88.0	**2.0**	7.5	19.1	**3.7**
7.9	0.41	2.8	0.70	**9.8**	2.49	1.47	12.49	4.01	56.9	**3.0**	15.4	13.3	**9.6**
9.9	0.17	1.4	0.58	**3.0**	0.23	0.33	4.33	3.19	83.0	**5.6**	33.0	0.0	**4.1**
9.8	0.00	0.0	0.62	**1.0**	-0.01	-0.40	-1.87	3.88	95.2	**4.6**	30.3	0.0	**6.5**
6.4	0.05	5.3	0.93	**1.5**	0.01	0.09	0.71	2.33	95.1	**5.0**	39.2	5.8	**4.6**
8.1	0.50	1.9	0.00	**4.4**	0.01	0.62	5.12	3.42	82.1	**4.6**	32.9	0.0	**4.3**
6.8	0.23	2.5	0.24	**5.0**	0.08	0.95	13.66	5.28	82.5	**4.3**	20.8	3.2	**2.8**
5.8	0.95	6.7	0.90	**1.0**	-0.01	-0.44	-5.19	3.99	92.9	**4.4**	14.2	0.0	**3.8**
3.7	5.76	23.2	0.24	**5.5**	0.09	1.02	8.29	3.34	72.9	**4.7**	23.8	0.8	**6.6**
9.6	0.00	0.0	-0.58	**3.0**	0.00	-0.72	-6.93	2.02	142.9	**7.4**	77.6	0.0	**6.5**
9.7	0.23	0.6	0.36	**4.6**	0.03	0.22	1.78	3.07	100.4	**5.3**	22.2	1.3	**6.4**
5.8	1.64	10.3	1.09	**3.4**	0.01	0.38	4.18	2.65	70.0	**4.8**	17.0	0.0	**2.3**
9.5	0.59	2.5	0.02	**8.1**	0.10	1.26	8.14	3.69	68.5	**4.6**	23.7	1.3	**7.9**
6.0	1.31	5.6	-0.14	**5.3**	0.08	1.35	14.47	4.44	83.9	**5.1**	19.0	0.9	**3.7**
8.4	3.11	4.2	0.01	**4.9**	0.32	0.83	3.74	2.64	59.0	**7.2**	72.7	1.5	**8.7**
9.6	0.44	1.6	0.00	**1.1**	-0.02	-0.51	-5.94	3.27	110.0	**6.5**	38.4	0.0	**3.3**
9.4	0.73	1.9	0.22	**1.6**	0.00	-0.04	-0.20	3.22	90.2	**4.3**	17.6	0.0	**6.3**
9.8	0.19	0.9	0.31	**3.9**	0.04	0.38	2.73	3.64	85.4	**4.1**	17.5	7.1	**6.5**
3.9	2.43	16.6	1.16	**3.7**	0.17	0.55	5.34	4.94	88.2	**2.5**	15.9	20.3	**6.6**
9.6	2.26	2.5	-0.08	**0.9**	-0.02	-0.34	-1.87	1.68	124.3	**5.4**	37.2	0.0	**6.9**
4.6	2.48	15.6	0.98	**1.7**	0.00	0.06	0.84	3.95	89.2	**5.5**	41.4	5.7	**1.0**
8.2	0.48	2.9	0.66	**4.1**	0.37	0.76	8.70	4.11	78.6	**5.2**	26.6	1.4	**4.4**
4.8	0.69	7.4	0.79	**4.1**	0.04	0.57	6.29	3.23	67.3	**3.5**	31.7	15.4	**4.8**
1.7	9.09	45.8	7.06	**1.2**	-0.05	-4.04	-44.26	9.73	104.7	**5.9**	57.9	13.4	**1.0**
6.9	1.01	5.6	1.19	**2.8**	0.03	0.26	3.60	2.79	85.3	**5.4**	39.9	2.8	**3.4**

Name	City	State	Rating	2016 Rating	2015 Rating	Total Assets ($Mil)	One Year Asset Growth	Asset Mix (As a % of Total Assets) Comm-ercial Loans	Cons-umer Loans	Mort-gage Loans	Secur-ities	Capital-ization Index	Net Worth Ratio
▲ Monroeville Boro Federal Credit Union	Monroeville	PA	**C-**	D+	D+	<1	-9.98	0.0	37.3	0.0	0.0	**10.0**	20.2
Monrovia City Employees FCU	Monrovia	CA	**C-**	C-	D+	3.5	-1.82	0.0	42.2	0.0	53.5	**10.0**	12.8
Montana Educators' Credit Union	Missoula	MT	**D+**	D+	C-	17.6	11.22	0.0	20.9	13.1	0.0	**6.3**	8.3
Montana Federal Credit Union	Great Falls	MT	**C+**	C+	B	239.0	5.94	0.1	31.6	6.9	9.9	**7.4**	9.4
Montana Health Federal Credit Union	Billings	MT	**D+**	D+	D+	25.4	0.05	0.0	53.3	2.9	0.0	**7.4**	9.3
Montcalm Public Employees Credit Union	Edmore	MI	**B-**	B-	B-	14.6	7.07	0.0	27.6	0.0	0.0	**10.0**	17.5
Montell Federal Credit Union	Westlake	LA	**C-**	C-	C	4.7	-3.99	0.0	38.9	0.0	0.0	**10.0**	28.2
Monterey Credit Union	Monterey	CA	**B+**	B+	B+	233.1	1.57	0.0	47.0	3.1	28.6	**10.0**	14.1
Montgomery County Employees FCU	Germantown	MD	**B**	B	B	135.4	14.77	4.7	32.9	22.8	9.2	**5.9**	8.0
Montgomery VA Federal Credit Union	Montgomery	AL	**C**	C	C	6.8	6.63	0.0	34.5	0.0	0.0	**10.0**	17.8
Montoursville Area Federal Credit Union	Montoursville	PA	**D+**	D+	D+	3.1	-10.21	0.0	37.9	0.0	0.0	**9.7**	10.8
Moog Employees Federal Credit Union	East Aurora	NY	**A**	A	A-	165.6	4.77	0.0	4.5	38.2	0.0	**10.0**	19.5
Moonlight Credit Union	Worthington	PA	**B+**	B+	B+	30.8	2.88	0.2	31.6	1.7	0.0	**10.0**	15.0
Moore County Schools FCU	Dumas	TX	**D**	D	D	7.6	-4.33	0.0	43.2	0.0	0.0	**10.0**	11.3
Moore West Federal Credit Union	San Leandro	CA	**D-**	D-	D	16.6	-3.25	0.0	11.5	2.6	54.8	**7.4**	9.3
MOPAC Employees Federal Credit Union	Palestine	TX	**C-**	C-	C-	15.2	-0.69	0.0	54.4	0.0	0.0	**9.1**	10.4
Morehead Community Federal Credit Union	Morehead	KY	**B-**	B-	C	32.9	5.23	0.0	22.0	14.0	0.0	**10.0**	11.0
Morgan City Federal Credit Union	Morgan City	LA	**D+**	D+	D+	6.6	0.99	0.0	48.9	0.0	26.6	**9.1**	10.4
Morgantown AES Federal Credit Union	Morgantown	WV	**D+**	D+	D+	42.6	-2.40	0.0	32.5	18.6	0.0	**6.0**	8.0
Morning Star Baptist FCU	Clairton	PA	**C+**	C+	C+	<1	-10.63	0.0	20.3	0.0	0.0	**10.0**	25.0
Morning Star Federal Credit Union	Tulsa	OK	**D-**	D-	D	<1	6.40	0.0	59.3	0.0	0.0	**10.0**	11.0
Morris Sheppard Texarkana FCU	Texarkana	TX	**D**	D	D+	7.8	5.59	0.0	63.6	0.0	0.0	**10.0**	11.7
▲ Morrison Employees Credit Union	Dubuque	IA	**C**	C-	C-	1.5	-7.37	0.0	11.9	0.0	0.0	**10.0**	34.3
Morrisons Cove 1st Federal Credit Union	Roaring Spring	PA	**C**	C	C-	41.3	6.27	0.0	17.6	1.6	0.0	**6.9**	8.9
Morrow County Federal Credit Union	Mount Gilead	OH	**C+**	C+	C	6.5	6.93	0.0	30.7	0.0	0.0	**10.0**	17.4
Morton Credit Union	South Hutchinson	KS	**C**	C	D+	4.1	7.07	0.0	58.6	0.0	0.0	**10.0**	13.5
Morton Federal Credit Union	Taunton	MA	**D**	D	D	9.4	6.83	0.0	12.0	21.2	1.1	**10.0**	12.8
Morton Lane Federal Credit Union	Buffalo	NY	**B+**	B+	B+	44.0	4.39	0.0	18.6	8.7	15.8	**10.0**	13.6
Morton Salt Credit Union	Rittman	OH	**D**	D	D	4.2	-2.51	0.0	40.7	0.0	42.7	**10.0**	18.3
Morton Weeks Federal Credit Union	New Iberia	LA	**C-**	C-	D+	9.8	-0.44	0.0	25.5	0.0	0.0	**8.7**	10.1
Mosaic Federal Credit Union	Harrisonburg	VA	**E-**	E-	E-	15.7	11.89	0.7	73.3	0.0	0.0	**4.6**	6.6
▼ Motion Federal Credit Union	Linden	NJ	**E-**	E	E-	75.6	-0.45	8.2	20.0	40.1	1.1	**3.9**	5.9
▲ Motor City Cooperative Credit Union	Clinton Township	MI	**C+**	C	D+	143.2	3.25	9.1	23.9	17.4	17.4	**10.0**	13.1
Motor Coach Employees Credit Union	East Saint Louis	IL	**D+**	D+	D+	2.4	14.94	0.0	41.5	0.0	0.0	**10.0**	16.4
Mount Carmel Baptist FCU	Philadelphia	PA	**D+**	D+	C-	<1	-3.17	0.0	16.4	0.0	0.0	**10.0**	28.1
▲ Mount Carmel Church Federal Credit Union	Houston	TX	**C-**	D+	D+	5.0	-3.98	0.0	35.6	0.0	0.0	**10.0**	16.6
Mount Gilead Federal Credit Union	Washington	DC	**C+**	C+	C-	<1	-8.06	0.0	31.6	0.0	0.0	**10.0**	14.0
Mount Lebanon Federal Credit Union	Baltimore	MD	**D-**	D-	D-	<1	4.25	0.0	71.1	0.0	0.0	**5.4**	7.4
Mount Olive Baptist Church FCU	Arlington	TX	**B-**	B-	B-	7.7	21.48	0.0	52.0	0.0	0.0	**10.0**	12.8
Mount Pleasant Area School Employees FCU	Mount Pleasant	PA	**C**	C	C	2.7	-0.84	0.0	27.4	0.0	0.0	**10.0**	15.1
▲ Mount Pleasant Baptist Church FCU	Alexandria	VA	**B**	B-	B-	<1	8.43	0.0	6.1	0.0	0.0	**10.0**	15.0
Mount Vernon Baptist Church Credit Union	Durham	NC	**D+**	D+	D	<1	-2.84	0.0	7.6	0.0	0.0	**10.0**	34.5
▼ Mount Vernon NY Postal Employees FCU	Mount Vernon	NY	**D+**	C-	D	1.7	-2.24	0.0	47.7	0.0	0.0	**10.0**	12.7
Mount Zion Indianapolis FCU	Indianapolis	IN	**D+**	D+	D+	<1	-4.63	0.0	53.8	0.0	0.0	**9.6**	10.8
Mount Zion Woodlawn Federal Credit Union	Cincinnati	OH	**D**	D	D	<1	-11.01	0.0	27.8	0.0	0.0	**7.4**	9.3
Mountain America Federal Credit Union	West Jordan	UT	**A-**	A-	A-	6456.6	19.53	8.2	45.3	29.1	0.5	**7.0**	9.0
Mountain Credit Union	Waynesville	NC	**B+**	B+	B+	190.8	5.65	0.0	36.3	9.6	0.2	**9.8**	10.9
Mountain Empire Federal Credit Union	Marion	VA	**C-**	C-	D	17.1	6.06	0.0	44.2	6.7	0.0	**6.8**	8.8
Mountain Gem Credit Union	Nampa	ID	**D**	D	D	20.3	1.31	0.0	73.5	4.9	0.0	**6.3**	8.3
▼ Mountain Heritage Federal Credit Union	Parkersburg	WV	**C-**	C	C	35.0	7.19	0.0	58.8	16.9	0.0	**8.3**	9.8
Mountain Lakes Community FCU	Piney Flats	TN	**D**	D	D+	24.2	-0.24	1.4	35.4	27.6	0.0	**6.8**	8.9
Mountain Laurel Federal Credit Union	Saint Marys	PA	**B+**	B+	B+	112.8	12.56	0.0	33.5	12.8	0.6	**10.0**	12.4
▼ Mountain River Credit Union	Salida	CO	**D**	D+	D	26.8	14.57	2.6	15.8	19.5	0.0	**5.2**	7.2
▼ Mountain Star Federal Credit Union	El Paso	TX	**D+**	C-	C-	31.7	6.90	0.0	28.5	0.0	0.0	**6.3**	8.3
Mountain States Credit Union	Johnson City	TN	**D**	D	D	18.7	12.67	3.3	46.7	18.3	0.0	**5.7**	7.7
Mountain West Federal Credit Union	Butte	MT	**B-**	B-	B-	8.2	12.74	0.0	41.8	0.0	0.0	**10.0**	26.3
MountainCrest Credit Union	Arlington	WA	**C**	C	C	97.8	4.83	0.0	48.2	15.7	4.7	**6.7**	8.7
▲ Mower County Catholic Parishes CU	Austin	MN	**C**	C-	C-	5.1	5.01	0.0	40.3	0.0	0.0	**10.0**	15.8
Mower County Employees Credit Union	Austin	MN	**C-**	C-	C-	5.7	4.98	0.0	57.9	0.0	0.0	**10.0**	20.8
MSBA Employees Federal Credit Union	Rockville Centre	NY	**E+**	E+	E+	5.7	-2.05	0.0	36.6	0.0	0.0	**2.0**	4.6

Asset Quality Index	Non-Performing Loans as a % of Total Loans	Non-Performing Loans as a % of Capital	Net Charge-Offs Avg Loans	Profitability Index	Net Income ($Mil)	Return on Assets	Return on Equity	Net Interest Spread	Overhead Efficiency Ratio	Liquidity Index	Liquidity Ratio	Hot Money Ratio	Stability Index
9.9	1.01	1.8	0.00	4.0	0.01	2.40	12.74	3.88	66.7	7.6	77.9	0.0	6.0
9.8	0.00	0.0	-0.81	4.3	0.01	1.51	11.90	2.88	79.2	4.3	15.0	0.0	5.5
8.3	0.25	1.7	0.00	3.9	0.03	0.73	8.58	3.63	80.1	5.1	28.8	3.4	3.3
9.1	0.46	3.2	0.23	2.8	0.05	0.09	0.97	2.60	90.8	5.4	36.9	1.6	5.9
4.1	0.13	12.4	0.02	2.2	0.01	0.08	0.85	3.98	98.2	3.7	10.9	3.2	3.9
8.6	1.51	2.7	0.00	6.1	0.03	0.93	5.21	3.04	70.9	5.1	25.1	2.6	5.7
5.7	7.67	12.7	0.00	6.2	0.01	1.01	3.66	4.03	73.8	4.9	29.4	0.0	4.3
7.1	0.76	4.1	0.90	4.1	0.25	0.43	3.13	4.17	81.7	4.0	5.4	1.1	7.7
8.2	0.50	4.1	0.41	5.0	0.19	0.58	7.22	4.16	86.4	4.6	21.7	3.5	5.1
7.6	2.62	5.8	1.32	2.6	0.00	-0.24	-1.32	5.57	96.5	6.7	63.8	0.0	6.9
9.8	0.10	0.6	0.00	0.9	0.00	-0.26	-2.39	4.78	105.4	5.5	40.4	0.0	4.6
10.0	0.30	0.9	0.05	7.3	0.53	1.28	6.56	2.44	48.0	4.6	27.5	0.8	9.1
9.9	0.08	0.3	0.16	6.3	0.09	1.17	8.08	3.31	65.0	4.7	30.2	3.9	7.8
5.3	3.24	14.6	0.10	1.1	0.00	0.11	0.94	2.67	89.1	4.5	32.7	3.1	5.3
10.0	0.14	0.3	0.27	0.2	-0.02	-0.38	-4.15	2.70	118.3	4.1	23.5	12.9	3.2
4.4	1.09	7.4	-0.14	2.3	0.00	0.05	0.51	4.60	99.5	4.3	26.0	4.8	5.0
7.3	0.73	3.7	0.45	4.7	0.08	0.97	8.84	2.98	83.3	4.9	63.3	12.5	5.5
7.0	0.37	2.1	0.30	2.6	0.01	0.31	2.94	4.10	92.7	4.1	17.3	0.0	4.7
8.6	0.05	0.4	0.86	1.6	0.02	0.17	2.12	2.83	89.6	4.5	18.1	1.0	2.7
6.4	13.46	10.7	0.00	9.3	0.00	2.38	9.52	2.60	33.3	5.5	13.3	0.0	5.0
0.6	7.02	47.2	0.00	5.7	0.00	1.37	13.11	3.93	60.0	2.2	15.7	21.4	6.5
4.9	1.54	9.3	0.00	0.6	0.00	0.10	0.88	3.05	97.1	4.3	24.8	0.0	5.3
10.0	0.00	0.0	0.00	2.0	0.00	0.27	0.79	1.51	100.0	6.4	50.7	0.0	6.9
9.0	0.71	2.1	0.32	2.7	0.03	0.28	3.05	2.38	82.6	6.1	32.5	0.0	4.3
7.5	2.23	4.8	1.25	7.0	0.02	1.07	6.10	4.16	69.2	5.4	39.2	0.0	5.0
8.4	0.34	1.6	-0.16	5.1	0.01	0.60	4.35	4.90	87.3	5.0	40.5	0.0	4.3
10.0	0.48	1.4	-0.12	0.1	-0.01	-0.30	-2.31	2.66	129.8	6.0	40.8	0.0	6.1
10.0	0.24	0.8	-0.08	4.7	0.06	0.55	4.24	3.01	81.3	4.4	11.9	0.0	7.2
9.7	0.26	0.6	-0.20	0.3	0.00	-0.19	-1.04	3.08	105.7	5.3	43.0	0.0	5.8
9.8	0.25	0.8	0.00	2.4	0.01	0.21	2.03	2.66	90.2	5.6	36.0	0.0	4.4
1.9	2.26	23.0	0.94	4.0	0.03	0.84	12.06	6.65	83.9	3.1	26.9	26.7	0.0
3.0	2.06	32.2	0.95	0.9	-0.02	-0.12	-2.44	4.18	93.3	3.9	21.1	1.5	0.3
8.1	0.60	3.1	0.28	3.3	0.25	0.69	5.33	4.09	77.3	3.4	5.2	3.4	7.4
9.2	0.10	0.3	1.96	0.6	0.00	-0.70	-4.10	6.59	108.7	6.2	43.7	0.0	5.2
8.8	5.76	3.5	17.52	0.5	0.00	-1.94	-6.84	4.18	100.0	7.9	79.6	0.0	6.5
9.0	0.34	0.9	-0.17	2.5	0.01	0.64	3.90	3.72	84.4	5.1	40.3	0.0	6.4
7.3	5.56	10.0	0.00	3.8	0.00	0.00	0.00	0.00	0.0	7.8	81.6	0.0	8.1
0.0	16.41	108.6	0.00	6.3	0.00	0.75	9.76	6.15	100.0	6.0	53.0	0.0	4.5
7.7	1.07	4.5	0.00	10.0	0.07	3.58	28.21	4.71	-15.5	6.5	51.2	0.0	5.7
10.0	0.00	0.0	0.00	3.7	0.00	0.45	2.92	1.59	57.1	7.2	62.0	0.0	7.7
10.0	0.00	0.0	0.00	9.5	0.00	2.29	14.81	0.00	100.0	8.6	105.9	0.0	6.3
9.6	7.69	1.6	-28.57	0.6	0.00	0.00	0.00	0.00	0.0	6.3	80.4	0.0	5.5
2.7	6.84	23.3	0.00	2.9	0.00	-0.24	-1.90	4.12	100.0	5.1	45.7	0.0	5.1
1.7	6.34	31.7	0.00	3.7	0.00	-0.51	-5.13	9.28	108.3	6.4	46.0	0.0	6.5
4.6	3.85	9.1	32.00	0.2	0.00	0.00	0.00	0.00	0.0	8.0	81.8	0.0	4.7
6.0	0.41	5.1	0.47	9.7	19.90	1.27	14.05	3.74	68.9	3.2	14.5	10.3	8.6
6.8	1.37	7.9	1.11	4.9	0.33	0.69	6.47	4.14	73.6	4.9	24.3	2.0	6.6
8.8	0.17	1.0	0.35	4.6	0.02	0.55	6.13	4.21	89.4	5.2	29.0	1.3	4.2
4.5	0.64	8.7	0.92	3.0	-0.01	-0.12	-1.43	4.88	91.3	3.8	16.5	3.8	2.3
2.1	2.54	19.8	1.12	5.5	0.06	0.69	6.80	5.12	71.8	3.9	17.3	2.4	4.8
6.2	0.69	5.1	0.27	2.3	0.04	0.61	6.98	3.75	94.2	3.7	24.1	4.3	2.3
9.4	0.47	2.1	0.23	4.7	0.22	0.80	6.37	3.29	75.1	5.5	34.8	0.3	8.0
5.6	2.22	13.1	0.03	0.3	-0.05	-0.71	-9.68	3.20	120.3	3.6	22.8	16.6	2.4
5.8	1.54	8.6	0.93	1.2	-0.05	-0.62	-7.02	3.97	105.9	6.3	43.2	3.5	3.0
8.5	0.00	0.0	0.33	2.3	0.01	0.28	3.61	4.44	91.1	4.0	26.9	7.6	2.6
9.4	0.41	0.8	0.37	8.4	0.02	1.01	3.71	5.32	82.5	5.7	46.2	0.0	5.7
7.1	0.27	3.0	0.17	4.7	0.20	0.81	9.64	4.18	78.4	4.6	21.6	1.9	3.9
9.2	0.59	1.6	0.54	4.5	0.02	1.17	7.49	3.35	69.1	5.1	47.2	0.0	4.3
7.9	0.00	0.0	1.26	2.3	0.00	-0.29	-1.35	3.91	100.0	3.3	30.8	15.1	7.5
3.0	5.05	32.1	0.00	2.3	0.00	0.28	6.08	5.14	91.3	5.5	29.2	0.0	1.0

Name	City	State	Rating	2016 Rating	2015 Rating	Total Assets ($Mil)	One Year Asset Growth	Asset Mix (As a % of Total Assets) Commercial Loans	Consumer Loans	Mortgage Loans	Securities	Capitalization Index	Net Worth Ratio
▼ MSD Federal Credit Union	Louisville	KY	**C-**	C	C+	5.4	5.71	0.0	51.0	0.0	0.0	**10.0**	19.8
▼ MSTC Federal Credit Union	Clinton	MS	**D**	D+	D	2.8	-4.44	0.0	16.9	0.0	0.2	**10.0**	13.4
MSU Federal Credit Union	Murray	KY	**D**	D	D	19.1	-3.36	0.0	40.3	0.0	0.0	**5.9**	7.9
Mt. Airy Baptist Church FCU	Washington	DC	**B-**	B-	C	1.2	-7.09	0.0	23.6	0.0	0.0	**10.0**	22.1
▼ Mt. Jezreel Federal Credit Union	Silver Spring	MD	**D+**	C-	D+	<1	11.96	0.0	1.7	0.0	0.0	**8.9**	10.3
Mt. Lebanon Federal Credit Union	Pittsburgh	PA	**B-**	B-	B-	10.4	-0.08	0.0	13.0	0.0	15.9	**10.0**	18.9
Mt. Rainier Federal Credit Union	Puyallup	WA	**C+**	C+	C+	13.7	9.71	0.0	35.8	0.0	0.0	**10.0**	12.0
Mt. Taylor Federal Credit Union	Grants	NM	**C**	C	C+	2.2	6.52	0.0	24.4	0.0	0.0	**10.0**	16.3
Mt. Zion Credit Union	Zion	IL	**C**	C	C	<1	-5.46	0.0	38.7	0.0	0.0	**10.0**	20.9
MTC Federal Credit Union	Greenville	SC	**A**	A	A	175.7	5.33	0.0	37.1	22.6	10.8	**10.0**	15.3
▼ MTCU	Midland	TX	**B-**	B+	B+	118.0	1.61	0.0	32.1	9.2	13.0	**8.0**	9.9
Muhlenberg Community Hospital CU	Greenville	KY	**C-**	C-	C	<1	10.49	0.0	19.6	0.0	0.0	**10.0**	16.2
▼ Muna Federal Credit Union	Meridian	MS	**C**	C+	C+	34.0	9.65	0.1	18.8	5.0	0.2	**8.9**	10.3
Muncie Federal Credit Union	Muncie	IN	**C+**	C+	C+	14.1	2.96	0.0	29.6	0.4	0.0	**10.0**	11.3
▲ Muncie Post Office Credit Union	Muncie	IN	**C**	C-	C-	<1	-2.76	0.0	64.3	0.0	0.0	**10.0**	21.1
Muni Employees Credit Union	Ottumwa	IA	**C-**	C-	D+	<1	1.14	0.0	82.9	0.0	0.0	**10.0**	13.6
Municipal Credit Union	Sioux City	IA	**C**	C	C	16.9	3.09	1.5	19.0	14.6	0.0	**7.0**	9.0
Municipal Credit Union	New York	NY	**C+**	C+	C	2641.2	7.87	0.3	31.2	28.2	11.5	**5.6**	7.6
Municipal Employees Credit Union	La Porte	IN	**D+**	D+	D+	1.2	13.38	0.0	64.9	0.0	0.0	**10.0**	17.3
Municipal Employees Federal Credit Union	Bogalusa	LA	**C**	C	C	1.3	1.64	0.0	17.5	0.0	0.0	**10.0**	21.1
Municipal Empls Credit Union of Baltimore, Inc.	Baltimore	MD	**B-**	B-	B-	1182.1	-0.08	2.8	29.0	25.2	25.8	**10.0**	11.4
Municipal Empls Credit Union of Oklahoma City	Oklahoma City	OK	**C+**	C+	B-	169.9	2.37	1.3	52.0	20.1	0.4	**6.2**	8.2
Munseetown Community FCU	Muncie	IN	**D**	D	D-	10.7	0.67	0.0	33.1	0.0	0.0	**6.4**	8.5
Musicians Federal Credit Union	Arlington	TX	**C-**	C-	D+	<1	-16.24	0.0	18.9	0.0	0.0	**10.0**	12.4
Musicians' Interguild Credit Union	Los Angeles	CA	**D**	D	D+	73.9	1.69	0.0	6.8	29.5	0.7	**4.6**	6.7
Muskegon Co-Op Federal Credit Union	Muskegon	MI	**B**	B	B	60.2	8.72	0.0	62.6	1.2	3.2	**10.0**	12.4
Muskegon Federal Credit Union	Muskegon	MI	**C**	C	C+	49.5	3.67	0.0	16.0	15.7	23.3	**9.8**	10.8
Muskegon Patternmakers FCU	Muskegon Heights	MI	**D+**	D+	D+	3.1	-0.42	0.0	47.6	0.0	30.7	**10.0**	28.3
Muskegon Saint Joseph FCU	Muskegon	MI	**C+**	C+	C	11.5	7.54	0.0	29.0	16.1	0.0	**10.0**	14.5
▼ Muskogee Federal Credit Union	Muskogee	OK	**D**	D+	D	70.2	1.46	0.0	37.0	7.1	0.0	**4.8**	6.8
▲ Mutual Credit Union	Vicksburg	MS	**B-**	C+	C+	204.7	5.10	0.0	21.0	14.2	30.2	**7.9**	9.9
Mutual First Federal Credit Union	Omaha	NE	**C-**	C-	C-	108.9	1.73	11.1	26.5	24.1	14.8	**5.9**	8.0
▼ Mutual Savings Credit Union	Hoover	AL	**C-**	C	D+	183.9	1.55	7.4	18.4	37.9	11.4	**6.6**	8.7
Mutual Savings Credit Union	Atlanta	GA	**C+**	C+	C+	78.6	9.69	2.1	25.5	21.3	7.2	**10.0**	11.3
Mutual Security Credit Union	Shelton	CT	**C**	C	C+	277.2	5.19	0.1	30.6	47.5	0.0	**5.6**	7.6
MUW Employees Federal Credit Union	Columbus	MS	**C-**	C-	C	4.1	6.93	0.0	39.2	0.0	12.4	**10.0**	16.3
MWD Federal Credit Union	Los Angeles	CA	**C**	C	C	47.5	6.56	0.0	20.7	7.7	15.3	**10.0**	12.0
MWRD Employees' Credit Union	Chicago	IL	**C+**	C+	C+	32.4	6.31	0.0	20.0	20.3	28.1	**10.0**	14.1
My Choice Federal Credit Union	Tulsa	OK	**E+**	E+	E+	1.7	1.90	0.0	71.0	0.0	0.0	**4.4**	6.4
▼ My Community Credit Union	Midland	TX	**B-**	B+	B+	345.7	7.74	1.2	49.2	11.8	5.3	**8.6**	10.2
▼ My Credit Union	Redwood City	CA	**D**	D+	D	33.9	0.20	12.1	25.9	31.6	2.8	**6.2**	8.2
My Credit Union	Watauga	TX	**D+**	D+	C-	48.5	2.12	0.0	38.9	12.8	0.0	**6.2**	8.2
▲ My Healthcare Federal Credit Union	Gainesville	FL	**B-**	C+	C+	26.2	2.29	0.0	39.2	5.1	0.0	**10.0**	15.9
My Pensacola Federal Credit Union	Pensacola	FL	**B+**	B+	B+	67.3	6.57	0.0	24.1	7.7	7.8	**10.0**	17.4
▼ My Personal Credit Union	Wyoming	MI	**C**	C+	B-	132.2	7.10	10.9	18.8	20.7	35.3	**6.5**	8.7
▼ MyCom Federal Credit Union	Pittsfield	MA	**C**	C+	C+	19.0	11.51	0.0	30.6	1.3	0.0	**10.0**	11.0
N A E Federal Credit Union	Chesapeake	VA	**B+**	B+	B+	105.4	12.59	1.1	61.4	4.6	8.8	**10.0**	14.6
N C P D Federal Credit Union	Plainview	NY	**A**	A	A	737.7	2.35	0.2	6.0	13.6	69.1	**10.0**	14.0
▲ N C S E Credit Union Inc.	Lovingston	VA	**C**	C-	D+	1.1	-7.59	0.0	36.0	0.0	0.0	**10.0**	20.2
▼ N Y Team Federal Credit Union	Hicksville	NY	**D**	C-	C-	37.5	-0.63	8.0	31.0	6.1	0.0	**5.8**	7.8
N. J. Latvian Federal Credit Union	Freehold	NJ	**C-**	C-	C-	10.7	2.21	0.0	0.8	0.7	92.8	**6.8**	12.2
N.B.A. Credit Union	Bristol	PA	**D+**	D+	D+	43.2	-0.47	3.7	10.5	44.3	6.1	**10.0**	14.8
▼ N.E.W. Credit Union	Oconto Falls	WI	**B-**	B	C	87.3	5.96	0.0	18.4	42.6	1.2	**10.0**	11.1
N.F.G. #2 Federal Credit Union	Warren	PA	**C+**	C+	C+	23.2	0.61	0.0	18.5	0.0	28.7	**10.0**	12.1
▼ N.G.H. Credit Union	Nashville	TN	**E+**	D-	D	6.9	2.98	4.4	50.3	4.2	0.0	**4.1**	6.1
N.G.P.L. Employees Credit Union	Saint Charles	IA	**C**	C	C	2.9	-12.13	0.0	11.0	0.0	0.0	**10.0**	26.8
N.H. Community Federal Credit Union	Claremont	NH	**E+**	E+	E+	9.6	6.51	0.0	28.0	6.8	0.0	**4.8**	6.8
N.I.C.E. Federal Credit Union	Saint Charles	IL	**D-**	D-	D-	1.6	8.29	0.0	56.9	0.0	0.0	**6.8**	8.8
N.J.T. Employees Federal Credit Union	Waldwick	NJ	**C-**	C-	C	13.4	10.73	0.0	21.8	0.0	0.0	**6.4**	8.4
N.O. Port Commission Employees CU	New Orleans	LA	**C-**	C-	D+	4.4	0.87	0.0	49.6	0.0	1.0	**10.0**	11.7

Asset Quality Index	Non-Performing Loans as a % of Total Loans	Non-Performing Loans as a % of Capital	Net Charge-Offs Avg Loans	Profitability Index	Net Income ($Mil)	Return on Assets	Return on Equity	Net Interest Spread	Overhead Efficiency Ratio	Liquidity Index	Liquidity Ratio	Hot Money Ratio	Stability Index
6.8	0.98	3.0	1.92	**2.3**	0.00	-0.30	-1.51	4.94	88.6	**5.3**	48.2	3.6	**6.3**
7.8	4.65	5.9	4.56	**0.1**	0.00	-0.42	-3.16	2.70	88.2	**6.9**	93.3	0.0	**4.5**
9.8	0.00	0.0	0.00	**1.4**	0.00	-0.04	-0.53	2.69	101.6	**4.6**	28.3	2.8	**3.2**
9.0	0.58	0.7	10.00	**8.2**	0.00	1.01	4.51	3.67	57.1	**7.3**	63.7	0.0	**5.7**
8.7	16.67	4.0	0.00	**1.1**	0.00	0.00	0.00	0.00	100.0	**8.0**	64.3	0.0	**3.7**
10.0	0.36	0.5	0.00	**3.5**	0.01	0.27	1.44	1.92	84.8	**5.1**	24.9	0.0	**7.8**
9.6	0.03	0.1	0.40	**3.8**	0.02	0.47	3.92	2.99	83.5	**5.6**	31.7	0.0	**6.6**
10.0	0.16	0.3	0.00	**2.1**	0.00	0.00	0.00	3.19	100.0	**6.9**	45.2	0.0	**7.4**
7.0	5.75	7.7	0.00	**8.9**	0.00	3.64	17.39	6.30	0.0	**7.3**	66.3	0.0	**5.0**
8.8	0.41	2.5	0.87	**6.8**	0.18	0.41	2.66	5.43	83.6	**4.5**	24.1	3.7	**9.4**
7.0	1.20	6.7	0.64	**2.0**	-0.03	-0.11	-1.30	3.81	95.0	**4.5**	26.2	11.3	**4.0**
10.0	0.65	0.7	0.00	**0.1**	0.00	-0.54	-3.10	2.81	83.3	**7.2**	59.1	0.0	**5.5**
7.6	0.82	3.0	1.86	**1.8**	-0.02	-0.22	-2.05	4.97	91.5	**7.0**	58.2	4.5	**4.1**
9.0	0.34	1.2	-0.82	**4.1**	0.01	0.40	3.53	2.94	88.5	**4.9**	30.1	3.5	**5.2**
8.0	1.13	3.1	0.00	**4.8**	0.00	1.98	9.47	8.44	76.5	**4.5**	20.0	0.0	**4.3**
5.9	1.53	8.7	0.00	**3.8**	0.00	0.57	4.12	4.58	85.7	**4.1**	19.7	0.0	**3.7**
9.9	0.22	1.0	0.05	**4.0**	0.02	0.51	5.56	3.15	84.8	**5.4**	30.5	0.0	**5.0**
5.7	1.20	15.1	0.73	**3.8**	2.86	0.45	9.91	5.05	87.7	**5.6**	29.1	0.9	**4.7**
2.6	5.51	20.3	0.00	**1.9**	0.00	-1.03	-5.80	3.78	133.3	**5.2**	38.5	0.0	**6.5**
10.0	0.00	0.0	0.00	**1.7**	0.00	0.00	0.00	2.52	116.7	**7.1**	55.2	0.0	**7.3**
6.1	1.72	10.8	0.94	**3.4**	1.51	0.51	4.59	3.59	81.4	**3.5**	15.9	6.7	**6.9**
4.5	0.94	10.5	1.95	**3.0**	-0.33	-0.77	-9.30	4.55	73.5	**2.6**	24.1	26.0	**4.5**
6.4	1.31	5.7	0.00	**2.4**	0.00	0.08	0.88	2.64	97.5	**4.6**	23.7	10.1	**2.3**
7.1	0.90	4.4	0.00	**2.0**	0.00	-0.60	-4.82	5.49	114.3	**5.3**	28.2	0.0	**5.4**
8.1	0.18	0.9	0.28	**1.2**	-0.02	-0.08	-1.22	2.80	103.3	**5.5**	56.0	14.1	**1.5**
6.8	0.65	3.9	0.81	**4.6**	0.04	0.25	1.94	4.19	85.6	**3.6**	19.9	7.2	**6.6**
10.0	0.12	0.4	1.40	**1.6**	-0.03	-0.24	-2.23	2.63	87.2	**4.2**	25.2	8.3	**5.2**
8.0	0.13	0.2	0.00	**0.4**	0.00	-0.39	-1.37	2.87	111.1	**5.5**	31.5	0.0	**6.2**
7.0	2.00	5.8	-1.03	**4.8**	0.02	0.71	4.85	2.44	70.6	**4.6**	12.0	0.0	**7.9**
6.1	0.61	7.3	0.41	**3.0**	0.05	0.31	5.83	2.86	82.4	**5.4**	33.9	0.4	**1.9**
9.6	0.19	1.2	0.29	**5.2**	0.64	1.27	14.74	3.20	73.9	**5.6**	31.3	0.7	**5.2**
8.0	0.60	4.5	0.49	**2.6**	0.03	0.11	1.40	3.89	90.7	**4.2**	24.2	3.8	**4.4**
3.7	1.10	25.4	0.76	**2.3**	0.00	0.00	0.03	3.67	91.1	**4.0**	15.6	4.9	**4.2**
9.1	0.60	2.9	0.29	**3.3**	0.08	0.41	3.57	2.89	75.9	**3.3**	31.0	15.3	**5.7**
6.1	0.86	11.8	0.51	**2.9**	0.06	0.09	1.19	3.78	87.5	**2.9**	9.8	6.8	**4.6**
3.6	8.25	21.5	8.05	**3.7**	-0.03	-3.10	-18.05	6.30	77.4	**6.4**	42.3	0.0	**6.2**
9.2	0.03	0.1	0.00	**2.0**	0.00	0.00	0.00	2.71	102.7	**5.0**	34.7	5.0	**5.7**
10.0	0.06	0.2	0.14	**2.6**	0.03	0.39	2.93	3.65	87.9	**5.2**	17.2	0.0	**6.9**
3.5	1.29	14.1	0.00	**0.7**	0.00	-0.24	-3.70	5.34	100.0	**4.4**	21.2	0.0	**1.3**
5.8	0.87	5.5	1.55	**2.4**	-0.12	-0.14	-1.33	3.65	78.0	**4.3**	23.5	7.5	**6.0**
7.2	0.52	4.0	0.21	**1.0**	-0.02	-0.22	-2.73	3.60	103.9	**3.8**	22.0	3.1	**3.2**
6.0	1.53	10.8	0.39	**2.3**	0.02	0.19	2.33	3.77	92.7	**5.4**	43.0	2.3	**3.8**
8.2	1.15	3.9	1.02	**4.8**	0.05	0.74	4.65	5.13	84.3	**5.1**	36.9	2.4	**5.7**
10.0	0.50	1.3	0.55	**3.4**	0.09	0.52	3.03	2.94	79.3	**5.8**	40.7	2.1	**7.3**
9.0	0.34	2.0	0.26	**2.7**	0.03	0.09	1.07	3.36	94.1	**4.4**	14.5	3.8	**5.5**
9.1	0.34	1.1	0.58	**1.6**	-0.02	-0.50	-4.38	3.51	101.7	**4.6**	22.8	3.5	**5.5**
8.4	0.49	2.0	0.55	**3.7**	0.10	0.37	2.76	5.18	87.8	**3.2**	18.6	17.6	**6.8**
9.3	1.69	2.8	0.18	**7.5**	2.03	1.11	8.37	1.83	36.5	**5.0**	12.6	0.0	**9.7**
7.1	4.39	7.5	0.00	**6.2**	0.00	1.52	7.48	5.26	66.7	**6.4**	66.7	0.0	**4.3**
0.3	14.58	112.9	0.02	**1.9**	0.01	0.08	1.89	6.11	82.5	**6.8**	50.1	0.0	**2.3**
7.5	14.55	3.4	0.00	**1.0**	-0.01	-0.41	-4.55	0.11	375.0	**5.5**	381.3	26.7	**4.1**
9.9	0.42	1.7	-0.03	**0.7**	0.01	0.09	0.63	3.46	97.6	**4.1**	16.7	1.9	**5.6**
7.2	1.09	6.4	0.03	**2.8**	0.06	0.27	2.35	3.33	90.8	**3.7**	22.6	3.4	**6.0**
10.0	0.87	1.9	0.25	**3.3**	0.02	0.39	3.14	2.78	83.0	**4.8**	16.5	1.4	**6.0**
3.0	1.82	15.6	5.82	**0.0**	-0.07	-4.28	-63.48	5.74	106.7	**5.9**	35.6	1.7	**3.1**
10.0	2.42	1.0	-9.92	**2.3**	0.00	0.40	1.54	1.67	75.0	**5.1**	16.4	0.0	**6.0**
4.5	0.95	9.6	0.06	**2.6**	0.01	0.34	4.91	4.68	91.1	**4.2**	17.3	0.0	**1.0**
5.0	0.59	3.9	1.55	**2.7**	0.00	0.51	5.63	9.22	93.8	**5.9**	38.9	0.0	**1.7**
9.0	0.84	2.1	0.13	**3.0**	0.01	0.18	2.14	4.56	52.9	**8.3**	84.5	0.0	**2.6**
5.9	2.05	8.4	0.00	**4.2**	0.01	0.54	4.65	3.80	85.1	**4.3**	15.9	0.0	**3.7**

	Name	City	State	Rating	2016 Rating	2015 Rating	Total Assets ($Mil)	One Year Asset Growth	Asset Mix (As a % of Total Assets) Comm-ercial Loans	Cons-umer Loans	Mort-gage Loans	Secur-ities	Capital-ization Index	Net Worth Ratio
	N.U.L. Federal Credit Union	New York	NY	**D**	D	C-	<1	-15.07	0.0	0.0	0.0	0.0	**10.0**	17.5
	N.W. Iowa Credit Union	Le Mars	IA	**B**	B	B	47.7	6.55	0.0	32.4	15.4	0.0	**10.0**	11.2
	N.Y.B. & FMC Federal Credit Union	Jersey City	NJ	**D**	D	D	6.0	-3.51	0.0	30.6	0.0	3.2	**10.0**	13.1
	Naft Federal Credit Union	Pharr	TX	**A-**	A-	B+	78.9	3.93	0.0	48.6	0.0	0.0	**10.0**	13.6
	Naheola Credit Union	Pennington	AL	**A-**	A-	A-	90.2	7.98	3.4	18.2	30.8	20.0	**10.0**	22.3
	Napfe Federal Credit Union	Washington	DC	**D**	D	D	3.0	-15.01	0.0	19.7	0.0	0.0	**10.0**	38.5
	NARC Federal Credit Union	Beltsville	MD	**D-**	D-	D-	21.9	-5.26	0.0	22.9	0.0	50.3	**5.3**	7.3
	NAS JRB Credit Union	New Orleans	LA	**C-**	C-	D	30.7	6.14	0.0	62.1	0.0	0.0	**6.9**	8.9
	NASA Federal Credit Union	Upper Marlboro	MD	**A-**	A-	A	2134.2	14.82	7.1	45.8	23.7	4.4	**8.3**	9.9
	Nascoga Federal Credit Union	Gainesville	TX	**C**	C	C	90.7	4.06	6.0	28.9	20.8	10.3	**6.3**	8.3
	Nashville Firemen's Credit Union	Nashville	TN	**B-**	B-	C+	23.9	5.61	0.0	56.2	1.0	0.8	**10.0**	16.7
	Nashville Post Office Credit Union	Nashville	TN	**C**	C	C-	69.8	-0.13	0.0	16.4	14.0	49.7	**10.0**	18.5
	Nashwauk Federal Credit Union	Nashwauk	MN	**D+**	D+	C-	5.7	10.29	0.0	29.5	2.9	13.5	**8.2**	9.8
	Nassau Educators Federal Credit Union	Westbury	NY	**B+**	B+	B+	2655.5	8.39	10.7	26.9	27.5	11.9	**8.2**	9.9
	Nassau Financial Federal Credit Union	Westbury	NY	**D+**	D+	D+	419.8	3.65	22.2	8.8	14.8	10.8	**7.1**	9.1
	Natchez-Adams Educators Credit Union	Natchez	MS	**C**	C	C+	1.4	-10.81	0.0	19.2	0.0	0.0	**10.0**	35.9
	Natco Credit Union	Richmond	IN	**B**	B	B	80.7	1.12	0.2	49.0	6.6	18.8	**10.0**	11.4
▲	Natco Employees Federal Credit Union	West Warwick	RI	**C**	C-	C	<1	5.02	0.0	20.9	0.0	0.0	**10.0**	14.8
	National Employees Federal Credit Union	Bluefield	WV	**C**	C	C	11.0	3.44	0.0	50.0	0.0	0.0	**10.0**	11.3
▼	National Geographic Federal Credit Union	Washington	DC	**D-**	D	D	12.5	-8.89	0.0	29.3	0.0	40.6	**9.4**	10.6
	National Institutes of Health FCU	Rockville	MD	**C**	C	C+	604.7	5.39	6.4	17.0	29.6	23.9	**6.1**	8.6
▼	National J.A.C.L. Credit Union	Salt Lake City	UT	**D**	D+	D+	31.7	5.05	3.7	19.7	16.0	10.2	**9.5**	10.7
	National Oilwell Varco Employees CU	Houston	TX	**B+**	B+	B+	15.3	-5.56	0.0	14.5	0.0	0.0	**10.0**	19.4
	Natrium Employees Federal Credit Union	Proctor	WV	**D**	D	D-	8.8	1.26	0.0	24.4	0.0	0.0	**6.0**	8.0
	Natural Resources Conservation Service FCU	Fort Worth	TX	**D**	D	D+	10.6	4.00	0.0	40.4	0.0	0.0	**10.0**	11.5
▲	Natural State Federal Credit Union	Searcy	AR	**C-**	D+	D+	5.5	3.16	0.0	62.3	0.0	0.0	**10.0**	15.8
	Navarro Credit Union	Corsicana	TX	**C+**	C+	C	3.2	-2.80	0.0	43.9	0.0	0.0	**10.0**	32.2
	Naveo Credit Union	Somerville	MA	**C**	C	C	126.2	6.04	9.9	13.2	38.3	13.5	**5.5**	7.5
▲	Navigant Credit Union	Smithfield	RI	**A-**	B+	B	1832.1	13.20	10.8	4.6	58.2	11.8	**10.0**	11.2
	Navigator Credit Union	Pascagoula	MS	**B+**	B+	A-	347.6	7.05	0.3	58.5	11.9	0.9	**10.0**	12.5
	Navy Army Community Credit Union	Corpus Christi	TX	**B+**	B+	A-	2594.7	8.03	2.9	45.5	35.4	1.2	**9.3**	10.6
	Navy Federal Credit Union	Vienna	VA	**A**	A	A	81547.5	8.49	0.6	35.0	33.4	18.1	**10.0**	11.7
	NBC (N.Y.) Employees FCU	New York	NY	**B**	B	B	36.8	3.86	0.8	5.6	26.8	33.4	**10.0**	12.6
	NCE Credit Union	Corpus Christi	TX	**C**	C	C	5.5	8.94	0.0	55.9	0.0	0.0	**10.0**	18.4
	NE PA Community Federal Credit Union	Stroudsburg	PA	**C**	C	D+	120.5	10.30	0.3	14.5	18.9	36.8	**6.0**	8.0
▼	NEA Federal Credit Union	Bardonia	NY	**D**	D+	C-	94.4	-9.33	15.3	11.4	17.8	7.8	**1.5**	4.5
	Nebo Credit Union	Springville	UT	**A-**	A-	A-	83.8	6.89	0.1	55.3	6.4	11.1	**10.0**	17.1
	Nebraska Energy Federal Credit Union	Columbus	NE	**A**	A	A	256.5	3.34	1.0	20.9	45.6	1.8	**10.0**	13.7
	Nebraska Rural Community FCU	Morrill	NE	**E+**	E+	E+	2.1	-3.22	0.0	35.2	20.2	0.0	**6.5**	8.5
	Nebraska Rural Electric Association CU	Lincoln	NE	**C**	C	C	6.3	-3.43	0.0	43.9	0.0	4.0	**10.0**	12.2
	Nebraska State Employees Credit Union	Lincoln	NE	**C-**	C-	C-	29.0	-2.52	0.0	18.0	6.3	0.0	**8.5**	10.0
	Neches Federal Credit Union	Port Neches	TX	**A**	A	A	500.7	7.26	5.0	44.4	19.9	4.0	**10.0**	13.9
	Neighborhood Community FCU	Omaha	NE	**C+**	C+	C+	24.9	2.28	0.0	20.0	0.2	0.0	**10.0**	13.6
	Neighborhood Credit Union	Dallas	TX	**A-**	A-	B+	614.4	3.89	0.0	50.3	4.7	6.7	**9.5**	10.7
▼	Neighborhood Trust Federal Credit Union	New York	NY	**D**	D+	C-	11.1	5.55	8.0	6.7	47.9	0.0	**9.0**	10.3
▼	Neighbors 1st FCU	Waynesboro	PA	**E-**	E	E+	11.0	2.24	0.0	18.6	1.3	8.2	**3.8**	5.8
	Neighbors Credit Union	Saint Louis	MO	**A**	A	A-	349.1	5.85	7.0	30.6	17.4	14.8	**10.0**	15.4
	Neighbors Federal Credit Union	Baton Rouge	LA	**B-**	B-	B-	823.8	9.02	2.4	60.3	8.6	2.1	**6.3**	8.3
	Neighbors United Federal Credit Union	Greenwood	SC	**B-**	B-	B	47.3	3.42	0.6	24.6	17.8	11.2	**10.0**	12.5
	Neiman Marcus Group Employees FCU	Dallas	TX	**C**	C	C+	13.0	1.34	0.0	48.4	0.0	0.0	**9.8**	10.8
	Nekoosa Credit Union	Nekoosa	WI	**C+**	C+	C+	21.8	2.91	3.2	5.4	38.2	0.0	**10.0**	24.6
	Neosho School Employees Credit Union	Neosho	MO	**C**	C	C-	2.3	1.21	0.0	50.2	0.0	0.0	**10.0**	14.4
	Nephi Western Employees FCU	Nephi	UT	**A-**	A-	A-	32.5	6.31	0.0	32.9	29.3	0.0	**10.0**	30.9
	NESC Federal Credit Union	Methuen	MA	**C+**	C+	C+	83.0	2.90	0.0	26.5	41.1	1.2	**7.6**	9.4
	Nestle (Freehold) Employees FCU	Freehold	NJ	**C+**	C+	C+	2.7	3.19	0.0	48.1	0.0	0.0	**10.0**	20.4
	Net Federal Credit Union	Scranton	PA	**B-**	B-	B-	188.7	2.19	0.0	14.5	4.7	31.8	**10.0**	15.0
▲	New Alliance Federal Credit Union	Ambridge	PA	**D+**	D	D	71.6	0.65	0.0	20.9	21.4	5.4	**8.4**	9.9
	New Bedford Credit Union	New Bedford	MA	**C**	C	C	122.7	1.97	0.0	16.4	27.4	11.5	**7.3**	9.2
▲	New Brunswick Postal FCU	Edison	NJ	**C**	C-	D+	12.0	-3.36	0.0	23.4	20.9	35.6	**10.0**	11.4
▼	New Castle Bellco Federal Credit Union	New Castle	PA	**D+**	C-	D+	11.6	-2.15	0.0	24.0	2.5	64.8	**9.7**	10.8

Asset Quality Index	Non-Performing Loans as a % of Total Loans	Non-Performing Loans as a % of Capital	Net Charge-Offs Avg Loans	Profitability Index	Net Income ($Mil)	Return on Assets	Return on Equity	Net Interest Spread	Overhead Efficiency Ratio	Liquidity Index	Liquidity Ratio	Hot Money Ratio	Stability Index
8.1	8.33	2.8	100.00	**1.1**	0.00	-1.04	-5.88	5.06	200.0	**8.9**	115.8	0.0	**4.7**
8.9	0.18	1.0	0.25	**7.7**	0.15	1.27	11.27	2.83	60.8	**4.6**	25.5	2.2	**6.8**
6.4	5.23	11.2	-2.47	**0.3**	-0.01	-0.33	-2.53	5.59	101.5	**6.9**	46.4	0.0	**5.0**
8.6	0.29	1.2	0.10	**7.0**	0.19	1.01	7.79	4.03	79.3	**5.5**	31.4	1.3	**7.9**
8.0	1.34	4.1	0.29	**9.0**	0.28	1.26	5.73	3.88	70.7	**3.6**	26.2	9.3	**8.2**
10.0	3.89	1.9	1.30	**0.0**	-0.01	-1.61	-4.16	3.11	157.9	**8.1**	131.4	1.0	**4.7**
1.7	1.00	39.2	1.67	**0.0**	-0.06	-1.12	-155.97	2.23	150.9	**6.7**	45.7	0.0	**1.0**
4.4	1.32	9.8	0.93	**5.0**	0.07	0.95	10.49	6.05	81.8	**4.9**	32.5	4.8	**4.1**
5.4	1.05	8.7	1.18	**7.7**	4.98	0.94	9.56	4.35	58.8	**3.0**	23.7	18.0	**7.8**
9.2	0.18	1.5	0.02	**2.7**	0.03	0.15	1.82	2.72	94.3	**3.6**	22.5	10.6	**4.2**
8.2	0.21	0.8	-0.05	**4.7**	0.03	0.50	2.92	4.44	88.9	**4.5**	28.2	7.2	**7.5**
9.5	0.32	2.0	0.22	**1.8**	0.01	0.06	0.33	2.53	96.3	**4.1**	41.2	17.9	**6.5**
9.4	0.23	1.0	0.00	**1.0**	0.00	-0.22	-2.13	3.15	107.0	**5.2**	30.8	0.0	**5.2**
7.3	0.68	5.9	0.27	**5.5**	5.26	0.80	8.44	2.81	65.7	**2.9**	10.9	11.9	**7.4**
1.7	5.96	43.4	0.14	**1.5**	0.04	0.04	0.42	2.10	90.2	**3.7**	16.0	7.6	**5.5**
9.4	2.89	1.5	14.24	**1.0**	-0.01	-3.87	-10.69	4.92	87.5	**7.0**	74.7	0.0	**5.5**
6.0	1.02	6.3	1.53	**3.4**	0.04	0.20	1.76	6.27	85.1	**4.5**	16.8	0.6	**5.5**
10.0	0.00	0.0	0.00	**2.2**	0.00	-1.71	-11.76	8.16	200.0	**8.3**	92.4	0.0	**5.9**
7.5	0.74	3.2	1.03	**3.3**	0.00	0.15	1.29	6.53	83.3	**5.5**	23.7	0.0	**5.1**
7.2	0.00	0.0	8.11	**0.0**	-0.02	-0.57	-5.40	3.45	116.4	**4.9**	26.3	1.0	**4.4**
6.8	0.92	7.4	0.98	**2.7**	0.11	0.07	0.96	2.97	92.7	**4.6**	16.6	4.9	**5.5**
9.9	0.17	0.7	0.21	**0.4**	-0.03	-0.42	-3.88	2.72	112.5	**4.8**	29.5	4.9	**5.2**
10.0	0.24	0.2	3.23	**5.0**	0.01	0.34	1.77	1.40	79.1	**7.1**	97.0	0.0	**6.4**
8.9	0.89	3.1	0.00	**2.4**	0.00	0.09	1.15	2.32	95.8	**6.2**	44.5	0.0	**2.3**
7.3	1.79	7.3	0.00	**0.0**	-0.02	-0.65	-5.58	2.67	121.0	**5.0**	63.7	6.0	**5.5**
8.1	0.03	0.1	-0.31	**4.3**	0.02	1.29	7.99	5.30	81.9	**4.7**	26.3	0.0	**6.4**
7.3	4.61	6.3	1.09	**10.0**	0.02	2.26	7.14	4.83	57.6	**5.4**	24.9	0.0	**5.7**
9.8	0.07	0.6	0.07	**2.7**	0.05	0.15	1.96	3.22	94.1	**4.2**	22.2	8.4	**4.9**
8.7	0.37	2.9	0.05	**5.5**	3.83	0.85	7.80	2.91	72.1	**2.6**	11.1	12.5	**8.7**
5.2	1.28	8.7	1.99	**5.1**	0.49	0.58	4.56	5.04	69.2	**3.4**	30.4	19.5	**7.4**
5.5	0.78	7.9	0.79	**6.3**	4.26	0.67	6.57	3.42	71.1	**1.9**	15.4	30.5	**8.0**
7.4	0.92	5.5	1.81	**9.8**	303.00	1.50	13.62	4.82	50.4	**2.9**	9.5	10.9	**9.6**
10.0	0.10	0.3	-0.03	**4.9**	0.06	0.62	4.77	3.02	81.1	**4.1**	17.0	3.6	**7.0**
8.4	0.00	0.0	0.12	**6.0**	0.01	0.96	5.22	5.54	87.2	**5.3**	39.1	5.7	**5.0**
7.6	1.28	6.1	0.40	**1.8**	0.01	0.05	0.58	2.89	91.7	**5.8**	39.5	5.0	**4.2**
0.3	11.78	100.4	3.90	**0.0**	-2.04	-8.57	-156.65	4.11	189.1	**4.2**	16.6	1.3	**1.9**
6.9	0.41	4.0	0.52	**9.1**	0.23	1.11	6.39	4.66	67.8	**3.3**	12.0	7.3	**9.4**
9.8	0.04	0.3	0.17	**7.2**	0.64	1.02	7.40	2.30	57.0	**3.7**	11.1	2.0	**9.1**
6.9	0.00	0.0	0.30	**2.3**	0.00	0.00	0.00	5.36	93.3	**3.9**	38.5	11.1	**1.7**
9.8	0.42	1.5	0.00	**1.9**	0.00	-0.06	-0.52	1.83	103.2	**4.4**	19.7	0.0	**6.3**
8.3	0.61	2.5	0.08	**2.6**	0.02	0.25	2.96	2.47	87.8	**5.8**	60.2	0.8	**3.8**
8.8	0.36	2.4	0.56	**7.7**	1.12	0.92	6.50	4.04	73.5	**3.3**	20.4	10.3	**9.3**
10.0	0.35	0.7	-0.49	**2.3**	0.01	0.10	0.71	2.41	96.7	**6.1**	42.0	0.0	**6.1**
7.3	0.56	3.6	0.68	**7.7**	1.54	1.02	9.52	3.77	70.9	**3.5**	21.6	12.8	**7.0**
5.4	1.53	11.2	2.07	**0.6**	-0.03	-1.13	-13.64	4.92	97.2	**5.8**	35.8	0.0	**4.1**
5.6	2.82	13.4	1.19	**0.4**	-0.02	-0.59	-9.83	3.31	106.0	**6.6**	40.8	0.0	**0.0**
9.2	0.64	2.6	0.61	**7.7**	0.88	1.03	6.67	3.43	76.4	**3.9**	14.7	5.0	**8.1**
6.8	0.35	3.7	0.72	**3.7**	0.88	0.43	5.51	3.24	78.6	**2.8**	17.1	18.6	**5.6**
6.3	1.81	7.4	0.78	**3.1**	0.02	0.20	1.56	4.82	90.7	**5.9**	39.6	6.2	**6.3**
5.9	1.18	4.9	0.99	**2.8**	0.00	-0.09	-0.85	4.44	83.8	**4.9**	17.0	0.0	**4.7**
10.0	0.02	0.0	0.00	**3.4**	0.03	0.54	2.17	2.74	81.3	**5.0**	38.5	2.1	**7.6**
4.6	4.49	15.9	0.00	**5.8**	0.00	0.52	3.55	3.84	85.0	**4.9**	28.8	0.0	**4.3**
9.2	0.16	0.4	-0.06	**9.3**	0.12	1.49	4.76	3.34	53.2	**4.6**	30.4	0.0	**8.0**
8.9	0.21	1.8	0.19	**3.8**	0.09	0.44	4.63	4.38	87.6	**3.8**	17.0	4.8	**4.5**
8.7	0.00	0.0	0.00	**5.8**	0.01	0.75	3.71	3.80	69.6	**4.5**	40.4	0.0	**5.0**
9.9	0.69	1.8	0.27	**2.5**	0.07	0.14	1.05	2.91	91.9	**5.1**	24.6	2.3	**7.8**
6.7	1.00	5.5	0.17	**1.6**	0.05	0.28	2.77	3.08	97.0	**4.5**	21.0	3.3	**3.7**
8.8	0.82	4.6	0.23	**2.3**	0.06	0.20	2.17	3.04	90.6	**4.9**	36.1	5.0	**5.7**
9.6	0.45	2.0	1.50	**2.2**	0.01	0.23	2.05	5.00	93.3	**4.3**	12.6	2.2	**4.9**
10.0	0.12	0.3	-0.12	**1.5**	0.00	0.00	0.00	2.02	100.0	**4.7**	17.8	1.0	**4.9**

Name	City	State	Rating	2016 Rating	2015 Rating	Total Assets ($Mil)	One Year Asset Growth	Asset Mix (As a % of Total Assets) Commercial Loans	Consumer Loans	Mortgage Loans	Securities	Capitalization Index	Net Worth Ratio
New Castle County Delaware Employees FCU	New Castle	DE	**D+**	D+	D+	23.3	3.79	0.0	12.8	0.0	0.0	**8.2**	9.8
New Castle County School Employees FCU	New Castle	DE	**D-**	D-	D-	47.0	3.77	0.0	36.8	0.2	0.0	**5.3**	7.3
▲ New Century Federal Credit Union	Joliet	IL	**C**	C-	D+	52.3	-1.79	0.4	14.7	8.3	2.9	**10.0**	12.1
New Community Federal Credit Union	Newark	NJ	**C+**	C+	C+	3.5	-0.54	37.5	1.3	50.5	0.0	**10.0**	12.1
New Covenant Dominion FCU	Bronx	NY	**C-**	C-	C-	1.1	6.91	0.0	30.6	0.0	0.0	**10.0**	12.1
New Cumberland Federal Credit Union	New Cumberland	PA	**C-**	C-	C-	153.2	4.62	0.0	33.5	18.4	18.8	**5.3**	7.3
New Dimensions Federal Credit Union	Waterville	ME	**C**	C	C-	89.7	12.86	7.4	36.3	38.3	0.0	**5.7**	7.7
New England Federal Credit Union	Williston	VT	**A-**	A-	B+	1207.9	6.08	8.1	12.2	48.9	18.0	**10.0**	12.3
New England Lee Federal Credit Union	Boston	MA	**C**	C	C-	3.8	-6.58	2.4	0.5	6.4	0.0	**10.0**	38.1
New England Teamsters FCU	Arlington	MA	**D+**	D+	D+	62.0	6.07	3.5	9.4	24.4	34.0	**10.0**	15.1
New Generations Federal Credit Union	Richmond	VA	**D**	D	D-	65.5	2.07	0.0	48.2	13.7	14.8	**4.8**	6.8
New Hampshire Federal Credit Union	Concord	NH	**B**	B	B	265.2	4.31	0.0	14.5	30.9	39.3	**10.0**	12.9
New Hampshire Postal Credit Union	Manchester	NH	**B-**	B-	B-	44.5	5.22	0.0	19.5	0.0	0.0	**10.0**	19.5
New Haven County Credit Union	North Haven	CT	**E-**	E-	E-	19.2	3.43	0.0	19.9	0.0	8.8	**3.2**	5.2
New Haven Firefighters Credit Union	New Haven	CT	**C+**	C+	C+	6.5	0.46	0.0	35.4	0.0	0.0	**10.0**	20.5
▲ New Haven Police and Municipal FCU	New Haven	CT	**C+**	C	C-	5.8	6.28	0.0	57.0	0.0	0.0	**10.0**	25.3
New Haven Teachers Federal Credit Union	New Haven	CT	**C**	C	C-	10.2	-3.51	0.0	10.4	0.0	0.0	**10.0**	26.3
New Horizon Credit Union	Danville	IL	**D+**	D+	D+	12.9	-1.01	0.0	49.3	4.1	0.0	**10.0**	11.7
New Horizon Federal Credit Union	Barberton	OH	**B-**	B-	B-	19.2	2.11	0.0	35.9	13.1	25.9	**9.4**	10.6
New Horizons Credit Union	Mobile	AL	**C+**	C+	B	224.2	-0.82	0.0	35.4	16.6	23.7	**4.2**	6.3
New Horizons Credit Union	West Point	MS	**C**	C	C	10.0	1.74	0.0	42.1	1.0	0.0	**10.0**	18.0
New Horizons Credit Union	Cincinnati	OH	**D**	D	D+	38.3	-2.98	9.8	35.2	30.3	1.9	**6.7**	8.7
New Jersey Community FCU	Moorestown	NJ	**E+**	E+	E+	9.0	1.58	0.0	14.7	26.2	0.0	**4.7**	6.7
▼ New Jersey Law & Public Safety CU	Trenton	NJ	**B-**	B	B	48.4	3.01	0.0	30.1	1.5	0.1	**10.0**	13.7
New Kensington Municipal FCU	New Kensington	PA	**C**	C	C	2.0	-2.17	0.0	27.1	6.5	0.0	**10.0**	23.7
▲ New Life Federal Credit Union	Philadelphia	PA	**C-**	D+	C-	<1	9.79	0.0	33.6	0.0	0.0	**10.0**	19.9
▼ New London Municipal Employees CU	New London	CT	**D**	D+	C-	3.1	-0.13	0.0	34.4	0.0	3.3	**10.0**	22.4
New Olivet Baptist Church Credit Union	Cordova	TN	**C**	C	C	<1	11.46	0.0	11.7	0.0	0.0	**10.0**	11.7
New Orleans Clerk & Checkers FCU	Metairie	LA	**C-**	C-	C	9.8	-3.42	0.0	19.7	28.2	0.0	**10.0**	15.0
New Orleans Firemen's FCU	Metairie	LA	**C+**	C+	C	163.0	1.90	1.9	54.4	11.2	9.0	**6.1**	8.1
New Orleans Police Department Empls CU	New Orleans	LA	**B+**	B+	B+	19.0	2.71	0.0	48.1	0.0	0.0	**10.0**	43.6
New Orleans Public Belt RR FCU	Metairie	LA	**C**	C	C	<1	-0.31	0.0	48.5	0.0	0.0	**10.0**	23.5
New Pilgrim Federal Credit Union	Birmingham	AL	**D-**	D-	D-	1.3	-2.69	0.0	45.3	0.0	0.0	**8.0**	9.6
New Rising Star Federal Credit Union	Detroit	MI	**C-**	C-	D+	<1	-7.21	0.0	25.2	0.0	0.0	**10.0**	13.6
New South Credit Union	Knoxville	TN	**B+**	B+	B+	56.2	20.96	0.2	33.5	13.2	0.0	**10.0**	14.9
New York State Employees FCU	New York	NY	**D**	D	D+	2.0	-17.84	0.0	60.2	0.0	0.0	**4.3**	6.3
New York Times Employees FCU	New York	NY	**C+**	C+	C	74.2	-0.43	5.5	11.7	23.0	18.2	**10.0**	17.2
New York University Federal Credit Union	New York	NY	**C**	C	C-	21.7	18.09	9.9	16.9	19.1	0.0	**6.3**	8.3
Newark Board of Education Employees CU	Newark	NJ	**D**	D	C-	28.9	-13.28	5.8	18.5	8.4	47.2	**10.0**	18.3
Newark Firemen Federal Credit Union	Newark	NJ	**D**	D	D+	17.3	-0.43	0.0	44.6	0.0	9.6	**10.0**	13.8
Newark Police Federal Credit Union	Newark	NJ	**C**	C	C+	6.1	5.16	0.0	46.3	0.0	0.1	**10.0**	22.8
▼ Newark Post Office Employees CU	Newark	NJ	**C-**	C	C	3.3	6.92	0.0	0.0	0.0	0.0	**10.0**	30.6
Newaygo County Service Employees CU	Fremont	MI	**D+**	D+	D	24.6	7.91	0.0	23.1	4.9	0.0	**5.6**	7.6
Newell Federal Credit Union	Newell	PA	**D**	D	D	5.3	0.63	0.0	39.2	0.0	0.0	**7.2**	9.1
▼ Newport News Municipal Employees CU	Newport News	VA	**D**	D+	D+	40.9	-0.77	3.1	24.7	22.2	33.1	**6.3**	8.7
Newport News Shipbuilding Employees' CU	Newport News	VA	**B**	B	B	1567.3	5.92	8.6	41.8	27.0	12.5	**10.0**	12.4
Newrizons Federal Credit Union	Hoquiam	WA	**C**	C	C	14.8	19.17	5.3	50.9	1.5	0.0	**9.8**	10.9
Newspaper Employees Credit Union	Albany	NY	**D+**	D+	C-	<1	-1.81	0.0	28.9	0.0	30.8	**10.0**	37.9
NGM Employees Federal Credit Union	Keene	NH	**D+**	D+	D+	5.5	0.09	0.0	49.5	0.0	31.0	**10.0**	11.4
Niagara Falls Air Force FCU	Niagara Falls	NY	**B-**	B-	B-	13.5	4.39	0.0	17.5	9.0	59.4	**10.0**	14.0
Niagara Falls Memorial Medical Ctr FCU	Niagara Falls	NY	**D**	D	D	4.2	-4.76	0.0	37.6	0.0	0.0	**5.2**	7.2
Niagara Falls Teachers FCU	Niagara Falls	NY	**C+**	C+	C	12.6	1.10	0.0	18.4	9.6	0.0	**10.0**	13.9
Niagara Frontier Federal Municipal CU	Niagara Falls	NY	**D**	D	D	2.8	2.05	0.0	46.8	0.0	0.0	**10.0**	14.8
Niagara Mohawk Power Core Troy East FCU	Troy	NY	**D**	D	D	3.9	6.97	0.0	65.2	0.0	0.0	**10.0**	12.3
▼ Niagara Regional Federal Credit Union	North Tonawanda	NY	**C**	C+	B-	30.9	8.23	0.8	16.1	31.5	27.0	**8.7**	10.2
Niagara's Choice Federal Credit Union	Niagara Falls	NY	**C+**	C+	C+	173.0	10.97	1.4	20.7	16.4	31.2	**6.3**	8.6
Niagara-Wheatfield Federal Credit Union	Sanborn	NY	**E+**	E+	E+	19.1	6.34	0.0	9.8	8.6	47.4	**4.4**	6.4
Nickel Steel Federal Credit Union	Lima	OH	**C+**	C+	C+	5.8	2.49	0.0	32.7	9.7	0.0	**10.0**	23.6
Nikkei Credit Union	Gardena	CA	**C+**	C+	C-	66.3	1.07	2.1	8.3	23.1	33.3	**10.0**	12.6
▼ Nishna Valley Credit Union	Atlantic	IA	**D+**	C-	C	33.4	4.95	6.5	31.9	10.8	0.0	**5.7**	7.7

Asset Quality Index	Non-Performing Loans as a % of Total Loans	Non-Performing Loans as a % of Capital	Net Charge-Offs Avg Loans	Profitability Index	Net Income ($Mil)	Return on Assets	Return on Equity	Net Interest Spread	Overhead Efficiency Ratio	Liquidity Index	Liquidity Ratio	Hot Money Ratio	Stability Index
8.8	0.08	0.2	0.25	**1.7**	0.00	0.07	0.70	2.34	97.7	**5.9**	41.3	1.2	**4.5**
6.3	1.48	7.7	1.28	**1.9**	0.04	0.37	5.06	3.96	91.6	**5.3**	30.4	0.0	**1.9**
10.0	0.14	0.3	0.14	**2.2**	0.03	0.23	1.90	2.37	88.7	**5.0**	33.6	3.2	**5.6**
9.0	0.10	0.5	0.00	**4.5**	0.00	0.24	1.90	4.17	97.6	**6.0**	58.3	0.0	**4.3**
3.7	13.68	34.8	0.00	**4.2**	0.00	0.83	6.15	12.31	73.9	**7.6**	73.2	0.0	**5.4**
9.5	0.23	1.9	0.35	**3.0**	0.17	0.44	6.05	3.57	84.8	**4.4**	21.5	4.6	**4.3**
4.3	1.32	13.5	0.29	**5.1**	0.11	0.50	6.58	4.78	83.2	**1.9**	15.2	25.9	**3.4**
9.0	0.48	2.9	0.18	**5.1**	2.15	0.72	6.06	2.77	76.6	**3.8**	14.9	7.0	**9.4**
10.0	0.00	0.0	0.00	**1.8**	0.00	0.31	0.83	1.53	83.3	**7.4**	119.2	0.0	**6.5**
8.1	1.20	4.0	0.73	**3.3**	1.54	10.18	72.43	2.94	29.3	**3.2**	11.6	17.5	**6.2**
3.9	0.66	8.0	2.88	**1.1**	0.02	0.13	1.89	4.93	77.9	**4.3**	16.3	4.5	**2.0**
10.0	0.03	0.1	0.05	**3.3**	0.21	0.32	2.44	2.33	88.1	**4.4**	27.7	4.5	**8.3**
10.0	0.04	0.1	-0.20	**2.9**	0.03	0.23	1.15	3.11	91.0	**7.3**	65.4	0.0	**7.2**
7.7	0.34	2.5	0.10	**1.2**	-0.04	-0.84	-15.40	3.56	118.6	**6.4**	47.1	0.9	**0.0**
9.9	0.87	1.5	0.00	**1.3**	-0.01	-0.86	-4.16	3.48	127.3	**4.7**	18.3	0.0	**7.7**
8.4	0.63	1.5	0.00	**7.5**	0.03	2.02	7.92	5.14	57.4	**5.4**	52.9	0.0	**5.0**
10.0	0.00	0.0	0.00	**2.3**	0.00	0.12	0.45	1.61	89.7	**7.1**	93.8	0.0	**7.2**
8.3	0.67	2.9	-0.46	**0.6**	-0.01	-0.19	-1.59	3.04	102.5	**5.0**	22.4	0.0	**5.3**
9.9	0.05	0.2	0.88	**3.4**	0.01	0.27	2.56	3.85	88.3	**4.8**	26.0	3.2	**5.5**
1.7	4.72	36.6	4.45	**4.6**	0.82	1.50	26.83	4.07	88.2	**4.9**	34.6	2.6	**3.1**
9.4	0.56	1.7	0.15	**4.0**	0.02	0.96	5.15	4.33	77.3	**4.9**	19.4	0.0	**7.0**
5.8	0.91	9.6	0.78	**0.7**	-0.02	-0.23	-2.65	4.66	100.9	**3.8**	20.5	5.3	**2.8**
4.9	1.41	9.6	0.58	**3.1**	0.01	0.45	6.69	4.35	89.7	**5.9**	49.9	0.0	**1.0**
9.9	0.38	1.5	1.46	**3.0**	0.00	-0.02	-0.12	4.04	88.5	**4.7**	32.6	2.6	**6.0**
9.6	0.00	0.0	0.00	**3.9**	0.01	0.98	4.18	3.64	77.8	**3.7**	30.9	0.0	**7.3**
1.7	23.16	31.5	0.00	**10.0**	0.00	3.21	15.69	10.87	33.3	**7.8**	80.6	0.0	**8.7**
9.7	0.00	0.0	-0.28	**0.2**	-0.01	-1.06	-4.61	4.40	124.1	**5.7**	36.7	0.0	**6.4**
9.7	0.00	0.0	0.00	**3.0**	0.00	0.00	0.00	4.60	100.0	**7.6**	71.0	0.0	**6.0**
6.5	2.21	7.7	0.00	**2.5**	0.01	0.53	3.54	4.65	83.2	**5.4**	34.2	0.0	**6.7**
4.5	1.27	12.3	1.36	**3.1**	0.12	0.28	3.52	6.30	80.7	**3.7**	14.3	6.3	**4.5**
8.7	0.33	0.4	0.00	**7.0**	0.09	1.82	4.22	4.89	54.0	**6.7**	87.1	0.0	**6.3**
8.7	0.00	0.0	1.24	**2.7**	0.00	0.00	0.00	12.42	100.0	**7.1**	69.1	0.0	**7.0**
0.0	12.54	58.5	0.00	**3.7**	0.00	0.96	9.92	5.27	79.0	**6.6**	54.0	0.0	**3.2**
0.3	38.46	62.5	0.00	**2.0**	0.00	0.00	0.00	14.81	100.0	**8.1**	87.6	0.0	**6.4**
9.7	0.01	1.1	0.07	**4.0**	0.06	0.49	3.10	3.36	85.9	**4.2**	22.1	4.8	**7.2**
0.0	9.33	66.9	0.00	**1.5**	-0.06	-10.93	-142.68	14.24	173.5	**5.9**	37.1	0.0	**3.3**
7.1	1.74	4.9	0.00	**2.0**	0.03	0.19	1.20	2.89	93.9	**5.5**	45.5	7.2	**6.7**
8.1	0.25	1.5	0.47	**7.0**	0.02	0.41	4.71	5.56	74.3	**6.0**	34.1	0.0	**4.3**
4.8	10.18	17.4	6.30	**0.5**	0.01	0.18	1.04	3.33	140.1	**5.4**	22.4	0.9	**4.7**
5.6	3.33	11.1	0.14	**0.6**	-0.01	-0.16	-1.17	4.18	101.7	**4.0**	10.0	3.2	**5.0**
7.7	2.27	4.4	0.42	**6.6**	0.02	1.06	4.61	7.73	80.9	**6.2**	43.1	0.0	**5.0**
6.8	3.10	4.4	0.00	**3.7**	0.00	-0.48	-1.56	11.76	108.5	**7.4**	80.2	0.0	**5.4**
7.6	0.52	2.8	0.00	**2.9**	0.03	0.47	6.29	3.47	90.2	**5.9**	57.3	0.0	**2.3**
9.2	0.23	0.9	0.00	**3.2**	0.01	0.69	7.52	3.58	87.9	**5.6**	43.5	0.0	**3.0**
7.7	0.54	3.3	0.19	**0.7**	-0.02	-0.22	-2.58	3.61	105.9	**5.1**	23.0	0.9	**3.0**
6.7	0.71	7.1	0.61	**3.3**	1.37	0.36	3.10	3.44	82.1	**3.9**	19.3	4.3	**8.3**
7.5	0.15	1.1	0.60	**5.2**	0.04	1.17	13.46	5.30	69.6	**4.0**	25.3	0.0	**3.3**
6.9	8.09	6.2	0.00	**1.0**	0.00	-1.00	-2.59	5.73	125.0	**7.6**	83.1	0.0	**5.7**
4.4	3.57	15.1	-0.13	**3.3**	0.01	0.37	3.17	4.25	72.0	**5.0**	17.3	0.0	**3.0**
10.0	0.22	0.5	-0.40	**2.7**	0.00	0.12	0.85	2.66	96.0	**5.1**	22.8	0.0	**7.0**
7.1	0.76	2.4	6.34	**3.5**	0.02	1.53	21.84	7.74	84.1	**7.5**	70.6	0.0	**2.3**
10.0	0.33	0.7	0.00	**2.8**	0.01	0.46	3.22	2.98	82.3	**6.4**	44.1	0.0	**6.8**
8.1	0.53	1.7	0.00	**0.0**	-0.01	-0.72	-4.76	3.05	133.3	**5.7**	32.3	0.0	**6.0**
6.6	0.74	3.7	-0.31	**0.0**	-0.04	-3.62	-27.94	5.12	141.0	**5.3**	27.7	0.0	**5.1**
6.5	1.14	6.6	0.36	**2.4**	0.02	0.20	1.92	3.32	94.4	**4.3**	24.2	3.3	**5.3**
6.9	1.09	6.6	0.38	**3.7**	0.26	0.61	7.28	3.16	72.6	**4.3**	12.0	0.3	**5.1**
6.5	0.03	7.4	11.72	**1.9**	0.00	0.04	0.66	2.56	98.9	**7.2**	41.5	0.0	**1.0**
9.7	0.59	1.2	0.44	**5.9**	0.01	0.48	2.07	3.80	79.0	**5.7**	60.3	0.0	**5.0**
10.0	0.08	0.2	0.05	**2.1**	0.00	-0.01	-0.10	2.12	96.7	**4.2**	17.2	6.5	**5.4**
5.8	1.41	8.2	0.18	**2.8**	0.01	0.17	2.18	3.46	96.0	**4.8**	22.2	0.0	**3.9**

Name	City	State	Rating	2016 Rating	2015 Rating	Total Assets ($Mil)	One Year Asset Growth	Asset Mix (As a % of Total Assets) Commercial Loans	Consumer Loans	Mortgage Loans	Securities	Capitalization Index	Net Worth Ratio
Nizari Progressive Federal Credit Union	Sugar Land	TX	A	A	A	139.2	18.88	7.5	42.0	29.8	10.1	10.0	13.2
NJ Gateway Federal Credit Union	Monmouth Junction	NJ	D+	D+	C-	28.2	2.63	0.0	6.9	5.9	37.9	9.2	10.5
NMA Federal Credit Union	Virginia Beach	VA	C	C	C-	63.1	1.65	0.3	52.6	1.7	21.6	7.2	9.2
Noble Federal Credit Union	Fresno	CA	A	A	A	698.2	8.80	0.3	60.1	6.9	10.4	9.6	10.8
NODA Federal Credit Union	Slidell	LA	C	C	C-	35.5	-0.33	0.0	29.4	9.1	0.7	10.0	18.0
None Suffer Lack FCU	Suitland	MD	B-	B-	C+	23.1	9.38	3.8	6.7	4.8	6.9	10.0	11.5
Nordstrom Federal Credit Union	Seattle	WA	C-	C-	C	53.4	1.09	0.0	34.2	0.0	25.8	6.1	8.2
Norfolk Community Federal Credit Union	Norfolk	MA	C+	C+	C	18.7	8.89	0.0	46.5	20.4	0.0	8.6	10.1
▼ Norfolk Fire Department FCU	Norfolk	VA	D+	C-	C-	22.4	-0.88	0.1	24.1	0.0	0.0	10.0	11.8
Norfolk Municipal Federal Credit Union	Norfolk	VA	D-	D-	D-	25.9	-4.29	0.0	26.8	4.0	0.6	8.7	10.1
Normal City Employees FCU	Normal	IL	E+	E+	D-	4.5	0.24	0.0	64.5	0.0	9.9	5.6	7.6
Norristown Bell Credit Union	Blue Bell	PA	C+	C+	B-	55.8	5.76	0.1	6.3	26.3	22.4	10.0	11.1
Norstar Federal Credit Union	Britton	SD	B+	B+	B+	37.3	1.78	19.5	19.2	24.2	0.0	10.0	14.3
NorState Federal Credit Union	Madawaska	ME	C+	C+	B-	182.1	2.16	19.5	17.8	51.4	6.3	10.0	12.7
▲ North Adams M.E. Federal Credit Union	North Adams	MA	D+	D	D+	1.7	2.60	0.0	48.4	0.0	0.0	10.0	24.8
▼ North Alabama Educators Credit Union	Huntsville	AL	C-	C	C	91.6	2.82	0.0	31.2	8.0	11.9	5.4	7.5
North Alabama Papermakers FCU	Stevenson	AL	C-	C-	C-	2.3	7.33	0.0	39.9	0.0	0.0	10.0	20.4
North Bay Credit Union	Santa Rosa	CA	C	C	C-	45.4	9.67	4.6	8.4	48.8	0.0	10.0	12.3
▲ North Carolina Community FCU	Goldsboro	NC	C-	D+	D	73.9	9.83	10.5	7.6	25.7	14.2	7.9	9.6
North Carolina Press Association FCU	Raleigh	NC	C+	C+	C+	8.0	7.62	0.0	16.0	9.4	0.0	10.0	13.1
North Central Area Credit Union	Houghton Lake	MI	C	C	C+	114.3	5.36	0.3	25.6	11.1	41.5	6.4	9.1
▲ North Coast Credit Union	Fairview Park	OH	D+	D	D	13.2	4.27	0.0	36.2	4.3	0.0	10.0	42.0
▲ North Coast Credit Union	Bellingham	WA	B+	B	B	233.2	5.70	18.2	20.6	39.9	18.1	7.9	9.9
North Country Federal Credit Union	South Burlington	VT	B	B	B	529.4	4.21	9.2	24.3	35.8	10.0	7.6	9.4
North County Credit Union	San Diego	CA	C-	C-	C+	68.7	3.29	1.2	32.9	21.7	3.3	7.4	9.3
North Districts Community Credit Union	Gibsonia	PA	B-	B-	B-	34.7	3.16	0.0	23.3	0.0	0.0	9.9	10.9
North East Kentucky Cap FCU	Olive Hill	KY	D	D	D	<1	-45.59	0.0	27.7	0.0	0.0	10.0	23.7
North East Texas Credit Union	Lone Star	TX	B-	B-	B	149.8	-0.62	7.7	16.4	25.3	24.8	9.7	11.1
North East Welch Federal Credit Union	North East	PA	C+	C+	C+	14.7	8.41	0.0	41.1	3.3	0.0	10.0	15.5
▼ North Franklin Federal Credit Union	Malone	NY	B+	A-	B	56.4	10.89	0.0	27.7	9.5	0.0	10.0	12.1
North Georgia Community FCU	Ringgold	GA	D+	D+	D+	19.7	10.48	0.0	47.3	2.3	0.0	6.1	8.1
North Georgia Credit Union	Toccoa	GA	B	B	B	56.0	7.13	0.0	27.2	39.0	0.0	9.6	10.7
North Iowa Community Credit Union	Mason City	IA	C-	C-	C-	64.5	4.31	1.3	40.8	22.8	1.4	9.0	10.3
North Jersey Federal Credit Union	Totowa	NJ	C-	C-	C-	231.3	0.19	6.3	9.2	16.2	19.4	8.4	10.2
North Little Rock Educator's FCU	North Little Rock	AR	D	D	D	1.1	1.00	0.0	12.8	0.0	0.0	10.0	11.9
North Main Credit Union	Cornelia	GA	B-	B-	B-	13.2	1.75	0.0	33.8	6.1	0.0	10.0	18.3
North Memorial Federal Credit Union	Robbinsdale	MN	C	C	C	38.2	5.35	0.0	33.7	10.1	2.0	8.1	9.7
North Mississippi Health Services Empls FCU	Tupelo	MS	C+	C+	C+	14.0	7.94	0.0	29.2	0.0	0.0	10.0	11.6
North Olmsted School Employees FCU	North Olmsted	OH	D-	D-	D	5.2	-1.72	0.0	18.9	1.9	52.6	9.4	10.6
North Penn Federal Credit Union	Colmar	PA	C-	C-	C-	17.3	6.34	0.0	14.0	0.0	32.0	7.6	9.4
North Platte Union Pacific Employee CU	North Platte	NE	B	B	B	35.4	4.38	0.0	49.8	0.0	8.3	10.0	15.2
North Sanpete Federal Credit Union	Fairview	UT	C-	C-	C-	<1	-12.51	0.0	79.5	0.0	0.0	10.0	25.1
▼ North Shore Federal Credit Union	Silver Bay	MN	B+	A-	A	156.9	7.77	8.7	8.0	58.8	2.7	10.0	14.8
North Side Community FCU	Chicago	IL	E+	E+	E+	8.7	-4.22	0.0	46.0	15.0	2.3	6.2	8.2
North Star Community Credit Union	Cherokee	IA	B-	B-	B-	86.6	2.27	1.3	34.8	16.5	4.5	9.3	10.5
▲ North Star Community Credit Union	Maddock	ND	A-	B+	B+	179.6	8.30	41.2	12.3	30.8	11.3	10.0	14.1
North Star Credit Union	Cook	MN	B	B	B	38.2	5.91	11.9	18.3	54.5	0.8	9.1	10.4
North Western Employees Credit Union	Council Bluffs	IA	C+	C+	C+	7.8	-1.05	0.0	43.3	0.0	0.0	10.0	18.7
Northampton Area School District Empls CU	Northampton	PA	C	C	C	9.3	4.76	0.0	23.7	0.0	25.0	10.0	14.5
Northampton V.A.F. Federal Credit Union	Leeds	MA	C-	C-	C-	7.5	0.48	0.0	27.7	0.0	0.0	10.0	13.1
Northeast Alabama Postal FCU	Anniston	AL	B-	B-	B-	12.5	1.74	0.0	30.6	32.5	0.0	10.0	18.9
Northeast Arkansas Federal Credit Union	Blytheville	AR	B+	B+	B	117.9	4.21	0.0	53.1	23.1	2.6	8.7	10.2
Northeast Community Credit Union	Elizabethton	TN	A	A	A	114.2	2.06	0.2	17.9	59.3	6.3	10.0	14.7
Northeast Community Federal Credit Union	San Francisco	CA	C-	C-	C	12.1	0.36	3.8	1.7	25.7	0.0	10.0	15.7
Northeast Credit Union	Portsmouth	NH	B	B	B	1138.5	4.93	0.8	59.2	17.6	0.0	9.5	10.7
Northeast Family Federal Credit Union	Manchester	CT	C+	C+	C+	79.4	6.59	0.4	11.7	18.1	5.9	7.4	9.2
Northeast Mississippi FCU	Amory	MS	C	C	C	5.0	11.58	0.0	39.9	24.1	0.0	10.0	16.1
Northeast Nebraska Federal Credit Union	Norfolk	NE	D+	D+	C-	9.9	0.96	0.0	44.5	10.4	0.0	9.1	10.4
Northeast Panhandle Teachers FCU	Perryton	TX	C+	C+	C+	22.5	-2.70	0.0	45.7	0.0	0.0	10.0	13.2
▲ Northeast Regional Credit Union	Hannibal	MO	C-	D+	C-	1.3	4.70	0.0	69.2	0.0	0.0	10.0	14.0

Asset Quality Index	Non-Performing Loans as a % of Total Loans	Non-Performing Loans as a % of Capital	Net Charge-Offs Avg Loans	Profitability Index	Net Income ($Mil)	Return on Assets	Return on Equity	Net Interest Spread	Overhead Efficiency Ratio	Liquidity Index	Liquidity Ratio	Hot Money Ratio	Stability Index
9.4	0.16	0.9	0.09	9.4	0.47	1.39	10.59	4.19	66.5	3.3	11.1	7.3	9.0
7.7	1.38	3.1	-0.29	1.3	0.00	0.01	0.14	2.26	98.8	4.9	16.9	0.0	3.8
4.4	1.71	10.7	1.04	3.6	0.08	0.48	5.30	4.35	78.7	3.3	13.9	15.6	3.5
6.8	0.50	3.8	0.72	5.4	1.01	0.59	5.44	4.03	79.6	3.6	15.3	6.8	7.9
9.2	0.97	2.1	0.41	1.9	0.01	0.15	0.81	2.76	92.1	5.2	30.5	0.0	7.0
10.0	0.00	0.0	0.00	4.6	0.04	0.77	6.72	1.40	70.1	6.4	44.2	0.0	7.0
8.3	0.42	2.5	1.09	1.0	-0.07	-0.55	-6.47	3.05	93.7	5.6	33.5	0.9	3.3
7.2	0.32	2.5	-0.09	6.5	0.04	0.84	8.37	4.13	76.3	4.2	34.4	11.1	5.0
10.0	0.11	0.3	1.02	0.9	-0.01	-0.23	-1.97	3.11	97.0	5.6	30.7	0.0	5.4
10.0	0.05	0.1	0.27	0.0	-0.06	-0.86	-8.28	2.98	103.4	6.7	50.6	1.0	3.1
7.1	0.51	4.1	-0.14	3.2	0.01	1.17	15.29	3.16	62.5	4.8	27.0	0.0	1.0
10.0	0.16	0.5	0.00	2.8	0.04	0.31	2.73	2.54	87.9	5.1	30.8	6.0	5.8
8.7	0.43	1.8	0.00	6.4	0.08	0.84	5.98	3.45	63.7	4.3	22.0	5.8	8.2
3.8	1.91	18.7	0.51	2.7	0.12	0.26	2.31	4.14	84.9	2.4	8.3	14.5	7.1
8.6	0.34	0.7	-0.45	1.8	0.00	0.70	2.80	4.14	106.3	5.3	30.1	0.0	5.7
8.8	0.43	2.5	0.09	2.2	0.02	0.07	0.88	2.85	96.6	5.2	27.8	1.4	2.9
9.6	0.00	0.0	0.00	1.4	0.00	-0.18	-0.85	4.38	100.0	6.4	40.4	0.0	6.5
9.7	0.07	0.4	0.13	2.4	0.01	0.12	1.03	3.70	93.2	3.2	25.5	8.4	6.8
6.4	1.95	8.7	0.29	2.3	0.07	0.37	3.85	3.29	88.7	4.7	25.8	5.0	4.3
10.0	0.35	0.6	1.32	6.9	0.02	1.02	7.74	1.70	58.6	6.6	80.0	1.5	5.7
9.3	0.40	2.0	1.16	1.6	-0.09	-0.31	-3.62	2.92	88.9	4.6	14.4	2.6	5.0
9.9	1.27	1.6	0.23	0.8	0.00	0.03	0.07	4.68	100.7	6.2	56.5	0.0	5.8
9.0	0.31	2.2	0.16	7.0	0.89	1.55	16.33	3.59	65.2	4.1	17.7	4.5	6.5
6.4	1.09	9.7	0.44	5.3	0.85	0.66	6.94	3.83	81.8	2.9	11.9	12.1	6.8
9.5	0.21	1.6	0.25	2.0	0.01	0.06	0.81	2.81	96.0	3.5	17.7	10.5	3.1
6.0	2.21	10.4	-0.02	3.8	0.05	0.53	4.79	3.30	79.8	5.7	43.0	0.5	6.1
9.5	2.33	2.7	0.00	0.0	0.00	-3.98	-21.62	8.00	200.0	8.0	89.4	0.0	4.9
7.6	0.53	4.2	0.01	3.5	0.11	0.29	2.66	3.58	88.5	4.5	15.5	4.6	7.3
8.6	1.05	3.4	0.36	4.1	0.02	0.63	4.07	3.87	75.7	4.7	27.5	2.0	6.8
9.2	0.15	0.7	1.39	3.4	0.00	0.02	0.18	3.51	72.3	6.5	58.6	3.1	6.4
5.4	0.56	4.9	0.56	0.6	-0.02	-0.46	-6.48	5.16	106.1	5.3	34.4	6.9	2.6
6.3	0.49	7.2	0.75	4.9	0.05	0.40	3.62	6.14	87.3	4.2	22.8	7.4	5.2
4.5	1.66	14.0	0.17	2.1	0.00	0.00	0.00	3.83	100.3	3.4	13.8	7.3	5.0
5.4	2.33	16.0	0.48	2.5	0.15	0.26	2.76	3.56	92.6	4.3	17.1	6.5	5.1
10.0	0.00	0.0	3.03	0.0	-0.01	-2.19	-17.78	2.49	300.0	7.7	60.4	0.0	6.1
9.1	0.88	2.6	0.65	2.5	0.00	0.09	0.50	4.69	97.6	5.6	45.1	0.0	6.5
7.3	0.63	4.8	0.13	3.3	0.03	0.31	3.15	4.02	89.5	4.1	17.5	5.4	5.0
10.0	0.31	0.8	0.10	3.2	0.01	0.29	2.46	2.05	84.4	6.2	53.5	0.0	5.9
4.7	6.11	13.4	0.00	1.1	0.00	0.08	0.73	3.51	97.6	6.2	30.8	0.0	3.8
8.3	0.89	2.0	0.00	3.0	0.01	0.33	3.46	2.57	88.3	6.0	33.7	0.0	4.3
5.8	2.10	8.0	0.00	4.3	0.05	0.56	3.67	2.54	81.3	4.3	23.5	6.3	8.0
7.9	0.00	0.0	0.00	1.8	0.00	0.00	0.00	3.00	100.0	3.7	14.1	0.0	6.2
6.2	1.16	9.5	0.20	4.5	0.29	0.75	5.07	3.35	77.9	4.1	21.2	6.3	9.4
2.2	2.15	29.7	1.17	0.4	-0.05	-2.21	-70.23	6.57	104.5	4.4	24.5	5.2	1.9
7.5	0.61	3.0	0.15	4.6	0.12	0.58	5.42	3.26	82.1	4.3	23.4	6.4	5.6
6.3	1.41	7.4	0.18	5.6	0.37	0.83	6.08	4.17	80.2	3.6	15.2	7.6	8.1
9.0	0.02	0.4	0.16	5.9	0.05	0.57	5.48	4.50	86.8	2.5	13.0	16.3	7.0
9.5	0.00	0.0	0.49	6.1	0.02	0.90	4.72	4.93	78.1	6.6	58.6	0.0	5.0
7.8	2.14	5.7	-0.11	4.1	0.01	0.44	2.98	2.25	68.8	4.9	23.5	0.0	7.9
9.8	0.24	0.6	0.16	2.6	0.01	0.38	2.85	1.82	77.4	4.9	22.1	0.0	6.0
8.4	0.89	5.2	0.00	5.6	0.03	0.87	4.58	3.43	74.0	4.3	49.9	12.1	7.6
6.2	0.55	5.3	0.19	7.7	0.38	1.33	14.20	3.65	71.7	3.3	9.1	2.8	6.9
6.9	1.11	7.6	0.08	9.6	0.37	1.28	8.82	3.70	64.4	3.6	18.4	7.0	10.0
3.6	9.64	25.2	0.44	2.7	0.00	0.03	0.26	2.82	99.1	4.7	49.2	38.4	6.5
8.2	0.22	1.7	0.42	5.0	2.65	0.95	9.02	2.93	76.4	3.1	16.6	11.7	7.8
8.3	0.53	2.4	0.68	2.8	0.04	0.19	2.08	2.89	92.7	4.4	14.1	1.3	4.3
5.3	2.83	13.9	0.21	8.1	0.02	1.44	9.00	5.13	66.1	3.6	28.8	10.9	4.3
6.3	1.06	5.9	1.50	2.9	0.01	0.33	3.11	3.87	83.2	4.9	27.3	0.0	5.1
8.6	0.42	1.6	0.03	3.2	0.03	0.45	3.36	2.14	77.7	5.4	47.1	0.0	6.6
5.9	0.85	4.7	-0.38	5.9	0.00	1.22	8.65	5.99	96.0	4.1	25.2	0.0	4.3

Name	City	State	Rating	2016 Rating	2015 Rating	Total Assets ($Mil)	One Year Asset Growth	Asset Mix (As a % of Total Assets) Commercial Loans	Consumer Loans	Mortgage Loans	Securities	Capitalization Index	Net Worth Ratio
Northeast Schools & Hospital CU	Newport	VT	**C**	C	C-	4.6	2.54	0.0	67.0	0.0	0.0	**10.0**	11.1
Northeast Texas Teachers FCU	Paris	TX	**C**	C	C+	24.8	1.65	0.0	28.3	1.4	0.0	**10.0**	13.8
Northeastern CT Healthcare Credit Union, Inc.	Putnam	CT	**C**	C	C	9.7	2.14	0.0	47.3	0.0	0.0	**10.0**	13.0
Northeastern Operating Engineers FCU	Whitestone	NY	**D+**	D+	D+	71.0	-4.42	1.5	2.1	58.8	11.6	**5.6**	7.6
Northeastern University FCU	Boston	MA	**D**	D	D	25.7	-7.44	0.0	22.4	29.6	0.0	**6.6**	8.6
Northern California Latvian Credit Union	San Francisco	CA	**C-**	C-	D	1.6	-2.32	0.0	3.5	0.0	47.8	**10.0**	16.0
Northern Chautauqua Federal Credit Union	Silver Creek	NY	**E+**	E+	D	3.7	-11.38	0.0	36.7	0.0	38.9	**5.4**	7.4
▲ Northern Colorado Credit Union	Greeley	CO	**C+**	C	B-	53.2	5.80	16.4	16.5	37.3	4.0	**10.0**	11.7
Northern Communities Credit Union	Duluth	MN	**D+**	D+	D	73.6	2.57	2.3	25.8	25.8	0.3	**5.2**	7.2
▼ Northern Eagle Federal Credit Union	Nett Lake	MN	**C+**	B-	B-	<1	5.20	0.0	44.3	0.0	0.0	**10.0**	15.0
Northern Energy Federal Credit Union	Mankato	MN	**D+**	D+	C-	3.1	24.04	0.0	66.2	0.0	0.0	**9.1**	10.4
Northern Federal Credit Union	Watertown	NY	**C+**	C+	C	240.9	6.20	2.8	18.8	31.9	0.0	**5.0**	7.0
Northern Hills Federal Credit Union	Sturgis	SD	**B-**	B-	B-	82.8	3.65	6.9	31.0	21.4	15.0	**8.9**	10.2
Northern Illinois Federal Credit Union	DeKalb	IL	**D**	D	E+	16.3	8.39	0.0	29.4	0.0	0.0	**4.8**	6.8
Northern Indiana Federal Credit Union	Merrillville	IN	**D**	D	D	35.5	5.18	0.0	20.1	12.5	0.7	**4.9**	7.0
Northern Kentucky Educators' FCU	Highland Heights	KY	**D**	D	D	18.7	1.50	5.3	33.1	0.0	0.0	**5.8**	7.8
Northern Lights Community FCU	Chatham	MI	**D+**	D+	D+	8.0	6.07	0.0	37.7	0.0	0.0	**7.9**	9.6
Northern Lights Federal Credit Union	Saint Johnsbury	VT	**C-**	C-	D+	21.5	7.56	0.0	42.4	2.4	0.0	**7.4**	9.3
▲ Northern Montana Hospital FCU	Havre	MT	**C-**	D+	C-	<1	6.05	0.0	43.9	0.0	0.0	**10.0**	12.0
Northern New Mexico School Employee FCU	Santa Fe	NM	**C-**	C-	C-	21.2	3.39	0.0	42.9	0.0	0.0	**7.8**	9.5
Northern Pacific Duluth FCU	Duluth	MN	**D**	D	D	2.1	-4.83	0.0	53.5	0.0	0.0	**10.0**	25.0
▼ Northern Paper Mills Credit Union	Green Bay	WI	**D+**	C-	C-	24.7	4.08	0.0	18.8	44.8	0.0	**10.0**	17.3
Northern Redwood Federal Credit Union	Arcata	CA	**D-**	D-	D	18.8	0.56	1.2	46.9	9.7	0.0	**5.4**	7.4
Northern Skies Federal Credit Union	Anchorage	AK	**B+**	B+	B+	116.5	18.13	0.0	40.0	2.3	0.4	**7.8**	9.5
Northern Star Credit Union, Inc.	Portsmouth	VA	**B-**	B-	B-	88.9	4.80	8.2	19.7	9.4	37.0	**10.0**	11.5
Northern States Power Company Empls FCU	Grand Forks	ND	**C-**	C-	D	1.3	-2.26	0.0	37.7	4.2	0.0	**8.2**	9.8
Northern States Power St. Paul CU	Saint Paul	MN	**C+**	C+	C+	48.1	0.26	0.0	32.4	13.9	22.5	**10.0**	13.4
▼ Northern Tier Federal Credit Union	Minot	ND	**C+**	B-	B-	125.3	3.21	9.7	36.0	6.9	8.2	**7.3**	9.2
▼ Northern United Federal Credit Union	Escanaba	MI	**D+**	C-	C-	20.0	-0.51	0.0	22.3	16.1	7.7	**10.0**	14.9
▼ Northern Valley Federal Credit Union	Grand Forks	ND	**C-**	C	C	15.3	2.84	0.0	34.2	0.5	0.0	**8.5**	10.0
Northland Area Federal Credit Union	Oscoda	MI	**A-**	A-	A-	348.1	7.23	13.4	20.2	44.5	14.2	**9.5**	10.6
▼ Northland Teachers Community CU	Gladstone	MO	**C**	C+	C-	10.1	0.95	0.0	15.2	0.0	0.0	**10.0**	13.1
▲ NorthPark Community Credit Union	Indianapolis	IN	**D**	D-	D-	56.4	-6.53	0.3	42.6	3.9	0.1	**5.4**	7.4
NorthRidge Community Credit Union	Hoyt Lakes	MN	**B**	B	B	42.4	8.58	0.5	31.0	25.2	14.6	**10.0**	12.5
▼ Northrop Grumman Federal Credit Union	Gardena	CA	**C+**	B-	B-	1104.6	5.50	1.0	18.7	22.8	43.3	**9.0**	11.1
▲ Northside Federal Credit Union	Atlanta	GA	**C-**	D+	D	15.3	7.01	0.0	52.3	0.0	0.0	**8.0**	9.7
Northside L Federal Credit Union	Broadview	IL	**D**	D	D	5.7	-7.53	0.0	51.3	0.0	0.0	**10.0**	15.5
▲ NorthStar Credit Union	Warrenville	IL	**A-**	B+	B	167.7	43.76	7.7	40.3	13.7	1.2	**10.0**	11.1
Northwest Adventist Federal Credit Union	Portland	OR	**C+**	C+	C+	31.4	5.87	0.0	23.6	37.9	1.6	**7.1**	9.1
▼ Northwest Arkansas Federal Credit Union	Fayetteville	AR	**E+**	D-	D-	10.4	-3.23	0.0	60.9	1.4	0.0	**5.9**	7.9
Northwest Christian Credit Union	Nampa	ID	**B-**	B-	B-	56.8	11.99	33.8	9.2	37.9	0.0	**8.0**	9.7
Northwest Community Credit Union	Morton Grove	IL	**D+**	D+	D+	59.3	0.21	3.3	17.3	35.2	9.6	**9.2**	10.5
Northwest Community Credit Union	Eugene	OR	**B**	B	B	1131.0	10.67	7.9	44.6	19.9	0.7	**7.1**	9.0
Northwest Consumers Federal Credit Union	Traverse City	MI	**C+**	C+	C+	18.9	4.90	0.5	45.0	23.1	0.0	**10.0**	11.8
Northwest Federal Credit Union	Herndon	VA	**B-**	B-	B	3220.5	4.88	4.8	39.3	23.2	23.7	**7.9**	9.8
Northwest Hills Credit Union	Torrington	CT	**D**	D	D-	31.8	2.45	0.0	25.9	9.7	0.0	**5.4**	7.4
Northwest Louisiana Federal Credit Union	Shreveport	LA	**C+**	C+	C	10.6	1.38	0.0	37.0	10.8	0.0	**10.0**	29.4
Northwest Missouri Regional Credit Union	Maryville	MO	**D+**	D+	D	8.7	6.18	0.0	61.6	0.1	0.0	**6.9**	8.9
Northwest Municipal Federal Credit Union	Des Plaines	IL	**C+**	C+	C	30.4	7.56	0.0	29.3	0.0	0.0	**6.9**	8.9
NorthWest Plus Credit Union	Everett	WA	**B+**	B+	B+	188.3	10.49	2.3	22.9	31.6	18.2	**9.3**	10.8
▼ Northwestern Energy Employees FCU	Butte	MT	**D-**	D	D	33.1	4.18	0.0	17.8	0.0	10.8	**7.4**	9.3
▼ Northwestern Federal Credit Union	Bryan	OH	**D**	D+	D+	12.6	6.70	0.0	31.2	0.0	0.0	**6.8**	8.8
Northwestern Mutual Credit Union	Milwaukee	WI	**B**	B	B	167.9	5.62	0.0	5.5	35.0	28.2	**10.0**	11.4
Northwood Federal Credit Union	Philadelphia	PA	**C+**	C+	C+	13.0	8.63	4.1	3.2	20.9	27.7	**10.0**	12.2
▲ Northwoods Community Credit Union	Park Falls	WI	**D**	D-	D-	73.6	0.34	2.8	36.2	16.4	2.3	**8.8**	10.2
▼ Northwoods Credit Union	Cloquet	MN	**B-**	B+	B+	92.8	14.39	0.0	34.3	23.6	8.8	**8.4**	9.9
▲ Norton-Troy Employees Credit Union	Watervliet	NY	**D+**	D	D+	7.6	-10.39	0.0	9.2	18.3	0.0	**10.0**	12.5
Norwalk Hospital Credit Union	Norwalk	CT	**D+**	D+	D	35.1	1.29	5.8	7.9	0.0	14.2	**7.2**	9.1
Norwalk Postal Employees FCU	Norwalk	CT	**D+**	D+	D	<1	1.89	0.0	63.0	0.0	0.0	**9.7**	11.0
▲ Norwesco Credit Union	Saint Francis	KS	**B-**	C+	C-	<1	-1.90	0.0	35.9	0.0	0.0	**10.0**	26.2

Asset Quality Index	Non-Performing Loans as a % of Total Loans	Non-Performing Loans as a % of Capital	Net Charge-Offs Avg Loans	Profitability Index	Net Income ($Mil)	Return on Assets	Return on Equity	Net Interest Spread	Overhead Efficiency Ratio	Liquidity Index	Liquidity Ratio	Hot Money Ratio	Stability Index
7.1	0.03	0.2	2.37	**6.9**	0.01	0.54	4.72	7.23	78.4	**5.6**	34.2	0.0	**4.3**
9.4	0.47	1.8	0.09	**1.8**	0.00	0.03	0.23	3.02	95.7	**6.3**	59.8	0.9	**6.7**
8.6	0.13	0.5	3.47	**2.7**	0.01	0.46	3.51	3.07	81.0	**4.4**	32.4	0.0	**5.9**
3.5	2.56	25.5	-0.05	**2.4**	0.03	0.18	2.37	3.09	92.2	**3.9**	16.0	0.0	**3.1**
5.9	1.43	9.0	1.57	**2.0**	0.01	0.15	1.82	3.83	92.7	**3.8**	45.2	15.7	**2.4**
9.8	11.11	2.5	0.00	**0.1**	-0.03	-7.47	-43.32	2.08	-47.4	**6.9**	63.7	0.0	**6.2**
5.2	2.44	15.4	-0.19	**2.4**	0.00	0.42	5.88	2.70	87.5	**4.3**	14.9	0.0	**1.0**
9.5	0.05	0.3	0.00	**3.2**	0.06	0.45	3.86	3.11	85.8	**4.1**	28.1	4.3	**6.7**
5.4	0.44	4.3	0.37	**2.6**	0.05	0.28	3.85	3.59	88.7	**4.5**	19.8	0.8	**2.6**
7.2	1.37	5.0	1.58	**3.7**	0.00	-0.96	-6.40	11.09	103.3	**6.0**	38.6	0.0	**8.5**
8.4	0.00	0.0	-0.19	**2.7**	0.00	0.39	3.74	3.24	86.4	**2.3**	29.3	26.8	**6.0**
6.6	0.52	8.5	0.29	**3.6**	0.08	0.14	1.93	4.58	91.2	**4.0**	12.2	0.1	**4.5**
7.6	0.32	2.3	0.24	**4.9**	0.12	0.57	5.51	3.85	84.2	**4.0**	17.9	3.4	**4.7**
8.4	0.41	2.5	-0.11	**3.4**	0.02	0.40	5.84	2.65	87.4	**5.7**	43.3	0.0	**2.3**
5.9	1.19	6.6	0.88	**2.5**	0.03	0.34	4.90	3.04	89.0	**5.3**	26.0	0.4	**2.2**
7.3	0.76	4.0	0.60	**1.8**	0.00	-0.02	-0.27	3.11	92.8	**5.9**	34.1	0.0	**3.1**
9.4	0.12	0.6	-0.30	**3.4**	0.00	0.10	1.04	4.31	98.9	**4.8**	25.9	5.2	**4.8**
7.9	0.08	0.7	0.05	**3.9**	0.01	0.23	2.42	4.83	95.4	**4.1**	14.7	3.1	**3.7**
9.2	1.00	3.5	0.00	**1.9**	0.00	0.60	4.88	5.38	100.0	**6.8**	49.8	0.0	**5.0**
7.8	0.39	2.0	0.16	**3.7**	0.02	0.38	4.25	3.78	88.7	**4.6**	16.8	0.5	**4.6**
7.8	0.06	0.2	0.00	**0.0**	-0.01	-1.75	-6.91	4.90	128.0	**3.7**	19.6	0.0	**5.8**
9.9	0.11	0.4	0.00	**0.9**	-0.02	-0.26	-1.50	3.26	108.3	**4.6**	30.5	0.5	**6.8**
6.7	0.00	2.5	0.14	**2.1**	0.01	0.11	1.45	4.33	94.4	**5.1**	32.9	0.0	**3.0**
6.0	0.61	7.2	0.52	**8.4**	0.33	1.16	12.13	4.71	70.8	**2.2**	25.4	44.2	**6.9**
5.9	1.56	14.6	0.67	**3.5**	0.08	0.37	3.22	4.96	86.0	**4.9**	17.2	1.8	**5.2**
9.4	0.00	0.0	0.00	**5.0**	0.00	1.22	12.80	2.59	50.0	**5.4**	38.6	0.0	**3.7**
6.5	1.89	7.5	0.77	**3.2**	0.05	0.45	3.43	3.01	86.3	**4.1**	21.6	2.4	**6.1**
5.9	0.73	7.9	0.44	**2.8**	-0.01	-0.02	-0.26	2.67	92.6	**2.2**	15.6	20.1	**4.9**
8.1	1.44	4.3	1.00	**0.7**	-0.03	-0.54	-3.61	3.74	102.9	**6.4**	38.8	0.0	**6.5**
8.9	0.00	1.9	1.40	**1.8**	-0.02	-0.56	-5.46	3.23	90.2	**4.4**	24.7	5.7	**5.5**
7.2	0.64	4.8	0.19	**5.9**	0.69	0.81	7.62	4.00	78.0	**3.7**	8.9	3.1	**7.6**
10.0	0.00	0.0	0.81	**1.4**	0.00	-0.12	-0.90	3.47	100.0	**5.4**	34.9	4.4	**6.6**
4.6	1.28	11.3	1.43	**0.8**	-0.02	-0.17	-2.16	4.28	87.0	**4.6**	27.3	3.2	**1.8**
7.2	0.99	5.8	0.17	**3.4**	0.01	0.09	0.68	4.35	95.1	**4.4**	18.8	3.0	**6.7**
10.0	0.33	1.6	0.27	**2.9**	0.43	0.16	1.51	2.53	87.6	**4.0**	28.9	11.2	**7.2**
5.7	0.74	4.0	2.00	**4.4**	0.03	0.78	8.17	4.89	62.2	**5.9**	40.5	0.0	**3.7**
4.6	4.26	13.0	1.72	**0.0**	-0.05	-3.41	-21.84	5.43	97.8	**5.5**	37.4	0.0	**4.7**
7.1	0.79	4.9	0.34	**6.2**	0.37	0.90	8.06	4.89	72.5	**3.8**	24.4	10.0	**6.3**
9.9	0.04	0.3	-0.04	**4.1**	0.05	0.67	7.23	3.45	85.4	**5.2**	39.6	3.3	**4.2**
4.2	0.58	8.2	0.65	**3.6**	0.00	0.08	0.98	4.41	89.9	**4.9**	25.3	0.0	**1.0**
5.9	1.16	5.8	0.02	**3.6**	0.06	0.41	4.26	3.11	87.5	**4.7**	14.8	2.2	**5.1**
9.7	0.14	0.8	-0.15	**1.4**	0.00	0.02	0.19	2.49	95.1	**2.9**	11.3	12.4	**4.6**
6.7	0.43	5.5	0.54	**4.4**	1.74	0.62	6.86	3.80	80.6	**2.6**	8.8	9.4	**6.2**
5.6	1.74	13.1	0.44	**6.5**	0.03	0.60	5.07	4.39	74.8	**4.0**	14.0	0.0	**5.0**
7.7	0.64	4.7	0.49	**4.5**	4.78	0.60	6.26	3.01	79.7	**2.2**	16.3	18.8	**7.0**
5.4	2.53	13.2	-0.26	**2.7**	0.03	0.32	4.30	3.74	86.6	**5.5**	28.3	0.4	**2.3**
9.3	0.83	1.4	0.45	**2.6**	0.01	0.30	1.03	4.25	113.8	**5.3**	47.8	7.4	**6.2**
6.3	0.02	2.7	0.00	**5.2**	0.02	0.71	7.78	5.70	87.5	**4.8**	22.8	0.0	**3.0**
9.8	0.24	1.2	-0.03	**4.5**	0.06	0.75	8.48	2.11	64.6	**4.4**	18.0	0.0	**4.4**
8.4	0.47	3.4	0.47	**5.0**	0.34	0.73	6.95	3.80	77.0	**4.3**	15.7	4.7	**6.4**
9.5	0.23	0.8	1.14	**0.1**	-0.06	-0.75	-7.75	2.58	113.9	**6.6**	52.3	0.0	**3.2**
6.5	1.88	7.0	0.39	**1.8**	0.00	0.13	1.44	2.56	95.2	**5.1**	37.1	6.2	**3.8**
10.0	0.00	0.0	0.00	**4.9**	0.30	0.76	6.51	2.08	67.2	**4.9**	23.2	1.9	**8.1**
6.3	5.31	12.0	0.00	**3.7**	0.00	-0.09	-0.76	3.02	103.5	**5.3**	46.5	10.3	**7.2**
5.7	1.25	9.0	-1.02	**2.4**	0.18	1.01	9.89	3.46	83.2	**5.1**	35.6	4.0	**3.2**
6.2	0.75	5.9	0.61	**1.9**	-0.15	-0.65	-6.41	4.96	102.9	**4.0**	22.6	5.5	**4.3**
7.6	3.02	6.5	0.00	**1.1**	0.00	0.15	1.26	2.11	92.1	**5.8**	67.5	0.0	**5.3**
5.5	4.17	14.1	-0.04	**1.5**	0.01	0.12	1.25	1.94	100.0	**5.0**	22.0	2.9	**3.4**
2.7	4.56	23.6	3.23	**6.7**	0.00	1.36	12.50	8.56	87.5	**6.0**	41.2	0.0	**5.0**
9.9	0.00	0.0	0.00	**7.8**	0.00	3.96	14.81	9.52	0.0	**7.8**	88.2	0.0	**5.7**

Name	City	State	Rating	2016 Rating	2015 Rating	Total Assets ($Mil)	One Year Asset Growth	Asset Mix (As a % of Total Assets) Commercial Loans	Consumer Loans	Mortgage Loans	Securities	Capitalization Index	Net Worth Ratio
Norwich Telops Federal Credit Union	Norwich	NY	**C-**	C-	C-	7.6	5.13	0.0	60.1	0.0	0.0	**10.0**	11.2
Norwin Teachers Federal Credit Union	North Huntingdon	PA	**D**	D	D	25.1	5.18	0.0	22.6	0.0	0.0	**5.9**	7.9
Norwood Town Employees FCU	Norwood	MA	**B-**	B-	C+	5.3	5.81	0.0	24.0	0.0	0.0	**10.0**	22.8
Noteworthy Federal Credit Union	Cleveland	OH	**D**	D	D	3.3	26.29	7.4	9.4	0.0	0.0	**5.7**	7.7
Notre Dame 2901 Federal Credit Union	Baltimore	MD	**C-**	C-	C-	1.9	5.79	0.0	8.8	0.0	0.0	**9.5**	10.7
Notre Dame Community FCU	Fall River	MA	**C**	C	C	49.8	4.25	2.9	2.9	26.6	49.0	**10.0**	12.1
Notre Dame Federal Credit Union	Notre Dame	IN	**B-**	B-	C	512.2	6.15	2.3	27.3	30.2	4.4	**6.0**	8.0
Nova Credit Union	Charlotte	NC	**B-**	B-	C+	114.3	33.48	0.0	25.6	27.3	24.1	**10.0**	15.6
Nova UA Federal Credit Union	Clifton	NJ	**B**	B	B	112.7	8.67	4.0	0.8	46.1	8.7	**10.0**	14.3
Novamont Employees Federal Credit Union	Kenova	WV	**D+**	D+	C-	<1	-7.87	0.0	63.2	0.0	0.0	**10.0**	19.9
Novartis Federal Credit Union	East Hanover	NJ	**B-**	B-	C+	132.8	-0.54	0.0	5.4	10.4	11.1	**8.0**	9.7
Novation Credit Union	Oakdale	MN	**B**	B	B	136.2	12.17	0.0	36.9	28.1	1.2	**5.8**	7.8
Novo Federal Credit Union	Norco	CA	**C**	C	C	9.8	16.14	0.0	70.1	0.0	0.0	**10.0**	14.4
NRL Federal Credit Union	Alexandria	VA	**C+**	C+	C+	465.9	2.69	0.0	19.6	31.1	29.9	**8.7**	10.3
NRS Community Development FCU	Birmingham	AL	**C-**	C-	C	1.5	39.81	0.0	67.3	0.0	0.0	**5.9**	7.9
NSWC Federal Credit Union	Dahlgren	VA	**D+**	D+	D	365.0	7.22	0.0	27.4	10.2	48.8	**6.0**	8.7
▼ NU Community Credit Union	Milton	PA	**D-**	D	C-	18.9	-2.72	0.0	37.6	0.6	0.0	**6.8**	8.8
Nucor Employees Credit Union	Florence	SC	**B**	B	B	38.6	8.64	0.0	49.9	0.9	0.0	**10.0**	14.6
Nucor Employees Federal Credit Union	Fort Payne	AL	**C-**	C-	C-	3.1	-5.86	0.0	41.4	0.0	0.0	**10.0**	22.6
Nueva Esperanza Community Credit Union	Toledo	OH	**D-**	D-	D-	1.9	11.97	0.0	56.3	3.8	0.0	**7.9**	9.7
NuMark Credit Union	Joliet	IL	**A-**	A-	A-	245.9	7.58	3.5	33.9	15.7	1.6	**10.0**	13.0
Numerica Credit Union	Spokane Valley	WA	**A-**	A-	A	1875.0	12.80	21.5	38.0	27.4	5.7	**8.9**	10.4
Nusenda Federal Credit Union	Albuquerque	NM	**A-**	A-	B+	1971.8	12.72	20.1	46.2	28.1	8.2	**9.1**	10.4
Nutmeg State Financial Credit Union	Rocky Hill	CT	**B+**	B+	B+	425.5	7.07	4.2	33.1	29.5	10.5	**10.0**	14.4
NuVision Federal Credit Union	Huntington Beach	CA	**B**	B	B	1549.0	9.20	10.4	25.7	38.9	16.0	**10.0**	11.7
NuVista Federal Credit Union	Montrose	CO	**D+**	D+	D+	84.1	-0.33	3.2	23.4	26.9	8.3	**5.5**	7.5
▲ NW Preferred Federal Credit Union	Tigard	OR	**B**	B-	B-	127.1	-0.91	21.8	23.8	25.3	7.7	**7.0**	9.0
NW Priority Credit Union	Portland	OR	**B-**	B-	C+	250.5	6.13	0.5	13.8	17.0	55.4	**10.0**	11.9
NYM Federal Credit Union	Brooklyn	NY	**B-**	B-	B-	17.9	5.62	2.9	20.3	0.0	3.1	**10.0**	15.5
Nymeo Federal Credit Union	Frederick	MD	**C+**	C+	A-	263.2	0.47	7.8	24.7	24.7	4.5	**8.8**	10.3
O And R Utilities Employees FCU	Monroe	NY	**D+**	D+	D	13.7	4.18	0.0	23.9	16.9	0.0	**10.0**	13.4
O Bee Credit Union	Tumwater	WA	**B-**	B-	B-	255.0	14.06	2.7	48.8	26.6	0.0	**5.7**	7.7
O'Neal Credit Union	Birmingham	AL	**C**	C	C	2.5	-0.92	0.0	62.5	0.0	0.0	**10.0**	24.6
O.F. Toalston Federal Credit Union	Logan	WV	**C+**	C+	C+	<1	-4.54	0.0	76.5	0.0	0.0	**10.0**	15.8
O.M.C. Employees' Credit Union	Charleston	TN	**C**	C	C	28.3	0.28	0.0	23.4	29.7	13.8	**6.8**	8.8
Oahe Federal Credit Union	Pierre	SD	**B-**	B-	B-	24.7	7.79	0.0	35.0	3.4	0.0	**10.0**	11.7
▲ Oahu Federal Credit Union	Honolulu	HI	**C+**	C	C	50.6	2.64	4.5	12.5	8.2	11.0	**10.0**	11.0
Oak Cliff Christian Federal Credit Union	Dallas	TX	**D+**	D+	D+	5.4	17.89	0.0	67.4	0.0	0.0	**6.7**	8.7
Oak Farms Employees Credit Union	Houston	TX	**C**	C	C	4.3	8.64	0.0	65.4	0.0	0.0	**10.0**	22.8
Oak Lawn Municipal Employees CU	Oak Lawn	IL	**D+**	D+	D	4.6	6.65	0.0	29.0	0.0	0.0	**8.3**	9.8
Oak Point Employees Credit Union	Belle Chasse	LA	**B-**	B-	B-	9.5	2.79	0.0	74.6	0.0	0.0	**10.0**	34.2
Oakdale Credit Union	Oakdale	WI	**C-**	C-	D+	68.1	4.30	1.7	24.8	38.0	0.0	**5.3**	7.3
Oakland County Credit Union	Waterford	MI	**A-**	A-	B+	342.9	9.73	0.0	25.4	16.3	14.9	**9.0**	10.4
▲ OAS Staff Federal Credit Union	Washington	DC	**C+**	C	C	214.0	10.38	2.2	5.0	34.4	24.4	**5.2**	7.2
Ocala Community Credit Union	Ocala	FL	**B-**	B-	B-	30.7	-0.76	0.0	32.3	9.9	37.1	**10.0**	11.6
▲ Ocean Communities Federal Credit Union	Biddeford	ME	**C**	C-	C-	171.7	5.04	7.7	24.6	36.9	8.6	**5.0**	7.0
Ocean County Employees FCU	Toms River	NJ	**D**	D	D+	1.5	-4.59	0.0	29.2	0.0	0.0	**9.7**	10.8
Ocean Crest Federal Credit Union	Signal Hill	CA	**D+**	D+	D+	38.4	8.01	3.8	13.5	16.4	25.4	**5.3**	7.3
▼ Ocean Financial Federal Credit Union	Oceanside	NY	**C+**	B-	B	316.7	3.88	8.9	10.1	27.7	27.2	**6.2**	8.8
Ocean Spray Employees FCU	Lakeville	MA	**C-**	C-	D+	11.6	5.10	0.0	26.7	15.5	0.0	**10.0**	12.1
OCNAC No 1 Federal Credit Union	Jersey City	NJ	**D+**	D+	D+	6.4	0.85	0.0	33.6	0.0	0.0	**10.0**	11.7
Odessa Employees Credit Union	Odessa	TX	**B**	B	B	16.3	-0.57	0.0	36.3	12.2	0.0	**10.0**	14.7
ODJFS Federal Credit Union	Columbus	OH	**D+**	D+	C-	10.4	3.76	0.0	41.6	1.9	21.3	**10.0**	11.4
Ohio Catholic Federal Credit Union	Garfield Heights	OH	**A-**	A-	A-	163.8	8.58	6.9	9.4	47.9	1.4	**10.0**	11.7
▼ Ohio County Public Schools FCU	Wheeling	WV	**D**	D+	C	5.2	-9.88	0.0	28.1	0.0	0.0	**10.0**	14.8
Ohio Educational Credit Union	Cleveland	OH	**C-**	C-	D+	132.6	2.88	17.0	35.5	11.1	3.5	**5.1**	7.2
Ohio Healthcare Federal Credit Union	Dublin	OH	**C+**	C+	C	82.4	9.50	0.0	53.8	5.9	5.5	**6.6**	8.6
Ohio Operating Engineers FCU	Cleveland	OH	**D**	D	D-	6.2	4.78	0.0	45.6	2.4	12.8	**6.3**	8.3
Ohio Teamsters Credit Union, Inc.	Independence	OH	**C**	C	C	13.8	0.12	0.6	26.5	15.4	19.7	**10.0**	26.9
Ohio University Credit Union	Athens	OH	**B**	B	B	343.3	6.95	10.6	21.5	36.2	9.7	**8.7**	10.2

Asset Quality Index	Non-Performing Loans as a % of Total Loans	Non-Performing Loans as a % of Capital	Net Charge-Offs Avg Loans	Profitability Index	Net Income ($Mil)	Return on Assets	Return on Equity	Net Interest Spread	Overhead Efficiency Ratio	Liquidity Index	Liquidity Ratio	Hot Money Ratio	Stability Index
7.3	0.72	3.8	-0.17	**2.7**	0.00	0.00	0.00	4.83	100.0	**5.3**	41.3	0.0	**5.7**
6.6	0.85	5.3	-0.06	**2.2**	0.01	0.16	2.02	2.92	94.7	**4.3**	17.6	1.9	**3.4**
8.9	0.08	0.2	0.00	**8.2**	0.01	0.99	4.36	4.33	75.0	**4.8**	35.3	0.0	**5.7**
5.8	0.29	3.0	0.00	**8.4**	0.01	1.40	17.81	6.58	82.0	**4.2**	38.7	3.4	**3.0**
6.3	11.30	9.2	0.00	**2.0**	0.00	0.21	1.97	0.83	100.0	**6.7**	42.4	0.0	**6.0**
10.0	0.03	0.1	0.07	**2.0**	0.00	0.02	0.21	2.31	99.1	**5.0**	34.8	10.3	**6.1**
7.1	0.59	5.8	0.38	**4.5**	0.91	0.72	9.21	3.76	79.0	**3.4**	12.8	9.6	**5.1**
7.6	1.42	5.3	0.52	**4.0**	0.22	0.77	5.07	4.58	82.6	**4.3**	14.3	4.1	**7.2**
10.0	0.00	0.0	-0.01	**1.8**	-0.17	-0.62	-4.29	2.14	158.8	**4.5**	56.1	20.1	**8.1**
6.7	0.00	0.0	2.67	**4.6**	0.00	1.37	6.82	2.42	50.0	**3.7**	5.2	0.0	**3.7**
8.3	1.20	3.4	0.83	**4.1**	0.26	0.82	8.25	2.25	66.5	**6.1**	42.7	3.7	**5.7**
9.0	0.19	2.1	0.11	**4.4**	0.17	0.50	6.34	3.44	86.3	**4.0**	12.3	0.7	**5.2**
8.4	0.00	0.0	0.34	**3.6**	0.01	0.30	1.99	6.20	96.0	**4.1**	31.9	4.7	**6.6**
9.3	0.51	2.8	0.39	**3.2**	0.32	0.27	2.71	3.02	81.4	**4.1**	19.9	2.5	**6.1**
4.2	0.66	5.2	0.00	**7.4**	0.01	2.63	31.86	8.28	69.0	**5.4**	34.4	0.0	**2.3**
7.1	1.33	7.4	1.14	**1.7**	0.12	0.13	1.62	2.74	77.5	**4.3**	12.6	4.3	**4.5**
3.5	3.44	21.2	1.48	**0.2**	-0.07	-1.54	-17.23	4.75	94.9	**5.3**	39.0	7.5	**4.7**
6.4	1.37	4.9	0.60	**5.2**	0.06	0.63	4.20	4.79	84.9	**6.3**	45.2	2.0	**7.5**
6.3	4.90	9.8	0.00	**2.8**	0.01	0.66	2.86	3.43	77.3	**6.2**	68.8	0.0	**6.8**
1.8	5.15	32.3	0.00	**3.7**	0.06	12.21	144.74	6.42	35.2	**4.3**	34.1	0.0	**1.7**
8.4	0.79	3.5	0.60	**5.5**	0.30	0.49	3.72	4.39	83.6	**3.7**	20.5	7.7	**8.6**
7.9	0.28	2.8	0.58	**6.6**	4.44	0.97	9.34	3.77	71.9	**2.6**	10.9	12.6	**8.0**
6.8	0.37	3.3	0.53	**7.0**	5.28	1.10	11.08	3.78	68.7	**3.5**	13.1	4.4	**7.6**
8.9	0.38	2.4	0.75	**4.0**	0.51	0.49	3.65	3.78	79.1	**2.8**	7.1	10.0	**7.7**
8.6	0.58	3.7	0.55	**4.6**	1.94	0.52	4.73	3.60	75.8	**3.4**	24.3	14.9	**8.1**
5.6	1.24	9.9	0.18	**2.7**	0.14	0.67	9.11	3.99	79.3	**4.4**	39.6	11.5	**2.3**
6.9	0.40	3.2	0.45	**4.6**	0.20	0.62	6.92	4.54	80.5	**4.0**	24.0	7.3	**5.4**
10.0	0.58	1.7	0.12	**3.5**	0.34	0.54	4.54	2.54	77.0	**4.8**	20.7	3.4	**7.4**
9.1	0.55	0.9	0.80	**4.3**	0.01	0.20	1.30	3.02	90.1	**5.6**	37.8	0.0	**7.5**
6.2	1.35	8.1	1.74	**3.4**	0.78	1.20	11.84	4.77	78.0	**4.0**	24.1	5.0	**5.5**
9.9	0.31	1.4	-0.09	**2.7**	0.02	0.68	5.03	4.09	90.2	**4.7**	27.4	2.6	**6.0**
5.9	0.36	6.7	0.93	**4.6**	0.35	0.55	7.06	4.12	74.4	**3.2**	11.9	5.0	**4.7**
6.3	3.43	8.3	0.26	**4.5**	0.00	0.65	2.64	5.77	85.2	**5.7**	36.6	0.0	**4.3**
5.7	1.39	6.0	0.00	**7.2**	0.00	0.94	5.48	9.70	88.9	**5.4**	49.8	0.0	**4.3**
9.8	0.01	0.0	0.12	**2.5**	0.04	0.63	7.10	2.40	74.1	**4.8**	26.8	1.9	**4.5**
8.4	0.31	2.1	0.06	**5.9**	0.06	0.98	8.27	3.75	73.3	**5.1**	29.2	0.6	**5.7**
10.0	0.32	1.0	0.05	**2.8**	0.04	0.29	2.67	2.51	87.3	**5.1**	29.0	0.9	**5.6**
4.5	0.90	6.6	0.00	**9.2**	0.02	1.84	21.19	3.73	69.2	**5.0**	33.7	0.0	**3.0**
6.2	1.62	4.9	0.13	**5.8**	0.01	0.85	3.68	6.50	85.5	**3.5**	27.7	15.1	**4.3**
10.0	0.00	0.0	0.00	**2.5**	0.01	0.44	4.42	2.44	80.8	**5.6**	33.2	0.0	**3.9**
6.1	2.82	5.8	0.00	**9.8**	0.06	2.61	7.68	3.74	18.4	**4.2**	40.6	0.0	**5.0**
5.2	0.90	13.3	0.18	**3.8**	0.06	0.36	4.91	3.76	86.0	**4.4**	20.5	1.6	**3.5**
9.4	0.36	2.6	0.48	**6.5**	0.61	0.72	7.23	3.81	79.7	**3.7**	10.7	3.9	**6.9**
7.3	0.77	7.1	0.12	**4.5**	0.62	1.18	16.16	3.39	66.2	**3.3**	34.8	19.5	**4.3**
9.4	0.43	1.7	0.19	**3.3**	0.04	0.55	4.73	3.23	79.9	**4.3**	19.1	2.7	**5.5**
6.6	0.70	7.4	0.56	**2.8**	0.15	0.36	5.15	3.70	86.8	**4.3**	19.9	5.0	**3.7**
6.9	1.52	3.8	9.02	**0.5**	-0.01	-2.39	-21.05	8.50	70.0	**7.1**	56.3	0.0	**3.9**
9.2	0.43	1.8	0.48	**1.1**	-0.01	-0.06	-0.86	2.95	101.4	**5.1**	17.4	0.0	**2.0**
5.2	1.79	13.7	0.45	**1.9**	-0.26	-0.33	-4.35	2.71	86.0	**4.5**	18.4	6.9	**5.0**
8.8	0.66	2.7	0.40	**1.7**	0.00	0.07	0.57	3.60	89.3	**4.9**	29.6	3.4	**5.4**
5.8	5.84	14.7	2.41	**2.5**	0.00	0.13	1.07	6.98	78.9	**6.7**	52.9	0.0	**5.5**
9.6	0.33	1.2	0.13	**3.2**	0.01	0.30	2.01	3.43	91.6	**5.3**	38.1	0.7	**7.3**
9.4	0.55	2.1	-0.34	**0.7**	-0.01	-0.28	-2.36	3.37	107.7	**6.0**	45.5	0.0	**4.9**
8.9	0.24	1.7	0.47	**6.5**	0.34	0.84	7.12	4.04	79.1	**3.6**	14.3	3.6	**7.6**
8.1	3.06	5.9	1.29	**0.2**	-0.04	-3.09	-19.95	3.53	181.6	**6.8**	60.4	0.0	**4.7**
6.3	0.85	9.1	0.24	**1.8**	0.02	0.05	0.64	3.18	93.7	**3.8**	12.2	1.8	**3.7**
5.5	0.64	5.3	0.26	**6.5**	0.24	1.18	13.68	4.99	80.1	**4.1**	14.3	0.3	**4.2**
6.3	0.29	1.9	1.50	**3.7**	0.00	-0.13	-1.55	3.77	80.0	**4.7**	42.9	0.0	**2.3**
7.1	5.70	8.5	3.47	**2.5**	0.00	0.00	0.00	3.95	100.0	**7.0**	65.0	0.0	**7.1**
7.8	0.62	4.0	0.27	**4.7**	0.57	0.67	6.59	3.43	83.4	**3.8**	18.3	7.3	**6.6**

	Name	City	State	Rating	2016 Rating	2015 Rating	Total Assets ($Mil)	One Year Asset Growth	Asset Mix (As a % of Total Assets) Commercial Loans	Consumer Loans	Mortgage Loans	Securities	Capitalization Index	Net Worth Ratio
▲	Ohio Valley Community Credit Union	Clarington	OH	**C**	C-	C-	136.5	3.81	5.2	21.6	23.4	26.1	**6.4**	8.7
▼	Ohio Valley Federal Credit Union	Batavia	OH	**D-**	D	D-	25.7	2.33	3.3	26.8	5.1	6.7	**6.2**	8.2
	Ohio's First Class Credit Union	Cleveland	OH	**C+**	C+	C-	42.3	6.40	0.0	63.0	0.0	8.2	**10.0**	15.2
	Oil Country Federal Credit Union	Titusville	PA	**D+**	D+	C-	18.7	-1.75	0.0	32.9	11.7	0.0	**10.0**	11.4
	OK Federal Credit Union	Bartlesville	OK	**C-**	C-	C-	21.0	4.45	0.0	42.6	0.0	0.0	**7.2**	9.1
	OK Members First Federal Credit Union	Tulsa	OK	**C**	C	C	21.0	-0.55	0.0	53.4	6.2	0.0	**10.0**	14.9
	Okaloosa County Teachers FCU	Crestview	FL	**C+**	C+	C+	81.3	7.13	0.0	29.1	8.7	10.1	**8.1**	9.8
	Oklahoma Central Credit Union	Tulsa	OK	**B-**	B-	B-	548.8	3.95	5.6	42.2	12.9	27.4	**10.0**	12.9
▲	Oklahoma Educators Credit Union	Oklahoma City	OK	**B+**	B	B	134.5	9.49	0.0	59.8	10.9	18.3	**6.9**	9.3
▼	Oklahoma Employees Credit Union	Oklahoma City	OK	**B+**	A-	A-	495.6	1.79	5.6	48.0	15.8	25.0	**10.0**	12.9
	Oklahoma Federal Credit Union	Oklahoma City	OK	**A**	A	A	122.3	4.95	0.2	51.0	15.4	17.4	**10.0**	13.6
	Olathe Federal Credit Union	Olathe	CO	**D-**	D-	D+	<1	-24.94	0.0	69.2	0.0	0.0	**10.0**	12.8
▲	Old Dominion University Credit Union, Inc.	Norfolk	VA	**D+**	D	D+	30.1	4.62	0.0	9.3	16.4	0.0	**7.2**	9.1
	Old Hickory Credit Union	Old Hickory	TN	**C**	C	D+	234.4	2.57	11.9	22.0	25.7	29.7	**6.7**	8.8
	Old Ocean Federal Credit Union	Old Ocean	TX	**C**	C	C	34.6	8.00	0.0	34.0	0.0	13.1	**6.4**	8.4
	Old South Federal Credit Union	Natchez	MS	**D**	D	D+	18.8	-0.56	0.0	28.3	0.0	0.0	**10.0**	13.1
	Old Spanish Trail Credit Union	Westlake	LA	**C-**	C-	D	9.2	0.04	0.0	36.8	0.0	0.0	**10.0**	17.7
	Old West Federal Credit Union	John Day	OR	**D+**	D+	D-	169.0	29.64	33.2	6.8	38.9	1.9	**8.5**	10.0
	Olean Area Federal Credit Union	Olean	NY	**A**	A	A	267.8	2.82	10.3	20.8	30.4	23.0	**10.0**	14.0
	Olean Teachers' and Postal FCU	Olean	NY	**D**	D	D+	18.8	6.95	0.0	16.8	18.1	28.6	**5.9**	7.9
	Olive View Employees FCU	Sylmar	CA	**A-**	A-	B+	43.7	8.61	0.0	41.1	0.0	4.5	**10.0**	21.0
	Olympia Credit Union	Olympia	WA	**C-**	C-	D+	37.2	9.87	1.6	42.8	12.0	13.8	**6.0**	8.1
	Omaha Douglas Federal Credit Union	Omaha	NE	**C+**	C+	C	33.8	4.85	0.0	24.8	5.1	0.0	**10.0**	11.3
	Omaha Federal Credit Union	Omaha	NE	**D+**	D+	C-	76.0	5.21	1.0	19.2	12.5	0.0	**5.8**	7.8
	Omaha Firefighters Credit Union	Omaha	NE	**B+**	B+	B+	59.1	4.21	0.0	17.1	5.7	3.2	**10.0**	16.2
	Omaha Police Federal Credit Union	Omaha	NE	**C-**	C-	C-	67.5	4.21	0.0	28.0	25.0	4.2	**6.0**	8.0
▲	Omaha Public Power District Empls FCU	Omaha	NE	**C+**	C	C-	30.1	-0.47	0.0	28.5	0.0	47.7	**10.0**	23.1
	Omega Federal Credit Union	Pittsburgh	PA	**C+**	C+	C+	103.5	5.04	3.2	23.0	9.1	14.9	**6.8**	8.8
	Omega Psi Phi Fraternity FCU	Lawrenceville	GA	**D+**	D+	D+	1.3	9.85	0.0	46.4	10.8	0.0	**7.1**	9.1
	Omni Community Credit Union	Battle Creek	MI	**A**	A	A-	383.1	9.17	8.1	29.1	14.1	41.0	**10.0**	13.6
	On Tap Credit Union	Golden	CO	**A**	A	A	236.9	4.85	4.4	34.5	27.1	9.7	**10.0**	11.1
	On The Grid Financial FCU	Atlanta	GA	**C+**	C+	C-	42.5	8.48	0.0	36.8	7.9	1.0	**10.0**	12.4
	One Community Federal Credit Union	Parkersburg	WV	**C**	C	C-	73.9	-0.56	0.2	25.2	28.9	0.0	**6.7**	8.7
▲	One Credit Union	Springfield	VT	**D+**	D	D+	146.7	3.03	2.2	27.9	27.3	11.2	**7.4**	9.4
	One Detroit Credit Union	Detroit	MI	**C+**	C+	C-	37.4	12.04	0.0	51.5	12.6	3.8	**10.0**	11.4
▼	One Federal Credit Union	Meadville	PA	**D+**	C-	C	76.6	6.14	0.8	57.8	6.5	0.1	**5.8**	7.8
	One Nevada Credit Union	Las Vegas	NV	**A**	A	A	870.5	9.35	7.9	30.5	16.2	5.1	**10.0**	11.7
	One Source Federal Credit Union	El Paso	TX	**D**	D	D+	92.5	-6.30	0.0	45.2	10.4	13.3	**5.0**	7.2
	One Thirteen Credit Union	Colorado Springs	CO	**E+**	E+	E+	9.1	9.50	0.0	42.3	0.0	0.0	**5.6**	7.6
	One Twenty Credit Union	Roslindale	MA	**C**	C	C-	<1	9.54	0.0	42.5	0.0	18.7	**10.0**	13.7
	One Vision Federal Credit Union	Clarksville	IN	**C+**	C+	C	54.6	4.75	0.0	18.4	13.3	0.0	**10.0**	11.5
	OneAZ Credit Union	Phoenix	AZ	**B+**	B+	A-	1981.1	7.33	11.7	29.5	30.5	18.9	**8.3**	10.0
	Oneida County Federal Credit Union	Utica	NY	**C-**	C-	C-	13.2	0.80	0.0	26.2	0.0	0.0	**9.0**	10.3
▼	Onomea Federal Credit Union	Papaikou	HI	**C-**	C	C-	16.7	3.55	0.0	29.3	10.6	40.3	**10.0**	17.6
	OnPoint Community Credit Union	Portland	OR	**A**	A	A	4776.9	17.83	3.2	23.6	32.0	18.9	**9.2**	10.6
	Ontario Montclair School Employees FCU	Ontario	CA	**B**	B	B	107.0	7.38	0.0	31.1	14.5	14.8	**8.7**	10.1
	Ontario Public Employees FCU	Ontario	CA	**D-**	D-	D	20.1	5.09	0.0	39.8	3.9	12.4	**5.3**	7.3
	Ontario Shores Federal Credit Union	Newfane	NY	**B-**	B-	B-	87.5	26.63	0.0	8.1	20.9	30.1	**5.8**	7.8
	OPC Federal Credit Union	Durkee	OR	**C**	C	C	2.6	5.64	0.0	58.3	0.0	0.0	**10.0**	15.0
	Operating Engineers Local #148 CU	Granite City	IL	**D+**	D+	C	17.2	-0.60	0.0	46.7	0.0	0.0	**10.0**	16.2
	Operating Engineers Local Union #3 FCU	Livermore	CA	**A**	A	A	1033.5	6.46	2.2	21.9	23.8	33.5	**10.0**	14.2
	Opp-Micolas Credit Union	Opp	AL	**D+**	D+	D	13.2	-3.40	0.4	9.6	16.1	0.0	**10.0**	24.6
	Opportunities Credit Union	Winooski	VT	**B**	B	B-	38.5	10.19	8.7	6.6	49.5	0.0	**10.0**	16.2
	Options Credit Union	Littleton	CO	**D-**	D-	D-	5.3	10.42	0.0	51.9	29.8	0.0	**5.4**	7.4
	Orange County Teachers Credit Union	Orange	TX	**C-**	C-	C-	1.8	-11.71	0.0	12.4	0.0	0.0	**10.0**	24.5
	Orange County's Credit Union	Santa Ana	CA	**A-**	A-	A-	1508.9	9.04	9.2	21.6	38.7	19.8	**7.8**	9.6
	Orange School Employees Credit Union	Pepper Pike	OH	**C**	C	C	3.2	2.35	0.0	23.5	0.0	6.2	**10.0**	20.3
	Oregon Community Credit Union	Eugene	OR	**B-**	B-	B-	1652.1	13.29	0.6	45.4	10.2	0.4	**5.8**	7.8
▲	Oregon Pioneer Federal Credit Union	Portland	OR	**C**	C-	D	26.4	8.98	0.5	12.2	23.2	22.8	**6.2**	8.2
	Oregon State Credit Union	Corvallis	OR	**A-**	A-	A-	1157.8	13.80	8.5	36.0	17.8	22.0	**9.0**	10.4

Asset Quality Index	Non-Performing Loans as a % of Total Loans	Non-Performing Loans as a % of Capital	Net Charge-Offs Avg Loans	Profitability Index	Net Income ($Mil)	Return on Assets	Return on Equity	Net Interest Spread	Overhead Efficiency Ratio	Liquidity Index	Liquidity Ratio	Hot Money Ratio	Stability Index
9.8	0.23	1.5	0.07	**2.8**	0.11	0.33	4.21	3.08	89.7	**4.2**	20.9	4.7	**4.3**
4.7	1.70	13.8	0.02	**1.5**	-0.01	-0.10	-1.14	3.45	102.0	**4.3**	24.3	3.0	**3.3**
6.1	1.56	6.8	0.97	**2.9**	0.03	0.27	1.73	4.86	89.2	**4.1**	13.7	0.0	**6.1**
9.4	0.68	2.7	0.45	**0.9**	0.01	0.24	2.07	3.62	101.1	**5.0**	19.3	2.0	**4.7**
6.2	0.11	5.2	0.83	**2.9**	0.01	0.12	1.26	3.13	80.2	**4.9**	38.5	9.7	**4.6**
7.0	0.34	1.8	0.15	**3.0**	0.02	0.40	2.70	3.50	90.7	**4.2**	32.0	3.9	**6.6**
5.9	1.61	8.8	1.16	**3.3**	0.07	0.34	3.45	3.40	88.2	**4.9**	34.4	4.4	**4.3**
7.4	0.92	4.3	0.65	**3.5**	0.69	0.51	3.98	3.60	77.9	**3.9**	19.4	5.8	**8.5**
7.0	0.32	3.6	0.59	**8.8**	0.46	1.37	15.56	4.56	61.4	**2.3**	5.4	14.8	**5.7**
7.8	0.45	3.0	0.46	**4.7**	0.74	0.60	4.97	2.86	74.7	**2.7**	6.7	14.3	**8.1**
8.5	0.23	1.2	0.54	**8.6**	0.34	1.14	8.59	3.24	63.1	**1.7**	20.3	32.4	**8.9**
7.8	0.88	4.4	0.00	**0.9**	0.00	0.00	0.00	4.51	100.0	**4.8**	34.3	0.0	**4.1**
1.7	10.79	37.2	1.46	**2.1**	0.00	0.03	0.29	2.63	98.5	**6.9**	62.1	0.0	**3.9**
8.5	0.51	2.9	0.47	**3.1**	0.22	0.38	4.33	3.21	82.3	**4.9**	28.9	2.0	**5.2**
7.4	0.57	4.1	0.09	**5.7**	0.11	1.28	14.90	4.20	77.3	**5.9**	41.8	1.3	**3.8**
7.2	2.57	7.3	2.62	**0.0**	-0.07	-1.44	-13.25	3.95	97.6	**6.8**	63.1	0.0	**5.0**
8.7	1.35	3.3	-0.20	**2.2**	0.01	0.22	1.23	3.67	95.1	**5.4**	66.5	0.0	**6.4**
2.2	1.32	34.5	-0.03	**2.1**	-0.17	-0.44	-4.77	5.34	111.0	**5.0**	26.1	2.2	**4.8**
9.2	0.42	1.7	0.32	**6.5**	0.64	0.97	6.88	2.94	68.9	**4.3**	28.0	5.5	**9.0**
6.8	0.18	0.8	-0.18	**1.7**	0.00	0.07	0.81	2.79	97.2	**5.9**	28.5	0.9	**3.9**
9.8	0.16	0.3	-0.02	**8.9**	0.12	1.12	5.23	3.83	68.9	**5.4**	41.1	4.6	**7.6**
8.9	0.26	2.1	0.16	**2.5**	0.00	0.03	0.40	3.21	91.1	**4.0**	25.0	2.8	**3.8**
9.0	0.88	2.6	1.18	**2.2**	0.00	0.05	0.42	2.85	93.6	**5.2**	32.4	2.5	**5.9**
4.0	1.36	15.1	1.33	**4.1**	0.04	0.20	2.49	3.79	88.3	**3.2**	30.5	16.4	**3.5**
10.0	0.10	0.3	-0.05	**4.4**	0.09	0.64	3.97	2.09	72.6	**5.8**	29.6	0.0	**7.8**
9.9	0.02	0.3	0.25	**2.0**	0.02	0.14	1.79	2.85	95.8	**4.7**	27.1	0.8	**3.9**
9.8	0.36	0.5	0.00	**2.6**	0.03	0.37	1.62	1.53	75.7	**4.8**	15.1	0.0	**7.3**
8.5	0.54	4.0	0.50	**3.5**	0.06	0.24	2.63	4.52	86.7	**5.9**	36.7	1.0	**5.6**
4.5	1.78	10.7	0.00	**7.8**	0.00	1.29	14.41	6.59	81.8	**5.3**	38.6	0.0	**3.0**
7.5	1.26	5.0	0.76	**7.3**	1.11	1.20	8.94	4.03	70.6	**3.9**	12.0	8.7	**8.4**
6.6	1.03	8.0	1.12	**4.9**	0.18	0.31	2.78	4.39	77.4	**4.0**	13.3	2.6	**7.7**
9.6	0.47	1.8	0.19	**3.0**	0.06	0.63	4.81	3.85	87.2	**5.6**	38.5	4.7	**6.5**
8.5	0.04	0.3	0.06	**2.8**	0.05	0.28	3.24	3.18	92.2	**4.6**	28.5	2.6	**4.5**
6.2	1.03	11.2	0.49	**1.7**	0.07	0.19	1.98	3.95	88.2	**4.2**	13.7	0.9	**4.9**
5.6	1.42	7.4	1.87	**4.0**	0.01	0.15	1.32	7.42	90.8	**4.3**	30.0	11.0	**5.3**
4.6	0.73	6.7	0.92	**2.7**	-0.01	-0.08	-0.94	4.11	88.2	**4.2**	17.6	3.7	**2.8**
9.3	0.54	2.1	1.03	**7.7**	1.80	0.84	7.17	4.49	82.9	**7.1**	50.8	1.1	**8.8**
4.1	1.45	10.7	0.76	**1.7**	0.17	0.73	10.46	4.20	89.4	**4.6**	36.7	11.5	**1.4**
4.4	1.85	12.6	0.08	**1.8**	0.00	0.04	0.58	4.35	99.1	**5.5**	44.4	0.0	**1.0**
9.8	0.00	0.0	0.00	**2.7**	0.00	0.00	0.00	2.38	100.0	**6.2**	56.4	0.0	**7.1**
10.0	0.05	0.1	0.46	**2.6**	0.03	0.21	1.79	2.64	94.4	**4.8**	26.7	2.2	**6.0**
8.4	0.17	2.2	0.31	**4.9**	2.52	0.52	5.64	3.22	85.0	**4.3**	18.2	1.5	**6.7**
8.5	0.98	2.6	0.21	**2.5**	0.01	0.34	3.24	3.27	82.2	**6.3**	32.6	1.1	**4.6**
10.0	0.16	0.4	0.05	**1.4**	-0.01	-0.12	-0.68	2.98	96.1	**4.7**	24.2	0.0	**6.6**
9.8	0.15	1.0	0.12	**8.1**	13.33	1.14	10.87	3.02	67.3	**4.9**	25.2	3.4	**8.3**
9.9	0.10	0.5	0.42	**4.3**	0.15	0.58	6.08	3.01	82.4	**4.5**	32.2	10.0	**6.1**
8.0	0.42	2.5	0.34	**1.1**	0.00	0.08	1.10	4.25	96.3	**5.5**	30.4	1.5	**2.9**
10.0	0.15	0.8	0.05	**4.9**	0.17	0.81	10.22	2.72	68.5	**5.3**	27.6	2.1	**4.0**
8.6	0.00	0.0	0.00	**5.3**	0.01	2.16	14.40	5.63	48.2	**6.0**	49.1	0.0	**5.0**
6.5	2.51	7.6	0.36	**0.8**	-0.01	-0.26	-1.58	2.92	86.4	**4.5**	29.0	3.3	**6.1**
9.8	0.37	1.7	0.23	**7.9**	4.59	1.79	12.68	3.30	59.2	**3.3**	16.8	13.2	**9.0**
7.6	1.90	7.6	-0.10	**0.9**	-0.01	-0.18	-0.74	3.20	105.9	**5.3**	40.8	0.5	**7.1**
5.8	1.10	8.5	1.20	**3.7**	-0.27	-2.89	-22.42	4.00	124.3	**4.4**	36.1	4.7	**7.7**
7.4	0.30	3.2	0.00	**4.1**	0.01	0.85	11.43	5.72	86.4	**3.3**	18.4	11.7	**1.7**
7.1	15.05	9.4	0.00	**2.2**	0.00	0.00	0.00	5.67	100.0	**8.6**	107.6	0.0	**5.6**
9.7	0.13	0.9	0.11	**6.0**	3.11	0.84	8.79	3.06	77.1	**4.2**	19.1	6.4	**7.9**
5.3	5.98	11.8	0.00	**5.5**	0.01	0.63	3.07	3.60	72.0	**5.5**	33.7	0.0	**4.3**
6.7	0.24	3.1	0.61	**4.1**	1.62	0.40	5.05	3.37	79.6	**4.1**	19.9	6.3	**5.6**
10.0	0.05	0.2	-0.11	**2.7**	0.01	0.14	1.65	3.36	96.6	**5.9**	35.8	0.9	**4.0**
9.1	0.27	2.0	0.18	**5.9**	2.29	0.81	7.76	3.14	77.2	**4.1**	16.3	1.3	**7.9**

	Name	City	State	Rating	2016 Rating	2015 Rating	Total Assets ($Mil)	One Year Asset Growth	Comm-ercial Loans	Cons-umer Loans	Mort-gage Loans	Secur-ities	Capital-ization Index	Net Worth Ratio
									Asset Mix (As a % of Total Assets)					
	Oregonians Credit Union	Milwaukie	OR	**B-**	B-	B-	311.0	2.28	6.6	23.7	15.9	36.8	**10.0**	12.2
▲	Orem City Employees Federal Credit Union	Orem	UT	**D**	D-	D+	3.7	1.29	0.0	30.7	0.0	31.6	**9.3**	10.5
	Organized Labor Credit Union	Modesto	CA	**D+**	D+	D	22.5	8.76	0.0	23.2	1.1	0.0	**5.6**	7.6
▲	Orion Federal Credit Union	Memphis	TN	**A**	A-	B	674.9	9.69	11.1	22.2	37.9	1.9	**10.0**	11.3
	Orlando Federal Credit Union	Orlando	FL	**B+**	B+	B+	227.5	10.94	1.1	33.8	17.6	8.8	**6.9**	8.9
	Orleans Parish Criminal Sheriff's CU	New Orleans	LA	**C+**	C+	C+	5.7	-4.09	0.0	21.7	0.0	0.0	**10.0**	33.1
	Orlex Government Employees Credit Union	Newport	VT	**E+**	E+	E+	5.9	-1.51	0.0	69.8	0.0	0.0	**6.5**	8.5
	ORNL Federal Credit Union	Oak Ridge	TN	**B+**	B+	B+	1911.6	8.27	3.9	29.4	32.7	8.2	**9.2**	10.5
	Oshkosh Community Credit Union	Oshkosh	WI	**D**	D	D+	18.3	-2.00	0.0	30.8	36.6	0.0	**6.5**	8.5
	Oshkosh Postal Employees Credit Union	Oshkosh	WI	**E+**	E+	D-	4.9	3.52	0.0	58.3	20.1	0.0	**6.7**	8.7
	Oshkosh Truck Credit Union	Oshkosh	WI	**C+**	C+	C	16.2	2.36	0.7	17.9	17.4	0.0	**10.0**	15.1
	OSU Institute of Technology FCU	Okmulgee	OK	**E+**	E+	E+	4.4	-9.30	0.0	24.2	0.9	0.0	**6.9**	8.9
	Oswego County Federal Credit Union	Oswego	NY	**D+**	D+	C	77.1	8.82	0.0	43.9	2.5	1.7	**5.7**	7.7
	Oswego Teachers Employees FCU	Oswego	NY	**B**	B	B	37.9	7.73	0.0	14.0	4.5	14.1	**9.4**	10.6
	Oteen VA Federal Credit Union	Asheville	NC	**D**	D	D	25.9	-2.13	0.0	13.6	6.0	0.0	**5.4**	7.4
	Otero County Teachers FCU	La Junta	CO	**D-**	D-	D+	4.3	5.20	0.0	29.8	0.0	0.0	**7.3**	9.2
	Otero Federal Credit Union	Alamogordo	NM	**B+**	B+	B+	307.0	2.87	0.0	34.2	9.0	31.5	**10.0**	13.7
	Otis Federal Credit Union	Jay	ME	**A**	A	A-	159.4	7.99	0.0	17.2	16.4	0.3	**10.0**	16.4
▼	OTS Employees Federal Credit Union	Honolulu	HI	**D+**	C-	C	13.1	-5.22	0.0	75.0	0.0	0.0	**10.0**	14.7
	Ottawa Hiway Credit Union	Ottawa	IL	**B-**	B-	C+	10.7	5.73	0.0	43.4	0.0	0.0	**10.0**	12.8
	Otter Tail Credit Union	Fergus Falls	MN	**D+**	D+	D	16.7	3.18	0.6	19.3	0.0	0.0	**6.0**	8.0
	OU Federal Credit Union	Norman	OK	**C**	C	C-	51.5	2.92	0.0	33.7	0.0	19.8	**5.8**	8.0
▼	Ouachita Valley Federal Credit Union	West Monroe	LA	**B+**	A-	A	215.1	3.12	3.5	45.3	9.9	4.3	**10.0**	12.4
	Ouachita Valley Health System FCU	Camden	AR	**D**	D	D+	<1	-1.02	0.0	54.6	0.0	0.0	**10.0**	22.7
	Our Community Credit Union	Shelton	WA	**A-**	A-	A	359.0	12.94	0.9	31.9	10.4	45.9	**9.7**	10.8
	OUR Credit Union	Royal Oak	MI	**B-**	B-	B-	243.4	5.34	9.9	26.9	24.2	31.1	**6.0**	8.8
▼	Our Family Social Credit Union	Omaha	NE	**D-**	D	D-	<1	1.95	0.0	50.6	0.0	0.0	**6.7**	8.7
	Our Lady of Snows Credit Union	Henley	MO	**D-**	D-	D-	4.8	-2.77	0.0	34.9	0.0	0.0	**6.4**	8.4
	Our Lady of the Angels FCU	Fall River	MA	**E+**	E+	E+	2.6	0.51	0.0	30.7	8.1	0.0	**6.0**	8.0
	Our Mother of Mercy Parish Houston FCU	Houston	TX	**D-**	D-	D-	2.1	-10.67	0.0	35.0	0.0	0.0	**9.9**	11.0
▼	Our Sunday Visitor Employees FCU	Huntington	IN	**C-**	C	C+	2.9	-1.58	0.0	82.5	0.0	0.0	**10.0**	12.9
	Outreach Community Federal Credit Union	Hermitage	TN	**C+**	C+	C+	19.6	4.73	0.0	30.5	12.0	0.0	**10.0**	12.9
	Owensboro Federal Credit Union	Owensboro	KY	**C-**	C-	D+	57.4	0.48	0.0	20.2	21.4	0.0	**10.0**	11.5
	Owosso WBC Federal Credit Union	Owosso	MI	**D+**	D+	D+	3.4	-1.78	0.0	49.4	0.0	0.0	**10.0**	17.8
	Oxford Federal Credit Union	Mexico	ME	**A**	A	A	175.5	9.00	1.2	27.5	36.3	0.6	**10.0**	14.5
	Ozark Federal Credit Union	Poplar Bluff	MO	**B**	B	B-	58.0	13.19	1.6	31.6	23.6	0.0	**8.3**	9.9
▲	P & S Credit Union	Salt Lake City	UT	**D+**	D	D	15.8	6.32	0.0	37.9	11.9	1.0	**6.1**	8.1
	P C Federal Credit Union	Port Allegany	PA	**C**	C	C	10.5	1.17	0.0	45.9	0.0	0.0	**10.0**	12.4
	P S E Federal Credit Union	Somerset	NJ	**C+**	C+	C+	11.8	3.81	0.0	43.9	0.0	0.0	**10.0**	11.8
	P&G Mehoopany Employees FCU	Tunkhannock	PA	**B**	B	C+	113.5	5.93	2.5	32.8	19.8	8.8	**6.9**	9.0
	P.A.C.E Kenner Federal Credit Union	Kenner	LA	**D+**	D+	D+	2.3	-11.05	0.0	39.3	11.2	0.0	**10.0**	14.4
	P.H.I. Federal Credit Union	Lafayette	LA	**D-**	D-	D-	8.5	-3.13	0.3	47.0	0.0	0.0	**6.2**	8.2
	P.I.A.S Credit Union	Nashville	TN	**C-**	C-	C-	5.3	1.43	0.0	36.6	5.6	0.0	**10.0**	18.8
	P.I.E. Credit Union	Houston	TX	**C**	C	C+	14.6	7.98	0.0	24.3	6.4	0.0	**10.0**	13.4
▼	P.N.G. Northern Federal Credit Union	Vandergrift	PA	**D**	D+	D+	3.9	2.44	0.0	74.5	0.0	0.0	**9.7**	10.8
▼	P.S. Local 821 Federal Credit Union	Jersey City	NJ	**C-**	C	C+	<1	-2.83	0.0	0.0	0.0	0.0	**10.0**	20.9
	P.V.H.M.C. Federal Credit Union	Pomona	CA	**C+**	C+	C+	10.3	-3.00	0.0	52.6	0.0	0.0	**10.0**	11.2
	PA Healthcare Credit Union	Sewickley	PA	**D+**	D+	C-	25.3	-0.66	0.0	18.1	0.0	73.6	**10.0**	12.3
▲	PAAC Transit Division FCU	Pittsburgh	PA	**C-**	D+	C-	27.9	-2.49	0.0	15.8	0.0	20.1	**10.0**	14.1
	Pace Federal Credit Union	Huntington	WV	**D**	D	D	7.7	2.10	0.0	35.0	0.0	0.0	**10.0**	15.1
▼	Pace Resources Federal Credit Union	York	PA	**D-**	D	D+	5.7	3.27	0.0	25.0	0.0	6.1	**6.9**	8.9
	Pacific Cascade Federal Credit Union	Eugene	OR	**C**	C	C+	108.8	9.43	0.0	49.4	10.8	6.0	**5.4**	7.4
	Pacific Community Credit Union	Fullerton	CA	**B**	B	B-	186.4	-0.69	2.4	25.0	9.1	17.2	**10.0**	15.3
▲	Pacific Crest Federal Credit Union	Klamath Falls	OR	**C+**	C	C+	169.1	5.28	6.5	37.1	17.9	1.2	**6.3**	8.3
	Pacific Federal Credit Union	Diamond Bar	CA	**D**	D	D+	18.2	2.83	1.1	20.7	0.0	0.0	**10.0**	16.2
	Pacific Horizon Credit Union	Springville	UT	**B-**	B-	C+	58.0	12.37	3.8	50.0	19.6	0.0	**8.4**	10.0
	Pacific Marine Credit Union	Oceanside	CA	**B**	B	B	792.0	5.90	1.6	32.9	28.8	19.1	**10.0**	13.9
▲	Pacific Northwest Ironworkers FCU	Portland	OR	**C+**	C	C-	23.5	11.80	0.0	70.1	0.0	0.0	**10.0**	11.1
	Pacific NW Federal Credit Union	Portland	OR	**B**	B	B	175.0	11.53	2.3	28.1	19.8	16.5	**6.1**	8.1
	Pacific Postal Credit Union	San Jose	CA	**B**	B	B	217.7	1.22	0.1	13.7	10.9	44.6	**10.0**	13.9

Asset Quality Index	Non-Performing Loans as a % of Total Loans	Non-Performing Loans as a % of Capital	Net Charge-Offs Avg Loans	Profitability Index	Net Income ($Mil)	Return on Assets	Return on Equity	Net Interest Spread	Overhead Efficiency Ratio	Liquidity Index	Liquidity Ratio	Hot Money Ratio	Stability Index
9.9	0.34	1.2	0.28	**3.0**	0.14	0.18	1.49	2.59	89.4	**5.6**	56.9	1.5	**7.4**
8.2	0.38	1.2	0.00	**0.7**	0.00	0.00	0.00	3.02	100.0	**4.9**	44.8	23.6	**4.5**
10.0	0.19	0.7	0.19	**1.7**	-0.01	-0.18	-2.34	2.76	104.7	**4.8**	21.1	0.0	**3.2**
8.9	0.28	2.5	0.34	**8.1**	2.19	1.32	11.65	3.54	71.6	**3.6**	11.8	2.6	**8.7**
9.1	0.25	2.0	1.40	**3.1**	0.26	0.46	5.14	5.91	83.4	**5.9**	35.1	1.2	**5.0**
9.8	3.80	2.4	0.92	**4.4**	0.01	0.50	1.49	2.98	84.6	**6.6**	57.1	0.0	**5.7**
3.9	0.99	9.3	0.09	**2.0**	-0.01	-0.41	-4.73	5.76	104.9	**4.6**	20.0	0.0	**1.0**
6.6	0.74	7.8	0.45	**4.2**	3.20	0.68	6.61	3.12	77.5	**3.5**	15.0	10.1	**7.5**
6.0	0.64	5.5	2.34	**3.4**	-0.01	-0.20	-2.30	4.73	84.4	**4.0**	24.0	9.5	**3.0**
3.5	1.83	15.9	-0.52	**2.1**	0.00	-0.08	-0.93	5.52	96.8	**4.2**	16.0	0.0	**1.0**
10.0	0.46	1.2	0.00	**2.4**	0.02	0.40	2.63	3.36	92.0	**5.7**	33.8	0.8	**7.0**
5.2	3.82	13.6	0.27	**2.5**	0.00	0.36	4.05	2.92	83.3	**5.5**	54.0	2.8	**1.0**
3.5	2.12	19.7	0.63	**4.8**	0.13	0.69	8.87	5.79	81.0	**3.8**	16.5	6.9	**3.7**
10.0	0.12	0.5	0.65	**4.5**	0.06	0.66	6.14	2.82	68.2	**5.2**	24.0	0.0	**5.8**
9.6	0.15	0.4	0.38	**0.6**	-0.03	-0.39	-5.14	2.44	113.0	**4.9**	37.0	12.3	**2.4**
6.5	2.44	9.4	-0.27	**0.5**	-0.01	-0.47	-5.01	3.96	116.7	**7.3**	70.4	0.0	**3.6**
9.7	0.27	1.7	0.50	**4.6**	0.50	0.67	4.84	2.98	78.0	**4.4**	24.6	5.2	**8.3**
9.2	1.15	2.9	0.13	**6.5**	0.45	1.14	6.93	2.60	64.8	**6.1**	71.1	4.6	**8.9**
0.9	8.62	32.1	1.55	**3.7**	-0.13	-3.89	-25.29	6.88	72.1	**4.3**	23.3	1.8	**6.9**
9.7	0.07	0.3	0.23	**4.4**	0.02	0.83	6.47	3.08	75.0	**4.9**	14.8	0.0	**6.4**
9.9	0.14	0.5	0.00	**1.6**	0.00	0.00	0.00	2.41	101.3	**6.3**	33.3	0.0	**3.3**
7.1	0.43	3.5	2.18	**2.4**	0.00	0.03	0.40	3.35	78.3	**5.6**	33.7	0.0	**2.6**
5.7	0.89	5.6	0.65	**4.3**	0.18	0.34	2.88	3.88	87.4	**3.8**	21.1	7.8	**7.8**
3.1	9.00	18.3	0.00	**2.9**	0.00	1.05	4.55	7.38	83.3	**6.2**	61.7	0.0	**5.0**
9.9	0.19	1.0	0.26	**5.9**	0.78	0.89	7.69	3.61	77.3	**5.0**	57.4	5.4	**7.1**
7.6	0.67	4.6	0.33	**3.0**	0.18	0.29	3.65	3.32	88.0	**4.0**	9.3	1.4	**5.2**
5.8	1.17	5.9	0.00	**2.0**	0.00	0.00	0.00	6.78	116.7	**6.3**	45.1	0.0	**1.7**
7.7	0.45	2.7	0.00	**3.3**	0.00	0.33	4.02	2.02	100.0	**4.4**	8.9	0.0	**2.3**
3.6	2.02	15.4	0.00	**2.2**	0.00	-0.16	-1.94	9.28	102.1	**5.2**	27.2	0.0	**1.0**
9.4	0.00	0.0	1.99	**0.3**	0.00	-0.56	-5.13	3.53	90.0	**5.5**	65.4	5.4	**3.6**
4.4	1.29	10.3	-1.13	**6.5**	0.02	2.94	22.16	4.96	52.9	**2.9**	10.1	10.1	**3.7**
9.8	0.00	0.0	-0.30	**2.4**	0.01	0.19	1.42	3.18	94.6	**4.3**	48.7	12.7	**6.2**
10.0	0.34	1.7	0.08	**1.6**	0.02	0.15	1.84	2.73	95.4	**5.6**	32.7	0.8	**4.6**
5.7	1.84	6.2	1.63	**2.2**	0.00	-0.23	-1.31	5.03	87.5	**4.8**	21.0	0.0	**6.4**
8.4	0.54	2.8	0.09	**8.7**	0.49	1.14	7.75	3.35	73.7	**3.1**	25.3	9.7	**9.1**
7.2	0.55	3.4	0.34	**4.3**	0.07	0.48	4.77	4.33	87.2	**4.4**	25.3	2.3	**5.0**
9.6	0.08	0.5	0.00	**1.9**	0.01	0.37	4.42	3.48	91.9	**4.5**	22.1	3.5	**3.7**
3.5	3.41	18.8	-0.16	**2.6**	0.01	0.23	1.85	4.41	93.9	**5.3**	36.1	2.2	**6.2**
5.5	4.19	14.3	0.08	**6.3**	0.02	0.79	6.73	2.00	57.9	**4.7**	28.6	0.0	**5.0**
7.0	1.24	8.1	0.54	**5.2**	0.22	0.81	8.92	4.20	75.7	**4.7**	24.1	1.6	**6.1**
7.2	0.77	5.5	0.00	**0.6**	0.00	-0.35	-2.40	3.66	100.0	**4.3**	29.5	0.0	**5.4**
7.9	0.19	1.4	0.00	**2.0**	0.00	-0.09	-1.15	3.73	101.3	**4.6**	29.9	0.0	**1.7**
9.4	0.41	1.6	0.00	**0.0**	-0.02	-1.38	-11.67	3.98	136.0	**4.9**	21.4	5.3	**6.0**
9.5	0.38	0.9	1.11	**1.0**	-0.01	-0.27	-2.04	2.02	101.4	**4.9**	25.5	3.0	**6.1**
0.7	3.64	26.8	0.60	**2.8**	0.00	0.00	0.00	5.01	100.0	**1.9**	19.5	50.6	**5.8**
9.4	0.00	0.0	8.37	**1.4**	-0.01	-5.79	-26.42	4.77	275.0	**7.0**	45.7	0.0	**5.7**
7.7	0.15	0.7	0.00	**4.4**	0.01	0.39	3.49	6.57	86.6	**6.6**	46.7	0.0	**6.2**
9.8	1.28	2.1	0.54	**0.9**	0.00	0.05	0.40	2.05	98.1	**5.0**	19.2	0.8	**4.8**
9.5	1.35	1.6	0.17	**1.9**	0.04	0.52	3.68	1.95	88.7	**6.0**	57.6	0.0	**5.3**
8.0	2.95	6.7	0.00	**0.6**	0.00	0.11	0.69	2.82	96.8	**5.4**	34.1	0.0	**5.4**
8.7	0.65	2.0	0.71	**1.0**	0.00	-0.14	-1.57	3.07	90.9	**6.2**	70.9	0.0	**2.5**
7.2	0.34	4.3	0.40	**3.0**	0.03	0.10	1.29	3.85	96.1	**4.6**	20.0	0.1	**4.4**
9.4	0.30	1.0	0.95	**3.7**	0.13	0.28	1.90	3.75	82.8	**5.3**	32.6	2.7	**7.2**
8.2	0.34	3.8	0.31	**3.7**	0.22	0.53	6.30	4.33	83.3	**4.6**	25.5	2.7	**4.8**
10.0	0.28	0.6	0.00	**0.6**	-0.01	-0.22	-1.55	3.02	108.6	**5.6**	29.6	2.8	**5.8**
5.2	0.56	4.5	0.59	**6.1**	0.11	0.78	8.20	3.88	79.2	**3.2**	26.0	15.5	**5.2**
9.6	0.41	2.1	0.50	**4.3**	0.86	0.44	3.21	3.50	86.0	**4.2**	14.4	5.3	**8.5**
3.8	1.11	16.2	-0.02	**10.0**	0.18	3.01	33.07	6.29	61.2	**2.7**	14.0	10.5	**6.0**
7.6	0.37	5.4	0.42	**6.5**	0.53	1.24	15.22	3.46	74.9	**5.0**	22.8	0.2	**5.2**
10.0	0.48	0.9	0.28	**4.0**	0.38	0.70	5.05	3.29	79.7	**6.2**	62.1	5.8	**7.6**

Name	City	State	Rating	2016 Rating	2015 Rating	Total Assets ($Mil)	One Year Asset Growth	Asset Mix (As a % of Total Assets) Commercial Loans	Consumer Loans	Mortgage Loans	Securities	Capitalization Index	Net Worth Ratio
Pacific Service Credit Union	Concord	CA	B-	B-	B-	1176.9	2.86	1.0	21.2	13.4	45.3	10.0	13.1
Pacific Spruce Federal Credit Union	Toledo	OR	D-	D-	D-	3.4	6.74	0.0	32.1	0.0	0.0	4.8	6.8
Pacific Transportation FCU	Gardena	CA	C-	C-	C	62.5	-5.18	1.2	14.5	38.8	12.9	10.0	19.4
Pacoima Development Federal Credit Union	Pacoima	CA	E+	E+	E+	4.4	0.43	19.8	15.1	29.3	0.0	0.0	2.9
Paducah Teachers Federal Credit Union	Paducah	KY	C-	C-	D+	10.3	5.65	0.0	68.6	0.0	0.0	10.0	11.4
Pagoda Federal Credit Union	Reading	PA	D-	D-	D-	25.8	2.45	0.0	23.0	15.4	0.0	5.0	7.0
PAHO/WHO Federal Credit Union	Washington	DC	B	B	B-	213.5	4.61	0.6	10.1	41.9	30.4	10.0	18.5
Pahranagat Valley Federal Credit Union	Alamo	NV	C+	C+	C+	23.3	6.20	2.1	21.4	20.5	0.0	9.6	10.7
▲ Painesville Credit Union	Painesville	OH	B	B-	B-	28.5	6.11	3.0	34.4	14.9	14.0	10.0	11.9
▲ Pakco Employees Federal Credit Union	Latrobe	PA	C	C-	C	<1	5.17	0.0	59.3	0.0	0.0	10.0	21.1
Palace City Federal Credit Union	Mitchell	SD	C+	C+	C+	11.3	5.04	0.0	27.4	0.0	0.0	10.0	11.5
▼ PALCO Federal Credit Union	Muncy	PA	C	C+	C	79.8	5.59	0.0	15.9	8.3	47.8	9.5	10.9
▼ Palisades Federal Credit Union	Pearl River	NY	D+	C-	C	200.4	26.22	3.1	11.8	23.9	27.3	7.4	9.9
Palmetto Citizens Federal Credit Union	Columbia	SC	A	A	A-	775.9	7.93	0.9	24.1	22.0	22.8	10.0	11.0
Palmetto First Federal Credit Union	Florence	SC	B	B	B	41.3	9.09	0.0	36.9	7.4	16.0	10.0	13.5
Palmetto Health Credit Union	Columbia	SC	A-	A-	A-	72.8	11.94	0.2	40.3	4.7	10.5	10.0	13.4
▼ Palmetto Trust Federal Credit Union	Columbia	SC	D-	D	D	18.4	4.05	0.0	39.6	1.0	18.4	5.9	7.9
PamCel Community Federal Credit Union	Pampa	TX	D	D	D	13.7	-4.74	0.0	23.1	0.0	0.0	10.0	16.0
Pampa Municipal Credit Union	Pampa	TX	D-	D-	E+	3.5	0.37	0.0	70.6	0.0	0.0	5.8	7.8
Pampa Teachers Federal Credit Union	Pampa	TX	C-	C-	C-	14.4	7.48	0.0	60.1	8.7	0.0	8.6	10.1
Pan Amoco Federal Credit Union	Metairie	LA	D	D	D+	10.4	3.85	0.0	39.1	0.0	42.2	8.0	9.7
Panhandle Educators Federal Credit Union	Panama City	FL	A	A	A	172.1	7.76	8.6	19.0	24.1	10.0	10.0	12.7
Panhandle Federal Credit Union	Wellington	KS	B	B	B-	52.7	1.72	0.4	8.9	30.1	0.0	10.0	15.6
▼ Pannonia Federal Credit Union	Feasterville Trevose	PA	C-	C	C	11.4	-9.25	8.7	2.8	70.9	0.0	10.0	37.6
Pantex Federal Credit Union	Borger	TX	B-	B-	B	229.8	0.89	0.0	15.1	3.0	63.5	10.0	17.1
▼ Paper Converters Local 286/1034 FCU	Philadelphia	PA	D	D+	D+	1.5	0.48	0.0	52.8	0.0	15.4	6.6	8.6
Par-Del Employees Federal Credit Union	Wyoming	PA	C-	C-	C-	8.7	-1.34	0.0	21.4	0.0	42.3	10.0	11.1
▼ Paradise Valley Federal Credit Union	National City	CA	C	C+	B	85.9	-0.18	9.3	14.2	24.2	0.0	10.0	11.1
Paramount Baptist Church FCU	Washington	DC	B-	B-	B-	<1	21.70	0.0	32.6	0.0	0.0	10.0	27.1
Parda Federal Credit Union	Auburn Hills	MI	B-	B-	B-	183.0	2.56	2.7	25.9	13.5	28.7	10.0	13.6
Paris District Credit Union	Paris	TX	C-	C-	D+	<1	31.21	0.0	31.2	0.0	0.0	10.0	15.2
Paris Highway Credit Union	Paris	IL	C	C	C	9.7	7.24	0.0	63.2	0.0	25.1	10.0	12.6
Parish Federal Credit Union	Toledo	OH	C	C	C	16.3	4.11	0.6	31.6	8.7	0.0	8.8	10.2
Parish Members Credit Union	Metamora	IL	D	D	D-	3.8	-0.68	0.0	29.6	0.0	0.0	8.4	10.0
▼ Parishioners Federal Credit Union	Torrance	CA	D+	C-	D	42.2	5.06	0.0	15.7	10.2	36.9	4.8	8.8
Park City Credit Union	Merrill	WI	B-	B-	B-	177.0	6.77	8.6	14.3	38.6	9.5	8.0	9.9
Park Community Credit Union, Inc.	Louisville	KY	B-	B-	B	830.0	2.92	3.0	35.0	25.6	3.9	8.1	9.8
▼ Park Manor Christian Church Credit Union	Chicago	IL	D	D+	C-	1.1	15.82	0.0	15.7	0.0	0.0	6.6	8.6
▼ Park Side Credit Union	Whitefish	MT	C	C+	B-	221.5	6.83	2.5	34.1	33.4	8.3	9.1	10.5
Park View Federal Credit Union	Harrisonburg	VA	B	B	B-	161.7	9.34	22.8	9.7	39.3	6.6	6.8	8.8
▼ Parker Community Credit Union	Janesville	WI	C-	C	C-	124.9	2.70	3.4	31.8	37.8	10.6	5.7	7.8
Parks Heritage Federal Credit Union	Glens Falls	NY	D+	D+	C	30.1	5.31	0.0	26.2	25.4	18.0	10.0	11.2
Parkside Credit Union	Livonia	MI	A-	A-	A-	118.4	5.98	3.2	23.9	14.2	17.7	10.0	13.3
Parkview Community Federal Credit Union	McKeesport	PA	C	C	C	44.4	10.45	0.0	29.4	0.0	20.0	10.0	12.1
Parkway Federal Credit Union	Redford	MI	D-	D-	D-	24.9	-0.14	2.7	14.6	23.0	0.0	8.6	10.1
Parlin Dupont Employees FCU	Sayreville	NJ	E+	E+	D	5.4	17.82	0.0	32.3	0.0	0.1	5.6	7.6
Parsons Federal Credit Union	Pasadena	CA	B+	B+	B+	214.2	-3.58	6.9	9.4	19.0	36.8	10.0	12.9
Parthenon Federal Credit Union	Nashville	TN	C-	C-	D+	14.9	-1.47	0.0	35.1	13.0	0.0	10.0	15.3
▲ Partner Colorado Credit Union	Arvada	CO	A-	B+	B+	348.4	11.95	1.1	58.4	8.1	3.1	10.0	11.1
Partners 1st Federal Credit Union	Fort Wayne	IN	C-	C-	C-	290.3	6.52	2.0	27.9	9.8	7.2	9.1	10.4
Partners Federal Credit Union	Burbank	CA	A-	A-	A-	1594.9	9.23	3.9	43.3	29.3	2.2	10.0	11.3
Partners Financial Federal Credit Union	Glen Allen	VA	D+	D+	D-	81.8	-4.13	0.0	36.3	26.3	14.1	5.5	7.6
Partnership Federal Credit Union	Arlington	VA	C-	C-	C-	156.2	3.18	0.0	29.8	18.9	12.0	6.6	8.6
Partnership Financial Credit Union	Morton Grove	IL	C-	C-	C-	179.7	3.68	0.6	11.3	16.3	0.7	7.6	9.4
Pasadena Federal Credit Union	Pasadena	CA	D+	D+	D+	163.8	4.29	2.5	15.7	14.9	29.3	8.1	9.8
Pasadena Municipal Federal Credit Union	Pasadena	TX	C+	C+	B-	12.4	7.86	0.0	38.8	0.0	0.0	10.0	17.2
Pasadena Postal Credit Union	Pasadena	TX	C-	C-	C-	2.4	36.41	0.0	84.7	0.0	0.0	10.0	14.1
Pasadena Service Federal Credit Union	Pasadena	CA	B-	B-	B-	116.7	8.91	7.0	30.6	24.7	21.3	7.1	9.1
Passaic Police Federal Credit Union	Passaic	NJ	C+	C+	C+	5.9	12.57	0.0	30.7	0.0	0.0	10.0	14.7
Passaic Postal Employees Credit Union	Passaic	NJ	D	D	D+	<1	-9.82	0.0	45.3	0.0	0.0	10.0	16.5

Asset Quality Index	Non-Performing Loans as a % of Total Loans	Non-Performing Loans as a % of Capital	Net Charge-Offs Avg Loans	Profitability Index	Net Income ($Mil)	Return on Assets	Return on Equity	Net Interest Spread	Overhead Efficiency Ratio	Liquidity Index	Liquidity Ratio	Hot Money Ratio	Stability Index
10.0	0.08	0.3	0.07	**3.6**	0.94	0.32	2.46	2.47	82.5	**4.3**	26.5	9.6	**8.2**
8.5	0.00	0.0	0.00	**0.0**	-0.01	-0.96	-13.56	3.18	125.8	**6.5**	61.6	0.0	**3.1**
7.5	1.91	5.5	0.36	**1.1**	0.04	0.23	1.19	3.42	94.9	**4.0**	22.7	7.2	**5.3**
0.3	11.16	600.0	5.71	**0.0**	-0.15	-13.21	-939.68	5.66	172.7	**3.2**	28.4	18.8	**1.3**
3.7	1.45	9.4	0.70	**7.4**	0.04	1.50	13.16	4.37	66.4	**3.9**	21.3	0.0	**3.7**
7.5	0.48	3.8	0.44	**1.7**	0.00	0.06	0.89	3.53	97.8	**6.2**	41.2	0.0	**1.7**
9.7	0.46	2.0	0.07	**4.9**	0.49	0.92	5.15	2.88	67.9	**3.8**	45.9	20.4	**8.5**
9.5	0.00	0.0	0.13	**6.0**	0.07	1.15	10.72	3.65	71.9	**3.6**	27.1	11.5	**5.7**
7.9	0.98	4.3	0.15	**7.2**	0.09	1.33	11.07	4.22	83.5	**4.1**	27.5	6.0	**6.1**
8.3	0.39	1.1	0.00	**3.8**	0.00	0.47	2.22	2.93	100.0	**5.9**	51.3	0.0	**6.1**
9.8	0.18	0.5	0.00	**3.0**	0.01	0.39	3.40	3.10	87.8	**6.2**	43.8	2.9	**6.3**
9.3	0.50	1.3	0.68	**1.4**	-0.21	-1.07	-9.68	2.40	125.5	**5.8**	35.6	1.8	**5.2**
7.2	0.93	7.9	0.41	**1.2**	-0.10	-0.21	-2.32	3.31	94.2	**3.5**	4.6	5.3	**5.1**
7.6	0.79	6.0	0.63	**7.8**	2.11	1.11	10.02	3.26	71.6	**4.8**	25.9	4.4	**8.6**
7.1	1.04	6.6	1.34	**5.6**	0.06	0.63	4.56	5.87	74.2	**5.9**	33.4	3.0	**6.4**
9.4	0.49	2.8	0.48	**10.0**	0.37	2.10	15.54	4.58	71.7	**5.2**	31.0	8.0	**8.0**
5.3	2.45	12.4	0.35	**1.6**	0.00	-0.09	-1.09	4.78	104.9	**6.5**	39.8	0.7	**2.8**
10.0	0.56	1.2	-0.08	**0.3**	-0.01	-0.18	-1.10	2.71	108.1	**5.4**	22.7	0.0	**5.8**
2.8	1.54	14.4	0.53	**3.7**	0.00	0.23	2.88	5.07	80.0	**4.2**	16.3	0.0	**1.0**
2.8	2.32	16.7	0.57	**5.2**	0.02	0.64	6.41	4.05	78.7	**2.9**	35.4	31.1	**5.5**
8.8	0.11	0.5	0.00	**1.2**	0.00	0.16	1.60	3.20	96.2	**5.1**	25.2	0.0	**4.0**
8.9	0.40	2.9	0.53	**8.3**	0.42	0.99	7.77	4.04	70.7	**4.8**	30.6	10.2	**8.7**
9.9	0.89	2.3	-0.02	**3.8**	0.07	0.50	3.17	2.13	78.8	**5.6**	58.1	3.9	**7.8**
9.4	1.23	2.4	0.00	**1.1**	-0.01	-0.39	-1.02	3.78	113.1	**4.8**	27.4	0.0	**6.8**
10.0	0.34	0.8	0.21	**2.9**	0.15	0.27	1.50	2.01	87.1	**5.5**	44.8	7.1	**8.0**
4.1	1.69	8.2	0.00	**2.1**	0.00	0.00	0.00	7.75	100.0	**6.0**	35.4	0.0	**1.0**
9.7	1.32	3.0	0.00	**2.6**	0.01	0.41	3.76	2.52	83.7	**6.4**	37.7	0.0	**5.3**
4.9	3.99	15.4	0.49	**1.7**	-0.01	-0.06	-0.53	2.72	98.3	**4.0**	48.5	27.4	**4.5**
7.1	7.14	8.3	0.00	**10.0**	0.00	3.23	11.11	6.45	0.0	**7.7**	88.3	0.0	**5.7**
8.1	1.32	4.7	0.53	**3.4**	0.18	0.39	2.91	3.87	86.5	**4.9**	18.1	1.1	**7.4**
9.8	0.00	0.0	0.00	**1.6**	0.00	-0.66	-4.40	4.61	125.0	**7.3**	72.6	0.0	**6.1**
8.3	0.01	0.1	0.06	**6.2**	0.03	1.38	10.92	3.27	56.6	**4.3**	41.4	0.0	**4.3**
7.9	0.29	2.5	0.38	**3.5**	0.02	0.42	4.11	3.27	89.9	**4.6**	25.3	1.9	**5.8**
6.1	1.11	3.2	1.02	**3.0**	0.00	0.32	3.19	2.92	84.0	**5.5**	25.8	0.0	**3.0**
10.0	0.11	0.5	0.00	**2.7**	0.04	0.42	6.07	2.86	87.5	**4.8**	16.7	1.7	**3.0**
6.0	0.94	7.0	0.01	**4.0**	0.22	0.51	5.22	3.94	87.1	**4.3**	12.2	0.6	**6.5**
7.2	0.32	4.7	0.36	**4.5**	1.49	0.73	8.20	3.34	81.2	**3.0**	6.9	7.2	**6.6**
6.5	3.55	7.5	0.00	**0.3**	0.00	-0.38	-4.40	2.66	125.0	**7.7**	67.3	0.0	**2.9**
7.5	0.51	4.6	0.46	**2.5**	0.02	0.03	0.28	4.09	90.9	**2.6**	8.4	12.6	**6.2**
7.7	0.29	3.1	0.02	**6.3**	0.41	1.02	11.78	4.07	74.4	**3.7**	16.6	7.0	**6.2**
6.9	0.54	6.4	0.27	**1.9**	-0.08	-0.25	-3.67	3.10	97.2	**3.0**	9.9	7.1	**3.3**
7.8	0.87	4.6	0.09	**1.1**	-0.01	-0.19	-1.67	4.15	102.6	**4.4**	20.4	6.9	**5.5**
9.7	0.50	1.5	0.41	**5.1**	0.22	0.75	5.55	3.72	84.6	**5.2**	32.4	2.1	**8.3**
9.7	0.32	1.2	0.34	**2.7**	0.04	0.41	3.30	3.44	87.5	**5.3**	30.9	0.0	**6.0**
6.3	2.78	10.2	-0.51	**0.0**	-0.06	-0.95	-9.08	3.10	127.3	**6.2**	60.9	1.7	**4.8**
5.8	0.69	9.6	4.14	**1.7**	0.00	0.23	2.93	5.00	93.0	**5.8**	32.4	0.0	**1.0**
10.0	0.03	0.2	0.06	**3.6**	0.21	0.39	3.05	2.41	85.6	**4.1**	24.7	7.3	**7.9**
9.9	0.04	0.1	0.22	**1.8**	0.00	0.08	0.53	3.13	96.9	**5.2**	28.7	1.8	**6.3**
7.1	0.56	3.7	0.47	**5.5**	1.31	1.57	13.80	3.51	73.3	**4.2**	23.9	8.8	**7.0**
9.9	0.30	1.2	0.68	**2.0**	0.09	0.12	1.13	3.10	91.3	**5.1**	26.0	0.7	**5.7**
7.1	0.82	6.7	0.65	**7.2**	3.84	0.98	8.62	4.03	72.5	**2.7**	10.5	12.1	**7.9**
5.6	1.32	11.4	0.31	**0.7**	-0.06	-0.27	-3.66	3.49	103.4	**4.2**	16.6	3.0	**2.7**
8.3	0.45	2.9	0.47	**2.0**	0.01	0.03	0.33	3.42	86.3	**4.5**	22.6	2.3	**4.8**
8.2	0.92	4.7	0.19	**2.5**	0.10	0.23	2.48	2.21	90.7	**5.1**	42.1	3.1	**5.4**
9.8	0.11	0.5	0.57	**1.2**	-0.08	-0.20	-2.02	2.56	96.2	**4.3**	25.2	10.0	**5.6**
9.8	0.00	0.0	0.16	**3.6**	0.02	0.66	3.76	2.20	70.2	**5.8**	43.7	0.0	**7.4**
6.7	0.20	1.2	0.00	**10.0**	0.01	2.29	15.85	8.45	70.5	**1.8**	14.8	30.4	**5.0**
9.1	0.38	2.5	0.30	**4.4**	0.14	0.50	5.34	4.06	86.8	**4.4**	26.4	3.8	**5.5**
8.6	1.26	2.6	2.15	**7.6**	0.01	0.82	5.55	1.56	42.9	**4.9**	33.0	0.0	**5.0**
4.8	3.42	9.2	9.76	**0.0**	0.00	-1.54	-9.30	5.21	133.3	**5.2**	28.4	0.0	**5.0**

Name	City	State	Rating	2016 Rating	2015 Rating	Total Assets ($Mil)	One Year Asset Growth	Asset Mix (As a % of Total Assets) Comm-ercial Loans	Cons-umer Loans	Mort-gage Loans	Secur-ities	Capital-ization Index	Net Worth Ratio
PATA Federal Credit Union	Pittsburgh	PA	**E+**	E+	E+	3.2	3.68	0.0	63.1	0.0	0.0	**5.0**	7.0
Patelco Credit Union	Pleasanton	CA	**A-**	A-	A	5681.6	12.18	7.2	19.0	39.6	24.1	**9.6**	10.8
Patent and Trademark Office FCU	Alexandria	VA	**D-**	D-	D	42.7	3.38	0.8	25.6	7.9	20.7	**4.3**	6.3
Paterson Police Federal Credit Union	Paterson	NJ	**C+**	C+	C+	5.3	2.62	0.0	25.7	0.0	0.0	**10.0**	16.1
Path Federal Credit Union	Jersey City	NJ	**B**	B	B	11.6	0.91	0.0	42.6	0.9	0.0	**10.0**	36.2
Pathway Credit Union	Cleveland	TN	**D-**	D-	D-	5.3	10.99	0.0	39.8	1.0	0.0	**7.9**	9.6
▲ Pathways Financial Credit Union, Inc.	Columbus	OH	**C**	C-	D	246.6	7.53	5.1	32.9	28.2	5.3	**8.0**	9.7
Patriot Credit Union	Saint Louis	MO	**D-**	D-	D-	9.5	5.08	0.0	44.0	0.0	0.0	**5.0**	7.0
Patriot Equity Credit Union	Jackson	TN	**D+**	D+	D	27.5	14.88	0.0	44.6	13.7	0.0	**10.0**	12.8
Patriot Federal Credit Union	Chambersburg	PA	**B**	B	B	580.5	7.53	1.6	38.3	19.9	17.3	**10.0**	12.7
Patterson Federal Credit Union	Arkadelphia	AR	**C-**	C-	C-	18.9	7.03	0.0	59.4	2.5	0.0	**8.3**	9.9
Patterson Pump Federal Credit Union	Toccoa	GA	**C**	C	C+	2.6	-1.09	0.0	26.7	0.0	0.0	**10.0**	16.8
▲ Paul Quinn Federal Credit Union	Jamaica	NY	**C-**	D+	D	<1	4.55	0.0	14.6	0.0	0.0	**10.0**	24.5
Pawtucket Credit Union	Pawtucket	RI	**B+**	B+	B+	2003.7	9.05	5.8	19.3	59.1	4.5	**7.6**	9.4
Pawtucket Municipal Employees FCU	Pawtucket	RI	**C**	C	C	4.2	0.36	0.0	62.1	0.0	15.5	**10.0**	14.5
PBA Federal Credit Union	Pine Bluff	AR	**C-**	C-	C-	10.1	-5.91	0.0	30.8	0.0	0.0	**10.0**	31.7
PCM Credit Union	Green Bay	WI	**A**	A	A	227.1	13.27	0.8	14.3	56.1	3.6	**10.0**	14.0
Peabody Municipal Federal Credit Union	Peabody	MA	**B-**	B-	C+	26.7	2.67	0.0	20.4	0.0	2.8	**10.0**	11.2
▲ Peach State Federal Credit Union	Lawrenceville	GA	**B**	B-	B-	355.6	14.22	14.9	23.4	26.4	10.1	**5.9**	8.1
▲ Pear Orchard Federal Credit Union	Beaumont	TX	**C-**	D+	D	<1	-5.10	0.0	66.1	0.0	0.0	**10.0**	19.7
Pearl Hawaii Federal Credit Union	Waipahu	HI	**C-**	C-	C-	346.2	1.38	2.2	19.3	14.2	49.0	**7.0**	9.7
Pearl Municipal Federal Credit Union	Pearl	MS	**B-**	B-	C+	1.3	11.17	0.0	42.4	0.0	0.0	**10.0**	17.2
Peco Federal Credit Union	Mineral Wells	TX	**D-**	D-	D-	5.0	-3.14	0.0	29.5	0.0	0.0	**6.3**	8.3
Pee Dee Federal Credit Union	Florence	SC	**A-**	A-	A-	29.2	5.50	0.0	44.5	18.4	0.0	**10.0**	17.6
Pelican State Credit Union	Baton Rouge	LA	**B+**	B+	B	308.3	14.64	2.7	44.1	16.1	2.6	**8.4**	10.0
Pen Air Federal Credit Union	Pensacola	FL	**A-**	A-	A-	1390.5	5.59	3.0	32.9	16.7	30.8	**10.0**	12.4
▲ Peninsula Community Federal Credit Union	Shelton	WA	**B**	B-	C	175.5	4.80	0.0	54.6	11.4	5.7	**6.2**	8.2
Peninsula Federal Credit Union	Escanaba	MI	**B-**	B-	B-	146.5	11.37	0.5	24.8	46.1	0.0	**10.0**	11.1
Peninsula General Hospital & Medical Ctr FCU	Salisbury	MD	**C-**	C-	C	3.3	8.41	0.0	45.9	0.0	0.0	**10.0**	20.9
Penlanco Federal Credit Union	Lancaster	PA	**C**	C	C	24.9	6.12	0.0	17.2	7.6	0.0	**10.0**	11.3
▼ Penn East Federal Credit Union	Scranton	PA	**C**	C+	C	170.4	15.54	8.3	33.2	1.8	10.7	**10.0**	11.6
Penn Hills Municipal FCU	Pittsburgh	PA	**B-**	B-	C+	2.3	-3.73	0.0	42.7	0.0	0.0	**10.0**	15.9
Penn South Cooperative FCU	New York	NY	**C-**	C-	D+	8.1	18.38	0.0	2.3	88.1	0.0	**8.1**	9.7
Penn State Federal Credit Union	Bellefonte	PA	**C-**	C-	C-	179.5	7.40	9.3	18.1	10.6	26.9	**5.8**	7.9
Penn Wilco Federal Credit Union	Wilkes-Barre	PA	**C**	C	C	12.3	-2.92	0.0	3.6	6.8	59.8	**10.0**	12.6
Penn-Trafford School Employees FCU	Trafford	PA	**C**	C	D+	4.7	1.42	0.8	44.6	0.0	0.0	**10.0**	11.4
Pennformer Community FCU	Canonsburg	PA	**D**	D	D	6.3	-4.18	0.0	20.7	0.0	0.0	**10.0**	23.3
▼ Pennington Municipal & County Empls CU	Thief River Falls	MN	**D+**	C-	C-	1.7	8.88	0.0	39.8	0.0	0.0	**9.6**	10.8
▼ Pennstar Federal Credit Union	Hermitage	PA	**C+**	B-	B-	42.3	2.58	0.0	24.4	8.2	1.9	**10.0**	16.5
Pennsylvania Central FCU	Harrisburg	PA	**D**	D	D	70.9	-7.84	0.0	60.7	10.6	2.1	**6.2**	8.2
Pennsylvania State Employees CU	Harrisburg	PA	**A-**	A-	B+	5009.9	8.78	0.6	44.9	19.6	6.7	**9.2**	10.5
Pennsylvania-American Water FCU	Bethel Park	PA	**D+**	D+	D	14.8	2.05	0.0	43.8	0.8	0.0	**6.9**	8.9
▼ PennTech Employees Federal Credit Union	Johnsonburg	PA	**D+**	C-	C-	11.1	2.61	0.0	38.0	0.0	14.0	**9.9**	11.0
Penobscot County Federal Credit Union	Old Town	ME	**C+**	C+	B-	69.8	21.76	3.7	38.1	24.0	0.0	**7.1**	9.1
Pensacola L&N Federal Credit Union	Pensacola	FL	**C**	C	C	8.2	0.77	0.0	60.1	0.2	0.0	**10.0**	17.7
Pentagon Federal Credit Union	Tysons	VA	**B+**	B+	B+	22400.5	12.45	0.2	23.3	51.6	6.0	**8.1**	9.9
People Driven Credit Union	Southfield	MI	**C**	C	C	260.7	4.89	3.1	35.8	15.4	22.4	**6.8**	9.0
▼ People First Federal Credit Union	Allentown	PA	**C-**	C	C-	564.1	10.45	5.6	32.3	17.1	28.6	**4.5**	7.4
People's Alliance Federal Credit Union	Hauppauge	NY	**C+**	C+	C+	263.1	3.67	11.5	36.1	15.3	17.2	**7.0**	9.0
People's Choice Federal Credit Union	Duryea	PA	**E+**	E+	E+	6.6	-18.45	0.0	34.4	0.0	25.6	**2.5**	4.8
People's Community Federal Credit Union	Vancouver	WA	**B**	B	B	206.9	5.76	16.8	4.6	27.9	29.9	**10.0**	11.4
People's Credit Union	Rayne	LA	**C**	C	C	25.5	-0.08	0.0	17.0	9.0	0.0	**10.0**	17.1
People's Credit Union	Middletown	RI	**B-**	B-	C+	468.3	6.90	10.4	22.5	53.9	4.7	**9.0**	10.4
People's Federal Credit Union	Amarillo	TX	**C**	C	C	181.3	2.63	0.0	41.8	1.3	28.5	**6.2**	8.2
People's First Federal Credit Union	Birmingham	AL	**D**	D	D+	4.2	-12.70	1.6	24.1	42.0	0.0	**10.0**	11.0
People's Trust Federal Credit Union	Houston	TX	**C+**	C+	B-	546.8	-0.90	11.8	34.4	17.7	12.8	**6.0**	8.1
Peoples Advantage Federal Credit Union	Petersburg	VA	**B-**	B-	C+	73.7	2.08	0.0	44.6	1.0	32.4	**10.0**	12.0
Peoples Choice Credit Union	Coffeyville	KS	**C**	C	C	7.4	-1.70	0.0	25.9	0.0	5.2	**10.0**	22.0
▼ Peoples Choice Credit Union	Medford	WI	**D**	D+	C-	31.5	3.04	8.6	25.8	37.3	12.5	**6.8**	8.9
Peoples Community Credit Union	Hopkins	MN	**C**	C	C	21.7	7.39	0.0	30.9	0.0	0.0	**10.0**	20.9

Asset Quality Index	Non-Performing Loans as a % of Total Loans	Non-Performing Loans as a % of Capital	Net Charge-Offs Avg Loans	Profitability Index	Net Income ($Mil)	Return on Assets	Return on Equity	Net Interest Spread	Overhead Efficiency Ratio	Liquidity Index	Liquidity Ratio	Hot Money Ratio	Stability Index
5.9	0.47	4.1	2.21	**2.9**	0.00	0.13	1.75	6.98	88.6	**5.7**	32.1	0.0	**1.0**
9.0	0.44	3.1	0.19	**5.6**	13.80	0.99	9.46	2.61	65.3	**3.9**	23.3	8.0	**9.3**
7.0	0.53	3.6	0.02	**1.9**	-0.01	-0.05	-0.74	3.02	91.3	**5.1**	22.5	0.0	**1.7**
10.0	0.92	1.5	0.00	**5.8**	0.02	1.15	7.09	3.34	61.5	**5.4**	23.2	0.0	**5.0**
8.8	2.95	4.0	1.61	**9.4**	0.04	1.21	3.35	5.30	65.2	**4.5**	29.3	0.0	**6.3**
6.3	0.80	3.6	-0.34	**1.0**	0.00	0.08	0.79	3.11	111.4	**5.5**	41.5	0.0	**3.6**
9.0	0.28	2.5	0.10	**3.2**	0.19	0.32	3.23	2.94	90.2	**4.1**	16.9	3.3	**6.1**
6.1	0.61	5.9	0.06	**1.9**	0.00	0.00	0.00	3.10	93.8	**4.8**	31.4	0.0	**1.0**
8.3	0.97	5.4	0.60	**0.7**	-0.02	-0.33	-2.50	3.76	93.8	**4.5**	26.4	2.7	**5.7**
8.3	0.58	3.6	0.54	**4.2**	0.95	0.67	6.02	3.45	77.6	**3.4**	18.6	8.4	**8.5**
4.1	1.30	10.7	0.32	**4.7**	0.03	0.71	7.14	4.35	86.5	**3.9**	21.5	4.3	**3.7**
8.6	1.74	2.9	1.54	**1.9**	0.00	-0.62	-3.71	3.41	110.5	**5.8**	37.4	0.0	**7.2**
10.0	0.00	0.0	0.00	**3.6**	0.00	1.26	5.06	3.11	100.0	**7.1**	66.0	0.0	**5.0**
9.6	0.06	1.2	0.18	**4.9**	3.21	0.65	6.88	2.26	68.8	**1.3**	7.5	24.2	**7.5**
8.2	0.72	3.0	0.00	**2.4**	0.00	0.00	0.00	4.83	95.6	**5.3**	41.8	0.0	**6.5**
9.9	1.48	1.6	0.00	**1.1**	-0.01	-0.32	-1.00	2.31	113.3	**5.3**	41.9	0.0	**6.3**
9.7	0.40	2.3	0.06	**6.4**	0.42	0.75	5.27	3.26	75.7	**3.4**	14.6	5.7	**9.3**
9.5	1.71	3.2	-0.07	**2.8**	0.01	0.18	1.61	2.76	84.5	**5.5**	29.8	6.3	**5.3**
6.6	0.93	8.1	0.58	**6.7**	2.63	3.05	38.46	5.76	59.8	**5.2**	27.1	2.1	**4.9**
4.5	3.94	13.0	0.00	**5.3**	0.00	0.89	4.65	6.43	80.0	**5.7**	37.8	0.0	**3.7**
10.0	0.32	1.6	0.82	**2.7**	0.30	0.34	3.84	2.83	77.0	**4.2**	15.8	5.3	**4.9**
9.5	0.16	0.4	0.61	**7.7**	0.00	0.63	3.64	6.35	80.0	**5.0**	61.5	14.0	**5.7**
3.0	6.59	27.7	1.62	**1.1**	0.00	0.16	1.93	5.25	96.6	**5.4**	31.6	0.0	**1.0**
9.6	0.03	0.1	0.23	**10.0**	0.16	2.27	12.82	5.91	66.4	**5.1**	31.0	1.3	**8.0**
5.9	1.11	8.5	2.45	**8.8**	1.60	2.11	21.39	6.76	67.6	**3.7**	15.2	6.4	**6.8**
9.0	0.54	3.0	0.76	**6.1**	3.60	1.05	8.64	3.34	67.3	**3.7**	23.9	13.2	**8.2**
8.3	0.25	2.4	0.33	**5.2**	0.41	0.95	11.64	3.47	75.5	**3.3**	7.2	2.3	**5.4**
8.0	0.52	4.0	0.16	**3.6**	0.13	0.36	3.22	3.64	84.9	**2.6**	13.1	13.1	**7.3**
4.2	6.06	12.0	8.89	**3.4**	0.00	-0.38	-1.75	8.74	46.5	**7.1**	70.3	0.0	**6.9**
10.0	0.04	0.1	0.00	**2.3**	0.02	0.29	2.57	1.20	73.1	**6.3**	50.4	0.1	**5.5**
7.1	1.20	7.1	0.24	**1.9**	-0.01	-0.02	-0.18	4.07	96.2	**4.6**	16.2	1.9	**6.2**
9.0	0.00	0.0	0.00	**9.0**	0.01	2.28	14.61	5.56	40.0	**6.2**	45.8	0.0	**5.7**
4.8	1.34	9.9	0.00	**9.8**	0.03	1.61	16.58	4.27	63.6	**3.7**	22.8	0.0	**4.3**
8.5	0.63	3.3	0.10	**3.1**	0.24	0.54	6.94	2.96	82.4	**5.1**	25.5	0.3	**4.6**
9.9	2.32	2.1	0.00	**2.4**	0.01	0.20	1.56	1.40	83.8	**6.8**	46.9	0.0	**5.9**
9.7	0.33	1.4	0.00	**3.9**	0.01	0.51	4.51	3.67	76.7	**6.4**	48.4	0.0	**5.8**
10.0	0.00	0.0	0.00	**0.0**	-0.03	-1.58	-6.72	2.64	163.2	**6.1**	42.8	0.0	**6.1**
9.2	0.00	0.0	0.00	**1.6**	0.00	0.00	0.00	4.23	100.0	**6.1**	39.4	0.0	**6.1**
9.1	1.44	3.1	0.08	**2.3**	0.01	0.05	0.29	2.13	92.6	**5.0**	23.0	0.9	**7.4**
5.9	0.35	3.1	0.13	**1.1**	0.00	0.02	0.19	3.44	99.4	**4.0**	13.8	1.8	**3.3**
8.2	0.54	3.6	0.80	**6.6**	12.79	1.04	9.82	4.24	64.1	**5.0**	30.9	5.3	**7.9**
6.5	1.28	6.4	0.00	**2.1**	0.01	0.16	1.83	3.61	89.7	**5.3**	31.0	0.0	**4.4**
8.3	0.63	2.2	0.74	**1.4**	0.00	-0.14	-1.31	2.35	101.6	**5.5**	55.8	5.7	**5.7**
5.4	0.59	9.1	0.18	**4.2**	0.10	0.56	7.10	5.14	87.6	**2.1**	20.0	20.8	**3.6**
6.2	1.43	5.1	0.44	**3.2**	0.00	0.05	0.28	5.99	92.2	**4.9**	32.6	5.6	**7.5**
9.0	0.37	3.5	0.44	**5.5**	42.12	0.77	7.95	2.39	55.6	**1.2**	4.2	26.1	**8.0**
7.3	0.57	6.6	0.66	**2.5**	0.08	0.13	1.53	3.85	91.2	**4.6**	19.6	2.3	**4.6**
7.2	0.63	5.8	0.49	**2.1**	0.06	0.04	0.66	3.63	91.6	**4.7**	25.7	5.2	**3.4**
6.2	1.33	10.9	1.31	**2.7**	0.04	0.07	0.97	3.95	84.1	**3.9**	22.0	7.2	**4.3**
0.3	5.46	55.9	6.69	**0.0**	-0.07	-4.10	-76.62	3.86	104.2	**4.9**	25.4	0.0	**0.3**
9.8	0.08	0.3	-0.07	**3.7**	0.19	0.37	3.27	2.88	85.9	**6.7**	40.1	1.9	**7.8**
9.4	1.18	2.7	0.95	**1.9**	0.01	0.13	0.73	2.23	86.1	**5.1**	29.8	0.0	**6.3**
8.0	0.33	3.3	0.86	**3.9**	0.85	0.73	8.07	3.49	72.3	**2.8**	8.8	9.9	**6.2**
7.3	0.80	6.0	0.53	**2.6**	0.08	0.18	2.16	2.94	89.7	**4.9**	22.7	3.7	**4.9**
7.6	1.24	7.8	-0.13	**0.0**	-0.02	-1.47	-12.85	4.78	132.6	**4.1**	23.7	10.4	**4.6**
8.1	0.49	3.8	0.96	**3.0**	0.40	0.31	3.71	3.53	72.3	**4.6**	17.5	2.9	**4.9**
6.8	1.26	6.9	2.10	**3.7**	0.00	0.01	0.13	5.74	77.7	**4.6**	25.4	5.5	**4.1**
9.5	0.35	0.4	1.97	**2.2**	0.00	-0.16	-0.74	3.53	82.4	**5.2**	19.3	0.0	**6.1**
5.7	1.07	8.3	-0.02	**0.8**	-0.02	-0.27	-3.00	3.31	108.6	**3.1**	19.5	11.4	**3.6**
8.0	0.81	3.1	0.35	**4.2**	0.04	0.65	3.10	5.75	86.8	**2.5**	6.6	11.6	**6.6**

Name	City	State	Rating	2016 Rating	2015 Rating	Total Assets ($Mil)	One Year Asset Growth	Asset Mix (As a % of Total Assets): Commercial Loans	Consumer Loans	Mortgage Loans	Securities	Capitalization Index	Net Worth Ratio
Peoples Credit Union	Springfield	CO	**B+**	B+	B	50.0	17.68	52.6	10.6	37.9	0.0	**10.0**	16.5
Peoples Credit Union	Webster City	IA	**B**	B	B-	52.0	64.51	0.6	30.4	6.1	18.5	**10.0**	13.6
Peoples Energy Credit Union	Chicago	IL	**C+**	C+	B-	35.6	0.53	0.0	23.0	0.0	0.0	**10.0**	13.7
Peoples Federal Credit Union	Nitro	WV	**D+**	D+	C-	92.0	4.05	4.0	38.8	18.8	0.8	**6.6**	8.7
▲ Peoples Independent Church FCU	Los Angeles	CA	**D+**	D	D	<1	-4.55	0.0	11.9	0.0	0.0	**6.3**	8.3
Peoples Natural Gas General Office Empls FCU	Pittsburgh	PA	**C**	C	C-	2.5	-9.18	0.0	14.5	0.0	0.0	**10.0**	19.9
▼ Peoples Transport Federal Credit Union	Mount Ephraim	NJ	**C-**	C	C	10.8	12.14	0.0	48.2	0.0	0.0	**9.0**	10.3
▼ Peoples-Neighborhood FCU	Washington	DC	**C**	C+	C+	<1	-7.23	0.0	0.7	0.0	0.0	**6.4**	8.4
PeoplesChoice Credit Union	Saco	ME	**C+**	C+	C	186.4	6.09	4.5	29.6	43.0	0.6	**6.4**	8.4
Peoria Bell Credit Union	Peoria	IL	**D+**	D+	C-	8.3	-2.33	0.0	44.5	0.0	0.0	**10.0**	32.2
Peoria City Employees Credit Union	Peoria	IL	**C-**	C-	C-	5.7	8.19	0.0	35.9	0.5	0.0	**10.0**	18.2
Peoria Fire Fighters Credit Union	Peoria	IL	**C+**	C+	C+	4.9	10.35	0.0	46.8	0.0	0.0	**10.0**	18.8
▼ Peoria Hiway Credit Union	Peoria	IL	**D+**	C-	C	3.3	4.73	0.0	68.3	0.0	0.0	**9.3**	10.5
Peoria Postal Employees Credit Union	Peoria	IL	**C+**	C+	C-	10.8	-1.53	0.0	50.3	0.0	8.3	**10.0**	22.1
Pepco Federal Credit Union	Washington	DC	**D+**	D+	D+	33.1	1.14	0.0	22.8	0.0	0.0	**7.8**	9.6
▼ Perfect Circle Credit Union	Hagerstown	IN	**C-**	C	C-	55.4	3.82	0.7	33.3	13.9	17.1	**8.3**	10.1
Peru Federal Credit Union	Peru	NY	**B-**	B-	B	17.7	1.07	0.0	28.3	18.9	0.0	**10.0**	15.7
Peru Municipal Credit Union	Peru	IL	**C-**	C-	D+	<1	-2.93	0.0	86.9	0.0	0.0	**10.0**	13.1
Petersburg Federal Reformatory Credit Union Inc	Hopewell	VA	**C+**	C+	C+	4.2	5.54	0.0	50.5	0.0	0.0	**10.0**	23.3
PFD Firefighters Credit Union Incorporated	Portsmouth	VA	**B+**	B+	B	27.2	4.96	0.9	49.7	22.8	0.0	**10.0**	13.6
PHB Employees Federal Credit Union	Fairview	PA	**C+**	C+	C+	7.0	16.75	0.0	31.1	0.0	0.0	**10.0**	16.6
Phenix Pride Federal Credit Union	Phenix City	AL	**C**	C	C-	9.2	4.99	0.0	70.0	2.7	0.0	**9.1**	10.4
▼ Phi Beta Sigma Federal Credit Union	Washington	DC	**D**	D+	D+	<1	1.14	0.0	53.1	0.0	0.0	**4.3**	6.3
Philadelphia Federal Credit Union	Philadelphia	PA	**A-**	A-	A-	1091.7	7.61	16.9	17.6	25.8	13.8	**10.0**	12.8
Philadelphia Gas Works Employees FCU	Philadelphia	PA	**D-**	D-	D	18.7	4.26	0.0	22.8	0.0	0.0	**4.1**	6.1
Philadelphia Letter Carriers FCU	Philadelphia	PA	**C**	C	D+	6.0	8.21	0.0	45.1	11.2	0.0	**10.0**	14.3
Philadelphia Mint Federal Credit Union	Philadelphia	PA	**D**	D	D	<1	-13.65	0.0	23.6	0.0	0.0	**10.0**	11.7
Philadelphia Post Office Employees CU	Yeadon	PA	**C-**	C-	C	2.6	-0.74	0.0	16.4	0.0	31.3	**10.0**	40.9
Picatinny Federal Credit Union	Dover	NJ	**C**	C	C+	339.7	5.68	0.4	10.8	18.0	40.3	**5.9**	8.1
Pickens Federal Credit Union	Pickens	SC	**B-**	B-	B-	22.3	8.33	10.8	15.6	12.3	0.0	**10.0**	14.7
Piedmont Advantage Credit Union	Winston-Salem	NC	**C+**	C+	C	348.3	6.05	0.0	53.6	18.0	2.0	**8.2**	9.8
Piedmont Credit Union	Statesville	NC	**D+**	D+	D+	4.6	-4.06	0.0	65.7	0.0	0.0	**10.0**	13.4
Piedmont Credit Union	Danville	VA	**D**	D	D+	63.9	8.85	0.7	44.0	4.8	2.0	**5.4**	7.4
▼ Piedmont Plus Federal Credit Union	Atlanta	GA	**D+**	C-	C+	32.7	-2.45	0.0	42.8	0.0	0.0	**10.0**	13.0
Pike Teachers Credit Union	Troy	AL	**C-**	C-	C-	7.9	-1.03	0.0	26.2	0.0	0.0	**10.0**	14.8
Pikes Peak Credit Union	Colorado Springs	CO	**B-**	B-	C+	84.9	8.93	0.8	60.2	13.3	0.5	**7.7**	9.5
Pilgrim Baptist Credit Union	Chicago	IL	**C-**	C-	C-	<1	-0.24	0.0	5.7	0.0	5.7	**10.0**	15.0
Pilgrim CUCC Federal Credit Union	Houston	TX	**D+**	D+	D-	1.1	-8.71	0.0	56.3	0.0	0.0	**8.8**	10.2
Pima Federal Credit Union	Tucson	AZ	**B+**	B+	B+	513.1	9.55	0.0	39.0	11.7	26.9	**8.4**	10.1
Pinal County Federal Credit Union	Casa Grande	AZ	**C+**	C+	C+	137.3	8.16	4.1	54.6	4.1	6.3	**5.0**	7.2
Pine Belt Federal Credit Union	Hattiesburg	MS	**B**	B	B	11.1	8.67	0.4	45.7	6.3	0.0	**10.0**	30.9
Pine Bluff Cotton Belt FCU	Pine Bluff	AR	**D+**	D+	D+	63.2	-3.47	0.5	26.0	27.9	0.0	**10.0**	12.3
▼ Pine Bluff Postal Federal Credit Union	Pine Bluff	AR	**D+**	C-	C	<1	-7.19	0.0	58.4	0.0	0.0	**10.0**	27.7
Pine Federal Credit Union	Pine Bluff	AR	**B+**	B+	B+	40.9	2.21	0.0	47.2	6.4	0.0	**10.0**	23.8
Pine Tree Community Credit Union	Grangeville	ID	**B-**	B-	B-	44.2	4.67	0.9	31.4	26.4	0.0	**9.5**	10.7
▼ Pinellas Federal Credit Union	Largo	FL	**C+**	B	B+	120.5	6.45	0.0	30.8	0.2	0.0	**10.0**	14.0
▼ Piney Hills Federal Credit Union	Simsboro	LA	**D+**	C-	C-	3.6	-4.53	0.0	49.2	1.4	0.0	**10.0**	15.7
▼ Pinn Memorial Federal Credit Union	Philadelphia	PA	**C**	C+	C+	<1	1.18	0.0	5.1	0.0	0.0	**10.0**	12.8
Pinnacle Credit Union	Atlanta	GA	**C-**	C-	D+	75.7	2.32	4.8	27.6	15.3	37.6	**4.9**	7.4
Pinnacle Federal Credit Union	Edison	NJ	**D-**	D-	D+	139.6	-7.00	36.0	14.6	16.6	0.0	**4.2**	6.3
Pinpoint Federal Credit Union	Milton	PA	**C+**	C+	C+	19.2	2.82	0.0	29.2	29.1	10.5	**10.0**	11.0
▲ Pioneer Community Federal Credit Union	Palisade	NE	**C-**	D+	D	3.1	-6.78	0.0	61.5	1.4	0.0	**9.9**	10.9
Pioneer Federal Credit Union	Mountain Home	ID	**B**	B	B	441.6	9.72	2.4	53.8	10.3	7.1	**6.7**	8.9
Pioneer Mutual Federal Credit Union	Sugar Land	TX	**A+**	A+	A+	133.8	6.29	3.6	34.3	16.7	0.0	**10.0**	15.5
Pioneer Valley Federal Credit Union	Springfield	MA	**B+**	B+	B+	66.6	2.65	0.0	35.8	26.4	0.0	**10.0**	11.3
Pioneer West Virginia FCU	Charleston	WV	**B-**	B-	B-	200.3	4.25	0.1	34.8	39.8	2.0	**8.1**	9.8
Pipefitters-Steamfitters Credit Union	Woodbury	MN	**C+**	C+	C+	35.2	2.42	2.9	34.1	8.3	6.4	**10.0**	12.1
Piscataway Township Employees FCU	Piscataway	NJ	**C**	C	C-	1.9	0.87	0.0	34.9	0.0	0.0	**10.0**	13.2
Pitney Bowes Employees FCU	Shelton	CT	**C-**	C-	C-	64.9	-2.51	3.4	10.4	9.5	3.1	**10.0**	15.9
▼ Pittsburgh City Hall Employees FCU	Pittsburgh	PA	**C**	C+	B-	53.2	6.05	0.0	16.6	0.0	52.7	**8.3**	10.9

Arrows denote recent upgrades ▲ or downgrades ▼

Asset Quality Index	Non-Performing Loans as a % of Total Loans	Non-Performing Loans as a % of Capital	Net Charge-Offs Avg Loans	Profitability Index	Net Income ($Mil)	Return on Assets	Return on Equity	Net Interest Spread	Overhead Efficiency Ratio	Liquidity Index	Liquidity Ratio	Hot Money Ratio	Stability Index
4.9	1.38	6.5	-0.12	**7.0**	0.04	0.31	1.90	4.28	82.3	**2.4**	19.1	21.2	**8.4**
6.7	1.54	6.4	2.88	**5.5**	0.02	0.18	1.30	3.88	75.1	**4.9**	31.3	5.4	**6.9**
10.0	0.78	1.4	-0.86	**2.8**	0.04	0.48	3.47	2.16	70.8	**4.8**	19.7	0.0	**5.2**
5.4	0.56	10.4	0.63	**1.2**	-0.06	-0.28	-3.15	3.64	95.0	**3.5**	14.3	10.2	**3.5**
7.1	10.00	12.5	0.00	**5.7**	0.00	0.00	0.00	10.81	100.0	**8.3**	93.5	0.0	**3.0**
9.8	3.64	2.5	0.00	**2.5**	0.00	0.48	2.45	1.74	50.0	**7.9**	80.4	0.0	**6.3**
4.4	2.62	10.3	1.19	**2.4**	-0.01	-0.30	-2.86	7.21	80.9	**5.8**	102.4	21.1	**6.3**
10.0	0.00	0.0	0.00	**3.9**	0.00	0.00	0.00	0.00	0.0	**6.2**	18.4	0.0	**3.0**
5.6	1.49	14.7	0.36	**3.1**	0.11	0.24	3.12	3.95	88.0	**2.7**	11.0	10.4	**4.9**
9.7	0.84	1.2	0.00	**0.4**	-0.01	-0.59	-1.79	2.78	103.6	**5.0**	31.8	0.0	**6.0**
9.9	0.91	1.8	-0.19	**1.9**	0.01	0.36	1.92	2.97	92.2	**6.3**	55.0	0.0	**6.4**
7.9	0.00	0.0	0.00	**3.9**	0.00	0.17	0.88	3.39	92.9	**6.3**	50.6	0.0	**7.8**
4.4	1.52	9.3	0.00	**4.9**	0.00	0.36	3.43	5.39	81.1	**4.0**	35.6	13.4	**3.0**
7.7	0.94	2.2	0.84	**2.5**	0.01	0.26	1.17	3.44	81.9	**4.8**	36.3	0.0	**6.6**
7.5	1.74	4.5	1.38	**1.6**	-0.01	-0.16	-1.64	3.49	91.3	**5.1**	35.4	11.9	**3.3**
6.2	1.06	6.0	0.68	**1.8**	-0.01	-0.06	-0.59	3.53	94.4	**4.2**	19.6	2.2	**4.5**
8.6	0.73	2.5	1.13	**4.2**	0.01	0.20	1.29	4.84	76.7	**4.7**	17.4	1.1	**6.1**
8.2	0.00	0.0	0.00	**3.8**	0.00	0.79	6.06	3.25	100.0	**3.1**	11.3	0.0	**7.1**
7.6	1.79	5.6	0.00	**5.7**	0.01	1.05	4.52	4.22	67.6	**4.6**	69.3	24.5	**4.3**
7.9	0.20	2.4	0.72	**4.7**	0.03	0.37	2.71	3.76	82.8	**3.8**	20.1	7.3	**7.2**
9.6	1.18	2.2	-0.18	**3.2**	0.00	0.12	0.69	3.64	87.3	**6.6**	59.4	0.0	**6.9**
4.9	0.15	4.1	0.84	**9.5**	0.03	1.31	12.25	10.14	70.5	**4.4**	18.0	1.4	**4.3**
1.1	6.95	32.1	67.65	**0.2**	-0.10	-83.94	-784.00	11.19	55.6	**6.3**	44.8	0.0	**5.4**
5.9	1.92	9.4	1.33	**6.0**	2.01	0.75	6.31	4.80	71.1	**5.4**	28.0	5.7	**8.6**
5.6	2.92	10.9	6.34	**1.6**	-0.01	-0.22	-3.50	5.09	92.3	**6.8**	35.8	0.0	**0.3**
6.8	1.16	4.7	0.00	**5.2**	0.02	1.10	7.55	6.39	84.0	**5.2**	29.0	0.0	**4.3**
6.4	1.43	6.2	0.00	**0.0**	-0.01	-3.15	-26.09	8.39	146.2	**6.3**	49.9	0.0	**5.0**
8.5	0.95	0.4	3.63	**2.0**	0.00	-0.16	-0.38	3.34	105.6	**7.1**	87.5	0.0	**7.3**
8.0	0.89	5.3	0.21	**2.6**	0.21	0.25	3.08	2.45	89.9	**4.5**	23.5	2.9	**5.1**
9.6	0.36	0.8	0.56	**3.5**	0.01	0.22	1.47	3.82	90.0	**7.1**	52.6	0.0	**6.8**
5.1	1.10	9.9	0.92	**3.7**	0.36	0.43	4.27	4.19	80.5	**3.9**	12.6	3.2	**5.5**
5.7	1.06	5.2	3.33	**1.3**	-0.02	-1.82	-13.31	5.19	90.7	**4.7**	25.1	0.0	**5.5**
3.2	2.74	26.5	2.61	**1.9**	-0.18	-1.17	-15.27	4.88	89.3	**4.9**	43.1	14.5	**3.2**
7.8	1.46	4.5	2.95	**0.4**	-0.09	-1.07	-8.20	4.82	102.1	**6.6**	47.1	1.8	**5.0**
6.1	7.13	13.8	0.00	**2.6**	0.01	0.35	2.39	2.33	84.2	**6.1**	39.3	0.0	**6.0**
6.2	0.44	3.4	0.28	**3.9**	0.07	0.35	3.69	2.80	79.3	**3.3**	23.4	13.7	**4.8**
7.7	8.89	5.9	0.00	**0.3**	0.00	-1.92	-12.70	1.59	300.0	**7.6**	61.8	0.0	**7.3**
7.5	0.31	1.6	-0.62	**0.9**	0.00	-0.38	-3.67	8.60	112.5	**6.1**	42.6	0.0	**4.6**
9.4	0.33	2.2	0.97	**4.7**	0.64	0.51	5.38	3.62	78.8	**4.4**	14.3	1.9	**6.0**
5.1	0.84	8.8	0.84	**2.9**	0.03	0.09	1.39	4.49	87.5	**4.4**	17.7	1.4	**3.3**
8.3	0.88	1.7	0.92	**7.7**	0.02	0.88	2.80	6.50	73.6	**3.9**	30.6	12.9	**6.3**
6.3	1.84	9.1	0.11	**1.0**	0.00	0.01	0.05	2.84	100.0	**3.8**	14.5	4.9	**5.9**
6.1	2.22	6.0	4.94	**1.0**	0.00	-1.83	-6.52	6.57	88.9	**5.1**	32.3	0.0	**6.8**
5.7	2.70	9.0	0.65	**6.8**	0.10	0.95	3.97	4.08	67.9	**5.2**	37.2	0.7	**7.4**
6.4	0.89	5.6	0.61	**4.9**	0.09	0.78	7.28	4.05	69.5	**3.4**	15.7	9.7	**5.6**
8.1	0.60	3.5	1.85	**1.2**	-0.05	-0.15	-1.09	3.21	89.2	**5.5**	48.4	3.3	**7.0**
6.7	0.38	4.8	0.00	**0.7**	-0.01	-0.79	-4.98	5.19	110.2	**6.0**	54.2	0.0	**6.3**
3.7	53.85	20.6	0.00	**2.5**	0.00	0.00	0.00	0.00	100.0	**7.8**	59.8	0.0	**7.4**
6.5	0.74	5.0	1.01	**3.2**	0.03	0.17	2.39	3.57	88.1	**4.3**	13.9	2.3	**2.2**
3.7	1.03	22.3	0.02	**0.8**	0.04	0.12	1.92	3.45	95.1	**3.6**	18.3	7.7	**1.9**
8.3	0.17	1.0	-0.15	**3.9**	0.03	0.57	5.16	3.81	85.0	**4.8**	29.7	1.2	**5.2**
4.8	0.49	3.0	0.70	**4.9**	0.00	0.51	4.76	5.91	90.0	**5.3**	34.2	0.0	**3.7**
5.9	0.64	6.9	0.43	**4.4**	0.71	0.64	7.44	3.15	78.7	**2.0**	9.3	21.7	**5.1**
9.6	0.27	1.0	-0.01	**7.0**	0.26	0.76	5.00	2.88	74.9	**5.1**	26.1	0.4	**9.6**
8.5	0.71	4.1	0.25	**7.0**	0.25	1.49	13.33	4.46	75.7	**3.3**	26.8	15.2	**6.2**
6.9	0.65	7.1	0.48	**4.7**	0.30	0.61	6.19	3.74	80.9	**3.1**	7.4	5.3	**6.2**
9.5	0.02	0.1	0.02	**2.7**	0.01	0.15	1.23	2.80	95.1	**4.2**	25.8	1.7	**6.5**
10.0	0.31	0.8	0.00	**2.2**	0.00	-0.22	-1.64	4.44	105.9	**6.3**	58.0	0.0	**5.9**
9.3	1.52	3.1	0.00	**1.7**	0.02	0.14	0.89	2.27	93.0	**5.3**	36.9	0.0	**6.6**
7.6	1.39	3.7	0.48	**2.4**	0.07	0.53	6.38	1.46	73.1	**4.9**	18.2	7.6	**4.9**

Name	City	State	Rating	2016 Rating	2015 Rating	Total Assets ($Mil)	One Year Asset Growth	Asset Mix (As a % of Total Assets): Commercial Loans	Consumer Loans	Mortgage Loans	Securities	Capitalization Index	Net Worth Ratio
Pittsburgh Federal Credit Union	Pittsburgh	PA	**D-**	D-	D	7.1	-2.87	0.0	33.9	0.0	0.0	**6.8**	8.8
Pittsburgh Firefighters' FCU	Pittsburgh	PA	**B+**	B+	B+	80.0	0.38	0.0	10.1	0.0	17.9	**10.0**	14.5
Pittsford Federal Credit Union	Pittsford	NY	**B**	B	B	386.4	2.78	0.0	7.1	48.1	13.6	**10.0**	11.0
▲ Plain Dealer Federal Credit Union	Cleveland	OH	**D+**	D	D+	15.9	-3.51	0.0	18.2	9.7	48.9	**10.0**	18.9
Plainfield Credit Union	Plainfield	NJ	**C**	C	C	1.4	-5.50	0.0	16.6	0.0	0.0	**10.0**	19.1
▼ Plainfield Police & Firemen's FCU	Plainfield	NJ	**D-**	D	D	3.6	-6.43	0.0	37.7	0.0	0.0	**9.7**	10.8
▼ Plains Federal Credit Union	Plainview	TX	**D**	D+	D+	3.9	-3.55	0.0	57.0	0.0	0.0	**10.0**	14.1
Planites Credit Union	Chicago	IL	**B-**	B-	C	33.3	2.48	0.0	13.3	20.4	0.0	**9.1**	10.4
Planters Federal Credit Union	Suffolk	VA	**D+**	D+	C-	4.4	-1.08	0.0	39.8	0.0	0.0	**10.0**	12.4
Platinum Federal Credit Union	Duluth	GA	**B-**	B-	B-	82.6	6.55	10.2	55.2	13.8	0.0	**6.6**	8.6
Plattsburgh City School District FCU	Plattsburgh	NY	**D+**	D+	D+	6.8	0.67	0.0	56.3	0.0	0.0	**10.0**	17.3
Plumbers & Fitters Local 675 FCU	Honolulu	HI	**C**	C	C-	2.6	1.33	0.0	20.1	0.0	0.0	**10.0**	11.7
Plumbers Local #27 Federal Credit Union	McKees Rocks	PA	**D-**	D-	D-	2.2	2.65	0.0	21.4	0.0	4.5	**8.1**	9.7
Plumbers Local 55 Federal Credit Union	Cleveland	OH	**C-**	C-	C-	3.1	-5.81	0.0	27.7	0.0	0.0	**10.0**	17.3
Plus Credit Union	Las Vegas	NV	**B+**	B+	A-	85.9	4.78	0.5	21.4	30.9	0.0	**10.0**	13.0
▼ Plus4 Credit Union	Houston	TX	**C**	C+	B-	119.1	8.24	0.0	52.0	1.3	0.0	**6.8**	8.8
Plymouth County Teachers FCU	West Wareham	MA	**D+**	D+	D	44.0	3.76	0.0	15.8	24.0	0.0	**7.9**	9.6
PMI Employees Federal Credit Union	Washington	DC	**D**	D	D	<1	-12.38	0.0	39.0	0.0	18.4	**10.0**	14.9
▼ Pocatello Simplot Credit Union	Pocatello	ID	**C+**	B-	C+	30.3	-2.61	0.0	31.3	8.1	1.1	**10.0**	19.4
Pocono Medical Center FCU	East Stroudsburg	PA	**D**	D	D	5.5	-2.88	0.0	30.4	0.0	23.9	**7.8**	9.5
Point Breeze Credit Union	Hunt Valley	MD	**B**	B	B	766.3	1.25	3.4	15.7	29.0	37.0	**10.0**	13.5
Point Loma Credit Union	San Diego	CA	**B-**	B-	C+	491.4	5.56	12.3	15.9	46.8	7.1	**6.1**	8.1
▲ Point West Credit Union	Portland	OR	**B-**	C+	C	103.9	7.74	1.0	55.7	5.4	10.8	**7.3**	9.2
Polam Federal Credit Union	Los Angeles	CA	**B**	B	B	58.3	6.05	4.7	2.1	46.3	0.8	**9.8**	10.9
▲ Polam Federal Credit Union	Redwood City	CA	**B+**	B	C-	73.6	3.88	10.8	0.8	44.0	0.0	**10.0**	11.8
Police and Fire Federal Credit Union	Philadelphia	PA	**A+**	A+	A+	4769.4	6.12	0.1	16.5	28.8	32.4	**10.0**	17.4
Police Credit Union	Sheboygan	WI	**C**	C	C	<1	-12.67	0.0	91.3	0.0	0.0	**10.0**	21.2
Police Federal Credit Union	Upper Marlboro	MD	**B**	B	B	145.2	0.27	0.0	27.9	22.9	31.1	**10.0**	13.1
Policemen's Federal Credit Union	South Bend	IN	**B**	B	B	58.3	0.28	0.0	26.7	12.9	0.0	**10.0**	14.6
Polish & Slavic Federal Credit Union	Brooklyn	NY	**B-**	B-	B-	1810.4	5.24	17.1	3.7	45.2	39.1	**7.4**	9.5
Polish National Credit Union	Chicopee	MA	**C+**	C+	C+	584.4	19.41	0.5	3.3	44.0	13.0	**10.0**	12.7
Polish-American Federal Credit Union	Troy	MI	**B+**	B+	B	112.4	7.13	2.4	5.9	58.3	0.8	**7.9**	9.6
▲ Polk County Credit Union	Des Moines	IA	**C+**	C	C-	5.3	4.41	0.0	77.8	0.0	0.0	**10.0**	16.4
Pollock Employees Credit Union	Dallas	TX	**D+**	D+	D+	4.7	-4.11	0.0	69.4	0.0	0.0	**10.0**	13.2
Poly Scientific Employees FCU	Blacksburg	VA	**C-**	C-	C-	8.7	-0.88	0.0	19.4	8.6	0.0	**10.0**	15.5
Pomona Postal Federal Credit Union	Pomona	CA	**C**	C	C	5.2	9.04	0.0	49.3	0.0	0.0	**10.0**	16.4
Pompano Beach City Employee Credit Union	Pompano Beach	FL	**B-**	B-	B	19.3	4.68	0.0	72.0	0.0	0.0	**10.0**	22.8
Pontiac Dwight Prison Employees CU	Pontiac	IL	**C**	C	C	6.0	2.09	0.0	36.7	0.0	0.0	**10.0**	12.5
POPA Federal Credit Union	Cerritos	CA	**B+**	B+	A-	219.3	6.13	0.4	32.1	25.4	16.3	**10.0**	11.9
Port Arthur Community FCU	Port Arthur	TX	**C**	C	C+	19.6	-1.66	0.0	47.3	13.9	0.0	**10.0**	11.9
▲ Port Arthur Teachers FCU	Port Arthur	TX	**C**	C-	C	29.9	4.67	0.0	26.0	0.0	0.0	**10.0**	12.3
Port Chester Teachers FCU	Rye Brook	NY	**D+**	D+	D+	33.7	1.64	0.0	17.3	0.0	31.5	**5.2**	7.2
Port City Federal Credit Union	Muskegon	MI	**C-**	C-	C-	30.3	2.28	0.0	12.1	22.8	0.0	**10.0**	13.1
Port Conneaut Federal Credit Union	Conneaut	OH	**C+**	C+	C	27.7	2.23	0.4	24.2	11.4	29.3	**10.0**	11.1
Port of Hampton Roads ILA FCU	Norfolk	VA	**D**	D	D+	6.4	1.75	0.0	46.7	0.0	0.0	**10.0**	21.9
Port of Houston Credit Union	Houston	TX	**C+**	C+	C+	6.8	9.86	0.0	69.1	0.0	0.0	**10.0**	23.3
Port of Houston Warehouse FCU	Houston	TX	**C+**	C+	C+	4.8	3.64	0.0	14.1	0.0	0.0	**10.0**	14.2
Port Terminal Federal Credit Union	Houston	TX	**C-**	C-	D+	9.9	-0.76	0.0	20.8	0.0	0.0	**10.0**	29.9
Port Washington Federal Credit Union	Port Washington	NY	**B+**	B+	B+	33.9	7.34	0.9	6.8	54.6	6.6	**10.0**	13.0
Port Washington Teachers FCU	Port Washington	NY	**C+**	C+	C-	11.6	1.30	0.0	11.4	0.0	0.0	**10.0**	29.5
PortAlliance Federal Credit Union	Norfolk	VA	**B-**	B-	B-	100.1	6.76	0.0	78.0	0.1	3.2	**8.9**	10.2
Porter Federal Credit Union	Denver	CO	**D+**	D+	D+	22.6	-1.12	0.0	12.8	6.9	0.0	**10.0**	15.8
Portland Federal Credit Union	Portland	MI	**B+**	B+	B+	310.6	9.72	1.8	28.4	30.9	2.6	**8.3**	9.9
▲ Portland Local 8 Federal Credit Union	Portland	OR	**C**	C-	D+	34.8	4.55	0.3	26.8	20.7	23.3	**6.4**	8.4
▲ Portsmouth Schools Federal Credit Union	Portsmouth	VA	**C-**	D+	C-	2.3	2.29	0.0	33.3	0.0	0.0	**10.0**	14.2
Portsmouth Virginia City Employees FCU	Portsmouth	VA	**E+**	E+	D-	1.7	-10.45	0.0	21.1	0.0	0.0	**3.6**	5.6
Post Community Credit Union	Battle Creek	MI	**B**	B	B-	90.2	6.11	6.4	14.8	50.4	0.0	**10.0**	11.5
Post Office Credit Union	Madison	WI	**C**	C	C	35.0	0.03	1.2	55.3	8.1	0.0	**10.0**	20.9
Post Office Credit Union of Maryland, Inc.	Baltimore	MD	**C**	C	C	32.7	0.85	0.0	14.0	0.0	78.4	**10.0**	27.0
▼ Post Office Employees FCU	Shreveport	LA	**E**	E+	D-	39.0	-6.15	0.5	20.8	17.7	11.7	**4.0**	6.0

Asset Quality Index	Non-Performing Loans as a % of Total Loans	Non-Performing Loans as a % of Capital	Net Charge-Offs Avg Loans	Profitability Index	Net Income ($Mil)	Return on Assets	Return on Equity	Net Interest Spread	Overhead Efficiency Ratio	Liquidity Index	Liquidity Ratio	Hot Money Ratio	Stability Index
4.6	2.22	17.4	1.30	**0.6**	-0.02	-0.97	-10.81	4.67	92.1	**4.6**	21.9	0.0	**2.8**
7.8	1.33	5.2	0.27	**3.7**	0.05	0.26	1.74	2.30	86.6	**6.2**	38.4	0.0	**7.1**
9.7	0.23	1.5	0.03	**3.5**	0.32	0.33	2.99	2.64	85.0	**4.1**	18.3	2.5	**7.6**
10.0	0.46	0.7	0.88	**1.0**	0.00	0.08	0.40	2.96	97.5	**6.2**	47.6	0.8	**5.7**
8.6	4.44	3.8	-3.48	**2.9**	0.00	0.00	0.00	2.54	100.0	**5.9**	48.6	0.0	**6.1**
0.3	16.50	54.3	4.37	**3.7**	0.00	-0.22	-2.05	5.13	107.1	**5.4**	32.6	0.0	**4.1**
8.1	0.20	2.8	0.98	**0.0**	-0.02	-1.62	-11.45	4.25	97.6	**3.6**	23.9	6.0	**5.7**
10.0	0.11	0.4	0.32	**4.2**	0.05	0.66	6.19	2.28	79.1	**4.0**	15.2	14.6	**5.5**
3.7	6.81	21.6	2.03	**2.1**	0.00	-0.09	-0.74	4.87	69.8	**5.7**	46.6	0.0	**4.9**
5.6	0.33	2.9	0.00	**7.8**	0.28	1.38	16.28	4.02	76.1	**4.0**	20.2	6.2	**5.7**
6.4	1.39	5.5	-0.08	**2.3**	0.01	0.36	2.05	4.36	91.0	**4.1**	16.3	3.9	**6.2**
10.0	0.00	0.0	0.00	**4.4**	0.01	0.77	6.62	2.08	63.6	**6.9**	61.9	0.0	**4.3**
1.7	15.65	35.4	-0.72	**0.8**	0.00	0.18	1.85	3.21	69.2	**6.6**	53.1	0.0	**3.6**
8.7	2.27	3.8	0.43	**1.2**	0.00	-0.25	-1.48	2.83	109.5	**4.9**	21.8	0.0	**6.2**
8.3	0.91	4.3	0.39	**3.6**	0.07	0.33	2.51	4.04	87.2	**5.6**	39.0	1.7	**6.4**
8.4	0.07	1.7	0.49	**1.2**	-0.20	-0.69	-10.63	4.27	96.0	**2.4**	16.3	19.8	**3.9**
8.5	0.59	3.3	0.17	**1.9**	0.05	0.44	4.58	3.44	87.6	**4.3**	28.2	3.7	**4.1**
9.9	0.00	0.0	0.00	**3.4**	0.00	1.45	9.76	3.72	33.3	**7.2**	70.8	0.0	**4.7**
8.4	0.81	2.1	2.13	**2.0**	-0.07	-0.90	-4.61	3.32	74.0	**4.7**	18.6	2.5	**7.1**
5.7	3.80	11.7	0.00	**2.9**	-0.01	-0.36	-3.77	2.61	94.4	**5.8**	53.9	0.0	**2.3**
9.4	0.56	2.4	0.52	**3.4**	0.46	0.24	1.81	2.76	78.4	**4.6**	16.2	2.7	**8.7**
9.6	0.15	1.5	0.12	**4.0**	0.43	0.35	4.34	3.50	87.9	**4.0**	16.7	5.0	**4.9**
7.4	0.44	4.6	-0.03	**5.1**	0.10	0.40	4.42	3.83	89.8	**4.3**	16.7	1.1	**5.5**
9.1	0.00	1.8	0.10	**4.6**	0.09	0.63	5.64	2.72	76.4	**3.2**	21.1	22.3	**6.4**
7.1	0.00	8.2	0.00	**5.6**	0.06	0.33	2.82	3.73	89.0	**5.5**	30.9	5.8	**6.7**
10.0	0.49	1.6	0.42	**9.5**	15.76	1.35	7.58	2.78	55.4	**5.3**	41.7	5.2	**10.0**
8.1	0.00	0.0	0.00	**6.2**	0.00	0.61	2.90	2.70	50.0	**3.5**	11.4	0.0	**5.0**
7.0	0.90	6.6	0.25	**4.1**	0.27	0.76	5.87	2.72	80.6	**3.4**	23.4	12.0	**7.5**
9.0	0.77	2.6	0.38	**4.2**	0.09	0.60	4.10	2.31	78.7	**4.4**	40.5	8.8	**7.2**
7.7	0.64	4.6	0.07	**3.9**	2.31	0.51	5.55	2.83	83.4	**3.9**	9.3	3.8	**6.5**
9.6	0.26	1.4	0.00	**2.6**	0.51	0.36	2.71	2.21	88.5	**3.3**	21.1	9.9	**8.5**
8.6	0.54	4.6	0.00	**5.9**	0.24	0.85	8.87	3.00	73.2	**3.9**	23.4	2.0	**6.3**
8.3	0.32	1.5	0.00	**7.6**	0.02	1.52	9.40	4.73	63.6	**4.8**	26.1	0.0	**5.0**
5.8	1.03	6.0	0.00	**1.6**	0.00	-0.26	-1.93	5.07	105.0	**3.9**	11.2	0.0	**6.0**
8.1	2.28	4.1	0.00	**1.6**	0.00	0.00	0.00	2.15	100.0	**5.9**	57.2	0.0	**6.5**
6.3	2.23	6.0	0.15	**4.6**	0.00	0.32	1.90	9.82	95.7	**6.9**	62.4	0.0	**4.3**
8.3	0.08	0.3	22.64	**4.6**	0.02	0.32	1.37	5.53	89.3	**3.0**	10.9	10.2	**7.8**
9.9	0.00	0.0	0.00	**1.9**	0.00	-0.07	-0.53	2.67	100.0	**6.7**	59.5	0.0	**6.6**
6.9	0.91	4.6	1.94	**3.7**	-0.01	-0.02	-0.17	3.91	92.5	**3.8**	16.6	10.9	**7.4**
6.7	0.82	4.1	0.33	**2.8**	0.02	0.33	2.76	4.10	87.7	**4.1**	36.0	14.9	**5.5**
9.0	1.12	2.8	0.49	**2.2**	0.04	0.57	4.60	2.96	85.2	**5.7**	40.7	0.8	**5.5**
10.0	0.23	0.7	-0.29	**2.1**	0.01	0.13	1.82	2.42	94.1	**7.0**	51.9	0.0	**2.8**
10.0	0.24	0.7	0.03	**2.0**	0.01	0.15	1.11	2.25	94.3	**4.7**	22.9	2.7	**6.5**
7.0	1.85	9.0	1.42	**0.7**	-0.07	-1.08	-9.38	4.01	96.4	**5.3**	32.6	2.6	**5.3**
6.7	1.58	3.7	5.00	**0.0**	-0.05	-3.10	-13.58	7.70	90.1	**6.5**	47.2	0.0	**5.4**
5.5	1.93	6.3	0.00	**9.7**	0.02	1.20	5.09	6.61	78.4	**4.2**	27.5	8.2	**5.0**
8.2	3.53	4.9	2.01	**6.1**	0.01	0.76	5.29	7.15	75.8	**8.0**	80.6	0.0	**5.0**
10.0	1.87	1.5	-0.17	**1.1**	0.00	-0.12	-0.41	2.42	104.6	**6.1**	81.2	0.0	**6.2**
10.0	0.19	1.2	0.10	**9.2**	0.14	1.72	13.19	3.27	54.6	**3.9**	13.4	0.0	**7.2**
10.0	0.12	0.1	0.00	**3.2**	0.01	0.45	1.52	2.68	88.1	**6.3**	47.4	0.0	**7.1**
5.7	1.15	8.3	1.01	**4.3**	0.07	0.28	2.78	6.10	81.0	**2.1**	24.3	54.3	**5.7**
10.0	0.34	0.5	-0.08	**1.5**	0.01	0.12	0.79	1.90	93.9	**5.7**	60.6	5.2	**6.6**
6.5	0.83	6.2	0.36	**6.1**	0.69	0.91	9.09	4.14	74.2	**3.6**	16.4	5.6	**6.8**
5.4	2.11	12.5	0.02	**8.2**	0.12	1.46	17.33	4.02	87.3	**4.1**	35.7	13.1	**3.2**
9.8	1.06	2.4	0.50	**1.3**	0.00	0.00	0.00	11.32	97.5	**7.6**	74.8	0.0	**5.5**
7.1	2.50	8.2	-1.00	**0.0**	-0.03	-5.81	-91.74	4.92	256.3	**7.6**	67.7	0.0	**2.4**
7.5	0.75	5.7	0.09	**4.7**	0.20	0.89	7.62	4.38	81.1	**4.5**	20.5	0.7	**5.5**
8.4	0.12	0.4	-0.03	**2.4**	0.01	0.16	0.77	2.97	95.0	**3.5**	25.1	3.7	**6.7**
10.0	1.48	0.8	1.40	**1.7**	0.00	0.04	0.14	1.75	98.2	**5.2**	16.7	0.0	**6.6**
1.7	4.96	44.2	0.59	**0.0**	-0.05	-0.56	-9.21	3.89	105.6	**5.4**	31.8	6.7	**0.0**

Name	City	State	Rating	2016 Rating	2015 Rating	Total Assets ($Mil)	One Year Asset Growth	Asset Mix (As a % of Total Assets) Comm-ercial Loans	Cons-umer Loans	Mort-gage Loans	Secur-ities	Capital-ization Index	Net Worth Ratio
▼ Post Office Employees' Credit Union	Metairie	LA	**C-**	C	C+	40.5	55.08	5.9	24.5	18.3	5.5	**10.0**	11.8
Post-Gazette Federal Credit Union	Clinton	PA	**C**	C	C+	11.6	-1.76	0.0	44.9	0.0	0.0	**10.0**	43.4
Postal & Community Credit Union	Saint Joseph	MO	**C-**	C-	C-	47.4	10.97	0.0	45.8	2.7	0.0	**5.9**	7.9
Postal Credit Union	Baton Rouge	LA	**C-**	C-	D+	28.5	3.64	0.0	29.7	15.9	20.0	**10.0**	17.6
Postal Credit Union	Meridian	MS	**C**	C	C	5.8	-3.31	0.0	11.1	0.0	0.0	**10.0**	16.3
Postal Employees Credit Union	Huntsville	AL	**C+**	C+	C	3.1	0.03	0.0	32.9	4.3	0.0	**10.0**	13.5
Postal Employees Credit Union	Yardville	NJ	**C+**	C+	B-	41.9	0.51	0.0	27.1	0.0	11.6	**10.0**	13.5
Postal Employees of Troy, N.Y. FCU	Troy	NY	**D**	D	D	1.4	-1.74	0.0	21.4	0.0	0.0	**10.0**	37.6
Postal Employees Regional FCU	Pawtucket	RI	**C**	C	C	6.2	-0.40	0.0	33.2	0.0	0.0	**10.0**	43.1
▲ Postal Family Credit Union	Cincinnati	OH	**C+**	C	C	60.7	-0.50	8.1	10.7	27.1	11.0	**10.0**	13.3
Postal Family Federal Credit Union	Fargo	ND	**D+**	D+	C	23.6	9.02	0.0	27.5	0.2	0.0	**9.7**	10.8
Postal Government Employees FCU	Providence	RI	**C-**	C-	C	45.1	2.51	0.0	15.8	26.7	0.0	**10.0**	11.7
PostCity Financial Credit Union	Long Beach	CA	**D+**	D+	C-	77.5	1.86	0.9	18.1	9.3	2.6	**10.0**	11.9
▼ Postel Family Credit Union	Wichita Falls	TX	**D+**	C-	C-	65.4	-3.40	1.2	27.4	27.5	2.8	**6.9**	8.9
Potlatch No. One Federal Credit Union	Lewiston	ID	**A-**	A-	A-	948.0	11.67	7.2	49.1	13.9	0.0	**7.3**	9.2
Potomac Federal Credit Union	Cumberland	MD	**B-**	B-	B-	24.5	1.71	0.0	58.5	11.4	0.0	**10.0**	14.4
Powell Schools Federal Credit Union	Powell	WY	**C-**	C-	D+	2.4	4.98	0.0	53.5	0.0	0.0	**7.7**	9.5
Power Co-Op Employees Credit Union	Humboldt	IA	**A-**	A-	B+	33.8	8.06	7.1	20.7	14.8	5.5	**10.0**	16.3
Power Credit Union	Pueblo	CO	**B**	B	B	89.3	3.34	0.7	42.1	10.7	5.4	**10.0**	11.8
Power Financial Credit Union	Pembroke Pines	FL	**C+**	C+	C+	652.1	13.44	7.1	11.0	46.0	17.3	**9.5**	11.1
Power One Federal Credit Union	Fort Wayne	IN	**C**	C	C+	15.7	-1.69	0.0	38.7	19.9	0.0	**9.1**	10.4
Powerco Federal Credit Union	Atlanta	GA	**C**	C	C	196.1	7.53	0.0	13.2	19.7	12.6	**10.0**	11.7
Powernet Credit Union	Tampa	FL	**C**	C	C+	83.6	7.30	3.3	12.9	29.0	31.7	**6.8**	8.8
PPG & Associates Federal Credit Union	Creighton	PA	**D**	D	D	22.1	-4.00	0.0	15.3	3.3	18.6	**10.0**	13.6
Prairie Federal Credit Union	Minot	ND	**A-**	A-	A	124.9	5.04	7.9	16.8	43.1	7.4	**10.0**	11.8
Prairie View Federal Credit Union	Prairie View	TX	**D-**	D-	D-	4.7	-4.96	0.0	32.0	0.0	0.0	**5.9**	8.0
Prairieland Federal Credit Union	Normal	IL	**B**	B	B	74.5	5.84	0.0	59.4	17.6	0.0	**10.0**	12.2
Precision Federal Credit Union	Keene	NH	**C+**	C+	C	16.9	5.91	0.0	11.7	34.5	0.0	**10.0**	12.9
Preferred Credit Union	Grand Rapids	MI	**A**	A	A	169.9	4.88	0.0	43.1	8.5	22.4	**10.0**	13.5
Premier America Credit Union	Chatsworth	CA	**A-**	A-	A-	2385.0	7.41	14.1	13.0	57.6	8.8	**8.4**	9.9
Premier Community Credit Union	Stockton	CA	**C**	C	C	144.4	4.34	6.7	21.3	15.5	29.3	**7.2**	9.4
Premier Credit Union	Des Moines	IA	**B+**	B+	B+	181.7	17.91	0.8	34.6	17.8	2.7	**7.9**	9.6
▼ Premier Federal Credit Union	Greensboro	NC	**B+**	A-	B+	183.9	4.55	2.8	44.7	4.0	8.2	**10.0**	13.4
Premier Financial Credit Union	New Holstein	WI	**C+**	C+	B	89.3	6.90	8.5	9.6	41.2	0.8	**8.7**	10.1
▲ Premier Members Credit Union	Boulder	CO	**B+**	B	C+	952.5	7.09	4.3	20.2	29.9	11.7	**9.4**	10.7
Premier Source Credit Union	East Longmeadow	MA	**D+**	D+	C-	69.2	-3.57	0.0	14.3	27.2	21.0	**10.0**	12.4
PremierOne Credit Union	San Jose	CA	**B-**	B-	B-	417.1	9.18	0.0	15.8	29.2	14.7	**6.9**	9.0
Prescott Federal Credit Union	Prescott	AZ	**C-**	C-	C-	8.3	21.47	0.0	46.5	0.0	0.0	**10.0**	12.3
Presidents Federal Credit Union	Cleves	OH	**C-**	C-	C-	11.7	0.62	2.5	41.8	0.0	0.0	**9.7**	10.8
Pressers Union Local 12 ILGWU CU	Boston	MA	**D+**	D+	C	<1	19.08	0.0	32.1	0.0	0.0	**7.9**	9.6
Prestige Community Credit Union	Dallas	TX	**B-**	B-	B-	93.2	15.03	49.8	20.6	0.8	1.9	**6.2**	8.2
Presto Lewiston Employees Credit Union	Lewiston	UT	**C**	C	C	<1	-2.60	0.0	71.8	0.0	0.0	**10.0**	26.7
Preston Federal Credit Union	Kingwood	WV	**B-**	B-	B-	25.2	1.66	0.0	19.6	8.5	0.0	**10.0**	12.4
Price Chopper Employees FCU	Schenectady	NY	**D-**	D-	D-	22.0	-6.34	0.0	10.0	4.3	0.0	**8.3**	9.9
Prime Care Credit Union	Norfolk	VA	**B-**	B-	B-	21.2	4.84	0.0	19.5	3.7	0.0	**10.0**	11.6
Prime Financial Credit Union	Cudahy	WI	**C+**	C+	C+	111.1	-0.12	3.1	49.0	29.4	0.0	**6.3**	8.3
Primesource Credit Union	Spokane	WA	**B+**	B+	B+	72.9	8.24	0.0	41.8	17.5	0.0	**10.0**	12.9
PrimeTrust Financial FCU	Muncie	IN	**C-**	C-	C	161.9	2.67	10.4	34.5	23.5	0.0	**8.6**	10.0
Primeway Federal Credit Union	Houston	TX	**C+**	C+	C+	474.4	1.71	3.8	44.8	17.4	9.0	**6.6**	8.7
▲ Prince George's Community FCU	Bowie	MD	**A-**	B+	B	167.7	5.70	5.5	29.0	19.1	9.9	**8.8**	10.2
Princeton Federal Credit Union	Princeton	NJ	**C-**	C-	D+	139.0	1.80	0.0	11.4	19.2	48.8	**8.5**	10.3
Printing Industries Credit Union	Riverside	CA	**D**	D	D-	24.1	0.07	0.0	65.9	12.3	0.0	**5.8**	7.8
Priority Credit Union	Orlando	FL	**D**	D	D+	69.1	-0.68	2.3	64.6	9.5	0.0	**5.5**	7.5
▼ Priority Federal Credit Union	Russellville	AR	**D-**	D	D-	9.7	-5.39	0.0	65.2	0.0	0.0	**6.2**	8.3
Priority First Federal Credit Union	DuBois	PA	**C+**	C+	C+	78.8	9.16	0.0	43.8	20.5	0.3	**6.9**	8.9
Priority One Credit Union	South Pasadena	CA	**C+**	C+	C+	162.9	2.76	0.0	19.4	16.2	39.7	**6.8**	9.3
Priority Plus Federal Credit Union	Wilmington	DE	**C+**	C+	C+	16.9	3.91	0.0	28.6	0.5	0.1	**10.0**	18.5
▼ PriorityONE Credit Union	Sunrise	FL	**C**	C+	B-	89.6	4.61	0.0	26.3	10.8	6.9	**7.7**	9.6
▼ Processors-Industrial Community CU	Granite City	IL	**D**	D+	D-	11.7	9.75	0.0	35.1	0.0	0.0	**6.3**	8.3
Procter & Gamble St. Louis Employees CU	Saint Louis	MO	**C-**	C-	C	<1	3.95	0.0	61.6	0.0	0.0	**10.0**	14.5

Asset Quality Index	Non-Performing Loans as a % of Total Loans	Non-Performing Loans as a % of Capital	Net Charge-Offs Avg Loans	Profitability Index	Net Income ($Mil)	Return on Assets	Return on Equity	Net Interest Spread	Overhead Efficiency Ratio	Liquidity Index	Liquidity Ratio	Hot Money Ratio	Stability Index
6.5	1.31	9.9	0.37	**1.5**	-0.03	-0.32	-2.73	4.80	105.4	**4.7**	24.0	0.9	**5.0**
8.7	3.05	3.4	-0.28	**3.0**	0.03	0.99	2.31	3.72	67.9	**5.0**	44.5	0.0	**5.4**
6.2	0.55	4.3	0.05	**3.3**	0.09	0.74	9.19	2.84	88.2	**4.1**	13.9	2.8	**3.0**
7.6	2.12	7.0	0.97	**1.3**	0.00	-0.01	-0.08	3.08	85.9	**5.2**	44.0	0.2	**6.8**
10.0	0.54	0.5	0.00	**2.3**	0.00	0.14	0.85	1.48	84.2	**5.6**	39.9	0.0	**6.8**
9.7	0.08	0.2	0.00	**4.6**	0.01	1.57	11.82	3.89	50.0	**5.7**	34.7	0.0	**6.8**
8.5	1.27	3.3	3.71	**1.1**	-0.06	-0.53	-3.94	2.21	104.7	**4.9**	43.2	13.2	**5.0**
10.0	0.00	0.0	-2.48	**0.0**	-0.01	-1.70	-4.50	2.63	175.0	**7.1**	93.8	0.0	**6.8**
9.9	1.24	1.2	-0.15	**2.6**	0.00	0.00	0.00	4.11	80.0	**6.3**	88.8	0.0	**5.8**
9.1	0.65	2.5	0.31	**2.8**	0.06	0.40	3.04	2.71	84.7	**5.3**	39.7	1.4	**6.2**
7.2	1.24	4.4	0.09	**1.8**	-0.01	-0.12	-1.10	3.63	101.4	**5.4**	26.6	1.2	**5.7**
1.7	10.62	43.1	0.72	**2.1**	0.03	0.30	2.59	3.31	88.6	**4.9**	35.5	6.9	**6.5**
9.9	0.77	2.2	0.55	**0.6**	-0.09	-0.48	-4.16	2.52	110.2	**5.2**	35.5	5.6	**5.5**
5.5	0.68	10.5	1.51	**1.5**	-0.08	-0.48	-5.30	3.81	84.0	**4.4**	22.6	5.4	**3.4**
6.1	0.41	4.2	0.75	**5.5**	1.37	0.59	6.85	3.59	73.0	**2.9**	16.2	15.2	**7.0**
8.4	0.00	0.0	0.73	**3.7**	-0.01	-0.21	-1.47	4.52	87.5	**3.7**	16.8	8.6	**6.2**
8.3	0.00	0.0	0.00	**6.8**	0.01	1.01	10.48	2.63	53.9	**4.7**	28.4	0.0	**3.7**
8.5	1.00	3.3	0.08	**9.5**	0.18	2.15	12.99	3.08	34.6	**4.5**	21.7	0.0	**8.0**
8.7	0.40	3.0	0.66	**5.0**	0.19	0.88	7.53	3.94	79.0	**3.2**	17.3	13.8	**5.5**
9.7	0.20	2.0	0.05	**3.0**	0.43	0.27	2.73	2.90	87.0	**4.8**	24.6	1.3	**6.6**
6.1	0.64	7.2	0.08	**2.6**	0.01	0.24	2.21	4.19	88.5	**4.6**	23.7	0.0	**5.4**
10.0	0.14	0.5	0.05	**2.3**	0.13	0.27	2.25	2.83	89.1	**6.7**	53.3	3.0	**7.5**
8.8	0.12	0.7	0.08	**2.4**	0.05	0.24	2.67	2.70	88.8	**4.4**	15.8	6.6	**4.3**
10.0	0.23	0.6	0.55	**0.2**	-0.01	-0.26	-2.42	2.66	110.9	**5.8**	36.2	1.9	**4.4**
6.9	0.96	8.3	-0.01	**6.0**	0.23	0.74	6.25	2.97	72.9	**3.8**	16.7	5.5	**7.6**
8.3	0.80	2.9	0.00	**1.5**	0.00	0.33	4.29	3.97	92.0	**6.0**	45.9	0.0	**1.0**
5.4	1.35	8.3	0.81	**5.1**	0.15	0.80	6.59	4.35	73.3	**2.7**	21.4	16.9	**6.2**
7.3	2.08	8.4	0.00	**2.2**	0.00	0.05	0.37	3.49	97.9	**5.3**	31.6	3.8	**6.7**
8.1	1.03	4.4	0.62	**6.5**	0.27	0.65	4.78	4.21	79.3	**4.6**	21.6	3.1	**8.6**
8.1	0.67	5.1	0.08	**5.8**	5.24	0.90	8.91	2.84	68.3	**2.9**	23.7	22.8	**8.5**
9.6	0.65	2.7	0.21	**2.8**	0.16	0.45	4.89	3.18	88.2	**5.3**	28.3	1.7	**5.5**
7.4	0.54	7.0	0.09	**5.0**	0.26	0.59	6.02	3.27	81.0	**2.7**	15.9	16.7	**7.3**
7.1	1.61	7.4	1.23	**4.6**	0.22	0.49	3.62	4.88	79.2	**4.3**	30.4	12.9	**7.2**
6.7	0.87	5.3	0.02	**2.1**	0.02	0.07	0.76	3.28	97.4	**4.6**	25.0	0.6	**4.4**
9.4	0.39	2.6	0.36	**5.4**	2.04	0.87	7.39	3.79	72.4	**4.1**	19.1	5.1	**7.5**
8.3	0.82	3.0	0.63	**0.6**	-0.01	-0.05	-0.38	3.30	98.0	**4.3**	20.0	5.1	**4.8**
10.0	0.13	0.8	0.20	**3.5**	0.36	0.35	3.77	3.22	83.5	**4.8**	25.8	2.9	**5.3**
6.8	1.37	4.8	2.07	**3.1**	0.01	0.30	2.35	4.40	81.4	**4.9**	32.5	0.0	**6.3**
2.8	4.17	25.7	3.40	**7.1**	0.01	0.24	2.22	6.51	79.9	**3.9**	32.2	13.4	**5.1**
10.0	0.00	0.0	0.00	**2.0**	0.00	0.00	0.00	7.69	100.0	**7.7**	75.2	0.0	**4.5**
5.7	0.34	3.2	1.30	**3.6**	0.10	0.46	5.66	3.71	79.0	**2.7**	22.2	21.0	**3.1**
8.2	0.00	0.0	0.00	**3.0**	0.00	0.00	0.00	6.99	100.0	**4.5**	28.5	0.0	**7.3**
8.8	1.32	3.1	0.11	**4.1**	0.02	0.39	3.09	1.99	67.4	**4.7**	25.8	4.1	**6.1**
9.9	0.74	1.1	0.96	**0.2**	-0.02	-0.40	-4.03	1.87	112.0	**6.0**	55.6	0.0	**3.6**
8.8	2.35	5.0	0.15	**2.7**	0.01	0.14	1.14	2.28	94.0	**6.5**	40.1	1.9	**6.0**
4.8	1.14	11.1	0.84	**3.2**	0.06	0.23	2.75	4.06	90.9	**3.9**	14.2	3.4	**4.6**
5.2	1.52	13.4	0.78	**3.7**	0.01	0.08	0.67	4.82	84.7	**2.5**	16.9	22.5	**7.2**
7.2	0.72	5.6	0.56	**1.8**	-0.03	-0.07	-0.79	4.40	94.4	**4.0**	19.3	6.1	**5.2**
6.3	0.84	8.6	0.95	**2.0**	-0.20	-0.17	-2.50	3.56	87.5	**3.2**	7.4	5.4	**3.6**
7.8	0.79	4.9	0.28	**6.5**	0.45	1.11	10.68	4.32	77.9	**4.4**	25.0	4.9	**7.0**
9.2	0.70	2.9	0.30	**2.0**	0.03	0.10	0.96	3.11	90.5	**4.2**	28.5	7.8	**5.6**
6.3	0.22	2.2	0.57	**5.2**	0.05	0.88	11.47	6.18	80.2	**3.3**	9.0	1.0	**3.0**
1.9	2.03	21.0	4.00	**2.2**	-0.50	-2.90	-36.78	5.18	81.4	**3.8**	17.4	6.0	**3.1**
2.4	1.21	18.9	2.12	**1.7**	-0.02	-0.65	-7.90	4.77	91.6	**4.8**	22.6	0.0	**1.0**
6.5	0.61	5.3	0.17	**4.1**	0.09	0.47	5.71	3.64	84.0	**4.3**	17.6	1.5	**3.8**
10.0	0.08	0.4	0.04	**3.6**	0.15	0.37	4.23	3.11	94.8	**4.7**	18.9	3.4	**5.3**
10.0	0.35	0.7	-0.06	**2.8**	0.01	0.31	1.67	3.18	91.5	**5.0**	23.9	0.0	**6.5**
7.5	0.68	4.0	0.90	**2.4**	0.02	0.10	1.09	4.11	93.7	**4.3**	23.0	1.2	**3.7**
6.5	1.70	6.6	2.08	**0.4**	-0.05	-1.92	-21.66	4.08	116.4	**6.2**	43.3	0.0	**3.5**
8.5	0.00	0.0	0.00	**1.8**	0.00	0.00	0.00	7.02	100.0	**5.9**	39.6	0.0	**6.0**

								Asset Mix (As a % of Total Assets)					
Name	City	State	Rating	2016 Rating	2015 Rating	Total Assets ($Mil)	One Year Asset Growth	Commercial Loans	Consumer Loans	Mortgage Loans	Securities	Capitalization Index	Net Worth Ratio
▼ Proctor Federal Credit Union	Proctor	MN	C+	B-	B-	39.0	7.74	0.0	29.7	12.8	0.0	9.5	10.7
Producers Employees' Credit Union	Columbus	OH	B-	B-	B-	<1	-2.71	0.0	39.8	0.0	0.0	10.0	17.0
Profed Federal Credit Union	Fort Wayne	IN	C+	C+	C	416.0	3.89	1.9	16.5	24.7	15.0	7.2	9.2
Professional Fire Fighters Credit Union	Shreveport	LA	B+	B+	B+	40.0	2.78	0.0	31.4	9.1	0.0	10.0	19.3
Professional Police Officers CU	Indianapolis	IN	B	B	B	41.4	2.28	0.0	21.4	4.9	20.8	10.0	14.5
▼ Profinance Federal Credit Union	Merrillville	IN	D+	C-	D+	13.9	-1.71	4.6	19.0	19.0	30.6	10.0	22.7
Progressions Credit Union	Spokane	WA	C+	C+	C+	57.5	3.12	0.0	50.4	15.8	2.0	7.2	9.1
▼ Progressive Credit Union	New York	NY	C	B-	B+	544.6	-14.30	89.9	0.1	17.3	0.0	10.0	31.1
Progressive Federal Credit Union	Mobile	AL	D+	D+	C-	6.1	4.89	0.0	23.5	1.5	0.0	10.0	20.7
▼ Projector Federal Credit Union	Melville	NY	D+	C-	D+	<1	-9.65	0.0	13.3	0.0	0.0	9.9	10.9
ProMedica Federal Credit Union	Toledo	OH	C+	C+	C+	56.1	8.66	0.0	37.0	2.9	34.0	10.0	11.5
▲ Promise Credit Union	Houston	TX	D+	D	D-	4.9	-9.12	0.0	62.9	0.0	0.0	10.0	13.0
▼ Proponent Federal Credit Union	Nutley	NJ	C+	B-	B-	512.5	0.81	7.8	13.0	40.8	23.3	9.7	11.3
Prospectors Federal Credit Union	Diamond Bar	CA	B-	B-	B-	69.6	4.71	5.8	27.1	20.7	29.5	10.0	11.7
Prospera Credit Union	Appleton	WI	B-	B-	B-	235.4	6.00	13.3	19.0	48.6	0.0	6.5	8.6
Providence Federal Credit Union	Milwaukie	OR	B+	B+	B	134.3	5.93	1.4	32.9	8.7	36.0	10.0	12.2
Provident Credit Union	Redwood City	CA	A-	A-	B+	2353.8	9.00	11.4	12.0	43.0	27.1	10.0	11.6
Provident Federal Credit Union	Dover	DE	D	D	D	10.4	1.20	0.0	46.4	2.0	0.0	10.0	15.1
Provo Police & Fire Department CU	Provo	UT	C-	C-	C-	2.8	1.22	0.0	56.3	0.0	0.0	10.0	11.8
PRR South Fork Federal Credit Union	South Fork	PA	C+	C+	C+	47.5	10.74	0.0	12.5	4.1	22.2	10.0	15.6
PSE Credit Union, Incorporated	Parma	OH	D+	D+	D-	132.0	4.27	0.2	35.4	6.1	26.2	5.5	7.8
▼ PSE&G Nuclear Employees FCU	Hancocks Bridge	NJ	D-	D	D-	9.4	-2.61	0.0	36.8	0.0	0.0	5.9	7.9
PSTC Employees Federal Credit Union	Upper Darby	PA	B	B	B-	36.1	2.29	1.1	21.0	30.0	1.7	10.0	17.1
Public Employees Credit Union	Waterloo	IA	B-	B-	B-	27.1	0.68	0.0	24.1	0.0	0.0	10.0	14.7
Public Employees Credit Union	Austin	TX	B-	B-	C+	329.0	5.43	0.0	48.1	3.8	25.5	6.0	8.3
Public Service Credit Union	Lone Tree	CO	A-	A-	A	2109.2	21.45	8.6	61.6	13.4	5.9	8.3	9.9
Public Service Credit Union	Fort Wayne	IN	B+	B+	B+	54.4	3.59	0.0	23.1	17.2	39.4	10.0	12.2
Public Service Credit Union	Romulus	MI	A-	A-	A-	250.0	53.22	6.2	36.7	16.7	19.6	10.0	11.5
Public Service Credit Union	Wausau	WI	C	C	C	12.4	-3.59	0.0	14.9	26.5	0.0	10.0	21.9
▲ Public Service E.D. Trenton FCU	Lawrence Township	NJ	D+	D	D	4.0	-1.80	0.0	9.3	0.0	0.0	10.0	30.3
▼ Public Service Edwardspt PL E FCU	Linton	IN	E+	D-	D	1.8	2.14	0.0	51.0	0.0	0.0	8.5	10.0
Public Service Federal Credit Union	Middlesex	NJ	B	B	B-	37.3	14.79	0.0	19.6	8.9	3.3	9.3	10.6
Public Service HC Employees FCU	Toms River	NJ	C-	C-	C-	8.7	0.35	0.0	24.5	0.5	67.5	10.0	28.9
▲ Public Service Plaza FCU	Newark	NJ	C	C-	C-	21.0	3.85	0.0	7.8	0.0	0.6	10.0	11.1
▼ Public Service Sewaren FCU	Sewaren	NJ	D-	D	D	<1	-18.03	0.0	4.2	0.0	0.0	8.4	10.0
Publix Employees Federal Credit Union	Lakeland	FL	A	A	A-	907.8	5.47	2.8	22.3	9.1	34.6	10.0	12.9
PUD Federal Credit Union	Longview	WA	C	C	C	7.7	2.29	0.0	45.6	0.0	1.3	10.0	15.7
Pueblo Government Agencies FCU	Pueblo	CO	C	C	C-	32.6	6.28	0.7	22.5	5.8	0.0	10.0	11.9
▼ Pueblo Horizons Federal Credit Union	Pueblo	CO	D	D+	D+	30.5	1.11	0.0	22.2	11.1	37.4	10.0	11.6
Puerto Rico Employee Groups FCU	Puerto Nuevo	PR	D	D	D+	2.6	-12.80	0.0	0.0	0.0	0.0	5.7	7.7
Puerto Rico Federal Credit Union	Caparra	PR	C+	C+	B-	133.5	1.65	1.0	30.3	10.9	33.9	10.0	16.6
▲ Puget Sound Cooperative Credit Union	Bellevue	WA	B+	B	C+	121.9	16.25	0.3	6.3	8.9	1.8	6.2	8.2
▼ Puget Sound Refinery FCU	Anacortes	WA	C	C+	C-	11.9	8.84	0.0	50.9	0.0	0.0	10.0	12.2
Purdue Federal Credit Union	West Lafayette	IN	B+	B+	B+	1131.4	9.76	14.9	12.0	48.0	15.3	6.6	8.6
Purity Dairies Employees FCU	Nashville	TN	C-	C-	C-	3.7	9.11	0.0	41.5	0.0	0.0	10.0	16.4
Putnam School Employees FCU	Eleanor	WV	B	B	B	12.3	-0.50	0.0	28.5	0.0	0.0	10.0	13.9
PWC Employees Credit Union	Woodbridge	VA	B+	B+	B+	57.2	3.83	0.0	27.5	0.6	39.3	10.0	13.3
▼ Pyramid Federal Credit Union	Tucson	AZ	C+	B-	C+	157.1	10.93	1.1	49.2	20.2	8.2	7.1	9.1
Qside Federal Credit Union	Queens Village	NY	D+	D+	C-	49.3	4.20	0.0	40.0	7.8	21.2	5.9	7.9
Quad Cities Postal Credit Union	Moline	IL	C-	C-	C-	7.0	-3.44	0.0	27.8	29.3	0.0	8.9	10.3
Quaker Oats Credit Union	Cedar Rapids	IA	C-	C-	C-	9.1	5.40	0.0	56.0	0.0	0.0	10.0	14.4
Qualstar Credit Union	Redmond	WA	A	A	A	483.7	14.44	1.7	27.1	17.1	6.2	10.0	12.3
▼ Qualtrust Credit Union	Irving	TX	D+	C-	C	200.8	3.30	0.0	32.0	18.8	4.4	7.1	9.1
Quantum Credit Union	Wichita	KS	C+	C+	C+	91.6	15.54	0.0	72.8	3.7	0.0	6.5	8.5
▼ Quay Schools Federal Credit Union	Tucumcari	NM	C-	C	C+	6.2	-3.43	0.0	53.6	0.0	0.0	10.0	18.3
Queen of Peace Arlington FCU	Arlington	VA	C	C	C	2.7	10.79	0.0	11.5	0.0	14.3	10.0	12.4
Queens Cluster Federal Credit Union	Hicksville	NY	C-	C-	C	<1	-15.99	17.1	9.1	0.0	0.0	6.9	8.9
Quest Federal Credit Union	Kenton	OH	B+	B+	B	112.0	16.06	7.4	18.4	31.0	2.6	7.5	9.4
Questa Credit Union	Questa	NM	B-	B-	B-	8.2	8.38	0.0	22.2	27.9	0.0	10.0	25.1
Quincy Credit Union	Quincy	MA	B+	B+	B+	513.2	5.79	0.0	15.7	38.6	23.6	10.0	13.0

Asset Quality Index	Non-Performing Loans as a % of Total Loans	Non-Performing Loans as a % of Capital	Net Charge-Offs Avg Loans	Profitability Index	Net Income ($Mil)	Return on Assets	Return on Equity	Net Interest Spread	Overhead Efficiency Ratio	Liquidity Index	Liquidity Ratio	Hot Money Ratio	Stability Index
6.3	0.72	6.4	0.16	**2.9**	0.01	0.09	0.86	3.24	97.7	**4.3**	38.6	4.6	**5.5**
7.6	2.94	6.4	0.00	**7.2**	0.00	0.59	3.45	2.84	50.0	**5.8**	53.0	0.0	**5.0**
9.8	0.26	2.0	0.05	**3.3**	0.38	0.38	4.06	2.80	91.1	**5.0**	27.8	0.9	**5.8**
9.4	0.86	2.4	0.00	**6.3**	0.08	0.78	4.02	3.21	73.6	**4.5**	53.8	21.7	**8.4**
10.0	0.17	0.4	0.27	**3.9**	0.08	0.74	5.11	2.54	74.8	**4.7**	20.4	2.6	**7.4**
6.2	5.14	9.7	0.74	**0.3**	-0.04	-1.29	-5.55	4.21	102.0	**5.6**	30.4	0.0	**6.2**
5.8	0.32	3.5	0.34	**3.6**	0.02	0.16	1.76	4.11	91.6	**2.9**	11.1	6.7	**4.2**
0.0	9.16	33.4	25.71	**0.0**	-25.60	-18.02	-57.58	2.51	77.7	**0.8**	15.1	39.7	**6.0**
7.2	5.47	9.5	-0.82	**0.7**	-0.02	-1.34	-6.28	5.78	112.3	**7.2**	64.3	0.0	**5.0**
10.0	0.00	0.0	0.00	**1.0**	0.00	-0.50	-4.44	0.70	150.0	**7.6**	72.7	0.0	**5.4**
9.8	0.16	0.6	0.37	**2.7**	0.03	0.19	1.62	3.08	93.7	**5.3**	32.7	2.7	**5.8**
3.4	3.52	19.7	0.00	**3.6**	-0.10	-8.21	-102.08	9.39	99.2	**4.6**	56.1	19.7	**3.0**
3.2	5.07	28.6	0.32	**1.3**	-2.96	-2.34	-20.85	3.39	81.8	**3.4**	15.8	7.5	**7.7**
9.7	0.13	0.6	0.34	**3.6**	0.08	0.44	3.79	2.97	85.9	**3.9**	18.7	10.8	**6.2**
7.4	0.31	3.9	0.09	**4.8**	0.35	0.59	7.25	3.34	84.6	**3.5**	16.1	10.2	**5.6**
9.7	0.20	0.9	0.23	**4.3**	0.16	0.48	4.03	3.12	81.9	**4.4**	20.4	2.0	**7.2**
9.7	0.05	0.3	0.06	**5.1**	3.90	0.67	5.72	2.45	80.2	**4.5**	22.1	2.8	**9.0**
8.0	0.96	3.0	0.44	**1.3**	0.00	0.16	1.02	4.96	93.8	**4.7**	25.4	5.0	**5.0**
5.1	1.35	6.1	0.00	**2.3**	0.00	0.00	0.00	4.37	100.0	**6.1**	42.8	0.0	**6.7**
10.0	0.21	0.2	-0.14	**2.1**	0.01	0.08	0.54	1.34	96.0	**6.0**	44.1	0.0	**6.6**
7.6	0.90	5.7	0.32	**1.8**	0.07	0.21	2.71	3.03	90.3	**5.0**	27.0	0.9	**3.9**
6.1	1.41	7.3	1.50	**2.3**	-0.05	-2.13	-26.18	4.29	95.0	**6.6**	46.5	0.0	**1.7**
6.2	3.96	11.1	2.59	**6.8**	0.11	1.18	7.06	4.81	67.0	**3.9**	39.7	25.5	**6.8**
9.8	0.00	0.0	-0.05	**3.1**	0.01	0.16	1.10	2.15	92.0	**4.5**	21.2	4.8	**7.5**
8.1	0.31	2.8	0.20	**3.8**	0.51	0.62	7.84	2.72	74.2	**4.2**	11.2	1.9	**4.8**
6.0	0.62	6.0	1.02	**7.4**	3.11	0.60	6.03	4.09	68.3	**2.9**	12.3	10.5	**7.7**
10.0	0.26	0.9	0.10	**4.0**	0.06	0.42	3.23	2.87	87.3	**5.1**	22.2	0.7	**6.4**
7.0	0.84	6.2	0.31	**5.6**	0.53	0.87	8.59	3.54	80.7	**4.1**	24.7	9.3	**7.1**
9.9	0.34	0.7	0.00	**2.2**	0.01	0.23	1.03	2.48	90.5	**4.4**	24.1	1.0	**7.3**
10.0	1.27	0.4	0.00	**0.7**	0.00	0.00	0.00	1.78	106.7	**5.6**	32.8	0.0	**5.4**
0.7	7.49	42.5	0.00	**0.5**	0.00	-0.69	-6.70	4.03	93.3	**5.4**	42.2	0.0	**4.2**
9.9	0.19	0.6	0.00	**7.6**	0.39	4.31	40.28	2.70	35.4	**4.4**	15.0	5.5	**5.8**
8.9	3.64	3.1	-0.89	**2.0**	0.00	0.05	0.16	3.37	85.5	**5.5**	30.9	0.0	**5.9**
10.0	0.15	0.2	1.31	**1.9**	0.01	0.23	2.07	1.03	76.9	**4.9**	3.0	0.0	**5.4**
8.4	0.00	0.0	0.00	**0.0**	0.00	-8.56	-76.19	0.00	0.0	**9.0**	109.9	0.0	**6.2**
9.2	0.61	2.1	0.13	**6.3**	2.27	1.02	8.11	3.12	72.4	**5.6**	31.9	5.5	**8.7**
8.5	0.00	0.0	0.00	**2.4**	0.00	0.21	1.32	2.54	97.7	**4.9**	49.6	5.0	**7.4**
8.5	0.33	4.4	0.19	**1.7**	0.00	0.00	0.00	3.02	99.3	**6.1**	50.4	1.2	**6.1**
9.1	0.56	3.5	0.42	**0.2**	-0.01	-0.11	-0.90	3.14	97.5	**5.3**	35.1	7.5	**5.1**
8.1	0.00	0.0	0.47	**0.0**	-0.04	-5.69	-67.29	7.23	96.8	**5.8**	37.6	0.0	**2.8**
9.8	0.37	1.0	0.20	**2.8**	0.14	0.41	2.52	2.40	78.7	**4.0**	12.1	9.2	**7.3**
7.9	0.22	2.2	0.12	**8.2**	0.29	0.98	12.29	3.75	75.7	**3.0**	17.2	10.1	**6.0**
8.3	0.26	2.5	2.35	**1.4**	-0.03	-0.93	-7.36	2.81	72.6	**5.0**	22.9	0.0	**6.7**
9.4	0.22	1.8	0.10	**5.4**	2.50	0.91	10.37	3.51	78.1	**4.3**	22.9	5.3	**6.8**
7.1	2.90	7.1	0.00	**2.7**	0.00	0.42	2.67	2.53	81.0	**5.1**	29.7	0.0	**6.2**
9.2	0.88	2.2	-0.93	**8.6**	0.04	1.24	8.99	3.17	48.7	**6.4**	40.8	0.0	**6.3**
10.0	0.43	1.1	-0.04	**5.0**	0.12	0.83	6.14	3.68	81.0	**6.4**	43.6	1.4	**6.3**
6.5	0.53	4.9	0.81	**2.3**	-0.09	-0.24	-2.79	4.36	88.0	**3.7**	16.8	7.6	**5.0**
7.7	0.43	2.8	1.23	**1.2**	-0.03	-0.26	-3.29	5.42	98.1	**4.4**	19.5	2.2	**2.4**
8.2	0.57	3.4	0.00	**2.9**	0.00	0.00	0.00	4.61	100.0	**5.0**	29.2	0.0	**5.6**
8.6	0.00	0.0	0.13	**2.4**	0.01	0.32	2.15	4.29	94.2	**4.8**	24.0	0.0	**6.8**
8.7	0.55	2.5	0.41	**7.8**	1.61	1.34	11.00	3.47	68.6	**4.5**	30.0	5.3	**8.3**
7.0	0.85	5.8	1.02	**0.1**	-0.57	-1.15	-12.37	3.38	104.0	**4.7**	28.0	2.4	**5.2**
4.3	0.98	9.5	0.87	**3.3**	0.07	0.33	3.82	4.21	73.2	**2.0**	10.7	18.1	**4.1**
0.3	11.11	42.1	-0.73	**6.0**	0.01	0.32	1.77	6.44	82.0	**4.3**	49.6	2.0	**7.6**
9.9	1.26	1.2	4.92	**3.6**	0.00	0.46	3.66	2.26	76.9	**5.5**	33.6	0.0	**6.5**
7.6	1.27	3.8	0.00	**2.8**	0.00	-1.66	-18.18	10.06	120.0	**7.5**	68.5	0.0	**7.4**
5.8	1.75	11.2	0.38	**4.6**	0.07	0.27	2.83	4.46	93.0	**4.9**	33.1	7.7	**6.2**
9.7	0.28	0.6	0.00	**8.6**	0.04	1.76	6.89	5.46	67.0	**5.8**	52.3	4.2	**5.7**
10.0	0.21	1.1	0.11	**5.0**	1.03	0.81	6.27	2.71	71.4	**4.0**	18.0	5.3	**8.2**

Name	City	State	Rating	2016 Rating	2015 Rating	Total Assets ($Mil)	One Year Asset Growth	Asset Mix (As a % of Total Assets) Comm-ercial Loans	Cons-umer Loans	Mort-gage Loans	Secur-ities	Capital-ization Index	Net Worth Ratio
Quincy Municipal Credit Union	Quincy	IL	**C**	C	C	3.5	-11.45	0.0	41.2	0.0	0.0	**10.0**	15.3
Quincy Postal Employees Credit Union	Quincy	IL	**D+**	D+	C-	2.1	-10.14	0.0	29.5	0.0	0.0	**10.0**	12.8
Quindaro Homes Federal Credit Union	Kansas City	KS	**D+**	D+	C-	<1	-10.88	0.0	0.0	0.0	0.0	**10.0**	27.7
Quorum Federal Credit Union	Purchase	NY	**D+**	D+	C	923.7	-4.90	9.1	7.9	26.7	7.2	**5.2**	7.3
▼ R T P Federal Credit Union	Durham	NC	**C-**	C	C	115.0	4.84	8.8	35.6	9.9	11.3	**6.5**	8.7
▲ R-G Federal Credit Union	Raymore	MO	**D+**	D	D	81.6	5.53	0.0	26.3	21.8	8.0	**5.8**	7.8
R-S Bellco Federal Credit Union	New Brighton	PA	**D-**	D-	E+	26.4	2.67	0.0	32.0	0.2	15.4	**4.5**	6.5
R.I.A. Federal Credit Union	Bettendorf	IA	**C+**	C+	C+	399.6	12.08	0.0	61.2	11.8	9.9	**7.2**	9.1
R.S.C. YO/CL Offices FCU	Youngstown	OH	**C-**	C-	C-	6.4	-1.20	0.0	17.8	0.3	60.0	**10.0**	12.5
R.T.A. Brooklyn Federal Credit Union	Cleveland	OH	**E+**	E+	E+	7.7	2.84	0.0	33.2	2.3	0.0	**4.2**	6.2
Rabun-Tallulah Federal Credit Union	Tiger	GA	**C+**	C+	C+	<1	-1.96	0.0	20.5	0.0	0.0	**10.0**	23.9
▼ Racine Municipal Employees Credit Union	Racine	WI	**C-**	C	C	13.8	-4.95	0.0	30.0	21.1	0.0	**10.0**	15.0
Radio Cab Credit Union	Portland	OR	**C+**	C+	C+	4.8	-0.91	1.2	1.2	0.0	0.0	**10.0**	17.8
Radio, Television & Communications FCU	New York	NY	**D**	D	D	3.7	-9.17	0.0	29.5	23.1	0.0	**10.0**	14.6
▼ Rafe Federal Credit Union	Riverside	CA	**D+**	C-	C	24.3	0.99	0.0	62.5	2.2	3.8	**10.0**	11.9
RAH Federal Credit Union	Randolph	MA	**C**	C	C-	16.0	4.43	0.0	27.9	31.6	0.0	**10.0**	11.9
Railroad & Industrial FCU	Tampa	FL	**B+**	B+	B+	327.4	7.87	0.2	18.9	5.6	34.7	**10.0**	11.3
Railroad Federal Credit Union	Irondale	AL	**C**	C	C	108.6	2.40	0.0	8.9	0.5	76.8	**10.0**	12.1
▼ Rails West Federal Credit Union	Chubbuck	ID	**D+**	C-	C-	61.0	6.21	0.0	39.0	21.0	0.0	**5.5**	7.5
Railway Credit Union	Mandan	ND	**A**	A	A-	103.6	8.45	9.8	27.9	15.8	10.6	**10.0**	13.3
Railway Employees Credit Union	Muscle Shoals	AL	**B-**	B-	C+	18.4	4.87	0.0	16.8	18.2	0.0	**10.0**	22.7
Rainbow Federal Credit Union	Lewiston	ME	**A-**	A-	B+	219.1	8.54	0.1	15.5	51.4	0.7	**10.0**	13.2
Raleigh County Educators FCU	Beckley	WV	**B-**	B-	B-	23.5	3.05	0.0	31.5	0.0	0.0	**10.0**	17.2
Raleigh County Federal Credit Union	Beckley	WV	**B**	B	B	11.8	8.26	0.0	57.2	0.0	0.0	**10.0**	11.6
Rancho Federal Credit Union	Downey	CA	**D+**	D+	D+	94.4	3.83	0.1	20.9	32.1	19.9	**5.2**	7.4
Randolph-Brooks Federal Credit Union	Live Oak	TX	**A+**	A+	A+	8126.9	14.03	5.0	35.6	27.5	15.4	**10.0**	11.6
▲ Rapides Federal Credit Union	Alexandria	LA	**D+**	D	D+	6.6	0.96	0.0	23.6	0.0	0.0	**10.0**	24.6
▼ Rapides General Hospital Employees FCU	Alexandria	LA	**C-**	C	C	12.2	1.22	0.0	26.4	0.5	0.0	**10.0**	13.1
▼ Raritan Bay Federal Credit Union	Sayreville	NJ	**D+**	C-	C-	87.8	7.21	0.0	25.0	2.1	43.4	**4.6**	6.8
Ravalli County Federal Credit Union	Hamilton	MT	**B**	B	B	43.9	10.01	0.8	16.8	19.6	33.2	**9.2**	10.4
Ravenswood Federal Credit Union	Ravenswood	WV	**C**	C	B-	32.8	-2.58	0.0	34.2	4.4	0.0	**10.0**	12.8
Ray Federal Credit Union	Kearny	AZ	**D**	D	D+	10.2	7.80	0.0	48.0	11.2	0.0	**8.9**	10.2
Raytown-Lee's Summit Community CU	Raytown	MO	**D**	D	D-	59.5	-3.17	0.0	74.1	2.9	0.0	**5.4**	7.4
Reading Berks School Employees CU	Reading	PA	**C**	C	C+	20.0	0.35	0.7	8.3	0.0	0.0	**10.0**	11.6
▼ Reading Federal Credit Union	Cincinnati	OH	**D**	D+	C-	6.8	-11.98	0.0	14.1	0.0	0.0	**10.0**	13.5
Reading Mass Town Employees FCU	Reading	MA	**D+**	D+	D	8.3	8.36	0.0	28.4	7.7	0.0	**10.0**	14.6
Reavis-Stickney Credit Union	Burbank	IL	**C-**	C-	D+	1.1	5.93	0.0	24.6	0.0	0.0	**8.4**	9.9
Red Canoe Credit Union	Longview	WA	**A-**	A-	B	719.6	7.10	9.9	29.2	36.6	5.7	**10.0**	12.1
Red Crown Federal Credit Union	Tulsa	OK	**B-**	B-	B-	189.7	6.89	3.0	57.7	13.9	6.6	**5.6**	7.7
Red Lake Co-Op Federal Credit Union	Red Lake Falls	MN	**D+**	D+	D+	6.6	-0.89	0.1	26.5	19.7	2.3	**8.2**	9.8
Red River Federal Credit Union	Altus	OK	**D+**	D+	C	81.8	6.29	1.3	37.1	10.0	31.3	**8.4**	10.5
Red River Federal Credit Union	Texarkana	TX	**A-**	A-	A-	801.2	7.55	12.0	38.6	20.0	10.1	**9.4**	10.6
▲ Red River Mill Employees FCU	Natchitoches	LA	**C**	C-	C-	8.7	8.44	0.4	62.2	0.1	1.3	**10.0**	18.6
Red Rocks Credit Union	Littleton	CO	**B**	B	B-	278.2	7.84	0.0	29.5	19.6	2.1	**7.4**	9.3
Red Wing Credit Union	Red Wing	MN	**B**	B	B	96.6	6.48	2.0	20.9	12.5	23.9	**8.4**	10.3
Redbrand Credit Union	Bartonville	IL	**B-**	B-	B-	60.1	6.77	0.0	31.3	7.2	16.7	**9.0**	10.3
Redeemer Federal Credit Union	Greenville	TX	**B**	B		<1	225.73	0.0	39.8	0.0	0.0	**10.0**	28.9
Rediform Niagara Falls NY FCU	Niagara Falls	NY	**D**	D	D+	10.8	5.59	0.0	29.9	13.0	0.1	**10.0**	14.5
Redlands City Employees FCU	Redlands	CA	**C-**	C-	D+	7.0	1.08	0.0	78.4	0.0	1.2	**10.0**	23.2
Redstone Federal Credit Union	Huntsville	AL	**B+**	B+	A-	4885.9	12.60	1.7	19.1	7.4	49.6	**8.4**	10.2
Redwood Credit Union	Santa Rosa	CA	**A**	A	A	3460.9	17.51	9.8	23.4	39.7	0.0	**10.0**	11.7
Reed Credit Union	Houston	TX	**D+**	D+	D+	16.5	-9.84	0.0	10.3	0.0	0.0	**10.0**	15.2
Reeves County Teachers Credit Union	Pecos	TX	**D+**	D+	D+	12.4	4.75	2.2	65.1	4.2	0.0	**7.6**	9.4
Refugio County Federal Credit Union	Refugio	TX	**B**	B	B	11.7	5.96	0.5	44.8	0.0	0.0	**10.0**	15.0
Regional Federal Credit Union	Hammond	IN	**C**	C	C-	134.8	1.95	1.2	16.9	13.1	55.6	**8.7**	10.4
Regional Medical Ctr Hopkins County Empls FCU	Madisonville	KY	**D+**	D+	C-	10.0	-0.49	0.0	28.5	0.0	0.0	**6.5**	8.5
Regional Members Federal Credit Union	Columbus	GA	**D+**	D+	D	8.7	0.09	0.0	42.2	0.0	1.7	**8.8**	10.2
Regional Water Authority Employees CU	New Haven	CT	**D+**	D+	C-	6.8	6.37	0.0	9.4	0.0	0.0	**9.2**	10.5
▲ Register Guard Federal Credit Union	Springfield	OR	**B-**	C+	C+	22.6	11.74	9.3	25.0	28.8	0.0	**10.0**	15.6
Reliance Credit Union	Kansas City	KS	**B-**	B-	B-	25.1	3.79	0.0	42.3	17.3	0.0	**10.0**	15.4

Asset Quality Index	Non-Performing Loans as a % of Total Loans	Non-Performing Loans as a % of Capital	Net Charge-Offs Avg Loans	Profitability Index	Net Income ($Mil)	Return on Assets	Return on Equity	Net Interest Spread	Overhead Efficiency Ratio	Liquidity Index	Liquidity Ratio	Hot Money Ratio	Stability Index
9.9	0.00	0.0	0.00	3.2	0.01	0.56	3.79	2.95	75.0	5.4	42.4	0.0	6.1
9.8	0.42	1.1	0.00	1.0	0.00	0.00	0.00	3.24	100.0	5.8	40.7	0.0	3.8
2.9	13.00	22.0	2.51	3.9	0.00	0.41	1.47	6.47	90.9	6.9	70.9	0.0	6.7
1.0	5.82	47.3	0.99	3.0	1.88	0.82	11.96	4.31	65.7	2.9	13.3	15.8	5.1
6.7	1.35	9.4	0.12	2.2	-0.01	-0.02	-0.25	3.18	95.9	4.8	21.0	1.6	5.7
7.2	0.46	5.3	0.57	3.7	0.46	2.27	29.77	3.39	56.8	5.0	26.1	0.6	2.2
7.5	0.33	3.0	0.41	1.0	0.00	0.05	0.79	3.08	96.0	5.0	30.9	1.5	2.1
5.6	0.78	8.3	0.77	3.6	0.44	0.45	4.80	3.71	79.7	3.2	7.2	4.4	5.1
8.6	0.50	0.9	0.00	2.7	0.00	0.25	2.00	1.58	82.6	5.5	33.1	0.0	6.4
1.7	6.32	37.1	0.72	0.3	-0.01	-0.48	-7.44	3.43	92.1	5.8	42.9	0.0	2.0
8.1	5.26	4.5	0.00	1.4	0.00	-0.62	-2.58	5.67	100.0	8.4	103.0	0.0	7.0
9.8	0.12	0.4	0.00	1.2	-0.01	-0.29	-1.93	2.95	108.4	4.3	23.7	1.7	6.9
8.9	0.00	0.0	0.61	5.2	0.01	0.71	4.23	3.51	53.5	5.3	55.3	0.0	5.0
5.9	3.48	12.2	16.92	0.0	-0.08	-8.45	-54.26	4.43	295.0	5.4	47.6	0.0	4.7
0.7	9.29	43.0	4.73	3.0	-0.10	-1.61	-13.06	10.12	72.1	4.1	28.3	7.6	6.2
8.7	0.98	5.7	0.00	2.7	0.01	0.30	2.54	3.40	90.8	4.4	20.6	0.7	6.1
8.2	1.64	4.7	0.59	4.1	0.41	0.50	4.66	2.70	77.2	5.6	40.5	10.9	6.5
10.0	0.42	0.6	0.25	1.7	0.00	0.01	0.12	1.15	97.2	4.2	11.1	11.3	6.8
5.8	1.00	8.9	0.31	2.9	0.01	0.07	0.97	3.97	96.8	4.3	20.0	1.0	3.0
9.2	0.11	1.8	0.22	8.5	0.28	1.08	8.10	3.63	71.8	3.2	13.3	9.7	9.7
10.0	0.18	0.3	-0.06	2.9	0.02	0.35	1.53	3.86	89.3	7.0	57.7	0.0	6.9
8.7	0.36	2.6	0.02	5.5	0.52	0.96	7.97	3.37	74.3	3.5	23.6	8.0	8.8
9.7	0.66	1.3	0.37	5.5	0.04	0.67	3.89	3.22	69.9	6.2	30.8	0.0	7.3
7.8	0.22	1.2	0.36	8.1	0.03	1.12	9.77	4.41	75.9	3.6	13.9	8.8	5.7
6.0	1.39	11.1	0.32	1.4	-0.03	-0.13	-1.83	3.70	98.8	4.3	14.7	2.2	2.7
9.2	0.33	2.1	0.28	7.2	20.63	1.04	8.75	2.87	70.6	3.6	16.5	5.8	10.0
9.9	0.49	0.6	0.42	1.3	0.01	0.37	1.49	3.01	86.5	6.3	45.2	0.0	5.9
9.4	0.76	2.4	0.40	1.1	-0.01	-0.20	-1.50	2.27	101.5	5.3	32.8	0.0	6.1
6.1	1.26	7.9	0.70	2.2	0.04	0.19	2.79	3.53	89.4	4.8	19.2	1.0	1.7
7.6	0.59	3.6	0.08	6.0	0.06	0.58	5.45	3.11	83.1	5.4	32.0	0.8	5.6
6.4	2.73	10.7	0.39	2.3	0.03	0.42	3.58	3.74	89.4	5.7	28.7	1.6	5.1
3.6	2.61	15.0	0.29	3.4	0.03	1.12	10.52	7.26	94.4	5.3	35.3	9.0	2.3
4.1	0.81	8.2	1.51	0.4	-0.26	-1.77	-23.20	3.20	101.9	3.5	14.7	8.0	2.8
7.1	2.78	7.3	0.00	1.8	-0.01	-0.12	-1.04	1.58	107.6	5.5	32.9	0.0	5.8
9.1	3.03	3.1	4.91	0.0	-0.01	-0.71	-5.19	1.92	90.9	4.1	27.1	13.6	3.9
10.0	0.59	1.6	0.00	0.6	0.00	-0.20	-1.32	2.82	105.9	6.1	61.9	0.0	6.4
10.0	0.00	0.0	0.00	2.9	0.00	0.73	7.48	2.91	60.0	7.0	74.1	0.0	4.6
8.6	0.30	2.5	0.29	5.3	1.30	0.73	5.94	3.95	76.7	3.8	12.6	5.4	8.8
6.0	0.43	6.5	0.36	4.4	0.16	0.34	4.71	3.66	86.5	3.2	14.8	11.4	4.0
7.8	0.29	2.0	0.00	4.7	0.01	0.54	5.60	4.08	84.9	4.7	23.5	0.0	3.7
6.0	0.98	7.0	0.64	1.3	0.04	0.20	2.03	2.97	89.2	4.3	12.2	2.6	3.7
7.3	0.40	3.9	0.78	6.9	2.20	1.12	10.46	4.02	65.0	3.8	25.5	15.9	7.4
6.9	0.93	3.0	0.24	7.2	0.06	2.98	13.15	5.09	62.0	3.7	8.8	0.0	5.0
7.9	0.43	4.5	0.52	4.1	0.24	0.35	3.81	4.23	80.9	3.3	17.4	12.3	6.3
7.4	0.65	3.9	0.09	5.0	0.16	0.69	6.93	3.07	77.8	4.7	18.1	0.7	5.5
6.2	1.40	6.8	0.99	3.8	0.06	0.43	4.64	4.26	82.8	5.2	25.2	1.1	4.1
9.9	0.00	0.0	0.00	9.8	0.05	38.64	129.34	4.32	11.9	7.6	80.8	0.0	6.3
7.8	1.37	4.5	0.83	0.0	-0.03	-1.13	-7.61	3.88	97.9	6.0	36.3	0.0	5.9
6.7	0.47	1.8	6.55	5.8	0.06	3.29	14.97	5.52	35.6	3.1	8.8	0.0	3.7
10.0	0.18	0.9	0.62	5.5	14.05	1.17	12.81	2.72	68.4	5.8	30.1	3.7	6.2
9.3	0.21	1.5	0.18	9.8	16.71	1.98	16.95	4.06	55.0	5.0	25.7	2.5	9.6
10.0	0.43	0.3	0.00	0.3	-0.02	-0.48	-3.19	1.89	123.5	5.6	43.3	0.0	5.6
1.4	4.20	32.8	0.00	5.4	0.02	0.80	8.36	5.57	86.7	4.2	17.3	0.0	5.2
7.4	2.06	7.0	0.00	5.3	0.03	0.87	5.77	3.34	64.2	5.7	53.2	0.0	7.7
10.0	0.53	1.7	0.12	2.5	0.05	0.16	1.60	2.75	91.9	5.5	44.5	0.8	5.7
9.4	0.00	0.0	0.00	2.0	0.01	0.20	2.35	3.52	95.3	6.0	41.2	0.0	1.7
5.3	2.22	11.3	0.00	3.7	0.01	0.38	3.65	3.77	89.5	4.1	29.7	4.2	3.0
10.0	0.09	0.1	0.00	1.5	0.00	0.00	0.00	1.66	96.4	4.9	21.8	0.0	5.3
9.3	0.63	2.1	0.32	6.6	0.15	2.85	17.51	6.09	61.9	6.0	44.4	3.4	6.3
8.7	0.91	3.7	0.15	3.8	0.04	0.57	3.65	3.82	76.2	4.0	9.0	1.2	6.6

	Name	City	State	Rating	2016 Rating	2015 Rating	Total Assets ($Mil)	One Year Asset Growth	Asset Mix (As a % of Total Assets) Comm-ercial Loans	Cons-umer Loans	Mort-gage Loans	Secur-ities	Capital-ization Index	Net Worth Ratio
	Reliance Federal Credit Union	King Of Prussia	PA	**D**	D	D+	27.4	18.52	2.6	22.2	1.9	4.8	**6.1**	8.1
	Reliant Community Federal Credit Union	Sodus	NY	**B-**	B-	B-	427.2	5.15	5.8	23.0	23.0	14.8	**7.2**	9.2
▲	Reliant Federal Credit Union	Casper	WY	**C+**	C	B-	122.3	3.02	0.4	44.7	10.3	10.8	**7.0**	9.1
	Remington Federal Credit Union	Ilion	NY	**C+**	C+	C-	41.4	0.54	0.0	28.0	2.7	23.4	**10.0**	12.8
	Reno City Employees Federal Credit Union	Reno	NV	**C-**	C-	D+	32.0	4.86	0.0	19.8	13.4	0.0	**6.3**	8.3
	Research 1166 Federal Credit Union	Paulsboro	NJ	**D**	D	D	17.5	-4.14	0.0	10.4	9.0	32.0	**6.6**	8.6
	Resource Federal Credit Union	Jackson	TN	**C-**	C-	D+	37.2	7.79	0.0	19.1	5.6	0.0	**6.3**	8.3
	Resource One Credit Union	Dallas	TX	**B+**	B+	A-	476.8	6.79	2.9	42.0	22.5	0.2	**7.2**	9.2
	Resurrection Lutheran FCU	Chicago	IL	**C**	C	C-	<1	13.64	0.0	26.0	0.0	0.0	**10.0**	23.0
	Revere Firefighters Credit Union	Revere	MA	**C**	C	C	6.6	4.30	0.0	18.3	0.0	2.8	**10.0**	14.5
▼	Revere Municipal Employees FCU	Revere	MA	**C-**	C	C-	11.2	3.69	0.0	52.2	0.0	0.0	**10.0**	12.8
	Rheem Arkansas Federal Credit Union	Fort Smith	AR	**D**	D	D+	5.4	0.49	0.0	59.9	0.0	0.0	**10.0**	15.0
	Rhode Island Credit Union	Providence	RI	**D+**	D+	C-	271.8	4.11	0.0	30.5	14.6	13.2	**8.7**	10.1
▼	Richfield-Bloomington Credit Union	Bloomington	MN	**C-**	C	B-	282.6	4.21	7.4	30.1	22.4	21.4	**6.2**	8.4
	Richland Federal Credit Union	Sidney	MT	**A-**	A-	A-	84.5	-4.18	30.7	6.2	15.4	3.9	**10.0**	12.7
	Richland Parish Schools FCU	Rayville	LA	**B-**	B-	C+	<1	4.54	0.0	30.3	0.0	0.0	**10.0**	18.7
	Richmond City Employees FCU	Richmond	IN	**D+**	D+	D+	6.0	14.02	0.0	39.0	0.0	8.5	**8.2**	9.8
	Richmond Heritage Federal Credit Union	Richmond	VA	**D-**	D-	D-	7.1	1.74	0.0	34.1	0.0	0.0	**5.7**	7.7
	Richmond Light Employees FCU	Richmond	IN	**D+**	D+	D+	1.0	-1.15	0.0	45.8	0.0	0.0	**10.0**	20.3
	Richmond Virginia Fire Police Credit Union, Inc.	Richmond	VA	**C-**	C-	C	20.8	0.02	0.0	39.9	0.0	0.0	**10.0**	12.3
	Riegel Federal Credit Union	Milford	NJ	**C**	C	C-	122.4	4.75	0.3	10.7	12.1	31.6	**10.0**	11.2
	Riegelwood Federal Credit Union	Riegelwood	NC	**C+**	C+	C	102.2	3.16	0.0	48.5	2.5	3.1	**10.0**	12.6
	Rig Employees Credit Union	Macon	GA	**C**	C	C	7.6	-0.12	0.0	43.5	0.0	0.0	**10.0**	29.6
	RIM Country Federal Credit Union	Snowflake	AZ	**C**	C	C	16.0	16.44	0.0	28.7	16.4	23.9	**8.3**	9.9
	Rimrock Credit Union	Billings	MT	**C**	C	C	39.1	6.09	0.1	18.1	2.5	0.0	**10.0**	14.8
	Rincones Presbyterian Credit Union	Chacon	NM	**D+**	D+	C-	4.1	14.05	0.0	48.2	0.0	0.0	**8.8**	10.2
	Rio Blanco Schools Federal Credit Union	Rangely	CO	**C+**	C+	B-	6.4	4.41	0.0	40.5	0.0	0.0	**10.0**	18.4
	Rio Grande Credit Union	Albuquerque	NM	**A**	A	A	313.5	10.85	1.0	53.4	10.4	8.8	**10.0**	13.6
	Rio Grande Federal Credit Union	Grand Junction	CO	**B**	B	B	51.8	6.00	4.5	16.0	12.0	0.0	**10.0**	18.0
	Rio Grande Valley Credit Union	Harlingen	TX	**C+**	C+	C+	94.0	6.86	0.0	36.4	7.7	22.7	**7.3**	9.2
	Ripco Credit Union	Rhinelander	WI	**B-**	B-	C+	123.1	5.76	3.5	24.3	16.1	13.4	**8.1**	9.9
	River Bend Federal Credit Union	South Bend	IN	**C**	C	C	5.7	3.05	0.0	40.5	4.3	0.0	**10.0**	15.4
	River Cities Community Credit Union	Atchison	KS	**E+**	E+	E+	3.6	10.34	0.0	80.4	0.0	0.0	**5.1**	7.1
	River Cities Credit Union	Alexandria	LA	**D-**	D-	D	8.2	-5.22	0.0	27.2	1.8	0.0	**8.0**	9.7
	River City Federal Credit Union	San Antonio	TX	**D-**	D-	D	119.3	-0.94	1.7	60.3	19.2	4.3	**4.1**	6.2
▲	River Community Credit Union	Ottumwa	IA	**B-**	C+	C	17.0	-2.04	1.6	44.0	6.8	1.3	**10.0**	14.9
	River Region Credit Union	Jefferson City	MO	**B**	B	B	194.5	4.40	1.1	54.9	11.5	4.8	**8.0**	9.7
	River Region Federal Credit Union	Lutcher	LA	**C+**	C+	C+	36.2	4.46	0.0	11.8	12.4	0.0	**10.0**	19.0
	River To River Credit Union	Vienna	IL	**D+**	D+	D+	18.7	2.86	0.0	32.3	0.7	0.0	**5.8**	7.8
	River Town Federal Credit Union	Fort Smith	AR	**D**	D	C-	12.9	-1.74	0.0	59.4	0.0	0.0	**9.9**	10.9
	River Valley Community FCU	Camden	AR	**D+**	D+	D+	43.3	5.54	0.2	48.3	12.5	0.0	**10.0**	11.3
	River Valley Credit Union	Ames	IA	**B+**	B+	B+	60.9	4.43	3.2	22.0	19.5	0.0	**10.0**	11.3
	River Valley Credit Union	Ada	MI	**D+**	D+	C-	96.7	3.96	3.1	24.4	8.7	12.6	**4.9**	6.9
	River Valley Credit Union	Miamisburg	OH	**C+**	C+	B-	330.2	1.66	12.7	53.2	24.0	3.3	**7.2**	9.2
	River Valley Credit Union	Brattleboro	VT	**C**	C	C-	98.3	8.99	4.5	17.7	34.3	0.0	**5.4**	7.4
	River Works Credit Union	Lynn	MA	**A-**	A-	A	107.8	-5.83	11.3	9.3	42.0	2.3	**10.0**	12.8
	River-Rail Community FCU	Casper	WY	**C-**	C-	D+	34.9	-5.51	3.6	36.2	20.8	0.0	**7.2**	9.1
▼	Riverdale Credit Union	Selma	AL	**B-**	B	B	76.2	10.62	0.0	67.1	5.6	0.3	**10.0**	12.6
	Riverfall Credit Union	Tuscaloosa	AL	**B+**	B+	B+	122.5	1.93	0.0	15.6	15.5	43.0	**10.0**	13.9
	Riverfork Federal Credit Union	Grand Forks	ND	**C**	C	C	24.2	0.15	0.0	37.0	0.0	0.0	**9.6**	10.7
▲	Riverfront Federal Credit Union	Reading	PA	**D**	D-	D	177.5	0.19	0.0	40.7	6.9	22.5	**6.4**	8.5
	Riverland Federal Credit Union	New Orleans	LA	**B-**	B-	B-	233.9	13.88	0.4	54.6	7.6	0.0	**6.0**	8.1
	Rivermark Community Credit Union	Beaverton	OR	**B+**	B+	B+	839.3	13.25	3.5	50.9	20.8	2.9	**6.7**	8.7
	Riverset Credit Union	Pittsburgh	PA	**B**	B	B	117.2	-0.95	0.0	42.5	28.0	3.4	**10.0**	21.5
▼	Riverside Beaver County FCU	Ellwood City	PA	**D-**	D	D	1.5	-0.46	0.0	33.5	0.0	0.0	**9.9**	11.0
	Riverside Community Credit Union	Kankakee	IL	**C**	C	C	30.3	1.85	0.0	18.5	18.3	2.8	**6.4**	8.4
	Riverside Community Federal Credit Union	Marion	IN	**B-**	B-	C+	37.9	6.48	13.9	50.1	9.7	0.0	**9.3**	10.6
	Riverside Federal Credit Union	Buffalo	NY	**D**	D	D-	55.9	-0.80	0.0	20.0	33.4	1.7	**7.4**	9.3
	Riverside Health System Employees CU	Newport News	VA	**C-**	C-	C-	8.8	2.70	0.0	43.9	0.0	0.0	**10.0**	16.3
▼	Rivertown Community Federal Credit Union	Grandville	MI	**C**	C+	C-	64.8	1.46	0.0	43.2	10.9	19.3	**10.0**	14.2

Asset Quality Index	Non-Performing Loans as a % of Total Loans	Non-Performing Loans as a % of Capital	Net Charge-Offs Avg Loans	Profitability Index	Net Income ($Mil)	Return on Assets	Return on Equity	Net Interest Spread	Overhead Efficiency Ratio	Liquidity Index	Liquidity Ratio	Hot Money Ratio	Stability Index
4.0	2.92	19.9	-0.42	**0.8**	-0.02	-0.28	-3.43	3.61	94.2	**4.3**	20.5	2.9	**1.8**
9.4	0.22	1.8	0.11	**3.6**	0.23	0.22	2.32	3.70	94.4	**4.2**	17.1	1.2	**6.4**
7.5	0.51	4.4	0.48	**3.3**	0.14	0.46	5.68	3.48	82.6	**4.1**	15.4	3.4	**5.1**
9.9	0.54	1.6	0.53	**3.5**	0.05	0.51	3.87	3.42	78.4	**5.7**	34.9	0.0	**5.9**
9.9	0.02	0.1	0.70	**2.1**	0.01	0.10	1.21	2.56	96.1	**5.4**	45.5	5.9	**3.3**
9.3	0.21	1.2	0.53	**0.9**	-0.01	-0.11	-1.59	2.72	102.7	**5.6**	33.3	0.0	**3.3**
10.0	0.19	0.7	0.04	**2.3**	0.02	0.23	2.73	2.44	94.0	**6.0**	38.2	3.3	**3.6**
7.3	0.48	4.2	1.27	**2.7**	-0.16	-0.14	-1.46	4.81	80.8	**3.7**	19.1	9.6	**5.4**
9.6	0.00	0.0	0.00	**2.4**	0.00	0.00	0.00	6.11	100.0	**6.8**	47.4	0.0	**7.3**
10.0	0.00	0.0	0.00	**1.7**	0.00	-0.06	-0.42	1.37	104.6	**4.9**	10.7	0.0	**7.0**
8.7	0.15	0.9	-0.09	**1.4**	-0.01	-0.25	-1.96	3.80	106.3	**4.5**	21.6	0.0	**7.0**
2.7	3.62	20.3	0.85	**0.4**	-0.01	-0.95	-5.95	5.45	102.6	**4.7**	27.9	3.6	**5.8**
9.9	0.16	1.1	0.23	**1.7**	0.09	0.13	1.38	3.48	93.1	**4.1**	18.5	2.0	**5.4**
6.5	1.03	8.2	0.70	**2.2**	0.32	0.46	5.64	3.42	85.9	**4.0**	16.5	2.6	**3.5**
6.6	2.29	8.0	0.11	**6.1**	0.18	0.87	7.06	2.89	70.3	**6.0**	48.9	1.0	**7.2**
10.0	0.44	0.6	0.00	**6.8**	0.00	1.03	5.67	5.27	75.0	**7.5**	87.0	0.0	**5.7**
9.6	0.19	0.8	0.00	**2.0**	0.00	-0.07	-0.68	3.47	102.3	**6.2**	37.7	0.0	**3.6**
5.7	2.53	11.4	1.28	**1.5**	-0.02	-1.32	-16.58	5.12	104.7	**5.4**	43.9	4.7	**1.0**
8.4	0.00	0.0	0.00	**1.2**	0.00	0.00	0.00	2.07	100.0	**5.0**	60.9	0.0	**6.5**
5.8	3.76	16.7	0.33	**2.4**	0.01	0.25	2.04	4.37	93.5	**5.0**	28.4	1.8	**4.5**
9.9	0.08	0.2	0.02	**2.5**	0.09	0.31	2.76	2.54	85.6	**5.9**	31.9	1.2	**6.8**
4.7	1.96	11.7	0.82	**2.9**	0.04	0.17	1.31	4.79	83.4	**4.3**	25.8	6.8	**7.2**
9.8	1.13	1.7	0.00	**2.3**	0.00	0.05	0.18	2.64	95.7	**5.7**	42.8	0.0	**7.5**
6.2	1.74	9.7	0.24	**4.5**	0.02	0.58	5.85	4.09	85.1	**4.3**	18.8	0.0	**4.3**
10.0	0.54	1.0	0.12	**2.4**	0.03	0.27	1.81	2.86	88.0	**6.0**	40.7	1.0	**6.5**
5.3	0.30	1.7	0.00	**4.8**	0.01	0.50	4.78	4.72	86.4	**5.5**	38.3	0.0	**3.7**
9.4	0.00	0.0	-0.36	**5.7**	0.02	0.94	5.13	3.33	68.8	**4.6**	22.2	1.9	**5.0**
7.5	0.54	3.4	1.30	**7.5**	0.63	0.82	5.94	4.58	67.8	**3.0**	22.6	18.4	**8.1**
9.9	0.18	0.5	0.02	**4.2**	0.07	0.52	2.89	2.70	80.2	**5.1**	49.9	12.4	**7.3**
7.3	0.62	3.8	0.34	**2.9**	0.05	0.22	2.37	3.77	92.6	**5.0**	24.2	1.1	**4.4**
7.2	1.29	6.6	0.11	**3.7**	0.17	0.54	5.54	3.44	86.6	**4.7**	27.6	2.1	**6.0**
8.2	1.21	3.7	0.29	**7.8**	0.02	1.56	10.23	4.29	64.6	**4.6**	40.5	2.7	**5.0**
2.1	2.79	29.2	0.92	**4.3**	0.01	0.80	11.07	5.50	80.8	**2.3**	15.3	19.7	**1.0**
7.9	0.33	1.4	0.11	**0.0**	-0.03	-1.56	-15.76	2.85	155.4	**5.6**	40.8	0.0	**3.4**
5.1	0.73	8.6	1.09	**0.5**	-0.16	-0.53	-8.60	4.32	90.1	**2.6**	7.2	9.2	**1.8**
9.7	0.24	1.0	-0.12	**5.0**	0.05	1.16	7.64	4.16	75.0	**5.0**	34.7	0.0	**6.7**
6.1	0.73	5.8	0.88	**6.4**	0.42	0.89	9.06	3.42	67.9	**2.7**	12.1	13.7	**6.4**
7.1	4.51	8.6	0.07	**2.5**	0.04	0.48	2.51	3.04	91.1	**7.0**	54.0	1.8	**6.4**
8.0	0.27	1.5	-0.05	**2.9**	0.01	0.15	1.92	3.16	95.8	**6.0**	41.4	1.5	**3.8**
5.0	0.97	6.9	0.45	**0.6**	-0.01	-0.34	-3.11	4.13	103.4	**4.1**	22.3	7.2	**4.4**
5.2	1.57	10.3	-0.07	**0.7**	-0.02	-0.22	-1.88	4.25	104.4	**4.3**	23.9	2.9	**5.8**
8.9	0.38	1.8	-0.02	**3.6**	0.04	0.29	2.57	2.63	82.1	**5.0**	31.9	2.8	**6.6**
4.4	2.22	13.4	5.95	**2.0**	0.10	0.43	6.02	3.30	89.9	**5.3**	25.9	0.6	**2.8**
7.2	0.29	3.0	0.41	**2.9**	0.33	0.40	4.20	3.02	81.6	**3.0**	10.3	6.8	**5.6**
5.2	0.84	11.3	0.49	**4.4**	0.08	0.31	4.22	5.33	88.0	**3.8**	11.2	0.4	**3.6**
7.3	1.33	6.4	0.56	**4.8**	0.10	0.38	2.97	4.09	87.4	**3.8**	39.4	20.7	**7.5**
5.1	1.35	11.7	-0.03	**2.9**	0.05	0.59	6.47	4.26	84.3	**2.9**	16.5	14.5	**4.0**
2.6	3.69	21.8	1.88	**7.5**	0.72	3.88	31.27	7.98	50.9	**3.1**	10.8	5.2	**5.8**
7.3	1.76	6.6	0.26	**2.7**	0.05	0.15	1.28	2.43	87.3	**4.0**	29.3	12.6	**7.7**
7.9	0.48	2.5	0.12	**4.5**	0.04	0.68	6.39	2.85	76.0	**5.8**	40.9	0.5	**5.3**
8.0	0.47	3.9	0.76	**1.3**	0.18	0.40	4.75	3.32	86.9	**5.0**	30.6	1.1	**3.8**
7.7	0.25	2.5	0.54	**4.3**	0.21	0.37	4.53	3.61	81.3	**4.3**	25.9	4.7	**5.2**
6.0	0.47	5.9	1.09	**5.7**	0.75	0.37	4.14	4.25	71.0	**3.1**	7.4	3.4	**6.6**
8.4	0.92	3.1	0.37	**4.2**	0.13	0.45	2.07	4.07	83.1	**4.3**	25.1	2.3	**7.7**
9.7	0.00	0.0	0.00	**0.0**	0.00	-0.80	-7.10	2.26	142.9	**5.9**	39.9	0.0	**4.6**
10.0	0.04	0.2	0.31	**2.7**	0.01	0.18	2.06	3.27	95.4	**5.3**	27.0	0.0	**4.0**
6.5	0.33	2.3	-0.11	**4.6**	0.08	0.83	7.77	3.42	83.2	**2.4**	24.9	22.3	**5.5**
6.4	1.07	6.4	0.01	**0.7**	0.00	-0.01	-0.15	3.22	94.8	**4.2**	23.8	4.1	**3.4**
9.2	0.21	0.6	1.96	**1.8**	-0.01	-0.37	-2.24	7.07	101.0	**7.1**	64.6	0.0	**6.2**
6.7	1.72	6.8	2.49	**1.2**	-0.19	-1.20	-8.23	4.99	74.4	**4.9**	26.9	1.6	**5.7**

								Asset Mix (As a % of Total Assets)					
Name	City	State	Rating	2016 Rating	2015 Rating	Total Assets ($Mil)	One Year Asset Growth	Commercial Loans	Consumer Loans	Mortgage Loans	Securities	Capitalization Index	Net Worth Ratio
▼ RiverTrace Federal Credit Union	Richmond	VA	D	D+	C-	23.8	-3.80	0.0	59.1	10.5	1.0	6.5	8.6
Rivertrust Federal Credit Union	Pearl	MS	B	B	B	176.1	-0.57	0.0	13.8	10.4	44.1	10.0	13.9
Riverview Community Federal Credit Union	Saint Clair	MI	C+	C+	C	29.6	3.70	2.2	27.4	13.1	11.5	6.7	8.7
Riverview Credit Union	South Saint Paul	MN	C	C	C-	5.5	5.08	0.0	34.9	13.5	0.0	10.0	17.8
Riverview Credit Union	Belpre	OH	C-	C-	C+	60.4	17.71	4.9	21.2	7.6	47.3	10.0	14.6
Riverways Federal Credit Union	Rolla	MO	C-	C-	C	45.1	5.62	8.4	27.6	36.2	2.7	6.4	8.4
▲ Roanoke Valley Community FCU	Roanoke	VA	B-	C+	C+	76.7	3.93	0.0	19.6	0.5	18.2	7.7	9.5
Roberts Dairy Employees FCU	Omaha	NE	D+	D+	D+	6.9	-4.44	0.0	41.1	0.0	0.0	10.0	26.8
Robins Financial Credit Union	Warner Robins	GA	A+	A+	A+	2322.3	6.57	3.6	36.7	14.4	28.6	10.0	17.1
▼ Rochester & Monroe County Employees FCU	Rochester	NY	D+	C-	C	25.5	-0.98	0.4	21.5	36.3	11.1	9.8	10.9
Rochester Area State Employees FCU	Rochester	NY	D+	D+	D	14.3	6.99	0.0	29.3	3.3	0.0	7.8	9.5
Rochester Polish Federal Credit Union	Rochester	NY	C	C	C	8.2	-2.60	0.0	4.4	20.9	0.0	10.0	17.5
Rock Community Federal Credit Union	Rock	MI	D	D	D-	7.5	16.97	0.0	26.4	0.7	0.0	5.7	7.7
▼ Rock Valley Federal Credit Union	Loves Park	IL	C+	B-	B-	101.4	8.43	3.0	42.9	23.8	2.9	8.1	9.7
Rockdale Federal Credit Union	Rockdale	TX	C	C	C	77.7	0.26	0.1	14.6	7.9	0.0	10.0	11.2
Rocket City Federal Credit Union	Huntsville	AL	C+	C+	B-	49.1	1.93	0.8	33.3	6.6	1.2	10.0	14.7
Rocket Federal Credit Union	McGregor	TX	D+	D+	D+	17.8	10.21	0.0	43.8	23.6	2.5	6.7	8.7
Rockford Bell Credit Union	Loves Park	IL	D+	D+	C-	33.9	7.46	0.0	30.1	31.5	0.0	10.0	14.3
Rockford Municipal Employees CU	Rockford	IL	C	C	C-	20.4	3.90	0.0	30.1	0.0	0.1	9.2	10.5
Rockland Employees Federal Credit Union	Spring Valley	NY	C-	C-	D+	37.4	3.98	0.0	47.0	14.6	6.2	6.9	8.9
Rockland Federal Credit Union	Rockland	MA	A-	A-	A-	1607.3	8.09	6.3	52.2	29.3	2.2	10.0	11.4
Rocky Mountain Credit Union	Helena	MT	B+	B+	A-	227.2	16.16	7.6	32.9	27.6	0.0	8.4	9.9
Rocky Mountain Law Enforcement FCU	Lone Tree	CO	A+	A+	A+	204.3	6.66	0.0	24.4	25.8	0.3	10.0	17.2
Rogers Employees Federal Credit Union	Rogers	CT	E+	E+	D-	4.3	-3.46	0.0	16.3	0.0	0.0	6.0	8.0
Rogue Credit Union	Medford	OR	A-	A-	A-	1340.7	17.96	8.0	40.9	16.8	14.8	7.4	9.4
Rogue River Community Credit Union	Sparta	MI	C+	C+	C	41.9	3.33	0.0	20.5	8.5	46.3	8.1	9.9
Rolling F Credit Union	Turlock	CA	C-	C-	C-	49.3	2.30	0.0	11.7	1.2	0.2	9.0	10.3
Rome Federal Credit Union	Rome	NY	D	D	D	20.6	8.55	0.0	26.9	18.3	0.0	5.7	7.7
▲ Rome Kraft Employees Credit Union	Rome	GA	C+	C	D+	15.7	-3.21	0.8	33.7	0.0	0.0	10.0	22.6
▲ Rome Teachers Federal Credit Union	Rome	NY	B-	C+	C+	37.8	3.88	0.0	25.5	9.9	8.7	10.0	12.8
Romeoville Community Credit Union	Romeoville	IL	D	D	E+	4.7	7.77	0.0	14.2	0.0	0.0	5.5	7.5
Romney Federal Credit Union	Romney	WV	C-	C-	C-	5.7	-5.60	0.0	47.0	0.4	0.0	10.0	14.1
Roper Corporation Employees Credit Union	Lafayette	GA	C+	C+	C+	1.9	9.81	0.0	1.4	0.0	0.0	10.0	14.5
Rose City Federal Credit Union	Thomasville	GA	C-	C-	C-	32.5	6.35	0.0	32.5	5.1	2.4	6.1	8.1
Roswell Community Federal Credit Union	Roswell	NM	B+	B+	B+	27.0	7.33	0.0	30.9	13.9	0.0	10.0	11.7
Route 1 Credit Union	Paris	IL	D	D	D+	4.0	-16.91	0.0	46.9	0.0	2.6	4.2	6.2
▼ Routt Schools Federal Credit Union	Steamboat Springs	CO	D-	D	D-	5.3	13.67	0.0	29.3	1.4	0.0	5.7	7.7
Royal Credit Union	Eau Claire	WI	A-	A-	A-	2111.5	18.05	32.3	28.8	37.7	0.6	9.0	10.3
RTA Hayden Federal Credit Union	East Cleveland	OH	C-	C-	C-	1.7	2.51	0.0	52.7	0.0	0.0	10.0	25.5
RTN Federal Credit Union	Waltham	MA	C+	C+	C+	893.7	5.19	4.2	11.7	32.6	32.5	9.9	11.0
▼ Rural Cooperatives Credit Union, Inc.	Louisville	KY	C	C+	C+	39.2	-0.61	7.9	37.5	5.0	0.0	10.0	12.5
Rushmore Electric Federal Credit Union	Rapid City	SD	C-	C-	C-	20.7	1.41	0.0	33.9	0.1	0.0	10.0	11.2
Russell Country Federal Credit Union	Great Falls	MT	C	C	C	68.8	7.94	0.0	36.0	10.2	0.0	7.8	9.6
▼ Rutgers Federal Credit Union	New Brunswick	NJ	D+	C-	C	92.3	2.89	7.8	14.5	17.3	16.7	5.2	7.2
Rutherford Postal District Employees FCU	Lakewood	NJ	E+	E+	E+	8.0	1.20	0.0	3.8	0.0	0.0	5.3	7.3
S And J School Employees FCU	Wintersville	OH	E+	E+	E+	3.6	4.80	0.0	54.9	0.0	0.0	4.0	6.0
S C H D District 7 Federal Credit Union	Orangeburg	SC	C+	C+	C	2.6	-0.89	0.0	56.2	0.0	0.0	10.0	21.6
S C I Federal Credit Union	Florence	SC	C	C	C+	16.5	0.72	0.0	42.9	2.3	0.0	10.0	18.0
S E A Credit Union	Richfield	UT	C	C	C	4.7	1.50	0.0	45.8	0.0	0.0	10.0	22.7
S E C U Credit Union	Keokuk	IA	C-	C-	C	2.1	-0.37	0.0	36.6	0.0	0.0	10.0	22.1
▼ S I Employees Federal Credit Union	Saratoga Springs	NY	C	C+	C+	<1	-4.10	0.0	28.7	0.0	0.0	10.0	29.7
S I Philadelphia Federal Credit Union	Philadelphia	PA	C-	C-	C-	<1	-5.98	0.0	6.4	0.0	0.0	10.0	34.1
S T O F F E Federal Credit Union	Solon	OH	C-	C-	C-	5.5	-1.77	0.0	63.2	0.0	0.0	10.0	21.7
S W E Federal Credit Union	Laird Hill	TX	D-	D-	D	1.4	14.15	0.0	60.0	0.0	0.0	5.4	7.5
▲ S.C. State Federal Credit Union	Columbia	SC	A	A-	A-	760.6	8.08	0.0	29.6	6.2	26.9	10.0	11.4
▼ S.F. Bay Area Educators Credit Union	San Francisco	CA	E+	D-	D-	19.8	1.80	0.0	21.8	16.9	0.0	4.9	6.9
S.F. Police Credit Union	San Francisco	CA	B+	B+	B+	865.6	6.10	7.7	12.6	42.7	17.7	10.0	14.1
S.M.S.D. Federal Credit Union	Buffalo	NY	C+	C+	C+	2.2	-0.37	0.0	32.9	0.0	0.0	10.0	17.9
Sabattus Regional Credit Union	Sabattus	ME	B-	B-	B	43.1	12.11	0.0	18.0	30.6	0.0	10.0	11.0
Sabine Federal Credit Union	Orange	TX	B-	B-	B-	184.2	5.19	0.0	37.4	18.5	18.0	10.0	11.6

Asset Quality Index	Non-Performing Loans as a % of Total Loans	Non-Performing Loans as a % of Capital	Net Charge-Offs / Avg Loans	Profitability Index	Net Income ($Mil)	Return on Assets	Return on Equity	Net Interest Spread	Overhead Efficiency Ratio	Liquidity Index	Liquidity Ratio	Hot Money Ratio	Stability Index
3.9	1.11	13.2	2.65	0.3	-0.14	-2.25	-25.73	5.03	91.5	3.7	16.0	0.0	3.0
10.0	0.16	1.7	0.53	3.6	0.20	0.45	3.41	2.01	73.1	4.3	15.6	9.8	7.8
6.7	1.13	6.1	0.09	3.9	0.02	0.33	3.72	4.06	98.6	5.5	29.7	1.9	4.1
9.6	0.13	0.5	0.00	2.7	0.00	0.07	0.41	4.35	98.3	4.8	36.0	2.3	7.3
9.4	0.26	0.7	0.24	1.8	0.02	0.14	0.91	2.20	94.9	4.6	23.1	4.4	5.5
5.9	0.58	5.7	0.21	4.8	0.04	0.38	5.09	4.74	86.4	3.5	12.2	5.3	3.4
8.1	0.59	2.8	0.14	4.7	0.15	0.81	8.51	3.68	77.7	5.9	30.9	0.4	4.1
9.7	0.82	1.4	2.26	0.6	0.00	-0.12	-0.43	3.06	101.7	4.7	26.4	0.0	6.4
9.7	0.26	1.1	0.37	9.5	11.05	1.94	11.56	3.02	48.7	4.5	18.0	5.4	10.0
8.3	0.29	2.0	0.56	1.1	-0.01	-0.18	-1.59	4.19	104.0	4.0	26.6	2.6	4.6
8.5	0.78	2.9	-0.08	1.3	0.00	-0.03	-0.29	2.61	98.9	5.9	38.0	0.0	4.4
10.0	0.00	0.0	0.00	2.3	0.00	0.20	1.12	1.91	89.5	6.1	69.7	2.3	6.4
8.6	0.80	3.0	0.00	3.1	0.01	0.27	3.50	3.88	88.6	7.2	58.7	0.0	2.3
6.1	0.84	9.2	0.69	2.1	-0.03	-0.11	-1.06	4.38	90.0	3.4	14.6	6.7	5.6
10.0	0.23	0.5	0.00	1.9	0.02	0.09	0.83	2.20	96.4	5.8	46.7	2.7	6.1
9.6	0.55	1.7	0.33	2.2	0.00	0.03	0.24	3.32	95.4	5.6	40.8	3.4	6.9
6.6	0.43	3.9	0.17	3.5	0.02	0.39	4.42	3.57	87.5	3.3	11.8	2.8	3.0
7.2	0.71	6.8	0.94	1.4	0.00	0.02	0.17	3.20	93.5	4.1	22.2	1.6	6.1
8.0	0.82	2.8	0.36	1.8	0.00	-0.02	-0.19	3.04	89.8	5.7	32.8	0.0	4.4
3.2	1.48	10.5	0.76	7.8	0.08	0.86	9.65	6.99	83.1	4.5	23.6	1.1	4.0
7.5	0.37	2.8	0.16	6.0	3.14	0.79	6.92	2.39	63.7	1.9	6.8	13.9	9.3
5.3	1.32	13.6	1.67	3.0	-0.01	-0.01	-0.09	4.01	89.2	3.6	15.7	7.7	6.4
10.0	0.10	0.4	0.17	8.6	0.55	1.09	6.21	3.99	75.0	4.6	36.7	9.4	9.7
7.5	1.35	3.1	0.51	0.0	-0.02	-1.42	-17.09	3.23	135.1	5.2	22.7	0.0	2.9
8.2	0.30	3.5	0.69	9.5	3.98	1.22	13.04	4.50	65.9	3.4	14.2	5.7	8.3
7.9	0.85	2.8	0.06	4.6	0.08	0.81	8.39	2.96	80.8	5.1	26.3	4.0	5.0
10.0	0.27	0.4	0.54	2.6	0.02	0.14	1.34	2.15	91.8	6.2	39.9	0.0	4.5
5.7	1.13	8.4	0.07	4.1	0.03	0.59	7.66	3.94	88.2	5.1	28.0	3.1	3.0
8.7	1.10	2.3	0.72	3.0	0.02	0.56	2.49	3.10	74.8	5.3	43.3	0.0	6.6
10.0	0.56	1.9	0.37	3.5	0.05	0.54	4.16	2.73	80.9	4.9	31.4	1.1	6.7
7.4	2.14	4.1	0.55	4.3	0.00	0.17	2.28	3.82	94.7	7.6	62.9	0.0	2.3
7.8	0.40	1.4	3.18	2.3	0.00	0.28	2.00	3.82	84.8	5.4	30.7	0.0	5.9
9.6	0.00	0.0	3.41	4.5	0.00	0.89	6.02	9.23	80.0	7.6	73.3	0.0	7.0
8.9	0.30	1.5	0.06	2.7	0.03	0.32	3.81	4.14	93.1	6.3	43.4	3.0	3.8
9.5	0.21	1.0	-0.03	6.9	0.06	0.85	7.29	3.91	81.0	2.9	13.6	16.0	6.6
0.0	7.83	54.3	6.53	0.4	-0.12	-11.49	-135.65	4.83	177.4	4.3	36.6	9.9	2.9
8.0	0.00	0.0	0.00	2.4	-0.02	-1.57	-19.14	3.38	90.0	5.0	36.6	0.0	1.7
8.6	0.20	1.5	0.22	7.7	5.79	1.12	10.81	3.29	74.6	3.4	13.4	9.5	8.3
6.9	2.05	4.7	1.20	2.8	0.00	0.24	0.91	6.51	95.8	6.0	51.1	0.0	6.7
9.1	0.50	2.6	0.19	2.8	0.93	0.42	4.31	2.78	83.1	3.4	15.2	13.3	6.8
7.2	1.28	5.2	0.99	1.4	-0.02	-0.25	-1.96	3.49	95.4	4.7	30.5	4.5	6.1
9.6	0.45	1.8	0.00	1.2	-0.01	-0.21	-1.89	2.30	108.2	4.1	22.7	5.3	5.7
8.6	0.16	1.0	0.25	2.5	0.05	0.29	2.93	2.85	91.7	4.5	26.1	4.1	4.9
2.6	4.93	33.7	0.49	2.1	-0.02	-0.07	-0.97	3.02	78.1	4.7	22.3	1.3	3.1
10.0	0.91	0.5	0.00	1.5	0.00	0.00	0.00	0.93	100.0	5.2	14.1	0.0	1.0
6.2	0.40	3.6	0.99	1.1	0.00	-0.34	-5.56	4.70	87.2	4.8	20.7	0.0	1.0
6.6	2.05	5.1	-0.54	10.0	0.01	2.05	9.51	6.63	67.5	4.9	45.0	5.9	5.0
9.2	0.44	2.4	1.21	2.1	0.00	-0.10	-0.54	3.75	93.2	5.3	33.9	0.9	6.5
5.7	3.23	7.7	-0.45	6.0	0.01	1.11	4.87	4.16	51.6	6.6	57.2	0.0	4.3
6.5	3.19	10.9	0.00	4.1	0.01	1.50	6.82	3.87	60.0	4.8	16.6	0.0	3.7
8.5	4.96	4.6	14.39	2.3	0.00	-3.29	-10.81	5.17	50.0	8.0	102.3	0.0	6.9
9.8	7.14	1.3	0.00	1.5	0.00	0.00	0.00	2.04	100.0	7.6	139.3	0.0	5.3
8.4	0.50	1.5	0.00	1.2	0.00	-0.15	-0.67	2.89	105.0	5.1	34.6	0.0	6.8
8.0	0.00	0.0	0.00	1.6	0.00	0.33	4.00	2.81	125.0	5.4	30.2	0.0	3.1
9.7	0.49	2.3	0.58	6.7	2.09	1.12	9.76	4.01	73.6	5.8	27.4	3.2	8.1
8.0	0.41	2.8	0.74	1.3	0.00	0.02	0.29	3.03	99.3	5.8	45.6	0.0	1.0
8.4	0.76	3.3	0.58	4.3	1.01	0.47	3.40	3.54	78.3	4.1	14.9	6.4	8.8
10.0	0.00	0.0	0.00	3.5	0.00	0.55	3.08	2.72	75.0	7.5	80.1	0.0	6.6
8.2	0.92	5.0	-0.08	3.8	0.04	0.40	3.54	3.22	91.0	4.9	27.7	0.6	5.9
8.2	0.27	1.8	0.52	3.9	0.36	0.78	6.68	3.60	73.8	4.0	16.5	6.3	7.1

Name	City	State	Rating	2016 Rating	2015 Rating	Total Assets ($Mil)	One Year Asset Growth	Asset Mix (As a % of Total Assets) Commercial Loans	Consumer Loans	Mortgage Loans	Securities	Capitalization Index	Net Worth Ratio
Sabine School Employees FCU	Many	LA	C	C	C	5.0	0.67	0.0	44.4	0.0	0.0	10.0	13.8
SAC Federal Credit Union	Papillion	NE	B-	B-	B-	886.9	4.63	7.7	63.8	21.1	0.0	6.4	8.4
Saco Valley Credit Union	Saco	ME	B+	B+	B+	111.3	6.26	1.1	15.1	49.1	0.0	9.0	10.4
Sacramento Credit Union	Sacramento	CA	A	A	A	449.1	8.19	4.5	26.5	10.8	10.7	10.0	13.2
Sacred Heart Federal Credit Union	Metairie	LA	D	D	D	1.1	-10.55	0.0	13.6	0.0	0.0	10.0	29.2
Sacred Heart Parish Hallettsville FCU	Hallettsville	TX	C+	C+	C+	40.0	-1.17	0.2	25.7	5.2	0.0	8.0	9.6
Safe 1 Credit Union	Bakersfield	CA	A	A	A	595.5	41.02	0.0	60.8	9.0	6.8	10.0	14.1
SAFE Credit Union	Folsom	CA	B-	B-	B-	2587.7	7.24	7.2	36.7	34.6	13.4	7.0	9.0
SAFE Credit Union	Beaumont	TX	D-	D-	D-	11.2	-1.01	0.0	36.6	0.4	0.0	8.2	9.8
Safe Federal Credit Union	Sumter	SC	B	B	B	1036.9	5.42	0.1	37.5	19.1	20.7	8.6	10.2
Safe Harbor Credit Union	Ludington	MI	B-	B-	C+	50.8	6.44	0.7	17.2	41.6	14.5	7.9	9.6
SafeAmerica Credit Union	Pleasanton	CA	C+	C+	B-	434.1	17.31	0.2	47.0	28.3	2.0	5.9	8.0
Safeway Federal Credit Union	Spokane	WA	B+	B+	B+	57.4	3.82	0.0	27.3	11.1	0.0	10.0	21.3
SAG-AFTRA Federal Credit Union	Burbank	CA	C-	C-	C+	236.5	2.65	7.8	15.8	23.1	26.3	6.0	8.0
Sagelink Credit Union	Durand	MI	B	B	B-	200.2	8.18	0.0	22.7	11.6	14.1	9.7	10.8
Saginaw County Employees Credit Union	Saginaw	MI	C-	C-	C-	36.3	5.06	0.9	15.0	23.1	0.0	6.6	8.6
Saginaw Medical Federal Credit Union	Saginaw	MI	B-	B-	B-	132.8	4.09	8.2	26.8	17.8	36.9	9.5	10.8
SAIF Federal Credit Union	Baton Rouge	LA	D	D	D-	9.6	-1.53	0.0	45.1	0.4	0.0	5.9	7.9
Saint Alphonsus Medical Credit Union	Boise	ID	D-	D-	E+	5.4	9.70	0.0	58.1	0.0	0.0	5.4	7.4
Saint Anthony Hospital FCU	Rockford	IL	D-	D-	D	4.5	3.86	0.0	34.8	0.0	0.0	6.4	8.4
Saint Dominics Federal Credit Union	Swansea	MA	B	B	B	29.8	1.14	0.0	12.7	22.3	0.0	10.0	16.0
▼ Saint Elizabeth Credit Union	Chicago	IL	D+	C-	C-	<1	-37.78	0.0	27.7	0.0	0.0	10.0	29.5
Saint Francis Employees FCU	Tulsa	OK	C	C	C-	42.0	16.76	0.0	24.0	0.0	3.9	4.8	6.9
Saint Gabriels Federal Credit Union	Washington	DC	D-	D-	D+	<1	1.89	0.0	16.9	0.0	0.0	8.4	9.9
Saint John AME Federal Credit Union	Niagara Falls	NY	D+	D+	D	<1	-0.53	0.0	37.6	0.0	0.0	10.0	14.5
Saint Lawrence Federal Credit Union	Ogdensburg	NY	B+	B+	B+	150.1	15.17	0.0	19.8	31.1	17.7	8.2	9.8
Saint Lukes Community FCU	Houston	TX	D+	D+	D+	1.4	4.83	0.0	14.7	0.0	0.0	7.3	9.2
Saint Norbert's Credit Union	Pittsburgh	PA	B-	B-	B-	<1	2.77	0.0	50.0	0.0	0.0	10.0	25.3
Saint Vincent Erie Federal Credit Union	Erie	PA	C-	C-	C-	15.2	1.20	0.0	16.0	9.6	0.0	7.6	9.4
Saint Vincent Hospital Credit Union	Worcester	MA	C-	C-	C-	13.5	3.94	0.0	26.5	0.0	22.9	6.6	8.6
Saint. Peter Paul Federal Credit Union	Brooklyn	NY	D	D	D	1.6	-7.42	0.0	8.7	0.0	0.0	10.0	20.8
Saints Margaret & Gregory FCU	South Euclid	OH	C-	C-	C	12.4	4.18	0.0	61.1	2.9	19.9	8.5	10.0
▲ Saker Shop Rite Federal Credit Union	Freehold	NJ	C-	D+	C-	7.6	2.18	0.0	21.7	0.0	64.9	10.0	21.6
Salal Credit Union	Seattle	WA	B+	B+	C+	513.4	12.87	11.0	35.2	34.5	15.2	6.6	8.8
▲ Salem Baptist Federal Credit Union	Jersey City	NJ	C+	C	C+	<1	1.95	0.0	8.3	0.0	0.0	10.0	21.7
Salem School System Credit Union	Salem	IL	C-	C-	D+	2.2	-7.21	0.0	48.0	0.0	0.0	10.0	23.2
Salem VA Medical Center FCU	Salem	VA	D+	D+	D+	85.0	4.29	0.0	46.8	4.3	0.0	5.9	7.9
Salina Interparochial Credit Union	Salina	KS	C+	C+	C+	17.1	3.54	0.0	52.3	0.0	0.0	10.0	26.6
Salina Municipal Credit Union	Salina	KS	D-	D-	D	2.1	-1.51	0.0	45.5	0.0	0.0	9.0	10.3
Salina Railroad Credit Union	Salina	KS	E+	E+	E+	<1	4.20	0.0	86.3	0.0	0.0	4.6	6.7
Salt Employees Federal Credit Union	Grand Saline	TX	C-	C-	C-	1.8	-6.76	0.0	43.6	0.0	0.0	10.0	37.4
San Angelo Federal Credit Union	San Angelo	TX	D	D	D	23.9	6.03	0.0	53.4	1.1	10.5	6.0	8.2
San Antonio Citizens FCU	San Antonio	FL	C+	C+	C+	201.7	9.36	7.0	20.9	21.4	36.6	6.0	8.7
San Diego County Credit Union	San Diego	CA	A+	A+	A+	8109.4	8.97	5.6	25.0	42.9	15.2	10.0	13.9
San Diego Firefighters FCU	San Diego	CA	C	C	C	99.4	5.46	3.1	12.4	30.8	35.7	5.6	7.6
▲ San Diego Metropolitan Credit Union	San Diego	CA	B+	B	B	267.8	2.80	4.2	14.5	21.3	6.4	8.1	9.7
San Fernando Valley Japanese CU	Northridge	CA	D	D	D	<1	-5.86	0.0	67.7	0.0	0.0	10.0	25.2
▼ San Francisco Federal Credit Union	San Francisco	CA	C+	B-	C+	1079.4	6.51	7.0	11.0	40.2	29.1	9.2	10.5
San Francisco Fire Credit Union	San Francisco	CA	B	B	B	1255.2	8.32	9.5	15.8	36.0	13.1	6.3	8.3
San Francisco Lee Federal Credit Union	San Francisco	CA	B-	B-	B-	11.7	-1.72	8.6	0.3	23.6	0.0	10.0	39.7
San Joaquin Power Employees Credit Union	Fresno	CA	B-	B-	B-	134.9	2.74	11.7	21.1	35.1	9.5	10.0	16.4
▲ San Juan Credit Union	Blanding	UT	C-	D+	D	18.8	11.14	0.3	52.4	0.9	0.0	6.4	8.4
San Juan Mountains Credit Union	Montrose	CO	C	C	C+	31.3	8.45	0.0	16.4	32.7	0.0	6.8	8.8
San Mateo City Employees FCU	San Mateo	CA	B	B	B	33.5	0.56	0.0	8.6	0.9	0.0	10.0	12.7
San Mateo Credit Union	Redwood City	CA	A-	A-	B+	975.6	9.88	1.8	31.8	30.9	14.0	8.1	9.8
San Patricio County Teachers FCU	Sinton	TX	C+	C+	B	32.7	2.59	0.0	59.2	3.0	0.0	10.0	11.9
San Tan Credit Union	Chandler	AZ	E+	E+	E+	10.1	0.56	0.0	58.2	0.0	0.0	4.8	6.8
Sandhills Federal Credit Union	Ulysses	KS	D	D	D+	1.1	3.68	0.0	52.4	0.0	0.0	10.0	13.7
Sandia Area Federal Credit Union	Albuquerque	NM	A-	A-	A-	641.7	11.58	7.2	70.4	13.4	0.3	9.9	10.9
Sandia Laboratory Federal Credit Union	Albuquerque	NM	B+	B+	A-	2413.6	6.09	8.3	15.8	28.2	39.5	9.3	10.8

Asset Quality Index	Non-Performing Loans as a % of Total Loans	Non-Performing Loans as a % of Capital	Net Charge-Offs Avg Loans	Profitability Index	Net Income ($Mil)	Return on Assets	Return on Equity	Net Interest Spread	Overhead Efficiency Ratio	Liquidity Index	Liquidity Ratio	Hot Money Ratio	Stability Index
6.5	2.58	8.4	0.00	**7.9**	0.02	1.38	9.97	3.45	57.5	**5.3**	61.0	0.0	**5.0**
4.7	1.18	11.1	0.76	**3.8**	0.59	0.27	3.17	3.36	77.5	**2.1**	8.5	14.6	**6.1**
9.9	0.17	1.9	0.02	**4.6**	0.16	0.56	5.57	3.22	84.1	**4.4**	37.5	4.9	**6.9**
9.5	0.18	0.7	0.02	**6.4**	1.03	0.93	7.01	2.60	79.1	**5.1**	29.6	2.6	**8.9**
5.1	14.13	11.6	0.00	**0.0**	0.00	-1.46	-4.98	1.92	180.0	**6.0**	79.1	0.0	**4.7**
9.4	0.06	0.3	0.31	**4.3**	0.05	0.53	5.45	2.84	75.7	**4.6**	36.5	2.2	**5.0**
8.0	0.41	2.3	0.47	**7.0**	1.49	1.14	7.78	2.99	59.1	**3.4**	19.1	14.7	**8.5**
9.5	0.22	2.0	0.24	**3.8**	3.49	0.55	6.05	2.80	81.3	**3.6**	16.6	5.3	**6.6**
6.4	1.39	5.2	0.09	**0.4**	-0.01	-0.39	-3.96	3.54	103.8	**5.9**	38.1	1.0	**3.6**
9.8	0.13	1.1	0.33	**4.5**	1.56	0.61	6.01	2.72	82.7	**4.4**	26.6	11.7	**7.2**
9.2	0.23	1.9	0.11	**7.6**	0.15	1.23	12.74	3.47	69.5	**3.3**	11.7	6.2	**5.4**
6.2	0.47	5.5	0.38	**4.0**	0.66	0.61	9.08	3.14	80.4	**2.6**	13.8	17.2	**3.6**
8.9	1.38	3.1	0.51	**4.4**	0.09	0.61	2.83	2.45	74.0	**4.8**	36.2	3.1	**7.5**
9.8	0.22	1.3	0.12	**2.2**	0.06	0.11	1.53	3.25	95.1	**5.3**	18.5	0.6	**3.5**
10.0	0.49	1.8	0.61	**3.8**	0.22	0.45	4.06	3.17	82.1	**5.5**	32.2	1.2	**7.3**
7.7	0.49	3.5	0.57	**3.4**	0.04	0.50	5.71	2.91	81.4	**4.7**	33.1	2.6	**3.9**
9.6	0.30	1.3	0.27	**3.4**	0.11	0.34	3.19	3.05	86.1	**4.6**	20.3	2.0	**6.9**
7.9	0.06	0.4	0.91	**1.8**	0.00	-0.08	-1.05	3.52	101.0	**3.8**	23.8	9.1	**1.7**
8.6	0.00	0.0	0.00	**3.1**	0.00	0.22	2.99	3.21	93.6	**5.0**	25.4	0.0	**2.3**
4.5	4.36	18.2	0.98	**0.9**	0.00	-0.19	-2.12	2.62	85.2	**6.4**	62.2	0.0	**3.2**
9.8	0.68	1.9	1.11	**3.1**	0.01	0.19	1.18	2.90	90.2	**3.6**	28.9	19.8	**6.7**
1.5	23.91	30.6	124.14	**2.5**	-0.01	-46.67	-136.59	6.90	100.0	**7.6**	84.8	0.0	**6.2**
9.1	0.57	2.0	0.19	**3.1**	0.03	0.35	4.75	2.50	89.9	**6.6**	41.4	2.2	**2.8**
1.7	22.62	38.8	-13.64	**2.5**	0.00	0.81	8.33	3.00	66.7	**6.0**	19.5	0.0	**3.5**
6.0	1.18	3.2	0.00	**1.8**	0.00	0.00	0.00	7.08	100.0	**6.9**	62.3	0.0	**5.7**
9.2	0.35	2.9	0.12	**6.1**	0.39	1.07	11.41	3.34	69.8	**3.1**	12.0	13.1	**6.6**
10.0	0.00	0.0	0.00	**3.0**	0.00	0.29	3.13	1.17	100.0	**6.5**	34.9	0.0	**3.0**
8.7	0.00	0.0	0.00	**10.0**	0.00	1.97	7.77	6.67	66.7	**5.7**	48.9	0.0	**6.3**
8.6	0.78	2.3	1.09	**1.9**	-0.01	-0.27	-2.79	3.14	91.4	**5.3**	25.1	0.0	**3.9**
10.0	0.20	0.8	0.70	**2.0**	0.00	0.03	0.34	3.62	95.2	**5.5**	25.6	0.0	**3.6**
10.0	0.00	0.0	0.00	**0.0**	0.00	-0.26	-1.23	1.53	120.0	**7.6**	92.3	0.0	**4.7**
7.9	0.10	0.6	0.92	**2.5**	0.01	0.26	2.60	3.10	88.0	**4.0**	20.2	0.0	**4.4**
9.1	2.20	2.0	10.46	**1.6**	-0.01	-0.27	-1.22	5.02	80.6	**6.0**	39.6	0.0	**5.0**
9.2	0.32	2.4	0.28	**6.8**	0.90	0.72	8.26	4.21	80.7	**3.5**	16.5	5.9	**6.2**
10.0	0.00	0.0	0.00	**5.2**	0.00	2.55	11.76	0.00	50.0	**8.6**	112.2	0.0	**7.4**
8.5	0.00	0.0	0.00	**1.7**	0.00	-0.18	-0.77	2.93	100.0	**4.9**	54.0	0.0	**6.3**
2.7	2.33	20.5	0.67	**1.5**	-0.01	-0.04	-0.57	4.43	90.0	**4.3**	25.0	3.2	**2.3**
6.1	3.41	6.3	1.25	**4.0**	0.03	0.59	2.21	3.02	46.9	**5.5**	66.9	6.1	**6.3**
8.1	0.36	1.8	0.00	**0.0**	-0.01	-0.98	-9.17	3.28	127.8	**5.0**	37.1	0.0	**4.5**
1.6	2.61	31.0	0.00	**1.7**	0.00	0.00	0.00	11.61	93.8	**1.3**	10.7	71.8	**1.0**
9.2	0.20	0.3	-0.41	**2.9**	0.00	0.44	1.18	4.05	93.8	**5.7**	69.9	0.0	**6.2**
6.5	0.23	2.2	0.11	**3.1**	0.02	0.27	3.35	3.92	94.0	**4.8**	28.3	6.4	**3.0**
9.7	0.13	1.6	0.19	**4.2**	0.34	0.68	8.43	3.23	78.5	**4.6**	15.0	6.2	**5.8**
9.7	0.26	1.3	0.17	**9.2**	25.02	1.25	9.00	2.59	59.4	**3.7**	26.7	13.3	**10.0**
10.0	0.02	0.1	0.00	**2.8**	0.09	0.37	4.71	2.70	86.7	**4.3**	27.8	10.7	**3.9**
6.5	0.87	5.8	0.10	**6.1**	0.60	0.89	9.25	5.08	89.4	**4.3**	21.6	5.7	**7.2**
8.4	0.00	0.0	0.00	**0.0**	0.00	-0.44	-1.79	3.13	120.0	**4.8**	40.9	0.0	**6.2**
7.1	0.93	7.8	0.42	**3.1**	0.82	0.30	2.86	3.02	75.4	**3.9**	27.3	10.1	**8.5**
7.4	0.57	5.7	0.37	**7.1**	5.13	1.66	20.28	3.45	68.2	**4.0**	16.5	7.0	**6.7**
10.0	0.00	0.0	0.00	**3.6**	0.01	0.31	0.78	2.07	80.0	**7.1**	95.1	4.7	**7.6**
9.3	0.10	0.4	0.05	**2.5**	0.03	0.08	0.51	1.37	91.5	**4.0**	12.1	0.0	**8.3**
4.6	1.15	6.8	0.56	**8.1**	0.10	2.19	25.98	7.78	76.0	**5.7**	43.3	5.4	**3.6**
6.6	0.24	1.5	0.30	**4.0**	0.05	0.60	6.71	3.84	85.9	**4.9**	32.0	4.1	**4.6**
6.7	6.51	10.3	0.93	**5.9**	0.12	1.41	10.99	2.34	37.9	**5.3**	34.2	0.0	**6.0**
9.8	0.17	1.2	0.25	**6.4**	2.44	1.02	10.36	3.50	74.6	**4.2**	19.3	5.2	**7.9**
4.4	0.02	12.1	1.27	**2.2**	-0.01	-0.11	-0.92	4.29	72.6	**2.6**	24.8	23.2	**5.0**
4.5	0.44	4.2	0.20	**2.3**	0.00	-0.04	-0.58	4.23	98.2	**5.2**	31.8	0.0	**1.0**
8.6	0.00	0.0	0.00	**0.0**	-0.07	-25.04	-182.05	-29.26	-24.1	**5.6**	50.7	10.3	**6.0**
7.4	0.30	2.9	0.15	**6.6**	1.31	0.83	7.86	2.29	69.2	**2.1**	10.9	15.9	**9.1**
9.0	0.50	3.2	0.17	**5.3**	4.95	0.83	8.58	2.29	66.2	**3.4**	10.9	12.5	**6.9**

								Asset Mix (As a % of Total Assets)					
Name	City	State	Rating	2016 Rating	2015 Rating	Total Assets ($Mil)	One Year Asset Growth	Commercial Loans	Consumer Loans	Mortgage Loans	Securities	Capitalization Index	Net Worth Ratio
Sandusky Ohio Edison Employee FCU	Sandusky	OH	**D+**	D+	D+	<1	17.13	0.0	34.2	0.0	0.0	**10.0**	16.1
Sangamo-Oconee Employees FCU	West Union	SC	**D**	D	D	4.0	2.99	0.0	19.2	0.0	0.0	**10.0**	19.5
Santa Ana Federal Credit Union	Santa Ana	CA	**C+**	C+	C	67.8	4.12	0.0	25.4	15.6	18.5	**6.4**	8.4
Santa Barbara County FCU	Santa Barbara	CA	**C-**	C-	C	44.5	9.08	0.0	11.0	2.5	11.1	**5.6**	7.6
Santa Barbara Teachers FCU	Santa Barbara	CA	**C+**	C+	C+	236.7	5.30	0.0	2.6	25.5	40.3	**8.5**	10.0
Santa Clara County Federal Credit Union	San Jose	CA	**B+**	B+	B	733.3	7.31	0.0	25.2	10.2	27.4	**6.8**	8.9
Santa Cruz Community Credit Union	Santa Cruz	CA	**B-**	B-	C-	114.8	6.24	11.7	28.9	22.3	4.0	**5.3**	7.3
Santa Fe Federal Credit Union	Amarillo	TX	**B+**	B+	A-	126.4	-0.44	0.0	43.5	0.1	28.7	**10.0**	13.7
Santa Maria Associated Employees FCU	Santa Maria	CA	**D-**	D-	D-	3.7	4.32	0.0	68.4	0.0	0.0	**6.4**	8.5
Santa Rosa County Federal Credit Union	Milton	FL	**B-**	B-	B-	122.6	7.72	0.0	26.1	6.3	14.4	**10.0**	11.3
Santee Cooper Credit Union	Moncks Corner	SC	**C+**	C+	C+	51.9	1.80	0.0	44.0	4.5	0.0	**8.4**	9.9
Santo Christo Federal Credit Union	Fall River	MA	**C-**	C-	C-	11.8	6.89	0.0	24.7	30.6	0.0	**8.5**	10.0
Sarasota Municipal Employees CU	Sarasota	FL	**B-**	B-	B-	30.4	4.16	0.0	27.8	0.1	0.0	**10.0**	11.1
Saratoga's Community FCU	Saratoga Springs	NY	**D-**	D-	E+	41.0	4.38	0.5	23.6	12.9	0.0	**4.4**	6.4
Sarco Federal Credit Union	Bethlehem	PA	**C-**	C-	C-	7.2	0.38	0.0	29.5	9.9	0.0	**10.0**	21.6
Sargent Federal Credit Union	Washington	DC	**E+**	E+	E+	<1	-4.05	0.0	44.2	0.0	0.0	**4.5**	6.5
Savannah Federal Credit Union	Savannah	GA	**C**	C	C	19.6	0.48	4.0	20.2	11.6	5.0	**10.0**	19.4
Savannah Postal Credit Union	Savannah	GA	**C+**	C+	B-	20.8	4.33	0.0	19.6	6.1	9.6	**10.0**	14.4
▼ Savannah Schools Federal Credit Union	Savannah	GA	**C**	C+	C+	30.3	6.68	0.5	29.4	2.3	0.0	**10.0**	12.2
Savastate Teachers Federal Credit Union	Savannah	GA	**C**	C	C	3.3	-10.77	0.0	30.7	0.0	0.0	**10.0**	18.5
SB Community Federal Credit Union	Muskegon	MI	**D**	D	D+	13.4	5.59	0.0	45.8	19.0	16.3	**6.4**	8.4
SC Telco Federal Credit Union	Greenville	SC	**A**	A	A	369.9	11.24	2.7	33.0	24.0	4.0	**10.0**	11.1
SCE Federal Credit Union	Irwindale	CA	**B-**	B-	B-	678.8	2.89	12.5	33.0	25.1	17.2	**8.1**	9.8
Scenic Community Credit Union	Hixson	TN	**B-**	B-	B-	122.3	5.31	4.8	33.9	17.3	0.0	**10.0**	12.4
▲ Scenic Falls Federal Credit Union	Idaho Falls	ID	**D+**	D	C-	64.2	-2.88	0.0	41.4	9.6	5.9	**6.1**	8.2
SCF Westchester NY Employees FCU	White Plains	NY	**C+**	C+	C-	1.6	8.77	0.0	10.6	0.0	0.0	**10.0**	20.4
▲ SCFE Credit Union, Inc.	Portsmouth	OH	**C**	C-	D	1.0	2.52	0.0	73.6	0.0	0.0	**10.0**	11.0
Schenectady County Employees FCU	Schenectady	NY	**E+**	E+	E+	4.2	-0.14	0.0	70.6	0.0	12.6	**5.7**	7.7
Schlumberger Employees Credit Union	Sugar Land	TX	**A+**	A+	A+	856.3	0.73	0.0	8.1	12.1	70.4	**10.0**	12.2
▼ Schneider Community Credit Union	Green Bay	WI	**C-**	C	C	21.8	6.18	0.0	50.6	9.6	0.0	**10.0**	14.7
Schofield Federal Credit Union	Wahiawa	HI	**B+**	B+	B+	33.1	-1.87	0.5	12.0	12.8	4.4	**10.0**	18.9
School District 218 Employees FCU	Oak Lawn	IL	**C-**	C-	D+	13.0	0.39	0.0	10.2	0.0	0.0	**6.9**	8.9
School District 3 Federal Credit Union	Colorado Springs	CO	**B-**	B-	B-	25.1	9.43	3.3	10.5	26.2	6.5	**10.0**	11.4
School Districts 162/163 Employees FCU	Park Forest	IL	**C-**	C-	C	2.0	7.73	0.0	11.8	0.0	0.0	**10.0**	19.7
School Employees Credit Union	Superior	WI	**C-**	C-	D+	2.7	2.28	0.0	41.3	0.0	0.0	**10.0**	12.5
School Empls Lorain County Credit Union, Inc.	Elyria	OH	**C-**	C-	C-	155.7	0.28	0.0	17.9	7.1	45.7	**8.6**	10.7
School Systems Federal Credit Union	Troy	NY	**C**	C	C	86.1	7.48	0.0	11.4	9.5	17.3	**5.3**	7.3
▲ Schools Federal Credit Union	Rancho Dominguez	CA	**B**	B-	C+	126.0	6.58	0.7	23.5	26.0	27.1	**10.0**	12.3
Schools Financial Credit Union	Sacramento	CA	**A-**	A-	A-	1842.9	7.94	3.7	45.0	11.8	26.7	**8.9**	10.2
SchoolsFirst Federal Credit Union	Santa Ana	CA	**A**	A	A	13639.1	11.56	0.6	21.9	22.1	40.6	**9.8**	10.9
Science Park Federal Credit Union	New Haven	CT	**D**	D	D	4.5	-4.40	0.0	28.7	0.0	0.0	**10.0**	26.7
Scient Federal Credit Union	Groton	CT	**C**	C	C	251.3	2.89	1.0	49.9	20.6	2.3	**6.4**	8.4
Scientific Research Partner's CU	Kansas City	MO	**E+**	E+	E+	1.2	12.72	0.0	57.2	0.0	0.0	**4.7**	6.8
Scott & White Employees Credit Union	Temple	TX	**D**	D	D	44.9	6.58	0.3	23.1	9.3	10.8	**4.0**	6.0
Scott Associates Credit Union, Inc.	Marysville	OH	**C-**	C-	C	10.8	2.33	0.9	41.4	0.0	0.0	**10.0**	13.1
Scott Credit Union	Edwardsville	IL	**B-**	B-	B-	1122.7	5.85	1.0	54.9	11.1	0.4	**6.9**	8.9
Scranton Times Downtown FCU	Scranton	PA	**D**	D	D	10.9	-9.16	6.1	10.8	48.9	0.0	**8.0**	9.6
Scurry County School FCU	Snyder	TX	**C+**	C+	B-	10.1	-5.25	0.0	39.1	0.0	0.0	**10.0**	17.8
Sea Air Federal Credit Union	Seal Beach	CA	**D**	D	D	135.6	-1.14	5.2	15.9	8.4	10.4	**10.0**	24.5
Sea Comm Federal Credit Union	Massena	NY	**A-**	A-	A-	537.1	6.01	3.0	20.8	17.1	40.6	**10.0**	13.4
Sea West Coast Guard FCU	Oakland	CA	**B**	B	B-	354.8	2.42	0.4	10.1	26.9	3.9	**10.0**	19.3
Seaboard Federal Credit Union	Bucksport	ME	**C+**	C+	C+	122.4	3.59	7.7	20.3	37.7	14.4	**7.4**	9.3
Seagoville Federal Credit Union	Seagoville	TX	**C+**	C+	C+	18.8	7.24	0.0	23.3	0.0	0.0	**10.0**	13.6
Seaport Federal Credit Union	Elizabeth	NJ	**B+**	B+	B+	69.4	4.53	0.0	29.1	12.7	0.6	**10.0**	14.6
Sears Spokane Employees FCU	Spokane	WA	**E+**	E+	E+	5.2	-2.97	0.0	34.5	6.2	0.0	**5.4**	7.4
▼ Seasons Federal Credit Union	Middletown	CT	**D**	D+	D+	163.4	-0.24	0.0	55.9	8.2	3.9	**5.1**	7.2
Seattle Metropolitan Credit Union	Seattle	WA	**B+**	B+	B+	785.7	16.37	8.1	19.9	31.2	9.1	**6.8**	9.1
Sebasticook Valley Federal Credit Union	Pittsfield	ME	**B**	B	B-	96.9	6.91	1.4	22.1	34.5	3.3	**8.2**	9.8
SECNY Federal Credit Union	Syracuse	NY	**B**	B	B	181.8	7.58	0.0	13.1	29.5	2.9	**5.7**	7.7
Section 705 Federal Credit Union	Lafayette	LA	**C+**	C+	C+	33.4	3.24	0.0	43.2	17.9	9.9	**8.7**	10.1

Asset Quality Index	Non-Performing Loans as a % of Total Loans	Non-Performing Loans as a % of Capital	Net Charge-Offs Avg Loans	Profitability Index	Net Income ($Mil)	Return on Assets	Return on Equity	Net Interest Spread	Overhead Efficiency Ratio	Liquidity Index	Liquidity Ratio	Hot Money Ratio	Stability Index
8.5	0.37	0.8	0.00	0.5	0.00	-0.54	-3.28	2.82	100.0	7.6	75.0	0.0	6.8
10.0	0.23	0.3	0.00	0.2	0.00	-0.40	-2.06	1.69	126.7	6.2	57.6	0.0	5.6
9.2	0.05	0.3	0.13	4.6	0.11	0.66	7.97	3.27	83.6	4.8	20.6	1.2	3.6
10.0	0.03	0.1	0.00	2.2	0.03	0.27	3.57	2.50	89.9	6.9	40.2	0.0	2.6
10.0	0.01	0.0	0.01	3.1	0.28	0.47	4.63	2.32	72.8	7.6	75.5	0.0	6.8
9.2	0.54	2.9	0.40	5.1	1.17	0.66	7.32	3.43	75.3	5.2	29.1	7.4	6.9
4.6	1.79	17.4	1.20	7.9	0.46	1.62	24.10	5.91	72.5	4.8	23.1	0.1	5.1
9.8	0.47	1.8	1.27	2.6	-0.05	-0.17	-1.25	3.57	83.7	3.3	14.2	17.4	6.5
3.9	1.67	12.7	0.82	1.7	0.00	-0.44	-5.13	4.58	113.8	5.6	33.7	0.0	1.0
9.1	0.45	2.3	0.29	3.8	0.15	0.51	4.47	2.83	87.7	5.0	29.6	3.9	7.6
6.9	0.46	2.9	-0.01	5.6	0.12	0.94	9.26	3.74	78.3	4.5	29.8	4.0	5.5
6.8	0.86	5.0	0.44	3.9	0.01	0.38	3.74	5.12	89.4	5.4	34.8	0.0	4.8
10.0	0.42	2.0	0.71	3.7	0.04	0.46	4.18	3.21	81.2	5.0	31.1	6.4	5.5
3.7	2.63	21.4	1.14	2.1	0.01	0.06	0.91	5.11	92.6	5.8	36.9	2.2	1.7
6.7	2.20	6.4	0.00	3.5	0.01	0.56	2.59	3.18	83.1	4.0	28.8	0.0	6.9
0.3	18.47	93.6	0.00	3.9	0.00	1.12	17.39	7.06	100.0	7.0	59.3	0.0	1.9
9.3	1.30	2.7	0.53	2.0	0.00	0.08	0.47	2.56	97.5	4.8	32.1	8.5	5.7
9.8	0.74	1.8	0.48	2.9	0.01	0.16	1.07	4.03	94.5	6.5	57.5	1.3	6.5
9.0	1.28	4.3	0.80	1.8	-0.02	-0.21	-1.72	5.32	97.6	6.5	49.6	0.4	5.9
9.8	0.39	0.6	0.74	3.5	0.01	1.08	5.99	3.41	66.7	6.6	82.6	0.0	5.3
6.7	0.29	2.3	0.30	1.7	-0.01	-0.27	-3.21	3.82	102.1	4.0	22.0	6.5	3.8
7.5	0.68	4.5	1.92	8.7	1.14	1.27	11.24	5.83	63.8	2.9	23.1	19.5	7.4
7.3	0.78	5.1	0.35	3.8	0.68	0.41	4.16	4.13	85.3	4.2	16.9	5.6	6.9
9.8	0.30	1.7	0.11	2.9	0.07	0.22	1.75	2.72	92.1	4.3	26.3	0.0	7.7
6.5	0.45	5.0	0.42	2.2	0.03	0.20	3.01	3.63	94.0	3.2	20.3	15.8	1.9
8.9	1.17	2.4	0.00	6.7	0.00	1.01	4.91	5.64	77.8	6.5	48.9	0.0	5.0
6.3	0.80	5.0	0.00	6.8	0.00	1.57	14.55	6.31	75.0	5.1	28.0	0.0	4.3
6.3	0.47	4.1	0.00	0.3	-0.01	-0.77	-9.67	4.37	118.2	4.5	17.7	0.0	2.5
10.0	0.47	0.8	0.39	9.5	3.05	1.45	11.83	2.15	45.4	5.1	19.7	2.2	9.3
8.5	0.26	1.2	0.32	0.6	-0.04	-0.74	-4.83	4.25	102.0	4.1	12.1	0.0	6.0
10.0	0.17	0.5	0.00	3.3	0.01	0.10	0.58	1.98	97.7	4.7	24.7	6.8	7.6
10.0	0.41	0.5	0.00	2.8	0.01	0.27	3.14	1.52	77.6	5.1	22.5	0.0	3.5
10.0	0.23	0.8	0.29	3.6	0.03	0.44	3.80	2.62	82.6	5.4	38.6	0.9	6.6
10.0	0.86	0.5	-1.62	0.8	0.00	-0.41	-2.05	2.27	144.4	7.5	69.5	0.0	5.2
7.7	1.63	5.6	0.00	1.8	0.00	0.00	0.00	3.53	100.0	6.7	49.5	0.0	6.4
9.4	0.81	2.8	0.50	2.2	0.09	0.23	2.29	2.70	86.3	4.8	26.1	3.5	6.1
6.4	1.66	8.3	0.00	2.6	0.04	0.18	2.43	2.26	92.3	5.7	36.0	1.2	3.3
10.0	0.45	1.8	0.21	6.0	3.06	10.09	88.81	3.55	28.3	5.0	29.0	3.1	7.2
8.4	0.33	2.2	0.48	6.2	4.68	1.03	10.07	2.81	62.1	4.0	13.5	3.3	7.9
9.8	0.48	2.1	0.45	5.5	26.05	0.78	7.10	2.56	67.0	3.9	26.5	15.2	8.9
9.6	2.80	3.1	1.50	0.0	-0.03	-2.94	-10.96	2.91	210.0	6.0	42.3	0.0	6.1
8.4	0.13	2.1	0.54	2.9	0.19	0.32	3.84	3.79	83.3	3.1	14.3	11.1	4.7
3.3	0.99	8.1	0.00	1.2	0.00	-0.33	-5.00	4.21	100.0	5.2	39.1	0.0	1.0
9.2	0.12	1.0	0.25	1.6	-0.02	-0.15	-3.45	3.42	101.3	5.9	34.7	0.3	2.0
7.9	1.38	4.6	0.49	1.7	0.00	-0.07	-0.56	3.31	89.7	4.9	31.2	1.1	5.9
5.9	0.69	5.3	0.83	5.5	2.82	1.02	11.46	3.52	69.9	4.3	22.5	7.7	6.6
1.7	4.72	42.6	0.00	1.3	0.00	-0.04	-0.38	4.32	100.9	5.4	38.2	0.0	3.7
6.8	2.77	6.9	1.07	3.2	0.01	0.43	2.44	4.34	74.8	3.0	30.9	21.2	5.1
10.0	1.23	1.4	0.49	0.2	-0.10	-0.30	-1.23	2.14	106.5	4.0	43.5	17.7	6.5
8.6	0.88	3.7	0.27	6.3	1.39	1.06	7.91	3.43	68.7	3.6	13.8	9.1	9.5
10.0	0.08	0.2	0.25	3.4	0.22	0.25	1.31	2.13	80.1	4.9	36.8	8.3	7.9
5.8	0.99	9.3	0.14	3.9	0.22	0.71	7.95	3.89	84.4	3.7	17.8	4.9	5.8
9.7	1.24	2.6	0.51	2.6	0.01	0.22	1.56	2.18	92.0	5.9	48.5	0.0	7.1
9.3	0.80	2.6	0.35	4.8	0.08	0.48	3.25	3.80	85.6	5.1	32.8	5.6	6.9
5.7	0.74	5.4	0.33	0.4	0.00	-0.08	-1.05	3.07	100.0	6.7	52.0	0.0	2.3
4.0	1.17	17.1	0.81	0.8	-0.22	-0.53	-8.81	4.38	95.8	2.7	3.8	8.0	3.0
8.0	0.34	2.9	0.32	3.5	0.53	0.28	3.07	3.56	88.1	3.7	11.2	5.7	5.4
6.0	0.86	9.2	0.29	4.6	0.11	0.46	4.67	3.92	82.2	2.8	8.9	11.0	5.2
9.9	0.31	2.4	0.11	4.1	0.28	0.64	8.17	3.06	79.9	4.5	22.5	3.3	5.3
4.7	1.64	12.4	0.43	3.0	0.02	0.26	2.61	4.03	89.7	3.8	15.3	3.1	4.6

Name	City	State	Rating	2016 Rating	2015 Rating	Total Assets ($Mil)	One Year Asset Growth	Asset Mix (As a % of Total Assets) Comm-ercial Loans	Cons-umer Loans	Mort-gage Loans	Secur-ities	Capital-ization Index	Net Worth Ratio
▼ Secured Advantage Federal Credit Union	Simpsonville	SC	**D+**	C-	C	79.7	-2.33	0.0	21.7	14.6	1.7	**10.0**	11.8
▼ Security Credit Union	Flint	MI	**C+**	B-	B-	437.7	5.20	2.9	34.4	8.1	17.0	**6.4**	8.5
Security First Federal Credit Union	Edinburg	TX	**D**	D	D+	361.8	-6.69	0.5	38.7	23.9	12.5	**5.9**	8.0
▲ Security Plus Federal Credit Union	Russellville	KY	**D+**	D	D	<1	-13.32	0.0	74.3	0.0	0.0	**10.0**	39.7
Security Service Federal Credit Union	San Antonio	TX	**B-**	B-	B-	9488.8	4.10	5.6	65.4	21.3	0.1	**6.3**	8.4
Securityplus Federal Credit Union	Woodlawn	MD	**C-**	C-	C-	389.0	6.04	10.1	35.1	21.1	20.5	**6.9**	8.9
SecurTrust Federal Credit Union	Southaven	MS	**B+**	B+	B+	22.3	13.58	0.1	49.7	15.3	0.0	**10.0**	20.3
SEG Federal Credit Union	Laurel	MT	**C**	C	C+	15.2	2.12	0.0	43.7	3.3	0.0	**10.0**	11.7
SEI Federal Credit Union	Pocatello	ID	**D+**	D+	D	19.6	6.90	0.0	49.5	0.0	0.0	**8.0**	9.7
SELCO Community Credit Union	Eugene	OR	**A-**	A-	A-	1485.6	10.54	12.3	45.0	21.5	8.1	**9.2**	10.5
▼ Select Employees Credit Union	Sterling	IL	**D**	D+	C-	44.4	4.31	0.0	26.7	24.8	0.0	**4.9**	6.9
Select Federal Credit Union	San Antonio	TX	**B**	B	B	41.3	3.53	4.2	59.7	14.6	0.0	**10.0**	15.3
Select Seven Federal Credit Union	Johnson City	TN	**B-**	B-	B-	52.9	5.05	0.0	61.5	16.9	0.0	**10.0**	11.7
Self Memorial Hospital FCU	Greenwood	SC	**C+**	C+	C+	14.6	1.37	0.0	47.6	0.0	0.0	**10.0**	12.1
Self Reliance Baltimore FCU	Baltimore	MD	**D**	D	E	17.7	-3.95	0.0	4.6	41.9	11.9	**6.9**	8.9
Self Reliance NY Federal Credit Union	New York	NY	**A**	A	A	1295.8	9.11	24.3	0.2	55.0	33.0	**10.0**	16.0
▲ Self-Help Credit Union	Durham	NC	**B**	B-	B-	758.9	2.83	8.0	6.7	54.9	5.1	**10.0**	14.1
▲ Self-Help Federal Credit Union	Durham	NC	**A-**	B+	B-	743.6	16.62	10.0	11.7	56.2	1.1	**10.0**	17.6
Selfreliance Ukrainian American FCU	Chicago	IL	**B+**	B+	A-	470.0	4.55	17.3	1.3	42.8	41.7	**10.0**	20.1
SELH Federal Credit Union	Mandeville	LA	**D**	D	D	3.2	-2.97	0.0	21.4	0.0	0.0	**10.0**	17.0
Seminole Public Schools FCU	Seminole	TX	**C-**	C-	C-	7.4	-3.76	0.0	34.2	0.6	0.0	**10.0**	20.6
▲ Seneca Nation of Indians FCU	Irving	NY	**E+**	E-	D	2.5	74.30	0.0	44.6	0.0	0.0	**7.1**	9.1
▼ Sentinel Federal Credit Union	Ellsworth AFB	SD	**B-**	B	B-	107.9	3.27	16.6	25.4	16.5	7.4	**7.4**	9.3
Sentry Credit Union	Stevens Point	WI	**B+**	B+	B+	97.2	5.04	0.0	15.7	35.3	0.0	**10.0**	15.0
▼ Sequoia Federal Credit Union	Redwood City	CA	**C-**	C	B-	31.6	8.49	0.0	12.2	20.7	0.0	**10.0**	11.2
▲ Service 1 Federal Credit Union	Norton Shores	MI	**A**	A-	A	116.5	7.44	0.0	36.4	9.3	2.7	**10.0**	16.0
Service 1st Credit Union	Greenville	TX	**C-**	C-	C-	57.4	5.11	0.0	41.8	5.7	0.0	**7.6**	9.4
Service 1st Federal Credit Union	Danville	PA	**B**	B	B	323.2	10.03	9.8	30.1	22.2	3.8	**5.9**	7.9
Service Credit Union	Portsmouth	NH	**B+**	B+	A-	3124.8	6.22	4.8	51.8	24.9	4.8	**10.0**	12.0
Service Credit Union	Green Bay	WI	**C-**	C-	C-	13.7	-10.90	0.0	29.8	8.7	0.0	**10.0**	17.9
Service First Federal Credit Union	Sioux Falls	SD	**C-**	C-	C-	156.9	7.94	5.0	49.1	12.3	10.8	**4.5**	6.8
Service One Credit Union, Inc.	Bowling Green	KY	**A**	A	B+	155.1	11.07	5.4	21.9	32.1	12.1	**9.5**	10.7
Service Plus Credit Union	Moline	IL	**B-**	B-	B-	22.0	3.95	0.0	20.4	39.0	0.0	**10.0**	13.1
Service Station Dealers FCU	Philadelphia	PA	**D**	D	D	<1	-8.93	0.0	56.9	0.0	0.0	**10.0**	49.8
Services Center Federal Credit Union	Yankton	SD	**B-**	B-	C+	63.6	7.55	0.6	18.5	16.7	6.0	**6.3**	8.3
Services Credit Union	Naperville	IL	**B**	B	B	<1	3.45	0.0	14.1	0.0	0.0	**10.0**	70.4
ServU Federal Credit Union	Painted Post	NY	**B+**	B+	A-	286.9	3.85	0.0	38.3	3.5	12.3	**10.0**	12.6
▲ Sesloc Federal Credit Union	San Luis Obispo	CA	**B**	B-	B	789.0	8.69	6.9	26.0	31.6	26.0	**6.4**	8.7
▼ Settlers Federal Credit Union	Bruce Crossing	MI	**C-**	C	C+	24.4	8.92	1.7	43.6	13.7	0.0	**8.0**	9.7
Seven Seventeen Credit Union	Warren	OH	**A**	A	A	950.5	5.38	9.8	24.7	39.5	10.7	**10.0**	13.8
Sevier County Schools FCU	Sevierville	TN	**C+**	C+	C+	10.9	4.96	0.0	33.4	0.0	0.0	**10.0**	13.9
▼ Sewerage & Water Board Employees FCU	New Orleans	LA	**D-**	D	D	6.8	3.37	0.0	45.6	0.0	0.0	**9.8**	10.9
Shacog Federal Credit Union	Carnegie	PA	**E+**	E+	E+	2.4	0.55	0.0	39.3	0.0	0.0	**5.0**	7.0
Shaker Heights Federal Credit Union	Shaker Heights	OH	**D+**	D+	D	2.1	2.00	0.0	28.3	0.0	21.1	**10.0**	13.2
Shambhala Credit Union	Boulder	CO	**D-**	D-	D-	2.3	1.62	0.0	29.6	8.5	0.0	**6.2**	8.2
Shamrock Federal Credit Union	Dumas	TX	**B-**	B-	C	51.5	3.75	0.0	62.7	0.0	0.0	**10.0**	12.8
▼ Shamrock Foods Federal Credit Union	Phoenix	AZ	**D-**	D	D	5.6	3.67	1.1	78.3	0.0	0.0	**6.5**	8.6
Share Advantage Credit Union	Duluth	MN	**C+**	C+	C	41.8	5.13	3.5	14.2	28.6	4.6	**6.7**	8.8
Shared Resources Credit Union	Pasadena	TX	**C+**	C+	C	28.7	6.21	0.0	53.1	12.0	0.0	**8.6**	10.1
Sharefax Credit Union, Inc.	Batavia	OH	**B-**	B-	B	369.9	5.20	3.0	27.4	20.4	21.3	**7.5**	9.3
▼ SharePoint Credit Union	Bloomington	MN	**B-**	B	B	200.0	4.00	6.4	22.1	26.2	16.2	**10.0**	11.9
Sharon Credit Union	Sharon	MA	**B**	B	B	557.3	9.66	4.4	11.1	52.7	16.8	**10.0**	11.0
Sharonview Federal Credit Union	Fort Mill	SC	**B+**	B+	A-	1400.7	14.60	0.2	28.3	46.9	4.3	**8.5**	10.0
Shaw University Federal Credit Union	Raleigh	NC	**D+**	D+	C-	<1	-4.84	0.0	40.9	0.0	0.0	**10.0**	24.4
Shaw-Ross Employees Credit Union	Miami	FL	**C+**	C+	C+	7.2	10.54	0.0	0.0	0.0	55.1	**9.6**	10.7
Shawnee TVA Employees FCU	West Paducah	KY	**C**	C	C-	6.3	-2.00	0.0	23.3	0.0	0.0	**10.0**	17.7
Sheboygan Area Credit Union	Sheboygan	WI	**B-**	B-	B-	49.6	8.83	1.5	32.4	13.4	0.0	**10.0**	11.2
▼ Sheet Metal Workers Federal Credit Union	Indianapolis	IN	**D-**	D	D-	8.0	11.49	0.0	31.5	0.0	0.0	**6.5**	8.5
▼ Shelby Community Federal Credit Union	Shelby	MT	**D**	D+	D	5.7	-6.15	0.0	24.0	0.0	0.0	**10.0**	18.4
▲ Shelby County Federal Credit Union	Memphis	TN	**B-**	C+	C+	59.6	1.53	0.0	41.7	1.1	6.3	**10.0**	15.2

Asset Quality Index	Non-Performing Loans as a % of Total Loans	Non-Performing Loans as a % of Capital	Net Charge-Offs Avg Loans	Profitability Index	Net Income ($Mil)	Return on Assets	Return on Equity	Net Interest Spread	Overhead Efficiency Ratio	Liquidity Index	Liquidity Ratio	Hot Money Ratio	Stability Index
9.2	0.91	3.1	0.40	**0.8**	-0.04	-0.22	-1.82	2.48	107.8	**5.0**	37.5	7.3	**5.3**
5.6	1.37	10.5	0.94	**2.8**	0.04	0.03	0.38	4.07	87.2	**4.6**	15.5	0.5	**4.7**
6.1	0.87	9.0	2.40	**0.5**	-0.39	-0.43	-5.55	4.44	77.9	**4.0**	16.7	7.0	**3.0**
8.0	0.68	1.2	0.00	**1.6**	0.00	0.50	1.27	5.99	83.3	**4.6**	42.7	0.0	**4.8**
4.2	1.28	13.4	1.20	**3.6**	6.63	0.28	3.36	3.14	67.4	**1.0**	7.3	29.9	**6.2**
6.0	1.29	10.1	0.31	**2.6**	0.20	0.21	2.63	3.27	88.2	**4.3**	26.8	1.7	**4.5**
6.2	1.41	5.2	0.00	**9.5**	0.10	1.92	9.31	6.09	65.8	**3.1**	32.2	17.2	**5.7**
5.5	1.98	10.2	0.75	**1.6**	-0.02	-0.54	-4.50	4.43	78.5	**5.0**	32.7	9.2	**6.0**
3.1	0.79	14.3	0.83	**5.3**	0.07	1.33	13.99	5.96	76.7	**3.5**	6.8	0.0	**3.0**
8.9	0.19	1.9	0.18	**6.4**	3.00	0.83	7.83	3.13	76.7	**3.9**	14.6	3.0	**8.2**
4.3	1.59	17.2	1.97	**3.6**	0.05	0.42	6.08	3.93	76.9	**5.9**	43.4	1.9	**2.3**
5.7	1.03	6.6	0.27	**9.7**	0.14	1.35	8.83	5.81	74.4	**1.4**	12.4	23.6	**7.8**
6.5	0.29	4.2	0.35	**2.8**	0.01	0.09	0.78	4.36	91.7	**1.6**	9.3	20.5	**6.0**
5.0	2.70	13.1	0.62	**4.0**	0.01	0.28	2.28	6.44	95.5	**6.0**	51.3	9.0	**5.9**
3.7	3.90	20.3	-0.03	**2.9**	0.02	0.36	4.07	2.86	87.4	**3.2**	31.3	19.6	**2.3**
9.4	0.34	1.4	0.00	**5.5**	2.36	0.74	4.68	1.63	51.1	**2.9**	28.1	32.3	**10.0**
5.2	1.95	12.8	0.44	**8.7**	2.40	1.27	12.57	4.67	61.5	**4.1**	27.7	14.4	**9.1**
6.2	0.72	8.6	0.34	**10.0**	3.63	1.99	29.72	6.39	61.7	**3.7**	28.2	17.5	**9.8**
7.6	1.12	4.6	0.13	**4.1**	0.58	0.50	2.47	2.66	81.0	**3.5**	8.0	12.0	**7.6**
7.2	3.78	6.0	8.80	**0.0**	-0.03	-3.56	-20.29	5.56	123.2	**7.0**	63.8	0.0	**5.0**
8.4	2.42	4.8	0.13	**1.8**	0.00	0.00	0.00	3.51	100.0	**6.1**	51.8	0.0	**7.0**
9.4	0.34	1.6	0.37	**0.0**	-0.08	-13.64	-118.35	3.52	290.0	**5.4**	71.1	17.0	**3.9**
6.4	0.93	7.0	0.44	**3.4**	0.01	0.04	0.44	3.78	87.5	**4.0**	18.2	2.3	**6.0**
10.0	0.13	0.5	0.00	**3.9**	0.11	0.48	3.14	2.47	80.2	**4.4**	32.1	2.6	**7.7**
9.5	0.84	2.6	-0.11	**1.2**	-0.01	-0.13	-1.13	3.13	100.0	**5.7**	33.6	0.0	**5.7**
9.4	0.48	1.7	0.13	**6.7**	0.33	1.15	7.05	3.45	77.8	**4.8**	30.3	3.3	**9.0**
7.8	0.57	3.0	0.48	**2.6**	0.05	0.32	3.35	2.91	83.4	**5.1**	22.0	0.2	**4.1**
8.1	0.33	3.8	0.28	**4.2**	0.30	0.37	4.60	3.63	88.9	**3.6**	14.3	4.4	**5.3**
8.3	0.21	1.6	0.40	**4.9**	5.46	0.71	6.14	2.79	75.7	**2.9**	16.0	15.6	**8.5**
10.0	0.00	0.0	0.00	**1.9**	0.00	0.03	0.16	2.21	98.7	**5.6**	43.5	0.0	**6.8**
4.4	0.57	15.7	0.04	**3.5**	0.16	0.40	7.52	3.22	91.6	**4.1**	14.5	1.8	**2.8**
8.0	0.71	3.9	0.50	**7.9**	0.49	1.30	11.86	3.84	72.2	**3.3**	14.8	10.6	**7.5**
10.0	0.10	0.5	-0.03	**3.3**	0.02	0.35	2.64	3.27	89.7	**4.6**	26.0	1.7	**6.4**
8.4	0.00	0.0	0.00	**0.0**	0.00	-3.21	-6.25	9.76	125.0	**6.9**	79.8	0.0	**5.5**
8.2	0.37	2.3	0.20	**3.7**	0.07	0.45	5.35	2.91	85.8	**4.8**	32.1	1.5	**4.5**
10.0	2.63	0.5	0.00	**10.0**	0.00	1.48	2.11	10.81	50.0	**9.6**	292.4	0.0	**7.0**
8.8	0.48	2.8	0.15	**4.6**	0.40	0.56	4.46	3.18	80.8	**4.5**	21.1	2.1	**8.4**
8.1	0.51	4.1	0.22	**4.6**	1.15	0.59	7.02	3.20	79.2	**4.1**	17.0	4.3	**6.1**
5.6	1.57	10.4	2.09	**4.7**	0.02	0.40	4.09	5.68	69.4	**3.8**	29.6	10.8	**3.7**
9.0	0.41	2.4	0.50	**7.8**	2.69	1.15	8.38	4.26	70.5	**3.7**	14.2	3.4	**9.9**
9.9	0.00	0.0	0.64	**3.5**	0.01	0.54	3.72	2.45	75.9	**6.3**	66.0	1.1	**7.6**
7.2	1.21	5.0	0.50	**0.1**	-0.02	-1.00	-9.05	5.74	113.1	**6.1**	46.0	0.0	**5.6**
7.2	0.75	4.2	0.00	**2.3**	0.00	0.00	0.00	3.26	100.0	**7.1**	63.8	0.0	**1.0**
1.7	19.52	38.9	0.00	**3.6**	0.00	0.56	4.29	4.14	81.3	**6.0**	68.0	0.0	**6.8**
9.6	0.00	0.0	0.00	**2.7**	0.00	-0.17	-2.09	6.20	100.0	**5.3**	28.9	0.0	**2.3**
7.2	0.54	2.9	-0.07	**3.7**	0.09	0.71	5.50	4.26	80.8	**4.4**	23.5	4.6	**6.8**
6.1	0.39	3.6	0.00	**2.6**	-0.01	-0.50	-5.80	5.19	106.7	**4.3**	17.4	0.0	**1.7**
8.3	0.68	4.6	0.00	**4.0**	0.03	0.29	3.31	3.21	91.6	**5.0**	27.9	1.4	**4.9**
5.1	1.20	8.0	0.55	**3.6**	0.02	0.32	3.06	4.58	87.6	**3.6**	27.4	8.5	**5.0**
7.8	0.65	4.6	0.47	**3.8**	0.59	0.65	7.32	1.91	75.8	**2.8**	25.5	21.7	**5.5**
8.5	0.54	3.3	0.17	**3.1**	0.08	0.15	1.28	3.35	93.4	**3.4**	12.7	8.1	**7.4**
9.9	0.14	0.9	0.00	**4.3**	0.86	0.63	5.65	2.73	72.0	**3.4**	17.7	8.8	**8.4**
7.8	0.42	4.0	1.05	**2.3**	-1.45	-0.42	-4.06	3.64	82.1	**1.5**	13.7	24.2	**6.2**
5.9	6.19	9.9	3.51	**3.0**	0.00	0.72	2.99	4.86	83.3	**6.5**	76.9	0.0	**5.0**
10.0	0.00	0.0	0.00	**2.2**	0.00	0.06	0.52	0.60	71.4	**8.2**	101.8	0.0	**4.3**
9.7	0.07	1.0	0.00	**2.1**	0.00	-0.13	-0.71	2.65	104.9	**4.5**	29.1	0.0	**6.9**
6.1	2.04	9.8	0.74	**4.5**	0.03	0.27	2.53	3.49	86.5	**4.5**	29.4	1.5	**6.0**
9.1	0.54	2.3	0.27	**1.4**	0.00	-0.05	-0.59	2.56	98.3	**5.4**	36.5	0.0	**3.0**
5.4	7.86	14.7	4.32	**0.1**	-0.01	-0.92	-4.96	3.24	91.1	**5.4**	37.4	0.0	**6.2**
8.6	1.13	3.3	0.50	**4.5**	0.17	1.14	7.50	3.49	76.8	**5.3**	28.4	4.4	**6.3**

Name	City	State	Rating	2016 Rating	2015 Rating	Total Assets ($Mil)	One Year Asset Growth	Asset Mix (As a % of Total Assets) Commercial Loans	Consumer Loans	Mortgage Loans	Securities	Capitalization Index	Net Worth Ratio
Shelby/Bolivar County FCU	Boyle	MS	**C+**	C+	C+	2.5	14.72	0.0	27.3	0.0	0.0	**10.0**	20.5
Shell Federal Credit Union	Deer Park	TX	**A-**	A-	A-	870.4	6.97	0.9	56.0	21.8	3.2	**8.3**	9.9
▼ Shell Geismar Federal Credit Union	Gonzales	LA	**C-**	C	C	30.5	3.06	0.0	39.5	1.8	21.2	**9.7**	11.0
▲ Shell Western States FCU	Martinez	CA	**C**	C-	D+	99.5	2.06	1.9	22.4	9.8	19.2	**6.7**	8.8
Shelter Insurance Federal Credit Union	Columbia	MO	**C+**	C+	C	31.5	3.31	0.0	21.7	0.0	19.7	**10.0**	11.2
Shenango China Area Federal Credit Union	New Castle	PA	**C**	C	C+	14.6	1.30	0.0	32.9	7.0	0.0	**10.0**	18.8
Sherchem Federal Credit Union	Ashtabula	OH	**C-**	C-	C-	2.8	-4.03	0.0	45.8	0.0	0.0	**10.0**	17.6
Sheridan Community Federal Credit Union	Sheridan	WY	**B**	B	B	49.5	16.53	1.2	77.9	3.4	0.0	**9.0**	10.3
Sherwin Federal Credit Union	Portland	TX	**D+**	D+	C-	8.4	-14.90	0.0	34.9	0.0	0.0	**10.0**	31.2
Sherwin Williams Employees Credit Union	South Holland	IL	**C-**	C-	D	31.4	0.20	0.0	24.8	2.9	27.9	**10.0**	14.3
▼ Shiloh Baptist Federal Credit Union	Waukegan	IL	**D+**	C-	C-	<1	1.01	0.0	25.4	0.0	0.0	**7.1**	9.0
▼ Shiloh Englewood Federal Credit Union	Chicago	IL	**C-**	C	C+	<1	-2.34	0.0	0.0	0.0	0.0	**10.0**	28.0
▲ Shipbuilders Credit Union	Manitowoc	WI	**A**	A-	B+	79.9	9.60	10.5	23.1	33.6	0.0	**10.0**	13.7
Shore to Shore Community FCU	Trenton	MI	**C-**	C-	C	59.2	8.30	0.3	24.6	5.7	24.7	**5.5**	7.5
Shoreline Credit Union	Two Rivers	WI	**C+**	C+	B-	93.0	1.81	4.8	28.0	30.0	12.8	**8.8**	10.2
Shoreline Federal Credit Union	Muskegon	MI	**D**	D	D-	17.7	-6.83	0.0	15.8	13.2	0.0	**6.4**	8.4
Show-Me Credit Union	Mexico	MO	**B**	B	B-	29.2	5.99	0.0	25.1	32.4	0.0	**10.0**	11.9
SHPE Federal Credit Union	Greensburg	LA	**E+**	E+	E+	3.0	4.01	0.0	47.5	0.0	0.0	**6.2**	8.2
▼ Shreveport Federal Credit Union	Shreveport	LA	**F**	E-	B	102.4	-7.88	0.1	57.0	17.4	0.0	**1.0**	4.3
▲ Shreveport Police Federal Credit Union	Shreveport	LA	**D**	D-	E+	5.6	-0.39	0.0	73.9	0.0	0.0	**6.9**	9.0
Shrewsbury Federal Credit Union	Shrewsbury	MA	**D+**	D+	D	142.9	7.65	1.6	13.9	22.7	22.2	**5.5**	7.6
Shuford Federal Credit Union	Hickory	NC	**C**	C	C-	23.9	3.80	0.2	30.5	20.6	1.1	**10.0**	11.5
Shyann Federal Credit Union	Cheyenne	WY	**D**	D	D+	8.6	-0.54	0.0	25.1	8.8	0.0	**10.0**	12.3
Sidney Federal Credit Union	Sidney	NY	**B+**	B+	B	462.2	7.66	1.2	34.6	8.2	26.7	**10.0**	12.8
▼ Sierra Central Credit Union	Yuba City	CA	**B+**	A-	A-	905.5	10.62	0.6	43.9	16.5	4.5	**9.9**	11.0
Sierra Pacific Federal Credit Union	Reno	NV	**B-**	B-	B-	120.8	6.28	2.3	43.4	0.3	5.5	**10.0**	12.1
▼ Signal Financial Federal Credit Union	Kensington	MD	**D+**	C-	C-	370.3	2.31	24.1	14.5	50.7	15.4	**8.1**	9.8
Signature Federal Credit Union	Alexandria	VA	**B+**	B+	A-	304.0	2.38	6.2	31.9	24.2	6.1	**10.0**	12.7
Signet Federal Credit Union	Paducah	KY	**A**	A	A-	247.1	4.95	3.2	15.1	26.2	31.1	**10.0**	16.7
Sikeston Public Schools Credit Union	Sikeston	MO	**C**	C	C	5.4	4.40	0.0	41.0	0.0	0.0	**10.0**	13.5
Sikorsky Financial Credit Union	Stratford	CT	**B-**	B-	B-	750.3	3.47	0.0	16.3	29.6	32.8	**9.7**	11.1
Silgan White Cap Credit Union	Downers Grove	IL	**D**	D	C-	2.8	-4.20	0.0	50.5	0.0	0.0	**10.0**	28.1
▲ Silver State Schools Credit Union	Las Vegas	NV	**C+**	C	C-	731.0	5.88	0.2	18.2	43.6	15.4	**6.0**	8.0
Silverado Credit Union	Angwin	CA	**D+**	D+	D+	43.1	2.89	7.0	6.6	64.6	0.0	**5.5**	7.5
Simplicity Credit Union	Marshfield	WI	**B+**	B+	B-	244.9	6.55	10.5	22.8	32.1	5.9	**8.5**	10.1
▼ Simplot Employees Credit Union	Caldwell	ID	**C**	C+	D+	19.7	5.69	0.0	52.1	0.0	6.5	**10.0**	15.4
▲ Simply Service Federal Credit Union	Belle Fourche	SD	**C**	C-	C+	15.3	0.57	0.0	21.8	5.0	0.0	**10.0**	13.7
Sing Sing Employees Federal Credit Union	Ossining	NY	**C+**	C+	C+	8.6	10.37	0.0	49.4	1.3	0.0	**10.0**	15.4
Singing River Federal Credit Union	Moss Point	MS	**C+**	C+	C	211.8	5.66	8.7	42.0	29.4	0.2	**6.4**	8.4
Sioux Empire Federal Credit Union	Sioux Falls	SD	**C+**	C+	C	106.0	7.62	0.2	35.0	6.0	0.0	**5.5**	7.5
Sioux Falls Federal Credit Union	Sioux Falls	SD	**A**	A	A-	262.9	8.31	6.0	29.3	6.9	1.9	**10.0**	11.5
▼ Sioux Valley Community Credit Union	Sioux City	IA	**B-**	B	C+	29.1	3.97	2.5	36.2	4.2	0.0	**10.0**	14.6
Sioux Valley Coop Federal Credit Union	Watertown	SD	**B**	B	B	18.3	12.31	0.0	53.9	0.0	0.0	**10.0**	21.1
Siouxland Federal Credit Union	South Sioux City	NE	**A-**	A-	A	180.0	5.70	3.9	33.7	33.4	0.0	**10.0**	14.7
Siskiyou Central Credit Union	Yreka	CA	**C**	C	C	66.6	11.17	0.0	29.5	1.4	18.9	**7.5**	9.4
Sisseton-Wahpeton Federal Credit Union	Agency Village	SD	**D+**	D+	C	4.3	-15.87	0.0	58.3	0.0	0.0	**10.0**	16.8
Sister's Hospital Employees FCU	Buffalo	NY	**D**	D	D	8.1	2.80	0.0	28.4	0.0	44.1	**5.9**	7.9
SIU Credit Union	Carbondale	IL	**B-**	B-	B-	338.0	6.26	6.8	45.6	10.8	17.3	**6.5**	8.5
SIUE Credit Union	Edwardsville	IL	**C-**	C-	D+	20.7	7.43	0.0	21.5	10.9	26.3	**5.8**	7.8
Sixth Avenue Baptist FCU	Birmingham	AL	**E+**	E+	E+	4.3	4.63	0.0	35.8	14.6	0.0	**6.2**	8.2
SJP Federal Credit Union	Buffalo	NY	**B-**	B-	C+	61.3	20.03	2.6	10.3	16.6	0.0	**6.6**	8.6
▼ Skel-Tex Credit Union	Skellytown	TX	**C-**	C	C+	5.9	-6.90	0.0	47.9	0.0	0.0	**10.0**	19.3
Sky Federal Credit Union	Livingston	MT	**C+**	C+	C	95.3	4.71	12.1	19.4	32.7	1.4	**7.3**	9.2
▲ Skyline Credit Union	Nashville	TN	**B-**	C+	C+	17.0	6.53	0.0	31.1	6.3	0.0	**10.0**	17.8
▼ Skyline Financial Federal Credit Union	Waterbury	CT	**C-**	C	D+	32.4	3.09	0.0	37.9	20.1	0.0	**10.0**	12.8
▼ SkyOne Federal Credit Union	Hawthorne	CA	**B-**	B+	B+	475.1	0.55	7.1	26.8	24.6	23.9	**8.7**	10.4
Skyward Credit Union	Wichita	KS	**A**	A	A	282.5	4.59	2.8	29.2	7.5	46.7	**10.0**	16.9
▼ SLO Credit Union	San Luis Obispo	CA	**C**	C+	C+	33.4	-2.92	0.0	7.2	0.8	41.1	**10.0**	16.5
▲ Sloan Public Schools FCU	Cheektowaga	NY	**D-**	E+	E+	2.2	-2.30	0.0	72.1	0.0	0.0	**5.8**	7.8
SM Federal Credit Union	Shawnee Mission	KS	**B**	B	B	66.9	4.21	0.0	7.3	67.5	4.6	**10.0**	16.4

Asset Quality Index	Non-Performing Loans as a % of Total Loans	Non-Performing Loans as a % of Capital	Net Charge-Offs Avg Loans	Profitability Index	Net Income ($Mil)	Return on Assets	Return on Equity	Net Interest Spread	Overhead Efficiency Ratio	Liquidity Index	Liquidity Ratio	Hot Money Ratio	Stability Index
9.2	1.02	1.5	1.46	**6.7**	0.01	1.05	4.64	12.05	76.2	**7.8**	82.4	0.0	**5.7**
6.8	0.46	3.8	0.58	**6.5**	2.25	1.06	11.22	4.05	70.6	**3.0**	9.5	9.9	**6.8**
7.9	0.37	1.9	1.64	**2.2**	0.01	0.17	1.59	3.91	86.1	**4.8**	19.2	1.6	**4.6**
8.5	0.65	2.4	0.00	**3.3**	0.20	0.77	9.06	1.96	74.0	**4.6**	26.2	1.5	**4.4**
10.0	0.15	0.3	-0.06	**2.7**	0.03	0.32	2.84	1.95	83.0	**6.6**	63.9	0.0	**5.8**
7.1	2.42	6.4	0.87	**1.9**	0.00	0.00	0.00	3.16	97.4	**4.7**	34.1	8.5	**6.6**
8.3	0.00	0.0	0.00	**2.0**	0.00	0.28	1.65	2.84	94.7	**4.6**	24.3	0.0	**7.0**
6.7	0.31	2.5	0.38	**6.3**	0.11	0.94	9.04	3.33	67.4	**1.3**	7.5	23.9	**5.7**
9.5	0.75	1.2	0.48	**0.3**	-0.01	-0.53	-1.68	3.76	112.2	**5.9**	52.9	0.0	**4.8**
7.3	3.72	7.5	2.17	**1.6**	0.01	0.13	0.89	3.14	88.6	**5.9**	40.5	0.4	**5.6**
10.0	0.00	0.0	0.00	**1.5**	0.00	0.00	0.00	1.61	200.0	**7.0**	79.0	0.0	**6.5**
10.0	0.00	0.0	0.00	**0.0**	0.00	-4.82	-16.90	-7.41	-200.0	**9.3**	135.2	0.0	**6.5**
9.6	0.24	1.2	-0.04	**8.9**	0.23	1.15	8.33	4.71	75.5	**3.8**	13.6	4.3	**7.6**
7.9	0.50	2.4	0.29	**2.6**	0.04	0.26	3.43	3.18	92.9	**5.3**	24.6	1.9	**2.7**
7.2	0.33	2.2	-0.05	**3.9**	0.17	0.73	7.11	3.77	86.3	**3.8**	12.2	2.1	**4.2**
9.7	0.40	1.6	0.19	**0.8**	0.01	0.14	1.62	3.00	97.0	**7.3**	66.4	0.0	**2.9**
8.5	0.97	5.0	0.04	**4.1**	0.05	0.73	6.16	4.08	85.5	**4.6**	29.1	6.1	**6.2**
0.7	6.80	41.4	0.91	**1.7**	0.00	-0.40	-4.88	5.87	75.6	**5.0**	22.0	0.0	**3.4**
0.0	2.03	53.3	1.02	**2.9**	-11.30	-43.21	-579.45	7.12	-27.1	**3.0**	22.9	17.6	**5.9**
5.2	0.43	3.6	0.34	**6.3**	0.03	1.82	20.41	5.81	66.2	**3.9**	14.3	0.0	**2.3**
9.1	0.45	3.3	0.01	**3.4**	0.21	0.60	8.74	2.92	81.2	**4.3**	18.0	2.6	**4.2**
6.3	2.13	13.5	0.26	**3.5**	0.02	0.41	3.49	5.24	89.1	**4.5**	27.2	4.2	**5.5**
9.9	0.00	0.0	0.59	**0.0**	-0.02	-0.85	-6.75	2.61	126.4	**6.2**	56.4	0.0	**6.1**
7.8	0.97	4.8	0.90	**4.0**	0.34	0.30	2.30	3.71	80.3	**4.2**	10.9	2.4	**8.2**
8.5	0.36	2.8	0.91	**4.7**	1.05	0.47	4.23	4.09	70.7	**4.5**	31.7	13.6	**8.0**
8.6	0.73	3.6	0.33	**2.7**	0.04	0.12	0.96	2.75	86.4	**4.4**	26.6	0.9	**7.6**
6.2	0.98	7.5	0.94	**1.3**	-0.14	-0.15	-1.54	3.48	88.3	**3.7**	20.2	7.7	**5.8**
9.2	0.42	2.7	0.37	**3.0**	0.07	0.09	0.74	3.38	88.5	**2.2**	17.3	24.8	**7.4**
8.8	1.14	3.4	0.19	**6.4**	0.57	0.94	5.60	2.72	61.5	**5.4**	30.8	1.9	**8.9**
9.5	0.17	0.6	0.51	**3.8**	0.01	0.52	3.85	2.00	72.0	**4.7**	43.1	10.2	**7.1**
10.0	0.29	1.4	0.39	**4.2**	1.10	0.60	5.48	2.94	77.9	**4.6**	12.6	2.3	**7.0**
5.5	5.42	9.0	-0.57	**0.7**	0.00	0.29	1.03	2.69	88.9	**4.9**	53.1	0.0	**5.1**
7.4	0.61	6.4	0.20	**9.3**	2.80	1.56	22.78	3.62	68.0	**4.8**	24.8	5.1	**6.8**
9.9	0.00	0.0	0.00	**2.1**	0.02	0.18	2.35	3.54	95.8	**4.1**	22.1	2.7	**3.1**
7.3	0.80	5.1	0.10	**4.5**	0.26	0.44	4.32	3.68	87.9	**4.5**	22.8	2.2	**7.3**
8.4	0.08	0.3	0.48	**1.9**	-0.02	-0.47	-3.04	4.21	96.4	**4.7**	28.1	1.4	**6.5**
9.7	0.31	0.9	0.07	**2.5**	0.02	0.45	3.26	2.92	102.2	**5.7**	52.1	4.7	**6.0**
5.6	2.83	8.8	0.00	**10.0**	0.04	1.87	12.04	6.76	67.1	**4.9**	29.0	0.0	**5.0**
4.9	1.26	16.3	0.85	**3.8**	0.19	0.36	4.24	4.47	82.5	**2.1**	15.9	26.2	**4.9**
8.3	0.66	4.0	0.08	**2.2**	-0.07	-0.27	-2.90	3.43	102.3	**5.4**	31.8	2.4	**5.6**
9.3	0.41	2.0	0.17	**6.2**	0.51	0.79	7.82	3.42	79.8	**4.9**	33.3	2.2	**7.4**
7.6	1.37	4.5	0.89	**1.9**	-0.02	-0.25	-1.70	3.31	104.0	**5.5**	44.4	0.0	**7.3**
5.5	1.95	6.4	0.18	**9.8**	0.11	2.33	11.18	4.26	45.1	**3.8**	19.6	0.0	**8.7**
8.2	0.54	2.6	0.03	**4.8**	0.15	0.35	2.30	3.50	89.3	**4.4**	31.6	5.0	**9.2**
9.5	0.26	1.1	0.08	**3.7**	0.10	0.60	6.28	2.86	83.4	**5.7**	28.8	0.0	**4.0**
5.8	2.61	7.9	-6.86	**0.4**	-0.05	-4.16	-24.57	10.57	117.3	**6.9**	80.8	0.0	**5.1**
10.0	0.04	0.2	1.36	**2.0**	0.00	-0.10	-1.25	2.50	102.1	**5.5**	22.6	0.0	**3.4**
4.9	1.33	9.7	0.73	**4.3**	0.44	0.53	6.06	3.01	80.6	**4.4**	21.7	3.7	**5.6**
9.6	0.28	1.5	0.05	**3.5**	0.02	0.37	4.76	3.49	92.2	**5.3**	28.4	1.5	**3.7**
2.8	3.93	26.5	-0.16	**3.1**	0.00	0.38	4.61	4.91	92.9	**5.2**	26.1	0.0	**1.0**
4.8	0.67	6.7	0.50	**9.8**	0.19	1.31	15.02	4.00	60.0	**1.5**	14.8	35.1	**5.9**
6.1	2.00	5.2	1.90	**2.3**	-0.01	-0.62	-3.15	3.04	95.2	**5.1**	34.9	0.0	**7.0**
4.6	0.34	13.9	-0.03	**3.9**	0.10	0.41	4.41	4.43	90.8	**3.5**	20.1	8.0	**4.1**
8.9	0.47	1.1	-0.22	**5.0**	0.04	1.04	5.86	2.99	76.9	**5.7**	41.2	0.0	**6.6**
9.4	0.27	1.2	2.66	**0.2**	-0.14	-1.72	-13.35	2.62	159.7	**4.4**	31.5	2.9	**6.1**
6.6	0.83	7.4	0.73	**1.6**	-0.15	-0.13	-1.31	3.38	87.8	**3.2**	15.0	13.3	**5.6**
9.0	1.09	3.4	0.27	**7.9**	0.97	1.39	9.03	2.95	59.6	**3.6**	5.6	11.1	**9.2**
10.0	0.50	0.3	0.00	**1.2**	-0.03	-0.30	-1.87	2.07	114.2	**5.8**	32.9	4.6	**6.8**
8.4	0.00	0.0	0.00	**4.0**	0.01	0.92	11.83	3.62	66.7	**5.1**	26.3	0.0	**1.7**
9.3	0.19	0.9	0.04	**4.5**	0.12	0.70	4.26	1.47	51.9	**3.0**	22.4	8.8	**8.0**

Name	City	State	Rating	2016 Rating	2015 Rating	Total Assets ($Mil)	One Year Asset Growth	Asset Mix (As a % of Total Assets) Commercial Loans	Consumer Loans	Mortgage Loans	Securities	Capitalization Index	Net Worth Ratio
SM Federal Credit Union	Philadelphia	PA	**D**	D	D	<1	-12.50	0.0	0.0	0.0	0.0	**9.1**	11.7
Smart Choice Credit Union	Cleveland	TN	**C**	C	C+	3.2	14.28	0.0	41.0	3.4	0.0	**8.1**	9.7
SMART Federal Credit Union	Columbus	OH	**C-**	C-	C-	31.4	2.06	0.0	27.6	0.0	14.2	**8.6**	10.1
Smart Financial Credit Union	Houston	TX	**B+**	B+	B+	663.0	1.34	11.1	33.7	20.9	15.5	**7.5**	9.4
▼ Smartchoice Credit Union	Spring Valley	IL	**D+**	C-	D+	<1	-1.42	0.0	49.2	0.0	0.0	**10.0**	21.9
Smith & Nephew Employees Credit Union	Memphis	TN	**C**	C	D+	8.6	1.15	0.0	27.1	0.0	0.0	**10.0**	16.5
SMMH Federal Credit Union	Pittsburgh	PA	**C**	C	C	5.2	-0.08	0.0	26.7	0.0	0.0	**10.0**	16.9
SMW 104 Federal Credit Union	San Leandro	CA	**C-**	C-	C-	88.7	2.11	0.0	23.0	0.0	0.0	**5.6**	7.6
▼ SMW Financial Credit Union	Lino Lakes	MN	**C-**	C	B-	79.1	3.57	1.2	47.1	19.4	0.0	**8.2**	9.8
Snake River Federal Credit Union	Twin Falls	ID	**C**	C	C	7.6	6.17	0.0	63.1	0.0	0.0	**10.0**	11.5
Sno Falls Credit Union	Snoqualmie	WA	**C**	C	C+	64.0	15.18	0.3	35.4	26.8	0.0	**5.1**	7.1
Snocope Credit Union	Everett	WA	**C**	C	C-	55.2	7.20	0.0	39.8	22.1	2.9	**6.3**	8.3
Social Security Credit Union	Birmingham	AL	**B-**	B-	C+	29.6	0.35	0.0	36.8	21.5	0.0	**10.0**	20.8
Softite Community Federal Credit Union	Martins Ferry	OH	**B-**	B-	B-	21.6	9.91	0.0	26.0	0.0	0.0	**10.0**	12.3
▼ Solano First Federal Credit Union	Fairfield	CA	**C-**	C	B-	144.8	11.43	3.9	40.0	14.1	12.3	**5.3**	7.3
Solarity Credit Union	Yakima	WA	**A**	A	A	721.5	12.86	7.9	19.9	30.4	7.8	**10.0**	13.7
Solidarity Community FCU	Kokomo	IN	**C+**	C+	C	228.5	5.34	1.2	52.5	10.4	8.6	**8.0**	9.7
Solon/Chagrin Falls Federal Credit Union	Solon	OH	**C+**	C+	C+	8.3	2.94	0.0	14.0	0.0	0.0	**10.0**	15.0
Solutions Federal Credit Union	Elmira	NY	**C**	C	C+	23.8	1.87	0.0	40.6	0.0	0.0	**9.0**	10.4
Somerset Federal Credit Union	Somerset	MA	**C+**	C+	C	141.5	3.45	2.6	5.7	47.4	31.4	**10.0**	15.1
Somerville Mass Firefighters FCU	Somerville	MA	**C+**	C+	C+	7.5	4.64	0.0	16.7	0.0	0.0	**10.0**	14.6
Somerville Municipal FCU	Somerville	MA	**B-**	B-	B-	41.2	7.21	0.0	9.0	29.2	0.0	**10.0**	14.3
Somerville School Employees FCU	Somerville	MA	**D+**	D+	D+	26.1	-2.25	0.0	4.4	0.0	0.0	**10.0**	15.6
▲ Sonoma Federal Credit Union	Santa Rosa	CA	**B-**	C+	C	25.7	11.58	0.6	10.3	14.8	0.0	**7.6**	9.4
▲ Soo Co-op Credit Union	Sault Sainte Marie	MI	**B**	B-	C+	170.9	5.19	0.8	33.6	16.4	11.2	**10.0**	11.3
Soo Line Credit Union	Savage	MN	**D+**	D+	D+	43.6	-0.06	0.2	39.1	10.1	17.9	**5.7**	7.7
Soo Select Credit Union	Thief River Falls	MN	**B-**	B-	B-	13.7	-1.39	0.0	34.4	0.0	0.0	**10.0**	12.4
▼ Sooper Credit Union	Arvada	CO	**C**	C+	C+	350.1	6.85	8.6	26.8	23.1	14.8	**9.5**	10.7
Soreng Employees Credit Union	Itasca	IL	**D+**	D+	D+	1.3	4.74	0.0	5.2	0.0	0.0	**10.0**	24.3
▼ Sorg Bay West Federal Credit Union	Middletown	OH	**E+**	D-	D	8.3	-1.01	1.1	33.0	14.4	0.0	**6.3**	8.3
Sound Credit Union	Tacoma	WA	**A**	A	A	1410.4	7.66	6.8	40.7	21.2	10.7	**10.0**	13.5
Soundview Financial Credit Union	Bethel	CT	**C+**	C+	C+	34.6	-1.40	0.0	26.1	0.0	1.2	**10.0**	12.0
Sourceone Credit Union	Chicago	IL	**D**	D	D	12.1	-3.65	0.0	11.7	0.0	0.0	**10.0**	13.7
South Atlantic Federal Credit Union	Boca Raton	FL	**C**	C	C-	14.4	8.39	0.0	39.6	0.0	0.0	**7.8**	9.6
South Bay Credit Union	Redondo Beach	CA	**A-**	A-	A-	95.5	8.47	7.2	28.8	36.4	3.8	**10.0**	11.4
South Bend Firefighters FCU	South Bend	IN	**A-**	A-	A-	39.7	3.59	0.0	38.9	15.7	0.0	**10.0**	24.5
South Bend Post Office Credit Union	South Bend	IN	**D+**	D+	D	9.0	-5.38	0.0	30.3	0.0	0.0	**10.0**	11.8
South Bend Transit Federal Credit Union	South Bend	IN	**C**	C	C	4.0	0.58	0.0	48.5	0.3	0.0	**10.0**	24.9
South Carolina Federal Credit Union	North Charleston	SC	**A-**	A-	A-	1634.9	11.65	2.1	30.2	33.5	0.2	**9.6**	10.7
South Carolina Methodist Conference CU	Columbia	SC	**D**	D	D	5.8	2.65	1.3	42.9	4.1	0.0	**7.8**	9.5
South Carolina National Guard FCU	Columbia	SC	**A-**	A-	A-	69.9	6.51	0.0	38.5	0.0	21.8	**10.0**	18.2
South Central Credit Union	Jackson	MI	**B-**	B-	C+	73.7	5.15	0.0	24.3	3.0	2.3	**10.0**	12.8
South Central Missouri Credit Union	Willow Springs	MO	**C+**	C+	C	12.2	2.22	0.0	21.9	0.0	0.0	**10.0**	12.3
South Charleston Employees FCU	South Charleston	WV	**B**	B	B	19.0	-2.28	0.0	24.4	3.3	0.0	**10.0**	40.6
South Coast ILWU Federal Credit Union	North Bend	OR	**C+**	C+	C	18.2	7.03	0.7	31.0	14.5	0.0	**10.0**	12.5
South Community Credit Union	Sullivan	MO	**D+**	D+	C-	8.8	0.52	0.9	55.7	0.0	0.0	**10.0**	11.3
South Division Credit Union	Evergreen Park	IL	**B-**	B-	B-	48.8	-0.65	4.9	21.9	9.5	2.1	**10.0**	11.9
South Florida Educational FCU	Miami	FL	**B-**	B-	B-	1083.9	7.99	0.0	14.5	4.6	47.5	**10.0**	18.4
South Florida Federal Credit Union	Miami	FL	**C+**	C+	C+	35.2	-3.74	0.0	35.3	1.9	8.7	**8.4**	10.0
South Hills Healthcare FCU	Pittsburgh	PA	**D-**	D-	D-	10.3	7.15	0.0	36.7	2.3	12.5	**6.4**	8.5
South Jennings Catholic FCU	Jennings	LA	**D**	D	D+	1.6	2.78	0.0	31.9	0.0	12.6	**10.0**	14.0
South Jersey Federal Credit Union	Deptford Township	NJ	**C**	C	C	362.5	5.33	0.2	21.6	15.3	31.6	**7.0**	9.0
South Jersey Gas Employees FCU	Folsom	NJ	**C**	C	C	10.6	0.48	0.0	21.9	0.0	0.0	**10.0**	22.0
South Louisiana Highway FCU	Bridge City	LA	**C-**	C-	C	6.2	-0.27	0.0	33.0	0.0	0.0	**10.0**	26.0
South Metro Federal Credit Union	Prior Lake	MN	**B-**	B-	B	113.6	9.54	7.1	24.3	12.6	19.5	**7.2**	9.3
South San Francisco City Employees FCU	South San Francisc	CA	**D**	D	D	3.2	4.95	0.0	14.5	0.0	0.0	**10.0**	14.7
South Sanpete Credit Union	Manti	UT	**D**	D	D+	1.0	14.51	0.0	52.2	0.0	0.0	**6.6**	8.6
South Shore Railroad Employees FCU	Michigan City	IN	**E+**	E+	E+	4.3	16.98	0.0	46.7	0.0	0.0	**3.9**	5.9
South Side Community FCU	Chicago	IL	**D-**	D-	D-	3.8	0.35	0.0	23.6	8.5	0.0	**5.3**	7.3
South Texas Area Resources Credit Union	Corpus Christi	TX	**C-**	C-	C	46.4	0.49	0.0	33.0	3.6	0.0	**10.0**	12.2

Asset Quality Index	Non-Performing Loans as a % of Total Loans	Non-Performing Loans as a % of Capital	Net Charge-Offs Avg Loans	Profitability Index	Net Income ($Mil)	Return on Assets	Return on Equity	Net Interest Spread	Overhead Efficiency Ratio	Liquidity Index	Liquidity Ratio	Hot Money Ratio	Stability Index
3.2	75.00	25.0	0.00	**1.0**	0.00	0.00	0.00	0.00	0.0	**9.1**	113.2	0.0	**6.8**
7.3	1.03	3.9	1.64	**7.9**	0.01	1.30	12.46	7.87	72.0	**6.6**	49.7	0.0	**4.3**
8.4	0.38	1.6	0.53	**1.8**	0.01	0.14	1.39	3.14	89.3	**5.0**	28.1	1.6	**4.8**
8.7	0.39	2.9	0.94	**3.2**	0.06	0.03	0.43	4.02	90.9	**4.9**	23.3	1.6	**5.3**
4.7	6.67	13.4	-1.58	**2.0**	0.00	-0.41	-1.88	4.69	112.5	**6.3**	42.7	0.0	**5.6**
8.8	1.96	3.4	1.70	**2.6**	0.01	0.24	1.41	3.70	92.4	**6.6**	65.8	1.4	**6.4**
9.0	1.79	2.8	1.41	**1.8**	0.00	0.00	0.00	2.03	104.2	**5.7**	32.9	0.0	**6.6**
9.8	0.14	0.6	0.42	**2.3**	0.06	0.29	3.75	2.32	96.8	**3.9**	27.9	10.8	**2.8**
5.9	0.36	4.0	0.64	**1.9**	-0.08	-0.41	-4.16	3.80	95.5	**2.8**	14.1	12.6	**4.2**
6.4	0.88	5.7	1.29	**6.2**	0.01	0.33	2.77	4.82	76.4	**3.3**	20.1	15.3	**4.3**
5.8	0.59	6.9	0.42	**3.6**	0.11	0.70	9.66	4.29	89.0	**3.8**	15.6	0.7	**1.7**
7.9	0.32	2.4	0.23	**3.9**	0.05	0.40	4.74	3.83	89.2	**3.9**	15.4	4.1	**4.0**
9.1	1.08	3.0	0.84	**3.5**	0.03	0.38	1.82	3.66	81.5	**4.6**	39.9	2.1	**6.9**
7.6	1.44	5.0	3.01	**3.7**	0.00	-0.02	-0.15	5.21	88.8	**5.8**	33.9	0.0	**6.3**
4.7	1.91	19.0	0.56	**1.7**	0.03	0.07	0.96	4.29	91.5	**4.6**	23.6	2.4	**3.9**
7.5	0.52	3.6	0.26	**5.9**	0.95	0.53	4.06	3.32	81.9	**4.3**	26.1	5.2	**9.4**
8.4	0.10	1.3	0.22	**3.1**	0.15	0.28	3.12	3.18	90.5	**4.4**	14.5	0.5	**5.7**
10.0	0.03	0.1	0.00	**4.7**	0.01	0.62	4.19	2.37	69.4	**4.5**	26.2	0.0	**7.8**
8.6	0.28	1.7	0.41	**3.0**	0.01	0.19	1.78	3.80	89.9	**4.7**	26.7	0.2	**5.3**
8.2	1.10	4.4	-0.01	**3.0**	0.14	0.39	2.75	3.17	89.0	**4.3**	25.9	4.9	**7.8**
10.0	0.00	0.0	0.00	**3.7**	0.01	0.75	5.14	2.13	61.1	**5.0**	20.8	0.0	**7.6**
10.0	0.21	0.7	0.06	**3.1**	0.02	0.24	1.64	2.49	90.0	**5.4**	44.9	4.2	**7.0**
9.7	0.52	1.2	0.00	**1.1**	0.00	-0.05	-0.30	2.00	102.4	**5.2**	53.6	2.7	**6.9**
8.9	0.14	1.0	0.00	**9.4**	0.09	1.31	14.35	3.82	67.9	**3.3**	23.7	8.6	**4.7**
9.0	0.30	2.1	0.10	**7.3**	0.57	1.35	12.05	3.72	73.6	**4.3**	18.3	3.6	**7.8**
4.0	1.77	17.7	0.06	**3.1**	0.02	0.22	2.89	3.40	94.7	**4.1**	21.9	0.3	**3.0**
9.4	0.14	0.5	1.10	**3.9**	0.00	0.09	0.71	3.86	98.0	**5.7**	37.2	0.9	**7.1**
9.0	0.29	2.5	0.95	**2.4**	0.30	0.34	3.19	3.96	80.5	**4.2**	14.2	3.7	**7.0**
8.8	16.88	4.1	-4.71	**0.5**	0.00	-0.32	-1.28	1.35	150.0	**5.8**	41.2	0.0	**5.2**
5.4	2.17	12.4	0.76	**1.6**	0.00	0.15	1.76	4.52	97.0	**4.4**	27.8	8.5	**1.0**
9.5	0.18	1.3	0.24	**9.8**	4.96	1.42	12.04	3.83	63.4	**4.4**	17.5	3.1	**10.0**
8.5	1.13	4.7	0.14	**2.5**	0.02	0.19	1.54	3.33	92.3	**4.7**	25.8	0.8	**5.4**
9.8	2.62	2.4	1.55	**0.2**	-0.02	-0.60	-4.34	2.01	127.7	**5.1**	16.8	0.0	**5.4**
8.1	0.44	1.8	0.07	**4.3**	0.01	0.35	3.51	4.71	78.6	**5.4**	27.3	0.0	**4.0**
8.5	0.31	2.1	0.53	**6.8**	0.15	0.64	6.07	4.11	76.0	**3.9**	19.4	6.2	**6.0**
9.7	0.64	1.7	0.00	**8.4**	0.13	1.34	5.47	3.13	61.5	**2.5**	22.5	20.3	**8.0**
8.6	1.18	3.1	0.28	**1.5**	0.01	0.36	3.04	3.03	91.9	**4.9**	31.7	0.0	**4.6**
5.5	3.23	6.4	-4.07	**3.1**	0.00	0.10	0.40	4.34	100.0	**4.7**	44.1	0.0	**3.0**
8.9	0.19	1.7	0.07	**5.8**	3.26	0.82	7.52	3.63	84.5	**4.1**	16.5	2.4	**7.0**
7.1	0.58	2.9	-0.14	**2.2**	0.01	0.35	3.66	5.13	89.9	**5.1**	39.7	3.3	**4.0**
9.7	0.41	1.0	0.56	**8.7**	0.24	1.40	7.92	4.51	67.8	**6.0**	45.2	9.2	**7.7**
9.1	0.72	2.8	0.39	**3.6**	0.11	0.62	4.78	2.69	81.7	**4.8**	21.7	2.3	**6.0**
9.9	0.14	0.3	0.67	**3.1**	0.01	0.36	2.96	2.08	80.7	**4.7**	10.7	0.0	**6.1**
10.0	2.16	1.6	0.42	**4.9**	0.03	0.72	1.76	2.96	72.8	**5.2**	56.8	11.5	**7.6**
9.9	0.13	0.5	0.67	**2.8**	0.01	0.25	1.95	3.22	92.1	**5.7**	59.9	0.0	**7.0**
7.2	0.55	2.9	-0.21	**1.8**	-0.01	-0.28	-2.41	4.09	110.0	**5.7**	36.3	0.0	**4.7**
8.7	1.35	4.2	0.32	**4.3**	0.08	0.63	6.14	4.21	86.4	**5.3**	23.0	1.0	**5.3**
10.0	0.21	0.3	0.31	**4.2**	1.86	0.71	3.79	3.02	78.7	**6.9**	40.7	4.2	**8.3**
5.7	1.40	11.0	0.66	**5.3**	0.02	0.21	2.18	4.64	90.2	**3.9**	14.1	6.6	**4.7**
5.8	2.10	9.2	0.99	**3.4**	0.01	0.40	4.68	2.89	82.2	**5.1**	23.6	0.0	**2.3**
5.4	2.47	6.4	-0.62	**1.9**	0.00	0.25	1.79	4.59	100.0	**5.8**	35.8	0.0	**5.5**
6.1	1.58	10.4	1.34	**2.6**	0.23	0.26	3.23	3.78	81.6	**4.5**	23.1	5.6	**4.5**
10.0	0.48	0.5	0.00	**2.7**	0.01	0.49	2.25	1.94	59.0	**7.3**	76.8	0.0	**5.9**
6.5	7.47	9.2	4.32	**3.3**	0.01	0.32	1.24	4.37	79.0	**6.4**	64.0	0.0	**6.3**
9.3	0.06	0.4	0.15	**3.7**	0.18	0.65	6.98	4.15	86.1	**3.2**	24.5	15.4	**6.2**
10.0	0.64	0.6	0.00	**0.0**	-0.01	-0.75	-5.00	1.88	172.7	**7.5**	96.4	0.0	**5.4**
8.1	0.00	0.0	0.00	**1.9**	0.00	0.00	0.00	2.21	80.0	**6.1**	40.1	0.0	**4.9**
0.7	5.11	42.1	1.81	**0.7**	-0.02	-1.55	-24.52	4.30	95.6	**6.0**	40.0	0.0	**1.0**
0.3	11.78	74.7	0.57	**0.3**	0.00	-0.43	-7.80	3.69	103.2	**6.2**	40.6	0.0	**4.4**
9.8	0.16	0.5	0.34	**1.0**	-0.01	-0.10	-0.85	2.75	103.1	**5.5**	34.8	3.0	**5.6**

Name	City	State	Rating	2016 Rating	2015 Rating	Total Assets ($Mil)	One Year Asset Growth	Asset Mix (As a % of Total Assets) Commercial Loans	Consumer Loans	Mortgage Loans	Securities	Capitalization Index	Net Worth Ratio
South Texas Federal Credit Union	McAllen	TX	**E-**	E-	D-	44.5	-7.91	0.0	62.2	2.9	12.8	**4.4**	6.4
South Texas Regional FCU	Laredo	TX	**E+**	E+	E+	7.4	-0.11	0.0	51.1	0.0	0.0	**5.9**	7.9
South Towns Community FCU	Lackawanna	NY	**D-**	D-	D-	16.1	4.95	0.0	14.5	15.5	32.8	**5.3**	7.3
Southbridge Credit Union	Southbridge	MA	**D+**	D+	D	181.7	6.85	15.7	16.6	48.8	11.2	**10.0**	11.7
▼ Southcoast Federal Credit Union	New Bedford	MA	**C**	C+	B-	49.2	-1.11	0.0	13.1	24.7	6.0	**10.0**	12.6
Southeast Federal Credit Union	Cornelia	GA	**A-**	A-	A-	65.7	12.17	1.0	36.5	30.6	0.0	**10.0**	15.0
Southeast Financial Credit Union	Franklin	TN	**D+**	D+	D+	384.6	0.69	9.2	34.5	22.0	0.3	**5.8**	7.8
▲ Southeast LA Veterans Health Care System FCU	New Orleans	LA	**C+**	C	C	1.6	4.16	0.0	73.7	0.0	0.0	**10.0**	16.0
Southeast Michigan State Employees FCU	Southfield	MI	**C**	C	C	35.4	2.50	0.0	25.4	1.5	17.9	**9.2**	10.7
Southeast Missouri Community CU	Park Hills	MO	**C-**	C-	C-	6.2	-2.12	0.0	51.6	0.0	0.0	**10.0**	12.4
Southeast Texas Employees FCU	Orange	TX	**D-**	D-	D-	9.5	4.19	0.0	48.3	0.0	0.0	**7.3**	9.2
▼ Southeastern Arizona FCU	Douglas	AZ	**C+**	B-	C	34.5	3.58	0.0	56.3	4.0	0.0	**10.0**	11.4
Southeastern Credit Union	Valdosta	GA	**B+**	B+	B	238.4	3.19	16.4	31.1	21.1	20.2	**7.7**	9.8
Southeastern Ohio Credit Union	Cambridge	OH	**B**	B	B	27.1	1.05	0.3	57.6	0.0	0.0	**10.0**	12.0
Southern Baptist Church of New York FCU	New York	NY	**D**	D	D	<1	-9.05	0.0	17.4	0.0	0.0	**10.0**	12.4
▼ Southern Chautauqua Federal Credit Union	Lakewood	NY	**C**	C+	B-	78.5	11.48	0.0	55.7	6.3	0.0	**5.8**	7.8
Southern Credit Union	Fayetteville	GA	**C**	C	C	380.2	5.91	0.4	25.4	7.4	27.2	**7.7**	10.0
Southern Credit Union	Chattanooga	TN	**C**	C	C	23.0	7.91	0.8	38.4	7.6	0.0	**10.0**	12.6
Southern Federal Credit Union	Houston	TX	**A-**	A-	A-	93.7	-1.86	0.0	46.0	0.0	0.0	**10.0**	28.5
▲ Southern Gas Federal Credit Union	Little Rock	AR	**D+**	D	D	5.8	-11.63	0.0	42.9	0.1	0.0	**10.0**	24.5
Southern Lakes Credit Union	Kenosha	WI	**D+**	D+	D+	88.6	0.90	2.3	47.9	15.0	13.2	**5.9**	8.0
▲ Southern Mass Credit Union	Fairhaven	MA	**C**	C-	C	205.7	0.72	0.5	11.1	31.4	18.8	**9.9**	10.9
Southern Middlesex County Teachers FCU	East Brunswick	NJ	**C-**	C-	C-	36.5	1.97	0.0	8.7	10.4	1.1	**7.0**	9.0
Southern Mississippi FCU	Hattiesburg	MS	**C-**	C-	D+	43.6	13.04	1.5	35.7	0.9	0.0	**7.4**	9.3
▲ Southern Pine Credit Union	Valdosta	GA	**B**	B-	B-	46.6	3.31	0.0	13.9	33.6	0.0	**10.0**	17.2
Southern Research Employees FCU	Birmingham	AL	**C-**	C-	C-	5.5	-3.12	0.0	2.8	1.4	0.0	**10.0**	25.9
Southern Security Federal Credit Union	Collierville	TN	**B-**	B-	B-	153.4	6.16	0.0	24.8	24.9	10.4	**8.3**	9.9
Southern Star Credit Union	Houston	TX	**D+**	D+	C+	23.3	0.94	0.0	36.0	6.4	0.0	**10.0**	15.0
Southern Teachers & Parents FCU	Baton Rouge	LA	**D+**	D+	C-	31.3	3.03	0.0	34.2	9.9	26.9	**5.7**	7.7
Southernmost Federal Credit Union	Key West	FL	**C+**	C+	C+	14.5	4.88	0.0	47.9	0.0	0.0	**10.0**	19.8
Southland Credit Union	Los Alamitos	CA	**C+**	C+	B-	753.3	27.07	10.0	27.2	27.2	13.8	**10.0**	11.3
Southland Federal Credit Union	Lufkin	TX	**B-**	B-	C	42.7	11.14	0.0	59.1	0.1	0.0	**10.0**	11.6
SouthPoint Financial Credit Union	Sleepy Eye	MN	**B+**	B+	B+	309.6	4.79	19.0	14.8	48.2	11.4	**10.0**	14.3
Southshop Federal Credit Union	Blue Island	IL	**B-**	B-	B-	13.6	-1.98	0.0	32.4	0.0	0.0	**10.0**	14.6
▼ Southwest 66 Credit Union	Odessa	TX	**B-**	B	B	78.3	-4.34	4.9	20.7	18.5	23.4	**10.0**	11.9
Southwest Airlines Federal Credit Union	Dallas	TX	**A**	A	A	485.5	18.54	0.0	42.4	16.6	11.2	**10.0**	11.4
Southwest Colorado Federal Credit Union	Durango	CO	**B**	B	B	51.4	12.96	0.4	12.8	8.1	0.0	**9.4**	10.6
Southwest Communities FCU	Carnegie	PA	**D**	D	D+	15.5	-0.97	0.0	22.1	18.1	0.0	**7.3**	9.2
▲ Southwest Counties School Employees CU	Neosho	MO	**D+**	D	D	2.1	-2.34	0.0	44.6	0.0	0.0	**8.1**	9.7
▼ Southwest Federal Credit Union	Albuquerque	NM	**D+**	C-	C	62.5	5.82	0.0	27.1	10.0	16.2	**5.6**	7.8
Southwest Financial Federal Credit Union	Dallas	TX	**B+**	B+	B+	62.7	7.12	0.0	73.4	1.9	0.4	**10.0**	16.0
▼ Southwest Health Care Credit Union	Phoenix	AZ	**D**	D+	D+	15.9	1.09	0.0	63.5	0.0	17.6	**7.3**	9.2
Southwest Heritage Credit Union	Odessa	TX	**B+**	B+	B+	123.8	11.93	13.2	40.0	16.8	2.0	**8.0**	9.7
Southwest Kansas Community Credit Union	Dodge City	KS	**D+**	D+	D	4.4	5.81	3.9	60.9	0.0	0.0	**10.0**	11.5
Southwest Louisiana Credit Union	Lake Charles	LA	**A-**	A-	A-	99.7	4.56	0.0	33.7	13.4	0.0	**10.0**	13.3
Southwest Montana Community FCU	Anaconda	MT	**C+**	C+	C+	109.1	2.87	1.3	15.5	24.8	18.9	**10.0**	13.2
Southwest Oklahoma Federal Credit Union	Lawton	OK	**B+**	B+	B+	93.8	3.20	1.1	22.1	5.3	49.7	**9.2**	10.8
Southwest Research Center FCU	San Antonio	TX	**C-**	C-	C	75.0	4.76	0.0	47.3	0.8	22.9	**6.2**	8.2
SP Trainmen Federal Credit Union	Houston	TX	**D**	D	D	3.4	-6.20	0.0	22.9	0.0	65.4	**10.0**	30.6
Space Age Federal Credit Union	Aurora	CO	**C**	C	C+	138.4	22.87	0.0	53.7	1.5	4.6	**7.1**	9.0
Space Age Tulsa Federal Credit Union	Tulsa	OK	**D+**	D+	C-	16.1	-4.95	0.0	32.7	0.0	0.0	**10.0**	16.2
Space City Credit Union	Houston	TX	**C**	C	C-	80.0	10.99	0.4	61.0	5.8	0.0	**7.5**	9.3
Space Coast Credit Union	Melbourne	FL	**A-**	A-	A-	4004.5	7.95	2.7	46.2	18.7	4.2	**10.0**	12.8
▲ Spartan Federal Credit Union	Spartanburg	SC	**B**	B-	B-	15.5	4.99	0.0	34.9	3.4	0.0	**10.0**	12.5
Spartanburg City Employees Credit Union	Spartanburg	SC	**C-**	C-	C-	4.8	4.10	0.0	49.7	0.0	0.0	**10.0**	23.6
SPC Brooklyn Federal Credit Union	Brooklyn	NY	**E+**	E+	D	<1	-0.66	0.0	20.0	0.0	0.0	**5.5**	7.5
SPC Credit Union	Hartsville	SC	**C+**	C+	C+	161.7	6.95	6.0	29.9	19.4	11.4	**7.0**	9.0
SPCO Credit Union	Houston	TX	**C-**	C-	C	40.0	7.81	0.7	29.3	38.5	8.1	**7.5**	9.3
SPE Federal Credit Union	State College	PA	**C-**	C-	D+	88.0	4.80	18.2	21.0	23.0	34.4	**5.2**	7.8
Special Metals Federal Credit Union	New Hartford	NY	**C+**	C+	C+	12.1	10.14	0.0	31.4	0.0	0.0	**10.0**	11.9

Asset Quality Index	Non-Performing Loans as a % of Total Loans	Non-Performing Loans as a % of Capital	Net Charge-Offs Avg Loans	Profitability Index	Net Income ($Mil)	Return on Assets	Return on Equity	Net Interest Spread	Overhead Efficiency Ratio	Liquidity Index	Liquidity Ratio	Hot Money Ratio	Stability Index
1.9	2.73	29.9	0.61	**1.5**	-0.02	-0.14	-2.23	4.38	95.7	**4.6**	23.9	0.0	**0.0**
4.2	1.10	8.8	1.05	**0.7**	0.00	-0.22	-2.71	3.64	106.1	**4.8**	36.0	0.0	**2.6**
6.0	1.52	7.6	0.00	**1.6**	0.00	-0.03	-0.34	2.93	101.8	**5.8**	28.6	0.0	**3.0**
6.8	0.78	5.1	0.17	**0.7**	-0.07	-0.15	-1.32	3.19	96.6	**2.7**	6.2	10.5	**7.4**
7.6	2.17	8.4	-0.03	**1.8**	-0.01	-0.04	-0.33	2.88	99.5	**5.7**	43.5	3.6	**6.0**
9.7	0.06	1.3	0.16	**7.8**	0.13	0.80	5.27	4.56	81.7	**3.8**	30.1	13.9	**8.0**
3.0	0.94	25.9	0.92	**2.1**	0.03	0.03	0.50	4.35	104.5	**3.3**	17.7	14.2	**3.5**
8.2	0.58	2.2	0.34	**8.0**	0.01	1.97	12.40	8.12	75.8	**4.4**	33.3	0.0	**5.0**
6.3	3.41	8.7	1.43	**2.4**	0.01	0.13	1.20	3.48	82.1	**5.3**	32.4	1.8	**4.5**
8.0	0.39	2.1	0.00	**2.4**	0.01	0.53	4.27	4.11	84.9	**4.5**	17.5	0.0	**6.1**
2.9	2.16	17.0	1.01	**4.3**	0.02	0.77	8.35	4.02	81.7	**2.9**	33.5	20.5	**1.7**
6.6	1.40	7.3	0.82	**2.2**	-0.05	-0.59	-4.94	3.53	93.1	**5.2**	29.8	2.0	**6.2**
9.1	0.33	2.2	0.92	**5.2**	0.40	0.68	7.14	3.76	78.2	**4.4**	17.5	5.9	**6.1**
4.8	2.78	13.0	0.99	**5.4**	0.01	0.17	1.36	5.07	77.1	**4.4**	19.2	0.0	**6.1**
1.3	45.71	50.0	0.00	**0.0**	0.00	-2.03	-15.38	3.48	100.0	**8.1**	96.6	0.0	**6.2**
3.1	1.96	17.6	1.50	**4.2**	0.07	0.34	4.26	5.91	72.9	**3.5**	23.7	9.2	**3.9**
9.9	0.09	0.4	0.29	**2.8**	0.13	0.14	1.42	2.58	93.8	**4.7**	18.5	3.2	**5.9**
7.2	1.67	7.2	0.69	**2.2**	0.02	0.30	2.37	3.41	88.7	**5.5**	48.8	0.9	**6.3**
5.9	2.75	5.9	1.10	**9.8**	0.36	1.57	5.48	3.73	42.2	**4.7**	57.5	7.0	**8.9**
9.4	0.13	0.3	0.00	**0.7**	0.00	-0.07	-0.28	4.40	101.7	**5.3**	42.4	0.0	**5.8**
7.0	0.27	2.3	0.20	**1.7**	0.02	0.08	0.98	2.87	94.0	**3.6**	9.9	3.4	**3.2**
9.8	0.39	2.0	0.09	**4.2**	0.56	1.10	9.59	2.67	72.0	**3.7**	18.9	4.3	**7.1**
9.1	0.58	1.7	0.49	**2.6**	0.02	0.19	2.08	2.19	87.0	**5.3**	29.9	2.0	**4.3**
2.8	3.35	31.9	0.96	**6.0**	0.07	0.69	7.29	6.27	80.4	**5.5**	38.4	6.6	**3.6**
7.5	1.97	5.9	0.15	**4.3**	0.09	0.77	4.47	2.60	70.2	**5.1**	27.2	0.0	**7.4**
10.0	0.00	0.0	1.41	**1.7**	0.00	0.07	0.28	1.27	100.0	**6.3**	40.9	0.0	**7.1**
9.1	0.44	2.7	0.21	**3.6**	0.18	0.46	5.28	3.30	87.0	**4.5**	22.5	5.4	**5.8**
7.1	2.07	7.5	1.10	**0.5**	-0.06	-1.08	-7.12	4.17	113.9	**5.0**	39.6	5.6	**5.3**
6.0	1.54	9.9	0.13	**3.0**	0.03	0.34	4.34	4.73	93.4	**5.2**	32.1	7.3	**3.3**
8.5	0.13	0.3	1.22	**2.3**	-0.01	-0.20	-0.98	6.05	98.9	**6.1**	50.8	7.4	**6.6**
7.9	0.88	5.0	0.60	**3.1**	0.38	0.22	2.03	3.50	87.8	**4.0**	18.5	9.3	**6.8**
2.4	2.92	23.9	0.66	**8.6**	0.11	1.03	9.18	4.58	62.6	**2.4**	20.3	22.6	**7.0**
8.5	0.67	3.5	0.04	**3.5**	0.29	0.37	2.62	3.25	89.0	**3.4**	8.7	5.1	**8.7**
6.8	4.41	9.9	1.77	**5.0**	0.02	0.51	3.46	3.80	61.8	**5.3**	23.5	0.0	**5.0**
5.8	2.62	15.6	0.55	**2.6**	0.04	0.19	1.65	3.71	91.1	**4.2**	21.7	8.6	**4.7**
8.7	0.43	2.9	0.60	**6.8**	0.91	0.77	7.26	3.82	75.0	**4.5**	23.4	2.5	**7.2**
10.0	0.00	0.3	0.03	**4.5**	0.08	0.64	6.07	2.37	74.8	**6.3**	43.7	1.4	**5.1**
3.9	3.11	18.1	0.27	**1.2**	0.00	0.00	0.00	3.72	102.0	**5.3**	33.4	1.4	**2.8**
8.1	0.11	0.5	0.00	**3.5**	0.00	0.59	6.03	4.23	76.5	**5.7**	32.6	0.0	**3.0**
6.1	0.50	8.2	0.52	**1.8**	0.00	0.00	0.00	3.89	98.5	**4.0**	19.4	6.0	**3.0**
7.0	0.84	3.6	2.09	**5.2**	0.09	0.60	3.65	4.62	72.7	**3.6**	22.2	6.6	**6.2**
4.2	1.82	13.0	1.65	**0.4**	-0.07	-1.66	-17.33	5.63	87.6	**3.5**	10.4	4.1	**3.7**
5.7	0.72	7.9	0.16	**6.0**	0.26	0.87	8.76	4.36	78.7	**3.2**	18.6	11.4	**6.5**
4.4	2.09	11.7	1.81	**2.5**	0.00	0.19	1.58	5.06	96.1	**5.1**	32.9	0.0	**5.7**
6.6	2.06	8.9	2.07	**7.3**	0.26	1.05	7.80	5.04	72.7	**4.9**	35.0	3.6	**6.7**
10.0	0.37	1.2	0.02	**2.6**	0.06	0.23	1.72	2.89	91.3	**5.1**	28.4	3.6	**8.2**
7.1	1.10	3.5	0.56	**4.1**	0.09	0.37	3.59	2.90	79.9	**5.2**	20.2	4.3	**4.9**
6.4	0.59	3.6	0.30	**1.6**	0.02	0.08	0.97	2.88	95.6	**4.7**	20.9	3.6	**2.4**
10.0	0.91	0.8	2.26	**0.0**	-0.01	-1.04	-3.40	3.85	110.0	**5.3**	20.9	0.0	**5.3**
5.5	0.50	6.8	0.36	**2.4**	0.01	0.03	0.33	4.11	95.3	**3.9**	27.9	6.5	**4.7**
8.7	1.83	5.1	-0.06	**0.4**	-0.02	-0.52	-3.87	3.52	116.8	**5.9**	42.9	1.5	**6.3**
4.7	0.69	7.1	0.46	**4.8**	0.09	0.46	5.20	4.56	86.3	**3.8**	18.4	10.7	**4.0**
5.6	0.85	7.3	0.71	**7.3**	9.11	0.93	7.39	3.55	67.5	**4.4**	20.3	2.0	**9.2**
9.3	0.73	2.6	0.31	**6.6**	0.06	1.44	11.52	5.16	77.7	**7.0**	57.9	0.0	**6.3**
8.5	0.00	0.0	0.29	**1.7**	0.00	-0.08	-0.35	3.73	100.0	**4.5**	18.1	0.0	**6.8**
0.3	21.93	55.6	0.00	**3.9**	0.00	0.90	11.76	3.91	100.0	**7.6**	82.0	0.0	**2.9**
7.9	0.29	4.1	0.27	**3.1**	0.14	0.35	4.75	4.21	91.1	**5.1**	27.7	2.3	**5.4**
6.3	0.86	6.2	0.69	**1.7**	0.03	0.28	3.02	4.19	89.0	**2.6**	29.2	30.5	**3.0**
6.0	0.84	6.4	0.33	**2.9**	0.12	0.55	7.58	4.09	84.6	**4.1**	10.2	0.5	**2.4**
7.1	2.12	9.7	-0.07	**2.8**	0.01	0.27	2.23	3.52	91.8	**5.7**	46.9	2.8	**4.9**

Name	City	State	Rating	2016 Rating	2015 Rating	Total Assets ($Mil)	One Year Asset Growth	Asset Mix (As a % of Total Assets) Commercial Loans	Consumer Loans	Mortgage Loans	Securities	Capitalization Index	Net Worth Ratio
SPELC Federal Credit Union	Lake Charles	LA	**E+**	E+	E+	11.0	-5.53	0.0	58.9	0.2	0.0	**5.9**	7.9
Spencerport Federal Credit Union	Spencerport	NY	**C-**	C-	C-	27.7	-0.70	0.0	31.6	10.4	25.8	**6.1**	8.1
▲ Sperry Associates Federal Credit Union	Garden City Park	NY	**C-**	D+	D	259.2	1.27	2.1	14.3	26.3	29.9	**5.0**	7.6
SPIRE Credit Union	Falcon Heights	MN	**B-**	B-	B-	932.2	10.23	9.1	28.1	31.3	14.0	**6.5**	8.6
Spirit Financial Credit Union	Levittown	PA	**B-**	B-	B-	49.2	3.86	0.0	7.6	4.1	18.6	**10.0**	14.1
Spirit of Alaska Federal Credit Union	Fairbanks	AK	**B+**	B+	B+	150.4	4.08	10.8	14.9	36.6	8.1	**9.9**	11.0
Spirit of America Federal Credit Union	Lincoln	NE	**C-**	C-	C-	43.1	7.26	0.0	17.5	0.1	0.0	**5.7**	7.7
Spojnia Credit Union	Scranton	PA	**D+**	D+	D+	14.0	-2.47	0.0	8.8	14.6	44.2	**10.0**	17.7
Spokane City Credit Union	Spokane	WA	**C+**	C+	C	37.5	6.38	0.0	33.5	10.6	0.0	**8.0**	9.7
▼ Spokane Federal Credit Union	Spokane	WA	**C+**	B-	C+	152.2	5.51	1.1	32.1	26.7	1.5	**7.5**	9.3
Spokane Firefighters Credit Union	Spokane	WA	**B**	B	B	50.0	8.92	0.4	21.3	31.0	27.1	**10.0**	15.9
Spokane Law Enforcement Credit Union	Spokane	WA	**B+**	B+	B	39.7	1.48	0.0	22.6	27.6	31.1	**10.0**	15.8
▲ Spokane Media Federal Credit Union	Spokane	WA	**D+**	D	D	11.4	5.36	0.0	31.0	13.9	0.0	**5.7**	7.7
Spokane Teachers Credit Union	Liberty Lake	WA	**A-**	A-	A-	2565.2	13.26	11.6	35.3	38.5	5.2	**9.3**	10.6
▼ Springdale P. P. G. Federal Credit Union	Springdale	PA	**D+**	C-	C-	1.0	-6.91	0.0	48.1	0.0	0.0	**10.0**	24.6
Springfield Catholic Credit Union	Springfield	MO	**D+**	D+	D+	3.9	-1.63	0.0	40.3	0.0	0.0	**10.0**	18.3
Springfield City Employees Credit Union	Springfield	IL	**C**	C	C	11.3	1.39	0.0	41.1	0.0	1.9	**10.0**	11.9
Springfield Firefighters Credit Union	Springfield	IL	**C+**	C+	C	3.6	-3.24	0.0	31.7	0.0	0.0	**10.0**	14.1
Springfield Postal Employees FCU	Springfield	OH	**D+**	D+	D+	4.7	-6.35	0.0	43.4	0.0	42.6	**10.0**	13.7
Springfield Street Railway Employees CU	Springfield	MA	**C+**	C+	C+	1.6	-0.63	0.0	37.0	0.0	0.0	**10.0**	23.6
Spruance Cellophane Credit Union	North Chesterfield	VA	**D-**	D-	D-	5.9	-2.76	0.0	34.6	7.2	0.0	**4.7**	6.7
SRI Federal Credit Union	Menlo Park	CA	**B-**	B-	C+	87.0	7.57	0.1	10.9	27.2	16.7	**6.7**	9.0
▲ SRP Federal Credit Union	North Augusta	SC	**A-**	B+	B	848.1	9.08	3.1	36.5	13.0	26.2	**7.4**	9.5
SRU Federal Credit Union	Slippery Rock	PA	**B**	B	B	45.1	6.37	0.7	10.2	13.5	43.5	**9.8**	10.9
SS Peter & Paul Federal Credit Union	Allentown	PA	**D+**	D+	D	<1	35.45	0.0	8.7	0.0	0.0	**10.0**	13.6
▲ SSMOK Employees Federal Credit Union	Oklahoma City	OK	**C-**	D+	D+	7.8	1.26	0.0	46.6	0.0	0.0	**10.0**	18.4
St Joseph's Hospital FCU	Tampa	FL	**B+**	B+	B+	55.0	42.46	0.0	34.6	0.1	9.1	**10.0**	11.6
St. Agnes Employees Credit Union	Fond du Lac	WI	**D-**	D-	D	7.3	2.62	0.0	43.5	1.5	0.0	**6.6**	8.6
St. Agnes Federal Credit Union	Baltimore	MD	**C-**	C-	C-	52.5	0.63	0.2	20.8	12.3	1.9	**7.5**	9.4
St. Andrew Kim Federal Credit Union	Palisades Park	NJ	**C**	C	C	2.0	-10.00	0.0	34.9	0.0	0.0	**10.0**	13.7
St. Ann's Arlington Federal Credit Union	Arlington	VA	**D+**	D+	C	3.8	18.73	0.0	7.0	5.8	0.0	**6.9**	8.9
▼ St. Anne Credit Union	New Bedford	MA	**D-**	D	D	17.1	0.69	0.0	21.0	37.5	15.0	**7.2**	9.5
St. Anne's Credit Union of Fall River	Fall River	MA	**C+**	C+	C	902.8	3.33	13.4	14.7	52.6	7.3	**8.3**	9.9
St. Anthony of New Bedford FCU	New Bedford	MA	**D**	D	D	11.1	1.48	0.0	13.6	8.9	0.0	**7.7**	9.5
St. Anthony of Padua FCU	Fall River	MA	**C+**	C+	C	26.0	-0.04	0.0	3.1	24.5	0.0	**10.0**	23.4
▲ St. Athanasius Credit Union	Jesup	IA	**C-**	D+	D	<1	-0.90	0.0	94.7	0.0	0.0	**10.0**	15.6
St. Augustine Credit Union	Benton	MO	**D-**	D-	D-	1.7	-0.12	0.0	48.6	0.0	0.0	**5.4**	7.4
St. Augustine Presbyterian FCU	Bronx	NY	**D-**	D-	D+	<1	1.96	0.0	3.9	0.0	30.8	**9.4**	10.6
St. Bernard Parish School Board Empls FCU	Chalmette	LA	**B-**	B-	B-	14.5	-2.86	0.0	27.1	0.0	44.0	**10.0**	25.9
St. Cloud Federal Credit Union	Saint Cloud	MN	**B**	B	B	161.3	8.54	1.3	32.0	22.5	0.0	**6.8**	8.8
▼ St. Colman & Affiliates FCU	Cleveland	OH	**E+**	D-	E+	7.0	6.63	0.0	42.4	0.0	0.0	**5.9**	7.9
St. Columbkille Federal Credit Union	Parma	OH	**C**	C	C	23.6	-4.80	0.0	9.5	18.0	23.6	**7.8**	9.5
St. Elizabeth Credit Union	Northampton	PA	**B-**	B-	B-	10.7	-1.28	0.0	4.9	7.5	0.0	**10.0**	18.6
St. Elizabeth Employees Credit Union	Appleton	WI	**C-**	C-	C-	4.6	5.29	0.0	43.7	6.1	0.0	**10.0**	14.8
St. Francis Federal Credit Union	Greenville	SC	**B-**	B-	B-	9.6	13.17	0.0	49.0	0.0	0.0	**10.0**	17.3
St. Francis Medical Center FCU	Honolulu	HI	**D**	D	D	9.9	3.97	0.0	64.0	0.0	0.0	**10.0**	13.7
St. Francis X Federal Credit Union	Petoskey	MI	**A**	A	A	132.5	11.54	3.2	7.8	37.8	27.2	**10.0**	14.7
St. Gregory Parish Credit Union	Chicago	IL	**E+**	E+	D	<1	3.91	0.0	19.4	0.0	0.0	**6.9**	8.9
St. Helen Federal Credit Union	Dayton	OH	**D-**	D-	D-	2.6	1.54	0.0	37.0	0.0	0.0	**7.1**	9.0
St. Helena Parish Credit Union	Chicago	IL	**D+**	D+	C-	<1	26.79	0.0	64.8	0.0	0.0	**8.3**	10.6
St. Helens Community FCU	Saint Helens	OR	**C+**	C+	C	221.9	13.43	22.0	26.4	37.6	9.6	**5.2**	7.3
St. James AME Church FCU	Miami	FL	**D+**	D+	D	<1	-18.77	0.0	5.3	0.0	0.0	**10.0**	27.4
St. James Hospital Employees FCU	Chicago Heights	IL	**D+**	D+	D	10.6	3.12	0.0	35.1	0.0	0.0	**7.0**	9.0
St. James Parish Credit Union	Cincinnati	OH	**C**	C	C	5.9	-4.62	0.0	38.7	0.0	4.3	**10.0**	15.8
St. Jean's Credit Union	Lynn	MA	**C**	C	C	222.8	3.81	4.3	15.0	44.6	1.3	**7.9**	9.6
St. Joe Valley Credit Union	Saint Maries	ID	**E+**	E+	E+	8.3	7.87	0.0	26.8	17.2	0.0	**3.7**	5.7
St. John Self-Help Federal Credit Union	Reserve	LA	**D**	D	D	1.2	-4.56	0.0	12.9	2.1	0.0	**10.0**	38.6
St. John United Federal Credit Union	Buffalo	NY	**C-**	C-	C-	1.1	-8.46	0.0	14.8	0.0	0.0	**10.0**	15.5
▼ St. Johns Buffalo Federal Credit Union	Buffalo	NY	**E+**	D-	D	4.4	7.50	0.0	36.2	7.2	32.4	**6.7**	8.7
St. Joseph Medical Center MD FCU	Towson	MD	**B-**	B-	B-	15.9	6.10	0.0	40.3	0.0	38.0	**10.0**	13.2

Arrows denote recent upgrades ▲ or downgrades ▼

Asset Quality Index	Non-Performing Loans as a % of Total Loans	Non-Performing Loans as a % of Capital	Net Charge-Offs Avg Loans	Profitability Index	Net Income ($Mil)	Return on Assets	Return on Equity	Net Interest Spread	Overhead Efficiency Ratio	Liquidity Index	Liquidity Ratio	Hot Money Ratio	Stability Index
5.8	0.29	2.4	0.22	**2.3**	0.00	0.11	1.39	3.23	86.0	**4.5**	20.9	0.1	**1.7**
7.8	0.30	2.3	0.64	**2.2**	0.01	0.15	1.79	3.17	89.2	**4.4**	20.5	0.0	**3.6**
3.7	2.91	24.5	0.05	**2.5**	0.08	0.13	1.86	2.51	92.7	**3.0**	4.8	11.2	**4.1**
8.5	0.36	3.1	0.09	**3.8**	1.31	0.58	6.67	2.77	86.6	**3.7**	9.1	1.5	**6.1**
9.7	0.86	2.3	0.37	**3.0**	0.02	0.19	1.33	2.66	93.5	**5.1**	27.9	2.8	**6.9**
6.1	0.66	6.8	0.22	**3.7**	0.16	0.42	3.79	4.39	90.9	**3.6**	18.1	3.4	**6.7**
9.2	0.28	1.5	-0.08	**2.8**	0.03	0.29	4.24	2.65	86.6	**4.9**	28.6	0.5	**3.0**
10.0	0.72	1.2	0.00	**1.0**	-0.01	-0.14	-0.80	2.22	107.1	**5.4**	29.0	2.2	**6.3**
6.7	0.58	4.4	0.14	**2.8**	0.01	0.11	1.10	3.66	95.2	**5.2**	38.5	2.7	**4.6**
7.0	0.70	5.7	0.69	**2.7**	-0.01	-0.01	-0.14	3.63	77.4	**3.8**	16.6	4.3	**6.1**
9.9	0.34	1.3	0.05	**4.9**	0.09	0.69	4.31	2.63	72.6	**4.3**	21.6	4.3	**7.4**
9.6	0.06	0.9	0.17	**3.0**	0.00	-0.02	-0.13	2.49	92.5	**3.8**	16.8	4.6	**7.1**
9.6	0.00	0.0	0.06	**3.4**	0.01	0.35	4.61	3.68	92.2	**4.9**	34.4	3.4	**3.3**
8.2	0.40	3.1	0.34	**5.9**	4.83	0.76	7.23	3.42	72.5	**2.6**	10.2	11.4	**8.5**
8.3	0.61	1.2	0.00	**0.7**	0.00	-0.39	-1.59	3.90	112.5	**5.9**	46.9	0.0	**5.4**
8.9	1.21	3.0	0.00	**0.5**	-0.01	-0.52	-2.82	3.88	111.8	**4.9**	29.9	0.0	**6.6**
7.5	0.97	4.6	-0.08	**1.8**	0.00	-0.14	-1.19	2.76	91.3	**5.8**	42.8	0.0	**6.2**
7.5	2.73	6.0	0.00	**5.1**	0.02	2.31	16.90	5.77	41.7	**7.3**	75.7	0.0	**4.3**
8.4	0.87	2.7	5.55	**0.0**	-0.03	-2.30	-16.49	3.49	97.6	**4.4**	20.7	0.0	**4.7**
9.9	0.17	0.3	0.00	**4.4**	0.00	0.51	2.17	6.61	85.7	**6.5**	53.9	0.0	**7.6**
9.6	0.12	0.8	0.00	**0.0**	-0.03	-1.93	-27.65	3.74	150.9	**4.8**	22.7	0.0	**2.6**
10.0	0.11	0.7	0.10	**5.8**	0.30	1.41	16.19	2.45	83.7	**4.0**	16.8	3.6	**4.2**
8.5	0.43	3.5	0.58	**7.7**	2.99	1.46	15.52	3.60	71.0	**5.1**	24.1	1.7	**7.2**
8.6	0.75	1.8	0.10	**4.6**	0.08	0.68	6.17	2.15	71.9	**5.7**	28.5	0.4	**5.6**
10.0	0.00	0.0	0.00	**2.3**	0.00	0.88	6.25	4.10	50.0	**8.2**	79.3	0.0	**6.1**
8.6	0.64	1.8	0.10	**1.6**	0.00	0.15	0.84	4.21	98.0	**4.8**	33.9	0.0	**6.2**
9.8	0.30	0.8	0.47	**3.7**	-0.14	-1.03	-7.84	3.59	76.2	**5.2**	44.9	13.8	**7.3**
8.1	0.00	0.0	2.27	**0.4**	-0.01	-0.44	-5.07	3.47	96.8	**6.2**	50.0	0.0	**4.1**
10.0	0.09	0.4	0.17	**2.0**	0.00	0.00	0.00	2.78	97.1	**4.6**	24.6	3.4	**4.4**
5.7	6.46	14.4	-0.57	**4.5**	0.00	0.00	0.00	8.51	106.7	**8.2**	118.7	0.0	**4.3**
9.9	0.29	1.1	0.00	**2.7**	0.00	0.33	3.59	1.92	80.0	**5.1**	13.4	0.0	**4.9**
8.1	0.08	0.5	1.07	**0.1**	-0.03	-0.73	-7.84	3.27	102.7	**5.1**	41.8	4.9	**4.3**
7.8	0.40	4.1	0.02	**3.8**	1.33	0.59	6.18	2.70	78.6	**2.5**	12.6	14.9	**7.2**
9.7	0.60	1.6	0.00	**1.4**	0.01	0.22	2.30	3.00	93.8	**5.3**	17.4	0.0	**4.2**
8.7	2.90	4.0	-0.05	**2.2**	0.01	0.14	0.59	2.16	94.1	**4.7**	27.7	6.7	**7.0**
4.9	1.59	8.5	0.00	**5.2**	0.00	1.20	7.84	5.39	77.8	**2.7**	7.2	0.0	**3.7**
7.2	0.00	0.0	0.00	**3.0**	0.00	0.24	3.28	2.40	66.7	**4.4**	18.8	0.0	**1.7**
3.7	75.00	27.3	0.00	**0.3**	0.00	0.00	0.00	0.00	0.0	**8.3**	105.4	0.0	**4.2**
9.1	0.75	1.0	0.29	**6.1**	0.03	0.88	3.42	2.96	68.6	**5.5**	36.5	1.2	**8.3**
7.2	0.68	5.3	0.25	**4.1**	0.13	0.32	3.55	3.05	91.4	**3.7**	14.6	3.5	**5.9**
6.7	1.57	8.6	-0.13	**2.7**	0.00	0.18	2.17	4.27	77.1	**5.4**	33.4	0.0	**1.0**
10.0	0.04	0.1	-0.11	**3.2**	0.02	0.39	4.12	1.93	78.6	**6.3**	49.7	0.0	**4.7**
10.0	0.00	0.0	0.00	**3.8**	0.01	0.37	2.00	1.95	79.6	**5.0**	21.0	0.0	**7.8**
9.7	0.09	0.3	0.00	**1.7**	0.00	0.00	0.00	3.67	100.0	**5.5**	32.8	0.0	**6.4**
8.6	0.00	0.0	0.08	**9.0**	0.03	1.35	7.84	4.68	74.2	**4.9**	28.1	3.1	**5.7**
0.0	16.13	56.3	1.78	**7.8**	0.02	0.69	5.04	6.80	52.3	**6.1**	45.6	0.0	**7.2**
9.0	0.01	2.1	0.00	**8.7**	0.35	1.08	7.29	3.25	71.1	**2.4**	12.9	17.5	**9.7**
5.5	2.08	4.7	24.00	**3.5**	0.00	0.95	12.12	2.08	50.0	**6.6**	82.9	0.0	**2.3**
4.8	3.81	15.6	0.00	**0.0**	-0.01	-0.93	-9.92	2.89	117.7	**5.7**	52.0	0.0	**3.3**
5.9	0.00	0.0	0.00	**6.1**	0.00	2.86	28.57	12.37	66.7	**5.9**	39.4	0.0	**3.7**
8.8	0.17	1.6	0.02	**4.8**	0.45	0.83	11.43	4.02	82.5	**3.7**	12.6	5.4	**3.8**
10.0	0.00	0.0	0.00	**0.9**	0.00	0.00	0.00	10.53	100.0	**8.9**	119.9	0.0	**5.7**
7.9	0.15	0.6	0.71	**2.2**	0.00	0.15	1.69	3.30	93.9	**4.8**	26.5	0.0	**3.8**
9.8	0.03	0.1	-0.13	**3.4**	0.00	0.27	1.72	3.60	92.7	**4.3**	19.2	0.0	**7.2**
9.2	0.23	1.8	0.07	**3.3**	0.29	0.54	5.37	3.06	86.8	**3.1**	15.5	14.0	**6.4**
3.7	3.15	28.5	0.00	**3.7**	0.02	0.73	12.88	3.52	78.9	**5.2**	33.0	0.0	**1.0**
10.0	0.98	0.4	3.74	**0.0**	-0.01	-1.61	-4.18	1.53	180.0	**7.1**	109.8	0.0	**5.6**
5.7	3.40	10.1	0.00	**3.0**	0.00	0.00	0.00	7.16	116.7	**7.9**	81.5	0.0	**5.6**
5.9	0.48	3.0	-0.16	**1.7**	0.00	0.18	2.07	4.37	87.9	**4.6**	10.4	0.0	**1.0**
8.6	1.22	3.7	-0.52	**4.2**	0.03	0.63	4.77	2.41	65.6	**4.8**	21.6	0.0	**6.8**

Name	City	State	Rating	2016 Rating	2015 Rating	Total Assets ($Mil)	One Year Asset Growth	Asset Mix (As a % of Total Assets) Commercial Loans	Consumer Loans	Mortgage Loans	Securities	Capitalization Index	Net Worth Ratio
St. Joseph Teachers' Credit Union	Saint Joseph	MO	**D-**	D-	D-	8.3	7.92	0.0	30.9	0.0	0.0	**5.4**	7.4
St. Josephs Canton Parish FCU	Canton	OH	**D-**	D-	D	52.4	9.99	1.8	23.2	3.9	8.1	**4.4**	6.4
St. Jude Credit Union	Chicago	IL	**C-**	C-	C-	<1	-5.83	0.0	34.5	0.0	0.0	**10.0**	25.3
St. Jules Credit Union	Lafayette	LA	**E+**	E+	D-	10.9	-2.35	0.0	33.9	4.6	2.3	**5.3**	7.3
St. Landry Parish Federal Credit Union	Opelousas	LA	**E+**	E+	E+	5.8	-10.27	0.0	18.5	13.3	0.0	**1.1**	4.3
▲ St. Louis Community Credit Union	Saint Louis	MO	**B+**	B	B	267.2	6.84	2.2	30.4	3.4	18.7	**10.0**	13.7
St. Louis Firefighters & Community CU	Saint Louis	MO	**D+**	D+	D+	17.9	2.62	0.0	18.4	0.0	3.4	**10.0**	13.3
▼ St. Louis Newspaper Carriers CU	Fenton	MO	**C-**	C	C	16.0	22.38	0.0	6.5	68.5	0.0	**6.9**	8.9
St. Louis Policemen's Credit Union	Saint Louis	MO	**C+**	C+	C+	18.9	0.01	0.0	25.4	0.0	1.7	**10.0**	16.6
St. Ludmila S Credit Union	Cedar Rapids	IA	**D+**	D+	D+	<1	2.89	0.0	61.4	0.0	0.0	**10.0**	27.9
St. Mark Credit Union	Chicago	IL	**C**	C	C	<1	8.54	0.0	9.4	0.0	0.0	**10.0**	13.5
▲ St. Marks Federal Credit Union	New York	NY	**D**	D-	D	<1	-35.84	0.0	0.0	0.0	0.0	**10.0**	13.5
St. Martin De Porres Parish FCU	Chicago	IL	**C-**	C-	C	<1	0.00	0.0	0.0	0.0	50.5	**10.0**	11.1
St. Mary Credit Union	Walsenburg	CO	**C-**	C-	C-	9.6	3.80	0.0	18.0	10.7	0.0	**10.0**	15.5
St. Mary Parish School Employees FCU	Franklin	LA	**C**	C	C-	<1	2.64	0.0	33.7	0.0	0.0	**10.0**	22.0
St. Mary's Bank Credit Union	Manchester	NH	**C**	C	C	979.6	6.66	9.8	43.4	30.2	2.1	**5.5**	7.5
St. Mary's Credit Union	Marlborough	MA	**C+**	C+	C	831.5	6.71	3.9	28.4	39.0	14.6	**8.0**	10.0
St. Marys & Affiliates Credit Union	Madison	WI	**C**	C	C	33.4	2.28	0.4	29.8	16.8	0.6	**9.2**	10.4
▼ St. Matthews Federal Credit Union	Virginia Beach	VA	**D+**	C-	C	5.9	-0.05	0.0	22.4	0.0	21.3	**10.0**	16.2
▲ St. Michael Federal Credit Union	Craig	CO	**D**	D-	D-	1.0	-5.48	0.0	19.6	0.0	0.0	**6.7**	8.8
St. Michaels Fall River FCU	Fall River	MA	**C+**	C+	C+	48.2	20.20	19.6	6.2	74.0	0.2	**7.6**	9.4
▼ St. Monica Federal Credit Union	Gary	IN	**C-**	C	C-	<1	-8.33	0.0	0.0	0.0	0.0	**10.0**	11.9
St. Nicholas Federal Credit Union	Wilkes-Barre	PA	**D**	D	D	4.6	-0.84	0.0	31.1	2.6	55.6	**10.0**	11.2
St. Paschal Baylons Federal Credit Union	Highland Heights	OH	**C-**	C-	C-	6.1	2.71	0.0	2.5	0.0	0.0	**10.0**	12.7
St. Patricks Parish Credit Union	Fairfield	VT	**D+**	D+	D	<1	1.62	0.0	38.7	0.0	0.0	**10.0**	11.6
St. Pats Employees Federal Credit Union	Missoula	MT	**D+**	D+	D+	4.5	19.85	0.0	43.7	0.0	0.0	**7.1**	9.1
▲ St. Paul A.M.E. Zion Church Credit Union	Cleveland	OH	**C**	C-	C-	<1	-1.59	0.0	22.7	0.0	0.0	**10.0**	21.5
St. Paul Federal Credit Union	Saint Paul	MN	**A**	A	A	158.0	9.04	1.4	32.0	28.9	6.3	**10.0**	12.7
▲ St. Pauls Federal Credit Union	Philadelphia	PA	**D+**	D	D+	<1	8.26	0.0	18.3	0.0	0.0	**10.0**	19.1
▲ St. Philip's Church Federal Credit Union	New York	NY	**C-**	D+	C	1.5	-6.20	0.0	1.9	0.0	0.0	**10.0**	26.4
St. Pius X Church Federal Credit Union	Rochester	NY	**C**	C	C+	79.8	17.99	0.6	27.7	24.7	15.5	**6.8**	8.8
St. Stephens Federal Credit Union	Houston	TX	**C+**	C+	C+	<1	-8.39	0.0	27.9	0.0	0.0	**10.0**	56.0
St. Tammany Federal Credit Union	Slidell	LA	**B-**	B-	B-	21.9	3.55	0.0	60.1	0.0	6.9	**10.0**	12.8
▲ St. Thomas Credit Union	Nashville	TN	**C**	C-	D-	26.4	0.33	0.0	33.5	24.7	0.0	**8.0**	9.7
St. Thomas Employee Federal Credit Union	Saint Paul	MN	**D+**	D+	D+	3.9	-1.48	0.0	43.2	0.0	20.8	**8.8**	10.2
St. Thomas Federal Credit Union	Charlotte Amalie	VI	**B+**	B+	B+	58.1	4.05	0.0	50.1	0.0	17.3	**10.0**	26.5
St. Thomas More Federal Credit Union	Arlington	VA	**C+**	C+	C-	<1	4.87	0.0	13.0	0.0	60.8	**10.0**	39.0
▼ St. Vincent's Medical Center FCU	Bridgeport	CT	**D**	D+	C-	21.0	3.45	0.0	12.4	0.0	69.9	**8.5**	10.9
Staley Credit Union	Decatur	IL	**C+**	C+	C+	132.7	1.91	0.5	36.8	33.8	5.1	**7.7**	9.5
Stamford Federal Credit Union	Stamford	CT	**C+**	C+	B-	59.9	3.83	2.0	21.5	13.7	0.0	**10.0**	11.0
Stamford Healthcare Credit Union, Inc.	Stamford	CT	**C+**	C+	C+	19.2	2.89	0.0	17.1	0.0	3.7	**9.0**	10.3
▼ Stamford Postal Employees FCU	Stamford	CT	**C-**	C	D+	12.2	2.83	0.0	24.9	0.0	50.0	**10.0**	27.6
Standard Register Federal Credit Union	Dayton	OH	**C-**	C-	C+	40.2	0.08	8.0	31.3	21.1	1.2	**10.0**	18.7
Standard Steel Employees FCU	Burnham	PA	**E+**	E+	E+	6.0	1.14	0.0	26.5	5.1	49.1	**4.7**	6.7
Stanford Federal Credit Union	Palo Alto	CA	**A-**	A-	A-	2211.6	12.23	12.8	6.0	47.6	27.8	**7.3**	9.2
▲ Stanwood Area Federal Credit Union	New Stanton	PA	**D+**	D	D-	12.3	0.18	0.0	24.8	0.0	0.0	**9.8**	10.9
Star Choice Credit Union	Bloomington	MN	**C**	C	C-	52.5	7.47	2.0	36.0	34.0	0.0	**6.5**	8.5
Star City Federal Credit Union	Roanoke	VA	**E+**	E+	E+	3.4	-4.69	0.0	60.3	0.0	0.0	**5.6**	7.6
Star Credit Union	Madison	WI	**B**	B	B-	<1	-5.71	0.0	0.0	0.0	0.0	**10.0**	66.7
Star Harbor Federal Credit Union	Rancho Dominguez	CA	**C**	C	D	14.4	-1.42	6.2	49.8	7.9	0.0	**10.0**	17.8
Star of Texas Credit Union	Austin	TX	**C+**	C+	C+	34.7	1.91	9.8	16.5	27.1	0.9	**10.0**	11.9
Star One Credit Union	Sunnyvale	CA	**B+**	B+	A-	9109.1	13.13	1.1	2.9	33.9	48.0	**8.5**	10.3
▲ Star Tech Federal Credit Union	Greenwood Village	CO	**C+**	C	C	8.5	4.45	0.0	42.6	0.0	0.0	**10.0**	18.1
▼ Star USA Federal Credit Union	Charleston	WV	**D**	D+	C-	156.7	-0.27	4.8	31.0	18.8	13.2	**6.7**	9.0
▼ Starcor Credit Union	Becker	MN	**D**	D+	C-	9.6	8.85	0.0	68.3	0.0	0.0	**10.0**	11.6
Stark Federal Credit Union	Canton	OH	**C+**	C+	C	124.4	5.63	5.3	28.3	9.5	1.6	**9.3**	10.5
Starr County Teachers FCU	Rio Grande City	TX	**B-**	B-	B-	29.2	1.63	0.0	33.9	0.0	0.0	**10.0**	16.4
State Agencies Federal Credit Union	Shreveport	LA	**B-**	B-	B-	9.7	0.77	0.0	29.9	9.6	0.0	**10.0**	24.2
State College Federal Credit Union	State College	PA	**C-**	C-	D+	17.1	7.71	0.0	27.5	20.6	13.7	**6.2**	8.2
State Credit Union	Charleston	WV	**A-**	A-	A-	67.0	5.53	0.0	25.7	27.3	2.8	**10.0**	13.9

Asset Quality Index	Non-Performing Loans as a % of Total Loans	Non-Performing Loans as a % of Capital	Net Charge-Offs Avg Loans	Profitability Index	Net Income ($Mil)	Return on Assets	Return on Equity	Net Interest Spread	Overhead Efficiency Ratio	Liquidity Index	Liquidity Ratio	Hot Money Ratio	Stability Index
5.9	1.29	9.8	0.52	**3.2**	0.00	0.20	2.64	3.58	89.7	**5.8**	37.0	0.0	**1.7**
6.9	0.83	4.1	1.55	**1.7**	-0.01	-0.10	-1.56	2.80	80.2	**6.2**	46.6	0.3	**1.3**
6.4	9.56	10.7	0.00	**2.4**	0.00	0.00	0.00	3.70	100.0	**7.1**	85.2	0.0	**7.2**
6.0	1.20	9.2	0.56	**0.8**	0.00	-0.07	-1.00	2.84	102.3	**5.3**	31.9	0.0	**2.2**
1.7	4.84	37.3	2.77	**0.0**	-0.03	-1.84	-41.22	4.06	121.1	**6.1**	54.1	0.0	**0.5**
8.8	0.90	2.9	2.12	**5.5**	0.69	1.07	8.40	4.27	79.7	**5.9**	33.3	1.7	**6.9**
9.8	0.80	1.8	1.81	**1.5**	0.01	0.22	1.67	3.60	94.3	**5.8**	31.8	1.4	**5.8**
10.0	0.09	0.8	0.00	**2.5**	0.01	0.21	2.26	1.14	80.5	**3.9**	9.3	0.0	**4.0**
10.0	0.79	1.4	0.14	**3.5**	0.03	0.68	4.10	2.61	77.5	**5.0**	15.4	0.0	**6.6**
3.4	9.13	19.0	0.00	**2.2**	0.00	0.00	0.00	2.64	100.0	**5.5**	33.7	0.0	**7.3**
10.0	0.00	0.0	0.00	**3.2**	0.00	0.59	4.30	2.49	50.0	**7.8**	82.3	0.0	**6.1**
10.0	NA	0.0	NA	**0.0**	0.00	-7.08	-50.00	0.00	0.0	**9.2**	113.5	0.0	**4.8**
8.4	0.00	0.0	0.00	**2.2**	0.00	0.00	0.00	2.67	100.0	**7.1**	45.6	0.0	**4.8**
8.3	2.27	4.0	-0.14	**2.3**	0.00	0.17	1.07	2.88	94.0	**6.4**	55.1	0.0	**6.8**
9.1	2.08	3.1	0.00	**3.7**	0.00	-0.92	-4.21	8.70	100.0	**7.3**	83.8	0.0	**5.5**
7.1	0.44	5.5	0.52	**3.3**	0.94	0.39	5.75	3.02	77.2	**3.3**	13.0	6.9	**4.3**
9.7	0.09	0.8	0.08	**3.5**	1.05	0.51	5.26	2.65	80.2	**2.6**	7.3	12.5	**7.2**
8.8	0.36	1.8	0.46	**2.4**	0.01	0.08	0.80	2.75	92.2	**5.3**	45.6	1.4	**5.0**
7.4	3.47	7.0	2.00	**0.5**	-0.02	-1.15	-7.02	5.97	100.0	**7.1**	53.9	0.0	**6.1**
7.9	0.32	1.0	0.00	**3.6**	0.00	0.80	9.09	1.83	50.0	**7.4**	76.4	0.0	**3.0**
4.0	1.44	13.0	-0.32	**6.1**	0.19	1.68	17.49	4.61	61.9	**3.3**	14.0	5.3	**4.1**
10.0	0.00	0.0	0.00	**1.2**	0.00	-2.21	-18.18	0.00	0.0	**7.7**	104.5	0.0	**6.2**
6.2	2.28	8.4	1.82	**0.6**	0.00	-0.09	-0.77	2.87	102.9	**4.7**	23.7	0.0	**4.9**
8.7	8.93	3.3	0.00	**2.3**	0.00	0.26	2.06	1.32	84.2	**6.1**	55.0	0.0	**5.4**
1.7	6.18	38.2	0.00	**5.7**	0.00	0.80	6.90	4.91	83.3	**4.3**	19.4	0.0	**7.1**
8.2	0.43	2.2	0.00	**5.2**	0.01	0.74	8.00	2.48	68.0	**3.8**	30.2	9.5	**3.0**
6.3	4.35	6.8	0.00	**5.9**	0.00	1.64	7.55	4.26	50.0	**7.1**	79.9	0.0	**4.3**
9.6	0.28	1.6	0.08	**8.1**	0.36	0.93	7.29	3.50	79.4	**4.1**	23.4	6.2	**9.3**
3.7	33.33	30.8	0.00	**1.1**	0.00	0.00	0.00	4.30	100.0	**7.9**	99.1	0.0	**6.5**
7.5	34.29	8.7	0.00	**1.5**	0.00	-0.28	-1.04	1.66	133.3	**8.3**	92.1	0.0	**7.3**
6.1	0.76	6.0	0.16	**3.3**	0.15	0.76	8.42	3.16	74.3	**2.9**	16.5	14.8	**3.4**
9.7	0.00	0.0	-1.41	**4.3**	0.00	1.03	1.85	5.25	62.5	**8.1**	150.0	0.0	**5.2**
7.5	0.77	3.6	-0.35	**9.2**	0.07	1.21	9.41	6.91	81.3	**4.9**	24.6	0.0	**6.3**
7.3	0.63	4.8	0.32	**2.9**	0.02	0.32	3.31	4.48	85.6	**3.4**	21.1	6.0	**4.1**
9.8	0.12	0.5	0.00	**3.0**	0.01	0.63	6.15	2.71	70.8	**5.0**	29.7	0.0	**5.2**
8.2	1.22	2.3	1.16	**3.6**	0.00	0.01	0.03	5.97	82.8	**4.7**	23.7	1.9	**6.5**
8.2	15.25	4.7	0.00	**5.8**	0.00	1.85	4.79	2.78	33.3	**7.0**	149.1	0.0	**5.0**
7.1	2.35	5.4	0.08	**0.9**	-0.02	-0.37	-3.60	2.48	111.4	**4.8**	12.4	1.2	**4.5**
9.4	0.19	1.9	0.15	**3.4**	0.18	0.54	7.27	3.73	86.7	**3.7**	11.0	3.1	**4.9**
6.8	0.95	4.7	0.06	**2.9**	0.04	0.26	2.38	3.97	85.8	**4.2**	30.6	3.1	**5.6**
10.0	0.31	0.6	-0.10	**3.0**	0.01	0.29	2.84	3.08	92.1	**5.4**	18.0	0.0	**5.3**
9.6	2.21	2.1	-0.62	**0.9**	-0.02	-0.69	-2.48	3.82	107.7	**6.1**	38.2	4.1	**6.5**
8.7	1.35	4.1	0.51	**1.6**	-0.01	-0.10	-0.53	3.65	100.2	**4.6**	20.5	1.9	**5.5**
9.0	0.40	2.0	0.00	**1.0**	0.00	0.07	1.00	3.21	95.8	**5.6**	34.7	0.0	**1.0**
9.7	0.05	0.3	0.05	**6.7**	5.25	0.97	10.47	2.74	64.2	**3.8**	25.1	12.4	**7.7**
7.1	1.06	3.8	0.50	**1.8**	0.01	0.36	3.31	3.49	82.1	**5.4**	35.0	0.0	**4.2**
8.6	0.21	2.0	0.54	**3.0**	0.02	0.17	1.97	4.05	82.7	**3.2**	8.2	2.6	**4.2**
5.8	0.59	4.3	0.58	**0.4**	-0.01	-0.60	-7.69	5.30	105.6	**5.6**	41.0	0.0	**1.8**
10.0	NA	0.0	NA	**6.2**	0.00	0.00	0.00	0.00	100.0	**9.4**	216.7	0.0	**3.2**
7.2	1.30	4.1	1.38	**3.4**	0.01	0.14	0.78	5.37	76.6	**5.4**	37.8	0.0	**6.2**
9.8	0.14	0.7	0.08	**2.9**	0.03	0.33	2.71	3.46	90.5	**5.4**	48.8	1.8	**5.9**
10.0	0.05	0.2	0.02	**5.0**	15.46	0.69	6.94	1.36	44.5	**5.0**	20.4	2.3	**8.1**
9.6	0.49	2.5	0.35	**5.1**	0.02	0.87	4.68	4.66	80.7	**5.0**	46.3	0.0	**5.0**
5.9	0.50	8.6	0.22	**0.9**	-0.06	-0.17	-1.87	3.46	100.0	**3.5**	9.9	6.1	**5.3**
2.7	2.90	20.8	0.24	**1.5**	-0.02	-0.97	-8.19	7.12	106.9	**3.4**	9.8	1.2	**6.2**
8.9	0.64	2.9	0.95	**3.7**	0.20	0.66	6.28	2.77	70.1	**5.7**	49.1	0.4	**6.6**
9.4	1.20	2.8	0.42	**3.8**	0.04	0.58	3.45	5.29	85.6	**6.6**	45.5	0.4	**7.1**
9.2	1.08	1.9	0.00	**9.3**	0.03	1.28	5.32	4.54	66.7	**5.1**	36.4	6.4	**5.7**
9.9	0.06	0.4	0.00	**3.9**	0.02	0.38	4.61	3.05	88.0	**4.6**	20.1	0.0	**3.7**
9.9	0.40	1.5	-0.02	**9.2**	0.21	1.26	9.00	3.56	68.7	**4.8**	31.3	0.4	**8.4**

Name	City	State	Rating	2016 Rating	2015 Rating	Total Assets ($Mil)	One Year Asset Growth	Asset Mix (As a % of Total Assets): Commercial Loans	Consumer Loans	Mortgage Loans	Securities	Capitalization Index	Net Worth Ratio
State CS Employees Federal Credit Union	Watertown	NY	C	C	C+	17.2	6.36	0.0	50.7	0.0	8.1	10.0	11.9
State Department Federal Credit Union	Alexandria	VA	B+	B+	B+	1834.3	4.61	0.8	16.1	30.1	37.3	7.7	9.7
▼ State Employees Community Credit Union	Alton	IL	D+	C-	C	5.5	-1.31	0.0	66.3	0.0	0.0	10.0	13.9
State Employees Credit Union	Santa Fe	NM	A	A	A	496.8	10.42	7.5	45.0	28.1	6.3	10.0	11.5
State Employees Federal Credit Union	Albany	NY	B-	B-	B-	3445.0	9.23	7.5	23.3	23.0	32.5	5.2	7.2
State Employees' Credit Union	Raleigh	NC	B-	B-	B-	36509.5	9.56	1.2	11.5	42.0	14.2	5.6	7.6
State Empls Credit Union of Maryland, Inc	Linthicum	MD	B	B	B	3374.7	10.95	4.4	30.8	40.3	3.5	7.8	9.5
State Farm Federal Credit Union	Bloomington	IL	B	B	B	4034.6	0.96	0.0	20.6	0.0	76.1	10.0	13.2
State Highway Credit Union	Union Gap	WA	C+	C+	C+	28.2	-0.76	3.3	24.1	28.7	0.0	10.0	16.2
State Highway Patrol FCU	Columbus	OH	B	B	B	63.9	3.46	0.0	26.5	10.6	11.0	10.0	12.5
State Police Credit Union Incorporated	Meriden	CT	B-	B-	B-	63.2	1.13	0.0	4.5	24.0	17.6	10.0	14.9
State University of NY Geneseo FCU	Geneseo	NY	C	C	C+	6.4	4.08	0.0	15.8	15.7	0.0	10.0	27.0
Statewide Federal Credit Union	Flowood	MS	B-	B-	B-	120.6	8.05	0.0	27.0	10.3	32.2	6.1	8.3
Stationery Credit Union	Saint Joseph	MO	C	C	C+	13.3	4.43	0.0	28.5	0.0	0.0	10.0	13.0
Steamfitters Phila Federal Credit Union	West Chester	PA	C-	C-	D+	1.2	-0.56	0.0	61.8	0.0	0.0	9.1	10.4
▲ STEC Federal Credit Union	Nursery	TX	C	C-	D	8.3	-0.45	0.0	24.3	0.0	0.0	10.0	13.8
▲ Steel Valley Federal Credit Union	Cleveland	OH	C-	D+	D	29.3	-3.75	0.0	37.8	17.1	2.5	6.1	8.1
Stephens County Community FCU	Toccoa	GA	D+	D+	D+	<1	3.07	0.0	6.0	0.0	0.0	6.9	9.5
▼ Stephens-Adamson Employees Credit Union	Clarksdale	MS	C-	C	C+	<1	-52.50	0.0	10.5	0.0	0.0	10.0	80.7
Stephens-Franklin Teachers FCU	Toccoa	GA	C	C	C	20.5	2.89	1.1	19.6	19.2	0.0	10.0	19.1
▲ Stepping Stones Community FCU	Wilmington	DE	C+	C	C+	1.8	25.81	0.0	3.8	0.0	0.0	10.0	19.8
▲ Sterling Federal Credit Union	Sterling	CO	A	A-	B+	137.2	1.96	7.3	11.9	14.4	10.0	10.0	15.4
Sterling Heights Community FCU	Sterling Heights	MI	D	D	D+	11.6	-7.58	0.0	28.9	14.9	44.3	10.0	11.8
Sterling United Federal Credit Union	Evansville	IN	C	C	C+	74.7	0.55	0.3	44.9	24.1	0.0	7.6	9.4
▼ Stewart's Federal Credit Union	Saratoga Springs	NY	C	C+	C+	16.4	58.70	0.0	22.3	0.0	0.0	6.8	8.8
▼ Stockton Community Federal Credit Union	Stockton	CA	D	D+	C-	5.6	4.33	0.0	22.0	0.0	0.0	7.7	9.5
Stoneham Municipal Employees FCU	Stoneham	MA	C+	C+	C	38.6	8.06	0.0	13.5	10.3	0.0	6.1	8.1
Stoppenbach Credit Union	Jefferson	WI	C-	C-	C-	1.3	-3.01	0.0	67.4	0.0	0.0	10.0	31.2
▲ Stoughton Town Employees FCU	Stoughton	MA	C-	D+	D	2.8	1.32	0.0	42.6	0.0	0.0	10.0	11.5
Stoughton U.S. Rubber Employees CU	Stoughton	WI	C-	C-	D+	1.2	-7.51	0.0	21.0	0.0	0.0	10.0	17.7
STP Employees Federal Credit Union	Duncansville	PA	C-	C-	C-	1.2	-10.74	0.0	72.6	0.0	0.0	10.0	15.4
Strait View Credit Union	Port Angeles	WA	B+	B+	B+	63.0	9.19	0.0	26.9	9.9	0.0	9.5	10.6
Straits Area Federal Credit Union	Cheboygan	MI	B-	B-	B-	86.2	6.17	0.2	23.2	13.4	37.5	6.8	9.0
Strategic Federal Credit Union	Sterling	VA	D-	D-	D-	18.8	2.07	0.0	25.1	10.9	0.0	5.2	7.2
Stratton Air National Guard FCU	Scotia	NY	C	C	C-	1.2	5.82	0.0	58.3	0.0	0.0	10.0	25.9
Streator Community Credit Union	Streator	IL	C	C	C	28.7	5.48	0.0	23.2	12.1	0.0	6.5	8.5
Streator Onized Credit Union	Streator	IL	A	A	A	221.6	6.22	0.0	57.0	11.8	2.8	10.0	13.3
Strip Steel Community FCU	Weirton	WV	C	C	C	46.3	4.55	0.0	18.2	12.0	23.5	10.0	19.5
Struthers Federal Credit Union	Struthers	OH	D-	D-	D	19.7	8.80	0.0	33.8	1.0	11.4	5.0	7.0
STSP Federal Credit Union	Mandeville	LA	D-	D-	D	<1	5.23	0.0	47.9	0.0	0.0	7.4	9.3
Subiaco Federal Credit Union	Subiaco	AR	C+	C+	B-	30.3	2.85	0.2	12.6	14.0	0.0	10.0	12.8
Suffolk Federal Credit Union	Medford	NY	C-	C-	C	1068.9	6.19	8.9	11.9	35.6	32.4	7.2	9.4
Sugar Growers Federal Credit Union	Santa Rosa	TX	C+	C+	C	2.5	-1.80	0.0	20.0	0.0	0.0	10.0	36.6
Sugar Valley Federal Credit Union	Scottsbluff	NE	C-	C-	C	8.2	-4.28	0.0	44.0	0.0	0.0	10.0	23.1
Sugardale Employees Credit Union	Canton	OH	D	D	D	4.0	-3.96	0.0	30.4	11.0	18.7	6.5	8.5
Suma Yonkers Federal Credit Union	Yonkers	NY	B	B	B	321.2	3.32	10.1	0.9	55.2	16.0	10.0	14.8
Summit Credit Union	Greensboro	NC	A-	A-	A-	231.1	22.38	1.4	35.0	22.9	4.7	10.0	12.1
Summit Credit Union	Madison	WI	A	A	A	2768.6	11.38	8.3	20.1	44.6	12.0	10.0	11.4
Summit Federal Credit Union	Rochester	NY	C+	C+	C+	859.5	8.09	0.0	58.6	20.9	1.0	7.6	9.4
Summit Federal Credit Union	Akron	OH	C	C	C	46.7	6.09	0.0	20.6	22.7	0.0	10.0	11.5
Summit Hampton Roads FCU	Norfolk	VA	D+	D+	C	12.7	-1.96	0.0	30.6	3.3	0.0	10.0	16.3
Summit Ridge Credit Union	Lee's Summit	MO	D-	D-	D-	16.3	0.41	0.0	50.5	0.0	0.0	6.6	8.6
Sumter City Credit Union	Sumter	SC	D+	D+	C-	3.1	6.07	0.0	47.4	0.0	0.0	10.0	14.3
Sun Community Federal Credit Union	El Centro	CA	B+	B+	B+	441.1	18.52	20.3	21.0	47.1	7.0	7.4	9.4
Sun Credit Union	Hollywood	FL	B-	B-	B	85.0	12.64	0.0	21.3	12.7	2.4	8.4	10.0
Sun East Federal Credit Union	Aston	PA	C	C	C	533.4	3.61	1.4	37.8	21.1	5.0	6.0	8.0
Sun Federal Credit Union	Maumee	OH	C-	C-	C+	482.9	-1.13	7.5	15.8	39.0	23.6	7.0	9.3
Sun Pacific Federal Credit Union	Richmond	CA	C-	C-	D	23.5	5.93	0.0	29.5	0.0	3.9	10.0	17.0
Suncoast Credit Union	Tampa	FL	B+	B+	B+	8421.3	14.91	0.5	35.3	24.5	20.9	6.3	8.4
Suncomp Employees Federal Credit Union	Bristol	VA	B	B	B	6.1	-0.26	0.0	68.4	0.0	0.0	10.0	51.6

Asset Quality Index	Non-Performing Loans as a % of Total Loans	Non-Performing Loans as a % of Capital	Net Charge-Offs Avg Loans	Profitability Index	Net Income ($Mil)	Return on Assets	Return on Equity	Net Interest Spread	Overhead Efficiency Ratio	Liquidity Index	Liquidity Ratio	Hot Money Ratio	Stability Index
7.7	0.47	2.6	-0.28	**2.0**	0.00	-0.05	-0.39	4.11	99.5	**5.0**	31.7	4.3	**5.8**
9.7	0.40	2.2	0.21	**4.6**	3.55	0.78	8.87	2.54	69.6	**4.1**	25.1	7.5	**6.7**
4.7	3.09	11.7	0.33	**3.3**	0.00	-0.30	-2.09	6.42	66.7	**5.2**	44.5	5.5	**3.0**
7.3	0.29	3.6	0.30	**8.1**	1.28	1.06	9.84	3.45	72.1	**3.6**	13.1	9.3	**8.7**
7.3	0.47	5.2	0.55	**4.3**	5.08	0.60	8.32	3.07	80.6	**4.5**	21.3	1.3	**5.3**
7.0	1.05	7.5	0.43	**3.9**	53.99	0.60	7.92	3.02	69.8	**5.9**	31.2	4.5	**6.8**
7.2	0.69	6.2	0.50	**3.9**	4.25	0.51	5.36	3.16	76.4	**3.1**	11.0	7.4	**6.4**
10.0	0.16	0.3	0.67	**4.8**	6.97	0.70	5.33	0.90	36.3	**5.6**	39.6	0.0	**8.0**
9.8	0.01	0.0	0.02	**3.2**	0.04	0.54	3.35	3.18	81.2	**5.1**	36.3	6.4	**7.5**
7.6	1.75	6.1	0.19	**3.9**	0.07	0.45	3.56	2.81	82.6	**4.2**	22.9	4.8	**6.0**
10.0	0.13	0.3	-0.04	**3.2**	0.04	0.23	1.58	2.18	86.1	**4.6**	26.1	3.0	**7.4**
10.0	0.49	0.6	0.00	**3.3**	0.01	0.50	1.85	3.57	83.7	**6.9**	87.4	0.0	**6.4**
9.8	0.27	1.4	0.24	**4.4**	0.22	0.74	9.27	3.36	85.4	**5.2**	23.3	0.0	**5.0**
9.9	0.33	0.8	-0.27	**3.8**	0.03	1.05	7.93	3.46	97.9	**5.4**	34.6	0.0	**5.5**
6.6	0.35	2.8	0.00	**4.5**	0.00	1.29	12.70	4.28	66.7	**3.3**	9.0	0.0	**3.7**
10.0	0.76	1.6	0.00	**5.3**	0.05	2.55	18.93	1.98	69.2	**5.5**	42.8	0.0	**5.0**
6.0	0.60	6.4	0.09	**5.2**	0.02	0.25	3.05	5.00	97.6	**5.2**	35.1	7.7	**2.7**
10.0	0.00	0.0	0.00	**2.0**	0.00	0.00	0.00	26.67	0.0	**8.8**	101.3	0.0	**4.5**
5.7	83.33	10.6	0.00	**0.0**	0.00	-13.33	-17.02	0.00	0.0	**9.7**	454.6	0.0	**6.2**
9.7	0.70	1.8	-0.08	**2.5**	0.03	0.49	2.57	3.27	83.2	**4.6**	21.9	1.4	**6.7**
9.5	17.65	3.4	5.80	**5.6**	0.02	3.44	17.65	1.74	50.0	**8.1**	114.8	0.0	**5.0**
9.8	0.02	0.1	0.04	**6.5**	0.52	1.54	10.00	2.60	52.8	**6.0**	37.8	1.7	**9.1**
7.7	1.57	5.6	3.56	**0.0**	-0.09	-3.07	-25.63	4.32	115.7	**4.6**	11.6	1.0	**4.3**
5.9	1.07	7.9	1.00	**2.4**	-0.03	-0.14	-1.48	3.69	83.8	**3.5**	17.8	11.8	**4.1**
7.5	1.72	6.1	0.31	**4.5**	0.03	0.65	7.80	4.57	77.1	**7.3**	54.8	0.0	**4.3**
8.2	0.74	2.4	0.00	**0.5**	0.00	-0.15	-1.51	3.75	107.0	**5.3**	12.9	0.0	**3.1**
10.0	0.00	0.0	0.00	**2.9**	0.03	0.28	3.33	2.29	88.5	**5.5**	37.0	1.6	**3.8**
4.5	4.33	10.0	0.41	**4.1**	0.00	0.63	2.00	6.91	76.5	**5.4**	37.1	0.0	**3.7**
9.2	0.99	3.6	0.00	**1.6**	0.00	0.29	2.45	2.16	85.7	**6.0**	51.5	0.0	**5.1**
9.9	1.18	1.3	0.00	**1.5**	0.00	0.00	0.00	1.91	100.0	**6.5**	54.2	0.0	**5.7**
6.4	1.23	5.9	0.00	**3.2**	0.00	0.34	2.17	3.59	87.5	**5.0**	27.5	0.0	**6.9**
9.1	0.00	0.1	0.25	**6.8**	0.15	0.98	9.78	4.50	68.4	**6.8**	49.0	3.1	**5.9**
6.0	0.80	7.9	0.63	**4.4**	0.13	0.62	7.09	3.60	79.8	**4.4**	12.7	3.8	**4.4**
6.2	1.21	10.1	0.10	**2.2**	0.01	0.19	2.67	3.17	90.9	**4.3**	20.8	0.0	**1.7**
8.6	0.00	0.0	0.00	**3.2**	0.00	0.33	1.35	3.38	87.5	**6.5**	55.8	0.0	**7.4**
9.5	0.19	0.8	0.70	**2.7**	0.01	0.17	1.97	2.74	91.2	**5.2**	26.2	4.2	**4.2**
8.3	0.41	2.4	0.44	**6.3**	0.43	0.80	5.94	3.63	76.6	**3.4**	26.5	12.2	**8.8**
10.0	0.24	1.4	-0.03	**2.7**	0.04	0.35	1.84	2.05	81.0	**5.3**	43.7	2.2	**6.4**
7.5	0.72	3.7	0.28	**3.4**	0.02	0.37	5.28	3.43	88.7	**6.3**	38.2	0.0	**2.3**
6.1	0.84	4.2	0.00	**2.1**	0.00	0.55	5.80	10.75	80.0	**6.4**	40.2	0.0	**3.2**
9.4	0.69	2.7	0.11	**2.5**	0.02	0.25	1.97	2.05	94.2	**4.7**	30.0	4.7	**6.2**
8.6	0.49	3.3	0.13	**2.1**	0.43	0.16	1.83	2.63	87.9	**3.8**	8.1	6.4	**6.3**
10.0	0.00	0.0	0.00	**5.7**	0.01	1.12	3.06	2.94	58.8	**5.9**	62.1	0.0	**5.0**
6.9	3.16	6.5	1.56	**2.1**	-0.01	-0.69	-3.10	3.34	97.2	**6.1**	53.7	0.0	**6.8**
4.0	1.62	7.6	4.16	**2.8**	0.00	0.00	0.00	5.14	93.2	**6.5**	51.7	0.0	**1.0**
5.9	2.97	12.4	0.00	**4.2**	0.45	0.57	3.83	1.96	67.1	**1.9**	14.6	24.7	**8.5**
7.0	0.18	1.4	1.06	**5.8**	0.18	0.33	2.83	5.19	80.5	**3.9**	20.7	8.3	**6.6**
8.1	0.64	4.2	0.31	**9.4**	8.63	1.27	11.21	3.04	63.3	**3.4**	13.7	6.8	**9.2**
7.7	0.29	2.8	0.25	**3.6**	0.91	0.43	4.80	2.98	84.8	**2.0**	7.0	13.7	**6.4**
9.9	0.36	1.6	0.31	**2.3**	0.04	0.30	2.61	2.91	90.4	**5.4**	44.3	0.3	**6.0**
10.0	0.68	1.5	0.00	**0.8**	-0.01	-0.38	-2.33	3.30	107.8	**6.0**	34.7	3.6	**5.2**
4.2	2.67	14.2	0.23	**0.7**	-0.01	-0.20	-2.28	3.90	96.5	**3.6**	16.6	11.3	**3.4**
8.5	0.19	0.7	0.50	**0.5**	0.00	-0.54	-3.64	3.96	118.2	**5.4**	53.2	11.3	**5.9**
9.2	0.10	1.4	0.22	**3.0**	0.03	0.03	0.34	3.38	95.6	**2.5**	20.3	22.2	**5.7**
8.3	0.28	2.3	0.40	**3.8**	0.10	0.50	4.86	2.76	90.9	**5.3**	35.9	1.6	**4.4**
6.8	0.75	8.7	0.26	**2.7**	0.04	0.03	0.36	3.09	93.5	**3.6**	19.1	9.7	**5.1**
5.9	1.52	11.7	0.45	**2.7**	0.42	0.35	4.11	3.01	85.7	**3.0**	9.4	12.2	**5.2**
8.9	0.89	2.1	0.32	**6.9**	0.10	1.72	10.03	4.49	74.5	**4.9**	31.5	2.1	**5.7**
7.5	0.57	4.8	0.75	**6.1**	16.92	0.82	9.74	2.41	64.8	**3.6**	18.9	8.0	**6.7**
8.4	1.36	1.8	0.67	**10.0**	0.05	3.19	6.19	5.23	43.5	**4.4**	48.6	0.0	**5.7**

	Name	City	State	Rating	2016 Rating	2015 Rating	Total Assets ($Mil)	One Year Asset Growth	Comm-ercial Loans	Cons-umer Loans	Mort-gage Loans	Secur-ities	Capital-ization Index	Net Worth Ratio
									Asset Mix (As a % of Total Assets)					
	Sunflower Federal Credit Union	Valley Center	KS	**D**	D	D	<1	4.14	0.0	87.9	0.0	0.0	**10.0**	19.4
	Sunflower UP Federal Credit Union	Marysville	KS	**D**	D	D	9.5	22.94	0.0	72.1	0.0	0.0	**5.8**	7.8
	Sunkist Employees Federal Credit Union	Valencia	CA	**D+**	D+	D+	4.8	-1.31	0.0	17.1	0.0	4.2	**10.0**	21.6
	Sunland Credit Union	Marianna	FL	**D+**	D+	D+	2.3	-5.21	0.0	65.6	0.0	0.0	**10.0**	28.8
	Sunlight Federal Credit Union	Cody	WY	**A**	A	A	106.1	-0.52	0.0	28.2	3.7	0.0	**10.0**	14.6
	Sunmark Federal Credit Union	Latham	NY	**B-**	B-	B-	585.3	14.10	10.7	21.9	38.4	0.4	**6.3**	8.3
	Sunnyside Credit Union	Sunnyside	UT	**D-**	D-	D+	2.7	-7.92	0.0	27.2	14.4	0.0	**8.6**	10.1
	Sunrise Family Credit Union	Bay City	MI	**C**	C	C	112.0	2.97	0.1	21.6	18.4	15.7	**6.7**	8.9
	Sunset Science Park Federal Credit Union	Portland	OR	**A-**	A-	B+	47.3	10.33	5.5	9.6	60.2	1.1	**10.0**	11.8
	SunState Federal Credit Union	Gainesville	FL	**A-**	A-	A-	398.4	12.86	12.2	32.2	30.9	10.2	**9.4**	10.9
	SunWest Educational Credit Union	Pueblo	CO	**B-**	B-	C+	125.7	7.47	3.6	30.6	21.3	0.6	**7.2**	9.2
	SunWest Federal Credit Union	Phoenix	AZ	**B-**	B-	B	345.1	10.66	0.0	57.7	0.3	15.0	**10.0**	12.9
	SUNY Fredonia Federal Credit Union	Fredonia	NY	**C+**	C+	C+	31.7	17.22	0.0	28.5	0.0	0.0	**8.2**	9.8
	Superior Choice Credit Union	Superior	WI	**A-**	A-	A-	380.4	12.01	16.8	13.3	55.6	1.4	**10.0**	11.1
▲	Superior Credit Union	Collegeville	PA	**D**	D-	E+	53.3	5.77	0.0	28.5	24.9	0.7	**5.6**	7.6
	Superior Credit Union, Inc.	Lima	OH	**A+**	A+	A+	685.4	15.01	10.8	16.3	34.5	15.6	**10.0**	14.1
	Superior Municipal Employees CU	Superior	WI	**C-**	C-	D+	3.3	8.97	0.0	61.8	0.0	0.0	**10.0**	16.4
▼	Superior Savings Credit Union	Massillon	OH	**D**	D+	D+	23.7	8.40	0.0	65.9	0.9	0.5	**6.8**	8.8
	Susquehanna Valley Federal Credit Union	Camp Hill	PA	**C-**	C-	C-	71.2	6.15	0.6	17.4	19.9	2.8	**5.7**	7.7
▲	Suwannee River Federal Credit Union	Live Oak	FL	**C+**	C	C+	18.2	4.68	0.0	23.0	17.8	0.0	**10.0**	11.3
	SwedishAmerican Federal Credit Union	Rockford	IL	**D**	D	D-	4.9	-1.36	0.0	23.7	0.0	0.0	**6.9**	8.9
	Sweeny Teachers Federal Credit Union	Sweeny	TX	**D**	D	D	3.1	-1.08	0.0	45.7	0.0	0.0	**8.9**	10.3
	Sweet Home Federal Credit Union	Amherst	NY	**D+**	D+	D+	32.4	9.47	0.0	14.7	18.7	5.0	**5.2**	7.2
	Sweetex Credit Union	Longview	TX	**C+**	C+	C+	11.4	-3.56	0.0	15.9	9.8	0.0	**10.0**	29.7
	Sweetwater Federal Credit Union	Rock Springs	WY	**C+**	C+	C	21.3	-1.17	0.0	14.8	5.8	0.0	**10.0**	12.7
	Sweetwater Regional Federal Credit Union	Sweetwater	TX	**C-**	C-	C	9.1	-10.61	0.4	33.2	0.4	0.0	**10.0**	17.2
	Swemp Federal Credit Union	Texarkana	TX	**C**	C	C-	10.1	7.87	0.0	59.7	0.0	0.0	**10.0**	15.5
	Swindell-Dressler Credit Union	Pittsburgh	PA	**D**	D	D+	5.8	-0.43	0.0	10.6	0.0	62.2	**10.0**	13.9
	Sycamore Federal Credit Union	Talladega	AL	**B**	B	B	18.7	16.16	0.0	31.7	36.8	0.0	**10.0**	19.6
▼	Sylvania Area Federal Credit Union	Sylvania	OH	**D+**	C-	C-	22.0	3.19	0.0	21.3	1.4	36.8	**7.4**	9.3
	Symphony Federal Credit Union	Boston	MA	**D**	D	E+	3.4	0.21	2.7	15.9	7.4	0.0	**8.1**	9.7
	Synergy Federal Credit Union	San Antonio	TX	**A**	A	A	239.0	-3.94	0.0	32.8	34.1	3.0	**10.0**	12.7
	Synergy Partners Credit Union	Chicago	IL	**C-**	C-	C-	13.2	0.38	0.0	20.3	0.0	0.0	**10.0**	18.9
	Syracuse Cooperative FCU	Syracuse	NY	**E-**	E-	E-	25.4	10.97	7.6	12.0	58.6	0.7	**5.0**	7.0
	Syracuse Fire Department Employees FCU	Syracuse	NY	**B+**	B+	B+	85.7	3.02	0.0	17.2	34.7	0.6	**10.0**	12.5
	Syracuse Postal Federal Credit Union	Syracuse	NY	**C-**	C-	C	14.2	5.21	0.8	16.8	0.0	0.0	**6.2**	8.2
	T & FS Employee Credit Union	Port Arthur	TX	**D+**	D+	D+	<1	-0.45	0.0	71.9	0.0	0.0	**10.0**	23.2
	T & P Longview Federal Credit Union	Longview	TX	**C+**	C+	B-	10.7	-2.07	0.0	54.3	11.0	0.0	**10.0**	19.0
	T H P Federal Credit Union	Terre Haute	IN	**D**	D	D	4.2	-6.87	0.0	64.4	0.0	0.0	**10.0**	21.9
	T&I Credit Union	Clawson	MI	**B-**	B-	C+	75.4	3.23	0.0	3.2	32.0	0.0	**10.0**	18.7
	T. H. D. District 17 Credit Union	Bryan	TX	**C**	C	C	3.0	-2.94	0.0	41.7	0.0	0.0	**10.0**	23.6
	T.C.W.H. #585 Federal Credit Union	Washington	PA	**D-**	D-	D-	<1	-2.01	0.0	65.4	0.0	0.0	**8.2**	10.0
	T.E.S. Regional Healthcare FCU	Shreveport	LA	**C-**	C-	C-	23.0	-4.45	0.0	17.8	7.0	0.0	**10.0**	16.3
▲	Tabernacle Federal Credit Union	Augusta	GA	**D+**	D	D	<1	3.23	0.0	19.8	0.0	0.0	**10.0**	20.3
▼	Tacoma Longshoremen Credit Union	Fife	WA	**B+**	A-	A-	91.3	7.57	0.0	11.7	6.8	0.0	**10.0**	11.5
	Tacoma Narrows Federal Credit Union	Ruston	WA	**C-**	C-	D+	9.0	7.08	0.0	27.6	2.1	0.0	**10.0**	13.9
	Taconnet Federal Credit Union	Winslow	ME	**C-**	C-	C	63.9	1.85	0.7	30.1	24.4	0.0	**5.0**	7.0
	Taft Employees Credit Union	Hahnville	LA	**C-**	C-	C-	2.6	0.92	0.0	43.8	0.0	0.0	**10.0**	20.2
▲	Tahquamenon Area Credit Union	Newberry	MI	**D+**	D	C	63.5	4.11	0.7	12.1	17.4	53.3	**7.8**	9.8
	Taleris Credit Union, Inc.	Cleveland	OH	**D**	D	D	75.2	10.43	13.6	39.3	22.0	10.9	**10.0**	14.6
	Tallahassee Federal Credit Union	Tallahassee	FL	**D**	D	D	4.8	-17.90	0.0	11.9	7.3	4.1	**10.0**	16.8
▲	Tallahassee-Leon Federal Credit Union	Tallahassee	FL	**C+**	C	C-	51.8	6.88	0.0	46.5	4.0	3.2	**8.0**	9.7
	Tampa Bay Federal Credit Union	Tampa	FL	**B+**	B+	B+	290.1	4.46	0.3	33.6	24.3	6.8	**8.5**	10.0
	Tampa Postal Federal Credit Union	Lutz	FL	**C-**	C-	C+	82.4	6.59	0.0	26.1	8.2	29.6	**10.0**	13.1
	Tandem Federal Credit Union	Warren	MI	**D**	D	D+	22.0	-1.23	0.0	21.7	4.0	61.8	**10.0**	18.8
	Tangipahoa Parish Teachers Credit Union	Amite	LA	**C+**	C+	C+	31.4	0.32	0.0	14.5	9.2	63.3	**10.0**	30.3
	Tanner Employees Credit Union	Salt Lake City	UT	**C-**	C-	D+	6.0	1.90	0.0	61.2	0.0	0.0	**10.0**	11.8
	Tapco Credit Union	Tacoma	WA	**B**	B	B-	356.6	9.14	12.3	37.1	24.8	12.1	**6.3**	8.3
▼	Tappan Community Credit Union, Inc.	Mansfield	OH	**C-**	C	C+	13.2	-5.06	0.0	7.9	0.0	1.4	**10.0**	22.2
▼	Tarrant County's Credit Union	Fort Worth	TX	**C-**	C	C+	85.1	3.44	0.1	62.2	7.9	0.0	**6.0**	8.0

Asset Quality Index	Non-Performing Loans as a % of Total Loans	Non-Performing Loans as a % of Capital	Net Charge-Offs Avg Loans	Profitability Index	Net Income ($Mil)	Return on Assets	Return on Equity	Net Interest Spread	Overhead Efficiency Ratio	Liquidity Index	Liquidity Ratio	Hot Money Ratio	Stability Index
0.0	23.87	95.0	0.00	**2.0**	0.00	0.00	0.00	7.16	100.0	**3.9**	16.7	0.0	**6.6**
4.5	0.75	7.9	0.00	**10.0**	0.04	1.95	24.51	6.04	70.1	**3.8**	11.5	0.0	**3.0**
10.0	0.12	0.1	0.49	**1.5**	0.00	0.17	0.77	2.53	90.0	**5.6**	38.4	0.0	**6.0**
3.4	7.26	16.2	-0.25	**5.5**	0.00	0.50	1.80	6.90	81.6	**5.0**	45.0	0.0	**5.3**
9.8	0.45	1.2	0.23	**6.6**	0.25	0.94	6.57	3.31	67.1	**5.1**	24.4	3.5	**9.1**
5.9	0.80	10.8	0.35	**4.9**	0.47	0.33	4.51	3.60	89.9	**2.5**	4.7	7.9	**5.6**
8.9	0.41	2.1	-0.27	**0.0**	-0.02	-3.16	-30.00	3.88	166.7	**5.5**	43.6	4.2	**3.8**
8.5	0.58	3.4	0.48	**2.6**	0.08	0.30	3.41	3.54	88.2	**5.3**	28.2	3.9	**4.9**
9.8	0.10	0.6	0.01	**9.7**	0.17	1.44	12.20	3.56	62.6	**3.3**	12.7	8.7	**7.3**
8.1	0.33	3.3	0.34	**7.3**	1.07	1.11	10.31	4.43	73.9	**3.7**	9.7	3.2	**7.6**
9.8	0.26	1.5	0.25	**4.5**	0.26	0.83	9.04	3.45	76.9	**5.3**	44.1	4.8	**5.9**
7.8	0.33	2.5	0.44	**3.3**	0.26	0.31	2.62	3.63	89.3	**3.4**	13.1	8.7	**6.8**
8.2	0.76	2.3	0.04	**5.9**	0.08	1.00	10.02	2.25	61.3	**5.9**	32.5	0.0	**4.8**
6.3	0.68	7.0	0.47	**9.1**	1.11	1.18	11.38	4.19	67.8	**2.4**	17.9	25.3	**8.5**
3.4	2.61	23.9	0.00	**2.6**	0.07	0.52	8.41	4.12	93.6	**4.6**	38.5	7.4	**2.3**
9.5	0.14	0.7	0.10	**8.7**	2.07	1.22	8.72	2.90	69.5	**4.8**	26.8	6.7	**10.0**
7.9	0.00	0.0	0.00	**1.6**	0.00	-0.24	-1.48	4.75	105.4	**3.8**	18.2	0.0	**6.5**
5.1	1.07	8.6	0.00	**2.5**	0.01	0.17	1.91	3.78	92.3	**2.0**	13.7	24.2	**2.3**
6.2	1.48	9.1	0.07	**3.1**	0.05	0.31	3.96	3.06	93.5	**4.6**	29.4	8.6	**2.9**
7.6	1.55	5.9	-0.10	**3.3**	0.02	0.36	3.13	3.77	91.5	**6.0**	43.1	0.8	**6.3**
7.5	1.26	3.5	0.00	**2.4**	0.00	0.08	0.91	2.66	96.9	**6.3**	49.4	0.0	**2.3**
8.3	0.06	0.3	0.00	**1.4**	0.00	0.00	0.00	4.27	100.0	**5.5**	36.4	0.0	**4.7**
10.0	0.15	0.9	0.05	**2.4**	0.02	0.24	3.26	3.53	90.8	**5.7**	33.1	0.3	**2.9**
10.0	0.00	0.0	0.00	**2.7**	0.01	0.31	1.07	2.38	85.1	**5.1**	36.6	1.9	**7.5**
10.0	0.75	1.5	0.87	**1.5**	-0.01	-0.17	-1.33	2.49	107.4	**5.9**	38.6	5.0	**6.4**
9.7	0.00	0.0	0.00	**1.1**	0.01	0.44	2.57	3.21	104.6	**5.4**	36.3	0.0	**4.7**
8.2	0.10	0.4	-0.29	**4.0**	0.01	0.48	3.07	2.75	82.1	**3.5**	25.7	7.4	**7.5**
10.0	0.15	0.1	0.00	**0.0**	-0.01	-0.85	-5.90	2.01	139.3	**4.5**	19.9	10.1	**5.0**
7.1	0.38	6.8	-0.06	**10.0**	0.14	3.05	15.69	6.37	51.5	**4.1**	15.6	0.0	**6.3**
7.7	1.07	3.5	0.75	**1.3**	-0.01	-0.20	-2.15	2.23	95.2	**5.3**	34.9	0.0	**3.4**
8.9	0.00	0.0	0.00	**2.2**	0.00	0.12	1.21	6.34	91.2	**4.8**	43.8	16.3	**3.6**
9.7	0.21	1.2	0.09	**7.0**	0.52	0.89	6.93	2.85	67.7	**3.7**	26.6	11.4	**9.2**
10.0	0.90	1.0	-0.16	**1.6**	0.00	-0.06	-0.32	2.42	90.3	**5.1**	30.1	4.6	**5.8**
0.3	9.42	221.4	0.15	**2.3**	0.00	-0.02	-0.38	5.03	98.9	**2.6**	14.1	17.0	**0.0**
7.9	0.94	4.3	0.09	**5.4**	0.18	0.83	6.61	3.34	71.7	**4.9**	27.7	3.9	**6.6**
9.2	0.90	1.9	0.46	**4.6**	0.02	0.62	6.69	2.47	68.2	**6.3**	31.9	0.0	**3.7**
6.9	0.30	0.9	2.35	**3.7**	0.01	4.10	17.91	14.81	79.3	**4.7**	33.5	0.0	**3.7**
5.5	2.15	8.3	0.00	**4.9**	0.01	0.48	2.56	5.09	86.3	**3.8**	23.1	5.6	**7.4**
8.2	0.00	0.0	0.00	**0.3**	-0.01	-0.48	-2.16	3.30	118.4	**4.4**	29.6	0.0	**6.3**
10.0	0.22	0.4	0.00	**3.1**	0.05	0.28	1.48	2.18	83.2	**6.2**	52.2	0.7	**7.8**
9.5	0.94	2.0	0.00	**2.5**	0.00	0.27	1.14	2.98	90.5	**4.4**	21.5	0.0	**7.2**
1.5	4.18	25.0	0.00	**1.8**	0.00	0.00	0.00	8.11	100.0	**5.8**	36.8	0.0	**4.8**
10.0	0.24	0.5	0.00	**1.8**	0.01	0.17	1.26	2.32	94.3	**5.3**	30.0	2.2	**6.5**
2.0	16.67	27.5	0.00	**4.2**	0.00	8.65	50.00	11.94	16.7	**7.8**	81.7	0.0	**5.0**
10.0	0.26	0.5	0.46	**4.3**	0.11	0.48	4.26	1.74	66.2	**5.1**	25.2	0.0	**5.7**
9.6	0.00	1.1	0.22	**1.5**	0.00	-0.04	-0.32	3.00	93.7	**4.8**	27.5	7.0	**6.1**
5.9	0.55	5.7	0.37	**2.1**	-0.05	-0.34	-4.75	4.90	94.3	**4.2**	19.0	5.8	**2.5**
7.0	2.25	5.1	2.03	**4.6**	0.00	0.46	2.26	4.51	80.0	**5.3**	59.8	0.0	**4.3**
8.8	0.11	1.2	0.06	**1.3**	-0.02	-0.11	-1.14	3.21	102.8	**4.9**	22.1	0.8	**3.9**
7.1	0.86	5.0	0.42	**0.5**	-0.05	-0.27	-1.95	3.82	109.9	**4.0**	11.5	1.1	**5.2**
10.0	0.17	0.2	0.00	**0.0**	-0.02	-1.29	-7.83	4.12	132.0	**5.7**	54.5	0.0	**4.7**
7.4	0.38	2.4	0.40	**6.3**	1.07	8.42	95.45	4.97	38.9	**5.3**	27.9	1.9	**4.0**
7.6	0.46	3.7	0.79	**5.1**	0.40	0.56	5.53	3.75	79.4	**4.5**	28.1	5.0	**6.3**
9.8	0.36	1.0	0.17	**1.9**	0.04	0.18	1.48	3.08	95.2	**4.3**	19.3	7.6	**5.1**
10.0	0.41	0.6	0.94	**0.5**	-0.01	-0.26	-1.35	3.31	102.9	**5.1**	20.9	2.6	**5.2**
9.7	3.08	2.5	-0.15	**3.2**	0.03	0.33	1.09	2.31	77.2	**6.1**	45.6	1.2	**6.9**
6.9	0.64	3.7	0.00	**6.0**	0.02	1.22	10.26	4.47	73.9	**4.5**	28.1	0.0	**4.3**
6.8	0.65	6.4	0.23	**4.9**	0.61	0.69	8.23	3.91	76.4	**4.6**	21.6	2.5	**5.5**
6.9	1.51	0.6	1.08	**1.6**	0.00	-0.09	-0.41	1.46	127.8	**5.8**	38.4	0.0	**5.7**
5.6	0.40	3.6	0.83	**2.3**	0.01	0.06	0.76	4.98	88.5	**3.4**	18.8	6.6	**2.5**

Name	City	State	Rating	2016 Rating	2015 Rating	Total Assets ($Mil)	One Year Asset Growth	Asset Mix (As a % of Total Assets) Comm-ercial Loans	Cons-umer Loans	Mort-gage Loans	Secur-ities	Capital-ization Index	Net Worth Ratio
Taunton Federal Credit Union	Taunton	MA	**A-**	A-	A-	147.2	2.33	10.1	21.3	44.0	2.5	**10.0**	13.1
Taupa Lithuanian Federal Credit Union	South Boston	MA	**D**	D	D	22.3	2.22	7.8	3.9	56.8	0.0	**7.1**	9.1
Tayco Employees Federal Credit Union	South Shore	KY	**D**	D	D	3.0	-8.32	0.0	19.9	0.0	0.0	**10.0**	31.3
Taylor Credit Union	Medford	WI	**C+**	C+	C-	55.5	3.12	2.1	23.9	38.2	0.0	**10.0**	11.2
Taylorville Community Credit Union	Taylorville	IL	**B**	B	B	53.6	14.42	0.1	28.4	36.9	0.0	**8.5**	10.0
Taylorville School Employees CU	Taylorville	IL	**C**	C	C	1.8	3.08	0.0	39.3	0.0	0.0	**10.0**	18.5
▲ Tazewell County Government Employees CU	Pekin	IL	**D+**	D	D-	1.6	-2.40	0.0	47.6	0.0	0.0	**10.0**	11.1
▲ Tazewell County School Employees CU	Pekin	IL	**C-**	D+	D	22.3	-4.81	0.0	15.1	0.7	0.9	**10.0**	12.6
TBA Credit Union	Traverse City	MI	**A**	A	A	195.3	7.59	6.0	40.6	25.8	5.8	**10.0**	14.0
▲ TBC Federal Credit Union	Richmond	VA	**C-**	D+	D+	<1	-3.60	0.0	36.6	0.0	0.0	**9.2**	10.5
TC Teachers Federal Credit Union	Texas City	TX	**D+**	D+	D	7.5	-7.04	0.0	25.7	0.0	0.0	**10.0**	17.7
▼ TCP Credit Union	Rural Hall	NC	**B-**	B	C+	11.8	-0.16	0.0	31.1	20.0	0.0	**10.0**	16.8
TCT Federal Credit Union	Ballston Spa	NY	**B-**	B-	B-	192.3	6.68	7.4	24.4	16.9	18.2	**5.8**	7.8
▲ TEA Federal Credit Union	Houma	LA	**D**	D-	E+	2.2	-4.49	0.0	45.5	0.0	0.0	**6.5**	8.5
Teachers Alliance Federal Credit Union	Longview	TX	**D**	D	D+	1.3	-5.07	0.0	31.6	0.0	0.0	**10.0**	27.4
Teachers Credit Union	South Bend	IN	**B-**	B-	B-	3109.4	6.39	7.9	49.3	31.9	6.8	**6.0**	8.1
Teachers Credit Union	Oklahoma City	OK	**C**	C	C	6.7	-2.31	0.0	20.7	0.0	0.0	**10.0**	36.4
Teachers Credit Union	Beloit	WI	**C-**	C-	C-	21.9	4.72	0.0	13.4	15.5	0.0	**10.0**	14.6
Teachers Federal Credit Union	Hauppauge	NY	**B**	B	B	5597.0	4.46	3.0	24.5	25.2	33.6	**9.0**	10.3
Team & Wheel Federal Credit Union	Winston-Salem	NC	**B-**	B-	B-	11.1	2.19	0.0	54.8	0.0	0.0	**10.0**	14.8
Team Financial Federal Credit Union	Houston	TX	**E+**	E+	E+	6.8	2.87	6.7	49.9	0.0	0.0	**5.9**	7.9
▲ Team First Federal Credit Union	Lancaster	PA	**C-**	D+	D+	10.0	-2.05	0.0	19.6	15.5	0.0	**10.0**	19.4
▼ Team One Credit Union	Saginaw	MI	**C**	C+	B-	504.1	2.58	11.3	32.4	30.6	15.0	**8.3**	9.9
Teamsters Council #37 FCU	Portland	OR	**B-**	B-	C+	57.4	1.63	0.5	23.2	12.9	0.0	**10.0**	13.0
Teamsters Credit Union	Detroit	MI	**C**	C	C	14.9	4.15	0.9	24.4	0.0	2.7	**10.0**	11.6
Teamsters Credit Union	Blaine	MN	**D**	D	D	11.5	9.36	0.0	39.1	0.0	0.0	**6.1**	8.1
▼ Teamsters Local #238 Credit Union	Cedar Rapids	IA	**D**	D+	D+	7.9	-2.19	0.0	38.1	0.0	0.0	**5.8**	11.5
Teamsters Local 30 Federal Credit Union	Jeannette	PA	**D-**	D-	D-	3.9	-0.20	0.0	50.9	0.0	0.0	**0.9**	4.1
Teamsters Local 697 Federal Credit Union	Wheeling	WV	**C-**	C-	C-	2.4	3.94	0.0	48.8	0.0	0.0	**10.0**	11.7
Teamsters Local 92 Federal Credit Union	Canton	OH	**D**	D	D-	2.1	-1.06	0.0	59.6	0.0	4.9	**7.4**	9.3
Teamsters Local Union #270 FCU	New Orleans	LA	**C+**	C+	C	<1	18.86	0.0	34.0	0.0	0.0	**10.0**	18.0
Teaneck Federal Credit Union	Teaneck	NJ	**D+**	D+	C-	13.3	8.42	0.0	8.0	4.0	0.0	**10.0**	14.1
Tech Credit Union	Crown Point	IN	**C-**	C-	C-	354.4	4.89	18.4	33.4	23.2	3.5	**5.9**	7.9
Technicolor Federal Credit Union	Burbank	CA	**C+**	C+	C+	53.1	3.48	2.2	19.0	60.2	7.1	**6.9**	9.0
▲ Technology Credit Union	San Jose	CA	**A-**	B+	B+	2280.6	7.70	8.2	8.5	45.4	19.3	**8.8**	10.4
Tee-Pak Credit Union	Danville	IL	**B-**	B-	B-	19.9	4.18	0.0	35.3	15.9	0.0	**10.0**	17.8
TEG Federal Credit Union	Poughkeepsie	NY	**B-**	B-	B-	268.2	8.35	7.8	34.3	21.7	10.3	**6.3**	8.3
Tel-U-Watt Federal Credit Union	Minot	ND	**E+**	E+	E+	5.2	2.83	0.0	45.9	0.0	0.0	**6.3**	8.3
Telbec Federal Credit Union	Beckley	WV	**B-**	B-	B	15.5	8.24	0.0	35.2	19.6	0.0	**10.0**	12.3
Telco Community Credit Union	Asheville	NC	**B+**	B+	A-	172.3	12.15	0.3	34.8	26.7	0.4	**7.3**	9.2
Telco Credit Union	Tarboro	NC	**D**	D	D	64.6	14.55	0.0	61.0	8.5	0.0	**10.0**	15.7
▲ Telco Plus Credit Union	Longview	TX	**C**	C-	C-	65.1	-1.29	0.0	30.1	16.8	2.8	**10.0**	13.7
Telco Roswell New Mexico FCU	Roswell	NM	**C+**	C+	C+	7.6	3.48	0.0	37.9	0.0	0.0	**10.0**	22.5
▼ Telco-Triad Community Credit Union	Sioux City	IA	**B-**	B	B-	88.3	0.35	0.1	46.0	5.0	0.0	**10.0**	12.2
▼ Telcoe Federal Credit Union	Little Rock	AR	**B+**	A-	A	353.1	1.31	0.4	12.4	12.9	63.1	**10.0**	21.2
Telcomm Credit Union	Springfield	MO	**A**	A	A-	148.2	6.67	0.4	18.3	9.8	35.2	**10.0**	13.9
Telhio Credit Union	Columbus	OH	**C**	C	C+	813.8	38.99	13.6	29.4	31.8	4.7	**6.3**	8.3
Temple Santa Fe Community Credit Union	Temple	TX	**D**	D	D-	16.7	2.81	0.0	34.5	10.0	0.0	**5.7**	7.7
Temple-Inland Federal Credit Union	Diboll	TX	**B-**	B-	B-	16.1	10.95	0.0	41.6	0.0	0.0	**10.0**	13.4
Tenn-Am Water Company FCU	Chattanooga	TN	**C-**	C-	C+	3.0	3.23	0.0	63.2	0.0	0.0	**10.0**	27.4
Tennessee Credit Union	Nashville	TN	**C-**	C-	C-	313.0	4.89	0.0	24.3	17.8	25.9	**7.2**	9.2
Tennessee Department of Safety CU	Nashville	TN	**C**	C	C	9.3	2.00	0.0	54.4	0.0	0.0	**10.0**	20.0
Tennessee Employees Credit Union	Nashville	TN	**C+**	C+	C+	16.4	-1.23	0.0	33.8	12.3	0.0	**10.0**	14.8
Tennessee Members 1st FCU	Oak Ridge	TN	**C-**	C-	C-	82.5	-1.74	0.6	16.7	15.7	38.7	**10.0**	11.7
Tennessee River Federal Credit Union	Counce	TN	**B-**	B-	B-	19.7	3.21	0.0	30.4	16.4	0.0	**10.0**	22.9
Tennessee Valley Federal Credit Union	Chattanooga	TN	**A**	A	A	1304.3	11.07	8.7	37.8	18.8	13.2	**10.0**	12.3
Terminal Credit Union	Metairie	LA	**B-**	B-	C+	17.4	-0.55	0.0	8.4	22.0	45.1	**10.0**	15.8
Terminals Federal Credit Union	Carteret	NJ	**C-**	C-	C-	<1	-4.46	0.0	34.8	0.5	0.0	**10.0**	28.0
Tesoro Northwest Federal Credit Union	Anacortes	WA	**C-**	C-	C-	13.3	-2.90	0.0	42.9	0.1	0.0	**10.0**	25.2
Tewksbury Federal Credit Union	Tewksbury	MA	**B**	B	B	60.8	11.23	0.0	17.6	10.9	6.4	**9.9**	11.0

Asset Quality Index	Non-Performing Loans as a % of Total Loans	Non-Performing Loans as a % of Capital	Net Charge-Offs Avg Loans	Profitability Index	Net Income ($Mil)	Return on Assets	Return on Equity	Net Interest Spread	Overhead Efficiency Ratio	Liquidity Index	Liquidity Ratio	Hot Money Ratio	Stability Index
6.0	1.45	8.6	1.11	**6.6**	0.23	0.64	4.89	4.85	76.6	**3.7**	17.0	7.4	**8.1**
4.0	1.95	16.8	0.24	**2.4**	0.00	0.05	0.60	2.62	89.3	**1.6**	12.8	29.3	**2.3**
10.0	0.00	0.0	0.63	**0.0**	0.00	-0.39	-1.26	2.25	116.7	**7.8**	91.2	0.0	**4.9**
8.5	0.54	3.2	0.05	**3.0**	0.03	0.19	1.67	3.71	92.1	**4.6**	26.2	1.9	**5.7**
8.3	0.16	1.4	0.65	**4.6**	0.08	0.62	6.03	3.97	79.3	**4.7**	27.6	1.0	**4.8**
9.3	1.58	3.1	0.00	**4.6**	0.00	0.92	4.91	2.64	63.6	**5.8**	33.4	0.0	**7.6**
5.0	1.59	7.7	2.43	**2.8**	0.00	0.51	4.57	5.34	82.4	**6.2**	45.2	0.0	**4.9**
10.0	1.10	1.4	-0.52	**1.4**	0.00	-0.04	-0.28	1.95	101.7	**5.3**	31.9	0.0	**6.5**
6.0	0.97	5.1	0.19	**5.9**	0.37	0.76	5.19	3.75	71.2	**3.4**	11.0	3.6	**9.2**
5.8	6.12	20.0	0.00	**8.6**	0.00	3.10	28.57	15.09	50.0	**7.5**	69.2	0.0	**4.3**
7.9	3.14	5.1	0.00	**0.5**	-0.01	-0.26	-1.51	3.06	108.9	**5.0**	18.8	0.0	**5.9**
8.7	0.79	2.3	5.08	**2.6**	-0.04	-1.49	-8.82	5.48	61.8	**6.0**	42.6	4.6	**6.3**
9.1	0.30	2.6	0.24	**4.5**	0.28	0.59	7.69	3.46	77.0	**3.5**	4.5	1.8	**5.0**
6.4	0.45	2.2	-0.35	**3.9**	0.00	0.53	6.38	6.04	90.6	**5.8**	39.6	0.0	**2.3**
3.5	19.72	21.9	-1.85	**3.7**	0.00	1.24	4.53	12.03	75.0	**7.9**	94.5	0.0	**3.0**
8.2	0.11	1.8	0.20	**3.9**	4.40	0.57	7.24	2.54	79.1	**2.9**	9.1	5.0	**6.1**
10.0	0.94	0.5	1.11	**2.4**	0.01	0.36	0.99	4.50	92.3	**5.2**	21.6	0.0	**5.8**
10.0	0.12	0.3	0.94	**1.7**	0.00	0.02	0.13	2.38	96.1	**5.4**	34.7	0.0	**7.0**
9.7	0.32	1.9	0.16	**4.3**	8.99	0.65	6.55	2.04	73.7	**3.5**	20.7	10.7	**8.2**
8.4	0.00	0.0	0.77	**3.1**	-0.01	-0.22	-1.46	5.32	95.2	**4.5**	30.8	1.1	**6.5**
2.3	2.99	27.8	0.29	**2.8**	0.01	0.29	3.77	6.01	95.7	**5.4**	37.2	0.0	**1.0**
10.0	0.26	0.5	0.62	**1.3**	0.00	0.04	0.21	2.88	97.4	**5.0**	18.6	1.2	**7.0**
6.6	0.69	5.6	0.46	**2.1**	0.34	0.27	2.74	3.66	88.5	**3.6**	15.7	5.8	**5.0**
10.0	0.07	0.2	0.39	**3.1**	0.05	0.32	2.47	2.95	87.2	**6.1**	69.4	6.5	**6.5**
9.8	0.62	1.5	0.46	**1.4**	-0.01	-0.19	-1.62	3.92	102.1	**6.3**	54.0	2.5	**5.4**
6.1	0.79	5.5	1.41	**2.5**	0.00	0.11	1.29	4.18	89.6	**4.0**	32.7	16.6	**2.3**
6.8	2.28	7.2	-0.52	**1.6**	0.00	-0.05	-0.44	2.99	101.2	**5.2**	36.0	0.0	**4.3**
6.8	0.37	4.0	0.00	**1.4**	0.00	0.31	7.59	5.05	91.8	**5.0**	24.7	0.0	**0.4**
5.2	2.70	10.4	0.00	**2.6**	0.00	0.00	0.00	8.15	100.0	**6.7**	53.8	0.0	**6.0**
8.5	0.16	1.0	0.00	**2.4**	0.00	0.00	0.00	5.19	96.7	**4.2**	38.6	13.7	**4.5**
7.7	2.90	5.2	0.00	**10.0**	0.00	1.53	8.28	12.46	81.8	**7.6**	79.6	0.0	**5.7**
9.7	1.63	1.5	2.43	**0.7**	-0.02	-0.58	-4.05	2.30	123.5	**5.6**	25.8	0.0	**5.4**
7.2	0.44	4.8	0.35	**2.7**	0.18	0.20	2.61	2.89	88.4	**3.7**	31.2	9.7	**4.8**
9.3	0.22	1.9	0.19	**3.8**	0.04	0.33	3.72	4.39	91.3	**2.5**	12.7	14.7	**4.8**
9.6	0.07	0.5	-0.01	**6.2**	6.13	1.09	10.71	3.00	63.7	**3.3**	11.6	6.2	**8.5**
9.3	0.81	2.4	0.26	**3.5**	0.00	-0.08	-0.45	4.16	94.6	**5.7**	40.5	0.6	**7.0**
5.9	1.02	11.3	0.66	**3.8**	0.06	0.09	1.21	4.56	89.9	**3.9**	17.6	8.3	**4.7**
3.8	1.76	12.0	0.00	**0.9**	-0.01	-1.07	-12.64	0.82	109.1	**4.3**	17.0	0.0	**4.2**
6.4	1.48	7.1	0.59	**8.0**	0.11	2.92	24.23	6.11	36.5	**5.6**	41.8	4.4	**5.7**
7.5	0.66	5.6	0.35	**7.2**	0.57	1.34	14.51	4.01	73.4	**4.3**	24.8	4.5	**6.7**
5.6	1.83	8.2	1.07	**0.0**	-0.11	-0.70	-4.33	3.21	116.6	**2.8**	24.3	23.5	**5.1**
9.0	0.49	2.1	0.91	**2.3**	0.07	0.43	3.30	3.14	94.5	**5.2**	37.8	2.6	**6.0**
5.6	1.19	8.1	2.06	**3.7**	0.00	-0.16	-0.70	4.94	88.2	**4.2**	102.4	35.0	**8.2**
7.5	0.67	4.2	0.23	**2.9**	0.00	0.01	0.08	4.13	96.1	**4.2**	25.0	3.1	**6.3**
10.0	0.16	0.2	-0.01	**4.0**	0.35	0.40	1.79	1.25	79.1	**4.3**	49.7	15.5	**9.3**
10.0	0.32	1.5	0.08	**6.7**	0.43	1.18	8.91	3.04	67.1	**4.3**	13.4	3.9	**8.9**
6.8	0.62	6.7	0.47	**2.7**	0.28	0.14	1.66	3.77	90.6	**3.3**	14.2	8.5	**5.2**
9.3	0.10	0.9	0.00	**1.9**	0.01	0.27	4.51	4.23	97.1	**4.3**	27.0	2.3	**2.2**
6.6	1.74	7.5	0.00	**4.6**	0.02	0.62	4.95	2.41	81.1	**4.7**	20.1	0.0	**7.4**
5.7	3.11	6.9	0.65	**3.4**	0.01	0.68	2.46	3.04	75.0	**4.6**	25.4	0.0	**7.2**
9.9	0.22	1.1	0.44	**2.2**	0.14	0.18	2.14	2.82	87.9	**5.6**	33.8	4.6	**5.3**
8.3	0.00	0.0	0.14	**3.2**	0.01	0.30	1.50	3.12	88.7	**3.0**	15.5	13.2	**7.7**
9.1	0.05	2.0	1.16	**3.3**	0.01	0.25	1.65	3.63	94.1	**4.4**	49.5	18.2	**6.4**
7.4	1.69	6.0	0.09	**1.5**	0.02	0.09	0.77	2.60	100.9	**4.8**	33.3	5.8	**4.9**
9.7	0.81	1.8	0.00	**4.2**	0.02	0.49	2.14	3.37	79.0	**4.2**	24.9	2.4	**7.4**
9.3	0.30	1.8	0.29	**7.9**	3.43	1.08	8.67	3.49	67.4	**5.3**	29.7	1.9	**9.2**
6.3	5.15	10.7	2.13	**5.5**	0.01	0.32	2.07	2.58	66.7	**4.2**	22.7	10.9	**5.0**
5.3	4.29	8.8	0.00	**7.8**	0.00	1.64	5.86	6.05	66.7	**6.2**	49.6	0.0	**5.0**
9.1	0.82	1.9	-0.05	**2.2**	0.00	0.06	0.24	4.29	109.1	**6.4**	48.9	0.0	**5.8**
5.3	1.35	7.3	-0.03	**3.9**	0.08	0.51	4.66	3.27	87.6	**3.7**	22.2	8.1	**5.4**

Name	City	State	Rating	2016 Rating	2015 Rating	Total Assets ($Mil)	One Year Asset Growth	Asset Mix (As a % of Total Assets) Commercial Loans	Consumer Loans	Mortgage Loans	Securities	Capitalization Index	Net Worth Ratio
▼ Tex-Mex Credit Union	Laredo	TX	**D+**	C-	C+	10.3	-5.02	0.0	38.0	0.0	0.0	**10.0**	24.4
Texaco of Houma Credit Union	Houma	LA	**D**	D	D+	4.6	-4.95	0.0	54.7	0.0	0.0	**10.0**	16.0
▲ Texans Credit Union	Richardson	TX	**D-**	E+	E-	1603.6	5.88	0.0	25.2	19.8	41.7	**1.0**	4.8
▼ Texar Federal Credit Union	Texarkana	TX	**B+**	A-	A	354.0	2.56	3.8	29.9	23.5	21.0	**10.0**	12.5
Texarkana Terminal Employees FCU	Texarkana	TX	**D-**	D-	D-	12.6	-12.81	0.0	55.0	0.0	0.0	**8.0**	9.7
Texas Associations of Professionals FCU	San Antonio	TX	**D+**	D+	C-	32.8	8.23	4.9	4.0	54.4	0.0	**6.3**	8.3
Texas Bay Credit Union	Houston	TX	**B+**	B+	B+	421.0	13.05	0.0	51.1	26.9	1.5	**8.1**	9.8
Texas Bridge Credit Union	Corpus Christi	TX	**C**	C	C-	56.2	5.66	1.2	42.5	7.3	0.0	**6.2**	8.2
Texas Community Federal Credit Union	Kingsville	TX	**C+**	C+	B-	16.9	10.33	0.0	55.3	0.0	0.0	**10.0**	12.6
Texas Dow Employees Credit Union	Lake Jackson	TX	**B-**	B-	B	3057.1	3.77	1.3	56.6	27.3	0.0	**5.8**	7.8
Texas DPS Credit Union	Austin	TX	**D+**	D+	D+	71.8	3.93	0.0	28.4	18.3	9.1	**5.9**	7.9
Texas Farm Bureau Federal Credit Union	Waco	TX	**C**	C	C	6.7	0.18	0.0	42.7	0.0	0.0	**10.0**	18.6
Texas Federal Credit Union	Dallas	TX	**D**	D	D	61.8	-0.11	0.0	29.4	21.4	14.5	**5.0**	7.0
Texas Gulf Carolina Employees CU	Aurora	NC	**C+**	C+	C	2.6	-0.81	0.0	33.7	1.9	0.0	**10.0**	34.4
Texas Health Credit Union	Austin	TX	**B**	B	B-	80.6	8.08	2.3	29.5	41.4	0.0	**9.7**	10.8
▼ Texas Health Resources Credit Union	Dallas	TX	**D-**	D	D+	18.4	-1.40	0.0	40.3	1.9	0.0	**5.9**	7.9
Texas Lee Federal Credit Union	Houston	TX	**C**	C	C	<1	114.94	0.0	16.6	0.0	0.0	**8.2**	9.8
Texas Partners Federal Credit Union	Killeen	TX	**D+**	D+	C-	158.0	7.78	0.0	19.1	5.1	22.2	**4.3**	6.3
▲ Texas People Federal Credit Union	Fort Worth	TX	**C**	C-	C	23.9	5.69	0.0	60.2	2.2	0.0	**10.0**	17.9
Texas Plains Federal Credit Union	Amarillo	TX	**B**	B	B	34.9	1.29	0.0	56.9	2.0	0.0	**10.0**	13.9
Texas Tech Federal Credit Union	Lubbock	TX	**A-**	A-	A-	130.8	8.88	0.0	38.1	19.1	0.1	**9.3**	10.6
Texas Telcom Credit Union	Dallas	TX	**B+**	B+	A-	58.8	-1.70	0.6	41.0	12.6	13.4	**10.0**	14.0
Texas Trust Credit Union	Arlington	TX	**B-**	B-	B-	1041.9	13.38	21.9	34.9	22.8	8.6	**9.2**	10.6
▼ Texas Workforce Credit Union	San Antonio	TX	**D-**	D	D-	9.9	-6.99	0.0	53.2	13.1	0.0	**7.8**	9.6
Texasgulf Federal Credit Union	Wharton	TX	**A-**	A-	A-	103.5	14.57	0.0	44.2	21.2	4.3	**10.0**	12.0
▼ Texell Credit Union	Temple	TX	**A-**	A	A	326.5	15.89	7.9	47.6	21.9	2.5	**9.4**	10.6
Texhillco School Employees FCU	Kerrville	TX	**E+**	E+	E-	15.3	4.27	0.0	58.9	4.1	0.0	**5.2**	7.2
Texoma Community Credit Union	Wichita Falls	TX	**A-**	A-	B+	127.1	7.68	1.4	46.3	15.9	0.0	**9.4**	10.6
Texoma Educators Federal Credit Union	Sherman	TX	**B-**	B-	B-	81.4	6.37	0.0	29.5	0.0	8.4	**10.0**	14.0
Texoma Federal Credit Union	Fritch	TX	**C+**	C+	C+	12.5	-1.96	0.0	25.4	0.0	0.0	**10.0**	19.5
TexStar Federal Credit Union	Kenedy	TX	**D+**	D+	D+	23.8	-2.30	0.0	13.0	1.7	0.0	**6.6**	8.6
Thd-6 Credit Union	Odessa	TX	**D**	D	D+	4.0	3.10	0.0	61.4	0.0	0.0	**10.0**	11.0
Thinkwise Federal Credit Union	San Bernardino	CA	**B+**	B+	B+	81.0	5.35	12.7	18.5	24.7	17.4	**10.0**	13.7
Thiokol Elkton Federal Credit Union	Elkton	MD	**C**	C	C	21.7	2.08	0.0	15.6	2.8	0.1	**10.0**	14.4
Third Coast Federal Credit Union	Corpus Christi	TX	**B**	B	B-	14.0	1.00	0.0	44.5	0.0	0.0	**10.0**	26.2
Third District Highway FCU	Lafayette	LA	**C**	C	C	15.1	-6.18	0.0	16.9	0.5	0.0	**10.0**	13.0
Thornapple Credit Union	Hastings	MI	**C**	C	C	26.4	12.10	0.0	45.7	18.3	1.3	**7.1**	9.1
Three Rivers Credit Union	Bainbridge	GA	**C**	C	C+	15.9	-1.10	0.0	31.2	7.0	0.0	**10.0**	11.0
Three Rivers Federal Credit Union	Fort Wayne	IN	**A**	A	A	897.7	9.31	10.8	22.5	30.0	18.9	**10.0**	13.6
Thrive Federal Credit Union	Muncie	IN	**C+**	C+	C	53.7	6.98	1.7	24.3	11.2	0.5	**10.0**	11.8
Thrivent Federal Credit Union	Appleton	WI	**C**	C	C+	552.8	7.87	25.4	5.1	39.9	22.2	**7.5**	9.6
Thunder Bay Area Credit Union	Alpena	MI	**D+**	D+	D+	24.4	4.77	6.5	30.6	24.3	11.0	**7.1**	9.1
Thunderbolt Area Federal Credit Union	Millville	NJ	**D+**	D+	D	21.7	3.64	0.0	18.1	3.6	3.0	**6.7**	8.8
▲ Ticonderoga Federal Credit Union	Ticonderoga	NY	**C**	C-	D+	101.8	6.38	0.1	15.4	6.2	45.7	**7.3**	9.6
Tidemark Federal Credit Union	Seaford	DE	**A**	A	A-	263.3	1.73	1.9	8.4	39.1	36.5	**10.0**	15.0
Timberland Federal Credit Union	DuBois	PA	**C+**	C+	C+	61.1	1.91	0.0	40.3	3.3	0.0	**8.4**	9.9
▼ Timberline Federal Credit Union	Crossett	AR	**D+**	C-	C-	80.0	0.30	5.4	21.8	18.5	22.2	**10.0**	19.9
Times Federal Credit Union	Honolulu	HI	**E+**	E+	E+	7.5	1.13	0.0	29.9	0.0	0.0	**5.7**	7.7
Times Free Press Credit Union	Chattanooga	TN	**C**	C	C	2.0	-5.92	0.0	68.2	0.0	0.0	**10.0**	32.9
Timken Aerospace Federal Credit Union	Lebanon	NH	**D+**	D+	C-	7.3	-0.46	0.0	44.1	0.1	1.7	**10.0**	11.8
Tin Mill Employees Federal Credit Union	Weirton	WV	**D**	D	D	18.0	-1.62	0.0	5.9	8.9	0.0	**10.0**	20.5
Tinker Federal Credit Union	Oklahoma City	OK	**B+**	B+	B+	3710.8	6.26	0.0	59.5	3.6	21.1	**9.1**	10.4
Tip of Texas Federal Credit Union	El Paso	TX	**D**	D	C-	23.6	6.38	0.0	36.8	6.3	0.0	**10.0**	14.5
Tippecanoe Federal Credit Union	Lafayette	IN	**C**	C	C-	14.0	7.06	0.0	33.3	0.0	0.0	**10.0**	11.8
Titan Federal Credit Union	Pleasant Gap	PA	**B-**	B-	C+	48.1	2.96	0.0	16.7	15.7	39.5	**10.0**	11.0
TLC Community Credit Union	Adrian	MI	**A**	A	A	461.3	7.69	2.1	19.0	23.2	38.8	**10.0**	14.0
TLCU Financial	Mishawaka	IN	**B-**	B-	B-	36.4	0.58	0.0	22.6	3.1	0.0	**10.0**	16.2
TMH Federal Credit Union	Tallahassee	FL	**B-**	B-	B	64.5	11.47	7.4	45.0	10.9	0.0	**8.5**	10.0
TNConnect Credit Union	Knoxville	TN	**D**	D	D	51.3	3.34	0.0	52.8	5.9	0.2	**6.0**	8.0
Tobacco Valley Teachers FCU	Enfield	CT	**C-**	C-	C-	45.5	7.81	0.0	18.7	8.0	39.6	**6.0**	8.1

Asset Quality Index	Non-Performing Loans as a % of Total Loans	Non-Performing Loans as a % of Capital	Net Charge-Offs Avg Loans	Profitability Index	Net Income ($Mil)	Return on Assets	Return on Equity	Net Interest Spread	Overhead Efficiency Ratio	Liquidity Index	Liquidity Ratio	Hot Money Ratio	Stability Index
8.8	1.12	2.3	0.88	**0.8**	-0.02	-0.74	-3.03	4.82	106.7	**3.4**	47.9	27.4	**5.7**
0.5	10.03	37.6	0.55	**1.9**	0.01	0.44	2.72	2.36	84.6	**4.2**	40.1	0.0	**5.0**
7.7	0.20	5.4	0.11	**8.5**	4.23	1.08	26.79	2.58	64.0	**4.8**	19.0	0.6	**5.2**
7.1	0.67	4.9	1.14	**4.7**	0.32	0.36	2.98	3.66	72.8	**2.3**	9.2	23.2	**6.9**
4.5	0.73	5.2	0.46	**1.2**	0.00	0.00	0.00	5.10	88.6	**2.8**	19.0	15.7	**3.0**
3.8	1.21	16.6	-0.03	**4.9**	0.05	0.56	6.87	4.27	87.9	**1.2**	8.4	27.9	**3.7**
5.1	1.11	10.3	1.39	**6.1**	0.59	0.58	5.77	5.00	71.5	**3.4**	16.3	7.5	**5.7**
7.4	0.46	2.9	0.45	**1.5**	-0.02	-0.16	-1.90	3.46	99.1	**4.5**	29.7	9.5	**3.6**
4.6	1.49	7.6	-0.46	**7.6**	0.08	2.03	15.89	7.30	81.6	**4.1**	32.9	7.8	**6.2**
4.5	0.86	10.8	0.80	**3.6**	2.34	0.31	3.95	4.07	76.0	**2.0**	7.0	13.0	**5.0**
7.5	0.51	3.5	0.00	**1.7**	0.01	0.06	0.78	2.70	93.7	**4.9**	28.8	0.6	**3.2**
9.6	0.32	0.8	0.00	**4.1**	0.01	0.35	1.94	3.79	87.3	**5.9**	58.7	0.0	**7.2**
7.7	0.48	3.6	0.21	**1.0**	-0.03	-0.16	-2.30	3.07	102.6	**4.6**	18.2	0.0	**1.8**
9.7	0.19	0.2	0.00	**4.2**	0.01	0.97	2.73	6.57	84.6	**4.8**	15.3	0.0	**5.8**
5.6	1.41	10.0	0.45	**4.9**	0.12	0.58	5.38	3.71	76.4	**3.2**	14.5	7.9	**5.6**
6.0	1.14	7.8	1.28	**1.2**	-0.02	-0.52	-6.53	4.59	94.2	**4.6**	33.1	0.0	**2.9**
8.7	0.00	0.0	0.00	**5.5**	0.00	1.91	14.55	3.29	50.0	**8.1**	140.0	0.0	**4.3**
8.6	0.41	2.7	1.50	**1.0**	-0.21	-0.54	-8.34	3.70	98.1	**6.6**	40.0	4.1	**1.3**
6.9	0.83	3.4	-0.62	**2.5**	0.02	0.40	2.16	4.30	101.8	**4.1**	25.4	6.7	**5.7**
6.1	0.74	5.8	0.81	**5.6**	0.07	0.82	5.82	5.58	83.2	**4.0**	28.9	8.0	**6.7**
7.9	0.41	3.0	0.29	**7.6**	0.22	0.69	6.61	4.16	90.6	**3.2**	7.7	6.3	**7.7**
7.0	0.82	5.0	1.13	**5.7**	0.06	0.38	3.00	3.45	71.7	**3.1**	26.5	22.6	**6.6**
7.9	0.08	4.2	0.31	**3.9**	1.30	0.50	5.21	2.82	81.5	**2.1**	7.1	18.3	**6.0**
4.3	1.36	11.1	0.56	**3.0**	0.02	0.65	6.81	4.44	70.9	**3.2**	25.0	14.2	**1.7**
7.8	0.54	3.2	0.28	**9.5**	0.43	1.72	14.13	3.32	53.3	**3.4**	20.9	11.8	**8.6**
5.6	0.97	7.4	1.01	**5.9**	0.38	0.48	4.40	3.96	77.7	**2.9**	17.0	15.9	**7.6**
4.4	1.08	11.4	0.74	**2.9**	0.01	0.24	3.30	5.96	89.8	**3.5**	13.2	3.4	**1.0**
6.3	0.52	5.1	0.42	**5.8**	0.18	0.56	5.22	4.44	80.7	**3.3**	16.2	12.6	**7.6**
9.8	0.59	1.4	0.09	**3.6**	0.12	0.62	4.37	2.47	79.3	**4.6**	15.8	2.0	**6.9**
6.5	5.26	9.4	0.00	**2.7**	0.01	0.26	1.32	2.33	85.7	**5.9**	78.6	1.0	**6.9**
10.0	0.13	0.2	0.10	**1.6**	-0.01	-0.10	-1.17	2.35	102.3	**4.9**	19.7	5.0	**3.7**
4.6	1.76	14.6	0.62	**1.1**	0.00	0.10	0.90	4.26	87.5	**4.7**	30.5	0.0	**5.4**
6.5	1.57	8.1	0.41	**2.5**	0.03	0.14	1.00	3.65	92.8	**4.9**	31.6	8.0	**6.3**
8.2	1.98	4.4	-0.13	**3.0**	0.02	0.34	2.72	2.57	84.6	**4.8**	27.6	2.8	**6.5**
8.7	1.80	4.6	2.53	**7.3**	0.03	0.81	3.07	9.47	70.8	**7.1**	67.3	0.0	**6.3**
9.7	1.71	2.9	0.23	**1.8**	0.00	0.03	0.20	1.83	98.5	**5.2**	30.7	0.0	**5.2**
3.1	2.05	17.6	-0.04	**9.9**	0.08	1.29	13.98	5.36	81.5	**4.4**	21.4	3.8	**5.4**
5.9	3.97	15.4	0.99	**2.1**	0.02	0.48	4.37	3.77	84.1	**3.7**	19.9	17.5	**4.9**
8.8	0.38	2.0	0.36	**8.0**	2.46	1.11	8.07	3.76	76.2	**3.5**	6.5	1.6	**10.0**
7.6	0.65	4.4	0.31	**2.8**	0.03	0.20	1.98	3.80	93.9	**4.3**	21.8	4.6	**4.8**
8.3	0.45	3.1	0.06	**3.0**	0.53	0.40	4.12	3.31	87.7	**4.3**	16.3	3.7	**6.8**
5.7	0.35	8.5	0.11	**1.9**	-0.03	-0.48	-5.19	3.52	100.9	**4.9**	21.2	0.0	**4.5**
6.2	3.10	9.8	-0.06	**3.9**	0.04	0.81	9.39	2.93	77.8	**5.7**	39.0	2.4	**3.7**
7.2	1.05	4.2	0.01	**2.8**	0.05	0.22	2.31	3.83	93.0	**5.4**	25.0	2.1	**4.5**
9.2	0.76	3.2	0.22	**5.9**	0.51	0.77	5.26	3.12	74.5	**3.8**	15.6	6.4	**8.6**
5.7	1.40	9.5	0.54	**2.8**	0.04	0.25	2.44	3.18	84.9	**4.9**	32.1	1.3	**4.4**
8.1	1.09	3.6	0.30	**0.4**	-0.12	-0.60	-3.23	3.21	112.0	**3.9**	18.9	10.1	**6.6**
7.8	1.01	3.7	-0.66	**2.4**	0.00	0.11	1.39	3.14	97.0	**6.2**	49.2	0.0	**1.0**
5.8	2.37	8.1	0.00	**4.2**	0.00	0.80	2.40	5.89	60.0	**5.4**	40.9	0.0	**3.7**
8.7	0.83	3.8	0.00	**0.7**	0.00	-0.17	-1.39	2.70	106.4	**4.6**	24.9	7.8	**5.5**
9.8	3.22	2.5	0.00	**0.4**	-0.02	-0.41	-1.95	1.89	125.7	**7.6**	88.5	0.0	**6.0**
6.2	0.79	5.5	0.94	**4.8**	5.46	0.60	5.71	2.94	67.0	**3.7**	15.8	6.8	**7.1**
7.8	1.76	5.2	2.12	**0.3**	-0.05	-0.90	-6.13	4.53	102.1	**4.4**	19.5	4.3	**5.0**
6.2	3.89	11.6	-0.16	**3.2**	0.02	0.67	5.60	2.50	77.2	**5.3**	39.5	0.0	**5.8**
8.4	0.63	2.1	0.14	**3.8**	0.06	0.50	4.49	1.76	69.7	**5.1**	27.0	0.0	**5.7**
9.9	0.17	0.9	0.18	**7.1**	1.11	0.98	7.29	2.75	73.7	**4.2**	25.5	6.6	**9.2**
10.0	0.92	1.7	-0.18	**3.0**	0.02	0.19	1.20	2.52	95.4	**5.9**	39.2	0.0	**7.1**
8.1	0.31	2.3	0.19	**5.9**	0.17	1.09	10.82	4.28	76.8	**5.3**	40.2	6.7	**4.2**
4.1	1.11	10.3	0.48	**2.5**	0.01	0.09	1.08	3.81	90.6	**3.9**	14.4	3.1	**2.9**
8.6	0.24	1.2	0.00	**2.4**	0.02	0.21	2.52	2.79	92.6	**5.4**	27.6	0.0	**3.4**

Name	City	State	Rating	2016 Rating	2015 Rating	Total Assets ($Mil)	One Year Asset Growth	Asset Mix (As a % of Total Assets) Commercial Loans	Consumer Loans	Mortgage Loans	Securities	Capitalization Index	Net Worth Ratio
Toledo Fire Fighters FCU	Toledo	OH	C	C	C	33.7	4.00	0.0	27.1	7.0	11.5	10.0	12.1
Toledo Metro Federal Credit Union	Toledo	OH	C+	C+	B-	54.8	18.44	0.0	48.4	8.1	16.5	7.1	9.1
Toledo Police Federal Credit Union	Toledo	OH	B-	B-	C+	36.9	5.18	0.0	24.5	9.7	1.4	9.0	10.3
Toledo Postal Empls Credit Union, Inc.	Toledo	OH	D+	D+	D+	4.6	-1.11	1.6	23.7	1.6	0.0	10.0	19.9
Toledo Teamsters Federal Credit Union	Toledo	OH	E+	E+	E+	4.3	-6.90	0.0	33.1	9.2	0.0	2.5	4.8
Toledo Urban Federal Credit Union	Toledo	OH	E+	E+	E+	6.8	10.35	0.9	62.1	7.1	0.0	4.3	6.3
Tolna Co-Operative Federal Credit Union	Tolna	ND	C-	C-	C-	1.1	-1.85	0.0	21.8	0.0	0.0	10.0	18.7
Tomah Area Credit Union	Tomah	WI	C-	C-	C	59.6	2.70	9.7	20.1	33.9	1.7	7.5	9.4
Tombigbee Federal Credit Union	Amory	MS	D+	D+	D	5.7	-1.87	0.0	23.3	0.0	0.0	10.0	13.6
Tompkins Employees Federal Credit Union	Ithaca	NY	C	C	C-	7.6	19.37	0.0	48.8	0.0	0.0	10.0	11.7
Tonawanda Community Federal Credit Union	Buffalo	NY	D+	D+	D+	30.0	9.30	0.0	15.3	15.4	42.9	5.4	7.4
Tonawanda Valley Federal Credit Union	Batavia	NY	C+	C+	C	103.3	6.61	0.0	17.0	17.3	3.2	6.2	8.2
▼ Tongass Federal Credit Union	Ketchikan	AK	B-	B	B-	71.2	1.61	16.4	17.7	27.2	12.3	6.4	8.4
▼ Topeka City Employees Credit Union	Topeka	KS	D+	C-	C-	9.7	-9.10	0.7	30.6	28.3	0.0	9.5	10.7
Topeka Firemen's Credit Union	Topeka	KS	C	C	C+	9.3	0.55	0.0	39.5	0.0	16.6	10.0	27.2
Topeka Police Credit Union	Topeka	KS	D+	D+	D	6.8	1.80	0.0	69.9	0.0	0.0	9.9	10.9
Topeka Post Office Credit Union	Topeka	KS	C+	C+	C+	8.2	13.55	0.0	27.9	6.2	0.0	10.0	21.7
TopLine Federal Credit Union	Maple Grove	MN	C+	C+	C+	404.6	4.47	3.7	30.1	20.2	25.6	7.4	9.6
TopMark Federal Credit Union	Lima	OH	B-	B-	C+	30.9	4.93	0.0	43.8	4.7	20.1	10.0	12.7
Torch Lake Federal Credit Union	Laurium	MI	D	D	D	7.8	10.41	0.0	44.7	2.8	0.0	6.9	8.9
Toro Employees Federal Credit Union	Bloomington	MN	B+	B+	B	27.9	-0.16	0.0	36.3	17.5	6.3	10.0	13.1
Torrance Community Federal Credit Union	Torrance	CA	C-	C-	C	129.1	5.98	0.4	11.8	6.7	54.0	5.4	7.5
Torrington Municipal & Teachers FCU	Torrington	CT	C+	C+	C	46.4	6.08	0.9	35.4	6.1	0.0	6.4	8.4
▲ Total Choice Federal Credit Union	Hahnville	LA	D+	D	D-	55.4	5.10	0.0	42.5	13.0	25.5	4.9	6.9
▼ Total Community Action FCU	New Orleans	LA	D	D+	C	<1	-24.40	0.0	52.5	0.0	0.0	10.0	20.3
Total Community Credit Union	Taylor	MI	C-	C-	D+	65.3	6.95	0.0	20.7	2.1	42.5	5.4	7.5
▼ Towanda School Employees FCU	Towanda	PA	C-	C	C+	<1	2.52	0.0	39.3	0.0	0.0	10.0	16.5
Tower Family Credit Union	Kalamazoo	MI	D-	D-	D-	8.4	2.83	0.0	23.2	0.0	63.7	6.5	8.5
▲ Tower Federal Credit Union	Laurel	MD	B	B-	B-	2978.9	3.65	0.0	36.6	14.8	14.1	10.0	11.2
Town & Country Credit Union	Minot	ND	A-	A-	B+	403.2	5.08	63.5	12.0	35.7	0.3	10.0	14.0
Town & Country Federal Credit Union	Scarborough	ME	B-	B-	B-	346.8	12.40	0.1	38.0	31.2	2.2	5.7	7.7
Town and Country Credit Union	Harlan	IA	C	C	B-	23.0	22.96	1.5	37.6	29.2	0.0	8.7	10.1
Town of Cheektowaga Federal Credit Union	Cheektowaga	NY	B+	B+	B+	21.4	6.31	0.0	10.6	21.4	9.1	10.0	14.0
▼ Town of Hempstead Employees FCU	North Baldwin	NY	D-	D	D+	125.1	3.26	8.1	11.0	18.9	15.3	4.9	6.9
Town of Palm Beach Federal Credit Union	West Palm Beach	FL	D+	D+	D+	2.8	1.13	0.0	46.7	0.0	0.0	9.2	10.5
▲ Towns-Union Educators' FCU	Young Harris	GA	D	D-	E+	2.5	11.34	0.0	45.1	0.0	0.0	5.6	7.6
▲ Towpath Credit Union	Fairlawn	OH	A-	B+	B-	127.5	7.73	2.7	38.7	7.2	22.8	10.0	11.9
▲ Trademark Federal Credit Union	Augusta	ME	C+	C	D	89.1	6.67	0.0	18.1	31.1	0.0	10.0	11.4
▲ Trades & Labor Federal Credit Union	Albert Lea	MN	C-	D+	D-	11.9	8.74	0.0	46.6	13.0	2.5	6.3	8.4
Tradesmen Community Credit Union	Des Moines	IA	B+	B+	B	55.0	11.11	3.8	30.2	8.9	13.1	10.0	13.5
Tradewinds Credit Union	Comstock Park	MI	E+	E+	D-	18.7	0.49	0.0	26.7	0.0	51.3	4.6	6.6
Trailhead Federal Credit Union	Portland	OR	C+	C+	C	113.7	9.29	2.5	17.3	15.3	19.6	5.9	8.3
Trans Texas Southwest Credit Union	San Angelo	TX	C+	C+	C+	44.4	-1.10	11.9	19.6	50.8	0.0	10.0	11.3
Transfiguration Manhattan FCU	New York	NY	D-	D-	D-	<1	-31.91	0.0	0.0	0.0	0.0	5.8	7.8
Transfiguration Parish FCU	Brooklyn	NY	D-	D-	D-	8.9	9.98	5.3	17.7	27.8	0.0	5.4	7.4
▲ Transit Authority Division B FCU	New York	NY	D	D-	E+	5.7	7.03	0.0	38.7	0.0	0.0	7.0	9.0
Transit Employees Federal Credit Union	Washington	DC	B-	B-	B+	100.0	-4.33	0.4	29.8	12.3	39.2	10.0	17.1
Transit Federal Credit Union	Valley Stream	NY	D+	D+	C-	14.0	1.98	0.0	14.2	0.0	2.0	10.0	11.8
Transit Operations Federal Credit Union	Minneapolis	MN	C+	C+	C	4.1	-2.76	0.0	29.3	0.0	0.0	10.0	15.7
Transit Workers Federal Credit Union	Philadelphia	PA	D	D	D	20.8	0.29	0.0	36.3	0.0	0.0	10.0	16.5
▼ Transportation Federal Credit Union	Alexandria	VA	C+	B-	B-	234.1	8.43	8.2	21.9	15.2	18.7	9.2	10.4
Transtar Federal Credit Union	Houston	TX	E	E	E-	33.6	-3.63	0.0	38.0	14.8	27.3	3.3	5.3
Transwest Credit Union	Salt Lake City	UT	B	B	B	134.0	5.76	1.9	22.2	39.4	7.9	5.9	7.9
Travis County Credit Union	Austin	TX	C-	C-	C-	32.5	8.64	0.0	26.1	20.5	8.6	5.2	7.2
Travis Credit Union	Vacaville	CA	A	A	A	2800.1	7.70	3.4	49.9	17.7	18.7	10.0	11.7
Treasury Department Federal Credit Union	Washington	DC	C	C	C+	172.1	-0.08	0.0	19.5	21.8	2.5	5.3	7.3
Treasury Employees Federal Credit Union	Jackson	MS	C-	C-	D+	10.1	5.89	0.0	9.9	0.0	0.0	7.8	9.5
▲ Tremont Credit Union	Braintree	MA	B-	C+	C	171.9	0.48	3.1	13.0	30.6	18.5	10.0	13.4
Trenton New Jersey Firemen FCU	Trenton	NJ	D+	D+	D	4.3	-1.34	0.0	21.8	0.0	0.0	10.0	15.0
Trenton Teachers Federal Credit Union	Hamilton Square	NJ	D+	D+	D	2.7	-2.58	0.0	11.0	0.0	0.0	8.1	9.8

Asset Quality Index	Non-Performing Loans as a % of Total Loans	Non-Performing Loans as a % of Capital	Net Charge-Offs Avg Loans	Profitability Index	Net Income ($Mil)	Return on Assets	Return on Equity	Net Interest Spread	Overhead Efficiency Ratio	Liquidity Index	Liquidity Ratio	Hot Money Ratio	Stability Index
10.0	0.44	1.4	0.00	**1.7**	-0.01	-0.12	-0.98	3.34	104.7	**6.9**	55.3	1.2	**6.5**
4.0	2.57	14.9	1.51	**3.7**	-0.08	-0.62	-6.60	5.34	89.5	**3.9**	37.1	25.9	**4.1**
9.5	0.16	1.9	0.17	**4.0**	0.05	0.53	4.96	3.16	82.7	**6.2**	43.8	1.4	**5.6**
10.0	0.76	1.1	0.00	**0.6**	0.00	-0.17	-0.87	3.21	105.3	**5.7**	31.0	0.0	**6.1**
5.0	1.57	13.6	0.58	**0.9**	-0.01	-0.57	-11.27	5.42	109.1	**5.8**	31.8	0.0	**0.6**
0.0	3.94	80.3	0.14	**6.8**	0.03	1.62	52.17	7.18	84.3	**4.0**	15.1	3.0	**3.1**
8.7	0.15	0.4	0.00	**1.7**	0.00	0.00	0.00	2.48	100.0	**5.2**	23.2	0.0	**6.8**
7.6	0.32	2.2	-0.01	**2.2**	0.03	0.17	1.80	3.08	95.3	**4.0**	17.8	2.6	**4.4**
7.1	2.97	6.8	0.47	**1.1**	0.00	0.21	1.56	2.75	85.4	**5.5**	41.5	0.0	**5.4**
8.3	0.16	0.8	-0.53	**4.5**	0.01	0.55	4.54	5.82	93.2	**5.5**	38.2	6.2	**4.3**
6.7	1.23	5.8	0.04	**3.1**	0.02	0.20	2.73	3.26	84.8	**5.5**	22.7	0.0	**3.0**
10.0	0.36	1.8	0.04	**3.7**	0.12	0.46	5.54	2.69	85.9	**5.5**	31.1	0.1	**5.3**
6.8	0.16	2.3	0.06	**4.5**	0.11	0.58	7.13	4.16	86.0	**3.9**	23.0	7.1	**4.5**
4.9	2.94	15.1	-0.24	**0.3**	-0.01	-0.29	-2.69	4.04	97.9	**5.6**	44.3	0.0	**4.5**
8.5	1.45	2.3	0.20	**2.9**	0.01	0.48	1.74	1.86	68.4	**5.1**	30.3	0.0	**7.5**
5.3	0.94	6.3	0.77	**2.2**	0.01	0.36	3.25	4.37	89.7	**3.2**	24.2	10.5	**5.1**
9.7	0.00	0.0	0.33	**3.7**	0.01	0.44	2.02	3.22	86.6	**5.5**	43.0	0.0	**7.2**
9.7	0.30	2.1	0.23	**2.9**	0.15	0.15	1.64	3.07	91.7	**3.9**	14.2	1.8	**5.7**
7.8	1.14	5.7	1.23	**4.3**	0.04	0.50	3.90	4.82	88.3	**4.4**	19.6	3.5	**5.9**
7.2	0.75	4.5	-0.36	**3.3**	0.01	0.37	4.01	3.95	91.9	**5.1**	19.2	0.0	**2.3**
9.7	0.28	1.6	0.60	**4.9**	0.03	0.49	3.76	4.18	77.8	**3.9**	15.4	1.7	**6.4**
10.0	0.26	1.1	0.42	**2.0**	0.07	0.21	2.83	2.49	88.1	**4.3**	20.9	8.6	**4.4**
7.4	0.62	3.5	0.20	**4.5**	0.07	0.57	6.71	3.64	85.1	**4.7**	22.7	1.6	**4.3**
5.9	0.82	7.4	0.49	**3.2**	0.06	0.48	6.76	3.46	83.6	**4.3**	22.6	2.7	**2.6**
2.6	8.00	18.2	0.00	**0.6**	-0.01	-3.27	-18.18	4.03	200.0	**6.5**	59.5	0.0	**4.7**
8.0	0.68	2.8	1.38	**2.7**	0.06	0.34	4.56	3.07	79.7	**5.8**	39.5	1.8	**2.8**
6.8	2.27	5.3	6.56	**1.9**	0.00	0.00	0.00	6.87	100.0	**7.3**	71.9	0.0	**5.7**
6.4	2.94	8.2	0.00	**0.0**	-0.02	-0.90	-10.47	2.51	119.1	**5.5**	24.4	0.0	**3.0**
7.8	0.67	5.1	0.38	**4.1**	3.67	0.50	4.70	3.02	73.8	**5.5**	36.3	1.7	**7.5**
5.1	0.71	5.5	0.00	**6.4**	0.21	0.22	1.51	4.18	93.3	**3.8**	23.7	10.3	**9.9**
6.2	1.11	11.2	0.37	**4.2**	0.39	0.46	5.91	4.48	84.8	**3.2**	9.9	6.0	**4.7**
7.6	0.05	5.3	0.04	**5.0**	0.04	0.75	7.29	5.07	83.3	**2.4**	9.4	14.3	**4.3**
9.2	0.97	3.2	0.00	**7.8**	0.06	1.07	7.55	3.23	67.6	**4.9**	17.4	0.7	**6.3**
0.3	2.23	50.3	-0.08	**1.5**	-0.04	-0.12	-6.04	2.76	89.1	**4.0**	20.5	5.1	**2.7**
5.7	1.00	4.2	0.00	**3.0**	0.00	0.15	1.38	4.70	96.6	**5.7**	49.7	0.0	**3.0**
8.7	0.00	0.0	0.35	**6.6**	0.01	1.67	21.51	4.60	60.0	**5.5**	39.9	0.0	**3.0**
7.7	1.14	5.9	0.94	**5.5**	0.26	0.82	6.77	4.83	76.0	**4.9**	26.0	1.8	**7.6**
9.7	0.39	2.0	0.00	**3.2**	0.09	0.41	3.53	3.26	87.0	**4.7**	35.6	4.6	**6.2**
8.0	0.15	1.3	0.00	**8.2**	0.05	1.65	19.38	4.82	73.1	**4.5**	26.5	3.7	**4.3**
7.4	1.23	5.0	0.28	**7.4**	0.15	1.10	8.05	3.73	73.3	**5.1**	33.3	3.6	**6.6**
8.9	0.31	1.7	0.42	**0.0**	-0.03	-0.63	-9.27	2.80	118.0	**5.1**	23.8	0.0	**2.1**
5.3	1.13	11.4	1.40	**2.8**	0.05	0.17	2.17	3.93	96.6	**4.8**	26.4	3.6	**4.5**
6.6	1.15	7.4	0.10	**3.5**	0.04	0.35	3.04	3.86	90.8	**2.0**	25.9	24.0	**6.3**
10.0	NA	0.0	NA	**0.0**	0.00	-5.13	-66.67	0.00	0.0	**8.0**	106.8	0.0	**3.2**
8.0	0.40	2.4	0.39	**2.7**	0.01	0.28	3.68	9.15	93.9	**6.9**	55.4	0.0	**1.7**
3.4	4.78	20.3	0.00	**8.4**	0.02	1.65	18.40	4.84	63.5	**6.0**	49.8	0.0	**3.0**
7.9	1.74	4.5	1.70	**2.9**	0.23	0.91	5.65	5.01	90.7	**4.3**	17.7	10.9	**5.3**
10.0	0.25	0.3	0.39	**0.6**	0.00	0.09	0.73	2.95	141.4	**6.4**	40.9	0.0	**5.2**
9.5	1.83	3.4	-0.33	**4.6**	0.01	0.49	3.15	4.09	81.0	**6.9**	66.6	0.0	**6.4**
9.0	1.84	4.0	0.90	**0.5**	-0.04	-0.76	-4.52	6.47	98.1	**7.0**	47.7	0.0	**5.0**
9.4	0.47	2.7	0.43	**2.2**	-0.10	-0.18	-1.88	3.75	94.5	**4.8**	29.5	10.0	**6.0**
6.8	0.43	4.2	0.88	**1.3**	-0.02	-0.18	-3.35	4.28	95.8	**4.5**	20.3	1.7	**0.7**
9.3	0.33	2.9	0.16	**6.0**	0.27	0.83	10.48	3.52	81.2	**3.1**	15.7	11.3	**6.2**
9.9	0.00	0.0	0.00	**2.8**	0.03	0.40	5.53	2.98	91.9	**4.4**	17.5	1.7	**3.1**
8.1	0.38	2.6	0.82	**5.6**	5.32	0.77	6.70	3.70	71.0	**3.5**	12.9	7.3	**8.2**
8.8	0.54	3.3	0.40	**2.5**	0.04	0.10	1.38	3.09	92.4	**5.4**	55.0	5.5	**3.5**
9.0	2.07	2.2	0.00	**2.4**	0.00	0.08	0.84	1.60	82.5	**5.1**	8.9	0.0	**4.9**
6.5	2.02	9.5	-0.03	**4.2**	0.22	0.51	4.21	3.71	88.3	**3.8**	10.3	1.8	**7.9**
9.4	2.51	3.7	0.00	**1.0**	0.00	-0.09	-0.61	2.96	105.0	**7.6**	76.8	0.0	**6.0**
6.8	5.33	5.7	-1.15	**1.4**	0.00	0.16	1.51	6.64	88.2	**8.4**	97.9	0.0	**3.0**

	Name	City	State	Rating	2016 Rating	2015 Rating	Total Assets ($Mil)	One Year Asset Growth	Asset Mix (As a % of Total Assets) Comm-ercial Loans	Cons-umer Loans	Mort-gage Loans	Secur-ities	Capital-ization Index	Net Worth Ratio
▲	Tri Ag West Virginia FCU	Morgantown	WV	**D-**	E+	E+	11.4	0.51	0.0	52.2	9.3	0.0	**5.9**	7.9
	Tri Boro Federal Credit Union	Munhall	PA	**C-**	C-	C-	98.1	-0.54	0.0	24.2	32.9	1.5	**10.0**	11.5
▲	Tri County Area Federal Credit Union	Pottstown	PA	**C-**	D+	C	128.4	8.77	5.8	24.3	25.7	4.2	**4.9**	6.9
	Tri State Area Federal Credit Union	Hoosick Falls	NY	**C**	C	C	23.4	2.73	2.5	21.1	19.9	32.8	**10.0**	14.0
	Tri State Rail Federal Credit Union	Erie	PA	**C**	C	C-	14.5	-4.45	0.0	23.8	3.7	0.0	**10.0**	21.1
	Tri-Cities Community FCU	Kennewick	WA	**B**	B	B	38.0	19.09	0.0	27.0	23.5	0.0	**9.4**	10.6
	Tri-Cities Credit Union	Grand Haven	MI	**C+**	C+	C+	33.9	8.54	0.0	22.8	9.2	22.4	**7.5**	9.3
	Tri-County Credit Union	Grinnell	KS	**C**	C	C	4.1	8.03	5.8	13.2	0.0	0.0	**10.0**	16.0
	Tri-County Credit Union	Panguitch	UT	**D+**	D+	C-	<1	1.94	0.0	46.2	0.0	0.0	**10.0**	28.5
	Tri-County Credit Union	Marinette	WI	**C-**	C-	C-	28.4	0.88	1.3	14.9	14.9	0.0	**10.0**	13.8
	Tri-County Federal Credit Union	Delevan	NY	**C**	C	C	4.1	2.64	0.0	37.7	0.0	0.0	**10.0**	18.6
	Tri-Lakes Federal Credit Union	Saranac Lake	NY	**D**	D	D	15.8	1.54	0.0	32.5	13.4	0.0	**5.2**	7.2
	Tri-Rivers Federal Credit Union	Montgomery	AL	**E-**	E-	E-	14.9	-8.51	0.1	55.8	0.9	0.0	**0.0**	2.2
	Tri-Town Teachers Federal Credit Union	Westport	CT	**D+**	D+	D+	21.5	11.07	0.0	23.6	44.4	0.0	**6.5**	8.5
	Tri-Valley Service Federal Credit Union	Pittsburgh	PA	**D**	D	E+	15.9	6.04	0.0	47.3	0.0	0.0	**5.7**	7.7
	Triad Partners Federal Credit Union	Greensboro	NC	**D+**	D+	D	31.7	-1.87	0.0	20.9	0.0	27.4	**10.0**	11.4
	Triangle Credit Union	Nashua	NH	**C+**	C+	C+	649.0	7.18	10.5	29.2	38.6	8.0	**5.4**	7.4
	Triangle Federal Credit Union	Columbus AFB	MS	**C+**	C+	C+	81.8	0.19	0.0	29.1	4.3	20.7	**7.2**	9.6
	Triboro Postal Federal Credit Union	Flushing	NY	**C+**	C+	C-	132.1	1.42	0.0	4.2	4.8	85.0	**10.0**	14.8
	TriCounty Federal Credit Union	Harlowton	MT	**C+**	C+	C+	1.2	2.65	0.0	61.1	0.0	0.0	**10.0**	12.2
	Trinity Baptist Church FCU	Florence	SC	**C**	C	C	2.4	-2.47	0.0	5.2	1.5	0.0	**10.0**	12.3
	Trinity U.C.C. Federal Credit Union	Chicago	IL	**C**	C	C-	2.9	-0.92	0.0	0.1	0.0	0.0	**10.0**	18.1
	Trinity Valley Teachers Credit Union	Palestine	TX	**B-**	B-	B-	28.8	6.24	0.0	14.1	0.8	0.0	**10.0**	25.5
	Triple C 16 Federal Credit Union	Baltimore	MD	**D**	D	D	3.4	-4.32	0.0	28.5	5.4	0.0	**10.0**	22.8
	Trius Federal Credit Union	Kearney	NE	**C-**	C-	C-	72.1	5.06	0.2	65.4	2.9	0.2	**5.6**	7.6
	TRMC Employees Credit Union	Orangeburg	SC	**C+**	C+	C+	5.3	2.95	0.0	79.8	0.0	0.0	**10.0**	19.7
	Trona Valley Community FCU	Green River	WY	**B+**	B+	B+	189.1	8.46	1.0	43.7	21.5	0.0	**9.9**	10.9
▼	Tropical Financial Credit Union	Miramar	FL	**B-**	B	B-	685.4	10.65	2.7	33.2	26.9	8.2	**6.3**	8.5
	Trouvaille Federal Credit Union	Philadelphia	PA	**C+**	C+	D	2.1	17.67	0.0	23.2	0.0	0.0	**9.5**	10.7
	Troy Area School Employees FCU	Troy	PA	**D+**	D+	D+	1.8	-5.44	0.0	20.1	0.0	20.1	**10.0**	12.4
	Troy Federal Credit Union	Troy	NY	**C**	C	C	2.8	-2.70	0.0	54.7	0.0	0.0	**10.0**	14.4
	Truchoice Federal Credit Union	Portland	ME	**A-**	A-	B+	120.9	11.46	0.0	42.0	20.4	0.0	**9.6**	10.7
	True North Federal Credit Union	Juneau	AK	**C+**	C+	C	141.2	1.93	9.8	29.7	25.4	1.2	**5.8**	7.9
▼	True Sky Credit Union	Oklahoma City	OK	**C**	C+	B-	594.7	2.43	0.1	35.5	16.5	29.1	**6.6**	8.9
	TrueCore Federal Credit Union	Newark	OH	**C+**	C+	C	164.7	4.27	4.5	17.9	31.1	2.0	**6.4**	8.4
	TruGrocer Federal Credit Union	Boise	ID	**C+**	C+	C+	260.2	2.80	0.0	11.7	17.3	4.3	**10.0**	19.1
	Truity Federal Credit Union	Bartlesville	OK	**B-**	B-	C+	796.8	2.06	4.4	49.2	21.3	11.2	**6.3**	8.4
	Truliant Federal Credit Union	Winston-Salem	NC	**B-**	B-	B	2192.6	9.27	7.2	41.8	21.2	9.3	**6.5**	8.6
	TruMark Financial Credit Union	Fort Washington	PA	**B+**	B+	B+	1994.8	14.51	6.5	14.2	31.5	20.0	**8.3**	10.1
	Trumbull County Postal Employees CU	Warren	OH	**C-**	C-	C-	1.1	-0.53	0.0	17.0	0.0	0.0	**10.0**	12.3
	Trumbull Credit Union	Trumbull	CT	**D+**	D+	D	3.5	-4.44	0.0	9.1	0.0	5.2	**7.8**	9.6
	TruNorth Federal Credit Union	Ishpeming	MI	**B**	B	B-	146.6	6.95	0.0	15.4	29.4	24.8	**6.8**	8.8
	TruPartner Credit Union, Inc.	Cincinnati	OH	**D+**	D+	C-	153.9	1.61	8.7	23.9	17.6	30.1	**8.3**	9.9
	TruService Community FCU	Little Rock	AR	**D+**	D+	D	36.0	-0.70	0.0	53.9	15.6	1.0	**6.5**	8.5
	Trust Federal Credit Union	Chattanooga	TN	**B-**	B-	C+	77.5	14.60	0.3	50.7	16.3	0.0	**9.8**	10.8
	TruStar Federal Credit Union	International Falls	MN	**A**	A	A	215.1	3.92	21.7	16.1	40.3	7.0	**10.0**	16.0
	TruStone Financial Federal Credit Union	Plymouth	MN	**A-**	A-	A-	1179.7	7.86	10.3	16.7	27.9	20.0	**8.9**	10.3
	TruWest Credit Union	Tempe	AZ	**B+**	B+	B+	991.1	5.53	8.8	45.4	30.5	2.1	**9.0**	10.4
	TSU Federal Credit Union	Nashville	TN	**C+**	C+	C+	1.6	0.06	0.0	64.1	0.0	0.0	**10.0**	15.5
	TTCU The Credit Union	Tulsa	OK	**A-**	A-	A-	1755.8	6.25	0.1	41.3	12.2	24.0	**10.0**	12.7
▲	Tucoemas Federal Credit Union	Visalia	CA	**C-**	D+	C-	232.9	2.95	0.0	48.7	13.8	6.4	**5.2**	7.2
▼	Tucson Federal Credit Union	Tucson	AZ	**B-**	B	B	436.9	10.98	2.2	52.6	10.4	18.2	**6.9**	8.9
	Tucson Old Pueblo Credit Union	Tucson	AZ	**C+**	C+	C-	145.1	2.60	1.1	28.6	17.6	13.2	**4.7**	7.0
▲	Tulane/Loyola Federal Credit Union	New Orleans	LA	**C-**	D+	D	19.0	-4.38	0.0	25.5	20.7	0.0	**9.2**	10.4
	Tulare County Federal Credit Union	Tulare	CA	**C-**	C-	C-	95.1	5.62	0.0	51.2	15.4	8.2	**5.2**	7.3
	Tulsa Federal Credit Union	Tulsa	OK	**C-**	C-	C-	721.8	0.05	4.1	30.4	21.5	21.6	**6.5**	8.8
▲	Turbine Federal Credit Union	Greenville	SC	**C-**	D+	D+	27.0	4.47	0.0	43.6	0.2	0.0	**10.0**	13.2
	Tuscaloosa County Credit Union	Tuscaloosa	AL	**D**	D	D	9.3	3.75	0.0	39.8	8.1	0.0	**7.1**	9.1
	Tuscaloosa Credit Union	Tuscaloosa	AL	**C+**	C+	C+	74.5	8.20	1.1	29.8	24.8	5.1	**7.8**	9.5
	Tuscaloosa Veterans Federal Credit Union	Tuscaloosa	AL	**B-**	B-	B-	39.6	2.71	2.6	9.0	19.6	0.0	**10.0**	11.4

Asset Quality Index	Non-Performing Loans as a % of Total Loans	Non-Performing Loans as a % of Capital	Net Charge-Offs Avg Loans	Profitability Index	Net Income ($Mil)	Return on Assets	Return on Equity	Net Interest Spread	Overhead Efficiency Ratio	Liquidity Index	Liquidity Ratio	Hot Money Ratio	Stability Index
2.8	0.96	9.4	-0.13	**5.6**	0.04	1.49	18.81	3.92	82.2	**3.7**	18.4	4.0	**2.3**
8.2	0.48	3.4	0.42	**1.8**	0.03	0.11	1.31	3.92	91.3	**4.0**	18.0	2.4	**4.3**
6.7	0.72	6.8	0.99	**2.0**	0.08	0.25	3.47	4.44	88.3	**4.4**	23.5	3.2	**3.0**
9.8	0.12	0.5	0.06	**2.7**	0.02	0.28	2.04	3.26	96.5	**4.6**	13.8	2.6	**7.1**
9.3	2.05	3.3	0.00	**1.9**	0.00	0.00	0.00	3.18	100.0	**5.8**	31.3	0.0	**6.9**
6.3	1.12	7.8	0.51	**9.8**	0.13	1.44	13.34	4.88	70.3	**3.7**	21.2	7.9	**6.4**
8.4	0.46	1.7	0.03	**4.9**	0.08	0.94	10.09	2.61	72.5	**6.5**	47.3	0.0	**4.9**
8.2	0.48	0.9	0.00	**4.7**	0.01	0.69	4.32	2.22	71.4	**5.0**	20.0	0.0	**4.3**
1.7	22.67	34.0	0.00	**2.5**	0.00	0.00	0.00	5.06	100.0	**7.3**	76.1	0.0	**6.9**
8.8	1.13	3.9	-0.03	**1.1**	-0.02	-0.33	-2.34	2.94	107.4	**5.2**	35.1	4.0	**7.0**
7.2	3.16	7.6	0.00	**3.3**	0.00	0.20	1.05	3.76	90.9	**6.0**	54.0	0.0	**7.6**
6.6	0.65	4.8	0.59	**4.6**	0.02	0.62	8.53	4.31	86.8	**4.9**	24.5	0.0	**3.0**
0.0	5.17	84.0	5.21	**0.0**	-0.52	-14.00	-369.95	4.87	263.9	**4.4**	22.1	8.3	**0.6**
7.4	0.35	3.2	0.18	**5.7**	0.05	0.95	11.14	4.79	75.2	**3.8**	21.2	7.4	**3.7**
6.7	0.33	2.0	1.49	**3.2**	0.02	0.51	6.60	4.58	87.2	**4.5**	16.6	1.5	**2.3**
8.7	1.45	3.9	-0.36	**1.1**	-0.01	-0.06	-0.72	2.36	109.1	**5.1**	24.9	3.0	**3.7**
8.3	0.16	2.0	0.09	**3.4**	0.73	0.46	6.43	2.52	81.8	**2.1**	13.0	15.4	**4.9**
6.2	1.28	6.6	2.24	**5.2**	0.18	0.91	9.94	4.04	73.9	**5.7**	28.7	1.7	**4.4**
10.0	2.61	1.8	0.27	**2.9**	0.18	0.54	4.05	1.43	67.8	**3.8**	16.5	16.9	**6.6**
6.4	0.00	0.0	2.24	**3.7**	-0.01	-1.99	-16.11	6.68	90.9	**5.1**	27.5	0.0	**6.8**
10.0	1.17	1.3	0.00	**2.5**	0.00	0.33	2.71	1.39	71.4	**6.3**	73.4	0.0	**6.2**
10.0	0.00	0.0	0.00	**2.4**	0.00	0.41	2.28	1.50	70.0	**6.4**	68.1	0.0	**7.1**
10.0	0.50	0.4	0.08	**3.2**	0.04	0.54	2.13	2.47	74.6	**6.3**	71.4	2.6	**6.3**
8.8	1.98	2.9	-0.90	**0.0**	-0.01	-1.64	-7.24	3.35	163.6	**6.5**	40.6	0.0	**5.0**
3.1	1.24	15.3	1.49	**4.6**	0.09	0.53	7.03	6.59	85.3	**3.9**	11.7	0.0	**2.3**
7.2	0.14	0.6	1.03	**10.0**	0.05	3.47	17.61	12.24	63.2	**4.9**	45.1	0.0	**5.7**
6.3	0.78	8.3	1.28	**4.2**	0.12	0.26	2.78	4.59	77.6	**3.2**	13.5	11.3	**5.5**
9.4	0.25	2.3	0.33	**3.4**	0.25	0.15	1.83	3.49	90.7	**4.4**	21.6	8.5	**5.2**
8.3	2.05	4.7	-1.48	**8.9**	0.01	1.88	20.00	13.09	84.3	**8.1**	84.0	0.0	**5.0**
6.4	5.11	8.0	30.93	**0.8**	-0.04	-9.50	-68.62	2.38	66.7	**7.2**	75.9	0.0	**6.4**
8.7	0.32	1.2	0.00	**2.1**	0.00	-0.28	-1.97	3.22	115.0	**4.6**	18.4	0.0	**7.4**
8.7	0.40	2.8	0.54	**6.4**	0.34	1.15	11.04	5.29	82.9	**4.3**	17.3	1.5	**6.2**
5.7	0.89	9.3	0.41	**2.8**	0.02	0.04	0.54	4.20	92.4	**3.9**	18.4	3.2	**4.9**
8.9	0.31	2.9	0.60	**2.4**	0.14	0.09	1.08	2.84	89.1	**3.8**	16.6	11.2	**5.7**
8.1	0.29	3.9	0.38	**3.2**	0.09	0.23	3.22	3.70	92.2	**4.7**	27.6	3.8	**3.6**
10.0	0.23	0.4	0.05	**2.3**	0.06	0.10	0.52	1.91	96.0	**6.0**	56.8	6.3	**7.9**
5.7	0.60	6.9	1.09	**4.0**	0.60	0.31	3.62	4.05	77.1	**3.7**	14.8	4.9	**5.9**
8.5	0.33	3.3	0.47	**3.8**	3.05	0.57	6.86	3.35	79.4	**3.5**	19.5	11.1	**5.8**
8.4	0.62	4.1	0.75	**3.8**	2.13	0.44	4.34	3.03	74.9	**3.7**	13.6	8.9	**6.5**
9.6	0.16	0.5	0.00	**1.5**	0.00	0.00	0.00	3.01	100.0	**5.7**	58.7	0.0	**6.9**
10.0	0.00	0.0	0.00	**1.8**	0.00	0.00	0.00	2.45	95.0	**5.3**	9.0	0.0	**4.6**
8.9	0.29	2.8	0.30	**4.8**	0.21	0.59	6.67	3.65	82.3	**5.0**	24.5	2.7	**5.6**
5.5	1.61	15.8	0.22	**1.7**	0.06	0.16	1.64	2.91	87.4	**4.2**	17.0	3.5	**5.5**
6.5	0.10	2.5	0.04	**2.7**	0.04	0.40	4.70	3.57	94.0	**3.0**	8.6	6.8	**3.8**
3.5	1.63	15.2	0.94	**3.8**	0.05	0.26	2.64	4.43	79.3	**3.7**	23.2	9.8	**3.8**
7.9	0.73	3.8	0.11	**5.9**	0.39	0.73	4.56	4.53	83.6	**3.7**	21.7	7.4	**9.3**
9.6	0.13	1.4	0.17	**7.3**	2.61	0.89	8.89	3.57	80.3	**3.7**	13.2	3.9	**8.0**
8.1	0.21	2.2	0.37	**3.5**	1.03	0.42	4.05	3.99	84.0	**2.9**	3.4	1.5	**6.7**
2.7	6.90	25.0	0.00	**7.8**	0.01	2.75	18.03	7.93	64.5	**4.4**	42.3	0.0	**6.3**
7.3	0.65	4.6	1.08	**6.1**	3.41	0.78	6.23	3.15	64.3	**2.9**	3.4	10.6	**8.7**
7.8	0.22	4.0	0.25	**2.2**	0.24	0.42	7.10	3.14	83.0	**4.2**	22.2	4.0	**3.0**
6.1	0.30	6.8	1.07	**3.8**	0.23	0.22	2.62	4.33	79.5	**4.4**	23.2	1.9	**4.8**
7.8	0.50	4.2	0.82	**2.6**	0.04	0.10	1.53	3.95	90.7	**4.3**	15.6	2.3	**2.9**
5.8	1.61	9.9	0.70	**2.0**	0.01	0.17	2.07	4.45	97.2	**6.1**	49.3	0.0	**3.7**
5.2	0.40	4.9	0.45	**3.3**	0.09	0.40	5.51	3.69	90.4	**3.7**	15.9	4.5	**3.1**
7.6	0.47	3.8	0.66	**2.3**	0.20	0.11	1.33	2.94	83.0	**3.1**	8.9	10.9	**5.3**
7.7	1.50	5.8	0.41	**2.4**	0.05	0.72	5.42	4.39	86.0	**5.1**	35.2	3.1	**5.7**
5.7	1.82	11.1	-0.35	**5.8**	0.01	0.57	6.20	4.62	97.8	**3.2**	24.6	18.6	**2.3**
6.6	0.75	5.6	0.27	**3.2**	0.03	0.16	1.83	3.18	92.6	**2.5**	19.9	27.5	**4.2**
8.0	1.49	4.5	2.16	**2.0**	-0.06	-0.58	-5.04	2.83	113.8	**5.8**	52.5	2.1	**4.9**

	Name	City	State	Rating	2016 Rating	2015 Rating	Total Assets ($Mil)	One Year Asset Growth	Comm-ercial Loans	Cons-umer Loans	Mort-gage Loans	Secur-ities	Capital-ization Index	Net Worth Ratio
	Tuscumbia Federal Credit Union	Tuscumbia	AL	**C+**	C+	C	1.4	-1.39	0.0	40.2	0.0	0.0	**10.0**	38.5
▲	Tuskegee Federal Credit Union	Tuskegee	AL	**D-**	E+	D	9.6	8.89	0.0	25.9	9.5	0.0	**6.4**	8.4
	TVA Allen Steam Plant FCU	Memphis	TN	**C-**	C-	C-	3.5	7.66	0.0	25.2	0.0	0.0	**10.0**	15.5
	TVA Community Credit Union	Muscle Shoals	AL	**A-**	A-	A-	314.6	1.05	0.0	12.9	16.9	51.3	**10.0**	14.3
	TVH Federal Credit Union	Tuskegee	AL	**C-**	C-	C-	4.7	2.03	0.0	48.5	0.0	0.0	**10.0**	25.7
	Twin Oaks Federal Credit Union	Apple Grove	WV	**D-**	D-	E+	5.4	5.54	0.0	70.7	0.4	0.0	**6.8**	8.8
▲	Twin Rivers Federal Credit Union	Massena	NY	**C+**	C	C	29.5	0.49	0.0	24.7	12.5	1.0	**10.0**	11.2
	Twin States Federal Credit Union	Columbus	MS	**D-**	D-	E+	6.1	16.16	0.0	72.5	0.0	0.0	**6.2**	8.2
	TwinStar Credit Union	Lacey	WA	**B+**	B+	B+	1215.9	12.55	5.3	37.2	12.5	6.8	**7.8**	9.6
	Two Harbors Federal Credit Union	Two Harbors	MN	**B+**	B+	B+	72.7	5.93	0.0	13.4	41.4	0.0	**10.0**	15.6
	TxDOT Credit Union	Abilene	TX	**C**	C	C-	12.8	-0.77	0.0	63.8	0.0	0.0	**10.0**	11.5
	Tyler City Employees Credit Union	Tyler	TX	**C+**	C+	C+	19.7	4.16	0.0	49.9	0.0	0.0	**10.0**	15.1
▲	Tyndall Federal Credit Union	Panama City	FL	**C**	C-	C+	1280.5	4.72	0.0	33.7	8.8	35.8	**8.1**	10.1
▼	U A P Employees Federal Credit Union	Forest	OH	**D+**	C-	C	1.1	0.56	0.0	31.3	0.0	0.0	**9.3**	10.5
	U OF P Federal Credit Union	Philadelphia	PA	**D**	D	D+	26.0	1.13	0.0	8.8	0.0	7.0	**8.1**	9.8
	U S Court House SDNY FCU	New York	NY	**C**	C	D+	3.4	6.60	0.0	78.9	0.0	0.0	**10.0**	22.6
	U S I Federal Credit Union	La Porte	TX	**B**	B	B	16.1	-1.89	0.0	25.4	0.0	0.0	**10.0**	29.9
	U S P L K Employees Federal Credit Union	Leavenworth	KS	**C+**	C+	C+	34.0	-1.91	0.0	15.3	14.4	2.2	**10.0**	12.2
▼	U S Pipe Bessemer Employees FCU	Bessemer	AL	**D**	D+	D+	2.8	0.00	0.0	20.2	0.0	0.0	**10.0**	28.2
	U T Federal Credit Union	Knoxville	TN	**B-**	B-	B-	259.7	6.38	14.5	39.9	29.4	8.7	**6.4**	8.5
	U T U Federal Credit Union	North Olmsted	OH	**D+**	D+	D+	2.3	-15.08	0.0	11.6	0.0	0.0	**10.0**	16.0
	U-1st Community Federal Credit Union	Carlsbad	NM	**C**	C	C	7.6	-18.47	0.4	36.4	0.1	0.0	**10.0**	13.3
	U-Haul Federal Credit Union	Phoenix	AZ	**D+**	D+	D+	6.4	4.27	0.0	42.4	0.0	0.0	**9.2**	10.5
	U. H. S. Employees Federal Credit Union	Johnson City	NY	**D+**	D+	D	18.1	5.70	0.0	26.9	0.0	0.0	**6.4**	8.4
	U. S. Employees Credit Union	Tomball	TX	**D+**	D+	D+	78.4	1.86	0.0	37.7	2.9	1.7	**5.8**	7.8
	U.A.L.U. 354 Federal Credit Union	Youngwood	PA	**D+**	D+	D	6.8	3.32	0.0	37.1	0.0	0.0	**10.0**	12.5
	U.F.C.W. Local #72 Federal Credit Union	Wyoming	PA	**D+**	D+	D	27.4	-2.29	0.0	6.1	7.2	42.4	**8.0**	9.7
	U.P. Catholic Credit Union	Marquette	MI	**A**	A	A-	168.9	6.19	13.4	18.2	21.6	37.7	**10.0**	14.5
	U.P. Connection Federal Credit Union	Omaha	NE	**C+**	C+	C	35.6	2.09	0.0	14.8	29.8	23.0	**10.0**	12.7
	U.P. Employees Federal Credit Union	North Little Rock	AR	**C-**	C-	C	4.2	-3.69	0.0	36.6	0.0	0.0	**10.0**	22.5
	U.P. State Credit Union	Escanaba	MI	**C**	C	C-	73.0	8.98	0.7	35.7	18.8	0.6	**6.1**	8.1
	U.P.S. Credit Union	Cincinnati	OH	**D+**	D+	D+	3.9	-0.94	0.0	44.1	0.0	0.0	**10.0**	16.5
	U.P.S. Employees Federal Credit Union	Ontario	CA	**C**	C	C	35.7	4.64	0.0	17.6	13.6	0.0	**6.7**	8.8
	U.S. Eagle Federal Credit Union	Albuquerque	NM	**B**	B	B	980.3	8.93	7.6	53.1	17.2	17.5	**8.0**	9.7
▼	U.S. Employees Credit Union	Chicago	IL	**C-**	C	C	84.2	-0.97	5.1	16.1	2.6	34.1	**10.0**	12.3
▼	U.S. Employees O.C. Federal Credit Union	Oklahoma City	OK	**B+**	A-	A-	157.0	7.03	0.0	55.8	14.3	14.6	**10.0**	12.4
	U.S. Postal Service Federal Credit Union	Clinton	MD	**B-**	B-	B-	213.2	3.07	0.0	24.3	17.3	15.6	**10.0**	11.4
	U.S.B. Employees Federal Credit Union	Wilmington	CA	**D**	D	D	2.3	0.48	0.0	11.5	0.0	17.4	**10.0**	26.5
	UARK Federal Credit Union	Fayetteville	AR	**B-**	B-	C+	57.4	8.20	0.0	56.2	9.5	0.0	**7.8**	9.5
	UAW MO-KAN Federal Credit Union	Kansas City	KS	**D+**	D+	C-	6.1	-2.03	0.0	57.4	0.0	0.0	**10.0**	13.0
	UBC Credit Union	Saint Louis	MO	**C-**	C-	D	2.8	34.67	0.0	29.0	0.0	0.0	**9.8**	10.9
	UBC Southern Council Of Ind Workers FCU	Sibley	LA	**C**	C	C	<1	8.15	0.0	68.5	0.0	0.0	**10.0**	35.7
▲	UCB Credit Union	Salt Lake City	UT	**D+**	D	C-	1.2	6.50	0.0	30.8	0.0	0.0	**10.0**	19.1
▲	UFCW Community Federal Credit Union	Wyoming	PA	**B**	B-	B-	128.1	2.94	1.0	26.7	16.1	0.0	**10.0**	11.2
▼	UFCW Local 1776 Federal Credit Union	Plymouth Meeting	PA	**D-**	D	D-	7.7	5.74	1.1	21.6	0.0	0.0	**5.8**	7.8
	UFCW Local 23 Federal Credit Union	Canonsburg	PA	**D**	D	D	8.6	-0.52	0.0	24.4	0.0	0.0	**10.0**	12.7
▲	UFirst Federal Credit Union	Plattsburgh	NY	**B+**	B	B	68.3	7.09	0.0	29.7	13.4	26.6	**10.0**	17.3
	Uintah Credit Union	Vernal	UT	**C-**	C-	C-	3.4	-3.26	0.0	31.9	0.0	0.0	**10.0**	14.3
	Ukrainian Federal Credit Union	Rochester	NY	**B-**	B-	B-	221.9	5.99	12.2	9.1	61.9	3.6	**7.1**	9.1
	Ukrainian Future Credit Union	Warren	MI	**B+**	B+	B+	86.0	2.41	5.4	2.5	28.2	10.8	**10.0**	12.5
	Ukrainian National Federal Credit Union	New York	NY	**C**	C	C	143.9	-1.50	15.2	0.9	53.3	8.6	**9.7**	10.8
▼	Ukrainian Selfreliance FCU	Philadelphia	PA	**C+**	B-	B-	306.4	13.28	10.0	1.4	56.3	24.6	**9.9**	11.1
	Ukrainian Selfreliance Michigan FCU	Warren	MI	**B+**	B+	B	119.3	2.55	1.0	2.8	18.5	34.8	**10.0**	11.5
▲	Ukrainian Selfreliance New England FCU	Wethersfield	CT	**D+**	D	D-	33.2	2.45	12.0	29.4	37.3	0.0	**6.1**	8.1
▲	Ukrainian Selfreliance of Western PA FCU	Pittsburgh	PA	**C**	C-	D	6.7	-2.23	0.0	4.8	20.6	0.0	**10.0**	14.9
	Ulster Federal Credit Union	Kingston	NY	**C-**	C-	C-	121.7	8.68	4.6	7.6	9.2	39.4	**5.7**	8.0
	UMassFive College Federal Credit Union	Hadley	MA	**B-**	B-	B-	459.9	6.81	0.0	23.8	26.9	16.7	**6.0**	8.1
	Umatilla County Federal Credit Union	Pendleton	OR	**B-**	B-	C+	47.7	3.72	0.0	12.5	15.1	0.0	**10.0**	11.0
▼	UMe Federal Credit Union	Burbank	CA	**B-**	B	B	204.7	12.30	2.3	9.0	22.7	17.9	**6.4**	8.4
▲	Umico Federal Credit Union	New Hartford	NY	**C-**	D+	D	7.6	0.93	0.0	47.1	0.0	0.0	**10.0**	11.3

Asset Quality Index	Non-Performing Loans as a % of Total Loans	Non-Performing Loans as a % of Capital	Net Charge-Offs Avg Loans	Profitability Index	Net Income ($Mil)	Return on Assets	Return on Equity	Net Interest Spread	Overhead Efficiency Ratio	Liquidity Index	Liquidity Ratio	Hot Money Ratio	Stability Index
9.3	0.68	0.9	0.00	**8.7**	0.01	1.78	4.65	6.21	70.0	**4.8**	16.3	0.0	**5.7**
3.0	2.19	32.7	0.67	**6.2**	0.02	0.79	13.94	7.19	86.2	**6.2**	52.1	9.3	**1.7**
7.8	3.18	5.8	0.00	**2.2**	0.00	0.35	2.19	2.17	83.3	**6.3**	69.8	0.0	**6.5**
9.6	0.35	2.4	0.25	**5.5**	0.69	0.89	6.59	2.53	67.6	**4.3**	10.0	7.5	**8.9**
7.8	1.52	2.8	1.38	**4.5**	0.03	2.33	8.99	7.58	66.3	**5.5**	40.3	0.0	**4.3**
2.9	0.74	6.7	0.00	**6.0**	0.01	0.91	10.30	6.43	85.5	**3.7**	17.0	0.0	**1.7**
9.8	0.02	0.1	-0.06	**3.6**	0.05	0.71	6.20	3.66	91.0	**6.1**	43.6	0.5	**5.8**
2.9	1.29	12.0	0.26	**8.3**	0.04	2.40	29.81	6.60	64.6	**2.8**	9.8	14.8	**1.7**
7.1	0.54	4.5	0.79	**4.3**	1.01	0.34	3.56	4.15	83.9	**4.3**	15.8	1.1	**6.9**
9.9	0.07	0.3	0.00	**3.9**	0.10	0.54	3.47	2.91	86.0	**3.4**	19.7	7.7	**7.6**
6.8	0.45	3.3	0.18	**5.8**	0.03	1.07	9.34	3.12	67.0	**0.9**	9.0	30.8	**5.0**
7.2	0.93	3.6	0.35	**3.2**	0.03	0.60	3.93	4.03	83.3	**4.9**	31.8	2.8	**7.0**
9.6	0.37	2.2	0.45	**2.6**	1.04	0.33	3.36	2.53	82.6	**4.6**	29.1	7.1	**6.2**
3.5	7.84	24.4	0.00	**2.8**	0.00	0.38	3.64	5.83	85.7	**6.9**	47.2	0.0	**5.0**
10.0	0.32	0.6	0.27	**0.3**	-0.03	-0.50	-5.04	2.95	114.3	**7.0**	49.2	0.0	**3.4**
8.3	0.00	0.0	-0.15	**4.7**	0.01	0.81	3.67	8.90	90.1	**4.2**	25.1	0.0	**4.3**
10.0	0.00	0.0	0.09	**4.0**	0.02	0.57	1.92	2.80	78.0	**5.2**	23.7	0.0	**7.6**
8.1	0.12	0.3	0.00	**3.3**	0.03	0.38	3.09	1.85	79.0	**4.8**	14.9	0.0	**6.1**
9.1	3.32	2.7	-0.57	**0.0**	-0.01	-0.72	-2.51	3.44	125.0	**6.7**	49.4	0.0	**5.5**
9.2	0.17	1.5	0.23	**4.3**	0.41	0.64	7.60	3.38	78.5	**4.0**	13.1	2.5	**5.5**
8.9	3.42	2.3	0.00	**3.6**	0.01	1.01	6.65	1.73	70.0	**6.1**	76.7	0.0	**5.2**
7.4	0.96	3.5	0.71	**5.6**	0.02	0.84	6.41	5.18	73.3	**6.3**	53.3	0.0	**4.3**
6.0	2.53	8.4	0.59	**2.2**	0.00	0.00	0.00	4.32	80.5	**6.0**	42.2	0.0	**6.2**
6.9	0.98	5.3	0.63	**1.6**	-0.02	-0.33	-3.94	3.49	83.7	**4.9**	32.9	2.3	**4.5**
7.9	0.52	3.0	-0.01	**1.8**	0.01	0.04	0.46	2.67	96.8	**4.2**	26.2	5.9	**2.7**
5.5	7.05	18.4	-6.22	**2.6**	0.01	0.42	3.34	3.05	79.3	**5.5**	50.5	0.0	**5.7**
9.6	0.19	1.2	0.36	**1.6**	0.01	0.10	1.07	2.10	88.3	**7.4**	50.7	0.0	**4.3**
7.7	0.73	4.3	0.09	**6.6**	0.41	0.97	6.73	3.40	74.1	**4.3**	14.3	3.5	**9.1**
10.0	0.27	1.0	-0.02	**2.6**	0.01	0.14	1.06	2.85	96.3	**4.2**	26.7	4.9	**5.9**
9.2	1.75	3.3	0.23	**0.9**	-0.01	-0.67	-2.93	5.65	111.3	**6.8**	52.9	0.0	**6.1**
5.0	1.48	13.8	0.50	**5.1**	0.11	0.62	7.63	5.09	80.8	**4.9**	25.3	1.5	**4.3**
8.9	1.11	3.3	0.00	**0.5**	-0.01	-0.83	-4.95	5.17	114.3	**6.1**	41.4	0.0	**6.2**
9.3	0.44	1.6	-0.21	**2.2**	0.01	0.16	1.81	3.03	95.9	**5.1**	26.4	4.4	**4.4**
5.2	0.74	7.7	0.94	**3.4**	0.52	0.22	2.21	3.33	70.2	**3.1**	6.8	7.7	**7.0**
8.1	3.72	6.7	0.91	**1.3**	0.06	0.30	2.36	2.59	58.6	**4.9**	27.5	1.7	**5.5**
6.3	0.63	5.2	0.59	**4.2**	0.08	0.22	1.96	3.61	82.6	**2.7**	6.5	12.7	**8.0**
8.9	0.73	3.6	1.62	**2.8**	0.16	0.29	2.56	3.03	91.0	**4.3**	27.4	3.1	**6.9**
9.3	7.20	3.0	0.00	**1.0**	0.00	0.18	0.66	2.62	92.9	**5.8**	39.8	0.0	**6.6**
6.0	0.43	3.1	0.18	**4.9**	0.11	0.78	8.08	3.67	83.6	**4.6**	17.5	1.2	**5.0**
1.8	6.24	32.5	-0.34	**3.0**	0.01	0.54	4.07	4.08	87.1	**4.5**	14.3	0.0	**6.3**
6.5	0.85	3.1	0.67	**7.2**	0.02	2.86	27.68	7.40	88.3	**6.8**	54.4	0.0	**4.3**
5.6	4.25	8.1	0.00	**7.9**	0.00	1.66	4.55	10.74	76.5	**5.0**	43.4	0.0	**4.3**
7.4	4.83	7.1	0.00	**1.1**	0.00	0.00	0.00	4.61	100.0	**7.6**	85.6	0.0	**5.4**
7.4	1.60	6.8	0.28	**4.0**	0.16	0.50	4.35	4.95	87.2	**5.7**	34.8	2.4	**7.0**
7.9	0.47	2.4	2.00	**3.3**	-0.02	-1.07	-13.09	5.18	106.4	**6.8**	61.2	0.0	**1.7**
3.7	5.32	20.0	1.36	**2.4**	0.01	0.52	4.02	4.29	85.2	**5.7**	37.6	0.0	**5.3**
9.5	0.14	0.7	0.27	**5.1**	0.14	0.86	7.36	4.36	81.8	**4.9**	19.5	0.0	**7.2**
9.7	0.00	0.0	-0.30	**1.8**	0.00	0.00	0.00	3.89	100.0	**7.2**	68.8	0.0	**6.6**
7.4	0.44	4.2	0.12	**3.3**	0.34	0.62	6.89	3.46	84.2	**1.3**	11.7	20.8	**5.9**
8.5	1.45	3.4	-0.22	**3.6**	0.06	0.27	2.22	1.92	104.8	**4.1**	28.9	10.4	**7.5**
6.3	1.51	8.6	0.02	**2.9**	0.09	0.25	2.30	2.62	90.0	**2.1**	17.7	28.2	**6.8**
9.9	0.02	0.1	0.00	**3.1**	0.21	0.28	2.67	1.85	85.8	**2.2**	35.6	33.2	**6.6**
9.0	1.95	4.4	0.03	**3.7**	0.08	0.28	2.74	1.76	84.9	**4.1**	27.9	12.3	**6.1**
6.8	0.55	4.6	0.07	**1.8**	0.01	0.13	1.65	3.71	95.4	**3.3**	24.1	9.5	**3.4**
10.0	0.00	0.0	0.00	**2.2**	0.01	0.29	2.01	2.68	87.2	**4.8**	24.6	8.1	**7.2**
7.4	1.36	7.4	0.17	**2.9**	0.12	0.39	5.00	3.33	84.9	**5.6**	25.6	2.5	**4.2**
7.4	0.83	7.6	0.09	**4.0**	0.56	0.50	6.15	3.68	83.0	**3.0**	13.9	11.4	**5.4**
9.3	0.48	2.1	-0.05	**3.8**	0.07	0.60	5.35	1.75	65.8	**4.6**	22.6	0.0	**6.3**
10.0	0.17	0.7	0.27	**3.9**	0.16	0.32	3.79	2.71	86.3	**4.7**	20.4	3.5	**4.6**
8.3	0.21	1.0	0.27	**2.1**	0.01	0.49	4.19	4.18	107.3	**5.9**	33.4	0.0	**5.5**

Name	City	State	Rating	2016 Rating	2015 Rating	Total Assets ($Mil)	One Year Asset Growth	Asset Mix (As a % of Total Assets) Commercial Loans	Consumer Loans	Mortgage Loans	Securities	Capitalization Index	Net Worth Ratio
UNCLE Credit Union	Livermore	CA	**B-**	B-	B-	381.8	13.97	6.2	19.2	41.0	10.1	**7.3**	9.2
UNI Credit Union	Cedar Falls	IA	**C+**	C+	C+	21.1	1.03	0.0	20.3	0.0	46.6	**10.0**	13.3
▲ Unified Communities Federal Credit Union	Belleville	MI	**D**	D-	E+	15.2	13.13	0.0	30.6	15.9	22.2	**5.8**	7.8
▲ Unified Homeowners of Illinois FCU	Chicago	IL	**C-**	D+	D+	<1	15.48	0.0	43.3	0.0	0.0	**10.0**	21.7
Unified People's Federal Credit Union	Cheyenne	WY	**A-**	A-	A-	46.9	8.62	0.0	22.1	0.1	4.0	**10.0**	20.0
UNIFY Financial Federal Credit Union	Torrance	CA	**B**	B	B	2734.1	21.95	6.1	28.0	32.9	19.2	**6.3**	8.5
Unilever Federal Credit Union	Englewood Cliffs	NJ	**C-**	C-	C-	47.6	4.12	0.0	6.6	51.9	0.7	**5.0**	7.0
▲ Union Baptist Church FCU	Fort Wayne	IN	**C**	C-	C	<1	-41.15	0.0	15.5	0.0	0.0	**10.0**	17.1
▼ Union Baptist Greenburgh FCU	White Plains	NY	**D**	D+	C-	<1	4.59	0.0	17.2	0.0	0.0	**10.0**	31.7
Union Building Trades FCU	Parsippany	NJ	**C**	C	C	75.9	1.34	0.0	19.4	12.7	1.8	**10.0**	13.1
▼ Union Congregational FCU	New York	NY	**C-**	C	C+	<1	0.00	0.0	0.4	0.0	0.0	**10.0**	21.4
Union County Employees FCU	Elizabeth	NJ	**C-**	C-	C-	8.5	2.23	0.0	31.0	0.0	10.4	**10.0**	13.8
▼ Union Federal Credit Union	Farmerville	LA	**C-**	C	D+	<1	1.78	0.0	16.8	0.0	0.0	**10.0**	30.0
Union Fidelity Federal Credit Union	Houston	TX	**B-**	B-	B-	20.7	-2.86	0.0	27.8	0.0	0.0	**10.0**	15.8
Union Memorial Credit Union	Saint Louis	MO	**D**	D	D	<1	-31.82	0.0	17.1	0.0	0.0	**10.0**	13.3
Union Of Poles In America Credit Union	Garfield Heights	OH	**C-**	C-	C-	<1	-12.10	0.0	32.1	0.0	0.0	**10.0**	15.9
Union Pacific California Employees FCU	Los Alamitos	CA	**D-**	D-	D	8.3	-5.85	0.0	38.7	10.4	0.0	**6.3**	8.3
▼ Union Pacific Employees Credit Union	Beaumont	TX	**C-**	C	C	3.9	-2.25	0.0	34.6	0.0	0.0	**10.0**	16.6
▼ Union Pacific Streamliner FCU	Omaha	NE	**E-**	E	E+	25.4	-0.18	2.0	42.4	4.8	0.0	**1.1**	4.3
Union Square Credit Union	Wichita Falls	TX	**B-**	B-	C+	349.6	1.50	6.1	25.5	39.5	14.7	**10.0**	12.2
Union Trades Federal Credit Union	Parkersburg	WV	**C+**	C+	C	24.0	-0.29	0.0	36.5	3.7	0.0	**10.0**	12.2
Union Yes Federal Credit Union	Orange	CA	**D-**	D-	E+	62.8	6.50	2.4	14.9	22.2	0.0	**0.8**	4.0
Unison Credit Union	Kaukauna	WI	**C**	C	C	203.0	1.10	0.3	21.0	38.3	15.2	**9.2**	10.5
United 1st Federal Credit Union	Kingsland	GA	**B+**	B+	B+	147.8	7.80	0.3	40.6	10.2	16.3	**9.2**	10.5
United Advantage Northwest FCU	Portland	OR	**C+**	C+	C	39.2	9.80	3.4	37.1	18.5	9.8	**6.9**	8.9
United America West Federal Credit Union	Panorama City	CA	**E+**	E+	E+	4.4	5.26	0.0	30.4	0.0	0.0	**5.1**	7.1
United Arkansas Federal Credit Union	Little Rock	AR	**B**	B	B	27.5	0.35	0.0	59.4	0.0	0.0	**10.0**	15.9
United Association Credit Union	Concord	CA	**C+**	C+	C+	6.2	-7.51	0.0	37.8	0.0	0.0	**10.0**	16.5
United Bay Community Credit Union	Bay City	MI	**C**	C	C-	194.8	3.42	0.5	28.7	22.4	18.8	**5.3**	7.5
United Business & Industry FCU	Plainville	CT	**D+**	D+	C-	100.5	0.09	0.0	48.8	10.6	6.4	**6.1**	8.1
United Catholics Federal Credit Union	West Covina	CA	**D-**	D-	D-	33.4	3.07	0.0	27.6	18.1	2.8	**4.2**	6.2
United Churches Credit Union	Taylor	MI	**D+**	D+	D	17.5	5.23	0.0	11.4	4.6	63.6	**5.6**	7.6
United Community Credit Union	Quincy	IL	**B**	B	C+	87.5	33.24	0.0	33.4	28.6	0.0	**10.0**	11.9
United Community Credit Union	Galena Park	TX	**B-**	B-	C	94.6	0.41	0.0	75.3	7.7	0.1	**8.0**	9.7
United Community Federal Credit Union	West Mifflin	PA	**D+**	D+	D	92.8	2.75	2.0	26.2	12.0	15.5	**9.1**	10.4
▼ United Consumers Credit Union	Independence	MO	**C**	C+	B-	142.8	7.94	3.1	38.7	17.4	0.2	**8.5**	10.0
United Credit Union	Council Bluffs	IA	**C-**	C-	C-	16.7	1.42	0.0	21.1	3.7	44.3	**7.8**	9.5
United Credit Union	Chicago	IL	**C**	C	D	179.2	2.05	0.1	25.1	14.4	19.0	**9.9**	11.0
United Credit Union	Ness City	KS	**D+**	D+	D	8.9	0.72	0.6	17.2	0.0	0.0	**6.8**	8.8
▲ United Credit Union	Mexico	MO	**A-**	B+	B+	171.6	6.32	2.0	30.6	21.5	8.7	**9.0**	10.4
▼ United Credit Union	Tyler	TX	**D**	D+	D+	30.2	-1.19	0.0	55.7	6.6	0.0	**6.3**	8.3
United Educators Credit Union	Apple Valley	MN	**C+**	C+	C+	179.0	6.67	0.0	19.7	6.3	13.0	**6.7**	8.9
United Employees Credit Union	Albert Lea	MN	**B-**	B-	B-	38.0	8.25	0.4	38.5	0.0	13.7	**10.0**	12.2
United Energy Credit Union	Humble	TX	**C-**	C-	C	26.5	2.59	0.0	47.0	0.4	0.0	**10.0**	17.6
▼ United Equity Credit Union	Decatur	IL	**C**	C+	B-	41.3	3.11	0.0	35.3	5.7	4.4	**9.5**	10.7
United Federal Credit Union	Saint Joseph	MI	**A-**	A-	A-	2304.1	12.94	12.1	31.6	41.3	3.2	**8.6**	10.1
United Federal Credit Union	Morgantown	WV	**A-**	A-	A-	87.3	1.79	7.8	14.4	41.0	1.1	**10.0**	19.1
▼ United Financial Credit Union	Saginaw	MI	**B-**	B	B	205.0	7.10	1.2	20.1	32.6	16.1	**7.6**	9.6
United Heritage Credit Union	Austin	TX	**B-**	B-	B-	918.1	4.27	9.8	36.5	37.0	4.3	**6.5**	8.6
United Hospital Center FCU	Bridgeport	WV	**B-**	B-	B-	11.8	2.56	0.0	30.2	0.0	0.0	**10.0**	13.9
United Investors Federal Credit Union	Linden	NJ	**D-**	D-	D-	3.9	-4.85	0.0	22.0	0.0	0.0	**6.5**	8.5
United Labor Credit Union	Kansas City	MO	**D+**	D+	D-	13.6	7.19	0.0	55.2	0.0	0.0	**6.7**	8.7
United Local Credit Union	Fresno	CA	**B-**	B-	B	114.5	2.18	6.4	50.5	21.8	1.1	**10.0**	16.8
United Members Federal Credit Union	Tulsa	OK	**C**	C	C	14.0	11.70	0.0	9.9	2.8	8.3	**10.0**	13.0
United Methodist Connectional FCU	Marietta	GA	**C**	C	C	28.6	2.83	7.1	36.8	20.6	0.0	**7.4**	9.3
United Methodist Federal Credit Union	Montclair	CA	**C+**	C+	C	91.9	2.35	8.9	11.7	25.6	8.4	**6.8**	8.8
United Methodist Financial Credit Union	North Canton	OH	**C+**	C+	C	87.2	2.82	27.1	7.2	32.2	39.7	**8.6**	10.6
United Methodist First Choice FCU	Rapid City	SD	**E+**	E+	E+	4.7	1.57	48.0	22.4	57.0	0.7	**5.9**	7.9
United Methodist of Mississippi FCU	Booneville	MS	**D-**	D-	D-	<1	-3.49	0.0	38.9	0.0	0.0	**4.8**	6.8
United Nations Federal Credit Union	Long Island City	NY	**B**	B	B	4850.9	9.05	1.6	11.3	35.0	43.7	**7.9**	9.9

Asset Quality Index	Non-Performing Loans as a % of Total Loans	Non-Performing Loans as a % of Capital	Net Charge-Offs Avg Loans	Profitability Index	Net Income ($Mil)	Return on Assets	Return on Equity	Net Interest Spread	Overhead Efficiency Ratio	Liquidity Index	Liquidity Ratio	Hot Money Ratio	Stability Index
9.8	0.06	0.5	0.08	**4.3**	0.78	0.84	9.51	3.48	81.6	**4.5**	20.8	2.8	**5.9**
9.1	0.47	1.1	-0.22	**2.8**	0.01	0.19	1.35	2.91	91.9	**5.7**	31.1	0.6	**6.4**
8.5	0.42	2.5	-0.37	**4.6**	0.00	0.03	0.34	3.83	100.0	**5.1**	22.2	0.0	**3.3**
6.1	3.57	6.8	0.00	**5.4**	0.05	55.49	325.42	12.70	31.4	**7.3**	75.6	0.0	**4.3**
10.0	0.94	1.5	-0.03	**7.1**	0.10	0.87	4.34	3.22	76.7	**6.1**	41.9	2.4	**8.2**
7.0	0.75	6.6	0.66	**3.1**	1.01	0.15	1.90	3.84	85.9	**3.7**	18.9	8.6	**5.2**
10.0	0.01	0.1	0.00	**2.5**	0.02	0.19	2.77	2.11	90.7	**2.6**	24.0	33.1	**3.2**
8.5	0.00	0.0	14.81	**6.5**	0.00	2.33	21.05	0.00	100.0	**8.5**	103.2	0.0	**5.0**
7.9	5.45	2.8	31.75	**0.0**	0.00	-3.81	-11.65	3.76	100.0	**8.3**	122.0	0.0	**8.0**
7.1	2.12	8.8	-0.05	**2.5**	0.06	0.29	2.23	3.71	92.9	**4.3**	20.2	4.1	**5.9**
10.0	0.00	0.0	0.00	**1.6**	0.00	0.00	0.00	7.84	50.0	**8.0**	73.6	0.0	**7.1**
7.3	2.76	6.1	0.95	**2.0**	0.00	0.14	1.02	4.95	72.0	**5.6**	19.5	0.0	**5.8**
6.1	5.58	8.3	-1.83	**2.7**	-0.01	-3.24	-10.73	4.08	177.8	**6.0**	73.0	0.0	**5.5**
10.0	0.60	1.8	0.64	**5.2**	0.03	0.64	4.06	3.92	75.5	**5.8**	44.5	4.8	**7.5**
3.7	18.18	21.1	0.00	**0.0**	0.00	-3.33	-26.67	0.00	0.0	**6.3**	44.0	0.0	**4.7**
7.5	2.99	7.3	0.00	**1.9**	0.00	0.00	0.00	2.04	100.0	**5.0**	51.8	0.0	**6.0**
7.3	0.51	3.0	2.17	**3.2**	0.02	1.01	12.35	5.94	87.9	**5.1**	30.6	0.0	**1.7**
9.4	0.00	0.0	1.28	**0.4**	-0.01	-1.23	-7.33	3.55	105.4	**5.4**	41.6	0.0	**6.0**
4.6	0.65	7.6	0.81	**3.3**	0.02	0.26	5.90	3.81	83.2	**5.7**	36.7	0.0	**0.0**
7.0	0.66	5.4	0.19	**3.8**	0.18	0.20	1.69	3.28	90.5	**3.3**	11.0	7.2	**7.1**
5.8	1.86	12.5	0.00	**6.2**	0.03	0.57	4.68	4.59	82.0	**4.4**	18.1	2.2	**5.0**
10.0	0.08	0.7	0.02	**2.0**	0.00	0.02	0.48	2.90	99.2	**6.0**	36.4	0.0	**1.9**
9.4	0.37	2.5	0.13	**2.9**	0.12	0.23	2.19	3.13	92.6	**4.3**	16.7	3.3	**6.8**
9.4	0.24	1.4	0.52	**3.7**	0.19	0.52	4.80	3.23	88.1	**4.5**	23.4	4.9	**6.1**
7.7	0.79	5.6	0.06	**4.4**	0.06	0.66	7.30	4.44	87.8	**4.3**	20.8	3.1	**4.9**
9.0	0.62	2.7	0.83	**0.0**	-0.01	-0.83	-11.36	3.96	98.2	**5.5**	37.1	0.0	**2.5**
8.2	0.10	0.4	0.49	**4.7**	0.04	0.52	3.23	3.74	73.4	**4.1**	23.0	2.0	**7.3**
9.9	0.00	0.0	0.00	**7.5**	0.02	1.31	7.94	2.48	79.2	**4.6**	33.3	0.0	**5.7**
6.7	0.86	6.5	0.47	**2.6**	0.06	0.12	1.67	3.71	92.5	**5.0**	29.3	1.7	**4.2**
7.9	0.29	3.1	0.27	**1.2**	-0.01	-0.04	-0.44	2.90	97.3	**3.8**	14.2	3.3	**3.7**
5.5	1.41	13.6	0.14	**2.3**	0.01	0.13	2.12	3.29	93.0	**4.3**	17.5	5.2	**1.7**
10.0	0.10	0.4	0.48	**2.9**	0.01	0.17	2.10	2.40	93.6	**5.7**	43.0	0.0	**2.8**
7.8	0.96	5.0	0.33	**7.3**	0.19	0.89	7.47	3.94	76.9	**4.4**	21.0	1.8	**4.8**
4.9	0.75	6.5	0.83	**5.2**	0.14	0.58	5.90	4.72	84.5	**3.0**	7.8	4.8	**4.8**
8.0	0.57	2.4	0.25	**1.5**	0.01	0.06	0.58	2.62	96.2	**5.4**	31.3	1.2	**4.4**
4.6	2.55	19.3	2.25	**0.8**	-0.33	-0.94	-9.21	3.91	83.2	**3.7**	20.2	7.3	**5.3**
8.3	0.82	2.6	0.38	**3.2**	0.02	0.39	4.05	2.80	85.9	**5.2**	25.4	3.8	**4.1**
9.1	0.64	2.2	0.90	**2.5**	0.14	0.32	2.85	3.38	82.0	**5.9**	41.0	3.8	**6.6**
9.9	0.00	0.0	0.00	**2.8**	0.01	0.27	3.06	2.29	88.5	**5.7**	53.8	7.0	**2.3**
8.2	0.52	3.3	0.57	**6.2**	0.45	1.06	11.31	4.02	74.7	**4.3**	25.1	3.4	**6.3**
3.2	1.21	15.4	0.92	**2.6**	0.00	0.05	0.73	6.21	89.3	**2.2**	15.9	21.8	**2.2**
8.3	0.31	2.4	0.73	**3.3**	0.15	0.35	3.93	3.28	82.0	**4.0**	14.1	2.4	**5.2**
9.9	0.26	1.0	0.00	**3.5**	0.03	0.36	2.86	2.28	86.0	**4.7**	34.3	1.5	**6.9**
7.9	1.08	3.0	0.78	**1.8**	0.01	0.09	0.51	4.23	96.8	**5.0**	52.5	9.5	**6.0**
7.5	0.74	3.6	0.56	**1.5**	0.01	0.14	1.27	3.28	88.4	**4.5**	19.5	4.1	**4.8**
7.0	0.57	4.8	0.85	**6.4**	5.76	1.01	10.07	4.23	66.8	**1.7**	4.7	14.0	**7.5**
6.8	2.78	9.6	0.30	**9.6**	0.29	1.34	7.01	4.09	67.3	**2.3**	23.1	21.5	**8.6**
8.0	0.49	3.1	1.34	**3.1**	-0.04	-0.07	-0.77	2.92	76.2	**3.1**	11.9	12.0	**5.7**
9.3	0.14	1.6	0.22	**4.2**	1.45	0.64	7.99	3.03	80.2	**3.0**	11.5	9.5	**6.1**
6.7	2.05	8.1	-0.09	**3.5**	0.01	0.31	2.19	2.48	86.5	**6.1**	37.9	0.0	**7.5**
6.5	1.85	8.5	0.00	**1.6**	0.00	-0.10	-1.21	3.73	103.1	**5.7**	26.1	0.0	**1.0**
4.9	0.88	6.2	0.97	**5.6**	0.02	0.69	7.88	6.60	81.7	**5.0**	31.0	2.7	**3.7**
8.4	0.11	0.7	0.06	**3.9**	0.13	0.47	2.76	3.54	84.0	**3.7**	21.3	11.9	**8.0**
9.0	0.99	1.1	0.40	**1.9**	0.01	0.14	1.10	1.74	92.4	**5.5**	24.7	0.0	**5.9**
9.0	0.22	1.6	-0.02	**2.5**	0.01	0.17	1.82	3.94	95.4	**4.0**	36.5	4.9	**4.6**
9.6	0.26	1.3	0.04	**4.8**	0.13	0.56	6.39	3.10	79.6	**3.8**	13.1	9.7	**3.7**
9.4	0.01	0.0	0.08	**2.7**	0.04	0.18	1.75	2.19	92.6	**4.2**	27.2	7.9	**5.0**
7.5	0.00	0.0	0.00	**1.8**	0.00	-0.09	-1.36	4.37	101.8	**4.2**	13.8	0.0	**1.0**
9.4	0.00	0.0	-0.88	**0.1**	0.00	-0.45	-6.56	3.27	112.5	**5.5**	55.7	0.0	**2.1**
9.1	0.65	3.5	0.30	**4.7**	8.60	0.72	7.73	2.74	72.2	**3.7**	20.5	9.3	**6.8**

Name	City	State	Rating	2016 Rating	2015 Rating	Total Assets ($Mil)	One Year Asset Growth	Comm-ercial Loans	Cons-umer Loans	Mort-gage Loans	Secur-ities	Capital-ization Index	Net Worth Ratio
								Asset Mix (As a % of Total Assets)					
United Neighborhood Federal Credit Union	Augusta	GA	**E+**	E+	D+	1.9	13.96	0.0	75.2	0.0	0.0	**7.0**	9.0
United Neighbors Federal Credit Union	Watertown	NY	**D+**	D+	D	6.3	-6.56	0.0	52.0	0.0	0.0	**9.7**	10.8
United Northwest Federal Credit Union	Norton	KS	**B+**	B+	B+	39.0	-3.43	4.6	27.9	15.6	0.8	**10.0**	15.5
United Poles Federal Credit Union	Perth Amboy	NJ	**C-**	C-	D-	40.0	6.63	1.0	10.6	51.2	23.2	**6.1**	8.2
United Police Federal Credit Union	Miami	FL	**C+**	C+	C	52.6	5.17	0.0	19.7	5.2	42.1	**10.0**	16.0
United Savers Trust Credit Union	Houston	TX	**E+**	E+	E+	6.2	-4.83	0.0	65.4	0.0	0.0	**5.3**	7.3
United Savings Credit Union	Fargo	ND	**A-**	A-	B+	59.8	16.46	6.8	32.3	31.1	0.0	**10.0**	15.6
United Southeast Federal Credit Union	Bristol	TN	**C+**	C+	B-	160.3	3.89	0.0	34.8	11.2	6.8	**10.0**	12.5
▲ United States Senate FCU	Alexandria	VA	**A**	A-	B+	637.9	4.91	14.1	17.7	21.5	12.3	**10.0**	11.4
▼ United Teletech Financial FCU	Tinton Falls	NJ	**D+**	C-	C	348.7	1.89	10.7	23.6	12.8	12.7	**7.0**	9.1
United Texas Federal Credit Union	San Antonio	TX	**B-**	B-	C	244.8	0.73	4.6	30.8	30.7	7.1	**6.6**	8.7
Unitedone Credit Union	Manitowoc	WI	**A**	A	A-	213.4	9.38	8.6	20.7	42.6	3.8	**10.0**	11.8
Unitus Community Credit Union	Portland	OR	**A-**	A-	B+	1088.0	8.17	6.8	34.9	29.7	16.1	**8.9**	10.3
Unity Catholic Federal Credit Union	Parma	OH	**C**	C	C-	71.4	1.50	0.3	33.5	14.2	23.7	**7.7**	9.5
Unity Credit Union	Warren	MI	**C+**	C+	C+	48.7	4.08	0.5	11.5	6.2	16.5	**10.0**	15.8
Unity Federal Credit Union	Oaklyn	NJ	**C**	C	C-	3.2	-1.88	0.0	49.1	0.0	0.0	**10.0**	18.9
▼ Unity One Credit Union	Fort Worth	TX	**C**	C+	C+	244.6	6.52	0.0	38.3	2.6	5.7	**5.3**	7.5
Universal 1 Credit Union	Dayton	OH	**C-**	C-	C-	425.1	5.67	0.9	61.1	7.4	7.1	**5.9**	8.0
Universal City Studios Credit Union	Burbank	CA	**C-**	C-	C	73.1	4.79	0.0	17.6	18.9	0.0	**6.3**	8.3
Universal Coop Federal Credit Union	Rio Grande	PR	**C-**	C-	D	25.4	8.44	0.0	37.5	16.0	11.2	**6.5**	8.6
Universal Credit Union	Independence	KS	**D**	D	D+	<1	-13.77	0.0	57.0	0.0	0.0	**10.0**	44.3
Universal Federal Credit Union	Huntington	WV	**C+**	C+	C+	83.4	1.74	0.0	16.7	18.8	0.3	**10.0**	13.3
University & Community FCU	Stillwater	OK	**B-**	B-	B	117.0	8.99	5.2	25.9	23.6	26.7	**7.3**	9.4
University & State Employees CU	San Diego	CA	**B+**	B+	B+	909.8	6.83	3.8	24.8	32.2	20.0	**7.3**	9.2
University Credit Union	Los Angeles	CA	**B**	B	B	614.1	9.31	0.8	13.0	22.5	35.0	**6.5**	8.7
University Credit Union	Miami	FL	**D+**	D+	D	206.5	4.15	1.9	13.5	8.4	22.4	**6.2**	8.7
University Credit Union	Orono	ME	**B-**	B-	B-	271.5	1.74	2.1	23.0	47.6	9.1	**7.6**	9.5
University Federal Credit Union	Grand Forks	ND	**B-**	B-	C+	33.2	7.20	0.0	23.8	0.0	0.0	**7.2**	9.2
University Federal Credit Union	Austin	TX	**B**	B	B	2206.4	7.77	2.8	37.6	38.5	2.0	**6.1**	8.1
University First Federal Credit Union	Salt Lake City	UT	**A-**	A-	A-	912.0	12.44	9.4	50.0	17.7	6.2	**8.9**	10.3
University of Hawaii FCU	Honolulu	HI	**A-**	A-	A-	611.7	4.99	4.6	6.3	11.9	54.8	**9.7**	11.5
University of Illinois Community CU	Champaign	IL	**B-**	B-	C+	331.1	7.84	0.1	51.9	17.5	2.3	**6.0**	8.0
University of Iowa Community CU	North Liberty	IA	**B+**	B+	B+	3965.3	18.40	16.8	27.7	47.5	0.4	**6.6**	8.6
University of Kentucky FCU	Lexington	KY	**A**	A	A	720.8	15.20	4.0	28.0	17.4	6.9	**9.8**	10.9
▼ University of Louisiana FCU	Lafayette	LA	**C**	C+	C+	45.4	1.79	0.0	26.6	21.3	5.3	**9.9**	11.0
University of Michigan Credit Union	Ann Arbor	MI	**B**	B	B	772.7	12.31	0.5	35.6	20.3	24.1	**6.8**	8.8
University of Nebraska FCU	Lincoln	NE	**C**	C	C-	101.0	7.18	0.1	22.2	17.3	11.8	**5.9**	8.0
University of Pennsylvania Students FCU	Philadelphia	PA	**C-**	C-	C	7.4	7.72	0.0	0.5	0.0	4.9	**9.3**	10.5
University of South Alabama FCU	Mobile	AL	**B-**	B-	C+	43.7	7.18	0.0	19.5	1.2	0.0	**8.0**	9.7
▼ University of Toledo FCU	Toledo	OH	**C-**	C	C	74.7	8.54	7.2	16.7	20.2	26.2	**9.0**	10.3
University of Virginia Community CU	Charlottesville	VA	**B+**	B+	A-	878.9	12.66	4.0	22.0	15.7	41.8	**8.5**	10.3
University of Wisconsin Credit Union	Madison	WI	**A-**	A-	B	2478.7	14.26	0.0	19.8	19.1	13.7	**7.0**	9.0
University Settlement FCU	New York	NY	**C-**	C-	D+	<1	6.75	0.0	29.8	0.0	0.0	**8.5**	10.0
UniWyo Federal Credit Union	Laramie	WY	**B-**	B-	B-	308.5	9.95	7.7	44.2	16.4	5.9	**8.7**	10.2
UNO Federal Credit Union	New Orleans	LA	**B**	B	B-	26.7	-3.12	0.0	40.6	2.9	0.0	**10.0**	11.8
▼ UP Arkansas Federal Credit Union	North Little Rock	AR	**C+**	B-	B	27.2	-2.04	0.0	54.5	4.7	0.0	**10.0**	16.5
Upper Cumberland Federal Credit Union	Crossville	TN	**B-**	B-	B-	60.8	9.04	0.0	35.3	29.0	0.3	**6.7**	8.7
▲ Upper Darby Belltelco FCU	Upper Darby	PA	**B-**	C+	C-	59.2	-0.55	0.9	8.3	6.6	48.4	**10.0**	12.4
▲ Upper Michigan Community Credit Union	Munising	MI	**C-**	D+	D+	35.9	1.73	1.0	24.8	20.7	0.0	**5.7**	7.7
UPS Employees Credit Union	Memphis	TN	**B+**	B+	B+	21.6	11.76	0.0	54.6	0.6	0.0	**10.0**	21.1
Upstate Federal Credit Union	Anderson	SC	**C+**	C+	C	55.7	14.82	0.0	60.5	0.1	0.0	**6.1**	8.1
Upstate Milk Employees FCU	Cheektowaga	NY	**E+**	E+	D-	2.9	1.34	0.0	32.2	0.0	55.2	**6.5**	8.5
▼ Upstate Telco Federal Credit Union	Gloversville	NY	**D**	D+	D+	5.0	-6.47	0.0	24.4	0.0	0.1	**10.0**	14.4
Upward Credit Union	Burlingame	CA	**C+**	C+	C	71.3	5.40	5.0	17.3	25.4	2.1	**7.4**	9.2
Urban Street Biscuit Wkrs FCU	Buffalo	NY	**C-**	C-	D+	<1	3.40	0.0	42.7	0.0	0.0	**10.0**	25.0
▼ Urban Upbound Federal Credit Union	Long Island City	NY	**D-**	D	D+	<1	23.95	0.0	7.2	0.0	0.0	**5.0**	7.0
Urbana Municipal Employees Credit Union	Urbana	IL	**D+**	D+	D	4.0	7.95	0.0	77.2	0.0	0.0	**7.2**	9.1
Urbana Postal Credit Union	Urbana	IL	**D+**	D+	D+	<1	-1.49	0.0	81.5	0.0	0.0	**10.0**	15.2
URE Federal Credit Union	East Pittsburgh	PA	**C-**	C-	C-	9.1	-1.73	0.0	49.0	0.0	0.0	**10.0**	16.7
URW Community Federal Credit Union	Danville	VA	**B**	B	B	171.7	12.17	1.5	67.6	10.8	0.0	**7.9**	9.6

Arrows denote recent upgrades ▲ or downgrades ▼

Asset Quality Index	Non-Performing Loans as a % of Total Loans	Non-Performing Loans as a % of Capital	Net Charge-Offs Avg Loans	Profitability Index	Net Income ($Mil)	Return on Assets	Return on Equity	Net Interest Spread	Overhead Efficiency Ratio	Liquidity Index	Liquidity Ratio	Hot Money Ratio	Stability Index
1.7	3.10	21.9	3.39	**3.5**	0.02	4.41	50.63	11.97	64.1	**4.6**	22.4	0.0	**1.0**
4.8	0.90	5.9	0.00	**5.5**	0.01	0.39	3.57	5.74	93.5	**4.5**	21.3	0.0	**3.0**
8.8	1.20	3.8	0.36	**5.7**	0.06	0.65	4.20	3.02	76.9	**4.2**	21.7	7.3	**7.8**
5.8	1.18	12.3	-0.06	**4.5**	0.05	0.51	6.26	3.61	89.4	**3.7**	15.2	2.0	**4.3**
9.4	0.32	1.0	-0.41	**3.1**	0.08	0.57	3.64	2.78	93.5	**4.6**	17.6	1.9	**7.0**
2.3	1.51	18.3	1.64	**0.0**	-0.03	-1.71	-23.23	5.38	102.0	**4.2**	13.6	0.0	**2.4**
7.9	0.89	4.6	0.05	**7.4**	0.12	0.79	5.05	4.61	79.4	**3.9**	20.5	5.4	**7.8**
8.4	0.52	2.7	0.35	**2.8**	0.09	0.22	1.71	3.21	87.9	**3.8**	17.6	6.4	**7.6**
9.6	0.13	0.7	0.31	**6.3**	1.54	0.98	8.51	4.84	72.1	**5.8**	35.0	4.2	**8.5**
2.8	2.83	29.2	2.44	**1.3**	0.03	0.04	0.44	4.23	86.8	**3.6**	9.9	3.0	**5.0**
7.5	0.49	4.8	0.14	**3.5**	0.26	0.43	5.60	3.36	93.2	**4.0**	18.4	8.8	**4.3**
8.3	0.53	3.2	0.28	**6.5**	0.40	0.78	6.43	3.88	84.0	**4.2**	21.0	3.3	**8.3**
9.5	0.15	1.2	0.13	**6.4**	2.46	0.92	8.76	3.11	74.7	**4.1**	16.9	4.5	**8.2**
5.0	2.19	13.5	0.65	**3.5**	0.08	0.46	4.90	3.71	79.5	**3.9**	15.4	3.1	**3.8**
9.9	1.41	2.0	0.14	**2.7**	0.03	0.23	1.42	2.36	90.8	**6.2**	53.7	1.5	**6.9**
8.7	0.00	0.0	0.42	**5.4**	0.01	0.75	3.94	5.99	87.5	**5.4**	51.6	0.0	**4.3**
6.7	0.63	7.0	0.59	**2.7**	0.03	0.04	0.56	4.41	88.0	**3.5**	8.6	3.6	**4.3**
5.1	1.00	9.3	0.91	**2.1**	0.28	0.27	3.33	3.32	84.6	**3.6**	21.5	9.9	**4.1**
7.8	0.20	1.7	0.60	**2.4**	0.01	0.06	0.80	4.38	89.4	**4.3**	16.4	6.5	**3.1**
2.6	3.22	27.1	1.41	**5.2**	0.05	0.83	9.75	5.48	72.6	**5.8**	37.8	3.5	**2.3**
6.5	2.83	3.5	-0.88	**0.0**	-0.01	-2.87	-6.76	5.43	160.0	**5.9**	77.0	0.0	**4.8**
8.8	1.18	3.5	-0.03	**2.3**	0.02	0.08	0.63	2.74	96.9	**5.3**	25.4	1.4	**6.8**
6.8	0.87	7.7	0.69	**3.8**	0.12	0.42	4.54	2.87	76.3	**4.4**	27.9	4.2	**5.7**
9.7	0.25	2.0	0.55	**3.7**	0.82	0.37	3.89	3.44	80.4	**4.4**	23.0	2.8	**6.7**
10.0	0.40	2.1	0.22	**4.4**	0.73	0.48	6.46	2.46	76.1	**5.3**	24.3	2.7	**5.6**
10.0	0.33	1.2	0.85	**1.2**	0.01	0.02	0.26	2.70	89.2	**5.2**	23.2	2.7	**3.6**
6.4	0.93	8.2	0.45	**3.9**	0.31	0.45	4.83	4.26	85.2	**3.2**	3.7	2.4	**6.1**
9.8	0.09	0.5	0.23	**5.4**	0.05	0.67	7.18	3.28	75.4	**4.6**	19.8	2.0	**5.1**
9.0	0.20	2.3	0.69	**4.9**	2.88	0.53	6.48	4.09	81.5	**3.9**	10.1	0.6	**5.8**
6.8	0.30	3.2	0.44	**6.8**	1.90	0.86	8.23	3.18	70.5	**3.1**	9.3	6.3	**8.2**
7.9	1.26	5.2	0.34	**5.4**	1.14	0.75	7.00	2.17	62.4	**4.2**	8.8	6.4	**7.9**
5.1	1.10	10.2	0.79	**3.7**	0.03	0.03	0.41	4.94	84.2	**3.8**	12.2	1.9	**4.9**
6.7	0.40	4.8	0.37	**9.5**	16.22	1.65	19.54	2.99	46.8	**0.6**	3.5	35.6	**8.0**
7.7	0.71	4.6	0.88	**8.3**	2.97	1.68	15.50	4.46	62.6	**2.7**	18.7	18.9	**8.4**
5.8	1.38	8.8	0.43	**2.7**	-0.01	-0.04	-0.53	4.34	92.3	**4.0**	18.7	6.7	**3.6**
6.9	0.91	7.5	0.58	**5.7**	1.62	0.86	9.69	3.56	72.9	**4.1**	13.9	3.3	**6.2**
10.0	0.16	0.9	0.06	**3.0**	0.08	0.30	3.79	2.97	91.3	**4.8**	19.4	1.1	**4.3**
10.0	0.00	0.0	0.00	**2.6**	0.01	0.44	4.56	1.87	80.0	**7.5**	67.3	0.0	**4.1**
8.2	1.17	2.8	0.59	**3.6**	0.06	0.51	5.23	2.12	82.3	**6.3**	45.0	1.0	**4.9**
8.0	0.72	2.8	0.33	**1.9**	-0.01	-0.04	-0.36	2.50	95.3	**5.2**	38.8	2.5	**4.7**
9.9	0.28	1.3	0.31	**5.0**	1.43	0.67	6.66	3.14	79.0	**4.6**	15.8	4.5	**6.5**
8.6	0.54	3.6	0.37	**9.5**	7.79	1.30	14.14	3.80	69.5	**5.5**	31.5	2.3	**7.5**
10.0	0.00	0.0	0.00	**2.8**	0.00	0.49	4.88	5.29	87.5	**6.6**	37.1	0.0	**5.4**
7.8	0.45	3.4	0.70	**3.8**	0.44	0.57	6.08	3.57	75.7	**3.2**	18.1	10.3	**6.2**
7.7	1.03	4.4	0.62	**3.4**	0.01	0.20	1.65	4.32	89.5	**6.1**	50.3	0.0	**6.0**
6.0	1.62	6.3	0.23	**1.9**	-0.01	-0.19	-1.16	3.84	98.3	**3.6**	23.4	7.2	**7.0**
7.0	0.24	4.4	0.25	**7.4**	0.15	1.00	11.19	5.02	80.1	**4.4**	18.7	1.6	**4.7**
7.3	3.04	8.6	0.07	**6.5**	0.22	1.48	12.01	2.83	85.9	**5.8**	39.6	4.9	**5.9**
6.4	0.70	5.2	0.05	**3.0**	0.04	0.45	5.84	3.79	89.2	**4.9**	24.8	0.9	**3.5**
8.3	0.35	1.0	0.74	**10.0**	0.10	1.88	8.75	6.42	70.9	**5.1**	25.5	0.2	**7.0**
5.7	0.43	4.4	0.52	**8.0**	0.18	1.36	16.53	5.25	79.2	**3.6**	19.1	11.0	**4.3**
6.5	1.64	6.4	-0.76	**0.8**	0.00	0.14	1.64	2.75	89.5	**5.1**	23.5	0.0	**2.4**
9.6	0.63	1.1	2.72	**0.0**	-0.02	-1.77	-12.10	3.52	118.8	**7.0**	51.2	0.0	**4.7**
9.0	0.21	1.2	0.27	**3.1**	0.06	0.32	3.42	3.55	89.8	**4.1**	17.0	2.2	**4.0**
9.7	1.20	2.0	0.00	**0.0**	0.00	-1.25	-4.92	3.17	150.0	**7.8**	176.9	0.0	**6.9**
8.6	0.00	0.0	0.00	**4.2**	0.01	4.23	59.02	5.41	11.1	**8.8**	101.8	0.0	**1.7**
6.5	0.13	1.0	0.63	**8.0**	0.02	2.18	23.60	5.71	61.1	**4.2**	16.8	0.0	**3.7**
2.2	5.35	27.5	0.00	**5.0**	0.00	1.27	8.63	6.15	75.0	**4.4**	20.0	0.0	**7.1**
5.2	2.97	9.9	0.15	**4.4**	0.01	0.35	2.10	4.17	87.4	**4.9**	33.8	0.0	**3.7**
4.4	1.40	12.6	1.32	**9.8**	0.62	1.47	15.27	6.04	59.4	**2.0**	15.4	24.8	**6.2**

Name	City	State	Rating	2016 Rating	2015 Rating	Total Assets ($Mil)	One Year Asset Growth	Asset Mix (As a % of Total Assets) Comm-ercial Loans	Cons-umer Loans	Mort-gage Loans	Secur-ities	Capital-ization Index	Net Worth Ratio
US #1364 Federal Credit Union	Merrillville	IN	**A-**	A-	A-	118.2	5.30	0.0	28.2	24.4	0.0	**8.7**	10.1
US Community Credit Union	Nashville	TN	**B**	B	B-	185.7	8.78	2.3	38.2	18.9	9.8	**10.0**	11.9
US Employees Federal Credit Union	Fairmont	WV	**D+**	D+	C-	<1	10.06	0.0	74.3	0.0	0.0	**10.0**	13.9
US Weather Bureau NY FCU	Bohemia	NY	**C-**	C-	C-	1.6	-6.42	0.0	3.9	0.0	0.0	**10.0**	13.3
USAgencies Credit Union	Portland	OR	**C+**	C+	C+	87.2	6.15	0.0	32.2	13.4	0.0	**7.9**	9.6
USAlliance Federal Credit Union	Rye	NY	**B-**	B-	B-	1238.9	7.67	2.2	13.6	31.0	1.2	**6.8**	8.8
USC Credit Union	Los Angeles	CA	**C+**	C+	B-	488.2	10.19	0.6	34.6	26.4	5.4	**5.7**	7.8
USEM Mena Federal Credit Union	Mena	AR	**C+**	C+	C+	2.1	-2.61	0.0	40.3	0.0	0.0	**10.0**	20.3
USF Federal Credit Union	Tampa	FL	**B-**	B-	B-	587.1	9.87	1.1	51.0	24.7	1.4	**8.8**	10.2
USNE Penitentiary Employees FCU	Lewisburg	PA	**C-**	C-	C-	13.2	0.81	0.0	28.8	0.0	53.7	**7.5**	9.3
Ussco Johnstown Federal Credit Union	Johnstown	PA	**C**	C	C	105.2	-0.02	5.9	24.8	8.7	21.8	**8.0**	9.8
USTC Employees Credit Union	Nashville	TN	**B-**	B-	B-	1.9	-11.51	0.0	84.9	0.0	0.0	**10.0**	20.8
USX Federal Credit Union	Cranberry Township	PA	**C+**	C+	B-	227.5	-0.52	0.1	39.3	21.5	22.3	**10.0**	14.2
Utah Community Federal Credit Union	Provo	UT	**A-**	A-	A-	1238.3	12.71	11.0	33.2	20.3	10.7	**8.7**	10.2
Utah Federal Credit Union	Salt Lake City	UT	**C+**	C+	C+	18.8	1.28	0.9	27.6	22.3	27.6	**10.0**	12.0
Utah First Federal Credit Union	Salt Lake City	UT	**A**	A	A	326.3	12.58	20.6	27.7	31.3	0.0	**9.7**	10.8
Utah Heritage Credit Union	Moroni	UT	**B-**	B-	C+	63.8	6.66	5.2	23.6	20.4	0.0	**7.9**	9.6
Utah Power Credit Union	Salt Lake City	UT	**A+**	A+	A+	625.7	7.34	0.5	16.1	18.0	51.2	**10.0**	13.2
Utah Prison Employees Credit Union	Draper	UT	**D-**	D-	D	3.7	-3.63	0.0	51.7	0.0	0.0	**6.2**	8.3
Utica District Telephone Employees FCU	Utica	NY	**B**	B	B	37.7	2.80	0.0	15.7	13.0	0.0	**10.0**	27.2
Utica Gas & Electric Employees FCU	New Hartford	NY	**B+**	B+	A-	63.5	7.47	1.9	12.5	32.1	26.7	**10.0**	17.6
Utica Police Department FCU	Utica	NY	**C-**	C-	C-	6.9	-1.34	0.0	47.5	0.5	42.1	**10.0**	17.3
Utilities Credit Union	Eau Claire	WI	**C-**	C-	C-	7.6	-7.62	0.0	26.1	0.0	0.0	**10.0**	11.9
Utilities Employees Credit Union	Wyomissing	PA	**B+**	B+	B+	1173.7	2.81	0.4	7.1	11.6	72.2	**10.0**	14.2
Utility District Credit Union	Oakland	CA	**C**	C	C	32.0	4.73	0.0	17.3	10.9	10.4	**6.2**	8.2
Utility Employees Federal Credit Union	Hoquiam	WA	**C**	C	C	3.6	-0.44	0.0	34.7	0.0	0.0	**10.0**	13.3
▲ V. Suarez Employees Federal Credit Union	Bayamon	PR	**D**	D-	E+	<1	-92.54	0.0	0.0	0.0	0.0	**10.0**	100.0
▼ V.A. Hospital Federal Credit Union	Little Rock	AR	**D**	D+	D	10.0	4.30	0.0	77.5	0.0	0.0	**6.8**	8.8
▲ V.A.C. Employees Federal Credit Union	Bath	NY	**C-**	D+	D+	25.4	3.29	0.0	14.1	1.5	68.2	**10.0**	16.2
VA Desert Pacific Federal Credit Union	Signal Hill	CA	**A-**	A-	A-	72.1	5.24	4.0	37.0	18.5	28.2	**10.0**	16.0
VA Pittsburgh Employees FCU	Pittsburgh	PA	**C**	C	D+	20.0	1.20	0.0	21.4	0.0	27.1	**10.0**	11.6
▼ VacationLand Federal Credit Union	Sandusky	OH	**B+**	A-	A-	210.7	9.82	11.1	32.1	20.4	12.7	**8.5**	10.1
Vah Lyons Employees Federal Credit Union	Lyons	NJ	**C+**	C+	B-	47.2	8.07	0.0	18.6	0.0	0.0	**8.3**	9.8
▲ Valdosta Teachers Federal Credit Union	Valdosta	GA	**C**	C-	C	10.1	6.10	0.0	38.0	2.4	0.0	**10.0**	14.4
Valex Federal Credit Union	Pineville	LA	**C**	C	C	18.9	-1.60	0.0	41.3	10.4	0.0	**9.6**	10.7
Valley 1st Community FCU	Monessen	PA	**C+**	C+	C+	84.7	-1.25	0.4	9.4	21.7	0.0	**10.0**	22.8
▼ Valley Bell Federal Credit Union	Charleston	WV	**C**	C+	C-	<1	-31.82	0.0	45.0	0.0	0.0	**10.0**	38.3
▲ Valley Board Federal Credit Union	Halltown	WV	**D+**	D	D	<1	9.02	0.0	56.6	0.0	0.0	**10.0**	26.2
Valley Catholic Federal Credit Union	Simsbury	CT	**D-**	D-	E+	<1	-0.66	0.0	70.5	0.0	0.0	**6.6**	8.6
Valley Communities Credit Union	Mosinee	WI	**B+**	B+	B	151.9	8.84	0.9	20.6	43.3	0.0	**10.0**	13.8
Valley Credit Union	Tuscumbia	AL	**B+**	B+	B+	71.8	3.61	0.2	20.9	15.0	26.1	**10.0**	16.3
Valley Credit Union	Salem	OR	**B**	B	B-	74.3	6.44	6.6	27.2	12.0	0.0	**9.8**	10.8
▲ Valley Educators Credit Union	Alamosa	CO	**D+**	D	D	5.2	0.08	0.0	54.1	0.0	0.0	**10.0**	11.1
Valley Federal Credit Union	Brownsville	TX	**B+**	B+	B+	69.4	5.00	0.0	50.2	2.7	0.0	**10.0**	14.5
Valley Federal Credit Union of Montana	Billings	MT	**A-**	A-	A-	238.5	10.22	0.0	48.3	7.5	0.0	**10.0**	11.1
Valley First Credit Union	Modesto	CA	**C+**	C+	B	609.0	4.33	0.7	45.5	6.2	20.4	**8.4**	10.1
Valley Gas Employees FCU	Jackson	MS	**D+**	D+	C-	5.9	-5.31	0.0	13.2	0.0	0.0	**10.0**	25.6
▲ Valley Hills Federal Credit Union	San Bernardino	CA	**C+**	C	C-	3.3	4.47	0.0	52.9	0.0	0.0	**10.0**	13.1
Valley Isle Community FCU	Kahului	HI	**C-**	C-	D+	117.3	1.26	0.0	21.1	7.0	21.4	**9.1**	10.4
Valley Oak Credit Union	Three Rivers	CA	**C-**	C-	C-	52.5	3.73	0.0	66.7	3.8	0.0	**7.5**	9.4
Valley One Community FCU	Steubenville	OH	**D+**	D+	D	33.9	4.09	0.5	12.1	5.1	24.4	**8.6**	10.0
Valley Pride Federal Credit Union	Kingston	PA	**D**	D	D	6.4	-2.29	0.0	15.5	0.0	14.8	**10.0**	16.1
Valley Wide Federal Credit Union	Vernal	UT	**D**	D	D	<1	6.54	0.0	65.2	0.0	0.0	**10.0**	17.8
▲ Valley Wide of PA Federal Credit Union	Tarentum	PA	**D+**	D	D+	1.3	-13.61	0.0	41.1	0.0	0.0	**10.0**	18.9
Valwood Park Federal Credit Union	Carrollton	TX	**C**	C	C+	21.9	4.40	0.6	51.6	1.0	0.0	**10.0**	14.6
Van Cortlandt Cooperative FCU	Bronx	NY	**C**	C	B+	75.7	-3.80	14.6	1.8	14.2	50.4	**8.4**	9.9
Vanderbilt University Employees CU	Nashville	TN	**C-**	C-	C-	39.3	5.97	0.0	11.9	4.5	0.0	**6.4**	8.4
▼ Vantage Credit Union	Bridgeton	MO	**C-**	C	C-	848.6	6.28	0.0	34.5	7.1	19.1	**5.9**	8.0
Vantage Point Federal Credit Union	Hopewell	VA	**B+**	B+	B+	34.9	4.42	0.0	24.2	7.1	26.2	**10.0**	12.6
▲ VAntage Trust Federal Credit Union	Wilkes-Barre	PA	**D+**	D	D-	59.2	-0.59	0.7	7.0	19.1	15.9	**6.4**	8.5

Asset Quality Index	Non-Performing Loans as a % of Total Loans	Non-Performing Loans as a % of Capital	Net Charge-Offs Avg Loans	Profitability Index	Net Income ($Mil)	Return on Assets	Return on Equity	Net Interest Spread	Overhead Efficiency Ratio	Liquidity Index	Liquidity Ratio	Hot Money Ratio	Stability Index
9.0	0.42	2.7	0.43	**5.9**	0.22	0.76	8.24	2.10	68.0	**3.2**	26.2	15.2	**7.3**
8.9	0.45	3.0	0.65	**3.8**	0.21	0.47	3.90	4.49	84.2	**3.8**	16.2	5.7	**7.5**
2.2	5.16	24.8	0.00	**3.8**	0.00	0.48	3.17	4.68	87.5	**5.0**	26.9	0.0	**7.2**
10.0	0.00	0.0	0.00	**1.8**	0.00	0.00	0.00	1.84	100.0	**5.5**	12.0	0.0	**6.4**
9.4	0.19	1.1	0.10	**3.3**	0.09	0.41	4.27	2.64	87.4	**5.0**	40.2	0.5	**5.1**
6.3	0.74	9.0	0.39	**6.1**	3.06	1.00	13.00	3.89	67.2	**2.1**	14.8	22.4	**6.2**
7.0	0.63	6.4	0.33	**3.8**	0.67	0.55	7.13	3.25	74.4	**3.5**	12.7	3.8	**4.9**
8.8	1.07	2.5	0.00	**7.3**	0.01	1.14	5.61	3.23	64.7	**4.8**	20.8	0.0	**5.0**
6.4	0.69	5.3	0.77	**4.3**	0.67	0.47	4.53	3.93	73.1	**3.9**	21.0	7.9	**6.8**
9.5	0.45	1.6	0.00	**2.6**	0.00	0.09	0.97	1.17	91.7	**4.9**	22.0	0.0	**4.3**
8.9	0.34	1.7	0.12	**2.7**	0.12	0.45	4.60	2.75	88.1	**4.4**	17.9	0.0	**6.3**
8.1	0.57	2.3	-0.26	**8.8**	0.01	1.04	5.22	7.68	97.0	**4.4**	24.5	0.0	**5.7**
6.4	1.93	9.5	0.60	**2.5**	0.12	0.22	1.52	4.46	86.9	**3.7**	11.5	2.4	**7.3**
8.8	0.30	1.9	0.32	**6.3**	1.55	0.51	4.97	3.25	79.6	**4.2**	13.5	3.1	**8.6**
9.7	0.18	0.9	0.34	**3.2**	0.01	0.28	2.31	3.12	91.6	**3.7**	13.3	6.4	**5.8**
8.6	0.38	2.9	0.34	**9.9**	1.18	1.49	13.63	4.93	69.3	**3.1**	14.7	12.8	**8.1**
5.5	1.20	8.6	0.14	**6.4**	0.14	0.92	9.50	4.45	79.9	**3.4**	27.4	17.3	**5.4**
10.0	0.15	0.7	0.11	**5.9**	1.21	0.79	6.12	1.80	61.2	**4.4**	14.3	0.8	**10.0**
5.0	0.65	4.4	1.15	**0.6**	0.00	-0.22	-2.60	4.59	102.6	**4.8**	37.0	0.0	**2.9**
9.9	0.63	1.2	1.13	**3.8**	0.03	0.31	1.16	2.95	70.9	**4.5**	19.6	2.4	**6.8**
6.5	2.59	9.4	0.08	**7.1**	0.15	0.98	5.97	3.17	69.1	**3.0**	14.0	11.7	**8.3**
4.8	4.67	12.0	0.23	**5.9**	0.02	1.03	6.03	2.63	50.0	**5.0**	26.7	0.0	**3.7**
10.0	0.35	1.4	0.21	**1.7**	0.00	0.05	0.44	2.36	88.1	**5.2**	34.9	0.0	**5.4**
10.0	0.26	0.5	0.17	**4.1**	1.73	0.60	4.47	1.62	65.2	**5.3**	32.0	2.0	**9.1**
9.8	0.30	1.1	0.49	**2.8**	0.01	0.14	1.67	2.74	89.5	**4.9**	10.9	0.4	**4.0**
9.8	0.00	0.0	0.00	**3.3**	0.00	0.34	2.52	2.23	81.3	**6.0**	40.5	0.0	**6.7**
10.0	NA	0.0	NA	**2.5**	0.00	0.00	0.00	NA	0.0	**4.0**	NA	101.0	**5.6**
4.7	0.91	8.5	0.05	**2.5**	-0.02	-0.72	-8.14	3.52	114.7	**2.6**	18.1	17.9	**2.3**
10.0	0.00	0.0	0.00	**1.5**	0.01	0.10	0.58	2.10	96.9	**5.2**	26.7	1.9	**7.1**
7.1	0.89	7.4	0.54	**6.8**	0.04	0.22	1.39	4.38	85.7	**4.1**	17.4	2.1	**8.9**
10.0	0.14	0.4	0.07	**1.7**	-0.02	-0.36	-3.42	3.06	108.5	**6.1**	45.9	0.0	**4.7**
8.1	0.44	2.9	0.40	**5.0**	0.26	0.50	4.95	3.84	83.8	**3.9**	15.7	4.2	**7.4**
8.0	2.44	4.5	2.17	**2.9**	0.03	0.21	2.16	1.94	77.9	**5.3**	17.9	0.0	**4.6**
9.8	0.00	0.0	-0.08	**2.8**	0.01	0.29	1.93	4.94	97.9	**5.6**	36.5	0.0	**5.9**
6.2	0.50	7.0	0.15	**3.5**	0.01	0.24	2.17	3.92	91.3	**4.8**	23.8	3.8	**5.7**
7.4	5.36	8.5	0.47	**3.0**	0.07	0.31	1.35	2.42	83.6	**5.0**	28.7	1.3	**6.3**
6.4	6.17	6.9	21.05	**3.7**	-0.01	-16.51	-52.94	10.96	250.0	**7.0**	88.3	0.0	**7.1**
8.5	0.00	0.0	0.00	**0.7**	0.00	0.00	0.00	11.11	100.0	**6.2**	53.3	0.0	**5.5**
4.9	1.31	9.7	3.20	**2.9**	0.00	0.45	5.13	5.99	92.3	**3.9**	17.7	0.0	**1.7**
8.4	0.56	3.9	0.04	**4.3**	0.16	0.43	3.07	3.77	87.8	**4.6**	29.1	2.4	**8.7**
6.9	0.84	8.3	0.28	**3.4**	0.08	0.47	2.89	3.33	83.1	**5.1**	38.5	7.4	**6.9**
5.7	1.36	9.0	1.10	**6.4**	0.18	0.97	8.89	4.18	70.1	**4.8**	27.1	6.5	**6.1**
1.9	5.23	29.5	2.18	**8.5**	0.02	1.25	11.41	6.35	79.0	**4.2**	31.4	8.6	**7.1**
7.1	0.91	3.5	1.59	**7.3**	0.16	0.97	6.59	6.27	80.9	**4.9**	34.4	4.0	**7.0**
6.4	0.41	4.4	0.60	**6.2**	0.54	0.93	8.25	4.19	73.0	**4.0**	17.9	3.5	**7.5**
8.7	0.18	1.0	0.37	**3.0**	0.24	0.16	1.57	3.25	91.8	**5.0**	24.5	3.8	**6.8**
10.0	0.12	0.1	0.00	**1.2**	0.00	-0.07	-0.27	2.10	107.1	**6.7**	70.5	0.0	**6.4**
8.5	0.33	1.4	-0.42	**6.7**	0.01	1.61	12.29	5.30	64.1	**5.5**	42.0	0.0	**5.0**
9.4	0.69	2.5	0.91	**3.0**	0.11	0.36	3.73	3.53	80.6	**4.9**	17.9	6.3	**5.9**
4.7	0.80	7.2	1.09	**1.0**	-0.09	-0.69	-7.19	4.84	96.7	**3.3**	16.4	10.3	**4.0**
7.4	1.13	3.4	0.34	**1.8**	0.02	0.18	1.96	2.52	88.5	**5.3**	26.1	0.0	**3.6**
9.6	2.12	2.0	3.22	**0.0**	-0.03	-1.71	-10.34	2.07	184.0	**7.8**	86.3	0.0	**5.2**
8.1	0.57	2.2	0.00	**0.1**	0.00	-0.82	-4.55	3.55	125.0	**5.5**	34.2	0.0	**5.8**
4.0	6.10	19.9	1.63	**6.5**	0.01	4.00	21.58	6.93	115.0	**4.9**	32.8	0.0	**3.7**
8.5	0.11	0.5	0.95	**2.3**	0.02	0.41	2.78	3.02	83.0	**4.8**	32.1	2.3	**6.4**
0.3	25.38	63.6	-0.02	**2.5**	0.11	0.56	5.64	2.02	73.9	**4.1**	13.6	8.4	**5.9**
9.3	0.27	1.3	0.00	**2.0**	0.00	0.01	0.12	3.15	97.3	**6.5**	45.4	0.0	**3.9**
7.0	0.70	5.7	1.38	**1.1**	-0.97	-0.46	-6.77	3.68	93.0	**5.2**	25.8	2.3	**4.0**
9.0	0.17	0.4	0.14	**3.7**	0.05	0.57	4.45	2.71	82.2	**5.1**	39.1	2.0	**5.2**
5.7	2.75	12.4	-0.04	**1.3**	0.00	0.01	0.18	2.73	102.2	**6.0**	36.6	0.7	**2.6**

								Asset Mix (As a % of Total Assets)					
Name	City	State	Rating	2016 Rating	2015 Rating	Total Assets ($Mil)	One Year Asset Growth	Comm-ercial Loans	Cons-umer Loans	Mort-gage Loans	Secur-ities	Capital-ization Index	Net Worth Ratio
Vantage West Credit Union	Tucson	AZ	**A-**	A-	A-	1743.2	9.71	6.5	59.2	24.8	0.3	**10.0**	11.6
VAPR Federal Credit Union	Guaynabo	PR	**C**	C	C-	223.8	5.77	0.0	55.9	3.4	26.9	**5.7**	7.8
Varex Federal Credit Union	Salt Lake City	UT	**C**	C	C	15.9	8.83	0.0	26.3	3.9	51.4	**10.0**	16.2
▼ Varick Memorial Federal Credit Union	Hempstead	NY	**E+**	D-	D-	<1	13.48	0.0	12.7	0.0	0.0	**3.8**	5.8
Vasco Federal Credit Union	Latrobe	PA	**C-**	C-	C-	24.5	2.73	0.0	11.9	0.0	3.7	**10.0**	11.4
Vatat Credit Union	Austin	TX	**C-**	C-	C-	7.5	4.03	0.0	61.2	0.0	0.0	**10.0**	16.6
Velma Federal Credit Union	Velma	OK	**D-**	D-	E+	3.0	13.61	0.0	50.9	0.0	0.0	**7.0**	9.0
Velocity Community Federal Credit Union	Palm Beach Garden	FL	**C+**	C+	C	333.9	6.65	0.0	24.0	15.5	42.6	**10.0**	11.8
▼ Velocity Credit Union	Austin	TX	**B+**	A-	A	854.5	3.48	0.3	63.6	1.1	6.9	**10.0**	12.5
Ventura County Credit Union	Ventura	CA	**C+**	C+	B	832.5	9.39	4.9	37.4	26.5	11.4	**6.0**	8.0
Veridian Credit Union	Waterloo	IA	**B+**	B+	A-	3215.9	8.93	5.8	36.3	31.3	8.6	**8.6**	10.0
Veritas Federal Credit Union	Franklin	TN	**C-**	C-	C	43.9	2.26	0.0	42.9	17.9	0.6	**6.8**	8.8
Verity Credit Union	Seattle	WA	**B+**	B+	B+	523.9	6.99	4.3	24.2	25.4	20.4	**6.6**	8.9
Vermilion School Employees Credit Union	Abbeville	LA	**C-**	C-	C-	14.7	1.76	0.0	19.8	0.0	0.0	**7.5**	9.3
Vermillion Federal Credit Union	Vermillion	SD	**B-**	B-	B-	17.0	-0.87	0.3	25.2	11.1	2.9	**10.0**	11.7
Vermont Federal Credit Union	Burlington	VT	**B-**	B-	B-	493.4	4.40	10.1	15.1	35.3	24.2	**6.5**	8.6
Vermont State Employees Credit Union	Montpelier	VT	**C+**	C+	C+	717.2	5.51	9.8	17.6	50.4	9.4	**6.7**	8.7
Vermont VA Federal Credit Union	White River Junctio	VT	**C-**	C-	D+	25.1	5.73	0.0	14.9	23.1	3.8	**7.8**	9.5
Verve, a Credit Union	Oshkosh	WI	**A-**	A-	A-	823.4	9.94	26.3	23.1	52.3	0.0	**10.0**	11.4
Via Credit Union	Marion	IN	**B**	B	B	344.1	7.62	0.5	36.1	19.2	29.4	**10.0**	12.3
Vibe Credit Union	Novi	MI	**B-**	B-	B-	534.3	6.81	6.4	10.7	44.7	13.0	**10.0**	13.0
Vibrant Credit Union	Moline	IL	**B**	B	B-	598.5	4.61	9.5	31.1	33.6	0.0	**8.7**	10.1
Vicksburg Railroad Credit Union	Vicksburg	MS	**D+**	D+	D+	11.5	-3.50	0.0	34.6	11.6	0.0	**10.0**	33.2
Vickswood Federal Credit Union	Vicksburg	MS	**C**	C	C+	11.2	2.42	0.0	18.0	0.0	0.0	**10.0**	22.4
Victor Valley Federal Credit Union	Victorville	CA	**E+**	E+	E+	9.8	4.92	0.0	19.0	0.0	0.0	**4.8**	6.8
▼ Victoria City-County Employees FCU	Victoria	TX	**D**	D+	C-	7.4	1.27	0.0	34.7	0.0	0.0	**10.0**	14.9
▲ Victoria Federal Credit Union	Victoria	TX	**C+**	C	D+	10.4	0.07	0.0	39.3	4.4	0.0	**10.0**	11.5
Victoria Teachers Federal Credit Union	Victoria	TX	**C+**	C+	C	15.3	-4.66	0.0	30.8	3.3	0.0	**10.0**	29.9
Vidor Teachers Federal Credit Union	Vidor	TX	**C**	C	C	3.1	-0.16	0.0	52.7	0.0	0.0	**10.0**	15.6
Vigo County Federal Credit Union	Terre Haute	IN	**D-**	D-	D-	37.4	3.92	0.0	55.8	1.4	15.7	**4.0**	6.0
Village Credit Union	Des Moines	IA	**B-**	B-	B-	13.3	16.84	2.9	35.5	24.3	0.0	**10.0**	12.4
Virginia Beach Postal FCU	Virginia Beach	VA	**C-**	C-	D+	7.8	2.96	0.0	48.5	0.0	0.0	**9.9**	11.0
Virginia Beach Schools FCU	Virginia Beach	VA	**D**	D	D+	96.5	5.81	3.3	23.3	4.6	26.6	**4.3**	6.8
Virginia Boxer Federal Credit Union	Richmond	VA	**D+**	D+	C-	2.7	-2.80	0.0	21.3	0.0	0.0	**10.0**	16.8
Virginia Coop Credit Union	Virginia	MN	**C-**	C-	C-	24.4	10.02	0.7	24.5	17.4	12.5	**5.9**	7.9
Virginia Credit Union, Inc.	Richmond	VA	**B+**	B+	B+	3388.2	11.20	2.5	38.9	22.6	27.9	**7.1**	9.1
Virginia Educators' Credit Union	Newport News	VA	**C+**	C+	C-	65.5	5.24	0.0	23.1	3.4	0.6	**8.2**	11.0
Virginia State University FCU	South Chesterfield	VA	**E**	E	E	8.6	3.33	2.4	55.1	6.9	0.0	**2.8**	4.9
Virginia Trailways Federal Credit Union	Charlottesville	VA	**D+**	D+	D+	2.3	-0.17	0.0	57.0	0.3	0.0	**9.4**	10.6
Virginia United Methodist Credit Union, Inc.	Glen Allen	VA	**D-**	D-	D-	15.7	-0.08	12.0	48.8	0.0	0.0	**6.7**	8.7
Viriva Community Credit Union	Warminster	PA	**C**	C	D+	68.4	8.06	12.2	11.7	21.6	25.7	**9.7**	11.2
▼ Vision Financial Federal Credit Union	Durham	NC	**D+**	C-	C	50.8	-3.30	0.0	54.2	0.0	0.0	**5.5**	7.5
Vision One Credit Union	Sacramento	CA	**B+**	B+	B+	68.6	3.24	46.3	0.0	2.3	0.0	**10.0**	14.4
Visionary Federal Credit Union	Bridgeville	PA	**D**	D	D	34.0	-3.73	0.5	29.1	0.0	29.0	**5.9**	7.9
Visions Federal Credit Union	Endicott	NY	**A-**	A-	A-	4011.2	13.36	11.6	16.1	33.4	33.2	**10.0**	12.4
Vital Federal Credit Union	Spartanburg	SC	**B**	B	B	49.2	11.12	5.9	57.1	5.9	0.0	**8.4**	9.9
Vitelco Employees Federal Credit Union	Charlotte Amalie	VI	**C-**	C-	C	2.0	2.83	0.0	47.1	0.0	0.0	**10.0**	21.9
▲ Vocal Credit Union	Helena	MT	**C-**	D+	D+	26.0	4.57	0.0	34.6	0.2	0.0	**5.9**	7.9
Vons Employees Federal Credit Union	El Monte	CA	**A+**	A+	A+	500.5	5.85	0.3	23.6	27.0	1.9	**10.0**	20.5
Voyage Federal Credit Union	Sioux Falls	SD	**B-**	B-	B-	90.4	7.56	7.3	35.8	26.5	1.9	**8.2**	9.8
Vue Community Credit Union	Bismarck	ND	**C+**	C+	B-	55.7	2.48	7.1	7.7	26.0	18.7	**9.8**	10.9
Vulcraft Employees Federal Credit Union	Saint Joe	IN	**C-**	C-	C	3.7	2.60	0.0	55.8	0.0	0.0	**10.0**	12.5
VyStar Credit Union	Jacksonville	FL	**B+**	B+	B+	6799.4	11.27	2.9	30.2	32.4	15.9	**6.7**	8.7
▼ W N M H Credit Union	Winfield	KS	**C-**	C	C+	1.8	4.93	0.0	74.8	0.0	0.0	**10.0**	12.6
W S P Credit Union	Waupun	WI	**D+**	D+	D+	2.8	-9.16	0.0	32.3	0.0	0.0	**10.0**	17.8
W T Community Federal Credit Union	Cincinnati	OH	**D-**	D-	D	4.2	26.22	0.0	71.6	0.0	0.0	**7.3**	9.2
W T N M Atlantic Federal Credit Union	Denver City	TX	**C-**	C-	D+	1.8	2.50	0.0	34.0	0.0	0.0	**10.0**	18.1
W-Bee Federal Credit Union	Wilkes-Barre	PA	**C-**	C-	C-	38.9	0.33	0.0	3.8	8.7	33.9	**5.4**	7.5
W.B.H. Employees Federal Credit Union	Paducah	KY	**C+**	C+	C+	13.3	-4.38	0.0	32.2	1.0	0.0	**10.0**	15.4
W.O.D. Federal Credit Union	Forty Fort	PA	**E+**	E+	E+	3.3	12.79	0.0	22.0	0.0	43.0	**4.9**	6.9

Asset Quality Index	Non-Performing Loans as a % of Total Loans	Non-Performing Loans as a % of Capital	Net Charge-Offs Avg Loans	Profitability Index	Net Income ($Mil)	Return on Assets	Return on Equity	Net Interest Spread	Overhead Efficiency Ratio	Liquidity Index	Liquidity Ratio	Hot Money Ratio	Stability Index
5.8	0.60	5.6	1.00	**6.5**	4.84	1.13	9.72	4.29	66.4	**3.0**	9.4	7.7	**8.7**
5.6	1.07	9.3	0.91	**2.8**	0.14	0.25	3.17	3.59	79.4	**3.2**	21.1	13.2	**4.6**
9.9	0.09	0.2	-0.25	**2.2**	0.00	0.05	0.31	2.37	99.0	**4.6**	16.4	0.9	**7.1**
0.3	32.76	57.6	0.00	**0.0**	0.00	-4.35	-69.57	6.78	100.0	**8.5**	91.8	0.0	**2.8**
9.8	1.18	2.5	0.13	**1.4**	-0.01	-0.15	-1.29	1.88	106.0	**5.8**	52.6	3.4	**5.7**
7.9	0.00	0.0	-0.07	**1.7**	0.00	0.00	0.00	3.51	103.1	**2.4**	25.5	17.8	**6.2**
2.1	2.68	17.8	0.21	**6.9**	0.01	1.08	11.99	4.96	75.0	**5.8**	38.3	0.0	**5.1**
9.9	0.22	0.8	0.40	**2.7**	0.14	0.17	1.38	3.16	92.6	**4.9**	25.9	0.7	**7.3**
5.3	1.22	9.5	1.77	**3.7**	-2.68	-1.26	-11.58	4.16	62.3	**3.0**	13.7	13.0	**8.6**
7.2	0.78	6.4	1.39	**2.0**	-0.26	-0.13	-1.53	3.85	78.0	**4.1**	19.9	5.7	**4.9**
7.5	0.54	4.8	0.27	**6.0**	8.53	1.08	10.72	2.84	70.4	**2.0**	8.5	16.4	**7.4**
5.8	0.57	4.3	1.00	**3.4**	0.05	0.46	5.35	5.32	85.6	**4.2**	26.9	6.9	**3.1**
8.9	0.24	2.4	0.53	**2.9**	0.06	0.05	0.55	3.66	93.3	**3.8**	12.1	4.1	**5.5**
8.8	0.85	2.2	0.00	**3.7**	0.03	0.72	7.67	2.10	79.7	**5.6**	36.3	0.0	**4.1**
9.2	0.05	0.2	0.05	**4.2**	0.03	0.73	6.09	3.27	79.8	**5.3**	36.2	0.0	**6.3**
7.6	0.61	4.6	0.32	**3.9**	0.59	0.48	5.64	2.86	85.0	**3.4**	9.8	9.0	**5.6**
6.0	1.00	9.3	0.19	**3.4**	0.59	0.33	3.83	3.33	89.0	**3.1**	9.6	4.1	**6.3**
9.6	0.07	0.3	-0.04	**2.9**	0.04	0.70	7.27	2.79	77.1	**5.0**	23.2	1.0	**4.0**
6.2	0.69	6.3	0.30	**7.3**	2.29	1.12	9.39	3.90	71.4	**2.7**	4.2	3.9	**8.9**
9.8	0.13	0.7	0.28	**4.4**	0.45	0.53	4.30	2.52	76.9	**4.4**	35.3	3.5	**7.5**
9.8	0.26	1.9	0.07	**2.4**	0.21	0.16	1.18	3.18	92.1	**4.5**	26.6	9.2	**7.9**
6.8	0.74	6.7	0.27	**4.4**	0.75	0.51	4.97	3.27	82.4	**4.1**	25.4	10.5	**8.2**
6.5	3.41	9.3	1.72	**1.6**	0.01	0.17	0.52	3.80	96.6	**4.7**	35.5	0.0	**6.0**
10.0	0.20	0.5	0.49	**1.9**	0.00	-0.04	-0.16	2.34	97.0	**5.5**	36.6	0.0	**6.7**
6.6	2.81	7.9	0.20	**0.4**	-0.01	-0.30	-4.17	2.54	112.1	**6.1**	31.3	0.0	**1.7**
7.3	1.54	6.5	0.68	**0.0**	-0.02	-0.99	-6.52	3.32	118.3	**4.9**	24.8	0.0	**5.8**
9.7	0.28	1.9	0.00	**2.9**	0.02	0.62	5.39	3.56	97.9	**5.3**	40.2	5.3	**4.8**
10.0	0.04	0.0	1.35	**3.0**	0.02	0.39	1.32	2.26	81.6	**5.7**	60.3	0.0	**7.3**
8.1	0.48	2.0	0.00	**2.8**	0.00	0.13	0.82	2.86	94.4	**3.6**	34.7	25.7	**7.3**
3.6	1.22	15.3	0.00	**4.7**	0.08	0.88	14.92	3.15	83.4	**4.7**	22.6	0.7	**2.1**
6.1	2.53	12.5	1.97	**4.6**	0.01	0.19	1.47	6.60	82.9	**5.1**	34.7	9.4	**6.5**
6.4	0.52	2.4	1.09	**3.6**	0.01	0.26	2.36	4.60	89.1	**5.0**	23.3	0.0	**5.3**
9.0	0.26	1.5	0.32	**0.9**	0.01	0.05	0.81	3.21	96.9	**5.4**	20.0	0.3	**1.7**
9.7	1.85	2.4	0.00	**0.5**	0.00	-0.30	-1.77	3.63	113.6	**5.4**	26.0	0.0	**5.5**
7.0	0.81	4.9	0.51	**3.6**	0.02	0.32	3.97	3.89	90.3	**5.0**	25.3	0.0	**3.0**
7.1	0.70	5.5	0.83	**4.7**	4.48	0.54	6.36	3.16	75.0	**3.2**	13.4	7.3	**5.5**
8.9	0.65	2.0	0.53	**3.8**	0.09	0.57	5.03	6.02	83.2	**7.9**	73.4	1.0	**5.4**
2.2	1.04	20.6	1.19	**3.5**	0.15	6.96	165.71	7.31	45.0	**4.7**	19.9	0.0	**0.2**
5.6	0.07	0.4	0.00	**4.5**	0.01	1.59	15.00	7.87	75.0	**5.6**	41.9	0.0	**3.0**
4.7	0.78	6.2	-0.12	**0.0**	-0.03	-0.66	-7.57	3.95	113.5	**3.6**	17.6	4.7	**3.4**
6.6	1.03	4.0	0.28	**2.2**	0.04	0.24	2.17	3.72	94.4	**4.9**	29.4	1.6	**5.3**
4.1	1.40	12.4	2.65	**0.0**	-0.30	-2.42	-30.59	5.34	76.9	**4.0**	32.1	14.2	**2.8**
6.0	0.00	0.0	-0.01	**6.9**	0.16	0.94	6.58	4.52	79.6	**2.1**	25.1	37.3	**8.6**
5.4	1.93	11.6	0.45	**1.8**	0.00	0.05	0.68	3.27	91.0	**5.5**	27.4	0.7	**2.2**
7.1	1.30	6.7	0.22	**5.0**	7.16	0.74	6.21	2.46	68.7	**3.4**	7.8	7.6	**8.8**
6.7	0.37	2.7	0.32	**6.4**	0.08	0.62	6.29	4.04	81.8	**3.8**	20.5	9.1	**5.2**
6.2	2.61	5.3	1.69	**3.0**	0.00	0.00	0.00	7.99	96.9	**6.6**	67.6	0.0	**6.8**
6.6	0.24	4.0	0.38	**4.2**	0.05	0.75	9.43	4.55	83.7	**4.2**	20.6	1.4	**3.2**
9.2	0.52	1.4	0.70	**8.1**	1.37	1.11	5.37	3.76	71.2	**3.7**	33.1	19.7	**8.8**
5.5	0.67	5.7	0.52	**4.9**	0.17	0.75	7.66	3.71	82.9	**3.7**	13.5	2.7	**5.3**
7.1	0.23	4.8	-0.11	**3.4**	0.07	0.49	4.58	3.06	86.4	**4.9**	30.0	0.9	**5.8**
7.0	0.63	3.2	0.00	**4.7**	0.01	0.78	6.13	3.67	64.3	**4.7**	27.0	0.0	**4.3**
9.1	0.29	2.4	0.40	**5.3**	14.02	0.84	9.62	2.87	70.2	**4.4**	25.7	7.3	**7.3**
5.0	2.34	13.7	1.72	**3.7**	0.00	-0.23	-1.78	4.11	81.8	**4.4**	24.4	0.0	**8.2**
5.4	7.93	15.3	1.90	**2.0**	0.00	0.14	0.82	2.17	71.4	**6.2**	70.5	0.0	**5.7**
1.6	3.14	27.3	2.07	**3.5**	0.01	0.59	6.30	4.20	68.9	**3.6**	13.4	0.0	**3.9**
4.6	7.74	18.3	2.17	**2.8**	0.00	0.00	0.00	4.33	89.5	**5.8**	69.9	0.0	**6.1**
10.0	0.02	0.0	0.00	**2.0**	0.01	0.12	1.66	1.94	88.2	**7.8**	63.4	0.0	**3.2**
9.8	0.00	0.0	0.48	**1.6**	0.00	0.03	0.20	3.24	96.5	**5.7**	37.4	1.0	**7.0**
9.3	0.11	0.4	0.00	**0.4**	0.00	-0.26	-3.54	3.42	109.5	**6.5**	35.4	0.0	**2.0**

Name	City	State	Rating	2016 Rating	2015 Rating	Total Assets ($Mil)	One Year Asset Growth	Asset Mix (As a % of Total Assets) Comm-ercial Loans	Cons-umer Loans	Mort-gage Loans	Secur-ities	Capital-ization Index	Net Worth Ratio
Wabellco Federal Credit Union	Washington	PA	**C-**	C-	D+	12.6	3.34	0.0	10.8	0.0	4.0	**8.4**	10.0
Waco Federal Credit Union	Waco	TX	**D**	D	D	16.3	7.27	0.0	25.1	1.0	0.0	**5.5**	7.5
▲ Waconized Federal Credit Union	Waco	TX	**C-**	D+	D	4.5	0.11	0.0	41.9	0.0	0.0	**10.0**	23.4
Wadena Federal Credit Union	Wadena	MN	**B-**	B-	B-	13.9	1.59	0.0	15.9	1.3	0.0	**10.0**	22.1
Waialua Federal Credit Union	Waialua	HI	**B-**	B-	C+	49.8	0.55	0.0	9.4	5.7	5.9	**10.0**	13.6
Wailuku Federal Credit Union	Kahului	HI	**A-**	A-	A-	50.9	3.63	7.6	11.4	22.3	3.0	**10.0**	14.9
Wakarusa Valley Credit Union	Lawrence	KS	**D**	D	D	3.4	-6.25	0.0	55.1	0.0	0.0	**10.0**	11.6
▲ Wakefern Federal Credit Union	Elizabeth	NJ	**D+**	D	D+	9.9	4.34	0.0	11.1	0.9	34.7	**10.0**	20.0
Wakefield Town Employees FCU	Wakefield	MA	**C**	C	C	3.8	6.31	0.0	27.7	0.0	0.0	**10.0**	14.2
▼ Wakota Federal Credit Union	South Saint Paul	MN	**C-**	C	C-	28.4	13.46	0.0	52.2	3.6	0.9	**6.9**	8.9
Walker County Educators FCU	Chickamauga	GA	**B-**	B-	B-	10.7	1.64	0.0	50.7	3.9	0.0	**10.0**	28.0
Walker County Federal Credit Union	Huntsville	TX	**B**	B	B-	31.5	7.49	0.0	47.8	0.0	1.9	**9.8**	10.9
Walled Lake School Employees FCU	Walled Lake	MI	**C+**	C+	C+	106.3	6.19	0.1	9.5	14.6	47.8	**9.5**	11.0
Waltham Municipal Employees Credit Union	Waltham	MA	**D+**	D+	D+	9.3	2.63	0.0	19.8	0.0	0.0	**10.0**	16.8
Walton County Teachers FCU	Defuniak Springs	FL	**D**	D	D	21.7	7.52	0.0	31.0	1.8	0.0	**5.5**	7.5
Wanigas Credit Union	Saginaw	MI	**A**	A	A	326.5	5.33	0.0	24.0	36.3	22.2	**10.0**	13.2
Ward County Credit Union	Monahans	TX	**D+**	D+	D+	16.0	1.07	0.7	22.7	0.0	60.0	**6.9**	8.9
▼ Ward Federal Credit Union	Philadelphia	PA	**E+**	D-	D-	<1	8.40	0.0	22.5	0.0	0.0	**6.5**	8.5
Ware County School Employees FCU	Waycross	GA	**D**	D	D-	4.3	-2.22	0.0	32.7	3.0	0.0	**7.2**	9.1
Warren Credit Union	Waterloo	IA	**C-**	C-	C	4.4	4.45	0.0	15.9	0.0	46.1	**10.0**	23.1
Warren Municipal Federal Credit Union	Warren	MI	**D-**	D-	E	17.3	-0.72	0.0	15.2	5.8	58.3	**4.9**	6.9
Wasatch Peaks Federal Credit Union	Ogden	UT	**B-**	B-	B-	299.8	5.42	13.6	26.2	28.3	4.8	**8.7**	10.1
Washington Area Teachers FCU	Washington	PA	**D-**	D-	C-	62.5	1.88	0.8	14.8	7.3	33.5	**6.6**	9.1
Washington County Teachers FCU	Hagerstown	MD	**B+**	B+	B+	65.0	5.83	0.0	16.8	12.5	0.0	**10.0**	13.7
▲ Washington Educational Association FCU	Franklinton	LA	**C**	C-	D	1.0	3.30	0.0	52.7	0.0	0.0	**10.0**	13.3
Washington Gas Light FCU	Springfield	VA	**D+**	D+	C	100.3	0.09	0.0	21.7	7.1	35.3	**10.0**	16.0
▼ Washington State Employees Credit Union	Olympia	WA	**B+**	A-	A-	2644.9	6.59	8.2	39.2	20.4	9.5	**9.0**	10.4
Washington Typographic FCU	Washington	DC	**E+**	E+	D	3.1	-8.88	0.0	51.0	0.0	0.0	**3.2**	5.2
Washtenaw Federal Credit Union	Ypsilanti	MI	**D+**	D+	C-	42.0	5.33	2.3	26.7	23.3	24.8	**5.5**	7.5
Water and Power Community Credit Union	Los Angeles	CA	**B**	B	B	627.9	8.92	1.2	13.7	23.5	46.3	**6.4**	8.4
Waterbury Connecticut Teacher FCU	Middlebury	CT	**B+**	B+	B+	232.5	-0.96	0.0	34.0	2.7	0.0	**10.0**	13.7
Waterbury Police Federal Credit Union	Waterbury	CT	**C-**	C-	D	6.4	7.23	0.0	32.4	0.0	0.0	**10.0**	13.2
Waterbury Postal Employees FCU	Waterbury	CT	**C**	C	C	11.2	1.44	0.0	13.6	0.0	0.0	**10.0**	20.2
▲ Waterfront Federal Credit Union	Seattle	WA	**C**	C-	C-	62.1	6.74	0.0	30.5	6.2	38.1	**5.3**	7.7
Waterloo Firemen's Credit Union	Waterloo	IA	**C-**	C-	C-	1.9	-6.83	0.0	78.9	0.0	0.0	**10.0**	13.7
Watertown Municipal Credit Union	Watertown	MA	**D+**	D+	D	11.6	-1.04	0.0	4.9	10.4	1.7	**10.0**	28.6
Watertown Postal Federal Credit Union	Watertown	NY	**D+**	D+	D	8.1	0.83	0.0	20.1	0.0	0.0	**9.2**	10.5
Watsonville Hospital FCU	Watsonville	CA	**C+**	C+	C	12.0	-3.06	0.0	25.9	0.0	0.0	**10.0**	12.5
Waukegan Municipal Employees CU	Waukegan	IL	**C**	C	C+	1.5	4.00	0.0	57.7	0.0	0.0	**10.0**	11.1
Wauna Federal Credit Union	Clatskanie	OR	**B**	B	B	222.6	11.91	9.4	34.8	33.3	12.0	**6.3**	8.3
Wave Federal Credit Union	Warwick	RI	**C+**	C+	C-	112.0	3.44	0.7	10.9	26.4	0.4	**10.0**	11.7
WAWA Employees Credit Union	Media	PA	**D+**	D+	D+	19.1	4.64	0.0	21.0	1.6	5.2	**5.6**	7.6
Way Credit Union	New Knoxville	OH	**D+**	D+	D+	13.6	-3.99	0.0	0.0	0.0	71.0	**6.8**	8.8
Waycose Federal Credit Union	Huntington	WV	**C-**	C-	C-	3.4	5.61	0.0	52.0	0.0	0.0	**10.0**	12.8
Wayland Temple Baptist FCU	Philadelphia	PA	**C**	C	C	<1	0.94	0.0	9.8	0.0	0.0	**10.0**	15.0
Wayne County Community FCU	Smithville	OH	**D**	D	D+	48.8	2.65	0.4	12.7	5.5	65.8	**5.4**	7.4
▲ Wayne County Federal Credit Union	Richmond	IN	**C-**	D+	D-	11.3	2.01	0.0	23.0	2.9	1.8	**6.6**	8.6
Wayne-Westland Federal Credit Union	Westland	MI	**C+**	C+	B-	98.1	6.93	0.7	19.9	7.6	47.3	**6.6**	9.3
Waynesboro Employees Credit Union, Inc.	Waynesboro	VA	**E+**	E+	D-	3.8	-4.39	0.0	54.5	0.0	0.0	**7.8**	9.6
WBRT Federal Credit Union	Port Allen	LA	**D+**	D+	D+	2.5	1.85	0.0	57.3	0.0	0.0	**10.0**	23.7
WCG Employees Credit Union	Martin	TN	**C-**	C-	C	1.0	2.85	0.0	62.5	0.0	0.0	**10.0**	17.9
▲ WCLA Credit Union	Olympia	WA	**B+**	B	B	54.9	14.82	82.2	0.8	9.8	8.6	**10.0**	11.9
WCU Credit Union	Decatur	AL	**C**	C	C-	24.8	2.38	0.0	37.9	8.1	12.1	**7.8**	9.6
▼ We Florida Financial	Margate	FL	**C**	C+	A-	538.0	1.76	2.2	34.9	12.5	15.3	**7.6**	9.5
WEA Credit Union	Madison	WI	**C**	C	D+	27.7	4.41	5.4	29.6	23.3	3.6	**9.9**	10.9
▼ Weatherhead CC Federal Credit Union	Columbia City	IN	**C-**	C	D	14.4	11.45	0.0	39.6	0.0	0.0	**8.3**	9.9
Weber State Federal Credit Union	Ogden	UT	**B**	B	B-	110.3	9.88	9.3	32.6	40.8	5.6	**7.9**	9.6
Webster City Municipal Credit Union	Webster City	IA	**C**	C	C-	<1	-1.91	0.0	29.5	0.0	0.0	**10.0**	34.3
Webster Federal Credit Union	Webster	NY	**D-**	D-	D-	16.2	8.58	0.0	32.8	5.3	0.0	**5.3**	7.3
Webster First Federal Credit Union	Worcester	MA	**A**	A	A	872.0	3.58	10.5	6.6	64.6	9.3	**10.0**	19.3

Asset Quality Index	Non-Performing Loans as a % of Total Loans	Non-Performing Loans as a % of Capital	Net Charge-Offs Avg Loans	Profitability Index	Net Income ($Mil)	Return on Assets	Return on Equity	Net Interest Spread	Overhead Efficiency Ratio	Liquidity Index	Liquidity Ratio	Hot Money Ratio	Stability Index
8.4	0.70	2.1	-0.10	**2.5**	0.01	0.38	3.83	2.37	89.2	**5.0**	17.8	0.0	**4.3**
9.8	0.00	0.0	0.00	**2.3**	0.00	0.05	0.65	3.39	98.7	**5.5**	37.0	8.5	**2.6**
7.6	2.63	5.7	1.39	**4.8**	0.01	0.89	3.81	5.89	79.0	**4.8**	32.1	0.0	**4.3**
8.4	5.69	4.8	-0.15	**3.7**	0.02	0.58	2.62	2.58	76.2	**6.0**	30.8	0.0	**7.2**
10.0	0.36	0.6	0.03	**3.8**	0.07	0.59	4.55	2.06	70.9	**5.0**	29.0	0.0	**6.4**
7.3	1.45	5.9	0.10	**5.9**	0.08	0.62	4.14	4.06	83.9	**3.2**	7.8	11.5	**7.7**
6.6	0.62	3.0	3.06	**1.2**	0.00	0.23	2.06	3.77	97.0	**3.4**	12.5	10.5	**4.2**
10.0	0.17	0.1	0.34	**1.0**	0.01	0.20	1.01	2.29	88.9	**5.5**	26.3	0.0	**5.3**
10.0	0.00	0.0	0.00	**2.3**	0.00	0.32	2.22	2.94	88.0	**4.8**	10.6	0.0	**6.7**
4.1	1.69	11.7	0.97	**4.2**	0.02	0.29	3.19	3.99	82.2	**3.7**	24.2	8.5	**3.7**
8.1	0.27	1.0	1.18	**6.1**	0.03	1.14	4.02	5.21	58.9	**3.9**	38.1	5.2	**5.7**
7.0	0.48	2.3	0.20	**6.7**	0.08	1.00	9.09	4.78	79.4	**5.7**	40.4	3.5	**5.5**
10.0	0.14	0.4	0.18	**3.4**	0.14	0.52	4.94	2.44	79.9	**5.0**	18.0	2.9	**6.7**
10.0	0.00	0.0	0.00	**1.0**	-0.01	-0.22	-1.28	2.37	110.6	**5.9**	38.1	0.0	**6.8**
6.2	1.13	5.5	-0.05	**1.9**	0.00	-0.08	-0.99	4.56	101.5	**7.0**	52.4	0.0	**3.4**
9.5	0.40	2.0	0.39	**5.9**	0.74	0.91	7.00	3.64	76.0	**3.8**	7.5	3.2	**8.7**
8.5	1.68	4.9	0.09	**1.7**	0.00	0.03	0.28	2.80	95.6	**4.5**	28.7	14.3	**3.8**
0.3	24.14	58.3	0.00	**1.6**	0.00	0.00	0.00	12.50	100.0	**8.1**	82.2	0.0	**2.8**
8.3	0.42	2.3	-0.16	**3.5**	0.00	0.37	4.08	3.67	90.6	**3.3**	34.7	26.4	**2.3**
8.3	0.39	0.5	-0.26	**2.3**	0.00	0.18	0.79	3.14	94.3	**5.2**	37.1	0.0	**7.2**
10.0	0.18	0.6	0.35	**1.2**	0.00	-0.07	-1.00	2.83	101.5	**5.0**	14.3	0.0	**1.7**
8.8	0.24	2.2	0.30	**3.8**	0.26	0.35	3.53	3.63	87.6	**3.4**	13.9	9.3	**6.2**
7.2	1.04	4.5	0.17	**0.3**	-0.08	-0.49	-5.62	3.38	112.5	**6.1**	47.9	2.8	**3.8**
9.9	0.73	1.8	0.33	**2.4**	-0.01	-0.07	-0.54	2.38	92.6	**7.2**	61.5	1.7	**7.1**
8.6	0.18	0.7	0.00	**4.7**	0.00	1.19	8.76	6.08	80.0	**4.8**	16.7	0.0	**4.3**
9.2	1.14	3.3	0.51	**1.2**	0.01	0.04	0.24	3.08	92.5	**4.3**	24.4	11.0	**5.9**
7.3	0.48	4.2	1.32	**5.2**	3.37	0.52	4.95	4.48	71.6	**4.0**	15.4	2.6	**7.9**
0.0	11.29	59.9	-1.49	**0.7**	-0.03	-3.75	-68.18	4.09	122.2	**5.4**	26.7	0.0	**2.8**
6.1	0.91	6.6	0.39	**1.1**	-0.01	-0.11	-1.39	3.43	98.3	**4.2**	14.6	1.2	**2.4**
8.2	0.83	3.8	0.53	**4.5**	1.17	0.76	9.20	3.16	76.8	**5.0**	17.0	3.6	**5.9**
9.8	0.42	2.4	0.19	**4.5**	0.34	0.58	4.34	3.25	77.6	**4.2**	30.3	2.1	**8.1**
8.4	1.24	3.4	-0.33	**2.1**	0.00	0.26	1.90	4.73	119.4	**6.9**	63.2	0.0	**5.8**
8.7	5.41	4.5	-0.21	**2.7**	0.02	0.65	3.21	2.24	72.2	**7.3**	61.8	0.0	**6.6**
9.6	0.04	0.3	0.30	**4.4**	0.11	0.74	10.19	3.67	82.4	**4.7**	23.1	0.4	**2.7**
8.1	0.00	0.0	0.00	**2.5**	0.00	0.21	1.56	2.52	90.9	**3.5**	17.6	0.0	**6.2**
10.0	0.42	0.2	0.00	**0.6**	-0.02	-0.62	-2.17	2.44	146.0	**7.5**	66.9	0.0	**6.8**
7.5	1.32	3.0	0.00	**2.8**	0.02	0.74	7.11	1.78	57.1	**5.2**	31.1	0.0	**4.2**
9.5	0.42	1.3	0.00	**5.4**	0.02	0.77	6.15	4.67	80.1	**4.6**	13.4	6.4	**5.6**
8.3	0.45	2.4	0.00	**4.6**	0.00	0.28	2.48	4.12	92.3	**5.1**	42.8	0.0	**4.3**
7.0	0.47	5.8	0.43	**4.5**	0.21	0.39	4.61	4.14	85.9	**3.3**	8.1	3.4	**5.6**
10.0	0.16	0.7	0.16	**2.8**	0.05	0.20	1.65	3.03	93.7	**4.7**	26.4	2.5	**6.8**
9.3	0.51	1.8	0.00	**2.5**	0.01	0.20	2.50	2.86	94.8	**7.0**	52.9	3.3	**3.4**
9.9	NA	0.0	NA	**1.8**	0.01	0.14	1.68	1.23	87.8	**6.0**	45.7	1.6	**1.2**
6.9	0.74	2.7	0.00	**5.0**	0.01	1.04	7.42	4.97	69.7	**6.0**	54.4	0.0	**4.3**
10.0	0.00	0.0	0.00	**1.8**	0.00	0.00	0.00	2.74	200.0	**8.1**	101.1	0.0	**7.5**
7.3	1.86	5.6	0.28	**0.7**	-0.01	-0.11	-1.44	2.21	96.4	**5.5**	33.8	1.8	**2.3**
10.0	0.00	0.0	0.00	**3.3**	0.03	0.91	11.39	2.49	69.5	**5.6**	32.7	0.0	**3.5**
5.9	2.04	10.6	0.65	**3.6**	0.13	0.56	6.40	2.96	84.1	**5.0**	18.3	3.2	**3.9**
2.0	3.79	21.3	2.46	**3.6**	0.00	0.42	4.42	5.92	94.2	**5.3**	43.2	0.0	**1.7**
3.8	7.58	19.8	1.33	**0.3**	-0.01	-2.29	-9.41	8.46	102.2	**6.2**	45.9	0.0	**5.4**
8.6	0.00	0.0	0.00	**1.5**	0.00	0.00	0.00	2.57	100.0	**5.5**	44.2	0.0	**7.1**
5.8	0.19	1.3	-0.01	**9.3**	0.23	1.69	14.15	3.82	50.7	**0.8**	9.7	52.4	**8.2**
9.7	0.06	0.3	0.38	**2.3**	0.01	0.11	1.18	3.74	93.6	**4.8**	22.1	5.4	**5.4**
6.7	1.14	7.7	1.91	**1.2**	-0.16	-0.12	-1.24	3.45	80.4	**3.6**	11.7	10.4	**5.5**
8.0	0.21	1.1	0.19	**2.9**	0.03	0.43	3.84	3.08	85.2	**4.8**	31.0	0.0	**5.4**
9.0	0.45	2.2	0.00	**2.0**	0.01	0.14	1.41	2.66	95.7	**5.1**	24.0	0.0	**4.7**
9.4	0.19	1.6	0.14	**4.2**	0.11	0.43	4.33	3.74	88.4	**3.0**	7.1	5.1	**6.1**
7.5	7.35	6.1	0.00	**5.6**	0.00	0.87	2.53	4.62	80.0	**4.9**	22.8	0.0	**4.3**
9.7	0.00	0.0	0.51	**1.1**	0.00	-0.08	-1.02	3.40	101.4	**5.0**	25.2	0.0	**2.8**
7.9	0.84	4.2	0.03	**9.2**	2.72	1.26	6.84	3.70	66.0	**3.1**	9.3	7.0	**10.0**

Name	City	State	Rating	2016 Rating	2015 Rating	Total Assets ($Mil)	One Year Asset Growth	Asset Mix (As a % of Total Assets) Commercial Loans	Consumer Loans	Mortgage Loans	Securities	Capitalization Index	Net Worth Ratio
Webster United Federal Credit Union	Minden	LA	D	D	D	4.1	-2.01	0.0	59.6	0.0	0.0	10.0	15.4
WEE Federal Credit Union	Parkersburg	WV	B-	B-	B-	18.2	4.68	0.0	22.1	14.1	0.0	10.0	11.0
Welcome Federal Credit Union	Morrisville	NC	C+	C+	C	88.7	-1.83	0.8	35.6	14.7	7.6	10.0	12.5
Weld Schools Credit Union	Greeley	CO	C+	C+	C	70.5	6.22	0.0	22.5	10.1	0.0	6.3	8.3
Wellesley Municipal Employees FCU	Wellesley	MA	D	D	D+	29.1	-1.92	0.0	18.3	13.1	0.0	9.6	10.7
Wellspring Federal Credit Union	Bridge City	TX	C-	C-	C	47.6	9.06	0.0	49.1	8.2	0.0	6.0	8.0
Wenatchee Valley Federal Credit Union	East Wenatchee	WA	D	D	D	32.8	5.49	0.0	26.2	2.6	5.2	5.2	7.2
▼ Weokie Credit Union	Oklahoma City	OK	B+	A-	B+	1104.6	6.69	9.3	20.4	30.2	35.0	10.0	11.0
Wepawaug-Flagg Federal Credit Union	Hamden	CT	C+	C+	B-	115.2	3.81	2.0	9.9	10.8	47.7	9.0	10.4
WEPCO Federal Credit Union	Bloomington	MD	C+	C+	C+	216.9	4.68	0.5	51.3	13.3	8.5	8.1	9.8
▲ WES Credit Union	Willoughby	OH	C-	D+	D	11.5	5.54	0.0	29.4	0.0	44.2	8.4	9.9
Wescom Central Credit Union	Pasadena	CA	B-	B-	B-	3646.0	10.01	2.9	15.0	30.0	35.8	5.1	7.6
Wesla Federal Credit Union	Shreveport	LA	D	D	D	83.0	1.38	0.0	15.8	4.6	0.0	10.0	14.9
West Branch Valley Federal Credit Union	Williamsport	PA	D+	D+	D	39.0	2.66	0.0	17.2	18.1	15.6	5.1	7.2
▼ West Coast Federal Employees CU	Sarasota	FL	D+	C-	C-	31.2	1.48	0.0	16.2	6.0	29.1	10.0	12.5
West Community Credit Union	O'Fallon	MO	B-	B-	B-	192.0	8.12	7.7	33.2	22.4	1.0	6.5	8.5
West Financial Credit Union	Medina	MN	C+	C+	C	28.4	5.85	4.5	16.7	33.4	0.0	7.8	9.5
West Hudson Teachers FCU	North Arlington	NJ	D+	D+	D	7.3	1.87	0.0	12.6	0.0	0.0	8.9	10.3
West Jefferson Federal Credit Union	Marrero	LA	E+	E+	E+	6.2	2.06	0.0	55.5	0.0	0.0	4.1	6.1
West Maui Community Federal Credit Union	Lahaina	HI	C-	C-	C-	38.2	5.28	0.0	18.4	0.0	16.3	10.0	21.1
West Metro Schools Credit Union	Hopkins	MN	B+	B+	B+	29.2	8.84	0.0	30.5	3.6	0.0	10.0	18.1
West Michigan Credit Union	Grand Rapids	MI	A	A	A	163.6	9.82	0.2	24.4	11.1	28.1	10.0	16.3
West Michigan Postal Service FCU	Muskegon	MI	E+	E+	E+	6.2	11.09	0.0	42.1	0.0	23.9	6.0	8.0
West Monroe Federal Credit Union	West Monroe	LA	D+	D+	D+	4.9	0.63	0.0	36.7	8.5	0.0	9.8	10.9
▲ West Oahu Community Federal Credit Union	Waianae	HI	B	B-	B-	41.2	10.14	0.0	14.6	5.7	13.4	10.0	12.2
West Orange Municipal FCU	West Orange	NJ	E+	E+	E+	6.8	-1.73	1.9	47.7	1.9	0.0	7.3	9.2
West Penn P&P Federal Credit Union	Beaver	PA	D+	D+	D+	11.6	0.26	0.0	19.4	3.7	0.0	10.0	16.9
▲ West Side Baptist Church FCU	Saint Louis	MO	C	C-	C	<1	-2.44	0.0	9.7	0.0	0.0	10.0	21.3
▲ West Springfield Federal Credit Union	West Springfield	MA	C-	D+	D+	29.3	4.50	0.0	9.4	7.6	27.9	6.0	8.0
West Tennessee Credit Union	Memphis	TN	D	D	D-	17.6	5.19	0.4	42.9	1.8	0.0	8.1	9.8
▼ West Texas Educators Credit Union	Odessa	TX	D+	C-	C-	54.2	-1.95	0.3	29.7	16.7	16.8	6.0	8.0
West Virginia Central Credit Union	Parkersburg	WV	A-	A-	B+	166.8	11.20	7.1	29.4	28.2	12.2	7.8	9.5
West Virginia Federal Credit Union	South Charleston	WV	C	C	C	144.7	-3.66	7.6	19.0	24.1	13.1	10.0	12.1
West Virginia State Convention CU	Hilltop	WV	D	D	D	<1	39.27	0.0	13.2	0.0	0.0	5.9	7.9
West York Area School District Empls FCU	York	PA	E+	E+	E+	5.0	2.59	0.0	24.4	0.8	0.0	6.1	8.1
West-Aircomm Federal Credit Union	Beaver	PA	C+	C+	C+	225.0	5.79	3.6	29.6	12.8	5.2	6.4	8.5
Westacres Credit Union	West Bloomfield	MI	C-	C-	D-	7.4	-5.08	0.0	3.8	20.7	32.2	10.0	11.8
Westar Federal Credit Union	Camillus	NY	C+	C+	C-	27.5	9.23	0.0	20.6	3.1	0.0	6.7	8.8
Westby Co-op Credit Union	Westby	WI	A	A	A-	456.5	6.57	38.9	19.6	40.8	7.1	10.0	15.7
WESTconsin Credit Union	Menomonie	WI	A-	A-	A-	1121.1	8.84	16.6	23.2	35.9	7.7	10.0	11.8
WestEdge Federal Credit Union	Bellingham	WA	C+	C+	B-	58.7	7.16	0.0	23.7	13.7	5.1	10.0	13.5
Westerly Community Credit Union	Westerly	RI	B-	B-	B-	257.2	9.77	11.1	7.6	57.0	3.2	7.0	9.1
Western Connecticut Federal Credit Union	Bethel	CT	E	E	E-	25.6	4.71	0.3	15.3	37.5	17.8	3.7	5.8
Western Cooperative Credit Union	Williston	ND	B+	B+	B+	328.6	-1.52	29.1	17.1	15.6	19.3	10.0	11.3
Western Districts Members Credit Union	Grand Rapids	MI	B+	B+	B+	40.5	2.35	0.0	17.5	12.1	44.2	10.0	18.0
Western Division Federal Credit Union	Williamsville	NY	B+	B+	B	141.7	4.20	0.0	12.8	18.1	3.7	10.0	14.8
Western Healthcare Federal Credit Union	Concord	CA	C	C	C+	39.9	6.10	9.7	33.9	26.4	0.0	6.6	8.6
▼ Western Heritage Credit Union	Alliance	NE	D+	C-	C	74.2	-9.80	0.0	43.0	9.0	15.6	7.3	9.4
Western Illinois Credit Union	Macomb	IL	C-	C-	C-	25.0	8.87	0.0	66.0	3.1	0.0	6.2	8.2
▲ Western Illinois School Employees CU	Quincy	IL	C	C-	C-	23.1	3.15	0.0	41.2	0.0	0.0	8.2	9.8
Western Indiana Credit Union	Sullivan	IN	C+	C+	C	24.5	4.43	46.2	4.8	42.5	0.0	10.0	15.0
Western New York Federal Credit Union	West Seneca	NY	B-	B-	B-	50.1	8.41	0.0	30.0	20.3	4.6	7.2	9.1
Western Region Federal Credit Union	Cleveland	OH	C+	C+	B-	14.0	2.68	0.0	38.4	0.0	30.3	10.0	14.3
▲ Western Rockies Federal Credit Union	Grand Junction	CO	D+	D	D+	124.8	6.50	0.5	26.4	13.6	33.4	5.6	8.3
Western Springs Federal Credit Union	Western Springs	IL	C	C	C	3.4	3.97	0.0	30.5	0.0	0.0	10.0	12.9
Western States Regional FCU	Los Angeles	CA	C+	C+	C+	<1	7.62	0.0	29.2	0.0	0.0	10.0	31.7
Western Sun Federal Credit Union	Broken Arrow	OK	B	B	B	167.2	9.76	0.2	54.3	2.8	0.0	10.0	11.7
Western Vista Federal Credit Union	Cheyenne	WY	B-	B-	B	144.0	-0.09	3.5	36.1	13.4	20.4	10.0	12.9
Westerra Credit Union	Denver	CO	B+	B+	B+	1473.8	7.40	8.5	42.3	24.9	10.2	10.0	11.5
WesTex Community Credit Union	Kermit	TX	A-	A-	B+	79.0	8.66	2.3	31.0	15.3	21.4	10.0	11.8

Arrows denote recent upgrades ▲ or downgrades ▼

Asset Quality Index	Non-Performing Loans as a % of Total Loans	Non-Performing Loans as a % of Capital	Net Charge-Offs Avg Loans	Profitability Index	Net Income ($Mil)	Return on Assets	Return on Equity	Net Interest Spread	Overhead Efficiency Ratio	Liquidity Index	Liquidity Ratio	Hot Money Ratio	Stability Index
3.3	4.55	16.2	-0.55	**0.0**	-0.03	-3.07	-19.44	5.35	69.2	**4.5**	15.0	0.0	**5.0**
6.4	3.62	11.8	0.06	**5.6**	0.04	0.95	8.47	4.02	73.8	**6.5**	58.3	6.6	**6.6**
6.8	1.81	9.2	0.25	**2.5**	0.03	0.15	1.16	4.33	94.5	**4.9**	28.0	0.9	**6.0**
9.9	0.05	0.3	-0.01	**4.2**	0.13	0.72	8.62	3.00	80.0	**5.2**	31.6	1.3	**4.2**
10.0	0.14	0.7	0.14	**1.3**	0.01	0.10	1.14	1.93	93.4	**4.7**	28.2	2.3	**4.1**
4.5	0.81	6.7	0.71	**3.1**	0.02	0.15	1.79	5.37	90.6	**4.1**	26.9	11.2	**3.0**
6.4	0.45	5.0	0.48	**0.9**	0.00	-0.01	-0.17	4.49	106.5	**6.0**	40.6	2.8	**2.1**
9.7	0.25	1.5	0.26	**4.9**	1.65	0.61	5.44	2.21	75.9	**4.6**	49.8	12.9	**8.3**
7.1	1.43	8.5	0.16	**3.2**	0.12	0.43	4.08	3.23	86.9	**5.0**	20.5	2.8	**6.7**
6.3	0.52	4.1	1.16	**1.9**	-0.16	-0.30	-3.19	3.91	77.6	**4.7**	22.4	1.4	**5.8**
6.8	1.94	5.7	0.82	**1.9**	0.00	0.07	0.69	2.68	96.3	**5.2**	25.8	0.0	**3.9**
9.6	0.28	2.2	0.17	**3.9**	4.08	0.48	6.63	3.00	88.1	**3.7**	16.0	9.7	**4.5**
10.0	0.69	1.5	0.89	**0.2**	-0.06	-0.27	-2.04	2.42	97.7	**5.4**	34.5	0.0	**5.2**
10.0	0.02	0.1	0.25	**2.1**	0.03	0.31	4.36	3.22	89.0	**4.5**	19.8	3.2	**2.8**
9.6	1.10	2.8	0.33	**0.7**	-0.02	-0.21	-1.69	3.30	106.1	**5.1**	18.9	0.9	**5.6**
6.6	0.78	8.2	0.30	**5.1**	0.32	0.67	8.62	4.61	81.2	**2.8**	5.0	4.0	**5.2**
7.3	0.54	4.1	0.17	**5.3**	0.04	0.56	5.82	5.26	87.4	**3.7**	11.9	3.2	**5.0**
6.1	6.93	10.3	0.00	**1.7**	0.00	0.00	0.00	2.95	94.9	**7.3**	60.6	0.0	**4.3**
0.7	3.84	35.4	0.00	**2.0**	0.00	0.07	1.06	4.28	97.5	**5.8**	36.5	0.0	**1.8**
10.0	0.20	0.2	0.06	**1.1**	0.01	0.06	0.31	2.41	97.3	**5.1**	33.0	3.7	**6.6**
9.9	0.71	1.8	0.51	**4.4**	0.03	0.47	2.58	3.36	79.7	**4.8**	41.5	3.7	**7.5**
9.6	0.71	2.0	0.43	**6.5**	0.37	0.92	5.57	3.20	71.9	**4.5**	21.2	2.9	**8.9**
7.1	0.87	7.1	1.42	**1.1**	-0.01	-0.39	-4.82	4.00	89.0	**3.5**	40.4	11.1	**1.0**
5.2	2.69	13.3	0.15	**2.7**	0.00	0.24	2.25	4.28	91.8	**4.9**	17.9	0.0	**5.7**
9.7	1.03	1.7	1.63	**4.6**	0.08	0.85	6.34	2.84	77.8	**6.6**	46.5	2.5	**5.6**
4.3	1.51	9.2	2.28	**2.6**	0.01	0.30	3.23	5.49	88.4	**4.4**	13.4	0.0	**1.7**
7.1	4.40	9.1	0.97	**1.2**	0.00	0.00	0.00	2.99	100.0	**6.3**	55.0	1.1	**6.6**
10.0	0.00	0.0	0.00	**4.6**	0.00	4.91	24.62	3.69	200.0	**8.1**	98.4	0.0	**5.4**
8.6	0.26	1.0	0.18	**2.4**	0.02	0.28	3.42	2.39	93.4	**5.5**	41.2	1.6	**3.1**
7.7	0.54	2.6	1.45	**0.3**	-0.02	-0.50	-5.10	3.50	92.8	**4.1**	26.5	9.8	**4.4**
5.8	1.50	8.6	1.82	**1.4**	-0.08	-0.60	-7.43	3.63	94.9	**4.7**	21.1	2.2	**2.5**
7.3	0.59	4.4	0.09	**7.0**	0.41	1.02	11.00	2.69	71.5	**3.9**	15.8	5.6	**7.0**
7.2	1.54	7.3	0.18	**2.0**	0.05	0.13	1.15	2.97	90.3	**4.2**	20.7	3.1	**7.0**
5.5	5.13	8.7	0.00	**4.9**	0.00	1.50	18.18	3.45	100.0	**8.0**	77.9	0.0	**2.3**
8.6	0.53	2.4	0.00	**1.6**	0.00	0.00	0.00	2.95	96.9	**6.1**	55.4	0.0	**2.8**
9.7	0.14	0.9	0.12	**2.8**	0.20	0.36	4.23	2.54	84.5	**4.5**	39.0	11.0	**5.3**
10.0	0.31	0.7	0.00	**0.6**	0.00	-0.22	-1.82	1.75	121.1	**7.1**	49.1	0.0	**5.2**
9.5	0.02	0.1	0.00	**3.9**	0.03	0.48	5.53	3.15	85.7	**4.8**	21.2	0.0	**4.6**
7.1	0.88	4.4	0.33	**9.8**	1.52	1.34	8.63	4.00	66.3	**3.4**	12.9	5.7	**9.6**
6.5	0.90	5.7	0.22	**6.9**	1.89	0.68	5.86	3.63	82.3	**3.8**	14.4	7.2	**9.4**
9.1	1.07	3.1	0.69	**3.1**	0.05	0.37	2.68	3.03	82.7	**4.5**	26.0	6.2	**6.4**
6.9	0.40	4.9	0.04	**4.1**	0.23	0.36	4.32	3.47	91.1	**2.5**	8.2	8.9	**5.8**
1.7	2.90	36.2	1.82	**2.5**	0.00	0.00	0.00	3.87	87.6	**3.9**	12.3	2.8	**0.0**
8.0	0.57	2.9	0.23	**3.8**	0.22	0.28	2.71	3.69	89.7	**5.3**	23.7	0.0	**7.1**
10.0	0.17	0.4	-0.08	**2.1**	-0.01	-0.06	-0.36	3.25	101.6	**5.5**	24.5	0.0	**7.3**
10.0	0.17	0.4	0.07	**4.5**	0.24	0.69	4.64	2.58	72.1	**5.4**	27.0	1.2	**8.5**
9.2	0.19	1.4	-0.03	**2.4**	-0.01	-0.10	-1.16	4.53	102.0	**4.6**	15.6	0.9	**3.4**
4.7	1.21	8.6	0.30	**1.1**	-0.08	-0.42	-4.62	3.89	98.0	**3.2**	18.9	13.0	**2.9**
7.0	0.37	3.0	0.05	**5.2**	0.03	0.53	6.33	3.50	76.9	**4.4**	19.3	0.1	**3.7**
6.0	2.08	8.4	0.38	**6.0**	0.06	1.00	10.21	2.01	49.1	**5.6**	56.1	0.0	**4.3**
5.0	0.81	4.1	0.00	**3.9**	0.02	0.40	2.63	3.50	88.3	**3.4**	18.1	11.5	**7.6**
7.0	0.65	4.1	0.13	**4.8**	0.06	0.48	5.12	4.05	87.1	**5.0**	24.2	1.3	**5.0**
9.5	0.91	2.4	0.58	**2.5**	0.00	0.03	0.20	4.25	96.0	**5.6**	34.8	1.9	**6.5**
9.5	0.42	2.8	0.82	**1.4**	0.00	0.01	0.14	3.44	88.4	**5.1**	19.2	1.5	**3.7**
6.9	4.59	10.8	0.00	**4.4**	0.01	0.82	6.39	2.58	65.0	**5.4**	34.0	0.0	**4.3**
10.0	0.87	0.8	0.00	**4.3**	0.00	0.52	1.59	3.15	60.0	**7.2**	102.6	0.0	**6.8**
3.6	2.09	15.9	0.83	**6.6**	0.33	0.80	6.85	4.26	69.3	**1.7**	18.9	26.4	**7.8**
7.3	1.21	6.2	0.21	**2.6**	0.00	-0.01	-0.09	3.55	91.7	**3.8**	11.8	7.3	**7.6**
9.5	0.10	0.7	0.17	**3.2**	0.88	0.24	2.03	2.71	92.6	**3.9**	21.0	7.6	**8.0**
9.1	0.41	2.2	1.17	**7.7**	0.18	0.93	8.70	4.36	77.8	**4.7**	34.2	12.4	**6.8**

Name	City	State	Rating	2016 Rating	2015 Rating	Total Assets ($Mil)	One Year Asset Growth	Asset Mix (As a % of Total Assets) Comm-ercial Loans	Cons-umer Loans	Mort-gage Loans	Secur-ities	Capital-ization Index	Net Worth Ratio
▼ Westex Federal Credit Union	Lubbock	TX	C	C+	B	64.5	3.62	0.0	26.9	5.4	11.1	10.0	11.1
Westmark Credit Union	Idaho Falls	ID	B-	B-	B	683.0	9.83	0.3	43.7	28.7	1.6	6.7	8.7
Westminster Federal Credit Union	Westminster	CO	C	C	C	35.2	-3.59	2.0	33.0	10.1	1.7	8.1	9.7
▲ Westmoreland Community FCU	Greensburg	PA	C	C-	D+	80.3	13.99	0.0	49.7	1.0	0.1	8.9	10.3
Westmoreland Water Federal Credit Union	Greensburg	PA	C+	C+	C+	18.0	2.23	0.1	22.2	0.0	0.0	10.0	12.5
Westport Federal Credit Union	Westport	MA	D-	D-	D	61.3	4.47	3.4	13.4	22.6	6.8	4.4	6.4
Westside Community Federal Credit Union	Churchville	NY	D	D	D	16.5	7.38	0.0	20.7	12.8	0.0	5.1	7.1
▼ WestStar Credit Union	Las Vegas	NV	B+	A-	A-	166.2	6.30	0.1	39.1	19.0	11.2	10.0	12.0
Wexford Community Credit Union	Cadillac	MI	C+	C+	C	54.6	6.49	0.0	32.0	4.6	44.0	6.0	8.0
▼ Weyco Community Credit Union	Plymouth	NC	D	D+	D	78.1	-2.51	2.4	9.1	16.4	12.1	10.0	12.2
Wharton County Teachers Credit Union	Wharton	TX	C	C	C	11.4	0.18	0.0	2.1	0.0	0.0	10.0	16.5
Whatcom Educational Credit Union	Bellingham	WA	A+	A+	A+	1423.7	12.70	15.5	25.0	47.3	0.8	10.0	15.1
Wheat State Credit Union	Wichita	KS	E-	E-	E-	21.7	3.60	1.0	59.6	10.3	0.0	4.2	6.2
Wheatland Federal Credit Union	Lancaster	PA	C-	C-	C-	55.4	0.70	0.7	37.8	28.9	2.2	7.2	9.1
Whetelco Federal Credit Union	Wheeling	WV	D+	D+	D+	3.7	-6.97	0.0	17.0	0.0	0.0	10.0	41.2
White County Federal Credit Union	Searcy	AR	E-	E-	D-	16.2	2.29	0.0	53.7	7.0	0.0	5.1	7.1
White Crown Federal Credit Union	Denver	CO	C	C	C	62.1	1.08	9.0	23.7	26.1	15.4	7.8	9.5
White Eagle Credit Union	Augusta	KS	A-	A-	A-	103.8	7.50	0.0	41.2	1.9	0.0	10.0	11.7
White Earth Reservation FCU	Mahnomen	MN	D+	D+	D-	2.1	5.35	0.0	34.6	0.0	0.0	10.0	16.9
White Gold Credit Union	Raceland	LA	D+	D+	C-	<1	-7.53	0.0	77.7	0.0	0.0	10.0	31.2
White Haven Center Employees FCU	White Haven	PA	D	D	D-	1.4	2.20	0.0	50.2	0.0	0.0	9.0	10.4
White Pine Credit Union	Pierce	ID	C-	C-	D+	8.1	3.03	0.0	45.6	0.0	0.0	10.0	12.9
▲ White Plains P O Employees FCU	White Plains	NY	D+	D	D+	1.2	-3.16	0.0	1.7	0.0	0.0	10.0	28.6
White River Credit Union	Rochester	VT	D	D	D-	37.8	6.49	0.0	25.4	27.3	19.6	5.3	7.3
White River Credit Union	Enumclaw	WA	A-	A-	A-	73.2	5.93	0.3	24.6	6.5	0.0	10.0	14.1
White Rock Federal Credit Union	Philadelphia	PA	C	C	C-	<1	2.76	0.0	8.3	0.0	18.2	8.0	9.7
White Rose Credit Union	York	PA	D	D	D-	74.1	8.40	0.2	30.2	17.8	18.3	6.9	8.9
White Sands Federal Credit Union	Las Cruces	NM	C+	C+	B-	304.3	5.57	0.0	47.3	14.1	18.7	6.3	8.3
Whitefish Credit Union Association	Whitefish	MT	A-	A-	A-	1382.3	3.72	9.2	1.7	47.2	38.8	10.0	12.5
Whitehall Credit Union	Columbus	OH	D	D	D	18.2	0.33	0.0	28.1	0.0	0.0	9.7	10.8
Whitesville Community Credit Union	Whitesville	KY	D+	D+	C	24.2	3.41	0.0	7.9	17.3	0.0	9.2	10.5
Whitewater Community Credit Union	Harrison	OH	D+	D+	D+	7.2	1.24	0.0	65.7	0.0	0.0	7.7	9.5
Whitewater Regional Federal Credit Union	Connersville	IN	C-	C-	C-	8.4	12.54	0.0	56.4	0.0	0.0	10.0	12.4
Whiting Refinery Federal Credit Union	Whiting	IN	B+	B+	B+	47.3	1.40	0.0	6.7	15.3	27.4	10.0	26.9
Wichita Falls Federal Credit Union	Wichita Falls	TX	C+	C+	C+	22.3	2.26	0.0	33.6	3.2	0.0	10.0	12.4
Wichita Falls Teachers FCU	Wichita Falls	TX	B	B	B	77.6	3.62	0.0	39.2	0.1	33.9	10.0	11.1
▲ Wichita Federal Credit Union	Wichita	KS	A-	B+	B	106.2	0.89	0.0	54.6	7.6	1.4	10.0	14.9
Widget Federal Credit Union	Erie	PA	C+	C+	C+	297.0	3.91	0.0	36.4	19.8	13.3	7.3	9.3
Wildfire Credit Union	Saginaw	MI	C+	C+	C+	752.8	5.81	5.3	16.8	34.1	35.4	10.0	12.3
Williamson County Catholic Credit Union	Herrin	IL	D-	D-	E+	2.2	0.64	0.0	76.4	0.0	0.0	6.2	8.3
Williamsport Teachers Credit Union	South Williamsport	PA	C+	C+	C	11.2	5.18	0.0	23.7	15.0	0.0	10.0	19.1
▲ Williamsville Federal Credit Union	Amherst	NY	D+	D	D	13.0	3.72	0.0	14.6	18.7	0.0	7.7	9.4
Willis Credit Union	Nashville	TN	B-	B-	B-	19.4	15.45	0.0	67.4	0.0	0.0	10.0	11.1
Willis Knighton Federal Credit Union	Shreveport	LA	B-	B-	B-	29.6	2.20	0.0	56.7	6.9	0.0	10.0	15.8
Willow Island Federal Credit Union	Saint Marys	WV	E+	E+	E+	9.0	0.66	0.0	58.8	0.0	0.0	5.3	7.3
Wilmac Employees' Credit Union	York	PA	C+	C+	C+	3.2	7.31	0.0	27.7	0.0	0.0	10.0	17.7
Wilmington Police & Fire FCU	Wilmington	DE	D	D	D	14.3	4.95	0.0	15.4	0.0	71.2	10.0	17.8
Win-Hood Co-Op Credit Union	Chicago	IL	C	C	C-	1.7	30.22	0.0	0.0	0.0	3.3	10.0	14.4
Winchester Federal Credit Union	Winchester	MA	D+	D+	D+	2.4	-2.14	0.0	41.2	0.0	0.0	10.0	14.4
Windsor Locks Federal Credit Union	Windsor Locks	CT	C-	C-	C	58.0	5.89	1.4	7.0	39.0	0.6	9.2	10.4
Windthorst Federal Credit Union	Windthorst	TX	B+	B+	B	49.7	-1.49	14.5	15.6	20.6	0.0	10.0	16.4
▲ Windward Community Federal Credit Union	Kailua	HI	C	C-	C-	88.8	-2.88	2.5	15.5	9.5	8.2	6.3	8.3
▲ Wings Financial Credit Union	Apple Valley	MN	A	A-	B+	4573.5	4.64	3.5	14.9	28.9	40.7	10.0	11.8
Winnebago Community Credit Union	Oshkosh	WI	B	B	B	96.2	5.43	0.0	13.7	52.7	0.0	9.3	10.5
▼ Winslow Community Federal Credit Union	Winslow	ME	C-	C	C	39.0	7.20	0.3	52.0	11.8	0.0	6.4	8.4
Winslow Santa Fe Credit Union	Winslow	AZ	B	B	B	15.0	10.59	0.0	22.0	0.0	0.0	10.0	12.2
Winslow School Employees FCU	Winslow	AZ	C	C	C	4.6	-1.83	0.0	46.3	0.0	0.0	10.0	14.2
WinSouth Credit Union	Gadsden	AL	C+	C+	C+	262.5	4.90	5.6	30.8	25.0	13.5	6.4	8.7
Winston-Salem Federal Credit Union	Winston-Salem	NC	B	B	B	64.9	0.72	0.5	38.1	25.4	2.6	10.0	12.7
Winthrop Area Federal Credit Union	Winthrop	ME	C+	C+	C+	65.4	4.21	0.0	18.7	34.7	0.0	8.4	10.0

Asset Quality Index	Non-Performing Loans as a % of Total Loans	Non-Performing Loans as a % of Capital	Net Charge-Offs Avg Loans	Profitability Index	Net Income ($Mil)	Return on Assets	Return on Equity	Net Interest Spread	Overhead Efficiency Ratio	Liquidity Index	Liquidity Ratio	Hot Money Ratio	Stability Index
9.4	0.67	2.6	-0.03	**1.9**	0.08	0.51	4.60	3.58	97.6	**5.5**	39.7	9.6	**4.5**
9.2	0.04	0.7	0.31	**2.8**	0.25	0.15	1.70	2.87	87.3	**2.2**	4.4	12.0	**6.2**
6.3	0.76	5.8	0.67	**3.6**	0.07	0.76	7.88	3.99	84.4	**4.3**	12.5	1.8	**4.7**
5.2	0.83	5.4	0.31	**3.5**	0.10	0.51	5.51	4.06	88.2	**4.4**	20.4	1.3	**3.7**
10.0	0.00	0.0	0.00	**4.3**	0.03	0.77	6.07	2.47	69.9	**5.4**	33.5	0.0	**6.5**
4.4	2.21	19.9	-0.03	**0.2**	-0.07	-0.45	-7.39	2.52	116.3	**4.8**	28.3	2.8	**1.4**
9.6	0.24	1.7	0.00	**1.3**	0.00	-0.05	-0.68	2.66	101.1	**5.1**	26.7	0.0	**2.8**
9.7	0.35	2.2	0.35	**4.0**	0.10	0.23	1.93	3.96	90.9	**4.9**	24.6	0.9	**7.7**
8.8	0.41	1.9	0.52	**3.4**	0.01	0.05	0.64	3.39	93.1	**5.3**	24.1	1.4	**3.5**
7.4	2.80	6.4	1.99	**0.2**	-0.14	-0.69	-5.71	2.39	101.4	**5.3**	32.0	5.7	**5.4**
10.0	0.33	0.1	0.00	**2.0**	0.00	0.00	0.00	1.42	102.8	**6.2**	32.7	0.0	**7.2**
9.3	0.13	0.8	0.24	**8.8**	4.35	1.25	8.14	3.62	72.1	**4.3**	18.3	0.6	**10.0**
0.7	4.48	48.0	1.32	**0.8**	-0.19	-3.49	-51.70	5.43	81.9	**3.0**	20.7	15.0	**0.0**
6.4	0.62	5.1	0.21	**1.9**	0.01	0.04	0.40	3.63	97.1	**3.6**	13.4	3.4	**4.3**
10.0	3.17	1.3	2.48	**0.7**	0.00	-0.21	-0.53	2.17	110.5	**4.9**	7.2	0.0	**5.5**
2.2	2.32	22.3	-0.38	**3.0**	0.02	0.60	8.39	4.49	78.4	**4.5**	25.6	0.0	**0.3**
9.6	0.15	0.9	-0.27	**2.5**	0.05	0.30	3.28	3.27	92.4	**4.8**	30.4	4.4	**5.3**
9.5	0.06	1.9	0.23	**7.0**	0.46	1.81	15.40	4.61	73.0	**4.9**	33.7	5.4	**6.8**
8.6	0.00	1.5	3.01	**8.4**	0.10	21.24	149.45	7.28	62.2	**6.5**	57.9	5.9	**5.7**
8.2	0.29	0.7	0.00	**0.8**	0.00	0.00	0.00	5.76	100.0	**4.5**	24.1	0.0	**5.6**
1.3	6.36	28.9	5.62	**8.6**	0.01	1.52	14.60	7.25	71.4	**6.8**	54.9	0.0	**4.5**
8.1	0.26	1.2	-0.08	**2.5**	0.00	0.00	0.00	3.69	100.0	**4.5**	41.7	11.3	**5.9**
9.9	0.00	0.0	0.00	**3.6**	0.02	5.94	21.11	2.36	33.3	**6.5**	48.0	0.0	**6.2**
7.0	0.50	4.0	0.24	**0.7**	-0.02	-0.21	-2.74	3.98	99.5	**4.6**	22.5	2.9	**2.6**
8.9	1.60	3.6	0.39	**6.8**	0.17	0.93	6.54	2.96	67.1	**5.3**	38.8	2.4	**7.1**
10.0	0.00	0.0	0.00	**4.7**	0.00	1.98	20.78	2.19	0.0	**6.1**	38.7	0.0	**3.7**
7.8	0.59	3.9	0.32	**0.4**	-0.08	-0.42	-4.65	4.02	96.5	**4.6**	23.0	0.0	**4.0**
7.9	0.39	3.1	0.41	**3.4**	0.27	0.35	4.22	3.21	79.8	**4.2**	13.7	5.0	**5.3**
7.2	0.25	7.3	0.01	**6.7**	3.62	1.05	8.61	2.41	56.7	**4.2**	12.6	0.0	**8.5**
7.6	0.92	3.7	-0.10	**0.9**	0.00	0.07	0.61	2.95	98.0	**5.1**	26.7	2.7	**4.6**
9.9	0.41	1.2	0.22	**2.0**	0.02	0.27	2.54	2.14	87.9	**5.8**	34.2	0.0	**5.4**
5.9	0.65	4.8	-0.08	**3.7**	0.01	0.28	2.94	3.75	93.6	**4.8**	23.2	0.0	**2.3**
7.0	0.38	1.7	-0.33	**4.1**	0.01	0.40	3.09	4.15	79.8	**5.3**	32.5	0.0	**3.7**
10.0	0.00	0.0	0.21	**4.6**	0.08	0.70	2.61	2.05	50.9	**4.9**	41.1	7.9	**7.1**
9.2	0.71	2.9	0.50	**3.8**	0.04	0.64	6.00	3.46	84.2	**4.8**	24.6	4.2	**5.5**
7.1	1.71	7.6	0.65	**4.1**	0.09	0.46	4.13	3.98	81.3	**4.4**	11.8	2.2	**5.3**
7.2	0.70	3.6	0.93	**6.9**	0.44	1.68	11.24	4.43	82.4	**3.9**	28.7	9.1	**7.5**
9.4	0.27	1.8	0.42	**3.0**	0.20	0.27	2.90	2.80	88.5	**3.6**	13.6	5.7	**5.9**
9.0	0.50	2.6	0.23	**2.9**	0.57	0.31	2.55	2.98	88.6	**2.9**	9.6	14.1	**8.3**
6.8	0.00	0.0	-0.88	**4.3**	0.00	0.74	8.94	4.11	83.3	**4.3**	19.6	0.0	**2.3**
10.0	0.00	0.0	0.41	**2.7**	0.01	0.26	1.32	2.54	86.3	**6.3**	49.6	0.0	**7.4**
10.0	0.04	0.2	0.00	**1.4**	0.01	0.25	2.62	2.56	89.5	**5.1**	24.1	0.0	**4.4**
8.2	0.04	0.7	0.43	**5.8**	0.02	0.33	2.78	4.85	84.6	**4.7**	38.6	13.9	**5.7**
6.1	0.44	5.2	0.13	**4.0**	0.03	0.34	2.15	3.47	87.8	**3.8**	16.2	7.7	**6.9**
1.5	2.70	26.4	1.55	**2.5**	0.00	0.18	2.45	4.50	92.7	**4.2**	33.3	10.2	**1.0**
9.5	1.19	2.4	0.00	**3.1**	0.00	0.25	1.41	2.64	83.3	**7.4**	75.7	0.0	**7.3**
10.0	1.24	1.2	0.81	**0.1**	-0.02	-0.59	-3.28	2.23	121.7	**5.6**	44.6	6.4	**5.2**
5.0	2.70	9.7	0.00	**7.6**	0.00	0.71	4.98	4.24	83.3	**6.2**	43.0	0.0	**8.1**
8.5	1.29	3.6	0.00	**1.1**	0.00	-0.17	-1.15	4.08	109.5	**5.4**	33.2	0.0	**7.1**
6.1	1.80	10.8	0.00	**2.3**	0.03	0.18	1.72	3.29	94.0	**3.9**	14.6	4.8	**4.9**
9.3	0.65	1.9	0.03	**4.6**	0.11	0.90	5.60	2.60	67.0	**4.1**	51.4	12.8	**7.7**
6.5	1.19	6.5	0.75	**3.4**	0.20	0.88	10.56	3.25	77.9	**4.8**	21.6	1.8	**3.3**
9.9	0.13	0.7	0.17	**6.8**	14.03	1.25	11.14	2.64	58.8	**3.8**	14.6	8.4	**8.9**
9.1	0.21	1.5	-0.01	**5.4**	0.20	0.83	7.79	3.14	80.1	**3.5**	20.1	6.0	**5.9**
5.7	0.55	4.9	0.15	**2.7**	-0.02	-0.16	-1.82	3.96	81.3	**3.4**	11.8	5.1	**4.0**
9.5	0.51	0.9	0.71	**4.5**	0.01	0.38	3.08	3.68	84.6	**7.6**	60.6	0.0	**6.0**
7.1	0.76	2.8	0.00	**4.1**	0.01	0.63	4.35	3.94	81.0	**5.0**	17.8	0.0	**7.1**
6.1	0.64	9.1	0.50	**3.5**	0.22	0.34	4.42	3.20	87.1	**3.9**	21.9	10.1	**4.4**
3.7	3.24	22.0	1.36	**3.7**	-0.02	-0.14	-1.06	5.73	87.4	**3.6**	13.1	7.0	**5.1**
7.6	0.08	3.2	0.22	**3.6**	0.08	0.48	4.76	3.02	81.7	**4.2**	38.4	10.0	**5.0**

	Name	City	State	Rating	2016 Rating	2015 Rating	Total Assets ($Mil)	One Year Asset Growth	Comm-ercial Loans	Cons-umer Loans	Mort-gage Loans	Secur-ities	Capital-ization Index	Net Worth Ratio
	Winthrop-University Hospital Empls FCU	Mineola	NY	**B+**	B+	B	32.7	4.63	0.0	30.8	0.0	0.0	**10.0**	11.5
	Wiregrass Federal Credit Union	Dothan	AL	**C-**	C-	D+	46.2	4.30	0.0	69.0	7.8	0.0	**6.9**	9.0
	Wiremen's Credit Union, Inc.	Parma	OH	**C+**	C+	C	27.1	2.23	0.0	23.2	6.6	25.1	**10.0**	22.0
	Wisconsin Latvian Credit Union, Incorporated	Milwaukee	WI	**C-**	C-	C	2.9	15.68	0.0	13.9	29.7	0.0	**8.9**	10.3
	Wisconsin Medical Credit Union	Green Bay	WI	**C-**	C-	C-	10.5	0.64	0.0	28.3	26.3	0.0	**8.2**	9.8
▼	Wit Federal Credit Union	Rochester	NY	**C-**	C	C-	18.4	42.55	0.8	39.0	10.9	0.0	**10.0**	11.1
	Witco Houston Employees Credit Union	Rosenberg	TX	**C-**	C-	C-	1.5	-1.57	0.0	73.3	0.0	0.0	**10.0**	22.5
	WJC Federal Credit Union	Damascus	VA	**D-**	D-	E+	4.1	8.67	0.0	72.0	0.0	0.0	**7.7**	9.5
	WNC Community Credit Union	Waynesville	NC	**B**	B	B-	80.5	4.82	0.0	6.9	40.2	8.0	**10.0**	15.3
▲	Woburn Municipal Federal Credit Union	Woburn	MA	**C-**	D+	D	43.3	-0.55	0.0	14.0	12.0	12.7	**6.5**	8.5
	Wolf Point Federal Credit Union	Wolf Point	MT	**B-**	B-	C+	12.9	-1.81	8.6	41.5	0.0	0.0	**10.0**	17.6
	Wood County Community FCU	Parkersburg	WV	**E+**	E+	E+	16.8	-7.21	0.0	36.5	4.6	0.0	**0.4**	3.5
	Wood County Employees Credit Union	Wisconsin Rapids	WI	**C**	C	C-	1.2	-2.25	0.0	81.4	0.0	0.0	**10.0**	14.5
	Woodco Federal Credit Union	Perrysburg	OH	**D+**	D+	D+	10.0	6.66	0.0	33.3	8.8	4.5	**7.6**	9.4
	Woodlawn Federal Credit Union	Pawtucket	RI	**E-**	E-	E-	14.0	1.86	14.5	19.2	27.0	0.0	**4.0**	6.0
	Woodmen Federal Credit Union	Omaha	NE	**C-**	C-	C-	9.5	8.41	0.0	17.6	11.7	0.0	**10.0**	12.9
	Woodstone Credit Union	Federal Way	WA	**D**	D	C-	101.6	3.25	1.8	58.4	7.1	7.8	**6.9**	8.9
	WOR Co Federal Credit Union	Pocomoke City	MD	**D**	D	D+	2.4	-2.67	0.0	20.4	0.0	0.0	**10.0**	12.6
▲	Worcester Credit Union	Worcester	MA	**C-**	D+	D	80.4	3.99	0.0	16.7	30.7	15.6	**7.4**	9.3
▼	Worcester Fire Department Credit Union	Worcester	MA	**D+**	C-	C-	39.4	0.83	0.0	11.3	8.6	6.9	**10.0**	13.8
	Worcester Police Department FCU	Worcester	MA	**C+**	C+	C+	16.7	9.67	0.0	46.9	20.8	0.0	**10.0**	12.0
	Workers Federal Credit Union	Stafford Springs	CT	**E-**	E-	E-	20.5	-4.23	0.0	25.8	12.3	0.0	**2.6**	4.9
	Workers' Credit Union	Fitchburg	MA	**A-**	A-	A	1542.4	14.55	7.3	11.2	39.1	22.9	**9.5**	11.0
	Workmen's Circle Credit Union	Savannah	GA	**A-**	A-	A-	71.8	13.31	47.1	1.7	50.3	3.9	**10.0**	19.1
	Worzalla Publishing Employees CU	Stevens Point	WI	**C-**	C-	C-	1.1	-4.90	0.0	15.0	0.0	0.0	**10.0**	22.5
	WR Grace Maryland Employees FCU	Curtis Bay	MD	**D**	D	D	3.4	-0.24	0.0	9.8	0.0	81.2	**8.7**	10.1
	Wright Credit Union	Toccoa	GA	**B-**	B-	B-	13.0	2.60	0.9	14.2	15.6	0.0	**10.0**	15.9
	Wright-Dunbar Area Credit Union	Dayton	OH	**D+**	D+	D	<1	34.14	0.0	11.2	0.0	0.0	**10.0**	12.0
	Wright-Patt Credit Union, Inc.	Beavercreek	OH	**A**	A	A	3625.2	11.46	4.1	43.5	20.8	9.3	**10.0**	11.6
	WSSC Federal Credit Union	Laurel	MD	**C-**	C-	C	27.1	10.09	0.0	48.2	0.0	0.0	**9.0**	10.3
	Wufface Federal Credit Union	Richmond	IN	**C-**	C-	D+	5.6	9.95	0.0	29.4	0.0	0.0	**7.4**	9.2
	WV National Guard Federal Credit Union	Charleston	WV	**B+**	B+	B+	44.1	2.89	0.0	25.3	4.5	0.0	**10.0**	11.6
	WVU Employees Federal Credit Union	Morgantown	WV	**B+**	B+	B	40.2	17.26	0.0	27.7	0.0	0.0	**9.3**	10.5
	WyHy Federal Credit Union	Cheyenne	WY	**A**	A	A	220.1	5.45	2.4	39.4	21.7	0.7	**10.0**	12.0
	Wymar Federal Credit Union	Geismar	LA	**A**	A	A	105.3	10.13	0.2	19.6	29.4	18.8	**10.0**	13.8
	Wyo Central Federal Credit Union	Casper	WY	**C-**	C-	C-	29.1	-1.86	1.0	35.5	8.7	0.0	**8.3**	9.9
	Wyochem Federal Credit Union	Green River	WY	**D+**	D+	D	21.0	7.78	0.0	51.8	0.0	0.0	**6.4**	8.4
	Wyoming Area Federal Credit Union	Wyoming	PA	**D**	D	D	8.2	1.49	0.0	2.1	0.0	57.8	**6.3**	8.3
	Wyoming Valley West Community FCU	Edwardsville	PA	**D**	D	D	10.2	3.51	3.4	19.9	0.0	16.9	**5.4**	7.6
	Wyrope Williamsport Federal Credit Union	South Williamsport	PA	**C**	C	C	34.8	6.69	0.0	18.3	0.8	52.3	**9.2**	10.4
	Xavier University Federal Credit Union	New Orleans	LA	**C-**	C-	D	2.0	-11.83	0.0	15.8	0.0	0.0	**10.0**	14.1
▼	Xceed Financial Federal Credit Union	El Segundo	CA	**D+**	C-	C	958.9	1.18	12.8	19.9	44.6	2.6	**7.7**	9.4
	XCEL Federal Credit Union	Bloomfield	NJ	**C+**	C+	C+	181.2	-3.40	6.2	40.7	13.7	5.1	**5.7**	7.8
	Xplore Federal Credit Union	New Orleans	LA	**B-**	B-	B-	153.9	-2.56	0.0	24.1	22.4	0.7	**6.7**	8.7
	Y-12 Federal Credit Union	Oak Ridge	TN	**B**	B	B	1090.2	12.36	4.3	43.9	31.1	6.9	**6.6**	8.7
	Yantis Federal Credit Union	Yantis	TX	**C**	C	C	24.5	1.48	4.4	9.8	29.0	0.0	**10.0**	14.3
	Yellowstone Federal Credit Union	Yellowstone Nation	WY	**E+**	E+	E+	4.4	-0.52	0.0	46.1	0.0	0.0	**4.6**	6.6
	Yoakum County Federal Credit Union	Plains	TX	**C+**	C+	C+	8.9	-3.00	0.0	37.1	0.0	0.0	**10.0**	18.5
	Yogaville Federal Credit Union	Buckingham	VA	**C+**	C+	C+	5.9	-1.30	0.0	6.8	23.7	0.0	**10.0**	16.4
	Yolo Federal Credit Union	Woodland	CA	**A-**	A-	A-	270.6	7.83	6.7	15.3	35.1	0.0	**9.0**	10.3
	Yonkers Postal Employees Credit Union	Yonkers	NY	**C**	C	C	8.1	1.04	0.0	25.1	0.0	56.0	**10.0**	17.2
	Yonkers Teachers Federal Credit Union	Yonkers	NY	**B-**	B-	B-	58.1	2.96	0.0	6.5	0.0	20.1	**10.0**	12.2
	York County Federal Credit Union	Sanford	ME	**B+**	B+	B+	280.1	15.18	2.5	25.4	38.6	2.3	**7.7**	9.5
	York Educational Federal Credit Union	York	PA	**D-**	D-	D	35.0	2.98	0.0	16.1	8.0	0.0	**4.9**	6.9
	Yorkville Community Federal Credit Union	Yorkville	OH	**D**	D	D+	10.5	0.96	0.0	28.1	0.0	0.0	**10.0**	13.4
	Youngstown City Schools Credit Union	Youngstown	OH	**C+**	C+	C+	8.9	1.91	0.0	31.1	0.0	1.7	**10.0**	30.8
	Your Choice Federal Credit Union	Altoona	PA	**D+**	D+	C-	11.9	7.90	0.0	18.7	5.6	21.0	**10.0**	11.6
	Your Hometown Federal Credit Union	Mayfield	KY	**D+**	D+	D+	19.7	1.46	0.0	14.4	24.1	0.0	**7.3**	9.2
	Your Legacy Federal Credit Union	Tiffin	OH	**C**	C	C	60.0	4.04	4.1	27.6	16.5	11.5	**7.2**	9.2
	YS Federal Credit Union	Yellow Springs	OH	**C-**	C-	C	18.6	14.20	0.0	11.9	0.0	6.7	**7.0**	9.0

Loan and securities columns show Asset Mix (As a % of Total Assets).

Asset Quality Index	Non-Performing Loans as a % of Total Loans	Non-Performing Loans as a % of Capital	Net Charge-Offs Avg Loans	Profitability Index	Net Income ($Mil)	Return on Assets	Return on Equity	Net Interest Spread	Overhead Efficiency Ratio	Liquidity Index	Liquidity Ratio	Hot Money Ratio	Stability Index
9.5	0.80	3.2	-0.02	8.0	0.06	0.77	6.69	5.56	76.2	5.7	51.9	10.1	6.1
4.7	0.84	8.4	0.35	5.0	0.12	1.04	11.58	4.59	79.2	2.8	12.4	10.8	3.8
9.0	1.76	3.1	1.43	2.8	0.04	0.57	2.63	2.65	78.5	4.7	14.8	0.0	6.9
9.9	0.16	0.9	0.00	2.1	0.00	0.28	2.74	2.67	84.2	4.8	39.3	0.0	5.8
6.7	0.85	5.3	0.00	3.6	0.01	0.31	3.13	3.84	93.6	4.3	19.0	0.0	5.6
6.9	0.94	6.2	0.20	1.3	-0.04	-0.88	-7.77	5.12	100.9	3.9	16.1	7.5	6.2
7.8	0.00	0.0	0.00	1.2	0.00	-0.53	-2.36	3.69	116.7	3.8	15.6	0.0	6.9
0.7	5.24	46.2	0.00	9.1	0.02	1.98	21.22	7.95	67.9	3.6	19.1	0.0	3.0
7.2	1.27	5.2	0.00	3.6	0.08	0.39	2.57	2.54	83.7	5.0	22.8	0.3	7.2
10.0	0.03	0.1	-0.03	2.1	0.02	0.16	1.84	2.63	93.0	4.8	27.6	1.6	3.9
7.4	2.48	6.9	0.06	7.9	0.06	1.96	11.06	4.09	70.8	5.8	57.6	2.1	6.3
0.3	9.93	61.8	-0.05	1.6	0.04	0.84	24.18	2.94	75.0	5.2	14.9	0.5	0.0
7.8	0.00	0.0	0.00	4.9	0.00	0.34	2.26	5.02	92.9	3.4	9.7	0.0	4.3
9.8	0.03	0.2	0.06	3.0	0.00	0.08	0.86	3.57	97.9	4.8	31.9	0.0	3.0
3.5	1.97	22.7	-0.25	1.7	0.00	0.12	1.92	5.80	101.4	5.7	45.6	10.8	0.0
10.0	0.06	0.2	0.00	1.8	0.00	0.13	0.98	2.92	97.4	5.4	26.0	1.4	7.3
7.3	0.27	2.7	1.10	0.3	-0.09	-0.34	-3.77	3.17	88.2	3.7	16.5	6.9	3.8
8.4	3.67	5.7	0.00	0.2	0.00	-0.68	-5.26	3.83	117.7	7.3	58.6	0.0	4.9
8.7	0.16	1.1	0.04	2.2	0.03	0.15	1.56	3.59	95.4	4.4	17.6	4.1	4.5
9.9	0.26	0.4	0.50	0.6	-0.03	-0.33	-2.35	2.08	108.6	4.6	16.2	5.5	6.2
8.6	0.00	0.0	0.58	2.6	0.00	0.07	0.60	3.97	96.8	3.7	17.1	7.4	6.6
4.9	0.69	16.5	0.19	1.0	0.00	0.02	0.40	4.05	101.7	4.3	25.2	4.9	0.0
7.7	0.58	4.3	1.92	5.6	3.23	0.85	7.95	2.96	69.6	1.9	17.9	22.4	8.7
7.7	0.02	0.1	0.00	9.8	0.34	1.94	10.13	3.51	31.9	4.8	29.6	6.5	9.7
10.0	0.00	0.0	0.00	1.5	0.00	0.00	0.00	1.90	100.0	6.7	42.9	0.0	7.1
10.0	0.00	0.0	0.00	0.0	-0.01	-0.86	-8.14	2.24	150.0	5.7	12.8	0.0	3.6
6.7	2.29	9.5	0.09	3.7	0.01	0.22	1.36	3.60	92.4	6.5	66.4	5.2	7.4
7.7	4.88	5.2	0.00	1.1	0.00	0.00	0.00	1.62	150.0	5.8	39.4	0.0	5.1
8.3	0.50	3.4	0.64	8.7	10.76	1.22	10.47	3.57	64.9	4.0	20.4	7.3	8.7
4.6	2.25	11.5	0.64	2.7	0.01	0.21	2.01	4.07	95.1	4.4	33.9	2.4	4.4
9.9	0.00	0.0	-0.88	3.9	0.01	0.82	8.58	3.18	93.6	6.8	44.5	0.0	3.7
9.9	0.33	1.0	-0.10	6.5	0.19	1.71	14.93	3.09	40.8	5.3	20.0	0.0	4.9
7.8	1.22	3.2	1.27	9.4	0.15	1.60	14.64	3.70	49.2	6.5	42.1	0.0	5.3
7.6	0.43	5.3	0.41	6.0	0.37	0.67	5.63	3.80	75.0	2.6	14.0	16.1	8.4
9.4	0.32	1.4	0.01	5.6	0.19	0.72	5.27	2.67	75.3	3.3	19.8	11.1	9.3
3.6	2.58	18.1	1.01	2.1	0.00	0.03	0.28	4.08	94.5	4.1	15.2	3.6	3.6
5.1	0.89	6.6	0.03	3.9	0.03	0.59	6.68	4.21	73.6	4.6	31.7	3.0	3.0
10.0	0.00	0.0	0.00	1.9	0.00	0.20	2.35	1.59	81.8	7.3	46.6	0.0	4.0
10.0	0.00	0.0	0.00	3.0	0.00	-0.12	-1.59	3.96	100.0	6.9	51.9	0.0	2.3
6.0	3.50	9.8	0.64	2.6	0.03	0.35	3.21	2.21	82.5	6.0	41.9	1.7	4.8
9.2	3.09	3.3	-3.31	1.5	0.00	0.00	0.00	1.53	88.9	6.9	97.5	0.0	5.5
7.2	0.57	5.2	0.69	1.4	0.26	0.11	1.14	3.45	90.8	2.9	11.6	10.8	6.2
3.2	2.31	25.0	0.71	3.9	0.19	0.41	6.39	4.73	78.4	2.3	8.6	16.7	3.5
9.9	0.16	0.9	0.39	3.8	0.13	0.33	3.77	3.26	85.5	4.9	26.1	1.8	5.9
6.7	0.48	6.3	0.88	6.9	2.84	1.04	13.81	3.29	62.0	1.7	5.8	18.8	6.3
9.4	0.06	1.4	0.12	2.7	0.02	0.37	2.63	3.49	86.7	3.4	25.6	15.3	6.9
5.8	1.36	9.2	0.00	2.1	0.00	0.19	2.77	3.58	93.8	4.9	24.2	0.0	1.0
9.4	0.02	0.1	-1.01	3.7	0.01	0.27	1.46	3.41	84.5	5.1	46.4	0.0	6.6
9.6	0.63	1.7	1.55	7.0	0.01	0.96	5.88	3.65	63.4	6.0	37.3	0.0	5.7
9.7	0.01	0.1	0.24	6.7	0.64	0.96	9.33	3.58	74.2	4.1	21.3	3.5	7.4
9.7	0.59	0.8	5.46	1.9	-0.05	-2.43	-13.92	3.11	89.7	5.4	24.0	0.0	6.6
9.8	3.71	2.1	0.09	3.0	0.04	0.28	2.33	1.30	72.7	5.1	11.5	0.0	5.7
8.0	0.44	3.5	0.24	6.0	0.55	0.82	8.59	4.56	78.1	3.3	16.9	11.0	6.4
7.9	0.31	2.2	0.08	2.3	0.05	0.57	8.86	3.18	81.7	4.5	22.9	1.3	2.3
6.3	5.88	11.9	0.12	0.0	-0.12	-4.52	-32.03	2.40	97.1	5.9	47.5	0.0	5.2
10.0	1.45	1.5	0.00	3.8	0.01	0.50	1.61	2.31	77.1	4.9	31.7	0.0	7.6
8.3	1.67	3.5	2.61	0.6	-0.01	-0.44	-3.75	2.76	93.6	5.3	24.1	0.0	5.0
6.6	0.84	3.9	0.00	1.2	-0.01	-0.18	-1.99	3.20	106.5	6.1	38.2	1.7	4.4
8.9	0.17	1.1	0.05	3.2	0.07	0.48	5.27	3.32	83.8	4.0	18.8	4.7	4.9
10.0	0.05	0.3	0.00	2.7	0.00	0.06	0.72	3.54	98.3	6.3	41.7	0.6	3.7

Name	City	State	Rating	2016 Rating	2015 Rating	Total Assets ($Mil)	One Year Asset Growth	Asset Mix (As a % of Total Assets) Comm-ercial Loans	Cons-umer Loans	Mort-gage Loans	Secur-ities	Capital-ization Index	Net Worth Ratio
Yuma County Federal Credit Union	Yuma	CO	**C+**	C+	C+	34.9	2.41	3.2	10.6	12.2	0.0	**10.0**	11.1
Zachary Community Federal Credit Union	Zachary	LA	**C**	C	C	<1	-2.37	0.0	33.5	0.0	0.0	**10.0**	34.5
Zeal Credit Union	Livonia	MI	**A**	A	A	582.2	6.11	0.0	25.4	17.2	40.8	**10.0**	14.7
Zellco Federal Credit Union	Bogalusa	LA	**A-**	A-	A-	59.6	2.35	1.0	26.0	22.4	0.0	**10.0**	34.4
ZIA Credit Union	Los Alamos	NM	**C+**	C+	C	139.4	3.24	0.0	25.8	32.7	11.8	**7.2**	9.2
Ziegler Federal Credit Union	Bloomington	MN	**C+**	C+	C+	4.4	-0.55	0.0	19.7	0.0	0.0	**10.0**	15.9
Zion Hill Baptist Church FCU	Los Angeles	CA	**D-**	D-	D	<1	-84.15	0.0	44.8	0.0	0.0	**10.0**	41.4

Asset Quality Index	Non-Performing Loans as a % of Total Loans	Non-Performing Loans as a % of Capital	Net Charge-Offs Avg Loans	Profitability Index	Net Income ($Mil)	Return on Assets	Return on Equity	Net Interest Spread	Overhead Efficiency Ratio	Liquidity Index	Liquidity Ratio	Hot Money Ratio	Stability Index
10.0	0.00	0.0	0.00	**3.1**	0.04	0.45	4.04	2.49	82.9	**4.7**	27.3	4.5	**6.1**
3.6	25.00	23.1	0.00	**7.0**	0.00	1.95	5.63	7.59	66.7	**7.4**	100.0	0.0	**8.0**
8.9	0.84	3.2	1.42	**7.2**	1.05	0.74	5.10	3.74	71.6	**4.1**	9.1	2.0	**9.9**
8.6	1.14	3.4	1.04	**8.3**	0.15	1.00	2.98	5.51	79.5	**6.8**	61.2	1.0	**7.7**
7.9	0.35	4.3	0.48	**3.8**	0.19	0.56	6.09	4.50	89.3	**3.2**	17.8	12.8	**5.6**
10.0	0.74	1.1	1.12	**3.0**	0.00	0.19	1.16	6.45	72.7	**8.0**	88.6	0.0	**6.4**
0.0	100.00	92.9	0.00	**0.0**	0.00	-44.44	-114.29	0.00	0.0	**7.6**	94.1	0.0	**4.7**

Section II

Weiss Recommended Credit Unions by State

A compilation of those

Credit Unions

receiving a Weiss Safety Rating
of A+, A, A-, or B+.

Institutions are ranked by Safety Rating
in each state where they have a branch location.

Section II Contents

This section provides a list of Weiss Recommended Credit Unions by state and contains all financial institutions receiving a Safety Rating of A+, A, A-, or B+. Recommended institutions are listed in each state in which they currently operate one or more branches. If a company is not on this list, it should not be automatically assumed that the firm is weak. Indeed, there are many firms that have not achieved a B+ or better rating but are in good condition with adequate resources to weather an average recession. Not being included in this list should not be construed as a recommendation to immediately withdraw deposits or cancel existing financial arrangements.

Institutions are ranked within each state by their Weiss Safety Rating, and then listed alphabetically by city. Companies with the same rating should be viewed as having the same relative safety regardless of their ranking in this table.

1. **Institution Name** The name under which the institution was chartered. A credit union's name can be very similar to, or the same as, the name of other companies which may not be on our Recommended List, so make sure you note the exact name, city, and state of the main branch listed here before acting on this recommendation.

2. **City** The city in which the institution's headquarters or main office is located. With the adoption of intrastate and interstate branching laws, many institutions operating in your area may actually be headquartered elsewhere. So, don't be surprised if the location cited is not in your particular city.

3. **State** The state in which the institution's headquarters or main office is located. With the adoption of interstate branching laws, some institutions operating in your area may actually be headquartered in another state. Even so, there are no restrictions on your ability to do business with an out-of-state institution.

4. **Telephone** The telephone number for the institution's headquarters, or main office. If the number listed is not in your area, or a local phone call, consult your local phone directory for the number of a location near you.

5. **Safety Rating** Weiss rating assigned to the institution at the time of publication. Our ratings are designed to distinguish levels of insolvency risk and are measured on a scale from A to F based upon a wide range of factors. Highly rated companies are, in our opinion, less likely to experience financial difficulties than lower rated firms. See *About Weiss Safety Ratings* for more information and a description of what each rating means.

Alabama

Rating: A

City	Name	Telephone
BIRMINGHAM	ACIPCO Federal Credit Union	(205) 328-4371
DECATUR	Family Security Credit Union	(256) 340-2000

Rating: A-

City	Name	Telephone
DOTHAN	Five Star Credit Union	(334) 793-7714
PENNINGTON	Naheola Credit Union	(205) 654-2370
MUSCLE SHOALS	TVA Community Credit Union	(256) 383-1019

Rating: B+

City	Name	Telephone
TUSCALOOSA	Alabama Credit Union	(205) 348-5944
GADSDEN	Alabama Teachers Credit Union	(256) 543-7040
BIRMINGHAM	Apco Employees Credit Union	(205) 226-6800
CHILDERSBURG	Coosa Pines Federal Credit Union	(256) 378-5559
RAINBOW CITY	Family Savings Credit Union	(256) 547-8190
ANNISTON	Fort McClellan Credit Union	(256) 237-2113
MUSCLE SHOALS	Listerhill Credit Union	(256) 383-9204
MONTGOMERY	Max Credit Union	(334) 260-2600
HUNTSVILLE	Redstone Federal Credit Union	(256) 837-6110
TUSCALOOSA	Riverfall Credit Union	(205) 759-1505
TUSCUMBIA	Valley Credit Union	(256) 381-4800

Alaska

City	Name	Telephone
Rating: A-		
FAIRBANKS	MAC Federal Credit Union	(907) 474-1291
Rating: B+		
ANCHORAGE	Credit Union 1	(907) 339-9485
PALMER	Matanuska Valley Federal Credit Union	(907) 745-4891
ANCHORAGE	Northern Skies Federal Credit Union	(907) 561-1407
FAIRBANKS	Spirit of Alaska Federal Credit Union	(907) 459-5900

Arizona

City	Name	Telephone
Rating:	**A**	
PHOENIX	Arizona Federal Credit Union	(602) 683-1000
PHOENIX	Desert Schools Federal Credit Union	(602) 433-7000
Rating:	**A-**	
TUCSON	Vantage West Credit Union	(520) 298-7882
Rating:	**B+**	
GLENDALE	Credit Union West	(602) 631-3200
TUCSON	Hughes Federal Credit Union	(520) 794-8341
PHOENIX	MariSol Federal Credit Union	(602) 252-6831
PHOENIX	OneAZ Credit Union	(602) 467-4081
TUCSON	Pima Federal Credit Union	(520) 887-5010
TEMPE	TruWest Credit Union	(480) 441-5900

Arkansas

City	Name	Telephone
Rating: A		
WARREN	Arkansas Superior Federal Credit Union	(870) 226-3534
Rating: B+		
LITTLE ROCK	Baptist Health Federal Credit Union	(501) 202-2373
BLYTHEVILLE	Northeast Arkansas Federal Credit Union	(870) 763-1111
PINE BLUFF	Pine Federal Credit Union	(870) 247-5100
LITTLE ROCK	Telcoe Federal Credit Union	(501) 375-5321

California

Rating: A+

City	Name	Telephone
SAN BERNARDINO	Arrowhead Central Credit Union	(909) 383-7300
LONG BEACH	Long Beach Firemen's Credit Union	(562) 597-0351
SAN DIEGO	San Diego County Credit Union	(877) 732-2848
EL MONTE	Vons Employees Federal Credit Union	(626) 444-1972

Rating: A

City	Name	Telephone
SANTA MONICA	California Lithuanian Credit Union	(310) 828-7095
ANAHEIM	Credit Union of Southern California	(866) 287-6225
FRESNO	Educational Employees Credit Union	(559) 437-7700
MONTEREY PARK	F&A Federal Credit Union	(323) 268-1226
ARCADIA	Foothill Federal Credit Union	(626) 445-0950
SACRAMENTO	Golden 1 Credit Union	(916) 732-2900
BURBANK	Logix Federal Credit Union	(800) 328-5328
CHATSWORTH	Matadors Community Credit Union	(818) 993-6328
SAN DIEGO	Mission Federal Credit Union	(858) 524-2850
FRESNO	Noble Federal Credit Union	(559) 252-5000
LIVERMORE	Operating Engineers Local Union #3 FCU	(925) 454-4000
SANTA ROSA	Redwood Credit Union	(707) 545-4000
SACRAMENTO	Sacramento Credit Union	(916) 444-6070
BAKERSFIELD	Safe 1 Credit Union	(661) 327-3818
SANTA ANA	SchoolsFirst Federal Credit Union	(714) 258-4000
VACAVILLE	Travis Credit Union	(707) 449-4000

Rating: A-

City	Name	Telephone
RIVERSIDE	Altura Credit Union	(888) 883-7228
SAN PEDRO	Bopti Federal Credit Union	(310) 832-0227
SAN DIEGO	California Coast Credit Union	(858) 495-1600
OAKLAND	Chevron Federal Credit Union	(800) 232-8101
EUREKA	Coast Central Credit Union	(707) 445-8801
GARBERVILLE	Community Credit Union of Southern Humboldt	(707) 923-2012
PASADENA	E-Central Credit Union	(626) 799-6000
HANFORD	Families & Schools Together FCU	(559) 584-0922
STOCKTON	Financial Center Credit Union	(209) 948-6024
MOUNTAIN VIEW	First Technology Federal Credit Union	(855) 855-8805
GLENDALE	Glendale Area Schools Credit Union	(818) 248-7425
WILMINGTON	I.L.W.U. Credit Union	(310) 834-6411
SYLMAR	Olive View Employees FCU	(818) 367-1057
SANTA ANA	Orange County's Credit Union	(714) 755-5900
BURBANK	Partners Federal Credit Union	(407) 354-5100
PLEASANTON	Patelco Credit Union	(800) 358-8228
CHATSWORTH	Premier America Credit Union	(818) 772-4000
REDWOOD CITY	Provident Credit Union	(650) 508-0300
REDWOOD CITY	San Mateo Credit Union	(650) 363-1725
SACRAMENTO	Schools Financial Credit Union	(916) 569-5400
REDONDO BEACH	South Bay Credit Union	(310) 374-3436
PALO ALTO	Stanford Federal Credit Union	(650) 723-2509
SAN JOSE	Technology Credit Union	(408) 467-2380
SIGNAL HILL	VA Desert Pacific Federal Credit Union	(562) 498-1250
WOODLAND	Yolo Federal Credit Union	(530) 668-2700

Rating: B+

City	Name	Telephone
SALINAS	allU.S. Credit Union	(831) 540-4627
LA HABRA	American First Credit Union	(800) 290-1112
RIVERSIDE	Bourns Employees Federal Credit Union	(951) 781-5600
SAN DIEGO	Cabrillo Credit Union	(858) 547-7400
SACRAMENTO	CAHP Credit Union	(916) 362-4191
TORRANCE	CalCom Federal Credit Union	(310) 371-4242
GLENDALE	California Credit Union	(800) 334-8788
LA CAÑADA FLINT	Caltech Employees Federal Credit Union	(818) 952-4444
UPLAND	Chaffey Federal Credit Union	(909) 986-4552
SAN DIMAS	Christian Community Credit Union	(626) 915-7551
LOMPOC	CoastHills Credit Union	(805) 733-7600
SAN JOSE	Commonwealth Central Credit Union	(408) 531-3100
LOS ANGELES	Farmers Insurance Group FCU	(800) 877-2345
LOS ANGELES	Firefighters First Federal Credit Union	(323) 254-1700
SACRAMENTO	First U.S. Community Credit Union	(916) 576-5700
TORRANCE	Honda Federal Credit Union	(310) 217-8600
BAKERSFIELD	Kern Schools Federal Credit Union	(661) 833-7900
HANFORD	Kings Federal Credit Union	(559) 582-4438
WESTMINSTER	LBS Financial Credit Union	(714) 893-5111
GLENDALE	Los Angeles Federal Credit Union	(818) 242-8640
OAKLAND	Matson Employees Federal Credit Union	(510) 628-4358
MERCED	Merced School Employees FCU	(209) 383-5550
SAN JOSE	Meriwest Credit Union	(408) 972-5222
STOCKTON	Mokelumne Federal Credit Union	(209) 938-1088
MONTEREY	Monterey Credit Union	(831) 647-1000
PASADENA	Parsons Federal Credit Union	(626) 440-7000
REDWOOD CITY	Polam Federal Credit Union	(650) 367-8940
CERRITOS	POPA Federal Credit Union	(562) 229-9181
SAN FRANCISCO	S.F. Police Credit Union	(415) 564-3800
SAN DIEGO	San Diego Metropolitan Credit Union	(619) 297-4835
SAN JOSE	Santa Clara County Federal Credit Union	(408) 282-0700
YUBA CITY	Sierra Central Credit Union	(800) 222-7228
SUNNYVALE	Star One Credit Union	(408) 543-5202
EL CENTRO	Sun Community Federal Credit Union	(760) 337-4200
SAN BERNARDINO	Thinkwise Federal Credit Union	(909) 882-2911
SAN DIEGO	University & State Employees CU	(858) 795-6100
SACRAMENTO	Vision One Credit Union	(916) 363-4293

Colorado

City	Name	Telephone
Rating: A+		
LONE TREE	Rocky Mountain Law Enforcement FCU	(303) 458-6660
Rating: A		
AURORA	Aurora Federal Credit Union	(303) 755-2572
GREENWOOD VIL	BellCo Credit Union	(303) 689-7800
LAKEWOOD	Credit Union of Denver	(303) 234-1700
BOULDER	Elevations Credit Union	(303) 443-4672
COLORADO SPRIN	Ent Credit Union	(719) 574-1100
GOLDEN	On Tap Credit Union	(303) 279-6414
STERLING	Sterling Federal Credit Union	(970) 522-0111
Rating: A-		
LITTLETON	Colorado Credit Union	(303) 978-2274
GRAND JUNCTION	Grand Junction Federal Credit Union	(970) 243-1370
PUEBLO	Minnequa Works Credit Union	(719) 544-6928
ARVADA	Partner Colorado Credit Union	(303) 422-6221
LONE TREE	Public Service Credit Union	(303) 691-2345
Rating: B+		
COLORADO SPRIN	Aventa Credit Union	(719) 482-7600
GRAND JUNCTION	Coloramo Federal Credit Union	(970) 243-7280
DENVER	Denver Community Credit Union	(303) 573-1170
CENTENNIAL	Metrum Community Credit Union	(303) 770-4468
SPRINGFIELD	Peoples Credit Union	(719) 523-6250
BOULDER	Premier Members Credit Union	(303) 657-7000
DENVER	Westerra Credit Union	(303) 321-4209

Connecticut

City	Name	Telephone
Rating:	**B+**	
ROCKY HILL	Nutmeg State Financial Credit Union	(860) 513-5000
MIDDLEBURY	Waterbury Connecticut Teacher FCU	(203) 758-9500

Delaware

Rating: A

City	Name	Telephone
SEAFORD	Tidemark Federal Credit Union	(302) 629-0100

District of Columbia

Rating: A-

City	Name	Telephone
WASHINGTON	Department of Labor Federal Credit Union	(202) 789-2901
WASHINGTON	IDB-IIC Federal Credit Union	(202) 623-3363

Florida

Rating: A

City	Name	Telephone
ROCKLEDGE	Community Credit Union of Florida	(321) 690-2328
JACKSONVILLE	Community First Credit Union of Florida	(904) 354-8537
WEST PALM BEAC	Guardians Credit Union	(561) 686-4006
MIAMI LAKES	JetStream Federal Credit Union	(305) 821-7060
JACKSONVILLE	JM Associates Federal Credit Union	(904) 378-4588
PANAMA CITY	Panhandle Educators Federal Credit Union	(850) 769-3306
LAKELAND	Publix Employees Federal Credit Union	(863) 683-6404

Rating: A-

City	Name	Telephone
DUNEDIN	Achieva Credit Union	(727) 431-7680
SUNRISE	BrightStar Credit Union	(954) 486-2728
JONESVILLE	Campus USA Credit Union	(352) 335-9090
TALLAHASSEE	First Commerce Credit Union	(850) 488-0035
GAINESVILLE	Florida Credit Union	(352) 377-4141
DELRAY BEACH	IBM Southeast Employees' Credit Union	(561) 982-4700
LAKELAND	MIDFLORIDA Credit Union	(863) 688-3733
PENSACOLA	Pen Air Federal Credit Union	(850) 505-3200
MELBOURNE	Space Coast Credit Union	(321) 752-2222
GAINESVILLE	SunState Federal Credit Union	(352) 381-5200

Rating: B+

City	Name	Telephone
MIAMI	Baptist Health South Florida FCU	(786) 257-2304
PENSACOLA	Central Credit Union of Florida	(850) 474-0970
CHIPLEY	Community South Credit Union	(850) 638-8376
SWEETWATER	Dade County Federal Credit Union	(305) 471-5080
CLEWISTON	Everglades Federal Credit Union	(863) 983-5141
ORLANDO	Fairwinds Credit Union	(407) 277-6030
JACKSONVILLE	First Florida Credit Union	(904) 359-6800
TALLAHASSEE	Florida State University Credit Union	(850) 224-4960
PENSACOLA	Gulf Winds Federal Credit Union	(850) 479-9601
MARIANNA	Jackson County Teachers Credit Union	(850) 526-4470
JACKSONVILLE	JAX Federal Credit Union	(904) 475-8000
BRADENTON	Manatee Community Federal Credit Union	(941) 748-7704
PENSACOLA	My Pensacola Federal Credit Union	(850) 432-9939
ORLANDO	Orlando Federal Credit Union	(407) 835-3500
TAMPA	Railroad & Industrial FCU	(813) 621-6661
TAMPA	St Joseph's Hospital FCU	(813) 870-4362
TAMPA	Suncoast Credit Union	(813) 621-7511
TAMPA	Tampa Bay Federal Credit Union	(813) 247-4414
JACKSONVILLE	VyStar Credit Union	(904) 777-6000

Georgia

City	Name	Telephone
Rating: A+		
WARNER ROBINS	Robins Financial Credit Union	(478) 923-3773
Rating: A		
MACON	CGR Credit Union	(478) 745-0494
ATLANTA	Delta Community Credit Union	(404) 715-4725
JESUP	Interstate Unlimited FCU	(912) 427-3904
Rating: A-		
WOODSTOCK	Credit Union of Georgia	(678) 322-2000
MARIETTA	LGE Community Credit Union	(770) 424-0060
MACON	Midsouth Community Federal Credit Union	(478) 471-9946
CORNELIA	Southeast Federal Credit Union	(706) 776-2145
SAVANNAH	Workmen's Circle Credit Union	(912) 356-9225
Rating: B+		
COLUMBUS	AFLAC Federal Credit Union	(706) 596-3239
JESUP	Altamaha Federal Credit Union	(912) 427-8924
DULUTH	Georgia United Credit Union	(770) 476-6400
BRUNSWICK	Marshland Community Federal Credit Union	(912) 279-2000
ALBANY	Members United Credit Union	(229) 439-1448
VALDOSTA	Southeastern Credit Union	(229) 244-2732
KINGSLAND	United 1st Federal Credit Union	(912) 729-2800

Guam

City	Name	Telephone
Rating: B+		
MAITE	Coast360 Federal Credit Union	(671) 477-8736

Hawaii

City	Name	Telephone
Rating:	**A**	
WAILUKU	Maui County Federal Credit Union	(808) 244-7968
Rating:	**A-**	
HONOLULU	Hawaii Federal Credit Union	(808) 847-1371
HONOLULU	Hawaiian Tel Federal Credit Union	(808) 832-8700
HONOLULU	University of Hawaii FCU	(808) 983-5500
KAHULUI	Wailuku Federal Credit Union	(808) 244-7981
Rating:	**B+**	
HILO	CU Hawaii Federal Credit Union	(808) 933-6700
HONOLULU	Hawaii Central Federal Credit Union	(808) 536-3677
HONOLULU	HawaiiUSA Federal Credit Union	(808) 534-4300
LIHUE	Kauai Community Federal Credit Union	(808) 245-6791
KAHULUI	Maui Federal Credit Union	(808) 873-5050
ELEELE	McBryde Federal Credit Union	(808) 335-3365
WAHIAWA	Schofield Federal Credit Union	(808) 624-9884

Idaho

Rating: A-

City	Name	Telephone
KAMIAH	Freedom Northwest Credit Union	(208) 935-0277
CHUBBUCK	Idaho Central Credit Union	(208) 239-3000
LEWISTON	Potlatch No. One Federal Credit Union	(208) 746-8900

Rating: B+

City	Name	Telephone
REXBURG	Beehive Federal Credit Union	(208) 656-1000
BOISE	Icon Credit Union	(208) 344-7948

Illinois

City	Name	Telephone
Rating: A		
OSWEGO	Earthmover Credit Union	(630) 844-4950
STREATOR	Streator Onized Credit Union	(815) 673-1589
Rating: A-		
GURNEE	Abbott Laboratories Employees CU	(847) 688-8000
VERNON HILLS	Baxter Credit Union	(800) 388-7000
OTTAWA	Financial Plus Credit Union	(815) 433-1496
BLOOMINGTON	IAA Credit Union	(309) 557-2541
SYCAMORE	Illinois Community Credit Union	(815) 895-4541
QUINCY	Members "FIRST" Community Credit Union	(217) 223-4377
WARRENVILLE	NorthStar Credit Union	(630) 393-7201
JOLIET	NuMark Credit Union	(815) 729-3211
Rating: B+		
BETHALTO	1st MidAmerica Credit Union	(618) 258-3168
ARLINGTON HEIG	A.A.E.C. Credit Union	(847) 392-1922
CHICAGO	Alliant Credit Union	(773) 462-2000
BELLEVILLE	Catholic & Community Credit Union	(618) 233-8073
PEORIA	Citizens Equity First Credit Union	(309) 633-7000
ELGIN	Corporate America Family Credit Union	(847) 214-2000
MOLINE	Deere Employees Credit Union	(309) 743-1000
ROCK ISLAND	Gas & Electric Credit Union	(309) 793-3610
NAPERVILLE	Healthcare Associates Credit Union	(630) 276-5555
SPRINGFIELD	Heartland Credit Union	(217) 726-8877
DECATUR	Land of Lincoln Credit Union	(217) 864-3030
MOLINE	Moline Municipal Credit Union	(309) 797-2185
CHICAGO	Selfreliance Ukrainian American FCU	(773) 328-7500

Indiana

City	Name	Telephone
Rating: A		
COLUMBUS	Centra Credit Union	(812) 376-9771
FORT WAYNE	Three Rivers Federal Credit Union	(260) 490-8328
Rating: A-		
ODON	Crane Credit Union	(812) 863-7000
KOKOMO	Financial Builders Federal Credit Union	(765) 455-0500
BLOOMINGTON	Indiana University Credit Union	(812) 855-7823
FORT WAYNE	Midwest America Federal Credit Union	(260) 482-3334
SOUTH BEND	South Bend Firefighters FCU	(574) 287-6161
MERRILLVILLE	US #1364 Federal Credit Union	(219) 769-1700
Rating: B+		
INDIANAPOLIS	Elements Financial Federal Credit Union	(317) 276-2105
TIPTON	Encompass Federal Credit Union	(765) 675-8848
EVANSVILLE	Evansville Federal Credit Union	(812) 424-2621
EVANSVILLE	Evansville Teachers Federal Credit Union	(812) 477-9271
FORT WAYNE	Public Service Credit Union	(260) 432-3433
WEST LAFAYETTE	Purdue Federal Credit Union	(765) 497-3328
WHITING	Whiting Refinery Federal Credit Union	(219) 659-3254

Iowa

City	Name	Telephone
Rating:	**A**	
CEDAR FALLS	Cedar Falls Community Credit Union	(319) 266-7531
FORT DODGE	Citizens Community Credit Union	(515) 955-5524
DUBUQUE	Dupaco Community Credit Union	(563) 557-7600
Rating:	**A-**	
CAMANCHE	1st Gateway Credit Union	(563) 243-4121
NEWTON	Advantage Credit Union	(641) 792-5660
DES MOINES	Des Moines Police Officers Credit Union	(515) 243-2677
ESTHERVILLE	Employees Credit Union	(712) 362-5897
DAVENPORT	Family Credit Union	(563) 388-8328
HIAWATHA	First Federal Credit Union	(319) 743-7806
HUMBOLDT	Power Co-Op Employees Credit Union	(515) 332-4096
Rating:	**B+**	
DUBUQUE	Alliant Credit Union	(563) 585-3737
BETTENDORF	Ascentra Credit Union	(563) 355-0152
JOHNSTON	Community Choice Credit Union	(515) 334-8100
FORT DODGE	Fort Dodge Family Credit Union	(515) 573-1160
OTTUMWA	Meridian Credit Union	(641) 684-4207
DES MOINES	Premier Credit Union	(515) 282-1611
AMES	River Valley Credit Union	(515) 232-1654
DES MOINES	Tradesmen Community Credit Union	(515) 243-8735
NORTH LIBERTY	University of Iowa Community CU	(319) 339-1000
WATERLOO	Veridian Credit Union	(319) 236-5600

Kansas

City	Name	Telephone
Rating: A		
WICHITA	Skyward Credit Union	(316) 517-6578
Rating: A-		
LENEXA	CommunityAmerica Credit Union	(913) 905-7001
WICHITA	Credit Union of America	(316) 265-3272
AUGUSTA	White Eagle Credit Union	(316) 775-7591
WICHITA	Wichita Federal Credit Union	(316) 941-0600
Rating: B+		
TOPEKA	Envista Credit Union	(785) 228-0149
BELOIT	Farmway Credit Union	(785) 738-2224
LEAVENWORTH	Frontier Community Credit Union	(913) 651-6575
TOPEKA	Kansas Blue Cross-Blue Shield CU	(785) 291-8774
PITTSBURG	Kansas Teachers Community Credit Union	(620) 231-5719
OVERLAND PARK	Mazuma Credit Union	(913) 574-5000
WICHITA	Meritrust Credit Union	(316) 683-1199
NORTON	United Northwest Federal Credit Union	(785) 877-5191

Kentucky

City	Name	Telephone
Rating: A+		
RADCLIFF	Fort Knox Federal Credit Union	(502) 942-0254
Rating: A		
PADUCAH	C-Plant Federal Credit Union	(270) 554-0287
BOWLING GREEN	Service One Credit Union, Inc.	(270) 796-8500
PADUCAH	Signet Federal Credit Union	(270) 443-5261
LEXINGTON	University of Kentucky FCU	(859) 264-4200
Rating: A-		
LOUISVILLE	Kentucky Telco Credit Union	(502) 459-3000
LOUISVILLE	L&N Federal Credit Union	(502) 368-5858
Rating: B+		
MIDDLESBORO	ARH Federal Credit Union	(606) 248-8566
ASHLAND	Ashland Credit Union	(606) 329-5489
LOUISVILLE	Autotruck Financial Credit Union	(502) 459-8981
FRANKFORT	Commonwealth Credit Union	(502) 564-4775
EDGEWOOD	Cove Federal Credit Union	(859) 292-9000
LOUISVILLE	Louisville Gas & Electric Company CU	(502) 627-3140
ASHLAND	Members Choice Credit Union	(606) 326-8000
LEXINGTON	Metro Employees Credit Union	(859) 258-3990

Louisiana

City	Name	Telephone
Rating: A		
BATON ROUGE	Department of Corrections Credit Union	(225) 342-6618
GEISMAR	Wymar Federal Credit Union	(225) 673-7191
Rating: A-		
BATON ROUGE	Baton Rouge Fire Department FCU	(225) 274-8383
LAPLACE	Louisiana Federal Credit Union	(985) 652-4990
LAKE CHARLES	Southwest Louisiana Credit Union	(337) 477-9190
BOGALUSA	Zellco Federal Credit Union	(985) 732-7522
Rating: B+		
BATON ROUGE	Baton Rouge Telco Federal Credit Union	(225) 924-8900
ALEXANDRIA	Cenla Federal Credit Union	(318) 445-7388
DERIDDER	First Street Federal Credit Union	(337) 463-3621
METAIRIE	Jefferson Financial Federal Credit Union	(504) 348-2424
NEW ORLEANS	Jefferson Parish Employees FCU	(504) 736-6144
LAFAYETTE	Lafayette Schools' Federal Credit Union	(337) 989-2800
LAFAYETTE	Maple Federal Credit Union	(337) 233-6264
NEW ORLEANS	New Orleans Police Department Empls CU	(504) 658-5570
WEST MONROE	Ouachita Valley Federal Credit Union	(318) 387-4592
BATON ROUGE	Pelican State Credit Union	(225) 408-6100
SHREVEPORT	Professional Fire Fighters Credit Union	(318) 603-0626

Maine

Rating: A

City	Name	Telephone
JAY	Otis Federal Credit Union	(207) 897-0900
MEXICO	Oxford Federal Credit Union	(207) 369-9976

Rating: A-

City	Name	Telephone
BRUNSWICK	Atlantic Regional Federal Credit Union	(207) 725-8728
SOUTH PORTLAN	Coast Line Credit Union	(207) 799-7245
PRESQUE ISLE	County Federal Credit Union	(207) 554-4700
SKOWHEGAN	Franklin-Somerset Federal Credit Union	(207) 474-3331
LEWISTON	Rainbow Federal Credit Union	(207) 784-5435
PORTLAND	Truchoice Federal Credit Union	(207) 772-0808

Rating: B+

City	Name	Telephone
FORT KENT	Acadia Federal Credit Union	(207) 834-6167
AUGUSTA	Capital Area Federal Credit Union	(207) 622-3442
FALMOUTH	Cumberland County Federal Credit Union	(207) 878-3441
GARDINER	Gardiner Federal Credit Union	(207) 582-2676
FREEPORT	Midcoast Federal Credit Union	(207) 865-4443
SACO	Saco Valley Credit Union	(207) 282-6169
SANFORD	York County Federal Credit Union	(207) 324-7511

Maryland

Rating: A

City	Name	Telephone
HYATTSVILLE	Library of Congress Federal Credit Union	(202) 707-5852

Rating: A-

City	Name	Telephone
BALTIMORE	Johns Hopkins Federal Credit Union	(410) 534-4500
LAUREL	Market USA Federal Credit Union	(301) 586-3400
UPPER MARLBOR	NASA Federal Credit Union	(301) 249-1800
BOWIE	Prince George's Community FCU	(301) 627-2666

Rating: B+

City	Name	Telephone
GREENBELT	Educational Systems Federal Credit Union	(301) 779-8500
LUTHERVILLE	First Financial of Maryland FCU	(410) 321-6060
CUMBERLAND	First Peoples Community FCU	(301) 784-3000
LARGO	Money One Federal Credit Union	(301) 925-4600
HAGERSTOWN	Washington County Teachers FCU	(301) 790-3131

Massachusetts

City	Name	Telephone
Rating: A		
SPRINGFIELD	Greater Springfield Credit Union	(413) 782-3161
WORCESTER	Webster First Federal Credit Union	(508) 671-5000
Rating: A-		
DORCHESTER	Boston Firefighters Credit Union	(617) 288-2420
MARLBOROUGH	Digital Federal Credit Union	(508) 263-6700
LYNN	River Works Credit Union	(781) 599-0096
ROCKLAND	Rockland Federal Credit Union	(781) 878-0232
TAUNTON	Taunton Federal Credit Union	(508) 824-6466
FITCHBURG	Workers' Credit Union	(978) 345-1021
Rating: B+		
NEEDHAM	Direct Federal Credit Union	(781) 455-6500
CAMBRIDGE	Harvard University Employees CU	(617) 495-4460
SPRINGFIELD	Pioneer Valley Federal Credit Union	(413) 733-2800
QUINCY	Quincy Credit Union	(617) 479-5558

Michigan

Rating: A

City	Name	Telephone
GRAND RAPIDS	AAC Credit Union	(616) 288-0288
SOUTHFIELD	Alliance Catholic Credit Union	(248) 663-4006
MUSKEGON	Best Financial Credit Union	(231) 733-1329
PLYMOUTH	Community Financial Credit Union	(734) 453-1200
GRAND BLANC	Dort Federal Credit Union	(810) 767-8390
MONROE	Education Plus Credit Union	(734) 242-3765
AUBURN HILLS	Genisys Credit Union	(248) 322-9800
BERRIEN SPRING	Honor Credit Union	(800) 442-2800
BATTLE CREEK	Kellogg Community Credit Union	(269) 968-9251
GRAND RAPIDS	Lake Michigan Credit Union	(616) 242-9790
MARSHALL	Marshall Community Credit Union	(269) 781-9885
CLINTON TOWNS	Michigan Schools and Government CU	(586) 263-8800
BATTLE CREEK	Omni Community Credit Union	(269) 441-1400
GRAND RAPIDS	Preferred Credit Union	(616) 942-9630
NORTON SHORES	Service 1 Federal Credit Union	(231) 739-5068
PETOSKEY	St. Francis X Federal Credit Union	(231) 347-8480
TRAVERSE CITY	TBA Credit Union	(231) 946-7090
ADRIAN	TLC Community Credit Union	(517) 263-9120
MARQUETTE	U.P. Catholic Credit Union	(906) 228-7080
SAGINAW	Wanigas Credit Union	(989) 759-5780
GRAND RAPIDS	West Michigan Credit Union	(616) 451-4567
LIVONIA	Zeal Credit Union	(800) 321-8570

Rating: A-

City	Name	Telephone
PARCHMENT	Advia Credit Union	(844) 238-4228
JACKSON	American 1 Credit Union	(517) 787-6510
ROCHESTER HILL	Chief Financial Federal Credit Union	(248) 253-7900
ROSEVILLE	Christian Financial Credit Union	(586) 772-6330
KALAMAZOO	Consumers Credit Union	(269) 345-7804
AUBURN HILLS	Cornerstone Community Financial CU	(248) 340-9310
DEARBORN	DFCU Financial	(313) 336-2700
BURTON	ELGA Credit Union	(810) 715-3542
FRANKENMUTH	Frankenmuth Credit Union	(989) 497-1600
MIDLAND	Members First Credit Union	(989) 835-5100
LATHRUP VILLAG	Michigan First Credit Union	(248) 443-4600
EAST LANSING	Michigan State University FCU	(517) 333-2424
OSCODA	Northland Area Federal Credit Union	(989) 739-1401
WATERFORD	Oakland County Credit Union	(248) 886-0144
LIVONIA	Parkside Credit Union	(734) 525-0700
ROMULUS	Public Service Credit Union	(734) 641-8400
SAINT JOSEPH	United Federal Credit Union	(269) 982-1400

Rating: B+

City	Name	Telephone
GRAND RAPIDS	Adventure Credit Union	(616) 243-0125
ALPENA	Alpena-Alcona Area Credit Union	(989) 356-3577
ROGERS CITY	Calcite Credit Union	(989) 734-4130
FARMINGTON HIL	Community Choice Credit Union	(877) 243-2528
KENTWOOD	Community West Credit Union	(616) 261-5657
LANSING	Consumers Professional Credit Union	(517) 372-2400
BUCHANAN	Country Heritage Credit Union	(269) 695-2334
JACKSON	CP Federal Credit Union	(517) 784-7101
MANISTEE	Filer Credit Union	(231) 723-3400
FLINT	Financial Plus Credit Union	(810) 244-2200
FIFE LAKE	Forest Area Federal Credit Union	(231) 879-4154
CLINTON TOWNS	FreeStar Financial Credit Union	(586) 466-7800
KALAMAZOO	KALSEE Credit Union	(269) 382-7800
TROY	Polish-American Federal Credit Union	(248) 619-0440
PORTLAND	Portland Federal Credit Union	(517) 647-7571
WARREN	Ukrainian Future Credit Union	(586) 757-1980
WARREN	Ukrainian Selfreliance Michigan FCU	(586) 756-3300
GRAND RAPIDS	Western Districts Members Credit Union	(616) 241-2516

Minnesota

City	Name	Telephone
Rating: A		
MONTEVIDEO	Co-Op Credit Union of Montevideo	(320) 269-2117
SAINT PAUL	St. Paul Federal Credit Union	(651) 772-8744
INTERNATIONAL F	TruStar Federal Credit Union	(218) 283-2000
APPLE VALLEY	Wings Financial Credit Union	(952) 997-8000
Rating: A-		
ROCHESTER	Mayo Employees Federal Credit Union	(507) 535-1460
MANKATO	Minnesota Valley Federal Credit Union	(507) 387-3055
PLYMOUTH	TruStone Financial Federal Credit Union	(763) 544-1517
Rating: B+		
COON RAPIDS	Anoka Hennepin Credit Union	(763) 422-0290
MELROSE	Central Minnesota Credit Union	(320) 256-3669
SAINT PAUL	City & County Credit Union	(651) 225-2700
BURNSVILLE	Firefly Federal Credit Union	(952) 736-5000
FULDA	Fulda Area Credit Union	(507) 425-2544
SAINT PAUL	Hiway Federal Credit Union	(651) 291-1515
WOODBURY	Ideal Credit Union	(651) 770-7000
CLOQUET	Members Cooperative Credit Union	(218) 879-3304
BAXTER	Mid Minnesota Federal Credit Union	(218) 829-0371
CAMBRIDGE	Minnco Credit Union	(763) 689-1071
SILVER BAY	North Shore Federal Credit Union	(218) 226-4401
SLEEPY EYE	SouthPoint Financial Credit Union	(507) 794-6712
BLOOMINGTON	Toro Employees Federal Credit Union	(952) 887-8041
TWO HARBORS	Two Harbors Federal Credit Union	(218) 834-2266
HOPKINS	West Metro Schools Credit Union	(952) 988-4165

Mississippi

City	Name	Telephone
Rating: A		
MERIDIAN	1st Mississippi Federal Credit Union	(601) 693-6873
LAUREL	Central Sunbelt Federal Credit Union	(601) 649-7181
BILOXI	Keesler Federal Credit Union	(228) 385-5500
RIDGELAND	Members Exchange Credit Union	(601) 922-3350
Rating: A-		
MONTICELLO	Ferguson Federal Credit Union	(601) 587-4037
GULFPORT	Gulf Coast Community FCU	(228) 539-7029
Rating: B+		
JACKSON	Mississippi Federal Credit Union	(601) 351-9200
PASCAGOULA	Navigator Credit Union	(228) 475-7300
SOUTHAVEN	SecurTrust Federal Credit Union	(662) 890-8760

Missouri

City	Name	Telephone
Rating:	**A+**	
SPRINGFIELD	CU Community Credit Union	(417) 865-3912
Rating:	**A**	
SAINT LOUIS	Century Credit Union	(314) 544-1818
SAINT LOUIS	Neighbors Credit Union	(314) 892-5400
SPRINGFIELD	Telcomm Credit Union	(417) 886-5355
Rating:	**A-**	
SPRINGFIELD	Assemblies of God Credit Union	(417) 831-4398
SAINT JOSEPH	Goetz Credit Union	(816) 232-8754
RICHMOND HEIGH	Health Care Family Credit Union	(314) 645-5851
MEXICO	United Credit Union	(573) 581-8651
Rating:	**B+**	
SPRINGFIELD	Blucurrent Credit Union	(417) 887-1983
SAINT LOUIS	First Missouri Credit Union	(314) 544-5050
JEFFERSON CITY	Missouri Electric Cooperatives Empls' CU	(573) 634-2595
SAINT LOUIS	St. Louis Community Credit Union	(314) 534-7610

Montana

City	Name	Telephone
Rating: A		
BILLINGS	Billings Federal Credit Union	(406) 248-1127
LIBBY	Lincoln County Credit Union	(406) 293-7771
Rating: A-		
BILLINGS	Altana Federal Credit Union	(406) 651-2328
SIDNEY	Richland Federal Credit Union	(406) 482-2704
BILLINGS	Valley Federal Credit Union of Montana	(406) 656-9100
WHITEFISH	Whitefish Credit Union Association	(406) 862-3525
Rating: B+		
SCOBEY	Daniels-Sheridan Federal Credit Union	(406) 487-5391
LEWISTOWN	Fergus Federal Credit Union	(406) 535-7478
GLENDIVE	Glendive BN Federal Credit Union	(406) 377-4250
CIRCLE	McCone County Federal Credit Union	(406) 485-2288
HELENA	Rocky Mountain Credit Union	(406) 449-2680

Nebraska

City	Name	Telephone
Rating: A		
OMAHA	Metro Health Services FCU	(402) 551-3052
COLUMBUS	Nebraska Energy Federal Credit Union	(402) 563-5900
Rating: A-		
LINCOLN	Liberty First Credit Union	(402) 465-1000
SOUTH SIOUX CIT	Siouxland Federal Credit Union	(402) 494-2073
Rating: B+		
ALLIANCE	Consumers Cooperative FCU	(308) 762-1871
COLUMBUS	Dale Employees Federal Credit Union	(402) 563-6207
OMAHA	Family Focus Federal Credit Union	(402) 933-0233
OMAHA	First Nebraska Credit Union	(402) 492-9100
OMAHA	Omaha Firefighters Credit Union	(402) 894-5005

Nevada

Rating: A

City	Name	Telephone
LAS VEGAS	Clark County Credit Union	(702) 228-2228
LAS VEGAS	One Nevada Credit Union	(702) 457-1000

Rating: A-

City	Name	Telephone
BOULDER CITY	Boulder Dam Credit Union	(702) 293-7777
CARSON CITY	Greater Nevada Credit Union	(775) 882-2060

Rating: B+

City	Name	Telephone
FALLON	Churchill County Federal Credit Union	(775) 423-7444
ELKO	Elko Federal Credit Union	(775) 738-4083
HAWTHORNE	Financial Horizons Credit Union	(775) 945-2421
RENO	Great Basin Federal Credit Union	(775) 333-4228
LAS VEGAS	Plus Credit Union	(702) 871-4746
LAS VEGAS	WestStar Credit Union	(702) 791-4777

New Hampshire

Rating: B+

City	Name	Telephone
PORTSMOUTH	Service Credit Union	(603) 422-8300

New Jersey

Rating: B+

City	Name	Telephone
HAMILTON	Central Jersey Police & Fire FCU	(609) 570-8155
ELIZABETH	Seaport Federal Credit Union	(908) 558-6124

New Mexico

City	Name	Telephone
Rating: A		
ALBUQUERQUE	Rio Grande Credit Union	(505) 262-1401
SANTA FE	State Employees Credit Union	(505) 983-7328
Rating: A-		
ARTESIA	Artesia Credit Union	(575) 748-9779
SANTA FE	Guadalupe Credit Union	(505) 982-8942
ALBUQUERQUE	Nusenda Federal Credit Union	(505) 889-7755
ALBUQUERQUE	Sandia Area Federal Credit Union	(505) 292-6343
Rating: B+		
BELEN	Belen Railway Employees Credit Union	(505) 864-4740
SANTA FE	Del Norte Credit Union	(505) 455-5228
TUCUMCARI	Everyone's Federal Credit Union	(575) 461-0433
ALBUQUERQUE	Kirtland Federal Credit Union	(505) 254-4369
ALAMOGORDO	LOCO Credit Union	(575) 437-3110
ALAMOGORDO	Otero Federal Credit Union	(575) 434-8500
ROSWELL	Roswell Community Federal Credit Union	(575) 623-7788
ALBUQUERQUE	Sandia Laboratory Federal Credit Union	(505) 293-0500

New York

City	Name	Telephone
Rating:	**A+**	
ROCHESTER	ESL Federal Credit Union	(585) 336-1000
Rating:	**A**	
EAST AURORA	Moog Employees Federal Credit Union	(716) 655-2360
PLAINVIEW	N C P D Federal Credit Union	(516) 938-0300
OLEAN	Olean Area Federal Credit Union	(716) 372-6607
NEW YORK	Self Reliance NY Federal Credit Union	(212) 473-7310
Rating:	**A-**	
ALBANY	Capital Communications FCU	(518) 458-2195
OSWEGO	Compass Federal Credit Union	(315) 342-5300
EAST SYRACUSE	Countryside Federal Credit Union	(315) 445-2300
SYRACUSE	Empower Federal Credit Union	(315) 477-2200
CORINTH	Hudson River Community Credit Union	(518) 654-9028
HAMBURG	Meridia Community Federal Credit Union	(716) 648-4411
MASSENA	Sea Comm Federal Credit Union	(315) 764-0566
ENDICOTT	Visions Federal Credit Union	(607) 754-7900
Rating:	**B+**	
NEW YORK	Actors Federal Credit Union	(212) 869-8926
ROCHESTER	Advantage Federal Credit Union	(585) 454-5900
ITHACA	CFCU Community Credit Union	(607) 257-8500
LATHAM	Community Resource Federal Credit Union	(518) 783-2211
PLATTSBURGH	Dannemora Federal Credit Union	(518) 825-0323
ROCHESTER	Family First of NY Federal Credit Union	(585) 586-8225
GLOVERSVILLE	First Choice Financial FCU	(518) 725-3191
NEW HARTFORD	First Source Federal Credit Union	(315) 735-8571
NEW HARTFORD	G.P.O. Federal Credit Union	(315) 724-1654
POUGHKEEPSIE	Hudson Valley Federal Credit Union	(845) 463-3011
BUFFALO	Morton Lane Federal Credit Union	(716) 837-2007
WESTBURY	Nassau Educators Federal Credit Union	(516) 561-0030
MALONE	North Franklin Federal Credit Union	(518) 483-8668
PORT WASHINGT	Port Washington Federal Credit Union	(516) 883-3537
OGDENSBURG	Saint Lawrence Federal Credit Union	(315) 393-3530
PAINTED POST	ServU Federal Credit Union	(607) 936-2293
SIDNEY	Sidney Federal Credit Union	(607) 561-7300
SYRACUSE	Syracuse Fire Department Employees FCU	(315) 471-4621
CHEEKTOWAGA	Town of Cheektowaga Federal Credit Union	(716) 686-3497
PLATTSBURGH	UFirst Federal Credit Union	(518) 324-5700
NEW HARTFORD	Utica Gas & Electric Employees FCU	(315) 733-1596
WILLIAMSVILLE	Western Division Federal Credit Union	(716) 632-9328
MINEOLA	Winthrop-University Hospital Empls FCU	(516) 493-9400

North Carolina

Rating: A-

City	Name	Telephone
CANTON	Champion Credit Union	(828) 648-1515
CHARLOTTE	Charlotte Metro Federal Credit Union	(704) 375-0183
DURHAM	Latino Community Credit Union	(919) 530-8800
DURHAM	Self-Help Federal Credit Union	(919) 956-4600
GREENSBORO	Summit Credit Union	(336) 662-6200

Rating: B+

City	Name	Telephone
WINSTON-SALEM	Allegacy Federal Credit Union	(336) 774-3400
RALEIGH	Coastal Federal Credit Union	(919) 420-8000
RALEIGH	Local Government Federal Credit Union	(919) 755-0534
WAYNESVILLE	Mountain Credit Union	(828) 456-8627
GREENSBORO	Premier Federal Credit Union	(336) 370-1286
ASHEVILLE	Telco Community Credit Union	(828) 252-6458

North Dakota

City	Name	Telephone
Rating: A		
MANDAN	Railway Credit Union	(701) 667-9500
Rating: A-		
MINOT	Affinity First Federal Credit Union	(701) 857-5541
BISMARCK	Capital Credit Union	(701) 255-0042
JAMESTOWN	First Community Credit Union	(701) 252-0360
MADDOCK	North Star Community Credit Union	(701) 438-2222
MINOT	Prairie Federal Credit Union	(701) 837-5353
MINOT	Town & Country Credit Union	(701) 852-2018
FARGO	United Savings Credit Union	(701) 235-2832
Rating: B+		
LAMOURE	LaMoure Credit Union	(701) 883-5241
WILLISTON	Western Cooperative Credit Union	(701) 572-4000

Ohio

City	Name	Telephone
Rating: A+		
LIMA	Superior Credit Union, Inc.	(419) 223-9746
Rating: A		
KETTERING	Day Air Credit Union	(937) 643-2160
FREMONT	Fremont Federal Credit Union	(419) 334-4434
WEST CHESTER	Kemba Credit Union	(513) 762-5070
GAHANNA	KEMBA Financial Credit Union	(614) 235-2395
WARREN	Seven Seventeen Credit Union	(330) 372-8100
BEAVERCREEK	Wright-Patt Credit Union, Inc.	(937) 912-7000
Rating: A-		
CINCINNATI	Cinfed Federal Credit Union	(513) 333-3835
DOVER	Dover-Phila Federal Credit Union	(330) 364-8874
CELINA	Dynamic Federal Credit Union	(419) 586-5522
GARFIELD HEIGHT	Ohio Catholic Federal Credit Union	(216) 663-8090
FAIRLAWN	Towpath Credit Union	(330) 664-4700
Rating: B+		
CINCINNATI	Children's Medical Center FCU	(513) 636-4470
YOUNGSTOWN	Doy Federal Credit Union	(330) 744-5680
CINCINNATI	General Electric Credit Union	(513) 243-4328
AKRON	GenFed Financial Credit Union	(330) 734-0225
CHILLICOTHE	Homeland Credit Union	(740) 775-3331
GREENVILLE	Members Choice Credit Union	(937) 548-0360
KENTON	Quest Federal Credit Union	(419) 674-4998
SANDUSKY	VacationLand Federal Credit Union	(419) 625-9025

Oklahoma

City	Name	Telephone
Rating: A		
OKLAHOMA CITY	Oklahoma Federal Credit Union	(405) 524-6467
Rating: A-		
TULSA	TTCU The Credit Union	(918) 743-9861
Rating: B+		
DUNCAN	Halliburton Employees FCU	(580) 255-3550
OKLAHOMA CITY	Oklahoma Educators Credit Union	(405) 722-2234
OKLAHOMA CITY	Oklahoma Employees Credit Union	(405) 606-6328
LAWTON	Southwest Oklahoma Federal Credit Union	(580) 353-0490
OKLAHOMA CITY	Tinker Federal Credit Union	(405) 732-0324
OKLAHOMA CITY	U.S. Employees O.C. Federal Credit Union	(405) 685-6200
OKLAHOMA CITY	Weokie Credit Union	(405) 235-3030

Oregon

Rating: A

City	Name	Telephone
PORTLAND	OnPoint Community Credit Union	(503) 228-7077

Rating: A-

City	Name	Telephone
ROSEBURG	Cascade Community Federal Credit Union	(541) 672-9000
MILWAUKIE	Clackamas Community Federal Credit Union	(503) 656-0671
CORVALLIS	Oregon State Credit Union	(541) 714-4000
MEDFORD	Rogue Credit Union	(541) 858-7328
EUGENE	SELCO Community Credit Union	(800) 445-4483
PORTLAND	Sunset Science Park Federal Credit Union	(503) 643-1335
PORTLAND	Unitus Community Credit Union	(503) 227-5571

Rating: B+

City	Name	Telephone
CLACKAMAS	Advantis Credit Union	(503) 785-2528
HOOD RIVER	Cascade Central Credit Union	(541) 387-9297
PORTLAND	Castparts Employees Federal Credit Union	(503) 771-2464
PORTLAND	Consolidated Federal Credit Union	(503) 232-8070
ONTARIO	Malheur Federal Credit Union	(541) 889-3149
MILWAUKIE	Providence Federal Credit Union	(503) 215-6090
BEAVERTON	Rivermark Community Credit Union	(503) 626-6600

Pennsylvania

City	Name	Telephone
Rating: A+		
PHILADELPHIA	Police and Fire Federal Credit Union	(215) 931-0300
Rating: A		
BUTLER	Butler Armco Employees Credit Union	(724) 284-2020
Rating: A-		
CLARION	Clarion Federal Credit Union	(814) 226-5032
WARMINSTER	Freedom Credit Union	(215) 612-5900
HARRISBURG	Pennsylvania State Employees CU	(800) 237-7328
PHILADELPHIA	Philadelphia Federal Credit Union	(215) 934-3500
Rating: B+		
RIDLEY PARK	BHCU	(610) 595-2929
HARRISBURG	Blue Chip Federal Credit Union	(717) 564-3081
POTTSVILLE	CACL Federal Credit Union	(570) 628-2400
WASHINGTON	Chrome Federal Credit Union	(724) 228-2030
EXTON	Citadel Federal Credit Union	(610) 380-6000
POTTSTOWN	Diamond Credit Union	(610) 326-5490
ALLENTOWN	First Class Federal Credit Union	(610) 439-4102
BETHLEHEM	First Commonwealth Federal Credit Union	(610) 821-2400
NEW CASTLE	GNC Community Federal Credit Union	(724) 652-5783
PITTSBURGH	Greater Pittsburgh Police FCU	(412) 922-4800
HAZLETON	Hazleton School Employees Credit Union	(570) 459-1611
ALLENTOWN	Lehigh Valley Educators Credit Union	(610) 820-0145
ALLENPORT	Mon Valley Community FCU	(724) 326-5632
WORTHINGTON	Moonlight Credit Union	(724) 297-3084
SAINT MARYS	Mountain Laurel Federal Credit Union	(814) 834-9518
PITTSBURGH	Pittsburgh Firefighters' FCU	(412) 928-8500
FORT WASHINGT	TruMark Financial Credit Union	(215) 953-5300
WYOMISSING	Utilities Employees Credit Union	(610) 927-4000

Puerto Rico

City	Name	Telephone
Rating: B+		
SAN JUAN	Caribe Federal Credit Union	(787) 474-5151

Rhode Island

City	Name	Telephone
Rating: A-		
SMITHFIELD	Navigant Credit Union	(401) 233-4300
Rating: B+		
PAWTUCKET	Pawtucket Credit Union	(401) 722-2212

South Carolina

Rating: A

City	Name	Telephone
COLUMBIA	AllSouth Federal Credit Union	(803) 736-3110
GREENVILLE	Greenville Heritage Federal Credit Union	(864) 467-4160
GREENVILLE	MTC Federal Credit Union	(864) 908-3469
COLUMBIA	Palmetto Citizens Federal Credit Union	(803) 779-1232
COLUMBIA	S.C. State Federal Credit Union	(803) 343-0300
GREENVILLE	SC Telco Federal Credit Union	(864) 232-5553

Rating: A-

City	Name	Telephone
SPARTANBURG	Carolina Foothills Federal Credit Union	(864) 585-6838
NORTH CHARLES	CPM Federal Credit Union	(843) 747-6376
LANCASTER	Founders Federal Credit Union	(800) 845-1614
GEORGETOWN	Georgetown Kraft Credit Union	(843) 546-8494
GREENVILLE	Greenville Federal Credit Union	(864) 235-6309
COLUMBIA	Palmetto Health Credit Union	(803) 978-2101
FLORENCE	Pee Dee Federal Credit Union	(843) 669-0461
NORTH CHARLES	South Carolina Federal Credit Union	(843) 797-8300
COLUMBIA	South Carolina National Guard FCU	(803) 799-1090
NORTH AUGUSTA	SRP Federal Credit Union	(803) 278-4851

Rating: B+

City	Name	Telephone
COLUMBIA	Carolina Collegiate Federal Credit Union	(803) 227-5555
MYRTLE BEACH	Carolina Trust Federal Credit Union	(843) 448-2133
ROCK HILL	Family Trust Federal Credit Union	(803) 367-4100
FORT MILL	Sharonview Federal Credit Union	(800) 462-4421

South Dakota

City	Name	Telephone
Rating: A		
SIOUX FALLS	Sioux Falls Federal Credit Union	(605) 334-2471
Rating: A-		
ABERDEEN	Aberdeen Federal Credit Union	(605) 225-2488
RAPID CITY	Black Hills Federal Credit Union	(605) 718-1818
HURON	Dakotaland Federal Credit Union	(605) 352-2845
Rating: B+		
BRITTON	Norstar Federal Credit Union	(605) 448-2292

Tennessee

Rating: A+

City	Name	Telephone
BARTLETT	First South Financial Credit Union	(901) 380-7400

Rating: A

City	Name	Telephone
TULLAHOMA	Ascend Federal Credit Union	(931) 455-5441
KINGSPORT	Eastman Credit Union	(423) 578-7676
SHELBYVILLE	Heritage South Community Credit Union	(931) 680-1400
JACKSON	Leaders Credit Union	(731) 664-1784
ELIZABETHTON	Northeast Community Credit Union	(423) 547-1200
MEMPHIS	Orion Federal Credit Union	(901) 385-5200
CHATTANOOGA	Tennessee Valley Federal Credit Union	(423) 634-3600

Rating: A-

City	Name	Telephone
KNOXVILLE	City Employees Credit Union	(865) 824-7200
MEMPHIS	FEDEX Employees Credit Association FCU	(901) 344-2500
MEMPHIS	L G & W Federal Credit Union	(901) 680-7995
MEMPHIS	Memphis City Employees Credit Union	(901) 321-1200
CORDOVA	Methodist Healthcare FCU	(901) 453-3500

Rating: B+

City	Name	Telephone
ERWIN	Clinchfield Federal Credit Union	(423) 743-9192
CLARKSVILLE	Fortera Federal Credit Union	(931) 431-6800
CAMDEN	Johnsonville TVA Employees Credit Union	(731) 584-7238
MEMPHIS	Kimberly Clark Credit Union	(901) 521-4646
KNOXVILLE	Knoxville TVA Employees Credit Union	(865) 544-5400
KNOXVILLE	New South Credit Union	(865) 523-0757
OAK RIDGE	ORNL Federal Credit Union	(865) 688-9555
MEMPHIS	UPS Employees Credit Union	(901) 396-2132

Texas

Rating: A+

City	Name	Telephone
LONGVIEW	East Texas Professional Credit Union	(903) 323-0230
CORPUS CHRISTI	Members First Credit Union	(361) 991-6178
SUGAR LAND	Pioneer Mutual Federal Credit Union	(281) 566-8000
LIVE OAK	Randolph-Brooks Federal Credit Union	(210) 945-3300
SUGAR LAND	Schlumberger Employees Credit Union	(281) 285-4551

Rating: A

City	Name	Telephone
AUSTIN	Austin Telco Federal Credit Union	(512) 302-5555
CORINTH	DATCU Credit Union	(940) 387-8585
AMARILLO	Education Credit Union	(806) 358-7777
FORT WORTH	EECU	(817) 882-0000
PASADENA	Gulf Coast Educators FCU	(281) 487-9333
HOUSTON	Harris County Federal Credit Union	(713) 755-5160
HOUSTON	Houston Police Federal Credit Union	(713) 986-0200
BEAUMONT	Mobiloil Federal Credit Union	(409) 892-1111
PORT NECHES	Neches Federal Credit Union	(409) 722-1174
SUGAR LAND	Nizari Progressive Federal Credit Union	(281) 921-8500
DALLAS	Southwest Airlines Federal Credit Union	(214) 357-5577
SAN ANTONIO	Synergy Federal Credit Union	(210) 345-2222

Rating: A-

City	Name	Telephone
LEAGUE CITY	Associated Credit Union of Texas	(409) 945-4474
BAY CITY	Baycel Federal Credit Union	(979) 244-3995
SLATON	Caprock Santa Fe Credit Union	(806) 828-5825
WACO	First Central Credit Union	(254) 776-9333
NEDERLAND	FivePoint Credit Union	(409) 962-8793
FORT WORTH	Fort Worth City Credit Union	(817) 732-2803
PHARR	Naft Federal Credit Union	(956) 787-2774
DALLAS	Neighborhood Credit Union	(214) 748-9393
TEXARKANA	Red River Federal Credit Union	(903) 793-7681
DEER PARK	Shell Federal Credit Union	(713) 844-1100
HOUSTON	Southern Federal Credit Union	(713) 232-7774
LUBBOCK	Texas Tech Federal Credit Union	(806) 742-3606
WHARTON	Texasgulf Federal Credit Union	(979) 282-2300
TEMPLE	Texell Credit Union	(254) 773-1604
WICHITA FALLS	Texoma Community Credit Union	(940) 851-4000
KERMIT	WesTex Community Credit Union	(432) 586-6631

Rating: B+

City	Name	Telephone
AUSTIN	A+ Federal Credit Union	(512) 302-6800
ABILENE	Abilene Teachers Federal Credit Union	(325) 677-2274
AUSTIN	Amplify Credit Union	(512) 836-5901
DALLAS	Baylor Health Care System Credit Union	(214) 820-2342
BIG SPRING	Big Spring Education Employees FCU	(432) 263-8393
DEL RIO	Border Federal Credit Union	(830) 774-2328
CLUTE	Brazosport Teachers Federal Credit Union	(979) 265-5333
MEXIA	Centex Citizens Credit Union	(254) 562-9296
RUSK	Cherokee County Federal Credit Union	(903) 683-2527
DALLAS	City Credit Union	(214) 515-0100
ODESSA	Complex Community Federal Credit Union	(432) 550-9126
TYLER	Cooperative Teachers Credit Union	(903) 561-2603
DALLAS	Credit Union Of Texas	(972) 263-9497
BEAUMONT	DuGood Federal Credit Union	(409) 899-3430
EDINBURG	Edinburg Teachers Credit Union	(956) 259-3511
BEAUMONT	Education First Federal Credit Union	(409) 898-3770
WACO	Educators Credit Union	(254) 776-7900
FLOYDADA	F C S Federal Credit Union	(806) 983-5126
ODESSA	First Basin Credit Union	(432) 333-5600
WACO	GENCO Federal Credit Union	(254) 776-9550
HEREFORD	Hereford Texas Federal Credit Union	(806) 364-1888
HOUSTON	Houston Texas Fire Fighters FCU	(713) 864-0959
TYLER	Kelly Community Federal Credit Union	(903) 597-7291
LAREDO	Laredo Federal Credit Union	(956) 722-3971
RICHARDSON	Lifetime Federal Credit Union	(972) 766-6732
LUFKIN	Lufkin Federal Credit Union	(936) 632-4397
PORT NECHES	MCT Credit Union	(409) 727-1446
WACO	Members Choice of Central Texas FCU	(254) 776-7070
HOUSTON	National Oilwell Varco Employees CU	(713) 634-3471
CORPUS CHRISTI	Navy Army Community Credit Union	(361) 986-4500
DALLAS	Resource One Credit Union	(214) 319-3100
AMARILLO	Santa Fe Federal Credit Union	(806) 373-0736
HOUSTON	Smart Financial Credit Union	(713) 850-1600
DALLAS	Southwest Financial Federal Credit Union	(214) 630-7111
ODESSA	Southwest Heritage Credit Union	(432) 367-8993
TEXARKANA	Texar Federal Credit Union	(903) 223-0000
HOUSTON	Texas Bay Credit Union	(713) 852-6700
DALLAS	Texas Telcom Credit Union	(214) 320-8818
BROWNSVILLE	Valley Federal Credit Union	(956) 546-3108
AUSTIN	Velocity Credit Union	(512) 469-7000
WINDTHORST	Windthorst Federal Credit Union	(940) 423-6776

Utah

City	Name	Telephone
Rating: A+		
SALT LAKE CITY	Utah Power Credit Union	(801) 708-8900
Rating: A		
BRIGHAM CITY	Box Elder County Federal Credit Union	(435) 723-3437
OGDEN	Goldenwest Federal Credit Union	(801) 621-4550
SALT LAKE CITY	Utah First Federal Credit Union	(801) 320-2600
Rating: A-		
RIVERDALE	America First Federal Credit Union	(801) 627-0900
WEST JORDAN	American United Family of Credit Unions, FCU	(801) 359-9600
WEST JORDAN	Cyprus Federal Credit Union	(801) 260-7600
SALT LAKE CITY	Hi-Land Credit Union	(801) 261-8909
WEST JORDAN	Mountain America Federal Credit Union	(801) 325-6228
SPRINGVILLE	Nebo Credit Union	(801) 491-3691
NEPHI	Nephi Western Employees FCU	(435) 623-1895
SALT LAKE CITY	University First Federal Credit Union	(801) 481-8800
PROVO	Utah Community Federal Credit Union	(801) 223-8188
Rating: B+		
SALT LAKE CITY	Granite Federal Credit Union	(801) 288-3000
BRIGHAM CITY	Members First Credit Union	(435) 723-5231

Vermont

City	Name	Telephone
Rating: A-		
WILLISTON	New England Federal Credit Union	(802) 879-8790
Rating: B+		
RUTLAND	Credit Union of Vermont	(802) 773-0027
RUTLAND	Heritage Family Federal Credit Union	(802) 775-4930
BARRE	Members Advantage Community Credit Union	(802) 479-9411

Virgin Islands of the U.S.

Rating: B+

City	Name	Telephone
CHARLOTTE AMAL	St. Thomas Federal Credit Union	(340) 774-1299

Virginia

City	Name	Telephone
Rating: A		
VIENNA	Navy Federal Credit Union	(703) 255-8000
ALEXANDRIA	United States Senate FCU	(202) 224-2967
Rating: A-		
FAIRFAX	Fairfax County Federal Credit Union	(703) 218-9900
ROANOKE	Freedom First Federal Credit Union	(540) 389-0244
Rating: B+		
FAIRFAX	Apple Federal Credit Union	(703) 788-4800
FALLS CHURCH	Arlington Community Federal Credit Union	(703) 526-0200
ROANOKE	Blue Eagle Credit Union	(540) 342-3429
RICHMOND	Credit Union Of Richmond Incorporated	(804) 355-9684
WAYNESBORO	Dupont Community Credit Union	(540) 946-3200
CHANTILLY	Justice Federal Credit Union	(703) 480-5300
ROANOKE	Member One Federal Credit Union	(540) 982-8811
CHESAPEAKE	N A E Federal Credit Union	(757) 410-2000
TYSONS	Pentagon Federal Credit Union	(703) 838-1000
PORTSMOUTH	PFD Firefighters Credit Union Incorporated	(757) 686-3051
WOODBRIDGE	PWC Employees Credit Union	(703) 680-1143
ALEXANDRIA	Signature Federal Credit Union	(703) 683-7300
ALEXANDRIA	State Department Federal Credit Union	(703) 706-5000
CHARLOTTESVILL	University of Virginia Community CU	(434) 964-2001
HOPEWELL	Vantage Point Federal Credit Union	(804) 541-1473
RICHMOND	Virginia Credit Union, Inc.	(804) 253-6000

Washington

Rating: A+

City	Name	Telephone
BELLINGHAM	Whatcom Educational Credit Union	(360) 676-1168

Rating: A

City	Name	Telephone
TUKWILA	Boeing Employees Credit Union	(206) 439-5700
ABERDEEN	Great Northwest Federal Credit Union	(360) 533-9990
REDMOND	Qualstar Credit Union	(425) 643-3400
YAKIMA	Solarity Credit Union	(509) 248-1720
TACOMA	Sound Credit Union	(253) 383-2016

Rating: A-

City	Name	Telephone
VANCOUVER	Columbia Credit Union	(360) 891-4000
VANCOUVER	IQ Credit Union	(360) 695-3441
BREMERTON	Kitsap Credit Union	(360) 662-2000
SPOKANE VALLEY	Numerica Credit Union	(509) 535-7613
SHELTON	Our Community Credit Union	(360) 426-9701
LONGVIEW	Red Canoe Credit Union	(800) 562-5611
LIBERTY LAKE	Spokane Teachers Credit Union	(509) 326-1954
ENUMCLAW	White River Credit Union	(360) 825-4833

Rating: B+

City	Name	Telephone
DUPONT	America's Federal Credit Union	(253) 964-3113
SPOKANE	Avista Corp. Credit Union	(509) 495-2000
KENT	Cascade Federal Credit Union	(425) 251-8888
RICHLAND	Gesa Credit Union	(509) 378-3100
SPOKANE VALLEY	Horizon Credit Union	(509) 928-6494
TUKWILA	Inspirus Credit Union	(206) 628-4010
BELLINGHAM	North Coast Credit Union	(360) 733-3982
EVERETT	NorthWest Plus Credit Union	(425) 297-1000
SPOKANE	Primesource Credit Union	(509) 838-6157
BELLEVUE	Puget Sound Cooperative Credit Union	(425) 283-5151
SPOKANE	Safeway Federal Credit Union	(509) 483-9416
SEATTLE	Salal Credit Union	(206) 298-9394
SEATTLE	Seattle Metropolitan Credit Union	(206) 398-5500
SPOKANE	Spokane Law Enforcement Credit Union	(509) 327-3244
PORT ANGELES	Strait View Credit Union	(360) 452-3883
FIFE	Tacoma Longshoremen Credit Union	(253) 272-0240
LACEY	TwinStar Credit Union	(360) 357-9911
SEATTLE	Verity Credit Union	(206) 440-9000
OLYMPIA	Washington State Employees Credit Union	(360) 943-7911
OLYMPIA	WCLA Credit Union	(360) 352-5033

West Virginia

City	Name	Telephone
Rating: A-		
CHARLESTON	State Credit Union	(304) 558-0566
MORGANTOWN	United Federal Credit Union	(304) 598-5010
PARKERSBURG	West Virginia Central Credit Union	(304) 485-4523
Rating: B+		
CHARLESTON	CAMC Federal Credit Union	(304) 388-5700
HUNTINGTON	Huntingtonized Federal Credit Union	(304) 528-2400
CHARLESTON	Members Choice WV Federal Credit Union	(304) 346-5242
CHARLESTON	WV National Guard Federal Credit Union	(304) 342-2422
MORGANTOWN	WVU Employees Federal Credit Union	(304) 293-5737

Wisconsin

Rating: A

City	Name	Telephone
WEST ALLIS	AppleTree Credit Union	(414) 546-7800
APPLETON	Community First Credit Union	(920) 830-7200
ANTIGO	Covantage Credit Union	(715) 627-4336
BELOIT	First Community Credit Union of Beloit	(608) 362-9077
WISCONSIN RAPI	Members' Advantage Credit Union	(715) 421-1610
GREEN BAY	PCM Credit Union	(920) 499-2831
MANITOWOC	Shipbuilders Credit Union	(920) 682-8500
MADISON	Summit Credit Union	(608) 243-5000
MANITOWOC	Unitedone Credit Union	(920) 684-0361
WESTBY	Westby Co-op Credit Union	(608) 634-3118

Rating: A-

City	Name	Telephone
ONALASKA	Altra Federal Credit Union	(608) 787-4500
MILWAUKEE	Aurora Credit Union	(414) 649-7949
GREEN BAY	Capital Credit Union	(920) 494-2828
RACINE	Educators Credit Union	(262) 886-5900
FORT ATKINSON	Fort Community Credit Union	(920) 563-7305
APPLETON	Fox Communities Credit Union	(920) 993-9000
EAU CLAIRE	Royal Credit Union	(715) 833-8111
SUPERIOR	Superior Choice Credit Union	(715) 392-5616
MADISON	University of Wisconsin Credit Union	(608) 232-5000
OSHKOSH	Verve, a Credit Union	(920) 236-7040
MENOMONIE	WESTconsin Credit Union	(715) 235-3403

Rating: B+

City	Name	Telephone
ARCADIA	Arcadia Credit Union	(608) 323-2126
MILWAUKEE	Brewery Credit Union	(414) 273-3170
NEENAH	CentralAlliance Credit Union	(920) 720-2572
WAUSAU	Cloverbelt Credit Union	(715) 842-5693
WAUSAU	Connexus Credit Union	(715) 847-4700
BLACK RIVER FAL	CO-OP Credit Union	(715) 284-5333
ONALASKA	Firefighters Credit Union	(608) 784-9480
WEST BEND	Glacier Hills Credit Union	(262) 338-1888
NEW BERLIN	Landmark Credit Union	(262) 796-4500
STEVENS POINT	Sentry Credit Union	(715) 346-6532
MARSHFIELD	Simplicity Credit Union	(715) 387-3702
MOSINEE	Valley Communities Credit Union	(715) 693-5770

Wyoming

City	Name	Telephone
Rating: A		
CODY	Sunlight Federal Credit Union	(307) 587-4915
CHEYENNE	WyHy Federal Credit Union	(307) 638-4200
Rating: A-		
CHEYENNE	Unified People's Federal Credit Union	(307) 632-1476
Rating: B+		
LANDER	Atlantic City Federal Credit Union	(307) 332-5151
CHEYENNE	Blue Federal Credit Union	(307) 432-5400
GREEN RIVER	Trona Valley Community FCU	(307) 875-9800

Section III

Rating Upgrades and Downgrades

A list of all

Credit Unions

receiving a rating upgrade or downgrade during the current quarter.

Section III Contents

This section identifies those institutions receiving a rating change since the previous edition of this publication, whether it be a rating upgrade, rating downgrade, newly rated company or the withdrawal of a rating. A rating upgrade or downgrade may entail a change from one letter grade to another, or it may mean the addition or deletion of a plus or minus sign within the same letter grade previously assigned to the company. Ratings are normally updated once each quarter of the year. In some instances, however, an institution's rating may be downgraded outside of the normal updates due to overriding circumstances.

1. **Institution Name** The name under which the institution was chartered. A company's name can be very similar to, or the same as, that of another, so verify the company's exact name, city, and state to make sure you are looking at the correct company.

2. **New Safety Rating** Weiss rating assigned to the institution at the time of publication. Our ratings are designed to distinguish levels of insolvency risk and are measured on a scale from A to F based upon a wide range of factors. Highly rated companies are, in our opinion, less likely to experience financial difficulties than lower rated firms. See *About Weiss Safety Ratings* for more information and a description of what each rating means.

3. **State** The state in which the institution's headquarters or main office is located.

4. **Date of Change** Date that rating was finalized.

New Ratings

Name	State	Date of Change
Rating: D+		
Farmers Credit Union	KS	06/12/17

Rating Upgrades

Rating: A

Name	State	Date of Change
C-Plant Federal Credit Union	KY	06/12/17
Department of Corrections Credit Union	LA	06/12/17
Elevations Credit Union	CO	06/12/17
Matadors Community Credit Union	CA	06/12/17
Orion Federal Credit Union	TN	06/12/17
S.C. State Federal Credit Union	SC	06/12/17
Service 1 Federal Credit Union	MI	06/12/17
Shipbuilders Credit Union	WI	06/12/17
Sterling Federal Credit Union	CO	06/12/17
United States Senate FCU	VA	06/12/17
Wings Financial Credit Union	MN	06/12/17

Rating: A-

Name	State	Date of Change
Community Credit Union of Southern Humboldt	CA	06/12/17
First Central Credit Union	TX	06/12/17
Guadalupe Credit Union	NM	06/12/17
Hawaii Federal Credit Union	HI	06/12/17
Market USA Federal Credit Union	MD	06/12/17
Members First Credit Union	MI	06/12/17
Navigant Credit Union	RI	06/12/17
North Star Community Credit Union	ND	06/12/17
NorthStar Credit Union	IL	06/12/17
Partner Colorado Credit Union	CO	06/12/17
Prince George's Community FCU	MD	06/12/17
Self-Help Federal Credit Union	NC	06/12/17
SRP Federal Credit Union	SC	06/12/17
Technology Credit Union	CA	06/12/17
Towpath Credit Union	OH	06/12/17
United Credit Union	MO	06/12/17
Wichita Federal Credit Union	KS	06/12/17

Rating: B+

Name	State	Date of Change
Altamaha Federal Credit Union	GA	06/12/17
Autotruck Financial Credit Union	KY	06/12/17
Central Minnesota Credit Union	MN	06/12/17
CentralAlliance Credit Union	WI	06/12/17
Community Choice Credit Union	IA	06/12/17
Kansas Teachers Community Credit Union	KS	06/12/17
Metro Employees Credit Union	KY	06/12/17
North Coast Credit Union	WA	06/12/17
Oklahoma Educators Credit Union	OK	06/12/17
Polam Federal Credit Union	CA	06/12/17
Premier Members Credit Union	CO	06/12/17
Puget Sound Cooperative Credit Union	WA	06/12/17
San Diego Metropolitan Credit Union	CA	06/12/17
St. Louis Community Credit Union	MO	06/12/17
UFirst Federal Credit Union	NY	06/12/17
WCLA Credit Union	WA	06/12/17

Rating: B

Name	State	Date of Change
AllCom Credit Union	MA	06/12/17
BCBST Employees Credit Union	TN	06/12/17
Calhoun-Liberty Employees Credit Union	FL	06/12/17
Detour Drummond Community Credit Union	MI	06/12/17
District of Columbia Teachers FCU	DC	06/12/17
EFCU Financial Federal Credit Union	LA	06/12/17
Elektra Federal Credit Union	NY	06/12/17
Emery Federal Credit Union	OH	06/12/17
Emporia State Federal Credit Union	KS	06/12/17
Federated Employees Credit Union	MN	06/12/17
Florida Hospital Credit Union	FL	06/12/17
GR Consumers Credit Union	MI	06/12/17
Greenwood Municipal Federal Credit Union	SC	06/12/17
Gulf Trust Credit Union	MS	06/12/17
Hawaii County Employees FCU	HI	06/12/17
Health Employees Federal Credit Union	NY	06/12/17
KUE Federal Credit Union	KY	06/12/17
Louisville Federal Credit Union	KY	06/12/17
Maine Savings Federal Credit Union	ME	06/12/17
Miami Federal Credit Union	FL	06/12/17
Mount Pleasant Baptist Church FCU	VA	06/12/17
NW Preferred Federal Credit Union	OR	06/12/17
Painesville Credit Union	OH	06/12/17
Peach State Federal Credit Union	GA	06/12/17
Peninsula Community Federal Credit Union	WA	06/12/17
Schools Federal Credit Union	CA	06/12/17
Self-Help Credit Union	NC	06/12/17
Sesloc Federal Credit Union	CA	06/12/17
Soo Co-op Credit Union	MI	06/12/17
Southern Pine Credit Union	GA	06/12/17
Spartan Federal Credit Union	SC	06/12/17
Tower Federal Credit Union	MD	06/12/17
UFCW Community Federal Credit Union	PA	06/12/17
West Oahu Community Federal Credit Union	HI	06/12/17

Rating: B-

Name	State	Date of Change
Aeroquip Credit Union	MI	06/12/17
Alabama Law Enforcement Credit Union	AL	06/12/17
Alternatives Federal Credit Union	NY	06/12/17
America's Christian Credit Union	CA	06/12/17
Ampot Federal Credit Union	MS	06/12/17
Arapahoe Credit Union	CO	06/12/17
Arkansas Federal Credit Union	AR	06/12/17
ASI Federal Credit Union	LA	06/12/17
Awakon Federal Credit Union	MI	06/12/17
Bergen Division Federal Credit Union	NJ	06/12/17
Blaw-Knox Credit Union	IL	06/12/17
C C S E Federal Credit Union	NY	06/12/17

Rating Upgrades

Name	State	Date of Change
Carpenters Federal Credit Union	MN	06/12/17
Citymark Federal Credit Union	PA	06/12/17
Commonwealth Utilities Employees CU	MA	06/12/17
Credit Union of Colorado, A FCU	CO	06/12/17
Dixie Line Credit Union	TN	06/12/17
Eagle Louisiana Federal Credit Union	LA	06/12/17
Financial Health Federal Credit Union	IN	06/12/17
Greater Eastern Credit Union	TN	06/12/17
Highway District 21 Federal Credit Union	TX	06/12/17
Kemba Indianapolis Credit Union	IN	06/12/17
Lancaster Red Rose Credit Union	PA	06/12/17
Linden New Jersey Police & Firemen FCU	NJ	06/12/17
Lisbon Community Federal Credit Union	ME	06/12/17
Loup Employees Credit Union	LA	06/12/17
Michigan Columbus Federal Credit Union	MI	06/12/17
Missouri Credit Union	MO	06/12/17
Monroe County Community Credit Union	MI	06/12/17
Mutual Credit Union	MS	06/12/17
My Healthcare Federal Credit Union	FL	06/12/17
Norwesco Credit Union	KS	06/12/17
Point West Credit Union	OR	06/12/17
Register Guard Federal Credit Union	OR	06/12/17
River Community Credit Union	IA	06/12/17
Roanoke Valley Community FCU	VA	06/12/17
Rome Teachers Federal Credit Union	NY	06/12/17
Shelby County Federal Credit Union	TN	06/12/17
Skyline Credit Union	TN	06/12/17
Sonoma Federal Credit Union	CA	06/12/17
Tremont Credit Union	MA	06/12/17
Upper Darby Belltelco FCU	PA	06/12/17

Rating: C+

Name	State	Date of Change
Allegan Community Federal Credit Union	MI	06/12/17
Athens Area Credit Union	WI	06/12/17
Baton Rouge City Parish Employees FCU	LA	06/12/17
Bay Cities Credit Union	CA	06/12/17
California Community Credit Union	CA	06/12/17
Chocolate Bayou Community FCU	TX	06/12/17
Common Cents Federal Credit Union	TX	06/12/17
Community Focus Federal Credit Union	MI	06/12/17
CSD Credit Union	MO	06/12/17
Diamond Valley Federal Credit Union	IN	06/12/17
East Idaho Credit Union	ID	06/12/17
Excel Federal Credit Union	GA	06/12/17
Gilt Edge Employees Federal Credit Union	OK	06/12/17
Great Neck School Employees FCU	NY	06/12/17
Hawaii First Federal Credit Union	HI	06/12/17
Jafari No-Interest Credit Union	TX	06/12/17
Latitude 32 Federal Credit Union	SC	06/12/17
Liberty Savings Federal Credit Union	NJ	06/12/17
Lormet Community Federal Credit Union	OH	06/12/17
Louchem Federal Credit Union	KY	06/12/17
M.P.D. Community Credit Union	TN	06/12/17
Midwest Operating Engineers Credit Union	IL	06/12/17
Motor City Cooperative Credit Union	MI	06/12/17
New Haven Police and Municipal FCU	CT	06/12/17
Northern Colorado Credit Union	CO	06/12/17
Oahu Federal Credit Union	HI	06/12/17
OAS Staff Federal Credit Union	DC	06/12/17
Omaha Public Power District Empls FCU	NE	06/12/17
Pacific Crest Federal Credit Union	OR	06/12/17
Pacific Northwest Ironworkers FCU	OR	06/12/17
Polk County Credit Union	IA	06/12/17
Postal Family Credit Union	OH	06/12/17
Reliant Federal Credit Union	WY	06/12/17
Rome Kraft Employees Credit Union	GA	06/12/17
Salem Baptist Federal Credit Union	NJ	06/12/17
Silver State Schools Credit Union	NV	06/12/17
Southeast LA Veterans Health Care System FCU	LA	06/12/17
Star Tech Federal Credit Union	CO	06/12/17
Stepping Stones Community FCU	DE	06/12/17
Suwannee River Federal Credit Union	FL	06/12/17
Tallahassee-Leon Federal Credit Union	FL	06/12/17
Trademark Federal Credit Union	ME	06/12/17
Twin Rivers Federal Credit Union	NY	06/12/17
Valley Hills Federal Credit Union	CA	06/12/17
Victoria Federal Credit Union	TX	06/12/17

Rating: C

Name	State	Date of Change
1st Class Express Credit Union	WI	06/12/17
1st Liberty Federal Credit Union	MT	06/12/17
Advanced Financial Federal Credit Union	NJ	06/12/17
Alive Credit Union	FL	06/12/17
Alloy Federal Credit Union	WV	06/12/17
Arkansas Health Center FCU	AR	06/12/17
Artesian City Federal Credit Union	GA	06/12/17
Astera Credit Union	MI	06/12/17
Bristol Virginia School System FCU	VA	06/12/17
Brownsville City Employees FCU	TX	06/12/17
Cal-Com Federal Credit Union	TX	06/12/17
Capital Area Taiwanese FCU	MD	06/12/17
Carter Federal Credit Union	LA	06/12/17
Centerville Clinics Employees FCU	PA	06/12/17
Chadron Federal Credit Union	NE	06/12/17
City Center Credit Union	UT	06/12/17
Community First Credit Union	OH	06/12/17
Cornerstone Credit Union	IL	06/12/17
Democrat P&L Federal Credit Union	AR	06/12/17
Doe Run Federal Credit Union	KY	06/12/17
Emerald Credit Union, Inc.	OH	06/12/17

Rating Upgrades

Name	State	Date of Change
Employee Resources Credit Union	TN	06/12/17
Encentus Federal Credit Union	OK	06/12/17
Fayette Federal Credit Union	WV	06/12/17
First Coast Federal Credit Union	FL	06/12/17
G P M Federal Credit Union	TX	06/12/17
Garden State Federal Credit Union	NJ	06/12/17
Grand Prairie Credit Union	TX	06/12/17
Green Mountain Credit Union	VT	06/12/17
Greensburg Teachers Credit Union	PA	06/12/17
Harvesters Federal Credit Union	FL	06/12/17
Iberville Federal Credit Union	LA	06/12/17
IBEW & United Workers FCU	OR	06/12/17
JACOM Credit Union	CA	06/12/17
Jefferson Credit Union	AL	06/12/17
Journey Federal Credit Union	MI	06/12/17
Kekaha Federal Credit Union	HI	06/12/17
LES Federal Credit Union	LA	06/12/17
Limoneira Federal Credit Union	CA	06/12/17
Louisville Metro Police Officers CU	KY	06/12/17
M G Employees Federal Credit Union	OH	06/12/17
M.A.B.C. Federal Credit Union	PA	06/12/17
Meadows Credit Union	IL	06/12/17
Members Choice Financial Credit Union	PA	06/12/17
Metro Wire Federal Credit Union	PA	06/12/17
Mid Plains Credit Union	KS	06/12/17
Middle Tennessee Federal Credit Union	TN	06/12/17
Monroe Telco Federal Credit Union	LA	06/12/17
Morrison Employees Credit Union	IA	06/12/17
Mower County Catholic Parishes CU	MN	06/12/17
Muncie Post Office Credit Union	IN	06/12/17
N C S E Credit Union Inc.	VA	06/12/17
Natco Employees Federal Credit Union	RI	06/12/17
New Brunswick Postal FCU	NJ	06/12/17
New Century Federal Credit Union	IL	06/12/17
Ocean Communities Federal Credit Union	ME	06/12/17
Ohio Valley Community Credit Union	OH	06/12/17
Oregon Pioneer Federal Credit Union	OR	06/12/17
Pakco Employees Federal Credit Union	PA	06/12/17
Pathways Financial Credit Union, Inc.	OH	06/12/17
Port Arthur Teachers FCU	TX	06/12/17
Portland Local 8 Federal Credit Union	OR	06/12/17
Public Service Plaza FCU	NJ	06/12/17
Red River Mill Employees FCU	LA	06/12/17
SCFE Credit Union, Inc.	OH	06/12/17
Shell Western States FCU	CA	06/12/17
Simply Service Federal Credit Union	SD	06/12/17
Southern Mass Credit Union	MA	06/12/17
St. Paul A.M.E. Zion Church Credit Union	OH	06/12/17
St. Thomas Credit Union	TN	06/12/17
STEC Federal Credit Union	TX	06/12/17
Telco Plus Credit Union	TX	06/12/17
Texas People Federal Credit Union	TX	06/12/17
Ticonderoga Federal Credit Union	NY	06/12/17
Tyndall Federal Credit Union	FL	06/12/17
Ukrainian Selfreliance of Western PA FCU	PA	06/12/17
Union Baptist Church FCU	IN	06/12/17
Valdosta Teachers Federal Credit Union	GA	06/12/17
Washington Educational Association FCU	LA	06/12/17
Waterfront Federal Credit Union	WA	06/12/17
West Side Baptist Church FCU	MO	06/12/17
Western Illinois School Employees CU	IL	06/12/17
Westmoreland Community FCU	PA	06/12/17
Windward Community Federal Credit Union	HI	06/12/17

Rating: C-

Name	State	Date of Change
5 Star Community Credit Union	IA	06/12/17
Aero Federal Credit Union	AZ	06/12/17
Alton Municipal Employees FCU	IL	06/12/17
American Chemical Society FCU	OH	06/12/17
Americo Federal Credit Union	PA	06/12/17
Borinquen Community Federal Credit Union	PR	06/12/17
Bradford Area School Employees FCU	PA	06/12/17
Bridgeport Post Office FCU	CT	06/12/17
Burns & McDonnell Credit Union	MO	06/12/17
Butler Heritage Federal Credit Union	OH	06/12/17
C.U.P. Federal Credit Union	UT	06/12/17
Cen Tex Manufacturing Credit Union	TX	06/12/17
Community Promise Federal Credit Union	MI	06/12/17
Connections Credit Union	ID	06/12/17
Cornerstone Community Credit Union	CT	06/12/17
Corrections Federal Credit Union	CA	06/12/17
District 58 Federal Credit Union	LA	06/12/17
Eagle One Federal Credit Union	DE	06/12/17
Eaton Employees Credit Union	MN	06/12/17
ELCA Federal Credit Union	IL	06/12/17
Evangelical Christian Credit Union	CA	06/12/17
Fidelis Federal Credit Union	NY	06/12/17
First NRV Federal Credit Union	VA	06/12/17
Forrest County Teachers FCU	MS	06/12/17
Generations Family Federal Credit Union	MI	06/12/17
Go Federal Credit Union	TX	06/12/17
Grand County Credit Union	UT	06/12/17
Hamakua Coast Community FCU	HI	06/12/17
Harrison Police & Firemen's FCU	NJ	06/12/17
Heartland Area Federal Credit Union	NE	06/12/17
Heekin Can Employees Credit Union	OH	06/12/17
Heritage Valley Federal Credit Union	PA	06/12/17
HMC (NJ) Federal Credit Union	NJ	06/12/17
Homefield Credit Union	MA	06/12/17
K.U.M.C. Credit Union	KS	06/12/17

Rating Upgrades

Name	State	Date of Change
Kaleida Health Federal Credit Union	NY	06/12/17
Lauhoff Employees Credit Union	IL	06/12/17
Local 520 UA Federal Credit Union	PA	06/12/17
Logan County School Employees FCU	WV	06/12/17
Maumee Educators Federal Credit Union	OH	06/12/17
McGraw Hill Federal Credit Union	NJ	06/12/17
Molokai Community Federal Credit Union	HI	06/12/17
Monarch Federal Credit Union	OH	06/12/17
Monroeville Boro Federal Credit Union	PA	06/12/17
Mount Carmel Church Federal Credit Union	TX	06/12/17
Natural State Federal Credit Union	AR	06/12/17
New Life Federal Credit Union	PA	06/12/17
North Carolina Community FCU	NC	06/12/17
Northeast Regional Credit Union	MO	06/12/17
Northern Montana Hospital FCU	MT	06/12/17
Northside Federal Credit Union	GA	06/12/17
PAAC Transit Division FCU	PA	06/12/17
Paul Quinn Federal Credit Union	NY	06/12/17
Pear Orchard Federal Credit Union	TX	06/12/17
Pioneer Community Federal Credit Union	NE	06/12/17
Portsmouth Schools Federal Credit Union	VA	06/12/17
Saker Shop Rite Federal Credit Union	NJ	06/12/17
San Juan Credit Union	UT	06/12/17
Sperry Associates Federal Credit Union	NY	06/12/17
SSMOK Employees Federal Credit Union	OK	06/12/17
St. Athanasius Credit Union	IA	06/12/17
St. Philip's Church Federal Credit Union	NY	06/12/17
Steel Valley Federal Credit Union	OH	06/12/17
Stoughton Town Employees FCU	MA	06/12/17
Tazewell County School Employees CU	IL	06/12/17
TBC Federal Credit Union	VA	06/12/17
Team First Federal Credit Union	PA	06/12/17
Trades & Labor Federal Credit Union	MN	06/12/17
Tri County Area Federal Credit Union	PA	06/12/17
Tucoemas Federal Credit Union	CA	06/12/17
Tulane/Loyola Federal Credit Union	LA	06/12/17
Turbine Federal Credit Union	SC	06/12/17
Umico Federal Credit Union	NY	06/12/17
Unified Homeowners of Illinois FCU	IL	06/12/17
Upper Michigan Community Credit Union	MI	06/12/17
V.A.C. Employees Federal Credit Union	NY	06/12/17
Vocal Credit Union	MT	06/12/17
Waconized Federal Credit Union	TX	06/12/17
Wayne County Federal Credit Union	IN	06/12/17
WES Credit Union	OH	06/12/17
West Springfield Federal Credit Union	MA	06/12/17
Woburn Municipal Federal Credit Union	MA	06/12/17
Worcester Credit Union	MA	06/12/17

Rating: D+

Name	State	Date of Change
Advance Financial Federal Credit Union	IN	06/12/17
Allwealth Federal Credit Union	OH	06/12/17
Antioch MB Federal Credit Union	IL	06/12/17
Belton Federal Credit Union	TX	06/12/17
Brantwood Credit Union	WI	06/12/17
C T A C And M Federal Credit Union	IL	06/12/17
Cherokee Strip Credit Union	OK	06/12/17
Chicago Avenue Garage FCU	IL	06/12/17
Citizens Choice Federal Credit Union	MS	06/12/17
Colton Federal Credit Union	CA	06/12/17
Continental Employees FCU	LA	06/12/17
Co-Operative Credit Union	KS	06/12/17
Cosden Federal Credit Union	TX	06/12/17
County Educators Federal Credit Union	NJ	06/12/17
ECU Credit Union	FL	06/12/17
EME Credit Union	PA	06/12/17
Emerald Coast Federal Credit Union	FL	06/12/17
Erie City Employees Federal Credit Union	PA	06/12/17
Ferko Maryland Federal Credit Union	MD	06/12/17
Fort Smith Municipal Employees FCU	AR	06/12/17
Franklin Johnstown Federal Credit Union	PA	06/12/17
General Portland Peninsular Empls FCU	OH	06/12/17
Generations Credit Union	WA	06/12/17
Generations Credit Union	IL	06/12/17
Hampton V. A. Federal Credit Union	VA	06/12/17
Hotel & Travel Industry FCU	HI	06/12/17
Israel Memorial AME Federal Credit Union	NJ	06/12/17
Junction Bell Federal Credit Union	CO	06/12/17
Keys Federal Credit Union	FL	06/12/17
Kraftsman Federal Credit Union	VA	06/12/17
Mahoning Valley Federal Credit Union	OH	06/12/17
New Alliance Federal Credit Union	PA	06/12/17
North Adams M.E. Federal Credit Union	MA	06/12/17
North Coast Credit Union	OH	06/12/17
Norton-Troy Employees Credit Union	NY	06/12/17
Old Dominion University Credit Union, Inc.	VA	06/12/17
One Credit Union	VT	06/12/17
P & S Credit Union	UT	06/12/17
Peoples Independent Church FCU	CA	06/12/17
Plain Dealer Federal Credit Union	OH	06/12/17
Promise Credit Union	TX	06/12/17
Public Service E.D. Trenton FCU	NJ	06/12/17
Rapides Federal Credit Union	LA	06/12/17
R-G Federal Credit Union	MO	06/12/17
Scenic Falls Federal Credit Union	ID	06/12/17
Security Plus Federal Credit Union	KY	06/12/17
Southern Gas Federal Credit Union	AR	06/12/17
Southwest Counties School Employees CU	MO	06/12/17
Spokane Media Federal Credit Union	WA	06/12/17
St. Pauls Federal Credit Union	PA	06/12/17

Rating Upgrades

Name	State	Date of Change
Stanwood Area Federal Credit Union	PA	06/12/17
Tabernacle Federal Credit Union	GA	06/12/17
Tahquamenon Area Credit Union	MI	06/12/17
Tazewell County Government Employees CU	IL	06/12/17
Total Choice Federal Credit Union	LA	06/12/17
UCB Credit Union	UT	06/12/17
Ukrainian Selfreliance New England FCU	CT	06/12/17
Valley Board Federal Credit Union	WV	06/12/17
Valley Educators Credit Union	CO	06/12/17
Valley Wide of PA Federal Credit Union	PA	06/12/17
VAntage Trust Federal Credit Union	PA	06/12/17
Wakefern Federal Credit Union	NJ	06/12/17
Western Rockies Federal Credit Union	CO	06/12/17
White Plains P O Employees FCU	NY	06/12/17
Williamsville Federal Credit Union	NY	06/12/17

Rating: D

Name	State	Date of Change
AFL-CIO Employees Federal Credit Union	DC	06/12/17
Ark City Teachers Credit Union	KS	06/12/17
BEKA Federal Credit Union	GA	06/12/17
Brewton Mill Federal Credit Union	AL	06/12/17
BSE Credit Union	OH	06/12/17
Buckeye State Credit Union Inc.	OH	06/12/17
City of Ukiah Employees Credit Union	CA	06/12/17
Coast-Tel Federal Credit Union	CA	06/12/17
Copper Basin Federal Credit Union	TN	06/12/17
Edison Credit Union	MO	06/12/17
Groton Municipal Employees FCU	CT	06/12/17
MCU Financial Center Credit Union	WI	06/12/17
NorthPark Community Credit Union	IN	06/12/17
Northwoods Community Credit Union	WI	06/12/17
Orem City Employees Federal Credit Union	UT	06/12/17
Riverfront Federal Credit Union	PA	06/12/17
Shreveport Police Federal Credit Union	LA	06/12/17
St. Marks Federal Credit Union	NY	06/12/17
St. Michael Federal Credit Union	CO	06/12/17
Superior Credit Union	PA	06/12/17
TEA Federal Credit Union	LA	06/12/17
Towns-Union Educators' FCU	GA	06/12/17
Transit Authority Division B FCU	NY	06/12/17
Unified Communities Federal Credit Union	MI	06/12/17
V. Suarez Employees Federal Credit Union	PR	06/12/17

Rating: D-

Name	State	Date of Change
Cogic Credit Union	LA	06/12/17
Eaton Employees Credit Union	IA	06/12/17
First Miami University Student FCU	OH	06/12/17
Sloan Public Schools FCU	NY	06/12/17
Texans Credit Union	TX	06/12/17
Tri Ag West Virginia FCU	WV	06/12/17

Name	State	Date of Change
Tuskegee Federal Credit Union	AL	06/12/17

Rating: E+

Name	State	Date of Change
Alabama One Credit Union	AL	06/12/17
Gateway Credit Union	TN	06/12/17
Green River Basin Federal Credit Union	WY	06/12/17
Long Island Community FCU	NY	06/12/17
Seneca Nation of Indians FCU	NY	06/12/17

Rating: E

Name	State	Date of Change
Chadwick Federal Credit Union	MA	06/12/17

Rating Downgrades

Name	State	Date of Change
Rating: A-		
Charlotte Metro Federal Credit Union	NC	06/12/17
Columbia Credit Union	WA	06/12/17
CPM Federal Credit Union	SC	06/12/17
Texell Credit Union	TX	06/12/17
Rating: B+		
Acadia Federal Credit Union	ME	06/12/17
Alabama Teachers Credit Union	AL	06/12/17
Beehive Federal Credit Union	ID	06/12/17
Border Federal Credit Union	TX	06/12/17
Cascade Federal Credit Union	WA	06/12/17
Centex Citizens Credit Union	TX	06/12/17
Citizens Equity First Credit Union	IL	06/12/17
City Credit Union	TX	06/12/17
Cloverbelt Credit Union	WI	06/12/17
CO-OP Credit Union	WI	06/12/17
Cooperative Teachers Credit Union	TX	06/12/17
Credit Union 1	AK	06/12/17
Georgia United Credit Union	GA	06/12/17
Kimberly Clark Credit Union	TN	06/12/17
Kirtland Federal Credit Union	NM	06/12/17
Maui Federal Credit Union	HI	06/12/17
Metrum Community Credit Union	CO	06/12/17
Midcoast Federal Credit Union	ME	06/12/17
Mississippi Federal Credit Union	MS	06/12/17
North Franklin Federal Credit Union	NY	06/12/17
North Shore Federal Credit Union	MN	06/12/17
Oklahoma Employees Credit Union	OK	06/12/17
Ouachita Valley Federal Credit Union	LA	06/12/17
Premier Federal Credit Union	NC	06/12/17
Sierra Central Credit Union	CA	06/12/17
Tacoma Longshoremen Credit Union	WA	06/12/17
Telcoe Federal Credit Union	AR	06/12/17
Texar Federal Credit Union	TX	06/12/17
U.S. Employees O.C. Federal Credit Union	OK	06/12/17
VacationLand Federal Credit Union	OH	06/12/17
Velocity Credit Union	TX	06/12/17
Washington State Employees Credit Union	WA	06/12/17
Weokie Credit Union	OK	06/12/17
WestStar Credit Union	NV	06/12/17
Rating: B		
4Front Credit Union	MI	06/12/17
Advantage One Credit Union	MI	06/12/17
Core Federal Credit Union	NY	06/12/17
Rating: B-		
Abilene Federal Credit Union	TX	06/12/17
ABNB Federal Credit Union	VA	06/12/17
Access Community Credit Union	TX	06/12/17
Alcon Employees Federal Credit Union	TX	06/12/17
Andrews Federal Credit Union	MD	06/12/17
Beacon Community Credit Union	KY	06/12/17
Canaan Credit Union	IL	06/12/17
CASE Credit Union	MI	06/12/17
Community Choice Credit Union	CO	06/12/17
Credit Union One	MI	06/12/17
DOCO Credit Union	GA	06/12/17
Essential Federal Credit Union	LA	06/12/17
EvergreenDIRECT Credit Union	WA	06/12/17
Family Financial Credit Union	MI	06/12/17
First Entertainment Credit Union	CA	06/12/17
First Heritage Federal Credit Union	NY	06/12/17
GHS Federal Credit Union	NY	06/12/17
Golden Plains Credit Union	KS	06/12/17
Great Erie Federal Credit Union	NY	06/12/17
Guthrie Federal Credit Union	PA	06/12/17
Heart of Louisiana Federal Credit Union	LA	06/12/17
KeyPoint Credit Union	CA	06/12/17
La Joya Area Federal Credit Union	TX	06/12/17
Magnolia Federal Credit Union	MS	06/12/17
McCoy Federal Credit Union	FL	06/12/17
Members Choice Credit Union	TX	06/12/17
MTCU	TX	06/12/17
My Community Credit Union	TX	06/12/17
N.E.W. Credit Union	WI	06/12/17
New Jersey Law & Public Safety CU	NJ	06/12/17
Northwoods Credit Union	MN	06/12/17
Riverdale Credit Union	AL	06/12/17
Sentinel Federal Credit Union	SD	06/12/17
SharePoint Credit Union	MN	06/12/17
Sioux Valley Community Credit Union	IA	06/12/17
SkyOne Federal Credit Union	CA	06/12/17
Southwest 66 Credit Union	TX	06/12/17
TCP Credit Union	NC	06/12/17
Telco-Triad Community Credit Union	IA	06/12/17
Tongass Federal Credit Union	AK	06/12/17
Tropical Financial Credit Union	FL	06/12/17
Tucson Federal Credit Union	AZ	06/12/17
UMe Federal Credit Union	CA	06/12/17
United Financial Credit Union	MI	06/12/17
Rating: C+		
Advantage Plus Federal Credit Union	ID	06/12/17
Altonized Community Federal Credit Union	IL	06/12/17
American Southwest Credit Union	AZ	06/12/17
Andovers Federal Credit Union	MA	06/12/17
Badger-Globe Credit Union	WI	06/12/17

Rating Downgrades

Name	State	Date of Change
Blue Flame Credit Union	NC	06/12/17
Buckeye Community Federal Credit Union	FL	06/12/17
Buffalo Service Credit Union	NY	06/12/17
Burbank City Federal Credit Union	CA	06/12/17
Caprock Federal Credit Union	TX	06/12/17
Chattanooga Area Schools FCU	TN	06/12/17
City and County Employees FCU	MN	06/12/17
Compass Financial Federal Credit Union	FL	06/12/17
Corpus Christi Postal Employees CU	TX	06/12/17
Corry Federal Credit Union	PA	06/12/17
Delaware State Police FCU	DE	06/12/17
Eagle Community Credit Union	CA	06/12/17
Family Community Credit Union	IA	06/12/17
First Baptist Church of Darby FCU	PA	06/12/17
First United Credit Union	MI	06/12/17
Gloucester Fire Department Credit Union	MA	06/12/17
Greater Iowa Credit Union	IA	06/12/17
Irving City Employees FCU	TX	06/12/17
Lewis Clark Credit Union	ID	06/12/17
LibertyOne Credit Union	TX	06/12/17
Michigan Legacy Credit Union	MI	06/12/17
Mid American Credit Union	KS	06/12/17
Northern Eagle Federal Credit Union	MN	06/12/17
Northern Tier Federal Credit Union	ND	06/12/17
Northrop Grumman Federal Credit Union	CA	06/12/17
Ocean Financial Federal Credit Union	NY	06/12/17
Pennstar Federal Credit Union	PA	06/12/17
Pinellas Federal Credit Union	FL	06/12/17
Pocatello Simplot Credit Union	ID	06/12/17
Proctor Federal Credit Union	MN	06/12/17
Proponent Federal Credit Union	NJ	06/12/17
Pyramid Federal Credit Union	AZ	06/12/17
Rock Valley Federal Credit Union	IL	06/12/17
San Francisco Federal Credit Union	CA	06/12/17
Security Credit Union	MI	06/12/17
Southeastern Arizona FCU	AZ	06/12/17
Spokane Federal Credit Union	WA	06/12/17
Transportation Federal Credit Union	VA	06/12/17
Ukrainian Selfreliance FCU	PA	06/12/17
UP Arkansas Federal Credit Union	AR	06/12/17

Rating: C

Name	State	Date of Change
121 Financial Credit Union	FL	06/12/17
Alabama Central Credit Union	AL	06/12/17
Ash Employees Credit Union	IL	06/12/17
Beacon Federal Credit Union	TX	06/12/17
Bowater Employees Credit Union	TN	06/12/17
Cabway Telco Federal Credit Union	WV	06/12/17
Central State Credit Union	CA	06/12/17
Columbus Metro Federal Credit Union	OH	06/12/17
Connect Credit Union	FL	06/12/17
Credit Union Advantage	MI	06/12/17
Dakota Plains Federal Credit Union	SD	06/12/17
Diversified Credit Union	MN	06/12/17
Division 10 Highway Employees' CU	MO	06/12/17
Dover Federal Credit Union	DE	06/12/17
Evanston Firemens Credit Union	IL	06/12/17
Falls Catholic Credit Union	OH	06/12/17
Farmers Federal Credit Union	FL	06/12/17
Fayette Federal Employees FCU	PA	06/12/17
FedChoice Federal Credit Union	MD	06/12/17
Fellowship Credit Union	CO	06/12/17
First Choice Credit Union, Inc.	OH	06/12/17
First Credit Union	AZ	06/12/17
First Tulsa Federal Credit Union	OK	06/12/17
Fond Du Lac Credit Union	WI	06/12/17
Frio County Federal Credit Union	TX	06/12/17
Generations Community FCU	TX	06/12/17
Global Credit Union	WA	06/12/17
Golmar Federal Credit Union	PR	06/12/17
Graphic Arts Credit Union	LA	06/12/17
Hartford Firefighters FCU	CT	06/12/17
Hartford Healthcare Federal Credit Union, Inc.	CT	06/12/17
Hercules Credit Union	UT	06/12/17
I.M. Detroit District Credit Union	MI	06/12/17
Kern Federal Credit Union	CA	06/12/17
Kone Employees Credit Union	IL	06/12/17
Lansing Postal Community Credit Union	MI	06/12/17
Last Federal Credit Union	NY	06/12/17
Lee Federal Credit Union	DC	06/12/17
Lion Federal Credit Union	AR	06/12/17
Livingston Parish Federal Credit Union	LA	06/12/17
Marriott Employees Federal Credit Union	MD	06/12/17
McDowell County Federal Credit Union	WV	06/12/17
Media Members Federal Credit Union	PA	06/12/17
Memorial Credit Union	TX	06/12/17
Mingo County Education FCU	WV	06/12/17
Muna Federal Credit Union	MS	06/12/17
My Personal Credit Union	MI	06/12/17
MyCom Federal Credit Union	MA	06/12/17
Niagara Regional Federal Credit Union	NY	06/12/17
Northland Teachers Community CU	MO	06/12/17
PALCO Federal Credit Union	PA	06/12/17
Paradise Valley Federal Credit Union	CA	06/12/17
Park Side Credit Union	MT	06/12/17
Penn East Federal Credit Union	PA	06/12/17
Peoples-Neighborhood FCU	DC	06/12/17
Pinn Memorial Federal Credit Union	PA	06/12/17
Pittsburgh City Hall Employees FCU	PA	06/12/17
Plus4 Credit Union	TX	06/12/17

Rating Downgrades

Name	State	Date of Change
PriorityONE Credit Union	FL	06/12/17
Progressive Credit Union	NY	06/12/17
Puget Sound Refinery FCU	WA	06/12/17
Rivertown Community Federal Credit Union	MI	06/12/17
Rural Cooperatives Credit Union, Inc.	KY	06/12/17
S I Employees Federal Credit Union	NY	06/12/17
Savannah Schools Federal Credit Union	GA	06/12/17
Simplot Employees Credit Union	ID	06/12/17
SLO Credit Union	CA	06/12/17
Sooper Credit Union	CO	06/12/17
Southcoast Federal Credit Union	MA	06/12/17
Southern Chautauqua Federal Credit Union	NY	06/12/17
Stewart's Federal Credit Union	NY	06/12/17
Team One Credit Union	MI	06/12/17
True Sky Credit Union	OK	06/12/17
United Consumers Credit Union	MO	06/12/17
United Equity Credit Union	IL	06/12/17
Unity One Credit Union	TX	06/12/17
University of Louisiana FCU	LA	06/12/17
Valley Bell Federal Credit Union	WV	06/12/17
We Florida Financial	FL	06/12/17
Westex Federal Credit Union	TX	06/12/17

Rating: C-

Name	State	Date of Change
ABCO Federal Credit Union	NJ	06/12/17
Adirondack Regional Federal Credit Union	NY	06/12/17
Airco Federal Credit Union	CA	06/12/17
Alden Credit Union	MA	06/12/17
Alps Federal Credit Union	AK	06/12/17
Anmed Health Federal Credit Union	SC	06/12/17
Argent Federal Credit Union	VA	06/12/17
Aspire Federal Credit Union	NJ	06/12/17
Bear Paw Credit Union	MT	06/12/17
Bethlehem 1st Federal Credit Union	PA	06/12/17
Cadets Federal Credit Union	NY	06/12/17
Carolina Community Federal Credit Union	NC	06/12/17
Carolina Federal Credit Union	NC	06/12/17
Central Oklahoma Federal Credit Union	OK	06/12/17
CHHE Federal Credit Union	WV	06/12/17
Chivaho Federal Credit Union	OH	06/12/17
Citizens Community Credit Union	ND	06/12/17
Citizens Federal Credit Union	TX	06/12/17
Communities of Abilene FCU	TX	06/12/17
Community 1st Credit Union	WA	06/12/17
Community United Credit Union	OH	06/12/17
CommunityWorks Federal Credit Union	SC	06/12/17
Cooperative Extension Service FCU	AR	06/12/17
County Schools Federal Credit Union	CA	06/12/17
Cowboy Country Federal Credit Union	TX	06/12/17
Decatur Postal Credit Union	IL	06/12/17
Enlighten Federal Credit Union	TN	06/12/17
Erie Metro Federal Credit Union	NY	06/12/17
Estacado Federal Credit Union	NM	06/12/17
Evolve Federal Credit Union	TX	06/12/17
Faith Cooperative Federal Credit Union	TX	06/12/17
Fontana Federal Credit Union	CA	06/12/17
Gary Police Department Employees FCU	IN	06/12/17
Gogebic County Federal Credit Union	MI	06/12/17
Greater Metro Federal Credit Union	NY	06/12/17
H&H Federal Credit Union	TX	06/12/17
Huntington C&O Railway Employees FCU	WV	06/12/17
IBEW 968 Federal Credit Union	WV	06/12/17
Insight Credit Union	FL	06/12/17
John Wesley Ame Zion Church FCU	DC	06/12/17
JSTC Employees Federal Credit Union	PA	06/12/17
Kennametal Orwell Employees FCU	OH	06/12/17
Lehrer Interests Credit Union	TX	06/12/17
LiFE Federal Credit Union	TX	06/12/17
LifeWay Credit Union	TN	06/12/17
Light Commerce Credit Union	TX	06/12/17
Los Angeles Lee Federal Credit Union	CA	06/12/17
Marine Federal Credit Union	NC	06/12/17
Maryvale Schools Federal Credit Union	NY	06/12/17
Matagorda County Credit Union	TX	06/12/17
MemberFocus Community Credit Union	MI	06/12/17
Members Advantage Credit Union	IN	06/12/17
Mountain Heritage Federal Credit Union	WV	06/12/17
MSD Federal Credit Union	KY	06/12/17
Mutual Savings Credit Union	AL	06/12/17
Newark Post Office Employees CU	NJ	06/12/17
North Alabama Educators Credit Union	AL	06/12/17
Northern Valley Federal Credit Union	ND	06/12/17
Onomea Federal Credit Union	HI	06/12/17
Our Sunday Visitor Employees FCU	IN	06/12/17
P.S. Local 821 Federal Credit Union	NJ	06/12/17
Pannonia Federal Credit Union	PA	06/12/17
Parker Community Credit Union	WI	06/12/17
People First Federal Credit Union	PA	06/12/17
Peoples Transport Federal Credit Union	NJ	06/12/17
Perfect Circle Credit Union	IN	06/12/17
Post Office Employees' Credit Union	LA	06/12/17
Quay Schools Federal Credit Union	NM	06/12/17
R T P Federal Credit Union	NC	06/12/17
Racine Municipal Employees Credit Union	WI	06/12/17
Rapides General Hospital Employees FCU	LA	06/12/17
Revere Municipal Employees FCU	MA	06/12/17
Richfield-Bloomington Credit Union	MN	06/12/17
Schneider Community Credit Union	WI	06/12/17
Sequoia Federal Credit Union	CA	06/12/17
Settlers Federal Credit Union	MI	06/12/17

Rating Downgrades

Name	State	Date of Change
Shell Geismar Federal Credit Union	LA	06/12/17
Shiloh Englewood Federal Credit Union	IL	06/12/17
Skel-Tex Credit Union	TX	06/12/17
Skyline Financial Federal Credit Union	CT	06/12/17
SMW Financial Credit Union	MN	06/12/17
Solano First Federal Credit Union	CA	06/12/17
St. Louis Newspaper Carriers CU	MO	06/12/17
St. Monica Federal Credit Union	IN	06/12/17
Stamford Postal Employees FCU	CT	06/12/17
Stephens-Adamson Employees Credit Union	MS	06/12/17
Tappan Community Credit Union, Inc.	OH	06/12/17
Tarrant County's Credit Union	TX	06/12/17
Towanda School Employees FCU	PA	06/12/17
U.S. Employees Credit Union	IL	06/12/17
Union Congregational FCU	NY	06/12/17
Union Federal Credit Union	LA	06/12/17
Union Pacific Employees Credit Union	TX	06/12/17
University of Toledo FCU	OH	06/12/17
Vantage Credit Union	MO	06/12/17
W N M H Credit Union	KS	06/12/17
Wakota Federal Credit Union	MN	06/12/17
Weatherhead CC Federal Credit Union	IN	06/12/17
Winslow Community Federal Credit Union	ME	06/12/17
Wit Federal Credit Union	NY	06/12/17

Rating: D+

Name	State	Date of Change
AL GAR Federal Credit Union	MD	06/12/17
Alhambra Credit Union	AZ	06/12/17
Alpine Community Credit Union	TX	06/12/17
Altier Credit Union	AZ	06/12/17
Atchison Village Credit Union	CA	06/12/17
Aurgroup Financial Credit Union	OH	06/12/17
Avenue Baptist Brotherhood FCU	LA	06/12/17
B.C.S. Community Credit Union	CO	06/12/17
B.O.N.D. Community Federal Credit Union	GA	06/12/17
Baraboo Municipal Employees Credit Union	WI	06/12/17
Bedford VA Federal Credit Union	MA	06/12/17
Berrien Teachers Federal Credit Union	GA	06/12/17
Billerica Municipal Employees CU	MA	06/12/17
Blackhawk Federal Credit Union	PA	06/12/17
Boston Customs Federal Credit Union	MA	06/12/17
Brassies Credit Union	AL	06/12/17
Brownfield Federal Credit Union	TX	06/12/17
Camden Firemen's Credit Union	NJ	06/12/17
Central Credit Union of Maryland	MD	06/12/17
Century Employees' Savings Fund CU	NC	06/12/17
Charleston County Teachers FCU	SC	06/12/17
Chesterfield Federal Credit Union	VA	06/12/17
Christ the King Parish FCU	KS	06/12/17
City of Firsts Community FCU	IN	06/12/17

Name	State	Date of Change
Clairton Works Federal Credit Union	PA	06/12/17
Clarksburg Area Postal Employees FCU	WV	06/12/17
Co-Lib Credit Union	MO	06/12/17
Cooperative Employees Credit Union	OK	06/12/17
Eastern Indiana Federal Credit Union	IN	06/12/17
Educational Community Credit Union	MO	06/12/17
Empire ONE Federal Credit Union	NY	06/12/17
Erie Community Federal Credit Union	OH	06/12/17
Ethicon Suture Credit Union	IL	06/12/17
FAB Church Federal Credit Union	GA	06/12/17
Fargo Federal Employee FCU	ND	06/12/17
FedFinancial Federal Credit Union	MD	06/12/17
First American Credit Union	AZ	06/12/17
Fisher Scientific Employees FCU	PA	06/12/17
Fort McPherson Credit Union	GA	06/12/17
Fremont First Central FCU	NE	06/12/17
Fresno Fire Department Credit Union	CA	06/12/17
G.E.M. Federal Credit Union	ND	06/12/17
Gale Credit Union	IL	06/12/17
GCA Federal Credit Union	LA	06/12/17
GHA Federal Credit Union	CT	06/12/17
Harris Employees Credit Union	GA	06/12/17
HealthNet Federal Credit Union	TN	06/12/17
Joliet Municipal Employees FCU	IL	06/12/17
Joy Employees Federal Credit Union	VA	06/12/17
KINZUA Federal Credit Union	PA	06/12/17
L C Municipal Federal Credit Union	LA	06/12/17
L. A. Electrical Workers Credit Union	CA	06/12/17
Lakes Community Credit Union	MI	06/12/17
Liberty Bay Credit Union	MA	06/12/17
Lomto Federal Credit Union	NY	06/12/17
Manchester Federal Credit Union	MA	06/12/17
MBFT Federal Credit Union	MD	06/12/17
McKesson Employees Federal Credit Union	CA	06/12/17
Medisys Employees Federal Credit Union	NY	06/12/17
Met Tran Federal Credit Union	TX	06/12/17
Methuen Federal Credit Union	MA	06/12/17
Mid-Atlantic Federal Credit Union	MD	06/12/17
Mid-Illini Credit Union	IL	06/12/17
Midwest Community Federal Credit Union	OH	06/12/17
Minerva Area Federal Credit Union	OH	06/12/17
Monmouth County Postal Employees CU	NJ	06/12/17
Mount Vernon NY Postal Employees FCU	NY	06/12/17
Mountain Star Federal Credit Union	TX	06/12/17
Mt. Jezreel Federal Credit Union	MD	06/12/17
New Castle Bellco Federal Credit Union	PA	06/12/17
Nishna Valley Credit Union	IA	06/12/17
Norfolk Fire Department FCU	VA	06/12/17
Northern Paper Mills Credit Union	WI	06/12/17
Northern United Federal Credit Union	MI	06/12/17

Rating Downgrades

Name	State	Date of Change
One Federal Credit Union	PA	06/12/17
OTS Employees Federal Credit Union	HI	06/12/17
Palisades Federal Credit Union	NY	06/12/17
Parishioners Federal Credit Union	CA	06/12/17
Pennington Municipal & County Empls CU	MN	06/12/17
PennTech Employees Federal Credit Union	PA	06/12/17
Peoria Hiway Credit Union	IL	06/12/17
Piedmont Plus Federal Credit Union	GA	06/12/17
Pine Bluff Postal Federal Credit Union	AR	06/12/17
Piney Hills Federal Credit Union	LA	06/12/17
Postel Family Credit Union	TX	06/12/17
Profinance Federal Credit Union	IN	06/12/17
Projector Federal Credit Union	NY	06/12/17
Qualtrust Credit Union	TX	06/12/17
Rafe Federal Credit Union	CA	06/12/17
Rails West Federal Credit Union	ID	06/12/17
Raritan Bay Federal Credit Union	NJ	06/12/17
Rochester & Monroe County Employees FCU	NY	06/12/17
Rutgers Federal Credit Union	NJ	06/12/17
Saint Elizabeth Credit Union	IL	06/12/17
Secured Advantage Federal Credit Union	SC	06/12/17
Shiloh Baptist Federal Credit Union	IL	06/12/17
Signal Financial Federal Credit Union	MD	06/12/17
Smartchoice Credit Union	IL	06/12/17
Southwest Federal Credit Union	NM	06/12/17
Springdale P. P. G. Federal Credit Union	PA	06/12/17
St. Matthews Federal Credit Union	VA	06/12/17
State Employees Community Credit Union	IL	06/12/17
Sylvania Area Federal Credit Union	OH	06/12/17
Tex-Mex Credit Union	TX	06/12/17
Timberline Federal Credit Union	AR	06/12/17
Topeka City Employees Credit Union	KS	06/12/17
U A P Employees Federal Credit Union	OH	06/12/17
United Teletech Financial FCU	NJ	06/12/17
Vision Financial Federal Credit Union	NC	06/12/17
West Coast Federal Employees CU	FL	06/12/17
West Texas Educators Credit Union	TX	06/12/17
Western Heritage Credit Union	NE	06/12/17
Worcester Fire Department Credit Union	MA	06/12/17
Xceed Financial Federal Credit Union	CA	06/12/17

Rating: D

Name	State	Date of Change
Advantage Financial Federal Credit Union	DC	06/12/17
Alcoa Municipal Employees FCU	TN	06/12/17
AME Church Federal Credit Union	LA	06/12/17
AP Federal Credit Union	OH	06/12/17
Associated School Employees Credit Union	OH	06/12/17
Auto Club Federal Credit Union	CA	06/12/17
Bayou City Federal Credit Union	TX	06/12/17
Bull Dog Federal Credit Union	MD	06/12/17
C & R Credit Union	KS	06/12/17
Cannon Federal Credit Union	NM	06/12/17
Central Texas Teachers Credit Union	TX	06/12/17
Champaign Postal Credit Union	IL	06/12/17
City of Clarksburg Federal Credit Union	WV	06/12/17
Cleveland Church of Christ FCU	OH	06/12/17
Commodore Perry Federal Credit Union	OH	06/12/17
Coshocton Federal Credit Union	OH	06/12/17
Cosmopolitan Federal Credit Union	IL	06/12/17
East Ohio Gas Cleveland Operating FCU	OH	06/12/17
Eastern Kentucky Federal Credit Union	KY	06/12/17
Finex Credit Union	CT	06/12/17
First Area Federal Credit Union	PA	06/12/17
First Cheyenne Federal Credit Union	WY	06/12/17
Focus Federal Credit Union	OK	06/12/17
Four Flags Area Credit Union	MI	06/12/17
Friends Federal Credit Union	OK	06/12/17
Generations Federal Credit Union	IN	06/12/17
Global 1 Federal Credit Union	NJ	06/12/17
Granco Federal Credit Union	WA	06/12/17
Greater Centennial Federal Credit Union	NY	06/12/17
Harrison County POE Federal Credit Union	MS	06/12/17
Hawaii Pacific Federal Credit Union	HI	06/12/17
Health Care of New Jersey FCU	NJ	06/12/17
Healthcare Plus Federal Credit Union	SD	06/12/17
Holsey Temple Federal Credit Union	PA	06/12/17
I F F Employees Federal Credit Union	NJ	06/12/17
IBEW Community Federal Credit Union	TX	06/12/17
ICI America Federal Credit Union	DE	06/12/17
Intercorp Credit Union	TX	06/12/17
InTouch Credit Union	TX	06/12/17
Israel Methcomm Federal Credit Union	IL	06/12/17
Keystone United Methodist FCU	PA	06/12/17
Latvian Federal Credit Union	NY	06/12/17
Lefors Federal Credit Union	TX	06/12/17
Lincoln National Federal Credit Union	NC	06/12/17
Lisbon Farmers Union Credit Union	ND	06/12/17
Louise Mills Federal Credit Union	MA	06/12/17
Madison County Federal Credit Union	IN	06/12/17
Mattel Federal Credit Union	CA	06/12/17
McComb Federal Credit Union	MS	06/12/17
McDonald Community Federal Credit Union	OH	06/12/17
MEA Credit Union	IL	06/12/17
MECU	GA	06/12/17
MembersOwn Credit Union	NE	06/12/17
Mountain River Credit Union	CO	06/12/17
MSTC Federal Credit Union	MS	06/12/17
Muskogee Federal Credit Union	OK	06/12/17
My Credit Union	CA	06/12/17
N Y Team Federal Credit Union	NY	06/12/17

Rating Downgrades

Name	State	Date of Change
National J.A.C.L. Credit Union	UT	06/12/17
NEA Federal Credit Union	NY	06/12/17
Neighborhood Trust Federal Credit Union	NY	06/12/17
New London Municipal Employees CU	CT	06/12/17
Newport News Municipal Employees CU	VA	06/12/17
Northwestern Federal Credit Union	OH	06/12/17
Ohio County Public Schools FCU	WV	06/12/17
P.N.G. Northern Federal Credit Union	PA	06/12/17
Paper Converters Local 286/1034 FCU	PA	06/12/17
Park Manor Christian Church Credit Union	IL	06/12/17
Peoples Choice Credit Union	WI	06/12/17
Phi Beta Sigma Federal Credit Union	DC	06/12/17
Plains Federal Credit Union	TX	06/12/17
Processors-Industrial Community CU	IL	06/12/17
Pueblo Horizons Federal Credit Union	CO	06/12/17
Reading Federal Credit Union	OH	06/12/17
RiverTrace Federal Credit Union	VA	06/12/17
Seasons Federal Credit Union	CT	06/12/17
Select Employees Credit Union	IL	06/12/17
Shelby Community Federal Credit Union	MT	06/12/17
Southwest Health Care Credit Union	AZ	06/12/17
St. Vincent's Medical Center FCU	CT	06/12/17
Star USA Federal Credit Union	WV	06/12/17
Starcor Credit Union	MN	06/12/17
Stockton Community Federal Credit Union	CA	06/12/17
Superior Savings Credit Union	OH	06/12/17
Teamsters Local #238 Credit Union	IA	06/12/17
Total Community Action FCU	LA	06/12/17
U S Pipe Bessemer Employees FCU	AL	06/12/17
Union Baptist Greenburgh FCU	NY	06/12/17
United Credit Union	TX	06/12/17
Upstate Telco Federal Credit Union	NY	06/12/17
V.A. Hospital Federal Credit Union	AR	06/12/17
Victoria City-County Employees FCU	TX	06/12/17
Weyco Community Credit Union	NC	06/12/17

Rating: D-

Name	State	Date of Change
American Baptist Association CU	TX	06/12/17
Baltimore Washington FCU	MD	06/12/17
Brentwood Baptist Church FCU	TX	06/12/17
Connecticut Federal Credit Union	CT	06/12/17
C-T Waco Federal Credit Union	TX	06/12/17
Dial Credit Union	IL	06/12/17
Eastpointe Community Credit Union	MI	06/12/17
First Jersey Credit Union	NJ	06/12/17
First Security Credit Union	IL	06/12/17
Focus Federal Credit Union	OH	06/12/17
Gates Chili Federal Credit Union	NY	06/12/17
GESB Sheet Metal Workers FCU	IN	06/12/17
Gideon Federal Credit Union	IL	06/12/17
GP Community Federal Credit Union	NY	06/12/17
Greater Wyoming Federal Credit Union	WY	06/12/17
Hardin County Hospital Employees CU	TN	06/12/17
Harrison Teachers Federal Credit Union	NY	06/12/17
Haxtun Community Federal Credit Union	CO	06/12/17
Homeport Federal Credit Union	TX	06/12/17
Houston Highway Credit Union	TX	06/12/17
IBEW 26 Federal Credit Union	MD	06/12/17
Kahuku Federal Credit Union	HI	06/12/17
Kaskaskia Valley Community Credit Union	IL	06/12/17
Lake Community Federal Credit Union	OH	06/12/17
M.W.P.H. Grand Lodge of Illinois FCU	IL	06/12/17
Merced Municipal Employees Credit Union	CA	06/12/17
Mid-Tex Federal Credit Union	TX	06/12/17
Missouri Baptist Credit Union	MO	06/12/17
National Geographic Federal Credit Union	DC	06/12/17
Northwestern Energy Employees FCU	MT	06/12/17
NU Community Credit Union	PA	06/12/17
Ohio Valley Federal Credit Union	OH	06/12/17
Our Family Social Credit Union	NE	06/12/17
Pace Resources Federal Credit Union	PA	06/12/17
Palmetto Trust Federal Credit Union	SC	06/12/17
Plainfield Police & Firemen's FCU	NJ	06/12/17
Priority Federal Credit Union	AR	06/12/17
PSE&G Nuclear Employees FCU	NJ	06/12/17
Public Service Sewaren FCU	NJ	06/12/17
Riverside Beaver County FCU	PA	06/12/17
Routt Schools Federal Credit Union	CO	06/12/17
Sewerage & Water Board Employees FCU	LA	06/12/17
Shamrock Foods Federal Credit Union	AZ	06/12/17
Sheet Metal Workers Federal Credit Union	IN	06/12/17
St. Anne Credit Union	MA	06/12/17
Texas Health Resources Credit Union	TX	06/12/17
Texas Workforce Credit Union	TX	06/12/17
Town of Hempstead Employees FCU	NY	06/12/17
UFCW Local 1776 Federal Credit Union	PA	06/12/17
Urban Upbound Federal Credit Union	NY	06/12/17

Rating: E+

Name	State	Date of Change
Bayer Credit Union	MO	06/12/17
Beacon Mutual Federal Credit Union	OH	06/12/17
Community First Credit Union	MO	06/12/17
Essex County Teachers FCU	NJ	06/12/17
Financial 1st Federal Credit Union	PA	06/12/17
First Baptist Church (Stratford) FCU	CT	06/12/17
Greater Galilee Baptist Credit Union	WI	06/12/17
Greece Community Federal Credit Union	NY	06/12/17
HealthPlus Federal Credit Union	MS	06/12/17
HSM Federal Credit Union	NC	06/12/17
Lake Superior Credit Union	MI	06/12/17

Rating Downgrades

Name	State	Date of Change
Lowell Municipal Employees FCU	MA	06/12/17
Members Financial Federal Credit Union	TX	06/12/17
N.G.H. Credit Union	TN	06/12/17
Northwest Arkansas Federal Credit Union	AR	06/12/17
Public Service Edwardspt PL E FCU	IN	06/12/17
S.F. Bay Area Educators Credit Union	CA	06/12/17
Sorg Bay West Federal Credit Union	OH	06/12/17
St. Colman & Affiliates FCU	OH	06/12/17
St. Johns Buffalo Federal Credit Union	NY	06/12/17
Varick Memorial Federal Credit Union	NY	06/12/17
Ward Federal Credit Union	PA	06/12/17

Rating: E

Name	State	Date of Change
Post Office Employees FCU	LA	06/12/17

Rating: E-

Name	State	Date of Change
1st University Credit Union	TX	06/12/17
First Unity Federal Credit Union	MS	06/12/17
Hamilton Horizons Federal Credit Union	NJ	06/12/17
Link Federal Credit Union	IN	06/12/17
Motion Federal Credit Union	NJ	06/12/17
Neighbors 1st FCU	PA	06/12/17
Union Pacific Streamliner FCU	NE	06/12/17

Rating: F

Name	State	Date of Change
Community United Federal Credit Union	GA	06/12/17
Shreveport Federal Credit Union	LA	06/12/17

Appendix

RECENT CREDIT UNION FAILURES
2017

Institution	Headquarters	Date of Failure	At Date of Failure	
			Total Assets ($Mil)	Safety Rating
Community United FCU	Waycross, GA	04/20/17	23.2	C (Fair)
Shreveport Federal Credit Union	Shreveport, LA	04/13/17	106.7	B (Good)
FCAMEC Federal Credit Union	Tallahassee, FL	03/17/17	1.77	D- (Weak)
Melrose CU	Briarwood, NY	02/10/17	1,950.00	C (Fair)

2016

Institution	Headquarters	Date of Failure	At Date of Failure	
			Total Assets ($Mil)	Safety Rating
First African Baptist Church FCU	Sharon Hill, PA	11/29/16	.77	E+ (Very Weak)
Valley State CU	Saginaw, MI	08/17/16	22.32	D- (Weak)
Cardozo Lodge FCU	Bensalem, PA	04/05/16	.23	D+ (Weak)
Chester Upland School Empl FCU	Chester, PA	04/05/16	.83	E+ (Very Weak)
Electrical Inspectors FCU	Bensalem, PA	04/05/16	.66	D (Weak)
OPS Empl FCU	Bensalem, PA	04/05/16	1.2	C- (Fair)
Servco FCU	Bensalem, PA	04/05/16	2.2	D+ (Weak)
Triangle Interests FCU	Bensalem, PA	04/05/16	.29	C- (Fair)
Veterans Health Administration CU	Detroit, MI	03/29/16	2.0	D+ (Weak)
Mildred Mitchell-Bateman Hospital FCU	Huntington, WV	02/24/16	.4	C+ (Fair)
CTK CU	Milwaukee, WI	02/05/16	.2	D- (Weak)
Cory Methodist Church CU	Cleveland, OH	02/04/16	1.7	D (Weak)
Clarkston Brandon Community CU	Clarkston, MI	01/13/16	68.8	C+ (Fair)

2015

Institution	Headquarters	Date of Failure	At Date of Failure: Total Assets ($Mil)	At Date of Failure: Safety Rating
First Hawaiian Homes FCU	Hoolehua, HI	12/9/15	3.2	C+ (Fair)
Helping Other People Excel FCU	Jackson, NJ	11/20/15	.6	C (Fair)
SWC Credit Union	Tampa, FL	9/24/15	1.9	D (Weak)
Bethex Federal Credit Union	Bronx, NY	9/18/15	12.9	D (Weak)
Montauk Credit Union	New York, NY	9/18/15	178.5	C (Fair)
SCICAP Credit Union	Chariton, IA	8/28/15	2.0	C (Fair)
Alabama One Credit Union	Tuscaloosa, AL	8/27/15	6.0	D+ (Weak)
Lakeside Federal Credit Union	Hammond, IN	7/16/15	8.9	D (Weak)
Trailblazer Federal Credit Union	Washington, PA	7/10/15	4.1	D (Weak)
New Bethel Federal Credit Union	Portsmouth, VA	4/30/15	.11	C- (Fair)
TLC Federal Credit Union	Tillamook, OR	4/30/15	109.0	D (Weak)
Montgomery County CU	Dayton, OH	4/23/15	27.3	D- (Weak)
North Dade Comm. Dev FCU	Miami Gardens, FL	3/31/15	3.0	C (Fair)
American Bakery Workers FCU	Philadelphia, PA	1/30/15	4.1	E+ (Very Weak)

2014

Institution	Headquarters	Date of Failure	At Date of Failure	
			Total Assets ($Mil)	Safety Rating
Metropolitan Church of God CU	Detroit, MI	12/03/14	0.1	E+ (Very Weak)
County & Municipal Empl CU	Edinburg, TX	10/10/14	40.3	C- (Fair)
Republic Hose Employees FCU	Youngstown, OH	09/30/14	.6	E+ (Very Weak)
Louden Depot Community CU	Fairfield, IA	09/05/14	5.0	C+ (Fair)
Bensenville Community CU	Bensenville, IL	07/31/14	14.0	E- (Very Weak)
IBEW Local 816 FCU	Paducah, KY	05/23/14	7.9	D (Weak)
Life Line Credit Union Inc	Richmond, VA	05/23/14	7.9	E+ (Very Weak)
Health One Credit Union	Detroit, MI	05/16/14	18.2	D (Weak)
St. Francis Campus Credit Union	Little Falls, MN	02/14/14	51.0	B (Good)
Parsons Pittsburgh CU	Parsons, KS	01/24/14	13.5	C- (Fair)

2013

Institution	Headquarters	Date of Failure	At Date of Failure	
			Total Assets ($Mil)	Safety Rating
Bagumbayan Credit Union	Chicago, IL	12/12/13	0.1	C- (Fair)
Polish Combatants Credit Union	Bedford, OH	11/22/13	0.1	B+ (Good)
Mayfair Federal Credit Union	Philadelphia, PA	11/1/13	14.3	C (Fair)
Craftsman Credit Union	Detroit, MI	09/06/13	24.1	D- (Weak)
Taupa Lithuanian Credit Union	Clevland, OH	07/15/13	23.6	C+ (Fair)
Ochsner Clinic FCU	New Orleans, LA	06/28/13	9.2	D- (Weak)
PEF Federal Credit Union	Highland Heights, OH	06/21/13	31.3	E- (Very Weak)
First Kingdom Community	Selma, AL	05/31/13	0.1	E+ (Very Weak)
Electrical Workers #527 FCU	Texas City, TX	05/23/13	0.6	E+ (Very Weak)
Lynrocten FCU	Lynchburg, VA	05/03/13	13.8	B (Good)
Shiloh of Alexandria FCU	Alexandria, VA	04/12/13	2.4	B (Good)
I.C.E Federal Credit Union	Inglewood, CA	03/15/13	3.4	D- (Weak)
Pepsi Cola FCU	Buena Park, CA	03/15/13	0.6	C- (Fair)
Amez United Credit Union	Detroit, MI	02/19/13	0.1	D+ (Weak)
NCP Community Development FCU	Norfolk, VA	02/08/13	2.0	D (Weak)
New Covenant Miss Bapt Church CU	Milwaukee, WI	01/07/13	0.5	E- (Very Weak)

2012

Institution	Headquarters	Date of Failure	At Date of Failure	
			Total Assets ($Mil)	Safety Rating
Olean Tile Employees FCU	Olean, NY	12/17/12	0.8	D- (Weak)
GIC FCU	Euclid, OH	12/13/12	15.5	B+ (Very Good)
Border Lodge Credit Union	Derby Line, VT	11/30/12	3.1	D (Weak)
Women's Southwest FCU	Dallas, TX	10/31/12	2.1	E+ (Very Weak)
El Paso's Federal Credit Union	El Paso, TX	9/28/12	471.0	D+ (Weak)
United Catholic Credit Union	Temperance, MI	08/09/12	0.2	C+ (Fair)
Trinity Credit Union	Trinidad, CO	07/27/12	4.0	D- (Weak)
USA One National Credit Union	Matteson, IL	06/05/12	37.9	E- (Very Weak)
Wausau Postal Employees CU	Wausau, WI	05/18/12	8.4	D- (Weak)
Shepherd's Federal Credit Union	Charlotte	03/26/12	0.6	C- (Fair)
Telesis Community Credit Union	Chatsworth	03/23/12	318.3	E+ (Very Weak)
AM Community Credit Union	Kenosha, WI	02/17/12	1.2	E+ (Very Weak)
Eastern New York FCU	Napanoch, NY	01/27/12	51.8	E- (Very Weak)
People for People Community Development CU	Philadelphia, PA	01/06/12	1.1	E+ (Very Weak)

How Do Banks and Credit Unions Differ?

Since credit unions first appeared in 1946, they have been touted as a low-cost, friendly alternative to banks. But with tightening margins, pressure to compete in technology, branch closures, and the introduction of a host of service fees — some even higher than those charged by banks — the distinction between banks and credit unions has been gradually narrowing. Following are the key differences between today's banks and credit unions.

	Banks	Credit Unions
Access	Practically anyone is free to open an account or request a loan from any bank. There are no membership requirements.	Credit unions are set up to serve the needs of a specific group who share a "common bond." In order to open an account or request a loan, you must demonstrate that you meet the credit union's common bond requirements.
Ownership	Banks are owned by one or more investors who determine the bank's policies and procedures. A bank's customers do not have direct input into how the bank is operated.	Although they may be sponsored by a corporation or other entity, credit unions are owned by their members through their funds on deposit. Therefore, each depositor has a voice in how the credit union is operated.
Dividends and Fees	Banks are for-profit organizations where the profits are used to pay dividends to the bank's investors or are reinvested in an effort to increase the bank's value to investors. In an effort to generate more profits, bank services and fees are typically more costly.	Credit unions are not-for-profit organizations. Any profits generated are returned to the credit union's members in the form of higher interest rates on deposits, lower loan rates, and free or low-cost services.
Management and Staffing	A bank's management and other staff are employees of the bank, hired directly or indirectly by its investors.	Credit unions are frequently run using elected members, volunteer staff, and staff provided by the credit union's sponsor. This helps to hold down costs.
Insurance	Banks are insured by the Federal Deposit Insurance Corporation, an agency of the federal government.	Credit unions are insured by the National Credit Union Share Insurance Fund, which is managed by the National Credit Union Administration, an agency of the federal government.

Glossary

This glossary contains the most important terms used in this publication.

ARM Adjustable-Rate Mortgage. This is a loan whose interest rate is tied to an index and is adjusted at a predetermined frequency. An ARM is subject to credit risk if interest rates rise and the borrower is unable to make the mortgage payment.

Average Recession A recession involving a decline in real GDP that is approximately equivalent to the average of the postwar recessions of 1957-58, 1960, 1970, 1974-75, 1980, 1981-82, 1990-1991, 2001, and 2007-2009. It is assumed, however, that in today's market, the financial losses suffered from a recession of that magnitude would be greater than those experienced in previous decades. (See also "Severe Recession.")

Board of Directors Group of volunteers charged with providing the general direction and control of the credit union. Officers of the credit union (chairman, vice chairman, etc.) are selected from the board membership.

Brokered Deposits Deposits that are brought into an institution through a broker. They are relatively costly, volatile funds that are more readily withdrawn from the institution if there is a loss of confidence or intense interest rate competition. Reliance on brokered deposits is usually a sign that the institution is having difficulty attracting deposits from its local geographic markets and could be a warning signal if other institutions in the same areas are not experiencing similar difficulties.

Bylaws A codification of the form of organization that the credit union takes and the governance of its day-to-day operations; federal credit unions are required to adopt a basic code approved by the National Credit Union Administration.

Capital A measure of a credit union's ability to withstand troubled times. A credit union's base capital represents the total of regular (statutory) reserves, other reserve accounts and undivided earnings. Regulatory capital includes all the above plus allowances for loan and investment losses. (See also "Core Capital")

Cash & Equivalents Cash plus highly liquid assets which can be readily converted to cash.

Core (Tier 1) Capital A measurement of capital defined by the federal regulatory agencies for evaluating an institution's degree of leverage. Core capital consists of the following: common stockholder's equity, preferred stockholder's equity up to certain limits, and retained earnings net of any intangible assets.

Corporate Credit Union A federal or state-chartered credit union that serves other credit unions, providing investment, short-term (liquidity) loans and other services to its member credit unions; they are sometimes refered to as "the credit union's credit union."

Credit Committee Optional internal committee of a credit union that considers applications for loans and lines of credit. In the event the credit union has delegated that authority to a loan officer, the credit committee ratifies the applications approved by the loan officer.

Credit Union A not-for-profit financial cooperative chartered by the state or federal government and, in most cases, insured by the federal government. It is owned by the members of the credit union. The coopereative is tied to a commonality of interest (such as employer, association or community) that the members or groups of members share.

Credit Union Service Organization An organization owned wholly or in part by one or more credit unions to provide service to the credit unions, their members, or both. (CUSO)

Critical Ranges Guidelines developed to help you evaluate the levels of each index contributing to a company's Weiss Safety Rating. The sum or average of these grades does not necessarily have a one-to-one correspondence with the final rating for an institution because the rating is derived from a wider range of more complex calculations.

CU A common acronym for credit unions.

CUNA Credit Union National Association. A national trade association based in Washington, D.C. and Miadison, Wisconson that serves credit unions.

CUSO Credit Union Service Organization (see above).

Dividend Funds paid to members based on account size and rates declared regularly (monthly, quarterly or annually) by the board of directors for various types of accounts. A dividend represents the payment by the credit union to the member for use of the member's funds.

Equity Total assets minus total liabilities. This is the "capital cushion" the institution has to fall back on in times of trouble. (See also "Capital.")

Field of Membership Definition of the type of membership generally served by the credit union, e.g.: "defense" credit unions primarily serve members of the armed forces; "education" credit unions primarily serve educators.

Safety Rating Weiss Safety Ratings, which grade institutions on a scale from A (Excellent) to F (Failed). Ratings are based on many factors, emphasizing capitalization, asset quality, profitability, liquidity, and stability.

FPR Financial Performance Report is a financial anaylysis report derived from Call Report data.

Goodwill The value of an institution as a going concern, meaning the value which exceeds book value on a balance sheet. It generally represents the value of a well-respected business name, good customer relations, high employee morale and other intangible factors which would be expected to translate into greater than normal earning power. In a bank or thrift acquisition, goodwill is the value paid by a buyer of the institution in excess of the value of the institution's equity because of these intangible factors.

Hot Money Individual deposits of $100,000 or more. These types of deposits are considered "hot money" because they tend to chase whoever is offering the best interest rates at the time and are thus relatively costly and fairly volatile sources of funds.

Loan Loss Reserves The amount of capital an institution sets aside to cover any potential losses due to the nonrepayment of loans.

National Credit Union Share Insurance Fund The federal share insurance fund for credit unions. The fund protects credit union members' shares (up to $250,000) in federal and federally insured, state-chartered credit unions. NCUSIF is backed by the full faith and credit of the United States.

NCUA National Credit Union Association. An independent federal agency that charters and supervises federal credit unions and insures savings in federal and most state-chartered credit unions.

Net Charge-offs The amount of foreclosed loans written off the institution's books since the beginning of the year, less any previous write-offs that were recovered during the year.

Net Interest Spread The difference between the interest income earned on the institution's loans and investments and the interest expense paid on its interest-bearing deposits and borrowings. This "spread" is most commonly analyzed as a percentage of average earning assets to show the institution's net return on income-generating assets.

Since the margin between interest earned and interest paid is generally where the company generates the majority of its income, this figure provides insight into the company's ability to effectively manage interest spreads. A low Net Interest Spread can be the result of poor loan and deposit pricing, high levels of nonaccruing loans, or poor asset/liability management.

Net Profit or Loss The bottom line income or loss the institution has sustained in its most recent reporting period.

Nonaccruing Loans Loans for which payments are past due and full repayment is doubtful. Interest income on these loans is no longer recorded on the income statement. (See also "Past Due Loans.")

Nonperforming Loans The sum of loans past due 90 days or more and nonaccruing loans. These are loans the institution made where full repayment is now doubtful. (See also "Past Due Loans" and "Nonaccruing Loans.")

Past Due Loans Loans for which payments are at least 90 days in arears. The institution continues to record income on these loans, even though none is actually being received, because it is expected that the borrower will eventually repay the loan in full. It is likely, however, that at least a portion of these loans will move into nonaccruing status. (See also "Nonaccruing Loans.")

Overhead Expense	Expenses of the institution other than interest expense, such as salaries and benefits of employees, rent and utility expenses, and data processing expenses. A certain amount of "fixed" overhead is required to operate a bank or thrift, so it is important that the institution leverage that overhead to the fullest extent in supporting its revenue-generating activities.
Par Value	The dollar equivalent of a share required to join a credit union. Par value is determined by the board and typically ranges from $5 to $25.
RBCR	See "Risk-Based Capital Ratio."
Restructured Loans	Loans whose terms have been modified in order to enable the borrower to make payments which he otherwise would be unable to make. Modifications could include a reduction in the interest rate or a lengthening of the time to maturity.
Risk-Based Capital Ratio	A ratio originally developed by the International Committee on Banking as a means of assessing the adequacy of an institution's capital in relation to the amount of credit risk on and off its balance sheet. (See also "Risk-weighted Assets.")
Risk-Weighted Assets	The sum of assets and certain off-balance sheet items after they have been individually adjusted for the level of credit risk they pose to the institution. Assets with close to no risk are weighted 0%; those with minor risk are weighted 20%; those with low risk, 50%; and those with normal or high risk, 100%.
R.O.A	Return on Assets calculated as net profit or loss as a percentage of average assets. This is the most commonly used measure of bank profitability.
R.O.E.	Return on Equity calculated as net profit or loss as a percentage of average equity. This represents the rate of return on the shareholders' investment.
Share Account	Refers to a regular share savings account or other account that isn't a share certificate account. A regular share account doesn't require a holder to maintain a balance greater than the par value or a notice of intent to withdraw (unless required in the bylaws). Shares are legally defined as equity and represent ownership.
Share Certificate Account	Account that earns dividends at a specified rate for a specified period of time, if held to maturity; and upon which a penalty may be assessed for premature withdrawal prior to maturity.
Share Draft (checking) Account	A dividend-earning account from which the holder is authorized to withdraw shares by means of a negotiable or transferable instrument or other order. (similar to a NOW account).
Sponsor	An organization (such as a corporation, religious congregation or association) that promotes the establishment or continuation of a credit union for its employees or members.
Stockholder's Equity	See "Equity."

Supervisory Committee Internal committee required for all federal credit unions and most state credit unions. Oversees the credit union's financial operations, conducts internal audits, may arrange for external audits, reports to board of directors and may suspend board members for malfeasance.

Total Assets Total resources of an institution, primarily composed of cash, securities (such as municipal and treasury bonds), loans, and fixed assets (such as real estate, buildings, and equipment).

Total Equity See "Equity."

Total Liabilities All debts owed by an institution. Normally, the largest liability of a bank or thrift is its deposits.

Trust Company A financial institution chartered to provide trust services (legal agreements to act for the benefit of another party), which may also be authorized to provide banking services.

Undivided Earnings Accumulated net income after distribution to members and provision for reserves required by law, plus or minus increases or decreases in other reserves (such as a special reserve for losses), plus or minus other authorized direct credits or charges for ad justments affecting prior period operations.